Ethan A. Andrews, Solomon Stoddard

A Grammar of the Latin Language

for the use of schools and colleges

Ethan A. Andrews, Solomon Stoddard

A Grammar of the Latin Language
for the use of schools and colleges

ISBN/EAN: 9783337087272

Printed in Europe, USA, Canada, Australia, Japan

Cover: Foto ©Paul-Georg Meister /pixelio.de

More available books at **www.hansebooks.com**

Andrews' Series of Latin School Books.

PUBLISHED BY CROCKER AND BREWSTER,
51 WASHINGTON STREET, BOSTON.

THE LATIN SCHOOL BOOKS prepared by Prof. E. A. ANDREWS, exclusive of his Latin-English Lexicon, founded on the Latin-German Lexicon of Dr. Freund, constitute two distinct series, adapted to different and distinct purposes. The basis of the First Series is Andrews' First Latin Book; of the Second, Andrews and Stoddard's Latin Grammar.

FIRST SERIES.

This Series is designed expressly for those who commence the study of Latin at a very early age, and for such as intend to pursue it to a limited extent only, or merely as subsidiary to the acquisition of a good English education. It consists of the following works, viz.:—

1. Andrews' First Latin Book; or Progressive Lessons in Reading and Writing Latin. This small volume contains most of the leading principles and grammatical forms of the Latin language, and, by the logical precision of its rules and definitions, is admirably fitted to serve as an introduction to the study of general grammar. The work is divided into lessons of convenient length, which are so arranged that the student will, in all cases, be prepared to enter upon the study of each successive lesson, by possessing a thorough knowledge of those which preceded it. The lessons generally consist of three parts:—1st. The statement of important principles in the form of rules or definitions, or the exhibition of orthographical or etymological forms; 2d. Exercises, designed to illustrate such principles or forms; and 3d. Questions, intended to assist the student in preparing his lesson. In addition to the grammatical lessons contained in this volume, a few pages of Reading Lessons are annexed, and these are followed by a Dictionary comprising all the Latin words contained in the work. This book is adapted to the use of all schools above the grade of primary schools, including also Academies and Female Seminaries. It is prepared in such a manner that it can be used with little difficulty by any intelligent parent or teacher, with no previous knowledge of the language.

2. The Latin Reader, with a Dictionary and Notes, containing explanations of difficult idioms, and numerous references to the Lessons contained in the First Latin Book.

3. The Viri Romæ, with a Dictionary and Notes, referring, like those of the Reader, to the First Latin Book. This series of three small volumes, if faithfully studied according to the directions contained in them, will not only render the student a very tolerable proficient in the principles of the Latin language and in the knowledge of its roots, from which so many words of his English language are derived, but will constitute the best preparation for a thorough study of the English grammar.

SECOND SERIES.

NOTE.—The "Latin Reader" and the "Viri Romæ," in this series, are the same as in the first series.

This Series is designed more especially for those who are intending to become thoroughly acquainted with the Latin language, and with the principal classical authors of that language. It consists of the following works:—

1. Latin Lessons. This small volume is designed for the younger classes of Latin students, who intend ultimately to take up the larger Grammar, but to whom that work would, at first, appear too formidable. It contains the prominent principles of Latin grammar, expressed in the same language as in the larger Grammar, and likewise Reading and Writing Lessons, with a Dictionary of the Latin words and phrases occurring in the Lessons.

NEW SERIES OF LATIN SCHOOL BOOKS.

2. Latin Grammar. Revised, with Corrections and Additions. A Grammar of the Latin Language, for the use of Schools and Colleges. By Professors E. A. ANDREWS and S. STODDARD. This work, which for many years has been the text-book in the department of Latin Grammar, claims the merit of having first introduced into the schools of this country the subject of grammatical analysis, which now occupies a conspicuous place in so many grammars of the English language. More than twenty years have elapsed since the first publication of this Grammar, and it is hardly necessary to say that its merits—placing it in a practical view, preëminently above every other Latin Grammar—have been so fully appreciated that it has been adopted as a Text Book in nearly every College and Seminary in the country. The present edition has not only been *thoroughly revised and corrected (two years of continuous labor having been devoted to its careful revision and to the purpose of rendering it conformable in all respects to the advanced position which it aims to occupy,*) but it contains at least *one third* more matter than the previous editions. To unite the acknowledged excellencies of the older English manuals, and of the more recent German grammars, was the special aim of the authors of this work; and to this end particular attention was directed:—1st. *To the preparation of more extended rules for the pronunciation of the language ;* 2d. *To a clear exposition of its inflectional changes ;* 3d. *To a proper basis of its syntax ;* and 4th. *To greater precision in rules and definitions.*

3. Questions on the Grammar. This little volume is intended to aid the student in preparing his lessons, and the teacher in conducting his recitations.

4. A Synopsis of Latin Grammar, comprising the Latin Paradigms, and the Principal Rules of Latin Etymology and Syntax. The few pages composing this work contain those portions of the Grammar to which the student has occasion to refer most frequently in the preparation of his daily lessons.

5. Latin Reader. The Reader, by means of two separate and distinct sets of notes, is equally adapted for use in connection either with the First Latin Book or the Latin Grammar.

6. Viri Romæ. This volume, like the Reader, is furnished with notes and references, both to the First Latin Book and to the Latin Grammar. The principal difference in the two sets of notes found in each of these volumes consists in the somewhat greater fulness of those which belong to the smaller series.

7. Latin Exercises. This work contains exercises in every department of the Latin Grammar, and is so arranged that it may be studied in connection with the Grammar through every stage of the preparatory course. It is designed to prepare the way for original composition in the Latin language, both in prose and verse.

8. A Key to Latin Exercises. This Key, in which all the exercises in the preceding volume are fully corrected, is intended for the use of teachers only.

9. Cæsar's Commentaries on the Gallic War, with a Dictionary and Notes. The text of this edition of Cæsar has been formed by reference to the best German editions. The Notes are principally grammatical. The Dictionary, which, like all the others in the series, was prepared with great labor, contains the usual significations of the words, together with an explanation of all such phrases as might otherwise perplex the student.

10. Sallust. Sallust's Jugurthine War and Conspiracy of Cataline, with a Dictionary and Notes. The text of this work, which was based upon that of Cortius, has been modified by reference to the best modern editions, especially by those of Kritz and Gerlach; and its orthography is, in

NEW SERIES OF LATIN SCHOOL BOOKS.

general, conformed to that of Pottier and Planche. The Dictionaries of Cæsar and Sallust connected with this series are original works, and, in connection with the Notes in each volume, furnish a very complete and satisfactory apparatus for the study of these two authors.

11. Ovid. Selections from the Metamorphoses and Heroides of Ovid, with Notes, Grammatical References, and Exercises in Scanning. These selections from Ovid are designed as an introduction to Latin poetry. They are accompanied with numerous brief notes explanatory of difficult phrases, of obscure historical or mythological allusions, and especially of grammatical difficulties. To these are added such Exercises in Scanning as serve fully to introduce the student to a knowledge of Latin prosody, and especially of the structure and laws of hexameter and pentameter verse.

12. Virgil. The Eclogues and Georgics of Virgil, with Notes and a Metrical Key. The text of this edition is, in general, that of Heyne as revised by Wagner. Particular attention has been given to the standard of prevalent usage, discarding the forms *is* for *es*, in the terminations of some accusatives plural, *quom* for *quum*, and the like, as they tend to embarrass the learner, while they give but a very imperfect idea of the peculiarities of the author's orthography, as will be seen by examination of the *Orthographia Virgiliana*, at the end of this edition. The notes are very numerous, and in their preparation the editor has drawn freely from the best commentaries on Virgil, both German and English, including those of Heyne, Wagner, Forbiger, Ladewig, Martyn, Keightley, Bryce, Conington and others. The notes contain many references to the Grammar, which will be found useful.

In announcing the Revised Edition of ANDREWS AND STODDARD'S LATIN GRAMMAR, the Publishers believe it to be quite unnecessary to speak of the merits of the work. The fact that in the space of about *Twenty Years*, SIXTY-FIVE EDITIONS, numbering above **Two Hundred Thousand Copies**, have been required for the purpose of meeting the steadily increasing demand for the work, sufficiently evinces the estimation in which it has been held. In preparing this Revised and Enlarged Edition, every portion of the original work has been reconsidered in the light of the experience of twenty years spent by the present editor in studies connected with this department of education, and with the aid of numerous publications in the same department, which, during this period, have issued from the European press. The results of this labor are apparent on almost every page, in new modifications of the old materials, and especially in such additional information in regard to its various topics as the present advanced state of classical education in this country seemed obviously to demand. The publishers commend this new edition to the attention of Teachers throughout the country, and express the hope that in its present form it will be deemed worthy of a continuance of the favor which it has so long received.

The following are extracts from a few of the many letters the Publishers have received from teachers from all parts of the country in commendation of this work:—

> The revised edition of Andrews and Stoddard's Latin Grammar is without doubt the best published in America. I have no doubt that the time is near at hand when this series of works will, by all lovers of the classics, be considered as the 'National Series.' The pronunciation is now by the same class considered the American Standard. I will hail with joy the day when every college and school in our country shall have adopted Prof. Andrews' series as the foundation of true classic knowledge. As such I consider it, and for that reason have I used it since I first knew its existence.—*Martin Armstrong, Potomac Seminary, Romney, Va.*

> Allow me to say, after a careful examination, that, in my judgment, it is the best manual of Latin Grammar to be found in the English language. In revising it the author has preserved the happy medium between saying too much and too little, so desirable for a Latin text-book for this country. In philosophical arrangement, simplicity of expression, and for brevity and fulness, it must entitle the author to the first rank in American classical scholarship. I shall use it in my classes, and recommend it to all teachers of Latin in this country —*N. E. Cobleigh, Professor of Ancient Languages and Literature, in Lawrence University, Appleton, Wis.*

NEW SERIES OF LATIN SCHOOL BOOKS.

I have reason to believe that the improvements, introduced into the last edition of Andrews and Stoddard's Latin Grammar by my respected and lamented friend Dr. Andrews, a little before his death, add very decidedly to the value of a work, which has done more to give the knowledge of that language to the youth of this country than any, perhaps than all others.—*Theodore W. Woolsey, President of Yale College, New Haven.*

No book, probably, has done more to improve classical training in American schools than Andrews and Stoddard's Latin Grammar. Its use is almost universal; and where it has not itself been adopted as a manual, it has made grammars of similar excellence necessary. The last edition, the sixty-fifth, was carefully revised by the lamented Dr. Andrews, not long before his death, by whom it was greatly enlarged by the incorporation of much valuable information, derived mainly from the last edition of the Latin Grammar of Professor Zumpt. It will therefore be found to be much improved as a repository of the principles and facts of the Latin language.—*Thomas A. Thacher, Professor of Latin in Yale College, New Haven.*

It is unnecessary to commend a Latin Grammar, which has been for twenty years in common use in our Colleges, and has generally superseded all others. The Revised Edition contains the results of the labors of Dr. Andrews, during all that time, on various Latin Classics, and on his great Latin Lexicon; and cannot, therefore, but be greatly improved.—*Edward Robinson, D. D., LL. D., Prof. of Biblical Literature in Union Theol. Seminary, New York City.*

I regard Andrews' and Stoddard's new Latin Grammar, as an exceedingly valuable work. It evidently contains the results of the Author's careful and long continued investigation, and from its fulness, clearness, and accuracy, will undoubtedly become the Standard Latin Grammar of this Continent. In Western New York, we have for a long time been using the earlier editions, and they have rapidly won upon the public regard. This new edition will give it a stronger claim upon our favor. It must rapidly supersede all others. I can unhesitatingly recommend the New Grammar as the best in use.—*Lewis H. Clark, Principal of Sodus Academy, Wayne Co., N. Y.*

I have looked over the new edition of the Grammar with great interest. It is now eighteen years since I introduced it into this college, and I have never felt inclined to change it for any other. The revision, without changing its general character, has added greatly to its fulness and completeness. It is now fully equal to Zumpt's in these respects, and far superior to it in adaptation to the class room. There is no *other* school grammar that can pretend to compare with it. I have introduced the new edition here and have no idea I shall ever wish to substitute another. The services of Prof. Andrews in the cause of classical learning in the United States cannot be over estimated.—*M. Sturgus, Professor in Hanover College, Indiana.*

I am willing to say that I am decidedly in favor of Andrews' Latin Series.—*Geo. Gan, Galesville University, Wisconsin.*

Andrews and Stoddard's Latin Grammar I consider decidedly the best Latin Grammar ever published.—*Ransom Norton, North Livermore, Maine.*

Such a work as Andrews and Stoddard's Revised Latin Grammar needs no recommendation, it speaks for itself.—*A. A. Keen, Professor of Greek and Latin, Tufts College, Medford, Ms.*

I have examined the revised edition of Andrews and Stoddard's Latin Grammar, and think it a complete success. I see it has all of Zumpt's merits and none of his defects, and welcome its advent with great pleasure.—*James M. Whiton, Hopkins Grammar School, New Haven, Conn.*

I have examined Andrews and Stoddard's Latin Grammar, and say, without hesitation, that the principles of the Latin language can be more easily and systematically acquired from it than any work I have ever seen. The arrangement and simplicity of its terms are such as to make it easily comprehended by the beginner, while, at the same time, its copiousness is sufficient for the most advanced student. The author has evidently noted and profited by the defects in this respect of most of the Latin Grammars now in use.—*C. W. Field, Mauch Chunk, Pa.*

The superior merits of the original work are too well known and appreciated to need any commendation from me. I have had some means of knowing how great pains and labor Dr. Andrews has bestowed upon this final revision and improvement of the work, and, therefore, was not unprepared to find its acknowledged excellence materially increased, and I do not hesitate to say, that its value has been greatly enhanced, and that it has been brought as near as practicable to the present state of philological science.—*John D. Philbrick, Superintendent of Public Schools, city of Boston.*

I have looked the Grammar through with much care and a great degree of satisfaction, and I unhesitatingly pronounce it superior to any Latin Grammar in method and manner of discussion, and happily adapted to the wants of both teachers and pupils.—*J. W. Simonds, Principal of New England Christian Institute, Andover, N. H.*

NEW SERIES OF LATIN SCHOOL BOOKS.

We have lately introduced the Revised Edition, and regard it as a great improvement upon former editions. We shall use it exclusively in future.—*E. Flint, Jr., Principal of Lee High School.*

After a due examination, I am happy to state that the Author has admirably accomplished the objects which he aimed at in making this last revision. He has added much that is in the highest degree valuable without materially changing the arrangement of the original work. The work appears to me well adapted to the daily use of our Classical Schools, and I shall hereafter direct my classes to use it.—*C. L. Cushman, Principal of Peabody High School, South Danvers, Ms.*

The Revised Grammar seems to me greatly improved and to be every thing a scholar could wish.—*Z. B. Sturgis, Charlestown, Indiana.*

I have subjected the Revised Edition to the test of actual use in the recitation room, and am persuaded that in its present form it decidedly surpasses every other Latin Grammar in point of adaptation to the wants of students in our Academies, High Schools and Colleges.—*William S. Palmer, Central High School, Cleveland, Ohio.*

I think Andrews' Series of Latin Works the most systematic and best arranged course I have ever seen,—and believe if our pupils would use them altogether, we should find them much better scholars. I shall use them wholly in my school.—*A. C. Stockin, Principal of Monmouth Academy, Maine.*

The examination of the Revised Edition has afforded me very great pleasure, and leads me to express the deep and sincere conviction that it is the most complete Grammar of the Latin language with which I am acquainted, and best adapted for ready consultation upon any subject connected with the study of Latin Authors. The paper, the typography, and the binding,—the whole style of publication—are such as to commend the good taste and judgment of the Publishers.—*J. R. Boyd, Principal of Maplewood Young Ladies Institute, Pittsfield, Mass.*

I find the Revised Edition to be just what is needed for a Latin Grammar,—clear, comprehensive, yet concise, in the subject matter. I shall introduce it as a permanent text-book.—*B. F. Dake, Principal of Clyde High School, Wayne Co., N. Y.*

I have carefully examined your Revised Edition throughout, particularly the Corrections and Additions. It now appears to me all that can be desired. It seems like parting with a familiar friend to lay aside the *old* edition, with its many excellencies, and adopt the *new*, but I shall cheerfully make the sacrifice for the greater benefit that will accrue to those commencing the study of Latin from time to time.—*J. H. Graham, Principal of Northfield Institution, Vermont.*

I thought before that the *old edition* was entitled to the appellation of "*The* Latin Grammar," but I perceive its value has been much increased by the numerous emendations and additions of Prof. Andrews. The Grammar is now fitted to be a complete hand-book for the Latin scholar during his whole course.—*E. W. Johnson, Canton Academy, Canton, N. Y.*

I unhesitatingly pronounce the Revised Edition of Andrews and Stoddard's Latin Grammar the best Grammar of the Latin Language, and shall certainly use my influence in its behalf.—*H. E. J. Clute, Edinboro', Pa.*

After a thorough examination, I have no hesitation in pronouncing it the best Latin Grammar for the purposes of the recitation room that I have ever examined. In its present form it ought certainly to displace a large majority of the Grammars in common use. Its rules of Syntax are expressed with accuracy and precision, and are in fact, what all rules ought to be, reliable guides to the learner.—*James W. Andrews, Principal of Hopewell Academy, Penn.*

Andrews and Stoddard's Latin Grammar, in the arrangement and adaptation to the learner, has excelled all others, and the revised edition is certainly a great improvement, and I do believe is better adapted to the wants of the student than any other. The whole seems to be critically revised and corrected. Prof. Andrews was truly the student's benefactor.—*M. L. Severance, North Troy, Vermont.*

It gives me great pleasure to bear my testimony to the superior merits of the Latin Grammar edited by Professor Andrews and Mr. Stoddard. I express most cheerfully, unhesitatingly, and decidedly, my preference of this Grammar to that of Adam, which has, for so long a time, kept almost undisputed sway in our schools.—*Dr. C. Beck, Cambridge.*

I know of no Grammar published in this country, which promises to answer so well the purposes of elementary classical instruction, and shall be glad to see it introduced into our best schools.—*Charles K. Dillaway, Boston.*

Your new Latin Grammar appears to me much better suited to the use of students than any other grammar I am acquainted with.—*Prof. Wm. M. Holland, Hartford, Ct.*

NEW SERIES OF LATIN SCHOOL BOOKS.

I have adopted the Latin Grammar of Andrews and Stoddard in the school under my charge, believing it better adapted, upon the whole, for elementary instruction than any similar work which I have examined. It combines the improvements of the recent German works on the subject with the best features of that old favorite of the schools, Dr. Adam's Latin Grammar.—*Henry Drisler, Professor of Latin in Columbia College.*

A careful review of the Revised Edition of Andrews and Stoddard's Latin Grammar, shows that this favorite text-book still continues to deserve the affections and confidence of Teachers and Pupils, incorporating as it does the results of Prof. Andrews' own constant study for many years with the investigations of English and German Philologists. No other Grammar is now so well fitted to meet the wants of the country as the rapid demand for it will show beyond doubt.—*A. S. Hartwell, University of St. Louis.*

This Grammar of the Latin Language, now universally pronounced *the very best*, is greatly improved by the corrections, revisions and additions of this revised edition. We do not believe a text-book was ever written which introduced so great an improvement in the method of teaching Latin, as this has done. We wish the revised edition the greatest success, which we are sure it merits.—*Rhode Island Schoolmaster.*

I have examined your revised edition with considerable care, and do not hesitate to pronounce it a great improvement upon the old editions, and as near perfection as we are likely to have. I have no doubt it will come into general use.—*A. Williams, Professor of Latin, Jefferson College, Canonsburg, Pa.*

I have been much interested in the Revised Edition. The improvement is very striking, and I shall no longer think of giving it up and putting Zumpt in its place. I am much pleased with the great improvement in the typography. You have given to our schools a book fifty per cent better in every respect, and I trust you will have your reward in largely increased sales.—*William J. Rolfe, Master of Oliver High School, Lawrence, Ms.*

I can with much pleasure say that your Grammar seems to me much better adapted to the present condition and wants of our schools than any one with which I am acquainted, and to supply that which has long been wanted—a good Latin Grammar for common use.—*F. Gardner, Principal of Boston Latin School.*

The Latin Grammar of Andrews and Stoddard is deserving, in my opinion, of the approbation which so many of our ablest teachers have bestowed upon it. It is believed that, of all the grammars before the public, this has greatly the advantage, in regard both to the excellence of its arrangement, and the accuracy and copiousness of its information.—*H. B. Hackett, Prof. of Biblical Literature in Newton Theological Seminary.*

The universal favor with which this Grammar is received was not unexpected. It will bear a thorough and discriminating examination. In the use of well-defined and expressive terms, especially in the syntax, we know of no Latin or Greek grammar which is to be compared to this.—*American Quarterly Register.*

These works will furnish a series of elementary publications for the study of Latin altogether in advance of any thing which has hitherto appeared, either in this country or in England.—*American Biblical Repository.*

I cheerfully and decidedly bear testimony to the superior excellence of Andrews and Stoddard's Latin Grammar to any manual of the kind with which I am acquainted. Every part bears the impress of a careful compiler. The *principles* of syntax are happily developed in the rules, whilst those relating to the moods and tenses supply an important deficiency in our former grammars. The rules of prosody are also clearly and fully exhibited.—*Rev. Lyman Coleman, Manchester, Vt.*

This work bears evident marks of great care and skill, and ripe and accurate scholarship in the authors. We cordially commend it to the student and teacher.—*Biblical Repository.*

Andrews and Stoddard's Latin Grammar is what I expected it would be—an excellent book. We cannot hesitate a moment in laying aside the books now in use, and introducing this.—*Rev. J. Penney, D. D., New York.*

Andrews and Stoddard's Latin Grammar bears throughout evidence of original and thorough investigation and sound criticism. It is, in my apprehension, so far as simplicity is concerned, on the one hand, and philosophical views and sound scholarship on the other, far preferable to other grammars; a work at the same time highly creditable to its authors and to our country.—*Professor A. Packard, Bowdoin College, Maine.*

I do not hesitate to pronounce Andrews and Stoddard's Latin Grammar superior to any other with which I am acquainted. I have never seen, any where, a greater amount of valuable matter compressed within limits equally narrow.—*Hon. John Hall, Principal of Ellington School, Conn.*

We have no hesitation in pronouncing this Grammar decidedly superior to any now in use.—*Boston Recorder.*

VALUABLE CLASSICAL WORKS.

Dr. Robinson's Gesenius.

Robinson's Hebrew Lexicon. Sixth Edition, Revised and Stereotyped. A Hebrew and English Lexicon of the Old Testament, including the Biblical Chaldee. Translated from the Latin of William Gesenius, late Professor of Theology in the University of Halle-Wittemberg. By EDWARD ROBINSON, D. D., LL. D., Professor of Biblical Literature in the Union Theological Seminary, New York. A new edition, with corrections and large additions, partly furnished by the author in manuscript, and partly condensed from his larger Thesaurus, as compiled by Roediger. These corrections and additions were made by Dr. Gesenius, during an interval of several years, while carrying his Thesaurus through the press, and were transcribed and furnished by him expressly for this edition. They will be found to be very numerous, every page having been materially corrected and enlarged, and a large number of articles having been re-written. It is printed on a new type, the face and cut of which is very beautiful, and has been highly commended and approved.

Dr. Robinson had already been trained to the business of lexicographical labor, when he began the translation of the present work. He is, in an uncommon degree, master of his own native tongue. He has diligence, patience, perseverance—yea, the iron diligence of Gesenius himself. For aught that I have yet been able to discover, all that can reasonably be expected or desired, has been done by the translator; not only as to rendering the work into English, but as to the manner and the accuracy of printing. The work will speak for itself, on the first opening. It does honor, in its appearance, to editor, printers, and publishers. I have only to add my hearty wish, that its beautiful white pages may be consulted and turned over, until they become thoroughly worn with the hands of the purchasers.—*Prof. Stuart, in the Biblical Repository.*

There is no lexicon in English that can be put on a level with Robinson's. I recommend the present as the best Lexicon of the Hebrew and Biblical Chaldee which an English scholar can have.—*Rev. Dr. Samuel Davidson, of London.*

Gesenius' Lexicon is known wherever Hebrew is studied. On the merits of this work criticism has long ago pronounced its verdict of approval.—*London Jewish Chronicle.*

This is a very beautiful and complete edition of the best Hebrew Lexicon ever yet produced. Gesenius, as a Hebrew philologist, is unequalled.—*London Clerical Journal.*

This is decidedly the most complete edition of Gesenius' Manual Hebrew Lexicon.—*London Journal of Sacred Literature.*

Robinson's Harmony of the Gospels, in Greek.

A Harmony of the Four Gospels, in Greek, according to the text of Hahn. Newly arranged, with Explanatory Notes, by EDWARD ROBINSON, D. D., LL. D., Professor of Biblical Literature in the Union Theological Seminary, New York. Revised Edition.

This work of Dr. Robinson confines itself to the legitimate sphere of a Harmony of the Gospels; and we do not hesitate to say that in this sphere it will be found to be all that a Harmony need or can be. The original text is printed with accuracy and elegance. It is a feast to the eyes to look upon a page of so much beauty. Its arrangement is distinguished for simplicity and convenience. No one will ever be able to comprehend the relations of the Gospels to each other, or acquire an exact knowledge of their contents, unless he studies them with the aid of a Harmony. The present work furnishes in this respect just the facility which is needed; and we trust that among its other effects, it will serve to direct attention more strongly to the importance of this mode of study.—*Prof. Hackett, of Newton Theological Seminary.*

Palmer's Arithmetic.

Arithmetic, Oral and Written, practically applied by means of Suggestive Questions. By THOMAS H. PALMER, Author of the Prize Essay on Education entitled the "Teacher's Manual," "The Moral Instructor," etc.

VALUABLE CLASSICAL WORKS.

Robinson's Harmony of the Gospels, in English.

A Harmony of the Four Gospels, in English, according to the common version; newly arranged, with Explanatory Notes. By EDWARD ROBINSON, D. D., LL. D.

The object of this work is to obtain a full and consecutive account of all the facts of our Lord's life and ministry. In order to do this, the four gospel narratives have been so brought together, as to present as nearly as possible the true chronological order, and where the same transaction is described by more than one writer, the different accounts are placed side by side, so as to fill out and supply each other. Such an arrangement affords the only full and perfect survey of all the testimony relating to any and every portion of our Lord's history. The evangelists are thus made their own best interpreters; and it is shown how wonderfully they are supplementary to each other in minute as well as in important particulars, and in this way is brought out fully and clearly the fundamental characteristics of their testimony, unity in diversity. To Bible classes, Sabbath schools, and all who love and seek the truth in their closets and in their families, this work will be found a useful assistant.

I have used "Robinson's English Harmony" in teaching a Bible Class. The result, in my own mind, is a conviction of the great merits of this work, and its adaptation to impart the highest life and interest to Bible Class exercises, and generally to the diligent study of the Gospel. It is much to be desired that every one accustomed to searching the Scriptures should have this invaluable aid.—*Rev. Dr. Skinner, New York.*

Robinson's Dictionary of the Bible.

Robinson's Bible Dictionary. A Dictionary for the use of Schools and Young Persons. By EDWARD ROBINSON, D. D., LL. D. Illustrated with Engravings on wood, and Maps of Canaan, Judea, Asia Minor, and the Peninsula of Mount Sinai, Idumea, etc.

Elements of Astronomy.

The Elements of Astronomy; or The World as it is and as it Appears. By the author of "Theory of Teaching," "Edward's First Lessons in Grammar," etc. Revised in manuscript by George P. Bond, Esq., of the Cambridge Observatory, to whom the author is also indebted for superintending its passage through the press.

Scott's Family Bible.

Scott's Family Bible. Boston Stereotype Edition. 6 vols. royal 8vo., containing all the Notes, Practical Observations, Marginal References, and Critical Remarks, as in the most approved London edition, with a line engraved likeness of the Author, Family Record, etc.

This Edition is the only one that has, or can have, the benefit of the final Additions and Emendations of the Author. The extent of these may be judged from the fact that upwards of *Four Hundred Pages of letter-press were added;* and as they consist chiefly of Critical Remarks, their importance to the Biblical student is at once apparent. The Preface to the entire work contains an elaborate and compendious view of the evidences that the Holy Scriptures were given by inspiration of God. Prefixed to each Book, both in the Old and New Testament, is an Introduction, or statement of its purport and intent. There are also copious Marginal References, with various Tables, a Theological Index, and a copious Topical Index.

☞ *Orders solicited.*

A

GRAMMAR

OF THE

LATIN LANGUAGE;

FOR THE

USE OF SCHOOLS AND COLLEGES.

BY

E. A. ANDREWS AND S. STODDARD.

ONE HUNDREDTH EDITION.

REVISED WITH CORRECTIONS AND ADDITIONS,
BY E. A. ANDREWS, LL. D.

BOSTON:
PUBLISHED BY CROCKER AND BREWSTER.
NEW YORK: A. S. BARNES & Co.
1868.

Entered according to Act of Congress, in the year 1857,
BY CROCKER AND BREWSTER,
In the Clerk's Office of the District Court of Massachusetts.

PREFACE.

As more than twenty years have elapsed, since the first publication of this Grammar, it can scarcely be necessary, in offering to the public a revised edition of the work, to make more than a passing allusion to its original plan or to the circumstances to which it owed its origin.

For some years previous to the date of its publication, the progress of classical learning in Europe, and particularly in Germany, had been such, as plainly to indicate the necessity of a corresponding advance in the manuals of Latin grammar employed in the schools of this country. Their deficiencies had indeed become so apparent, that various attempts had already been made to furnish a remedy by means of translations of German grammars; but none of these, however excellent in many respects, had seemed to be fully adapted to the purpose for which they were intended.

To unite the acknowledged excellencies of the older English manuals and of the more recent German grammars was the special aim of the authors of this work; and to this end their attention was directed, first to the preparation of more extended rules for the pronunciation of the language, secondly to a clearer exposition of its inflectional changes, thirdly to the proper basis of its syntax, and fourthly to greater precision in its rules and definitions.

The system of rules for the division and accentuation of Latin words, prepared in pursuance of the plan which has just been specified, was accordingly more copious than any previously found in the Latin grammars in common use in this country. For the purpose also of preventing the formation of erroneous habits of pronunciation in the early part of the student's course, the penultimate quantities of all Latin words occurring in the Grammar were carefully marked, unless determinable by some general rule, and the paradigms were divided and accented in such a manner as to indicate their true pronunciation.

In their treatment of Latin etymology, the authors aimed to render its study less a mere exercise of memory, and in a greater degree an efficient aid in the general cultivation of the mental powers. The principal means adopted for this purpose consisted in the practical distinction, every where made in treating inflected words, between the root, or ground-form, and the termination.

The third prominent peculiarity of the original work was its direct derivation of the rules of Syntax from the logical analysis of sentences, and its distinct specification of the particular use of each of the several words of which a sentence is composed. This method of treating syntax—a method previously unknown in the schools of this country—has, since that period, been extensively adopted, and in some instances greatly extended, particularly in a portion of the English grammars recently published in this country, and has probably contributed more to the advancement of grammatical science, than any other innovation of modern times.

The errors noticed in the original work have been corrected, as successive editions have issued from the press, but no opportunity has occurred, until the present, of thoroughly revising it in every part. Two years of continuous labor have now been devoted to its revision, and to the purpose of rendering it conformable in all respects to the advanced position which it originally aspired to occupy.

In all the modifications which have now been made, I have aimed to accomplish these two purposes—to preserve, as far as possible, the identity of the work, and at the same time to bring it as near, as should be practicable, to the present state of philological science. Hence, while I have made no changes either in language or arrangement, but such as appeared to me quite necessary, I have omitted none which logical accuracy or requisite fulness of explanation seemed to demand. In doing even this it soon became evident, that the changes and additions must be more numerous, than would well consist with the convenient use of the old and the new editions in the same classes. Though not insensible of the trouble occasioned to the teacher by alterations in a familiar text-book, I could not but suppose, that such modifications as the progress of the last twenty years had rendered necessary, would still be welcomed by him, notwithstanding the personal inconvenience arising from the disturbance of his previous associations. To his pupils, who will have known no other form of the Grammar, than that in which it now appears, the work, it is believed, will not only be as easy of comprehension in its new, as in its old form, but in its practical application far more satisfactory.

Of the minor changes and additions occurring on almost every page, and even of the occasional rearrangement of small portions of the materials, it is unnecessary to speak particularly. The student familiar with former editions will at once detect these slight modifications, and note them in his memory for future use; and though he may fail to find a rule, exception, or remark on the page where he has been wont to see it, he will still meet with it in the same relative position,—in the same section and subdivision of the section in which it formerly appeared.

In the department of Orthoëpy will now be found some account of the Continental mode of pronouncing Latin; and, by means of the joint exhibition of this and of the English methods, the student will be able to use the Grammar with equal facility, whether choosing to adhere to the usual pronunciation of English and American scholars, or preferring that of the continental schools.

In the Etymology of nouns, no other alteration need be specified, except the introduction, in the third declension, of "Rules for forming the nominative singular from the root." These are copied, in a modified form, from the editor's First Latin Book. In themselves they are of considerable utility in showing the mutual relations between the sounds of certain letters, and they are also closely connected with corresponding changes in some of the verbal roots. In the Etymology of adjectives, besides the minor modifications already alluded to, a few changes in arrangement have been made in those sections which relate to Comparison. To pronouns have been added some remarks on Pronominal Adjectives, which seemed to require a more particular notice, than they had heretofore received, both in their relation to each other and to the Adverbial Correlatives. The Etymology of particles has been treated somewhat more fully than in former editions—a fulness especially observable in relation to adverbs and conjunctions, and which was rendered necessary by the more extended treatment of those particles in the revised Syntax.

In almost every section of the Syntax the student will meet with modifications and especially with additions, which, as in other parts of the work, are introduced in such a manner as seldom to interfere with the references made to former editions in the series based upon this Grammar. The principal exception to the latter remark is to be found in sections 247—251, which relate to certain uses of the ablative.

A comparison of the Prosody in the present and former editions will show, that it has been revised with minute care in every part. Similar attention has also been given to the Appendix, in which will be found some additions relating to Roman Money, Weights and Measures. For the greater convenience of he student the Index in this edition has been much enlarged.

In conclusion, I would briefly indicate the principal sources from which have been derived the various additions and corrections, to which allusion has been made. In preparing the original work, the earlier editions of Zumpt's Grammar were consulted at almost every step, and while frequent use was made of the grammars of Scheller, Grant, Adam, Ruddiman, Hickie and others, the treatises of Zumpt were even then regarded as the most valuable embodiment of the principles of Latin philology. It was therefore natural and almost unavoidable, in revising a work which had in so many points received both its form and its substance from the earlier labors of that distinguished grammarian, to look to his maturer works for many of the materials by means of which our original sketch should be made more complete. Accordingly I have constantly consulted the last edition c his Grammar, translated by Dr. Schmitz, and have freely incorporated in this edition such of its materials, as were suited to my purpose. In most cases his ideas have been either expressed in my own language, or in language so modified as to suit the general plan of my work. In the Etymology, and not unfrequently in the Syntax also, the copious Grammar of Ramshorn has furnished valuable materials; and the Grammars of Key and of Kühner, the latter translated by Prof. Champlin, have been consulted with profit and satisfaction. In the sections comprising conjunctions, and especially in those relating to grammatical analysis, I am happy to acknowledge my indebtedness to Prof. S. S. Greene of Brown University. To the sources already specified I must add the Latin Lexicon of Dr. Freund, in editing a translation of which I had frequent occasion to note such matters as promised to be of utility in the revision of this Grammar. The additions in the Appendix relating to Roman money, etc., are taken principally from Dr. Riddle's translation of Dr. Freund's School Dictionary. To these references I will only add, that such other notes relating to Latin philology, as I have made during the past twenty years, so far as they were adapted to my purpose, have either been used in my former occasional corrections, or are incorporated in the present edition.

In taking a final leave of the earliest of the elementary Latin works with which my name has been associated, and with which, in my own mind, must ever be connected the pleasant memory of my early friend and associate, Prof. Stoddard, I trust I shall be pardoned in commending it once more to the kind indulgence of the teachers of this country, and in expressing the hope that, in its present form, it will be deemed not altogether unworthy of a continuance of the favor which it has so long received. I cannot indeed venture to indulge the hope, that all the imperfections of the work have even now been removed, or that, in my attempts to render it more perfect, I may not sometimes have fallen into new errors; but this I can truly say that since its first publication I have devoted much time to its revision, and have sought to manifest my sense of the kindness with which it has been received, by doing all in my power to render it less unworthy of public favor.

E. A. ANDREWS.

New Britain, Conn., Oct., 1857.

CONTENTS.

ORTHOGRAPHY.

	Page
Letters	9
Division of letters	10
Diphthongs	10
Punctuation	10

ORTHOËPY.

	Page
Continental pronunciation	11
English pronunciation	11
Sounds of the letters	11
—— of the vowels	11
—— of the diphthongs	12
—— of the consonants	13
Quantity of syllables	14
Accentuation	15
Latin accents	15
English accents	16
Division of words into syllables	16

ETYMOLOGY.

	Page
NOUNS	19
Gender	20
Number	22
Cases	23
Declensions	23
First declension	25
Greek nouns	26
Second declension	26
Greek nouns	29
Third declension	29
Formation of nom. sing.	30
Rules for the gender	33
—— oblique cases	36
Greek nouns	45
Fourth declension	45
Fifth declension	47
Declension of compound nouns	47
Irregular nouns	48
Variable nouns	48
Defective nouns	49
Redundant nouns	54
Derivation of nouns	56
Composition of nouns	60
ADJECTIVES	61
Adjectives of the first and second declensions	62
Adjectives of the third declension	64
Rules for the oblique cases	67
Irregular adjectives	69
Defective adjectives	69
Redundant adjectives	69
Numeral adjectives	70
Comparison of adjectives	74
Irregular comparison	75
Defective comparison	76
Derivation of adjectives	78
Composition of adjectives	81
PRONOUNS	82
Substantive pronouns	82
Adjective pronouns	83
Demonstrative pronouns	83
Intensive pronouns	85
Relative pronouns	86
Interrogative pronouns	87
Indefinite pronouns	88
Possessive pronouns	89
Patrial pronouns	90
Pronominal adjectives	90
VERBS	91
Voices	91
Moods	92
Tenses	93
Numbers	95
Persons	95
Participles, gerunds, and supines	95
Conjugation	96
Table of terminations	98
Sum	100
Prosum, Possum, etc.	102
First conjugation	103
Second conjugation	108
Third conjugation	111
Fourth conjugation	116
Deponent verbs	120
Remarks on the conjugations	121
Periphrastic conjugations	123
General rules of conjugation	124
Formation of second and third roots	125
First conjugation	125
Second conjugation	129
Third conjugation	131
Fourth conjugation	139
Irregular verbs	140
Defective verbs	145
Impersonal verbs	147

CONTENTS.

	Page
Redundant verbs	150
Derivation of verbs	152
Composition of verbs	154
Particles	155
ADVERBS	155
Derivation of adverbs	160
Composition of adverbs	162
Comparison of adverbs	163
PREPOSITIONS	163
Prepositions in composition	167
CONJUNCTIONS	170
INTERJECTIONS	176

SYNTAX.

Sentences and Propositions	177
Subject	178
Predicate	181
Apposition	183
Adjectives	184
Relatives	189
Demonstratives, etc.	193
Reflexives	198
Nominative	200
Subject-nominative and verb	200
Predicate-nominative	205
Genitive	206
Genitive after nouns	206
———— after partitives	211
———— after adjectives	214
———— after verbs	216
———— of place	221
———— after particles	222
Dative	222
Dative after adjectives	222
———— after verbs	225
———— after particles	230
Accusative	231
Accusative after verbs	231
———— after prepositions	237
———— of time and space	239
———— of place	240
———— after adjectives, adverbs and interjections	241
Subject-accusative	242
Vocative	243
Ablative	243
Ablative after prepositions	243
———— after certain nouns, adjectives and verbs	244
———— of cause, etc.	246
———— of price	252
———— of time	252
———— of place	254
———— after comparatives	255
———— absolute	258
Connection of tenses	261
Indicative mood	263
Subjunctive mood	265

	Page
Protasis and apodosis	268
Subjunctive after particles	269
———— after *qui*	275
———— in indirect questions	278
———— in inserted clauses	279
Imperative mood	281
Infinitive mood	282
Participles	292
Gerunds and gerundives	296
Supines	299
Adverbs	300
Prepositions	303
Conjunctions	304
Interjections	306
Arrangement	306
Arrangement of words	306
———— of clauses	310
Analysis	312
Parsing	313

PROSODY.

Quantity	319
General rules	319
Special rules	322
First and middle syllables	322
Derivative words	322
Compound words	324
Increment of nouns	325
Increment of verbs	329
Penults and antepenults	331
Final syllables	336
Versification	341
Feet	341
Metre	342
Verses	342
Figures of prosody	343
Arsis and thesis	346
Cæsura	347
Different kinds of metre	347
Dactylic metre	347
Anapæstic metre	350
Iambic metre	351
Trochaic metre	353
Choriambic metre	354
Ionic metre	355
Compound metres	356
Combination of verses	356
Horatian metres	357
Key to the odes of Horace	359

APPENDIX.

Grammatical figures	361
Tropes and figures of rhetoric	363
Roman mode of reckoning time	367
———— money, weight, etc.	370
Abbreviations	374
Different ages of Roman literature	374
Writers of the different ages	375
INDEX	378

LATIN GRAMMAR.

§ 1. The Latin language is the language spoken by the ancient Romans. Latin Grammar teaches the principles of the Latin language. These relate,
1. To its written characters;
2. To its pronunciation;
3. To the classification and derivation of its words;
4. To the construction of its sentences;
5. To the quantity of its syllables, and its versification.

The first part is called Orthography; the second, Orthoëpy; the third, Etymology; the fourth, Syntax; and the fifth, Prosody.

ORTHOGRAPHY.

§ 2. Orthography treats of the letters, and other characters of written language, and the proper mode of spelling words.

1. The Latin alphabet consists of twenty-five letters. They have the same names as the corresponding characters in English. They are A, a; B, b; C, c; D, d; E, e; F, f; G, g; H, h; I, i; J, j; K, k; L, l; M, m; N, n; O, o; P, p; Q, q; R, r; S, s; T, t; U, u; V, v; X, x; Y, y; Z, z.
2. The Romans used only the capital letters.
3. *I* and *j* were anciently but one character, as were likewise *u* and *v*.
4. *W* is not found in Latin words, and *k* occurs only at the beginning of a few words before *a*, and even in these *c* is commonly used, except in their abbreviated form; as, *K* or *Kal.* for *Kalendæ* or *Calendæ,* the Calends.
5. *Y* and *z* are found only in words derived from the Greek.
6. *H*, though called a letter, only denotes a breathing, or aspiration.

DIVISION OF LETTERS.

§ 3. Letters are divided into *vowels* and *consonants*.

1. The vowels are .... *a, e, i, o, u, y.*

The consonants are divided into
- Liquids, ... *l, m, n, r.*
- Mutes,
  - Labials, ... *p, b, f, v.*
  - Palatals, ... *c, g, k, q, j.*
  - Linguals, ... *t, d.*
- Sibilant, ... *s.*
- Double consonants, ... *x, z.*
- Aspirate, ... *h.*

2. *X* is equivalent to *cs* or *gs; z* to *ts* or *ds;* and, except in compound words, the double consonant is always written, instead of the letters which it represents. In some Greek words *x* is equivalent to *chs*.

DIPHTHONGS.

§ 4. Two vowels, in immediate succession, in the same syllable, are called a *diphthong*.

The diphthongs are *ae, ai, au, ei, eu, oe, oi, ua, ue, ui, uo, uu,* and *yi. Ae* and *oe* are frequently written together, *œ, æ.*

PUNCTUATION.

§ 5. The only mark of punctuation used by the ancients was a point, which denoted pauses of different length, according as it was placed at the top, the middle, or the bottom of the line. The moderns use the same marks of punctuation, in writing and printing Latin, as in their own languages, and assign to them the same power.

Marks of *quantity* and of *accent* are sometimes found in Latin authors, especially in elementary works:—

1. There are three marks of quantity, viz. ˘, ¯, ⁎; the first denotes that the vowel over which it stands is short; the second, that it is long; the third, that it is doubtful, that is, sometimes long and sometimes short.

2. There are also three written accents—the acute (´), the grave (`), and the circumflex (^). These were used by the old grammarians to denote the rising and sinking of the voice in the Roman mode of pronouncing words. (See §§ 14 and 15.) In modern elementary Latin works, the acute marks the emphatic syllable of a word, (§ 16); the grave distinguishes certain particles from other words spelled in the same manner; as, *quòd*, because; *quod*, which; and the circumflex is placed over certain penultimate and final syllables that are formed by contraction.

The diæresis (¨) denotes that the vowel over which it stands does not form a diphthong with the preceding vowel; as, *aër*, the air. It is used principally with *ae, ai,* and *oe.*

ORTHOËPY.

§ 6. Orthoëpy treats of the right pronunciation of words.

The ancient pronunciation of the Latin language being in a great measure lost, the learned, in modern times, have applied to it those principles which regulate the pronunciation of their own languages; and hence has arisen, in different countries, a great diversity of practice.

The various systems now prevalent in Europe, may, however, be reduced to two—the *Continental* and the *English*—the former prevailing, with only slight diversities, in most of the countries of continental Europe, and the latter in England. Their principal difference is found in the pronunciation of the vowels and diphthongs, since, in both methods, the consonants are pronounced in nearly the same manner.

THE CONTINENTAL METHOD.

[According to this system, each of the vowels, when standing at the end of a syllable, is considered as having but one sound, which, however, may be either short or long. Thus,

Short ă, as in hat.	Long ō, as in no.
Long ā, as in father.	Short ŭ, as in tub.
Short ĕ, as in met.	Long ū, as in full.
Long ē, as in there.	æ or œ, as *e* in there.
Short ĭ, as in sit.	au, as *ou* in our.
Long ī, as in machine.	eu, as in feudal.
Short ŏ, as in not.	ei, as *i* in ice.

REMARK. These sounds are sometimes slightly modified when followed by a consonant in the same syllable.]

THE ENGLISH METHOD.

In the following rules for dividing and pronouncing Latin words, regard has been had both to English analogy and to the laws of Latin accentuation. See § 14 and 15. The basis of this system is that which is exhibited by Walker in his "Pronunciation of Greek and Latin Proper Names." To pronounce correctly, according to this method, a knowledge of the following particulars is requisite:—

1. Of the *sounds* of the letters in all their combinations.
2. Of the *quantities* of the penultimate and final syllables.
3. Of the place of the *accent*, both primary and secondary.
4. Of the mode of dividing words into *syllables*.

OF THE SOUNDS OF THE LETTERS.

I. OF THE VOWELS.

§ 7. A vowel, when ending an accented syllable, has always its long English sound; as,

pa'-ter, de'-dit, vi'-vus, to'-tus, tu'-ba, Ty'-rus; in which the accented vowels are pronounced as in *fatal, metre, vital, total, tutor, tyrant*.

1. *A*, at the end of an unaccented syllable, has nearly the sound of *a* in *father* or in *ah*, but less distinct or prolonged; as, *mu'-sa, e-pis'-tŏ-la, a-cer'-bus, Pal-a-mē'-des;* pronounced *mu'-zah*, etc.

2. *E*, *o*, and *u*, at the end of an unaccented syllable, have nearly the same sound as when accented, but shorter and less distinct; as, *re'-te, vo'-lo, u'-su-i.*

3. (*a*.) *I* final has always its long sound; as, *qui, au'-di, le-gā'-ti.*

Rem. 1. The final *i* of *tibi* and *sibi* has its short sound.

(*b*.) *I*, at the end of an unaccented syllable not final, has an indistinct sound like short *e*; as, *Fa'-bi-us* (fă'-be-us), *phi-los'-ŏ-phus* (phelos'-o-phus).

Exc. *I* has its long sound in the first syllable of a word the second of which is accented, when it either stands alone before a consonant, as in *i-dŏ'-ne-us*, or ends a syllable before a vowel, as in *fi-ē'-bam.*

Rem. 2. *Y* is always pronounced like *i* in the same situation.

§ 8. A vowel has always its *short* English sound, when followed by a consonant in the same syllable; as,

mag'-nus, reg'-num, fin'-go, hoc, fus'-tis, cyg'nus, in which the vowels are pronounced as in *magnet, seldom, finish, copy, lustre, symbol.*

EXCEPTION 1. *A*, when it follows *qu* before *dr* and *rt*, has the sounds of *a* in *quadrant* and in *quart;* as, *qua'-dro, quad-ra-gin'-ta, quar'-tus*. In other connections *a* before *r* has the sound of *a* in *part;* as, *par-tĭ-ceps, ar'-ma;* except when followed by another *r*, as in *par-ri-cĭ'-da.*

Exc. 2. *Es*, at the end of a word, is pronounced like the English word *ease;* as, *ig'-nes, au'-des.*

Exc. 3. *Os*, at the end of plural cases, is pronounced like *ose* in *dose;* as, *nos, il'-los, dom'-ĭ-nos.*

Exc. 4. *Post* is pronounced like the same word in English; so also are its compounds; as, *post'-quam, post'-e-a;* but not its derivatives; as, *pos-trē'-mus.*

Exc. 5. *E, i* and *y* before final *r*, or before *r* in a syllable not final, when followed in the next syllable by any other consonant, except *r*, have the sound of *e* and *i* in the English words *her* and *fir;* as, *fer, feri, fer'-tĭ-lis; hir, hir'-cus, myr'-tus.*

II. OF THE DIPHTHONGS.

§ 9. *Ae* and *oe* are always diphthongs unless separated by diæresis. They are pronounced as *e* would be in the same situation; as, *œ'-tas, œs'-tas, pœ'-na, œs'-trum.*

1. *Ai, ei, oi*, and *yi*, usually have the vowels pronounced separately. When they are accented, and followed by another vowel, the *i* is pronounced like initial *y*, and the vowel before it has its long sound; as, *Maia, Pompeius, Troia, Harpyia;* pronounced *Ma'-ya, Pom-pe'-yus, Tro'-ya, Har-py'-ya.*

§ 10, 11. SOUNDS OF THE CONSONANTS. 13

REMARK 1. *Ei*, when a diphthong and not followed by another vowel, is pronounced like *i*; as in *hei, om'-neis*.

2. *Au*, when a diphthong, is pronounced like *aw*; as, *laus, au'-rum*, pronounced *laws*, etc.

REM. 2. In the termination of Greek proper names, the letters *au* are pronounced separately; as, *Men-e-lā-us*.

3. *Eu*, when a diphthong, is pronounced like long *u*; as, *heu, Orpheus* (or'-phuse), *Eu-phrā-tes*.

REM. 3. The letters *eu* are pronounced separately in the terminations *eus* and *eum* of *Latin* nouns, and of all adjectives, whether Greek or Latin, except *neuter*; as, *ur'-ce-us, me'-us, me'-um, e'-um*. In other situations they form a diphthong; as, *Eu-rŏ'-pa, Thē'-seus, e'-heu*.

4. *Ua, ue, ui, uo, uu*, when diphthongs, are pronounced like *wa, we*, etc.; as, *lin'-gua, quĕ'-ror, sua'-de-o, quŏ'-tus, ĕ'-quus*. They are always diphthongs after *q*, usually also after *g*, and often after *s*.

5. *Ui* in *cui* and *huic*, when monosyllables, is pronounced like *wi*, and by some like long *i*.

III. OF THE CONSONANTS.

§ **10.** The consonants have, in general, the same power in Latin as in English words.

The following cases, however, require particular attention.

C.

C has the sound of *s* before *e, i*, and *y*, and the diphthongs *æ, œ*, and *eu*; as, *ce'-do, ci'-bus, Cæ'-sar, cœ'-lum, ceu, Cy'-rus*. In other situations, it has the sound of *k*; as, *Ca'-to, cru'-dus, lac*.

1. *Ch* has always the sound of *k*; as, *charta* (kar'-tah), *machĭna* (mak'-ĕ-nah).

EXC. *C*, following or ending an accented syllable, before *i* followed by a vowel, and also before *eu* and *yo*, has the sound of *sh*; as, *socia* (so'-she-ah), *caduceus* (ca-du'she-us), *Sicyon* (sish'-e-on).

REMARK. In the pronunciation of the ancient Romans, the hard sound of *c* and *g* seems to have been retained in all their combinations.

G.

G has its soft sound, like *j*, before *e, i*, and *y*, and the diphthongs *æ* and *œ*; as *ge'-nus, ag'-i-lis, Gy'-ges, Gœ-tū'-li*. In other situations, it has its hard sound, as in *bag, go*.

EXC. When *g* comes before *g* soft, it coalesces with it in sound; as, *agger* (aj'-er), *exaggeratio* (ex-aj-e-ra'-she-o).

S.

§ **11.** *S* has generally its hissing sound, as in *so, thus*.

EXC. 1. (*a*.) When *si* followed by a vowel is immediately preceded by a consonant in an accented syllable, the *s* has the sound of *sh*; as, *Per'-si-a* (per'-she-a).

(*b.*) But when *si* or *zi* followed by a vowel is immediately preceded by an accented vowel, the *s* or *z* has the sound of *zh*; as, *As-pa'-si-a* (as-pa'-zhe-ah), *Su-ba'-zi-a* (su-ba'-zhe-ah).

NOTE. In a few proper names, *s* preceded by a vowel in an accented syllable and followed by *i* before another vowel, has the sound, not of *zh*, but of *sh*; as, *A'-si-a* (a'-she-a): so *Sosia*, *Theodosia*, *Lysias*.

EXC. 2. *S*, at the end of a word, after *e*, *œ*, *au*, *b*, *m*, *n*, and *r*, has the sound of *z*; as, *res*, *œs*, *laus*, *trabs*, *hi"-ems*, *lens*, *Mars*.

English analogy has also occasioned the *s* in *Cœ'-sar*, *cœ-sŭ'-ra*, *mi'-ser*, *mu'-sa*, *re-sid'-u-um*, *cau'-sa*, *ro'-sa*, and their derivatives, and in some other words, to take the sound of *z*. *Cœs-a-re'-a*, and the oblique cases of *Cæsar*, retain the hissing sound; so likewise the compounds of *trans*; as, *trans'-e-o*.

T.

§ **12.** 1. *T*, following or ending an accented syllable before *i* followed by a vowel, has the sound of *sh*; as, *ratio* (ra'-she-o), *Sulpitius* (sul-pish'-e-us).

EXC. *T*, in such case, retains its hard sound (*a*) after *s*, *t*, or *x*; as, *Sal-lus'-ti-us*, *Brut'-ti-i*, *Sex'-ti-us*: (*b*) in proper names in *tion* and *tyon*; as, *Eu-ryt'-i-on*, *Am-phic'-ty-on*; and (*c*) in old infinitives in *er*; as, *flec'-ti-er*, for *flec'-ti*.

X.

2. *X*, at the beginning of a syllable, has the sound of *z*; at the end, that of *ks*; as, *Xenŏphon* (zen'-o-phon); *axis* (ak'-sis).

EXC. 1. When *ex* or *ux* is followed by a vowel in an accented syllable, *x* has the sound of *gz*; as, *exemplum* (eg-zem'-plum), *ux-o'-ri-us* (ug-zo'-re-us), *inexhaustus* (in-eg-zaus'-tus).

EXC. 2. *X*, ending an accented syllable before *i* followed by a vowel, and before *u* ending a syllable, has the power of *ksh*; as, *noxius* (nok'-she-us), *pexui* (pek'-shu-i).

REMARK. *Ch* and *ph*, before *th*, in the beginning of a word, are silent; as, *Chthonia* (tho'-ni-a), *Phthia* (thi'-a). Also in the following combinations of consonants, in the beginning of words of Greek origin, the first letter is not sounded:—*mne-mon'-i-ca*, *gna'-vus*, *tmc'-sis*, *Cte'-si-as*, *Ptol-e-mœ'-us*, *psal'-lo*.

OF THE QUANTITIES OF THE PENULTIMATE AND FINAL SYLLABLES.

§ **13.** 1. The *quantity* of a syllable is the relative time occupied in pronouncing it.

2. A *short* syllable requires, in pronunciation, half the time of a *long* one.

REM. The *penultimate* syllable, or *penult*, is the last syllable but one. The *antepenult* is the last syllable but two.

The quantity of a syllable is generally to be learned from the rules of prosody, §§ 282—801; but for the convenience of the student, the following general rules are here inserted:—

3. A vowel before another vowel or *h* is short.

4. Diphthongs, not beginning with *u*, are long.

§ 14, 15. ACCENTUATION. 15

5. A vowel before *x, z, j,* or any two consonants, except a mute followed by a liquid, is long by *position,* as it is called.

6. A vowel naturally short before a mute followed by a liquid is common, *i. e.* either long or short.

In this Grammar, when the quantity of a penult is determined by one of the preceding rules, it is not marked; in other cases, except in dissyllables, the proper mark is written over its vowel.

To pronounce Latin words correctly, it is necessary to ascertain the quantities of their last two syllables only; and the rules for the quantities of final syllables would, for this purpose, be unnecessary, but for the occasional addition of enclitics. As these are generally monosyllables, and, for the purpose of accentuation, are considered as parts of the words to which they are annexed, they cause the final syllable of the original word to become the penult of the compound. But as the enclitics begin with a consonant, the final vowels of all words ending with a consonant, if previously short, are, by the addition of an enclitic, made long by position. It is necessary, therefore, to learn the quantities of those final syllables *only* which end with a *vowel.*

OF ACCENTUATION.

I. OF LATIN ACCENTS.

§ 14. 1. Accent, in Latin, signifies the rising and falling of the voice in pronouncing the syllables of a Latin word. It is a general rule of the Latin language, that every word has its accent. The enclitics, however, have no accent of their own, but they modify the accent of the words to which they are annexed, and prepositions lose their accent, when they precede the cases which they govern.

2. The Latin language has three accents, the acute (′), or rising tone, the grave (`), or falling tone, and the circumflex (ˆ), composed of the acute and the grave, i. e. of the rising and the falling tone.

3. A monosyllable, when short by nature, takes the acute, when long by nature, the circumflex accent; as, *pix, et, pars; dôs, jûs, spês.*

4. In words of two syllables, the penult is always accented; as, *pă′-ter, mā′-ter, pen′-na.*

REM. 1. Words of two syllables have the circumflex accent, when the vowel of the penult is naturally long and that of the last syllable short; as, *Rō-mă, mū-să, lū-cĕ, jū-ris;* if otherwise, they have the acute; as, *hŏ′-mŏ, dĕ′-ăs, Rō′-mă* (abl.), and *ar′-tĕ,* in which *a* is long only by position.

5. In words of more than two syllables, if the *penult* is *long,* it is accented; but if it is *short,* the accent is on the *antepenult;* as, *a-mī′-cus, dom′-ĭ-nus.*

REM. 2. When the accent of a word of more than two syllables falls upon the penult, it may be either the circumflex or the acute according as the last syllable is short or long. The antepenult can take no accent except the acute, and in no case can the accent be drawn farther back than to the antepenult.

EXC. Vocatives of the second declension in *i,* instead of *ie,* from nominatives in *ius,* and genitives in *i,* instead of *ii,* are accented as they would be, if the rejected letters were annexed, i. e. with the acute upon the penult, even when it is short; as, *Vir-gil′-i; Va-lē′-ri, in-gĕ′-ni.* So, also, the compounds of *facio* with words which are not prepositions; as, *cal-e-fă′-cit, tep-e-fă′-cit.*

§ 15. If the penult is *common,* the accent, in prose, is upon the *antepenult;* as, *vol′-ŭ-cris, phar′-ĕ-tra, ib′-ĭ-que:* but genitives in *ius,* in which *i* is common, accent their *penult* in prose; as *u-nī′-us, is-tī′-us.*

REM. 3. All the syllables of a Latin word, except that on which the acute or circumflex accent falls, are supposed to have the grave accent, and were pronounced with the lower tone.

1. The rules for the *accentuation* of compound and simple words are the same; as, *se'-cum, sub'-e-o.*
2. In accentuation, the enclitics *que, ne, ve,* and also those which are annexed to pronouns,* are accounted constituent parts of the words to which they are subjoined; as, *ĭ'-ta, ĭt'-ă-que; vĭ'-rum, vi-rum'-que.*

II. OF ENGLISH ACCENTS.

§ 16. Accent, in English, is a particular stress of voice upon certain syllables of words. Cf. § 5, 2.

According to the English method of pronouncing Latin, a word may have two, three, or even four accents. That accent which is nearest to the termination of the word, and which always corresponds in position with the Latin accent, is called the *primary* or *principal* accent, and the *secondary* accent is that which next precedes the primary. The *third* and *fourth* accents, in like manner, precede the secondary, and are subject in all respects to the same rules; as, *pă'-ter, mā'-ter, ser-mŏ'-nes, dom'-ĭ-nis; pe-rĭc'-ŭ-lum, con''-ju-ra'-ti-o, op'''-por-tu''-ni-tā'-tes, ex-er''''-ci-ta'''-ti-on''-i-bus'-que.*

1. If only two syllables precede the primary accent, the secondary accent is on the first; as, *mod''-e-rā'-tus, tol''-e-rab'-ĭ-lis.*
2. If three or four syllables stand before the primary accent, the secondary accent is placed, sometimes on the first, and sometimes on the second syllable; as, *de-mon''-stra-ban'-tur, ad''-o-les-cen'-ti-a.*
3. Some words which have only four syllables before the primary accent, and all which have more than four, have *three* accents; as, *mod'''-e-ra''-ti-ō'-nis, tol'''-e-ra-bil''-i-ō'-rem, ex-er'''-ci-ta''-ti-ō'-nis.*

DIVISION OF WORDS INTO SYLLABLES.

VOWELS.

§ 17. Every Latin word is to be divided into as many syllables, as it has separate vowels and diphthongs.

REMARK. In the following rules, the term *vowel* includes not only single vowels, but diphthongs; and when a particular vowel is mentioned, a diphthong, also, ending with that vowel is intended.

CONSONANTS.

SPECIAL RULES.

§ 18. REMARK. The following special rules, relating to particular letters or to particular combinations of letters, are in all cases to be regarded rather than the general rules, §§ 19—23, when the latter are inconsistent with the former.

1. *H,* when standing alone between two vowels, is always joined to the vowel that follows it.

Thus, *mi'-hi, tra'-hĕ-re, co'-hors, co''-hor-ta'-ti-o.*

---

* These are *te, met, pte, ce, cine,* and *dem;* as, *tute, egŏmet, meapte, hicce, hiccine, idem*

2. *Ch*, *ph*, and *th*, in the division of words into syllables, are considered, not as separate letters, but as single aspirated mutes, and hence are never separated.

Thus, *A-chil'-les, Ach"-ra-dī'-na, Neph'-ē-le, Tē'-thys.*

3. *Gl*, *tl*, and *thl*, when standing alone between any two vowels, unless the first be *u*, and *bl* after *u* are always separated.

Thus, *Æg'-le, Ag-lau'-rus, At'-las, ath-let'-i-cus;—Pub'-li-us, Pub-lic'-ŏ-la, res-pub'-li-ca.*

4. In writing syllables, *x*, when standing alone between two vowels, is united to the vowel before it, but, in pronouncing such syllables, its elementary sounds are separated.

Thus, *sax'-um* (snk'-sum); *ax-il'-la* (ak-sil'-lah); *ex-em'-plum* (eg-zem'-plum); *ux-o'-ri-us* (ug-zo'-re-us).

GENERAL RULES.

I. SIMPLE WORDS.

§ 19. A.—*A single Consonant between two Vowels.*

1. A single consonant, or a mute with *l* or *r*, between the *last two vowels* of a word, or between the vowels of any two *unaccented* syllables, must be joined to the latter vowel.

Thus, *t* in *pă'-ter* and *au'-tem; th* in *œ'-ther; cl* in *Hi-er'-ŏ-cles; q* in *ā'-qua; cr* in *ā'-cris* and *vol'-ŭ-cris; chr* in *a'-chras; r* in *tol"-e-ra-bil'-i-us; m* in *et"-y-mo-lŏ'-gi-a; l* in *am"-bu-lā-tŏ'-ri-us;* and *gr* in *per"-e-gri-na'-ti-o*. Respecting *ch* and *th* cf. § 18, 2.

Exc. *Tib'-i* and *sib'-i* are commonly excepted.

§ **20**. 2. A single consonant, or a mute with *l* or *r*, *before* the vowel of an accented syllable, must be joined to the accented vowel.

Thus, *t* in *i-tin'-ĕ-ra; d* in *vi-dē'-to; th* in *œ-the'-ri-us; cl* in *Eu-cli'-des* and *Her"-a-clē'-a; gr* in *a-gres'-tis* and *a-gric'-ŏ-la; pr* in *ca-prē'-ŏ-ius; q* in *a-quā'-ri-us;* and *phr* in *Eu-phrā'tes.*

§ **21**. 3. A single consonant *after* the vowel of any accented syllable, except a penult, must be joined to the accented vowel.

Thus, *m* in *dom'-i-nus* and *dom"-i-na'-ti-o; t* in *pat'-ĕ-ra; th* in *Scyth'-i-a;* and *q* in *aq'-ui-la* (ak'-we-lah), and *Aq"-ui-ta'-ni-a* (ak"-we-ta'-ne-ah).

4. When a mute with *l* or *r* follows the vowel of any accented syllable, except the penult, the mute is to be joined to the accented vowel.

Thus, *cr* in *ac'-ri-ter, ac"-ri-mo'-ni-a; tr* in *det"-ri-men'-tum; pr* in *cap'-ri-pes, cap"-ri-mul'-gus, phl* in *Paph"-la-go'-ni-a;* and *phr* in *Aph"-ro-dis'-i-a.* Respecting *phl* and *phr* cf. § 18, 2.

EXCEPTIONS TO THE 3D AND 4TH RULES.

Exc. 1. A single consonant, or a mute with *l* or *r*, after an accented *a*, *e*, or *o*, and before two vowels the first of which is *e*, *i*, or *y*, must be joined to the syllable following the accent.

Thus, *d* in *ra'-di-us, tæ'-di-um, me"-di-ā'-tor;* r in *hæ'-re-o, (n"-ry-ā'-tes*, ch in *bra'-chi-um;* q in *re'-qui-es, re"-qui-es'-co;* tr in *pa'-tri-us, Œ-nō'-tri-a,* and r and *l* in *ce"-re-ā'-li-a.*

Exc. 2. A single consonant or a mute with *l* or *r*, after an accented *u*, must be joined to the vowel following it.

Thus, r in *lu'-ri-dus, au'-re-us;* cr in *Eu'-cri-tus;* gl in *ju'-glans;* and *pl* in *Nau'-pli-us, du'-pli-co,* and *du"-pli-ca'-ti-o.* Cf. § 18, 3.

§ **22.** B.—*Two Consonants between two Vowels.*

Any two consonants, except a mute followed by *l* or *r* in the cases before mentioned, when standing between two vowels, must be separated.

Thus, rp in *cor'-pus,* rm in *for'-ma* and *ger-mā'nus;* rv in *ca-ter'-va;* sc in *ad-o-les'-cens;* nn in *an'-nus;* phth in *aph'-tha;* cch in *Bac'-chus* and *Bac"-cha-nā'-li-a;* and thl in *ath-lĕ'-ta.*

C.—*Three or four Consonants between two Vowels.*

1. When three consonants stand between any two vowels, the last, or, if that be *l* or *r* after a mute, the two last, are joined to the latter vowel.

Thus, mpt in *emp'-tor,* ad-emp'-ti-o; str in *fe-nes'-tra;* mpl in *ex-em'-plum;* rthr in *ar-thri'-tis.*

2. When four consonants stand between two vowels, two are joined to each vowel; as, nstr in *trans-trum.*

II. COMPOUND WORDS.

§ **23.** 1. In dividing a compound word into syllables the component parts are to be separated, if the former part ends with a consonant; as, *ab-es'-se, in'-ers, cir'-cum-er'-ro, su'-pĕr-est, sub'-ĭ-tus, præ-ter'-e-a, trans'-ĭ-tur, sub'-stru-o.* So, also, if a consonant is inserted to prevent hiatus, it is joined to the preceding vowel; as, *prod'-e-o, red'-e-o, sed-it'-i-o.*

2. But if the former part either ends with a vowel, or has dropped its termination, it is to be divided like a simple word; as, *def'-ĕ-ro, dil'-ĭ-gens, be-nev'-o-lus, præs'-to, eg'-ŏ-met;—po'-tes, po-tes'-tis, an"ĭ-mad-ver'-to, ve'-ne-o* (from *venum, eo*), *mag-nan'-ĭ-m s, am-bā'-ges, lon-gæ'-vus.*

ETYMOLOGY.

§ **24.** 1. Etymology treats of the different classes of words, their derivation, and their various inflections.

2. The classes, into which words are divided in reference to their signification are called *Parts of Speech.*

3. The parts of speech in Latin are eight—*Substantive* or *Noun*, *Adjective*, *Pronoun*, *Verb*, *Adverb*, *Preposition*, *Conjunction*, and *Interjection*.

4. The first four are *inflected*; the last four, which are sometimes called *Particles*, are *not inflected*, except that some adverbs change their termination to express comparison.

REM. Substantives, pronouns, and adjectives are often included by grammarians under the general term *nouns*; but, in this Grammar, the word *noun* is used as synonymous with *substantive* only.

§ **25.** 1. To verbs belong *Participles*, *Gerunds*, and *Supines*, which partake of the meaning of the verb, and the inflection of the noun.

2. *Inflection*, in Latin grammar, signifies a change in the termination of a word. It is of three kinds—*declension*, *conjugation*, and *comparison*.

3. Nouns, adjectives, pronouns, participles, gerunds, and supines, are *declined*; verbs are *conjugated*, and adjectives and adverbs are *compared*.

NOUNS.

§ **26.** 1. A substantive or noun is the *name* of an object.

2. A *proper* noun is the name of an individual object; as, *Cæsar*; *Rōma*, Rome; *Tibĕris*, the Tiber.

3. A *common* or *appellative* noun is the name of a class of objects, to each of which it is alike applicable; as, *hŏmo*, man or a man; *avis*, a bird; *quercus*, an oak; *leo*, a lion; *mendacium*, a falsehood.

4. A *collective* noun is one which, in the singular number, denotes a collection of individuals; as, *exercĭtus*, an army.

REM. 1. The following are examples of nouns used as collectives, viz. *exercĭtus*, *gens*, *juventus*, *multitūdo*, *nobilĭtas*, *plebs*, *popŭlus*, *turba*, *vis*, and *vulgus*.

5. An *abstract* noun is the name of a quality, action, or other attribute; as, *bonĭtas*, goodness; *gaudium*, joy; *festinatio*, haste.

REM. 2. A *concrete*, in distinction from an abstract noun, is one which denotes an object that has an actual and independent existence; as, *Rōma*, *hŏmo*, *popŭlus*, *ferrum*.

6. A *material* noun is the name of a substance considered in the gross; as, *lignum*, wood; *ferrum*, iron; *cĭbus*, food.

REM. 3. Proper, abstract, and material nouns become common, when employed to denote one or more of a class of objects. A verb in the infinitive mood is often used as an abstract noun.

7. To nouns belong *gender*, *number*, and *case*.

REM. 4. Adjectives and participles have likewise different genders, numbers, and cases, corresponding to those of nouns.

GENDER.

§ 27. 1. The gender of a noun is its distinction in regard to sex.

2. Nouns have three genders—the *masculine*, the *feminine*, and the *neuter*.

3. The gender of Latin nouns is either *natural* or *grammatical*.

4. Those nouns are naturally masculine or feminine, which are used to designate the sexes; as, *vir*, a man; *mulier*, a woman.

5. Those are grammatically masculine or feminine, which, though denoting objects that are neither male nor female, take adjectives of the form appropriated to nouns denoting the sexes.

Thus, *domĭnus*, a lord, is naturally masculine, because it denotes a male; but *sermo*, speech, is grammatically masculine, because, though not indicative of sex, it takes an adjective of that form which is appropriated to nouns denoting males.

6. The grammatical gender of Latin nouns depends either on their signification, or on their declension and termination. The following are the general rules of gender, in reference to *signification*. Many exceptions to them, on account of *termination*, occur: these will be specified under the several declensions.

§ 28. MASCULINES. 1. Names, proper and appellative, of all male beings are masculine; as, *Homērus*, Homer; *păter*, a father; *consul*, a consul; *ĕquus*, a horse.

As proper names usually follow the gender of the general name under which they are comprehended; hence,

2. Names of rivers, winds, and months, are masculine, because *fluvius*, *ventus*, and *mensis*, are masculine; as, *Tibĕris*, the Tiber; *Aquĭlo*, the north wind; *Aprīlis*, April.

Exc. *Styx* and some names of rivers in *a* and *e* are feminine. §§ 62, and 41, 1.

3. Names of mountains are sometimes masculine, because *mons* is masculine; as, *Othrys*, a mountain of Thessaly; but they usually follow the gender of their termination; as, *hic** Atlas, haec Ida, hoc Soracte*.

§ 29. FEMININES. 1. Names, proper and appellative, of all female beings are feminine; as, *Helĕna*, Helen; *māter*, a mother; *juvenca*, a heifer.

2. Names of countries, towns, trees, plants, ships, islands, poems, and gems, are feminine; because *terra*, *urbs*, *arbor*, *planta*, *nāvis*, *insŭla*, *fabŭla*, and *gemma*, are feminine; as,

Ægyptus, Egypt; *Corinthus*, Corinth; *pirus*, a pear-tree; *nardus*, spikenard; *Centaurus*, the ship Centaur; *Sămos*, the name of an island; *Eunŭchus*, the Eunuch, a comedy of Terence; *amethystus*, an amethyst.

Exc. Names of countries and islands in *um*, *i*, and (plur.) *a*, *ōrum*, are neuter.—Names of towns in *i*, *ōrum*; four in *o*, *ōnis*, viz. *Trusino*, *Hippo*, *Narbo*, and *Sulmo*, with *Tunes*, *Taras*, and *Canōpus*, are masculine. Names of towns in *um* or *on*, *i*, and (plur.) *a*, *ōrum*; those in *e* and *ur* of the third declension, indeclinable nouns in *i* and *y*, and some barbarous names, as *Suthul*, *Hispal* and *Gadir* are neuter.—Names of trees and plants in *er* of the third declension, (§ 60), with *baccar* and *rōbur* are neuter. A few names in *us*, *i*, (§ 50), with *oleaster*, *pinaster*, *Styrax* and *unĕdo* are masculine.—A few names of gems in *us*, *i*, are also masculine.

---

* To distinguish the gender of Latin nouns, grammarians write *hic* before the masculine, *haec* before the feminine, and *hoc* before the neuter.

§ 30–32.   COMMON AND DOUBTFUL GENDER.   21

§ 30. COMMON AND DOUBTFUL GENDER. Some words are either masculine or feminine. These, if they denote things animate, are said to be of the *common* gender; if things inanimate, of the *doubtful* gender.

Of the former are *părens*, a parent; *bos*, an ox or cow: of the latter, *finis*, an end.

The following nouns are of the common gender:—

Adolescens, *a youth.*	Exsul, *an exile.*	Palumbes, *a wood-pigeon.*
Affīnis, *a relative by marriage.*	Grus, *a crane.*	Părens, *a parent.*
	Hospes, *a guest, a host.*	Par, *a mate.*
Ales, *a bird.*	Hostis, *an enemy.*	Præses, *a president.*
Antistes, *a chief priest.*	Index, *an informer.*	Præsul, *a chief priest.*
Auctor, *an author.*	Infans, *an infant.*	Princeps, *a prince or princess.*
Augur, *an augur.*	Interpres, *an interpreter.*	
Bos, *an ox or cow.*	Jūdex, *a judge.*	Serpens, *a serpent.*
Cănis, *a dog.*	Juvĕnis, *a youth.*	Sacerdos, *a priest or priestess.*
Cīvis, *a citizen.*	Martyr, *a martyr.*	
Cōmes, *a companion.*	Mīles, *a soldier.*	Satelles, *a life-guard.*
Conjux, *a spouse.*	Municeps, *a burgess.*	Sus, *a swine.*
Consors, *a consort.*	Mus, *a mouse.*	Testis, *a witness.*
Convīva, *a guest.*	Nēmo, *nobody.*	Vātes, *a prophet.*
Custos, *a keeper.*	Obses, *a hostage.*	Verna, *a slave.*
Dux, *a leader.*	Patruēlis, *a cousin.*	Vindex, *an avenger.*

The following hexameters contain nearly all the above nouns:—

Conjux, *atque* părens, princeps, pătruēlis, *et* infans,
Affīnis, vindex, jūdex, dux, mīlēs, *et* hostis,
Augŭr, *et* antistes, juvĕnis, convīva, săcerdōs,
Mūnĭ-*que*-ceps, vātēs, adolescens, cīvis, *et* auctor,
Custōs, nēmo, cōmes, testis, sus, bōs-*que*, cănis-*que*,
Pro consorte tŏrī par, præsul, verna, sătelles,
Mus-*que* obses, consors, interprĕs, *et* exsŭl, *et* hospes.

§ 31. 1. When nouns of the common gender denote males, they take a masculine adjective; when they denote females, a feminine.

2. The following are either masculine or feminine in sense, but masculine only in grammatical construction:—

Artĭfex, *an artist.*	Fur, *a thief.*	Lătro, *a robber.*
Auspex, *a soothsayer.*	Hēres, *an heir.*	Libĕri, *children.*
Eques, *a horseman.*	Hŏmo, *a man or woman.*	Pĕdes, *a footman.*

To these may be added personal appellatives of the first declension; as, *advĕna*, a stranger; and some gentile nouns; as, *Persa*, a Persian.

§ 32. 1. The following, though masculine or feminine in sense, are feminine only in construction:—

Copiæ, *troops.*	Opĕræ, *laborers.*	Vigĭlæ, *watchmen.*
Custodiæ, *guards.*	Prōles, \} *offspring.*	
Excubiæ, *sentinels.*	Subŏles,	

2. Some nouns, signifying persons, are neuter, both in their termination and construction; as,

Acroāma, *a buffoon.* Mancipium, } *a slave.* Scortum, } *a prostitute.*
Auxilia, *auxiliaries.* Servitium, Prostibŭlum,

3. (*a.*) In some personal appellatives masculines and feminines are distinguished by different terminations affixed to the same root. The masculines end in *us, er, o, tor,* etc.; the feminines in *a* or *trix*, as, *cŏquus, cŏqua; magister, magistra; lēno, lēna; inventor, inventrix; tibīcen, tibicīna; ăvus, avia; rex, regīna; poëta, poëtria.*

(*b.*) So also in some names of animals; as, *ĕquus, ĕqua; gallus, gallīna; leo, lea* and *leaena.* Sometimes the words are wholly different; as, *taurus, vacca.*

4. Some names of animals are sometimes masculine and sometimes feminine without regard to difference of sex; as, *anguis, serpens, dāma, talpa, tigris, colŭber* and *colŭbra,* etc.

§ **33.** EPICENES. Names of animals which include both sexes, but admit of an adjective of one gender only, are called *epicene.* These commonly follow the gender of their terminations.

Thus, *passer,* a sparrow, *corvus,* a raven, are masculine; *aquila,* an eagle, *vulpes,* a fox, are feminine; though each of them is used to denote both sexes.

NOTE. This class includes the names of animals, in which the distinction of sex is seldom attended to. When it is necessary to mark the sex, *mas* or *femina* is usually added.

§ **34.** NEUTERS. Nouns which are neither masculine nor feminine, are said to be of the neuter gender; such are,

1. All indeclinable nouns; as, *fas, nĕfas, nihil, gummi, pondo.*

2. Names of letters; as, *o longum,* long *o.* But these are sometimes feminine, *litĕra* being understood.

3. Words used merely as such, without reference to their meaning: as, *pater est dissyllăbum; pater* is dissyllabic.

4. All infinitives, imperatives, clauses of sentences, adverbs, and other particles, used substantively; as *scire tuum,* your knowledge; *ultĭmum vale,* the last farewell; *hoc diu,* this (word) *diu.*

REMARK. 1. Words derived from the Greek retain the gender which they have in that language.

REM. 2. Some nouns have different genders in the singular and plural, and are called *heterogeneous* nouns. See § 92.

NUMBER.

§ **35.** 1. (*a.*) Number, in nouns, is the form by which they denote whether they represent one object or more than one.

(*b.*) Latin nouns have two numbers,—the *singular* and the *plural,* —which are distinguished by their terminations. The singular number denotes one object; the plural, more than one.

PERSON.

2. The person of a noun or pronoun is the character sustained by the object which it represents, as being the speaker, the person addressed, or the person or thing spoken of.

Hence there are three persons. The speaker is of the *first* person, the person addressed is of the *second* person, and the person or thing spoken of is of the *third* person.

CASES.

§ 36. Many of the relations of objects, which, in English, are denoted by prepositions, are, in Latin, expressed by a change of termination.

Cases are those terminations of nouns, which denote their relations to other words. Latin nouns have six cases; viz. *Nominative, Genitive, Dative, Accusative, Vocative,* and *Ablative.*

REMARK. Though there are six cases in each number, no noun has in each number so many different terminations.

§ 37. 1. The nominative denotes the relation of a *subject* to a finite verb; as, ego *scribo, I* write. Caius *dicit, Caius* says.

2. The genitive denotes *origin, possession,* and many other relations, which, in English, are expressed by the preposition *of* or by the *possessive* case; as, *Vita Cæsăris,* the life *of Cæsar,* or *Cæsar's* life.

3. The dative denotes that *to* or *for* which any thing is, or is done; as, *Ille* mihi *librum dedit,* He gave the book *to me.*

4. The accusative is either the *object* of an active verb, or of certain prepositions, or the *subject* of an infinitive.

5. The vocative is the form appropriated to the name of any object which is addressed.

6. The ablative denotes *privation,* and many other relations, especially those expressed in English by the prepositions *with, from, in,* or *by.*

REMARK. The nominative and vocative are sometimes called *casus recti,* i. e. the uninflected cases; and the others, *casus obliqui;* i. e. the oblique or inflected cases.

DECLENSIONS.

§ 38. The regular forming of the several cases in both numbers, by annexing the appropriate terminations to the root, is called *declension.*

The Latin language has five declensions or modes of declining nouns, distinguished by the termination of the genitive singular, which, in the first declension, ends in *æ,* in the second in *i,* in the third in *is,* in the fourth in *ūs,* and in the fifth in *ei*

§ 39. The following table exhibits a comparative view of the terminations or case-endings of the five declensions.

TERMINATIONS.

Singular.

	I.	II. M.	II. N.	III. M.	III. N.	IV. M.	IV. N.	V
Nom.	ă,	ŭs, ĕr,	ŭm,	ŏr, etc. ĕ, etc.		ŭs,	ū,	ēs,
Gen.	æ,	ī,		ĭs,		ūs,	ū,	eï,
Dat.	æ,	ō,		ī,		uī,	ū,	eï,
Acc.	ăm	ŭm,		ĕm,(ĭm), ĕ, etc.		ŭm,	ū,	ĕm,
Voc.	ă,	ĕ, ĕr,	ŭm,	ŏr, etc. ĕ, etc.		ŭs,	ū,	ēs,
Abl.	ā.	ō.		ĕ, (ī.)		ū.		ē.

Plural.

	I.	II. M.	II. N.	III. M.	III. N.	IV. M.	IV. N.	V
Nom.	æ,	ī,	ă,	ēs,	ă, (iă),	ūs,	uă,	ēs,
Gen.	ārŭm,	ōrŭm,		ŭm, (iŭm),		uŭm,		ērŭm,
Dat.	īs,	īs,		ĭbŭs,		ĭbŭs, (ŭbŭs),		ēbŭs,
Acc.	ās,	ōs,	ă,	ēs,	ă, (iă),	ūs,	uă,	ēs,
Voc.	æ,	ī,	ă,	ēs,	ă, (iă),	ūs,	uă,	ēs,
Abl.	īs.	īs.		ĭbŭs.		ĭbŭs, (ŭbŭs).		ēbŭs.

Remarks.

§ 40. 1. The terminations of the nominative, in the third declension, are very numerous. See §§ 55, 58, 62, 66.

2. The accusative singular of masculines and feminines, always ends in *m*.

3. The vocative singular is like the nominative in all Latin nouns, except those in *us* of the second declension.

4. The nominative and vocative plural always end alike.

5. The genitive plural always ends in *um*.

6. The dative and ablative plural always end alike;—in the 1st and 2d declensions, in *is*; in the 3d, 4th, and 5th, in *bus*.

7. The accusative plural of masculines and feminines, always ends in *s*.

8. Nouns of the neuter gender have the accusative and vocative like the nominative, in both numbers; and these cases, in the plural, always end in *a*.

9. The 1st and 5th declensions contain no nouns of the neuter gender, and the 4th and 5th contain no proper names.

10. Every inflected word consists of two parts—a *root*, and a *termination*. The root or *crude form*, is the part which is not changed by inflection. The termination is the part annexed to the root. The root of a *declined* word may be found by removing the termination of any of its oblique cases. The case commonly selected for this purpose is the genitive singular.

11. The preceding table exhibits terminations only. In the fifth declension, the *e* of the final syllable, though unchanged, is considered as belonging to the termination.

FIRST DECLENSION.

§ 41. Nouns of the first declension end in *ă, ē, ās, ēs*. Those in *a* and *e* are feminine; those in *as* and *es* are masculine.

Latin nouns of the first declension end only in *a*. They are thus declined:—

	Singular.			Plural.	
Nom.	mū'-să,	a muse;	Nom.	mu'-sæ,	muses;
Gen.	mu'-sæ,	of a muse;	Gen.	mu-sā'-rŭm,	of muses,
Dat.	mu'-sæ,	to a muse:	Dat.	mu'-sis,	to muses
Acc.	mu'-săm,	a muse;	Acc.	mu'-sās,	muses
Voc.	mu'-să,	O muse;	Voc.	mu'-sæ,	O muses,
Abl.	mu'-să,	with a muse.	Abl.	mu'-sis,	with muses.

In like manner decline

Au'-la, *a hall.*   Lit'-ĕ-ra, *a letter.*   Sa-git'-ta, *an arrow.*
Cu'-ra, *care.*   Lus-cin'-i-a, *a nightingale.*   Stel'-la, *a star.*
Ga'-le-a, *a helmet.*   Mach'-ĭ-na, *a machine.*   Tŏ'-ga, *a gown.*
In'-sŭ-la, *an island.*   Pen'-na, *a feather, a quill.*   Vi'-a, *a way.*

NOTE. As the Latin language has no article, appellative nouns may be rendered either with or without the English articles *a, an,* or *the,* according to their connection.

EXCEPTIONS IN GENDER.

§ 42. 1. Names proper and appellative of men, as, *Sulla, Cinna; poëta,* a poet; *nauta,* a sailor; and names of rivers, though ending in *a,* are masculine: § 28, 1 and 2. But the following names of rivers have been used as feminine: viz. *Albŭla, Allia, Druentia, Garumna, Himĕra, Matrŏna, Mosella, Trebia. Lēthe* is always feminine.

Ossa and *Œta,* names of mountains, are masculine or feminine.

2. *Hadria,* the Adriatic sea, *dāma* in Virgil and Statius, and *talpa* in Virgil, are masculine.

EXCEPTIONS IN DECLENSION.

§ 43. *Genitive singular.* 1. The poets sometimes formed the genitive singular in *āī;* as, *aula,* gen. *aulāī*.

2. *Familia,* after *păter, māter, filius,* or *filia,* usually forms its genitive in *as;* as, *mater-familias,* the mistress of a family; gen. *matris-familias;* nom. plur. *matres-familias* or *familiārum.* Some other words anciently formed their genitive in the same manner.

Genitive plural. The genitive plural of patronymics in *es,* of several compounds in *cŏla* and *gĕna,* and of some names of nations, is sometimes, especially in poetry, formed in *um* instead of *ārum;* as, *Æneădum, Cælicŏlum, terrigĕnum, Lapĭthum.* So *amphŏrum, drachmum,* for *amphorārum, drachmārum.*

Dative and Ablative plural. The following nouns have sometimes *ābus* instead of *is,* in the dative and ablative plural, especially when it is necessary to distinguish them from the same cases of masculines in *us* of the second declension having the same root; as, *filiis et filiābus,* to sons and daughters.

Dea, *a goddess.* Equa, *a mare.*
Filia, *a daughter.* Mula, *a she mule.*

The use of a similar termination in *anĭma, asĭna, libertă, nătă, conserva,* and some other words, rests on inferior authority.

GREEK NOUNS.

§ 44. Nouns of the first declension in *ē, ās,* and *ēs,* and some also in *ă,* are Greek. Greek nouns in *ă* are declined like *musa,* except that they sometimes have *ān* in the accusative singular; as, *Ossa;* acc. *Ossam,* or *Ossan.*

Greek nouns in *e, as,* and *es,* are thus declined in the singular number:—

N. Pe-nel′-ŏ-pē,	*N.* Æ-nē′-ās,	*N.* An-chī′-sēs,
G. Pe-nel′-ŏ-pēs,	*G.* Æ-nē′-æ,	*G.* An-chī′-sæ,
D. Pe-nel′-ŏ-pæ,	*D.* Æ-nē′-æ,	*D.* An-chī′-sæ,
Ac. Pe-nel′-ŏ-pēn,	*Ac.* Æ-nē′-ăm *or* ān,	*Ac.* An-chī′-sēn,
V. Pe-nel′-ŏ-pē,	*V.* Æ-nē′-ă,	*V.* An-chī′-sē *or* ā,
Ab. Pe-nel′-ŏ-pē.	*Ab.* Æ-nē′-ă.	*Ab.* An-chī′-sā *or* ē.

§ 45. In like manner decline

Al′-o-e, *aloes.* Ti-ă′-ras, *a turban.*
E-pit′-ŏ-me, *an abridgment.* Co-mē′-tes, *a comet.*
This′-be. Dy-nas′-tes, *a ruler.*
Bo′-rĕ-as, *the north wind.* Pri-am′-ĭ-des, *a son of Priam.*
Mi′-das. Py-rī′-tes, *a kind of stone.*

1. Most proper names in *es,* except patronymics, follow the third declension; but in the accusative they often have both *em* and *en,* and in the vocative both *es* and *e.* See §§ 80, IV, and 81.

2. Greek nouns of the first declension, which admit of a plural, are declined in that number like the plural of *musa.*

3. The Latins frequently change the terminations of Greek nouns in *ēs* and *ē* into *ā;* as, *Atrides, Atrida,* a son of Atreus; *Perses, Persa,* a Persian; *geomĕtres, geomĕtra,* a geometrician; *Circe, Circa; epitŏme, epitŏma; grammatĭce, grammatĭca,* grammar; *rhetorĭce, rhetorĭca,* oratory.—So also *tiăras, tiăra.*

SECOND DECLENSION.

§ 46. Nouns of the second declension end in *ĕr, ĭr, ŭs, ŭm, os, on.* Those ending in *um* and *on* are neuter; the rest are masculine.

Nouns in *er, us,* and *um,* are thus declined:—

SINGULAR.

	A lord.	*A son-in-law.*	*A field.*	*A kingdom.*
N.	dŏm′-ĭ-nŭs,	gĕ′-nĕr,	ă′-gĕr,	reg′-nŭm,
G.	dom′-ĭ-nī,	gen′-ĕ-rī,	a′-grī,	reg′-nī,
D.	dom′-ĭ-nō,	gen′-ĕ-rō,	a′-grō,	reg′-nō,
Ac.	dom′-ĭ-nŭm,	gen′-ĕ-rŭm,	a′-grŭm,	reg′-nŭm,
V.	dom′-ĭ-nĕ,	ge′-nĕr,	a′-gĕr,	reg′-nŭm,
Ab.	dom′-ĭ-nō.	gen′-ĕrō.	a′-grō.	reg′-nō.

§ 47-49.   SECOND DECLENSION.—EXCEPTIONS.   27

PLURAL.

N.	dom'-ĭ-nī,	ger'-ĕ-rī,	a'-grī,	reg'-nă,
G.	dom-i-nō'-rŭm,	gen-e-rō'-rŭm,	a-grō'-rŭm,	reg'-nō'-rŭm,
D.	dom'-ĭ-nīs,	gen'-ĕ-rīs,	a'-grīs,	reg'-nīs,
Ac.	dom'-ĭ-nŏs,	gen'-ĕ-rōs,	a'-grōs,	reg'-nă,
V.	dom'-ĭ-nī,	gen'-ĕ-rī,	a'-grī,	reg'-nă,
Ab.	dom'-ĭ-nīs.	gen'-ĕ-rīs.	a'-grīs.	reg'-nīs.

Like *dominus* decline

An'-ĭ-mus, *the mind.*   Fŏ'-cus, *a hearth.*   Nu'-mĕ-rus, *a number.*
Clĭp'-e-us, *a shield.*   Gla'-di-us, *a sword.*   O-ce'-ă-nus, *the ocean.*
Cor'-vus, *a raven.*   Lū'-cus, *a grove.*   Trŏ'-chus, *a trundling-hoop.*

NOTE. Nouns in *us* of the second declension are the only Latin nouns, whose nominative and vocative singular differ in form. See § 40, R. 3.

§ **47.** A few nouns in *er*, like *gener*, add the terminations to the nominative singular, as a root. They are the compounds of *gĕro* and *fĕro;* as, *armĭger, -ĕri,* an armor-bearer;. *Lucĭfer, -ĕri,* the morning star; and the following:—

A-dul'-ter, *an adulterer.*   Lī'-ber, *Bacchus.*   Pu'-er, *a boy.*
Cel'-tĭ-bĕr, *a Celtiberian.*   Lĭb'-ĕ-ri, (*plur.*), *children.*   Sŏ'-cer, *a father-in-law.*
I'-ber, *a Spaniard.*   Pres'-bў-ter, *an elder.*   Ves'-per, *the evening.*

Mul'-cĭ-ber, Vulcan, sometimes has this form.

§ **48.** 1. All other nouns in *er* reject the *e* in adding the terminations, (§ 322, 4), and are declined like *ager;* thus,

A'-per, *a wild boar.*   Lĭ'-ber, *a book.*   Al-ex-an'-der.
Aus'-ter, *the south wind.*   Ma-gis'-ter, *a master.*   Is'-ter.
Fă'-ber, *a workman.*   On'-ă-ger, *a wild ass.*   Teu'-cer.

2. *Vir,* a man, with its compounds, and the patrial *Trēvir,* (the only nouns in *ir,*) are declined like *gener.*

Like *regnum* decline

An'-trum, *a cave.*   Ex-em'-plum, *an example.*   Præ-sid'-i-um, *a defence*
A'-tri-um, *a hall.*   Ne-go'-ti-um,* *a business.*   Sax'-um, *a rock.*
Bel'-lum, *war.*   Ni'-trum, *natron.*   Scep'-trum, *a sceptre.*

EXCEPTIONS IN GENDER.

§ **49.** 1. The following nouns in *us* and *os* are feminine:—

Abyssus, *a bottomless pit.*   Dialectos, *a dialect.*   Miltos, *vermilion.*
Alvus, *the belly.*   Diphthongus, *a diphthong.*   Phărus(os), *a light-house.*
Antidŏtus, *an antidote.*   Dŏmus, *a house, home.*   Plinthus, *the base of a column.*
Arctos(us), *the Northern Bear.*   Erēmus, *a desert.*
Carbăsus, *a sail.*   Hūmus, *the ground.*   Vannus, *a corn-fan.*

2. Greek nouns in *ŏdus* (ἡ ὁδός), and *metros,* are likewise feminine; as, *synŏdus,* an assembly; *diametros,* a diameter.

---

* Pronounced ne-go'-she-um. See § 12.

SECOND DECLENSION.—EXCEPTIONS. § 50–53.

§ 50. Names of countries, towns, trees, plants, etc. are feminine. See § 29, 2.

Yet the following names of plants are masculine:—

Acanthus, *bear's-foot.*
Amarantus, *amaranth.*
Asparagus, *asparagus.*
Calamus, *a reed.*
Carduus, *a thistle.*
Dumus, *a bramble.*

Ebulus, *an elder.*
Helleborus, *hellebore.*
Intubus, *endive.*
Juncus, *a bulrush.*
Raphanus, *a radish.*
Rhamnos, *buck-thorn.*

Rubus, *a blackberry-bush.*
Tribulus, *a caltrops.*

And sometimes
Amaracus, *marjoram.*
Cytisus, *snail-clover.*

Oleaster and pinaster, names of trees, are also masculine.

The following names of gems are also masculine:—

Beryllus, *a beryl.*
Carbunculus, *a carbuncle.*

Chrysoprasus, *chrysoprase.*
Opalus, *opal.*

So also,
Pyropus, *gold-bronze.*

Chrysolithus, *chrysolite*, and smaragdus, *an emerald*, are doubtful.
Names of females in *um* are feminine; § 29, 1; as, *mea Glycerium*, Ter.
Names of trees and plants in *um* are generally neuter; as, *apium*, parsley; *aconitum*, wolf's bane.
Canopus, Pontus, Hellespontus, Isthmus, and all plural names in *i* of countries and towns are masculine. *Abydus(os)* is doubtful.
Names of countries and towns ending in *um*, or, if plural, in *a*, are neuter; as, *Ilium* or *Ilion; Ecbatana, ōrum.*

§ 51. The following are doubtful, but more frequently masculine:—

Balanus, *a date.*
Barbitos, *a lute.*

Grossus, *an unripe fig.*
Pampinus, *a vine-leaf.*

Phaselus, *a light vessel.*

Atomus, an atom, and colus, a distaff, are doubtful, but more frequently feminine.

Pelagus, the sea, and virus, poison, are neuter.
Vulgus, the common people, is neuter, and rarely masculine.

EXCEPTIONS IN DECLENSION.

§ 52. *Genitive singular.* When the genitive singular ends in *ii*, the poets frequently contract it into *i*; as, *ingeni*, for *ingenii*.

Vocative singular. The vocative of nouns in *us* is sometimes like the nominative, especially in poetry; as, *fluvius, Latinus*, in Virgil. So, *audi tu, populus Albānus.* Liv.

Proper names in *ius* omit *e* in the vocative; as, *Horatius, Horāti; Virgilius, Virgili.*

Filius, a son, and *genius*, a guardian angel, make also *fili* and *geni*. Other nouns in *ius*, including patrials and possessives derived from proper names, form their vocative regularly in *e*; as, *Delius, Delie; Tirynthius, Tirynthie; Laertius, Laertie.*

§ 53. *Genitive plural.* The genitive plural of some nouns of the second declension, especially of those which denote money, weight and measure, is commonly formed in *um*, instead of *ōrum*: § 322, 4.

Such are particularly *nummum, sestertium, denarium, medimnum, jugerum, modium, talentum.* The same form occurs in other words, especially in poetry; as, *deum, liberum, Danaum;* etc., and sometimes *om* is found instead of *un*; as, *Achivum.* Virg. Cf. § 322, 8.

Deüs, *a god*, is thus declined:—

Singular.		Plural.	
N.	de'-us,	N.	di'-i, di, *or* de'-i,
G.	de'-i,	G.	de-ō'-rum,
D.	de'-o,	D.	di'-is, dis, *or* de'-is,
Ac.	de'-um,	Ac.	de'-os,
V.	de'-us,	V.	di'-i, di, *or* de'-i,
Ab.	de'-o.	Ab.	di'-is, dis, *or* de'-is.

Jĕsus, or Iĕsus, the name of the Savior, has *um* in the accusative, and *u* in all the other oblique cases.

GREEK NOUNS.

§ 54. 1. *Os* and *on*, in the second declension, are Greek terminations, and are commonly changed, in Latin, into *us* and *um*; but sometimes both forms are in use; as, *Alphēos*, and *Alphēus*; *Ilion* and *Ilium*. Greek names in *ros* after a consonant commonly change *ros* into *er*; as, *Alexandros, Alexander; Teucros, Teucer.* In a few words *ros* is changed to *rus*; as, *Codrus, hydrus,* and once in Virgil, *Teucrus.*

Greek nouns are thus declined in the singular number:—

	Singular.		Barbiton, *a lyre.*	
N.	Dē'-lŏs,	Andrŏ'-ge-ōs,	N.	bar'-bĭ-tŏn,
G.	De'-li,	An-dro'-ge-ō, *or* I,	G.	bar'-bĭ-tĭ,
D.	De'-lō,	An-dro'-ge-ō,	D.	bar'-bĭ-tō,
Ac.	De'-lŏn *or* ŭm,	An-dro'-ge-ō, *or* ōn,	Ac.	bar'-bĭ-tŏn,
V.	De'-lĕ,	An-dro'-ge-ōs,	V.	bar'-bĭ-tŏn,
Ab.	De'-lō.	An-dro'-ge-ō.	Ab.	bar'-bĭ-tō.

2. The plurals of Greek nouns in *os* and *on* are declined like those of *dominus* and *regnum*; but the nominative plural of nouns in *os* sometimes ends in *œ*, as, *canephŏræ*.

3. In early writers some nouns in *os* have a genitive in *ū* (*ov*); as, *Menandrū*. Ter.

4. A genitive plural in *ōn*, instead of *ōrum*, occurs in the titles of books and in some names of places; as, *Georgicōn*; *Philēnōn aræ.* Sall.

5. Greek proper names in *eus* (see § 9, R. 8), are declined like *dominus*, except that the vocative ends in *eu*; but sometimes in the genitive, dative, and accusative also, they retain the Greek form, viz. gen. *ĕŏs*, dat. *ĕī* (contracted *ēī*), acc. *ĕā* or *ĕā*, and are of the third declension. See §§ 86, and 806, (1.) So in Lucretius the neuter *pelăgus* (Greek πέλαγος, *εος*) has an accusative plural *pelăgē* for *pelagea* after the third declension. § 83, 1.—See also respecting a genitive in *i* of some proper nouns in *es*, § 73, Rem.—*Panthū* occurs in Virgil, A. 2, 822, as the vocative of *Panthūs*. Cf. § 81.

THIRD DECLENSION.

§ 55. The number of final letters, in this declension, is twelve. Five are vowels—*a, e, i, o, y;* and seven are consonants—*c, l, n, r, s, t, x.* The number of its final syllables exceeds fifty.

REM. The following terminations belong exclusively to Greek nouns; viz. *ma i y, ăn, in, ŏn, ўn, er, ŷr, ys, eus, yx, inx, ynx,* and plurals in *e*.

Mode of declining Nouns of the Third Declension.

To decline a word properly, in this declension, it is necessary to know its gender, its nominative singular, and one of its oblique cases; since the root of the cases is not always found entire and unchanged in the nominative. The case usually selected for this purpose is the genitive singular. The formation of the accusative singular, and of the nominative, accusative, and vocative plural, depends upon the gender: if it is masculine or feminine, these cases have one form; if neuter, another.

§ 56. The student should first fix well in his memory the terminations of one of these forms. He should next learn the nominative and genitive singular of the wo. ? which is to be declined. If *is* be removed from the genitive, the remainder will always a the root of the oblique cases, and by annexing their terminations to this root, the wou ' declined; thus, *rupes*, genitive (found in the dictionary) *rupis*, root *rup*, dative *rupi*, so *ars*, gen. *artis*, root *art*, dat. *arti*, etc.; *opus*, gen. *opĕris*, root *opĕr*, dat. *opĕri*, etc.

RULES FOR FORMING THE NOMINATIVE SINGULAR OF THE THIRD DECLENSION FROM THE ROOT.

I. Roots ending in *c, g; b, m, p; u, t, d,* and some in *r,* add *s* to form the nominative; as, *trăbis, trabs; hiĕmis, hiems; gruis, grus.*

REMARK 1. *T, d* and *r* before *s* are dropped; as, *nepōtis, nepos; laudis, laus; floris, flos.* So *bovis, bos,* drops *v.*

REM. 2. *C* and *g* before *s* form *x;* as, *vocis, vox; regis, rex.* So *vs* forms *x* in *nivis, nix.* Cf. §§ 3, 2, and 171, 1.

REM. 3. Short *i* in the root before *c, b, p, t,* is commonly changed to *ĕ;* as, *pollĭcis, pollex; cœlĭbis, cœlebs; princĭpis, princeps; comĭtis, comes.* So *ŭ* is changed to *ĕ* in *aucŭpis, auceps.*

REM. 4. Short *ĕ* or *ŏ* before *r* in neuters is changed to *ŭ;* as, *genĕris, genŭs; tempŏris, tempŭs.*

REM. 5. Short *ĕ* before *r* is changed to *i* in the masculines *cinĕris, cinis; cucumĕris, cucumis; pulvĕris, pulvis; vomĕris, vomis.*

REM. 6. A few and those mostly monosyllabic roots of masculines and feminines, not increasing in the genitive, add *es* or *is,* instead of *s* alone; as, gen. *rūpis,* nom. *rūpes;* gen. *auris,* nom. *auris.*

REM. 7. A few neuters add *ĕ* to the root to form the nominative; as, *rētis, rĕtĕ; măris, mărĕ.*

II. To roots ending in *l* and *n,* to some in *r* and *s,* and to those of most neuters in *t,* no addition is made in forming the nominative; as, *animālis, animal; canŏnis, cănon; honōris, hŏnor; assis, as.*

REMARK 1. Final *ŏn* and *ĭn* in the roots of masculines and feminines, become *o* in the nominative; as, *sermōnis, sermo; arundĭnis, arundo.*

REM. 2. Final *ĭn* in the roots of neuters becomes *ĕn* in the nominative; as, *flumĭnis, flūmĕn.* So also in the masculines, *oscen, pecten, tibīcen* and *tubīcen.*

REM. 3. *Tr* and *br* at the end of a root, take *ĕ* between them in the nominative; as, *patris, păter; imbris, imber.* Cf. §§ 108, 48, and 106.

REM. 4. Short *ŏ* is changed to *ŭ* in *ebŏris, ĕbŭr; femŏris, fĕmŭr; jecŏris, jĕcŭr;* and *robŏris, rŏbŭr.*

REM. 5. In the roots of neuters *at* drops *t,* and *it* becomes *ut* in the nominative; as, *poematis, poēma; capĭtis, caput.*

REM. 6. Roots of this class ending in repeated consonants drop one of them in the nominative; as, *fellis, fel; farris, far; assis, as; bessis, bes.*

§ 57. THIRD DECLENSION. 31

The following are the two forms of termination in this declension:—

	Singular.			Plural	
	Masc. and Fem.	Neut.		Masc. and Fem.	Neut.
N.	*	*	N.	ēs,	ă, (iă),
G.	ĭs,	ĭs,	G.	ŭm, (iŭm),	ŭm, (iŭm),
D.	ī,	ī,	D.	ĭbŭs,	ĭbŭs,
Ac.	ĕm, (ĭm),	*	Ac.	ēs,	ă, (iă),
V.	*	*	V.	ēs,	ă, (iă),
Ab.	ĕ, (ī).	ĕ, (ī).	Ab.	ĭbŭs.	ĭbŭs.

The asterisk stands for the nominative, and for those cases which are like it.

§ **57.** The following are examples of the most common forms of nouns of this declension, declined through all their cases.

Hŏnor, *honor;* masc.

	Singular.	Plural.
N.	ho'-nor,	ho-nō'-res,
G.	ho-nō'-ris,	ho-nō'-rum,
D.	ho-nō'-ri,	ho-nor'-ĭ-bus,
Ac.	ho-nō'-rem,	ho-nō'-res,
V.	ho'-nor,	ho-nō'-res,
Ab.	ho-nō'-re.	ho-nor'-ĭ-bus.

Turris, *a tower;* fem.

	Singular.	Plural.
N.	tur'-ris,	tur'-res,
G.	tur'-ris,	tur'-ri-um,
D.	tur'-ri,	tur'-rĭ-bus,
Ac.	tur'-rim, rem,	tur'-res,
V.	tur'-ris,	tur'-res,
Ab.	tur'-ri, *or* re.	tur'-rĭ-bus.

Rūpes, *a rock;* fem.

	Singular.	Plural.
N.	ru'-pes,	ru'-pes,
G.	ru'-pis,	ru'-pi-um,
D.	ru'-pi,	ru'-pĭ-bus,
Ac.	ru'-pem,	ru'-pes,
V.	ru'-pes,	ru'-pes,
Ab.	ru'-pe.	ru'-pĭ-bus.

Nox, *night;* fem.

	Singular.	Plural.
N.	nox,	noc'-tes,
G.	noc'-tis,	noc'-ti-um,*
D.	noc'-ti,	noc'-tĭ-bus,
Ac.	noc'-tem,	noc'-tes,
V.	nox,	noc'-tes,
Ab.	noc'-te.	noc'-tĭ-bus.

Ars, *art;* fem.

	Singular.	Plural.
N.	ars,	ar'-tes,
G.	ar'-tis,	ar'-ti-um,*
D.	ar'-ti,	ar'-tĭ-bus,
Ac.	ar'-tem,	ar'-tes,
V.	ars,	ar'-tes,
Ab.	ar'-te.	ar'-tĭ-bus.

Miles, *a soldier;* com. gen.

	Singular.	Plural.
N.	mi'-les,	mil'-ĭ-tes,
G.	mil'-ĭ-tis,	mil'-ĭ-tum,
D.	mil'-ĭ-ti,	mi-lit'-ĭ-bus,
Ac.	mil'-ĭ-tem,	mil'-ĭ-tes,
V.	mi'-les,	mil'-ĭ-tes,
Ab.	mil'-ĭ-te.	mi-lit'-ĭ-bus.

Sermo, *speech;* masc.

	Singular.	Plural.
N.	ser'-mo,	ser-mō'-nes,
G.	ser-mō'-nis,	ser-mō'-num,
D.	ser-mō'-ni,	ser-mon'-ĭ-bus,
Ac.	ser-mō'-nem,	ser-mō'-nes,
V.	ser'-mo,	ser-mō'-nes,
Ab.	ser-mō'-ne.	ser-mon'-ĭ-bus.

Păter, *a father;* masc.

	Singular.	Plural.
N.	pa'-ter,	pa'-tres,
G.	pa'-tris,	pa'-trum,
D.	pa'-tri,	pat'rĭ-bus,
Ac.	pa'-trem,	pa'-tres,
V.	pa'-ter,	pa'-tres,
Ab.	pa'-tre.	pat'-rĭ-bus.

* Pronounced *ar'-she-um, noc'-she-um.* See § 12.

THIRD DECLENSION. § 57

Sĕdĭle, *a seat;* neut.

	Singular.	Plural.
N.	se-dĭ′-le,	se-dĭl′-ĭ-a,
G.	se-dĭ′-lis,	se-dĭl′-ĭ-um,
D.	se-dĭ′-li,	se-dĭl′-ĭ-bus,
Ac.	se-dĭ′-le,	se-dĭl′-ĭ-a,
V.	se-dĭ′-le,	se-dĭl′-ĭ-a,
Ab.	se-dĭ′-li.	se-dĭl′-ĭ-bus.

Virgo, *a virgin.* fem.

	Singular.	Plural.
N.	vir′-go,	vir′-gĭ-nes,
G.	vir′-gĭ-nis,	vir′-gĭ-num,
D.	vir′-gĭ-ni,	vir-gin′-ĭ-bus,
Ac.	vir′-gĭ-nem,	vir′-gĭ-nes,
V.	vir′-go,	vir′-gĭ-nes,
Ab.	vir′-gĭ-ne.	vir-gin′-ĭ-bus.

Carmen, *a verse;* neut.

	Singular.	Plural.
N.	car′-men,	car′-mĭ-na,
G.	car′-mĭ-nis,	car′-mĭ-num,
D.	car′-mĭ-ni,	car-min′-ĭ-bus,
Ac.	car′-men,	car′-mĭ-na,
V.	car′-men,	car′-mĭ-na,
Ab.	car′-mĭ-ne.	car-min′-ĭ-bus.

Anĭmal, *an animal;* neut.

	Singular.	Plural.
N.	ăn′-ĭ-mal,	an-i-ma′-li-a,
G.	an-i-mā′-lis,	an-i-ma′-li-um,
D.	an-i-mā′-li,	an-i-mal′-ĭ-bus.
Ac.	an′-ĭ-mal,	an-i-ma′-li-a,
V.	an′-ĭ-mal,	an-i-ma′-li-a,
Ab.	an-i-mā′-li.	an-i-mal′-ĭ-bus.

Iter, *a journey:* neut.

	Singular.	Plural.
N.	i′-ter,	i-tin′-ĕ-ra,
G.	i-tin′-ĕ-ris,	i-tin′-ĕ-rum,
D.	i-tin′-ĕ-ri,	it-i-ner′-ĭ-bus,
Ac.	i′-ter,	i-tin′-ĕ-ra,
V.	i′-ter,	i-tin′-ĕ-ra,
Ab.	i-tin′-ĕ-re.	it-i-ner′-ĭ-bus.

Opus, *work;* neut.

	Singular.	Plural.
N.	ŏ′-pus,	op′-ĕ-ra,
G.	op′-ĕ-ris,	op′-ĕ-rum,
D.	op′-ĕ-ri,	o-per′-ĭ-bus,
Ac.	o′-pus,	op′-ĕ-ra,
V.	o′-pus,	op′-ĕ-ra,
Ab.	op′-ĕ-re.	o-per′-ĭ-bus.

Lŭpis, *a stone;* masc.

	Singular.	Plural.
N.	la′-pis,	lap′-ĭ-des,
G.	lap′-ĭ-dis,	lap′-ĭ-dum,
D.	lap′-ĭ-di,	la-pid′-ĭ-bus,
Ac.	lap′-ĭ-dem,	lap′-ĭ-des,
V.	la′-pis,	lap′-ĭ-des,
Ab.	lap′-ĭ-de.	la-pid′-ĭ-bus.

Căput, *a head;* neut.

	Singular.	Plural.
N.	ca′-put,	cap′-ĭ-ta,
G.	cap′-ĭ-tis,	cap′-ĭ-tum,
D.	cap′-ĭ-ti,	ca-pit′-ĭ-bus,
Ac.	ca′-put,	cap′-ĭ-ta,
V.	ca′-put,	cap′-ĭ-ta,
Ab.	cap′-ĭ-te.	ca-pit′-ĭ-bus.

Poëma, *a poem;* neut.

	Singular.	Plural.
N.	po-ē′-ma,	po-em′-ă-ta,
G.	po-em′-ă-tis,	po-em′-ă-tum,
D.	po-em′-ă-ti,	po-e-mat′-ĭ-bus, *or* po-em′-ă-tis,
Ac.	po-ē′-ma,	po-em′-ă-ta,
V.	po-ē′-ma,	po-em′-ă-ta,
Ab.	po-em′-ĭ-te.	po-e-mat′-ĭ-bus, *or* po-em′-ă-tis.

Rules for the Gender of Nouns of the Third Declension

§ 58. Nouns whose gender is determined by their signification, according to the general rules, § 28—34, are not included in the following rules and exceptions.

MASCULINES.

Nouns ending in *o*, *er*, *or*, *es* increasing in the genitive, *os*, and *n*, are masculine; as,

sermo, speech; *dolor*, pain; *flos*, a flower; *carcer*, a prison; *pes*, a foot; *cănon*, a rule.

Exceptions in O.

§ 59. 1. Abstract and collective nouns in *io* are feminine; as, *ratio*, reason; *legio*, a legion.

REM. 1. But numerals in *io*; as, *binio*, *trinio*, etc., except *unio*, unity, are masculine.

2. Nouns in *do* and *go*, of more than two syllables, are feminine, as, *arundo*, a reed; *imāgo*, an image. So also *grando*, hail. But *comĕdo*, a glutton; *unĕdo*, the arbute tree; and *harpăgo*, a grappling-hook, are masculine.

REM. 2. *Margo*, the brink of a river, is doubtful. *Cupīdo*, desire, is often masculine in poetry, but in prose is always feminine.
3. *Căro*, flesh, and Greek nouns in *o*, are feminine; as, *ēcho*, an echo. *Būbo*, the owl, is once feminine, Virg. A. 4, 462.

Exceptions in ER.

§ 60. 1. *Laver*, a water plant, and *tūber*, the tuber tree, are feminine, but when the latter denotes the fruit, it is masculine. *Linter*, a boat, is feminine, and once, in Tibullus, masculine. *Siser*, skirret, is neuter in the singular, but masculine in the plural.

2. The following, in *er*, are neuter:—

Acer, *a maple-tree.*	Papāver, *a poppy.*	Tūber, *a swelling.*
Cadāver, *a dead body.*	Piper, *pepper.*	Uber, *a teat.*
Cicer, *a vetch.*	Siler, *an osier.*	Ver, *the spring.*
Iter, *a journey.*	Spinther, *a clasp.*	Verber, *a scourge.*
Lāser, *assafetida.*	Sūber, *a cork-tree.*	Zingiber, *ginger.*

Exceptions in OR.

§ 61. *Arbor*, a tree, is feminine! *ădor*, spelt; *æquor*, the sea; *marmor*, *cor*, the heart, are neuter.

Exceptions in ES increasing in the genitive.

1. The following are feminine:—

Compes, *a fetter.*	Quies, *and* Requies, *rest.*	Teges, *a mat.*
Merces, *a reward.*	Inquies, *restlessness.*	
Merges, *a sheaf of corn.*	Seges, *growing corn.*	

2. *Ales*, a bird; *comes*, a companion; *hospes*, a guest; *interpres*, an interpreter; *miles*, a soldier; *obses* a hostage; *præses*, a president; and *satelles*, a life-guard, are common, § 30. *Æs*, brass, is neuter.

Exceptions in OS.

3. *Arbos*, a tree; *cos*, a whetstone; *dos*, a dowry; *eos*, the morning; and rarely *nĕpos*, a grandchild, are feminine: *sacerdos*, *custos*, and *bos* are common, § 30: *ŏs*, the mouth, and *ŏs*, a bone, are neuter; as are also the Greek words *ĕpos*, epic poetry; and *mĕlos*, melody.

Exceptions in N.

4. Nouns in *men* with four in *n* are neuter—*glūten*, glue; *inguen*, the groin *pollen*, fine flour; and *unguen*, ointment.
5. Four nouns in *on* are feminine—*aĕdon*, a nightingale; *halcyon*, a kingfisher; *icon*, am image; and *sindon*, muslin.

FEMININES.

§ 62. Nouns ending in *as*, *es* not increasing in the genitive, *is*, *ys*, *aus*, *s* preceded by a consonant, and *x*, are feminine; as,

aetas, age; *nūbes*, a cloud; *ăvis*, a bird; *chlămys*, a cloak; *laus*, praise; *trabs*, a beam; *pax*, peace.

Exceptions in AS.

1. *Mas*, a male, *vas*, a surety, and *as*, a piece of money, or any unit divisible into twelve parts, are masculine. Greek nouns in *as*, *antis*, are also masculine; as, *adămas*, adamant. So also *Mĕlas*, the name of a river, § 28, 2. *Arcas* and *Nŏmas* are common.—2. *Vas*, a vessel, the indeclinable nouns, *fas* and *nĕfas*, and Greek nouns in *as*, *ătis*, are neuter; as, *artocreas*, a meat-pie; *bucĕras*, a species of herb.

Exceptions in ES not increasing in the genitive.

3. *Acināces*, a scimitar, and *cōles* or *cōlis*, a stalk, are masculine. *Antistes*, *palumbes*, *vātes*, and *vepres*, are masculine or feminine. *Cacoëthes*, *hippomănes*, *nepenthes*, and *panāces*, Greek words, are neuter.

Exceptions in IS.

§ 63. 1. Latin nouns in *nis* are masculine or doubtful.

(1.) Masc. *Crīnis*, hair; *ignis*, fire; *pānis*, bread; *mānes*, (plur.), departed spirits.—(2.) Masc. or fem. *Amnis*, a river; *cĭnis*, ashes; *fīnis*, an end; *clŭnis*, the haunch; *cănis*, a dog; *fūnis*, a rope. The plurals, *cinĕres*, the ashes of the dead, and *fīnes*, boundaries, are always masculine.

2. The following are common or doubtful:—

Anguis, *a snake*.	Corbis, *a basket*.	Tigris, *a tiger*.
Callis, *a path*.	Pollis, *fine flour*.	Torquis, *a chain*.
Canālis, *a conduit pipe*.	Pulvis, *dust*.	
Contubernālis, *a comrade*.	Scrŏbis, *a ditch*.	

3. The following are masculine:—

Axis, *an axle*.	Cenchris, *a serpent*.	Follis, *a pair of bellows*.
Aquālis, *a water-pot*.	Collis, *a hill*.	Fustis, *a club*.
Cassis, *a net*.	Cucŭmis, *a cucumber*.	Glis, *a dormouse*.
Caulis, or ⎱ *a stalk*.	Ensis, *a sword*.	Lăpis, *a stone*.
Cōlis, ⎰	Fascis, *a bundle*.	Lemŭres, pl., *spectres*.

§ 64, 65.   THIRD DECLENSION.—GENDER.   35

Mensis, *a month.*	Sanguis, *blood.*		Sentis, *a brier.*
Mugilis, *a mullet.*	Semis, *or*		Sodālis, *a companion.*
Orbis, *a circle.*	Semissis,		Torris, *a firebrand.*
Piscis, *a fish.*	Bessis,	compounds	Unguis, *a nail.*
Postis, *a post.*	Centussis,	of *as.*	Vectis, *a lever.*
Quiris, *a Roman.*	Decussis,		Vermis, *a worm.*
Samnis, *a Samnite.*	Tressis,		Vomis, *a ploughshare.*

4. Names of male beings, rivers, and months in *is* are masculine; as, *Dis*, Pluto; *Anūbis*, an Egyptian deity; *Tigris*, the river Tigris; *Aprilis*, April. See § 28.

Exceptions in YS.

Names of rivers and mountains in *ys* are masculine; as, *Hălys*, *Othrys.* See § 28, 2 and 3

Exceptions in S preceded by a consonant.

§ **64.** 1. *Dens*, a tooth; *fons*, a fountain; *mons*, a mountain; and *pons*, a bridge, are masculine. So also are *auceps*, a bird-catcher; *chălybs*, steel; *cliens*, a client; *ellops*, a kind of fish; *ĕpops*, a hoopoe; *gryps*, a griffin; *hydrops*, the dropsy; *mĕrops*, a kind of bird. *Rudens*, a rope, is masculine and very rarely feminine.

2. The following nouns also are masculine, viz. (*a.*) these which are properly adjectives—*confluens* and *torrens*, scil. *amnis*; *occidens* and *oriens*, scil. *sol*; (*b.*) compounds of *dens*—*tridens*, a trident, and *bidens*, a two-pronged mattock;—but *bidens*, a sheep, is feminine; (*c.*) the parts of *as* ending in *ns*; as, *sextans*, *quadrans*, *triens*, *dodrans*, and *dextans.*

3. The following are common or doubtful:—

Adeps, *grouse.*	Seps, *a kind of serpent.*	Serpens, *a serpent.*
Forceps, *pincers.*	Scrobs, *a ditch.*	Stirps, *the trunk of a tree.*

Animans an animal, which is properly an adjective, is masculine, feminine, or neuter.

Exceptions in X.

§ **65.** 1. AX. *Anthrax*, cinnabar; *cŏrax*, a raven; *cordax*, a kind of dance; *drōpax*, an ointment; *stўrax*, a kind of tree; *thōrax*, a breast-plate; and *Atax*, the river Aude, are masculine; *limax*, a snail, is common.

2. EX. Nouns in *ex* are masculine, except *fæx*, *forfex*, *lex*, *nex*, *prex*, (obsolete in nom. and gen. sing.), and *supellex*, which are feminine; to which add (§ 29) *cārex*, *ilex*, *mūrex*, *pellex*, and *vitex*. *Atriplex* is neuter and very rarely masculine or feminine. *Alex*, a fish-pickle; *cortex*, bark; *imbrex*, a gutter-tile; *ōbex*, a bolt; and *silex*, a flint, are doubtful: *sĕnex*, an old person; *grex*, a herd; *rūmex*, sorrel; and *pūmex*, pumice-stone, are masculine and very rarely feminine.

3. IX. *Cĭlix*, a cup; *fornix*, an arch; *phœnix*, a kind of bird; and *spādix*, a palm-branch, are masculine: *lărix*, the larch-tree; *perdix*, a partridge; and *vārix*, a swollen vein, are masculine or feminine.

4. OX. *Box* and *ĕsox*, names of fishes, are masculine.

5. UX. *Trădux*, a vine-branch, is masculine.

6. YX. *Bombyx*, a silk-worm; *călyx*, the bud of a flower; *coccyx*, a cuckoo; *ŏryx*, a wild goat, and names of mountains in *yx*, as *Eryx*, are masculine. *Onyx*, a box made of the onyx-stone, and *sardŏnyx*, a precious stone; also, *calx*, the heel, and *calx*, lime; *lynx*, a lynx, and *sandyx*, a kind of color, are masculine or feminine.

NOTE. *Bombyx*, when it signifies silk, is doubtful.

7. *Quincunx*, *septunx*, *dĕcunx*, *deunx*, parts of *as*, are masculine.

NEUTERS.

§ 66. Nouns ending in *a, e, i, y, c, l, t, ar, ur, us,* and *men,* are neuter; as,

diadēma, a crown; *rēte,* a net; *hydromēli,* mead; *lac,* milk; *vectīgal,* revenue *cāput,* the head; *calcar,* a spur; *guttur,* the throat; *pectus,* the breast; and *flūmen,* a river.

Exceptions in L, C, and E.

Mūgil, a mullet, and *sol,* the sun, are masculine. *Sal,* salt, is masculine or neuter in the singular; but, in the plural, it is always masculine. *Lac* is neuter and rarely masculine. *Præneste* is neuter, and once in Virgil feminine.

Exceptions in AR and UR.

§ 67. *Furfur,* bran; *sălar,* a trout; *turtur,* a turtle dove; and *vultur,* a vulture, are masculine.

Exceptions in US.

1. *Lĕpus,* a hare; and Greek nouns in *pus* (πούς), are masculine; as, *tripus,* a tripod; but *lagōpus,* a kind of bird, is feminine.
2. Nouns in *us,* having *ūtis,* or *ūdis,* in the genitive, are feminine; as, *juventus,* youth; *incus,* an anvil.
3. *Pecus, -ŭdis,* a brute animal, and *tellus,* the earth, are feminine. *Pessinus,* and *Selinus,* names of towns, are also feminine. See § 29.
4. *Grus,* a crane; *mus,* a mouse; and *sus,* a swine, are masculine or feminine.
5. *Rhus,* sumach, is masculine, and rarely feminine.

RULES FOR THE OBLIQUE CASES OF NOUNS OF THE THIRD DECLENSION.

GENITIVE SINGULAR.

§ 68. 1. The genitive singular of the third declension of *Latin* nouns always ends in *is,* in *Greek* nouns it sometimes ends in *os* and *us.*

A.

2. Nouns in *a* form their genitive in *ătis;* as, *di-a-dē'-ma, di-a-dem'-ă-tis,* a crown; *dog'-ma, dog'-mă-tis,* an opinion.

E.

3. Nouns in *e* change *e* into *is;* as, *rĕ'-te, rĕ'-tis,* a net; *se-di'-le, se-dĭ'-lis,* a seat.

I.

4. Nouns in *i* are of Greek origin, and are generally indeclinable; but *hydrom'-ĕ-li,* mead, has *hyd-ro-mel'-ĭ-tis* in the genitive.

O.

§ 69. Nouns in *o* form their genitive in *ōnis;* as, *ser'-mo, ser mō'-nis,* speech; *pā'-vo, pa-vō'-nis,* a peacock.

§ 70, 71.   THIRD DECLENSION.—GENITIVE.   37

REMARK. Patrials in *o* have *ŏnis*; as, *Macĕdo, -ŏnis*; but some have *ōnis*, as, *Eburōnes*, etc. See 3d exception to increments in O, § 287.

EXC. 1. Nouns in *do* and *go* form their genitive in *ĭnis*; as, *a-run'-do, a-run'-dĭ-nis*, a reed; *i-mă'-go, i-mag'-ĭ-nis*, an image.

But four dissyllables—*cūdo, ūdo, ligo* and *mango*; and three trisyllables—*comēdo, unēdo*, and *harpăgo*, have *ŏnis*.

EXC. 2. The following nouns, also, have *ĭnis*:—*Apollo; hŏmo*, a man; *nēmo*, nobody; and *turbo*, a whirlwind.

Căro, flesh, has, by syncope, *carnis*. *Anio*, the name of a river, has *Aniĕnis*; *Nerio*, the wife of Mars, *Neriĕnis*; from the old nominatives, *Anien*, and *Neriĕnes*.

EXC. 3. Some Greek nouns in *o* form their genitive in *ūs*, and their other cases singular, in *o*; as, *Dido*, gen. *Didus*, dat. *Dido*, etc.; *Argo, -us*; but they are sometimes declined regularly; as, *Dido, Didōnis*.

Y.

Greek nouns in *y* have their genitive in *yos*; as, *misy, misȳos*, or, by contraction, *misys*.

C.

§ **70.** The only nouns in *c* are *ā'-lec, a-lē'-cis*, fish-brine, and *lac, lac'-tis*, milk.

L. N. R.

Nouns in *l, n*, and *r*, form their genitive by adding *is*; as, *con'-sul, con'-sŭ-lis*, a consul; *că'-non, can'-ŏ-nis*, a rule; *hŏ'-nor, ho-nō'-ris*, honor.

So, An'-i-mal, an-i-mă'-lis, *an animal*.   Cal'-car, cal-cā'-ris, *a spur*.
Vi'-gil, vig'-i-lis, *a watchman*.   Car'-cer, car'-cĕ-ris, *a prison*.
Ti'-tan, Ti-tă'-nis, *Titan*.   A'-mor, a-mŏ'-ris, *love*.
Si'-ren, Si-rē'-nis, *a Siren*.   Gut'-tur, gut'-tŭ-ris, *the throat*.
Del'-phin, del-phĭ'-nis, *a dolphin*.   Mar'-tyr, mar'-tȳ-ris, *a martyr*.

Exceptions in L.

Fel, gall, and *mel*, honey, double *l* before *is*, making *fellis* and *mellis*.

Exceptions in N.

§ **71.** 1. Neuters in *en* form their genitive in *ĭnis*; as, *flū'-men, flŭ'-mĭ-nis*, a river; *glū'-ten, glu'-tĭ-nis*, glue.

The following masculines, also, form their genitive in *inis*:—*oscen*, a bird which forbided by its notes; *pecten*, a comb; *tibicen*, a piper; and *tubicen*, a trumpeter.

2. Some Greek nouns in *ōn* form their genitive in *ontis*; as, *Laomĕdon, Laomĕdontis*. Some in *in* and *yn* add *is* or *os*; as, *Trăchin*, or *Trăchyn, Trachĭnis* or *Trachȳnos*.

Exceptions in R.

1. Nouns in *ter* drop *e* in the genitive; as, *pă'-ter, pa'-tris*, a father. So also *imber*, a shower, and names of months in *ber*; as, *October, Octōbris*.

4

But *crāter*, a cup; *sōtēr*, a savior; and *lāter*, a brick, retain *e* in the genitive.

2. *Far*, a kind of corn, has *farris*; *hĕpar*, the liver, *hepătis*; *Lar* or *Lars*, *Lartis*; *iter*, a journey, has *itinĕris* from the old nominative *itiner*; *Jupĭter Jŏvis*; and *cor*, the heart, *cordis*.

3. These four in *ur* have *ŏris* in the genitive:—*ĕbur*, ivory; *fĕmur*, the thigh; *jĕcur*, the liver; *rōbur*, strength.

Fĕmur has also *femĭnis*, and *jĕcur*, *jecinŏris*, and *jocinŏris*.

AS.

§ 72. Nouns in *as* form their genitive in *ātis*; as, *æ'-tas*, *æ-tā'-tis*, age; *pī'-ĕ-tas*, *pi-e-tā'-tis*, piety.

Exc. 1. *As* has *assis*; *mās*, a male, *māris*; *vas*, a surety, *vădis*; and *vās*, a vessel, *vāsis*. *Anas*, a duck, has *anătis*.

Exc. 2. Greek nouns in *as* form their genitive according to their gender; the masculines in *antis*, the feminines in *ădis* or *ădos*, and the neuters in *ătis*; as, *adămas*, *-antis*, adamant; *lampas*, *-ădis*, a lamp; *Pallas*, *-ădis* or *-ădos*; *bucĕras*, *-ătis*, a species of herb. *Arcas*, an Arcadian, and *Nŏmas*, a Numidian, which are of the common gender, form their genitive in *ădis*. *Mĕlas*, the name of a river, has *Melănis*.

ES.

§ 73. 1. Nouns in *es* form their genitive by changing *es* into *is*, *ĭtis*, *ĕtis*, or *ētis*; as, *rū'-pes*, *ru'-pis*, a rock; *mī'-les*, *mil'-ĭ-tis*, a soldier; *sĕ'-ges*, *seg'-ĕ-tis*, growing corn; *qui'-es*, *qui-ē'-tis*, rest.

REMARK. A few Greek proper names in *es* (gen. *is*) sometimes form their genitive in *ei*, or, by contraction, *i*, after the second declension; as, *Achilles*, *is*, *ei* or *-i*: and a few in *æ* after the first declension; as, *Orestes*, *is* or *æ*.

2. Those which make *ĭtis* are,

Ales, *a bird*.	Gurges, *a whirlpool*.	Poples, *the ham*.
Ames, *a fowler's staff*.	Hospes, *a guest*.	Satelles, *a lifeguard*.
Antistes, *a priest*.	Limes, *a limit*.	Stipes, *the stock of a tree*.
Cæspes, *a turf*.	Merges, *a sheaf of corn*.	Termes, *an olive bough*.
Cōmes, *a companion*.	Miles, *a soldier*.	Trames, *a by-path*.
Eques, *a horseman*.	Palmes, *a vine-branch*.	Veles, *a skirmisher*.
Fomes, *touchwood*.	Pedes, *a foot-soldier*.	

3. The following have *ĕtis*:—*abies*, a fir-tree; *aries*, a ram; *indiges*, a man deified; *interpres*, an interpreter; *paries*, a wall; *sĕges*, a corn-field; and *tĕges*, a mat.

4. The following have *ētis*:—*Cēbes*; *Cres*, a Cretan; *lēbes*, a caldron; *magnes*, a loadstone; *quies* and *requies*, rest; *inquies*, restlessness; and *tāpes* (used only in acc. and abl.), tapestry.—Some Greek proper names have either *ētis* or *is* in the genitive; as, *Chrēmes*, *-ētis*, or *-is*. *Dăres*, *-ētis*, or *-is*.

Exc. 1. *Obses*, a hostage, and *præses*, a president, have *ĭdis*. *Hēres*, an heir, and *merces*, a reward, have *ēdis*; *pes*, a foot, and its compounds, have *ĕdis*.

Exc. 2. *Cĕres* has *Cerēris*; *bes*, *bessis*; *præs*, *prædis*; and *æs*, *æris*.

IS.

§ 74. Nouns in *is* have their genitive the same as the nominative; as, *au'-ris*, *au'-ris*, the ear; *ă'-vis*, *ă'-vis*, a bird.

§ 75, 76.   THIRD DECLENSION.—GENITIVE.   39

Exc. 1. The following have the genitive in *ĕris*:—*cĭnis*, ashes; *pulvis*, dust; *vŏmis* or *vŏmer*, a ploughshare.   *Cucŭmis*, a cucumber, has *ĕris* and rarely *is*.

Exc. 2. The following have *ĭdis*:—*căpis*, a cup; *cassis*, a helmet; *cuspis*, a point; *lăpis*, a stone; and *prōmulsis*, an antepast.

Exc. 3. Two have *ĭnis*:—*pollis*, fine flour, and *sanguis* or *sanguen*, blood.

Exc. 4. Four have *ītis*:—*Dis*, Pluto; *lis*, strife; *Quīris*, a Roman; and *Samnis*, a Samnite.

Exc. 5. *Glis*, a dormouse, has *glīris*.

GREEK NOUNS.

1. Greek nouns in *is*, whose genitive ends in *ios* or *eos*, (ιος or ως), form their genitive in Latin in *is*; as (a.) verbals in *sis*; as, *basis*, *mathēsis*, etc. (b.) compounds of *polis* (πόλις); as, *metropōlis*, *Neapŏlis*, etc.; and (c.) a few other proper names, as *Charybdis*, *Lachēsis*, *Syrtis*, etc. In some nouns of this class the Greek genitive is sometimes found; as, *Nemĕsis*, *Nemesios*.

2. Greek nouns in *is*, whose Greek genitive is in *ĭdos* (ιδος), form their Latin genitive in *ĭdis*; as, *ægis*, *aspis*, *ephemĕris*, *pyrămis*, *tyrannis*, *Æneis*, *Iris*, *Nereis*, etc. *Tigris* has both *is* and *ĭdis*; and in some other words of this class later writers use *is* instead of *ĭdis*.

3. *Chăris* has *Charĭtis*; *Salămis*, *Salamīnis*, and *Simŏis*, *Simoentis*.

OS.

§ 75. Nouns in *ōs* form their genitive in *ōris* or *ōtis*; as, *flos, flō'-ris*, a flower; *nĕ'-pos, ne-pō'-tis*, a grandchild.

The following have *ōris*:—

Flos, *a flower*.	Lăbos or lăbor, *labor*.	Os, *the mouth*.
Glos, *a husband's sister*.	Lĕpos or lĕpor, *wit*.	Ros, *dew*.
Hŏnos or hŏnor, *honor*.	Mos, *a custom*.	

Arbos or *arbor*, a tree, has *ōris*.

The following have *ōtis*:—

Cos, *a whetstone*.	Monocĕros, *a unicorn*.	Nĕpos, *a grandchild*.
Dos, *a dowry*.	Rhinocĕros, *a rhinoceros*.	Sacerdos, *a priest*.

Exc. 1. *Custos*, a keeper, has *custōdis*; *bos*, an ox, *bŏvis*; and *ŏs*, a bone, *ossis*.

Exc. 2. Some Greek nouns in *os* have *ōis* in the genitive; as, *hēros*, a hero; *Mīnos*; *Tros*, a Trojan; and some Greek neuters in *os* are used in the third declension in the nominative and accusative only; as, *Argos*, *cētos*, *ĕpos*, *mĕlos*.

US.

§ 76. 1. Nouns in *ŭs* form their genitive in *ĕris* or *ōris*; as, *gĕ'nus, gen'-ĕ-ris*, a kind; *tem'-pus, tem'-pŏ-ris*, time.

2. Those which make *ĕris* are, *ăcus*, (chaff), *fœdus*, *fūnus*, *gĕnus*, *glŏmus*, *lătus*, *mūnus*, *ŏlus*, *ŏnus*, *ŏpus*, *pondus*, *rūdus*, *scĕlus*, *sīdus*, *ulcus*, *vellus*, *viscus* and *vulnus*. In early writers *pignus* has sometimes *pignĕris*.

3. Those which make *ōris* are, *corpus*, *dĕcus*, *dedĕcus*, *facĭnus*, *fēnus*, *frigus*, *lĕpus*, *lītus*, *nĕmus*, *pectus*, *pĕcus*, *pĕnus*, *pignus*, *stercus*, *tempus*, and *tergus*.

Exc. 1. These three in *ūs* have *ŭdis*:—*incūs*, an anvil; *pălūs*, a morass; and *subscūs*, a dove-tail. *Pĕcūs*, a brute animal, has *pecūdis*.

Exc. 2. These five have *ūtis*:—*juventūs*, youth; *sălūs*, safety; *senectūs*, old age; *servĭtūs*, slavery *virtūs*, virtue.

Exc. 3. Monosyllables in *ūs* have *ūris*; as, *crus*, the leg; *jus*, right; *jus*, broth; *mus*, a mouse; *pus*, matter; *rus*, the country; *tus*, frankincense; except *grus*, and *sus*, which have *gruis*, and *suis*; and *rhus*, which has *rhois* or *roris*. *Tellus*, the earth, has *tellūris*; and *Ligus* or *Ligur*, a Ligurian, has *Ligūris*.

Exc. 4. *Fraus*, fraud, and *laus*, praise, have *fraudis*, *laudis*.

Exc. 5. Greek nouns in *pūs* (πούς) have *ŏdis*; as, *tripus*, *tripŏdis*, a tripod; *Œdĭpus*, *-ŏdis*; but this is sometimes of the second declension.

Exc. 6. Some Greek names of cities in *us* have *untis*; as, *Amāthus*, *Amathuntis*. So *Trapĕzus*, *Opus*, *Pessinus*, and *Selīnus*.

Exc. 7. Greek nouns ending in *eus* are all proper names, and have their genitive in *eos*; as, *Orpheus*, *-eos*. But these nouns are found also in the second declension; as, *Orpheus*, *-ĕi* or *-ī*. Cf. § 64, 5.

YS.

§ 77. 1. Nouns in *ys* are Greek, and make their genitive in *ўis* (contracted *ўs*), or, as in Greek, *yos* (υος); as,

Cŏtys, gen. *Cotyis* or *Cotys*; *Tēthys*, *-yis* or *ўos*. So *Atys*, *Cāpys*, *Erinnys*, *Hălys*, *Oūrys*. A few have *ўdis*; as, *chlāmys*, *chlamŷdis*.

S preceded by a consonant.

2. Nouns in *s*, with a consonant before it, form their genitive by changing *s* into *is* or *tis*; as, *trabs*, *trā'-bis*, a beam; *hi'-ems*, *hi'-ĕ-mis*, winter; *pars*, *par'-tis*, a part; *frons*, *fron'-tis*, the forehead.

(1.) Those in *bs*, *ms*, and *ps*; as, *scrobs*, *hiems*, *surps*, change *s* into *is*; except *gryps*, a griffin, which has *grўphis*.

REMARK. Compounds in *ceps* from *căpio* have *ĭpis*; as, *princeps*, *princĭpis*, a prince. But *auceps* has *aucŭpis*.

(2.) Those in *ls*, *ns*, and *rs*, as, *puls*, *gens*, *ars*, change *s* into *tis*.

Exc. 1. The following in *ns* change *s* into *dis*:—*frons*, foliage: *glans*, an acorn; *juglans*, a walnut; *lens*, a nit; and *libripens*, a weigher.

Exc. 2. *Tiryns*, a town of Argolis, has *Tirynthis* in the genitive.

T.

§ 78. 1. Nouns in *t* form their genitive in *ĭtis*. They are, *căput*, the head, gen. *cap'-ĭ-tis*; and its compounds, *occĭput* and *sincĭput*.

X.

2. Nouns in *x* form their genitive by resolving *x* into *cs* or *gs*, and inserting *i* before *s*; as, *vox* (*vocs*) *vō'-cis*, the voice; *lex* (*legs*) *lē'-gis*, a law.

(1.) Latin nouns in *ax* have *ācis*; as, *fornax*, *fornācis*, except *fax*, *făcis*. Most Greek nouns in *ax* have *ăcis*; as, *thōrax*, *thorācis*; a few have *ācis*; as, *cŏrax*, *corācis*; and Greek names of men in *nax* have *nactis*; as, *Astyănax*, *Astyanactis*.

(2.) Nouns in *ex* have *ĭcis*; as, *jūdex*, *judĭcis*: *ŏbex* has *obĭcis* or *objĭcis*; and *vibex*, *vibĭcis*. *Nex*, *prex*, (nom. obs.), *rĕsex* and *senĭsex* have *ĕcis*; *ălex*, *narthex*, and *vervex* have *ēcis*, and *fax*, *făcis*. *Lex* and *rex* have *ēgis*; *aquilex* and *grex* have *ĭgis*; *rēmex* has *remĭgis*; *sĕnex*, *sĕnis*; and *supellex*, *supellectĭlis*.

(3.) Nouns in *ix* have *ĭcis*; as, *cervix, cervīcis*; and less frequently *ĭcis*; as, *călix, calĭcis*. But *nix* has *nivis*; *strix*, foreign names of men, and gentile nouns in *rix* have *īgis*; as, *Bitŭrix, Dumnŏrix*, etc.

(4.) Nouns in *ox* have *ŏcis*; as, *vox, vōcis*; but *Cappădox* has *Cappadŏcis*; *Allŏbrox, Allobrŏgis*; and *nox, noctis*.

(5.) Of nouns in *ux, crux, dux, trādux*, and *nux* have *ŭcis*; *lux* and *Pollux, ūcis.—Conjux* has *conjŭgis, frux* (nom. obs.) *frūgis*, and *faux, faucis*.

(6.) *Yx*, a Greek termination, has *ўcis, ўcis*, or *ўgis, ўgis*. *Onyx* and *sardŏnyx*, in which *x* is equivalent to *chs* (§ 3, 2) have *ўchis*; as, *ŏnyx, onўchis*.

DATIVE SINGULAR.

§ 79. The dative singular ends in *i*; as, *sermo*, dat. *sermōni*.

Anciently it also ended in *e*; as, *morte dătus*. Varro in Gellius. So *ære* for *æri*, Cic. and Liv.; and *jūre* for *jūri*. Liv.

ACCUSATIVE SINGULAR.

(*a.*) The accusative singular of all neuter nouns is like the nominative.

(*b.*) The accusative singular of masculines and feminines, ends in *em*. Yet some Latin nouns in *is*, which do not increase in the genitive, have *im*, and some Greek nouns have *im, in*, or *a*.

1. Many proper names in *is*, denoting places, rivers, or gods, have the accusative singular in *im*; as, *Hispălis, Tibĕris, Anūbis*; so also *Albis, Athĕsis, Bætis, Arar* or *Arăris, Bilbĭlis, Apis, Osīris, Syrtis*, etc. These sometimes, also, make the accusative in *in*; as, *Albin. Scaldis* has *in* and *em*, and *Līris, im, in*, and *em. Līger* has *Ligĕrim*.

2. The following also have the accusative in *im*:—

Amussis, *a mason's rule.*   Mephītis, *foul air.*   Sināpis, *mustard.*
Būris, *a plough-tail.*   Pelvis, *a basin.*   Sĭtis, *thirst.*
Cannăbis, *hemp.*   Rāvis, *hoarseness.*   Tussis, *a cough.*
Cucŭmis, (gen. -is), *a cucumber.* Secūris, *an axe.*   Vis, *strength.*

3. These have *im*, and sometimes *em*:—
Febris, *a fever.*   Puppis, *the stern.*   Restis, *a rope.*   Turris, *a tower.*

But these have *em*, and rarely *im*:—
Bipennis, *a battle-axe.*   Nāvis, *a ship.*   Sementis, *a sowing.*
Clāvis, *a key.*   Præsēpis, *a stall.*   Strigĭlis, *a flesh-brush.*
Messis, *a harvest.*

4. *Lens* and *pars* have rarely *lentim* and *partim*; and *crātim* from *crates*, is found in Plautus.

5. Early writers formed the accusative of some other nouns in *im*.

Accusative of Greek Nouns.

§ 80. The accusative singular of masculine and feminine Greek nouns sometimes retains the Greek terminations *in* and *a*, but often ends, as in Latin, in *em* or *im*.

I. Masculine and feminine Greek nouns, whose genitive increases in *is* or *os*, *impure*, that is, with a consonant going before, have their accusative in *em* or *a*; as, *lampas, lampădis* (Greek -*δος*) *lampăda*; *chlămys, chlamўdis, chlamўdem*, or -*ӯda*; *Helicon, Helicōnis, Helicōna*.

REMARK. In like manner these three, which have *is* pure in the genitive—*Trōs, Trōis, Trōem,* and *Trōa,* a Trojan; *hēros,* a hero; and *Mĭnos,* a king of Crete.—*Aĕr,* the air; *œther,* the sky; *delphin,* a dolphin; and *pœan,* a hymn, have usually *a*; as, *aĕra, œthĕra, delphīna, pœāna. Pan,* a god, has only *a.*

EXC. 1. Masculines in *is,* whose genitive increases in *is* or *os* impure, have their accusative in *im* or *in*; sometimes in *idem*; *Părĭs, Parĭdis*; *Parim,* or *Paridem.*

EXC. 2. Feminines in *is,* increasing impurely in the genitive, though they usually follow the rule, have sometimes *im* or *in*; as, *Elis, Elĭdis*; *Elin* or *Elĭdem.* So *tigris,* gen. *is* or *ĭdis*; acc. *tigrim* or *tigrin.*

II. Masculine and feminine Greek nouns in *is* not increasing, and in *ys,* gen. *yos,* form their accusative by changing the *s* of the nominative into *m* or *n*; as, *Charybdis,* (gen. Lat. *-is,* Gr. εως), acc. *Charybdim* or *-in*; *Hălys, -yis* or *-yos, Halym* or *-yn.* So *rhus,* gen. *rhois,* has *rhun* or *rhum.*

III. Proper names ending in the diphthong *eus,* gen. *ĕi* and *ĕos,* have the accusative in *ea*; as, *T'hēseus, Thesea*; *Tȳdeus, Tydea.* See § 54, 5.

IV. Some Greek proper names in *es,* whose genitive is in *is,* have in Latin, along with the accusative in *em,* the termination *en,* as if of the first declension; as, *Achilles, Achillen*; *Xerxes, Xerxen*; *Sophŏcles, Sophŏclen.* Cf. § 45, 1. Some also, which have either *ētis* or *is* in the genitive, have, besides *ētem, ēta,* or *em,* the termination *en*; as, *Chrēmes, Thāles.*

VOCATIVE SINGULAR.

§ 81. The vocative is like the nominative.

REMARK. Many Greek nouns, however, particularly proper names, drop *s* of the nominative to form the vocative; as, *Daphnis, Daphni*; *Tēthys, Tethy*; *Melampus, Melampu*; *Orpheus, Orpheu.* Proper names in *es* (gen. *is*) sometimes have a vocative in *ē,* after the first declension; as, *Socrătes, Socrăte.* § 45, 1.

ABLATIVE SINGULAR.

§ 82. The ablative singular commonly ends in *e.*

EXC. 1. (*a.*) Neuters in *e, al,* and *ar,* have the ablative in *i*; as, *sedīle, sedīli*; *anĭmal, animāli*; *calcar, calcāri.*

(*b.*) But names of towns in *e,* and the following neuters in *ar,* have *e* in the ablative; viz. *baccar,* an herb; *far,* corn; *hēpar,* the liver; *jūbar,* a sunbeam; *nectar,* nectar; *par,* a pair; *sal,* salt. *Rēte,* a net, has either *e* or *i*; and *măre,* the sea, has sometimes in poetry *mare* in the ablative.

EXC. 2. (*a.*) Nouns which have *im* alone, or both *im* and *in* in the accusative, and names of months in *er* or *is,* have *i* in the ablative; as, *vis, vim, vi*; *Tibĕris, -im, i*; *December, Decembri*; *Aprilis, Aprili.*

(*b.*) But *Bœtis, cannăbis,* and *sĭnāpis,* have *e* or *i.* *Tigris,* the tiger, has *tigride*; as a river it has both *Tigrīde* and *Tigri.*

EXC. 3. (*a.*) Nouns which have *em* or *im* in the accusative, have their ablative in *e* or *i*; as, *turris, turre* or *turri.*

(*b.*) So *Elis,* acc. *Elĭdem* and *Elin,* has *Elĭde* or *Eli.* But *restis,* and most Greek nouns with *ĭdis* in the genitive, have *e* only; as, *Părĭs, -ĭdis, -ĭde.*

EXC. 4. (*a.*) Adjectives in *is,* used as nouns, have commonly *i* in the ablative, but sometimes *e*; as, *familiāris,* a friend; *natālis,* a birthday; *sodālis,* a companion; *trirēmis,* a trireme.—Participles in *ns,* used as nouns, have commonly *e* in the ablative, bu *contĭnens* has *i.*

(*b.*) When adjectives in *is* become proper names, they always have *e*; as *Juvenālis, Juvenāle*. *Affinis* and *ædīlis* have generally *e*; as have always *juvĕnis*, a youth; *rūdis*, a rod; and *volŭcris*, a bird.

Exc. 5. (*a.*) The following, though they have only *em* in the accusative, have *e* or *i* in the ablative, but most of them have oftener *e* than *i*:—

Amnis,	Collis,	Ignis,	Pars,	Supellex,
Anguis,	Convallis,	Imber,	Postis,	Tridens,
Avis,	Corbis,	Mugilis,	Pŭgil,	Unguis,
Bilis,	Finis,	Orbis,	Sordes,	Vectis,
Civis,.	Fustis,	Ovis,	Sors,	Vesper.
Classis,				

(*b.*) *Occĭput* has only *i*, and *rus* has either *e* or *i*; but *rure* commonly signifies from the country, and *ruri*, in the country. *Mel* has rarely *i*.

(*c.*) So also names of towns, when denoting the place where any thing is said to be, or to be done, have the ablative in *i*; as, *Carthagĭni*, at Carthage; so, *Anxŭri* and *Lacedæmŏni*, and, in the most ancient writers, many other nouns occur with this termination in the ablative. *Canālis* has *i*, and very rarely *e*.

Exc. 6. Nouns in *ys*, which have *ym* or *yn* in the accusative, have their ablative in *ye* or *y*; as, *Atys, Atye*, or *Aty*.

NOMINATIVE PLURAL.

§ **83.** I. The nominative plural of masculines and feminines ends in *es*; as, *sermōnes, rūpes*:—but neuters have *a*, and those whose ablative singular ends in *i* only, or in *e* and *i*, have *ia*; as, *căput, capĭta; sedīle, sedīlia; rēte, retia. Aplustre* has both *a* and *ia*.

1. Some Greek neuters in *os* have *ē* in the nominative plural; as, *mĕlos;* nom. plural, *mele;* (in Greek μέλεα, by contraction μέλη). So *Tempe*.

GENITIVE PLURAL.

II. The genitive plural commonly ends in *um;* sometimes in *ium*.

1. Nouns which, in the ablative singular, have *i* only, or both *e* and *i*, make the genitive plural in *ium;* as, *sedīle, sedīli, sedilium; turris, turre* or *turri, turrium*.

2. Nouns in *es* and *is*, which do not increase in the genitive singular, have *ium;* as, *nūbes, nubium; hostis, hostium*.

Exc. *Cănis, juvĕnis, fŏris, mugĭlis, prōles, strues*, and *vātes*, have *um;* so oftener have *ăpis, strigĭlis,* and *volŭcris;* less frequently *mensis, sēdes*, and, in the poets only, *ambāges, cædes, clādes, vepres*, and *cœlestis*.

3. Monosyllables ending in two consonants have *ium* in the genitive plural; as, *urbs, urbium; gens, gentium; arx, arcium*.

Exc. *Lynx, sphinx*, and *ops* (nom. obsolete) have *um*.

Most monosyllables in *s* and *x* pure have *um*, but the following have *ium; dos, mas, glis, lis, os (ossis), faux*, (nom. obs.) *nix, nox, strix, vis*, generally *fraus* and *mus;* so also *fur* and *ren*, and sometimes *lar*.

4. Nouns of two or more syllables, in *ns* or *rs*, and names of nations in *as*, have commonly *ium*, but sometimes *um*; as, *cliens, clientium* or *clientum, Arpīnas, Arpīnatium*.

(1.) Other nouns in *as* generally have *um*, but sometimes *ium*; as, *ætas*, *æta̅-tum* or *ætatium*. *Penățs* and *optima̅tes* have usually *ium*.

5. The following have *ium:—ca̅ro, compes, linter, imber, u̅ter, venter, Samnis, Quiris,* and usually *Insu̅ber. Fornax* and *pălus* have sometimes *ium*.

6. Greek nouns have generally *um*; as, *gĭgas, gigantum; Arabs, Arăbum; Thrax, Thra̅cum;*—but a few, used as titles of books, have sometimes *ŏn*; as, *Epigramma, epigramma̅tōn; Metamorphōsis, -eōn*. The patrial *Maleōn* also is found in Curtius, 4, 13.

REMARK 1. *Bos* has *boum* in the genitive plural.

REM. 2. Nouns which want the singular, form the genitive plural as if they were complete; as, *ma̅nes, manium; cœlĭtes, cœlĭtum; ilia, ilium;* as if from *ma̅nis, cœles,* and *ile*. So also names of feasts in *alia*; as, *Saturnalia Saturna̅lium;* but these have sometimes *ōrum* after the second declension. *Ales* has sometimes, by epenthesis, *alĭtuum*. See § 322, 3.

DATIVE AND ABLATIVE PLURAL.

§ 84. The dative and ablative plural end in *ĭbus*.

EXC. 1. *Bos* has *bŏbus* and *bu̅bus*, by contraction, for *borĭbus; sus* has *su̅bus* by syncope, for *suĭbus*. § 322, 5, and 4.

EXC. 2. Greek nouns in *ma* have the dative and ablative plural more frequently in *is* than in *ibus;* as, *poëma, poemătis,* or *poematĭbus*.

EXC. 3. The poets sometimes form the dative plural of Greek nouns, that increase in the genitive, in *si,* and, before a vowel, in *sin;* as, *herōis, heroĭdis; heroĭsi,* or *heroĭsin*. Ovid. So in Quintilian, *Metamorphosĕsi*.

ACCUSATIVE PLURAL.

§ 85. The accusative plural ends, like the nominative, in *ēs, ă, iă*.

EXC. 1. The accusative plural of masculines and feminines, whose genitive plural ends in *ium,* anciently ended in *is* or *ēis,* instead of *es;* as, *partes,* gen. *partium,* acc. *partēis* or *partēs*.

EXC. 2. Greek masculines and feminines, whose genitive increases in *is* or *os* impure, have their accusative in *as;* as, *lampas, lampădis, lampădas*. So also *hēros, herōis, herōas,* and some barbarian names of nations have a similar form; as, *Brigantas, Allobrŏgas*.

Jupĭter, and *vis,* strength, are thus declined :— .

Singular.	Singular.	Plural.
N. Ju'-pĭ-ter,	*N.* vis,	vī'-res,
G. Jŏ'-vis,	*G.* vis,	vir'-i-um,
D. Jŏ'-vi,	*D.* —	vir'-ĭ-bus,
Ac. Jŏ'-vem,	*Ac.* vim,	vī'-res,
V. Ju'-pĭ-ter,	*V.* vis,	vī'-res,
Ab. Jŏ'-ve.	*Ab.* v̄.	vir'-ĭ-bus.

§ 86. The following table exhibits the principal forms of Greek nouns of the third declension:—

	Nom.	Gen.	Dat.	Acc.	Voc.	Abl.
S.	Lampas,	-ădis, -ădos,	-ădi,	-ădem, -ăda,	-as,	-ăde.
Pl.	-ădes,	-ădum,	-adĭbus,	-ădes, -ădas,	-ădes,	-adĭbus.
S.	Hēros,	-ōis,	-ōi,	-ōem, -ōa,	-os,	-ōe.
Pl.	-ōes,	-ōum,	-oĭbus,	-ōes, -ōas,	-ōes,	-oĭbus.
	Chĕlys,	-y̆is, y̆os,	-y̆i,	-ym, -yn,	-y,	-y̆e or y.
	Poēsis,	-is, -ios, -ĕos,	-i,	-im, -in,	-i,	-i.
	Achilles,	-is, -ei, -i, -ĕos,	-i,	-em, -ĕa, ēn,	-es, -ē,	-e or -i.
	Orpheus,	-ĕos,	-ĕi,	-ĕa,	-eu,	See § 54.
	Aër,	-ĕris,	-ĕri,	-ĕra,	-er,	-ĕre.
	Dīdō,	-ūs,	-ō,	-ō,	-ō,	-ō.

FOURTH DECLENSION.

§ 87. Nouns of the fourth declension end in *us* and *u*. Those in *us* are masculine; those in *u* are neuter, and, except in the genitive, are indeclinable in the singular.

Nouns of this declension are thus declined:—

Fructus, *fruit.*

Singular.	Plural.
N. fruc'-tŭs,	fruc'-tūs,
G. fruc'-tūs,	fruc'-tu-ŭm,
D. fruc'-tu-ī,	fruc'-tĭ-bŭs,
Ac. fruc'-tŭm,	fruc'-tūs,
V. fruc'-tŭs,	fruc'-tūs,
Ab. fruc'-tū.	fruc'-tĭ-bŭs.

Cornu, *a horn.*

Singular.	Plural.
N. cor'-nū,	cor'-nu-ă,
G. cor'-nūs,	cor'-nu-ŭm,
D. cor'-nū,	cor'-nĭ-bŭs,
Ac. cor'-nū,	cor'-nu-ă,
V. cor'-nū,	cor'-nu-ă,
Ab. cor'-nū.	cor'-nĭ-bŭs.

In like manner decline

Can'-tus, *a song.*
Cur'-rus, *a chariot.*
Ex-er'-cĭ-tus, *an army.*
Fluc'-tus, *a wave.*
Luc'-tus, *grief.*
Mō'-tus, *motion.*
Se-nā'-tus, *the senate.*
Gĕ'-lu, *ice.* (in sing.)
Vĕ'-ru, *a spit.*

EXCEPTIONS IN GENDER.

§ 88. 1. The following are feminine:—

Acus, *a needle.*
Dŏmus, *a house.*
Ficus, *a fig.*
Manus, *a hand.*
Porticus, *a gallery.*
Tribus, *a tribe.*

Cŏlus, a distaff, and the plurals *Quinquātrus*, a feast of Minerva, and *Idus*, the Ides, are also feminine. So *noctu*, by night, found only in the ablative singular

Pĕnus, a store of provisions, when of the fourth declension, is masculine or feminine. *Sĕcus*, sex, is neuter; see § 94. *Spĕcus*, a den, is masculine and rarely feminine or neuter.

2. Some personal appellatives, and names of trees, are feminine by signification; as,

Anus, nŭrus, socrus;—cornus, laurus, and *quercus. Myrtus* also is feminine and rarely masculine. See § 29, 1 and 2.

EXCEPTIONS IN DECLENSION.

§ 89. *Dŏmus,* a house, is partly of the fourth declension, and partly of the second. It is thus declined:—

Singular.	Plural.
N. do'-mŭs,	do'-mūs,
G. do'-mūs, *or* do'-mī,	dom'-u-ŭm, *or* do-mō'-rŭm,
D. dom'-u-ī, *or* do'-mō,	dom'-ĭ-bŭs,
Ac. do'-mŭm,	do'-mūs, *or* do'-mōs,
V. do'-mŭs,	do'-mūs,
Ab. do'-mō.	dom'-ĭ-bŭs.

(*a.*) *Domŭs,* in the genitive, signifies, of a house; *domī* commonly signifies, at home. The ablative *domu* is found in Plautus, and in ancient inscriptions. In the genitive and accusative plural the forms of the second declension are more used than those of the fourth.

(*b.*) *Cornus,* a cornel-tree; *ficus,* a fig, or a fig-tree; *laurus,* a laurel; and *myrtus,* a myrtle, are sometimes of the second declension. *Pĕnus* is of the second, third or fourth declension.

(*c.*) Some nouns in *u* have also forms in *us* and *um;* as, *cornu, cornus,* or *cornum.* Adjectives, compounds of *manus,* are of the first and second declensions.

REMARK 1. Nouns of this declension anciently belonged to the third, and were formed by contraction, thus:—

Singular.	Plural.
N. fructŭs,	frutuēs, ūs,
G. fructuĭs, -ūs,	fructuŭm, -ŭm,
D. fructui, -ū,	fructuĭbŭs, -ŭbŭs, *or* -ĭbŭs,
Ac. fructuĕm, -ŭm,	fructuēs, ūs,
V. fructŭs,	fructuēs, -ūs,
Ab. fructuĕ, -ū.	fructuĭbŭs, -ŭbŭs, *or* -ĭbŭs.

2. The genitive singular in *is* is sometimes found in ancient authors; as, *anuis,* Ter. A genitive in *i,* after the second declension, also occurs; as, *senātus, senātī; tumultus, tumulti.* Sall.

3. The contracted form of the dative in *u* is not often used; yet it sometimes occurs, especially in Cæsar, and in the poets.

4. The contracted form of the genitive plural in *um* rarely occurs.

5. The following nouns have *ŭbus* in the dative and ablative plural:—

| Acus, *a needle.* | Artus, *a joint.* | Partus, *a birth.* | Spĕcus, *a den.* |
| Arcus, *a bow.* | Lăcus, *a lake.* | Pĕcu, *a flock.* | Tribus, *a tribe.* |

Gĕnu, a knee; *portus,* a arbor; *tonitrus,* thunder; and *vĕru,* a spit, have *ibus* or *ŭbus.*

FIFTH DECLENSION.

§ 90. Nouns of the fifth declension end in ēs, and are of feminine gender.

They are thus declined:—

Res, *a thing.*		Dies, *a day.*	
Singular.	*Plural.*	*Singular.*	*Plural.*
N. rēs,	rēs,	N. dĭ'-ēs,	dĭ'-ēs,
G. rĕ'-ī,	rē'-rŭm,	G. di-ē'-ī,	di-ē'-rŭm,
D. rĕ'-ī,	rē'-bŭs,	D. di-ē'-ī,	di-ē'-bŭs,
Ac. rĕm,	rēs,	Ac. dĭ'-ĕm,	dĭ'-ēs,
V. rēs,	rēs,	V. dĭ'-ēs,	dĭ'-ēs,
Ab. rē.	rē'-bŭs.	Ab. dĭ'-ē.	di-ē'-bŭs.

REMARK. Nouns of this declension, like those of the fourth, seem to have belonged originally to the third declension.

EXCEPTIONS IN GENDER.

1. *Dies*, a day, is masculine or feminine in the singular, and always masculine in the plural; *meridies*, mid-day, is masculine only.

NOTE. *Dies* is seldom feminine, in good prose writers, except when it denotes duration of time, or a day fixed and determined.

EXCEPTIONS IN DECLENSION.

2. The genitive and dative singular sometimes end in *ē* or in *ī*, instead of *ei*; as, gen. *diē* for *diēi*, Virg.; *fīde* for *fidei*, Hor.; *acie* for *aciēi*, Cæs.—gen. *plēbi* for *plebēi*, Liv.—dat. *fīde* for *fidei*, Hor., *pernicie*, Liv., and *pernicii*, Nep., for *perniciēi*. The genitive *rabiēs* contracted for *rabieis*, after the third declension, is found in Lucretius.

REMARK 1. There are only about eighty nouns of this declension, and of these only two, *res* and *dies*, are complete in the plural. *Acies, effigies, eluvies, facies, glacies, progenies, series, species, spes*, want the genitive, dative, and ablative plural, and the rest want the plural altogether.

REM. 2. All nouns of this declension end in *ies*, except four—*fīdes*, faith, *res*, a thing; *spes*, hope; and *plēbes*, the common people;—and all nouns in *ies* are of this declension, except *abies, aries, paries, quies*, and *requies*, which are of the third declension.

DECLENSION OF COMPOUND NOUNS.

§ 91. When a compound noun consists of two nominatives, both parts are declined; but when one part is a nominative, and the other an oblique case, the nominative only is declined. Of the former kind are *respublica*, a commonwealth, and *jusjurandum*, an oath; of the latter, *mater-familias*, a mistress of a family. Cf. § 43, 2.

Singular.	*Plural.*
N. V. res-pŭb'-lĭ-ca,	N. V. res-pub'-lĭ-cæ,
G. D. re-i-pub'-lĭ-cæ,	G. re-rum-pub-li-cā'-rum,
Ac. rem-pub'-lĭ-cam,	D. Ab. re-bus-pub'-lĭ-cis,
Ab. re-pub'-lĭ-cā.	Ac. res-pub'-lĭ-cas.

	Singular	Plural		Singular
N.	jus-ju-ran'-dum,	ju-ra-ju-ran'-da,	N.	ma-ter-fa-mil'-i-as,
G.	ju-ris-ju-ran'-di,		G.	ma-tris-fa-mil'-i-as,
D.	ju-ri-ju-ran'-do,		D.	ma-tri-fa-mil'-i-as,
Ac.	jus-ju-ran'-dum,	ju-ra-ju-ran'-da,	Ac.	ma-trem-fa-mil'-i-as,
V.	jus-ju-ran'-dum,	ju-ra-ju-ran'-da.	V.	ma-ter-fa-mil'-i-as,
Ab.	ju-re-ju-ran'-do.		Ab.	ma-tre-fa-mil'-i-as, *etc.*

NOTE. The preceding compounds are divided and pronounced like the simple words of which they are compounded.

IRREGULAR NOUNS.

§ 92. Irregular nouns are divided into three classes— *Variable, Defective,* and *Redundant.*

I. VARIABLE NOUNS.

A noun is variable, which, in some of its parts, changes either its gender or declension or both.

Nouns which vary in gender are called *heterogeneous;* those which vary in declension are called *heteroclites.*

Heterogeneous Nouns.

1. Masculine in the singular, and neuter in the plural; as,

Avernus, Dindўmus, Ismărus, Massĭcus, Mœnălus, Pangœus, Tartărus, Taygĕtus; plur. *Averna,* etc.

2. Masculine in the singular, and masculine or neuter in the plural; as,

jŏcus, a jest; plur. *jŏci,* or *jŏca;—lŏcus,* a place; plur. *lŏci,* passages in books, topics, places; *lŏca,* places;—*sibĭlus,* a hissing; plur. *sibĭla,* rarely *sibĭli;—intŭbus,* endive; plur. *intŭbi* or *intŭba.*

3. Feminine in the singular, and neuter in the plural; as,

carbăsus, a species of flax; plur. *carbăsa,* very rarely *carbăsi,* sails, etc., made of it;—*Hierosolўma, -æ,* Jerusalem; plur. *Hierosolўma, -ōrum.*

4. Neuter in the singular, and masculine in the plural; as,

cœlum, heaven; plur. *cœli;—Elysium;* plur. *Elysii;—Argos;* plur. *Argi.* So *siser,* neut., plur. *siseres,* masc.

5. Neuter in the singular, and masculine or neuter in the plural; as,

frēnum, a bridle; plur. *frēni* or *frēna;—rastrum,* a rake; plur. *rastri,* or, more rarely, *rastra;—pugillar,* a writing tablet; plur. *pugillāres* or *pugillaria.*

6. Neuter in the singular, and feminine in the plural; as,

epŭlum, a feast; plur. *epŭlæ;—balneum,* a bath; plur. *balneæ* or *balnea;—nundĭnum,* a market-day; plur. *nundĭnæ,* a fair.

7. Feminine or neuter in the singular, and feminine in the plural; as,

delicia or *delicium,* delight; plur. *deliciæ.*

Heteroclites.

§ 93. 1. Second or third declension in the singular, and third in the plural; as,

nom. and acc. *jugĕrum*, an acre; gen. *jugĕri* or *jugĕris*; abl. *jugĕro* and *jugĕre*; plur., nom., and acc. *jugĕra*; gen. *jugĕrum*; abl. *jugĕris* and *jugeribus*.

2. Third declension in the singular, and second in the plural; as,

vās, a vessel; plur. *vāsa, ōrum*. *Ancīle*, a shield, has sometimes *anciliōrum*, in the genitive plural.

NOTE. Variable nouns seem anciently to have been redundant, and to have retained a part of each of their original forms. Thus, *vāsa, -ōrum*, properly comes from *vāsum, -i*, but the latter, together with the plural of *vas, vāsis*, became obsolete.

II. DEFECTIVE NOUNS.

§ 94. Nouns are defective either in case or in number.

1. Nouns defective in case may want either one or more cases. Some are altogether indeclinable, and are called *aptotes*.

Such are *pondo*, a pound; most nouns in *i*; as, *gummi*, gum: foreign words; as, *Aaron, Jacob: sēmis*, a half; *git*, a kind of plant; the singular of *mille*, a thousand; words put for nouns; as, *velle suum*, for *sua voluntas*, his own inclination; and names of the letters of the alphabet.

A noun which is found in one case only, is called a *Monoptote*; if found in two cases, a *Diptote*; if in three, a *Triptote*; if in four, a *Tetraptote*; and if in five, a *Pentaptote*.

The following list contains most nouns defective in case. Those which occur but once in Latin authors are distinguished by an asterisk:—

*Abactus, acc. pl.; a driving away.
Accītu, abl.; a calling for.
Admissu, abl.; admission.
Admonītu, abl.; admonition.
Æs, not used in gen. pl.
Afflātu, abl.; an addressing;—pl. afflātus, -ĭbus.
Algus, nom.; algum, acc.; algu, abl.; cold.
Ambāge, abl.: a going around;—pl. entire.
*Amissum, acc.; a loss.
Aplustre, nom. and acc.; the flag of a ship;—pl. aplustria, or aplustra.
Arbitrātus, nom.; -um, acc.; -u, abl.; judgment.
Arcessitu, abl.; a sending for.
Astu, nom., acc.; a city.
Astus, nom.; astu, abl.; craft;—astus, acc. pl.
Cacoēthes, nom., acc.; an evil custom;—cacoēthe, nom. pl.; -e, and -es, acc. pl.
Canities, nom. -em, acc.; -e, abl.

Cētos, acc.; a whale;—cēte, nom. and acc. pl.; cetis, dat.
Chãos, nom. acc.; chao, abl.; chaos.
Cassem, acc.; casse, abl.; a net;—pl. entire.
Circumspectus, nom.; -um; -u; a looking around.
Coactu, abl.; constraint.
Cœlĭte, abl.; pl. entire; inhabitants of heaven.
*Commutātum, acc.; an alteration.
Compĕdis, gen.; compĕde, abl.; a fetter;—pl. compĕdes, -ium, -ĭbus.
Concessu, abl.; permission.
Condiscipulātu, abl.; companionship at school.
Crātim, or -em, acc.; -e, abl.; a hurdle;—pl. crates, -ium, -ĭbus.
Cupressu, abl.; a cypress.
Daps, nom., scarcely used; dăpis, gen. etc. pl. dapes, -ĭbus; a feast.
*Dătu, abl.; a giving.
Derīsus, -ui, dat.; -um, acc.; -u, abl.; ridicule.

DEFECTIVE NOUNS. § 94.

Despicatui, *dat.*; *contempt.*
Dica, *nom.*; dicam, *acc.*; *a legal process;*—dicas, *acc. pl.*
Dicis, *gen.*; *as,* dicis gratiā, *for form's sake.*
Ditiōnis, *gen.*; -i, *dat.*; -em, *acc.*; -e, *abl.*; *power.*
Diu, *abl.*; *in the day time.*
Divisui, *dat.*; *a dividing.*
Ebur, *ivory;*—not used in the plural.
*Efflagitātu, *abl.*; *importunity.*
*Ejectus, *nom.*; *a throwing out.*
Epos, *nom.* and *acc.*; *an epic poem.*
Ergo, *abl.* (or *adv.*); *for the sake.*
Essĕdas, *acc. pl.*; *war chariots.*
Evectus, *nom.*; *a carrying out.*
Fæx, *dregs,* wants *gen. pl.*
Famĕ, *abl.*; *hunger.*
Far, *corn,* not used in the *gen., dat.,* and *abl. pl.*
Fas, *nom.*; *acc.*; *right.*
Fauce, *abl.*; *the throat;*—*pl.* entire.
Fax, *a torch,* wants *gen. pl.*
Fel, *gall,* wants *gen. pl.*
Feminis, *gen.*; -i, *dat.*; -e, *abl.*; *the thigh;*—*pl.* femina, -ibus.
Flictu, *abl.*; *a striking.*
Fŏris, *nom.* and *gen.*; -em, *acc*; -e, *abl.*; *a door;*—*pl.* entire.
Fors, *nom.*; -tis, *gen.*; -tem, *acc.*; -te, *abl.*; *chance.*
*Frustratui, *abl.*; *a deceiving.*
Frux, *fruit,* *nom.* scarcely used;—frūgis, *gen.,* etc.
Fulgetras, *acc. pl.*; *lightning.*
Gausāpe, *nom., acc., abl.*; *a rough garment;*—gausāpa, *acc. pl.*
Glos, *nom.*; *a husband's sister.*
Grātes, *acc. pl.*;—gratibus, *abl.*; *thanks.*
Hebdomădam, *acc.*; *a week.*
Hiems, *winter,* not used in *gen., dat.,* and *abl. pl.*
Hippomănes, *nom.* and *acc.*
*Hir, *nom.*; *the palm of the hand.*
Hortātu, *abl.*; *an exhorting;*—*pl.* hortatibus.
Impĕtis, *gen.*; -e, *abl.*; *a shock;*—*pl.* impetibus.
Incitas, or -a, *acc. pl.*; *as,* ad incitas redactus, *reduced to a strait.*
*Inconsultu, *abl.*; *without advice.*
*Indultu, *abl.*; *indulgence.*
Inferiæ, *nom. pl.*; -as, *acc*; -is, *abl.*; *sacrifices to the dead.*
Infitias, *acc. pl.*; *a denial;* *as,* ire infitias, *to deny.*
Iugratiis, *abl. pl.,* (used adverbially); *against one's will.*
Injussu, *abl.*; *without command.*
'nquies, *nom.*; *restlessness.*
Instar, *nom., acc.*: *a likeness.*

Interdiu, *abl.* (or *adv.*); *in the day time.*
*Invitātu, *abl.*; *an invitation.*
Irrisui, *dat.*; -um, *acc.*; -u, *abl.*; *derision.*
Jŏvis, *nom.,* rarely used;—*pl.* Joves.
Jugĕris, *gen.*; -e, *abl.*; *an acre;*—*pl.* jugĕra, -um, -ibus.
Jussu, *abl.*; *command.*
Lābes, *a spot,* wants *gen. pl.*
Lūcu, *abl.*; *day-light.*
*Ludificatui, *dat.*; *a mockery.*
Lux, *light,* wants the *gen. pl.*
Mandātu, *abl.*; *a command.*
Māne, *nom., acc.*; *mane,* or rarely -i, *abl.*; *the morning.*
Mel, *honey,* not used in *gen., dat.,* and *abl. pl.*
Mĕlos, *nom., acc.*; melo, *dat.*; *melody;* —mĕle, *nom., acc. pl.*
Mētus, *fear,* not used in *gen., dat.,* and *abl. pl.*
Missu, *abl.*; *a sending;*—*pl.* missus, -ibus.
Monitu, *abl.*; *admonition;*—*pl.* monitus.
Nātu, *abl.*; *by birth.*
Nauci, *gen.,* with non; *as,* homo non nauci, *a man of no account.*
Nĕfas, *nom., acc.*; *wickedness.*
Nēmo, *nobody,* wants the *voc.* and the *pl.*
Nepenthes, *nom., acc.*; *an herb.*
Nex, *death,* wants the *voc.;*—nĕces, *nom., acc. pl.*
Nihil, or nihilum, *nom.* and *acc.*; -i, *gen.*; -o, *abl.*; *nothing.*
Noctu, *abl.*; *by night.*
Nuptui, *dat.*; -um, *acc.*; -u, *abl.*; *marriage.*
Obex, *nom.*; -icem, *acc.*; -ice, or -jice, *abl.*; *a bolt;*—*pl.* obices, -jicibus.
Objectum, *acc.*; -u, *abl.*; *an interposition;*—*pl.* objectus.
Obtentui, *dat.*; -um, *acc.*; -u, *abl.*; *a pretext.*
Opis, *gen.*; ŏpem, *acc.*; ŏpe, *abl.*; *help;*—*pl.* entire.
Oppositu, *abl.*; *an opposing;*—*pl.* oppositus, *acc.*
Opus, *nom., acc.*; *need.*
Os, *the mouth,* wants the *gen. pl.*
Panăces, *nom.*; -is, *gen.*; -e, *abl.*; *an herb.*
Pax, *peace,* wants *gen. pl.*
Peccātu, *abl.*; *a fault.*
Pecudis, *gen.*; -i, *dat.*; -em, *acc.*; -e, *abl.*;—*pl.* entire.
Pelăge, *acc. pl.* of pelăgus; *the sea.*
Permissu, *abl.*; -um, *acc.*; *permission.*
Piscātus, *nom.*; -i, *gen.*; -um, *acc.* -u, *abl.*; *a fishing.*

§ 95. DEFECTIVE NOUNS.

Pix, *pitch*; pĭces, *acc. pl.*
Pondo, *abl.*; *in weight.* Cf. § 94, 1.
Prĕci, *dat.*; -em, *acc.*; -e, *abl.*; *prayer* —*pl.* entire.
Prōcer; *nom.*; -em, *acc.*; *a peer*;—*pl.* entire.
Promptu, *abl.*, *readiness.*
Pus wants *gen. dat.* and *abl. pl.*
Relātum, *acc.*;—u, *abl.*; *a recital.*
Repetundārum, *gen. pl.*; -is, *abl.*; *money taken by extortion.*
Rogātu, *abl.*; *a request.*
Ros, *dew*, wants *gen. pl.*
Rus, *the country*, wants *gen.*, *dat.*, and *abl. pl.*
Satias, *nom.*; -ātem, *acc.*; āte, *abl.*; *satiety.*
Sĕcus, *nom.*, *acc.*; *sex.*
Situs, *nom.*; -um, *acc.*; -u, *abl.*; *situation*;—sĭtus, *nom.* and *acc. pl.*
Sĭtus, *nom.*; -ūs, *gen.*; -um, *acc.*; -u, *abl.*; *rust*;—sĭtus, *acc. pl.*
Sol, *the sun*, wants *gen. pl.*
Sordis, *gen.*; -em, *acc.*; -e and -i, *abl*; *filth*;—*pl.* sordes,-ium, etc.
Spontis, *gen.*; -e, *abl.*; *of one's own accord.*
Subŏles, *offspring*, wants *gen. pl.*

Suppetiæ, *nom. pl.*; -as, *acc.*; *supplies.*
Tābum, *nom.*; -i, *gen.*; -o, *abl.*; *corrupt matter.*
Tempe, *nom. acc. voc. pl.*; *a vale in Thessaly.*
Tus wants *gen.*, *dat.*, and *abl. pl.*
Vĕnui and -o, *dat.*; um, *acc.*; -o, *abl.*; *sale.*
Veprem, *acc.*; -e, *abl.*; *a brier*;—*pl.* entire.
Verbĕris, *gen.*; -e, *abl.*; *a stripe*;—*pl.* verbĕra, um, Ibus.
Vesper, *nom.*; -um, *acc.*-; -e, -i, *or* -o, *abl.*; *the evening.*
Vespĕrn, *nom.*; -am, *acc.*; -ā, *abl.*; *the evening.*
Vicis, *gen.*; -i, *dat.*; -em, *acc.*; -e, *abl.*; *change*;—*pl.* entire, except *gen.*
Virus, *nom.*; -i, *gen.*; -us, *acc.*; -o, *abl.*; *poison.*
Vis, *gen.* and *dat.* rare; *strength; pl.* vires, -ium, etc. See § 85.
Viscus, *nom.*; -ĕris, *gen.*; -ĕre, *abl.*; *an internal organ. pl.* viscĕra, eto.
Vocātu, *abl.*; *a calling*;—vocātus, *acc. pl.*

REMARK 1. To these may be added nouns of the fifth declension, which either want the plural, as most of them are abstract nouns, or have in that number only the nominative, accusative, and vocative. *Res* and *dies*, however, have the plural entire. Cf. § 90, R. 1.

REM. 2. For the use of the vocative, also, of many nouns, no classical authority can be found.

§ **95.** 2. Nouns defective in number, want either the plural or the singular.

(*a*) Many nouns want the plural from the nature of the things which they express. Such are generally names of persons, most names of places (except those which have only the plural), the names of herbs, of the arts, most material and abstract nouns; but these may have a plural when used as common nouns, (§ 26, R. 3.), and many others.

REM. In Latin the plural of abstract nouns is often used to denote the existence of the quality, attribute, etc. in different objects, or the repetition of an action; and in poetry such plurals are used for the sake of emphasis or metre. See § 98.

The following list contains many of the *nouns which want the plural*, and also some, marked *p*, which are included in the above classes, but are sometimes used in the plural.

Aconītum, *wolfsbane*, p.
Adoren, *a military reward*
Aēr, *the air*, p.
Æs, *brass, money*, p.
Æther, *the sky.*
Ævum, *age, lifetime*, p.
Album, *an album.*
Allium, *garlic*, p.
Amicitia, *friendship*, p.
Argilla, *white clay.*
Avēna, *oats*, p.
Balaustium, *the flower of the pomegranate.*
Balsāmum, *balsam*, p.
Barathrum, *a gulf.*
Callum, *hardened skin*, p.
Călor, *heat*, p.

52 DEFECTIVE NOUNS. § 96

Carduus, *a thistle*, p.
Caro, *flesh*, p.
Cera, *wax*, p.
Cestus, *a girdle*.
Cicuta, *hemlock*, p.
Cœnum, *mud*.
Contagium, *contagion*, ‖.
Crocum, *saffron*.
Crocus, *saffron*, p.
Cruor, *blood*, p.
Cutis, *the skin*, p.
Diluculum, *the dawn*.
Ebur, *ivory*.
Electrum, *amber*, p.
Far, *corn*, p.
Fel, *gall*, p.
Fervor, *heat*, p.
Fides, *faith*.
Fimus, *dung*.
Fuga, *flight*, p.
Fumus, *smoke*, p.
Furor, *madness*, p.
Galla, *an oak-apple*, p.
Gelu, *frost*.
Glarea, *gravel*.
Gloria, *glory*, p.
Glastum, *woad*.
Gluten, *or*
Glutinum, *glue*.
Gypsum, *white plaster*.
Hepar, *the liver*.
Hesperus, *the evening star*.
Hilum, *a little thing*.
Hordeum, *barley*, p.
Humus, *the ground*.
Indoles, *native quality*, p.
Ira, *anger*, p.
Jubar, *radiance*.
Jus, *justice, law*, p.
Justitium, *a law vacation*.

Lac, *milk*.
Lætitia, *joy*, p.
Languor, *faintness*, p.
Lardum, *bacon*, p.
Latex, *liquor*, p.
Letum, *death*.
Lignum, *wood*, p.
Limus, *mud*.
Liquor, *liquor*, p.
Lues, *a plague*.
Lutum, *clay*, p.
Lux, *light*, p.
Macellum, *the shambles*.
Mane, *the morning*.
Marmor, *marble*, p.
Mel, *honey*, p.
Meridies, *mid-day*.
Mors, *death*, p.
Munditia, *neatness*, p.
Mundus, *female ornaments*.
Muscus, *moss*.
Nectar, *nectar*.
Nemo, *no man*.
Nequitia, *wickedness*, p.
Nihilum, *nihil, or nil, nothing*.
Nitrum, *natron*.
Oblivio, *forgetfulness*, p.
Omasum, *bullock's tripe*.
Opium, *opium*.
Palea, *chaff*, p.
Pax, *peace*, p.
Penum, *and*
Penus, *provisions*, p.
Piper, *pepper*.
Pix, *pitch*, p.
Pontus, *the sea*.
Prolubium, *desire*.
Pubes, *the youth*.
Pulvis, *dust*, p.

Purpura, *purple*, p.
Quies, *rest*, p.
Ros, *dew*, p.
Rubor, *redness*, p.
Sabulo, *and*
Sabulum, *gravel*.
Sal, *salt*.
Salum, *the sea*.
Salus, *safety*.
Sanguis, *blood*.
Scrupulum, *a scruple*, p.
Senium, *old age*.
Siler, *an osier*.
Sinapi, *mustard*.
Siser, *skirret*, p
Sitis, *thirst*.
Sol, *the sun*, p.
Sopor, *sleep*, p.
Specimen, *an example*.
Spuma, *foam*, p.
Sulfur, *sulphur*, p.
Supellex, *furniture*.
Tabes, *a consumption*.
Tabum, *corrupt matter*.
Tellus, *the earth*.
Terror, *terror*, p.
Thymum, *thyme*, p.
Tribulus, *a thistle*, p.
Tristitia, *sadness*.
Ver, *spring*.
Vespera, *the evening*.
Veternus, *lethargy*.
Vigor, *strength*, p.
Vinum, *wine*, p.
Virus, *poison*.
Viscum, *and*
Viscus, *bird-lime*.
Vitrum, *woad*.
Vulgus, *the common people*.
Zingiber, *ginger*.

§ 96. (*b*). The names of festivals and games, and several names of places and books, want the singular; as, *Bacchanalia*, a festival of Bacchus; *Olympia*, the Olympic games; *Bucolica*, a book of pastorals; and the following names of places:—

Acroceraunia,	Baiæ,	Fundi,	Locri,	Susa,
Amyclæ,	Ceraunia,	Gabii,	Parisii,	Syracusæ,
Artaxata,	Ecbatana,	Gades,	Philippi,	Thermopylæ,
Athenæ,	Esquiliæ,	Gemoniæ,	Puteoli,	Veii.

NOTE. Some of those in *i* properly signify the people.

The following list contains most other *nouns which want the singular*, and also some, marked *s*, which are rarely used in that number:—

Acta, *records*.
Adversaria, *a memorandum-book*.
Æstiva, sc. castra, *summer quarters*.

Alpes, *the Alps*, s.
Annales, *annals*, s.
Antæ, *door-posts*.
Antes, *rows*.
Antiæ, *a forelock*.

Apinæ, *trifles*.
Argutiæ, *witticisms*, s.
Arma, *arms*.
Artus, *the joints*, s.
Bellaria, *sweetmeats*.

§ 97. DEFECTIVE NOUNS. 58

Bigæ, *a two-horse chariot*, s.
Braccæ, *breeches.*
Branchiæ, *the gills of fishes.*
Brevia, *shallow places.*
Calendæ, *the Calends.*
Cancelli, *balustrades.*
Cāni, *gray hairs.*
Casses, *a hunter's net*, s.
Caulæ, *sheep-folds.*
Celĕres, *the body-guard of the Roman kings.*
Cibaria, *victuals*, s.
Clitellæ, *a pack-saddle.*
Codicilli, *a writing.*
Cœlites, *the gods*, s.
Crepundia, *a rattle.*
Cunabŭla, *and*
Cūnæ, *a cradle.*
Cyclădes, *the Cyclades*, s.
Decĭmæ, *tithes*, s.
Dīræ, *the Furies*, s.
Divitiæ, *riches.*
Druīdes, *the Druids.*
Dryădes, *the Dryads*, s.
Epŭlæ, *a banquet*, s.
Eumenĭdes, *the Furies*, s.
Excubiæ, *watches.*
Exsequiæ, *funeral rites.*
Exta, *entrails.*
Exuviæ, *spoils.*
Facetiæ, *pleasantry*, s.
Feriæ, *holidays*, s.
Fīdes, *a stringed instrument*, s.
Flabra, *blasts.*
Fraces, *the lees of oil.*
Frāga, *strawberries*, s.
Geminī, *twins*, s.
Gĕnæ, *cheeks*, s.
Gerræ, *trifles.*
Grātes, *thanks.*
Habēnæ, *reins*, s.
Hiberna, sc. castra, *winter quarters.*
Hyădes, *the Hyades*, s.
Idus, *the ides of a month.*
Ilia, *the flank.*
Incunabŭla, *a cradle.*
Indutiæ, *a truce.*

Induviæ, *clothes.*
Ineptiæ, *fooleries*, s.
Infĕri, *the dead.*
Inferiæ, *sacrifices in honor of the dead.*
Insecta, *insects.*
Insidiæ, *an ambuscade*, s.
Justa, *funeral rites.*
Lactes, *small entrails*, s.
Lamenta, *lamentations.*
Lapicidīnæ, *a stone quarry.*
Latebræ, *a hiding place*, s.
Laurīces, *young rabbits.*
Lautia, *presents to foreign ambassadors.*
Lemŭres, *hobgoblins.*
Lendes, *nits*
Libĕri, *children*, s.
Lucĕres, *a division of the Roman cavalry.*
Magalia, *cottages.*
Majōres, *ancestors.*
Mānes, *the shades*, s.
Manubiæ, *spoils of war.*
Mapalia, *huts*, s.
Minaciæ, *and*
Minæ, *threats.*
Minōres, *posterity.*
Mœnia, *the walls of a city*, s.
Multitia, *garments finely wrought.*
Munia, *official duties.*
Naiădes, *water-nymphs*, s.
Nāres, *the nostrils*, s.
Natāles, *parentage.*
Nātes, *the haunches*, s.
Nōmæ, *corroding sores or ulcers.*, s.
Nōnæ, *the nones of a month.* § 326, 1.
Nūgæ, *jests, nonsense.*
Nundĭnæ, *the weekly market.*
Nuptiæ, *a marriage.*
Oblīvia, *forgetfulness*, s.
Offuciæ, *cheats*, s.
Optimātes, *the aristocratic party*, s.

Palearia, *the dewlap*, s.
Pandectæ, *the pandects*
Parietīnæ, *old walls.*
Partes, *a party*, s.
Pascua, *pastures*, s.
Penātes, *household gods*, s.
Phalĕræ, *trappings.*
Philtra, *love potions.*
Pleiădes, *the Pleiads* or *seven stars*, s.
Postĕri, *posterity.*
Præbia, *an amulet.*
Præcordia, *the diaphragm, the entrails.*
Primitiæ, *first fruits.*
Procĕres, *nobles*, s.
Pugillaria, *or -ares, writing-tablets*, s.
Quadrīgæ, *a team of four horses*, s.
Quirītes, *Roman citizens*, s.
Quisquiliæ, *refuse.*
Reliquiæ, *the remains*, s.
Salebræ, *rugged roads*, s.
Salīnæ, *salt pits.*
Scālæ, *a ladder*, s.
Scatebræ, *a spring*, s.
Scōpæ, *a broom.*
Scruta, *old stuff.*
Sentes, *thorns*, s.
Sponsalia, *espousals.*
Statīva, sc. castra, *a stationary camp.*
Supĕri, *the gods above.*
Talaria, *winged shoes.*
Tenebræ, *darkness*, s.
Tesca, *rough places.*
Thermæ, *warm baths.*
Tormĭna, *colic-pains.*
Transtra, *seats for rowers*, s.
Trīcæ, *trifles, toys.*
Utensilia, *utensils.*
Valvæ, *folding doors*, s.
Vepres, *brambles*, s.
Vergiliæ, *the seven stars.*
Vindiciæ, *a legal claim*, s.
Virgulta, *bushes.*

§ 97. The following usually differ in meaning in the different numbers.

Ædes, -is, *a temple.*
Ædes, -ium, *a house.*
Aqua, *water.*
Aquæ, *medicinal springs.*
Auxilium, *aid.*
Auxilia, *auxiliary troops.*

Bŏnum, *a good thing.*
Bŏna, *property.*
Carcer, *a prison.*
Carcĕres, *the barriers of a race-course*
Castrum, *a castle.*

Castra, *a camp.*
Comitium, *a part of the Roman forum.*
Comitia, *an assembly for election.*
Copia, *plenty.*

6*

Copiæ, *troops, forces.*
Cupedia, -æ, *daintiness.*
Cupediæ, -ārum, *and*
Cupedia, -ōrum, *dainties.*
Facultas, *ability.*
Facultātes, *property.*
Fastus, -ūs, *pride.*
Fastus, -uum, *and*
Fasti, -ōrum, *a calendar.*
Fortūna, *Fortune.*
Fortūnæ, *wealth.*
Furfur, *bran.*
Furfūres, *dandruff.*
Gratia, *favor.*
Gratiæ, *thanks.*

Impedimentum, *a hinderance.*
Impedimenta, *baggage.*
Litĕra, *a letter of the alphabet.*
Litĕræ, *an epistle.*
Lūdus, *pastime.*
Lūdi, *public games.*
Lustrum, *a morass.*
Lustra, *a haunt* or *den of wild beasts.*
Mos, *custom.*
Mōres, *manners.*
Nāris, *a nostril.*
Nāres, *the nose.*

Natālis, *a birthday.*
Natāles, *birth, lineage.*
Opĕra, *work, labor.*
Opĕræ, *workmen.*
Opis, gen. *power.*
Opes, -um, *means, wealth.*
Plăga, *a region, tract.*
Plăgæ, *nets, toils.*
Principium, *a beginning.*
Principia, *the general's -quarters.*
Rostrum, *a beak, prow.*
Rostra, *the Rostra.*
Sal, *salt.*
Sāles, *witticisms.*

§ **98.** The following plurals, with a few others, are sometimes used in poetry, especially in the nominative and accusative, instead of the singular, for the sake of emphasis or metre.

Æquŏra, *the sea.*
Alta, *the sea.*
Animi, *courage.*
Auræ, *the air.*
Carīnæ, *a keel.*
Cervīces, *the neck.*
Colla, *the neck.*
Cŏmæ, *the hair.*
Connubia, *marriage.*
Corda, *the heart.*
Corpŏra, *a body.*
Crepuscŭla, *twilight.*
Currūs, *a chariot.*
Exsilia, *banishment.*
Frigŏra, *cold.*
Gaudia, *joy.*
Gramĭna, *grass.*
Guttŭra, *the throat.*

Hymenæi, *marriage.*
Ignes, *love.*
Inguĭna, *the groin.*
Iræ, *anger.*
Jejunia, *fasting.*
Jŭbæ, *a mane.*
Limĭna, *a threshold.*
Litŏra, *a shore.*
Mensæ, *a service or course of dishes.*
Neniæ, *a funeral dirge.*
Numĭna, *the divinity.*
Odia, *hatred.*
Ora, *the mouth, the countenance.*
Oræ, *confines.*
Ortus, *a rising, the east.*
Otia, *ease, leisure.*

Pectŏra, *the breast.*
Reditūs, *a return.*
Regna, *a kingdom.*
Rictūs, *the jaws.*
Robŏra, *strength.*
Silentia, *silence.*
Sinūs, *the bosom of a Roman garment.*
Tædæ, *a torch.*
Tempŏra, *time.*
Terga, *the back.*
Thalămi, *marriage* or *marriage-bed.*
Tŏri, *a bed, a couch.*
Tūra, *frankincense.*
Viæ, *a journey.*
Vultus, *the countenance.*

III. REDUNDANT NOUNS.

§ **99.** Nouns are redundant either in termination, in declension, in gender, or in two or more of these respects.

1. In termination: (*a.*) of the nominative; as, *arbor*, and *arbos*, a tree: (*b.*) of the oblique cases; as, *tigris*,; gen. *tigris*, or *-ĭdis*; a tiger.

2. In declension; as, *laurus*; gen. *-i*, or *-ūs*; a laurel.

3. In gender; as, *vulgus*, masc. or neut.; the common people.

4. In termination and declension; as, *senecta*, *-æ*, and *senectus*, *-ūtis*; old age.

5. In termination and gender; as *pileus*, masc., and *pileum*, neut.; a hat.

6. In declension and gender; as *pĕnus*, *-i* or *ūs*, masc. or fem., and *pĕnus*, *-ŏris*, neut.; a store of provisions. *Spĕcus*, *-ūs* or *-i*, masc. fem. or neut.; a cave.

7. In termination, declension, and gender; as, *menda*, *-æ*, fem. and *mendum*, *-i*, neut.; a fault.

§ 99. REDUNDANT NOUNS.

The following list contains most *Redundant Nouns* of the above classes:—

Acinus, -um, *and* -a, *a berry.*
Adagium, *and* -io, *a proverb.*
Admonitio, -um, *and* -us, *ūs, a reminding.*
Æthra, *and* æther, *the clear sky.*
Affectio, *and* -us, *ūs, affection.*
Agamemno, *and* -on, *Agamemnon.*
Alabaster, *tri, and pl.* -tra, *ōrum, an alabaster box.*
Alimonia, *and* -um, *aliment.*
Alluvio, *and* -es, *a flood.*
Alvearium, *and* -āre, *a bee-hive.*
Amarācus, *and* -um, *marjoram.*
Amygdāla, *and* -um, *an almond.*
Anfractum, *and* -us, *ūs, a winding.*
Angiportum, *and* -us, *ūs, a narrow lane or alley.*
Antidōtus, *and* -um, *an antidote.*
Aranea, *and* -us, *i, a spider.*
Arar, *and* Arāris, *the river Arar.*
Arbor, *and* -os, *a tree.*
Architectus, *and* -on, *an architect.*
Arcus, -ūs, *and* i, *a bow.*
Attagēna, *and* -gen, *a moor-hen.*
Avaritia, *and* -ies, *avarice.*
Augmentum, *and* -men, *an increase.*
Baccar, *and* -āris, *a kind of herb.*
Bacŭlus, *and* -um, *a staff.*
Balteus, *and* -um, *a belt.*
Barbaria, *and* -ies, *barbarism.*
Barbĭtus, *and* -on, *a harp.*
Batillus, *and* -um, *a fire-shovel.*
Blanditia, *and* -ies, *flattery.*
Buccĭna, *and* -um, *a trumpet.*
Būra, *and* -is, *a plough-tail.*
Buxus, *and* -um, *the box-tree.*
Cæpa, *and* cæpe, *an onion.*
Calamister, *tri, and* -trum, *a crisping-pin.*
Callus, *and* -um, *hardened skin.*
Cancer, *cri, or* ěris, *a crab.*
Canitia, *and* -ies, *hoariness.*
Cāpus, *and* cāpo, *a capon.*
Carrus, *and* -um, *a kind of waggon.*
Cassĭda, *and* -cassis, *a helmet.*
Catīnus, *and* -um, *a bowl, dish.*
Chirogrăphus, *and* -um, *a hand-writing.*
Cingŭla, -us, *and* -um, *a girdle.*
Clipeus, *and* -um, *a shield.*
Cochlearium, -ar, *and* -āre, *a spoon.*
Colluvio, *and* -ies, *filth.*
Commentarius, *and* -um, *a journal.*
Compāges, *and* -go, *a joining.*
Conātum, *and* -us, *ūs, an attempt.*
Concinnĭtas, *and* -tūdo, *neatness.*
Consortium, *and* -io, *partnership.*
Contagium, -io, *and* -es, *contact.*
Cornum, -us, *i, or* ūs, *a cornel tree.*
Costos, *i, and* -um, *a kind of shrub.*

Cratēra, *and* crāter, *a bowl.*
Crŏcus, *and* -um, *saffron.*
Crystallus, *and* -um, *crystal.*
Cubĭtus, *and* -um, *the elbow.*
Cupidĭtas, *and* -pĭdo, *desire.*
Cupressus, *i, or* ūs, *a cypress-tree.*
Delicia, *and* -um, *delight.*
Delphīnus, *and* delphin, *a dolphin.*
Dictamnus, *and* -um, *dittany.*
Diluvium, -o, *and* -ies, *a deluge.*
Dōmus, *i, or* ūs, *a house.*
Dorsus, *and* -um, *the back.*
Duritia, *and* -ies, *hardness.*
Effigia, *and* -ies, *an image.*
Elegia, *and* -on, *i, an elegy.*
Elěphantus, *and* -phas, *an elephant.*
Epitōma, *and* -e, *an abridgment.*
Essĕda, *and* -um, *a chariot.*
Evander, *dri, and* -drus, *Evander.*
Eventum, *and* -us, *ūs, an event.*
Exemplar, *and* -āre, *a pattern.*
Ficus, *i, or* ūs, *a fig-tree.*
Fĭmus, *and* -um, *dung.*
Frētum, *and* -us, *ūs, a strait.*
Fulgetra, *and* -um, *lightning.*
Galērus, *and* -um, *a hat, cap.*
Ganea, *and* -um, *an eating-house.*
Gausăpa, -es, -e, *and* -um, *frieze.*
Gibba, -us, *and* -er, *ěri, a hump.*
Glutĭnum, *and* -ten, *glue.*
Gobius, *and* -io, *a gudgeon.*
Grammatĭca, *and* -e, *grammar.*
Grus, *gruis, and* gruis, *is, a crane.*
Hebdomăda, *and* -mas, *a week.*
Hellebŏrus, *and* -um, *hellebore.*
Hŏnor, *and* hŏnos, *honor.*
Hyssōpus, *and* -um, *hyssop.*
Ilios, -um, *and* -on, *Troy.*
Incestum, *and* -us, *ūs, incest.*
Intŭbus, *and* -um, *endive.*
Jugŭlus, *and* -um, *the throat.*
Juventa, -us, *ūtis, and* -as, *youth.*
Lăbor, *and* lăbos, *labor.*
Lacerta, *and* -us, *a lizard.*
Laurus, *i, or* ūs, *a laurel.*
Lěpor, *and* lěpos, *wit.*
Ligur, *and* -us, *ŭris, a Ligurian.*
Lupīnus, *and* -um, *a lupine.*
Luxuria, *and* -ies, *luxury.*
Mæander, -dros, *and* -drus, *Mæander.*
Margarīta, *and* -um, *a pearl.*
Materia, *and* -ies, *materials.*
Medimnus, *and* -um, *a measure.*
Menda, *and* -um, *a fault.*
Modius, *and* -um, *a measure.*
Mollitia, *and* -ies, *softness.*
Momentum, *and* -men, *influence.*
Mūgil, *and* -ĭlis, *a mullet.*
Mulcĭber, *ěri, or* ěris, *Vulcan.*

Mulctra, *and* -um, *a milk-pail.*
Munditia, *and* -ies, *neatness.*
Muria, *and* -ies, *brine or pickle.*
Myrtus, *i* or *ūs, a myrtle.*
Nardus, *and* -um, *nard.*
Nāsus, *and* -um, *the nose.*
Necessitas, *and* -ūdo, *necessity.*
Nequitia, *and* -ies, *worthlessness.*
Notitia, *and* -ies, *knowledge.*
Oblivium, *and* -io, *forgetfulness.*
Obsidium, *and* -io, *a siege.*
Œdĭpus, *i,* or *ŏdis, Œdipus.*
Ostrea, *and* -um, *an oyster.*
Palātus, *and* -um, *the palate.*
Palumba, -us, *and* -es, *a pigeon.*
Papȳrus, *and* -um, *papyrus.*
Paupertas, *and* -ies, *poverty.*
Pāvus, *and* pāvo, *a peacock.*
Pĕnus, *i, -ŏris,* or *ūs,* and pĕnum, *provisions.*
Peplus, *and* -um, *a veil.*
Perseus, *ei,* or *eos, Perseus.*
Pileus, *and* -um, *a hat.*
Pīnus, *i,* or *ūs, a pine-tree.*
Pistrīna, *and* -um *a bake-house.*
Planitia, *and* -ies, *a plain.*
Plāto, *and* Plāton, *Plato.*
Plebs, *and* plēbes, *ei, the common people.*
Porrus, *and* -um, *a leek.*
Postulātum, *and* -io, *a request.*
Præsēpia, -ium, -es, *or* -is, *and* -e, *a stable.*
Prætextum, *and* -us, *ūs, a pretext.*
Prosapia, *and* -ies, *lineage.*
Rāpa, *and* -um, *a turnip.*
Requies, *ētis* or *ĕi, rest.*
Rēte, *and* rētis, *a net.*
Reticŭlus, *and* -um, *a small net.*

Rictum, *and* -us, *ūs, the open mouth.*
Sævitia, -ūdo *and* -ies, *ferocity.*
Sāgus, *and* -um, *a military cloak.*
Sanguis, *and* sanguen, *blood.*
Satrāpes, *and* satraps, *a satrap.*
Scabritia, *and* -ies, *roughness.*
Scorpius, -os, *and* -io, *a scorpion.*
Segmentum, *and* -men, *a piece.*
Segnitia, *and* -ies, *sloth.*
Senecta, *and* -us, *old age.*
Sequester, *tri,* or *tris, a trustee.*
Sesāma, *and* -um, *sesame.*
Sibīlus, *and* -a, *ōrum, a hissing.*
Sināpi, *and* -is, *mustard.*
Sinus, *and* -um, *a goblet.*
Spărus, *and* -a, *ōrum, a spear.*
Spurcitia, *and* -ies, *filthiness.*
Stramentum, *and* -men, *straw.*
Suffimentum, *and* -men, *fumigation.*
Suggestus, *and* -um, *a pulpit, stage.*
Suppārus, *and* -um, *a linen garment.*
Supplicium, -icamentum, *and* -icatio *a public supplication.*
Tapētum, -ēte, *and* -es, *tapestry.*
Teneritas, *and* -tūdo, *softness.*
Tergum, *and* -us, *ŏris, the back.*
Tiāra, *and* -as, *a turban.*
Tignus, *and* -um, *a beam, timber.*
Tigris, *is,* or *ĭdis, a tiger.*
Titānus, *and* Titan, *Titan.*
Tonitruum, *and* -trus, *ūs, thunder.*
Torāle, *and* -al, *a bed-covering.*
Trabes, *and* trabs, *a beam.*
Tribŭla, *and* -um, *a threshing sledge.*
Vespĕra, -per, *ĕri* and *ĕris, the evening.*
Vinaceus, *and* -a, *ōrum, a grape-stone.*
Viscus, *and* -um, *the mistletoe.*
Vulgus, masc. and neut., *the common people.*

REMARK 1. To these may be added some other verbals in *us* and *io*, and Greek nouns in *o* and *on*; as, *Dio* and *Dion;* also some Greek nouns in *es* and *ē*, which have Latin forms in *a;* as, *Atrides* and *Atrida.* See § 45.

REM. 2. Some proper names of places also are redundant in number; as, *Argos* and *Argi; Fidēna* and *Fidēnæ; Thēbe* and *Thēbæ.*

NOTE. The different forms of most words in the above list are not equally common, and some are rarely used, or only in particular cases.

DERIVATION OF NOUNS.

§ 100. Nouns are derived from other nouns, from adjectives, and from verbs.

I. FROM NOUNS.

From nouns are derived the following classes:—

1. A *patronymic* is the name of a person, derived from that of his father or other ancestor, or of the founder of his nation.

§ 100. DERIVATION OF NOUNS.

NOTE 1. Patronymics are properly Greek nouns, and have been borrowed from that language by the Latin poets.

(a.) Masculine patronymics end in ĭdes, īdes, ădes, and ĭădes.

(1.) Nouns in us of the second declension, and those nouns of the third declension, whose root ends in a short syllable, form their patronymics in ĭdes; as, *Priămus, Priamĭdes; Agamemnŏn*, gen. ŏnis, *Agamemnŏnĭdes*.

(2.) Nouns in ēus and cles form their patronymics in īdes; as, *A-trēus, Atrīdes; Hērăcles* (i. e. Hercules,) *Heraclīdes*.

REM. 1. *Ænīdes*, in Virg. A. 9, 653, is formed in like manner, as if from *Ænēus*, instead of *Ænēas*.

(3.) Nouns in ăs and ēs of the first declension form their patronymics in ădes, as *Ænĕas, Æneădes; Hippŏtēs, Hippŏtădes*.

(4.) Nouns in ius of the second declension, and those nouns of the third declension, whose root ends in a long vowel, form their patronymics in ĭădes; as, *Thestius, Thestĭădes; Amphitryŏ* (gen. ŏnis), *Amphitryonĭădes*.

REM 2. A few nouns also of the first declension have patronymics in ĭădes; as, *Anchīses, Anchisĭădes*.

(b.) Feminine patronymics end in is, ēis, and ias, and correspond in termination to the masculines, viz. is to ĭdes, ēis to īdes, and ias to ĭădes; as, *Tyndărus*, masc. *Tyndarĭdes*, fem. *Tyndăris; Nēreus*, masc. *Nerĕĭdes*, fem. *Nerēis; Thestius*, masc. *Thestĭădes*, fem. *Thestias*.

REM. 3. A few feminines are found in īne, or iŏne; as, *Nerīne, Acrisiŏne*, from *Nereus* and *Acrisius*.

NOTE 2. Patronymics in des and ne are of the first declension; those in is and as, of the third.

2. A *patrial* or *gentile* noun is derived from the name of a country; and denotes an inhabitant of that country; as,

Trōs, a Trojan man; *Trōas*, a Trojan woman: *Macĕdo*, a Macedonian; *Samnis*, a Samnite; from *Trŏja, Macedonia*, and *Samnium*.

NOTE 3. Most patrials are properly adjectives, relating to a noun understood; as, *hŏmo, civis*, etc. See § 128, 6.

3. A *diminutive* signifies a small thing of the kind denoted by the primitive; as, *lĭber*, a book; *libellus*, a little book.

Diminutives generally end in *ŭlus, ŭla, ŭlum*, or *cŭlus, cŭla, cŭlum*, according as the primitive is masculine, feminine, or neuter.

A. 1. If the primitive is of the first or second declension, or its root ends in c, g, d, or t after a vowel, the diminutive is formed by annexing *ŭlus, a, um* to the root; as, *arŭla, servŭlus, puerŭlus, scutŭlum, cornĭcŭla, regŭlus, capĭtŭlum, mercedŭla*; from *āra, servus, puer, scūtum, cornix*, (-icis), *rex*, (*rēgis*), *căput*, (-itis), *merces*, (-ēdis.)

2. Primitives of the first or second declension whose root ends in e or i, instead of *ŭlus, a, um*, add *ŏlus, a, um*; as, *filiŏlus, gloriŏla, horreŏlum*; from *filius, gloria, horreum*.

3. Primitives of the first or second declension whose root ends in l, n, or r, form diminutives by contraction in *ellus, a, um*, and some in *illus, a, um*; as, *ocellus, asellus, libellus, lucellum*; from *oculus, asina, liber, lucrum*; and *sigillum, tigillum*, from *signum, tignum*.

B. 1 If the primitive is of the third, fourth, or fifth declension, the diminutive is formed in *cŭlus*, (or *icŭlus*), *a, um*.

2. Primitives of the third declension whose nominative ends in r, or in os or us from roots ending in r annex *culus* to the nominative; as, *fraterculus, soror-*

cŭla osculum, corpusculum; from *p͞ater, s͞oror, ōs,* (*ōris*), *corpus,* (*-ŏris*).—So also primitives in *es* and *is,* but these drop the *s* of the nominative; as, *ignicŭlus, nŭbecŭla, diecŭla;* from *ignis, nŭbes, dies.*

3. Primitives of other terminations of the third declension, and those of the fourth, add *ĭcŭlus* to the root; as, *ponticŭlus, coticŭla, ossicŭlum, versicŭlus, cornicŭlum;* from *pons, cos, ŏs,* (*ossis*), *versus, cornu.*

4. Primitives in *o,* (*inis* or *ōnis*), in adding *cŭlus, a, um,* change the final vowel of the root (*i* or *o*) into *u;* as, *homuncŭlus, sermuncŭlus;* from *hŏmo* and *sermo;* and a few primitives of other terminations form similar diminutives; as, *avuncŭlus, domuncŭla;* from *ăvus* and *dŏmus.*

C. 1. A few diminutives end in *uleus,* as, *equuleus, aculeus;* from *ĕquus* and *ăcus;* and a few also in *io;* as, *homuncio, senecio,* from *hŏmo* and *sĕnex.*

2. Diminutives are sometimes formed from other diminutives; as, *asellŭlus,* from *ăsellus;* sometimes two or more diminutives with different terminations are formed from the same primitive, as, *homuncŭlus, homullus,* and *homuncio;* from *hŏmo;* and sometimes the primitive undergoes euphonic changes; as *rumuscŭlus,* from *rūmor.*

REM. Some diminutives differ in gender from their primitives; as *ranuncŭlus, scamillus,* from *rāna* and *scamnum.*

4. (*a.*) An **amplificative** is a personal appellation denoting an excess of that which is expressed by its primitive; as,

Capito, one who has a large head: so *naso, labeo, bucco, fronto, mento,* one who has a large nose, lips, or cheeks, a broad forehead or long chin; from *căput, năsus, labia, bucca, frons,* and *mentum.*

(*b.*) A few personal appellatives in *io* denote the trade or profession to which a person belongs; as, *ludio,* an actor; *pellio,* a furrier; from *lūdus,* and *pellis.*

5. The termination *ium* added to the root of a noun, indicates the office or condition, and often, derivatively, an assemblage of the individuals denoted by the primitive; as, *collegium,* colleagueship, and thence an assembly of colleagues; *servitium,* servitude, and collectively the servants; so *sacerdotium,* and *ministerium;* from *collēga, servus, sacerdos,* and *minister.*

6. The termination *imonium* is added to the root of a few nouns, denoting something derived from the primitives, or imparting to it its peculiar character: as, *testimonium,* testimony; so *vadimonium, patrimonium, matrimonium;* from *testis, văs* (*vădis*), *păter,* and *māter.*

7. The termination *ētum,* added to the root of names of plants, denotes a place where they grow in abundance; as, *quercētum, laurētum, olivētum,* from *quercus, laurus,* and *oliva.*

So, also, *æscŭlētum, dumētum, myrtētum,* and by analogy *saxētum.* But some drop *e;* as, *carectum, salictum, virgultum,* and *arbustum.*

8. The termination *ărium,* added to the root of a noun, denotes a receptacle of the things signified by the primitive; as, *aviārium,* an aviary; *plantārium,* a nursery; from *ăvis,* a bird, and *planta,* a plant.

9. The termination *īle,* added to the root of names of animals, marks the place where they are kept; as, *bovile,* a stall for oxen; so *caprīle, ovīle;* from *bōs,* an ox, *căper,* a goat, and *ŏvis,* a sheep.

NOTE 1. This class and the preceding are properly neuter adjectives.

NOTE 2. Abstract nouns are derived either from adjectives or from verbs. See § 26, 5.

II. FROM ADJECTIVES.

§ 101. 1. Abstract nouns are formed by adding the termination *ĭtas, ĭtūdo, ia, itia* or *ities, ēdo,* and *imōnia* to the root of the primitive

2. Abstracts in *ĭtas*, (equivalent to the English *ty* or *ity*), are formed from adjectives of each declension ; as, *cupidĭtas, tenerĭtas, celerĭtas, crudelĭtas, felĭcĭtas*; from *cupĭdus, tĕner, cĕler, crudēlis*, and *fēlix*.

(1.) When the root ends in *i*, the abstract is formed in *ĕtas*; as, *piĕtas*, from *pius*; and when it ends in *t*, *as* only is added ; as, *honestas* from *honestus*.

(2.) In a few abstracts *i* before *tas* is dropped ; as, *libertas, juventas*, from *liber, juvĕnis*. In *facultas* and *difficultas*, from *facĭlis, difficĭlis*, there is a change also in the root-vowel from *i* to *u*.

(3.) A few abstracts are formed in *ĭtus* or *tus*, instead of *ĭtas*; as, *servĭtus, juventus*, from *servus* and *juvĕnis*. See § 76, Exc. 2.

3. Abstracts in *itūdo* are formed from adjectives in *us*, and some from adjectives of the third declension of two or three terminations; as, *magnitūdo, altitūdo, fortitūdo, acritūdo*, from *magnus, altus, fortis, ācer*. Polysyllabic adjectives in *tus*, generally form their abstracts by adding *ūdo* instead of *itūdo* to their root; as, *consuetūdo*, from *consuētus*.

4. Abstracts in *ia* (equivalent to the English *ce* or *cy*,) are for the most part formed from adjectives of one termination ; as, *clementia, constantia, impudentia*, from *clemens, constans, impŭdens*. But some adjectives in *us* and *er*, including verbals in *cundus*, likewise form their verbals in *ia ;* as, *miseria, angustia, facundia*, from *miser, angustus, facundus*.

5. Abstracts in *itia* and *ities* are formed from adjectives in *us* and *is ;* as, *justitia, tristitia, duritia*, and *durities, segnitia* and *segnities*, from *justus, tristis, dūrus*, and *segnis*.

6. A few abstracts are formed in *ēdo*, and a few in *imōnia ;* and sometimes two or more abstracts of different terminations are formed from the same adjective ; as, *acrĭtas, acritūdo, acrēdo*, and *acrimonia*, from *ācer*. In such case those in *itūdo* and *imonia* seem to be more intensive in signification than those in *itas*.

REMARK. Adjectives, as distinguished from the abstracts which are formed from them, are called *concretes*.

III. FROM VERBS.

§ 102. Nouns derived from verbs are called *verbal* nouns.

The following are the principal classes :—

1. Abstract nouns expressing the action or condition denoted by a verb, especially by a neuter verb, are formed by annexing *or* to their first root ; as, *ămor*, love ; *făvor*, favor ; *mæror*, grief ; *splendor*, brightness; from *ămo, făveo, mæreo*, and *splendeo*.

2. (*a*.) Abstracts are also formed from many verbs by annexing *ium* to the first or to the third root ; as, *colloquium*, a conference ; *gaudium*, joy ; *exordium*, a beginning ; *exitium*, destruction ; *solatium*, consolation ; from *collŏquor, gaudeo, exordior, exeo* and *sōlor*.

3. Some verbal abstracts are formed by annexing *ēla, imōnia*, or *imōnium*, to the first root of the verb ; as, *querēla* and *querimonia*, a complaint ; *suadēla*, persuasion ; from *quĕror* and *suadeo*.

4. (*a*.) The terminations *men* and *mentum*, added to the first root of the verb, generally with a connecting vowel, denote the thing to which the action belongs, both actively and passively, or a means for the performance of the action ; as, *fulmen* from *fulgeo, flūmen* from *fluo, agmen* from *ăgo, solāmen* from *sōlor, documentum* from *dŏceo, blandimentum* from *blandior*.

(*b*.) The final consonant of the root is often dropped, and the preceding and connecting vowels contracted into one syllable ; as, *ăgo*, (*ăgĭmen*,) *agmen ; fŏveo*, (*fŏvimentum*,) *fōmentum*.

(*c.*) Some words of this class have no primitive verb in use; as, *atramentum,* ink; but, in this case, the connecting vowel seems to imply its reference to such a verb as *atrāre,* to blacken.

5. (*a.*) The terminations *ŭlum, bŭlum, cŭlum; brum, crum, trum,* annexed to the first root of a verb, denote an instrument for performing the act expressed by the verb, or a place for its performance; as, *cingŭlum, opercŭlum, ventbŭlum, ventilābrum, fulcrum, spectrum,* from *cingo, opĕrio, vĕnor, ventĭlo, fulcio, spĕcio.*

(*b.*) Sometimes *cŭlum* is contracted into *clum*; as, *vinclum* for *vincŭlum.* Sometimes, also, *s* is inserted before *trum*; as, *rostrum,* from *rōdo,* and a connecting vowel is placed before this and some of the other terminations; as, *arātrum, stabŭlum, cubicŭlum,* from *āro, sto,* and *cŭbo.*

(*c.*) Some words of this kind are formed from nouns; as, *acetabŭlum,* a vinegar cruet; *turibŭlum,* a censer; from *acetum* and *tus.*

6. (*a.*) Nouns formed by adding *or* and *rix* to the third root of the verb, denote respectively the male and female agent of the action expressed by the verb; as, *adjūtor, adjūtrix,* an assistant; *fautor, fautrix,* a favorer; *victor, victrix,* a conqueror; from *adjŭvo (adjūt-), făveo (faut-), vinco (vict-).* They are often likewise used as adjectives. The feminine form is less common than the masculine, and when the third root of the verb ends in *s,* the feminine is sometimes formed in *trix*; as, *tondeo (tons-) tonstrix.*

(*b.*) Some nouns in *tor* are formed immediately from other nouns; as, *viātor,* a traveller; *janitor,* a door-keeper; from *via* and *janua.* In *meretrix* from *mereo,* *i* of the third root becomes *e.*

(*c.*) The agent of a few verbs is denoted by the terminations *a* and *o* annexed to the first root; as, *conviva,* a guest; *advĕna,* a stranger; *scriba,* a scribe; *erro,* a vagrant; *bibo,* a drunkard; *comĕdo,* a glutton, from *convīvo, advĕnio,* etc.

7. Many abstract nouns are formed by annexing *io* and *us* (gen. *ūs*) to the third root of a verb; as, *actio,* an action; *lectio,* reading; from *ăgo (act-), lĕgo (lect-);—cantus,* singing; *visus,* sight; *ūsus,* use; from *căno (cant-), video (vis-), ūtor (ūs-).*

REMARK 1. Nouns of both forms, and of like signification, are frequently derived from the same verb; as, *concursio* and *concursus,* a running together; *mōtio* and *mōtus,* etc.

REM. 2. Nouns formed by adding the termination *ūra* to the third root of a verb, sometimes have the same signification as those in *io* and *us,* and sometimes denote the result of an action; as, *positūra,* position; *vinctūra,* a binding together; from *pōno,* and *vincio;* and the termination *ēla* has sometimes the same meaning; as, *querēla,* complaint; *loquēla,* speech, from *quĕror* and *lŏquor.*

NOTE. One of these forms is generally used to the exclusion of the others, and when two or more are found, they are usually employed in somewhat different senses.

8. The termination *ōrium,* added to the third root of a verb, denotes the place where the action of the verb is performed; as, *audītōrium,* a lecture-room; *condĭtōrium,* a repository; from *audio* and *condo.*

COMPOSITION OF NOUNS.

§ 103. Compound nouns are formed variously:—

1. Of two nouns; as, *rupicapra,* a wild goat, of *rūpes* and *capra.* In some words, compounded of two nouns, the former is a genitive; as, *senatūsconsultum,* a decree of the senate; *jurisconsultus,* a lawyer; in others, both parts are declined; as, *respublica, jusjurandum.* See § 91.

2. Of a noun and a verb; as, *artĭfex,* an artist, of *ars* and *făcio; fidĭcen,* a harper of *fides* and *căno; agricŏla,* a husbandman, of *ăger* and *cŏlo.*

3. Of an adjective and a noun; as, *æquinoctium*, the equinox, of *æquus* and *nox; millepēda*, a millepede, of *mille* and *pes*.

In *duumvir, triumvir, decemvir, centumvir*, the numeral adjective is in the genitive plural.

REMARK 1. When the former part of a compound word is a noun or an adjective, it usually ends in *i*; as, *artĭfex, rupĭcapra, agricŏla*, etc. If the second word begins with a vowel, an elision takes place; as, *quinquennium*, of *quinque* and *annus; magnanĭmus*, of *magnus* and *anĭmus*.

4. Of an adverb and a noun; as, *nĕfas*, wickedness; *nĕmo*, nobody; of *ne, fas*, and *hŏmo*. So *biduum*, of *bis* and *dies*.

5. Of a preposition and a noun; as, *incuria*, want of care, of *in* and *cūra*. So *intervallum*, an interval; *præcordia*, the diaphragm; *proverbium*, a proverb; *subsellium*, a low seat; *superficies*, a surface.

REM. 2. When the former part is a preposition, its final consonant is sometimes changed, to adapt it to that which follows it: as, *ignobĭlis, illepĭdus, imprudentia, irrumpo*, of *in* and *nobĭlis, lepĭdus*, etc. See § 196.

ADJECTIVES.

§ 104. An adjective is a word which qualifies or limits the meaning of a substantive.

Adjectives may be divided, according to their *signification*, into various classes; as denoting,

1. Character or quality; as, *bŏnus*, good; *albus*, white; *amīcus*, friendly.
2. State or condition; as, *fēlix*, happy; *dives*, rich.
3. Possession; as, *herīlis*, a master's; *patrius*, a father's.
4. Quantity; as, *magnus*, great; *tōtus*, entire; *parvus*, small.
5. Number; as, *ūnus*, one; *secundus*, second; *tot*, so many; *quot*, as many. These are called *numerals*.
6. Time; as, *annuus*, yearly; *hesternus*, of yesterday; *bīmus*, of two years; *trimestris*, of three months.
7. Place; as, *altus*, high; *vicīnus*, near; *aërius*, aërial; *terrestris*, terrestrial.
8. Material; as, *aureus*, golden; *fagineus*, beechen; *terrēnus*, earthen.
9. Part; as, *nullus*, no one; *aliquis*, some one. These are called *partitives*.
10. Country; as, *Romānus*, Roman; *Arpīnas* of *Arpīnum*. These are called *patrials*.
11. Diminution; as, *parvŭlus*, from *parvus*, small; *misellus*, from *miser*, miserable. These are called *diminutives*.
12. Amplification; as, *vinōsus* and *vinolentus*, much given to wine; *aurītus*, having long ears. These are called *amplificatives*.
13. Relation; as, *arĭdus*, desirous of; *mĕmor*, mindful of; *insuētus*. These are called *relatives*.
14. Interrogation; as, *quantus?* how great; *qualis?* of what kind; *quot?* how many? *quotus?* of what number? These are called *interrogatives*; and, when not used interrogatively, they are called *correlatives*.
15. Specification; as, *tālis*, such; *tantus*, so great; *tot*, so many. These are called *demonstratives*.

DECLENSION OF ADJECTIVES.

§ 105. 1. Adjectives are declined like substantives, and are either of the first and second declensions, or of the third only.

ADJECTIVES OF THE FIRST AND SECOND DECLENSIONS.

2. The masculine of adjectives belonging to the first and second declensions, ends either in *us* or in *er*. The feminine and neuter are formed respectively by annexing *a* and *um* to the root of the masculine. The masculine in *us* is declined like *dŏmĭnus;* that in *er* like *gĕner* or *ăger;* the feminine always like *mūsa;* and the neuter like *regnum*.

REMARK 1. The masculine of one adjective, *sătur, -ŭra, -ŭrum,* full, ends in *ur*, and is declined like *gĕner*.

Bŏnŭs, *good.*

Singular.

	Masc.	*Fem.*	*Neut.*
N.	bo'-nŭs,	bo'-nă,	bo'-nŭm,
G.	bo'-nī,	bo'-næ,	bo'-nī,
D.	bo'-nō,	bo'-næ,	bo'-nō,
Ac.	bo'-nŭm,	bo'-năm,	bo'-nŭm,
V.	bo'-nĕ,	bo'-nă,	bo'-nŭm,
Ab.	bo'-nō.	bo'-nā.	bo'-nō.

Plural.

N.	bo'-nī,	bo'-næ,	bo'-nă,
G.	bo-nō'-rŭm,	bo-nā'-rŭm,	bo-nō'-rŭm,
D.	bo'-nīs,	bo'-nīs,	bo'-nīs,
Ac.	bo'-nōs,	bo'-nās,	bo'-nă,
V.	bo'-nī,	bo'-næ,	bo'-nă,
Ab.	bo'-nīs.	bo'-nīs.	bo'-nīs.

In like manner decline

Al'-tus, *high.*   Fī'-dus, *faithful.*   Lon'-gus, *long.*
A-vā'-rus, *covetous.*   Im'-prŏ-bus, *wicked.*   Plē'-nus, *full.*
Be-nig'-nus, *kind.*   In-ī'-quus, *unjust.*   Tac'-ĭ-tus, *silent.*

REM. 2. Like *bŏnus* are also declined all participles in *us;* as,
A-mā'-tus.   Am-a-tū'-rus.   A-man'-dus.

Rem. 3. The masculine of the vocative singular of adjectives in *us* is sometimes like the nominative; as, *O vir fortis atque amīcus.* Hor. *Meus* has both *mi* and *meus*.

REM. 4. The genitive plural of distributive numerals ends commonly in *ăm* instead of *ōrum;* as, *crassitūdĕ binŭm digitōrum.* Plin.

§ 106 ADJECTIVES—FIRST AND SECOND DECLENSIONS. 63

3. Tĕner, *tender.*

Singular.

	Masc.	Fem.	Neut.
N.	te´-nĕr,	ten´-ĕ-ră,	ten´-ĕ-rŭm,
G.	ten´-ĕ-rī,	ten´-ĕ-ræ,	ten´-ĕ-rī,
D.	ten´-ĕ-rō,	ten´-ĕ-ræ,	ten´-ĕ-rō,
Ac.	ten´-ĕ-rŭm,	ten´-ĕ-răm,	ten´-ĕ-rŭm,
V.	te´-nĕr,	ten´-ĕ-ră,	ten´-ĕ-rŭm,
Ab.	ten´-ĕ-rō.	ten´-ĕ-rā.	ten´-ĕ-rō.

Plural.

N.	ten´-ĕ-rī,	ten´-ĕ-ræ,	ten´-ĕ-ră,
G.	ten-e-rō´-rŭm,	ten-e-rā´-rŭm,	ten-e-rō´-rŭm,
D.	ten´-ĕ-rīs,	ten´-ĕ-rīs,	ten´-ĕ-rīs,
Ac.	ten´-ĕ-rōs,	ten´-ĕ-rās,	ten´-ĕ-ră,
V.	ten´-ĕ-rī,	ten´-ĕ-ræ,	ten´-ĕ-ră,
Ab.	ten´-ĕ-rīs.	ten´-ĕ-rīs.	ten´-ĕ-rīs.

In like manner are declined

As´-per, *rough.*   Lă´-cer, *torn.*   Pros´-per, *prosperous.*
Ex´-ter, *foreign.*   Lī´-ber, *free.*   Să´-tur, *full.*
Gib´-ber, *crook-backed.*   Mi´-ser, *wretched.*

So also *alter*, except in the genitive and dative singular (see § 107), *semifer* and the compounds of *gero* and *fero*; as, *laniger, opifer.*

NOTE. Prosper is less frequent than *prospĕrus*, and *exter* is scarcely used in the nominative singular masculine.

§ **106.** The other adjectives in *er* drop *e* in declension; as,

Pĭger, *slothful.*

Singular.

	Masc.	Fem.	Neut.
N.	pĭ´-gĕr,	pĭ´-gră,	pĭ´-grŭm,
G.	pĭ´-grī,	pĭ´-græ,	pĭ´-grī,
D.	pĭ´-grō,	pĭ´-græ,	pĭ´-grō,
Ac.	pĭ´-grŭm,	pĭ´-grăm,	pĭ´-grŭm,
V.	pĭ´-gĕr,	pĭ´-gră,	pĭ´-grŭm,
Ab.	pĭ´-grō.	pĭ´-grā.	pĭ´-grō.

Plural.

N.	pĭ´-grī,	pĭ´-græ,	pĭ´-gră,
G.	pi-grō´-rŭm,	pi-grā´-rum,	pi-grō´-rŭm,
D.	pĭ´-grīs,	pĭ´-grīs,	pĭ´-grīs,
Ac.	pĭ´-grōs,	pĭ´-grās,	pĭ´-gră,
V.	pĭ´-grī,	pĭ´-græ,	pĭ´-gră,
Ab.	pĭ´-grīs.	pĭ´-grīs.	pĭ´-grīs.

In like manner decline

Æ'-ger, *sick.* Mă'-cer, *lean.* Scă'-ber, *rough.*
A'-ter, *black.* Nĭ'-ger, *black.* Si-nis'-ter, *left.*
Crē'-ber, *frequent.* Pul'-cher, *fair.* Tē'-ter, *foul.*
Glă'-ber, *smooth.* Rŭ'-ber, *red.* Vă'-fer, *crafty.*
In'-tĕ-ger, *entire.* Să'-cer, *sacred.*

Dexter, right, has *-tra, -trum*, and less frequently *-tĕra, -tĕrum.*

§ 107.

Six adjectives in *us*, and three in *er*, have their genitive singular in *ius*, and their dative in *ī*, in all the genders:—

Alius, *another.* Tōtus, *whole.* Alter, -tĕra, -tĕrum, *the other.*
Nullus, *no one.* Ullus, *any.* Uter, -tra, -trum, *which of the two.*
Sōlus, *alone.* Unus, *one.* Neuter, -tra, -trum, *neither.*

To these may be added the other compounds of *uter*,—namely, *uterque*, each of two; *utercumque, uterlibet,* and *utervis,* which of the two you please; gen. *utriusque,* etc.—also, *alterŭter,* one of two; gen. *alterutrius,* and sometimes *alterius utrius;* dat. *alterutri.* So *alteruterque,* and *unusquisque.* See § 139, 4.

Nullus, sōlus, tōtus, ullus, and *ūnus* are thus declined:—

Singular.

	Masc.	Fem.	Neut.
N.	ū'-nŭs,	ū'-nă,	ū'-nŭm,
G.	u-nī'-ŭs,*	u-nī'-ŭs,	u-nī'-ŭs,
D.	u'-nī,	u'-nī,	u'-nī,
Ac.	u'-nŭm,	u'-năm,	u'-nŭm,
V.	u'-nĕ,	u'-nă,	u'-nŭm,
Ab.	u'-nō.	u'-nā.	u'-nō.

The plural is regular, like that of *bŏnus.*

REMARK 1. *Alius* has *aliud* in the nominative and accusative singular neuter, and in the genitive *alīus,* contracted for *aliius.*

REM. 2. Except in the genitive and dative singular, *alter* is declined like *tĕner,* and *uter* and *neuter* like *piger.*

REM. 3. Some of these adjectives, in early writers, and occasionally even in Cicero, Cæsar, and Nepos, form their genitive and dative regularly, like *bŏnus, tĕner,* or *piger.*

ADJECTIVES OF THE THIRD DECLENSION.

§ 108.

Some adjectives of the third declension have three terminations in the nominative singular; some two; and others only one.

I. Those of three terminations end in *er,* masc.; *is,* fem.; and *e,* neut.; and are thus declined:—

Acer, *sharp.*

Singular.

	Masc.	Fem.	Neut.
N.	ā'-cĕr,	ā-crĭs,	ā'-crĕ,
G.	a'-crĭs,	a'-crĭs,	a'-crĭs,
D.	a'-crī,	a'-crī,	a'-crī,
Ac.	a'-crĕm,	a'-crĕm,	a'-crĕ,
V.	a'-cĕr,	a'-crĭs,	a'-crĕ,
Ab.	a'-crī.	a'-crī.	a'-crī.

---

* See § 15.

§ 109, 110.   ADJECTIVES—THIRD DECLENSION.   35

Plural.

	M.	F.	N.
N.	a'-crēs,	a'-crēs,	a'-cri-ă,
G.	a'-cri-ŭm,	a'-cri-um,	a'-cri-ŭm,
D.	ac'-rĭ-bŭs,	ac'-rĭ-bŭs,	ac'-rĭ-bŭs,
Ac.	a'-crēs,	a'-crēs,	a'-cri-ă,
V.	a'-crēs,	a'-crēs,	a'-cri-ă,
Ab.	ac'-rĭ-bŭs.	ac'-rĭ-bŭs.	ac'-rĭ-bŭs.

In like manner are declined the following;—

A.'-ăcer, *cheerful.*   Pa-lus'-ter, *marshy.*   Sil-ves'-ter, *woody.*
Cam-pes'-ter, *champaign.*   Pe-des'-ter, *on foot.*   Ter-res'-ter, *terrestrial.*
Cel'-ĕ-ber, *famous.*   Pŭ'-ter, *rotten.*   Vol'-ŭ-cer, *winged.*
E-ques'-ter, *equestrian.*   Sa-lū'-ber, *wholesome.*

To these add names of months in *-ber*, used as adjectives; as, *Octōber*, etc. (cf. § 71), and *cĕler*, swift, which has *celĕris, celĕre*; gen. *celĕris*, etc.

REMARK 1. The termination *er* was anciently sometimes feminine; as, *volŭcer fama*. Petr.: and, on the other hand, the masculine often ends in *is*; as, *collis silvestris*, Cæs.

REM. 2. *Volŭcer* has *um* in the genitive plural.

§ **109.** II. Adjectives of two terminations end in *is* for the masculine and feminine, and *e* for the neuter, except comparatives, which end in *or* and *us*.

Those in *is, e*, are thus declined:—

Mītis *mild.*

Singular.   *Plural.*

	M. & F.	N.		M. & F.	N.
N.	mi'-tĭs,	mi'-tĕ,	N.	mi'-tēs,	mit'-i-ă,*
G.	mi'-tĭs,	mi'-tĭs,	G.	mit'-i-ŭm,*	mit'-i-ŭm,
D.	mi'-tī,	mi'-tī,	D.	mit'-ĭ-bŭs,	mit'-ĭ-bŭs,
Ac.	mi'-tĕm,	mi'-tĕ,	Ac.	mi'-tēs,	mit'-i-ă,
V.	mi'-tĭs,	mi'-tĕ,	V.	mi'-tēs,	mit'-i-ă,
Ab.	mi'-tī.	mi'-tī.	Ab.	mit'-ĭ-bŭs.	mit'-ĭ-bŭs.

In like manner decline

Ag'-ĭ-lis, *active.*   Dul'-cis, *sweet.*   In-col'-ŭ-mis, *safe.*
Brĕ'-vis, *short.*   For'-tis, *brave.*   Mi-rab'-ĭ-lis, *wonderful.*
Cru-dē'-lis, *cruel.*   Grā'-vis, *heavy.*   Om'-nis, *all.*

Tres, three, is declined like the plural of *mitis*.

NOTE. Several adjectives of this class have forms also in *us, a, um*. See § 116.

§ **110.** (*a.*) All comparatives, except *plus*, more, are thus declined:—

---

* Pronounced *mish'-e-a*, etc. See § 12.

Mitior,* *milder.*

Singular.

	M. & F.	N.
N.	mit'-i-ŏr,	mit'-i-ŭs,
G.	mit-i-ō'-rĭs,	mit-i-ō'-rĭs,
D.	mit-i-ō'-rī,	mit-i-ō'-rī,
Ac.	mit-i-ō'-rĕm,	mit'-i-ŭs,
V.	mit'-i-ŏr,	mit'-i-ŭs,
Ab.	mit-i-ō'-rĕ, *or* -rī.	mit-i-ō'-rĕ, *or* -rī.

Plural.

	M. & F.	N.
N.	mit-i-ō'-rēs,	mit-i-ō'-ră,
G.	mit-i-ō'-rŭm,	mit-i-ō'-rŭm,
D.	mit-i-or'-ĭ-bŭs,	mit-i-or'-ĭ-bŭs,
Ac.	mit-i-ō'-rēs,	mit-i-ō'-ră,
V.	mit-i-ō'-rēs,	mit-i-ō'-ră,
Ab.	mit-i-or'-ĭ-bŭs.	mit-i-or'-ĭ-bŭs.

In like manner decline

A'-ti-or, *higher.*
A ı-da'-ci-or, *bolder.*
B:e'-vi-or, *shorter.*
Cru-de'-li-or, *more cruel.*
Dul'-ci-or, *sweeter.*
Fe-lic'-i-or, *happier.*
Fe-ro'-ci-or, *fiercer.*
For'-ti-or, *braver.*
Gra'-vi-or, *heavier.*
Pru-den'-ti-or, *more prudent.*
U-be'-ri-or, *more fertile.*

Plūs, *more,* is thus declined:—

Singular.

	N.
N.	plus,
G.	plū'-rĭs,
D.	———,
Ac.	plus,
V.	———,
Ab.	(plū'-rĕ, *obs.*)

Plural.

	M. & F.	N.
N.	plū'-rēs,	plū'-ră, *rarely* plu -ri-ă,
G.	plu'-ri-ŭm,	plu'-ri-ŭm,
D.	plu'-rĭ-bŭs,	plu'-rĭ-bŭs,
Ac.	plū'-rēs,	plū'-ră,
V.	———,	———,
Ab.	plu'-rĭ-bŭs.	plu'rĭ-bŭs.

So, but in the plural number only, *complūres,* a great many.

§ 111. III. Other adjectives of the third declension have but one termination in the nominative singular for all genders. They all end in *l, r, s,* or *x,* and increase in the genitive.

They are thus declined:—

Fēlix, *happy.*

Singular.

	M. & F.	N.
N.	fe'-lix,	fe'-lix,
G.	fe-lī'-cĭs,	fe-lī'-cĭs,
D.	fe-li'-cī,	fe-li'-cī,
Ac.	fe-lī'-cĕm,	fe'-lix,
V.	fe'-lix,	fe'-lix,
Ab.	fe-li'-cĕ, *or* -cī.	fe-li'-cĕ, *or* -cī.

---

* Pronounced *mish'-e-or,* etc. See § 12.

§112. ADJECTIVES—OBLIQUE CASES. 67

Plural.

	M. & F.	N.
N.	fe-lī′-cēs,	fe-lic′-i-ă,*
G.	fe-lic′-i-ŭm,*	fe-lic′-i-ŭm,
D.	fe-lic′-I-bŭs,	fe-lic′-I-bŭs,
Ac.	fe-lī′-cēs,	fe-lic′-i-ă,
V.	fe-lī′-cēs,	fe-lic′-i-ă,
Ab.	fe-lic′-I-bŭs.	fe-lic′-I-bŭs.

Præsens, *present.*
Singular.

	M. & F.	N.
N.	præ′-sens,	præ′-sens,
G.	præ-sen′-tĭs,	præ-sen′-tĭs,
D.	præ-sen′-tī,	præ-sen′-tī,
Ac.	præ-sen′-tĕm,	præ′-sens,
V.	præ′-sens,	præ′-sens,
Ab.	præ-sen′-tĕ, *or* -tī.	præ-sen′-tĕ, *or* -tī.

Plural.

N.	præ-sen′-tēs,	præ-sen′-ti-ă,†
G.	præ-sen′-ti-ŭm,	præ-sen′-ti-ŭm,
D.	præ-sen′-tĭ-bŭs,	præ-sen′-tĭ-bŭs,
Ac.	præ-sen′-tēs,	præ-sen′-ti-ă,
V.	præ-sen′-tēs,	præ-sen′-tĭ-ă,
Ab.	præ-sen′-tĭ-bŭs.	præ-sen′-tĭ-bŭs.

In like manner decline

Au′-dax, -ācis, *bold.*
Com′-pos, -ĭtis, *master of.*
Fĕ′-rox, -ōcis, *fierce.*
In′-gens, -tis, *huge.*

Par′-tĭ-ceps, -ĭpis, *participant.*
Præ′-pes, -ĕtis, *swift.*
Prū′-dens, -tis, *prudent.*

Sol′-lers, -tis, *shrewd.*
Sos′-pes, -ĭtis, *safe.*
Sup′-plex, -Icis, *suppliant.*

REMARK. All present participles are declined like *præsens;* as, A′-mans. Mŏ′-nens. Rĕ′-gens. Ca′-pi-ens. Au′-di-ens.

NOTE. A few adjectives of one termination have redundant forms in *us, a, um;* see § 116.

RULES FOR THE OBLIQUE CASES OF ADJECTIVES OF THE THIRD DECLENSION.

GENITIVE SINGULAR.

§ 112. Most adjectives of the third declension form their genitive singular like nouns of the same termination.

The following may here be specified:—
1. Of those in *es* (cf. § 73) some have *-ĕtis*; as, *hĕbes, perpes, propes,* and *tĕres--inquies* and *locŭples* have *-ĕtis*;—some have *-itis*; as, *dives, sospes,* and *superstes*;—some have *-ĭdis*; as, *dēses,* and *rēses*;—*bipes,* and *tripes* have *-pĕdis*;—*pūbes* cas *pubĕris,* and *impubes, impubĕris* and *impubis.*

---

* Pronounced *fe-lish′-e-um* etc   See § 10, Exc., and § 7., 3, (b.)
† Pronounced *pre-zen′-she-a,* etc

2. *Compos* and *impos* have *-ōtis*, and *exos, exossis.*—*Exlex* has *exlēgis, pernox* has *pernoctis* (§ 78), *præcox, præcōcis*, and *rĕdux, redūcis.* — *Cœlebs* has *cœlĭbis* (§ 77); *intercus, intercŭtis*, and *vĕtus, vetĕris*. Those in *ceps* which are compounds of *căput*, have *-cipitis*; as, *anceps, præceps* (§ 78, 1); but the compounds of *ceps* from *căpio* have *-ĭpis*; as, *particeps, particĭpis.*—Those in *cors*, compounds of *cor*, have *-cordis*; as, *concors, concordis* (§ 71, Exc. 2).— *Mĕmor* and *immĕmor* have *-ŏris*.

ABLATIVE SINGULAR.

§ 113. 1. Adjectives which have *e* in the nominative singular neuter have only *i* in the ablative.

Exc. 1. The ablatives *bimestre, cœleste*, and *perenne* are found in Ovid, and *cognomine* in Virgil.

2. Comparatives and participles in *ns*, when used as participles, especially in the ablative absolute, have rather *e* than *i;* but participial adjectives in *ns* have rather *i* than *e*.

3. Adjectives of one termination have either *e* or *i* in the ablative.

Exc. 2. The following adjectives of one termination have only *e* in the ablative:—
Bicorpor, bipes, cælebs, compos, dēses, discŏlor, hospes, impos, impūbes, juvĕnis, locŭples, pauper, princeps, pūber *or* pūbes, senex, sospes, superstes, tricorpor, tricuspis, *and* tripes.

Exc. 3. The following adjectives of one termination have only *i* in the ablative:—
Anceps, concors, discors, hĕbes, immĕmor, Iners, ingens, Inops, mĕmor, par, præceps, rŏcens, rĕpens, vigil, and most adjectives in *x*, especially those in *plex*.

Rem. 1. *Inerte* occurs in Ovid, *recente* in Ovid and Catullus, and *præcipe* in Ennius.

Rem. 2. *Præsens*, when used of things, makes the ablative in *i;* when used of persons, it has *e*.

NOMINATIVE, ACCUSATIVE, AND GENITIVE PLURAL

§ 114. 1. The neuter of the nominative and accusative plural ends in *ia*, and the genitive plural of all genders in *ium;* but comparatives in *or*, with *vĕtus*, old, and *ūber*, fertile, have *a*, and *um*.

2. The accusative plural of masculine and feminine adjectives, whose genitive plural ends in *ium*, anciently ended in *is* or *ēis*, instead of *ēs*. Cf. § 85, Exc. 1.

Exc. 1. Those adjectives that have only *e* in the ablative singular, have *um* in the genitive plural.

Exc. 2. Compounds of *făcio, căpio*, and of such nouns as make *um* in their genitive plural, with *cĕler, compar, cicur, dives, mĕmor, immĕmor, præpes, supplex*, and *vigil*, make their genitive plural in *um*.

Exc. 3. *Dis, locuples, sons*, and *insons* have either *um* or *ium*. The poets and the later prose writers sometimes form the genitive plural of other adjectives and of participles in *ns*, by syncope, in *um*, instead of *ium;* as, *cælestum*, Virg. Ovid, etc.

IRREGULAR ADJECTIVES.

§ 115. Some adjectives are defective, others redundant.

DEFECTIVE ADJECTIVES.

1. (*a.*) Many adjectives denoting personal qualities or attributes want the neuter gender, unless when occasionally joined to a neuter substantive used figuratively. Such are the following:—

Bicorpor, bĭpes, cælebs, compos, consors, degĕner, dīves, impos, impūbes, industrius, ĭnops, insons, invītus, juvĕnis, locuples, mĕmor, pauper, particeps princeps, pūber, *or* pūbes, rĕdux, sĕnex, sons, sospes, superstes, supplex, tricorpor, vĭgil.

(*b.*) *Victrix* and *ultrix* are feminine in the singular, seldom neuter; in the plural, they are feminine and neuter. Such verbals partake of the nature both of substantives and adjectives, and correspond to masculines in *tor*. See § 102, 6, (*a.*)

2. The following want the genitive plural, and are rarely used in the neuter gender:—

Concŏlor, dēses, hĕbes, perpes, rēses, tĕres, versicŏlor.

3. The names of months, which are properly adjectives, have only the masculine and feminine genders.

4. Some adjectives are wholly indeclinable.

Such are *frŭgi*, temperate; *nĕquam*, worthless; *săt* or *sătis*, sufficient; the plurals *aliquot*, *tŏt*, *quŏt*, *totĭdem*, *quotquot*; and the cardinal numbers from *quatuor* to *centum* inclusive, and also *mille*. Cf. § 118, 1, and 6, (*b.*)

5. The following adjectives are used only in certain cases: —

Bilĭcem, *acc.*; *doubly-tissued*. Cetĕra, cetĕrum, *the rest*, wants the nom. sing. masc. Decemplĭcem, *acc.*; *tenfold*. Exspes, *nom.*; *hopeless*. Inquies, *nom.*; -ētem, *acc.*; -ēte, *abl.*; *restless*. Mactus, *and* macte, *nom.*; macte, *acc.*; *honored*; —macti, *nom. plur.* Necesse, *and* necessum, *nom., acc.*; *necessary.* Plus, *nom., acc.*; plūris, *gen.*; *more*;—*pl.* plūres, -a, *nom. acc.*; -ium *gen.*; ĭbus, *dat., abl.* Cf. § 110. Postĕra, postĕrum, *coming after*, wants the nom. sing. masc. Pŏtis, *nom. sing.* and *pl.*, all genders; *able*. Pŏte, *nom. sing.*, for potest; *possible*. Septemplĭcis, *gen.*; -ce, *abl.*; *seven-fold*. Sĭremps, *and* sĭrempse, *nom.* and *acc.*, *alike.* Tantundem, *nom. acc.*; tantīdem, *gen.*; tantandem, *acc.*; *so much* Trilĭcem, *acc.*; *trebly-tissued*; trilĭces, *nom.* and *acc. pl.*

REDUNDANT ADJECTIVES.

§ 116. The following adjectives are redundant in termination and declension. Those marked *r* are more rarely used.

Acclīvis, *and* -us, *r, ascending.*
Auxiliāris, *and* -ius, *auxiliary.*
Bijŭgis, *and* -us, *yoked two together.*
Declīvis, *and* -us, *r, descending.*
Exanĭmis, *and* -us, *r, lifeless.*
Hilāris, *and* -us, *cheerful.*
Imbecillis, *r, and* -us, *weak.*
Impūbes, *and* -is, *r,* -is *or* -ĕris, *not grown up.*
Inermis, *and* -us, *r, unarmed.*
Infrēnis, *and* -us, *unbridled.*

Inquies, *and* -ētus, *restless.*
Joculāris, *and* -ius, *r, laughable.*
Multijŭgis, *r, and* -us, *yoked many together.*
Opŭlens, *and* -lentus, *rich.*
Præcox, -cŏquis, *and* -cŏquus, *early ripe.*
Proclīvis, *and* -us, *r, sloping.*
Quadrijŭgis, *and* -us, *yoked four together.*
Seminĭmis, *and* -us, *half alive.*

Semiernais, *and* -us, *half armed.*
Semisomnis, *and* -us, *r, half asleep.*
Singulāris, *and* -ius, *single.*

Sublīmis, *and* -us, *r, high.*
Unanĭmis, *r, and* -us, *unanimous.*
Viŏlens, *r, and* -lentus, *violent.*

To these may be added some adjectives in *er* and *is;* as, *salūber* and *-bris,* *celĕber* and *-bris.* Cf. § 108, R. 1.

NUMERAL ADJECTIVES.

§ 117. Numeral adjectives are divided into three principal classes—*Cardinal, Ordinal,* and *Distributive.*

I. Cardinal numbers are those which simply denote the number of things, in answer to the question *Quot?* 'How many?' They are,

1.	Unus,	*one.*	I.
2.	Duo,	*two.*	II.
3.	Tres,	*three.*	III.
4.	Quătuor,	*four.*	IIII. *or* IV.
5.	Quinque,	*five.*	V.
6.	Sex,	*six.*	VI.
7.	Septem,	*seven.*	VII.
8.	Octo,	*eight*	VIII.
9.	Nŏvem,	*nine.*	VIIII. *or* IX.
10.	Dĕcem,	*ten.*	X.
11.	Undĕcim,	*eleven.*	XI.
12.	Duodĕcim,	*twelve.*	XII.
13.	Tredĕcim,	*thirteen.*	XIII.
14.	Quatuordĕcim,	*fourteen.*	XIIII. *or* XIV.
15.	Quindĕcim,	*fifteen.*	XV.
16.	Sedĕcim, *or* sexdĕcim,	*sixteen.*	XVI.
17.	Septendĕcim,	*seventeen.*	XVII.
18.	Octodĕcim,	*eighteen.*	XVIII.
19.	Novendĕcim,	*nineteen.*	XVIIII. *or* XIX.
20.	Viginti,	*twenty.*	XX.
21	Viginti unus, *or* unus et viginti,	*twenty-one.*	XXI.
22.	Viginti duo, *or* duo et viginti, etc.,	*twenty-two.*	XXII.
30.	Triginta,	*thirty.*	XXX.
40.	Quădrāginta,	*forty.*	XXXX. *or* XL.
50.	Quinquaginta,	*fifty.*	L.
60.	Sexaginta,	*sixty.*	LX.
70.	Septuaginta,	*seventy.*	LXX.
80.	Octoginta, *or* octuaginta,	*eighty.*	LXXX.
90.	Nōnāginta,	*ninety.*	LXXXX. *or* XC.
100.	Centum,	*a hundred.*	C.
101.	Centum unus, *or* centum et unus, etc.,	*a hundred and one*	CI.
200.	Dŭcenti, -æ, a,	*two hundred.*	CC.
300.	Trĕcenti, etc.,	*three hundred.*	CCC.
400.	Quadringenti,	*four hundred.*	CCCC, *or* CD.
500.	Quingenti,	*five hundred.*	IƆ, *or* D.
600.	Sexcenti,	*six hundred.*	IƆC, *or* DC.
700.	Septingenti,	*seven hundred.*	IƆCC, *or* DCC.
800.	Octingenti,	*eight hundred.*	IƆCCC, *or* DCCC.
900.	Nongenti,	*nine hundred.*	IƆCCCC, *or* DCCCC
1000.	Mille,	*a thousand.*	CIƆ, *or* M.
2000.	Duo millia, *or* bis mille,	*two thousand.*	CIƆCIƆ, *or* MM.

5000	Quinque millia, *or* quinquies mille,	*five thousand.*	IƆƆ.
10000	Decem millia, *or* decies mille,	*ten thousand.*	CCIƆƆ.
50000.	Quinquaginta millia, *or* quinquagies mille,	*fifty thousand.*	IƆƆƆ.
100000.	Centum millia, *or* centies mille,	*a hundred thousand.*	CCCIƆƆƆ.

§ **118.** 1. The first three cardinal numbers are declined; from four to a hundred inclusive they are indeclinable; those denoting hundreds are declined like the plural of *bŏnus*.

For the declension of *ūnus* and *tres*, see §§ 107 and 109.

Duo is thus declined:—

Plural.

	M.	*F.*	*N.*
N.	dŭ'-o,	du'-æ,	dŭ'-o,
G.	du-ŏ'-rum,	du-ā'-rum,	du-ŏ'-rum,
D.	du-ŏ'-bus,	du-ā'-bus,	du-ŏ'-bus,
Ac.	du'-os, *or* du'-o,	du'-as,	du'-o,
V.	du'-o,	du'-æ,	du'-o,
Ab.	du-ŏ'-bus.	du-ā'-bus.	du-ŏ'-bus.

REMARK 1. *Duŏrum, duărum*, are often contracted into *duûm*, especially in compounds; as, *duŭmvir*, and when joined with *millium.—Ambo*, both, which partakes of the nature of a numeral and of a pronoun, is declined like *duo*.

2. The cardinal numbers, except *ūnus* and *mille*, are used in the plural only.

REM. 2. The plural of *unus* is used with nouns which have no singular, or whose singular has a different sense from the plural; as, *unæ nuptiæ*, one marriage; *una castra*, one camp. It is used also with nouns denoting several things considered as one whole; as, *una vestimenta*, one suit of clothes. So also, when it takes the signification of "alone" or "the same"; as, *uni Ubii*, the Ubians alone; *unis moribus vivĕre*,—with the same manners.

3. (*a.*) Thirteen, sixteen, seventeen, eighteen, and nineteen, are often expressed by two numbers, the greater of which usually precedes, united by *et*; thus, *dĕcem et tres, dĕcem et nŏvem*, or, omitting *et, dĕcem nŏvem*. *Octodĕcim* has no good authority. See *infra*, 4.

(*b.*) From twenty to a hundred, the smaller number with *et* is put first, or the greater without *et*; as, *unus et viginti*, or *viginti unus*. Above one hundred, the greater precedes, with or without *et*; as, *centum et unus*, or *centum unus*, *trecenti sexaginta sex*, or *trecenti et sexaginta sex*. *Et* is never twice used, but the poets sometimes take *ac, atque, or que*, instead of *et*.

4. For eighteen, twenty-eight, etc., and for nineteen, twenty-nine, etc. (excepting sixty-eight, sixty-nine, and ninety-eight), a subtractive expression is more frequent than the additive form; as, *duodeviginti*, two from twenty; *undeviginti*, one from twenty; *duodetriginta, undetriginta*, etc. Neither *un* (*unus*) nor *duo* can be declined in these combinations. The additive forms for thirty-eight, etc. to ninety-eight, and for forty-nine, etc. to ninety-nine, except those for sixty-nine, seem not to occur.

5. (*a.*) Thousands are generally expressed by prefixing the smaller cardinal numbers to *millia;* as, *dĕcem millia*, ten thousand; *ducenta millia*, two hundred thousand. As there is in Latin no unit above *mille*, a thousand, the higher units of modern numeration are expressed by prefixing the numeral adverbs to the

combination *centēna millia;* as, *decies centēna millia,* a million; *centies centēna millia,* ten millions. In such combinations *centēna millia* is sometimes omitted; as, *decies, scil. centēna millia.*

(*b.*) The poets sometimes make use of numeral adverbs in expressing smaller numbers; as, *bis sex* for *duodĕcim; bis centum* for *ducĕnti,* etc.

6. *Mille* is used either as a substantive or as an adjective.

(*a.*) When taken substantively, it is indeclinable in the singular number, and, in the plural, has *millia, millium, millĭbus,* etc.; as, *mille homĭnum,* a thousand men; *duo millia homĭnum,* two thousand men, etc. When *mille* is a substantive, the things numbered are put in the genitive, as in the preceding examples, unless a declined numeral comes between; as, *habuit tria millia trecentos milites.*

(*b.*) As an adjective, *mille* is plural only, and indeclinable: as, *mille homines,* a thousand men; *cum bis mille hominibus,* with two thousand men.

7. Capitals were used by the Romans to mark numbers. The letters employed for this purpose were C. I. L. V. X., which are, therefore, called *Numeral Letters.* I. denotes *one;* V. *five;* X. *ten;* L. *fifty;* and C. *a hundred.* By the various combinations of these five letters, all the different numbers are expressed.

(*a.*) The repetition of a numeral letter repeats its value. Thus, II. signifies *two;* III. *three;* XX. *twenty;* XXX. *thirty;* CC. *two hundred,* etc. But V. and L. are never repeated.

(*b.*) When a letter of a less value is placed before a letter of a greater value, the less takes away its value from the greater; but being placed after, it adds its value to the greater; thus,

IV. Four.	V. Five.	VI. Six.
IX. Nine.	X. Ten.	XI. Eleven.
XL. Forty.	L. Fifty.	LX. Sixty.
XC. Ninety.	C. A hundred.	CX. A hundred and ten.

(*c.*) *A thousand* was marked thus, CIƆ, which, in later times, was contracted into M. *Five hundred* is marked thus, IƆ, or, by contraction, D.

(*d.*) The annexing of the *apostrophus* or inverted C (Ɔ) to IƆ makes its value ten times greater; thus, IƆƆ marks *five thousand;* and IƆƆƆ, *fifty thousand.*

(*e.*) The prefixing of C, together with the annexing of Ɔ, to the number CIƆ, makes its value ten times greater; thus, CCIƆƆ denotes *ten thousand;* and CCCIƆƆƆ, *a hundred thousand.* The Romans, according to Pliny, proceeded no further in this method of notation. If they had occasion to express a larger number, they did it by repetition; thus, CCCIƆƆƆ, CCCIƆƆƆ, signified *two hundred thousand,* etc.

(*f.*) We sometimes find *thousands* expressed by a straight line drawn over the top of the numeral letters. Thus, I̅I̅I̅. denotes *three thousand;* X̅., *ten thousand.*

§ **119.** II. *Ordinal* numbers are such as denote order or rank, and answer to the question, *Quŏtus?* Which of the numbers? They all end in *us,* and are declined like *bŏnus;* as, *prīmus,* first; *secundus,* second.

III. *Distributive* numbers are those which indicate an equal division among several persons or things, and answer to the question, *Quotēni?* How many apiece? as, *singŭli,* one by one, or, one to each; *bīni,* two by two, or two to each, etc. They are always used in the plural, and are declined like the plural of *bŏnus,* except that they usually have *ûm* instead of *ōrum* in the genitive plural. Cf. § 105, R. 4.

NUMERAL ADJECTIVES.

The following table contains the ordinal and distributive numbers, and the corresponding numeral adverbs, which answer to the question, *Quoties?* How many times?—

	Ordinal.	Distributive.	Numeral Adverbs.
1.	Prīmus, *first*.	Singŭli, *one by one*.	Sĕmel, *once*.
2.	Sĕcundus, *second*.	Bīni, *two by two*.	Bis, *twice*.
3.	Tertius, *third*.	Terni, *or* trīni.	Ter, *thrice*.
4.	Quartus, *fourth*.	Quaterni.	Quăter, *four times*.
5.	Quintus, *fifth*.	Quini.	Quinquies.
6.	Sextus, *sixth*.	Sēni.	Sexies.
7.	Septĭmus, *seventh*.	Septēni.	Septies.
8.	Octāvus, *eighth*.	Octōni.	Octies.
9.	Nōnus, *ninth*.	Novēni.	Novies.
10.	Decĭmus, *tenth*, etc.	Dēni.	Děcies.
11.	Undecĭmus.	Undēni.	Undecies.
12.	Duodecĭmus.	Duodēni.	Duodecies.
13.	Tertius decĭmus.	Terni dēni.	Terdecies.
14.	Quartus decĭmus.	Quaterni dēni.	Quatuordecies.
15.	Quintus decĭmus.	Quini dēni.	Quindecies.
16.	Sextus decĭmus.	Sēni dēni.	Sedecies.
17.	Septĭmus decĭmus.	Septēni dēni.	Decies et septies.
18.	Octāvus decĭmus.	Octōni dēni.	Duodevicies.
19.	Nōnus decĭmus.	Novēni dēni.	Undevicies.
20.	Vicēsĭmus, *or* vigesĭmus.	Vicēni.	Vicies.
21.	Vicesĭmus prīmus.	Vicēni singŭli.	Semel et vicies.
22.	Vicesĭmus secundus.	Vicēni bīni, etc.	Bis et vicies, etc.
30.	Tricesĭmus, *or* trigesĭmus.	Tricēni.	Tricies.
40.	Quadragesĭmus.	Quadragēni.	Quadragies.
50.	Quinquagesĭmus.	Quinquagēni.	Quinquagies.
60.	Sexagesĭmus.	Sexagēni.	Sexagies.
70.	Septuagesĭmus.	Septuagēni.	Septuagies.
80.	Octogesĭmus.	Octogēni.	Octogies.
90.	Nonagesĭmus.	Nonagēni.	Nonagies.
100.	Centesĭmus.	Centēni.	Centies.
200.	Ducentesĭmus.	Ducēni.	Ducenties.
300.	Trecentesĭmus.	Trecēni, *or* trecentēni.	Trecenties, *or* tricenties.
400.	Quadringentesĭmus	Quadringēni, *or* quadringentēni.	Quadringenties.
500.	Quingentesĭmus.	Quingēni.	Quingenties.
600.	Sexcentesĭmus.	Sexcēni, *or* sexcentēni.	Sexcenties.
700.	Septingentesĭmus.	Septingēni.	Septingenties.
800.	Octingentesĭmus.	Octingēni.	Octingenties.
900.	Nongentesĭmus.	Nongēni.	Noningenties.
1000.	Millesĭmus.	Millēni, *or* singŭla millia.	Millies.
2000.	Bis millesĭmus.	Bis millēni, *or* bina millia.	Bis millies.

§ 120. 1. In the ordinals, instead of *primus*, prior is used, if only two are spoken of. *Alter* is often used for *secundus*.

2. (*a.*) From thirteenth to nineteenth, the smaller number is usually put first, without *et*; as, *tertius decimus*, but sometimes the greater with or without *et*; as, *decimus et tertius*, or *decimus tertius*.

(*b.*) Twenty-first, thirty-first, etc., are often expressed by *unus et vicesimus, unus et tricesimus*, etc., one and twentieth, etc.; and twenty-second, etc., by *duo*, or *alter et vicesimus*, etc., in which *duo* is not changed. In the other compound numerals, the larger precedes without *et*, or the smaller with *et*; as, *vicesimus quartus*, or *quartus et vicesimus*.

(*c.*) For eighteenth, etc., to fifty-eighth, and for nineteenth, etc. to fifty-ninth, the subtractive forms, *duodevicesimus*, etc., and *undevicesimus*, etc., are often used.

3. In the distributives, eighteen, thirty-eight, forty-eight, and nineteen and twenty-nine, are often expressed by the subtractives *duodeviceni*, etc., *undeviceni*, etc.

4. (*a.*) Distributives are sometimes used by the poets for cardinal numbers; as, *bina spicula*, two darts. Virg. So likewise in prose, with nouns that want the singular; as, *binæ nuptiæ*, two weddings.

(*b.*) The singular of some distributives is used in the sense of multiplicatives; as, *binus*, twofold. So *ternus, quinus, septēnus*.

5. In the numeral adverbs, for the intermediate numbers 21, 22, etc., the larger number also may be put first, either with or without *et*; and for twenty-eight times and thirty-nine times, *duodetricies* and *undequadragies* are found.

§ **121.** To the preceding classes may be added the following:—

1. *Multiplicatives*, which denote how many fold, in answer to the question, *quotŭplex?* They all end in *plex*, and are declined like *fēlix*; as,

Simplex, *single.* Quincŭplex, *fivefold.*
Dŭplex, *twofold*, or *double.* Septemplex, *sevenfold.*
Triplex, *threefold.* Decemplex, *tenfold.*
Quadrŭplex, *fourfold.* Centŭplex, *a hundred fold.*

2. *Proportionals*, which denote how many times one thing is greater than another; as, *dŭplus, a, um,* twice as great; so *triplus, quadrŭplus, octŭplus, decŭplus.* They are generally found only in the neuter.

3. *Temporals*, which denote time; as, *bīmus, a, um*, two years old; so *trīmus, quadrīmus*, etc. Also, *biennis*, lasting two years, biennial; so *quadriennis, quinquennis*, etc. So also, *bimestris*, of two months' continuance; *trimestris*, etc., *biduus*, etc. To these may be added certain nouns, compounds of *annus* and *dies* with the cardinal numbers; as, *biennium, triennium*, etc., a period of two, etc. years; *biduum, triduum*, etc., a period of two, etc. days.

4. Adjectives in *arius*, derived from the distributives, and denoting of how many equal parts or units a thing consists; as, *binarius*, of two parts; *ternarius*, etc.

5. *Interrogatives*; as, *quot*, how many? *quŏtus*, of what number? *quotēni*, how many each? *quoties*, how many times? Their correlatives are *tot, totidem*, so many; *aliquot*, some; which, with *quot*, are indeclinable; and the adverbs, *toties*, so often; *aliquoties*, several times.

6. *Fractional expressions*, which denote the parts of a thing. These are expressed in Latin by *pars* with *dimidia, tertia, quarta*, etc. Thus, ½, *dimidia pars*; ⅓, *tertia pars*, etc. When the number of parts into which a thing is divided exceeds by one only the parts mentioned, as in ⅔, ¾, etc. the fraction is expressed simply by *duæ, tres*, etc. *partes*, denoting two out of three, three out of four, etc.

COMPARISON OF ADJECTIVES.

§ **122.** 1. Adjectives may be divided into two classes—those which denote a *variable*, and those which denote an *invariable*, quality or limitation.

Thus, *bŏnus*, good, *altus*, high, and *opācus*, dark, denote variable attributes; but *æneus*, brazen, *triplex*, threefold, and *diurnus*, daily, do not admit of different degrees in their signification.

2. The *comparison* of an adjective is the expression of its quality in different degrees.

§ 123-125.   ADJECTIVES.—IRREGULAR COMPARISON.   75

3. There are three degrees of comparison—the *positive*, the *comparative*, and the *superlative*.

4. The positive simply denotes a quality, without reference to other degrees of the same quality; as, *altus*, high; *mitis*, mild.

5. The comparative denotes that a quality belongs to one of two objects, or sets of objects, in a greater degree than to the other; as, *altior*, higher; *mitior*, milder.

6. The superlative denotes that a quality belongs to one of several objects, or sets of objects, in a greater degree than to any of the rest; as, *altissimus*, highest; *mitissimus*, mildest.

REM. 1. Sometimes also the comparative denotes that a quality, at different times or in other circumstances, belongs in different degrees to the *same* object as, *est sapientior quam fuit*, he is wiser than he was.

REM. 2. The comparative sometimes expresses the proportion between two qualities of the same object; as, *est doctior quam sapientior*, he is more learned than wise; that is, his learning is greater than his wisdom.

REM. 3. The comparative is also used elliptically instead of our 'too' or rather'; as, *vivit liberius*, he lives too freely, or, rather freely. Cf. § 256, R. 9

REM. 4. The superlative, like the positive with *per*, (cf. § 127, 2), often indicates a high degree of a quality without direct comparison with the same quality in other objects; as, *amicus carissimus*, a very dear friend.

§ **123**. 1. Degrees of a quality *inferior* to the positive may be denoted by the adverbs *minus*, less; *minime*, least, prefixed to the positive; as, *jucundus*, pleasant; *minus jucundus*, less pleasant; *minime jucundus*, least pleasant.

2. A small degree of a quality is indicated by *sub* prefixed to the positive; as, *amarus*, bitter; *subamarus*, bitterish, or, somewhat bitter.

3. An *equal* degree of a quality may be denoted by *tam* followed by *quam* *æque* followed by *ac, sic* followed by *ut*, etc.; as, *hebes, æque ac pecus*, as stupid as a brute.

§ **124**. 1. The comparative and superlative in Latin, as in English, are denoted either by peculiar terminations, or by certain adverbs prefixed to the positive. Cf. § 127, 1.

2. The terminational comparative ends in   Masc. *ior*,   Fem. *ior*,   Neut *ius*; the terminational superlative in *issimus, issima, issimum*.

3. These terminations are added to the root of the positive; as,
*al*tus, *al*tior, *al*tissimus;   high, higher, highest.
*mi*tis, *mi*tior, *mi*tissimus;   mild, milder, mildest.
felix, (gen. *felicis*,) *felici*or, *felici*ssimus;   happy, happier, happiest.

In like manner compare

Arc'-tus, *strait.*   Cru-dē'-lis, *cruel.*   Cā'-pax, *capacious.*
Cā'-rus, *dear.*   Fer'-tĭ-lis, *fertile.*   Clē'-mens, (*gen.* -tis) *merciful.*
Doc'-tus, *learned.*   Lĕ'-vis, *light.*   In'-ers, (*gen.* -tis), *sluggish.*

IRREGULAR COMPARISON.

§ **125**. 1. Adjectives in *er* form their superlative by adding *rimus* to that termination; as, *acer*, active; gen. *acris*; comparative, *acrior*; superlative, *acerrimus*.

In like manner, *pauper, pauperrĭmus.* *Vĕtus* has a similar superlative, *veterrĭmus,* from the old collateral form *vĕter.*

2. Six adjectives in *lis* form their superlative by adding *lĭmus* to the root:—

Facĭlis,	facilior,	facillĭmus,	*easy.*
Difficĭlis,	difficilior,	difficillĭmus,	*difficult.*
Gracĭlis,	gracilior,	gracillĭmus,	*slender.*
Humĭlis,	humilior,	humillĭmus,	*low.*
Simĭlis,	similior,	simillĭmus,	*like.*
Dissimĭlis,	dissimilior,	dissimillĭmus,	*unlike.*

Imbecillus or *imbecillis,* weak, has two forms, *imbecillissĭmus* and *imbecillĭmus.*

3. (*a.*) Five adjectives in *fĭcus* (from *făcio*) derive their comparatives and superlatives from supposed forms in *ens*:—

Benefĭcus,	beneficentior,	beneficentissĭmus,	*beneficent.*
Honorifĭcus,	honorificentior,	honorificentissĭmus,	*honorable.*
Magnifĭcus,	magnificentior,	magnificentissĭmus,	*splendid.*
Munifĭcus,	munificentior,	munificentissĭmus,	*liberal.*
Malefĭcus,	——,	maleficentissĭmus,	*hurtful.*

(*b.*) Adjectives in *dĭcens* and *vŏlens* form their comparatives and superlatives regularly; but instead of those positives, forms in *dĭcus* and *vŏlus* are more common; as,

Maledĭcens *or* dĭcus, maledicentior, maledicentissĭmus, *slanderous.*
Benevŏlens, *or* -vŏlus, benevolentior, benevolentissĭmus, *benevolent.*

4. These five have regular comparatives, but irregular superlatives:—

Dexter,	dexterior,	dextĭmus,	*right.*
Extĕra, (*fem.*)	exterior,	extrēmus, *or* extĭmus,	*outward.*
Postĕra, (*fem.*)	posterior,	postrēmus, *or* postŭmus,	*hind.*
Infĕrus,	inferior,	infĭmus, *or* īmus,	*below.*
Supĕrus,	superior,	suprēmus, *or* summus,	*above.*

REMARK 1. The nominative singular of *postĕra* does not occur in the masculine, and that of *extĕra* wants good authority.

5. The following are very irregular in comparison:—

Bŏnus,	melior,	optĭmus,	*good,*	*better,*	*best.*
Mălus,	pējor,	pessĭmus,	*bad,*	*worse,*	*worst.*
Magnus,	mājor,	maxĭmus,	*great,*	*greater,*	*greatest.*
Parvus,	mĭnor,	minĭmus,	*little,*	*less,*	*least.*
Multus,	——,	plurĭmus, }			
Multa,	——,	plurīma, }	*much,*	*more,*	*most.*
Multum,	plus,*	plurĭmum, }			
Nēquam,	nequior,	nequissĭmus,	*worthless,* etc.		
Frūgi,	frugalior,	frugalissĭmus,	*frugal,* etc.		

REM. 2. All these, except *magnus,* whose regular forms are contracted, either form their comparatives and superlatives from obsolete adjectives, or take them from other words of similar signification.

DEFECTIVE COMPARISON.

§ **126.** 1. Seven adjectives want the positive:—

Citerior, citĭmus, *nearer.* Prior, primus, *former.*
Deterior, deterrĭmus, *worse.* Propior, proxĭmus, *nearer.*
Interior, intĭmus, *inner.* Ulterior, ultĭmus, *farther.*
Ocior, ocissĭmus, *swifter.*

---

* See § 110.

2. Eight want the terminational comparative:—

Consultus, consultissimus, *skilful.*
Inclŭtus, inclutissĭmus, *renowned.*
Invictus, invictissĭmus, *invincible.*
Invītus, invitissĭmus, *unwilling.*
Merĭtus, meritissĭmus, (very rare,) *deserving.*

Par, parissĭmus, (very rare), *equal.*
Persuāsus, persuasissĭmum (neuter) *persuaded.*
Sācer, sacerrĭmus, *sacred.*

3. Eight have very rarely the terminational comparative:—

Aprīcus, apricissĭmus, *sunny.*
Bellus, bellissĭmus, *fine.*
Cōmis, comissĭmus, *courteous.*
Diversus, diversissĭmus, *different.*

Falsus, falsissĭmus, *false.*
Fīdus, fidissĭmus, *faithful.*
Nŏvus, novissĭmus, *new.*
Vĕtus, veterrĭmus, *old.*

4. The following want the terminational superlative:—

Adolescens, adolescentior, *young.*
Agrestis, agrestior, *rustic.*
Alăcer, alacrior, *active.*
Ater, atrior, *black.*
Cæcus, cæcior, *blind.*
Dēses, desidior, *inactive.*
Diuturnus, diuturnior, *lasting.*
Infinītus, infinitior, *unlimited.*
Ingens, ingentior, *great.*
Jejūnus, jejunior, *fasting.*
Juvĕnis, junior, *young.*
Licens, licentior, *unrestrained.*
Longinquus, longinquior, *distant.*
Opīmus, opimior, *rich.*

Proclīvis, proclivior, *sloping.*
Prŏnus, pronior, *bending down.*
Protervus, protervior, *violent.*
——— sequior, *worse.*
Propinquus, propinquior, *near.*
Salutāris, salutarior, *salutary.*
Sătis, *sufficient;* satius, *preferable.*
Sătur, saturior, *full.*
Sĕnex, senior, *old.*
Silvestris, silvestrior, *woody.*
Sinister, sinisterior, *left.*
Supīnus, supinior, *lying on the back.*
Surdus, surdior, *deaf.*
Tĕres, teretior, *round.*

REMARK 1. The superlative of *juvĕnis* and *adolescens* is supplied by *minĭmus nātu,* youngest; and that of *sĕnex* by *maxĭmus nātu,* oldest. The comparatives *minor nātu* and *major nātu* sometimes also occur.

REM. 2. Most adjectives also in *ilis, ilis, ālis,* and *bĭlis,* have no terminational superlative.

5. Many variable adjectives have no terminational comparative or superlative. Such are,

(*a.*) Adjectives in *bundus, īmus, ĭnus* (except *divīnus*), *ŏrus,* most in *ĭvus,* and in *us* pure (except *-quus.*) Yet *arduus, assiduus, egregius, exiguus, industrius, perpetuus, pius, strenuus,* and *vacuus,* have sometimes a terminational comparison. So, dropping *i, noxior, innoxior, sobrior.*

(*b.*) The following—*almus, calvus, cānus, cicur, claudus, degĕner, delīrus, dispar, egēnus, impar, impĭger, invĭdus, lăcer, mĕmor, mīrus, nŭdus, præcox, prædĭves, rŭdis, salvus, sospes, superstes, vulgāris,* and some others.

§ **127.** 1. The comparative and superlative may also be formed by prefixing to the positive the adverbs *măgis,* more, and *maxĭme,* most; as, *idoneus,* fit; *magis idoneus, maxĭme idoneus.*

2. Various degrees of a quality above the positive are expressed by *admŏdum, aliquanto, apprīme, bĕne, imprimis, multum, oppĭdo, perquam,* and *valde,* and also by *per* compounded with the positive; as, *difficĭlis,* difficult; *perdifficĭlis,* very difficult. To a few adjectives *præ* is in like manner prefixed; as, *prædūrus,* very hard.

3. The force of the comparative is increased by prefixing *etiam,* even, still, *or* yet; and that of both comparative and superlative, by

prefixing *longe* or *multo*, much, far; as, longe *nobilissĭmus;* longe *melior iter* multo *facilius;* multo *maxĭma pars.*

4. *Vel*, 'even', and *quam*, with or without *possum*, 'as much as possible', before the superlative, render it more emphatic; as, *Cicĕro vel optĭmus oratōrum Romanōrum.* Quam *maxĭmum* potest *milĭtum numĕrum collĭgit;* quam *doctissĭmus*, extremely learned; quam *celerrĭme*, as speedily as possible.

NOTE 1. Instead of *quam* with *possum*, *quantus* is sometimes used, in the same case as the superlative; as, Quantis *maxĭmis* potuit *itinerĭbus contendit.*

NOTE 2. *Unus*, with or without *omnium*, is sometimes added to superlatives to increase their force; as, *Hoc ego* ūno omnium *plurĭmum ūtor.* Cic. *Urbem* ūnam *mihi amicissĭmam declināvi*, Id. It is used in like manner with *excello.*

5. All adjectives whose signification admits of different degrees, if they have no terminational comparison, may be compared by means of adverbs.

6. Instead of the comparative and superlative degrees, the positive with the prepositions *præ, ante, præter,* or *supra*, is sometimes used; as, *præ nobis beātus*, happier than we. Cic. *Ante alias pulchritudĭne insignis*, most beautiful. Liv. Sometimes the preposition is used in connection with the superlative; as, *Ante alios pulcherrĭmus omnes.* Virg.

7. Among adjectives which denote an invariable quality or limitation, and which, therefore, cannot be compared, are those denoting matter, time, number, possession, country, part, interrogation; also compounds of *jŭgum, somnus, gĕro,* and *fĕro,* and many others.

DERIVATION OF ADJECTIVES.

§ **128.** Derivative adjectives are formed chiefly from nouns, from other adjectives, and from verbs.

I. Those derived from nouns and adjectives are called *denominatives.* The following are the principal classes:—

1. (*a.*) The termination *ĕus*, added to the root, denotes the material of which a thing is made, and sometimes similarity; as, *aureus*, golden; *argenteus*, of silver; *ligneus*, wooden; *vitreus*, of glass; *virgineus*, maidenly; from *aurum*, *argentum*, etc. See § 9, Rem. 3.

(*b.*) Some adjectives of this kind have a double form in *neus* and *nus;* as, *eburneus* and *eburnus*, of ivory.

(*c.*) The termination *inus* has the same meaning; as, *adamantĭnus*, of adamant; *cedrĭnus*, of cedar; from *adāmas* and *cedrus.* So, also, *ēnus;* as, *terrēnus*, of earth, from *terra.*

(*d.*) The termination *ēus* or *īus* (Greek ιος), and also *ĭcus*, belong to adjectives formed from Greek names of men, and denote 'of' or 'pertaining to'; as, *Achillēus, Sophoclēus, Aristotelīus, Platonĭcus; Pythagorēus* and *Pythagorĭcus; Homerĭus* and *Homerĭcus.* Names in *ias* make adjectives in *iăcus;* as, *Archias, Archiăcus.* Sometimes, though rarely in the purest Latin authors, adjectives in *ēus* or *ĭus* are formed from Latin names; as, *Marcellīa* or *-ĕa*, a festival in honor of the Marcelli.

2. (*a.*) The terminations *ālis, āris, ārius, ilis, atĭlis, ĭcius, ĭcus, ius, ĕus,* and *inus,* denote 'belonging,' 'pertaining,' or 'relating to'; as, *capitālis*, relating to the life; from *capŭt*

§ 128. ADJECTIVES—DERIVATION.

So *comitiālis, regālis; Apollināris, consulāris, populāris; argentarius; civīlis, hostīlis, juvenīlis; aquatīlis, fluviatīlis; tribunicius, patricius; bellicus, civicus, Germanicus; accusatorius, imperatorius, regius; Hectorēus; canīnus, equīnus, ferīnus, masculīnus;* from *comitia, rex, Apollo, consul, popŭlus, argentum, civis,* etc.

(*b.*) The termination *ilis* sometimes expresses character; as, *hostīlis,* hostile; *puerīlis,* boyish; from *hostis* and *puer.*

(*c.*) The termination *inus* belongs especially to derivatives from names of animals, and other living beings.

3. The termination *arius,* as a substantive, scil. *faber,* etc., generally denotes profession or occupation; as, *argentarius,* a silversmith; from *argentum;—coriarius, statuarius;* from *corium* and *statua.* When added to numeral adjectives, it denotes how many equal parts a thing contains. See § 121, 4.

4. The terminations *ōsus* and *lentus* denote abundance, fulness; as, *animōsus,* full of courage; *fraudulentus,* given to fraud; from *animus* and *fraus.* So *lapidōsus, vinōsus, portuōsus, turbulentus, sanguinolentus, violentus.* Before *lentus,* a connecting vowel is inserted, which is commonly *u,* but sometimes *o.*

NOTE.—Adjectives of this class are called *amplificatives.* See § 104, 12.

5. From adjectives are formed *diminutives* in *ulus, culus,* etc., in the same manner as from nouns; as, *dulcicŭlus,* sweetish; from *dulcis.* So *lentŭlus, misellus, parvŭlus,* etc. See § 100, 3, and § 104, 11. Diminutives are sometimes formed from comparatives; as, *majuscŭlus, duriuscŭlus,* somewhat great, somewhat hard, etc. Double diminutives are formed from *paucus,* viz *pauxillus* and *pauxillŭlus;* and from *bŏnus,* (*bĕnus*) are formed *bellus* and *bellŭlus.*

6. (*a.*) From the names of places, and especially of towns, are derived *patrial* adjectives in *ensis, inus, as,* and *ānus,* denoting of or belonging to such places.

(*b.*) Thus from *Cannæ* is formed *Cannensis;* from *Sulmo, Sulmonensis.* In like manner, from *castra* and *circus* come *castrensis, circensis.* But *Athēnæ* makes *Atheniensis;* and some Greek towns in *ia* and *ea* drop *i* and *e* in their adjectives; as, *Antiochensis, Nicomedensis.*

(*c.*) Those in *inus* are formed from names of places ending in *ia* and *ium;* as, *Aricia, Aricīnus; Caudium, Caudīnus; Capitolium, Capitolīnus; Latium, Latīnus.* Some names of towns, of Greek origin, with other terminations, also form adjectives in *inus;* as, *Tarentum, Tarentīnus.*

(*d.*) Most of those in *as* are formed from nouns in *um;* some from nouns in *a;* as, *Arpīnum, Arpīnas; Capēna, Capēnas.*

(*e.*) Those in *ānus* are formed from names of towns of the first declension, or from certain common nouns; as, *Alba, Albānus; Rōma, Romānus; Cūmæ, Cumānus; Thēbæ, Thebānus;* also from some of the second declension; as, *Tuscŭlum, Tusculānus; Fundi, Fundānus:—fons, fontānus; mons, montānus; urbs, urbānus; oppĭdum, oppidānus.*

(*f.*) Adjectives with the terminations *ānus, iānus,* and *inus* are formed from names of men; as, *Sulla, Sullānus; Tullius, Tulliānus; Jugurtha, Jugurthīnus.*

(*g.*) Greek names of towns in *polis* form patrial adjectives in *politānus;* as, *Neapŏlis, Neapolitānus.*

(*h.*) Greek names of towns generally form patrials in *ius;* as, *Rhodus, Rhodius; Lacedæmon, Lacedæmonius;*—but those in *a* form them in *æus;* as, *Larissa, Larissæus; Smyrna, Smyrnæus.*

(*i.*) From many patrials; as, *Britannus, Gallus, Afer, Persa, Arabs,* etc., adjectives are formed in *icus* and *ius;* as, *Britannicus, Gallicus, Africus, Persicus, Arabicus;* so *Syrus, Syrius; Thrax, Thracius.*

7. A large class of derivative adjectives, though formed from nouns, have the terminations of perfect participles. They generally signify *wearing* or *furnished with;* as,

alātus, winged; *barbātus,* bearded; *galeātus,* helmeted; *aurītus,* long-eared; *turrītus,* turreted, *cornūtus,* horned; from *ala, barba, galea, auris,* etc.

8. The termination *aneus*, annexed to the root of an adjective or participle in *us*, expresses a resemblance to the quality denoted by the primitive; as, *supervacāneus*, of a superfluous nature.

§ 129. II. Adjectives derived from verbs are called *verbal* adjectives. Such are the following classes:—

1. The termination *bundus*, added to the first root of the verb, with a connecting vowel, which is commonly that of the verb, (see § 150, 5,) has the general meaning of the present participle; as,

errābundus, moribundus, from *erro, morior*, equivalent to *errans, moriens*.

(*a.*) In many the meaning is somewhat strengthened; as, *gratulābundus*, full of congratulations; *lacrimābundus*, weeping profusely.

(*b.*) Most verbals in *bundus* are from verbs of the first conjugation, a few from those of the third, and but one from the second and fourth respectively, viz. *pudībundus* and *lascivībundus*.

(*c.*) Some verbal adjectives in *cundus* have a similar sense; as, *rubīcundus, verēcundus*, from *rubeo* and *vereor*.

2. The termination *ĭdus*, added to the root, especially of neuter verbs, denotes the quality or state expressed by the verb; as,

algĭdus, cold; *calĭdus*, warm; *madĭdus*, moist; *rapĭdus*, rapid; from *algeo, caleo, madeo, rapio*.

3. The termination *uus*, also, denotes the quality expressed by the verb; and adjectives in *uus* derived from active verbs take a passive meaning; as,

congruus, agreeing, from *congruo*; so, *assiduus, nocuus, innocuus:—irriguus*, well watered; *conspicuus*, visible; from *irrigo, conspicio*.

4. (*a.*) The terminations *ĭlis* and *bĭlis*, added to the root of a verb, with its connecting vowel, denote passively, capability, or desert; as,

amabĭlis, worthy to be loved; *credibĭlis*, deserving credit; *placabĭlis*, easy to be appeased; *agĭlis*, active; *ductĭlis*, ductile; from *amo, credo, plāco; ăgo, dūco*. They are rarely active; as, *horribĭlis, terribĭlis, fertĭlis; aër per cuncta meabĭlis*. Plin.

(*b.*) In adjectives of these forms, derived from verbs of the third conjugation, the connecting vowel is *i*; sometimes, also, in those from verbs of the second conjugation, in these and other forms, *i* is used instead of *e*; as, *horribĭlis, terribĭlis*, from *horreo* and *terreo*.

(*c.*) These terminations, with the connecting vowel, are sometimes added to the third root; as, *flexĭlis, flexibĭlis; coctĭlis, coctibĭlis*, from *flecto (flex-)*, etc.

5. The termination *icius* or *itius*, added to the third root of the verb, has a passive sense; as, *fictitius*, feigned; *conductitius*, to be hired; from *fingo (fict-)*, etc.

6. The termination *ax*, added to the root of a verb, denotes an inclination, often one that is faulty; as,

audax, audacious; *lŏquax*, talkative; *răpax*, rapacious; from *audeo, lŏquor răpio*.

7. The termination *ivus*, annexed to the third root of a verb, denotes fitness or ability to produce the action expressed by the verb as, *disjunctīvus*, disjunctive, from *disjungo*.

§ 130, 131.   ADJECTIVES—COMPOSITION.   81

8. Verbals in *tŏr* and *trix*, (see § 102, 6, (*a*.), are often used as adjectives, especially in poetry; as, *victor exercĭtus, victrīces littĕræ*. In the plural they become adjectives of three terminations; as, *victōres, victrīces, victrīcia*. So also *hospes*, especially by the later poets, is used as an adjective, having *hospĭta* in the feminine singular and also in the neuter plural.

§ **130.** III. Adjectives derived from participles, and retaining their form, are called *participial adjectives*; as, *ămans*, fond of; *doctus*, learned.

IV. Some adjectives are derived from adverbs; as, *crastĭnus*, of to-morrow; *hodiernus*, of this day; from *cras* and *hodie*.

V. Some adjectives are derived from prepositions; as, *contrarius*, contrary, from *contra*; *postĕrus*, subsequent, from *post*.

COMPOSITION OF ADJECTIVES.

§ **131.** Compound adjectives are formed variously:—

1. Of two nouns; as, *capripes*, goat-footed—of *căper* and *pes*; *ignicŏmus*, having fiery hair—of *ignis* and *cŏma*.

NOTE.—See, respecting the connecting short **i**, in case the first part of the compound is a noun or an adjective, § 103, Rem. 1.

2. Of a noun and an adjective; as, *noctivăgus*, wandering in the night—of *nox* and *văgus*. So *lucifŭgax*, shunning the light—of *lux* and *fugax*.

3. Of a noun and a verb; as, *cornĭger*, bearing horns—of *cornu* and *gĕro*; *letĭfer*, bringing death—of *lētum* and *fĕro*. So *carnivŏrus, causidĭcus, ignivŏmus, lucifŭgus, particeps*.

4. Of an adjective and a noun; as, *æquævus*, of the same age—of *æquus* and *ævum*; *celerĭpes*, swift-footed—of *celer* and *pes*. So *centimănus, decennis, magnanĭmus, miserĭcors, unanĭmis*.

5. Of two adjectives; as, *centumgemĭnus*, a hundred-fold; *multicăvus*, having many cavities; *quīntusdecĭmus*, the fifteenth.

6. Of an adjective and a verb; as, *brevĭlŏquens*, speaking briefly—of *brĕvis* and *lŏquor*; *magnifĭcus*, magnificent—of *magnus* and *făcio*.

7. Of an adjective and a termination; as, *qualiscumque, quotcumque, uterque*.

8. Of an adverb and a noun; as, *bicorpor*, two-bodied—of *bis* and *corpus*.

9. Of an adverb and an adjective; as, *maledĭcax*, slanderous—of *măle* and *dīcax*. So *antemeridiānus*, before mid-day.

10. Of an adverb and a verb; as, *benefĭcus*, beneficent—of *bĕne* and *făcio*; *malevŏlus*, malevolent—of *măle* and *vŏlo*.

11. Of a preposition and a noun; as, *āmens*, mad—of *a* and *mens*. So *consors, decŏlor, deformis, implūmis, inermis*.

12. Of a preposition and an adjective; as, *concăvus*, concave; *infīdus*, unfaithful. So *improvĭdus, percărus, prædīves, subalbĭdus*.

13. Of a preposition and a verb; as, *continuus*, uninterrupted—of *con* and *teneo*; *insciens*, ignorant—of *in* and *scio*. So *præcipuus, promiscuus, substillus, superstes*.

REMARK. When the former part is a preposition, its final consonant is sometimes changed, to adapt it to the consonant which follows it, as, *imprūdens*—of *in* and *prūdens* See § 196; and cf. § 103, R. 2.

PRONOUNS.

§ 132. 1. A pronoun is a word which supplies the place of a noun.

2. There are eighteen simple pronouns:—

Ego, *I.*	Hic, *this, the latter.*	Suus, *his, hers, its,* etc.
Tu, *thou.*	Is, *that* or *he.*	Cujus? *whose?*
Sui, *of himself,* etc.	Quis? *who?*	Noster, *our.*
Ille, *that, the former.*	Qui, *who.*	Vester, *your.*
Ipse, *himself.*	Meus, *my.*	Nostras, *of our country.*
Iste, *that, that of yours.*	Tuus, *thy.*	Cujas? *of what country*

3. *Ego, tu,* and *sui,* and commonly also *quis* and its compounds, are substantives: the other pronouns, both simple and compound, are adjectives, but are often by ellipsis used as substantives.

4. *Ego, tu,* and *sui* are commonly called *personal pronouns.* They are a species of appellatives (§ 26, 3,) of general application. *Ego* is used by a speaker to designate himself; *tu,* to designate the person whom he addresses. Hence *ego* is of the first person, *tu* of the second. (§ 85, 2.) *Sui* is of the third person, and has always a reflexive signification, referring to the subject of the sentence. The oblique cases of *ego* and *tu* are also used reflexively, when the subject of the proposition is of the first or second person.

5. The remaining pronouns, except *quis* and its compounds, are adjectives, as they serve to limit the meaning of substantives; and they are pronouns, because, like substantive pronouns, they may designate any object in certain situations or circumstances.

6. *Meus, tuus, suus, noster, vester,* and *cujus,* have the same extent of signification as the pronouns from which they are derived, and are equivalent to the genitive cases of their primitives.

7. Pronouns, like substantives and adjectives, are declined; but most of them want the vocative. *Sui,* from the nature of its signification, wants also the nominative in both numbers.

8. The substantive pronouns take the gender of the objects which they denote. The adjective pronouns, like adjectives, have three genders.

SUBSTANTIVE PRONOUNS.

§ 133. The substantive pronouns are thus declined:—

Singular.

N. ĕ'-gŏ, *I.*	tū, *thou.*	
G. me'-ī, *of me.*	tu'-ī, *of thee.*	su'-ī, *of himself, herself, itself.*
D. mĭ'-hĭ, *to me.*	tĭb'-ī,* *to thee.*	sĭb'-ī,* *to himself,* etc.
Ac. mē, *me.*	tē, *thee.*	sē, *himself,* etc.
V. ———	tū, *O thou.*	
Ab. mē, *with me.*	tē, *with thee.*	sē, *with himself,* etc.

*See § 19, 1, Exc.

§ 134.   ADJECTIVE PRONOUNS.   83

Plural.

N.	nōs, *we.*	vōs, *ye* or *you.*	
G.	{nos'-trum / or nos'-trī,} *of us*	{ves'-trum or / ves'-trī,} *of you.*	suī, *of themselves.*
D.	nō'-bĭs, *to us.*	vō'-bĭs, *to you.*	sĭb'-ĭ, *to themselves.*
Ac.	nōs, *us.*	vōs, *you.*	sē, *themselves.*
V.		vōs, *O ye* or *you.*	
Ab.	nō'-bĭs, *with us.*	vō'-bĭs, *with you.*	sē, *with themselves.*

REMARK 1. *Mĕ* and *mī* are ancient forms for *mihi.* So *min'* for *mihine*, Pers. 1, 2.

REM. 2. The syllable *met* is sometimes annexed to the substantive pronouns, in an intensive sense, either with or without *ipse;* as, *egŏmet,* I myself; *mihimet ipsi,* for myself. It is not annexed, however, to the genitives plural, nor to *tu* in the nominative or vocative. In these cases of *tu, tŭtĕ* or *tŭtĕmet* is used. In the accusative and ablative the reduplicated forms *mēmē* and *tētĕ* in the singular, and *sēsē* in both numbers, are employed intensively. *Mepte,* intensive, *med* and *ted,* for *me* and *te,* and *mis* and *tis* for *mei* and *tui,* occur in the comic writers.

☞ *Nostrum* and *vestrum* are contracted from *nostrōrum, nostrārum,* and *vestrōrum, vestrārum.* Respecting the difference in the use of *nostrum* and *nostri, vestrum* and *vestri,* see § 212, R. 2, N. 2.

4. The preposition *cum* is affixed to the ablative of these pronouns in both numbers; as, *mēcum, nobiscum,* etc. Cf. § 136, R. 1.

ADJECTIVE PRONOUNS.

§ **134.** Adjective pronouns may be divided into the following classes:—*demonstrative, intensive, relative, interrogative, indefinite, possessive,* and *patrial.*

NOTE. Some pronouns belong to two of these classes.

DEMONSTRATIVE PRONOUNS.

Demonstrative pronouns are such as specify what object is meant.

They are *ille, iste, hic,* and *is,* and their compounds, and are thus declined:—

	Singular.			*Plural.*		
	M.	*F.*	*N.*	*M.*	*F.*	*N.*
N.	il'-lĕ,	il'-lă,	il'-lŭd,	il'-lī,	il'-læ,	il'-lă,
G.	il-lī'-us,*	il-lī'-us,	il-lī'-us,	il-lō'-rum,	il-lā'-rum,	il-lō'-rum,
D.	il'-lī,	il'-lī,	il'-lī,	il'-līs,	il'-līs,	il'-līs,
Ac.	il'-lum,	il'-lam,	il'-lŭd,	il'-lōs,	il'-lās,	il'-lă,
V.	il'-lĕ,	il'-lă,	il'-lŭd,	il'-lī,	il'-læ,	il'-lă,
Ab.	il'-lō.	il'-lā.	il'-lō.	il'-līs.	il'-līs.	il'-līs.

* See § 15, 1.

DEMONSTRATIVE PRONOUNS.

Iste is declined like *ille*.

	Singular.			Plural.	
	M.	F.	N.	M.	F.	N.
N.	hĭc,	hæc,	hŏc,	hī,	hæ,	hæc,
G.	hū′-jŭs,	hū′-jŭs,	hū′-jŭs,	hō′-rum,	hā′-rum,	hō′-rum,
D.	huic*,	huic,	huic,	his,	his,	his,
Ac.	hunc,	hanc,	hŏc,	hōs,	hās,	hæc,
V.	hĭc,	hæc,	hŏc,	hī,	hæ,	hæc,
Ab.	hōc.	hāc.	hōc.	his.	his.	his.

	Singular.			Plural.		
	M.	F.	N.	M.	F	N.
N.	ĭs,	e′-ă,	ĭd,	ī′-ī,	e′-æ,	e′-ă,
G.	ē′-jŭs,	ē′-jŭs,	ē′-jŭs,	e-ō′-rum,	e-ā′rum,	e-ō′-rum,
D.	e′-ī,	e′-ī,	e′-ī,	ī′-īs *or* e′-īs,	ī′-īs *or* e′-īs,	ī′-īs *or* e′-īs,
Ac.	e′-um,	e′-am,	ĭd,	e′-ōs,	e′-ās,	e′-ă,
V.	——	——	——			
Ab.	e′-ō.	e′-ā.	e′-ō.	ī′-īs *or* e′-īs.	ī′-īs *or* e′-īs.	ī′-īs *or* e′-īs.

REMARK 1. Instead of *ille*, *ollus* was anciently used; whence *olli* masc. plur. in Virgil. *Illæ* fem., for *illius* and *illi*, is found in Lucretius and Cato, as also in Cato, *hæ* for *huic* fem.; *hice* for *hi*, and *hæc* for *hæ* in Plautus and Terence. *Im* for *eum*, is found in the Twelve Tables; *eii* for *ei*, and *ibus* and *iibus* for *iis*, in Plautus; *eæ*, fem., for *ei*, and *eābus* for *iis*, in Cato.

REM. 2. From *ecce*, lo! with *ille*, *iste*, and *is*, are formed, in colloquial language, nom., *ecca; eccilla, eccillud;* acc. sing., *eccum, eccam; eccillum* (by syncope *ellum*), *eccillam; eccistam;* acc. plur., *eccos, ecca.*

REM. 3. *Istic* and *illic* are compounded of *iste hic*, and *ille hic;* or, as some say, of *iste ce*, and *ille ce*. The former sometimes retains the aspirate, as *isthic*. They are more emphatic than *ille* and *iste*.

Istic is thus declined:—

	Singular.			Plural.		
	M.	F.	N.	M.	F.	N.
N.	ĭs′-tĭc,	ĭs′-tæc,	ĭs′-tŏc, *or* ĭs′-tŭc,	N. ——	ĭs′-tæc,	
Ac.	ĭs′-tunc,	ĭs′-tanc,	ĭs′-tŏc, *or* ĭs′-tŭc,	Ac. ——	——	ĭs′-tæc.
Ab.	ĭs′-tōc.	ĭs′-tāc.	ĭs′tŏc.			

Illic is declined in the same manner.

REM. 4. *Ce*, intensive, is sometimes added to the several cases of *hic*, and rarely to some cases of the other demonstrative pronouns; as, *hujusce, huncce, hancce, hocce, hice, hæce* or *hæc, horunc, harumce, harunce,* or *harunc, hosce, hasce, hisce; illiusce, illāce, illosce, illasce, illisce; istāce, istisce; ejusce, iisce.* When *ne*, interrogative, is also annexed, *ce* becomes *ci;* as, *hæccine, hoscine, hiscine; istuccine, istaccine, istuscine; illiccine, illanccine.*

REM. 5. *Modi*, the genitive of *modus*, annexed to the genitive singular of demonstrative and relative pronouns, imparts to them the signification of adjectives of quality; as, *hujusmodi* or *hujuscemodi*, like *talis*, of this sort, such; *illiusmodi* and *istiusmodi*, of that sort; *cujusmodi*, of what sort, like *qualis; cu-*

---

*See § 9, 5.

§ 135.   INTENSIVE PRONOUNS.   85

juscemŏdi, cujusquemŏdi, cujusmodicumque, of what kind soever; *cujusdammŏdi,* of some kind.   So also *istimŏdi, cuimŏdi* and *cuicuimŏdi,* instead of *istiusmŏdi, cujusmŏdi,* etc.

REM. 6. The suffix *dem* is annexed to *is,* forming *idem,* "the same," which is thus declined:—

	Singular.		
	M.	*F.*	*N.*
N.	ĭ'-dem,	e'-ă-dem,	ĭ'-dem,
G.	e-jus'-dem,	e-jus'-dem,	e-jus'-dem,
D.	e-ī'-dem,	e-ī'-dem,	e-ī'-dem,
Ac.	e-un'-dem,	e-an'-dem,	ĭ'-dem,
V.	——	——	——
Ab.	e-ō'-dem.	e-ā'-dem.	e-ō'-dem.

	Plural.		
	M.	*F.*	*N.*
N.	i-ī'-dem,	e-æ'-dem,	e'-ă-dem,
G.	e-o-run'-dem,	e-a-run'-dem,	e-o-run'-dem,
D.	e-is'-dem, *or* i-is'-dem,	e-is'-dem, *or* i-is'-dem,	e-is'-dem, *or* i-is'-dem,
Ac.	e-os'-dem,	e-as'-dem,	e'-ă-dem,
V.	——	——	——
Ab.	e-is'-dem, *or* i-is'-dem.	e-is'-dem, *or* i-is'-dem.	e-is'dem, *or* i-is'-dem.

NOTE 1. In compound pronouns, *m* before *d* is changed into *n;* as, *eundem, eorundem,* etc.

NOTE 2. In Sallust *isdem,* and in Palladius *hisdem* occur for *iisdem;* and Ennius in Cicero has *eademmet* for *eddem.*

INTENSIVE PRONOUNS.

§ **135.** Intensive pronouns are such as serve to render an object emphatic.

To this class belong *ipse,* and the intensive compounds already mentioned.   See §§ 133, R. 2, and 134, R. 4.

Ipse is compounded of *is* and the suffix *pse,* and is thus declined:—

	Singular.			Plural.		
	M.	*F.*	*N.*	*M.*	*F.*	*N.*
N.	ip'-sĕ,	ip'-să,	ip'-sum,	ip'-sī,	ip'-sæ,	ip'-să,
G.	ip-sī'-us,	ip-sī'-us,	ip-sī'-us,	ip-sō'-rum,	ip-sā'-rum,	ip-sō'-rum,
D.	ip'-sī,	ip'-sī,	ip'-sī,	ip'-sīs,	ip'-sīs,	ip'-sīs,
Ac.	ip'-sum,	ip'-sam,	ip'-sum,	ip'-sōs,	ip'-sās,	ip'-să,
V.	ip'-sĕ,	ip'-să,	ip'-sum,	ip'-sī,	ip'-sæ,	ip'-să,
Ab.	ip'-sō.	ip'-sā.	ip'-sō.	ip'-sīs.	ip'-sīs.	ip'-sīs.

REMARK 1. *Ipse* is commonly subjoined to nouns or pronouns; as, *Jupiter ipse, tu ipse,* Jupiter himself, etc.; and hence is sometimes called the *adjunctive* pronoun.

REM. 2. A nominative *ipsus,* occurs in early writers, and a superlative *ipsissimus,* his very self, is found in Plautus.

REM. 3. In old writers the *is* of *ipse* is declined, while *pse* remains undeclined; as, *eapse,* (nom. and abl.), *eampse,* and *eopse,* instead of *ipsa, ipsam* and *ipso.*   So also *reapse,* . e. *re eapse,* "in fact."

8

RELATIVE PRONOUNS.

§ 136. Relative pronouns are such as relate to a preceding noun or pronoun.

1. They are *qui*, who, and the compounds *quicumque* and *quisquis*, whoever. The latter are called *general* relatives.

2. In a general sense, the demonstrative pronouns are often relatives; but the name is commonly appropriated to those above specified. They serve to introduce a proposition, limiting or explaining a preceding noun or pronoun, to which they relate, and which is called the *antecedent*.

Qui is thus declined:—

	Singular.			Plural.		
	M.	*F.*	*N.*	*M.*	*F.*	*N.*
N.	quĭ,	quæ,	quŏd,	quĭ,	quæ,	quæ,
G.	cū´-jŭs,	cū´-jŭs,	cū´-jŭs,	quō´-rum,	quā´-rum,	quō´-rum,
D.	cui,*	cui,	cui,	quī´-bŭs,	quī´-bŭs,	quī´-bŭs,
Ac.	quem,	quam,	quŏd,	quōs,	quās,	quæ,
V.						
Ab.	quō.	quā.	quō.	quī´-bŭs.	quī´-bŭs.	quī´-bŭs.

REMARK 1. *Quī* is sometimes used for the ablative singular, in all genders and rarely also for the ablative plural. To the ablatives *quo, qua, qui,* and *quibus, cum* is commonly annexed, cf. § 133, 4. Cicero uses *quicum* for *quōcum*, when an indefinite person is meant.

REM. 2. *Queis* (monosyllabic, § 9, R. 1), and *quīs* are sometimes used in the dative and ablative plural for *quibus*. *Cūjus* and *cui* were anciently written *quŏjus* and *quoi*: and, instead of the genitive *cūjus*, a relative adjective *cūjus, a, um*, very rarely occurs.

3. *Quicumque*, (or *quicunque*), is declined like *qui*.

REM. 3. *Qui* is sometimes separated from *cumque* by the interposition of one or more words; as, *quæ me cumque vocant terræ*. Virg. A similar separation sometimes occurs in the other compounds of *cumque*.

4. *Quisquis* is thus declined:—

	Singular.			Plural.
	M.	*F.*	*N.*	*M.*
N.	quĭs´-quĭs,	quĭs´-quĭs,†	quĭd´-quĭd,	N. quī´-quī,
Ac.	quem´-quem,	——	quĭd´-quĭd,	D. qui-bŭs´-qui-bus,
Ab.	quō´-quō.	quā´-quā.	quō´-quō.	

REM. 4. *Quicquid* is sometimes used for *quidquid*. *Quīquī* for *quisquis* occurs in Plautus; and *quidquid* is used adjectively in Cato R. R. 48.

---

* See § 9, 5; and cf. § 306, (1.)   † Cf. § 137, R. (1.)

INTERROGATIVE PRONOUNS.

§ 137. Interrogative pronouns are such as serve to inquire which of a number of objects is intended.

They are

Quis? }
Quisnam? } *who? what?*
Qui? }
Quinam? } *which? what?*

Ecquis? }
Ecquisnam? }
Numquis? } *is any one?*
Numquisnam, }

Cūjus? *whose?*
Cūjas? *of what country?*

1. *Quis* is commonly used substantively; *qui*, adjectively. The interrogative *qui* is declined like *qui* the relative.

Quis is thus declined:—

	Singular.			Plural.		
	M.	*F.*	*N.*	*M.*	*F.*	*N.*
N.	quĭs,	quæ,	quĭd,	qui,	quæ,	quæ,
G.	cū´-jŭs,	cū´-jŭs,	cū´-jŭs,	quō´-rum,	quā´-rum,	quō´-rum,
D.	cui,	cui,	cui,	quī´-bŭs,	quī´-bŭs,	quī´-bŭs,
Ac.	quem,	quam,	quĭd,	quōs,	quās,	quæ,
V.	—					
Ab.	quō.	quā.	quō.	quī´-bŭs.	quī´-bŭs.	quī´-bŭs.

REMARK (1.) *Quis* is sometimes used by comic writers in the feminine, and even in the neuter. *Quisnam, quisque* and *quisquam* also occur as feminine.

REM. (2.) *Qui* is used for the ablative of *quis* in all genders, as it is for that of the relative *qui*. Cf. § 136, R. 1.

REM. (3.) *Quis* and *qui* have sometimes the signification of the indefinite pronoun *aliquis* (some one, any one), especially after the conjunctions *ec* (for *en*), *si, ne, neu, nisi, num;* and after relatives, as *quo, quanto,* etc. Sometimes *quis* and *qui* are used in the sense of *qualis?* what sort?'

2. The compounds *quisnam* and *quinam* have respectively the signification and declension of the interrogatives *quis* and *qui*. In the poets *nam* sometimes stands before *quis*. Virg. G. 4, 445.

3. *Ecquis* and *numquis* are declined and used like *quis;* but are sometimes adjectives. Virg. Ecl. 10, 28: Cic. Att. 13, 8.

REM. (4.) *Ecqua* is sometimes found in the nominative singular feminine; and the neuter plural of *numquis* is *numqua*.

REM. (5.) *Ecqui* and *numqui* also occur, declined like the interrogative *qui*, and, like that, used adjectively.

4. *Ecquisnam* and *numquisnam* are declined like *ecquis;* but are found only in the singular;—the former in the nominative in all genders, and in the ablative masculine; the latter in the nominative masculine and accusative neuter. In the nominative feminine and in the ablative, the former is used adjectively.

5. The interrogative *cujus* is also defective:—

	Singular.			Plural.
	M.	F.	N.	F.
N.	cū'-jŭs,	cū'-jă,	cū'-jum,	N. cū'-jæ,
Ac.	cū'-jum,	cū'-jam,	——	Ac. cū'-jās.
Ab.	——	cū'-jā.	——	

6. *Cūjās* is declined like an adjective of one termination; *căjas, cujātis*. See § 139, 4.

NOTE. The interrogative pronouns are used not only in direct questions but in such dependent clauses also, as contain only an indirect question; as, e.g. in the direct question, *quis est?* who is he? in the indirect, *nescio quis sit*, I know not who he is. *Qui*, in this sense, is found for *quis*; as, *qui sit apĕrit*, he discloses who he is. Cf. § 265, N.

INDEFINITE PRONOUNS.

§ 138. Indefinite pronouns are such as denote an object in a general manner, without indicating a particular individual. They are

Alĭquis, *some one.* Quisquam, *any one.* Quĭdam, *a certain one.*
Sīquis, *if any.* Quispiam, *some one.* Quilĭbet, ⎫ *any one you*
Nĕquis, *lest any.* Unusquisque, *each.* Quĭvis, ⎭ *please.*
Quisque, *every one.* Aliquipiam, *any, some.* Quis *and* qui, § 137, R. (3.)

NOTE. *Siquis* and *nequis* are commonly written separately, *si quis* and *ne quis:* so also *unus quisque*.

1. *Alĭquis* is thus declined:—

	Singular.		
	M.	F.	N.
N.	al'-ĭ-quis,	al'-ĭ-qua,	al'-ĭ-quod, *or* -quid,
G.	al-i-cū'-jus,	al-i-cū'-jus,	al-i-cū'-jus,
D.	al'-ĭ-cui,	al'-ĭ-cui,	al'-ĭ-cui,
Ac.	al'-ĭ-quem,	al'-ĭ-quam,	al'-ĭ-quod, *or* -quid,
V.	——	——	——
Ab	al'-ĭ-quo.	al'-ĭ-quā.	al'-ĭ-quo.

	Plural.		
	M.	F.	N.
N.	al'-ĭ-qui,	al'-ĭ-quæ,	al'-ĭ-qua,
G.	al-i-quō'-rum,	al-i-quā'-rum,	al-i-quō'-rum,
D.	a-liq'-uĭ-bus,*	a-liq'-uĭ-bus,	a-liq'-uĭ-bus,
Ac.	al'-ĭ-quos,	al'-ĭ-quas,	al'-ĭ-qua,
V.	——	——	——
Ab.	a-liq'-uĭ-bus.	a-liq'-uĭ-bus.	a-liq'-uĭ-bus.

* Pronounced *a-lik'-wĕ-bus*. See §§ 9, 4, and 21, 3

2. *Siquis* and *nēquis* are declined in the same manner; but they sometimes have *quæ* in the fem. singular and neut. plural.

(*a.*) *Aliquis*, in the nominative singular masculine, is used both as a substantive and as an adjective;—*aliqui*, as an adjective, but is nearly obsolete. *Aliquæ* in the fem. sing. occurs as an adjective in Lucretius, 4, 2, 64. *Siqui*, and *nēqui*, which are properly adjectives, are used also substantively for *siqui* and *nēquis*, and in the nominative singular masculine these two forms are equivalent. The ablatives *aliqui* and *siqui* also occur.

(*b.*) *Aliquid*, *siquid*, and *nēquid*, like *quid*, are used substantively; *aliquod*, etc., like *quod*, are used adjectively.

3. *Quisque, quisquam,* and *quispiam,* are declined like *quis*.

(*a.*) In the neuter singular, however, *quisque* has *quodque, quidque,* or *quicque;* *quisquam* has *quidquam* or *quicquam;* and *quispiam* has *quodpiam, quidpiam,* or *quippiam.* The forms *quidque* or *quicque, quidpiam* or *quippiam* are used substantively.

(*b.*) *Quisquam* wants the feminine (except *quamquam*, Plaut. Mil. 4, 2, 68), and also the plural, and, with a few exceptions in Plautus, it is always used substantively, its place as an adjective being supplied by *ullus*. *Quispiam* is scarcely used in the plural, except in the nominative feminine, *quæpiam*.

4. *Unusquisque* is compounded of *unus* and *quisque*, which are often written separately, and both words are declined.

Thus *unusquisque, uniuscujusque, unicuique, unumquemque,* etc. The neuter is *unumquodque,* or *unumquidque.* It has no plural. *Unumquidquid* for *unumquidque* occurs in Plautus and Lucretius.

5. *Quīdam, quilĭbet,* and *quīvis,* are declined like *qui,* except that they have both *quod* and *quid* in the neuter, the former used adjectively, the latter substantively.

NOTE. *Quĭdam* has usually *n* before *d* in the accusative singular and genitive plural; as, *quendam, quorundam,* etc. Cf. § 134, NOTE 1.

POSSESSIVE PRONOUNS.

§ **139.** 1. The possessive are derived from the genitives of the substantive pronouns, and of *quis*, and designate something belonging to their primitives.

They are *meus, tuus, suus, noster, vester,* and *cūjus*. *Meus, tuus,* and *suus,* are declined like *bŏnus;* but *meus* has in the vocative singular masculine *mi,* and very rarely *meus*. Cf. § 105, R. 3. In late writers *mi* occurs also in the feminine and neuter.

2. *Cūjus* also is declined like *bŏnus;* but is defective. See § 137, 5. It occurs only in early Latin and in legal phraseology.

3. *Noster* and *vester* are declined like *pĭger*. See § 106.

REMARK 1. The terminations *pte* and *met* intensive are sometimes annexed to possessive pronouns, especially to the ablative singular; as, *suopte pondĕre* by its own weight; *suapte manu,* by his own hand. So *nostrapte culpā; suumple amicum; meamet culpā*. The suffix *met* is usually followed by *ipse;* as, *Hannibal suāmet ipse fraude captus abiit.* Liv.; but Sallust has *meamet facta dicĕre*.

REM. 2. *Suus,* like its primitive *sui,* has always a reflexive signification, referring to the subject of the sentence. *Meus, tuus, noster,* and *vester,* are also used reflexively, when the subject of the proposition is of the first or second person. See § 132, 4.

PATRIAL PRONOUNS.

4. (*a.*) These are *nostras* and *cūjas*. See §§ 100, 2, and 128, 6. They are declined like adjectives of one termination; as, *nostras, nostrātis*, but both are defective.

(*b.*) *Nostras* is found in the nominative and genitive singular, in the nominative plural, (masc. and fem., *nostrātes*, neut. *nostratia*), and in the ablative, (*nostratĭbus*). *Cūjas* or *quōjas* occurs in the nominative, genitive and accusative (*cujātem* masc.) singular, and in the nominative plural, masc. (*cujātes*). Cf. § 137, 6.—*Nostrātis* and *cujātis* (or *quojātis*) also occur in the nominative.

PRONOMINAL ADJECTIVES.

5. To the adjective pronouns may be added certain adjectives of so general a meaning, that they partake, in some degree, of the character of pronouns. Of this kind are:—

(1.) (*a.*) *Alius, ullus, nullus*, and *nonnullus*, which answer to the question, *who?*

(*b.*) *Alter, neuter, alterŭter, utervis*, and *uterlĭbet*, which answer to the question, *ŭter?* which of two?

(2.) Adjectives denoting quality, size, or number, in a general way. These stand in relation to one another, and are hence called *correlatives*.

REMARK. The *relatives* and *interrogatives* of this class begin with *qu*, and are alike in form. The *indefinites* are formed from the relatives by prefixing *ali*. The *demonstratives* begin with *t*, and are sometimes strengthened by *dem*. A *general relative*, having a meaning more general than the relative, is formed by doubling the simple relative, or by affixing to it the termination *cumque*. A *general indefinite* is formed by annexing *libet* or *vis* to the relative.

(3.) Their mutual relation is denoted by the following table, with which may be compared the *adverbial correlatives*, § 191, R. 1.

Interrog.	Demonstr.	Relat.	Relat. general.	Indefin.	Indef genera.
quālis?	tālis,	quālis,	qualis-qualis, qualiscumque.		qualislĭbet,
quantus?	tantus, tantundem,	quantus,	quantus-quantus, quantuscumque,	aliquantus,	quantuslĭbet
quŏt?	tŏt, totĭdem,	quŏt,	quot-quot, quotcumque,	alĭquot,	quotlĭbet,
quōtus?	tōtus,	quōtus,	quotuscumque,	(aliquŏtus),	.
		Diminutives.			
quantŭlus?	tantŭlus.	——.	quantuluscumque.	aliquantŭlum.	——.

NOTE 1. The suffix *cumque*, which is used in forming general relatives, is composed of the relative adverb *cum* (*quum*) and the suffix *que*, expressive of universality, as in *quisque* and in adverbs, (see § 191). *Cumque*, therefore, originally signified 'whenever.' When attached to a relative, whether a pronoun, adjective, or adverb, it renders the relative meaning more general; as, *qui*, who; *quicumque*, whoever; or, every one who.

NOTE 2. *Cujusmŏdi* is sometimes used for *qualis*, and *hujusmŏdi, istiusmŏdi, ejusmŏdi* and *ejusdemŏdi* for *tālis*. Cf. § 134, R. 5.

VERBS.

§ **140.** A verb is a word by which something is affirmed of a person or thing.

1. That of which any thing is affirmed is called the *subject* of the verb. (2.) That which is affirmed of the subject is called the *predicate*. Cf. § 201.

3. A verb either expresses an action or state; as, *puer legit*, the boy *reads*; *aqua* calet, the water *is warm*;—or it connects an attribute with a subject; as, *terra* est *rotunda*, the earth *is* round.

4. All verbs belong to the former of these classes, except *sum*, I am, the most common use of which is, to connect an attribute with a subject. When so used, it is called the *copŭla*.

§ **141.** Verbs are either *active* or *neuter*.

NOTE. Active and neuter verbs are sometimes called *transitive* and *intransitive*; and verbs of motion are by some grammarians divided into *active-transitive* and *active-intransitive*, according as they require, or do not require, an object after them.

I. An *active* or *transitive verb* expresses such an action as requires the addition of an object to complete the sense; as, *amo te*, I love thee; *sequitur consŭlem*, he follows the consul.

II. A *neuter* or *intransitive verb* expresses such an action or state, as does not require the addition of an object to complete the sense; as, *equus currit*, the horse runs; *gradior*, I walk.

REMARK 1. Many verbs, in Latin, are considered as neuter, which are usually translated into English by active verbs. Thus *indulgeo*, I indulge, *noceo*, I hurt, *pareo*, I obey, are reckoned among neuter verbs. In strictness, such Latin verbs denote rather a state than an action, and their sense would be more exactly expressed by the verb *to be* with an adjective; as, 'I am indulgent, I am hurtful,' etc. Some verbs in Latin, which do not usually take an object after them, are yet active, since the object is omitted by ellipsis. Thus *credo* properly signifies *to intrust*, and, in this sense, takes an object; as, *credo tibi salūtem meam*, I intrust my safety to you; but by ellipsis it usually means *to believe*; as, *crede mihi*, believe me.

To verbs belong *voices*, *moods*, *tenses*, *numbers*, and *persons*.

VOICES.

(*a.*) Voice, in verbs, is the form by which they denote the relation of the agent to the action of the verb.

(*b.*) Most active Latin verbs have, for this purpose, two forms which are called the *active* and *passive voices*.

1. A verb in the *active voice* represents the agent as *acting upon* some person or thing, called the *object*; as, *puer legit librum*, the boy *is reading* a book.

2. A verb in the *passive voice* represents the object as *acted upon* by the agent; as, *liber legĭtur a puĕro*, a book *is read* by the boy.

REM. 2. By comparing the two preceding examples, it will be seen that they have the same meaning. The passive voice may thus be substituted at pleasure for the active, by making the object of the active the subject of the passive, and placing the subject of the active in the ablative case, with or without the preposition *a* or *ab*, according as it is a voluntary or involuntary agent. The active form is used to direct the attention especially to the agent as acting; the passive, chiefly to exhibit the object as acted upon. In the one case the object, in the other the agent, is frequently omitted, and left indefinite; as, *puer legit*, the boy is reading, scil. *librum, litĕras*, etc., a book, a letter, etc.; *virtus laudātur*, virtue is praised, scil. *ab hominibus*, by men.

The two voices are distinguished from each other by peculiar terminations. Cf. § 152.

§ **142.** 1. Neuter verbs have, in general, only the form of the active voice. They are, however, sometimes used impersonally in the passive voice. See § 184, 2.

2. The neuter verbs *audeo*, I dare, *fīdo*, I trust, *gaudeo*, I rejoice, and *soleo*, I am wont, have the passive form in the perfect and its cognate tenses; as *ausus sum*, I dared. Hence these verbs are called *neuter passives*, or *semideponents*.

3. The neuter verbs *vapŭlo*, I am beaten, and *vēneo*, I am sold, have an active form, but a passive meaning, and are hence called *neutral passives.*

4. (*a.*) *Deponent* verbs have a transitive or intransitive signification with only the passive form. They are called *deponent verbs*, from *depōno*, to lay aside, as having laid aside their active form, and their passive signification; as, *sĕquor*, I follow; *mŏrior*, I die.

(*b.*) Some deponent verbs have both an active and a passive signification, especially in the perfect participle. These are sometimes called *common verbs*. Cf. § 162, 17.

MOODS.

§ **143.** (*a.*) Moods (or modes) are forms of the verb, which denote the relation of the action or state, expressed by the verb, to the mind of the speaker or to some other action.

(*b.*) Latin verbs have four moods—the *indicative*, the *subjunctive*, the *imperative*, and the *infinitive*.

1. The *indicative* mood is used in independent and absolute *assertions* and *inquiries;* as, *amo*, I love; *audisne?* dost thou hear?

2. The *subjunctive* mood is used to express an action or state simply as conceived by the mind; as, *si me obsĕcret, redībo;* if he entreat me, I will return.

3. The *imperative* mood is used in commanding, exhorting, or entreating; as, *ama*, love thou ; *amanto*, they shall love.

4. The *infinitive* mood is used to denote an action or state indefinitely, without limiting it to any person or thing as its subject; as, *virtus est vitium* fugĕre, *to shun* vice is a virtue.

TENSES.

§ 144. Tenses are forms of the verb, denoting the *time* of the action or state expressed by the verb.

1. Time admits of a threefold division, into present, past and future; and, in each of these times, an action may be represented either as going on, or as completed. From these two divisions arise the six tenses of a Latin verb, each of which is distinguished by its peculiar terminations.

2. They are called the *present, imperfect, future, perfect, pluperfect,* and *future perfect* tenses.

Present (action) *amo,* I love, *or* am loving; *Present tense.*
Past { not com- } *amābam,* 1 was loving; *Imperfect tense.*
Future (pleted;) *amābo,* I shall love, *or* be loving; *Future tense.*
Present (action) *amāvi,* I have loved; *Perfect tense.*
Past { com- } *amavĕram,* I had loved; *Pluperfect tense.*
Future (pleted;) *amavĕro,* I shall have loved; *Future perfect tense.*

3. There is the same number of tenses in the passive voice, in which actions not completed are represented by simple forms of the verb, and those which are completed by compound forms.

Present (action) *amor,* I am loved; *Present tense.*
Past { not com- } *amābar,* I was loved; *Imperfect tense.*
Future (pleted;) *amābor,* I shall be loved; *Future tense.*
Present (action) *amātus sum,* or *fui,* I have been loved; *Perfect tense.*
Past { com- } *auātus eram,* or *fuĕram,* I had been loved; *Pluperfect.*
Future (pleted;) *amātus ero,* or *fuĕro,* I shall have been loved; *Future Perfect.*

§ 145. I. The *present tense* represents an action as now going on, and not completed; as, *ămo,* I love, *or* am loving.

1. Any existing custom, or general truth, may be expressed by this tense as, *apud Parthos, signum datur tympāno;* among the Parthians, the signal is given by a drum. A general truth is sometimes also expressed by the perfect.

2. The present tense may also denote an action which has existed for some time, and which still exists; as, *tot annos bella gero;* for so many years I have waged, and am still waging war.

3. The present tense is often in narration used for the perfect indefinite. It is then called the *historical present;* as, *desiliunt ex equis, provŏlant in primum;* they dismount, they fly forward to the front.

II. The *imperfect tense* represents an action as going on at some past time, but not then completed; as, *amābam,* I was loving.

1. The imperfect sometimes denotes repeated or customary past action; as, *legēbam,* I was wont to read.

2. It may also denote an action which had existed for some time, and which was still existing at a certain past time; as, *audiēbat jamdūdum verba;* he had long heard, and was still hearing the words.

3. In letters, and with reference not to the time of their being written, but to that of their being read, the imperfect is sometimes used for the present as, *expectabam*, I was expecting, (i. e. when I wrote).

4. The imperfect also sometimes denotes the *intending, preparing,* or *attempting* to act at a definite past time.

III. The *future tense* denotes that an action will be going on hereafter, but without reference to its completion; as, *amābo,* I shall love, *or* shall be loving.

IV. The *perfect tense* represents an action either as just completed, or as completed in some indefinite past time; as, *amāvi,* I have loved, *or* I loved.

REMARK. In the former sense, it is called the *perfect definite;* in the latter, the *perfect indefinite, historical perfect,* or *aorist.*

V. The *pluperfect tense* represents a past action as completed, at or before the time of some other past action or event; as, *littĕras* scripsĕram, *quum nuncius vēnit ; I had written* the letter, when the messenger arrived.

VI. The *future perfect tense* denotes that an action will be completed, at or before the time of some other future action or event; as, *quum cœnavĕro, proficiscar ;* when *I shall have supped,* I will go.

NOTE 1. This tense is often, but improperly, called the *future subjunctive.* It has the signification of the indicative mood, and corresponds to the *second future* in English.

NOTE 2. The imperfect, historical perfect, and pluperfect tenses are sometimes called *preterites* or the *preterite tenses.*

NOTE 3. The present, imperfect, and future tenses passive, in English, do not express the exact sense of those tenses in Latin, as denoting an action which is, was, or will be, going on at a certain time. Thus *laudor* signifies, not 'I am praised,' but 'I am in the act of being praised, or, if such an expression is admissible, 'I am being praised.'

REMARK 1. The six tenses above enumerated are found only in the indicative mood.

REM. 2. The subjunctive mood, in the regular conjugation, has the present and past, but no future tenses.

NOTE 4. The tenses of the subjunctive mood have less definiteness of meaning, in regard to time, than those of the indicative. Thus the present and perfect, besides their common signs, *may* or *can, may have* or *can have,* must, in certain connections, be translated by *might, could, would,* or *should; might have, could have,* etc. The tenses of this mood must often, also, be translated by the corresponding tenses of the indicative. For a more particular account of the signification of each of the tenses of the subjunctive mood, see § 260.

REM. 3. The imperative mood has two tenses—a present and a future; the former for that which is to be done at once, and the latter for that which is to be done in future.

REM. 4. The infinitive mood has three tenses—the present, the perfect, and the future; the first of which denotes an incomplete, the second a completed action, and the last an action to be performed.

NUMBERS.

§ 146. Number, in verbs, is the form by which the *unity* or *plurality* of their subject is denoted. Hence verbs, like nouns, have two numbers—the *singular* and the *plural.* Cf. § 35, 1.

PERSONS.

§ 147. Person, in verbs, is the form by which they denote the person of their subject. Hence in each number there are three persons—the *first, second,* and *third.* Cf. § 35, 2.

1. The imperative *present* has only the second person in both numbers. The imperative *future* has in each number the second and third persons, but in the singular they have both the same form, *-to* in the active, and *-tor* in the passive voice.

2. As the signification of the infinitive mood is not limited to any subject, it admits no change to express either number or person.

3. The following are the terminations of the different persons of each number, in the indicative and subjunctive moods, in both voices:—

Person.	Active.			Passive.		
	1.	2.	3.	1.	2.	3.
Singular.	o, i, *or* m,	s,	t;	r,	ris,	tur;
Plural.	mus,	tis,	nt.	mur,	mini,	ntur.

These may be called *personal* terminations.

REMARK 1. The perfect indicative active is irregular in the second person singular and plural, which end in *sti* and *stis,* and in one of the forms of the third person plural, which ends in *re.*

REM. 2. The passive form above given belongs to the simple tenses only.

REM. 3. The pronouns of the first and second persons, *ego, nos; tu* and *vos,* are seldom expressed in Latin as subjects of a finite verb, the several persons being sufficiently distinguished by the terminations of the verb.

PARTICIPLES, GERUNDS, AND SUPINES.

§ 148. 1. A participle is a word derived from a verb, and partaking of its meaning, but having the form of an adjective.

(1.) Like a verb, it has different *voices* and *tenses;* like an adjective, it has *declension** and *gender;* and like both, it has two *numbers.*

(2.) Active verbs have usually *four* participles—two in the active voice, a present and a future; as, *amans,* loving; *amaturus,* about to love;—and two in the passive voice, a perfect and a future; as, *amatus,* loved, *or* having been loved; *amandus,* to be loved.

---

* See §§ 105, R. 2; and 111, R.

(3.) Neuter verbs have usually only the participles of the active voice.

(4.) Deponent verbs, both active and neuter, may have the participles of both voices.

2. (*a.*) *Gerunds* are verbal nouns, used only in the oblique cases, and expressing the action or state of the verb; as, *amandi*, of loving, etc.

(*b.*) Like other abstract nouns, they are found only in the singular number, and by their cases supply the place of a declinable present infinitive active.

3. *Supines* also are verbal nouns of the fourth declension in the accusative and ablative singular; as, *amātum*, to love; *amātu*, to be loved.

REMARK. These also serve in certain connections to supply the place of the infinitive present both active and passive. The supine in *um* is called the *former* supine; that in *u*, the *latter*. The former is commonly used in an active, the latter in a passive sense.

CONJUGATION.

§ 149. 1. The conjugation of a verb is the regular formation and arrangement of its several parts, according to their voices, moods, tenses, numbers, and persons.

2. There are four conjugations, which are characterized by the vowel before *re* in the present of the infinitive active.

    In the first conjugation, it is *ā* long;
    In the second, ... *ē* long;
    In the third, ... *ĕ* short;
    In the fourth, ... *ī* long.

EXCEPTION. *Do*, *dăre*, to give, and such of its compounds as are of the first conjugation, have *ă* short before *re*.

§ 150. A verb, like a noun, consists of two parts—the *root*, and the *termination*. Cf. § 40, R. 10.

1. The *first* or *general* root of a verb consists of those letters that are found in every part. This root may always be found by removing the termination of the present infinitive.

2. There are also two special roots, the first of which is found in the perfect, and is called the *second* root; the other, found in the supine or perfect participle, is called the *third* root.

3. In regular verbs of the first, second, and fourth conjugations, the *second* root is formed by adding, respectively, *āv*, *u*, and *īv*, to the *general* root; and the *third* root by a similar addition of *āt*, *ĭt*, and *ĭt*.

REMARK. Many verbs, in each of the conjugations, form their second and third roots irregularly.

4. In the third conjugation, the second root either is the same as the first, or is formed from it by adding *s*; the third root is formed by adding *t*. See § 171.

NOTE. In the second and fourth conjugations, *e* and *i* before *o* are considered as belonging not to the root, but to the termination. In verbs whose second or third roots are formed irregularly, the general root often undergoes some change in the parts derived from them.

5. The vowel which unites the general root with the remaining letters of the verb, is called the *connecting* vowel. Each conjugation, except the third, is, in a great degree, distinguished by a peculiar connecting vowel, which is the same as characterizes the infinitives. See § 149, 2.

(*a*.) In the third conjugation, the connecting vowel is generally *ĕ* or *ĭ*. In the second and fourth conjugations, and in verbs in *io* of the third, a second connecting vowel is sometimes added to that which characterizes the conjugation; as, *a* in *docent*, *u* in *capiunt*, etc.

(*b*.) In verbs whose second and third roots are formed irregularly, the connecting vowel often disappears, or is changed in the parts derived from those roots; but it is almost always found in the parts derived from the first root.

§ **151.** 1. From the *first* root are derived, in each voice, the present, imperfect, and future indicative; the present and imperfect subjunctive; the imperative, and the present infinitive. From this root are derived also the present participle, the gerund, and the future participle passive.

2. From the *second* root are derived, in the active voice, the perfect, pluperfect, and future perfect indicative; the perfect and pluperfect subjunctive, and the perfect infinitive.

3. (*a*.) From the *third* root are derived, in the active voice, the supine in *um*, and the future participle; the latter of which, with the verb *esse*, constitutes the future infinitive active.

(*b*.) From this root are derived, in the passive voice, the supine in *u*, and the perfect participle; from the latter of which, with the verb *sum*, are formed all the tenses which in the active are derived from the second root. The future infinitive passive is formed from the supine in *um*, and *iri*, the present infinitive passive of the verb *eo*, to go.

4. The present and perfect indicative, the supine in *um*, and the present infinitive, are called the *principal parts* of the verb, because from the first three the several roots are ascertained, and from the last, the characteristic vowel of the conjugation. In the passive voice, the principal parts are the present indicative and infinitive, and the perfect participle.

NOTE. As the supine in *um* is wanting in most verbs, the third root must often be determined from the perfect participle, or the future participle active.

§ **152.** The following table exhibits a connected view of the verbal terminations, in all the conjugations. By annexing these to the several roots, all the parts of a verb may be formed.

VERBS.—TERMINATIONS. § 152

Terminations added to the First Root.

ACTIVE VOICE.

INDICATIVE MOOD.

Present Tense.

Conjugation	SINGULAR. Persons.			PLURAL. Persons.		
	1.	2.	3.	1.	2.	3.
1. -ābam,	-o,	-ās,	-āt;	-āmŭs,	-ātĭs,	-ant.
2. -ēbam,	-eo,	-ēs,	-ĕt;	-ēmŭs,	-ētĭs,	-ent.
3. -ēbam,	-o,	-ĭs,	-ĭt;	-ĭmŭs,	-ĭtĭs,	-unt.
4. -iēbam,	-io,	-īs,	-ĭt;	-īmŭs,	-ītĭs,	-iunt.

Imperfect.

1. -ābam,	-ābās,	-ābăt;	-ābāmŭs,	-ābātĭs,	-ābant.
2. -ēbam,	-ēbās,	-ēbăt;	-ēbāmŭs,	-ēbātĭs,	-ēbant.
3. -ēbam,	-ēbās,	-ēbăt;	-ēbāmŭs,	-ēbātĭs,	-ēbant.
4. -iēbam,	-iēbās,	-iēbăt;	-iēbāmŭs,	-iēbātĭs,	-iēbant.

Future.

1. -ābo,	-ābĭs,	-ābĭt;	-ābĭmŭs,	-ābĭtĭs,	-ābunt.
2. -ēbo,	-ēbĭs,	-ēbĭt;	-ēbĭmŭs,	-ēbĭtĭs,	-ēbunt.
3. -am,	-ēs,	-ĕt;	-ēmŭs,	-ētĭs,	-ent.
4. -iam,	-iēs,	-iĕt;	-iēmŭs,	-iētĭs,	-ient.

SUBJUNCTIVE MOOD.

Present Tense.

1. -em,	-ēs,	-ĕt;	-ēmŭs,	-ētĭs,	-ent.
2. -eam,	-eās,	-eăt;	-eāmŭs,	-eātĭs,	-eant.
3. -am,	-ās,	-ăt;	-āmŭs,	-ātĭs,	-ant.
4. -iam,	-iās,	-iăt;	-iāmŭs,	-iātĭs,	-iant.

PASSIVE VOICE.

INDICATIVE MOOD.

Present Tense.

SINGULAR. Persons.			PLURAL. Persons.		
1.	2.	3.	1.	2.	3.
-ŏr,	-ārĭs or -ārĕ,	-ātŭr;	-āmŭr,	-amĭnī,	-antŭr.
-eor,	-ērĭs or -ērĕ,	-ētŭr;	-ēmŭr,	-emĭnī,	-entŭr.
-ŏr,	-ĕrĭs or -ĕrĕ,	-ĭtŭr;	-ĭmŭr,	-imĭnī,	-untŭr.
-iŏr,	-īrĭs or -īrĕ,	-ītŭr;	-īmŭr,	-imĭnī,	-iuntŭr.

Imperfect.

1. -ābăr,	-ābārĭs or -ābārĕ,	-ābātŭr;	-ābāmŭr,	-abamĭnī,	-abantŭr.
2. -ēbăr,	-ēbārĭs or -ēbārĕ,	-ēbātŭr;	-ēbāmŭr,	-ebamĭnī,	-ebantŭr.
3. -ēbăr,	-ēbārĭs or -ēbārĕ,	-ēbātŭr;	-ēbāmŭr,	-ebamĭnī,	-ebantŭr.
4. -iēbăr,	-iēbārĭs or -iēbārĕ,	-iēbātŭr;	-iēbāmŭr,	-iebamĭnī,	-iebantŭr.

Future.

1. -ābŏr,	-ābĕrĭs or -ābĕrĕ,	-ābĭtŭr;	-ābĭmŭr,	-abimĭnī,	-abuntŭr.
2. -ēbŏr,	-ēbĕrĭs or -ēbĕrĕ,	-ēbĭtŭr;	-ēbĭmŭr,	-ebimĭnī,	-ebuntŭr.
3. -ăr,	-ērĭs or -ērĕ,	-ētŭr;	-ēmŭr,	-emĭnī,	-entŭr.
4. -iăr,	-iērĭs or -iērĕ,	-iētŭr;	-iēmŭr,	-iemĭnī,	-ientŭr.

SUBJUNCTIVE MOOD.

Present Tense.

1. -ĕr,	-ērĭs or -ērĕ,	-ētŭr;	-ēmŭr,	-emĭnī,	-entŭr.
2. -eăr,	-eārĭs or -eārĕ,	-eātŭr;	-eāmŭr,	-eamĭnī,	-eantŭr.
3. -ăr,	-ārĭs or -ārĕ,	-ātŭr;	-āmŭr,	-amĭnī,	-antŭr.
4. -iăr,	-iārĭs or -iārĕ,	-iātŭr;	-iāmŭr,	-iamĭnī,	-iantŭr.

§ 152. VERBS.—TERMINATIONS.

ACTIVE VOICE.

Present.
1. -ō, -ās, -āt, -āmus, -ātis, -ant.
2. -eō, -ēs, -ēt, -ēmus, -ētis, -ent.
3. -ō, -is, -it, -imus, -itis, -unt.
4. -iō, -īs, -it, -īmus, -ītis, -iunt.

Imperfect.
1. -ābam, -ābās, -ābāt, -ābāmus, -ābātis, -ābant.
2. -ēbam, -ēbās, -ēbāt, -ēbāmus, -ēbātis, -ēbant.
3. -ēbam, -ēbās, -ēbāt, -ēbāmus, -ēbātis, -ēbant.
4. -iēbam, -iēbās, -iēbāt, -iēbāmus, -iēbātis, -iēbant.

Future.
1. -ābō, -ābis, -ābit; -ābimus, -ābitis, -ābunt.
2. -ēbō, -ēbis, -ēbit; -ēbimus, -ēbitis, -ēbunt.
3. -am, -ēs, -et; -ēmus, -ētis, -ent.
4. -iam, -iēs, -iet; -iēmus, -iētis, -ient.

IMPERATIVE MOOD.

Present.
1. -ā, -āte; -ātō, -ātōte, -antō.
2. -ē, -ēte; -ētō, -ētōte, -entō.
3. -e, -ite; -itō, -itōte, -untō.
4. -ī, -īte; -ītō, -ītōte, -iuntō.

Future.
1. -ātō, -ātōte, -antō.
2. -ētō, -ētōte, -entō.
3. -itō, -itōte, -untō.
4. -ītō, -ītōte, -iuntō.

INFIN. Pres. 1. -āre, 2. -ēre, 3. -ere, 4. -īre.

PART. Pres. 1. -āns, 2. -ēns, 3. -ēns, 4. -iēns.

GER. 1. -andī, 2. -endī, 3. -endī, 4. -iendī.

NOTE. Verbs in *io* of the third conjugation have two connecting vowels in all the parts in which they occur in verbs of the fourth conjugation, and these vowels are the same in both.

Terminations added to the Second and Third Roots.

The terminations of the tenses which are formed from the second and third roots, are the same in all the conjugations. Thus:—

ACTIVE VOICE.—SECOND ROOT.

INDICATIVE MOOD.

Singular. *Plural.*

Perf. -ī, -istī, -it; -imus, -istis, -ērunt or -ēre.
Plup. -eram, -erās, -erat; -erāmus, -erātis, -erant.
Fut. perf. -erō, -eris, -erit; -erimus, -eritis, -erint.

SUBJUNCTIVE MOOD.

Perf. -erim, -eris, -erit; -erimus, -eritis, -erint.
Plup. -issem, -issēs, -isset; -issēmus, -issētis, -issent.

INFIN. Perf. -isse. PART. Fut. -ūrūs. F. SUP. -um.

PASSIVE VOICE.—THIRD ROOT.

Singular.

Perf.   -ŭs sum *or* fuī,   -ŭs sim   *or* fuerim,   -ŭs sis   *or* fueris, etc.
Plup.   -ŭs eram *or* fueram, -ŭs essem *or* fuissem, -ŭs essēs *or* fuissēs, etc.
Fut. perf. -ŭs erō *or* fuerō, -ŭs erō   *or* fueris, -ŭs eris *or* fueris, etc.

INFIN. Perf. -ŭs esse *or* fuisse. PART. Perf. -ŭs. INF. Fut. -um īrī. L. SUP. -ū.

THIRD ROOT. INF. Fut. -ūrūs esse.

REMARK 1. In analyzing a verb, the voice, person, and number, are ascertained by the *personal* terminations. See § 147, 3. The conjugation, mood, and tense, are, in general, determined by the letter or letters which intervene between the root of the verb and the personal terminations. Thus in *amabamus, mus* denotes that the verb is of the act.ve voice, plural number, and first person; *ba* denotes that it is of the indicative mood, imperfect tense; and the connecting vowel *a* determines it to be of the first conjugation. So in *amaremini, mini* denotes the passive voice, plural number, and second person; *re*, the subjunctive mood, imperfect tense; and *a*, as before, the first conjugation.

REM. 2. Sometimes, the part between the root of the verb and the personal termination, does not precisely determine the conjugation, mood, and tense, but only within certain limits. In such cases, the conjugation may be learned, by finding the present tense in the dictionary, and if two forms are alike in the same conjugation, they can only be distinguished by the sense. Thus *amēmus* and *docēmus* have the same termination; but, as *amo* is of the first, and *doceo* of the second conjugation, the former is determined to be the subjunctive, the latter the indicative, present. *Regar* may be either the future indicative, or the present subjunctive—*bibĭmus* either the present or the perfect indicative.

§ **153.** SUM, I am, is called an *auxiliary* verb, because it is used, in conjunction with participles, to supply the want of simple forms in other verbs. From its denoting existence, it is sometimes called the *substantive* verb.

REMARK. *Sum* is very irregular in those parts which, in other verbs, are formed from the first root. Its imperfect and future tenses, except in the third person plural of the latter, have the form of a pluperfect and future perfect. It is thus conjugated:—

PRINCIPAL PARTS.

Pres. Indic.	*Pres. Infin.*	*Perf. Indic.*	*Fut. Part.*
Sum,	es'-sĕ,	fu'-ī,	fŭ'-tū'-rŭs.

INDICATIVE MOOD.

Present Tense.

SINGULAR. — PLURAL.

Person.
1. sum, *I am*,   sŭ'-mŭs, *we are*,
2. ĕs, *thou art*,*   es'-tĭs, *ye*† *are*,
3. est, *he is*;   sunt, *they are*.

Imperfect.

1. ĕ'-ram, *I was*,   ĕ-rā'-mŭs, *we were*,
2. ĕ'-rās, *thou wast*,   ĕ-rā'-tĭs, *ye were*,
3. ĕ'-răt, *he was*;   ĕ'-rant, *they were*.

Future. *shall, or will.*

1. ĕ'-rŏ, *I shall be*,   ĕr'-ĭ-mŭs, *we shall be*,
2. ĕ'-rĭs, *thou wilt be*,   ĕr'-ĭ-tĭs, *ye will be*,
3. ĕ'-rĭt, *he will be*;   ĕ'-runt, *they will be*.

---

* In the second person singular in English, the plural form *you* is commonly used except in solemn discourse; as, *tu es*, you are.

† The plural pronoun of the second person is either *ye* or *you*.

§ 153.

Perfect. have been, or was.

1. fu'-ĭ, *I have been,* fu'-ĭ-mŭs, *we have been,*
2. fu-is'-tĭ, *thou hast been,* fu-is'-tĭs, *ye have been,*
3. fu'-ĭt, *he has been;* fu-ē'-runt or rŏ, *they have been.*

Pluperfect.

1. fu'-ĕ-ram, *I had been,* fu-e-rā'-mŭs, *we had been,*
2. fu'-ĕ-rās, *thou hadst been,* fu-e-rā'-tĭs, *ye had been,*
3. fu'-ĕ-răt, *he had been;* fu'-ĕ-rant, *they had been.*

Future Perfect. *shall or will have.*

1. fu'-ĕ-rŏ, *I shall have been,* fu-er'-ĭ-mŭs, *we shall have been*
2. fu'-ĕ-rĭs, *thou wilt have been,* fu-er'-ĭ-tĭs, *ye will have been,*
3. fu'-ĕ-rĭt, *he will have been;* fu'-ĕ-rint, *they will have been.*

SUBJUNCTIVE MOOD.

Present. *may, or can.*

1. sim, *I may be,* sī'-mŭs, *we may be,*
2. sīs, *thou mayst be,* sī'-tĭs, *ye may be,*
3. sĭt, *he may be* sint, *they may be.*

Imperfect. *might, could, would, or should.*

1. es'-sem, *I would be,* es-sē'-mŭs, *we would be,*
2. es'-sēs, *thou wouldst be,* es-sē'-tĭs, *ye would be,*
3. es'-sĕt, *he would be;* es'-sent, *they would be.*

Perfect.

1. fu'-ĕ-rim, *I may have been,* fu-ĕr'-ĭ-mus, *we may have been,*
2. fu'-ĕ-rĭs, *thou mayst have been,* fu-ĕr'-ĭ-tĭs, *ye may have been,*
3. fu'-ĕ-rĭt, *he may have been;* fu'-ĕ-rint, *they may have been.*

Pluperfect. *might, could, would, or should have.*

1. fu-is'-sem, *I would have been,* fu-is-sē'-mŭs, *we would have been,*
2. fu-is'-sēs, *thou wouldst have been,* fu-is-sē'-tĭs, *ye would have been,*
3. fu-is'-sĕt, *he would have been;* fu-is'-sent, *they would have been.*

IMPERATIVE MOOD.

Pres. 1. ĕs, *be thou,* es'-tĕ, *be ye.*
Fut. 2. es'-tŏ, *thou shalt be* es-tō'-tĕ, *ye shall be,*
    3. es'-tŏ, *let him be;* sun'-tŏ, *let them be.*

INFINITIVE MOOD.

Present. es'-sĕ, *to be.*
Perfect. fu-is'-sĕ, *to have been.*
Future. fŭ-tū'-rŭs (ă, um), es'-sĕ, *or* fŏ'-rĕ, *to be about to be.*

PARTICIPLE.

Future. fŭ-tū'-rus, a, um, *about to be.*

§ 154. REMARK 1. A present participle *ens* seems to have been anciently in use, and is still found in the compounds *absens, præsens,* and *potens*.

REM. 2. The perfect *fui*, and its derivative tenses, are formed from an obsolete *fuo*, whence come also the participle *futūrus*, an old subjunctive present *fuam, fuas, fuat*; ——, ——, *fuant,* and the forms *fuvĭmus*, perf. ind., *fuvĕrint,* perf. subj., and *fuvisset,* plup. subj.

REM. 3. From *fuo* appear also to be derived the following:—

Subj. imperf. fŏ'-rem, fŏ'-rēs, fŏ'-rĕt; ——, —— fŏ'-rent.
Inf. pres. fŏ'-rĕ.

These forms seem to have been contracted from *fuĕrem*, etc., and *fuĕre*. *Fŏrem* is equivalent in meaning to *essem*, but the infinitive *fŏre* has, in most cases, acquired a future signification, equivalent to *futūrus esse*.

REM. 4. *Siem, sies, siet, sient,* for *sim, sis, sit, sint,* are found in ancient writers, as are also *escit* for *erit, escunt* for *erunt, ese, esĕtis,* and *esent,* for *esse, essĕtis,* and *essent*.

REM. 5. Like *sum* are conjugated its compounds, *absum, adsum, dēsum, insum, intersum, obsum, præsum, subsum,* and *supersum*.

REM. 6. PROSUM, from the old form *prōd* for *prō*, and *sum*, has *d* after *pro*, when the simple verb begins with *e*; as,

Ind. pres. prŏ'-sum, prŏd'-es, prŏd'-est, etc.
— *imperf.* prod'-ĕ-ram, prod'-ĕ-rās, etc.

REM. 7. (*a.*) POSSUM is compounded of *pŏtis*, able, and *sum*. They are sometimes written separately, and then *pŏtis* is the same in all genders and numbers.

(*b.*) In composition, *is* is omitted in *pŏtis*, and *t*, as in other cases, coming before *s*, is changed into *s*. In the infinitive, and imperfect subjunctive, *es* of the simple verb is dropped, as is also *f* at the beginning of the second root. In every other respect *possum* is conjugated like *sum*, wherever it is found; but the imperative, and the parts derived from the third root, are wanting.

Pres. Indic.   *Pres. Infin.*   *Perf. Indic.*
Pos'-sum,   pos'-sĕ,   pŏt'-u-ī,   *I can,* or *I am able.*

INDICATIVE.   **SUBJUNCTIVE.**

Present.

pos'-sum, pŏs'-tĕs, pŏ'-test;   pos'-sim, pos'-sīs, pos'-sīt;
pos'-sŭ-mŭs, pŏ-tes'-tĭs, pos'-sunt.   pos-sī'-mŭs, pos-sī'-tĭs, pos'-sint.

Imperfect.

pŏt'-ĕ-ram, pot'-ĕ-rās, pot'-ĕ-răt;   pos'-sem, pos'-sēs, pos'-sĕt;
pŏt-ĕ-rā'-mŭs, -ĕ-rā'-tĭs, -ĕ-rant.   pos-sē'-mŭs, -sē'-tĭs, pos'-sent.

Future.

pŏt'-ĕ-rō, pŏt'-ĕ-rĭs, pŏt'-ĕ-rĭt;
pŏ-tĕr'-ĭ-mŭs, po-tĕr'-ĭ-tĭs, pot'-ĕ-runt.

Perfect.

pŏt'-u-ī, pŏt-u-is'-tī, pŏt'-u-ĭt;   pŏ-tu'-ĕ-rim, -ĕ-rĭs, -ĕ-rĭt;
pŏ-tu'-ĭ-mŭs, -is'-tĭs, -ĕ-runt *or* -ē'rĕ.   pŏt-u-ĕr'-ĭ-mŭs, -ĭ-tĭs, -ĕ-rint.

VERBS.—FIRST CONJUGATION. ACTIVE.

Pluperfect.

pŏ-tŭ'-ĕ-ram, -ĕ-rās, -ĕ-rāt; pŏt-u-is'-sem, -is'-sēs, -is'-sĕt;
pŏt-u-ĕ-rā'-mŭs, -ĕ-rā'-tĭs, -ĕ-rant. pŏt-u-is-sē'-mŭs, -is-sē'-tĭs, -is'-sent.

Future Perfect.

pŏ-tŭ'-ĕ-rŏ, pŏ-tŭ'-ĕ-rĭs, pŏ-tŭ'-ĕ-rĭt;
pŏt-u-ĕr'-ĭ-mŭs, pŏt-u-ĕr'-ĭ-tis, pŏ-tŭ'-ĕ-rint.

(No Imperative.)

INFINITIVE.	PARTICIPIAL ADJECTIVE.
Pres. pos'-sĕ. *Perf.* pŏt-u-is'-sĕ.	pŏ'-tens, *able.*

NOTE. The following forms are also found; *potissum* for *possum*, *potessunt* for *possunt*, *potessim* and *possiem* for *possim*, *possies*, *possiet* and *potessit* for *possit* and *possit*, *potessem* for *possem*, *potesse* for *posse*, and before a passive infinitive the passive forms *potestur* for *potest*, *poterātur* for *poterat*, and *possētur* for *posset*.—*Potis* and *pote* without *est* are sometimes used for *potest*.

§ 155. FIRST CONJUGATION.

ACTIVE VOICE.

PRINCIPAL PARTS.

Pres. Ind.	*Pres. Inf.*	*Perf. Ind.*	*Supine.*
A'-mŏ,	ă-mā'-rĕ,	ă-mā'-vi,	ă-mā'-tum.

INDICATIVE MOOD.

Present. *love, do love, am loving.*

Sing.	ă'-mŏ,	*I love,*
	ă'-mās,	*thou lovest,*
	ă'-măt,	*he loves;*
Plur.	ă-mā'-mŭs,	*we love,*
	ă-mā'-tĭs,	*ye love,*
	ă'-mant,	*they love.*

Imperfect. *was loving, loved, did love.*

Sing.	ă-mā'-bam,	*I was loving,*
	ă-mā'-bās,	*thou wast loving,*
	ă-mā'-băt,	*he was loving;*
Plur.	ăm-ā-bā'-mŭs,	*we were loving,*
	ăm-ā-bā'-tĭs,	*ye were loving,*
	ă-mā'-bant,	*they were loving.*

Future. *shall, or will.*

Sing.	ă-mā'-bŏ,	*I shall love,*
	ă-mā'-bĭs,	*thou wilt love,*
	ă-mā'-bĭt,	*he will love;*
Plur.	ă-māb'-ĭ-mŭs,	*we shall love,*
	ă-māb'-ĭ-tis,	*ye will love,*
	ă-mā'-bunt,	*they will love.*

Perfect. *loved*, or *have loved.*

Sing. ă-mā'-vi,   *I have loved,*
ăm-ā-vis'-tī,   *thou hast loved,*
ă-mā'-vĭt,   *he has loved;*
Plur. ă-māv'-ĭ-mŭs,   *we have loved,*
ăm-ā-vis'-tis,   *ye have loved,*
ăm-ā-vē'-runt *or* -rĕ,   *they have loved.*

Pluperfect. *had.*

Sing. ă-māv'-ĕ-ram,   *I had loved,*
ă-māv'-ĕ-rās,   *thou hadst loved,*
ă-māv'-ĕ-răt,   *he had loved;*
Plur. ă-māv-ĕ-rā'-mŭs,   *we had loved,*
ă-māv-ĕ-rā'-tis,   *ye had loved,*
ă-māv'-ĕ-rant,   *they had loved.*

Future Perfect. *shall,* or *will have.*

Sing. ă-māv'-ĕ-rŏ,   *I shall have loved,*
ă-māv'-ĕ-rĭs,   *thou wilt have loved,*
ă-māv'-ĕ-rĭt,   *he will have loved;*
Plur. ăm-ā-vĕr'-ĭ-mŭs,   *we shall have loved,*
ăm-ā-vĕr'-ĭ-tis,   *ye will have loved,*
ă-māv'-ĕ-rint,   *they will have loved*

SUBJUNCTIVE MOOD,

Present. *may,* or *can.*

Sing. ă'-mem,   *I may love,*
ă'-mēs,   *thou mayst love,*
ă'-mĕt,   *he may love;*
Plur. ă-mē'-mŭs,   *we may love,*
ă-mē'-tis,   *ye may love,*
ă'-ment,   *they may love.*

Imperfect. *might, could, would,* or *should.*

Sing. ă-mā'-rem,   *I would love,*
ă-mā'-rēs,   *thou wouldst love,*
ă-mā'-rĕt,   *he would love;*
Plur. ăm-ā-rē'-mŭs,   *we would love,*
ăm-ā-rē'-tis,   *ye would love,*
ă-mā'-rent,   *they would love.*

Perfect. *may,* or *can have.*

Sing. ă-māv'-ĕ-rim,   *I may have loved,*
ă-māv'-ĕ-rĭs,   *thou mayst have loved,*
ă-māv'-ĕ-rĭt,   *he may have loved;*
Plur. ăm-ā-vĕr'-ĭ-mŭs,   *we may have loved,*
ăm-ā-vĕr'-ĭ-tis,   *ye may have loved,*
ă-māv'-ĕ-rint,   *they may have loved*

§ 156.   VERBS.—FIRST CONJUGATION, PASSIVE.   105

Pluperfect. *might, could, would,* or *should have.*

Sing. ăm-ā-vĭs′-sem,   *I would have loved,*
ăm-ā-vĭs′-sēs,   *thou wouldst have loved,*
ăm-ā-vĭs′-sĕt,   *he would have loved;*
Plur. ăm-ā-vĭs-sē′-mŭs,   *we would have loved,*
ăm-ā-vĭs-sē′-tĭs,   *ye would have loved,*
ăm-ā-vĭs′-sent,   *they would have loved.*

IMPERATIVE MOOD.

Pres. Sing. ă′-mā,   *love thou;*
Plur. ă-mā′-tĕ,   *love ye.*
Fut. Sing. ă-mā′-tŏ,   *thou shalt love,*
ă-mā′-tŏ,   *he shall love;*
Plur. ăm-ā-tō′-tĕ,   *ye shall love,*
ă-man′-tŏ,   *they shall love*

INFINITIVE MOOD.

Present. ă-mā′-rĕ,   *to love.*
Perfect. ăm-ā-vĭs′-sĕ,   *to have loved.*
Future. ăm-ā-tū′-rŭs, (ă, um,) es′-sĕ,   *to be about to love.*

PARTICIPLES.

Present. ă′-mans,   *loving.*
Future. ăm-ā-tū′-rŭs, ă, um,   *about to love.*

GERUND.

G. ă-man′-dī,   *of loving,*
D. ă-man′-dŏ,   *for loving,*
Ac. ă-man′-dum,   *loving,*
Ab. ă-man′-dŏ,   *by loving.*

SUPINE.

Former. ă-mā′-tum,   *to love.*

§ 156. PASSIVE VOICE.

PRINCIPAL PARTS.

Pres. Indic.   *Pres. Infin.*   *Perf. Part.*
A′-mor,   ă-mā′-rī,   ă-mā′-tŭs.

VERBS.—FIRST CONJUGATION, PASSIVE. §156

INDICATIVE MOOD.

Present. *am.*

Sing.	ă'-mŏr,	I am loved,
	ă-mā'-rĭs *or* -rĕ,	thou art loved,
	ă-mā'-tŭr,	he is loved;
Plur.	ă-mā'-mŭr,	we are loved,
	ă-mām'-ĭ-nī,	ye are loved,
	ă-man'-tŭr,	they are loved.

Imperfect. *was.*

Sing.	ă-mā'-băr,	I was loved,
	ăm-ă-bā'-rĭs *or* -rĕ,	thou wast loved,
	ăm-ă-bā'-tŭr,	he was loved;
Plur.	ăm-ă-bā'-mŭr,	we were loved,
	ăm-ă-bām'-ĭ-nī,	ye were loved,
	ăm-ă-ban'-tŭr,	they were loved.

Future. *shall,* or *will be.*

Sing.	ă-mā'-bŏr,	I shall be loved,
	ă-māb'-ĕ-rĭs *or* -rĕ,	thou wilt be loved,
	ă-māb'-ĭ-tŭr,	he will be loved;
Plur.	ă-māb'-ĭ-mŭr,	we shall be loved,
	ăm-ă-bĭm'-ĭ-nī,	ye will be loved,
	ăm-ă-bun'-tŭr,	they will be loved.

Perfect. *have been,* or *was.*

Sing.	ă-mā'-tŭs sum *or* fu'-ī,	I have been loved,
	ă-mā'-tŭs ĕs *or* fu-is'-tī,	thou hast been loved,
	ă-mā'-tŭs est *or* fu'-ĭt,	he has been loved;
Plur.	ă-mā'-tī sŭ'-mŭs *or* fu'-ĭ-mŭs,	we have been loved,
	ă-mā'-tī es'-tĭs *or* fu-is'-tĭs,	ye have been loved,
	ă-mā'-tī sunt, fu'ē'-runt *or* -rĕ,	they have been loved

Pluperfect. *had been.*

Sing.	ă-mā'-tŭs ĕ'-ram *or* fu'-ĕ-ram,	I had been loved,
	ă-mā'-tŭs ĕ'-rās *or* fu'-ĕ-rās,	thou hadst been loved,
	ă-mā'-tŭs ĕ'-răt *or* fu'-ĕ-răt,	he had been loved;
Plur.	ă-mā'-tī ĕ-rā'-mŭs *or* fu-ĕ-rā'-mŭs,	we had been loved,
	ă-mā'-tī ĕ-rā'-tĭs *or* fu-ĕ-rā'-tĭs,	ye had been loved,
	ă-mā'-tī ĕ'-rant *or* fu'-ĕ-rant,	they had been loved.

Future Perfect. *shall have been.*

Sing.	ă-mā'-tŭs ĕ'-rŏ *or* fu'-ĕ-rŏ,	I shall have been loved,
	ă-mā'-tŭs ĕ'-rĭs ōr fu'-ĕ-rĭs,	thou wilt have been loved,
	ă-mā'-tŭs ĕ'-rĭt *or* fu'-ĕ-rĭt,	he will have been loved;
Plur.	ă-mā'-tī ĕr-ĭ-mŭs *or* fu-ĕr'-ĭ-mŭs	we shall have been loved,
	ă-mā'-tī ĕr'-ĭ-tĭs *or* fu-ĕr'-ĭ-tĭs,	ye will have been loved,
	ă-mā'-tī ĕ'-runt *or* fu'-ĕ-rint,	they will have been loved.

SUBJUNCTIVE MOOD.

Present. *may, or can be.*

Sing. ă'-mĕr, — *I may be loved,*
ă-mē'-rĭs *or* -rĕ, — *thou mayst be loved,*
ă-mē'-tŭr, — *he may be loved;*
Plur. ă-mē'-mŭr, — *we may be loved,*
ă-mēm'-ĭ-nī, — *ye may be loved,*
ă-men'-tŭr, — *they may be loved.*

Imperfect. *might, could, would, or should be.*

Sing. ă-mā'-rĕr, — *I would be loved,*
ăm-ā-rē'-rĭs *or* -rĕ, — *thou wouldst be loved,*
ăm-ā-rē'-tŭr, — *he would be loved;*
Plur. ăm-ā-rē'-mŭr, — *we would be loved,*
ăm-ā-rēm'-ĭ-nī, — *ye would be loved,*
ăm-ā-ren'-tŭr, — *they would be loved.*

Perfect. *may have been.*

Sing. ă-mā'-tŭs sim *or* fu'-ĕ-rim, — *I may have been loved,*
ă-mā'-tŭs sis *or* fu'-ĕ-rĭs, — *thou mayst have been loved,*
ă-mā'-tŭs sit *or* fu'-ĕ-rĭt, — *he may have been loved,*
Plur. ă-mā'-tī sī'-mŭs *or* fu-er'-ĭ-mŭs, — *we may have been loved,*
ă-mā'-tī sī'-tĭs *or* fu-er'-ĭ-tĭs, — *ye may have been loved,*
ă-mā'-tī sint *or* fu'-ĕ-rint, — *they may have been loved.*

Pluperfect. *might, could, would, or should have been.*

Sing. ă-mā'-tŭs es'-sem *or* fu-is'-sem, — *I would have been loved,*
ă-mā'-tŭs es'-sēs *or* fu-is'-sēs, — *thou wouldst have been loved,*
ă-mā'-tŭs es'-sĕt *or* fu-is'-sĕt, — *he would have been loved;*
Plur. ă-mā'-tī es-sē'-mŭs *or* fu-is-sē'-mŭs, — *we would have been loved,*
ă-mā'-tī es-sē'-tĭs *or* fu-is-sē'-tĭs, — *ye would have been loved,*
ă-mā'-tī es'-sent *or* fu-is'-sent, — *they would have been loved*

IMPERATIVE MOOD.

Pres. Sing. ă-mā'-rĕ, — *be thou loved;*
Plur. ă-măm'-ĭ-nī, — *be ye loved.*
Fut. Sing. ă-mā'-tŏr, — *thou shalt be loved,*
ă-mā'-tŏr, — *he shall be loved;*
Plur. (ăm-ā-bĭm-ĭ-nī, — *ye shall be loved),*
ă-man'-tŏr, — *they shall be loved.*

INFINITIVE MOOD.

Present. ă-mā'-rī, — *to be loved.*
Perfect. ă-mā'-tŭs es'-sĕ *or* fu-is'-sĕ, — *to have been loved.*
Future. ă-mā'-tum ī'-rī, — *to be about to be loved.*

PARTICIPLES.

Perfect. ă-mā´-tŭs,   loved, or having been loved.
Future. ă-man´-dŭs, to be loved.

SUPINE.

Latter. ă-mā´-tū,   to be loved.

FORMATION OF THE TENSES.

From the first root, *am*, are derived

	Active.	Passive.
Ind. pres.	amo,	amor.
— imperf.	am*ā*bam,	am*ā*bar.
— fut.	am*ā*bo,	am*ā*bor.
Subj. pres.	amem,	amer.
— imperf.	am*ā*rem,	am*ā*rer.
Imperat. pres.	am*ā*,	am*ā*re.
——— fut.	am*ā*to,	am*ā*tor.
Inf. pres.	am*ā*re,	am*ā*ri.
Part. pres.	amans,	
— fut.		am*a*ndus.
Gerund.	amandi.	

From the second root, *amav*, are derived

Active.	Passive.
Ind. perf. amāvi,	amātus sum, etc.
— plup. amavĕram,	amātus eram, etc.
— fut. perf. amavĕro,	amātus ero, etc.
Subj. perf. amavĕrim,	amātus sim, etc.
— plup. amavissem,	amātus essem, eto
Inf. perf. amavisse,	amātus esse, etc.

From the third root,
Inf. fut. amatūrus esse, amātum iri.
Part. fut. amatūrus.
— perf.   amātus.
Form. sup. amātum. Lat. sup. amātu.

From the third root *amat*, are derived

§ 157. SECOND CONJUGATION.

ACTIVE VOICE.   PASSIVE VOICE.
       PRINCIPAL PARTS.

Pres. Ind. mŏ´-ne-ŏ.	*Pres. Ind.* mŏ´-ne-ŏr.
Pres. Inf. mŏ-nē´-rĕ.	*Pres. Inf.* mŏ-nē´-rī.
Perf. Ind. mŏn´-u-ī.	*Perf. Part.* mŏn´-ĭ-tŭs.
Supine. mŏn´-ĭ-tum.	

INDICATIVE MOOD.
Present.

I advise.   *I am advised.*
Sing. mŏ´-ne-ŏ,   Sing. mŏ-ne-ŏr,
      mŏ´-nēs,   mŏ-nē´-rĭs *or* -rĕ,
      mŏ´-nĕt;   mŏ-nē´-tŭr;
Plur. mŏ-nē´-mŭs,   Plur. mŏ-nē´-mŭr,
      mŏ-nē´-tĭs,   mŏ-nēm´-ĭ-nī,
      mŏ´-nent.   mŏ-nen´-tŭr.

Imperfect.

I was advising.   *I was advised.*
S. mŏ-nē´-bam,   S. mŏ-nē´-băr,
   mŏ-nē´-bās,   mŏn-ē-bā´-rĭs *or* -rĕ,
   mŏ-nē´-băt;   mŏn-ē-bā´-tŭr;
P. mŏn-ē-bā´-mŭs,   P. mŏn-ē-bā´-mŭr,
   mŏn-ē-bā´-tĭs,   mŏn-ē-bām´-ĭ-nī,
   mŏ-nē´-bant.   mŏn-ē-ban´-tŭr.

§ 157. VERBS.—SECOND CONJUGATION.

ACTIVE.   PASSIVE.

Future.

I shall or *will advise.* | *I shall* or *will be advised.*
S. mŏ-nē'-bŏ, | S. mŏ-nē'-bŏr,
   mŏ-nē'-bĭs, | mŏ-nēb'-ĕ-rĭs *or* -rĕ,
   mŏ-nē'-bĭt; | mŏ-nēb'-ĭ-tŭr;
P. mŏ-nēb'-ĭ-mŭs, | P. mŏ-nēb'-ĭ-mŭr,
   mŏ-nēb'-ĭ-tĭs,| mŏn-ē-bĭm'-ĭ-nī,
   mŏ-nē'-bunt. | mŏn-ē-bun'-tŭr.

Perfect.

I advised or *have advised.* | *I was* or *have been advised.*
S. mŏn'-u-ī, | S. mŏn'-ĭ-tŭs sum *or* fu'-ī,
   mŏn-u-ĭs'-tī, | mŏn'-ĭ-tŭs ĕs *or* fu-ĭs'-tī,
   mŏn'-u-ĭt; | mŏn'-ĭ-tŭs est *or* fu'-ĭt;
P. mŏ-nu'-ĭ-mŭs, | P. mŏn'-ĭ-tī sŭ'-mŭs *or* fu'-ĭ-mŭs,
   mŏn-u-ĭs'-tĭs, | mŏn'-ĭ-tī es'-tĭs *or* fu-ĭs'-tĭs,
   mŏn-u-ē'-runt *or* -rĕ. | mŏn'-ĭ-tī sunt, fu-ē'-runt *or* -rĕ-

Pluperfect.

I had advised. | *I had been advised.*
S. mŏ-nu'-ĕ-ram, | S. mŏn'-ĭ-tŭs ĕ'-ram *or* fu'-ĕ-ram,
   mŏ-nu'-ĕ-rās, | mŏn'-ĭ-tŭs ĕ'-rās *or* fu'-ĕ-rās,
   mŏ-nu'-ĕ-răt; | mŏn'-ĭ-tŭs ĕ'-răt *or* fu'-ĕ-răt;
P. mŏn-u-ĕ-rā'-mŭs, | P. mŏn'ĭ-tī ĕ-rā'-mŭs *or* fu-e-rā'-mŭs,
   mŏn-u-ĕ-rā'-tĭs,| mŏn'-ĭ-tī ĕ-rā'-tĭs *or* fu-e-rā'-tĭs,
   mŏ-nu ĕ-rant. | mŏn'-ĭ-tī ĕ'-rant *or* fu'-ĕ-rant.

Future Perfect.

I shall have advised. | *I shall have been advised.*
S. mŏ-nu'-ĕ-rŏ, | S. mŏn'-ĭ-tŭs ĕ'-rŏ *or* fu'-ĕ-rŏ,
   mŏ-nu'-ĕ-rĭs, | mŏn'-ĭ-tŭs ĕ'-rĭs *or* fu'-ĕ-rĭs,
   mŏ-nu'-ĕ-rĭt; | mŏn'-ĭ-tŭs ĕ'-rĭt *or* fu'-ĕ-rĭt;
P. mŏn-u-ĕr'-ĭ-mŭs, | P. mŏn'-ĭ-tī ĕr'-ĭ-mŭs *or* fu-ĕr'-ĭ-mŭs,
   mŏn-u-ĕr'-ĭ-tĭs,| mŏn'-ĭ-tī ĕr'-ĭ-tĭs *or* fu-ĕr'-ĭ-tĭs,
   mŏ-nu'-ĕ-rint. | mŏn'-ĭ-tī ĕ'-runt *or* fu'-ĕ-rint.

SUBJUNCTIVE MOOD.

Present.

I may or *can advise.* | *I may* or *can be advised.*
S. mŏ'-ne-am, | S. mŏ'-ne-ăr,
   mŏ'-ne-ās, | mŏ-ne-ā'-rĭs *or* -rĕ,
   mŏ'-ne-ăt; | mŏ-ne-ā'-tŭr;
P. mŏ-ne-ā'-mŭs, | P. mŏ-ne-ā'-mŭr,
   mŏ-ne-ā'-tĭs,| mŏ-ne-ām'-ĭ-nī,
   mŏ'-ne-ant. | mŏ-ne-an'-tŭr.

VERBS.—SECOND CONJUGATION. §157

ACTIVE.	PASSIVE
Imperfect.	
I might, could, would, or *should advise.*	*I might, could, would,* or *should be advised.*
S. mŏ-nē'-rem,	S. mŏ-nē'-rĕr,
mŏ-nē'-rēs,	mŏn-ē-rē'-rĭs *or* -rĕ,
mŏ-nē'-rĕt;	mŏn-ē-rē'-tŭr;
P. mŏn-ē-rē'-mŭs,	P. mŏn-ē-rē'-mŭr,
mŏn-ē-rē'-tĭs,	mŏn-ē-rēm'-ĭ-nī,
mŏ-nē'-rent.	mŏn-ē-ren'-tŭr.
Perfect.	
I may have advised.	*I may have been advised.*
S. mŏ-nŭ'-ĕ-rim,	S. mŏn'-ĭ-tŭs sim *or* fu'-ĕ-rim,
mŏ-nŭ'-ĕ-rĭs,	mŏn'-ĭ-tŭs sis *or* fu'-ĕ-rĭs,
mŏ-nŭ'-ĕ-rĭt;	mŏn'-ĭ-tŭs sĭt *or* fu'-ĕ-rĭt;
P. mŏn-u-ĕr'-ĭ-mŭs,	P. mŏn'-ĭ-tī sī'-mŭs *or* fu-ĕr'-ĭ-mŭs,
mŏn-u-ĕr'-ĭ-tĭs,	mŏn'-ĭ-tī sī'-tĭs *or* fu-ĕr'-ĭ-tĭs,
mŏ-nŭ'-ĕ-rint.	mŏn'-ĭ-tī sint *or* fu'-ĕ-rint.
Pluperfect.	
I might, could, would, or *should have advised.*	*I might, could, would,* or *should have been advised.*
S. mŏn-u-is'-sem,	S. mŏn'-ĭ-tŭs es'-sem *or* fu-is'-sem,
mŏn-u-is'-sēs,	mŏn'-ĭ-tŭs es'-sēs *or* fu-is'-sēs,
mŏn-u-is'-sĕt;	mŏn'-ĭ-tŭs es'-sĕt *or* fu-is'-sĕt;
P. mŏn-u-is-sē'-mŭs,	P. mŏn'-ĭ-tī es-sē'-mŭs *or* fu-is-sē'-mŭs,
mŏn-u-is-sē'-tĭs,	mŏn'-ĭ-tī es-sē'-tis *or* fu-is-sē'-tĭs,
mŏn-u-is'-sent.	mŏn'-ĭ-tī es'-sent *or* fu-is'-sent.

IMPERATIVE MOOD.

Pres. S. mŏ'-nĕ, *advise thou;*	*Pres.* S. mŏ-nē'-rĕ, *be thou advised;*
P. mŏ-nē'-tĕ, *advise ye.*	P. mŏ-nēm'-ĭ-nī, *be ye advised.*
Fut. S. mŏ-nē'-tō, *thou shalt advise,*	*Fut.* S. mŏ-nē'-tŏr, *thou shalt be advised,*
mŏ-nē'-tō, *he shall advise;*	mŏ-nē'-tŏr, *he shall be advised;*
P. mŏn-ē-tō'-tĕ, *ye shall advise,*	P. (mŏn-ē-bĭm'-ĭ-nī, *ye shall be advised,*)
mŏ-nen'-tō, *they shall advise.*	mŏ-nēn'-tŏr, *they shall be advised.*

INFINITIVE MOOD.

Pres. mŏ-nē'-rĕ, *to advise.*	*Pres.* mŏ-nē'-rī, *to be advised.*
Perf. mŏn-u-is'-sĕ, *to have advised.*	*Perf.* mŏn'-ĭ-tŭs es'-sĕ *or* fu-is'-sĕ, *to have been advised.*
Fut. mŏn-ĭ-tū'-rŭs es'-sĕ, *to be about to advise.*	*Fut.* mŏn'-ĭ-tum ī'-rī, *to be about to be advised.*

§ 158. VERBS.—THIRD CONJUGATION. 111

ACTIVE.   PASSIVE.

PARTICIPLES.

Pres. mŏ′-nens, *advising.* | *Perf.* mŏn′-ĭ-tŭs, *advised.*
Fut. mŏn-ĭ-tū′-rŭs, *about to advise.* | *Fut.* mŏ-nen′-dŭs, *to be advised.*

GERUND.

G. mŏ-nen′-dī, *of advising,*
D. mŏ-nen′-dŏ, etc.
Ac. mŏ-nen′-dum,
Ab. mŏ-nen′-dŏ.

SUPINES.

Former. mŏn′-ĭ-tum, *to advise.* | *Latter.* mŏn′-ĭ-tū, *to be advised.*

FORMATION OF THE TENSES.

From the first root, *mon*, are derived,

	Active.	Passive.
Ind. pres.	moneo,	mŏneor.
— *imperf.*	monēbam,	monēbar.
— *fut.*	monēbo,	monēbor.
Subj. pres.	moneam,	monear.
— *imperf.*	monerem,	monerer.
Imperat. pres.	mone,	monēre.
— *fut.*	moneto,	monētor.
Inf. pres.	monēre,	monēri.
Part. pres.	monens,	
— *fut.*		monendus.
Gerund.	monendi.	

From the second root, *monu*, are derived,

	Active.
Ind. perf.	monui,
— *plup.*	monueram,
— *fut. perf.*	monuero,
Subj. perf.	monuerim,
— *plup.*	monuissem,
Inf. perf.	monuisse,

From the third root, *monit*, are derived,

Passive.
monitus sum, etc.
monitus eram, etc.
monitus ero, etc.
monitus sim, etc.
monitus essem, etc.
monitus esse, etc.

From the third root,
Inf. fut. monitūrus esse,   monitum iri.
Part. fut. monitūrus,
— *perf.*   monitus.
Form. Sup. monitum. *Lat. Sup.* monitu.

§ 158. THIRD CONJUGATION.

PRINCIPAL PARTS.

Pres. Ind. rĕ′-gŏ. | *Pres. Ind.* rĕ′-gŏr.
Pres. Inf. rĕg′-ĕ-rĕ. | *Pres. Inf.* rĕ′-gī.
Perf. Ind. rex′-ī. | *Perf. Part.* rec′-tŭs.
Supine. rec′-tum.

INDICATIVE MOOD.

Present.

I rule. | *I am ruled.*

Sing. rĕ′-gŏ, | Sing. rĕ′-gŏr,
      rĕ′-gĭs, | rĕg-ĕ-rĭs *or* -rĕ,
      rĕ′-gĭt; | rĕg′-ĭ-tŭr;
Plur. rĕg′-ĭ-mŭs, | Plur. rĕg′-ĭ-mŭr,
      rĕg′-ĭ-tĭs, | rĕ-gĭm′-ĭ-nī,
      rĕ′-gunt. | rĕ-gun′-tŭr.

ACTIVE.	PASSIVE
Imperfect.	
I was ruling.	*I was ruled.*
S. rĕ-gē´-bam,	S. rĕ-gē´-băr,
rĕ-gē´-bās,	rĕg-ē-bā´-rĭs *or* -rĕ,
rĕ-gē´-băt;	rĕg-ē-bā´-tŭr;
P. rĕg-ē-bā´-mŭs,	P. rĕg-ē-bā´-mŭr,
rĕg-ē-bā´-tĭs,	rĕg-ē-bām´-ĭ-nĭ,
rĕ-gē´-bant.	rĕg-ē-ban´-tŭr.
Future.	
I shall or will rule.	*I shall or will be ruled.*
S. rĕ´-gam,	S. rĕ´-găr,
rĕ´-gēs,	rĕ-gē´-rĭs *or* -rĕ,
rĕ´-gĕt;	rĕ-gē´-tŭr;
P. rĕ-gē´-mŭs,	P. rĕ-gē´-mŭr,
rĕ-gē´-tĭs,	rĕ-gēm´-ĭ-nĭ,
rĕ´-gent.	rĕ-gen´-tŭr.
Perfect.	
I ruled or have ruled.	*I was or have been ruled.*
S. rex´-ī,	S. rec´-tŭs sum *or* fu´-ī,
rex-is´-tī,	rec´-tŭs ĕs *or* fu-is´-tī,
rex´-ĭt;	rec´-tŭs est *or* fu´-ĭt;
P. rex´-ĭ-mŭs,	P. rec´-tī sŭ´-mŭs *or* fu´-ĭ-mŭs,
rex-is´-tĭs,	rec´-tī es´-tĭs *or* fu-is´-tĭs,
rex-ē´-runt *or* -rĕ.	rec´-tī sunt, fu-ē´-runt *or* -re
Pluperfect.	
I had ruled.	*I had been ruled.*
S. rex´-ĕ-ram,	S. rec´-tŭs ĕ´-ram *or* fu´-ĕ-ram,
rex´-ĕ-rās,	rec´-tŭs ĕ´-rās *or* fu´-ĕ-rās,
rex´-ĕ-răt;	rec´-tŭs ĕ´-răt *or* fu´-ĕ-răt;
P. rex-ĕ-rā´-mŭs	P. rec´-tī ĕ-rā´-mŭs *or* fu-ĕ-rā´-mŭs,
rex-ĕ-rā´-tĭs,	rec´-tī ĕ-rā´-tĭs *or* fu-ĕ-rā´-tĭs,
rex´-ĕ-rant.	rec´-tī ĕ´-rant *or* fu´-ĕ-rant.
Future Perfect.	
I shall have ruled	*I shall have been ruled.*
S. rex´-ĕ-rŏ,	S. rec´-tŭs ĕ´-rŏ *or* fu´-ĕ-rŏ,
rex´-ĕ-rĭs,	rec´-tŭs ĕ´-rĭs *or* fu´-ĕ-rĭs,
rex´-ĕ-rĭt;	rec´-tŭs ĕ´-rĭt *or* fu´ ĕ-rĭt;
P. rex-ĕr´-ĭ-mŭs,	P. rec´-tī ĕr´-ĭ-mŭs *or* fu-ĕr´-ĭ-mŭs,
rex-ĕr´-ĭ-tĭs,	rec´-tī ĕr´-ĭ-tĭs *or* fu-ĕr´-ĭ-tĭs,
rex´-ĕ-rint.	rec´-tī ĕ´-runt *or* fu´-ĕ-rint.

§ 158.   VERBS.—THIRD CONJUGATION.

ACTIVE.   PASSIVE.
              SUBJUNCTIVE MOOD.
                   Present.

I may or can rule.   *I may or can be ruled.*
  S. rĕ'-gam,   S. rĕ'-găr,
     rĕ'-gās,   rĕ-gā'-rĭs *or* -rē,
     rĕ'-găt;   rĕ-gā'-tŭr;
  P. rĕ-gā'-mŭs,   P. rĕ-gā'-mŭr,
     rĕ-gā'-tĭs,   rĕ-gŭm'-ĭ-nī,
     rĕ'-gant.   rĕ-gan'-tŭr.

                   Imperfect.

*I might, could, would, or should   I might, could, would, or should
         rule.*   be ruled.*
  S. rĕg'-ĕ-rem,   S. rĕg'-ĕ-rĕr,
     rĕg'-ĕ-rēs,   rĕg-ĕ-rē'-rĭs *or* -rē,
     rĕg'-ĕ-rĕt;   rĕg-ĕ-rē'-tŭr;
  P. rĕg-ĕ-rē'-mŭs,   P. rĕg-ĕ-rē'-mŭr,
     rĕg-ĕ-rē'-tĭs,   rĕg-ĕ-rēm'-ĭ-nī,
     rĕg'-ĕ-rent.   rĕg-ĕ-ren'-tŭr.

                   Perfect.

I may have ruled.   *I may have been ruled.*
  S. rex'-ĕ-rim,   S. rec'-tŭs sim *or* fu'-ĕ-rim,
     rex'-ĕ-rĭs,   rec'-tŭs sīs *or* fu'-ĕ-rĭs,
     rex'-ĕ-rĭt;   rec'-tŭs sit *or* fu'-ĕ-rĭt;
  P. rex-ĕr'-ĭ-mŭs,   P. rec'-tī si'-mŭs *or* fu-ĕr'-ĭ-mŭs,
     rex-ĕr'-ĭ-tĭs,   rec'-tī sī'-tĭs *or* fu-ĕr'-ĭ-tĭs,
     rex'-ĕ-rint.   rec'-tī sint *or* fu'-ĕ-rint.

                   Pluperfect.

*I might, could, would, or   I might, could, would, or should have
   should have ruled.*   been ruled.*
  S. rex-is'-sem,   S. rec'-tŭs es'-sem *or* fu-is'-sem,
     rex-is'-sēs,   rec'-tŭs es'-sēs *or* fu-is'-sēs,
     rex-is'-sĕt;   rec'-tŭs es'-sĕt *or* fu-is'-sĕt;
  P. rex-is-sē'-mŭs,   P. rec'-tī es-sē'-mŭs *or* fu-is-sē'-mŭs,
     rex-is-sē'-tĭs,   rec'-tī es-sē'-tĭs *or* fu-is-sē'-tĭs,
     rex-is'-sent.   rec'-tī es'-sent *or* fu-is'-sent.

              IMPERATIVE MOOD.

Pres. S. rĕ'-gĕ, *rule thou,*   *Pres.* S. rĕg'-ĕ-rĕ, *be thou ruled;*
       P. rĕg'-ĭ-tĕ, *rule ye.*   P. rĕ-gĭm'-ĭ-nī, *be ye ruled.*
Fut. S. rĕg'-ĭ-tŏ, *thou shalt rule,* *Fut.* S. rĕg'-ĭ-tŏr, *thou shalt be ruled,*
       rĕg'-ĭ-tŏ, *he shall rule;*   rĕg'-ĭ-tŏr, *he shall be ruled,*
       P. rĕg-ĭ-tō'-tĕ, *ye shall rule,*   P. (rĕ-gĭm'-ĭ-nī, *ye shall, etc.*)
       rĕ-gun'tŏ, *they shall rule.*   rĕ-gun'-tŏr, *they shall, etc.*

10*

VERBS.—THIRD CONJUGATION.

ACTIVE.   PASSIVE.

INFINITIVE MOOD.

Pres. rĕg'-ĕ-rĕ, *to rule.*   *Pres.* rĕ'-gī, *to be ruled.*
Perf. rex-is'-sĕ, *to have ruled.*   *Perf.* rec'-tŭs es'-sĕ *or* fu-is'-sĕ, *to have been ruled.*
Fut. rec-tū'-rŭs es'-se, *to be about to rule.*   *Fut.* rec'-tum ī'-rī, *to be about to be ruled.*

PARTICIPLES.

Pres. rĕ'-gens, *ruling.*   *Perf.* rec'-tŭs, *ruled.*
Fut. rec-tū'-rŭs, *about to rule.*   *Fut.* rĕ-gen'-dŭs, *to be ruled.*

GERUND.

G. rĕ-gen'-dī, *of ruling.*
D. rĕ-gen'-dŏ, *etc.*
Ac. rĕ-gen'-dum,
Ab. rĕ-gen'-dŏ.

SUPINES.

Former. rec'-tum, *to rule.*   *Latter.* rec'-tū, *to be ruled.*

FORMATION OF THE TENSES.

From the first root, *reg*, are derived,			From the second root, *rex*, are derived,		From the third root, *rect.* are derived,
	Active.	Passive.		Active.	Passive.
Ind. pres.	rego,	regor.	Ind. perf.	rexi,	rectus sum, etc.
— imperf.	regēbam,	regēbar.	— plup.	rexĕram,	rectus eram, etc.
— fut.	regam,	regar.	— fut. perf.	rexĕro,	rectus ero, etc.
Subj. pres.	regam,	regar.	Subj. perf.	rexĕrim,	rectus sim, etc.
— imperf.	regĕrem	regĕrer.	— plup.	rexissem,	rectus essem, etc.
Imperat. pres.	rege,	regĕre.	Inf. perf.	rexisse.	rectus esse, etc.
— fut.	regĭto,	regĭtor	From the third root,		
Inf. pres.	regĕre,	regi.	Inf. fut.	rectūrus esse,	rectum iri.
Part. pres.	regens,		Part. fut.	rectūrus.	
— fut.		regendus.	— perf.		rectus.
Gerund.	regendi.		Form. Sup. rectum.		Lat. Sup. rectu.

§ 159. VERBS IN *IO* OF THE THIRD CONJUGATION.

Verbs in *io* of the third conjugation, in tenses formed from the first root, have, as connecting vowels, *ia, ie, io,* or *iu,* wherever the same occur in the fourth conjugation; but where they have only a single connecting vowel, it is the same which characterizes other verbs of the third conjugation. They are all conjugated like *căpĭo.*

§ 159. VERBS.—THIRD CONJUGATION.

ACTIVE.   PASSIVE.

PRINCIPAL PARTS.

Pres. Ind. că'-pi-ŏ, *to take.*	*Pres. Ind.* că'-pi-ŏr, *to be taken.*
Pres. Inf. căp'-ĕ-rĕ.	*Pres. Inf.* că'-pī.
Perf. Ind. cē'-pī.	*Perf. Part.* cap'-tŭs.
Supine. cap'-tum.	

INDICATIVE MOOD.

Present.

S. că'-pi-ŏ,	S. că'-pi-ŏr,
că'-pĭs,	căp'-ĕ-rĭs *or* -rĕ,
că'-pĭt;	căp'-ĭ-tŭr;
P. căp'-ĭ-mŭs,	P. căp'-ĭ-mŭr,
căp'-ĭ-tĭs,	că-pĭm'-ĭ-nī,
că'-pi-unt.	că-pi-un'-tŭr.

Imperfect.

S. că-pi-ē'-bam,	S. că-pi-ē'-băr,
că-pi-ē'-bās,	că-pi-ē-bā'-rĭs *or* -rĕ,
că-pi-ē'-băt;	că-pi-ē-bā'-tŭr;
P. că-pi-ē-bā'-mŭs,	P. că-pi-ē-bā'-mŭr,
că-pi-ē-bā'-tĭs,	că-pi-ē-bām'-ĭ-nī,
că-pi-ē'-bant.	că-pi-ē-ban'-tŭr.

Future.

S. că'-pi-am,	S. că'-pi-ăr,
că'-pi-ēs,	că-pi-ē'-rĭs *or* -rĕ,
că'-pi-ĕt;	că-pi-ē'-tŭr;
P. că-pi-ē'-mŭs,	P. că-pi-ē'-mŭr,
că-pi-ē'-tĭs,	că-pi-ēm'-ĭ-ni,
că'-pi-ent.	că-pi-en'-tŭr.

The parts formed from the second and third roots being entirely regular, only a synopsis of them is given.

Perf. cē'-pī.	*Perf.* cap'-tŭs sum *or* fu'-ī.
Plup. cēp'-ĕ-ram.	*Plup.* cap'-tŭs ĕ'-ram *or* fu'-ĕ-ram.
Fut. perf. cēp'-ĕ-rŏ.	*Fut. perf.* cap'-tŭs ĕ'-rŏ *or* fu'-ĕ-rŏ.

SUBJUNCTIVE MOOD.

Present.

S. că'-pi-am,	S. că'-pi-ăr,
că'-pi-ās,	că-pi-ā'-rĭs *or* -rĕ,
că'-pi-ăt;	că-pi-ā'-tŭr;
P. că-pi-ā'-mŭs,	P. că-pi-ā'-mŭr,
că-pi-ā'-tĭs,	că-pi-ām'-ĭ-nī,
că'-pi-ant.	că-pi-an'-tŭr.

VERBS.—FOURTH CONJUGATION   § 160.

ACTIVE.   PASSIVE.

Imperfect.

S. căp'-ĕ-rem,   S. căp'-ĕ-rĕr,
   căp'-ĕ-rēs,   căp-ĕ-rē'-ris or -rĕ,
   căp'-ĕ-rĕt;   căp-ĕ-rē'-tŭr;
P. căp-ĕ-rē'-mŭs,   P. căp-ĕ-rē'-mŭr,
   căp-ĕ-rē'-tĭs,   căp-ĕ-rēm'-ĭ-nĭ,
   căp'-ĕ-rent.   căp-ĕ-ren'-tŭr.

Perf. cēp'-ĕ-rim. | *Perf.* cap'-tŭs sim *or* fu'-ĕ-rim.
Plup. cē-pis'-sem. | *Plup.* cap'-tŭs es'-sem *or* fu-is'-sem.

IMPERATIVE MOOD.

Pres. 2. S. că'-pĕ;   P. 2. căp'-ĭ-tŏ. | S. căp'-ĕ-rĕ; P. că-pĭm'-ĭ-nĭ.
Fut. 2. căp'-ĭ-tŏ,   căp-ĭ-tō-tĕ, | căp'-ĭ-tŏr, (că-pĭ-ēm'-ĭ-nĭ,)
— 3. căp'-ĭ-tŏ;   că-pi-un'-tŏ. | căp'-ĭ-tŏr; că-pi-un'-tŏr.

INFINITIVE MOOD.

Pres. căp'-ĕ-rĕ. | *Pres.* că'-pī.
Perf. cē-pis'-sĕ. | *Perf.* cap'-tŭs es'-sĕ *or* fu-is'-sĕ.
Fut. cap-tū'-rŭs es'-sĕ. | *Fut.* cap'-tum ĭ'-ri.

PARTICIPLES.

Pres. că'-pi-ens. | *Perf.* cap'-tŭs.
Fut. cap-tū'-rŭs. | *Fut.* că-pi-en'-dŭs.

GERUND.

G. că-pi-en'-dī, etc.

SUPINES.

Former. cap'-tum. | *Latter.* cap'-tū.

§ 160. FOURTH CONJUGATION.

PRINCIPAL PARTS.

Pres. Ind. au'-di-ŏ. | *Pres. Ind.* au'-di-ŏr.
Pres. Inf. au-dī'-rĕ. | *Pres. Inf.* au-dī'-rī.
Perf. Ind. au-dī'-vī. | *Perf. Part.* au-dī'-tŭs.
Supine. au-dī'-tum.

§ 160. VERBS.—FOURTH CONJUGATION.

ACTIVE.   PASSIVE.
           INDICATIVE MOOD.
              Present.

I hear.   *I am heard.*
S. au'-di-ŏ,   S. au'-di-ŏr,
   au'-dīs,   au-dī'-rĭs *or* -rĕ,
   au'dĭt;   au-dī'-tŭr;
P. au-dī'-mŭs,   P. au-dī'-mŭr,
   au'-dī'-tĭs,   au-dīm'-ĭ-nī,
   au'-di-unt.   au-di-un'-tŭr.

              Imperfect.

I was hearing.   *I was heard.*
S. au-di-ē'-bam,   S. au-di-ē'-băr,
   au-di-ē'-bās,   au-di-ē-bā'-rĭs *or* -rĕ,
   au-di-ē'-băt;   au-di-ē-bā'-tŭr;
P. au-di-ē-bā'-mŭs,   P. au-di-ē-bā'-mŭr,
   au-di-ē-bā'-tĭs,   au-di-ē-bām'-ĭ-nī,
   au-di-ē-bant.   au-di-ē-ban'-tŭr.

              Future.

I shall or *will hear.*   *I shall* or *will be heard.*
S. au'-di-am,   S. au'-di-ăr,
   au'-di-ēs,   au-di-ē'-rĭs *or* -rĕ,
   au'-di-ĕt;   au-di-ē'-tŭr;
P. au-di-ē'-mŭs,   P. au-di-ē'-mŭr,
   au-di-ē'-tĭs,   au-di-ēm'-ĭ-nī,
   au'-di-ent.   au-di-en'-tŭr.

              Perfect.

I heard or *have heard.*   *I have been* or *was heard.*
S. au-dī'-vī,   S. au-dī'-tŭs sum *or* fu'-ī,
   au-dī-vĭs'-tī,   au-dī'-tŭs ĕs *or* fu-is'-tī,
   au-dī'-vĭt;   au-dī'-tŭs est *or* fu'-ĭt;
P. au-dīv'-ĭ-mŭs,   P. au-dī'-tī sŭ'-mŭs *or* fu'-ĭ-mŭs,
   au-di-vĭs'-tĭs,   au-dī'-tī es'-tĭs *or* fu-is'-tĭs,
   au-di-vē'-runt *or* -rĕ.   au-dī'-tī sunt, fu-ē'-runt *or* -rĕ

              Pluperfect.

I had heard.   *I had been heard.*
S. au-dīv'-ĕ-ram,   S. au-dī'-tŭs ĕ'-ram *or* fu'-ĕ-ram,
   au-dīv'-ĕ-rās,   au-dī'-tŭs ĕ'-rās *or* fu'-ĕ-rās,
   au-dīv'-ĕ-rŭt;   au-dī'-tŭs ĕ'-răt *or* fu'-ĕ-răt;
P. au-dīv-ĕ-rā'-mŭs,   P. au-dī'-tī ĕ-rā'-mŭs *or* fu-ĕ-rā'-mŭs,
   au-dīv-ĕ-rā'-tĭs,   au-dī'-tī ĕ-rā'-tĭs *or* fu-ĕ-rā'-tĭs,
   au-dīv'-ĕ-rant.   au-dī'-tī ĕ'-rant *or* fu'-ĕ-rant.

VERBS.—FOURTH CONJUGATION. § 160.

ACTIVE.	PASSIVE
Future Perfect.	
I shall have heard.	*I shall have been heard.*
S. au-dīv'-ĕ-rŏ,	S. au-dī'-tŭs ĕ'-rŏ *or* fu'-ĕ-rŏ,
au-dīv'-ĕ-rĭs,	au-dī'-tŭs ĕ'-rĭs *or* fu'-ĕ-rĭs,
au-dīv'-ĕ-rĭt;	au-dī'-tŭs ĕ'-rĭt *or* fu'-ĕ-rĭt;
P. au-di-vĕr'-ĭ-mŭs,	P. au-dī'-tī ĕr'-ĭ-mŭs *or* fu-ĕr'-ĭ-mŭs,
au-di-vĕr'-ĭ-tĭs,	au-dī'-tī ĕr'-ĭ-tĭs *or* fu-ĕr'-ĭ-tis,
au-dīv'-ĕ-rint.	au-dī'-tī ĕ'-runt *or* fu'-ĕ-rint.

SUBJUNCTIVE MOOD.

Present.

I may or can hear.	*I may or can be heard.*
S. au'-di-am,	S. au'-di-ăr,
au'-di-ās,	au-di-ā'-rĭs *or* -rĕ,
au'-di-ăt;	au-di-ā'-tŭr;
P. au-di-ā'-mŭs,	P. au-di-ā'-mŭr,
au-di-ā'-tĭs,	au-di-ām'-ĭ-nī,
au'-di-ant.	au-di-an'-tŭr.

Imperfect.

I might, could, would, or should hear.	*I might, could, would, or should be heard.*
S. au-dī'-rem,	S. au-dī'-rĕr,
au-dī'-rēs,	au-di-rē'-rĭs *or* -rĕ,
au-dī'-rĕt;	au-di-rē'-tŭr;
P. au-di-rē'-mŭs,	P. au-di-rē'-mŭr,
au-di-rē'-tĭs,	au-di-rēm'-ĭ-nī,
au-dī'-rent.	au-di-ren'-tŭr.

Perfect.

I may have heard.	*I may have been heard.*
S. au-dīv'-ĕ-rim,	S. au-dī'-tŭs sim *or* fu'-ĕ-rim,
au-dīv'-ĕ-rĭs,	au-dī'-tŭs sis *or* fu'-ĕ-rĭs,
au-dīv'-ĕ-rĭt;	au-dī'-tŭs sit *or* fu'-ĕ-rĭt;
P. au-di-vĕr'-ĭ-mŭs,	P. au-dī'-tī sī'-mŭs *or* fu-ĕr'-ĭ-mŭs,
au-di-vĕr'-ĭ-tĭs,	au-dī'-tī sī'-tĭs *or* fu-ĕr'-ĭ-tis,
au-dīv'-ĕ-rint.	au-dī'-tī sint *or* fu'-ĕ-rint.

Pluperfect.

I might, could, would, or should have heard.	*I might, could, would, or should have been heard.*
S. au-di-vis'-sem,	S. au-dī'-tŭs es'-sem *or* fu-is'-sem,
au-di-vis'-sēs,	au-dī'-tŭs es'-sēs *or* fu-is'-sēs,
au-di-vis'-sĕt;	au-dī'-tŭs es'-sĕt *or* fu-is'-sĕt;
P. au-di-vis-sē'-mŭs,	P. au-dī'-ti es-sē'-mŭs *or* fu-is-sē'-mŭs,
au-di-vis-sē'-tĭs,	au-dī'-ti es-sē'-tĭs *or* fu-is-sē'-tĭs,
au-di-vis'-sent.	au-dī'-ti es'-sent *or* fu-is'-sent

VERBS.—FOURTH CONJUGATION.

ACTIVE.	PASSIVE.

IMPERATIVE MOOD.

Pres. S. au'-dī, *hear thou;* *P.* au-dī'-tĕ, *hear ye.* *Fut. S.* au-dī'-tŏ, *thou shalt hear,* au-dī'-tŏ, *he shall hear;* *P.* au-di-tō'-tĕ, *ye shall hear,* au-di-un'-tŏ, *they shall hear.*	*Pres. S.* au-dī'-rĕ, *be th. u heard,* *P.* au-dim'-ĭ-nī, *be ye heard.* *Fut. S.* au-dī'-tŏr, *thou shalt be heard,* au-dī'-tŏr, *he shall be heard;* *P.* (au-di-ēm'-ĭ-nī, *ye shall be heard,*) au-dī-un'-tŏr, *they shall be heard.*

INFINITIVE MOOD.

Pres. au-dī'-rĕ, *to hear.* *Perf.* au-dī-vis'-sĕ, *to have heard.* *Fut.* au-dī-tū'-rŭs es-sĕ, *to be about to hear.*	*Pres.* au-dī'-rī, *to be heard.* *Perf.* au-dī'-tŭs es'-sĕ *or* fu—is'-sĕ, *to have been heard.* *Fut.* au-dī'-tum ĭ'-rī, *to be about to be heard.*

PARTICIPLES.

Pres. au'-di-ēns, *hearing.* *Fut.* au-dī-tū'-rŭs, *about to hear.*	*Perf.* au-dī'-tŭs, *heard.* *Fut.* au-di-en'-dŭs, *to be heard.*

GERUND.

G. au-di-en'-dī, *of hearing.*
D. au-di-en'-dŏ, etc.
Ac. au-di-en'-dum,
Ab. au-di-en'-dŏ.

SUPINES.

Former. au-dī'-tum, *to hear.*	*Latter.* au-dī'-tū, *to be heard.*

FORMATION OF THE TENSES.

From the first root, *aud,* are derived,

	Active.	Passive.
Ind. pres.	audio,	audior.
— *imperf.*	audiēbam,	audiēbar.
— *fut.*	audiam,	audiar.
Subj. pres.	audiam,	audiar.
— *imperf.*	audirem,	audirer.
Imperat. pres.	audi,	audire.
—— *fut.*	audito,	auditor.
Inf. pres.	audire,	audiri.
Part. pres.	audiens,	
—— *fut.*		audiendus.
Gerund.	audiendi.	

From the second root, *audiv,* are derived,

	Active.
Ind. perf.	audivi,
— *plup.*	audiveram,
— *fut. perf.*	audivero,
Subj. perf.	audiverim,
— *plup.*	audivissem,
Inf. perf.	audivisse,

From the third root, *audit,* are derived,

	Passive.
	auditus sum, etc.
	auditus eram, etc.
	auditus ero, etc.
	auditus sim, etc.
	auditus essem, etc
	auditus esse, etc.

From the third root,
Inf. fut. auditūrus esse, auditum iri.
Part. fut. auditūrus.
—— *perf.*   auditus.
Form. sup. auditum   *Lat. sup.* auditu.

DEPONENT VERBS.

§ 161. Deponent verbs are conjugated like the passive voice, and have also all the participles and participial formations of the active voice. Neuter deponent verbs, however, want the future passive participle, except that the neuter in *dum* is sometimes used impersonally. See § 184, 3.

The following is an example of an active deponent verb of the first conjugation :—

PRINCIPAL PARTS.

Mǐ'-rŏr, mǐ-rā'-rī, mǐ-rā'-tŭs, *to admire.*

INDICATIVE MOOD.

Pres.	mǐ'-rŏr, mǐ-rā'-rǐs, etc.	*I admire,* etc.
Imperf.	mǐ-rā'-bǎr, etc.	*I was admiring.*
Fut.	mǐ-rā'-bŏr,	*I shall admire.*
Perf.	mǐ-rā'-tŭs sum *or* fu'-ī,	*I have admired.*
Plup.	mǐ-rā'-tŭs ĕ'-ram *or* fu'-ĕ-ram,	*I had admired.*
Fut. Perf.	mǐ-rā'-tŭs ĕ'-ro *or* fu'-ĕ-ro,	*I shall have admired.*

SUBJUNCTIVE MOOD.

Pres.	mǐ'-rĕr, mǐ-rē'-rǐs, etc.	*I may admire,* etc.
Imperf.	mǐ-rā'-rĕr,	*I would admire.*
Perf.	mǐ-rā'-tŭs sim *or* fu'-ĕ-rim,	*I may have admired.*
Plup.	mǐ-rā'-tŭs es'-sem *or* fu-is'-sem,	*I would have admired.*

IMPERATIVE MOOD.

Pres. S. mǐ-rā'-rĕ, *admire thou;*	*P.* mǐ-rām'-ǐ-nǐ, *admire ye.*
Fut. S. mǐ-rā'-tŏr, *thou shalt admire,*	*P.* (mǐr-ā-bǐm'-ǐ-nǐ, *ye shall,* etc.)
mǐ-rā'-tŏr, *he shall admire;*	mǐ-ran'-tŏr, *they shall,* etc.

INFINITIVE MOOD.

Pres.	mǐ-rā'-rī,	*to admire.*
Perf.	mǐ-rā'-tŭs es'-sĕ *or* fu-is'-sĕ,	*to have admired.*
Fut. Act.	mǐr-ā-tū'-rŭs es'-sĕ,	*to be about to admire.*
Fut. Pass.	mǐ-rā'-tum ī'-rī,	*to be about to be admired.*

PARTICIPLES.

Pres.	mǐ'-rans,	*admiring.*
Perf.	mǐ-rā'-tŭs,	*having admired.*
Fut. Act.	mǐr-ā-tū'-rŭs,	*about to admire.*
Fut. Pass.	mǐ-ran'-dŭs,	*to be admired.*

GERUND.

G. mǐ-ran'-dī, *of admiring,* etc.

SUPINES.

Former mǐ-rā'-tum, *to admire.* | *Latter.* mǐ-rā'-tū, *to be admired.*

Remarks on the Conjugations.

Of the Tenses formed from the First Root.

§ 162. 1. A few words in the present subjunctive of the first and third conjugations, in the earlier writers and in the poets, end in *im*, *is*, *ĭt*, etc.; as, *ĕdim*, *ĕdis*, *ĕdĭt*, *edĭmus; comĕdim, comĕdis, comĕdĭt;* for *edam*, etc. *comĕdăm*, etc.; *duim, duis, duit, duint;* and *perduim, perduis, perduit, perduint;* for *dem*, etc. *perdam*, etc. from old forms *duo* and *perduo*, for *do* and *perdo:* so *creduis, creduit*, and also *creduam, creduas, creduat*, for *credam*, etc. from the old form *creduo*, for *credo*. The form in *im*, etc. was retained as the regular form in *sim* and *velim*, from *sum* and *volo*, and in their compounds.

2. The imperfect indicative in the fourth conjugation, sometimes, especially in the more ancient writers, ends in *ībam* and *ībar*, for *iēbam* and *iēbar*, and the future in *ībo* and *ībor*, for *iam* and *iar;* as, *vestībat*, Virg., *largībar*, Propert. for *vestiēbat, largiēbar; scībo, opperībor*, for *sciam, opperiar*. *Ibam* and *ibo* were retained as the regular forms of *eo, queo*, and *nequeo*. Cf. § 182.

3. The termination *re*, in the second person singular of the passive voice, is rare in the present, but common in the other simple tenses.

4. The imperatives of *dīco, dūco, făcio*, and *fĕro*, are usually written *dic, duc, fac*, and *fer;* in like manner their compounds, except those compounds of *făcio* which change *a* into *i;* as, *effĭce, confĭce;* but *calfăce* also is found in Cicero; and in old writers *dice, edice, adūce, indīce, dūce, abdūce, redūce, tradūce*, and *făce*. *Inger* for *ingĕre* is rare. *Scio* has not *sci*, but its place is supplied by *scīto*, and *scitōte* is preferred to *scīte*.

5. In the imperative future of the passive voice, but especially of deponents, early writers and their imitators sometimes used the active instead of the passive form; as, *arbitrāto, amplexāto, utito, nitīto;* for *arbitrātor*, etc.; and *censento, utunto, tuento*, etc. for *censentor*, etc.—In the second and third persons singular occur, also, forms in *-mīno;* as, *hortamĭno, veremĭno, fruimĭno;* for *hortātor*, etc.

6. The syllable *er* was often added to the present infinitive passive by early writers and especially by the poets; as, *amarier* for *amāri, dicier* for *dici*.

Of the Tenses formed from the Second Root.

7. (*a.*) When the second root ends in *v*, a syncopation and contraction often occur in the tenses formed from it, by omitting *v*, and sinking the first vowel of the termination in the final vowel of the root, when followed, in the fourth conjugation, by *s*, and in the other conjugations, by *s* or *r;* as, *audissem* for *audivissem, amasti* for *amavisti, implērunt* for *implevērunt, nōram* and *nosse* for *novĕram* and *novisse*.

(*b.*) When the second root ends in *iv*, *v* is often omitted without contraction; as, *audiĕro* for *audivĕro; audiisse* for *audivisse*.

(*c.*) When this root ends in *s* or *x*, especially in the third conjugation, the syllables *is, iss*, and *sis*, are sometimes omitted in the termination of tenses derived from it; as, *evasti* for *evasisti, extinxti* for *extinxisti, divisse* for *divisisse; extinxem* for *extinxissem, surrexe* for *surrexisse; accestis* for *accessistis, jussi* for *jussisti; dixti* for *dixisti*. So *fuxem* for *(facsissem,* i. e.*) fecissem*.

(*d.*) In the perfect of the first, second, and fourth conjugations, a syncope sometimes occurs in the last syllable of the root and the following syllable of the termination, especially in the third person singular; as, *fumăt, audit, cŭpit;* for *fumāvit, audivit, cupivit*. So, also, but rarely, in the first person; as, *sepĕli, enarrāmus;* for *sepelivi, enarrāvimus*.

8. In the third person plural of the perfect indicative active, the form in *ēre* is less common than that in *ērunt*, especially in prose.

9. Ancient forms of a future perfect in *so*, a perfect and pluperfect subjunctive in *sim* and *sem*, and a perfect infinitive in *se* sometimes occur. They may, in general, be formed by adding these terminations to the second root of the verb; as, *recepso, emissim, ausim* from the obsolete perfect, *ausi*, from *audeo, confexim* and *promissem: divisse* and *promisse*. But when the root ends in *x*, and frequently when it ends in *s*, only *o, im, em,* and *e,* etc. are added; as, *jusso, dixis; intellexes, percepset; surrexe, sumse. V*, at the end of the root, in the first conjugation, is changed into *s*; as, *levasso, locassim. U*, at the end of the root, in the second conjugation, is changed into *es*; as, *habesso, licessit*. Sometimes the vowel of the present is retained in these forms, though changed in the other parts derived from the second root; as, *capso, faxo (facso), faxim (fucsim)*.

NOTE. *Faxo* expresses determination, ' I will,' or, ' I am resolved, to make, cause,' etc. The subjunctive *faxit*, etc., expresses a solemn wish; as, *dii immortāles faxint. Ausim*, etc. express doubt or hesitation, ' I might venture,' etc. The perfect in *sim* is used also in connection with the present subjunctive; as, *quæso uti tu calamitātes prohibessis, defendas, averruncesque.* Cato.

10. In the ancient Latin a few examples occur of a future passive of similar form; as, *turbassitur, jussitur*, instead of *turbātum fuĕrit*, and *jussus fuĕrit.*—A future infinitive active in *sēre* is also found, in the first conjugation, which is formed by adding that termination to the second root, changing, as before, *v* into *s*; as, *expugnassēre, impetrassēre*, for *expugnatūrum esse*, etc.

Of the Tenses formed from the Third Root.

11. The supine in *um*, though called one of the principal parts of the verb, belongs in fact to very few verbs, the whole number which have this supine not amounting to three hundred. The part called in dictionaries the supine in *um* must therefore, in most cases, be considered as the neuter gender of the perfect participle.

12. In the compound tenses of the indicative and subjunctive moods, the participle is always in the nominative case, but it is used in both numbers, and in all genders, to correspond with the number and gender of the subject of the verb; as, *amātus, -a, -um, est; amāti, -æ, -a, sunt*, etc.

(1.) *Fui, fuĕram, fuĕrim, fuissem*, and *fuisse*, are seldom used in the compound tenses of deponent verbs, and not so often as *sum*, etc., in those of other verbs, but when used they have generally the same sense. It is to be remarked, however, that *fui* with the perfect participle usually denotes that which has been, but which no longer exists. In the pluperfect subjunctive, *fŏrem*, etc., for *essem*, etc., are sometimes found.

(2.) But as the perfect participle may be used in the sense of an adjective, expressing a permanent state, (see § 162, 22), if then connected with the tenses of *sum* its meaning is different from that of the participle in the same connection; *epistŏla scripta est*, when *scripta* is a participle, signifies, the letter *has been* written, but if *scripta* is an adjective, the meaning of the expression is, the letter *is* written, and *epistŏla scripta fuit*, in this case, would signify, the letter *has been* written, or, *has existed* as a written one, implying that it no longer exists.

13. The participles in the perfect and future infinitive, are used only in the nominative and accusative, but in all genders and in both numbers; as, *amātus, -a, -um, esse* or *fuisse; amātum, -am, -um, esse* or *fuisse; amāti, -æ, -a, esse* or *fuisse; amātos, -as, -a, esse* or *fuisse;* and so of the others. With the infinitive *fuisse, amātus*, etc. are generally to be considered as participial adjectives

(1.) These participles in combination with *esse* are sometimes used as indeclinable; as, *cohortes ad me missum facias.* Cic. *Ad me, mea Terentia, scribis te vicum venditurum.* Id.

Periphrastic Conjugations.

14. The participle in *rus*, joined to the tenses of the verb *sum*, denotes either *intention*, or *being upon the point* of doing something. This form of the verb is called the *active periphrastic conjugation*.

REMARK 1. As the performance of the act depends either on the will of the subject, on that of others, or upon circumstances, we may say, in English, in the first case, 'I intend,' and in the others, 'I am to,' or 'I am about to' (be or do any thing).

INDICATIVE.

Pres.	amatūrus sum,	*I am about to love.*
Imperf.	amatūrus eram,	*I was about to love.*
Fut.	amatūrus ero,	*I shall be about to love.*
Perf.	amatūrus fui,	*I was or have been about to love.*
Plup.	amatūrus fuĕram,	*I had been about to love.*

SUBJUNCTIVE.

Pres.	amatūrus sim,	*I may be about to love.*
Imperf.	amatūrus essem,	*I would be about to love.*
Perf.	amatūrus fuĕrim,	*I may have been about to love.*
Plup.	amatūrus fuissem,	*I would have been about to love.*

INFINITIVE.

Pres.	amatūrus esse,	*to be about to love.*
Perf.	amatūrus fuisse,	*to have been about to love.*

REM. 2. *Fuĕro* is scarcely used in connection with the participle in *rus*.

REM. 3. *Amatūrus sim* and *amatūrus essem* serve also as subjunctives to the future *amābo*. The infinitive *amatūrus fuisse* answers to the English, 'I should have loved,' so that in hypothetical sentences it supplies the place of an infinitive of the pluperfect subjunctive.

REM. 4. In the passive, the fact that an act is about to be performed is expressed by a longer circumlocution: as, *in eo est*, or *futūrum est, ut epistŏla scribātur*, a letter is about to be written. So *in eo erat*, etc., through all the tenses.

15. The participle in *dus*, with the verb *sum*, expresses *necessity* or *propriety*; as, *amandus sum*, I must be loved, *or* deserve to be loved. With the various moods and tenses of *sum*, it forms a *passive* periphrastic conjugation;—thus:

INDICATIVE.		SUBJUNCTIVE.	
Pres.	amandus sum,	*Pres.*	amandus sim,
Imperf.	amandus ĕram,	*Imperf.*	amandus essem,
Fut.	amandus ĕro,	*Perf.*	amandus fuĕrim,
Perf.	amandus fui,	*Plup.*	amandus fuissem.
Plup.	amandus fuĕram,		
Fut. Perf.	amandus fuĕro.	INFINITIVE.	
		Pres.	amandus esse,
		Perf	amandus fuisse.

REM. 5. The neuter of the participle in *dus* with *est* and the dative of a person, expresses the necessity of performing the action on the part of that person as, *mihi scribendum est* I must write, etc., and so through all the tenses.

Participles.

16. The following perfect participles of neuter verbs, like those of active deponents, are translated by active participles:—*cœnātus,* having supped; *pōtus,* having drunk; *pransus,* having dined; and sometimes *jurātus,* having sworn. So also *adultus, coalĭtus, conspirātus, interĭtus, occāsus, obsolētus,* and *crētus.*

For the active meaning of *ōsus* and its compounds, see § 183, 1.

17. (*a.*) The perfect participles of some deponent verbs have both an active and a passive sense; as, *adeptus libertātem,* having obtained liberty, *or adeptā libertāte,* liberty having been obtained. Cf. § 142, 4, (*b.*)

So *abominātus, comitātus, commentātus, complexus, confessus, contestātus, detestātus, dignātus, dimensus, effātus, emensus, ementītus, emerĭtus, expertus, execrātus, interpretātus, largītus, machinātus, meditātus, mercātus, meiātus, oblītus, opinātus, orsus, pactus, partītus, perfunctus, periclitātus, pollicĭtus, populātus, depopulātus, stipulātus, testātus, ultus, venerātus.*

(*b.*) The participle in *dus,* of deponent verbs, is commonly passive.

18. The perfect participles of neuter passive verbs have the signification of the active voice; as, *gavīsus,* having rejoiced. But *ausus* is used both in an active and a passive sense.

19. The genitive plural of participles in *rus* is seldom used, except that of *futūrus. Venturōrum* is found in Ovid, *exiturārum, transiturārum* and *periturōrum* in Seneca, and *moriturōrum* in Augustine.

20. In the third and fourth conjugations, the gerund and future passive participle (including deponents) sometimes end in *undum* and *undus,* instead of *endum* and *endus,* especially when *i* precedes; as, *faciundum, audiundum, scribundus. Potior* has usually *potiundus.*

21. Many present and perfect participles are compounded with *in,* signifying *not,* whose verbs do not admit of such composition; they thus become adjectives; as, *insciens,* ignorant; *imparātus,* unprepared.

22. Participles, when they do not express distinctions of time, become adjectives, and as such are compared; as, *amans,* loving; *amantior, amantissimus.* They sometimes also become substantives; as, *præfectus,* a commander; *ausum,* an attempt; *commissum,* an offence.

NOTE. Many words derived from substantives, with the terminations of participles, *ātus, ĭtus,* and *ūtus,* are yet adjectives; as, *alātus,* winged; *turrītus,* turreted, etc. See § 128, 7.

GENERAL RULES OF CONJUGATION.

§ **163.** 1. Verbs which have *a* in the first root have it also in the third, even when it is changed in the second; as, *făcio, factum hăbeo, habĭtum.*

2. The connecting vowel is often omitted in the second root, and in such cases, if *v* follows, it is changed into *u*. This happens in most verbs of the second conjugation.

REMARK. Some verbs of the first, second, and third conjugations prefix to the second root their initial consonant with the vowel which follows it, or with *ĕ*; as, *curro, cŭcurri; fallo, fĕfelli.* This prefix is called a *reduplication.*

NOTE 1. *Spondeo* and *sto* lose *s* in the second syllable, making *spŏpondī* and *stĕti.* For the verbs that take a reduplication, see §§ 165, R. 2; 168, N. 2; 171, EXC. 1,(*b.*)

3. Verbs which want the second root commonly want the third root also.

4. Compound verbs form their second and third roots like the simple verbs of which they are compounded; as, *audio, audīvi, audītum; exaudio, exaudīvi, exaudītum.*

NOTE 2. Some compound verbs, however, are defective, whose simples are complete, and some are complete, whose simples are defective.

EXC. 1. Compound verbs omit the reduplication; but the compounds of *do, sto, disco, posco,* and some of those of *curro,* retain it.

EXC. 2. Verbs which, in composition, change *a* into *e* in the first root, (see § 189, 1,) retain *e* in the second and third roots of the compound; as, *scando, scandi, scansum; descendo, descendi, descensum.*

EXC. 3. (*a.*) When *a*, *œ*, or *e*, in the first root of the simple verb, is changed in the compound into *i*, (see § 189, 2,) the same is retained in the second and third roots, in case the third root of the simple verb is a dissyllable; as, *hăbeo, hăbui, hăbĭtum; prohĭbeo, prohĭbui, prohĭbĭtum.*

(*b.*) But if the third root is a monosyllable, the second root of the compound has usually the same vowel as that of the simple, but sometimes changes *a* or *e* into *i*, and the third root has *e*; as, *făcio, fēci, factum; confĭcio, confēci, confectum; tĕneo, tĕnui, tentum; retĭneo, retĭnui, retentum; răpio, răpui, raptum; abrĭpio, abrĭpui, abreptum.*

NOTE 3. The compounds of *cădo, ăgo, frango, pango,* and *tango,* retain *a* in the third root. See § 172.

EXC. 4. The compounds of *părio,* (*ĕre*), and some of the compounds of *do* and *cŭbo,* are of different conjugations from their simple verbs. See *do, cŭbo* and *părio* in §§ 165 and 172.

A few other exceptions will be noticed in the following lists.

FORMATION OF SECOND AND THIRD ROOTS.

FIRST CONJUGATION.

§ 164. In regular verbs of this conjugation, the second root ends in *āv*, and the third in *āt;* as, *amo, amāvi, amātum.*

The following list contains such regular verbs of this conjugation as are of most frequent occurrence.

126 VERBS.—SECOND AND THIRD ROOTS. § 164.

NOTE. In this and subsequent lists, those verbs which are marked * are said to have no perfect participle; those marked † to have no present participle. A dash (—) after the present, denotes that there is no second root. The participles in *rus* and *dus*, and the supines in *um* and *u* which are in use, are indicated respectively by the letters r., d., m., and u. *Abundo*, for example, has no perfect participle, no supine, no participle in *dus*; but it has a present participle, and a participle in *rus*.

In the lists of irregular verbs, those compounds only are given, whose conjugation differs from that of their simples.

When *p.* is subjoined to a deponent verb, it denotes that some of the parts which have commonly an active meaning, are used either actively and passively, or passively alone. Such verbs are by some grammarians called *common*. Cf. § 142, 4, (b.)

*Abundo, r. *to overflow*.
Accūso, m. r. d. *to accuse*.
†Adumbro, *to delineate*.
Ædifĭco, r. d. *to build*.
Æquo, r. d. *to level*.
Æstĭmo, r. d. *to value*.
*Ambŭlo, m. d. *to walk*.
Amo, r. d. *to love*.
†Amplio, d. *to enlarge*.
Appello, d. *to call*.
Apto, d. *to fit*.
Aro, r. d. *to plough*.
*†Ausculto, *to listen*.
*†Autŭmo, *to assert*.
†Basio, —, d. *to kiss*.
*Bello, m. r. d. *to wage war*.
Beo, *to bless*.
Boo, *to bellow*.
†Brĕvio, *to shorten*.
†Cæco, *to blind*.
†Cælo, *to carve*.
†Calceo, d. *to shoe*.
*†Calcĭtro, *to kick*.
Canto, m. *to sing*.
Capto, m. r. d. *to seize*.
†Castīgo, m. d. *to chastise*.
Celĕbro, d. *to celebrate*.
Celo, d. *to conceal*.
Cesso, d. *to cease*.
Certo, r. d. *to strive*.
Clamo, *to shout*.
Cogĭto, d. *to think*.
Concĭlio, r. d. *to conciliate*.
Consīdĕro, r. d. *to consider*.
Cremo, d. *to burn*.—concrĕmo, r.
†Creo, r. d. *to create*.
Crucio, d. *to torment*.
Culpo, r. d. *to blame*.
†Cuneo, d. *to wedge in*.
Curo, r. d. *to care for*.
Damno, m. r. d. *to condemn*.
Decŏro, d. *to adorn*.
*Delĭneo, *to delineate*.
Desīdĕro, r. d. *to desire*.

Destĭno, d. *to design*.
Dico, nf. r. d. *to dedicate*.
Dicto, *to dictate*.
†Dolo, *to hew*.
Dono, r. d. *to bestow*.
Duplĭco, r. d. *to double*.
Duro, r. *to harden*.
†Effĭgio, *to portray*.
†Enucleo, *to explain*.
Equĭto, *to ride*.
Erro, *to wander*.
Existĭmo, n. r. d. *to think*.
Explōro, m. d. *to search*.
Exsŭlo, m. r. *to be banished*.
Fabrĭco, d. *to frame*.
†Fatīgo, r. d. *to weary*.
Festīno, r. *to hasten*.
Firmo, r. d. *to strengthen*.
Flagĭto, m. d. *to demand*.
*Flagro, r. *to be on fire*.—conflagro, r.—deflagro.
Flo, d. *to blow*.
Formo, r. d. *to form*.
Foro, d. *to bore*.
†Fraudo, d. *to defraud*.
†Freno, *to bridle*.
†Frio, —, *to crumble*.
Fugo, r. d. *to put to flight*.
†Fundo, r. *to found*.
†Furio, —, *to madden*.
†Galeo, —, *to put on a helmet*.
Gesto, d. *to bear*.
Glacio, —, *to congeal*.
Gravo, d. *to weigh down*.
Gusto, d. *to taste*.
Habĭto, m. d. *to dwell*.
*Halo, —, *to breathe*.
Hiĕmo, m. *to winter*.
*Hio, d. *to gape*.
†Humo, r. d. *to bury*.
Ignōro, r. d. *to be ignorant of*.
Impĕro, r. d. *to command*.
†Impetro, r. d. *to obtain*.
Inchŏo, *to begin*.
Indāgo, r. d. *to trace out*.

Indĭco, m. r. d. *to show*.
†Inēbrio, —, *to inebriate*.
Initio, *to initiate*.
Inquĭno, *to pollute*.
Instauro, d. *to renew*.
Intro, r. d. *to enter*.
Invīto, d. *to invite*.
Irrīto, r. d. *to irritate*.
Itĕro, u. d. *to do again*.
Jacto, r. d. *to throw*.
Judĭco, r. d. *to judge*.
Jugo, d. *to couple*.
Jugŭlo, m. d. *to butcher*.
Juro, d. *to swear*.
Labōro, r. d. *to labor*.
Lacĕro, d. *to tear*.
*Lacto, *to suckle*.
†Lanio, d. *to tear in pieces*.
Latro, *to bark*.
Laudo, r. d. *to praise*.
Laxo, d. *to loose*.
†Lego, *to depute*.
Levo, r. d. *to lighten*.
Libĕro, r. d. *to free*.
Libo, d. *to pour out*.
Ligo, *to bind*.
†Liquo, d. *to melt*.
Lito, *to appease*.
Loco, r. d. *to place*.
Lustro, d. *to survey*.
Luxŭrio, *to be luxuriant*.
Macto, d. *to sacrifice*.
Macŭlo, *to spot, stain*.
Mando, r. d. *to command*.
Mandūco, *to chew*.
*Mano, d. *to flow*.
Matūro, d. *to ripen*.
Memŏro, u. d. *to tell*.
*Meo, *to go*.
*Migro, u. r. d. *to depart*.
*Milĭto, m. r. *to serve as a soldier*.
†Minio, d. *to paint red*.
Ministro, d. *to serve*.
Mitĭgo, d. *to pacify*.
Monstro, r. *to show*.—†demonstro, d.
Muto, r. d. *to change*.

§ 165. VERBS.—SECOND AND THIRD ROOTS. 127

Narro, r. d. *to tell.*
Nato, m. r. *to swim.*
*Nauseo, *to be sea-sick*
†Navigo, r. d. *to sail.*
Navo, r. d. *to perform.*
Nego, m. r. d. *to deny.*
*No, *to swim.*
Nomino, r. d. *to name.*
Noto, d. *to mark.*
Novo, r. d. *to renew.*
Nudo, d. *to make bare.*
Nuncupo, r. d. *to name*
Nuntio, m. r. *to tell.—* renuntio, d.
*Nuto, r. *to nod.*
Obsecro, m. r. d. *to beseech.*
Obtrunco, r. *to kill.*
Onero, r. d. *to load.*
Opto, d. *to wish.*
†Orbo, r. *to bereave.*
Orno, r. d. *to adorn.*
Oro, m. r. d. *to beg.*
Paco, d. *to subdue.*
Paro, r. d. *to prepare.*
  comparo, d. *to compare.*
Patro, r. d. *to perform.*
*Pecco, r. d. *to sin.*
†Pio, d. *to propitiate.*
Placo, r. d. *to appease.*
Ploro, m. d. *to bewail.*
Porto, u. r. d. *to carry.*
Postulo, m. r. d. *to demand.*
Privo, d. *to deprive.*
Probo, m. u. r. d. *to approve.*—comprobo, m.
Profligo, d. *to rout.*
Propero, d. *to hasten.*
*†Propino, *to drink to.*
Propitio, d. *to appease.*
Pugno, r. d. *to fight.*
Pulso, d. *to beat.*
Purgo, u. r. d. *to cleanse.*

Puto, d. *to reckon.*
Quasso, d. *to shake.*
Radio, *to emit rays.*
Rapto, d. *to drag away.*
Recupero, m. r. d. *to recover.*
Recuso, r. d. *to refuse.*
Redundo, *to overflow.*
Regno, r. d. *to rule.*
†Repudio, r. d. *to reject.*
Resero, d. *to unlock.*
*†Retalio, —, *to retaliate.*
Rigo, *to water.*
Rogo, m. r. d. *to ask.*
Roto, *to whirl around.*
Sacrifico, m. *to sacrifice.*
Sacro, d. *to consecrate.*
†Sagino, d. *to fatten.*
Salto, r. *to dance.*
Saluto, m. r. d. *to salute.*
Sano, r. d. *to heal.*
Satio, *to satiate.*
†Saturo, *to fill.*
Saucio, d. *to wound.*
*Secundo, *to prosper.*
Sedo, m. d. *to allay.*
Servo, r. d. *to keep.*
*†Sibilo, r. *to hiss.*
Sicco, d. *to dry.*
Signo, r. d. *to mark out.—* assigno, m.
Simulo, r. d. *to pretend.*
Socio, d. *to associate.*
*Somnio, *to dream.*
Specto, m. r. d. *to behold.*
Spero, r. d. *to hope.*
*Spiro, *to breathe.*—conspiro. — exspiro, r.— suspiro, d.
Spolio, m. d. *to rob.*
Spumo, *to foam.*
Stillo, *to drop.*
Stimulo, *to goad.*
Stipo, *to stuff.*

Sudo, *to sweat.*
Suffoco, *to strangle.*
Sugillo, d. *to taunt.*
Supero, r. d. *to overcome.*
Suppedito, *to afford.*
*Supplico, m. *to supplicate.*
*Susurro, *to whisper.*
Tardo, *to delay.*
Taxo, d. *to rate.*
Temero, d. *to defile.*
Tempero, r. d. *to temper* —obtempero, r. *to obey.*
Tento, m. r. d. *to try.*
Terebro, *to bore.*
Termino, r. d. *to limit.*
Titubo, *to stagger.*
Tolero, u. r. d. *to bear.*
Tracto, u. d. *to handle.*
*†Tripudio, *to dance.*
Triumpho, r. *to triumph.*
Trucido, r. d. *to kill.*
Turbo, d. *to disturb.*
*Vaco, *to be at leisure.*
*Vapulo, m. d. *to be beaten.* Cf. § 142, 3.
Vario, *to diversify.*
Vasto, d. *to lay waste.*
Vellico, *to pluck.*
Verbero, r. d. *to beat.*
*Vestigo, *to search for*
Vexo, d. *to tease.*
Vibro, d. *to brandish.*
Vigilo, *to watch.*
Violo, m. r. d. *to violate.*
Vitio, d. *to vitiate.*
Vito, u. d. *to shun.*
Ululo, *to howl.*
Umbro, r. *to shade.*
Voco, r. d. *to call.*
*Volo, *to fly.*
Voro, r. *to devour.*
Vulgo, r. d. *to publish.*
Vulnero, d. *to wound.*

§ **165.** The following verbs of the first conjugation are either irregular or defective.

*Crepo, crepui, *to make a noise.* *discrepo, -ui, *or* -avi. increpo, -ui *or* -avi, -itum *or* -atum. *†percrepo, —. *†recrepo, —.

*Cubo, cubui, (*perf. subj.* cubaris; *inf.* cubasse), cubitum (*sup.*), *to recline.* incubo, -ui *or* avi, d. *Those compounds of* cubo *which take* m *before* b, *are of the third conjugation.*

Do, dedi, datum, m. r. d. *to give.—* So circumdo, pessumdo, satisdo, *and*

venumdo; *the other compounds of* do *are of the third conjugation. See* § 163, Exc. 1.

Domo, domui, domitum, r. d. *to tame.*

Frico, fricui, frictum *or* fricatum, d. *to rub.* confrico, —, -atum. So infrico. defrico, —, -atum *or* -ctum.

Juvo, juvi, jutum, r. d., *also* juvaturus, *to help.* adjuvo, -juvi, -jutum, m. r. d. *also* adjuvaturus.

*Labo, labasse, *to totter.*

Lăvo, lāvi, *rar.* lăvāvi, lavātum, lautum or lōtum; *(sup.)* lautum *or* lavātum, lavatūrus, d. *to wash.* Lăvo *is also sometimes of the third conjugation.*
*Mĭco, mĭcŭi, d. *to glitter.* dĭmĭco, -āvi *or* -ui, -atūrus. *emĭco, -ui, -atūrus. *intermĭco, —. *promĭco, —, d.
Nĕco, necāvi *or* necui, necātum, r. d. *to kill.* euĕco, -āvi *or* -ui, -ātum, *or* -ctum, d. †internĕco, —, -ātum.
*†Nexo, —, *to tie.*
Plĭco, —, plicātum, *to fold.* duplĭco, -āvi, -ātum, r. d. multiplĭco *and* replĭco *have* -āvi, -ātum. *supplĭco, -āvi, m. r. applĭco, -āvi *or* -ui, -ātum *or* -ĭtum, -itūrus. *So* implĭco, —complĭco, -ui, -ĭtum *or* ātum. explĭco, -āvi *or* -ui, -ātum *or* -ĭtum, -atūrus *or* -itūrus.
Pōto, potāvi, potātum *or* pōtum, r. r. m. m. d. *to drink.* †epōto, -āvi, -um. —*perpōto, -āvi.
Sĕco, secui, sectum, secatūrus, d. *to cut.*—*circumsĕco, —. *intersĕco —, d. *persĕco, -ui. præsĕco, -ui, -tum *or* -ātum. *So* resĕco, d.
*Sŏno, sonui, -atūrus, d. *to sound.* *consŏno, -ni. *So* ex-, in-, per-, præ-sŏno. *resŏno, -āvi. *assŏno, —. *So* circumsŏno *and* dissŏno.
*Sto, stĕti, statūrus, *to stand.* *antesto, -stĕti. *So* circumsto, intersto, supersto.—*Its compounds with nonosyllabic prepositions have* stĭti; as, *consto, -stĭti, -statūrus. *So* exsto, insto, obsto, persto. *præsto, -stĭti, -statūrus, d. *adsto *or* asto, -stĭti, -stitūrus. *prosto, -stĭti. *So* resto, restĭti: *but subj. perf.* restāvĕrit, Propert, 2, 34, 53. *disto, —. *So* substo *and* supersto.
*Tŏno, tonui, *to thunder. So* circumtŏno. attŏno, -ui, -ĭtum. intŏno, -ui, -ātum. *retŏno, —.
Vĕto, vetui, *rarely* āvi, vetĭtum, *to forbid.*

REMARK 1. The principal irregularity, in verbs of the first and second conjugations, consists in the omission of the connecting vowel in the second root, and the change of the long vowels *ā* and *ē* in the third root into *i*. The *v* remaining at the end of the second root, when it follows a consonant, is pronounced as *u*; as, *cubo*, (*cubāri*, by syncope *cubvi*), i. e. *cubui*; (*cubātum*, by change of the connecting vowel,) *cubĭtum.* Sometimes in the first conjugation, and very frequently in the second, the connecting vowel is omitted in the third root also; as, *juro*, (*āre*) *jūvi*, *jūtum*; *teneo*, (*ēre*) *tĕnui*, *tentum.* In the second conjugation several verbs whose general root ends in *d* and *g*, and a few others of different terminations, form either their second or third root or both, like verbs of the third conjugation, by adding *s*; as, *rideo*, *rīsi*, *rīsum*.

REM. 2. The verbs of the first conjugation whose perfects take a reduplication are *do*, *sto*, and their compounds.

REM. 3. The following verbs in *eo* are of the first conjugation, viz. *beo, calceo, creo, cuneo, enucleo, illaqueo, collineo, delineo, meo, nauseo, screo*; *eo* and its compounds are of the fourth.

§ 166.

All deponent verbs, of the first conjugation, are regular, and are conjugated like *mīror*, § 161; as,

Abomĭnor, d. *to abhor.*
Adūlor, d. *to flatter.*
Æmŭlor, d. *to rival.*
Ancillor, *to be a handmaid.*
*Aprĭcor, *to bask in the sun.*
Arbĭtror, r. d. *to think.*
Aspernor, d. p. *to despise.*
Aucŭpor, r. p. *to hunt after.*
Auxĭlior, p. *to help.*
Aversor, d. *to dislike.*
Bacchor, p *to revel.*
Calumnior, *to censure unfairly.*
Causor, *to allege.*
*Comissor, m. *to revel.*
Comĭtor, p. *to accompany.*
Conciōnor, *to harangue.*
*Confabŭlor, m. *to converse together.*
Cōnor, d. *to endeavor.*
ᴸConspĭcor, *to see.*
Contemplor, d. p. *to view attentively.*
Crimĭnor, m. p. *to complain of.*
Cunctor, d. p. *to delay.*
Deprĕcor, m. r. d. p. *to deprecate.*
*†Diglădior, *to fence.*
Dignor, d. p. *to deem worthy.*
Domĭnor, p. *to rule.*
Epŭlor, r. d. *to feast.*
*Famŭlor, m. *to wait on.*
Fatur, (defect.) n. d. p. *to speak. See* § 183, 6.
†Fērior, r. *to keep holiday.*
*Frumentor, m. *to forage.*
Fūror, m. *to steal.*
Glōrior, r. d. *to boast.*
Gratŭlor, m. d. *to congratulate.*

§ 167.   VERBS.—SECOND AND THIRD ROOTS.   129

Hariŏlor, to practise soothsaying.
Hortor, d. to encourage.
Imĭtor, u. r. d. to imitate.
Indignor, d. to disdain.
Infĭtior, d. to deny.
Insector, to pursue.
Insĭdior, r. d. to lie in wait for.
Interprĕtor, p. to explain.
Jacŭlor, p. to hurl.
Jŏcor, to jest.
Lætor, r. d. p. to rejoice.
Lamentor, d. p. to bewail.
*†Lignor, m. to gather wood.
Luctor, d. to wrestle.
Medĭcor, r d. p. to heal.
Medĭtor, p to meditate.
Mercor, m. r. d. p. to buy.
Minor, to threaten.
Miror, u. r. d. to admire.
Miserŏr, d. to pity.
Modĕror, u. d. to govern.

Modŭlor, d. p. to modulate.
Mŏror, r. d. to delay.
†Mūtuor, p. to borrow.
Negōtior, r. to traffic.
*†Nūgor, p. to trifle.
Obsōnor, m. to cater.
Obtestor, p. to beseech.
Opĕror, to work.
Opīnor, u. r. d. to think.
Opitŭlor, m. to help.
†Otior, to be at leisure.
Pabŭlor, m. d. to graze.
Pālor, to wander about.
Percontor, m. to inquire.
Periclĭtor, d. p. to try.
†Piscor, m. to fish.
Popŭlor, r. d. p. to lay waste.
Prædor, m. p. to plunder.
Precor, m. u. r. d. to pray.
Prœlior, to fight.
Recordor, d. to recollect.
Rīmor, d. to search.
Rixor, to quarrel.

*Rustĭcor, to live in the country.
Seiscĭtor, m. p. to inquire.
*Scītor, m. to ask.
Scrūtor, p. to search.
Sōlor, d. to comfort.
Spātior, to walk about.
Specŭlor, m. r. d. to spy out.
†Stipŭlor, p. to bargain, stipulate.
†Suāvior, d. to kiss.
Suspĭcor, to suspect.
Testifĭcor, p. to testify.
Testor, d. p. to testify. do detestor.
Tūtor, to defend.
Vāgor, to wander.
Venĕror, d. p. to venerate, worship.
Vēnor, m. p. to hunt.
Versor, to be employed.
Vocifĕror, to bawl.

NOTE. Some deponents of the first conjugation are derived from nouns, and signify being or practising that which the noun denotes; as, ancillāri, to be a handmaid; hariolāri, to practise soothsaying; from ancilla and hariŏlus.

SECOND CONJUGATION.

§ 167. Verbs of the second conjugation end in eo, and form their second and third roots in u and ĭt; as, moneo, monui, monĭtum.

The following list contains most of the regular verbs of this conjugation, and many also which want the second and third roots:—

*Aceo, to be sour.
*Ægreo, —, to be sick.
*Albeo, —, to be white.
*Arceo, d. to drive away; part. adj. arctus or artus. The compounds change a into e; as, coerceo, d. to restrain. exerceo, r. d. to exercise.
*Areo, to be dry.
*Aveo, —, to covet.
*Cāleo, r. to be warm.
*Calleo, —, to be hardened. *percalleo, to know well.
*Calveo, —, to be bald.
*Candeo. to be white.
*Cāneo to be hoary.
*Careo, r. d. to want.
*Cevco —, to j'wn.

*Clāreo, —, to be bright.
*Clueo, —, to be famous.
*Denseo, —, to thicken.
*Diribeo, — to sort the voting tablets.
*Doleo, r. d. to grieve.
*Egeo, r. to want.
*Emineo, to rise above.
*Flacceo, to droop.
*Flāveo, — to be yellow.
*Flōreo, to blossom.
*Fœteo, — to be fetid.
*Frigeo, —, to be cold.
*Frondeo, —, to bear leaves.
Hăbeo, r. d. to have. The compounds, except posthăbeo, change ă into I; as. ad-, ex-, pro-hibeo. cohĭbeo, d. to restrain. inhĭbeo, d. to hinder.

*†perhĭbeo, d. to report.
†posthăbeo, to postpone.
præbeo, (for præhĭbeo), r. d. to afford.
*præhĭbeo, —. dŭbeo, (for dehăbeo), r. d. to owe.
*Hĕbeo, —, to be dull.
*Horreo, d. to be rough.
*Hūmeo. —. to be moist.
*Jăceo, r. to lie.
*Lucteo, —, to suck.
*Langueo, —, to be faint
*Lāteo, to lie hid.
*Lenteo, —, to be slow.
*Lĭceo, to be valued.
*Līveo, —, to be livid.
*Măceo, —, to be lean.
*Mādeo, to be wet.
*Mareo, —, to grieve.
Mĕreo, r. to deserve.

130 VERBS.—SECOND AND THIRD ROOTS. § 168

†commĕreo, *to fully deserve.* †dēmĕreo, d. *to earn.* †emĕreo, *to serve out one's time.* *†permĕreo, —, *to go through service.* promĕreo, *to deserve.*
Mŏneo, r. d. *to advise.* admŏneo, m. r. d. *to remind.* commŏneo, *to impress upon.* præmŏneo, *to forewarn.*
*Mūceo, —, *to be mouldy.*
*Nigreo, —, *to be black.*
*Niteo, *to shine.*
Nŏceo, m ~. *to hurt.*
*Oleo, *to smell.*
*Palleo, *to be pale.*

*Pāreo, m. r. d. *to obey.*
*Pāteo, *to be open.*
Plăceo, *to please.*
*Polleo, —, *to be able.*
*Pūteo, *to stink.*
*Putreo, *to be putrid.*
*Renīdeo, —, *to glitter.*
*Rīgeo, *to be stiff.*
*Rŭbeo, *to be red.*
*Scăteo, —, *to gush forth.*
*Sĕneo, —, *to be old.*
*Sĭleo, d. *to be silent.*
*Sordeo, —, *to be filthy.*
*Splendeo, —, *to shine.*
*Squāleo, —, *to be foul.*
*Strīdeo, —, *to creak.*
*Stŭdeo, d. *to study.*
*Stŭpeo, *to be amazed.*

*Sueo, —, *to be wont.*
Tăceo, r. d. *to be silent.*
*Tĕpeo, *to be warm.*
Terreo, d. *to terrify.* So deterreo, *to deter.* †absterreo, *to deter.* †conterreo, †exterreo, †perterreo, *to frighten.*
*Tĭmeo, d. *to fear.*
*Torpeo, —, *to be stiff.*
*Tŭmeo, *to swell.*
*Vălco, r. *to be able.*
*Vĕgeo, —, *to arouse.*
*Vieo, —, *to plait.* Pa. viētus, *shriveled.*
*Vīgeo, *to flourish.*
*Vīreo, *to be green.*
*Uveo, —, *to be moist.*

§ 168. The following verbs of the second conjugation are irregular in their second or third roots or in both.

NOTE 1. As the proper form of verbs of the first conjugation is, *o, āvi, ātum,* of the fourth *io, īvi, ītum,* so that of the second would be *eo, ēvi, ētum.* Very few of the latter conjugation, however, retain this form, but most of them, as noticed in § 165, Rem. 1, drop in the second root the connecting vowel, *ē,* and those in *veo* drop *vē*; as, *cāreo, (cāvēri) cāvi, (cāvētum* or *cārītum) cautum.* Others, imitating the form of those verbs of the third conjugation whose general root ends in a consonant, add *s* to form the second and third roots. Cf. § 165, Rem. 1, and § 171.

NOTE 2. Four verbs of the second conjugation take a reduplication in the parts formed from the second root, viz. *mordeo, pendeo, spondeo,* and *tondeo.* See § 163, Rem.

Abŏleo, -ēvi, -ītum, r. d. *to efface.*
*Algeo, alsi, *to be cold.*
Ardeo, arsi, arsum, r. *to burn.*
Audeo, ausus sum, (*rarely* ausi, *whence* ausim, § 183, R. 1,) r. d. *to dare.*
Augeo, auxi, auctum, r. d. *to increase.*
Căveo, cāvi, cautum, m. d. *to beware.*
Censeo, censui, censum, d. *to think.* recenseo, -ui, -um *or* -ītum. *perceuseo, -ni. *succenseo, -ui, d.
Cieo, cīvi, cītum, *to excite.* There is a cognate form, cio, *of the fourth conjugation, both of the simple verb and of its compounds. The penult of the participles* excitus *and* concitus *is common, and that of* accītus *is always long.*
*Connīveo, -nīvi, *to wink at.*
Dēleo, -ēvi, -ētum, d. *to blot out.*
Dŏceo, docui, doctum, d. *to teach.*
*Făveo, fāvi, fautūrus, *to favor.*
*Ferveo, ferbui, *to boil. Sometimes* fervo, vi, *of the third conjugation.*
Fleo, flēvi, flētum, r. d. *to weep.*
Fŏveo, fōvi, fōtum, d. *to cherish.*

*Fulgeo, fulsi, *to shine.* Fulgo, *of the third conjugation, is also in use.*
Gaudeo, gavīsus sum, r. *to rejoice.* § 142, 2.
*Hæreo, hæsi, hæsūrus, *to stick.* So ad-, co-, in-, ob- hæreo; *but* *subhæreo, —.
Indulgeo, indulsi, indultum, r. d. *to indulge.*
Jŭbeo, jussi, jussum, r. d. *to order.*
*Lūceo, luxi, *to shine.* pollūceo, -luxi -luctum.
*Lūgeo, luxi, d. *to mourn.*
*Măneo, mansi, mansum, m. r. d. *to remain.*
Misceo, miscui, mistum *or* mixtum. mistūrus, d. *to mix.*
Mordeo, momordi morsum, d. *to bite.* remordeo, -di, -morsum, r.
Mŏveo, mōvi, mōtum, r. d. *to move.*
Mulceo, mulsi, mulsum, d. *to soothe.* permulceo, permulsi, permulsum *and* permulctum, *to rub gently.*
*Mulgeo, mulsi *or* mulxi, *to milk.* emulgeo, —, emulsum, *to milk out.*

Neo, nēvi, nētum, *to spin.*
*Păveo, pāvi, d. *to fear.*
*Pendeo, pependi, *to hang.* *impendeo, —. propendeo, —, propensum.
Pleo, (*obsolete*). compleo, -ēvi, -ētum, *to fill.* So the other compounds.
Prandeo, prandi, pransum, r. *to dine.*
Rideo, risi, rīsum, m. r. d. *to laugh.*
*Sĕdeo, sēdi, sessum, m. r. *to sit.*
The compounds with monosyllabic prepositions change ĕ into ī, in the first root; as, insīdeo, insēdi, insessum. *dissīdeo, -sēdi. So præsīdeo, and rarely circumsīdeo.
Sŏleo, solĭtus sum *and rarely* solui, *to be accustomed.* § 142, 2.
*Sorbeo, sorbui, *to suck in.* So *exsorbeo: but* *resorbeo, —. *absorbeo, -sorbui *or* -sorpsi.

Spondeo, spopondi, sponsum *o promise.* See § 168, Rem.
*Strīdeo, idi, *to whiz.*
Suādeo, suāsi, suāsum, r. d. *to advise.*
Tĕneo, tĕnui, tentum, r. d. *to hold.* The compounds change ĕ into i in the first and second roots; as, detineo, detinui, detentum. *attineo, -tinui. So pertineo.
Tergeo, tersi, tersum, *to wipe.* Tergo, *of the third conjugation, is also in use.*
Tondeo, tŏtondi, tonsum, *to shear.* The compounds have the perfect tondi.
Torqueo, torsi, tortum, d. *to twist.*
Torreo, torrui, tostum, *to roast.*
*Turgeo, tursi, *to swell.*
*Urgeo *or* urgueo, ursi, d. *to urge.*
Vĭdeo, vĭdi, vīsum, m. u. r. d. *to see.*
Vŏveo, vōvi, vōtum, d. *to vow.*

§ 169. *Impersonal Verbs of the Second Conjugation.*

Dĕcet, decuit, *it becomes.*
Libet, libuit *or* libitum est, *it pleases, is agreeable.*
Licet, licuit *or* licitum est, *it is lawful,* or *permitted.*
Liquet, liquit, *it is clear, evident.*
Mĭsĕret, miseruit *or* miserĭtum est, *it moves to pity;* miseret me, *I pity.*
Oportet, oportuit, *it behooves.*

Pĭget, piguit *or* pigĭtum est, d. *it troubles, grieves.*
Pœnĭtet, pœnituit, pœnitūrus, d. *it repents;* pœnitet me, *I regret.*
Pŭdet, puduit *or* pudĭtum est, d.; *it shames;* pudet me, *I am ashamed.*
Tædet, tæduit *or* tæsum est, *it disgusts or wearies.* pertædet, pertæsum est.

NOTE. *Lŭbet* is sometimes written for *libet*, especially in the comic writers.

§ 170. *Deponent Verbs of the Second Conjugation.*

Fătĕor, fassus, r. d. p. *to confess.* The compounds change ă into i in the first root, and into e in the third; as, confĭteor, confessus, d. p. *to acknowledge.* *†diffĭteor, *to deny.* profĭteor, professus, d. p. *to declare.*
Licĕor, licĭtus, *to bid a price.*

*Mĕdĕor, d. *to cure.*
Mĕreor, merĭtus, *to deserve.*
Misĕreor, miserĭtus *or* misertus, *to pity.*
Pollĭceor, pollicĭtus, p. *to promise.*
Reor, rātus, *to think, suppose.*
Tueor, tuĭtus, d. p. *to protect.*
Vĕreor, verĭtus, d. p. *to fear.*

THIRD CONJUGATION.

§ 171.
In the third conjugation, when the first root ends with a consonant, the second root is regularly formed by adding *s*; when it ends with a vowel, the first and second roots are the same: the third root is formed by adding *t*; as, carpo, **carpsi**, carptum; arguo, argui, argūtum.

In annexing *s* and *t*, certain changes occur in the final consonant of the root:—

1. The palatals *c, g, qu,* and also *h*, at the end of the first root, form with *s* the double letter *x*; in the third root, *c* remains, and the others are changed into *c* before *t*; as, dico, (dicsi, i. e.), dixi, dictum; rego (regsi, i. e.), rexi, rectum; veho, vexi, rectum; cŏquo, coxi, coctum.

NOTE. *Fluo* and *struo* form their second and third roots after the analogy of verbs whose first root ends in a palatal or *h*.

2. *B* is changed into *p* before *s* and *t*; as, *scribo, scripsi, scriptum*.

3. *D* and *t*, before *s*, are either dropped, or changed into *s*; as, *claudo, clausi; cēdo, cessi; mitto, misi*. Cf. § 56, I, Rem. 1. After *m*, *p* is sometimes inserted before *s* and *t*; as, *sūmo, sumpsi, sumptum*. *R* is changed to *s* before *s* and *t* in *gĕro* and *ūro*.

4. Some other consonants are dropped, or changed into *s*, in certain verbs.

EXC. 1. Many verbs whose first root ends in a consonant, do not add *s* to form the second root.

(*a*.) Of these, some have the second root the same as the first, but the vowel of the second root, if a monosyllable, is long; as,

Bĭbo,	Excūdo,	Īco,	Mando,	Scăbo,	Solvo,	Verro,
Edo,	Fŏdio,	Lambo,	Prehendo,	Scando,	Strīdo,	Verto,
Emo,	Fŭgio,	Lĕgo,	Psallo,	Sīdo,	Tollo,	Volvo;

to which add the compounds of the obsolete *cando*, *fendo*, and *nuo*.

(*b*.) Some make a change in the first root. Of these, some change a vowel, some drop a consonant, some prefix a reduplication, others admit two or more of these changes; as,

Ago, ēgi.	Căpio, cēpi.	Făcio, fēci.
Findo, fĭdi.	Frango, frēgi.	Fundo, fūdi.
Jăcio, jēci.	Linquo, liqui.	Rumpo, rūpi.
Scindo, scĭdi.	Sisto, stĭti.	Vinco, vīci.

Those which have a reduplication are

Cădo, cĕcĭdi.	Cædo, cĕcĭdi.	Căno, cĕcĭni.
Curro, cŭcurri.	Disco, dĭdĭci.	Fallo, fĕfelli.
Păgo, (*obs*.) pĕpĭgi	Parco, pĕperci.	Pārio, pĕpĕri.
and pēgi.	Pĕdo, pĕpēdi.	Pello, pĕpŭli.
Pendo, pĕpendi.	Posco, pŏposci.	Pungo, pŭpŭgi.
Tango, tĕtĭgi.	Tendo, tĕtendi.	Tundo, tŭtŭdi.

EXC. 2. Some, after the analogy of the second conjugation, add *u* to the first root of the verb; as,

Alo, alui, etc.	Consŭlo,	Gĕmo,	Răpio,	Trĕmo,
Cŏlo,	Depso,	Gĕno, (*obs*.)	Strĕpo,	Vŏlo,
Compesco,	Frĕmo,	Mŏlo,	Texo,	Vŏmo.

Mĕto, messui; and *pŏno, pŏsui*; add *su*, with a change in the root.

EXC. 3. The following, after the analogy of the fourth conjugation, add *iv* to the first root:—

| Arcesso, | Cŭpio, | Lăcesso, | Rŭdo, | Tĕro, *dropping* ĕ. |
| Căpesso, | Incesso, | Pĕto, | Quæro, *with a change of* r *into* s. |

EXC. 4. The following add *v*, with a change in the root; those in *no* and *sco* dropping *n* and *sc*, and those having *er* before *n* changing it to *rē* or *rā*:—

| Cresco, | Pasco, | Scisco, | Sperno, | Lĭno, | Sĕro, |
| Nosco, | Quiesco, | Cerno, | Sterno, | Sĭno, | *to sow*. |

EXC. 5. (*a*.) The third root of verbs whose first root ends in *d* or *t*, and some in *g*, add *s*, instead of *t*, to the root, either dropping the *d, t,* and *g*, or changing them into *s*; as, *claudo, clausum; defendo, dēfensum; cēdo, cessum; flecto, flexum; figo, fixum*. But the compounds of *do* add *ĭt*; as, *perdo, perdĭtum*.

§ 172.   VERBS.—SECOND AND THIRD ROOTS.

(b.) The following, also, add s, with a change of the root:—

Excello,   Fallo,   Pello,   Spargo,   Verro.
Percello, Mergo,   Premo,   Vello,

Exc. 6. The following add t, with a change of the root; those having n, nc, ng, nqu, or mp at the end of the first root dropping n and m in the third:—

Cerno,   Fingo,   Gero,   Sero,   Sperno, Stringo, Uro,
Colo,   Frango, Rumpo,   Sisto,   Sterno, Tero,   Vinco;

to which add the compounds of *linquo*, and verbs in *sco* with the second root in *v*; the latter drop *sc* before *t*; as, *nosco, novi, notum*; except *pasco*, which drops *c* only.

Exc. 7. (a.) The following have *ŭi*:—

Bibo,   Elicio,   Molo,   Pono, *with a change of* ōn *into* ŏs.
Geno, (*obs. form of* gigno,) Vomo,   Sino, *dropping* n.

(b.) The following, like verbs of the fourth conjugation, add *ii* to the first root:—

Arcesso,   Cupio,   Peto,   Tero, *dropping* e.
Facesso,   Lacesso, Quæro, *with a change of* r *into* s.

For other irregularities occurring in this conjugation, see § 172-174.

§ **172.** The following list contains most of the simple verbs, both regular and irregular, in the third conjugation, with such of their compounds as require particular notice:—

Acuo, acui, acutum, d. *to sharpen.*
Ago, egi, actum, r. d. *to drive.* So circumago, cogo, *and* perago. *ambigo,* —, *to doubt.* So satago. *The other compounds change* a *into* i, *in the first root;* as, exigo, exegi, exactum, *to drive out.* *prodigo, -egi, *to squander.* See § 189, 2.
Alo, alui, altum, *and later* alitum, d. *to nourish.*
*Ango, anxi, *to strangle.*
Arguo, argui, argutum, d. *to convict.*
Arcesso, -cessivi, -cessitum, r. d. *to call for. Pass. inf.* arcessiri *or* arcessi.
*Batuo, batui, d. *to beat.*
Bibo, bibi, bibitum, d. *to drink.*
*Cado, cecidi, casurus, *to fall. The compounds change* a *into* i, *in the first root, and drop the reduplication;* as, occido, -cidi, -casum, r. *to set.*
Cædo, cecidi, cæsum, r. d. *to cut. The compounds change* æ *into* i, *and drop the reduplication;* as, occido, -cidi, -cisum.
Cando, (*obsolete,*) *synonymous with* candeo *of the second conjugation. Hence* accendo, -cendi, -censum, d. *to kindle.* So incendo, succendo.
*Cano, cecini, d. *to sing. The compounds change* a *into* i; *as,* *concino,

-cinui. So occino, præcino. *accino, —. So incino, intercino, succino, recino.
*Capesso, -ivi, r. d. *to undertake.*
Capio, cepi, captum, r. d. *to take. So* antecapio. *The other compounds change* a *into* i, *in the first root, and into* e *in the third; as,* decipio, decepi, deceptum.
Carpo, carpsi, carptum, d. *to pluck. The compounds change* a *into* e; *as,* decerpo, decerpsi, deceptum.
Cedo, cessi, cessum, r. *to yield.*
Cello, (*obsolete.*) excello, -cellui, -celsum, *to excel.* *antecello, —. *So* præcello, recello. percello, -culi, -culsum, *to strike.*
Cerno, crevi, cretum, d. *to decree.*
*Cerno, —. *to see.*
Cingo, cinxi, cinctum, d. *to gird.*
*Clango, —, *to clang.*
Claudo, clausi, clansum, r. d. *to shut. The compounds change* au *into* u; *as,* occludo, occlusi, occlusum, *to shut up.*
*†Claudo, —, *to limp.*
*†Clepo, clepsi, *rarely* clepi, *to steal.*
Colo, colui, cultum, d. *to till.* †occulo, -cului, -cultum, d. *to hide.*
Como, compsi, comptum, *to deck.*
*Compesco, -pescui, *to restrain.*

12

Consŭlo, -sŭlui, -sultum, m. r. d. *to consult.*
Cŏquo, coxi, coctum, m. d. *to cook.*
Crēdo, crēdĭdi, crēdĭtum, r. d. *to believe.*
*Cresco, crēvi, *to grow.* concresco, -crēvi, -crētum.
Cūbo *is of the first conjugation.* Cf. § 165. *accumbo, -cŭbui, *to lie down. So the other compounds which insert* m.
*Cūdo, —, *to forge.* excūdo, -cūdi, -cūsum, d. *to stamp.*
Cŭpĭo, cŭpīvi, cŭpĭtum, d. *to desire. Subj. imperf.* cŭpīret. *Lucr.* 1, 72.
*Curro, cŭcurri, cursūrus, *to run.* concurro, succurro, *and* transcurro, *drop the reduplication; the other compounds sometimes drop, and sometimes retain it; as,* dĕcurro, dĕcurri, *and* dĕcŭcurri, dĕcursum. *antĕcurro, —. So circumcurro.*
*Dēgo, dēgi, d. *to live.*
Dēmo, dempsi, demptum, r. d. *to take away.*
†Depso, depsui, depstum, *to knead.*
Dīco, dixi, dictum, u. r. d. *to say.*
*Disco, dĭdĭci, discitūrus, d. *to learn.*
*Dispesco, —, *to separate.*
Dīvĭdo, dīvīsi, dīvīsum, r. d. *to divide.*
Do *is of the first conjugation.* abdo, -dĭdi, -dĭtum, d. *to hide.* So condo, indo, addo, -dĭdi, -dĭtum, r. d. *to add.* So dēdo, ēdo, prōdo, reddo, trādo, vendo. †dīdo, -dĭdi, -dĭtum, *to distribute.* So abdo, subdo, perdo, -dĭdi, -dĭtum, m. r. d. abscondo, -di *or* -dĭdi, -dĭtum *or* -sum.
Dūco, duxi, ductum, m. r. d. *to lead.*
Edo, ēdi, ēsum, m. u. r. d. *to eat.*
Exuo, exui, exūtum, d. *to strip off.*
Emo, ēmi, emptum, r. d. *to buy.* So coemo. *The other compounds change* ĕ *to* ī; as, exĭmo, -ēmi, -emptum.
Făcesso, -cessi, -cessītum, *to execute.*
Făcio, fēci, factum, m. u. r. d. *to do. Compounded with a preposition, it changes* ă *into* ĭ *in the first root, and into* e *in the third, makes* -fĭce *in the imperative, and has a regular passive. Compounded with other words, it retains* ă *when of this conjugation, makes* făc *in the imperative, and has the passive,* fīo, factum. *See* § 180.
Fallo, fĕfelli, falsum, d. *to deceive.*
*refello, -felli, d. *to refute.*
Fendo, (*obsolete.*) dēfendo, -fendi, -fensum, m. u. r. d. *to defend.* offendo, -fendi, -fensum, d. *to offend.*
Fĕro, tŭli, lātum, r. d. *to bear. See* § 179. *A perfect* tĕtŭli *is rare. Its compounds are* affĕro attŭli, allātum;

aufĕro, abstŭli, ablātum; diffĕro, distŭli, dilātum; confĕro, contŭli, collātum; infĕro, intŭli, illātum; offĕro, obtŭli, oblātum; effĕro, extŭli, elātum; suffĕro, sustŭli, sublātum; *and* circum-, per-, trans-, dē-, prō-, antĕ-, præfĕro, -tŭli, -lātum.
*Fervo, vi, *to boil.* Cf. ferveo, 2d *conj.*
Fīdo, —, fīsus, *to trust.* *See* § 162, 18. confīdo, confīsus sum *or* confīdi, *to rely on.* diffīdo, diffī.us sum, *to distrust.*
Fīgo, fixi, fixum, r. *rarely* fictum, *to fix.*
Findo, fĭdi, fissum, d. *to cleave.*
Fingo, finxi, fictum, d. *to feign.*
Flecto, flexi, flexum, r. d. *to bend.*
*Flīgo, flīxi, *to dash.* So conflīgo. afflīgo, -flixi, -flictum, *to afflict.* So inflīgo. proflīgo *is of the first conjugation.*
Fluo, fluxi, fluxum, (fluctum, *obs.*) r. *to flow.*
Fŏdio, fōdi, fossum, d. *to dig. Old pres. inf. pass.* fŏdīri: *so also* effŏdīri.
Frango, frēgi, fractum, r. d. *to break. The compounds change* a *into* i, *in the first root; as,* infringo, infrēgi, infractum, *to break in upon.*
*Frĕmo, frĕmui, d. *to roar, howl.*
Frendo, —, frēsum *or* fressum, *to gnash.*
Frīgo, frixi, frictum, *rarely* frixum, *to roast.*
*Fŭgio, fŭgi, fŭgĭtūrus, d. *to flee.*
*Fulgo, —, *to flash.*
Fundo, fūdi, fūsum, r. d. *to pour.*
*Fŭro, —, *to rage.*
*Gĕmo, gĕmui, d. *to groan.*
Gĕro, gessi, gestum, r. d. *to bear.*
Gigno, (*obsolete* gĕno,) gĕnui, gĕnĭtum, r. d. *to beget.*
*Glisco, —, *to grow.*
*Glūbo, —, *to peel.* deglūbo, —, -gluptum.
Gruo, (*obsolete.*) *congruo, -grui, *to agree.* So ingruo.
Ico, ĭci, ictum, r. *to strike.*
Imbuo, imbui, imbūtum, d. *to imbue.*
*Incesso, -cessīvi *or* -cessi, *to attack.*
†Induo, indui, indūtum, *to put on.*
Jăcio, jēci, jactum, d. *to cast. The compounds change* ă *into* ĭ *in the first root, and into* e *in the third.* (§ 163, *Exc.* 3); *as,* rejĭcio, rejēci, rejectum.
Jungo, junxi, junctum, r. d. *to join.*
Lăcesso, -cessīvi, -cessītum, r. d. *to provoke.*
Lăcio, (*obsolete.*) *The compounds change* ă *into* ĭ; *as,* allĭcio, -lexi, -lectum, d. *to allure.* So illĭcio, pellĭcio. ēlĭcio, -lĭcui, -lĭcĭtum, *to draw out.*

§ 172. VERBS.—SECOND AND THIRD ROOTS. 135

Lædo, læsi, læsum, m. r. *to hurt.* *The compounds change æ into ī; as,* illīdo, illīsi, illīsum, *to dash against.*
*Lambo, lambi, *to lick.*
Lĕgo, lēgi, lectum, r. d. *to read.* So allĕgo, perlĕgo, prælĕgo, relĕgo, sublĕgo, *and* translĕgo; *the other compounds change* ĕ *into* ī; *as,* collīgo, collēgi, collectum, *to collect. But the following add* s *to form the second root;* § 171, 1; dilīgo, -lexi, -lectum, *to love.* intellīgo, -lexi, -lectum, u. r. d. *to understand.* neglīgo, -lexi, -lectum, r. d. *to neglect.*
Lingo, —, linctum, d. *to lick.* *delingo, —, *to lick up.*
Lino, līvi *or* lēvi, litum, d. *to daub.*
*Linquo, līqui, d. *to leave.* relinquo, -līqui, -lictum, r. d. delinquo, -līqui, -lictum. *So* derelinquo.
Lūdo, lūsi, lūsum, m. r. *to play.*
*Luo, lui, luitūrus, d. *to atone.* abluo, -lui, -lūtum, r. d. diluo, -lui, -lūtum, d. *So* eluo.
Mando, mandi, mansum, d. *to chew.*
Mergo, mersi, mersum, r. d. *to dip.* *So* immergo; *but pres. inf. pass.* immergēri, Col. 5, 9, 3.
Mĕto, messui, messum, d. *to reap.*
Mĕtuo, metui, metūtum, d. *to fear.*
*Mingo, minxi, mictum, (*sup.*) *to make water.*
Minuo, minui, minūtum, d. *to lessen.*
Mitto, misi, missum, r. d. *to send.*
Molo, molui, molĭtum, *to grind.*
Mungo, (*obsolete.*) emungo, -munxi, -munctum, *to wipe the nose.*
Necto, nexi, nexum, d. *to knit.* hinecto, -nexui, -nexum. *So* annecto, connecto.
*Ningo *or* -guo, ninxi, *to snow.*
Nosco, nōvi, nōtum, d. *to learn.* agnosco, -nōvi, -nĭtum, d. *to recognize.* cognosco, -nōvi, -nĭtum, u. r. d. *to know.* *So* recognosco. *internosco, nōvi, *to distinguish between.* præcognosco, —, præcognĭtum, *to fore-know.* *dignosco, —. *So* prænosco. ignosco, -nōvi, -nōtum, d. *to pardon.*
Nūbo, nupsi, *or* nupta sum, nuptum, m. r. *to marry.*
Nuo, (*obsolete,*) *to nod.* *abnuo, -nui, -nuitūrus, d. *to refuse.* *annuo, -nui. *So* innuo, renuo.
*Olo, ōlui, *to smell.*
Pando, —, passum *or* pansum, *to open.* *So* expando. dispando, —, -pansum.
Pago, (*obs. the same as* paco *whence* pāciscor,) pĕpĭgi, pactum, *to bargain:* *hence*
Pango, panxi *or* pēgi, pactum panctū-

rus, d. *to drive in.* compingo, -pēgi, -pactum. *So* impingo. *oppango, -pēgi. *depango, —. *So* repango, suppingo.
*Parco, pĕperci *rarely* parsi, parsūrus, *to spare.* *Some of the compounds change a to* e; as, *comparco *or* comperco. *imperco, —.
Pario, pĕpĕri, partum, pārĭtūrus, d. *to bring forth.* *The compounds are of the fourth conjugation.*
Pasco, pāvi, pastum, m. r. d. *to feed.*
Pecto, —, pexum, *and* pectĭtum, d. *to comb.* *So* depecto. repecto.
*Pēdo, pĕpēdi. *oppēdo, —.
Pello, pĕpŭli, pulsum, d. *to drive.* *Its compounds are not reduplicated.*
Pendo, pĕpendi, pensum, r. *to weigh.* *The compounds drop the reduplication. See* § 163, *Exc.* 1.
Pĕto, petīvi, petītum, m. u. r. d. *to ask.*
Pingo, pinxi, pictum, *to paint.*
Pinso, pinsi, pinsĭtum, pinsum *or* pistum, *to pound.*
*Plango, planxi, planctūrus, *to lament.*
Plaudo, plausi, plausum, d. *to clap, applaud.* *So* applaudo. *†circumplaudo, —. *The other compounds change* au *into* ō.
Plecto, —, plexum, d. *to twine.*
*Pluo, plui *or* plūvi, *to rain.*
Pōno, pōsui, (*anciently* posīvi), pŏsĭtum, r. d. *to place.*
*†Porricio, —, *to offer sacrifice.*
*Posco, pŏposci, d. *to demand.*
Prehendo, }
Prendo,   } -di, -sum, r. d. *to seize.*
Prĕmo, pressi, pressum, r. d. *to press.* *The compounds change* ĕ *into* ī, *in the first root; as,* imprĭmo, impressi, impressum, *to impress.*
Prōmo, prompsi, promptum, r. d. *to bring out.*
*Psallo, psalli, *to play on a stringed instrument.*
Pungo, pŭpŭgi, punctum, *to prick.* compungo, -punxi, -punctum. *So* dispungo, expungo. interpungo, —, -punctum. *repungo, —.
Quæro, quæsīvi, quæsītum, m. r. d. *to seek.* *The compounds change* æ *into* ī; *as,* requīro, requisīvi, requisītum, *to seek again.*
Quătio, —, quassum, *to shake.* *The compounds change* quă *into* cŭ; *as,* concŭtio, -cussi, -cussum, d. discŭtio, -cussi, -cussum, r. d.
Quiesco, quiēvi, quiētum, r. d. *to rest.*
Rādo, rāsi, rāsum, d. *to shave.*
Rapio, rapui, raptum, r. d. *to snatch.* *The compounds change* ă *into* ĭ *in the*

first and second roots, and into e in the third; as, dirĭpio, -rĭpui, -reptum, m. r. So erĭpio *and* præripio.

Rĕgo, rexi, rectum, r. d. *to rule.* The *compounds change* ĕ *into* ĭ, *in the first root; as,* dirĭgo, direxi, directum. *pergo, (for* perrĭgo), perrexi, r. *to go forward.* surgo (*for* surrĭgo), surrexi, surrectum, r. d. *to rise.* So porrĭgo (*for* prorĭgo), *to stretch out.*

*Rĕpo, repsi, *to creep.*

Rōdo, rōsi, rōsum, r. *to gnaw.* ab-, ar-, e-, ob-, præ-rōdo, *want the perfect.*

*Rŭdo, rudīvi, *to bray.*

Rumpo, rūpi, ruptum, r. d. *to break.*

Ruo, rui, rŭtum, ruitūrus, *to fall.* dīruo, -rui, -rŭtum, d. So obruo.
*corruo, -rui. So irruo.

*Sapio, sapīvi, *to be wise.* The *compounds change* ă *into* ĭ; *as,* *resĭpio, -sĭpīvi *or* -sĭpui. *desĭpio, —, *to be silly.*

*†Scăbo, scābi, *to scratch.*

Scalpo, scalpsi, scalptum, *to engrave.*

Sălo *or* sallo, — salsum, *to salt.*

*Scando, —, d. *to climb.* The *compounds change* a *into* e; *as,* ascendo, ascendi, ascensum, r. d. descendo, descendi, (*anciently* descendĭdi,) descensum.

Scindo, scĭdi, (*anciently* sciscĭdi), scissum, d. *to cut.*

Scisco, scīvi, scītum, d. *to ordain.*

Scrībo, scripsi, scriptum, r. d. *to write.*

Sculpo, sculpsi, sculptum, d. *to carve.*

Sĕro, sēvi, sătum, r. d. *to sow.* consĕro, -sēvi, -sĭtum. So insĕro, r., *and* obsĕro.

Sĕro, —, sertum, *to entwine.* Its *compounds have* -sĕrui; *as,* assĕro, -sĕrui, -sertum, r.

*Serpo, serpsi, *to creep.*

*Sīdo, sīdi, *to settle.* Its *compounds have generally* sēdi, sessum, *from* sedeo.

*Sīno, sīvi, sītūrus, *to permit.* desīno, desīvi, desĭtum, r. § 284, R. 3, Exc. 2.

Sisto, stĭti, stătum, *to stop.* *absisto, -stĭti. So the *other compounds; but* circumsisto *wants the perfect.*

Solvo, solvi, sŏlūtum, r. d. *to loose.*

Spargo, sparsi, sparsum, r. d. *to spread.* The *compounds change* a *into* e; *as,* respergo, -spersi, -spersum; *but with* circum *and* in, a *sometimes remains.*

Spĕcio, (*obsolete.*) The *compounds change* ĕ *into* ĭ, *in the first root; as,* aspĭcio, aspexi, aspectum, d. *to look at.* inspĭcio, inspexi, inspectum. r. d.

Spcrno, sprēvi, sprētum, d. *to despise.*

*†Spuo, spui, *to spit.* *respuo, respui, d.

Stătuo, stătui, stătūtum, d. *to place.* The *compounds change* ă *into* ĭ; *as,* instĭtuo, instĭtui, instĭtūtum, *to institute.*

Sterno, strāvi, strātum, d. *to strew.*

*Sternuo, sternui, *to sneeze.*

*Sterto, —, *to snore.* *†desterto, destertui.

*Stinguo, —, *to extinguish.* distinguo, distinxi, distinctum. So exstinguo, r. d.

*Strĕpo, strĕpui, *to make a noise.*

*Strīdo, strīdi, *to creak.*

Stringo, strinxi, strictum, r. d. *to bind or tie tight.*

Struo, struxi, structum, d. *to build.*

Sūgo, suxi, suctum, *to suck.*

Sūmo, sumpsi, sumptum, r. d. *to take.*

Suo, —, sūtum, d. *to sew.* So consuo, dissuo, insuo, -sui, sūtum. *assuo, —.

Tāgo, (*very rare*), *to touch.* Hence

Tango, tĕtĭgi, tactum, r. d. *to touch.* The *compounds change* a *into* ĭ *in the first root, and drop the reduplication; as,* contingo, contĭgi, contactum, r.

Tĕgo, texi, tectum, r. d. *to cover.*

*Temno, —, d. *to despise.* contemno, -tempsi, -temptum, d.

Tendo, tĕtendi, tentum *or* tensum, *to stretch.* The *compounds drop the reduplication; as,* extendo, -tendi, -tentum *or* -tensum. So in-, os-, *and* retendo. detendo *has* tensum. The *other compounds have* tentum.

*†Tergo, tersi, tersum, *to wipe.* Tergeo, *of the second conjugation has the same second and third roots.*

Tĕro, trīvi, trītum, d. *to rub.*

Texo, texui, textum, d. *to weave.*

Tingo *or* tinguo, tinxi, tinctum, r. d. *to moisten, tinge.*

*Tollo, *anciently* tĕtŭli, *rarely* tolli, d. *to raise.* The *perfect and supine* sustŭli *and* sublātum *from* suffĕro *take the place of the perfect and supine of* tollo *and* sustollo. *sustollo, —, r. *to raise up, to take away.* *attollo, —. So extollo.

Trăho, traxi, tractum, r. d. *to draw.*

*Trĕmo, trĕmui, d. *to tremble.*

Trĭbuo, trĭbui, trĭbūtum, r. d. *to ascribe.*

Trūdo, trūsi, trūsum, *to thrust.*

Tundo, tŭtŭdi, tunsum *or* tūsum, *to beat.* The *compounds drop the reduplication, and have* tūsum. Yet contunsum, detunsum, obtunsum, *and* retunsum, *are also found.*

Ungo, (or -guo), unxi, unctum, d. *to anoint.*

§ 173. VERBS.—SECOND AND THIRD ROOTS. 137

Uro, ussi, ustum, d. *to burn.*
*Vādo, —, *to go.* So supervādo. *The other compounds have* vāsi; *as,* *evādo, evāsi, r. *So* pervādo; *also* invādo, r. d.
Vĕho, vexi, vectum, r. *to carry.*
Vello, velli *or* vulsi, vulsum, d. *to pluck.* So avello, d., divello, evello, d., revello, revelli, revulsum. *The other compounds have* velli *only, except* intervello, *which has* vulsi.

*Vergo, versi, *to incline.*
Verro, —, versum, d. *to brush.*
Verto, verti, versum, r. d. *to turn.* See § 174, *Note.*
Vinco, vici, victum, r. d. *to conquer.*
*Viso, —, d. *to visit.*
*Vivo, vixi, victūrus, d. *to live.*
*Volo, vŏlui, velle (*for* volĕre), *to be willing.* See § 178.
Volvo, volvi, vŏlūtum, d. *to roll.*
Vŏmo, vŏmui, vŏmĭtum, r. d. *to vomit*

REMARK. Those verbs in *io* (and deponents in *ior*), of the third conjugation, which are conjugated like *capio* (page 115) are, *căpio, cŭpio, făcio, fŏdio, fŭgio, jăcio, părio, quătio, răpio, săpio,* compounds of *lăcio* and *spĕcio*, and *grădior, mŏrior, pătior,* and *mŏrior*: but compare *mŏrior* in § 174, and *ŏrior*, and *pŏtior* in § 177.

Inceptive Verbs.

§ **173.** Inceptive verbs in general either want the third root, or adopt that of their primitives: (see § 187, II, 2). Of those derived from nouns and adjectives, some want the second root, and some form it by adding *u* to the root of the primitive.

In the following list, those verbs to which *s* is added, have a simple verb in use from which they are formed:—

*Acesco, ăcui, s. *to grow sour.*
*Ægresco, *to grow sick.*
*Albesco, —, s. *to grow white.*
*Alesco, —, s. *to grow.* coalesco, -alui, -alitum, *to grow together.*
*Ardesco, arsi, s. *to take fire.*
*Aresco, —, s. *to grow dry.* *exaresco, -arui. So inaresco, peraresco.
*Augesco, auxi, s. *to increase.*
*Calesco, călui, s. *to grow warm.*
*Calvesco, —, s. *to become bald.*
*Candesco, candui, s. *to grow white.*
*Cānesco, cānui, s. *to become hoary.*
*Claresco, clārui, s. *to become bright.*
*Condormisco, -dormīvi, s. *to go to sleep.*
*Conticesco, -ticui, *to become silent.*
*Crebresco, crēbui *and* crebrui, *to increase.*
*Crudesco, crūdui, *to become violent.*
*Ditesco, —, *to grow rich.*
*Dulcesco, —, *to grow sweet.*
*Dūresco, dūrui, *to grow hard.*
*Evilesco, evīlui, *to become worthless.*
*Extimesco, -timui, *to fear greatly.*
*Fātisco, —, *to gape.*
*Flaccesco, flaccui, s. *to wilt.*
*Fervesco, ferbui, s. *to grow hot.*
*Floresco, flōrui, s. *to begin to flourish.*
*Frācesco, frācui, *to grow rancid.*
*Frigesco, —, s. *to grow cold.* *perfrigesco, -frixi. So refrigesco.

*Frondesco, —, s. *to put forth leaves.*
*Fruticesco, —, *to put forth shoots.*
*Gĕlasco, —, s. *to freeze.* So *congĕlasco, s. *to congeal.*
*Gĕmisco, —, s. *to begin to sigh.*
*Gemmasco, —, *to begin to bud.*
*Gĕnĕrasco, —, s. *to be produced.*
*Grandesco, —, *to grow large.*
*Grăvesco, —, *to grow heavy.*
*Hæresco, —, s. *to adhere.*
*Hĕbesco, —, s. *to grow dull.*
*Horresco, horrui, s. *to grow rough.*
*Hūmesco, —, s. *to grow moist.*
*Ignesco, —, *to become inflamed.*
*Indŏlesco, -dŏlui, d. *to be grieved.*
*Insŏlesco, —, *to become haughty.*
*Intĕgrasco, —, *to be renewed.*
*Jŭvĕnesco, —, *to grow young.*
*Languesco, langui, s. *to grow languid.*
*Lăpidesco, —, *to become stone.*
*Lātesco, —, *to grow broad.*
*Lătesco, *to be concealed.* s. *delĭtesco -lĭtui; *oblītesco, -lĭtui.
*Lentesco, —, *to become soft.*
*Liquesco, —, s. *to become liquid* *dēliquesco, -licui.
*Lūcesco, —, s. *to grow light, to dawn*
*Lŭtesco, —, s. *to become muddy.*
*Măcesco, —, s. } *to grow lean.*
*Macresco, —,
  *remacresco, -macrui.
*Mădesco, mădui, s. *to grow moist.*

*Marcesco, —, s. *to pine away.*
*Māturesco, mātūrui, *to ripen.*
*Mīsĕresco, mĭsĕrui, s. *to pity.*
*Mītesco, —, *to grow mild.*
*Mollesco, —, s. *to grow soft.*
*Mūtesco, —, *to become dumb.* *obmūtesco, obmūtui.
*Nigresco, nigrui, s. *to grow black.*
*Nĭtesco, nĭtui, s. *to grow bright.*
*Nōtesco, nōtui, *to become known.*
*Obbrūtesco, —, *to become brutish.*
*Obdormisco, —, s. *to fall asleep.*
*Obsurdesco, -surdui, *to grow deaf.*
*Occallesco, -callui, *to become callous.*
*Olesco, (*scarcely used.*) *ăbŏlesco, -ŏlēvi, s. *to cease.* ădŏlesco, -ōlēvi, -ultum, s. *to grow up.* exŏlesco, -ōlēvi, -ōlētum, *to grow out of date.* So obsŏlesco. Inŏlesco, -ōlēvi, -ōlitum, d. *to grow in or on.*
*Pallesco, pallui, s. *to grow pale.*
*Pătesco, pătui, s. *to be opened.*
*Păvesco, păvi, s. *to grow fearful.*
*Pertĭmesco, -tĭmui, d. *to fear greatly.*
*Pinguesco, —, *to grow fat.*
*Pūbesco, —, *to come to maturity.*
*Puĕrasco, —, *to become a boy.*
*Pūtesco, —, s. } *to become putrid.*
*Putresco, —, s. }
*Rāresco, —, *to become thin.*
*Rĕsĭpisco, -sĭpui, s. *to recover one's senses.*
*Rĭgesco, rĭgui, s. *to grow cold.*
*Rūbesco, rŭbui, s. *to grow red.* *ērŭbesco, -rŭbui, d.

*Sānesco, —, *to become sound.* *consānesco, -sānui.
*Sĕnesco, sĕnui, s. d. *to grow old.* & consĕnesco.
*Sentisco, —, s. *to perceive.*
*Siccesco, —, *to become dry.*
*Sĭlesco, sĭlui, s. *to grow silent.*
*Solĭdesco, —, *to become solid.*
*Sordesco, sordui, s. *to become filthy.*
*Splendesco, splendui, s. *to become bright.*
*Spūmesco, —, *to begin to foam.*
*Stĕrĭlesco, —, *to become barren.*
*Stŭpesco, stŭpui, s. *to become astonished.*
Suesco, suēvi, suētum, s. *to become accustomed.*
*Tābesco, tābui, s. *to waste away.*
*Tĕnĕresco and -asco, —, *to become tender.*
*Tĕpesco, tĕpui, s. *to grow warm.*
*Torpesco, torpui, s. *to grow torpid.*
*Trĕmisco, —, s. *to begin to tremble.*
*Tŭmesco, tŭmui, s. } *to begin to swell.*
*Turgesco, —, s. }
*Uvesco, —, *to become moist.*
*Vălesco, —, s. *to become strong.*
*Vānesco, —, *to vanish.* *ēvānesco, ēvānui.
*Vĕtĕrasco, vĕtĕrāvi, *to grow old.*
*Vĭresco, virui, s. *to grow green.*
*Vīvesco, vixi, s. *to come to life.* *rĕvīvisco, -vixi.

§ 174. *Deponent Verbs of the Third Conjugation.*

Apiscor, aptus, *to get.* The compounds change ă into I in the first root, and into e in the third; as, ădĭpiscor, ădeptus. So indĭpiscor.
Expergiscor, experrectus, *to awake.*
*Fātiscor, *to gape or crack open.* The compounds change ă into ĕ; as, dēfĕtiscor, -fessus.
Fruor, fruĭtus or fructus, fruĭtūrus, d. *to enjoy.*
Fungor, functus, r. d. *to perform.*
Grădior, gressus, *to walk.* The compounds change ă into ĕ; as, aggrĕdior, aggressus, r. d. *Inf. pres.* aggrĕdi and aggrĕdīri; so, progrĕdi and progrĕdīri; and *pres. ind.* ēgrĕditur, *Plaut.*
*Irascor, *to be angry.*
Lābor, lapsus, r. *to fall.*
*Liquor, *to melt, flow.*
Lŏquor, lŏcūtus, r. d. *to speak.*
Mĭniscor, (*obsolete.*) commĭniscor, commentus, p. *to invent.* *remĭniscor, *to remember.*

Mŏrior, (mŏri, rarely mŏrīri,) mortuus, morĭtūrus, d. *to die.* So ēmŏrīri, *Plaut. for* emŏri.
Nanciscor, nactus or nanctus *to obtain.*
Nascor, nātus, nascĭtūrus, u. *to be born.*
Nītor, nixus or nīsus, nīsūrus, *to lean upon.*
Oblīviscor, oblītus, d. p. *to forget.*
Păciscor, pactus, d. *to bargain.* So dēpăciscor.
Pătior, passus, r. d. *to suffer.* perpĕtior -pessus.
From plecto, *to twine,* come, amplector, amplexus, d. p. complector, complexus, p. So circumplector.
Profĭciscor, profectus, r. *to depart.*
Quĕror, questus, m. u. d. *to complain.*
*Ringor, *to snarl.*
Sĕquor, sĕcūtus, r. d. *to follow.*
Tuor, tūtus, *to protect.*
*Vescor, d. *to eat.*
Ulciscor, ultus, m. d. p. *to avenge.*
Utor, ūsus, r. d. *to use.*

§ 175, 176.   VERBS.—SECOND AND THIRD ROOTS.   139

NOTE. *Divertor, prævertor, revertor*, compounds of *verto*, are used as deponents in the present and imperfect tenses; *revertor* also, sometimes, in the perfect.

FOURTH CONJUGATION.

§ 175. Verbs of the fourth conjugation regularly form their second root in *iv*, and their third in *it;* as, aud*io*. audīv*i*, audītum.

The following list contains most regular verbs of this conjugation :—

Audio, -ivi or -ii, m. u. r. d. *to hear.*
*Cio, civi, *to excite.* Cf. cieo, § 168.
Condio, -ivi or -ii, *to season.*
Custodio, -ivi or -ii, d. *to guard.*
*Dormio, -ivi or -ii, m. r. d. *to sleep.*
Erudio, -ivi or -ii, d. *to instruct.*
Expedio, -ivi or -ii, d. *to disentangle.*
Finio, -ivi or -ii, r. d. *to finish.*
*Gestio, -ivi or -ii, *to exult; desire.*
Impedio, -ivi or -ii, r. d. *to entangle.*
Insanio, -ivi or -ii, *to be mad.*
Irretio, -ivi or ii, *to ensnare.*
Lenio, -ivi or ii, d. *to mitigate.*
Mollio, -ivi or -ii, d. *to soften.*

*Mugio, -ivi or -ii, *to bellow.*
Munio, -ivi or -ii, r. d. *to fortify.*
Mutio, -ivi, *to mutter.*
Nutrio, -ivi or -ii, d. *to nourish.*
Partio, -ivi or -ii, r. *to divide.*
Polio, -ivi, d. *to polish.*
Punio, -ivi or -ii, d. *to punish.*
Redimio, -ivi, *to crown.*
Scio, -ivi, u. r. *to know.*
Servio, -ivi or -ii, m. r. d. *to serve.*
Sopio, -ivi or -ii, *to lull asleep.*
Stabilio, -ivi or -ii, *to establish.*
Tinnio, -ivi or -ii, r. *to tinkle.*
Vestio, -ivi or -ii, *to clothe.*

§ 176. The following list contains those verbs of the fourth conjugation which form their second and third roots irregularly, and those which want either or both of them.

REMARK. The principal irregularity in verbs of the fourth conjugation arises from following the analogy of those verbs of the third conjugation whose first root ends in a consonant; as, *sopio, sepsi, septum*. A few become irregular by syncope; as, *venio, veni, ventum*.

Amicio, -ui or -xi, amictum, d. *to clothe.*
*Balbutio, —, *to stammer.*
Bullio, ii, itum, *to bubble.*
*Cæcutio, —, *to be dim-sighted.*
*Cambio, —, *to exchange.*
*Dementio, —, *to be mad.*
Effutio, —, *to babble.*
Eo, ivi or ii, itum, r. d. *to go.* The compounds have only ii *in the perfect*, except obeo, præeo, and subeo, which have ivi *or* ii. All the compounds want the supine and perfect participles, except adeo, ambio, ineo, obeo, prætereo, subeo, circumeo or circueo redeo, transeo, and *†veneo, venii r. (from venum eo), to be sold.*
Farcio, farsi, fartum *or* farctum, *to cram.* The compounds generally change n *to* e; as, refercio, -fersi, -fertum, but con- and ef-, -farcio and -fercio.
Fastidio, -ii, -itum, d. *to loathe.*
*Ferio, —, d. *to strike.*

*Ferocio, —, *to be fierce.*
Fulcio, fulsi, fultum, d. *to prop up.*
*Gannio, —, *to yelp, bark.*
*Glocio, —, *to cluck as a hen.*
*Glutio, ivi, or glutii, *to swallow.*
Grandio, —, *to make great.*
*Grunnio, grunnii, *to grunt.*
Haurio, hausi, rar. haurii, haustum, rar. hausitum, hausturus, hansurus, u. d. *to draw.*
*Hinnio, —, *to neigh.*
*Ineptio, —, *to trifle.*
*Lascivio, lascivii, *to be wanton.*
*Ligurio, ligurii, *to feed delicately.*
*Lippio, —, r. *to be blear-eyed.*
*Obedio, obedii, r. *to obey.*
Pario *is of the third conjugation, but its compounds are of the fourth, changing* ă *to* ĕ; *as,* aperio, aperui, apertum, r. d. *to open. So* operio, operui, comperi, compertum, *rarely dep.* comperior, *to find out. So* reperio r. d.

Păvio, —, păvītum, *to beat.*
*Prūrio, —, *to itch.*
Queo, quīvi *or* quii, quĭtum, *to be able.*
  So *nĕqueo.
*Raucio, —, r. *to be hoarse.*
*Rŭgio, —, *to roar as a lion.*
Sævio, sævii, ĭtum, r. *to rage.*
*Săgio, —, *to perceive keenly.*
*Sălio, sălui *or* sălii, *to leap. The compounds change* ă *into* ĭ; *as,* *absĭlio, —. *So* circumsĭlio. *assīlio, -ui. *So* dissĭlio, insĭlio. *dĕsĭlio, -ui *or* -ŭ. *So* exsĭlio, rĕsĭlio, subsĭlio. *transĭlio, -ui *or* -īvi, d. *So* prōsĭlio.
Sălio, —, ītum, r. d. *to salt.*
Sancio, sauxi, sancītum *or* sanctum, d. *to ratify, sanction.*

Sarcio, sarsi, sartum, d. *to patch.*
Sarrio, -īvi *or* -ui, sarrītum, d. *to weed, hoe.*
*Scătūrio, —, *to gush out.*
Sentio, sensi. sensum, r. *to feel.*
Sĕpĕlio, sĕpĕlīvi *or* -ii, *rar.* sĕpĕli, sĕpultum, r. d. *to bury.*
Sĕpio, sepsi, septum, d. *to hedge in.*
*Singultio, —, *to sob, hiccup.*
*Sĭtio, sĭtii, *to thirst.*
Suffio, -ii, -ītum, d. *to fumigate.*
*Tussio, —, *to cough.*
*Văgio, văgii, *to cry.*
Vĕnio, vēni, ventum, r. *to come.*
Vincio, vinxi, vinctum, r. d. *to bind.*

Note. Desiderative verbs want both the second and third roots, except these three;—*ĕsŭrio, —, ĕsŭritus, r. to desire to eat; *nuptŭrio, -īvi, to desire to marry; *partŭrio, -īvi, to be in travail. See § 187, II. 3.

§ **177.** *Deponent Verbs of the Fourth Conjugation.*

Assentior, assensus, r. d. p. *to assent.*
Blandior, blandītus, *to flatter.*
Largior, largītus, p. *to give, bestow.*
Mentior, mentītus, r. p. *to lie.*
Mētior, mensus *or* mētītus, d. p. *to measure.*
Mōlior, mōlītus, d. *to strive, toil.*
Ordior, orsus, d. p. *to begin.*
Orior, ortus, orītūrus, d. *to spring up.* *Except in the present infinitive, this verb seems to be of the third conjugation.*

Pĕrior, (*obs. whence* pĕrītus.) exper̆ior, expertus, r. d. *to try.* oppĕrior, oppertus *or* oppĕrītus, d. *to wait for.*
Partior, partītus, d. *to divide.*
Pŏtior, pŏtītus, r. d. *to obtain, enjoy.* *In the poets the present indicative and imperfect subjunctive are sometimes of the third conjugation.*
Sortior, sortītus, r. *to cast lots.*

IRREGULAR VERBS.

§ **178.** Irregular verbs are such as deviate from the common forms in some of the parts derived from the first root.

They are *sum, vŏlo, fĕro, ĕdo, fīo, eo, queo,* and their compounds.

Sum and its compounds have already been conjugated. See § 153. In the conjugation of the rest, the parts which are irregular are fully exhibited, but a synopsis only, of the other parts is, in general, given. Some parts of *volo* and of its compounds are wanting.

1. *Volo* is irregular only in the present of the indicative and infinitive, and in the present and imperfect of the subjunctive.

REMARK. It is made irregular partly by syncope, and partly by a change in the vowel of the root. In the present infinitive also and in the imperfect subjunctive, after *ĕ* was dropped, *r* following *l* was changed into *l*; as, *velĕre* (velre) *velle* ; *velĕrem* (velrem) *vellem.*

Pres. Indic.	Pres. Infin.	Perf. Indic.	
vŏ′-lŏ,	vel′-lĕ,	vŏl′-u-ī,	*to be willing, to wish.*

§ 178. IRREGULAR VERBS. 141

INDICATIVE.

Pres. S. vŏ'-lŏ, vīs, vult; *Perf.*   vŏl'-u-ī.
   P. vŏl'-ŭ-mŭs, vul'-tĭs, vŏ'-lunt. *Plup.*   vŏ-lu'-ĕ-ram
Imperf. vŏ-lē'-bam, vŏ-lē'-bās, etc. *Fut. perf.* vŏ-lu'-ĕ-rŏ.
Fut. vŏ'-lam, vŏ'-lēs, etc.

SUBJUNCTIVE.

Pres. S. vĕ'-lim, vĕ'-līs, vĕ'-līt; *Perf.* vŏ-lu'-ĕ-rim.
   P. vĕ-lī'-mŭs, vĕ-lī'-tĭs, vĕ'-lint. *Plup.* vŏl-u-is'-sem.
Imperf. S. vel'-lem, vel'-lēs, vel'-lĕt;
   P. vel-lē'-mŭs, vel-lē'-tĭs, vel'-lent.

INFINITIVE.   PARTICIPLE.

Pres. vel'-lĕ.   *Pres.* vŏ'-lens.
Perf. vŏl-u-is'-sĕ.

NOTE. *Volt* and *voltis*, for *vult* and *vultis*, and *vin'*, for *visne* are found in Plautus and other ancient authors.

2. *Nōlo* is compounded of the obsolete *nē* (for *non*) and *vŏlo*. The *v* of *vŏlo* after *nē* is dropped, and the vowels (*ē ŏ*) are contracted into *ō*.

Pres. Indic.   *Pres. Infin.*   *Perf. Indic.*
nō'-lŏ,   nol'-lĕ,   nōl'-u-ī,   *to be unwilling.*

INDICATIVE.

Pres. S. nō'-lŏ, non'-vīs, non'-vult; *Perf.*   nōl'-u-ī.
   P. nōl'-ŭ-mŭs, non-vul'-tĭs, nō'-lunt. *Plup.*   nō-lu'-ĕ-ram.
Imperf. nō-lē'-bam, -bās, -băt, etc. *Fut. perf.* nō-lu'-ĕ-rŏ.
Fut. nō'-lam, -lēs, -lĕt, etc.

SUBJUNCTIVE.

Pres. S. nō'-lim, nō'-līs, nō'-lit; *Perf.* nō-lu'-ĕ-rim.
   P. nō-lī'-mŭs, nō-lī'-tĭs, nō'-lint. *Plup.* nōl-u-is'-sem.
Imperf. S. nol'-lem, nol'-lēs, nol'-lĕt;
   P. nol-lē'-mŭs, nol-lē'-tĭs, nol'-lent.

IMPERATIVE.

     Present.   *Future.*
Sing. 2. nō'-li; *Plur.* nō-li-tĕ. *Sing.* 2. nō-li-tŏ, *Plur.* nōl-i-tō'-tĕ,
                          3. nō-li'-tŏ;   nō-lun'-tō

INFINITIVE.   PARTICIPLE.

Pres. nol'-lĕ.   *Pres.* nō'-lens.
Perf. nōl-u-is'-sĕ.

NOTE. In *non-vis, non-vult*, etc. of the present, *non* takes the place of *ne*, but *nĕvis* and *nĕvolt* also occur in Plautus.

3. *Mālo* is compounded of *măgis* and *vŏlo*. In composition *măgis* drops its final syllable, and *vŏlo* its *v*. The vowels (*ă ŏ*) are then contracted into *ā*.

Pres. Indic.	Pres. Infin.	Perf. Indic.
mā'-lŏ,	mal'-lĕ,	māl'-u-ī, *to prefer.*

INDICATIVE.

Pres. S. mā'-lŏ, mā'-vīs, mā'-vult; *Perf.* māl'-u-ī.
P. māl'-ŭ-mŭs, mā-vul'-tĭs, mā'-lunt. *Plup.* mā-lu'-ĕ-ram.
Imperf. mā-lē'-bam, -bās, *etc.* *Fut. perf.* mā-lu'-ĕ-rŏ.
Fut. mā'-lam, -lēs, *etc.*

SUBJUNCTIVE.

Pres. S. mā'-lim, mā'-līs, mā'-līt; *Perf.* mā-lu'-ĕ-rim.
P. mā-li'-mŭs, mā-li'-tĭs, mā'-lint. *Plup.* māl-u-is'-sem.
Imperf. S. mal'-lem, mal'-lēs, mal'-lĕt;
P. mal-lē'-mŭs, mal-lē'-tĭs, mal'-lent.

INFINITIVE.

Pres. mal'-lĕ. Perf. māl-u-ĭs'-sĕ.

NOTE. *Māvŏlo, māvŏlunt; māvŏlet; māvĕlim, māvĕlis, māvĕlit;* and *māvellem;* for *mălo, mălunt,* etc., occur in Plautus.

§ 179. *Fĕro* is irregular in two respects:—1. Its second and third roots are not derived from the first, but from otherwise obsolete verbs, viz. *tŭlo* for *tollo*, and *tlao*, sup. *tlātum*, by aphœresis, *lātum*:— 2. In the present infinitive active, in the imperfect subjunctive, and in certain parts of the present indicative and imperative, of both voices, the connecting vowel is omitted. In the present infinitive passive, *r* is doubled.

ACTIVE VOICE.   PASSIVE VOICE.

Pres. Indic. fĕ'-rŏ, (*to bear.*) *Pres. Indic.* fĕ'-rŏr, (*to be borne.*)
Pres. Infin. fer'-rĕ, *Pres. Infin.* fer'-rī,
Perf. Indic. tŭ'-lī, *Perf. Part.* lā'-tŭs.
Supine. lā'-tum.

INDICATIVE.
Present.

S fĕ'-rŏ, fers, fert; fĕ'-rŏr, fer'-rĭs *or* -rĕ, fer'-tŭr;
P fĕr'-ĭ-mŭs, fer'-tĭs, fĕ'-runt. fĕr'-ĭ-mŭr, fĕ-rĭm'-ĭ-nī, fĕ-run'-tŭr

Imperf. fĕ-rē'-bam. *Imperf.* fĕ-rē'-bar.
Fut. fĕ'-ram, -rēs, *etc.* *Fut.* fĕ'-rār -rē'-rĭs *or* -rē'-rĕ, *etc*
Perf. tŭ'-lī. *Perf.* lā'-tŭs sum *or* fu'-ī.
Plup. tŭ'lĕ-ram. *Plup.* lā'-tŭs ĕ'-ram *or* fu'-ĕ-ram.
Fut. perf. tŭ'-lĕ-rŏ. *Fut. perf.* lā'-tŭs ĕ'-rŏ *or* fu'-ĕ-rŏ.

§ 180. IRREGULAR VERBS.

SUBJUNCTIVE.

Pres. fĕ'-ram, -rās, etc. *Pres.* fĕ'-răr, -rā'-rĭs or -r.í rĕ, etc.
Imperf. fer'-rem, -rēs, etc. *Imperf.* fer'-rĕr, -rē'-rĭs, etc.
Perf. tŭ'-lĕ-rim. *Perf.* lā'-tŭs sim or fu'-ĕ-rim.
Plup. tŭ-lis'-sem. *Plup.* lā'-tŭs es'-sem or fu-is'-sem.

IMPERATIVE.

Pres. S. fĕr,   *P.* fer'-tŏ.   *Pres. S.* fer'-rĕ,   *P.* fĕ-rĭm'-ĭ-nī.
Fut. S. fer'-tŏ,   *P.* fer-tō'-tĕ,
      fer'-tŏ;   fĕ-run'-tŏ.   *Fut. S.* fer'-tŏr,   *F.* (fĕ-rēm'-ĭ-nī.)
                                       fer'-tŏr.   fĕ-run'-tŏr.

INFINITIVE.

Pres. fer'-rĕ. *Pres.* fer'-rī.
Perf. tŭ-lis'-sĕ. *Perf.* lā'-tus es'-sĕ or fu-is'-sĕ.
Fut. lā-tū'-rŭs es'-sĕ. *Fut.* lā'-tum ī'-rī.

PARTICIPLES.

Pres. fĕ'-rens. *Perf.* lā'-tŭs.
Fut. lā-tū'-rŭs. *Fut.* fĕ-ren'-dŭs.

GERUND.

fĕ-ren'-dī, etc.

SUPINES.

Former. lā'-tum.   *Latter.* lā'-tū.

NOTE. In the comic writers the following reduplicated forms are found in parts derived from the second root, viz. *tetăli, tetulisti, tetŭlit, tetulĕrunt; tetulĕro, tetulĕrit; tetulissem,* and *tetulisse.*

§ **180.** *Fio,* 'to become,' is properly a neuter verb of the third conjugation, having only the parts derived from the first root; but it is used also as a passive of *făcio*, from which it takes those parts of the passive which are derived from the third root, together with the participle in *dus*. The infinitive present has been changed from the regular form *fiĕrĕ* to *fiĕrī.*

Pres. Indic.   *Pres. Infin.*   *Perf. Part.*
fī'-ŏ,   fī'-ĕ-rī,   fac'-tŭs,   *to be made* or *to become.*

INDICATIVE.

Pres. S. fī'-ŏ, fīs, fīt;   *Perf.*   fac'-tŭs sum or fu'-ī.
     P. fī-mŭs, fī'-tĭs, fī'-unt. *Plup.* fac'-tŭs ĕ'-ram or fu'-ĕ-ram.
Imperf. fī-ē'-bam, fī-ē'-bās, etc. *Fut. perf.* fac'-tŭs ĕ'-rŏ or fu'-ĕ-rŏ.
Fut.   fī'-am, fī'-ēs, etc.

SUBJUNCTIVE.

Pres fī'-am, fī'-ās, etc.   *Perf.* fac'-tŭs sim or fu'-ĕ-rim.
Imp. fī'-ĕ-rem, -ĕ'-rēs, etc. *Plup.* fac'-tŭs es'-sem or fu-is'-sem.

144　　　　　　IRREGULAR VERBS.　　　　　§ 181.

IMPERATIVE.	INFINITIVE.

Pres. Sing. fī;　*Plur.* fī´-tĕ.　　*Pres.* fī´-ĕ-rī.
　　　　　　　　　　　　　　　Perf. fac´-tŭs es´-sĕ *or* fu-is´-sĕ.
　　　　　　　　　　　　　　　Fut. fac´-tum ī´-rī.

PARTICIPLES.	SUPINE.

Perf. fac´-tŭs.　　　　　　　*Latter.* fac´-tū.
Fut.　fă-ci-en´-dŭs.

NOTE. The compounds of *făcio* which retain *a*, have also *fīo* in the passive; as, *calefăcio*, to warm; passive, *calefīo*; but those which change *a* into *i* form the passive regularly. (Cf. *facio* in the list, § 172.) Yet *confit*, *dēfit*, and *infit*, occur. See § 183, 12, 13, 14.

§ 181. *Edo*, to eat, is conjugated regularly as a verb of the third conjugation; but in the present of the indicative, imperative, and infinitive moods, and in the imperfect of the subjunctive, it has also forms similar to those of the corresponding tenses of *sum*:— Thus.

INDICATIVE.
Present.

S. ĕ´-dŏ,　　　ĕ´-dĭs,　　　ĕ´-dĭt,
　　(*or*　ēs,　　　　est);
P. ĕd´-ĭ-mŭs,　ĕd´-ĭ-tĭs,　ĕ´-dunt.
　　(*or*　es´-tĭs),

SUBJUNCTIVE.
Imperfect.

S. ĕd´-ĕ-rem,　ĕd´-ĕ-rēs,　ĕd´-ĕ-rĕt,
(*or* es´-sem,　es´-sēs,　　es´-sĕt);
P. ĕd-ĕ-rē´-mŭs,　ĕd-ĕ-rē´-tĭs,　ĕd´-ĕ-rent,
(*or* es-sē´-mŭs,　es-sē´-tĭs,　es´-sent).

IMPERATIVE.

Pres. S. ĕ´-dĕ,　　　P. ĕd´-ī-tĕ,
　　(*or* ēs;　　　　es´-tĕ).
Fut. S. ĕd´-ĭ-tŏ,　　P. ĕd-ĭ-tō´-tĕ, ĕ-dun´-tŏ.
　　(*or* es´-tŏ,　　es-tō´-tĕ).

INFINITIVE.
Pres ĕd´-ĕ-rĕ, (*or* es´-sĕ).

PASSIVE.

Pres.　　ĕd´-ĭ-tŭr,　　(*or* es´-tŭr).
Imperf.　ĕd-ĕ-rē´-tŭr,　(*or* es-sē´-tŭr).

NOTE. (*a.*) In the present subjunctive, *edim*, *edīs*, etc., are found, for *edam* *edās*, etc.

(*b.*) In the compounds of *ĕdo*, also, forms resembling those of *sum* occur Ambĕdo has the participles *ambens* and *ambēsus*; *comĕdo* has *comēsus*, *comesurus* and rarely *comestus*; and *adĕdo* and *exĕdo* have *adēsus* and *exēsus*.

§ **182.** *Eo* is irregular in the parts which, in other verbs are formed from the first root, except the imperfect subjunctive and the present infinitive. In these, and in the parts formed from the second and third roots, it is a regular verb of the fourth conjugation.

NOTE. *Eo* has no first root, and the parts usually derived from that root, consist, in this verb, of terminations only.

Pres. Indic.   Pres. Infin.   Perf. Indic.   Perf. Part.
e'-ŏ,   ĭ'-rĕ,   ĭ'-vī,   ĭ'-tum,   *to go.*

INDICATIVE.

Pres.   S e'-ŏ, īs, ĭt ;   Fut.   ĭ'-bŏ, ĭ'-bĭs, ĭ'-bĭt, *etc.*
        P. ī'-mŭs, ī'-tĭs, e'-unt. Perf. ĭ'-vī, ĭ-vĭs'-tī, ĭ'-vĭt, *etc.*
Imperf. S. ī'-bam, ī'-bās, ī'-băt ; Plup. ĭv'-ĕ-ram, ĭv'-ĕ-rās, *etc.*
        P. ī-bā'-mŭs, *etc.*   Fut. perf. ĭv'-ĕ-rŏ, ĭv'-ĕ-rĭs, *etc.*

SUBJUNCTIVE.

Pres.   e'-am, e'-ās, e'-ăt, *etc.*   Perf. ĭv'-ĕ-rim, ĭv'-ĕ-rĭs, *etc.*
Imperf. ī'-rem, ī'-rēs, ī'-rĕt, *etc.* Plup. ī-vĭs'-sem, ī-vĭs'-sēs, *etc*

IMPERATIVE.

Pres. S. i,   P. ī'-tē.
Fut. 2. ī'-tŏ,   ī-tŏ'-tĕ,
      3. ī'-tŏ ;   e-un'-tŏ.

INFINITIVE.

Pres. ī'-rĕ.
Perf. ī-vĭs'-sĕ.
Fut. ī-tū'-rŭs es'-sĕ.

PARTICIPLES.

Pres. ī'-ens, (*gen.* e-un'-tĭs.)
Fut. ī-tū'-rŭs, a, um.

GERUND.

e-un'-dī,
e-un'-dŏ, *etc.*

REMARK 1. In some of the compounds the forms *eam, ies, iet* occur, though rarely, in the future; as, *redeam, redies, abiet, exiet, prodient. Istis, issem,* and *isse,* are formed by contraction for *ivistis, ivissem,* and *ivisse.* See § 162, 7.

REM. 2. In the passive voice are found the infinitive *Iri,* and the third persons singular *itur, ibātur, ibītur, itum est,* etc.; *eātur, irētur, eundum est,* etc., which are used impersonally. See § 184, 2, (*a.*)

REM. 3. The compounds of *eo,* including *vēneo,* are conjugated like the simple verb, but most of them have *ii* in the perfect rather than *ivi.* See under *eo* in § 176. *Adeo, anteeo, ineo, prætĕreo, sŭbeo,* and *transeo,* being used actively, are found in the passive voice. *Iniĕtur* occurs as a future passive of *ineo. Ambio* is regular, like *audio,* but has either *ambibat* or *ambībat.*

NOTE. *Queo,* I can, and *nequeo,* I cannot, are conjugated like *eo,* but they want the imperative mood and the gerund, and their participles rarely occur. They are sometimes found in the passive voice, before an infinitive passive.

DEFECTIVE VERBS.

§ **183.** (1.) Defective verbs are those which are not used in certain tenses, numbers, or persons.

REMARK. There are many verbs which are not found in all the tenses, numbers, and persons, exhibited in the paradigms. Some, not originally defective, are accounted so, because they do not occur in the classics now extant. Others are in their nature defective. Thus, the first and second persons of the passive voice must be wanting in many verbs, from the nature of their signification.

DEFECTIVE VERBS. § 183

(2.) The following list contains such verbs as are remarkable for wanting many of their parts:—

1. Odi, *I hate*.
2. Cœpi, *I have begun*.
3. Memini, *I remember*.
4. Aio, } *I say*.
5. Inquam, }
6. Fāri, *to speak*.
7. Quæso, *I pray*.
8. Ave, } *hail*, or
9. Salve, } *farewell*.
10. Apăge, *begone*.
11. Cĕdo, *tell*, or *give me*
12. Confit, *it is done*.
13. Dēfit, *it is wanting*.
14. Infit, *he begins*.
15. Ovat, *he rejoices*.

1. *Odi, cœpi*, and *memini* are used chiefly in the perfect and in the other parts formed from the second root, and are thence called *preteritive* verbs. *Odi* has also a deponent form in the perfect:— Thus,

    IND. *perf.* ō'-di *or* ō'-sus sum; *plup.* ōd'-ĕ-ram; *fut. perf.* ōd'-ĕ-ro.
    SUBJ. *perf.* ōd'-ĕ-rim; *plup.* ō-dis'-sem.
    INF. *perf.* ō-dis'-se; *fut.* ō-sū'-rum es'-se.
    PART. *fut.* ō-sū'-rus; *perf.* ō'-sus.

NOTE 1. *Exōsus* and *pĕrōsus*, like *ōsus*, are used actively. *Odivit*, for *ōdit*, occurs, M. Anton. in Cic. Phil. 13, 19: and *odiendi* in Appuleius.

2.   IND. *perf.* cœ'-pi; *plup.* cœp'-ĕ-ram; *fut. perf.* cœp'-ĕ-ro.
    SUBJ. *perf.* cœp'-ĕ-rim; *plup.* cœ-pis'-sem.
    INF. *perf.* cœ-pis'-se; *fut.* cœp-tū'-rum es'-se.
    PART. *fut.* cœp-tū'-rus; *perf.* cœp'-tus.

NOTE 2. In Plautus are found a present, *cœpio*, present subjunctive, *cœpiam*, and infinitive, *capĕre*. Before an infinitive passive, *cœptus est*, etc., rather than *cœpi*, etc., are commonly used.

3.   IND. *perf.* mĕm'-ĭ-ni; *plup.* mĕ-mĭn'-ĕ-ram; *fut. perf.* mĕ-mĭn'-ĕ-ro.
    SUBJ. *perf.* mĕ-mĭn'-ĕ-rim; *plup.* mĕm-ĭ-nis'-sem.
    INF. *perf.* mĕm-ĭ-nis'-se.
    IMPERAT. 2 *pers. S.* mĕ-men'-to; *P.* mĕm-en-tō'-tĕ.

NOTE 3. *Odi* and *memini* have, in the perfect, the sense of the present, and, in the pluperfect and future perfect, the sense of the imperfect and future, as, *fugiet atque odĕrit*. Cic. In this respect. *nōvi*, I know, the perfect of *nosco*, to learn, and *consuēvi*, I am wont, the perfect of *consuesco*, I accustom myself, agree with *ōdi* and *memini*.

4.   IND. *pres.* ai'-o,* a'-is, a'-it; ——, ——, ai'-unt.*
    —— *imp.* ai-ē'-bam, ai-ē'-bās, ai-ē'-băt; ai-ē-bā'-mŭs, ai-ē-bā'-tĭs, ai-ē'-bant.
    SUBJ. *pres.* ——, ai'-ās, ai'-ăt; ——, ——, ai'-ant.
    IMPERAT. *pres.* a'-i.   PART. *pres.* ai'-ens.

NOTE 4. *Ais* with *ne* is contracted to *ain'* like *viden'*, *ābin'*: for *videsne*, *visne*. The comic writers use the imperfect *aibas*, *aibat* and *aibant*, which are dissyllabic.

5.   IND. *pres.* in'-quam, in'-quĭs, in'-quĭt; in'-quĭ-mŭs, in'-quĭ-tĭs, in'-quĭ-unt.
    —— *imp.* ——, in-quĭ-ē'-bāt, *and* in-quī'-bāt; ——, ——, in-quĭ-ē'-bant
    —— *fut.* ——, in'-quĭ-ēs, in'-quĭ-ĕt; ——, ——, ——.
    —— *perf.* ——, in-quĭs'-tī, in-quĭt; ——, ——, ——.
    SUBJ. *pres.* ——, in'-quĭ-ās, in'-quĭ-ăt; ——, in-quĭ-ā'-tĭs, in'-quĭ-ant.
    IMPERAT. in'-quĕ, in'-quī-to.

6.   IND. *pres.* ——, ——, fā'-tŭr; *fut.* fā'-bŏr, ——, fāb'-ĭ-tŭr.
    —— *perf.* fātus est; *plup.* fātus ĕram.
    IMPERAT. fā'-rĕ.   PART. *pres.* fans; *perf.* fā'-tŭs; *fut.* fan'-dŭs.
    INFIN. *pres.* fā'-rī *or* fā'-rĭ-ĕr.   GERUND. *gen.* fan'-dī; *abl.* fan'-dō.
    SUPINE, fā'-tū.

---

* Pronounced a'-yo, a'-yunt, etc., wherever the diphthong *ai* is followed by a vowel. See § 9, 1

§ 184. IMPERSONAL VERBS. 147

Interfāri has the forms *interfātur, interfāta est, interfāri, interfans,* and *interfātus.*—*Effāri* has *effābor, effabēre, effātus est, effāti sunt;* imperat *effāre; effāri, effātus, effandus, effando; effātu.*—*Præfāri* occurs in the following forms, *præfātur, præfāmur; præfabantur; præfārer præfarentur; præfāti sumus; præfātus fuēro;* imperat. *præfāto, præfāmino; præfans, præfātus, præfandus; præfando.*—*Profāri* has *profātur, profāta est, profāta sunt, profātus* and *profans.*

7. IND. *pres.* quæ'-so, ——, quæ'-sĭt; quæs'-ŭ-mŭs, ——, ——.
INF. *pres.* quæs'-ĕ-rĕ.

8. ᵛ T. ă'-vē, ă-vē'-tĕ; ă-vē'-to. INF. ă-vē'-rĕ.
Avēre and *salvēre* are often used with *jŭbeo.*

9. IND. *pres.* sal'-ve-o; *fut.* sal-vē'-bĭs. INF. *pres.* sal-vē'-rĕ.
IMPERAT. sal'-vē, sal-vē'-tĕ; sal-vē'-to.

10. IMPERAT. ăp'-ă-gĕ. So *age* with a subject either singular or plural.

11. IMPERAT *sing.* cĕ'-do; *pl.* cet'-tĕ *for* cĕd'-ĭ-tĕ. *Hence* cēdodum.

12. IND. *pres.* con'-fĭt; *fut.* con-fī'-et.
SUBJ. *pres.* con-fī'-ăt; *imperf.* con-fī'-ĕ-rĕt. INF. *pres.* con-fī'-ĕ-rī.

13. IND. *pres.* dē'-fĭt; *pl.* dē-fī'-unt; *fut.* dē-fī'-ĕt. SUBJ. *pres.* dē-fī'-ăt.
INF. *pres.* dē-fī'-ĕ-rī. So ef-fī'-ĕ-rī, *and* in-ter-fī'-ĕ-rī. *Plaut.;* and in-ter-fī'-at. *Lucr.*

14. IND. *pres.* in'-fĭt; *pl.* in-fī'-unt.

15. IND. *pres.* ŏ'-văt. SUBJ. *pres.* ŏ'-vĕt; *imperf.* ŏ-vā'-rĕt.
PART. *pres.* ŏ'-vans; *perf.* ō-vā'-tŭs; *fut.* ŏv-ā-tū'-rŭs. GERUND, ŏ-van'-dī.

REMARK 1. Among defective verbs are sometimes, also, included the following:—*Fŏrem, fŏres,* etc., *fŏrĕ,* (see § 154, R. 3.) *Ausim, ausis, ausit; ausint. Faxo* and *fuxim, faxis, faxit; faximus, faxitis, faxint. Faxem.* The form in o is an old future perfect; that in *im* a perfect, and that in *em* a pluperfect subjunctive. See § 162, 7, (*c.*), and 9.

REM. 2. In the present tense, the first person singular, *fŭro,* to be mad, and *dor* and *der,* from *do,* to give, are not used. So in the imperative *scī, cŭpe* and *polle,* from *scio, cŭpio,* and *polleo,* do not occur.

REM. 3. A few words, sometimes classed with defectives, are formed by contraction from a verb and the conjunction *si;* as, *sis* for *si vis, sultis* for *si vultis, sōdes* for *si audes* (for *audies.*)

IMPERSONAL VERBS.

§ 184. (*a.*) Impersonal verbs are those which are used only in the third person singular, and do not admit of a *personal* subject.

(*b.*) The subject of an impersonal verb in the active voice is, for the most part, either an infinitive, or an infinitive or subjunctive clause; but in English the neuter pronoun, *it,* commonly stands before the verb, and represents such clause; as, *me delectat* scribĕre, *it* delights me *to write.* Sometimes an accusative depending on an impersonal verb takes, in English, the place of a subject; as, *me miseret tui,* I pity thee.

1. Impersonal verbs in the active voice are conjugated in the several conjugations like *delectat,* it delights; *decet,* it becomes; *contingit,* it happens; *evenit,* it happens; thus:—

IMPERSONAL VERBS. § 184.

	1st Conj.	2d Conj.	3d Conj.	4th Conj.
IND. Pres.	delectat,	dŏcet,	contingit,	ᴠĕnit,
Imp.	delectābat,	decēbat,	contingēbat,	ᴠeniēbat,
Fut.	delectābit,	decēbit,	continget,	ᴠeniet,
Perf.	delectāvit,	decuit,	contĭgit,	evēnit,
Plup.	delectāvĕrat,	decuĕrat,	contigĕrat,	evenĕrat,
Fut. perf.	delectāvĕrit.	decuĕrit.	contigĕrit.	evenĕrit
SUB. Pres.	delectet,	deceat,	contingat,	eveniat,
Imp.	delectāret,	decēret,	contingĕret,	evenīret,
Perf.	delectāvĕrit,	decuĕrit,	contigĕrit,	evenĕrit,
Plup.	delectāvisset.	decuisset.	contigisset.	evenisset.
INF. Pres.	delectāre,	decēre,	contingĕre,	evenīre,
Perf.	delectavisse.	decuisse.	contigisse.	evenisse.

2. (*a.*) Most *neuter* and many *active* verbs may be used impersonally in the passive voice, by changing the personal subject of the active voice into an ablative with the preposition *a* or *ab*; as,

Illi pugnant; or *pugnātur ab illis,* they fight. *Illi quærunt,* or *quæritur ab illis,* they ask. Cf. § 141, Rem. 2.

(*b.*) In the passive form, the subject in English is, commonly, either the *agent,* expressed or understood, or an *abstract* noun formed from the verb; as,

Pugnātum est, we, they, etc. fought; or, the *battle* was fought. *Concurritur,* the *people* run together; or, there is a *concourse.*

(*c.*) Sometimes the English subject in the passive form is, in Latin, an oblique case dependent on the verb; as, *favētur tibi,* thou art favored.

The following are the forms of impersonal verbs in the several conjugations of the passive voice:—

INDICATIVE MOOD.

Pres.	pugnātur,	favētur,	currĭtur,	venītur,
Imp.	pugnabātur,	favebātur,	currebātur,	veniebātur,
Fut.	pugnābitur,	favēbitur,	currētur,	veniētur,
Perf.	pugnātum est *or* fuit,	fautum est *or* fuit,	cursum est *or* fuit,	ventum est *or* fuit,
Plup.	pugnātum ĕrat *or* fuĕrat,	fautum ĕrat *or* fuĕrat,	cursum ĕrat *or* fuĕrat,	ventum ĕrat *or* fuĕrat,
Fut. p.	pugnātum ĕrit *or* fuĕrit.	fautum ĕrit *or* fuĕrit.	cursum ĕrit *or* fuĕrit.	ventum ĕrit *or* fuĕrit.

SUBJUNCTIVE MOOD.

Pres	pugnētur,	faveātur,	currātur,	veniātur,
Imp.	pugnarētur,	faverētur,	currerētur,	venirētur,
Perf.	pugnātum sit *or* fuĕrit,	fautum sit *or* fuĕrit,	cursum sit *or* fuĕrit,	ventum sit *or* fuĕrit,
Plup.	pugnātum esset *or* fuisset.	fautum esset *or* fuisset.	cursum esset *or* fuisset.	ventum esset *or* fuisset.

INFINITIVE MOOD.

Pres.	pugnāri	favēri,	curri,	venīri,
Perf.	pugnātum esse *or* fuisse,	fautum esse *or* fuisse,	cursum esse *or* fuisse,	ventum esse *or* fuisse,
Fut.	pugnātum iri.	fautum iri.	cursum iri.	ventum iri.

§ 184. IMPERSONAL VERBS. 149

3. In like manner, in the periphrastic conjugation, the neuter gender of the participle in *dus*, both of active and neuter verbs, is used impersonally with *est*, etc., and the *dative* of the person; as, *mihi scribendum fuit*, I have been obliged to write; *moriendum est omnibus*, all must die. See § 162, 15, R. 5.

REMARK 1. Grammarians usually reckon only ten real impersonal verbs, all of which are of the second conjugation, viz. *decet, libet, licet, liquet, miseret, oportet, piget, pænitet, pudet,* and *tædet.* (See § 169.) Four of these, *decet, libet, licet,* and *liquet* occur also in the third person plural, but without personal subjects. There seems, however, to be no good reason for distinguishing the verbs above enumerated from other impersonal verbs. The following are such other verbs as are most commonly used impersonally:—

(*a.*) In the first conjugation:—

Constat, *it is evident.*
Jŭvat, *it delights.*
Præstat, *it is better.*
Restat, *it remains.*
Stat, *it is resolved.*

Văcat, *there is leisure.*
Certātur, *there is a contention.*
Peccātur, *a fault is committed.*

Pugnātur, *a battle is fought.*
Stătur, *they stand firm.*

(*b.*) In the second conjugation:—

Appāret, *it appears.*
Attĭnet, *it belongs to.*
Displĭcet, *it displeases.*
Dŏlet, *it grieves.*
Miserētur, *it distresses.*
Pătet, *it is plain.*

Pertĭnet, *it pertains.*
Plăcet, *it pleases.*
Flētur, *we,* etc. *weep,* or, *there is weeping.*
Nocētur, *injury is inflicted.*

Persuadētur, *he, they,* etc. *are persuaded.*
Pertæsum est, *he, they,* etc. *are disgusted with.*
Silētur, *silence is maintained.*

(*c.*) In the third conjugation:—

Accĭdit, *it happens.*
Condūcit, *it is useful.*
Contĭngit, *it happens.*
Fallit, or } *it escapes me;*
Fŭgit me, } *I do not know.*

Miserescit, *it distresses.*
Sufficit, *it suffices.*
Credĭtur, *it is believed.*
Currĭtur, *people run.*

Desĭnĭtur, *there is an end.*
Scribĭtur, *it is written.*
Vivĭtur, *we,* etc. *live.*

(*d.*) In the fourth conjugation:—

Convĕnit, *it is agreed upon; it is fit.*
Evĕnit, *it happens.*

Expĕdit, *it is expedient.*
Dormītur, *we, they,* etc. *sleep.*

Scītur, *it is known.*
Itur, *they,* etc. *go.*
Venītur, *they,* etc. *come.*

(*e.*) Among irregular verbs:—

Fit, *it happens.*
Intĕrest, *it concerns.*
Obest, *it is hurtful.*

Prætĕrit me, *it is unknown to me.*
Prōdest, *it avails.*

Rĕfert, *it concerns.*
Sŭbit, *it occurs.*
Supĕrest, *it remains.*

(*f.*) To these may be added verbs signifying the state of the weather, or the operations of nature. The subject of these may be *Jupiter, deus,* or *cælum,* which are sometimes expressed. Of this kind are the following:—

Fulget,   }
Fulgŭrat,   } *it lightens.*
Fulmĭnat,   }
Gĕlat, *it freezes.*
Grandĭnat *it hails.*

Lapĭdat, *it rains stones.*
Lucescit,   } *it grows light.*
Illucescit, }
Ningit, *it snows.*
Pluit, *it rains.*

Tŏnat, *it thunders.*
Vesperascit,   }
Advesperascit, } *evening approaches.*
Invesperascit,   }

Lapĭdat, ningit, and *pluit* are also used impersonally in the passive voice.

Rem. 2. Impersonal verbs, not being used in the imperative, take the subjunctive in its stead; as, *delectet*, let it delight. In the passive voice, their perfect participles are used only in the neuter.

Rem. 3. Most of the impersonal verbs want participles, gerunds, and supines; but *pœnitet* has a present participle, futures in *rus* and *dus*, and the gerund. *Pudet* and *piget* have also the gerund and future passive participle.

Rem. 4. Most of the above verbs are also used personally, but frequently in a somewhat different sense; as, *ut Tiberis inter eos et pons interesset*, so that the Tiber and bridge were between them.

REDUNDANT VERBS.

§ 185. Redundant verbs are those which have different forms to express the same meaning.

Verbs may be redundant in *termination ;* as, *fabrĭco* and *fabrĭcor*, to frame ;—in conjugation ; as, *lăvo, -āre*, and *lăvo, -ĕre*, to wash ;— or in certain tenses ; as, *ōdi* and *ōsus sum*, I hate.

1. The following deponent verbs, besides their passive form, have an active form in *o*, of the same meaning, but which is, in general, rarely used. A few, however, which are marked r., occur more rarely than the corresponding forms in *o*.

Abomĭnor, *to abhor.*	Fabrĭcor, *to frame.*	Oscĭtor, *to gape.*
Adūlor, *to flatter.*	Fenĕror, *to lend on interest.*	Pacifĭcor, r. *to make a peace.*
Altercor, *to dispute.*		
Amplexor, *to embrace.*	Fluctuor, *to fluctuate.*	Palpor, *to caress.*
Arbĭtror, *to suppose.*	Frustror, *to disappoint.*	Partĭor, *to divide.*
Argūtor, *to prate.*	Frutĭcor, *to sprout.*	Popŭlor, *to lay waste.*
Assentior, *to assent.*	Impertior, r. *to impart.*	Pūnior, *to punish.*
Aucŭpor, *to hunt after.*	Jurgor, *to quarrel.*	Rumĭnor, *to ruminate.*
Augŭror, *to foretell.*	Lacrĭmor, r. *to weep.*	Sciscĭtor, *to inquire.*
Aurīgor, *to drive a chariot.*	Ludifĭcor, *to ridicule.*	Sortĭor, *to cast lots.*
Auspĭcor, *to take the auspices.*	Luxŭrior, r, *to be rank.*	Stabŭlor, *to stable.*
	Medĭcor, *to heal.*	Tueor, *to defend.*
Cachinnor, r. *to laugh aloud.*	Mĕreor, *to deserve.*	Tumultuor, *to be in confusion.*
	Mētor, *to measure.*	
Comĭtor, *to accompany.*	Misĕreor, *to commiserate.*	Tūtor, *to defend.*
Commentor, *to deliberate.*	Modĕror, *to moderate.*	Ūtor, *to use.*
Convīvor, *to feast together.*	Munĕror, r. *to bestow.*	Urīnor, *to dive.*
Cunctor, (cont.), *to delay.*	Nictor, r. *to wink.*	Velifĭcor, *to set sail.*
Dignor, *to deem worthy.*	Nūtrior, r. *to nourish.*	Venĕror, *to reverence.*
Depascor, *to feed upon.*	Obsōnor, *to cater.*	Vocifĕror, *to bawl.*
Elucubror, *to elaborate.*	Opīnor, *to suppose.*	

2. The following verbs are redundant in conjugation:—

Boo, -āre,	} *to roar.*	Fulgeo, -ēre,	} *to shine.*	Sŏno, -āre,	} *to sound.*
Boo, -ĕre, r.		Fulgo, -ĕre, r.		Sŏno, -ĕre, r.	
Bullo, -āre,	} *to boil.*	Lăvo, -āre,	} *to wash.*	Strīdeo, -ēre,	} *to creak.*
Bullio, -īre,		Lăvo, -ĕre, r.		Strīdo, -ĕre,	
Cieo, -ēre,	} *to excite.*	Līno, -ĕre,	} *to anoint.*	Tergeo, -ēre,	} *to wipe.*
Cio, -īre, r.		Līnio, -īre, r.		Tergo, -ĕre,	
Denso, -āre,	} *to thicken.*	Nicto, -āre,	} *to wink.*	Tueor, -ēri,	} *to protect*
Denseo, -ēre,		Nicto, -ĕre,		Tuor, -i, r.	
Ferveo, -ēre,	} *to boil.*	Sălo, -ĕre,	} *to salt.*		
Fervo, -ĕre,		Sallio, -īre,		*Those marked* r. *are rarely used.*	
Fŏdio, -ĕre,	} *to dig.*	Scāteo, -ēre,	} *to abound.*		
Fŏdio, -īre, r.		Scāto, -ĕre, r.			

§ 186.   REDUNDANT VERBS.   151

Morior, oriar, and *potior*, also, are redundant in conjugation in certain parts See in lists §§ 174 and 177.

§ **186.** 1. Some verbs are spelled alike, or nearly alike, but differ in conjugation, quantity, pronunciation, or signification, or in two or more of these respects.

Such are the following:—

Abdĭco, -āre, *to abdicate.*
Abdĭco, -ĕre, *to refuse.*
Accīdo, -ĕre, *to fall upon.*
Accīdo, -ĕre, *to cut down.*
Addo, -ĕre, *to add.*
Adeo, -īre, *to go to.*
Aggĕro, -āre, *to heap up.*
Aggĕro, -ĕre, *to heap upon.*
Allēgo, -āre, *to depute.*
Allĕgo, -ĕre, *to choose.*
Appello, -āre, *to call.*
Appello, -ĕre, *to drive to.*
Cădo, -ĕre, *to fall.*
Cædo, -ĕre, *to cut.*
Cēdo, -ĕre, *to yield.*
Căleo, -ēre, *to be hot.*
Calleo, -ēre, *to be hard.*
Căno, -ĕre, *to sing.*
Cāneo, -ēre, *to be gray.*
Căreo, -ēre, *to want.*
Căro, -ĕre, *to card wool.*
Cēlo, -āre, *to conceal.*
Cælo, -āre, *to carve.*
Censeo, -ēre, *to think.*
Sentio, -īre, *to feel.*
Claudo, -ĕre, *to shut.*
Claudo, -ēre, *to be lame.*
Collīgo, -āre, *to bind together.*
Collĭgo, -ĕre, *to collect.*
Cōlo, -āre, *to strain.*
Cŏlo, -ĕre, *to cultivate.*
Compello, āre, *to accost.*
Compello, -ĕre, *to force.*
Concīdo, -ĕre, *to cut to pieces.*
Concĭdo, -ĕre, *to fall.*
Conscendo, -ĕre, *to embark.*
Conscindo, -ĕre, *to tear to pieces.*
Consterno,-āre, *to terrify.*
Consterno, -ĕre, *to strew over.*
Decīdo, -ĕre, *to fall down.*
Decĭdo, -ĕre, *to cut off.*
Decĭpio, -ĕre, *to deceive.*
Desĭpio, -ĕre, *to dote.*
Delīgo, -āre, *to tie up.*
Delĭgo, -ĕre, *to choose.*
Dilīgo, -ĕre, *to love.*
Dīco, -ĕre, *to say.*
Dĭco, -āre, *to dedicate.*

Edo, -ĕre, *to eat.*
Edo, -ĕre, *to publish.*
Edūco, -āre, *to educate.*
Edūco, -ĕre, *to draw out.*
Effĕro, -āre, *to make wild.*
Effĕro, -re, *to carry out.*
Excīdo, -ĕre, *to fall out.*
Excĭdo, -ĕre, *to cut off.*
Ferio, -īre, *to strike.*
Fero, -re, *to bear.*
Ferior,-āri, *to keep holiday.*
Frigeo, -ēre, *to be cold.*
Frigo, -ĕre, *to fry.*
Fŭgo, -āre, *to put to flight.*
Fŭgio, -ĕre, *to fly.*
Fundo, -āre, *to found.*
Fundo, -ĕre, *to pour out.*
Incīdo, -ĕre, *to fall into.*
Incĭdo, ĕre, *to cut into.*
Indĭco, -āre, *to show.*
Indīco, ĕre, *to proclaim.*
Inficio, -ĕre, *to stain.*
Infĭtior, -āri, *to deny.*
Intercīdo, -ĕre, *to happen.*
Intercĭdo, -ĕre, *to cut asunder.*
Jăceo, -ēre, *to lie.*
Jăcio, -ĕre, *to throw.*
Lābo, -āre, *to totter.*
Lābor, -i, *to glide.*
Lacto, -āre, *to suckle.*
Lacto, -āre, *to deceive.*
Lēgo, -āre, *to depute.*
Lĕgo, -ĕre, *to read.*
Liceo, -ēre, *to be lawful.*
Liceor, -ēri, *to bid for.*
Liquo, -āre, *to melt.*
Liqueo, -ēre, *to be manifest.*
Liquor, -i, *to melt.*
Māno, -āre, *to flow.*
Maneo, -ēre, *to stay.*
Mando, -āre, *to command.*
Mando, -ĕre, *to eat.*
Mēto, -ĕre, *to reap.*
Mētor, -āri, *to measure.*
Mētior, -īri, *to measure.*
Metuo, -ĕre, *to fear.*
Miseror, -āri, *to pity.*
Misĕreor, -ēri, *to pity.*
Mŏror, -āri, *to delay.*
Morior, -i, *to die.*
Nĭteo, -ēre, *to glitter.*

Nītor, -i, *to strive.*
Obsĕro, -āre, *to lock up.*
Obsĕro, -ĕre, *to sow.*
Occīdo, -ĕre, *to fall.*
Occĭdo, -ĕre, *to kill.*
Opĕrio, -īre, *to cover.*
Opĕror, -āri, *to work.*
Oppĕrior, -īri, *to wait for.*
Pando, -ĕre, *to bend.*
Pando, -ĕre, *to extend.*
Păro, -āre, *to prepare.*
Pāreo, -ēre, *to appear.*
Părio, -ĕre, *to bring forth.*
Părio, -āre, *to balance.*
Pendeo, -ēre, *to hang.*
Pendo, -ĕre, *to weigh.*
Percōlo, -āre, *to filter.*
Percŏlo, -ĕre, *to adorn.*
Permăneo, -ēre, *to remain.*
Permāno, -āre, *to flow through.*
Prædīco, -āre, *to publish.*
Prædīco, -ĕre, *to foretell.*
Prōdo, -ĕre, *to betray.*
Prōdeo, -īre, *to come forth.*
Recēdo, -ĕre, *to retire.*
Recīdo, -ĕre, *to fall back.*
Recĭdo, -ĕre, *to cut off.*
Reddo, -ĕre, *to restore.*
Redeo, -īre, *to return.*
Refĕro, -re, *to bring back.*
Refĕrio, -īre, *to strike back.*
Relēgo, -āre, *to remove.*
Relĕgo, -ĕre, *to read over.*
Sēdo, -āre, *to allay.*
Sĕdeo, -ēre, *to sit.*
Sīdo, -ĕre, *to sink.*
Sĕro, -ĕre, *to sow.*
Sĕro, -ĕre, *to entwine.*
Succīdo, -ĕre, *to fall under.*
Succīdo, -ĕre, *to cut down.*
Vādo, -ĕre, *to go.*
Vădor, -āri, *to bind over by bail.*
Vēneo, -īre, *to be sold.*
Venio, -īre, *to come.*
Vēnor, -āri, *to hunt.*
Vincio, -īre, *to bind.*
Vinco, -ĕre, *to conquer.*
Vŏlo, -āre, *to fly.*
Vŏlo, velle, *to be willing.*

2. Different verbs have sometimes the same perfect; as,

Aceo, acui, *to be sour.*
Acuo, acui, *to sharpen.*
Cresco, crēvi, *to grow.*
Cerno, crēvi, *to decree.*
Fulgeo, fulsi, *to shine.*
Fulcio, fulsi, *to prop.*
Lūceo, luxi, *to shine.*
Lūgeo, luxi, *to mourn.*
Mulceo, mulsi, *to soothe.*
Mulgeo, mulsi, *to milk.*
Păveo, păvi, *to fear.*
Pasco, păvi, *to feed.*
Pendeo, pĕpendi, *to hang.*
Pendo, pĕpendi, *to weigh.*

To these add some of the compounds of *sto* and *sisto*.

3. Different verbs have sometimes, also, the same supine or perfect participle; as,

Frico, frictum, *to rub.*
Frigo, frictum, *to roast.*
Maneo, mansum, *to remain.*
Mando, mansum, *to chew.*
Pango, pactum, *to drive in.*
Paciscor, pactus, *to bargain.*
Pando, passum, *to extend.*
Pătior, passus, *to suffer.*
Tĕneo, tentum, *to hold.*
Tendo, tentum, *to stretch.*
Verro, versum, *to brush.*
Verto, versum, *to turn.*

DERIVATION OF VERBS.

§ 187. Verbs are derived either from nouns, from adjectives, or from other verbs.

I. Verbs derived from nouns or adjectives are called *denominatives.*

1. (*a.*) Active denominatives are generally of the first conjugation; those which are neuter, of the second. They are usually formed by adding respectively *o* and *eo* to the root; as,

FROM NOUNS.

Actives.
Armo, *to arm,* (arma.)
Fraudo, *to defraud,* (fraus.)
Nomino, *to name,* (nomen.)
Numĕro, *to number,* (numĕrus.)

Neuters.
Flōreo, *to bloom,* (flos.)
Frondeo, *to produce leaves,* (frons.)
Lūceo, *to shine,* (lux.)
Vireo, *to flourish,* (vis.)

FROM ADJECTIVES.

Albo, *to whiten,* (albus.)
Celebro, *to frequent,* (celĕber.)
Libĕro, *to free,* (līber.)
Albeo, *to be white,* (albus.)
Calveo, *to be bald,* (calvus.)
Flāveo, *to be yellow,* (flāvus.)

(*b.*) Sometimes a preposition is prefixed in forming the derivative; as,

Concervo, *to heap together,* (acervus.)
Excăvo, *to excavate,* (căvus.)
Exstirpo, *to extirpate,* (stirps.)
Illāqueo, *to insnare,* (lăqueus.)

2. Many deponents of the first conjugation, derived from nouns, express the exercise of the character, office, etc., denoted by the primitive; as, *architector,* to build; *comitor,* to accompany; *fūror,* to steal; from *architectus, cōmes,* and *fūr.*

3. Such as denote resemblance or imitation are called *imitatives;* as, *cornicor,* to imitate a crow, from *cornix; Græcor,* to imitate the Greeks. Some of these end in *isso;* as, *patrisso,* to imitate a father.

II. Verbs derived from other verbs are either *frequentatives, inceptives, desideratives, diminutives,* or *intensives.*

§ 187　　　　　DERIVATION OF VERBS.　　　　　153

1. *Frequentatives* express a repetition, or an increase of the action expressed by the primitive.

(*a.*) They are all of the first conjugation, and are formed by adding to the third root; as, *dŏmo*, (*dŏmĭt-*) *dŏmĭto*. So *adjŭvo*, *adjŭto*, *dīco*, *dicto*; *gĕro*, *gesto*. In verbs of the first conjugation, *āt* of the root is often changed into *ĭt*; as, *clāmo*, to cry, (*clamāt-*) *clamĭto*, to cry frequently.

(*b.*) A few frequentatives are formed by adding *ĭto* to the first root of the primitive; as, *ăgo* (*ăg-*) *ăgĭto*. So *lăteo*, *lătĭto*; *nosco*, *noscĭto*; *quæro*, *quærĭto*.

(*c.*) Frequentatives, from primitives of the second, third, and fourth conjugations, sometimes serve again as primitives, from which new frequentatives are formed; as, *dīco*, *dicto*, *dictĭto*; *curro*, *curso*, *cursĭto*; *vĕnio*, *vento*, *ventĭto*. Sometimes the second or intermediate form is not in use.

(*d.*) Some frequentatives are deponent; as, *minĭtor*, from *mĭnor* (*mināt-*); *versor*, from *verto* (*vers-*). So *amplexor*, *sector*, *lŏquĭtor*, from *amplector*, *sĕquor*, and *lŏquor*.

(*e.*) When verbs of this class express simply an *increase* of the action denoted by the primitive, they are, by some grammarians, called *intensives*.

2. *Inceptives*, or *inchoatives* mark the beginning of the action or state expressed by the primitive.

(*a.*) They all end in *sco*, and are formed by adding that termination to the root of the primitive, with its connecting vowel, which, in the third conjugation, is *i*; as, *căleo*, to be hot; *călesco*, to grow hot. So *lăbo*, (*āre*), *lābasco*; *ingĕmo*, (*ĕre*), *ingĕmisco*; *obdormio*, (*īre*), *obdormisco*. *Hisco* is contracted for *hiasco*, from *hio*, (*āre*).

(*b.*) Most inceptives are formed from verbs of the second conjugation.

(*c.*) Some inceptives are formed from nouns and adjectives by adding *asco* or *esco* to the root; as, *puerasco*, from *puer*; *juvenesco*, from *juvenis*.

NOTE. Inceptives are all neuter, and of the third conjugation. See § 173. Some verbs in *sco*, which are not inceptives, are active; as, *disco*, *posco*.

3. *Desideratives* express a desire of doing the act denoted by the primitive.

(*a.*) They are formed from the third root, by adding *ŭrio*; as, *cœno*, to sup, (*cœnāt*,) *cœnātŭrio*, to desire to sup.

(*b.*) Desideratives are all of the fourth conjugation. See § 176, Note.

(*c.*) Verbs in *ūrio*, having *u* long, are not desideratives; as, *prūrio*, *ligūrio*.

4. *Diminutives* denote a feeble or trifling action. They are formed by adding *illo* to the root of the primitive; as, *conscrībillo*, to scribble, from *conscrībo*.

They are few in number, and are all of the first conjugation.

5. *Intensives* denote eager action. They are usually formed by adding *so*, *esso*, or *isso* to the root of the primitive; as, *făcesso*, to act earnestly—from *făcio*.

So *căpesso*, *incesso*, from *căpio* and *incēdo*. *Concŭpisco*, to desire greatly, though in form an inceptive, is, in its signification, an intensive.

NOTE. Verbs of all these classes have sometimes simply the meaning of their primitives.

COMPOSITION OF VERBS.

§ 188. Verbs are compounded variously:—

1. Of a noun and a verb; as, *ædifico, belligero, lucrifacio.* See § 103, R. 1.
2. Of an adjective and a verb; as, *amplifico, multiplico.*
3. Of two verbs; as, *calefacio, madefacio, patefacio.*

REM. In verbs of this class, the first part, which is a verb of the second conjugation, loses its final *o*; the second part is always the verb *facio.*

4. Of an adverb and a verb; as, *benefacio, maledico, satago, nolo, negligo.*
5. Of a preposition and a verb; as, *adduco, excolo, prodo, subrepo, discerno, sejungo.*
6. Of a preposition and a noun, as, *pernocto, irretio.*

§ 189. In composition with particles, the vowels *a* and *e* and the diphthong *æ* in the radical syllable of the simple verb are often changed in the compound.

1. The following simple verbs in composition change *a* into *e*:—

Arceo,	Carpo,	Farcio,	Jacto,	Pario,	Patro,	Spargo,
Candeo,	Damno,	Fatiscor,	Lacto,	Partio,	Sacro,	Tracto.
Capto,	Fallo,	Gradior,	Mando,	Patior,	Scando,	

EXC. *A* is retained in *amando, præmando, desacro,* and *retracto; prædamno,* and *pertracto* sometimes also occur. *A* is also changed into *e* in *occento* from *canto,* and *anhelo* from *halo; comperco* also is found.

2. The following, in the first root, change *ă* and *ĕ* into *ĭ*; viz.

ăgo, cădo, ĕgeo, ĕmo, frango, pango, prĕmo, rĕgo, sĕdeo, spĕcio, tango.

3. These change *ă* and *ĕ*, in the first and second roots, into *ĭ*; viz.

sălio, *to leap,* săpio, tăceo, *and* tĕneo.

4. These change *ă* into *ĭ*, and *æ* into *ī*, in all the roots; viz.

hăbeo, lăcio, lăteo, plăceo, stătuo; cædo, lædo, *and* quæro.

5. The following change *ă*, in the first root, into *ĭ*, and in the third root into *e*; viz.

căno, căpio, făteor, jăcio, răpio, *and* ăpiscor.

EXC. (*a.*) *A* is retained in *circumago, perago, satago; antehabeo, posthabeo, dipango, repango, compliceo,* and *perpliceo. Occano* and *recano* also sometimes occur. *E* is retained in *coëmo, circumsedeo,* and *supersedeo. Antecapio* and *anticipo* are both used; so also are *superjacio* and *superjicio.*

(*b.*) *Cōgo* and *dēgo* are formed, by contraction, from *con, de,* and *ago; dēmo, prōmo* and *sūmo,* from *de, pro, sub,* and *ĕmo; præbeo,* and perhaps *debeo,* from *præ, de,* and *habeo; pergo* and *surgo,* from *per, sub,* and *rĕgo.*

NOTE 1. *Facio,* compounded with a preposition, changes *a* into *i* in the first root, and into *e* in the third; as, *afficio, affeci, affectum.* Some compounds of *facio* with nouns and adjectives, change *a* into *i,* and also drop *i* before *o,* and are of the first conjugation; as, *significo, lætifico, magnifico. Specio* forms some compounds in the same manner; as, *conspicor* and *suspicor.*

NOTE 2. *Lego,* compounded with *con, de, di, e, inter, nec,* and *se,* changes *e* into *i,* in the first root; as, *colligo, negligo,* etc.; but with *ad, præ, per, re, sub,* and *trans,* it retains *ĕ*; as, *allĕgo.*

NOTE 3. *Calco* and *salto,* in composition, change *a* into *u*; as, *inculco, insulto. Plaudo* changes *au* into *ō*; as, *explōdo;* except *applaudo. Audio* changes *au* into *ē* in *obēdio. Causo, claudo,* and *quatio,* drop *a*: as, *accuso, recludo, percutio. Juro* changes *u* into *e* in *dejero* and *pejero,* but *dejuro,* also, is in use.

§ 190, 191.   ADVERBS.   155

NOTE 4. In the compounds of *căveo*, *măneo*, and *trăh* *ă* remains unchanged, and so also does *æ* in the compounds of *hæreo*.

NOTE 5. The simple verbs with which the following are compounded are not used:—

Dēfendo,	Impĕdio,	Confūto,	Instīgo,	Connīveo,	
Offendo,	Imbuo,	Rĕfūto,	Impleo,	Percello,	
Expĕrior,	Compello, (-āre,)	Ingruo,	Compleo,	Induo,	and some
Expĕdio,	Appello, (-āre,)	Congruo,	Rĕnīdeo,	Exuo,	others.

For the changes produced in prepositions by composition with verbs see § 196.

PARTICLES.

§ 190. 1. *Particles* are those parts of speech which are neither declined nor conjugated. They are divided into four classes—*adverbs, prepositions, conjunctions,* and *interjections.*

NOTE. A word may sometimes belong to two or more of these classes, according to its connection.

ADVERBS.

2. An adverb is a particle used to modify or limit the meaning of a verb, an adjective, or another adverb; as,

Bĕne et sapienter dixit, he spoke *well* and *wisely*; *Cănis ēgrĕgie fĭdēlis*, a remarkably faithful dog; *Nimis valde laudāre*, to praise *too* much. Compare § 277, R. 1.

3. Adverbs, in regard to their *signification,* are divided into various classes; as, adverbs of *place, time, manner,* etc:, and some belong to either class according to their connection.

4. In regard to their *etymology,* adverbs are either *primitive* or *derivative.*

REMARK. Among primitive adverbs are here classed not only such as cannot be traced to any more remote root, but also all which are not included in the regular classes of derivative adverbs hereafter mentioned.

PRIMITIVE ADVERBS.

§ 191. The primitive adverbs are few in number, when compared with the derivatives, and most of them are contained in the following lists marked I, II, and III.

I. Adverbs of *Place* and *Order*.

ădeo, *so far, as far*.	ălĭcūbi, *somewhere*.	ălĭquōversum, *toward some place*.
ădhūc, *to this place*.	ălĭoundĕ, *from some place*.	ălĭundĕ, *from another place*.
adversŭs, } *opposite*,	ălĭō, *to another place*.	
adversum, } *over against*,	ălĭquā, *in some way*.	circā, } *around*.
exadversŭs,—um, } *toward*.	ălĭorsum, *toward another place*.	circum, }
ăliā, *by another way*.		circĭter, *on every side*.
ălĭās, *in another place*.	ălĭquō, *to some place*.	circumcircā *all around*.
ălĭbi, *elsewhere*.		

citrā, *on this side.*
citro, *hither.*
contrā, *over against.*
cōram, *before.*
dehinc, *henceforth.*
deinceps, *successively.*
deindĕ, *after that.*
dēnīquĕ, *finally.*
dēnuo, *again.*
deorsum, *downward.*
dextrorsum, *toward the right.*
eā, *that way.*
eādem, *the same way.*
eō, *to that place, thither.*
eōdem, *to the same place.*
exindĕ, *after that.*
extrā, *without.*
extrinsĕcŭs, *from without.*
fŏrās, *out of doors.*
fŏrĭs, *without.*
hāc, *this way.*
hactĕnŭs, *thus far.*
hīc, *here.*
hinc, *hence.*
hūc, *hither.*
hūcusquĕ, *thus far.*
horsum, *hitherward.*
ĭbi, *there.*
ĭbĭdem, *in the same place.*
illāc, *that way.*
illīc, *there.*
illinc, *thence.*
illō, *thither.*
illorsum, *thitherward.*
illūc, *thither.*
indĕ, *thence.*
indĭdem, *from the same place.*

īnfrā, *below, beneath.*
ĭnĭbi, *in that place.*
intrinsĕcŭs, *from within*
intrā, intro,
introrsum, } *within.*
intŭs,
istāc, *that way.*
istīc, *there.*
istinc, *thence.*
istō, istūc, *thither.*
juxtā, *near, alike.*
nĕcŭbi, *lest any where.*
neutro, *to neither side.*
neutrūbi, *to neither place, to neither side.*
nullĭbi,
nusquam, } *no where.*
pēnĭtŭs, *within.*
pōnĕ, post, *behind, back.*
porro, *onward.*
prŏcŭl, *far.*
prŏpĕ, proptĕr, *near.*
prorsum, *forward.*
prōtĭnŭs, *onward.*
quā? *in which way?*
quāquā, } *what way*
quācumque, } *soever.*
quāquĕ, *wheresoever.*
quālĭbĕt,
quāvīs, } *in every way.*
quō? *whither?*
quoād,
quousquĕ, } *how far.*
quōpiam,
quōquam, } *to some place.*
quōquō, } *whither-*
quōcumquĕ, } *soever.*
quōquōversŭs, *toward every side.*

quorsum? *whitherward?*
quōvīs,
quōlĭbĕt, } *to every place.*
retro,
retrorsum, } *backward, back.*
rursum,
sīcŭbi, *if any where.*
sīcundĕ, *if from any place.*
sinistrorsum, *toward the left.*
subtĕr, *beneath.*
sŭpĕr, suprā, *above, on top.*
sursum, *upward.*
tum, *then, in the next place.*
ŭbi? *where?*
ŭbicumquĕ, } *wherever,*
ŭbiūbi, } *wheresoever.*
ŭbĭlĭbĕt,
ŭbīquĕ, } *any where,*
ŭbīvīs, } *every where.*
ultrā, ultro, *beyond.*
undĕ? *whence?*
undĕlĭbĕt,
undēvīs, } *from every*
undīquĕ, } *where.*
undeundĕ, } *whence-*
undĕcumquĕ, } *soever.*
uspiam, } *somewhere,*
usquam, } *any where.*
usquĕ, *all the way.*
usquĕquāquĕ, *in all ways.*
utrimquĕ, *on both sides.*
utrō? *which way?*
utrōbī? *in which place?*
utrōbīquĕ, *in both places.*
utrōquĕ, *to both sides.*
utrōquĕversum, *toward both sides.*

REMARK 1. (*a.*) The interrogative adverbs of place, *ŭbi?* where? *undĕ?* whence? *quō?* whither? and *quā?* in what way? have relation to other adverbs formed in a similar manner, thus constituting a system of *adverbial correlatives* similar to that of the pronominal adjectives. See § 139, 5, (3.)

(*b.*) As in the case of the pronominal correlatives, the *interrogative* and *relative* forms are alike, beginning with *u* or *qu.* The *demonstratives* are formed from *is*, which is strengthened by *dem*, and the *indefinite* from *ăliquis*. The *general relatives* and the *general indefinites* or *universals*, like those of the pronominal adjectives, are made, the former by doubling the simple relatives or by appending to them the termination *cumquĕ*, 'soever,' and the latter by adding *quĕ*, *vīs*, or *lĭbĕt*. Thus:

Interrog.	Demonstr.	Relat.	Gen. Relat.	Indefin.	Gen. Indefin
ŭbi?	ĭbi, ĭbĭdem,	ŭbi,	ŭbiŭbi, ŭbicumquĕ,	ălĭcŭbi,	ŭbīquĕ, ŭbīvīs, ŭbĭlĭbĕt,
undĕ?	indĕ, indĭdem,	undĕ,	undeundĕ, undĕcumquĕ,	ălĭcundĕ,	undīquĕ, undēvīs, undĕlĭbĕt,
quō?	eō, eōdem,	quō,	quōquō, quōcumquĕ,	ălĭquō,	quōvīs, quōlĭbĕt,
quā?	eā, eādem.	quā.	quāquā, quācumquĕ.	ălĭquā.	quāvīs. quālĭbĕt.

(c.) To those answering to *ŭbĭ?* may be added *ălĭbĭ, nullĭbĭ,* and *ĭnĭbĭ,* the latter being a strengthened form of *ĭbĭ.* In like manner *ălĭundĕ, utrĭnquĕ, intrinsĕcŭs,* and *extrinsĕcŭs* may be added to those answering to *undĕ?* and *ălĭō* to those answering to *quō?* So also to *utrō?* answer *utrōquĕ* and *neutro.*

(d.) The demonstratives *ĭbĭ, indĕ,* and *ĕō* are used only in reference to relative sentences which precede; but more definite demonstratives are formed from the pronouns *hīc, istĕ,* and *illĕ,* answering in like manner to *ŭbĭ? undĕ?* and *quō?* These together with the preceding correlatives are, in the following table, arranged respectively under their several interrogatives *ŭbĭ? undĕ? quō? quā?* and *quorsum?*—Thus:

ŭbi?	undĕ?	quō?	quā?	quorsum?
hīc,	hinc,	hūc,	hāc,	horsum,
istīc,	istinc,	istūc,	istāc,	istorsum,
illīc,	illinc,	illūc,	illāc,	illorsum,
ĭbĭ,	indĕ,	eō,	eā,	———,
ĭbĭdem,	indĭdem,	eōdem,	eādem,	———,
ălĭbĭ,	ălĭundĕ,	ălĭō,	ălĭā,	ălĭorsum,
ălĭcŭbĭ.	ălĭcundĕ.	ălĭquō.	ălĭquā.	ălĭquŏversum.

(e.) *Hīc, hinc, hūc,* refer to the place of the speaker; *istīc, istinc, istūc,* to the place of the second person or person addressed; and *illīc, illinc, illūc,* to that of the third person or the person or thing spoken of. Cf. § 207, R. 23, (a.) and (d.)

(f.) The interrogative adverbs *ŭbĭ, undĕ, quō, quā,* etc. are often used without a question, simply as adverbs of place; as, *In eam partem itŭros, atque* ibi *futŭros Helvetios,* ŭbi *eos Cæsar constituisset.*

(g.) In consequence of a transfer of their meaning, some of the adverbs of place, as, *hīc, ĭbĭ, ŭbi, hinc, indĕ, hactĕnŭs,* etc., become also adverbs of time, and some of them are used also as conjunctions.

II. Adverbs of *Time.*

actūtum, *immediately.*
abhinc, *from this time.*
ădeō, *so long (as).*
ădhūc, *until now, still.*
ălĭās, *at another time.*
ălĭquamdĭū, *for awhile.*
ălĭquandō, *at some time.*
ălĭquŏtĭēs, *several times.*
antĕ, } *before,*
anteā, } *previously.*
antĕhāc, *formerly.*
bĭs, *twice.* (see § 119).
circĭtĕr, *about, near.*
crās, *tomorrow.*
cum *or* quum, *when.*
deinceps, *in succession.*
deindĕ *or* dein, } *thereupon,*
exindĕ *or* exin, } *afterward.*
dehinc, *from this time.*
dēmum, *at length.*
dēnĭque, *lastly.*
dĭū, *long.*
dūdum, *previously.*
eousquĕ, *so long.*
hĕrĕ *or* hĕrī, *yesterday.*
hīc, *here, hereupon.*
hinc, *from this time, since.*
hŏdĭē, *to-day.*
ĭbĭ, *then, thereupon.*
dentĭdem, *now and then, repeatedly.*

illĭcō, *immediately.*
inde, *after that, then.*
interdum, *sometimes.*
intĕrim, *meanwhile.*
ĭtĕrum, *again.*
jam, *now, already.*
jamdĭū, }
jamdūdum, } *long ago.*
jamjam, *presently.*
jamprīdem, *long since.*
mŏdo, *just now.*
mox, *soon after.*
nondum, *not yet.*
nonnumquam, *sometimes.*
nūdĭŭs tertĭŭs, *three days ago.*
nunc, *now.*
numquam, *never.*
nŭpĕr, *lately.*
ōlim, *formerly.*
parumpĕr, } *for a short*
paulispĕr, } *time.*
pĕrendĭē, *two days hence.*
porro, *hereafter, in future.*
post, posteā, *afterwards.*
posthāc, *hereafter.*
postrīdĭē, *the day after.*
pridem, *long since.*
pridĭē, *the day before.*
prōtĭnŭs, *instantly.*

quamdĭū? *how long?*
quandō? *when?*
quandōcumquĕ, *whenever.*
quandōquĕ, *at some time.*
quătĕr, *four times.*
quŏad? }
quousquĕ? } *how long?*
quondam, *formerly.*
quŏtĭdĭē, *daily.*
quŏtĭēs? *how often?*
quum *or* cum, *when.*
rursŭs, *again.*
sæpĕ, *often.*
sĕmel, *once.*
sempĕr, *always.*
stătim, *immediately.*
sŭbindĕ, *immediately, now and then.*
tamdĭū, *so long.*
tandem, *at length.*
tantispĕr, *for so long.*
tĕr, *thrice.*
tŏtĭēs, *so often.*
tum, tunc, *then.*
ŭbĭ, *when, as soon as.*
umquam, *ever.*
usquĕ, *until, ever.*
ŭt *or* ŭtĭ, *as, or soon as, when.*

III. Adverbs of Manner, Quality, Degree, etc.

ădĕō, *so, to that degree.*
admŏdum, *very much.*
ălĭtĕr, *otherwise.*
ceu, *as, like as.*
cūr? *why?*
duntaxăt, *only, at least.*
ĕtĭam, *also, truly, yes.*
ĕtĭamnunc,
ĕtĭamtum, } *also, besides.*
fĕrē,
fermē, } *almost, nearly.*
fortassĕ, *perhaps.*
frustrā, *in vain.*
grātīs, *freely.*
haud, *not.*
haudquāquam, *by no means.*
hūcusquĕ, *so far.*
ĭdentĭdem, *constantly.*
immō, *nay, on the contrary.*
ĭtă, *so.*
ĭtem, *just so, also.*
ĭtĭdem, *in like manner.*
juxtā, *equally, alike.*
măgis, *more.*
mŏdo, *only.*
næ or nē, *truly, verily.*
nē, *not.*
nĕdum, *much less.*
nempĕ, *truly, forsooth.*
nēquāquam, } *by no*
neutīquam, } *means.*
nīmīrum, *certainly, to be sure.*

nĭmīs, } *too much.*
nĭmium, }
nōn, *not.*
omnīno, *altogether, only.*
pænĕ, *almost.*
pălam, *openly.*
părĭtĕr, *equally.*
părum, *too little.*
paulātim, *by degrees.*
pĕnĭtŭs, *wholly.*
pĕrindē, } *just as,*
prŏindē, } *as though.*
perquam, *very much.*
plērumquĕ, *for the most part, commonly.*
pŏtĭŭs, *rather.*
porro, *moreover, then.*
prætĕr, *beyond, except.*
præsertim, *particularly.*
prŏfecto, *truly.*
prŏpĕ, *almost, near.*
prŏpĕmŏdum, *almost.*
prorsŭs, *wholly.*
quam, *how much, as.*
quamobrem, *wherefore.*
quārē? *why? wherefore?*
quăsi, *as if, as it were.*
quemadmŏdum, *as.*
quĭdem, } *indeed.*
ĕquĭdem, }
quōmŏdō? *how? in what manner?*
quŏquĕ, *also.*
rītĕ, *duly.*
saltem, *at least.*

sānē, *truly.*
săt, } *enough.*
sătĭs, }
sătĭŭs, *rather.*
scīlĭcĕt, *truly, to wit.*
sĕcŭs *otherwise.*
seorsum, } *separately.*
seorsŭs, }
sīc, *so.*
sīcŭt, } *so as, as.*
sīcŭtī, }
sĭmŭl, *together.*
singillātim, *one by one.*
sōlum, *only, alone.*
tam, *so, so much.*
tamquam, *like, as if.*
tantŏpĕrĕ, *so greatly.*
tantum, *so much, only.*
tantummŏdō, *only.*
tĕmĕrē, *at random.*
ūnā, *together.*
usquĕquāquĕ, *in all points, in all ways.*
ŭt, } *as.*
ŭtī, }
ŭtĭquĕ, *at any rate, certainly.*
utpŏtē, *as, inasmuch as.*
valdē, *very much.*
vĕl, *even.*
vĕlŭt, } *as, like as, for*
vĕlŭtī, } *example.*
vĭcissim, *in turn, again.*
vĭdēlĭcĕt, *clearly, to wit.*
vix, *scarcely.*

REM. 2. Adverbs denoting quality, manner, etc., are sometimes divided into those of, 1. Quality; as, *bĕnē, mălē.* 2. Certainty; as, *certē, plānē.* 3. Contingence; as, *fortē.* 4. Negation; as, *haud, nōn, nē, immō.* 5. Affirmation; as, *næ, quidem, ŭtĭquĕ, nempĕ.* 6. Swearing; as, *herclē.* 7. Explaining; as, *vĭdēlĭcĕt, utpŏtē.* 8. Separation; as, *seorsum.* 9. Joining together; as, *simŭl, ūnā.* 10. Interrogation; as, *cūr? quārē?* 11. Quantity or degree; as, *sătĭs, ădeō.* 12. Excess; as, *perquam, maxĭmē.* 13. Defect; as, *părum, pænē.* 14. Preference; as, *pŏtĭŭs, sătĭŭs.* 15. Likeness; as, *ĭtă, sīc.* 16. Unlikeness; as, *ălĭtĕr.* 17. Exclusion; as, *tantum, sōlum.*

REM. 3. *Non* is the ordinary Latin negation. *Haud* signifies either 'not at all,' or 'not exactly.' It is used by the comic and later writers in all combinations, but in the authors of the best age its use is more especially limited to its connection with adjectives and adverbs denoting a measure; as, *haud multum, haud magnum, haud parvus, haud mediocris, haud paulo, haud procul, haud longe,* especially *haud sāne* in connection with other words; as, *haud sāne făcĭle, res haud sāne diffĭcĭlis, haud sāne intellĭgo;* also *haud quisquam, haud umquam, haud quāquam.* With verbs *haud* is scarcely used until Livy and Tacitus, except in the common phrase *haud scio an,* which is equivalent to *nescio an.*—*Nē,* (or *nī*) is the primitive Latin negative particle, signifying *no* or *not.* It is used in this sense and as an adverb, (*a*) with *quidem* to make an emphatic negation of the word standing between them: as, *nē in oppidis quidem,* not even in the towns; (*b*) in composition as in *nescio, nefas, neuter* etc.; (*c*) with imperatives and subjunctives used as imperatives; as, *Nĕ pŭĕri, nē tanta animis assuescite bella.* Virg. So, also, in wishes and asseverations; as, *Nē id Jupiter sinĕret,* may Jupiter forbid it. Liv. *Ne vivam, si scio,* may I die, if I know. Cic.; and in concessive and restrictive clauses; as, *Ne fuĕrit,* suppose there was not. Cic. *Sint misericordes in furtbus ærarii, ne illis sanguinem nostram largiantur,* only let them not, etc. Cic. So *dum ne, dummŏdo ne, mŏdo ne, dum quīdem ne;* and in intentional clauses with *ut.*—*Immo,* as a negative, substitutes something stronger in the place of the preceding statement, which is denied; as, *Causa igitur non bona est? Immo optima, sed,* etc. Cic. It may often be translated by 'nay,' or 'nay even.'

REM. 4. *Quidem* gives particular emphasis to a word or an idea, and then answers to our 'certainly' or 'indeed,' but frequently, especially with a pronoun, it merely adds emphasis. *Equidem,* which is considered as a compound of *ego* and *quidem,* is used exclusively in this sense by Cicero, Virgil, and Horace, but by other and particularly by later writers it is used like *quidem.*— *Nempe,* 'surely,' is often used ironically, when we refute a person by concessions which he is obliged to make, or by deductions. In other connections it may be translated 'namely.'

REM. 5. *Sic, ită, tam,* as also *tantŏpĕre,* and *ădeŏ* signify 'so.' *Sic* is more particularly the demonstrative 'so,' or 'thus'; as, *sic se res habet. Ita* defines or limits more accurately, and is equivalent to our 'in such a manner,' or 'only in so far'; as, *ita defendĭto, ut neminem lædas.* Frequently, however, *ita* has the signification of *sic,* but *sic* has not the limiting sense of *ita.*— *Tam,* 'so much,' generally stands before adjectives and adverbs, and increases the degree; before vowels *tantopĕre* is generally used instead of *tam.*— *Adeo,* 'to that degree' or 'point,' increases the expression to a certain end or result. Hence it forms the transition to the conclusion of an argument or to the essential part of a thing; and Cicero employs it to introduce the proofs of what he has previously alleged; as, *Id adeo ex ipso senātus consulto cognoscite,* and always in such case puts *adeo* after a pronoun.

REM. 6. *Umquam,* 'ever,' and *'usquam,* 'somewhere,' like *quisquam,* require a negation in the sentence, and thus become equivalent to *numquam* and *nusquam.* A negative question, however, may supply the place of a negative proposition; as, *num tu eum umquam vidisti?*—*Uspiam,* like *quispiam,* is not negative, but is the same as *alicŭbi,* but strengthened, just as *quispiam* is the same as *aliquis.* So, also, *quŏpiam* is used affirmatively, and *quŏquam* negatively.—*Jam,* with a negative, answers to our 'longer'; as, *Nihil jam spēro,* I no longer hope for any thing. When used to connect sentences it signifies 'further,' or 'now.'—*Usque* is commonly accompanied by the prepositions *ad, in, ab,* or *ex.* It rarely signifies 'ever and anon'; as, *Natūram expellas furcā, tamen usque recurret.* Hor.—*Nūper, mŏdo,* and *mox* are relative and indefinite.—*Dūdum,* 'previously,' or 'before,' in relation to a time which has just passed away, may often be translated 'just before.'—*Jamdūdum* signifies 'long before,' or 'long since.' With the poets *jamdūdum* contains the idea of impatience, and signifies 'without delay,' 'forthwith'; as, *Jamdūdum sumite pœnas.* Virg.—*Tandem,* 'at length,' also expresses the impatience with which a question is put.

REM. 7. *Tunc* is 'then,' 'at that time,' in opposition to *nunc,* 'now': *Tum* is 'then,' as the correlative of *quum,* 'when;' as, *quum omnes adessent, tum ille exorsus est dicĕre,* when all were present, then he began to speak. Without a relative sentence *tum* signifies 'hereupon,' or 'thereupon'; but a relative sentence may always be supplied. The same difference exists between *etiam nunc* and *etiam tum,* 'still,' or 'yet'; and between *nunc ipsum* and *tum ipsum; quummaxime* and *tummaxime,* 'just,' or 'even then'; for *etiam nunc, nunc ipsum* and *quum maxime* refer to the present; but *etiamtum, tum ipsum,* and *tummaxime,* to the past.

DERIVATION OF ADVERBS.

§ 192. Adverbs are derived from nouns, adjectives, pronouns, and participles.

I. From Nouns.

1. Of these a few end in *im* (generally *ātim*), and denote manner; as,

grĕgātim, in herds; *membrātim*, limb by limb; *vĭcissātim*, or more frequently, *vĭcissim*, by turns; from *grex, membrum,* and *vĭcis.*

2. Some end in *ĭtus*, and denote origin or manner; as,

cælĭtus, from heaven; *fundĭtus*, from the bottom; *rādīcĭtus*, by the roots; from *cælum, fundus,* and *rādix.*

3. Some are merely the different cases of nouns used adverbially; as,

(*a.*) Some adverbs of time; as, *mānĕ, noctū, dĭū, tempŏre* or *tempŏri, ĭnĭtĭō, princĭpĭō, mŏdo.*—(*b.*) Adverbs of place; as, *fŏris, fŏrās.*—(*c.*) Adverbs of manner; as, *spontĕ, fortĕ, grātis* or *grātiis, ingrātiis, vulgō, partim.*

II. From Adjectives and Participles.

By far the greater number of derivative adverbs come from adjectives and participles (present and perfect), and end in *ē* and *tĕr.*

1. Adverbs derived from adjectives and participles of the second declension, are formed by adding *ē* to the root; as,

ægrē, scarcely; *altē*, high; *lībĕrē*, freely; *longē*, far; *mĭsĕrē*, miserably; *plēnē*, fully; *doctē*, learnedly; *ornātē*, elegantly; from *æger, altus, liber, longus, miser, plēnus, doctus,* and *ornātus.* *Bĕnē*, well, is from *bŏnus,* or an older form *bĕnus.*

REMARK. A few adverbs in *e* differ in meaning from their adjectives; as, *sānē*, certainly; *valdē*, very; from *sānus*, sound, well; and *vălĭdus*, strong.

Exc. 1. A few adverbs derived from adjectives and participles of the second declension, add *ĭtĕr, ĭtus, im,* or *ātim* to the root; as,

nāvĭtĕr, actively; *antīquĭtus*, anciently; *dīvīnĭtus*, divinely; *prīvātim*, privately; *tuātim*, after your manner; *singŭlātim, singillātim, sigillātim,* or *singultim*, severally; *cæsim, carptim, sensim, stătim,* etc. from *nāvus, antīquus, dīvīnus, prīvātus, tuus, singŭli, cæsus, carptus,* etc.

Exc. 2. Some adverbs are formed with two or more of the above terminations with the same meaning; as, *dūrē, dūrĭtĕr; firmē, firmĭtĕr; nāvē, nāvĭtĕr; largē, largĭtĕr; lūcŭlentē, lūcŭlentĕr; turbŭlentē, turbŭlentĕr:* so *cautē* and *cautim; hūmānē, hūmānĭtĕr,* and *hūmānĭtus; pūblĭcē* and *pūblĭcĭtus.*

2. Adverbs derived from adjectives and participles of the third declension, are formed by adding *ĭtĕr* to the root, except when it ends in *t*, in which case *ĕr* only is added; as,

ācrĭtĕr, sharply; *fēlĭcĭtĕr*, happily; *turpĭtĕr*, basely;—*ēlĕgantĕr*, elegantly, *prūdentĕr*, prudently; *āmantĕr*, lovingly; *prŏpĕrantĕr*, hastily; from *ācer, fēlix, turpis, ēlĕgans, prūdens, āmans,* and *prŏpĕrans.* So also from the obsolete *ălis* for *ălĭus*, and *prŏpis*, (neuter *prŏpe*), come *ălĭtĕr* and *prŏpĭtĕr* for *prŏpĭtĕr.*

Exc. From *audax* comes by syncope *audactĕr;* from *fortis* comes *fortĭtĕr;* from *omnis, omnīno;* from *ūber, ūbertim;* and from *nēquam, nēquĭtĕr.*

§ 192.   DERIVATION OF ADVERBS.   161

3. From the cardinal numerals are formed numeral adverbs in *tēs*; as,

quinquiēs, dĕciēs, from *quinquĕ* and *dĕcem.* So *tŏtiēs* and *quŏtiēs*, from *tŏt* and *quŏt.* See § 119.

4. Some adverbs are merely certain cases of adjectives. Such are,

(*a.*) Ablatives in *ō*, from adjectives and participles of the second declension as, *citŏ,* quickly; *contĭnuŏ,* immediately; *falsŏ,* falsely; *crēbrō,* frequently; *mĕrĭtō,* deservedly; *nēcōpīnātō,* unexpectedly; *fortuĭtō,* by chance; *auspĭcātō,* auspiciously; *consultō,* designedly; and a few in *ā* from adjectives of the first declension; as, *rectā,* straight on; *ūnā,* together. In like manner, *rĕpentē,* suddenly, from *rĕpens*; and *pĕregre* or *pĕregri,* from *pĕrĕger.*

(*b.*) Nominatives or accusatives of the third declension in the neuter singular; as, *făcĭlĕ, diffĭcĭlĕ, rĕcens, sublīmĕ,* and *impūnĕ*; and some also of the second declension; as, *cētĕrum, plērumquĕ, multum, plūrĭmum, pŏtissĭmum, paulum, nĭmĭum, pārum,* and the numeral adverbs, *prīmum, ĭtĕrum, tertium, quartum,* etc. which have also the termination in *ō,* and so also *postrēmum (ō),* and *ultĭmum (ō).* The neuter plural sometimes occurs also, especially in poetry; as, *multā gemĕre; tristiā ululāre; crēbrā ferīre.*

(*c.*) Accusatives of the first declension; as, *bĭfăriam, trĭfăriam, multĭfăriam, omnĭfăriam,* etc. scil. *partem.*

Note 1. The forms in *ē* and *ō* from adjectives of the second declension have generally the same meaning, but *vērē* and *vēro* have a somewhat different sense. *Vērē,* truly, is the regular adverb of *vērŭs,* true; but *vēro* is used in answers, in the sense of 'in truth,' or 'certainly.' In this use it is added to the verb used in the question; as, *adfuistĭnĕ hĕrĭ in convivio?* The affirmative answer is *ego vēro adfui,* or without the verb, *ego vēro,* and negatively, *mĭnĭmē vēro;* and as *vēro* thus merely indicates a reply, it is often untranslatable into English.—*Certŏ,* on the other hand, usually takes the meaning of the adjective *certus,* while *certē* often signifies 'at least'; as, *victi sŭmus, aut, si dignĭtas vinci non pŏtest, fracti certē;* but *certē* is frequently used in the sense of 'certainly,' especially in the phrase *certē scio.*

Note 2. Some adjectives, from the nature of their signification, have no corresponding adverbs. Of some others, also, none occur in the classics. Such are *āmens, dīrŭs, discors, guārŭs, rŭdĭs, trux, imbellĭs, immōbĭlĭs,* and similar compounds. In place of the adverbs formed from *vĕtŭs* and *fīdŭs, vĕtustē* and *antīquē* are used for the former, and *fīdēlĭter* for the latter, from *vĕtustŭs, antĭquŭs,* and *fīdēlis.*

III. From the adjective pronouns are derived adverbs of place, etc. (See § 191, Rem. 1.)

Remark. The terminations *ō* and *ūc* denote the place *whither,* instead of the accusative of the pronoun with a preposition; as, *eō* for *ad eum lŏcum; hūc* for *ad hunc lŏcum;* the terminations *dē* and *inc* denote the place *from which;* 1 and *ic,* the place *in which;* and *ā* and *āc,* the place *by* or *through which;* as, *eā; viā* or *parte* being understood.

IV. (*a.*) A few adverbs are derived from prepositions; as, *subtŭs,* beneath; from *sŭb; proptĕr,* near; from *prŏpē.* (*b.*) *Mordicūs* and *versŭs* are derived from the verbs *mordeo* and *verto.*

Remark. Diminutives are formed from a few adverbs; as, *clam, clancŭlum; prīmum, prīmŭlum; cĕlĕriŭs, cĕlĕriuscŭlē; sæpiŭs, sæpiuscŭlē; bĕnĕ, bellĕ, bellissĭmē,*

COMPOSITION OF ADVERBS.

§ 193. Adverbs are compounded variously:—

1. Of an adjective and a noun; as, *postrīdĭē, quŏtĭdĭē, magnŏpĕrē, maxĭmŏpĕrē, summŏpĕrē, quantŏpĕrē, tantŏpĕrē, tantummŏdō, sōlummŏdō, multĭmŏdis, quŏtannīs*—of *postĕrō dĭē, magnō ŏpĕrē*, etc.
2. Of a pronoun and a noun; as, *hŏdĭē, quārē, quōmŏdō*—of *hōc dĭē, quā rē*, etc.
3. Of an adverb and a noun; as, *nūdĭŭs, sæpĕnŭmĕrō*—of *nunc dies*, etc.
4. Of a preposition and a noun; as, *commĭnŭs, ēmĭnŭs, illĭco, ōbĭter, extemplō, ŏbvĭam, postmŏdō, admŏdum, prŏpĕdiem*—of *con, e*, and *mănŭs; in* and *lŏcŭs*; etc.
5. Of an adjective and a pronoun; as, *ălĭōquī* or *ălĭōquin, cētĕrōquī* or *cētĕrōquin*—of *ălĭŭs* and *quī*, i. e. *ălĭō quō (mŏdo)*, etc.
6. Of a pronoun and an adverb; as, *ălĭquamdiū, ălĭcŭbĭ*—of *ălĭquis, dĭū*, and *ŭbi; nēquāquam* and *nēquicquam*—of *nē* and *quisquam*.
7. Of two verbs; as, *īlĭcĕt, scīlĭcĕt vĭdēlĭcĕt* of *īre, scīre, vĭdēre*, and *lĭcĕt*.
8. Of an adverb and a verb; as, *quōlĭbĕt, ŭbĭvīs, undēlĭbĕt*. So *deinceps*—from *dein* and *căpio; duntaxat*—from *dum* and *taxo*.
9. Of a participle with various parts of speech; as, *deorsum, dextrorsum, horsum, retrorsum, sursum*—of *dē, dexter, hīc, retro, sŭper*, and *vorsŭs* or *versŭs*.
10. Of two adverbs; as, *jamdūdum, quamdĭū, tamdĭū, cummaxĭmē, tummaxĭmē quousquĕ, sīcŭt*.
11. Of a preposition and an adjective; as, *dēnuo, imprīmis, cumprīmis, apprīmē, incassum*—of *dē nŏvō, in prīmis*, etc.
12. Of a preposition and a pronoun; as, *quaproptĕr, posteā, intĕreā, prætĕreā, hactĕnŭs, quātĕnŭs, ălĭquātĕnŭs, eātĕnŭs*—ot *propter quæ, post ea* or *eam*, etc.
13. Of a preposition and an adverb; as, *ăbhinc, ădhūc, dērĕpentĕ, intĕrĭbĭ, intĕrdĭū, interdum, persæpē*.
14. Of two or three prepositions; as, *insŭpĕr, prŏtĭnŭs, indĕ, dein, deindĕ, pĕrindĕ*.
15. Of a conjunction and an adverb; as, *nēcŭbi, sīcŭbi*—of *nē, sī*, and *ălĭcŭbi*.
16. Of an adverb and a termination scarcely used except in composition; as, *ĭbīdem, părumpĕr, quandōcumquĕ, ŭbīquĕ, utcumquĕ*.
17. Of three different parts of speech; as, *forsĭtăn*—of *fors, sĭt, ăn, quemadmŏdum, quamobrem*, etc.
18. Of an adverb and an adjective; as, *nīmīrum, utpŏtĕ*.
19. Of an adjective and a verb; as, *quantumvīs, quantumlĭbĕt*.

Signification of certain Compound and Derivative Adverbs.

1. The adverbs *contĭnuo, prŏtĭnus, stătim, confestim, sŭbĭto, rĕpente* and *dērĕpente, actūtum, illĭco, ĭlĭcĕt, extemplo,* signify in general 'directly' or 'immediately'; but, strictly, *contĭnuo* means, 'immediately after'; *stătim,* 'without delay'; *confestim,* 'directly'; *sŭbĭto,* 'suddenly, unexpectedly'; *prŏtĭnus,* 'farther,' viz. in the same direction, and hence, 'without interruption'; *rĕpente* and *dērĕpente,* 'at once,' opposed to *sensim,* 'gradually,' (see Cic. Off. 1, 33); *actūtum,* 'instantaneously,' i. q. *eōdem actū; illĭco,* and more rarely *ilĭcet,* 'forthwith, the instant,' (Virg. Æn. 2, 424, Cic. Mur. 10); so also *extemplo,* (Liv. 41, 1).

2. *Præsertim, præcĭpue, imprīmis, cumprīmis, apprīme,* are generally translated 'principally,' but, properly, *præsertim* is 'particularly,' and sets forth a particular circumstance with emphasis; *præcĭpue,* from *præcĭpio,* has reference to privilege, and signifies 'especially'; *imprīmis* and *cumprīmis,* signify 'principally,' or 'in preference to others'; and *apprīme,* 'before all,' 'very.' is used

in pure Latin to qualify and strengthen only adjectives. *Admŏdum* properly signifies 'according to measure,' that is, 'in as great a measure as can be,' 'very, exceedingly.' With numerals it denotes approximation, 'about.' *Admŏdum nihil* and *admŏdum nullus* signify 'nothing at all' and 'no one at all.'

3. *Mŏdo* is the usual equivalent for 'only.' *Sōlum*, 'alone,' 'merely,' points to something higher or greater. *Tantum*, 'only,' 'merely,' intimates that something else was expected. The significations of *sōlum* and *tantum* are strengthened by *mŏdo*, forming *sōlummŏdo* and *tantummŏdo*. *Duntaxat*, 'only, solely,' is not joined with verbs. It also signifies 'at least,' denoting a limitation to a particular point. *Saltem* also signifies 'at least,' but denotes the reduction of a demand to a minimum; as, *Eripe mihi hunc dolōrem, aut minue saltem*.

4. *Frustrā* implies a disappointed expectation; as in *frustra suscipĕre labōres*. *Nēquicquam* denotes the absence of success, as in Hor. Carm. 1, 3, 21. *Incassum*, composed of *in* and *cassum*, 'hollow' or 'empty,' signifies 'to no purpose'; as, *tela incassum jacĕre*.

COMPARISON OF ADVERBS.

§ 194. 1. Adverbs derived from adjectives with the terminations *ē* and *tĕr*, and most of those in *o*, are compared like their primitives.

2. The comparative, like the neuter comparative of the adjective, ends in *iŭs;* the superlative is formed from the superlative of the adjective by changing *ŭs* into *e;* as,

dūrē, dūriŭs, dūrissimē; făcĭlē, făcĭliŭs, făcĭlimē; ācrĭtĕr, ācriŭs, ācerrĭmē; rārō, rāriŭs, rārissĭme; mātūrē, mātūriŭs, mātūrissime or *māturrime.*

3. Some adverbs have superlatives in *ō* or *um;* as, *mĕrĭtissimō, plūrĭmum, prīmō* or *prīmum, pŏtissĭmum.*

4. If the comparison of the adjective is irregular or defective, (see §§ 125, 126), that of the adverb is so likewise; as,

bĕnē, mĕliŭs, optĭmē; mălĕ, pĕjŭs, pessĭmē; părum, minŭs, minĭme; multum, plūs, plūrĭmum; —, priŭs, prīmō or *prīmum; —, ŏciŭs, ŏcissĭme; —, dētĕriŭs, dēterrĭme; —, pŏtiŭs, pŏtissĭne* or *pŏtissĭmum; mĕrĭtō, —, mĕrĭtissĭmo; sătĭs, sătiŭs, —. Măgĭs, maxĭmē,* (from *magnŭs,*) has no positive; *nūpĕr, nūperrĭme,* has no comparative. *Prŏpē, prŏpiŭs, proxĭme;* the adjective *prŏpĭŏr* has no positive in use. The regular adverb in the positive degree from *ūbĕr* is wanting, its place being supplied by *ūbertim,* but *ūbĕriŭs* and *ūberrĭmē* are used. So instead of *tristĭtĕr, tristē,* the neuter of *tristis,* is used, but the comparative *tristiŭs* is regular; and from *sōcors* only *sōcordiŭs,* the comparative, is in use.

5. *Diū* and *sæpĕ,* though not derived from adjectives, are yet compared;— *diū, diūtiŭs, diūtissĭme; sæpē, sæpiŭs, sæpissĭme.* A comparative *tempĕriŭs,* from *tempĕri* or *tempŏri,* also sometimes occurs. So *sĕcŭs, sĕciŭs.*

6. Adverbs, like adjectives, are sometimes compared by prefixing *măgĭs* and *maxĭmē;* as, *măgĭs apertē, maxĭmē accommŏdātē.*

PREPOSITIONS.

§ 195. 1. A preposition is a particle which expresses the relation between a noun or pronoun and some preceding word.

2. Prepositions express the relations of persons or things, either to one another, or to actions and conditions; as, *ămor meus erga te,* my love toward thee; *eo ad te,* I go to thee.

3. Some prepositions have the noun or pronoun which follows them in the accusative, some, in the ablative, and some, in either the accusative or the ablative.

4. Twenty-six prepositions have an accusative after them:—

ăd, *to, towards, at, for.*
adversŭs, } *against,*
adversum, } *towards.*
antĕ, *before.*
ăpŭd, *at, with, near, before, in presence of.*
circā, } *around, about.*
circum, }
circĭtĕr; *about, near.*
cĭs, } *on this side, within.*
cĭtrā, }
contrā, *against, opposite.*
ergā, *towards, opposite.*

extrā, *without, beyond.*
infrā, *under, beneath.*
intĕr, *between, among, during.*
intrā, *within.*
juxtā, *near to, next to.*
ŏb, *for, on account of, before.*
pĕnĕs, *in the power of, with.*
pĕr, *through, throughout, by, during.*
pōnĕ, *behind.*

post, *after, since, behind.*
prætĕr, *past, before, against, beyond, besides.*
prŏpĕ, *near by, nigh.*
proptĕr, *near, on account of.*
sĕcundum, *after, behind, along, next to, according to.*
suprā, *above, over.*
trans, *over, beyond.*
ultrā, *beyond.*

5. Eleven prepositions have after them an ablative:—

ā, }
ăb, } *from, after, by.*
abs, }
absquĕ, *without, but for.*
cōram, *before, in presence of.*
cum, *with.*

dē, *from, down from, after, of, concerning.*
ē, } *out of, from, of, by,*
ex, } *after.*
pălam, *before, in presence of.*

præ, *before, for, on account of, in comparison with.*
prō, *before, for, instead of, according to.*
sĭnĕ, *without.*
tĕnŭs, *as far as, up to.*

6. Five prepositions take after them sometimes an accusative, and sometimes an ablative:—

clam, *without the knowledge of.*
In, *in, on; to, into, against.*

sŭb, *under, about, near.*
subtĕr, *under, beneath.*

sŭpĕr, *above, over; upon concerning.*

REMARK 1. Prepositions are so called, because they are generally *placed before* the noun or pronoun whose relation they express. They sometimes, however, stand after it. Cf. § 279, 10.

REM. 2. *A* is used only before consonants; *ab* before vowels, and frequently before consonants, though rarely before labials: *abs* is obsolete, except in the phrase *abs te.*
E is used only before consonants, *ex* before both vowels and consonants.

REM. 3. *Versŭs,* which follows its noun, (cf. § 235, R. 3), *usquĕ,* and *exadversŭs* (*.um*), sometimes take an accusative, *simŭl* and *prŏcŭl,* an ablative, and are then by some called prepositions. *Sĕcŭs,* with an accusative, occurs in Pliny and Cato.

REM. 4. Many of the prepositions, especially those which denote place, are also used as adverbs. Cf. § 191.

Signification and Use of certain Prepositions.

REM. 5. (*a.*) *Ad* denotes direction, and answers to the questions Whither? and Till when? as, *Venio ad te. Sophocles ad summam senectutem tragœdias fecit.* Cic. It also denotes a fixed time; as, *ad hōram,* at the hour; *ad tempus aliquid facĕre,*—at the right time. But sometimes *ad tempus* denotes 'for a time.' Sometimes, also, *ad* denotes the approach of time; as, *ad lūcem, ad vespĕram, ad extrēmum,* towards day-break, etc.; and also the actual arrival of a time; as, *ad prima signa vēris profectus,* at the first sign of Spring.

§ 195.   PREPOSITIONS.   165

(b.) In answer to the question Where? ăd signifies 'near' a place as, ăd urbem esse; ăd portas urbis; pugna navālis ăd Tenēdum. It is used like in, 'at,' in such phrases as ăd ædem Bellōnæ, or, without ædem, ăd Opis; negotium habēre ăd portum.—With numerals it may be rendered 'to the amount of' or 'nearly'; as, ăd ducentos. It is also used like circĭtĕr without any case; as, Occīsis ăd homĭnum millĭbus quatuor.—The phrase omnes ăd ūnum signifies, 'all without exception,' 'every one.'

(c.) Ad often denotes an object or purpose, and hence comes its signification of 'in respect to'; as, hŏmo ăd labōres belli impĭger. It is also used in figurative relations to denote a model, standard, or object of comparison, where we say 'according to,' or 'in comparison with'; as, ăd mŏdum, ăd effĭgiem, ăd simĭlĭtudĭnem, ăd speciem alicūjus rei; ăd normam, etc. ăd voluntātem alicūjus facĕre alĭquid. Ad verbum signifies, 'word for word'; nihil ăd hanc rem, 'nothing in comparison with this thing.'

Rem. 6. *Apŭd* expresses nearness to, and was primarily used of persons as ăd was applied to things. Apŭd also denotes rest, and ăd direction, motion, etc. Hence it signifies 'with,' both literally and figuratively. With names of places it signifies 'near,' like ăd; as, Mălĕ pugnātum est ăpŭd Caudium. But in early writers, ăpŭd is used for in; as, Augustus ăpŭd urbem Nōlam extinctus est,—at Nola.—With me, te, se, or the name of a person, it signifies 'at the house' or 'dwelling of'; as, Fuisti ăpŭd Læcam illā nocte.—Before appellatives of persons having authority in regard to any matter, it is translated 'before,' 'in the presence of'; as, ăpŭd judĭces, ăpŭd prætōrem, ăpŭd popŭlum.—It is also used with names of authors, instead of in with the name of their works; as, Apŭd Xenophontem, but we cannot say in Xenophonte.

Rem. 7. *Adversŭs, contrā,* and *ergā* signify 'opposite to.' Contrā denotes hostility, like our 'against'; ergā, a friendly disposition, 'towards'; and adversŭs is used in either sense. But ergā sometimes occurs in a hostile sense.

Rem. 8. *Intrā* signifies 'within,' in regard both to time and place. In regard to place it is used in answer to both questions Where? and Whither? It denotes time either as an entire period, when it is equivalent to 'during,' or as 'unfinished,' when it corresponds with 'under,' or 'before the expiration of.'

Rem. 9. *Pĕr*, denoting place, signifies, 'through,' and also 'in,' in the sense of 'throughout.'—With the accusative of persons it signifies 'through,' 'by the instrumentality of.' It often expresses the manner; as, pĕr litĕras, by letter; pĕr injuriam, pĕr scĕlus, with injustice, criminally; pĕr iram, from or in anger; pĕr simulatiōnem, pĕr speciem, pĕr causam, under the pretext; pĕr occasiōnem, on the occasion; pĕr ridĭcŭlum, in a ridiculous manner.—It sometimes signifies 'on account of'; as, pĕr valetudĭnem, on account of illness.—Pĕr me licet,—so far as I am concerned.

Rem. 10. *A* or *ăb*, denoting time, is used with nouns, both abstract and concrete, with the same general meaning; as, ā prīmā ætāte, ăb ineunte ætāte, ăb initio ætātis, ăb infantiā, ā pueritiā, ăb adolescentiā; and, ā puĕro, ā puĕris, ăb adolescentŭlo, ăb infante, all of which signify 'from an early age.' So also, ā parvis, ā parvŭlo, ā tenĕro, ā tenĕris unguicŭlis, which expressions are of Greek origin.—Ab initio, ā principio, ā prīmo, properly denote the space of time from the beginning down to a certain point; as, Urbem Rōmam ā principio rēges habuēre, i. e. for a certain period after its foundation. But frequently ăb initio is equivalent to initio, in the beginning.—The adherents or followers of a school are often named from its head; as, ā Platone, ăb Aristotĕle, etc.—In comic writers ăb is sometimes used instead of the genitive; as, ancilla ăb Andriā.—In a figurative sense it signifies 'with regard to'; as, ăb equitātu firmus.—With names of persons it also denotes relationship, and signifies 'on the side of'; as, Augustus ā matre Magnum Pompeium artissĭmo contingēbat grădu,—on his mother's side.—Stătim, confestim, rēcens ăb alĭquā re, 'immediately after.'—Ab itinĕre alĭquid facĕre, to do a thing while on a journey.

Rem. 11. *Cum* is used not only to designate accompanying persons but also accompanying circumstances; as, cum alĭquo ire; hostes cum detrimento sunt *depulsi.* It signifies also 'in,' i. e. 'dressed in'; as, *cum tunīcā pullā sedēre.* With verbs implying hostility, it signifies with,' in the sense of 'against'; as, *cum aliquo bellum gerĕre; cum aliquo quĕri* to complain of or against.

REM. 12. *Dē* commonly signifies 'concerning,' 'about.' Hence *traditur dē Homēro* is very different from *traditur ăb Homēro;* in the former, Homer is the object, in the latter the agent.—In the epistolary style, when a new subject is touched upon, *dē* signifies 'in regard to,' 'as respects'; as, *dē frātre, confīdo ita esse, ut semper volui.*—It often signifies 'down from'; and also 'of,' in a partitive sense; as, *hŏmo dē plēbe, ūnus dē popŭlo.*—From its partitive signification arises its use in denoting time; as, *in comitium dē nocte venīre*, i. e. even by night, or spending a part of the night in coming; hence *multā dē nocte, mediā dē nocte,* 'in the depth of night,' 'in the middle of the night.'—In other cases, also, it is used for *ex* or *ăb;* as, *Audīvi hoc dē parente meo puer.* Cic.; especially in connection with *emĕre, mercāri, conducĕre. Triumphum agĕre dē Gallis* and *ex Gallis* are used indiscriminately—Sometimes, like *sĕcundum,* it signifies 'in accordance with,' 'after'; as, *dē consilio meo:*—sometimes it denotes the manner of an action; as, *dēnuo, dē integro,* afresh; *dē improviso,* unexpectedly; *dē industriā,* purposely:—*quā dē re, quā dē causā, quibus dē causis,* for which reason or reasons.

REM. 13. *Ex*, 'from,' 'out of.' *Ex ĕquo pugnāre,* to fight on horseback; so *ex itinĕre scribĕre: ex adverso, ē regiōne,* opposite; *ex omni parte,* in or from all parts.—*Ex vino* or *ex ăquā coquĕre* or *bibĕre,* i. e. 'with wine,' etc. are medical expressions.—It sometimes denotes manner; as, *ex animo laudāre,* to praise heartily; *ex sententiā* and *ex voluntāte,* according to one's wish.—It is also, like *dē*, used in a partitive sense; as, *ūnus ē plēbe, ūnus ē multis.*

REM. 14. *In*, with the accusative, signifying 'to' or 'into,' denotes the point towards which motion proceeds; as, *in ædem ire;* or the direction in which a thing extends; as, *decem pĕdes in altitudĭnem,* in height; so, also, it denotes figuratively the object towards which an action is directed, either with a friendly or a hostile design; as, *amor in patriam, odium in malos cives, in milĭtes liberālis'; oratio in aliquem,* a speech against some one.—It also denotes a purpose; as, *pecunia data est in rem militārem. Pax data Philippo in has lēges est,* on these conditions.—With words denoting time, it expresses a predetermination of that time, like 'for'; as, *invitāre aliquem in postĕrum diem,* for the following day. *In diem vivĕre,* to live only for the day; *in futūrum, in postĕrum, in reliquum,* for the future; *in æternum, in perpetuum,* forever; *in præsens,* for the present: with all these adjectives *tempus* may be supplied. *In* with *singŭli,* expressed or understood, denotes a distribution, and may be translated 'to,' 'for,' 'on,' 'over.'—*In singŭlos dies,* or simply *in dies,* with comparatives and verbs denoting increase, signifies 'from day to day.'— In some phrases it denotes the manner of an action; as, *servīlem in mŏdum, mirum in mŏdum;* so *in universum,* in general; *in commūne,* in common; *in vicem,* alternately, or, instead of; *in alicūjus lŏcum aliquid petĕre,* in the place, or, instead of.

REM. 15. *In*, with the ablative, signifies 'in,' 'on,' 'upon,' and answers to the question, Where? When a number or quantity is indicated, it signifies 'among,' and is equivalent to *intĕr*. It may sometimes be translated 'with,' or 'notwithstanding'; as, *In summā copiā oratōrum, nēmo tămen Cicerōnis laudem æquāvit.*—With nouns which by themselves denote time, such as *secŭlum, annus, mensis, dies, nox, vesper,* etc., the time, in answer to the question When? is expressed by the simple ablative; but *in* is used with words which acquire the signification of time only by such connection; as, *in consulātu in principio, in bello;* but even with these *in* is sometimes omitted, but is usually retained in connection with the gerund or gerundive; as, *in legendo, in legendis libris. In præsenti,* or *in præsentiā,* signifies 'at the present moment,' 'for the present.'—*Ex in eo, ut aliquid fiat* signifies that something is on the point of happening.

PREPOSITIONS IN COMPOSITION.

§ 196. Most of the prepositions are used also in forming compound words. In composition, they may be considered either in reference to their form, or their force.

I. (*a.*) Prepositions in composition sometimes retain their final consonants, and sometimes change them, to adapt them to the sounds of the initial consonants of the words with which they are compounded. In some words, both forms are in use; in others, the final consonant or consonants are omitted.

1. *A*, in composition, is used before *m* and *v*; as, *āmŏveo, āvello*, and sometimes before *f* in *āfui* and *āfŏre*, for *abfui* and *abfŏre*. *Ab* is used before vowels, and before *d, f, h, j, l, n, r*, and *s*; as, *abjūro, abrŏgo*, etc. *Abs* occurs only before *c, q*, and *t*; as, *abscondo, absque, abstineo*. In *aspello, aspernor*, and *asporto*, the *b* of *abs* is dropped; in *aufĕro* and *aufugio*, it is changed into *u*.

2. *Ad* remains unchanged before vowels and before *b, d, h, m, v*. It often changes *d* into *c, f, g, l, n, p, r, s, t*, before those letters respectively; as, *cccēdo, affĕro, aggrĕdior, alli go, annītor, appōno, arrĭgo, assĕquor, attollo*. Its *d* is usually omitted before *s* followed by a consonant, and before *gn*; as, *aspergo, aspĭcio, agnosco, agnātus*. Before *q*, the *d* is changed into *c*; as, *acquiro*.

3. *Ante* remains unchanged, except in *antīcipo* and *antisto*, where it changes *e* to *i*; but *antesto* also occurs.

4. *Circum* in composition remains unchanged, only in *circŭmeo* and its derivatives the *m* is often dropped; as, *circueo, circuitus*, etc.

5. *Cum* (in composition, *com*), retains *m* before *b, m, p*; as, *combĭbo, commĭtto, compōno*: before *l, n, r*, its *m* is changed into those letters respectively; as, *collĭgo, connītor, corripĭo*: before other consonants, it becomes *n*; as, *condūco, conjungo*. Before a vowel, *gn* or *h*, *m* is commonly omitted; as, *cŏeo, coopio, cognosco, cohabĭto*; but it is sometimes retained; as, *comēdo, cōmes, cōmĭtor*. In *cōgo* and *cōgito* a contraction also takes place; as, *cōĭgo, cōgo*, etc. In *combūro*, *b* is inserted.

6. *Ex* is prefixed to vowels, and to *c, h, p, q, s, t*; as, *exeo, exĭgo, excurro, exhĭbeo, expĕdio*. Before *f, x* is assimilated, and also rarely becomes *ec*; as, *effĕro*, or *ecfĕro*. *S* after *x* is often omitted; as, *exĕquor*, for *exsĕquor*; in *excidium* (from *exscindo*), *s* is regularly dropped. *E* is prefixed to the other consonants; as, *ēbibo, ēdico*, except in *eclex*. Before these however, with the exception of *n* and *r*, *ex* is sometimes used; as, *exmŏveo*. *E* is sometimes used before *p*; as, *ēpōto*.

7. *In* remains unchanged before a vowel. Before *b, m, p*, it changes *n* into *m*; as, *imbuo, immitto, impōno*: before *l* and *r*, *n* is assimilated; as, *illĭgo, irrētio*: before *gn*, *n* is omitted; as, *ignārus*. Before the other consonants *in* is unchanged. In some compounds, *in* retains *d* before a vowel, from an ancient form *indu*; as, *indigĕna, indigeo, indolesco*. So anciently *induperātor*, for *imperātor*.

8. *Inter* remains unchanged, except in *intellĭgo* and its derivatives, in which *r* before *l* is assimilated.

9. *Ob* remains unchanged before vowels and generally before consonants. Its *b* is assimilated before *c, f, g, p*; as, *occurro, offĭcio, oggannio, oppēto*. In *ŏmitto*, *b* is dropped. An ancient form *obs*, analogous to *abs* for *ab*, is implied in *obsolesco*, from the ample verb *oleo*, and in *ostendo*, for *obstendo*.

10. *Per* is unchanged in composition, except in *pellicio* and sometimes in *pellūceo*, in which *r* is assimilated before *l*. In *pējĕro*, *r* is dropped.

11. *Post* remains unchanged, except in *pōmarium* and *pōmĕridiānus*, in which *st* is dropped.

12. *Præ* and *præter* in composition remain unchanged, except that *præ* is shortened before a vowel. Cf. § 283, II Exc. 1.

13. *Prō* has sometimes its vowel shortened, (cf. § 285, 2, Exc. 5) and, to avoid hiatus, it sometimes takes *d* before a vowel; as, *prōdeo, prōdesse, prŏdigo*. Before verbs beginning with *r* and *l*, *pro* sometimes becomes *por* and *pol*; as, *porrigo, polliceor*.

14. *Sŭb* in composition remains unchanged before a vowel and before *b, d, j, l, n, s, t, v*. Before *c, f, g, m, p, r*, its *b* is regularly assimilated; as, *succēdo, suffēro, suggēro, summŏveo, supplico, surrīpio*. Before *c, p,* and *t*, it sometimes takes the form *sus* from *subs*, analogous to *abs* and *obs*; as, *suscīpio, suspendo, sustollo*: *b* is omitted before *s*, followed by a consonant; as, *suspīcio*.

15. *Subter* and *sŭper* in composition remain unchanged.

16. *Trans* remains unchanged before a vowel. It omits *s* before *s*; as, *transcendo*: in *trādo, trādūco, trājicio*, and *trāno, ns* is commonly omitted.

(*b.*) The following words are called *inseparable prepositions*, because they are found only in composition:—

Ambĭ or amb, (Greek ἀμφί), *around, about*.   Rĕd or rĕ, *again, back*.   Vē, *not*.
Dĭs or dī, *asunder*.   Sē, *apart, aside*.

1. *Amb* is always used before a vowel; as, *ambāges, ambarvālis, ambĕdo, ambīgo, ambio, ambūro*: except *ampulla, āmicio*, and *ānhelo*. Before consonants it has the forms *ambi*; as, *ambidens, ambifāriam, ambŭrium: am*; as, *amplector, amputo*: or *an*; as, *anceps, anfractus, anquiro*.

2. *Dĭs* is prefixed to words beginning with *c, p, q, s* before a vowel, *t*, and *h*; as, *discŭtio, dispōno, disquiro, distendo, dishisco:* but *disertus* is formed from *dissēro*; before *f, s* is changed into *f*; as, *diffēro*: in *dīrĭmo*, and *diribeo* (from *dis habeo*), *s* becomes *r*. *Dī* is prefixed to the other consonants, and to *s* when followed by a consonant; as, *didūco, dīmitto, distinguo, displĭcio*. But both *dīs* and *dī* are used before *j*; as, *disjungo, dījūdĭco*, and before *r* in *rumpo*.

3. *Rĕd* is used before a vowel or *h*; *rĕ* before a consonant; as, *rĕdāmo, rĕdeo, rĕdhībeo, rĕdĭgo, rĕdŏleo, rĕdundo; —rĕjĭcio, rĕpōno, rĕvertor*. But *rĕd* is used before *do*; as, *reddo*. The connecting vowel *i* is found in *rĕdivīvus*; and in the poetical forms *relligio, relliquiæ*, and sometimes in *reccĭdo* the *d* is assimilated. In later writers *re* is sometimes found before a vowel or *h*.

4. *Sē* and *vē* are prefixed without change; as, *sēcēdo, sēcūrus; vēgrandis, vēcors*.

§ 197. II. Prepositions in composition usually add their own signification to that of the word with which they are united; but sometimes they give to the compound a meaning different from that of its simples. The following are their most common significations:—

1. *A,* or *ab, away, from, down; entirely; un-*. With verbs it denotes removal, disappearance, absence; as, *aufĕro, abūtor, absum*. With adjectives it denotes absence, privation; as, *āmens, absŏnus*.

2. *Ad, to, toward; at, by*. In composition with verbs *ăd* denotes (*a*) *motion to*, (not *into*), as, *accēdo*; (*b*) *addition*, as, *ascrībo*; (*c*) *nearness*, as, *assideo*; (*d*) *assent, favor*, as, *annuo, arrīdeo*; (*e*) *repetition* and hence *intensity*, as, *accīdo*; (*f*) *at, in consequence of*, as, *urrīgo*. It is sometimes augmentative, rarely inchoative.

3. *Ambĭ*, around, about, on both sides.

4. *Circum*, around, about, on all sides.

5. *Cŏm* or *cŏn*, together, entirely. In composition with verbs it denotes (*a*) *union*, as, *concurro, consŭlo*; (*b*) *completeness*, as, *comburo, confĭcio*; (*c*) *with effort*, as, *conjĭcio, conclāmo*; (*d*) *in harmony*, as, *consŏno, consentio*; (*e*) *on or over*, like the English *be-*, as, *collīno*, to besmear.

6. *Contra*, against, opposite.

7. *Dē*, off, away, through, over, down; entirely; very, extremely. With verbs *dē* denotes (*a*) *down*; as, dēmitto; (*b*) *removal*; as, dētondeo; (*c*) *absence*; as, dēsum, dehābeo; (*d*) *prevention*; as, dēhortor; (*e*) *unfriendly feeling*; as, despicio, dērideo.—With adjectives *dē* denotes (*a*) *down*; as, dēclīvis; (*b*) *without*; as, dēmens.

8. *Dis*, asunder, apart, in pieces, in two; dis-, un-; very greatly. With verbs *dis* denotes (*a*) *division*; as, dīvĭdo, dīlābor; (*b*) *difference*; as, discrĕpo, dissentio; (*c*) *the reverse of the simple notion*; as, displĭceo, diffīdo; (*d*) *intensity*; as, dīlaudo.—With adjectives *dis* denotes *difference*; as, discŏlor, discors.

9. *E*, or *ex*, out, forth, away, upward, without, -less, un-; utterly, completely, very. With verbs it denotes (*a*) *out*; as, exeo, eximo, ēlăbōro; (*b*) *removal of something*; as, ēdormio; (*c*) *publicity*; as, ēdīco; (*d*) *ascent*; as, exsisto; (*e*) *completeness*; as, ēdisco, exūro; (*f*) with denominative verbs, *change of character*; as, expio, effĕro (āre); (*g*) *removal of what is expressed by the noun whence the verb is derived*; as ēnōdo; (*h*) *the reversal of the fundamental idea*; as, explīco; (*i*) *distance*; as, exaudio.—With adjectives formed from substantives it denotes *absence*; as, exsomnis.

10. *In*, with verbs, signifies in, on, at; into, against; as, *inhăbĭto*, *induo*, *ingĕmo*, *ineo*, *illīdo*. With adjectives, un-, in-, im-, il-, ir-, not; as, *ignōtus*, *inhospĭtālis*, *immortālis*. Some of its compounds have contrary significations, according as they are participles or adjectives; as, *intectus*, *part*., covered, *adj.*, uncovered.

11. *Inter*, between, among, at intervals.

12. *Ob*, with verbs, signifies to, towards; as, *ŏbeo*, *ostendo*; against; as, *obluctor*, *obnuntio*; at, before; as, *ŏbambŭlo*, *obversor*; upon; as, *occulco*; over; as, *obdūco*.

13. *Per*, with verbs, denotes, through, thoroughly, perfectly, quite; as, *perdūco*, *perfĭcio*, *perdo*: with adjectives, through, very; as, *pernox*, *perlĕvis*.

14. *Post*, after, behind.

15. *Præ* in composition with verbs denotes (*a*) *before* in place; as, *præmitto*; (*b*) *by* or *past*; as, *præfluo*; (*c*) *in command*; as, *præsum*, *præfĭcio*; (*d*) *superiority*; as, *præsto*; (*e*) *before* in time; as, *prædīco*, *præcerpo*; *at the extremity*; as, *præūro*.—With adjectives, (*a*) *before* in place or time; as, *præceps*, *præscius*; (*b*) *very*; as, *præaltus*, *præclārus*.

16. *Præter*, past, by, beyond, besides.

17. *Prō*, before, forward, forth, away, down; for; openly; as, *prōlūdo*, *porrĭgo*, *prŏterreo*, *prōtĕro*, *prōcūro*, *prōfĭteor*.

18. *Rĕ*, again, against, back, re-, un-, away; greatly; as, *rĕflōresco*, *rĕpendo*, *rĕfĕrio*, *rĕfĭgo*, *rĕcondo*.

19. *Sē*, without, aside, apart; as, *sēcūro*, *sēpōno*, *sēcēdo*, *sēcūrus*.

20. *Sŭb* up, from below upwards, under. With verbs *sŭb* also signifies (*a*) *assistance*; as, subvenio; (*b*) *succession*; as, succīno; (*c*) *in place of*; as, suffīcio; (*d*) *near*; as, subsum; (*e*) *secretly*, *clandestinely*; as, surrĭpio, subdūco; (*f*) *somewhat*, *a little*; as, subrĭdeo, sŭbaccūso.—With adjectives it signifies, *slightly*, *rather*; as, sŭbobscūrus, sŭbabsurdus, sŭbăcĭdus.

21. *Subter*, beneath, under, from under, secretly, privately.

22. *Sŭper*, above, over, left over, remaining, super-; as, *sŭpersĕdeo*, *sŭpersum*, *sŭperstes*, *sŭpervăcāneus*.

23. *Trans*, over, across, through; beyond; as, *trādo*, *transeo*, *transfīgo*, *transalpīnus*.

24. *Vĕ*, not, without; very; as, *vēgrandis*, *vēcors*; *vēpallĭdus*.

REMARK. In composition the preposition seems often to add nothing to the signification of the word with which it is compounded.

15

CONJUNCTIONS.

§ 198. A conjunction is a particle which connects words or propositions.

The most usual conjunctions are,

ătque, } *and, as; than.*
ăc, }
ăc si, *as if.*
ădeo, *so that, so.*
ăn, } *whether.*
anne, }
annon, *whether or not.*
antĕquam, *before.*
ăt, ast, *but.*
ăt ĕnim, *but indeed.*
atquī, *but.*
attămĕn, *but yet.*
aut, *either, or.*
aut...aut, *either...or.*
autem, *but.*
cētĕrum, *but, however.*
ceu, *as, like as, as if.*
cum *or* quum, *since.*
dōnĕc, *as long as, until.*
dum, *provided, while, as long as, until.*
dummŏdo, *if but, if only.*
ĕnimvēro, *in very deed.*
ĕnim, } *for.*
ĕtĕnim, }
eō, *therefore.*
ĕquidem, *indeed.*
ergo, *therefore.*
ĕt, *and.*
ĕt...ĕt } *both...and;*
ĕt...quĕ, } *as well...as.*
ĕt...nĕque *or* nĕc, *on the one hand, but not on the other.*
ĕtiam, *also.*
ĕtiamsī, } *although,*
etsī, } *though.*
iccirco, }
ideo, } *therefore.*
igĭtŭr, }
ĭtăquĕ, }
licĕt, *though, although.*
mŏdo, *provided.*
nam, namquĕ, *for.*

nē, *lest, that not.*
-nĕ, *whether.*
nĕque *or* nĕc, *neither, nor.*
nĕque...nĕque, }
nĕc...nĕc, } *neither,*
nĕque...nĕc, } *...nor.*
nĕc...nĕque,
necnĕ, *or not.*
nĕque, *neither, nor.*
nĕquĕ *or* nĕc...ĕt, } *not*
nĕquĕ *or* nĕc...quĕ, } *on the one hand, but on the other.*
nēve *or* neu, *nor, and not.*
nēve...nēve, } *neither...*
neu...neu, } *nor.*
nī, nĭsī, *unless.*
num, *whether.*
præut, *in comparison with.*
prout, *according as, just as, as.*
proinde, *hence, therefore.*
proptĕreā, *therefore, for that reason.*
postquam, *after, since.*
priusquam, *before.*
quam, *as, than.*
quamvis, *although.*
quando, quandŏquĭdem, *whereas, since.*
quamquam, *although.*
quāpropter, }
quārē, }
quamobrem, } *wherefore.*
quōcircā, }
quantumvis, } *although,*
quamlĭbet, } *however.*
quăsi, *as if, just as.*
-quĕ, *and.*
-quĕ...ĕt, } *both...and;*
-quĕ...quĕ, } *as well...as.*
quia, *because.*
quīn, *but that, that not.*
quippĕ, *because.*

quŏ, *in order that.*
quoăd, *as long as, until.*
quŏd, *because, but.*
quodsī, *but if.*
quŏmĭnus, *that not.*
quŏniam, *since, because.*
quŏquĕ, *also.*
quum *or* cum, *when, since because.*
quum...tum, *both...and.*
sĕd, *but.*
sīcŭt, } *so as, just as, as.*
sīcŭtī, }
sī, *if.*
sī mŏdo, *if only.*
sĭmŭl, } *as soon*
sĭmŭlăc (-atquĕ) } *as.*
sīn, *but if, if however.*
sīvĕ *or* seu, *or if.*
sīvĕ...sīvĕ, } *whether...or.*
seu...seu, }
sīquĭdem, *if indeed, since.*
tămĕn, *however, still.*
tămetsī, *although.*
tamquam, *as if.*
tum...tum, *both...and.*
undĕ, *whence.*
ŭt, } *that, as that, so that,*
ŭtī, } *to the end that.*
ŭt sī, *as if.*
utrum, *whether.*
-vĕ, } *either, or.*
vĕl, }
vĕl...vĕl, *either...or.*
vĕlŭt, } *even as, just as,*
vĕlŭtī, } *like as.*
vēro, *truly, but indeed.*
vērum, *but.*
vēruntămĕn, *yet, notwithstanding.*
vērum-ĕnim vēro, *but indeed.*

Conjunctions, according to their different uses, are divided into two general classes,—coördinate and subordinate.

1. **Coördinate conjunctions**, are such as join coördinate or similar constructions; as,

Luna et stellæ fulgebant, The moon *and* the stars were shining. *Concidunt venti, fugiuntque nubes,* The winds subside, *and* the clouds disperse. *Difficile factu est, sed conabor tamen,* It is difficult to accomplish *but still* I will try.

§ 198. CONJUNCTIONS. 171

Coördinate conjunctions include the following subdivisions, viz. *copulative, disjunctive, adversative, illative,* and most of the *causal* conjunctions.

II. Subordinate conjunctions are such as join dissimilar constructions; as,

Edo, *ut vivam,* I eat that I may live. Pyrrhus rex in itinere incidit in canem, qui interfecti hominis corpus custodiebat. *Mergi pullos in aquam jussit, ut biberent,* quoniam *esse nollent.*

Subordinate conjunctions include all those connectives which unite subordinate or dependent clauses. These are the *concessive, illative, final, conditional, interrogative,* and *temporal* conjunctions, and the *causals quod, quum, quoniam,* etc. To these may be added also the relatives whether pronouns, adjectives, or adverbs.

The following paragraphs contain a specification of the several conjunctions comprised in each of the preceding subdivisions, and remarks respecting their particular import and use as connectives.

1. COPULATIVE conjunctions connect things that are to be considered jointly; as, *ĕt, āc, atquĕ,* the enclitic *quĕ,* which, combined with the negation belonging to the verb, becomes *nĕquĕ* or *nĕc,* and, the negation being doubled, *nĕc nōn* or *nĕquĕ nōn,* it becomes again affirmative and equivalent to *ĕt.* To these are to be added *ĕtiam* and *quŏquĕ,* with the adverbials *item* and *itidem.*

REMARK. (a.) *Et* and *quĕ* differ in this, *ĕt* connects things which are conceived as different, and *quĕ* adds what belongs to, or naturally flows from them. *Et,* therefore, is copulative and *quĕ* adjunctive. Hence, in an enumeration of words, *quĕ* frequently connects the last of the series, and by its means the preceding idea is extended without the addition of any thing which is generically different. In connecting propositions *quĕ* denotes a consequence, and is equivalent to 'and therefore.'

(b.) *Ac* never stands before vowels, *atquĕ* chiefly before vowels, but also before consonants.—*Atquĕ,* being formed of *ăd* and *quĕ,* properly signifies 'and also,' 'and in addition,' thus putting things on an equality, but giving emphasis to the latter. In the beginning of a proposition, which is explanatory of that which precedes, *atquĕ* or *ăc* introduces a thing with great weight, and may be rendered 'now'; and in answers; as, *Cognostine hos versus? Ac memoriter,* it is rendered 'yes, and that.' *Ac* being an abridged form of *atquĕ* loses somewhat of its power in connecting single words, and its use alternates with that of *ĕt*; it is preferred in subdivisions, whereas the main propositions are connected by *ĕt.*

(c.) *Nĕquĕ,* compounded of the ancient *nĕ* for *nōn* and *quĕ,* is used for *ĕt nōn. Et nōn* itself is used, when only one idea or one word of a proposition is to be negatived; as, *patior* et non *moleste fero*; and also when our '*and not*' is used for 'and not rather' to correct an improper supposition; as, *Si quam Rubrius injuriam suo nomine ac non impulsu tuo fecisset.* Cic. *Et nōn* is commonly found also in the second clause of a sentence when *ĕt* precedes, but *nĕquĕ,* also, is often used in this case. *Nĕc nōn* or *nĕquĕ nōn,* in classical prose, is not used like *ĕt* to connect nouns, but only to join propositions, and the two words are separated. In later writers, however, they are not separated and are equivalent to *ĕt.*

(d.) *Etiam* has a wider extent than *quŏquĕ,* for it contains the idea of our 'even,' and it also adds a new circumstance, whereas *quŏquĕ* denotes the addition of a thing of a similar kind. Hence *ĕtiam* is properly used to connect sentences, while *quŏquĕ* refers to a single word. *Etiam* signifies 'and further,' *quŏquĕ,* 'and so,' 'also.' *Quŏquĕ* always follows the word to which it refers, *ĕtiam* in similar cases is usually placed before it, but when it connects propositions its place is arbitrary. *Et,* too, in classical prose, is sometimes used in the sense of 'also.' So often is *non modo—sed ĕt,* 'not only—but also,' or 'but even.'

(e.) Copulative conjunctions are often repeated in the sense of 'both—and,' 'as well—as,' 'not only—but also.' *Et—et* is of common occurrence; so, in later writers, but rarely in Cicero, *ět—quě*; *quě—ět* connect single words, but not in Cicero; *quě—quě*, occur for the most part only in poetry, or in connection with the relative.—Negative propositions are connected in English by 'neither—nor,' and in Latin by *nĕquĕ—nĕquĕ, nĕc—nĕc, nĕquĕ—nĕc*, and rarely by *nĕc—nĕquĕ*. Propositions, one of which is negative and the other affirmative 'on the one hand—but not on the other,' or, 'not on the one hand—but on the other,' are connected by *ĕt—nĕquĕ* or *nĕc*, *nĕquĕ* or *nĕc—ĕt*, and occasionally by *nĕc* or *nĕquĕ—quĕ*.

2. DISJUNCTIVE conjunctions connect things that are to be considered separately; as, *aut, věl*, the enclitic *vě*, and *sivě* or *seu*.

REMARK. (a.) *Aut* and *vĕl* differ in this; *aut* indicates a difference of the object, *vĕl*, a difference of expression, i. e. *aut* is objective, *vĕl*, subjective. *Vĕl* is connected with the verb *velle*, and is generally repeated, *vĕl—vĕl*, 'choose this or choose this,' and the single *vĕl* is used by Cicero only to correct a preceding expression, and commonly combined with *dicam, pŏtius*, or *ĕtiam*.— Hence by ellipsis *vĕl* has acquired the signification of the adverb, 'even,' and so enhances the signification of the word modified by it; as, *Quum Sophŏcles vel optime scripsĕrit Electram*, where *bĕne* is to be supplied before *vel*, and the latter is used for the purpose of correcting the preceding expression. Cf. § 127, 4. By means of its derivation from *velle* it has, also, the signification of 'for example' or 'to take a case,' for which *vĕlŭt* is more frequently used.—(b.) *Vĕ*, the apocopated *vĕl*, leaves the choice free between two or more things, and in later but good prose *vĕl* is used in the same manner.

(c.) *Sivĕ* commonly retains the meaning of *si*, and is then the same as *vĕl si*, but sometimes loses it, and is then equivalent to *vĕl*, denoting a difference of name; as, *Vocabŭlum sivĕ appellatio.* Quint. The form *seu* is rarely used by Cicero except in the combination *seu pŏtius*.—(d.) *Aut* and *vĕ* serve to continue the negation in negative sentences, where we use 'nor'; as, *nŏn—aut*, where *nŏn—nĕquĕ* also may be used. They are used also in negative questions; as, *Num leges nostras moresvĕ novit?* Cic.; and after comparatives; as, *Doctrina paulo aspĕrior, quam veritas aut natūra patiātur.* Cic. It is only when both ideas are to be united into one that a copulative is used instead of *aut* and *vĕ*.—

(e.) 'Either—or' is expressed in Latin by *aut—aut*, denoting an opposition between two things, one of which excludes the other, or by *vĕl—vĕl*, denoting that the opposition is immaterial in respect to the result, so that the one need not exclude the other; as, *Vel imperatōre vel milite me utimini.* Sall.—*Sivĕ—sivĕ* is the same as *vĕl si—vĕl si*, and retains the meaning of *vĕl—vĕl*. If nouns only are opposed to each other, an uncertainty is expressed as to how a thing is to be called; as, *Crētum leges, quas sive Jupiter sive Minos sanxit;* i. e. I do not know whether I am to say Jupiter or Minos.

3. COMPARATIVE conjunctions express a comparison. These are, *ŭt* or *ŭti, sicŭt, vĕlŭt, proŭt, præŭt*, the poetical *ceu, quam, tamquam*, (with and without *si*), *quăsi, ŭt si, āc si*, with *ăc* and *atquĕ*, when they signify 'as.'

REMARK. *Ac* and *atquĕ* signify 'as' or 'than' after adverbs and adjectives which denote similarity or dissimilarity; as, *æquĕ, juxtā, pār* and *pārĭtĕr, pĕrindĕ* and *proindĕ, pro eō, sĭmĭlis* and *simĭlĭter, dissimĭlis, tālis, tŏtĭdem, ălius* and *ălĭtĕr, contrā, sēcŭs, contrārius.*— *Quam* is rarely used after these words, except when a negative particle is joined with *alius*; as, *Virtus nihil aliud est, quam*, etc.; and *ĕt* and *quĕ* do not occur in this connection.—*Ac* is used for *quam*, after comparatives, in poetry and occasionally by late prose writers; as, *Artius atque hedera*. Hor. *Insānius* ac *si.* Id.

4. CONCESSIVE conjunctions express a concession, with the general signification 'although.' These are *etsi, ĕtiamsi, tămetsi*, or *tămĕnetsi quamquam, quamvis, quantumvis, quamlĭbĕt, licĕt, ŭt* in the sense of 'even if' or 'although,' and *quum* when it signifies 'although.'

REMARK. *Tămĕn* and other particles signifying 'yet,' 'still,' are the correlatives of the concessive conjunctions; as, *Ut desint vires, tămen est laudanda voluntas.* Ovid. The adverb *quidem* becomes a concessive conjunction, when it is used to connect propositions and is followed by *sĕd*.— *Quamquam* in absolute sentences, sometimes refers to something preceding, which it limits and partly nullifies; as, Quamquam *quid loquor?* Yet why do I speak?

5. CONDITIONAL conjunctions express a condition, their fundamental signification being 'if.' These are *sī, sīn, nĭsī* or *nī, sī mŏdŏ, dummŏdŏ,* 'if only,' 'if but,' (for which *dum* and *mŏdo* are also used alone), *dummŏdŏ nē,* or simply *mŏdo nē* or *dumnē*.

REMARK. (*a*.) In order to indicate the connection with a preceding proposition, the relative *quŏd,* which in such case loses its signification as a pronoun, and may be rendered, 'nay,' 'now,' 'and,' or 'then,' is frequently put before *sī* and sometimes before *nĭsī* and *etsī,* so that *quodsī* may be regarded as one word, signifying 'now if,' 'but if,' or 'if then.' It serves especially to introduce something assumed as true, from which further inferences may be drawn.' It sometimes signifies 'although.' *Quodnisi* signifies 'if then—not,' and *quodĕtsī*, 'nay, even if.' *Quŏd* is found also before *quum, ŭbī, quiă, quŏniam, nē, ŭtĭnam,* and even before the relative pronoun.

(*b*.) *Nī* and *nĭsī* limit a statement by introducing an exception, and thus differ from *sī nōn,* which introduces a negative case. It is often immaterial whether *nĭsī* or *sī nōn* is used, but the difference is still essential. *Sī nōn* is used when single words are opposed to one another, and in this case *sī mĭnŭs* may be used instead of *sī nōn*.—If after an affirmative proposition its negative opposite is added without a verb, our 'but if not' is commonly expressed in prose by *sī mĭnŭs* or *sīn mĭnŭs* or *sīn ălĭter;* as, *Educ tecum etiam omnes tuos;* si minus, *quam plurimos.* Cic.; rarely by *sī nōn*.

6. ILLATIVE conjunctions express an inference or conclusion, with the general signification of 'therefore,' 'consequently.' These are *ergo, igĭtŭr, ĭtăquĕ, eō, ĭdeo, iccirco, proindĕ, proptĕrĕā,* and the relative conjunctions, *quaproptĕr, quārē, quamobrem, quōcircā, undĕ,* 'wherefore.'

REMARK. *Ergo* and *ĭgĭtŭr* denote a logical inference.—*Ĭtăquĕ,* 'and thus,' expresses the relation of cause in facts.—*Ideo, iccirco,* and *proptĕrĕā,* 'on this account,' express the agreement between intention and action.—*Eō,* 'on this account,' or 'for this purpose,' is more frequently an adverb of place.— *Proindĕ,* 'consequently,' implies an exhortation.—*Undĕ,* 'whence,' is properly an adverb of place.—*Adeo,* 'so that,' or simply 'so,' is also properly an adverb. *Hinc,* 'hence,' and *indĕ,* 'thence,' continue to be adverbs.

7. CAUSAL conjunctions express a cause or reason, with the general signification of 'for' and 'because.' These are *nam, namquĕ, ĕnim, ĕtĕnim, quĭă, quŏd, quŏniam, quippĕ, quum, quando, quandŏquĭdem sĭquĭdem;* and the adverbs *nĭmīrum, nempĕ, scīlĭcĕt,* and *vĭdēlĭcĕt*.

REMARK. (*a*.) *Nam* is used at the beginning of a proposition, *ĕnim,* after the first or second word. *Nam* introduces an objective reason, and *ĕnim* merely a subjective one. There is the same difference between *namquĕ* and *ĕtĕnim. Namquĕ,* however, though constantly standing at the beginning of a proposition in Cicero, Cæsar, and Nepos, is in later writers often put after the beginning. *Enim* in the sense of *āt ĕnim* or *sĕd ĕnim* is sometimes, by comic writers, put at the beginning of a proposition.—*Nam, ĕnim,* and *ĕtĕnim* are often used in the sense of 'namely,' or 'to wit,' to introduce an explanation of something going before. *Nĭmīrum, vĭdēlĭcĕt,* and *scīlĭcĕt* likewise answer to our 'namely' or 'viz.' *Nĭmīrum,* compounded of *nī* and *mīrum,* and signifying a wonder if not,' is used as a connective in the sense of 'undoubtedly' or surely,' and implies strong confidence in the truth of the proposition with which it is connected.—*Vĭdēlĭcĕt* and *scīlĭcĕt* introduce an explanation, with this difference that *vĭdēlĭcĕt* generally indicates the true, and *scīlĭcĕt* a wrong explanation. Sometimes, however, *nam, ĕnim, ĕtĕnim, nĭmīrum,* and *vĭdēlĭcĕt* are used in an ironical sense, and *scīlĭcĕt* introduces a true reason.—*Nempĕ* surely,' often assumes a sarcastic meaning when another person's concession is taken for the purpose of refuting him.—(*b*.) *Quiă* and *quŏd* indicate a definite and conclusive reason, *quŏniam*, (i. e. *quum jam*), a motive.—*Ideo, iccirco, proptĕreā quŏd*, and *quiă*, are used without any essential difference, except that *quiă* introduces a more strict and logical reason, whereas *quŏniam*, signifying 'now as,' introduces important circumstances.—*Quando, quandŏquidem*, anc *siquidem* approach nearer to *quŏniam* than to *quiă*, as they introduce only subjective reasons. *Quandŏquidem* denotes a reason implied in a circumstance previously mentioned; *siquidem*, a reason implied in a concession. In *siquidem* the meaning of *si* is generally dropped, but it sometimes remains, and then *si* and *quidem* should be written as separate words; as, *O fortunātam rempublicam*, si quidem *hanc sentĭnam ejecĕrit.* Cic.— *Quippĕ*, with the relative pronoun or with *quum*, introduces a subjective reason. When used elliptically without a verb it signifies 'forsooth' or 'indeed.' Sometimes it is followed by a sentence with *ĕnim*, and in this way gradually acquires the signification of *nam*.

8. FINAL conjunctions express a purpose, object, or result, with the signification of 'in order that,' or 'in order that not.' These are *ŭt* or *ŭtī*, *quŏ*, *nĕ* or *ŭt nĕ*, *nĕvĕ* or *neu*, *quīn* and *quŏminŭs*.

REMARK. *Ŭt*, as a conjunction indicates either a result or a purpose, 'so that,' and 'in order that.' When indicating a result, if a negative is added to it, it becomes *ŭt nōn*; when indicating a purpose, if the negative is added, it, becomes *nē* or *ŭt nĕ*, but *ŭt nōn* also is very rarely used for *nē*.—*Nēvĕ* (i. e. *vĕl nĕ*) signifies either 'or in order that not,' or 'and in order that not.' *Ŭt nē* is a pleonasm, not differing perceptibly from *nē*. It is used more frequently by Cicero than by other writers. *Quŏ nē* for *nē* occurs once in Horace.

9. ADVERSATIVE conjunctions, express opposition, with the signification of 'but.' These are *sĕd*, *autem*, *vĕrum*, *vĕro*, *ăt* (poetical *ast*), *ăt ĕnim*, *atquī*, *tămen*, *attămen*, *sedtămen*, *vĕruntămen*, *ăt vĕro* (*ĕnimvĕro*), *vĕrumĕnim*, *vĕrum*, *vĕro*, *cĕtĕrum*.

REMARK. (*a.*) *Sĕd* denotes a direct opposition, and interrupts the narrative or argument; *autem* marks a transition, and denotes at once a connection and an opposition. *Porro*, 'further,' denotes progression and transition but not opposition, except in later authors.— *Vĕrum* has a similar relation to *vĕro* as *sĕd* to *autem*. *Vĕrum*, while it denotes opposition, contains also an explanation. *Vĕr:* connects things which are different, but denotes the point in favor of which the decision should be. It thus forms the transition to something more important as in the phrase, *Illud vero plane non est ferendum*, i. e. that which I am about to mention. In affirmative answers *vĕro* is often added to the verb; as, *Dasne? Do vĕro.* Hence, when the protasis supplies the place of a question, it is sometimes introduced into the apodosis merely to show that it contains an answer. Hence also *vĕro* alone signifies 'yes,' like *sānĕ*, *ĭtă*, and *ĕtiam*.—*Enimvĕro*, 'yes, truly,' 'in truth,' does not denote opposition. It sometimes, like *vĕro*, forms the transition to that which is most important. The compound *vĕrum ĕnimvĕro* denotes the most emphatic opposition.

(*b.*) *At* denotes that that which is opposed is equivalent to that which precedes. It frequently follows *si*, in the sense of 'yet,' or 'at least'; as, *etsi non sapientissimus, at amicissimus*. It is especially used to denote objections whether of the speaker himself or of others. *At ĕnim* introduces a reason for the objection implied in *at*.—By *atquī*, 'but still,' 'but yet,' or 'nevertheless,' we admit what precedes, but oppose something else to it; as, *Magnum narras, vix credibile.* Atqui *sic habet.* Hor. So, also, when that which is admitted, is made use of to prove the contrary. Finally, *atquī* is used in syllogisms, when a thing is assumed which had before been left undecided; in this case it does not denote a direct opposition of facts, and may be translated by 'now,' 'but,' 'but now.'— *Cĕtĕrum*, properly 'as for the rest,' is often used by later writers for *sĕd*.— *Contra ea*, in the sense of 'on the other hand,' is used as a conjunction. So *ŏdeo* with a pronoun, when it may be translated 'just,' 'precisely,' 'even,' 'indeed,' or an intensive 'and.'

10. TEMPORAL conjunctions, express time. These are *quum*, *quum primum*, *ŭt*, *ŭt primum*, *ŭbī*, *postquam*, *antĕquam*, and *priusquam*, *quando*, *simŭlāc* or *simŭlatque*, or *simŭl* alone, *cum quĕ aum*, *dōnĕc*, *quoad*.

§ 198. CONJUNCTIONS 175

REMARK. *Ut* and *ŭbi*, as particles of time, signify 'when.' *Dum*, *dōnĕc*, and *quoad* signify either 'as long as,' or 'until.' *Dum* often precedes *intĕrea* or *intĕrim*, and both *dum* and *donĕc* are often preceded by the adverbs *usquĕ*, *usquĕ eō* or *usquĕ adeo*.

11. INTERROGATIVE conjunctions indicate a question. These are, *num utrum*, *ăn*, and the enclitic *nĕ*. This, when attached to the three preceding particles, forming *numnĕ*, *utrumnĕ*, and *annĕ*, does not affect their meaning. With *nōn* it forms a special interrogative particle *nonnĕ*. To these add *ec* and *ĕn*, as they appear in *ecquis*, *ecquando*, and *ĕnumquam*, and *numquid* and *ecquid*, when used simply as interrogative particles.

REMARK. (*a*.) The interrogative particles have no distinct meaning by themselves in direct questions, but only serve to give to a proposition the form of a question. In direct speech the interrogative particles are sometimes omitted, but in indirect questions they are indispensable, except in the case of a double question, where the first particle is sometimes omitted.—*Ecquid* and *numquid*, as interrogative particles, have the meaning of *num*, *quid* in this case having no meaning, but they must be carefully distinguished from the interrogative pronouns *ecquid* and *numquid*. *En*, or when followed by a *q*, *ec* is, like *num*, *nĕ*, and *ăn*, an interrogative particle, but is always prefixed to some other interrogative word.

(*b*.) In direct questions, *num* and its compounds *numnĕ*, *numnam*, *numquid*, *numquidnam*, and the compounds with *ĕn* or *ec* suppose that the answer will be 'no'; as, *Num putas me tam dementem fuisse?* But *ecquid* is sometimes used in an affirmative sense. In general the negative sense of these particles does not appear in indirect questions.

(*c*.) *Nĕ* properly denotes simply a question, but it is used sometimes affirmatively and sometimes negatively. When *nĕ* is attached, not to the principal verb but to some other word, a negative sense is produced; as, *mene istud potuisse facĕre putas?* Do you believe that I would have done that? The answer expected is 'no.' When attached to the principal verb *nĕ* often gives the affirmative meaning, and the answer expected is 'yes.'—*Nonnĕ* is the sign of an affirmative question; as, *Canis nonne lupo similis est?*—*Utrum*, in accordance with its derivation from *ūter*, which of two, is used only in double questions whether consisting of two or more. It is sometimes accompanied by *nĕ*, which is usually separated from it by one or more words; as, *Utrum*, *lucearnne an praedicem?* In later writers, however, *utrumnĕ* is united into one word. *Nĕ* is rarely appended to interrogative adjectives, but examples of such use are sometimes found in poetry; as, *uternĕ*; *quonĕ malo*; *quantanĕ*. In a few passages it is even attached to the relative pronoun.

(*d*.) *An* is not used as a sign of an indirect question before the silver age; when so used it answers to 'whether.' It is used by Cicero exclusively in a second or opposite question, where we use 'or'; as, *Si sitis*, *nihil intĕrest* utrum *aqua sit*, an *vinum*; *nec refert*, utrum *sit aureum pocŭlum*, an *vitreum*, an *manus concāva*. Sen. In direct interrogations, when no interrogative clause precedes, *in*, *annĕ*, *ăn vēro* are likewise used in the sense of 'or,' that is in such a manner that a preceding interrogation is supplied by the mind; as, *Invitus te offendi*, an *putas me delectāri laedendis hominibus?* Here we may supply before *an putas*, etc. the sentence, 'Do you believe this?'—*An*, after a preceding question, is rendered by 'not,' and it then indicates that the answer cannot be doubtful; as, *A rebus gerendis senectus abstrāhit. Quibus?* An *his*, *quae geruntur juventūte ac viribus?* Is it not from those kinds of business, which? etc. Here we may suppose *aliisne?* to be supplied before *an his?* Is it from other kinds of business, or from those? etc. Such questions may be introduced by *nonnĕ*, but without allusion to an opposite question, which is implied in *ăn*.

(*e*.) To the rule that *ăn*, in indirect questions, is used exclusively to indicate a second or opposite question, there is one great exception, for it is employed in single indirect questions after such expressions as *dubĭto*, *dubium est*, *incertum est*; *delibĕro*, *haesĭto*, and especially after *nescio* or *haud scio*, all of which denote uncertainty, but with an inclination to the affirmative; as, *Si per se virtus sine fortūna ponderanda sit dubĭto hvnc primum omnium ponam,* If virtue is to be estimated without reference to its success, I am not certain whether I should not prefer this man to all others. Nep. It is not Latin to say *dubĭto annon* for *dubĭto an.—Nescio an,* or *haud scio an* are used quite in the sense of 'perhaps,' so that they are followed by the negatives *nullus, nēmo, nunquam,* instead of *ullus, quisquam* and *umquam.* When the principal verb is omitted, *ăn* is often used in the sense of *aut;* as, *Themistocles, quum ei Simonides,* an *quis alius, artem memoriæ polliceretur,* etc. In such cases *incertum est* is understood, and in Tacitus is often supplied.—The conjunction *sĭ* is sometimes used in indirect interrogations instead of *num,* like the Greek *ei,* and it is so used by Cicero after the verb *expĕrior.*

NOTE 1. The conjunctions *-ne, -que, -ve,* are not used alone, but are always affixed to some other word, and are hence called *enclitics.*

NOTE 2. Some words here classed with conjunctions are also used as adverbs, and many classed as adverbs are likewise conjunctions; that is, they at the same time qualify verbs, etc., and connect propositions; as, *Cetēris in rebus, quum venit calamĭtas,* tum *detrimentum accipĭtur,* In other concerns, *when* misfortune comes, *then* damage is received.

NOTE 3. Conjunctions, like adverbs, are variously compounded with other parts of speech, and with each other; as, *atque,* (i. e. *adque*), *iccirco* or *idcirco,* (i. e. *id-circa*), *ideo, namque,* etc. In some, compounded of an adverb and a conjunction, each of the simple words retains its meaning, and properly belongs to its own class; a*c, etiam (et jam)* and now; *itdque,* and so; *neque* or *nec,* and not.

INTERJECTIONS.

§ 199. An interjection is a particle used in exclamation, and expressing some emotion of the mind.

The most usual interjections are,

ăh! *ah! alas!*
ăha! *aha! ah! haha!*
ăpăgĕ! *away! begone!*
ătăt! *or* atatte! *oh! ah! alas! lo!*
au! *or* hau! *oh! ah!*
eccĕ! *lo! see! behold!*
ĕhem! *ha! what!*
ĕheu! *ah! alas!*
ĕho! ehodum! *ho! soho!*
eiă! *or* heiă! *ah! ah ha! indeed!*
ōn! *lo! see! behold!*
eu! *well done! bravo!*
eugĕ! *well done! good!*
euax! } *huzzah! hurrah!*
euœ! }
ha! *hold! ho!*
ha! ha! he! *ha! ha!*
hei! *ah! wo! alas!*

hem! *oho! indeed! well! hah! alas! alack!*
heu! *oh! ah! alas!*
heus! *ho! ho there! hark! halloa!*
hui! *hah! ho! oh!*
iŏ! *ho! hurrah! huzzah!*
ō! *o! oh! ah!*
ōh! *oh! o! ah!*
ŏhē! *ho! halloa! ho there!*
ŏho! *oho! aha!*
oi! *hoy! alas!*
păpæ! *strange! wonderful!*
phui! *foh! fugh!*
phy! *pish! tush!*
prŏ! *or* prŏh! *oh! ah!*
st! *hist! whist! hush!*
tatæ! *so! strange!*
væ! *ah! alas! woe!*
vah! vaha! *ah! alas! oh!*

REMARK 1. An interjection sometimes denotes several different emotions. Thus *vah* is used to express wonder, grief, joy, and anger.

REM. 2. Other parts of speech may sometimes be regarded as interjections; as, *pax!* be still! So *indignum, infandum, malum, misĕrum, miserabĭle, nĕfas,* when used as expressions of astonishment, grief, or horror; and *macte* and *macti,* as expressions of approbation. In like manner the adverbs *næ, profecto, cito, bĕne, belle;* the verbs *quæso, precor, ōro, obsecro, amābo, āge, āgĭte, cĕdo, sōdes,* (for *si audes*), *sis, sultis,* (for *si vis* and *si vultis*), *ăgēsis, ăgĕdum,* and *ăgĭte dum,* and the interrogative *quid?* what? used as exclamations.

Rem. 3. With the interjections may also be classed the following invocations of the gods: *hercŭles, hercŭle, hercle;* or *mehercŭles, mehercŭle, mehercle, medius fidius, mecastor, ecastor, ecēre, pol, edepol, equirīne, per deum, per deum immortālem, per deos, per Jŏvem, prō* (or *prōh*) *Jūpĭter, prō dii immortāles, prō deum fidem, prō deum atque homĭnum fidem, prō deum immortālium* (scil. *fidem*), etc.

SYNTAX.

§ **200.** 1. Syntax treats of the construction of sentences.

2. A sentence is a thought expressed in words; as, *Cānes latrant,* The dogs bark.

3. All sentences are either

(1.) DECLARATIVE; as, *Venti spīrant,* The winds blow:—

(2.) INTERROGATIVE; as, *Spīrantne venti?* Do the winds blow?—

(3.) EXCLAMATORY; as, *Quam vehĕmenter spīrant venti!* How fiercely the winds blow!—or

(4.) IMPERATIVE; as, *Venti, spīrāte,* Blow, winds.

4. The mood of the verb in the first three classes of sentences is either the indicative or the subjunctive; in imperative sentences it is either the imperative or the subjunctive.

5. A sentence may consist either of one proposition or of two or more propositions connected together.

PROPOSITIONS.

§ **201.** 1. A proposition consists of a *subject* and a *predicate.*

2. The subject of a proposition is that of which something is affirmed.

3. The predicate is that which is affirmed of the subject.

Thus, in the proposition, *Equus currit,* The horse runs, *ĕquus* is the subject and *currit* is the predicate.

NOTE. The word *affirm,* as here used, includes all the various significations of the verb, as expressed in the several moods.

4. Propositions are either *principal* or *subordinate.*

5. A principal proposition is one which makes complete sense by itself; as,

Phōcion fuit perpetuo pauper, *quum ditissimus esse posset,* Phocion was always poor, though he might have been very rich.

6. A subordinate proposition is one which, by means of a subordinate conjunction, is made to depend upon or limit some part of another proposition; as,

Phŏcion fuit perpĕtuo pauper, quum ditissĭmus esse posset, Phocion was always poor, *though he might have been very rich.*

7. Subordinate propositions are used either as *substantives, adjectives,* or *adverbs,* and are accordingly called *substantive, adjective* or *adverbial propositions* or *clauses.*

8. Substantive clauses are connected with the propositions on which they depend by means of the final conjunctions *ut, ne, quo, quin,* etc., sometimes by *quod,* and in clauses containing an indirect question, by interrogative pronouns, adjectives, adverbs and conjunctions. See §§ 262 and 265.

REMARK. A dependent substantive clause often takes the form of the accusative with the infinitive and in that case has no connective; as, *Gaudeo te valēre.*

9. Adjective clauses are connected by means of relatives, both pronouns and pronominal adjectives; as, *qui, quālis, quantus,* etc. Adverbial clauses are connected either by relative adverbs of place and time, (§ 191, R. 1, (*b.*),) or by temporal, conditional, concessive, comparative, and sometimes by causal conjunctions.

10. A sentence consisting of one proposition is called a *simple sentence*; as,

Cădunt fŏlia, The leaves fall. *Semirămis Babylōnem condĭdit.*

11. A sentence consisting of a principal and one or more subordinate propositions is called a *complex* sentence; as,

Qui fit, ut nēmo contentus vivat? How happens it, that no one lives content? *Quis ego sim, me rogĭtas,* You ask me, who I am.

12. A sentence consisting of two or more principal propositions, either alone or in connection with one or more subordinate propositions, is called a *compound* sentence; as,

Spirant venti et cădunt fŏlia, The winds blow, and the leaves fall.

13. The propositions composing a complex or a compound sentence are called its *members* or *clauses;* the principal proposition is called the *leading clause,* its subject, the *leading subject,* and its verb, the *leading verb.*

SUBJECT.

§ **202.** 1. The subject also is either *simple, complex,* or *compound.*

2. The simple subject, which is also called the *grammatical* subject, is either a noun or some word standing for a noun; as,

Aves *vŏlant, Birds* fly. Tu *lĕgis, Thou* readest. A *est vōcālis, A* is a vowel. Mentiri *est turpe, To lie* is base.

3. The complex subject, called also the *logical* subject, consists of the simple subject with its modifications; as,

Conscientia bĕne actæ vītæ *est jūcundissima, The consciousness of a well spent life* is very pleasant. Here *conscientia* is the grammatical, and *conscientia bĕne actæ vītæ* the complex, subject.

4. The compound subject consists of two or more simple or complex subjects to which a single predicate belongs; as,

Lūna *et* stellæ *fulgēbant*, *The moon* and *stars* were shining. Grammătĭce *ac* mūsĭcæ *junctæ fuērunt*, *Grammar* and *music* were united. Semper hŏnos nōmenque tuum laudesque mănēbunt.

REMARK. Words are said to *modify* or *limit* other words, when they serve to explain, describe, define, enlarge, restrict, or otherwise qualify their meaning.

5. Every sentence must contain a subject and a predicate, called its *principal* or *essential* parts: any sentence may also receive additions to these, called its *subordinate* parts.

Complex or Modified Subject.

6. The complex subject is formed by adding other words to the simple subject. All additions to the subject, like the subject itself, are either *simple, complex,* or *compound.*

I. *Simple additions.* The subject may be modified by adding:—

1. A *single word*:—

(1.) A noun in the same case; as,

Nos consŭles *dēsŭmus,* We *consuls* are remiss. *Mūcius* augur *multa narrāvit,* Mucius *the augur* related many things.

(2.) A noun or pronoun in an oblique case, modifying or limiting the subject; as,

Amor multĭtūdĭnis *commŏvētur,* The love *of the multitude* is excited. *Cura* mei, Care *for me.* Vīrĭbus *usus,* Need *of strength.*

(3.) An adjective, adjective pronoun, or participle; as,

Fŭgit invĭda *ætas, Envious* time flies. Mea *māter est bēnigna. Dūcit agmĭna* Penthēsĭlēa fūrens. Lĭtĕra scripta mănet.

2. A *phrase* consisting of a preposition and its case; as,

Sŏpor in grāmĭne. *Oppĭda* sĭne præsĭdĭo. *Receptio* ad te.

3. A dependent adjective *clause* introduced by *qui, quālis, quantus,* etc.; as,

Lĕve fit, quod bĕne fertur, *ŏnus,* The burden, *which is borne well,* becomes light. *Lĭtĕræ,* quas scripsisti, *acceptæ sunt. Ut,* quālis (ille) hăbēri vellet, tālis esset. Tanta est inter eos, quanta maxĭma esse pŏtest, *mōrum distantĭa.*

II. *Complex additions.* The subject may be modified:—

1. By a *word* to which other words are added.

(1.) When the word to which other words are added is a noun or pronoun, it may be modified in any of the ways above mentioned.

(2.) When it is an adjective it may be modified:—

(*a.*) By an adverb either simple or modified; as,

Erat exspectātĭo valde *magna. Præsĭdium* non nĭmis *firmum.*

(*b.*) By a noun in an oblique case; as,

Major pĭĕtāte, Superior *in piety.* Contentiōnis *cŭpĭdus,* Fond *of contention.* Patri sĭmĭlis, Like his father. *Nūdus* membra. *Jŭvĕnes* patre *digni.*

(*c.*) By an infinitive, a gerund, or a supine; as,

Insuētus vinci, Not accustomed *to be conquered.* Vēnandi *stŭdiōsus*, Fond of hunting. *Mīrābĭle* dictu, Wonderful *to tell.*

(*d.*) By a phrase consisting of a preposition and its case; as,

Rŭdis in rēpublĭcā, Unskilled *in civil affairs.* Ab ĕquĭtātu *fīrmus.* *Cēler* in pugnam. *Prōnus* ad fĭdem.

(*e.*) By a subordinate clause; as,

Mĕlior est certa pax, quam spērāta victōria, A certain peace is better *than an expected victory.* *Dŭbius sum,* quid fāciam.

(3.) When it is a participle, it may be modified like a verb. See § 203.

2. By a *phrase* consisting of a preposition and its case to which other words are added; as,

De victōria Cæsăris *fāma perfertur,* A report *concerning Cæsar's victory* is brought.

REMARK 1. As the case following the preposition is that of a noun or pronoun, it may be modified like the subject in any of the foregoing ways.

REM. 2. The preposition itself may be modified by an adverb, or by a noun or adjective in an oblique case; as,

Longe *ultra,* Far beyond. Multo *ante noctem,* Long before night. Sexennio *post Vēios captos,* Six years after the capture of Veii.

3. By a *subordinate clause,* to whose subject or predicate other words are added.

REMARK. These additions may be of the same form as those added to the principal subject or predicate of the sentence.

III. *Compound additions.* The subject may be modified:—

1. By two or more nouns in the same case as the subject, connected by a coördinate conjunction; as,

Consŭles, Brūtus *et* Collatīnus, The consuls, *Brutus* and *Collatinus.*

2. By two or more oblique cases of a noun or pronoun connected coördinately; as,

Vītæque nĕcisque *pŏtestas.* Pĕrīcŭlōrum *et* lăbōrum *incĭtāmentum.*

3. By two or more adjectives, adjective pronouns, or participles, connected coördinately; as,

Grăve *bellum* perdiŭturnum*que.* *Anĭmi* tĕnĕri *atque* molles.

4. By two or more adjective clauses connected coördinately; as,

Et qui fēcēre, *et* qui facta ăliōrum scripsēre, *multi laudantur.* Sall.

5. By two or more of the preceding modifications connected coördinately; as,

Genus homĭnum agreste, sine legĭbus, sine imperio, libĕrum, *atque* solūtum.

REM. 1. A modified grammatical subject, considered as one complex idea, may itself be modified; as,

Omnia tua consĭlia, All thy counsels. Here *omnia* modifies, not *consĭlia,* but the complex idea expressed by *tua consĭlia.* So Trĭginta *nāves longa.* Præpŏtens *finitĭmus rex.*

REM. 2. An infinitive, with the words connected with it, may be the logical subject of a proposition; as,

Virtus est vitium fugere, *To shun vice* is a virtue.

REM. 3. A clause, or any member consisting of two or more clauses, may be the logical subject of a proposition; as,

E cœlo descendit ' Nosce te ipsum.' *Æquum est*, ut hoc facies.

REM. 4. The noun or pronoun which is the subject of a proposition is put in the nominative, when the verb of the predicate is a finite verb; but when the verb is in the infinitive, the subject is put in the accusative.

NOTE 1. A verb in any mood, except the infinitive, is called a *finite* verb.

NOTE 2. In the following pages, when the term *subject* or *predicate* is used alone, the grammatical subject or predicate is intended.

PREDICATE.

§ 203. 1. The predicate, like the subject, is either *simple, complex,* or *compound.*

2. The simple predicate, which is also called the *grammatical* predicate, is either a single finite verb, or the copula *sum* with a noun, adjective, and rarely with an adverb; as,

Sol lucet, The sun *shines. Multa animalia* repunt, Many animals *creep* Brevis est *võ· upous,* Pleasure *is brief. Europa* est peninsula, Europe *is a peninsula.* Rectissime sunt *apud te omnia.*

3. The complex predicate, called also the *logical* predicate, consists of the simple predicate with its modifications; as,

Scipio fudit Annibalis copias, Scipio *routed the forces of Hannibal.* Here *fudit* is the grammatical, and *fudit Annibalis copias* the logical predicate.— So, *Romulus* Romanæ conditor urbis fuit.

4. The compound predicate consists of two or more simple or complex predicates belonging to the same subject; as,

Probitas laudatur *et* alget, Honesty *is praised* and *neglected.* Leti vis rapuit, rapletque gentes. *Lucius Catilina* fuit magna vi et animi et corporis, *sed* ingenio malo pravoque.

Complex or Modified Predicate.

5. The complex predicate is formed by adding other words to the simple predicate. All additions to the predicate, like the predicate itself, are either simple, complex, or compound.

I. *Simple additions.* The predicate may be modified by adding:—

1. A *single word;—*

(1.) A noun or adjective in the same case as the subject. This occurs after certain neuter verbs and passive verbs of naming, calling, etc. (See § 210, R. 3.); as,

Servus fit libertinus, The slave becomes a *freedman. Servius Tullius* rex est declaratus. *Aristides* justus *est appellatus. Incedo* regina.

(2.) A noun or pronoun in an oblique case; as,

Spe *vivimus,* We live *by hope. Deus regit* mundum, God rules *the world.*

(3.) An adverb either simple or modified; as,

Sæpe *vēnit*, He came *often*. *Festīna* lente, Hasten *slowly*. *Lĭtĕræ făcĭle dĭscuntur*. *Chrĕmes* nĭmis grăvĭter *crŭciat ădŏlescentŭlum*.

(4.) An infinitive mood; as,

Cŭpit discere, He desires *to learn*. *Audeo* dĭcĕre. *Ver* esse *cœpĕrat*.

2. A *phrase* consisting of a preposition and its case; as, *Vēnit* ad urbem, He came *to the city*.

3. A dependent substantive or adverbial *clause*; as,

Vĕreor ne reprĕhendar, I fear *that I shall be blamed*. *Zēnōnem*, quum **Athēnis** essem, *audiēbam frĕquenter*. *Făc* cōgītes.

II. *Complex additions.* The predicate may be modified:—

1. By a *word* to which other words are added.

REMARK. These words are the same as in the corresponding cases of complex additions to the subject. See § 202, II.

2. By a *phrase* consisting of a preposition and its case, to which other words are added. See complex additions to the subject, § 202.

3. By a subordinate *clause*, to whose subject or predicate other words are added. See complex subject, § 202, II, 3.

REM. 2. Each of the words constituting a proposition may be modified by two or more additions not dependent on, nor connected with each other, and consisting either of single words, phrases, or dependent clauses; as, Agamemnōnis belli *glōria*. Pătermum *ŏdium* erga Rōmānos. *Mens* sibi *conscia* recti. Mea maxime *intĕrest*, te *vălēre*. *Ago* tibi grātias. Meipsum inertiæ *condemno*. Eos hoc *mŏneo*. In quo te *accūso*. *Mŏnet* eum, ut suspīciōnes vītet.

III. *Compound additions.* 1. The predicate may be modified by two or more words, phrases, or clauses, joined together by a coördinate conjunction. See Compound additions to the subject, § 202, III

2. The leading verb is usually either in the indicative or imperative mood, but sometimes in the subjunctive or the historical infinitive.

3. The members of a compound sentence are connected by coördinate conjunctions; those of a complex sentence by some relative word, or by a subordinate conjunction.

4. Instead of a dependent clause connected by a conjunction, a noun and participle, or two nouns, sometimes stand as an abridged proposition; as,

Bello confecto *discessit*, i. e. *quum bellum confectum esset, discessit*, The war being finished, or when the war was finished, he departed. *Nil despērandum*, Teucro dūce.

5. An infinitive may be modified like the verb of a predicate.

6. *Agreement* is the correspondence of one word with another in gender, number, case, or person.

7. A word is said to *govern* another, when it requires it to be put in a certain case or mood.

8. A word is said to *depend* on another, when its case, gender number, mood, tense, or person, is determined by that word.

9. A word is said to *follow* another, when it depends upon it in construction, whatever may be its position in the sentence.

APPOSITION.

§ 204. A noun, annexed to another noun or to a pronoun, and denoting the same person or thing, is put in the same case as,

Urbs Rōma, The city *Rome. Nos* consŭles, We *consuls.* So *Apud Herodŏtum, patrem històriæ, sunt innumerabĭles fabŭlæ,* In Herodotus, the *father* of history, etc. Cic. *Lapides* silices, *flint* stones. Liv. *Ante me* consŭlem, Before I was *consul. Fons cui nōmen* Arethūsa *est.* Cic.

REMARK 1. (*a.*) A noun, thus annexed to another, is said to be in *apposition* to it. It is generally added for the sake of explanation, identification, or description; sometimes it denotes character or purpose; as, *Ejus fŭgæ comĭtem me adjunxi,* I added myself, *as a companion* of his flight; and sometimes the time, cause, reason, etc., of an action; as, *Alexander* puer, Alexander *when a boy. Cato* sěnex *scribĕre historiam instituit.* Suet.

(*b.*) A noun in apposition, like an adjective used as an epithet, (§ 205, N. 2,) assumes the attribute denoted by it as belonging to the noun which it limits, while the predicate-nominative *affirms* it. Hence both nouns belong to the same part of the sentence, whether subject or predicate. In cases of apposition, there seems to be an ellipsis of the ancient participle *ens,* being; *qui est,* who is; *qui vocātur,* who is called; or the like.

REM. 2. If the annexed noun has a form of the same gender as the other noun, it takes that form; as, *Usus* magister *egrĕgius.* Plin. *Philosŏphia* magistra *vitæ.* Cic. If the annexed noun is of the common gender, the adjective qualifying it takes the gender of the preceding noun; as, *Laurus* fidissĭma custos.

REM. 3. The annexed noun sometimes differs from the other in gender or in number; as, *Duo* fulmĭna *belli, Scipiadas,* clādem *Libyæ.* Virg. *Mitylēnæ,* urbs *nobĭlis.* Cic. *Tulliŏla,* deliciæ *nostræ.* Id.;—and sometimes in both; as, *Nate, meæ* vīres. Virg. *Nos,* animæ *viles, inhumāta infletāque* turba. Id.

REM. 4. The substantive pronoun is sometimes omitted before the word in apposition to it; as, Consul *dixi,* scil. *ego;* (I) the consul said. And instead of the substantive pronoun, a possessive adjective pronoun is sometimes used; as, Tua *dŏmus, tālis viri.* Cic. See § 211, R. 3, (*b.*)

REM. 5. A noun may be in apposition to two or more nouns, and, in such case, is usually put in the plural; as, *M. Antonius, C. Cassius,* tribūni *plēbis,* M. Antonius, C. Cassius, tribunes of the people. Cæs. *Publius et Servius* Sullæ, *Servi filii.* Sall. *Tib. et Gaius* Gracchi. Cic. *Oratiōnes L. et C.* Aureliōrum Orestārum. Id. But sometimes in the singular; as, Cn. et L. Domitius. Cic.

(1.) So when the nouns are connected by *cum,* the annexed noun taking the case of the former; as, *Dicæarchum vero cum Aristoxĕno, doctos sāne* homĭnes, *omittāmus.* Cic.

(2.) If the nouns are proper names of different genders, a masculine noun is annexed rather than a feminine, when both forms exist; as, *Ad Ptolemæum Cleopatramque* rēges *legāti missi sunt.* Liv.

REM. 6. The annexed noun is sometimes in the genitive; as, *Urbem* Patāvi *ccāvit,* The city of Patavium. Virg. *Plurĭmus* Eridāni *amnis.* Id. *Arbŏrem* fici *numquam vidĕrat.* Cic. *In oppĭdo* Antiochĭæ. Id. Rupĭli *et* Persi *par.* Hor.

REM. 7. The name of a town in the genitive occurs with an ablative in apposition to it; as, *Corinthi Achaiæ* urbe; At Corinth, a city of Achaia. Tac. *Antiochiæ, celĕbri* urbe. Cic. See § 221, Note, and § 254, Rem. 3.

REM. 8. (*a.*) A proper name, after *nōmen* or *cognōmen,* with a verb followed by a dative, is put in apposition either to *nōmen,* etc., or to the dative, the latter by a species of attraction; as, *Fons, cui nōmen* Arethūsa *est.* Cic. *Stirps virilis, cui* Ascanium *parentes dixēre nōmen.* Liv. *Nōmen* Arctūro *est mihi,* I have the name Arcturus. Plaut. *Cui nunc cognōmen* Iūlo *addĭtur.* Virg. *Cui Igerio indĭtum nōmen.* Liv.—(*b.*) The name may also be put in the genitive; as, *Nōmen Mercŭrii est mihi.* Plaut. Q. *Metellus, cui* Macedonici *nōmen indĭtum erat.* Vell. Cf. R. 6.—(*c.*) In *Illa œtas, cui fecĭnus* Aurea *nōmen*, Ov. Met. 15, 96, *Aurea* is used as an indeclinable noun, instead of *Auream* (scil. *œtātem*); or *Aureœ* dat. (scil. *œtāti.*)

REM. 9. A *clause* may supply the place of one of the nouns; as, *Cōgĭtet* oratōrem institui—*rem arduam*, Let him reflect that an orator is training—a difficult thing. Quint.—So also a neuter adjective used substantively; as, Triste *lŭpus stabŭlis*, The wolf, a sad thing to the folds. Virg. Vărium *et* mutabīle *semper femina.* Id.

REM. 10. Sometimes the former noun denotes a whole, and its parts are expressed by nouns in apposition to it; as, *Onerāriœ*, pars *maxĭma ad Ægimūrum*,—*aliœ adversus urbem ipsam delātœ sunt,* The ships of burden were carried, the greatest part, to Ægimurus,—others opposite to the city itself. Liv. *Pictōres et poëtœ suum* quisque *ŏpus a. vulgo considerāvi vult.* Cic. In the construction of the ablative absolute, *quisque* remains in the nominative, though the word to which it is in apposition is in the ablative; as, *Multis sibi* quisque *impěrium petentĭbus.* Sall. J. 18. So also, in Liv. 26, 29, *quisque* remains in the nominative although the word to which it is in apposition is in the accusative with the infinitive.

To this rule may be subjoined that which relates to the agreement of interrogative and responsive words.

REM. 11. The principal noun or pronoun in the answer to a question, must be in the same case as the corresponding interrogative word; as,

Quis *hĕrus est tĭbi?* Amphitruo, scil. *est.* Who is your master? Amphitruo (is.) Plaut. Quid *quœris?* Librum, scil. *quœro.* What are you looking for? A book. Quŏtā *hŏrā venisti?* Sextā. At what hour did you come? At the sixth.

NOTE 1. Instead of the genitive of a substantive pronoun, the corresponding possessive pronoun is often used, agreeing with its noun; as, Cūjus *est lĭber?* Meus, (not *Mei.*) (See § 211, Rem. 3, (*b.*)) So *cūjum* for genitive *cūjus?* Cūjum *pĕcus? an Melibœi? Non; verum Ægōnis.* Virg.

NOTE 2. Sometimes the rules of syntax require the responsive to be in a different case from that of the interrogative; as, Quanti *emisti? Vigĭnti* minis. *Damnatusne ĕs* furti? *Imo ălio* crimine. See §§ 214, R. 1, and 217, R. 2.

ADJECTIVES.

§ 205. Adjectives, adjective pronouns, and participles, agree with their nouns, in gender, number, and case; as,

Bŏnus vir, A good man. *Bŏnos vĭros,* Good men.
Benigna māter, A kind mother. *Vānœ lĕges,* Useless laws.
Triste bellum, A sad war. *Mināciă verba,* Threatening words.
Spe amissā, Hope being lost. *Hœc res,* This thing.
So, *Mea māter est benigna.*
Hœc lĕges vānœ sunt.

NOTE 1. Adjectives, according to their meaning, (§ 104), are divided into two classes—*qualifying* and *limiting*—the former denoting some *property* or *quality* of a noun; as, a *wise* man, lead is *heavy*; the latter *defining* or *restricting* its meaning; as, *this* man, *ten* cities. To the former class belong such adjectives as denote a property or quality, including all participles and participal adjectives; to the latter, the adjective pronouns, pronominal adjectives, and numerals.

§ 205.   SYNTAX.—ADJECTIVES.   185

NOTE 2. An adjective, participle, or pronoun, may either be used as an epithet to modify a noun, or, with the copula *sum*, may constitute a predicate In the former case the quality is *assumed*, in the latter it is *asserted*. In both cases, the rule for their agreement is, in general, the same. See § 210, R. 1.

NOTE 3. Any word or combination of words added to a noun to modify or limit its meaning is of the nature of an adjective.

NOTE 4. In the following remarks, the word *adjective* is to be considered as including participles, either alone or combined with the auxiliary *sum*, and also adjective pronouns, unless the contrary is intimated.

REMARK 1. An adjective agrees also with a substantive pronoun, taking its gender from that of the noun for which the pronoun stands; as, *Ipse capellas æger āgo*, scil. *ĕgo, Melibœus;* Virg. *Fortunāte puer, tu nunc eris* alter *ab illo.* Id. *Ut se tōtum ei trādĕret.* Nep. *O me misĕrum* (spoken by a man), *misĕram me* (spoken by a woman). So *salvi sŭmus, salvæ sŭmus,* scil. *nos,* masculine or feminine.—In general propositions which include both sexes, the pronouns are considered masculine; as, *Nos frūges consūmĕre* nāti. Hor.

REM. 2. An adjective may belong to each of two or more nouns, and in such case is put in the plural. If the nouns are of the same gender, the adjective agrees with them in gender, as well as in number; as,

Lŭpus et agnus sĭti compulsi, A wolf and a lamb, constrained by thirst. Phæd. *Sicilia Sardiniăque* amissæ. Liv.

When the nouns are of different genders,

(1.) If they denote living things, the adjective is masculine rather than feminine; as,

Păter mīhi et māter mortui *sunt,* My father and mother are dead. Ter. So also *uterque* in the singular. *Procumbit* uterque, scil. *Deucălion et Pyrrha.* Ovid.

(2.) If they denote things without life, the adjective is generally neuter; as,

His gĕnus, œtas, eloquentia prŏpe æquālia *fuēre,* Their family, age, and eloquence, were nearly equal. Sall. *Regna, impĕria, nobilitātes, honōres, divitiæ in cāsu* sita *sunt.* Cic. *Huic bella, rapinæ, discordia civīlis,* grāta *fuēre.* Sall. *Anima atque animus, quamvis* integra *rĕcens in corpus eunt.* Lucr.

NOTE. When nouns denoting things without life are of the *same* gender (either masculine or feminine), but of different numbers, the adjective is sometimes neuter; as, *Crœso et vita et patrimōnii partes, et urbs Barce* concessa *sunt.* Just.; sometimes also when both nouns are in the singular number; as, *Plerosque velocitas et rēgio hostĭbus ignāra* tutāta *sunt.* Sall. *Nox atque præda* remorāta *sunt.* Id.

(3.) If one of the nouns denotes an animate, and another an inanimate thing, the adjective is sometimes neuter, and sometimes takes the gender of that which has life ; as,

Numīdæ atque signa militāria obscurāti *sunt,* The Numidians and the military standards were concealed. Sall. *Romāni rēgem regnumque Macedŏniæ* sua *futūra sciunt.* Liv. *Jūne, făc* æternos *păcem pacisque ministros.* Ovid.

EXC. to REM. 2. The adjective often agrees with the nearest noun, and is understood with the rest; as,

Sŏciis et rēge recepto, Our companions and king having been recovered. Virg. *Agri* omnes *et māria.* Cic. *Cognitum est salūtem, libĕros, fāmam, fortūnas esse* cārissimas. Cic.

16*

NOTE. A noun in the singular, followed by an ablative with *cum*, has sometimes a plural adjective, the gender being the same as if the nouns were connected by *et*; as, *Filiam cum filio accitos.* Liv. *Ilia cum Lauso de Numitore sati.* Ovid. *Filium Alexandri cum matre in arcem* custodiendos *mittit.* Just.

REM. 3. (1.) **An adjective qualifying a collective noun is often put in the plural, taking the gender of the individuals which the noun denotes**; as,

Pars certare părāti, A part, prepared to contend. Virg. *Pars per agros dīlapsi. ..... suam quisque spem* exsĕquentes. Liv. *Supplex turba ērant sine jūdĭce tūti.* Ovid. This construction always occurs when the collective noun is the subject of a plural verb. See § 209, R. 11.

(2.) Sometimes, though rarely, an adjective in the *singular* takes the gender of the individuals; as, *Pars* arduus *altis* pulvĕrŭlentus *ĕquis fŭrit.* Virg. *Pars una dūcum*—fractus *morbo.* Ovid.

(3.) Sometimes other nouns, which only in a figurative sense denote human beings, have by *synĕsis* an adjective of a different gender from their own, referring to the words which they include; as, *Lătium Căpuăque agro* mulctāti Latium and Capua were deprived of their land. Liv. *Căpĭta conjūrātiōnis virgis* cǣsi *ac sēcūri* percussi *sunt.* Id. *Auxilia* irāti. Id. So after *millia*; as, *Duo millia Tyriōrum, crūcibus* affixi. Curt. Cf. § 323, 3, (4.)

REM. 4. **Two adjectives in the singular are sometimes joined to a plural noun**; as, *Măria Tyrrhēnum atque* Adriāticum, The Tuscan and Adriatic seas. Liv. *Cum lĕgiōnibus sĕcundā et* tertiā. Liv. *Circa portas* Collīnam Esquilīnamque. Id. But sometimes the noun is in the singular; as, *Inter Esquilīnam Collīnamque* portam. Id. *Lĕgio Martia et quarta.* In comic writers, an adjective or participle in the singular is sometimes used with a plural pronoun; as, *Nōbis prǣsente.* Plaut. *Absente nōbis.* Ter.

REM. 5. **A participle which should regularly agree with the subject of a proposition, when placed after the noun of the predicate,** (a) sometimes takes the gender and number of the latter; as, *Non omnis error stultitia est* dicenda, Not every error is to be called folly. Cic. *Gens universa Vĕnĕti* appellāti. Liv. (b.) Sometimes also it agrees with a noun following the subject and in apposition to it; as, *Cōrinthum, patres vestri, tōtius Grǣciæ* lūmen, exstinctum *esse vŏluĕrunt.* Cic.; or (c) with the noun of a subordinate sentence; as, *Illōrum urbem ut* prōpugnăcŭlum oppōsitum *esse barbăris.* Nep.

REM. 6. **When the subject of an infinitive is omitted after a dative of the same signification,** (§ 239, R. 1,) **an adjective in the predicate, belonging to that subject, is sometimes put in the dative**; as, *Mihi* negligenti *esse non licuit*, i. e. *me negligentem esse mihi non licuit.* Cic. *Da mihi* justo sanctōque *vidēri.* Hor. A noun is sometimes expressed with the adjective; as, *Vōbis nĕcesse est* fortibus *esse viris.* Liv. But the adjective often agrees with the omitted subject; as, *Expĕdit* bōnas *esse vōbis*, scil. *vos.* Ter. *Si civi Rōmāno licet esse* Gādītānum. Cic.

REM. 7. (1.) **An adjective is often used alone, especially in the plural, the noun, with which it agrees, being understood**; as,

Bŏni sunt rāri, scil. *hŏmĭnes*, Good (men) are rare. *Cæsar snos misit, scl. milĭtes*, Cæsar sent his (soldiers). *Dextra*, scil. *mănus*, The right (hand). *Implextur pinguis* fĕrīnæ, scil. *carnis.* Virg. *Hiberna*, scil. *castra. Altum* scil. *mare. Quartāna*, scil. *febris. Inmortāles*, scil. *Dii.* Lucr. *Amantium*, scil. *hŏmĭnum.* Ter. *Illum* indignanti *sĭmilem, simīlemque* minanti *aspĭcĕres*, scil. *hŏmĭni.* Virg. *Tibi* primas *dĕfĕro*, scil. *partes.* Cic. *Respīce* prætĕrĭtum, scil. *tempus*, which is often omitted, as in *ex quo, ex eo*, and *ex illo*, scil. *tempŏre. Cognōsci ex* meōrum *omnium litĕris*, scil. *amīcōrum.* Cic. So patrial adjectives; as, *Missi ad* Parthum Armēniumque *lēgāti* scil. *rēgem. In* Tuscŭlāno, scil. *prædio.*

§ 205. SYNTAX.—ADJECTIVES. 137

NOTE 1. The noun to be supplied with masculine adjectives is commonly *hŏmĭnes*, but when they are posessives, it is oftener *ămīci, mīlĭtes, cīves,* or *prŏpinqui*.

NOTE 2. The noun to be supplied is often contained in a preceding clause.

(2.) An adjective in the neuter gender, without a noun, is often used substantively, where, in English, the word *thing* or *things* is to be supplied; as,

Bŏnum, a good thing; *mălum,* a bad thing, or, an evil. So *hŏnestum, vērum, turpe ;* and in the plural, *bŏna, măla, turpia, lēvia, cœlestia,* etc. *Lăbor omnia vincit,* Labor overcomes all things. Virg.

NOTE 1. The Latins generally preferred adding *res* to an adjective, to using its neuter as a substantive. But sometimes, when *res* is used, an adjective or pronoun referring to it is put in the neuter instead of the feminine; as, *Eārum rērum* utrumque. Cic. *Hūmānārum rērum fortūna* plērăque *rēgit.* Sall. *Illud te rŏgo, sumptui ne parcas ullā in re,* quod *ad valetūdĭnem ŏpus sit.* Cic. *Omnium rērum mors est* extrēmum. Cic.

NOTE 2. Instead of *thing* or *things,* other words may sometimes be supplied, as the sense requires. With a preposition, neuter adjectives form adverbial phrases; as, *A primo,* At first. Plaut. *Per mūtua,* Mutually. Virg. *In primis,* In the first place. *Ad hoc,* or *Ad hæc,* Moreover, besides.

(3.) Adjectives used substantively often have other adjectives agreeing with them; as, *Alia omnia,* All other (things.) Plin. *Inĭquissimi* mei, My greatest enemies. *Familiāris* meus. Cic. *Inīquus* noster. Id. *Justa fūnebria.* Liv. *Jŏvis omnia* plēna. scil. sunt. Virg.

REM. 8. (*a.*) Imperatives, infinitives, adverbs, clauses, and words considered merely as such, may be used substantively, and take a neuter adjective in the singular number; as, *Suprēmum vāle dixit,* He pronounced a last farewell. Ovid. *Dulce et decōrum est* pro patriā mŏri. Hor. *Velle suum cuique est.* Pers. *Cras istud quando vēnit?* Mart. J. *Rĕdībo actūtum.* A. *Id actūtum diu est.* Plaut. *Excepto quod non simul esses, cētĕra lætus.* Hor. (*b.*) In the poets and later prose writers the adjective, as in Greek, is sometimes in the neuter plural; as, *Ut Æneas pĕlăgo jactētur*—nōta *ŭbi.* Virg.

REM. 9. (*a.*) Adjectives and adjective pronouns, instead of agreeing with their nouns, are sometimes put in the neuter gender, with a partitive signification, and their nouns in the genitive; as, *Multum tempŏris,* for *multum tempus ;* much time. *Id rei,* for *ea res ;* that thing. So, plus *ēlŏquentiæ,* the other form not being admissible with *plus.* (See § 110, (*b.*) Neuter adjectives are used in like manner in the plural; as, *Vāna rērum,* for *vānæ res.* Hor. *Plērăque hūmānārum rērum.* Sall. Cf. § 212, R. 3, N. 4. But in some such examples, the adjective seems to be used substantively, according to Rem. 7, (2); as, *Acūta belli.* Hor. *Tellūris* ŏperta. Virg. *Summa pectŏris.*

NOTE. The adjectives thus used partitively in the singular, for the most part, signify quantity. See § 212, Rem. 3, Note 1.

REM. 10. A neuter adjective is sometimes used adverbially in the nominative or accusative, both singular and plural; as, *Dulce rīdentem Lălăgen amăbo, dulce lŏquentem.* Hor. *Magnum strīdens.* Virg. *Arma* horrendum *sŏnuēre.* Id. *Multa deos venerāti sunt.* Cic. *Hŏdie aut* summum *cras.* Id. See § 192, II. 4, (*b.*)

REM. 11. (*a.*) A noun is sometimes used as an adjective; as, *Nēmo miles Rŏmānus,* No Roman soldier. Liv. *Nēmo fēre adŏlescens.* Cic. *Vir* nēmo *bŏnus.* Id. Cf. § 207, R. 31, (*c.*) *Tiberim* accŏlis *flŭviis orbātum.* Tac. *Incŏla turba.* Ovid. The poets use in this manner the Greek patronymics in *as* and *is ;* as, *Pēlias hasta.* Ovid. *Laurus Parnāsis.* Id. *Ursa Libystis.* Virg. Cf. also § 129, 8.

(*b.*) An adverb is also sometimes used as an adjective; as, *Neque enim ignāri sŭmus* ante *malōrum ·* i. e. *antiquōrum* or *præterĭtōrum.* Virg. Nunc *hŏminum mōres* Plaut.

REM. 12. (*a.*) An adjective or adjective pronoun, used partiti·ely, stands alone, and commonly takes the gender of the genitive plural, which depends upon it; but when it is preceded by a noun of a different gender, to which it refers, it usually takes that gender, but sometimes that of the genitive; as, *Elĕphanto belluārum* nulla *est prūdentior*, No beast is wiser than the elephant. Cic. *Indus, qui est omnium flūmĭnum* maxĭmus. Cic. Vēlōcissĭmum *omnium ănĭmālium est delphīnus*. Plin. See § 212, Rem. 2.—(*b.*) So also with *de, ex, in, ăpud, inter*, etc., with the ablative or accusative instead of the partitive genitive. See § 212, R. 2, N. 4.

(*c.*) When a *collective* noun follows in the genitive singular, (§ 212, R. 2.) the adjective takes the gender of the individuals which compose it; as, *Vir fortissĭmus nostræ cīvĭtātis*, The bravest man of our state. Cic. Maxĭmus *stirpis* Liv.

REM. 13. (*a*) When a possessive pronoun or adjective is used instead of the genitive of its primitive or of its corresponding noun (see § 211, R. 3, (*b.*) and (*c.*) and R. 4), an adjective agreeing with that genitive is sometimes joined with such possessive; as, Sōlius meum *peccātum corrĭgi non pŏtest*, The fault of me alone cannot be corrected. Cic. Noster duōrum *ēventus*. Liv. Tuum ipsīus *stŭdium*. Cic. *Pugna* Rōmāna *stăbĭlis suo pondĕre* incumbentium *in hostem*. Liv.

(*b.*) Sometimes a noun in the genitive is expressed, in apposition to the substantive pronoun for which the possessive stands; as, *Pectus tuum*, hŏmĭnis *simplĭcis*. Cic.

REM. 14. An adjective, properly belonging to the genitive, is sometimes made to agree with the noun on which the genitive depends, and *vice versā*; as, *Ædĭfĭcātĭōnis* tuæ *consĭlium* for *tuum*, Your design of building. Cic. *Accūsantes* vĭŏlāti *hospĭtii fædus*, for *vĭŏlātum*. Liv. *Ad* mājōra *inĭtia rērum dūcentĭbus fātis*, for *mājōrum*. Id. Iis *nōmĭnĭbus cīvĭtātum, quĭbus ex cīvĭtātĭbus*, etc., for *eārum cīvĭtātum*. Cæs.

REM. 15. (*a.*) An adjective agreeing with a noun is sometimes used, instead of an adverb qualifying a verb, especially in poetry; as, *Ecce vēnit Tĕlămon prŏpĕrus*, Lo, Telamon comes in haste. Ovid. Læti *pācem ăgĭtābāmus*, for *læte*. Sall. *Ænēas se* mātūtīnus *ăgēbat*, for *māne*. Virg. *Nec lŭpus grĕgĭbus* nocturnus *ŏbambŭlat*, i. e. by night. Id.

(*b.*) So *nullus* is used for *non*; as, *Mĕmĭni tămetsi* nullus *mŏneas*, Though you do not suggest it. Ter. *Sextus ab armis* nullus *discēdit*. Cic. *Prior, prīmus, princeps, prŏpior, proxĭmus, sōlus, ūnus, ultĭmus, multus, tōtus*, and some others, are used instead of their neuters, adverbially; as, Priōri *Rēmo augŭrium vēnisse fertur*. Liv. *Hispānia* postrēma *omnium prōvinciārum perdŏmĭta est* Liv. *Scævŏla* sōlos *nŏvem menses Asiæ præfuit*, Only nine months. Cic. Unum *hoc dīco*, This only I say. Id. This is sometimes done, for want of an adverb of appropriate meaning; as, Prōnus *cĕcĭdit*. Ovid. Frĕquentes *convēnērant*. Sall.

(*c.*) In such expressions, *tu*, in the nominative, sometimes takes an adjective in the vocative, and *vice versā*; as, *Sic rēnias* hŏdierne. Tibull. *Salve*, prīmus *omnium pārens patriæ* appellāte. Plin.

REM. 16. (*a.*) A noun is often qualified by two or more adjectives; and sometimes the complex idea, formed by a noun with one or more adjectives, is itself qualified by other adjectives, which agree in gender, etc. with the noun.

(*b.*) When several adjectives, each independently of the other, qualify a noun, if they precede it, they are almost always connected by one or more conjunctions; as, *Multā* et *vărĭā* et *cōpĭōsā ōrātĭōne*. Cic. If they follow it, the conjunction is sometimes expressed, and sometimes omitted; as, *Vir altus* et *excellens*. Cic. *Actio, vărĭa, vĕhĕmens, plēna vērĭtātis*. Id.

(*c.*) But when one of the adjectives qualifies the noun, and another the complex idea formed by the first with the noun, the conjunction is always omitted; as, Pĕrīcŭlōsissĭmum *cīvīle bellum*, A most dangerous civil war. Cic. Mălam *dŏmestĭcam disciplīnam*. Id. So with three or more adjectives; Externos multos clāros viros nōmĭnārem. Cic. Cf. § 202, III., R. 1.

REM. '17. The first part, last part, middle part, etc., of any place or time are generally expressed in Latin by the adjectives *primus, medius, ultimus, extremus, intimus, infimus, imus, summus, supremus reliquus,* and *cetera;* as,

Media nox, The middle of the night. *Summa arbor,* The top of a tree. *Supremos montes,* The summits of the mountains. But these adjectives frequently occur without this signification; as, *Ab extremo complexu,* From the last embrace. Cic. *Infimo loco natus,* Of the lowest rank. Id.

REM. 18. The participle of the compound tenses of verbs, used impersonally in the passive voice, is neuter; as, Ventum *est.* Cic. Itum *est in viscera terræ* Ovid. Scribendum *est mihi.* See § 184, 2 and 3.

RELATIVES.

§ 206. REM. 19. (*a.*) Relatives agree with their antecedents in gender, number, and person, but their case depends on the construction of the clause to which they belong; as,

Puer qui *legit,* The boy who reads. *Ædificium* quod *exstruxit,* The house which he built. *Literæ* quas *dedi,* The letter which I gave. *Non sum* qualis *eram,* I am not such as I was. Hor. So *Deus* cujus *munere vivimus,* cui *nullus est similis,* quem *colimus,* a quo *facta sunt omnia,* est *æternus.* Addictus *Hermippo, et ab* hoc *ductus est.* Aquilo, quantus *frangit ilices.* Hor.

NOTE 1. This rule includes all adjectives and adjective pronouns which relate to a noun in a preceding clause. Its more common application, however, is to the construction of the demonstrative pronouns and the relative *qui.*

NOTE 2. When a pronoun refers to the mere words of a sentence, it is said to be used *logically.* *Qui* and *is* are so used, and sometimes also *hic* and *ille.*

(*b.*) The relative may be considered as placed between two cases of the same noun, either expressed or understood, with the former of which it agrees in gender, number, and person, and with the latter in gender, number, and case.

(1.) Sometimes both nouns are expressed; as,

Erant omnino duo itinera, quibus itineribus *domo exire possent,* There were only two *routes,* by which *routes* they could leave home. Cæs. *Crudelissimæ* bello, quale bellum *nulla umquam barbaria gessit.* Cic. But it is most frequent with the word *dies;* as, *Fore in armis certo die,* qui dies *futurus erat,* etc. Cic. The repetition of the substantive is necessary, when, for any reason, it becomes doubtful to which of two or more preceding substantives the relative refers.

(2.) Usually the antecedent noun only is expressed; as,

Animum *rege,* qui, *nisi paret, imperat,* Govern your passions, which rule unless they obey. Hor. *Tantæ* multitudinis, quantam *capit urbs nostra, concursus est ad me factus.* Cic. Quot *capitum vivunt, totidem studiorum* millia. Hor.

(3.) Sometimes the *latter* noun only is expressed, especially when the relative clause, as is frequently the case, precedes that of the antecedent; as,

Quibus *de rebus ad m— scripsisti, coram videbimus;* scil. *de rebus,* In regard to the things of which you wrote to me, we will consider when we meet. Cic. *In* quem *primum egressi sunt* locum, *Troja vocatur;* scil, *locus.* Liv. Quanta vi expetunt, *tanta defendunt.* Qualesque risus eram ridisse viros, *ex ordine tales aspicio.* Ovid.

(*a.*) The place of the antecedent is sometimes supplied by a demonstrative pronoun; as, *Ad quas res aptissimi erimus, in iis potissimum elaborabimus.* Cic. But the demonstrative is often omitted when its case is the same as that of the relative, and not unfrequently, also, when the cases are different. When the relative clause precedes that of the antecedent, *is* is expressed only for the sake of emphasis. Hence we find such sentences as, *Maximum ornamentum amicitiæ tollit, qui ex eā tollit verecundiam.* Cic. *Terra quod accēpit, numquam sine ūsūrā reddit.* Id.—The demonstrative adjectives and adverbs are in like manner often omitted before their corresponding relatives; *tālis* before *quālis, tantus* before *quantus, inde* before *unde, ibi* before *ūbi*, etc.

(*b.*) Sometimes the latter noun only is expressed, even when the relative clause does not precede; as, *Quis non mālārum quas āmor cūras hăbet, hæc inter obliviscitur?* Hor.

(4.) Sometimes neither noun is expressed; this happens especially when the antecedent is designedly left indefinite, or when it is a substantive pronoun; as,

Qui *běne lătuit, běne vixit,* scil. *hŏmo,* (He) who has well escaped notice, has lived well. Ovid. *Sunt quos currĭcŭlo pulvěrem Olympĭcum collēgisse jŭvat,* scil. *hŏmĭnes,* There are whom it delights, i. e. Some delight. Hor. *Non hăbeo quod te accūsem,* scil. *id propter quod.* Cic. *Non sŏlum săpĭens vidēris, qui hinc absis, sed ětiam beātus,* scil. *tu.* Cic.

(5.) The relative is sometimes either entirely omitted; as, *Urbs antīqua fuit; Tўrii tēnuēre colōni,* scil. *quam* or *eam,* There was an ancient city (which) Tyrian colonists possessed, Virg.; or, if once expressed, is afterwards omitted even when, if supplied, its case would be different; as, *Bocchus cum pĕdĭtĭbus, quos filius ējus adduxĕrat, něque in priōre pugnā adfuērant, Rōmānos invādunt, for et qui non in priōre,* etc. Sall.

(6.) (*a.*) The relative sometimes takes the case of the antecedent, instead of its own proper case; as, *Quum scrības et ăliquid āgas eōrum,* quōrum *consuesti,* for *quæ.* Cic. *Raptim quibus quisque pōtĕrat ēlātis, exībant,* for *iis, quæ quisque efferre pōtĕrat, ēlātis.* Liv.

(*b.*) The antecedent likewise sometimes takes the case of the relative, the substantive either preceding or following the pronoun; as, *Urbem quam stătuo vestra est,* for *urbs.* Virg. *Eunūchum quem dĕdisti nōbis, quas turbas dĕdit!* for *Eunūchus.* Ter. *Naucrătem quem convēnīre volui, in nāvi non ĕrat.* Plaut. *Atque ălii, quōrum cōmædia prisca virōrum est, for atque ălii viri, quōrum est.* Hor. *Illi, scripta quibus cōmædia prisca viris est,* for *illi vĭ-i, quibus.* Id. *Quos pŭĕros misĕram, ĕpistŏlam mihi attŭlērunt.* Cic.

These constructions are said to occur by *attraction.*

(7.) (*a.*) An adjective, which properly belongs to the antecedent, is sometimes placed in the relative clause, and agrees with the relative; as, *Inter jŏcos, quos incondĭtos jăciunt,* for *jŏcos incondĭtos, quos,* etc. Amidst the rude jests which they utter. Liv. *Verbis, quæ magna vŏlant.* Virg. *Călōre, quem multum hăbet.* Cic.

(*b.*) This is the common position of the adjective, when it is a *numeral,* a *comparative,* or a *superlative;* as, *Nocte* quam *in terris* ultimam *ēgit,* The last night which he spent upon earth. *Æsculāpius, qui primus vulnus obligărisse* dicitur. Cic. *Consiliis pāre, quæ nunc pulcherrĭma Nautes dat sēnior,* Listen to the excellent advice, which, etc. Virg. Some instances occur in which an adjective belonging to the relative clause, is placed in that of the antecedent; as, *Quum vēnissent ad răda* Volaterrāna, *quæ nōmĭnantur,* Which are called Volaterran. Cic.

(8.) When to the relative or demonstrative is joined a noun explanatory of its antecedent, but of a different gender or number, the relative or demonstrative usually agrees with that noun; as,

Santōnes non longe a Tŏlōsātium finibus absunt, quæ civĭtas *est in prōvinciā*. The Santones are not far distant from the borders of the Tolosates, which state is in the province. Cæs. *Ante comitia*, quod tempus *haud longe ăbĕrat*. Sall. *Rōmæ fănum Diănæ pŏpŭli Lătini cum pŏpŭlo Rōmāno fĕcĕrunt; ea ĕrat confessio căput rērum Rōmam esse*; i. e. that thing or that act. Liv. *Si omnia făcienda sunt, quæ ămĭci vēlint, non ămīcītiæ* tales, *sed* conjūrātiōnes *pŭtandæ sunt*; i. e. such things or such connections. Cic. So, Ista *quĭdem* vis, Surely this is force. *Ea ipsa causa belli fuit*, for *id ipsum*. Hither also may be referred such explanatory sentences as, Qui *meus* āmor *in te est*, Such is my love for you. Cic.

(9.) If the relative refers to one of two nouns, denoting the same object, but of different genders, it agrees with either; as,

Flūmen est Arar quod *in Rhŏdānum influit*. Cæs. *Ad flūmen Oxum pervertun mi*, qui *turbidus semper est*. Curt.

(10.) When, in a relative clause containing the verb *sum* or a verb of naming, esteeming, etc., a predicate-noun occurs of a different gender from the antecedent, the relative commonly agrees with the latter; but when the preceding noun is to be explained and distinguished from another, the relative agrees with the former; as,

Nātūræ vultus *quem dixēre Chaos*, The appearance of nature which they called chaos. Ovid. Genus *hŏmĭnum* quod *Hĭlōtes vŏcātur*. Nep. *Anĭmal*, quem *vŏcāmus* hŏmĭnem, The animal whom we call man. Cic. *Lŏcus in carcĕre*, quod Tulliānum *appellātur*. Sall. *Pĕcūniārum conquisĭtio*; eos esse belli civīlis nervos *dictĭtans Muciānus*. Tac.

(11.) The relative sometimes agrees with a noun, either equivalent in sense to the antecedent, or only implied in the preceding clause; as,

Abundantia cārum rērum, quæ *mortāles prīma pŭtant*, An abundance of those things, which mortals esteem most important. Sall. Cf. § 205, R. 7, (2.) N. 1. But sometimes when a neuter adjective used substantively has preceded, *res* with a relative follows; as, Permulta *sunt, quæ dici possunt*, quā re *intelligātur*. Cic. *Fātāle monstrum*, quæ, etc., scil. *Cleŏpātra*. Hor. Cf. § 323, 3, (4.)

(*a.*) A relative or demonstrative pronoun, referring to a collective noun, or to a noun which only in a figurative sense denotes a human being, sometimes takes the gender and number of the individuals which the noun implies; as, *Equitātum*, quos. Sall. *Gĕnus*, qui *prĕmuntur*. Cic. *Sĕnātus—ii*. Sall.

(*b.*) A pronoun in the plural often follows a noun in the singular, referring not only to the noun but to the class of persons or things to which it belongs, as, *Dēmŏcrĭtum ŏmittāmus; nihil est enim ăpud istos, quod*, etc. i. e. with Democritus and his followers. Cic. *Dionȳsius nĕgāvit se jūre illo nigro quod cœna cāput ĕrat, dēlectātum. Tum* is, qui illa *coxĕrat*, etc. Id.

(12.) The antecedent is sometimes implied in a possessive pronoun; as, *Omnes laudāre fortūnas mens*, qui *nātum tāli ingĕnio præditum hăbērem*; scil. *mei*, All were extolling *my* fortune, *who*, etc. Ter. *Id* mea *mĭnĭme rĕfert*, qui *sum nātu maxĭmus*. Id. Nostrum consilium *laudandum est*, qui *nŏluĕrim*, etc. Cic.; cr in a possessive adjective; as, *Servīli tŭmultu*, quos, etc. Cæs.

(13.) (*a.*) Sometimes the antecedent is a proposition; the relative then is commonly neuter; as, *Postrēmo*, quod *difficillĭmum inter mortāles, glōriā invidiam vīcisti*, Finally, you have overcome envy with glory, *which*, among men is most difficult. Sall. *Equidem exspectābam jam tuas litĕras, idque cum multis*. Cic.

(*b.*) In such instances, *id* is generally placed before the relative pronoun, referring to the idea in the antecedent clause; as, *Sive*, id *quod constat, Plātōnis stŭdiōsus audiendi fuit*. Cic. *Diem consŭmi vŏlĭbant*, id *quod fĕcĕrunt*. Id.

(*c.*) Sometimes *is*, referring to a clause, agrees with a noun following; as, *Idem velle atque idem nolle, ea dēmum firma ămīcītia est*. Sall.

(14.) *Quod* relating to a preceding statement, and serving the purpose of transition, is often placed at the beginning of a sentence after a period, where it may be translated by 'nay,' 'now,' or 'and.' It is thus use l especially before *si, etsi,* and *nisi;* as, Quodsi *illinc inānis prŏfūgisses, tămen ista tua fŭga nĕfāria jūdicārētur,* i. e. and even if you had fled without taking any thing with you, still, etc. Cic. Verr. 1, 14. *Quodsi,* 'if then,' is especially used in introducing something assumed as true, from which further inferences may be drawn. Sometimes also it is equivalent to 'although.' *Quodnisi* signifies 'if then—not'; as, Quodnisi *ĕgo meo adventu illīus cōnātus ăliquantŭlum repressissem, tam multos,* etc. *Quŏdetsi* is 'nay, even if'; as, *Quŏdetsi ingĕniis magnis præditi quidam dicendi cōpiam sine rătiōne consĕquentur, ars tămen est dux certior.*—*Quod* is found also before *quum, ŭbi, quia, quŏniam, nĕ* and *ŭtĭnam,* where the conjunction alone would seem to be sufficient; as, Quod *ŭtĭnam illum, cūjus impio făcĭnŏre in has misĕrias prōjectus sum, eădem hæc simŭlantem vĭdeam.* Sall. It is so used even before a relative in Cic. Phil. 10, 4, *fin.*—*Quod,* in such examples, seems to be an accusative, with *propter* or *ad* understood.

(15.) (*a.*) A relative is always plural, when referring to two or more nouns in the singular. If the nouns are of different genders, the gender of the relative is determined by Rem. 2, page 185; as, *Ninus et Sĕmirămis,* qui *Băbȳlōna condĭdĕrant,* Ninus and Semiramis, who had founded Babylon. Vell. *Crēbro fŭndli et libicĭne,* quæ *sibi sumpsĕrat.* Cic. *Ex summā lætitiā atque lascīviā,* quæ *diŭturna quies pĕpĕrĕrat.* Sall. *Nāves et captīvos* quæ *ad Chium capta ĕrant.* Liv.

(*b.*) If the antecedents are of different persons, the relative follows the first person rather than the second or third, and the second rather than the third; as, *Tu et pāter,* qui *in convivio ĕrātis. Ego et tu, qui ĕrāmus.* Cf. § 209, R. 12, (7.)

(16.) The relative adjectives *quŏt, quantus, quālis,* are construed like the relative *qui.* They have generally, in the antecedent clause, the corresponding demonstrative words, *tŏt, tantus, tālis;* but these are also often omitted. Frequently also the order of the clauses is reversed, so that the relative clause precedes the demonstrative.

(17.) *Qui,* at the beginning of a sentence, is often translated like a demonstrative; as, Quæ *quum ita sint,* Since *these* (things) are so. Cic.

(18.) The relative *qui* with *sum* and either a nominative or the ablative of quality, is used in explanatory clauses, instead of *pro,* 'in accordance with,' or 'according to'; thus, instead of *Tū,* pro *tuā prŭdentiā, quid optĭmum factu sit, vĭdēbis.* Cic., we may say, *quæ tua est prŭdentia,* or, *quā prŭdentiā ĕs.* So, *Vĕlis tantummŏdo,* quæ *tua virtus, expugnābis.* Hor. Quā prūdentiā es, *nihil te fŭgiet.* Cic.

(19.) A relative clause is sometimes used for the purpose of denoting by circumlocution the person of the agent in a definite but not permanent condition; as, *Ii,* qui *audiunt,* or *qui adsunt,* i. e. the hearers, the persons present. So also, a relative clause is used for the English expression 'above mentioned'; as, *Ex libris quos dixi* or *quos ante* (*supra*) *laudāvi:* and the English 'so called,' or 'what is called,' is expressed by *quem, quam, quod vŏcant,* or by *qui, quæ, quod vŏcātur, dicĭtur,* etc.; as, *Nec Hermas hos, quos vŏcant, impōni* (*Athēnis*) *licēbat.* Cic. *Vestra,* quæ *dicĭtur, vīta, mors est.* Id.

(20.) Relative and demonstrative adverbs (see § 191, R. 1), are frequently used instead of relative and demonstrative pronouns with prepositions; as, *Is,* unde *te audisse dicis,* i. e. *a quo.* Cic. *Divĭtiæ ăpud illos sunt, aut ŭbi illi vŏlunt,* i. e. *ăpud quos.* Sall. *Huic ab ădŏlescentiā bella intestīna, cædes, răpīnæ, discordia civīlis, grāta fuere,* Ibique *jŭventūtem exercuit,* i. e. *in iis,* in these things. Sall.

(21.) With *quam qui* and the superlative after *tam* the verb of the relative clause is sometimes omitted; as, *Tam mihi grātum id ĕrit, quam quod grātissimum.* Cic. *Tam ĕnim sum ămīcus reipūblĭcæ, quam qui maxime.* Id. *Tam sum mitis, quam qui lēnissĭmus.* Id. So also with *ut qui* without *tam;* as, *Te semper sic colam et tuēbor, ut quem dīligentissĭme.* Id.

DEMONSTRATIVES.

§ 207. . REM. 20. The oblique cases of the personal pronoun of the third person (*him, her*, etc.) are commonly expressed in prose by the oblique cases of *is, ea, id*. *Hic* and *ille*, however, being more emphatic, take the place of *is, ea, id*, in lyric poetry, and occasionally in prose also, when particular emphasis is intended. The cases of *ipse, ipsa, ipsum*, also, are employed for this purpose, when the individuality of the person is to be distinctly expressed. In reflexive sentences, the oblique cases of the pronoun of the third person, are regularly supplied by *sui, sibi, se*; and it is only when the person of the leading subject is to be referred to with particular emphasis, that *ipse* is used instead of *sui*.

REM. 21. The demonstrative pronouns, *is* and *ille*, are sometimes used, especially with *quidem*, where a corresponding word in English is unnecessary; as, *Sapientiæ studium vetus* id quidem *in nostris, sed tamen*, etc. Cic. *O hŏmĭnem semper* illum quidem *mihi aptum, nunc vero etiam suāvem*. Id. *Quem neque fĭdes, neque jusjūrandum, neque* illum *misĕrĭcordia, repressit*, Whom neither fidelity, nor an oath, nor pity, has restrained. Ter. *Is* when used for the sake of emphasis seems sometimes in English to be superfluous; as, *Măle se res hăbet, quum, quod virtūte effĭci debet*, id *tentātur pĕcūniā*. Cic.

REM. 22. *Sic, ita, id, hoc, illud*, are often used redundantly as a preliminary announcement of a subsequent proposition, and are added to the verb on which this proposition depends; as, Sic *a majōribus suis accipěrant, tanta pŏpŭli Rōmāni esse benefĭcia, ut*, etc. Cic. *Te* illud *admŏneo, ut quŏtidie medĭtēre, resistendum esse irăcundiæ*. Id. Hoc *tibi persuadeas vĕlim, me nihil ōmisisse*, I wish you to be persuaded of this—that I have omitted nothing. These pleonastic additions have generally no influence on the construction of propositions, but in a few instances they are followed by *ut*; as, *De cūjus dicendi cōpiā* sic *accĭpĭmus, ut*, etc. Cic. Ita *enim dĕfĭnit, ut perturbātio sit*, etc. Id. In the phrase *hoc, illud*, or *id ăgĕre ut*, the pronoun is established by custom and is necessary. See § 273, 1, (*a*.)

REM. 23. (*a.*) *Hic* 'this' refers to what is near to the speaker either in place or time, *ille* 'that' to what is more remote. Hence *hic* sometimes refers to the speaker himself, and *hic hŏmo* is then the same as *ěgo*. On this account *hic* is sometimes called the demonstrative of the first person. When reference is made to two things previously mentioned, *hic* commonly refers to the latter, *ille* to the former, and the pronouns are arranged in the same order, as the objects to which they relate; as, *Ignāvia corpus hĕbĕtat, labor firmat*; illa *mātūram senectūtem*, hic *longam adŏlescentiam reddit*, Sloth enervates the body, labor strengthens it; the former produces premature old age, the latter protracted youth. Cels.

(*b.*) But the order is often reversed, so that *hic* refers to the object first mentioned, and *ille* to the one mentioned last; as, *Sic deus et virgo est*; hic *spe cĕler*, illa *timōre*. Ovid. So when *alter...alter*, 'the one...the other,' refer to two things mentioned before, the previous order is sometimes observed and sometimes reversed; but wherever there is ambiguity the order is reversed, so that the first *alter* refers to the last object. Sometimes *hic...hic* are used instead of *hic . ille*. So *ille...ille* sometimes denote 'the one...the other.'

(*c.*) *Hic* and *ille* have the same relation to time present and past as *nunc* and *tunc*, see § 277; and hence whatever, in speaking of present time, is expressed by *hic* and its derivative adverbs, *hic, hinc, huc*, and *adhuc*, is expressed by *ille* and its derivatives, when it is spoken of as belonging to past time.

REM. 24. *Ille*, when not in opposition to *hic*, is often used to denote that which is of general notoriety; as, *Magno illi Alexandro simillĭmus*, Very like Alexander *the* Great. Vell. *Medea illa*, The celebrated Medea. Cic. Hence *ille* is sometimes added to other pronouns, to refer to something discussed before; as, *Acēbunt risěre, quis ille tot per annos ŏpes nostras sprevisset*. Tac. *Ille* is sometimes translated *this*; as, *Unum illud dico*, This only I say. Cic. *Ille* sometimes marks a change of persons, and may then be translated 'the other,' as, *Vercingetorix obviam Caesari proficiscitur.* 'Ille (scil. *Caesar*) *oppidum Noviodūnum oppugnāre instituĕrat.* Caes.

REM. 25. *Iste* properly refers to the person addressed, and for this reason is called the demonstrative of the second person.—*Ille* refers to the person spoken of, and is hence called the demonstrative of the third person. Thus *iste liber* is thy book, but *ille liber* is the book of which we are speaking. Hence, in letters, *hic* and its derivatives are used of the writer; *iste* and its derivatives of the person addressed; *ille*, etc., of some other person or thing. See § 191, R. 1, (e.) *Iste* from its frequent forensic use, and its application to the opponent, often denotes contempt.

REM. 26. (*a*.) *Is* does not, like *hic, ille,* and *iste,* denote the place or order of the object to which it relates, but either refers without particular emphasis to something already mentioned or to something which is to be defined by the relative *qui*. *Hic, is,* or *ille,* may be used in this way before the relative, but only *hic* or *is* after it; as, *Qui dŏcet, is discit,* or *hic discit,* but not *ille discit,* unless some individual is referred to.

(*b*.) *Is* before a relative or *ut* has sometimes the sense of *tālis,* such, denoting a class; as, *Nĕque ĕnim tu* is *es, qui quid sis nescins,* Nor are you such a person, as not to know what you are. Cic.; sometimes it has the force of *idem;* as, *vos* —*ii.* Cic. Manil. 12.

(*c*.) If the noun to which *is* refers is to receive some additional predicate, we must use *et is, atque is, isque, et is quidem,* and with a negative *nec is;* as, *Vincŭla vēro, et ea sempiternă,* etc. Cic. *Unā in dŏmo, et ea quidem angusta,* etc. Id. *Adŏlescentes ăliquot,* nec ii *tĕnui lŏco orti,* etc. Liv. *Sed is* is used when the additional predicate is opposed to the preceding; as, *Sĕvĕritātem in sĕnectūte prŏbo,* sed eam, *sicut ălia, mŏdĭcam.* Cic. The neuter *et id,* or *idque,* serves to introduce an addition to the preceding proposition; as, *Quamquam te, Marce fili, annum jam audientem Crătippum,* idque *Athēnis,* etc.

(*d*.) *Is* is not expressed when it would be in the same oblique case as the preceding noun to which it refers; as, *Pāter ămat libĕros et tămen castigat. Multos illustrat fortūna, dum vexat.*

(*e*.) When in English 'that' or 'those' is used instead of the repetition of the preceding substantive, *is* is never used in Latin, and *ille* only in later authors. In such cases the noun is commonly not repeated in Latin, and no pronoun is used in its place; as, *Philippus hostium mānus sæpe vitāvit, suōrum effugĕre non văluit,* those of his own subjects. Curt. Sometimes the substantive is repeated; as, *Judicia civitātis cum judiciis principis certant.* Vell. Sometimes a possessive adjective is used instead of the genitive depending on the omitted substantive; as, *Terentii făbŭlas stŭdiōse lĕgo,* Plautinis *minus dĕlector:* and sometimes instead of the genitive or a possessive adjective the name of the person itself is put in the case which the verb governs; as, *Si cum Lycurgo et Drăcōne et Sŏlōne nostras lĕges conferre volueritis.* Cic.—In Cicero *hic* and *ille,* when the preceding substantive is understood, retain their demonstrative signification, and therefore do not merely supply the place of the omitted substantive; as, *Nullam ĕnim virtus ăliam mercēdem dĕsĭdĕrat, praeter hanc,* i. e. the one of which I am speaking. Cic.

REM. 27. (*a*.) *Idem,* as denoting a subject which stands in equal relations to two different predicates, often supplies the place of *item* or *ĕtiam,* 'also,' 'at the same time,' or of *tămen,* 'yet,' if the things are apparently inconsistent; as, *Mūsici, qui ĕrant quondam* iidem *poëtæ,* Musicians, who formerly were poets also. Cic. *Euphrātes et Tigris magno āquārum divortio iter percurrunt;* iidem (and yet) *paulātim in arctius coĕunt.*

(*b*.) *Et ipse,* on the other hand, denotes that the same predicate belongs to two subjects. It is rendered by 'too' or 'also'; as, *Antōnīnus Commŏdus nihil pāternum hăbuit, nisi quod contra Germānos fēliciter* et ipse *pugnārit,* for *item* or *ipse quōque.* Eutr.—So, also, *nec ipse* is used in the sense of 'neither'; as, *Primis rĕpulsis Măharbal cum majōre rōbŏre virōrum missus* nec ipse *ĕruptiŏnem cohortium sustinuit.* Liv.

(c.) *Idem* is sometimes repeated in the sense of 'at once,' denoting the union of qualities which might be thought incompatible; as, *Fuēre quidam qui iidem ornāte iidem versūte dicĕrent*, There have been some who could speak at once elegantly and artfully. Cic.
(d.) '*The same as*' is variously expressed in Latin, by *idem* with *qui*, *ac* or *atque*, *quam*, *quāsi*, *ut* or *cum*; as, *Verres* idem *est* qui *fuit semper*, Verres is the same as he has always been. Cic. *Vita est* eādem *ac fuit*. Liv. *Dispūtātiōnem expōnĭmus* iisdem *fĕre verbis ut actum est.* Cic. Eandem *constituit pŏtestātem* quam *si*, etc. Cic. Eōdem *lŏco res est*, quăsi *ea pēcūnia lēgāta non esset*. Id. *Hunc ĕgo* eōdem *mēcum patre gĕnĭtum*, etc. So also poetically with the *dative*; as, Eūdem ăliis *sōpītu' quiĕte est*. Lucr. Cf. § 222, R. 7.

IPSE, INTENSIVE OR ADJUNCTIVE.

REM. 28. (a.) *Ipse*, when used with a substantive pronoun taken reflexively, agrees either with such pronoun or with the subject of the proposition, according as either is emphatic; as, *Agam per me ipse*, I will do it myself. Cic. *Non ĕgeo mĕdĭcīnā* (i. e. *ut ălii me consōlĕntur*); *me* ipse *consōlor*. Cic. *Accūsando eum, a cūjus crūdēlĭtāte* vosmet ipsi *armis vindĭcastis*. Liv.—*Cn. Pompeium omnĭbus, Lentŭlum* mihi ipsi antĕpōno. Cic. *Fac ut te* ipsum *custōdias*. Id. *Dēforme est de se* ipsum *prædicāre*. Id.—But Cicero often construes *ipse* as the subject, even where the emphasis belongs to the object; as, *Quid est nēgōtii continēre eos, quibus præsis, si te* ipse *contĭneas?*
(b.) When *ipse* is joined with a possessive pronoun used reflexively, it usually takes the case of the subject; as, *Meam* ipse *lēgem nēglĭgo*; not *meam ipsius*, according to § 211, R. 3, (a). So, *Si ex scrīptis cognosci* ipsi *suis pŏtuissent*. Cic. *Eam fraudem vestrā* ipsi *virtūte rītustis*. Liv. But the genitive is necessary when the possessive does not refer to the subject; as, *Tuā* ipsius *causā hoc fēci*. And it is sometimes found where the case of the subject should be used; as, *Conjectūram de tuo* ipsius *stūdio cēpĕris*, instead of *ipse*.—(c.) *Ipse* is sometimes used as reflexive without *sui*; as, *Omnes bŏni, quantum in* ipsis *fuit, Cæsărem occīdērunt*. Cic.
(d.) *Ipse*, with nouns denoting time or number, expresses exactness, and may be rendered, 'just,' 'precisely'; or 'very,' 'only'; as, *Dyrrhăchio sum prŏfectus* ipso *illo die, quo lex est dăta de nōbis*, on the very day. Cic. *Trīginta dies ĕrant* ipsi, *quum has dăbam littĕras, per quos nullas a vōbis accēpĕram*, just thirty days. Id. *Et quisquam dŭbĭtābĭt—quam făcile impĕrio atque exercĭtu sŏcius et vectīgālia conservātūrus sit, qui* ipso *nōmĭne ac rūmōre dēfendĕrit*, by his very name, or, by his name only. Id.

GENERAL RELATIVES.

REM. 29. *Quicumque, quisquis*, and the other general relatives (see § 139, 5, R., are, in classical prose, always connected with a verb, and form the protasis. *Quicumque* is commonly used as an adjective, and *quisquis* as a substantive; but the neuter *quodcumque* is used as a substantive with a following genitive; as, *Quodcumque militum*; and, on the other hand, *quisquis* is rarely an adjective; as, *Quisquis ĕrit vītæ cŏlor*. Hor.; and even the neuter *quidquid* is used in the same manner; as, *Quisquis hŏnos tŭmŭli, quidquid sōlāmen hŭmandi* est. Virg. *Quicumque* seems sometimes even in Cicero equivalent to *omnis* or *quīvis*; as, *Quæ sānāri pŏtĕrunt*, quācumque *rătiōne sānābo*, What can be cured, I will cure by every possible means. Cic. Yet *possum* is rather to be supplied;—'in whatever way I can.' But in later writers *quicumque* is frequently used in the absolute sense for *quīvis* or *quīlĭbet*; as, *Cicĕrōnem cuicumque eōrum fortiter oppōsuĕrim*. Quint. *Quāliscumque* and *quantuscumque* are likewise used in an absolute sense by ellipsis; as, *Tu non concŭpisces quantīcumque ad lībertātem pervĕnīre?* At any price, be it ever so high. Sen. So *quisquis* is occasionally used, not as a relative, but as an indefinite pronoun. *Sīquis* often seems to stand as a relative, like the Greek εἴτις for ὅστις, 'whoever'; but it always contains the idea of 'perhaps'; as, *Nūda fĕre Alpium căcūmĭna sunt, et si quid est păbŭli, ŏbruunt nives* Liv.

INDEFINITE PRONOUNS.

REM. 30. (*a*.) *Aliquis* and *quispiam* are particular and affirmative, corresponding to the English *some one*; as, *Hērēdĭtas est pĕcūnia, quæ morte ălĭcūjus ad* quempiam *pervēnit jūre,* An inheritance is property which, at the death of some one, falls to some (other) one by law. Cic. *Multi sine doctrīnā* ăliquid *omnium gĕnĕrum et artium consĕquuntur.* Id.

(*b*.) *Aliquis* is more emphatic than the indefinite pronoun *quis.* (See § 137, (3.)) Hence *aliquis* stands by itself, but *quis* is commonly connected with certain conjunctions or relative words, but these are sometimes separated from it by one or more words. Sometimes, however, *quis* is used without such conjunctions or relatives; as, *Morbus aut ĕgestas aut* quid *ejusmŏdi.* Cic. *Dētrăhĕre* quid *de ăliquo.* Id. *Injūriam* cui *făcĕre.* Id. So, *Dixērit* quis, Some one might say. But even after those conjunctions which usually require *quis, ăliquis* is used when employed antithetically and of course emphatically; as, *Tĭmēbat Pompeius omnia,* ne ăliquid *vos tĭmērĕtis.* Cic. In English the emphasis of *ăliquis* is sometimes expressed by 'really'; as, *Sensus mŏriendi,* si aliquis *esse pŏtest, is ad exĭguum tempus dūrat.* Cic.—*Quispiam,* also, is sometimes used like *quis* after *si,* etc., and sometimes stands alone; as, *Quærĕt fortasse quispiam.*

REM. 31. (*a.*) *Quisquam,* 'any one,' and *ullus,* 'any,' are universal. Like *umquam* and *usquam* they are used in propositions which involve a universal negative, or which express an interrogation with a negative force, or a condition (usually with *si* or *quasi*); also, after comparatives, after the adverb *vix,* and the preposition *sine;* as. *Nĕque ex castris Cătilīnæ* quisquam *omnium discessĕrat* Nor had any one departed from the camp of Catiline. Sall. *Nĕc ullo cāsu pŏtest contingĕre, ut ulla intermissio fīat offĭcii.* Cic. *An* quisquam *pŏtest sine perturbātiōne mentis īrasci?* Id. *Tētrior hic tyrannus Syrācūsānis fuit, quam* quisquam *supĕriōrum.* Id. *Vix* quidquam *spei est.* Sen. But after the dependent negative particles *ne, nēve,* and the negative interrogative particle *num, quis* and not *quisquam* is used.

(*b*.) But *quisquam* and *ullus* after *si* are often used not in a negative sense, but instead of *aliquis* or *quis,* serving only to increase the indefiniteness which would be implied in the latter pronouns; as, *Aut ĕnim nēmo, quod quidem măgis crēdo, aut,* si quisquam, *ille săpiens fuit,* if any man. Cic. Hence, ultimately, even without *si,* where the indefiniteness is to be made emphatic, *quisquam, ullus, umquam* and *usquam* were used; as, *Quamdiu* quisquam *ĕrit, qui te dĕfendĕre audeat, vīves.* Cic. *Bellum maxime omnium mĕmŏrābĭle, quæ* umquam *gesta sunt, scriptūrus sum.* Tac.

(*c*.) *Ullus* is properly an adjective, but *quisquam* is commonly used without a noun, except it is a word denoting a person; as, *Cuiquam cīvi,* To any citizen. *Cūjusquam ōrātōris ēlōquentiam.* Hence *quisquam* corresponds to the substantive *nēmo* and *ullus* to the adjective *nullus.* *Nēmo* is often used with other substantives denoting male persons so as to become equivalent to the adjective *nullus;* as, *nēmo pictor, nēmo ădŏlescens,* and even *hōmo nēmo.* Cic. *Quisquam* is sometimes used in a similar manner: as, *quisquam hōmo, quisquam cīvis.* On the other hand *nullus* and *ullus* are used as substantives instead of *nēmo* and *quisquam,* especially the genitive *nullius* and the ablative *nullo.*

REM. 82. (*a.*) *Alius,* like *ullus,* though properly an adjective, is sometimes used like a pronoun. It is often repeated, or joined with an adverb derived from it, in the same proposition, which may be translated by two separate propositions, commencing respectively with 'one...another'; as, Aliud ăliis *vidētur optimum,* One thing seems best to one, another to another. Cic. Aliis ălinde *pĕrīcŭlum est,* Danger threatens one from one source, another from another; *or,* Danger threatens different persons from different sources. Ter. *Diŏnȳsium Alĭter cum ăliis de nōbis lŏcūtum audĭībam.* Cic.—*Alter* is used in the same manner when only *two* persons are spoken of, but there are no adverbs derived from it; as, Alter *in* altĕrum *causam confĕrunt,* They accuse each other.

(*b*.) *Alius,* repeated in *diffĕrent* propositions, is also translated 'one...another'; as, Aliud *ăgĭtur,* aliud *sĭmŭlātur,* One thing is done, another pretended. Cic. Alter *loquĭtur,* ălter *scrībit,* like *ălĭter ac* or *atque,* He speaks otherwise than he writes. So *Aliud lŏquĭtur, ăliud scrībit.*

(c.) *Uterque*, 'each of two,' is always used by Cicero in the singular number, when only two individuals are spoken of. Its plural, *utrīque*, is used only when each of two parties consists of several individuals; as, *Măcĕdōnes— Tўrii, utrīque.* But in other good prose writers the plural *utrīque* is occasionally used in speaking of only two; as, *Utrīque Diŏnÿsii.* Nep. Cf. § 209, R. 11, (4.)

REM. 33. (a.) *Quĭdăm* differs from *ălĭquis* by implying that a person or thing, though indefinitely described, is definitely known; as, *Quĭdam de collēgis nostris*, A certain one of our colleagues. Cic. *Scis me quŏdam tempŏre Mĕtăpontum vĕnisse tēcum.* Id.

(b.) *Quĭdam* is sometimes used for *some*, as opposed to *the whole*, or to *others*; as, *Excessērunt urbe* quĭdam, ălii *mortem sibi consciverunt*, Some departed from the city, others destroyed themselves. Liv. Hence it is used to soften an expression, where in English we say 'so to speak,' etc.; as, *Milvo est* quoddam *bellum nătūrāle cum corvo*, A kind of natural warfare. Cic. *Fuit ĕnim illud* quoddam *cæcum tempus servĭtūtis*. Id. *Etĕnim omnes artes quæ ad hūmānĭtātem pertĭnent, hăbent* quoddam *commūne vincŭlum et quăsi cognātiōne* quādam *inter se contĭnentur.* Id.—*Tamquam* is used for the same purpose, and also *ut ita dicam*.

REM. 34. *Quīvis* and *quilĭbet*, 'any one,' and *ūnusquisque*, 'each,' are universal and absolute; as, *Omnia sunt ejusmŏdi* quivis *ut perspĭcēre possit*, All are of such a nature that any one can perceive. Cic. *Hic ăpud mājōres nostros adhĭbēbātur pĕrītus*, nunc quilĭbet. Id. *Nātūra* ūnumquemque *trăhit ad discendum.* A negative joined with them denies only the universality which they imply; as, *Non* cuivis *homĭni contingit ădīre Cŏrinthum*, i. e. not to every man without distinction. Hor. *Cuiquam* would have made the negation universal.

REM. 35. (a.) *Quisque* signifies *each, every one*, distributively or relatively, and generally stands without a noun; as, *Quod* cuique *oblĭgit, id* quisque *tĕneat*, Let each one keep what has fallen to each. Cic. Hence it is used particularly after relative and interrogative pronouns and adverbs; as, *Scīpio pollicētur sĭbi magnæ cūræ fōre, ut omnia civĭtātĭbus*, quæ cūjusque *fuissent, restĭtuērentur.* Cic. *Ut prædīci posset*, quid cuique *ĕventūrum, et* quo quisque *făto nātus esset.* Id. *Cur fīat* quidque *quæris: recte omnīno.* Id. *Quo quisque est sollertior, hoc dŏcet lăbōriōsius.* Id. *Ut quisque optĭme dīcit, ita maxĭme dicendi diffĭcultātem tīmet.* Id. And hence the expression *quŏtusquisque* in the sense of 'how few among all.' It is also used distributively after numerals; as, *Dĕcĭmus* quisque *sorte lectus*, Every tenth man. Quinto quōque *anno*, In every fifth year. So also after *suus*; as, *Sui* cuique *libĕri cārissĭmi:* suum cuique *plăcet.* (Respecting the order of the words, cf. § 279, 14: and respecting *quisque* in the nominative in apposition to a noun or pronoun in the ablative absolute or in the accusative with the infinitive, see § 204, R. 10.)

(b.) *Quisque* with a superlative, either in the singular or the plural, denotes universality, and is generally equivalent to *omnes* with the positive; as, *doctissĭmus quisque*, Every learned man, i. e. all the learned; but often, also, in connection with the verb, it retains the idea of a reciprocal comparison, and is to be rendered by the superlative; as, *In omni arte* optimum quidque *rărissĭmum*, The best is the rarest. Cic. *Altissĭma* quæque *flūmĭna mĭnĭmo sŏno lăbuntur*, The deepest rivers flow with the least sound. Curt. With *primus*, it denotes the *first possible;* as, *Prīmo quōque tempŏre*, As soon as possible. Cic.

POSSESSIVES.

REM. 36. (a.) The possessive pronouns *meus, tuus, suus, noster*, and *vester*, are joined to nouns, to indicate an action or possession of the persons denoted by their primitives; as, *Tūtus ămor* meus *est tĭbi*, My love is secure to you. Ovid. *Tuam vĭcem dŏlēre sŏleo.* Cic.—These pronouns, as in English, when belonging to two substantives, are generally expressed but once, even when the substantives are of different genders; as, *ămor tuus ac jūdĭcium de me.*

(b.) But these pronouns are sometimes used when the persons to which they refer are the *objects* of an action, feeling, etc.; as, *Nam nĕque* tuā *nĕglĭgentiā, nĕque ŏdio id fĕcit* tuo, For he did it neither through neglect nor hatred *of you.* Ter. See § 211, R. 3.

(*c*) The possessive pronouns, especially when used as reflexives, are often omitted; as, *Quo rĕvertar? in patriam?* scil. *meam*, Whither shall I return? to (my) country? Ovid. *Dextrā mūnĕra porrexit*, scil. *suā*. Id. But they are expressed when emphasis or contrast is intended, where in English 'own' might be added to the pronoun; as, *Ego non dicam, tămen id pŏtŭritis cum ănĭmis* vestris *cōgĭtāre.* Cic.

(*d.*) When besides the person of the subject, that of a remote object also occurs in the proposition, the possessive pronoun will refer to the latter; as, *Patris ănĭmum mihi rĕconciliasti*, i. e. *patris mei ănĭmum* rather than *tui.*

(*e.*) As reflexives, *meus*, etc., are translated my, thy, his, her, its, our, your, their; or my own, thy own, his own, etc.

THE REFLEXIVES *SUI* AND *SUUS*.

§ 208. REM. 37. (*a.*) *Sui* and *suus* properly refer to the subject of the proposition in which they stand; as,

Oppĭdāni *făcĭnus in* se *ac* suos *fœdum consciscunt*, The citizens decide on a foul crime against themselves and their friends. Liv.

(*b.*) They continue to be used in successive clauses, if the subject remains the same; as,

Ipse se *quisque dilĭgit, non ut ălĭquam a se ipse mercēdem exĭgat cārĭtātis* suæ, *sed quod per* se sĭbi *quisque cārus est.* Cic.

(1.) In dependent clauses, in which the subject does not remain the same, the reflexives are commonly used in references to the leading subject, when the thoughts, language, purposes, etc., of that subject are stated; as,

Ariŏvistus prædĭcāvit, non sēse *Gallis, sed Gallos* sĭbi *bellum intŭlisse*, Ariovistus declared that he had not made war upon the Gauls, but the Gauls upon him. Cæs. *Hŏmērum Cŏlŏphōnii cĭvem esse dīcunt* suum, The Colophonians say that Homer is their citizen. Cic. *Tўrannus pĕtīvit ut se ad ămīcĭtiam tertium ascrībĕrent.* Id. But sometimes, to avoid ambiguity, the cases of *is* or *ille* are used in such clauses in references to the leading subject; as, *Helvētii sēse Allobrŏges vi coactūros existĭmābant, ut per* suos *fines eos ire pătĕrentur.* Cæs. Here *suos* refers to the subject of the dependent clause, and *eos* to *Helvētii*, the subject of the leading clause. And sometimes, even in the same dependent clause, two reflexive pronouns are used, referring to different persons; as, *Scўthæ pĕtēbant ut rēgis* sui *fīliam mātrĭmōnio* sĭbi *jungĕret.* Curt.

(2.) If, however, the leading subject, whose thoughts, etc., are expressed, is indefinite, the reflexives relate to the subject of a dependent clause; as,

Mēdēam prædicant (scil. *hŏmĭnes*) *in fŭgā frātris* sui *membra in iis lŏcis, quā se pārens persĕquĕrētur, dissĭpāvisse.* Cic. *Ipsum rēgem trādunt ŏpĕrātum his sacris se abdĭdisse.* Liv.

(3.) (*a.*) When the leading verb is in the passive voice, the reflexive often refers not to its subject, but to that which would be its subject in the active voice; as,

A Cæsāre invītor ut sim sĭbi *lēgātus*, i. e. *Cæsar me invītat*, I am invited by Cæsar to become his lieutenant. Cic.

(*b.*) So when the subject is a thing without life, the reflexive may relate to some other word in the sentence, which denotes a thing having life; as,

Cănum tam fĭda custōdia quid signĭfĭcat ăliud, nisi se *ad hŏmĭnum commŏdĭtātes esse gĕnĕrātos?* Cic.

(4.) Instead of *sui* and *suus*, whether referring to a leading or a subordinate subject, *ipse* is sometimes used, to avoid ambiguity from the similarity of both numbers of *sui*, and also to mark more emphatically than *suus*, the person to whom it relates; as,

Jugurtha *legatos misit, qui ipsi liberisque vitam peterent*, Jugurtha sent ambassadors to ask life for himself and his children. Sall. *Ea molestissime ferre homines debent, quæ* ipsorum *culpa contracta sunt.*

(5.) In the plural number, with *inter*, *se* only is used, if the person or thing referred to is in the nominative or accusative; *se* or *ipse*, if in any other case; as,

Fratres *inter* se *quum forma, tum moribus similes*, Brothers resembling each other both in person and character. Cic. *Feras inter sese conciliat natura.* Cic. *Incidunt aliqua a doctis etiam inter ipsos mutuo reprehensa.* Quint.

(6.) (*a.*) When reference is made not to the subject of the proposition, but to some other person or thing, *hic*, *is*, or *ille*, is generally used, except in the cases above specified; as,

Themistocles servum ad Xerxem *misit, ut ei nuntiaret, suis verbis, adversarios ejus in fuga esse*, Themistocles sent his servant to Xerxes, to inform him (Xerxes), in his ('Themistocles') name, that his (Xerxes') enemies were upon the point of flight. Nep.

(*b.*) But when no ambiguity would arise, and especially when the verb is of the first or second person, *sui* and *suus* sometimes take the place of the demonstrative pronouns; as,

Suam *rem* sibi *salvam sistam*, I will restore his property entire to him. Plaut.

(*c.*) On the contrary, the demonstratives are sometimes used for the reflexives; as,

Helvetii *persuadent Rauracis, ut una cum iis proficiscantur*, The Helvetii persuade the Rauraci to go with them. Cæs.—In some instances, a reflexive and a demonstrative are used in reference to the same person; as, *Ita se gessit* (scil. *Ligarius*) *ut ei pacem esse expediret.* Cic. *C. Claudii orantis pro sui fratris parentisque ejus manes.* Liv.—Sometimes the reflexives refer to different subjects in the same sentence; as, *Ariovistus respondit, neminem secum sine sua pernicie contendisse* (Cæs.); where *se* refers to Ariovistus, and *sua* to *neminem*.

(7.) (*a.*) *Suus* often refers to a word in the predicate of a sentence, and is then usually placed after it; as,

Hunc *cives* sui *ex urbe ejecerunt*, Him his fellow-citizens banished from the city. Cic. *Titurius quum procul* Ambiorigem, suos *cohortantem, conspexisset.* Cæs.

(*b.*) *Suus*, and not *hujus*, is used when a noun is omitted; as,

Octavius *quem* sui (scil. amici) *Cæsarem salutabant*, Octavius, whom his followers saluted as Cæsar.

(*c.*) *Suus* is also commonly used when two nouns are coupled by *cum* but not when they are connected by a conjunction; as,

Ptolemæus *amicos Demetrii cum* suis *rebus dimisit*, Ptolemy dismissed the friends of Demetrius with their effects. Just.

(8.) *Suus* sometimes denotes *fit, favorable;* as,

Sunt et sua *dona parenti*, There are likewise for my father suitable presents. Virg. *Ut liberator ille populi Romani opprimitur tempora* sua. Liv. *Alphenus ætebatur populo sane suo.* Cic. Sometimes it signifies *peculiar;* as, *Molles* sua *tura Sabæi*, scil. *mittunt*, i. e. the frankincense for which their country was famous. Virg. *Fessosque sopor* suus *occupat artus.* Id.

NOMINATIVE.

SUBJECT-NOMINATIVE AND VERB.

§ 209. (*a.*) The noun or pronoun which is the subject of a finite verb is put in the nominative.

NOTE 1. (*a.*) A verb in any mood except the infinitive is called a finite verb. (*b.*) In historical writing the nominative is sometimes joined with the present infinitive instead of the imperfect indicative. Cf. R. 5.

(*b.*) A verb agrees with its subject-nominative, in number and person; as,

Ego lĕgo, I read.   *Nos lĕgĭmus,* We read.
Tu scrībis, Thou writest. *Vos scrībĭtis,* You write.
Equus currĭt, The horse runs. *Equi currunt,* Horses run.

NOTE 2. The imperative singular is sometimes used in addressing several persons; as, *Huc nātas adjice septem,* scil. *vos, Thēbaidos.* Ovid. Met. 6, 182. So Adde *dēfectiōnem Italiæ,* scil. *vos, milĭtes.* Liv. 26, 41.

REMARK 1. (*a.*) The nominatives *ĕgo, tu, nos, vos,* are seldom expressed, the termination of the verb sufficiently marking the person; as,

Cūpio, I desire; *vīcis,* thou livest; *hăbēmus,* we have. See § 147, 3.

(*b.*) But when emphasis or opposition is intended, the nominatives of the first and second persons are expressed; as, *Ego rēges ējēci,* vos *tӯrannos introdūcĭtis,* I banished kings, you introduce tyrants. Auct. ad Her. Nos, nos, *dico ăperte, consŭles dēsŭmus,* Cic. *Tu es patrōnus,* tu *pāter.* Ter. In indignant questions and addresses *tu* is expressed; as, *Tu in fŏrum prōdīre,* tu *lūcem conspicĕre,* tu *in hōrum conspectum vĕnīre cŏnāris?* Auct. ad Her.

REM. 2. The nominative of the third person is often omitted:—

(1.) When it has been expressed in a preceding proposition:—

(*a.*) As nominative; as, *Mōsa prōfluit ex monte Vōsĕgo, et in Ocĕănum influit.* Cæs.; or (*b.*) in an oblique case; as, *Cursōrem misērunt, ut id nuntiāret,* scil. *cursor.* Nep.: or (*c*) in a possessive adjective; as, *Et vĕreor quo se Junōnia vertant Hospĭtia; haud tanto* cessābit *cardĭne rērum,* scil. *illa,* i. e. *Junō.* Virg. Æn. 1. 672.

(2.) When it is a general word for *person* or *thing:*—

Thus *hŏmĭnes* is often omitted before *aiunt, dīcunt, fĕrunt,* etc.; as, *Ut aiunt* As they say. Cic. *Maxĭme admīrantur eum, qui pĕcūniā non mŏvētur.* Id — Sĭ *bĕne est, bĕne* hăbet or *bĕne* ăgĭtur, It is well; as, *Si rales,* bĕne *est, ego rateo* Cic. *Quum mĕlius est, grātŭlor dis.* Afran. Optŭme hăbet, Nothing can be better. Plaut. *Bĕne* hăbet: *jacta sunt fundāmenta dēfensiōnis.* Cic. *Bĕne* ăgĭtur *pro noxia.* Plaut.

NOTE 3. This omission of the nominative is common in the clause preceding a relative; as, *Qui Bāvium non ŏdit, ămet tua carmĭna, Mævī,* scil. *hŏmo,* Let him who hates not Bavius, love your verses, Mævius. Virg. *Vastātur agri quod inter urbem ac Fidēnas est,* scil. *id spătium.* Liv. *Sunt quos jŭvat...*scil. *hŏmĭnes,* There are (those) whom it delights. Hor. *Est qui nec vĕtĕris pōcŭla Massĭci spernit,* scil. *hŏmo.* Hor. Here *sunt quos* and *est qui* are equivalent to *quidam, ălĭquis,* or *ălĭqui.* So, *Est quod gaudeas,* There is (reason) why you should rejoice. Cic. *Nĕque ĕrat cur fallĕre vellent.* Ovid. *Est ubi id văleat.* Cic. *Est, quum non est sătius,* etc. Auct. ad Her. In the latter cases the adverbs are equivalent to *in quo,* scil. *loco, tempŏre.*

§ 209   SYNTAX.—SUBJECT-NOMINATIVE.   201

REM. 3 (1.) The nominative is *wanting* before verbs denoting the state of the weather, or the operations of nature; as,

Fulgŭrat, It lightens. Plin. *Ningit,* It snows. Virg. *Lūcescĭbat,* It was growing light. Liv. *Jam advesperascit.* Cic.

(2.) The nominative is also wanting before the third person singular of the passive of neuter verbs, and of active verbs used impersonally; as,

Făvētur tĭbi a me, Thou art favored by me. *Ejus ōrātiōni vĕhĕmenter ab omnĭbus* reclāmātum est. Cic. Proinde ut bĕne *vīvītur,* diu *vīrĭtur.* Plaut. *Ad exĭtum* ventum est. Sen. Actum est *de impĕrio.* See § 184, 2: and cf. § 229, R. 5, (*b.*)

NOTE 4. A nominative, however, is expressed before the passive of some neuter verbs, which, in the active voice, are followed by an accusative; as, *Pugna pugnāta est.* Cic. See § 232, (1.)

(3.) It is wanting also before the neuter of the future passive participle with *est;* as,

Si vis me flēre dŏlendum est *primum ipsi tĭbi,* If you wish me to weep, you yourself must first grieve. Hor. Orandum est, *ut sit mens sāna in corpŏre sāno.* Juv. *Ad villam* revertendum est. Cic.

(4.) The nominative is also wanting before the impersonal verbs *mĭsĕret, pœnĭtet, pŭdet, tædet,* and *pĭget;* as,

Eos ineptiārum pœnĭtet, They repent of their follies. Cic. *Mĭsĕret te āliōrum, tui te nec mĭsĕret nec pŭdet.* Plaut. *Me cīvĭtātis mōrum pĭget tædetque.* Sall.— In such examples, the sense will sometimes permit us to supply *fortūna, condĭtio, mĕmŏria,* etc. So in the expression, *Vēnit in mentem,* It came into mind as, *In mentem vēnit de spĕcŭlo,* scil. *cōgĭtātio,* etc. Plaut.—An infinitive or a subjunctive clause sometimes forms the subject of these verbs; as, *Te id nullo mŏdo pŭduit fācĕre,* To do that by no means shamed you. Ter. *Nŏn pœnĭtet me,* quantum prŏfēcĕrim. Cic.

(5.) The subject of the verb is sometimes an infinitive or a neuter participle (either alone or with other words), one or more propositions, or an adverb. (Cf. § 202, R. 2 and 3: and § 274, R. 5, (*b.*)) The verb is then in the third person singular; as,

Vācāre culpā magnum est sōlātium, To be free from fault is a great consolation. *Nĕque est te fallĕre quidquam,* To deceive you in any thing is not (possible.) Virg. *Mentīri non est meum.* Plaut. Te non istud audīvisse *mīrum est,* That you have not heard that is wonderful. Cic. 'Summum jus, summa injūria,' *factum est jam trītum sermōne prōverbium.* Id. *Ni dĕgĕnĕrātum in āliis huic quōque dĕcŏri effēcisset.* Liv. (Cf. § 274, R. 5, (*b.*)) *Sin est ut velis mănēre illum apud te.* Ter. *Nec prŏfuit Hȳdræ* crescĕre per damnum, gĕmĭnasque resūmĕre vires. Ovid. *Dic mĭhi,* cras istud, *Postŭme, quando vĕnit?* Tell me, Postumus, when does that to-morrow come? Mart. *Parumne campis atque Neptūno super fūsum est Lătīni sanguĭnis?* Hor.

(*a.*) This construction is especially common with impersonal verbs; as, Ōrātōrem irasci *non dĕcet,* That an orator should be angry, is not becoming. Cic. Hoc *fĭĕri et ŏportet et ŏpus est.* Id. *Me pĕdĭbus dĕlectat* claudĕre verba, Hor. *Intĕrest omnium* recte făcĕre. Cic. *Cāsu accĭdit,* ut, id quod Rōmæ audīĕrat primus nuntiāret. Id. Sometimes a neuter pronoun is interposed between a proposition and its verb; as, *Impūne făcĕre quæ libet,* id est *rēgem esse.* Sall. Cf. § 206, (13,) (*a.*)

(6.) The nominative is also wanting before *pŏtest, cœpit* or *cœptum est, incĭpit, dēsĭnit, dĕbet, sŏlet,* and *vĭdētur,* when followed by the infinitive of an impersonal verb; as,

Pĭgēre eum facti cœpit, It began to repent him (i. e. he began to repent) of his conduct. Just. *Săpientia est ūna, quā præceptrīce, in tranquillĭtāte vivi pŏtest*. Cic. *Tædēre sŏlet ăcārōs impendĭi*. Quint.

REM. 4. The *verb* is sometimes omitted; as,

Di mĕliōra piis, scil. *dent* or *vĕlint*, May the gods grant better things to the pious. Virg. *Hōrum hæc hactĕnus*, scil. *diximus*. Cic. *Pertĭneo* is understood in such expressions as *nihil ad me, nihil ad rem; Quid hoc ad Epicūrum?* What does this concern Epicurus? *Quorsus hæc?* i. e. *quorsus hæc pertĭnent?* What is that for?—*Părābo* is to be supplied, in *Quo mihi hanc rem?* Of what use is this to me? and, *Unde mihi aliquam rem?* Whence am I to get any thing? as, *Quo mihi bibliōthĕcas?* Sen. *Unde mihi lăpĭdem?* Hor. A tense of *făcio* is often to be supplied, as in *Recte ille, mĕlius hi; Bĕne Chrȳsippus, qui dŏcet*. Cic *Nihil per vim umquam Clōdius, omnia per vim Mĭlo*. Id. *Quæ quum dixisset Cotta finem*. Id. So, also in the phrases *nihil aliud quam; quid aliud quam; nihil præterquam*, which signify ' merely '; as, *Tisaphernes nihil aliud quam bellum compărāvit*. Nep. This verb is in like manner omitted with *nihil amplius quam; nihil minus quam*, and in the phrase *si nihil aliud*.—*Ait* or *inquit* is sometimes omitted in introducing the direct words of another, and more frequently in relating a connected conversation; as, *Tum ille; hic ĕgo; huic ĕgo. Dīcit* is sometimes omitted in quoting a person's words; as, *Scīte Chrȳsippus: ut gladii causā vāgīnam, sic præter mundum cētĕra omnia aliōrum causā esse gĕnĕrāta*. Cic. —After *per* in adjurations *ōro, rŏgo* or *prĕcor* is often omitted; as, *Per ĕgo vos deos patrios, vindicāte ab ultimo dedĕcŏre nōmen gentemque Persārum*; i. e. *per deos patrios vos ōro, vindicāte*. Curt. This omission is most common with the copula *sum*; as, *Nam Pŏlȳdōrus ĕgo*, scil. *sum*, For I am Polydorus. Virg. And so *est* and *sunt* are often omitted with predicate adjectives, and especially in proverbial phrases; as, *Quot hŏmĭnes tot sententiæ*. Ter. *Omnia præclāra rāra*, scil. *sunt*. Cic. So also *est* and *sunt* are often omitted in the compound tenses of the passive voice; as, *Agro mulctāti*, scil. *sunt*. Liv. Cf. § 270, R. 3.

NOTE 5. In Latin, as in English, a verb is often joined to one of two connected nominatives and understood with the other, and that even when the persons are different; as, *măgis ĕgo te ămo, quam tu me*, scil. *ămas*. After a negative verb a corresponding positive verb is sometimes to be supplied; as, after *nĕgo, dīco*, after *vĕto, jŭbeo*, and in this case *et* takes the signification of *sed*. Cf. § 323, 1, (2.), (b.).

NOTE 6. Sometimes, when the verb of an appended proposition is omitted, its subject is attracted to the case of a noun in the leading proposition with which is joined a participle of the omitted verb; as, *Hannĭbal Minŭcium, măgistrum ĕquĭtum, pāri ac* dictātōrem *dŏlo* prŏductum *in prœlium, fŭgāvit*, i. e. *pāri ac* dictātor *dŏlo* prŏductus fuĕrat. Nep. Hann. 5. So Liv. 34, 32.

REM. 5. In the historic style the nominative is sometimes found with the present infinitive; as,

Intĕrim quŏtĭdie Cæsar Æduos frūmentum flāgĭtāre, Meanwhile Cæsar was daily demanding corn of the Ædui. Cæs. *Nos păvĭdi* trĕpĭdāre *mĕtu*. Virg. *Id horrendum* ferri. Id.

NOTE 7. The infinitive in this construction is called the *historical infinitive*, and is used instead of the imperfect indicative to express in a lively manner a continued or repeated action or condition.

REM. 6. The relative *qui* may refer to an antecedent either of the first, second, or third person; and its verb takes the person of the antecedent; as,

Ĕgo qui lĕgo, I who *read*. *Tu qui* scrībis, Thou who *writest*. *Equus qui* currit, The horse which *runs*. *Vos qui* quærītis, You who *ask*.

REM. 7. (a.). Verbs in the first person plural, and the second person singular, are sometimes used to express general truths; as,

Quam multa fácimus causā ămĭcōrum! How many things we do (i. e. men do) for the sake of friends! Cic. *Si vis me flēre, dŏlendum est prīmum ipsi tibi,* Whoever wishes me, etc. Hor.

(*b.*) *Nos* is often used for *ĕgo*, and *noster* for *meus*; and even when the pronoun is not expressed, the verb is frequently put in the first person plural instead of the first person singular. The genitive *nostri* is used for *mei*, but *nostrûm* always expresses a real plurality.

REM. 8. The accusative is sometimes used for the nominative by attraction. See § 206, (6.) (*b.*)

REM. 9. The verb sometimes agrees with the *predicate-nominative*, especially if it precedes the verb; as, *Amantium irœ ămōris* integrātio est, The quarrels of lovers are a renewal of love. Ter. *Lōca, quæ proxima Carthāginem, Nŭmĭdĭa* appellātur. Sall. And sometimes it agrees with the nearest subject of a subordinate sentence; as, *Sed ei cārĭōra semper omnia, quam dĕcus atque pŭdīcĭtia fuit.* Sall. Cat. 25.

REM. 10. In cases of apposition, the verb commonly agrees with the noun which is to be explained; as, *Tulliŏla, dēlĭciæ nostræ, jlāgĭtat.* Cic. But sometimes the verb agrees, not with the principal nominative, but with a nearer noun in apposition to it; as, *Tungri, cīvitas Galliæ, fontem* hăbet *insignem*, The Tungri, a state of Gaul, has a remarkable fountain. Plin. *Cŏrĭoli* oppidum captum (est). Liv.

REM. 11. A collective noun has sometimes, especially in poetry, a plural verb; as,

Pars ĕpŭlis ŏnĕrant mensas, Part load the tables with food. Virg. *Turba ruunt.* Ovid. *Atria turba tĕnent; vēniunt lĕve vulgus euntque.* Id.

(1.) (*a.*) A plural verb, joined to a collective noun, usually expresses the action, etc., of the *individuals* which that noun denotes. In Cicero, Sallust, and Cæsar, this construction scarcely occurs in simple sentences; but it is often used, when the subject of the verb is expressed not in its own, but in a preceding clause; as, *Hoc idem gĕnĕri hūmāno ēvĕnit, quod in terrā* collŏcāti sint, becuuse they (scil. *hŏmĭnes*) live on earth. Cic. In Livy it occurs more frequently; as, *Locros omnis multĭtŭdo* ăbeunt.

(*b.*) Abstract nouns are sometimes used collectively, instead of their concretes; as, *nōbĭlĭtas* for *nōbĭles, jŭventus* for *jŭvĕnes, vīcīnia* for *vīcīni, servĭtium* for *servi, lĕvis armātūra* for *lĕvĭter armāti*, etc. (*c.*) *Miles, ĕques, pĕdes*, and similar words are sometimes used collectively for the soldiery, the cavalry, etc.

(2.) When two or more clauses have the same collective noun as their subject, the verb is frequently singular in the former, and plural in the latter; as, *Jam ne nocte quidem turba ex eo lŏco* dīlābēbātur, *refractūrosque carcĕrem* minābantur. Liv. *Gens eādem, quæ te crūdēli Daunia bello* insĕquĭtur, *nos si* pellant, *nihil abfŏre crēdunt.* Virg.

(3.) *Tantum*, followed by a genitive plural, has sometimes a plural verb, like a collective noun; as, *Quid huc* tantum *hŏmĭnum incēdunt?* Why are so many men coming hither? Plaut.

(4.) A plural verb is sometimes used, though not by Cicero, after *ŭterque* and *quisque, pars...pars, ălius...ălium,* and *alter...altĕrum,* on account of the idea of plurality which they involve; as, *Uterque eōrum ex castris exercĭtum ēdūcunt,* Each of them leads his army from the camp. Cæs. *Intimus quisque lībertōrum* vincti abreptīque (sunt). Tac. *Alius ălium, ut prœlium* incĭpiant, circumspectant. Liv. Cf. § 207, R. 32, (*c.*)

NOTE 8. This construction may be explained by passages like the following, in which the plural is placed first, and then the singular, denoting its parts; *Cētĕri, suo quisque tempŏre,* ădĕrunt. Liv. *Dēcemvĭri perturbāti ălius* in *ăliam partem castrōrum* discurrunt. Id. See § 204, R. 10.

REM. 12. Two or more nominatives singular, not in apposition, generally have a plural verb; as,

Furor īrāque mentem præcipitant, Fury and rage hurry in (my) mind. Virg. *Dum ætas, mētus, māgister, prohibēbant.* Ter.

(1.) If the predicate belongs to the several nominatives jointly, the verb is always plural; as, *Grammătice quondam ac mūsīce junctæ fuērunt.* Quint.

(2.) A verb in the singular is often used after several nominatives singular, especially if they denote things without life; as,

Mens ĕnim, et rătio et consĭlium in sĕnĭbus est. Cic. *Bĕnĕfĭcentia, lībĕrālĭtas, bŏnĭtas, justĭtia fundĭtus* tollĭtur. Id.

NOTE 9. This construction is most common when the several nominatives, as in the preceding examples, constitute, as it were, but one idea. So also the compound subject *Sĕnātus pŏpŭlusque Rōmānus* has always a predicate in the singular. The same construction sometimes, especially in the poets, occurs with names of persons; as, *Gorgĭas, Thrăsŷmăchus, Prōtăgŏras, Prŏdĭcus, Hippĭas in hŏnōre* fuit. Cic. *Quin et Prōmĕtheus et Pēlŏpis părens dulci labōrum dēcīpītu. sōno.* Hor. When the nominatives denote both persons and things, the verb is commonly plural; as, *Coitio cōnsŭlum et Pompeius* obsunt. Liv.

(3.) When one of the nouns is plural, the verb is generally so; but sometimes it is singular, when the plural noun does not immediately precede it; as, *Dii te pĕnātes patrĭīque, et patris* Imāgo, *et dōmus rēgia, et in dōmo rēgāle sŏlium, et nōmen Tarquĭnium* creat vōcat*pue rēgem.* Liv.

(4.) When each of the nominatives is preceded by *et* or *tum*, the verb agrees with the last; as, *Hoc et* rătio *et* doctis, *et* necessitas *barbăris*, et mos *gentĭbus, et fĕris* nātūra *ipsa* præscripsit, This, reason has dictated to the learned, and necessity to barbarians, and custom to nations, and nature itself to wild beasts Cic. *Et ego, et Cĭcĕro meus* flāgĭtābit. Id. *Tum* ætas vīres*que, tum ărīta* glōria *ūnĭmum* stīmŭlābat. Liv. So when the subject consists of two infinitives; as, *Et fācĕre, et* pāti *fortia, Rōmānum* est. Cic. *Unus et alter* always takes a singular verb; as, *Dīcit ūnus et alter brĕvīter.* Cic. *Unus et alter* assultur *pannus.* Hor.

(5.) When the nominatives are connected by *aut*, sometimes the plural, but commonly the singular, is used; as,

Si Sōcrătes aut Antisthĕnes dīcĕret, If Socrates or Antisthenes should say. Cic *Ut quosque stŭdium prīvătim aut grātia* occŭpāvērunt. Liv.

(*a.*) The plural is *necessary* with disjunctives, if the subject includes the first or second person; as, *Quod in Dĕcemvĭris nĕque ĕgo nĕque Cæsar* hăbĭti essēmus. Cic.—(*b.*) With *aut...aut* and *nec...nec* the singular is preferred, but with *seu...seu* and *tam...quam* the verb is in the plural.

(6.) A nominative singular, joined to an ablative by the preposition *cum*, sometimes has a singular but more frequently a plural verb; as, *Dŏmĭtĭus cum Messālā certus esse* vĭdēbātur. Cic. *Bocchus, cum pĕdĭtĭbus, postrēmam Rōmānōrum aciem* invādunt, Bocchus, with his foot-soldiers, attacks the rear of the Roman army. Sall. *Ipse dux, cum ălĭquot* princĭpĭbus, căpiuntur. Liv.

(7.) If the nominatives are of different persons, the verb is of the first person rather than the second or third, and of the second rather than the third; as,

Si tu et Tullia vălētis, *ĕgo et Cĭcĕro* vălēmus, If you and Tullia *are well,* Cicero and I *are well.* Cic. *Hæc nĕque ĕgo nĕque tu* fēcīmus. Ter *Ego pŏpŭlusque Rōmānus bellum* jūdico făcioque. Liv.

(*a.*) Yet sometimes the verb agrees in number and person with the nearest nominative, and is understood with the other; as, *Vos ipsi et sĕnātus frĕquens* restĭtit. This is always the case when the action of the verb is qualified with reference to each nominative separately; as, *Ego mĭsĕre tu fēlīcĭter vīvis.*

REM. 13. The interjections *en, ecce,* and *O,* are sometimes followed by the nominative; as,

En Priămus! Lo Priam! Virg. *En ĕgo, vester Ascănius.* Id. *Ecce hŏmo Catiĕnus!* Cic. *Ecce tuæ litĕræ.* Id. *O vir fortis atque amīcus!* Ter.

PREDICATE-NOMINATIVE.

§ 210. A noun in the predicate, after a verb neuter or passive, is put in the same case as the subject, when it denotes the same person or thing; as,

(*a.*) When the subject is in the nominative; *Ira furor brĕvis est,* Anger is a short madness. Hor. *Ego rŏcor Lyconides,* I am called Lyconides. Plaut. *Ego incēdo regina,* I walk a queen. Virg. *Caius et Lūcius* frātres *fuĕrunt.* Cic.— So (*b.*) when the subject is in the accusative with the infinitive; *Judicem me esse vŏlo.* Cic.

(*c.*) Sometimes also a *dative,* denoting the same object, both precedes and follows a verb neuter or passive. See § 227, N.—And (*d.*) a predicate ablative sometimes follows passive participles of *choosing, naming,* etc.; as, *Consulĭbus certiōrĭbus factis.* Liv. See § 257, R. 11.

(*e.*) If the predicate noun has a form of the same gender as the subject, it takes that form; as, *Licentia* corruptrix *est mōrum.* Cf. § 204, R. 2.—(*f.*) But if the subject is neuter, the noun of the predicate, if it has both a masculine and a feminine form, takes the former; as, *Tempus vitæ* măgister *est.*

(*g.*) An infinitive may supply the place of a predicate nominative. See § 269, R. 4.

REMARK 1. (*a.*) Adjectives, adjective pronouns, and participles, standing in the predicate, after verbs neuter or passive, and relating to the subject, agree with it in gender, number, and case.

(*b.*) When the subject consists of two or more nouns, the gender and number of such predicate adjectives are determined by § 205, R. 2.

REM. 2. (*a.*) The noun in the predicate sometimes differs in gender and number from the subject; as, Sanguis *ĕrant lăcrimæ,* Her tears were blood. Ovid. *Captīvi mīlĭtum* præda *fuĕrunt.* Liv.

(*b.*) So when a subject in the singular is followed by an ablative with *cum,* the predicate is plural; as, Exsūles *esse jŭbet L. Tarquinium cum conjŭge et libĕris.* Liv.

REM. 3. The verbs which most frequently have a noun, etc., in the predicate agreeing in case, etc., with their subject, are:—

(1.) The *copula sum;* as, *Ego Jŏvis sum* fīlius. Plaut. *Disce esse* păter. Ter. The predicate with *sum* may be an adverb of place, manner, etc.; as, *Quod est* longe ălĭter. Cic. Rectissime *sunt ăpud te omnia,* Every thing with you is in a very good condition. Id.; or a noun in an oblique case; as, *Nūmen illae* tūre *est.* Ovid. *Sunt* nōbis *mitia pōma.* Virg.

(2.) Certain neuter verbs denoting *existence, position, motion,* etc.; as, *vivo, exsisto, appāreo, cădo, eo, evādo, fŭgio, incēdo, jăceo, măneo, sĕdeo, sto, vĕnio,* etc. Thus, *Rex circuĭbat* pĕdes, The king went round on foot. Plin. *Quos judicābat non posse* orātōres *evādĕre.* Cic. *Ego huic causæ* patrōnus *exstĭti.* Cic. *Qui fit, ut nēmo* contentus *vivat?*

(3.) The passive of verbs denoting,

(*a.*) To *name* or *call;* as, *appellor, dicor, nōminor, nuncŭpor, perhibeor, salūtor, scrībor, inscrībor, vŏcor.* Thus, *Cognōmine Justus est appellātus,* He was called by the surname Just. Nep. *Aristæus ŏlīvæ dicitur* inventor. Cic.

(n.) To *choose, render, appoint*, or *constitute;* as, *constituor, creor dechiror, designor, eligor, fio, reddor, renuncior*. Thus, *Dux a Rōmānis electus est Q. Fābius. Postquam* ephēbus *factus est.* Nep. *Certior factus sum.*

(i.) To *esteem* or *reckon;* as, *censeor, cognoscor, crēdor, deprēhendor existimor, dūcor, fēror, hăbeor, jūdicor, memoror, numeror, pūtor, rĕpērior, vĭdeor.* Thus, *Credēbar sanguinis* auctor *ĕgo.* Ovid. *Mālim vidēri* timĭdus *quam părum* prūdens. Cic.

NOTE 1. With several passives of the last class, when followed by a predicate-nominative, etc., an infinitive of *sum* is expressed or understood; as, Amens *nihi* fuisse *videor*, I think I was beside myself. Cic. But the dative of the first person is sometimes omitted after *videor*; as, *Sătis dŏcuisse vĭdeor.* Id.—*Atilius* prūdens esse *pŭtābātur.* Id. So with *dīcor* (to be said), and *perhĭbeor;* as, *Vērus patriæ dīcĕris* esse *pāter.* Mart. *Hoc ne* lŏcūtus *sine mercēde existīmer.* Phæd..

NOTE 2. *Audio* is sometimes used by the poets like *appellor;* as, *Tu* rexque pāter*que audisti cōram.* Hor.

REM. 4. A predicate-nominative is used after many other verbs to denote a *purpose, time,* or *circumstance* of the action; as, Cōmes *addĭtus Æŏlĭdes,* Æolides was added as a companion. Virg. *Lŭpus ŏbambŭlat* nocturnus. Id. *Appăret liquido* sublimis *in æthĕre Nīsus.* Id. So with an active verb; *Audīvi hoc* puer. Cic. *Săpiens nil făcit* invītus. Id. *Rempŭblĭcam dēfendi* ădŏlescens. Id. Cf. § 204, R. 1.

NOTE 3. Instead of the predicate-nominative, a dative of the end or purpose sometimes occurs (see § 227); sometimes an ablative with *pro;* as, *audācia* pro mūro *est;* and sometimes the ablatives *lŏco* or *in nŭmero* with a genitive; as, *ille est mihi* pārentis lŏco; *in* hostium nŭmero *hăbētur.*

REM. 5. The noun *ŏpus,* signifying 'need,' is often used as a predicate after *sum.* It is, in such cases, translated by the adjectives *needful, necessary,* etc.; as, *Dux nōbis et auctor* ŏpus *est.* Cic. *Multi* ŏpus *sunt bŏves.* Varr. *(Dixit)* *aurum et ancillas* ŏpus *esse.* Ter. *Usus* also is occasionally so construed.

REM. 6. When the pronoun, which is the subject of an infinitive, is omitted, the case of the predicate is sometimes, in the poets, *attracted* into that of the subject of the verb on which the infinitive depends; as, Uxor *invicti Jŏvis esse nescis,* i. e. *te esse uxōrem.* Hor. *Rĕtŭlit Ajax esse Jŏvis* prōnĕpos. Ovid.

GENITIVE.

GENITIVE AFTER NOUNS.

§ **211.** A noun which limits the meaning of another noun, denoting a different person or thing, is put in the genitive; as,

Amor glōriæ, Love of glory; *Arma Achillis,* The arms of Achilles; *Păter patriæ,* The father of the country; *Vĭtium iræ,* The vice of anger; *Nĕmŏrum custōs,* The guardian of the groves; *Amor hăbendi,* Love of possessing.

NOTE 1 In the first example, *ămor* denotes love in general; *glōriæ* limits the affection to the particular object, glory. Such universally is the effect of the genitive, depending upon a noun. Hence the limitation of a noun by a genitive resembles that which is effected by an adjective. In each the noun limited constitutes with its limitation only a single idea.

REMARK 1. The genitive denotes various relations, the most common of which are those of *Source;* as, *Rădii sōlis,* The rays of the sun;—*Cause;* as, *Dŏlor pŏdagræ,* The pain of the gout;—*Effect;* as, *Artifex mundi,* The Creator of the world;—*Connection:* as, *Pater consŭlis,* The father of the consul;—*Possession;* as, *Dŏmus Cæsăris,* The house of Cæsar;—*Object;* as *Cōgĭtātio aliēnĭus rei,* A thought of something;—*Purpose;* as, *Appărātus triumphi,* Preparation for a triumph;— A *whole;* as, *Pars hŏmĭnum,* A part of men; this is called the *partitive* genitive;—*Character* or *Quality*; as, *Adolescens summæ audāciæ*, A youth of the greatest boldness;—*Material* or *Component Parts*; as, *Montes auri*, Mountains of gold; *Acervus scūtōrum*, A heap of shields;—*Time*; as, *Frūmentum diērum dĕcem*, Corn for ten days. Sall.

REM. 2. The genitive is called *subjective* or *active*, when it denotes either that *to which a thing belongs*, or the *subject* of the action, feeling, etc., implied in the noun which it limits. It is called *objective* or *passive*, when it denotes the *object* affected by such action, or towards which such feeling is directed; as,

Subjective.	Objective.
Facta virōrum, Deeds of men.	*Odium vĭtii*, Hatred of vice.
Dŏlor ănĭmi, Grief of mind.	*Amor virtūtis*, Love of virtue.
Jūnōnis ira, The anger of Juno.	*Dĕsĭdĕrium ōtii*, Desire of leisure.

(*a.*) Whether a genitive is subjective or objective is to be determined by the meaning of the words, and by their connection. Thus, *prŏvĭdentia Dĕi* signifies God's providence, or that exercised by him; *timor Dĕi*, the fear of God, or that exercised towards him. The same or similar words, in different connections, may express both significations. Thus, *mĕtus hostium*, fear of the enemy, may mean, either the fear felt by the enemy, or that felt by their opponents. So *vulnus Ulixis* (Virg. Æn. 2, 436.) denotes the wound which Ulysses had given; *vulnus Ænĕæ*, (Id. Æn. 12, 323.) that which Æneas had received.

(*b.*) The relation expressed by the English *possessive case* is subjective, while that denoted by *of* with its case is either subjective or objective.

(*c.*) The objective genitive is of very extensive use in Latin in the limitation of verbal nouns and adjectives, whatever may be the construction of the verbs from which such nouns and adjectives are derived, whether they take an accusative or some other case or even a preposition.

(*d.*) When ambiguity would arise from the use of the objective genitive, a preposition with an accusative or ablative is commonly used; as, *Amor in rempūblĭcam*, for *reipūblĭcæ*, Love to the state. Cic. *Odium erga Rōmānos*, for *Rōmānōrum*. Nep. *Cūra de sălūte patriæ*, for *sălūtis*. Cic. *Prædātor ex sŏciis*, for *sŏciōrum*. Sall. Sometimes both constructions are combined; as, *Rĕvĕrentia adversus hŏmĭnes et optĭmi cūjusque et rĕlĭquōrum*. Cic. Off. 1, 28.

NOTE. A limiting genitive is sometimes used instead of a noun in apposition, especially with *vox, nōmen, verbum*, etc.; as, *vox vŏluptātis*, the word pleasure; *nōmen* ămīcĭtiæ, the word *ămīcĭtia*; *dŏmĭni appellātio*. This is usual when the genus is defined by the species; as, *arbor fīci*, a fig-tree; *flos vĭŏlæ*, a violet; *virtus* continentiæ, the virtue of abstinence: and in geographical names; as, *oppidum* Antiŏchīæ. Cf. § 204, R. 6.—Cicero frequently uses a genitive in this manner with *gĕnus* and *causa*; as, *Unum gĕnus est eōrum, qui*, etc. *Duæ sunt causæ, ūna pŭdōris, altĕra scĕlĕris*.—So, also, the genitive of gerunds; as, *Triste est nōmen ipsum* cărendi, The very word *to want* is sad. Cic.

REM. 3. (*a.*) A substantive pronoun in the genitive, limiting the meaning of a noun, is commonly objective; as,

Cūra mei, Care for me. Ovid. *Pars tui*, Part of thee. Id. *Vestri cūram ăgĭte*. Curt. This genitive is used especially with verbal substantives in *or, ix* and *io*; as, *Accūsātor mei*. Cic. *Nĭmia æstĭmātio sui*. Id. *Rătiōnem et sui et ăliōrum hăbēre*. Id.

(*b.*) Instead of the *subjective* or *possessive* genitive of a substantive pronoun, the corresponding adjective pronoun is commonly used; as,

Liber meus, not *liber mei*, my book. *Cūra mea*, My care, *i. e.* the care exercised by me. Cic. *Tuas litĕras exspecto*. Id. Yet the subjective genitive of a substantive pronoun sometimes occurs; as, *Tui ūnīus stŭdĭo*, By the zeal of yourself alone. Cic.

(c) And not unfrequently, also, an adjective pronoun occurs instead of the *objective* genitive; as, *Meā injūriā*, Injury to me. Sall. So, *Invidia tua*, Envy of thee. *Fidūcia tuā*, Confidence in thee. Plaut. *Spes mea*, The hope placed in me. With *causā* the adjective pronoun, and never the genitive, is used as, *Meā causā*, For my sake. Plaut.

REM. 4. (*a.*) Instead, also, of the subjective genitive of a *noun*, a possessive adjective is often used; as, *Causa rēgia*, for *causa rēgis*. Cic. Hĕrīlis *filius*, for *hĕri filius*. Id. Evandrius *ensis*, for *Evandri*. Virg. Hercŭleus *labor*, for *Hercŭlis*. Hor. Cīvīlis *furor*, for *civium*. Hor. So, also, for the *objective* genitive, *Metus* hostīlis, Fear of the enemy. Sall.

(*b.*) The genitive of the person implied in the adjective pronoun or possessive adjective, or an adjective agreeing with such genitive, is sometimes added as an apposition; as, Vestrā ipsorum *causā hoc feci*. In the poets and later prose writers a participle also is found agreeing with such implied genitive; as, *Mea scripta vulgo recitāre* timentis. Hor. Cf. § 204, R. 4, and § 205, R. 13.

REM. 5. In the predicate after *sum*, and sometimes after other verbs, the dative is used like the objective genitive; as,

Idem amor exitium pecŏri (est), *pecŏrisque* māgistro. Virg. *Vitis ut arbŏribus decori est, ut vitibus ūvæ—Tu decus omne tuis*. Virg. In this passage the dative *decori* and the nominative *decus* are used with no difference of meaning. Cf. § 227, R. 4. *Auctor fui senātui*. Cic. *Muræna legātus Lūcullo fuit*. Id. *Erit ille mihi semper deus*. Virg. *Huic causæ patrōnus exstīti*. Cic. *Huic ego me bello ducem proflteor*. Id. *Se tertium (esse) cui fātum foret urbis pŏtīri*. Id.—*Cum P. Africāno senātus ēgit, ut legātus frātri proflciscerētur*. Id. *Cæsar legimenta gāleis mīlites ex riminibus facere jūbet*. Cæs. *Trinobantibus Cæsar imperat—frumentum exercitui*. Id. *Quod neque insidiæ consŭli procedēbant*. Sall. *Quem exitum tantis mālis sperārent?* Id. *Sanctus vir et ex sententia ambōbus*, scil. *qui fuit*. Id. See § 227, R. 4.

NOTE. The dative in the preceding examples has been thought by some grammarians to depend on the nouns connected with it; as, *exitium, decus, auctor, legātus, deus, patrōnus*, etc.; by others it has been held to depend on these nouns in connection with the verbs, and not upon either separately; but the better opinion seems to be that, which makes such datives grammatically dependent upon the verbs only, though logically connected also with the nouns.

(1.) Instead, also, of the *possessive* genitive, a dative of the person may follow a verb, when its act has relation to the body or possessions of such person; as,

Sese omnes flentes Cæsari ad pedes projēcērunt, They all, weeping, cast themselves at the feet of Cæsar. Cæs. Cui *corpus porrigitur*, For whom the body, *i. e.* whose body, is extended. Virg. *Tum vero exarsit juveni dolor ossibus ingens*. Id. *Transfigitur scūtum* Pulfioni. Cæs.

REM. 6. When the limiting noun denotes a *property, character,* or *quality*, it has an adjective agreeing with it, and is put either in the genitive or the ablative; as,

Vir exempli recti, A man of correct example. Liv. *Adolescens summæ audāciæ*, A youth of the greatest boldness. Sall. *Fossa pedum viginti*, A ditch of twenty feet, (i. e. in width). Cæs. *Hamilcar secum duxit filium Hannibalem annōrum novem*. Nep. *Athēnienses diligunt Periclem*, spectātæ virtūtis *virum*. Just. *Quinquāgīnta annōrum imperium*. Id. *Iter unius diēi*. Cic. Pulchritūdine eximiā *femina*, A woman of exquisite beauty. Cic. Maxīmo natu *filius*, The eldest son. Nep. *L. Catilina fuit magnā vi et animi et corpŏris, sed ingenio malo pravōque*. Sall. *Spelunca* infinitā altitūdine. Cic.—Sometimes both constructions occur in the same proposition; as, *Lentulum nostrum*, eximiā spe, summæ virtūtis *adolescentem*. Cic.

§ 211. SYNTAX.—GENITIVE AFTER NOUNS. 209

(1.) A genitive sometimes supplies the place of the adjective; and the noun denoting the property, etc., is then always put in the ablative; as, *Est bos cervi figūrā,*...of the form of a stag. Caes. *Uri spĕcie et cŏlōre tauri.* Id. *Frūtex palmi altitūdĭne.* Plin. *Clāvi digiti pollĭcis crassitūdĭne.* Caes.

(2.) All the qualities and attributes of persons and things, whether inherent or accidental, may be thus expressed by the genitive and ablative of quality, provided the substantives are *immediately* connected; as, *fossa quindĕcim pĕdum; hŏmo antīquā virtūte.* It hence follows that such genitives and ablatives, when used to express duration of time or extent of space, are distinguished from the cases in which the accusative is required, since the latter case always follows adjectives or verbs; as, *fossa quindĕcim pĕdes* lāta: *puer dĕcem annos* nātus. Cf. § 236.

(3.) Whether the genitive or the ablative of quality is preferable in particular cases, can frequently be determined only by reference to classical authority; but, in general, the genitive is used more frequently to express inherent qualities than such as are merely accidental, while the ablative is used indifferently for either purpose. In speaking of transitory qualities or conditions the ablative is always used; as, *Magno timōre sum,* I am in great fear. Cic. *Bŏno ănĭmo sum.* Id. *Quanto fuĕrim dŏlōre memĭnisti.* Id. *Maxĭmo honōre Servius Tullius ĕrat.* Liv. With plural substantives the genitive is rare; while in expressions of measure it is used rather than the ablative.

(4.) An accusative instead of a genitive of quality is used with *sĕcus* (sex), *gĕnus* and *pondo*; as, *Libĕrōrum căpĭtum vīrīle sĕcus ad dĕcem millia capta,* i. e. of the male sex, instead of *sexūs virīlis.* Liv. So *gĕnus,* when joined with a pronoun, as *hoc, id, illud, quod,* or with *omne,* is used for *hūjus, ĕjus, omnis,* etc., *gĕnĕris;* as, *Orātiōnes aut ălĭquid* id gĕnus *scrībĕre,*—of that kind. Cic. *Concrēdĕre nūgas* hoc gĕnus. Hor. So *pondo* is joined as an indeclinable word to the accusatives *lībrum* and *lībras;* as, *Dictātor corōnam auream* lībram pondo *in Capitōlio Jŏvi dōnum pŏsuit,*...a pound in weight. Liv. Cf. § 236, R. 7.

(5.) The genitive *mŏdi* with an adjective pronoun supplies the place of a pronoun of quality; as, *cūjusmŏdi lĭbri,* the same as *quāles lĭbri,* what kind of books; *hūjusmŏdi lĭbri,* i. e. *tāles lĭbri,* such books. So, also, *gĕnĕris* is used, but less frequently.

(6.) With the genitive of measure are often connected such ablatives as *longitūdĭne, lātĭtūdĭne,* etc., or *in longĭtūdĭnem,* etc.; as, *fossa dĕcem pĕdum lātĭtūdĭne;* but the genitive does not depend on these words.

(7.) *Sum* may be followed by either the genitive or the ablative of quality with an ellipsis of the word limited, which, with the genitive, is *hŏmo, res, negōtium, prŏprium* or *prŏprius,* etc., and with the ablative, *prædĭtus, instructus, ornātus,* etc. Cf. Rem. 8, and §§ 244, and 249, I..

REM. 7. (1.) The limited noun is sometimes omitted; as, *O misĕræ sortis!* scil. *homĭnes;* O (men) of wretched fortune! Lucan. *Ad Diānæ,* scil. *ædem.* Ter. *Hectŏris Andromăche,* scil. *uxor.* Virg. *Suspiciōnis vītandæ,* scil. *causā.* Tac. So *fīlius* or *fīlia;* as, *Hannĭbal Gisgōnis.*

(2.) The omitted noun may sometimes be supplied from the preceding words; as, *Cūjum pĕcus? an Mēlibœi? Non; vērum Ægōnis,* scil. *pĕcus.* Virg. An adjective is often expressed referring to the noun omitted; as, *Nullam virtus īliam mercēdem dēsĭdĕrat, præter hanc* (scil. *mercēdem*) *laudis.* Cic.

REM. 8. The limited noun is often wanting in the predicate of a sentence after *sum.* This usually happens,

(1.) When it has been previously expressed; as,

Hæc dŏmus est Cæsăris, This house is Cæsar's. *Nōmen auræ tam sæpe vocātum esse pŭtans Nymphæ.* Ovid. *Nāves ŏnĕrāriăs, quăr ӗm mĭnor nulla ĕrat duum villium amphŏrum,* i. e. *quārum mĭnor nulla ĕrat quam* 1 āvis *duum,* etc. Cic.

(2.) When it is a general word denoting a person, an animal, etc. as,

Thŭcy̆dĭdes, qui ejusdem œtātis fuit, scil. *hŏmo,* Thucydides, who was of the same age. Nep. *Multum ei dĕtraxit, quod ăliēnœ ĕrat cīvĭtātis,* scil. *hŏmo* or *cīvis* Id. *Prīmum stīpendium mĕruit annōrum dĕcem septemque,* scil. *ădŏlescens.* Id. *Summi ut sint lăbōris effĭciunt,* scil. *ănĭmālia.* Cœs. (*Claudius*) *somni brĕvissĭmi ĕrat.* Suet. *Mĭrā sum ălăcrĭtāte.* Cic. *Vulgus ingĕnio mōbĭli ĕrat.* Sall. *Non est jūris sui,* He is not his own master. Lucan. *Pŏtestātis suœ esse.* Liv. *Suārumque rērum ĕrant.* Id. Cf. Rem. 6, (7.)

(3.) When it is a general word denoting *thing,* for which, in English, the words *part, property, duty, office, business, characteristic,* etc. are commonly supplied; as,

Tĕmĕrĭtas est flōrentis œtātis, prūdentia sĕnectūtis, Rashness is (the characteristic) of youth, prudence of old age. Cic. *Est hoc Gallicœ consuētūdĭnis.* Cœs. So, *stultĭtiœ est; est ērŭtātis,* etc., which are equivalent to *stultĭtia est, lĕvĭtas est. Omnia hostium ĕrant. A paucis ĕmi, quod multōrum esset.* Sall.

(*a.*) This happens especially when the subject of the verb is an infinitive, or an entire clause, in which case, instead of the genitive of the personal pronouns, *mei, tui,* etc., the neuters of the possessives, *meum, tuum,* etc., are used; as, *Ădŏlescentis est mājōres nătu rĕvĕrēri,* It is (the duty) of a youth to reverence the aged. Ovid. *Cŭjusvis hŏmĭnis est errāre, nullīus nisi insĭpientis in errōre persĕvĕrāre.* Cic. *Paupĕris est nŭmĕrāre pĕcus.* Ovid. So especially *mōris est;* as, *Nĕgāvit mōris esse Grœcōrum, ut in convīvio vĭrōrum accumbĕrent mŭlĭĕres,* the same us *mōrem esse Grœcōrum.* Cic. *Nĭhil tam œquandœ libertātis esse.* Liv. So when the verb is omitted; *Tămen officii duxit, exōrāre patrem,* scil. *esse.* Suet. *Non est mentīri* meum. Ter. *Tuum est, M. Cāto, vidēre quid ăgātur.*

(*b.*) Instead of the genitive of a substantive, also, the neuter of a possessive adjective derived from it is sometimes used; as, *Hūmānum est errāre,* To err is human. Ter. *Et făcĕre et păti fortia* Rōmānum *est.* Liv.

(4.) The same construction sometimes occurs after *făcio,* and some other verbs mentioned in § 230, *esse* being understood; as, *Asia Rōmānōrum facta est,* Asia became (a possession) of the Romans. Just. *Agrum suœ dĭtiōnis fĕcisse.* Liv.

(5.) The limited noun is sometimes wanting, when it is a general word, though not in the predicate after *sum;* as, *Magni formīca lăbōris,* scil. *ănĭmal,* The ant (an animal) of great labor. Hor. So *Si vĕnit in mentem pŏtestātis tuœ* scil. *mĕmōria,* or the like. Cic.

NOTE. When the noun which is wanting denotes a *thing,* grammarians sometimes supply *nĕgōtium, officium, mūnus, ŏpus, res, causa,* etc. It is an instance of a construction common in Latin, to omit a noun when a general idea is intended. See § 205 Rem. 7, (2.)

REM. 9. The *limiting* noun also is sometimes omitted; as,

Tria millia, scil. *passuum.* In most cases of this kind, an adjective, adjective pronoun, or participle, is expressed in the genitive.

REM. 10. Two genitives sometimes limit the same noun, one of which is commonly subjective, and the other objective; as,

Ăgămemnŏnis belli glōria, Agamemnon's glory in war. Nep. *Illius admĭnistrātio prōvinciœ.* Cic. *Eōrum diērum consuētūdĭne ĭtĭnĕris nostri exercĭtūs perspectā.* Cœs. *Orbĭtas reipūblĭcœ tălium vĭrōrum.* Cic. *Pro vĕtĕrĭbus* Helvētiōrum *injūriis* pŏpŭli Rōmāni. Cœs.

REM. 11. *Opus* and *ūsus* are rarely limited by a genitive or accusative, but generally by an ablative, of the thing needed; as,

Argenti ŏpus fuit, There was need of money. Liv. *Ad consĭlium pensandum tempŏris ŏpus esse.* Id. *Prooemii non semper ūsus est.* Quint. *Si quo ŏpĕrœ ŏbrum ūsus est.* Liv. *Puĕro ŏpus est* cibum. Plaut. *Usus est* hŏmĭnem *œtātum.* Id. See § 243.

§ 212.   SYNTAX.—GENITIVE AFTER PARTITIVES.   211

REM. 12 The relation denoted by the genitive in Latin, is generally expressed, in English, by *of*, or by the possessive case. Cf. R. 2, (*b*.) The objective genitive may often be rendered by some other preposition; as,

Rĕmĕdium dŏlōris, A remedy for pain. *Injūria patris*, Injury to a father. *Descensus Averni*, The descent to Avernus. *Ira belli*, Anger on account of the war. *Pŏtestas rei*, Power in or over a thing.

NOTE. Certain limitations of nouns are made by the accusative with a preposition, and by the ablative, either with or without a preposition. Cf. § 202, 6, I. and II.

GENITIVE AFTER PARTITIVES.

§ **212.** Nouns, adjectives, adjective pronouns, and adverbs, denoting a part, are followed by a genitive denoting the whole; as,

Pars civitātis, A part of the state. *Nulla sŏrōrum*, No one of the sisters. *Aliquis philŏsŏphŏrum*, Some one of the philosophers. *Quis mortālium?* Who of mortals? *Major jŭvĕnum*, The elder of the youths. *Doctissimus Rōmānōrum*, The most learned of the Romans. *Multum pĕcūniæ*, Much (of) money. *Satis ĕlŏquentiæ*, Enough of eloquence. *Ubinam gentium sŭmus?* Where on earth are we?

NOTE. The genitive thus governed denotes either a *number*, of which the partitive designates one or more individuals; or a *whole*, of which the partitive designates a portion. In the latter sense, the genitive of common and abstract nouns commonly follows either the neuter of adjectives and adjective pronouns, or adverbs; and that of material nouns depends on substantives signifying quantity, weight or measure; as, *mĕdimnum tritici*, a bushel of wheat; *libra farris*; *jūgĕrum agri*; *magna vis auri*.

REMARK 1. Nouns denoting a part are *pars*, *nemo*, *nihil*, etc., and also nouns denoting measure, weight, etc.; as, *mŏdius*, *mĕdimnum*, and *libra*; as,

Nēmo nostrum, No one of us. *Maxima pars hŏminum*. *Nihil hūmānārum rērum*. Cic. *Dimidium militum*. Liv. *Mĕdimnum tritici*. Cic.

REM. 2. Adjectives and adjective pronouns, denoting a part of a number, including partitives and words used partitively, comparatives, superlatives, and numerals, are followed by the genitive plural, or by the genitive singular of a collective noun.

(1.) Partitives (§104, 9,); as, *ullus*, *nullus*, *sōlus*, *alius*, *uter*, *uterque*, *utercumque*, *utervis*, *uterlibet*, *neuter*, *alter*, *alterūter*, *aliquis*, *quidam*, *quispiam*, *quisquis*, *quisque*, *quisquam*, *quicumque*, *unusquisque*, *quis?* *qui?* *quot?* *quotus?* *quotusquisque?* *tot*, *aliquot*, *nonnulli*, *plērique*, *multi*, *pauci*, *medius*. Thus, *Quisquis deōrum*, Whoever of the gods. Ovid. *Consulum alter*, One of the consuls. Liv. *Multi hŏminum*, Many men. Plin. *Et medius jŭvĕnum ibat;* i. e. between. Ovid. For the gender of adjectives used partitively, see § 205, R. 12.

(2.) Words used partitively; as, *Expĕditi militum*, The light-armed (of the) soldiers. Liv. *Dilecti equitum* . Id. *Vĕtĕres Rōmānōrum ducum*. Vell. *Superi deōrum*, The gods above. Hor. *Sancte deōrum*. Virg. *Dĭgĕnĕres cănum* Plin. *Piscium fēminæ*. Id.

(3.) Comparatives and superlatives; as, *Doctior jŭvĕnum*. *Oratōrum præstantissimus*. *Eloquentissimus Rōmānōrum*. *Optimus omnium*.

(4.) Numerals, both cardinal and ordinal; also the distributive *singŭli*; as, *Equitum centum quinquaginta interfecti*, A hundred and fifty of the horsemen were killed. Curt. *Sapientum octavus*. Hor. *Singŭlos vestrum*. Curt.

(*b*.) The meaning is often nearly the same, whether the partitive adjective agrees in case and number with a noun, or takes such noun after it a the genitive; as, *Doctissimus Rŏmānōrum*, or, *doctissĭmus Rōmānus: Alter consŭl m*, or *alter consul*. But the genitive cannot be used, when the adjective includes the s me number of things as that of which the whole consists; as, *Vĕniāmus ad vīvos*, qui duo *sŭpersunt*; not *quōrum duo*, since these are all, though we say in English, 'of whom two survive.'

NOTE 1. (*a*.) The comparative with the genitive denotes one of *two* individuals or classes; the superlative denotes a part of a number greater than two; as, *Mājor frātrum*, The elder of two brothers. *Maxĭmus frātrum*, The eldest of three or more.

(*b*.) In like manner, *ŭter*, *alter*, and *neuter*, generally refer to two; *quis*, *ălius*, and *nullus*, to a whole consisting of more than two; as, *Ŭter nostrum?* Which of us (two?) *Quis vestrum?* Which of you (three or more?)

NOTE 2. *Nostrum* and *vestrum* are used as partitive genitives, in preference to *nostri* and *vestri*, and are always joined with *omnium* even when the genitive is a subjective one; as, *Patria, quæ commūnis est* omnium nostrum *părens*. Cic. But *vestrum* sometimes occurs in other connections also without a partitive meaning; as, *Quis ĕrit tam cŭpĭdus vestrum*. Cic.

NOTE 3. The partitive word is sometimes omitted; as, *Fies nōbĭlium tu quŏque fontium*, scil. *ūnus*. Hor. *Centies sestertium*, scil. *centēna millia*.

NOTE 4. The noun denoting the whole, after a partitive word, is often put in the ablative, with the prepositions *de, e, ex*, or *in*, or in the accusative, with *ăpŭd* or *intĕr*; as, *Nēmo* de iis. *Alter* ex censōribus. Liv. *Unus* ex multis. Cic. *Acerrĭmus* ex sensibus. Id. *Thăles, qui săpientissĭmus* in septem *fuit*. Id. *Primus* inter omnes. Virg *Crœsus* inter rēges *ŏpŭlentissĭmus*. Sen. Apud Helvētios *nōbĭlissĭmus*.

NOTE 5. The whole and its parts are frequently placed in apposition, distributively; as, Interfectōres, pars *in fŏrum*, pars *Sўrācūsas pergunt*. Liv. See § 204, R. 10.

NOTE 6. *Cuncti* and *omnes*, like partitives, are sometimes followed by a genitive plural; as, *Attălus* Macĕdŏnum *fēre omnĭbus persuāsit*, Attălus persuaded almost all the Macedonians. Liv. *Cunctos* homĭnum. Ovid. *Cunctas* prōvinciārum. Plin.

NOTE 7. In the following passage, the genitive singular seems to be used like that of a collective noun: *Tōtius autem* injustitiæ *nulla căpĭtālior est*, etc. Cic. Off. 1, 13. The phrase *Rem nullo mŏdo prŏbābĭlem omnium* (Cic. Nat. Deor. 1, 27,) seems to be used for *Rem nullo omnium mŏdōrum prŏbābĭlem*.

REM. 3. The genitive denoting a whole, may depend on a neuter adjective or adjective pronoun. With these the genitive singular is commonly used; as,

Plus ĕlŏquentiæ, More (of) eloquence. *Tantum fĭdei*, So much fidelity. *In tempŏris*, That time. *Ad hoc ætātis*. Sometimes the genitive plural; as, *Id misĕriārum*. Ter. *Armōrum quantum*. Cæs.

NOTE 1. (*a*.) Most neuter adjectives used partitively denote quantity; as, *tantum, quantum, ălĭquantum, plūs, mĭnus, mĭnĭmum, dīmĭdĭum, multum, nimium, paulum, plūrĭmum, rĕliquum*; with the compounds and diminutives, *tantŭlum, tantundem, quantŭlum, quantŭlumcumque*, etc.; to which add *mĕdium, summum, ultĭmum, ăliud*, etc. The pronouns thus used are *hoc, id, illud, istud, idem, quod*, and *quid*, with their compounds, *ălĭquid, quidquid, quippiam, quidquam, quodcumque*.

(*b*.) Most of these adjectives and pronouns may either agree with their nouns, or take a genitive; but the latter is more common. *Tantum, quantum, ălĭquantum*, and *plūs*, when they denote quantity, are used with a genitive only, as are also *quid* and its compounds, when they denote a part, sort, etc., and *quŏd* in the sense of *quantum*. Thus, *Quantum crēvit Nilus, tantum* spni *in mānum est*. Sen. *Quid* mulĭĕris *uxōrem hăbes?* What kind of a woman... Ter.

§ 212.   SYNTAX.—GENITIVE AFTER PARTITIVES.   213

Aliquid formæ. Cic. *Quid hoc* rei *est?* What does this mean? Ter. *Quod* auri, *quod* argenti, *quod* ornamentōrum *fuit, id Verres abstŭlit.*

NOTE 2. Neuter adjectives and pronouns, when followed by a genitive, are to be accounted substantives, and in this construction are found only in the nominative and accusative.

NOTE 3. Sometimes the genitive after these adjectives and pronouns is a neuter adjective, of the second declension, without a noun; as, *Tantum bŏni,* So much good. *Si quid hăbes* nŏvi, If you have any thing new. Cic. *Quid rĕliqui est?* Ter. *Nihil* is also used with such a genitive; as, *Nihil sincēri,* No sincerity. Cic. This construction occurs very rarely with neuter adjectives in *i* of the third declension, and only in connection with neuters of the second declension; as, *Si quidquam non dīco* civīlis *sed hūmāni esset.* Liv.

NOTE 4. In the poets and in the prose writers later than Cicero, neuter adjectives in the *plural* number are sometimes followed by a genitive, either singular or plural, with a partitive signification; as, *Extrēma impĕrii,* The frontiers of the empire. Tac. *Pontes et* viārum *angusta,* The bridges and the narrow parts of the roads. Id. *Opāca lŏcōrum.* Virg. *Antīqua fœdĕrum.* Liv *Cuncta campōrum.* Tac. *Exercent colles, atque hōrum aspernma pascunt.* Virg Cf. § 205, R. 9.

REM. 4. The adverbs *săt, sătis, părum, nĭmis, ăbunde, largĭter, affātim,* and *partim,* used partitively, are often followed by a genitive; as,

Sat rătiōnis, Enough of reason. Virg. *Sătis ēlŏquentiæ, părum săpientiæ,* Enough of eloquence, (yet) but little wisdom. Sall. *Nĭmis insĭdiārum.* Cic. *Terrōris et fraudis ăbunde est.* Virg. *Auri et argenti largĭter.* Plaut. *Cōpiārum affātim.* Liv. *Quum partim illōrum mihi fămiliārissĭmi essent.* Cic.

NOTE 1. The above words, though generally adverbs, seem, in this use, rather to be nouns or adjectives.

NOTE 2. (*a*.) The genitives *gentium, terrārum, lŏci,* and *lŏcōrum,* with certain adverbs of place, strengthen their meaning; as, *Usquam terrārum.* Just. *Usquam gentium,* Any where whatever. Plaut. *Ubi terrārum sŭmus?* Where in the world are we? Cic. *Abīre quo terrārum possent.* Liv. *Ubi sit lŏci.* Plin. *Eo lŏci,* equivalent to *eo lŏco,* In that place. Tac. *Eōdem lŏci res est.* Cic. *Nescīre quo* lŏci *esset.* Id. But the last three examples might perhaps more properly be referred to Rem. 3.

(*b.*) The adverbs of place thus used are *ŭbi, ubĭnam, ŭbicumque, ŭbiŭbi, ŭbivis, ubīque, unde, usquam, nusquam, quo, quōcunique, quōvis, quōquo, ălĭquo, hīc, hŭc, eo, eōdem. Lŏci* also occurs after *ĭbi* and *ibĭdem; gentium* after *longe;* as, *Ibi lŏci,* In that place. Plin. *Abes longe gentium.* Cic. So, *minĭme gentium,* By no means. Ter. *Vicīniæ* in the genitive is used by the comic writers after *hic* and *huc;* as, *Hic proxĭmæ vicīniæ.* Plaut. *Huc vicīniæ.* Ter. Cf. § 221, R. 3, (4.)

NOTE 3. *Huc, eo, quo,* when used figuratively to express a degree, are joined also with other genitives; as, *Eo insŏlentiæ fŭrōrisque prŏcessit,* He advanced to such a degree of insolence and madness. Plin. *Huc ĕnim mălōrum ventum est.* Curt. *Huccĭne rērum vĕnĭmus?* Have we come to this? Pers. *Eo misĕriārum vĕnīre,* To such a pitch of misery. Sall. *Quo* āmentiæ *prōgressi sītis.* Liv.

NOTE 4. The genitives *lŏci, lŏcōrum,* and *tempŏris,* appear to be redundant after the adverbs *adhuc, inde, intĕrea, postea, tum,* and *tunc,* in expressions denoting time; as, *Adhuc lŏcōrum,* Till now. Plaut. *Inde lŏci,* After that. Lucr. *Intĕrea 'ŏci,* In the mean time. Ter. *Postea lŏci,* Afterwards. Sall. *Tum tempŏris,* and *tunc tempŏris,* At that time. Just. *Lŏcōrum* also occurs after *id,* denoting time; as, *Ad id locōrum,* Up to that time. Sall. Cf. R. 3.

NOTE 5. When the genitive *ējus* occurs after *quoad,* in such connections as the following: *Quoad ējus făcĕre pŏtĕris.* Cic.; or passively, *Quoad ējus fĭeri possit,* As far as may be. Cic.; the *ējus* refers to the preceding clause; literally as much of it as possible.

NOTE 6. *Prĭdie* and *postrĭdie*, though reckoned adverbs, are followed by a genitive, depending on the noun *dies* contained in them; as, *Pridie ějus diēi*, lit. On the day before that day, i. e. The day before. Cic. *Prĭdie insidiārum*, The day before the ambush. Tac. *Postrĭdie ējus diēi*, The next day. Cæs. When they are followed by an accusative, *ante* or *post* is understood. Cf. § 238, 1, (b.)

NOTE 7. Adverbs in the superlative degree, like their adjectives, are followed by a genitive; as, *Optime omnium*, Best of all. Cic.

GENITIVE AFTER ADJECTIVES.

§ 213. A noun, limiting the meaning of an adjective, is put in the objective genitive, to denote the relation expressed in English by *of, in,* or *in respect to* ; as,

Avĭdus laudis, Desirous *of praise.*   *Plēna* timōris, Full *of fear.*
Appĕtens glōriæ, Eager *for glory.*   *Egēnus* aquæ, Destitute *of water.*
Mēmor virtūtis, Mindful *of virtue.*   *Doctus* fandi, Skilful *in speaking.*

So, *Nescia mens* fāti, The mind ignorant *in regard to fate.* Virg. *Inpŏtens* iræ, lit. Powerless *in respect to anger,* i. e. unable to control it. Liv. *Hŏmines expertes* vēritātis, Men destitute *of truth.* Cic. Lactis *ăbundans*, Abounding *in milk.* Virg. *Terra fĕrax* arbŏrum, Land productive *of trees.* Plin. *Tĕnax* prŏpŏsĭti vir, A man tenacious *of his purpose.* Hor. *Æger* animi, Sick *in mind.* Liv. *Locus mĕdius* juguli suminĭque lăcerti, i. e. between. Ovid. *Mŏrum diversus.* Tac. *Opĕrum sŏlūtus.* Hor. *Liber libōrum.* Id. *Intĕger* vitæ scĕlŏrisque pūrus, Upright *in life,* and free *from wickedness.* Hor. Vini *pollens Liber.* Plaut.

From the above examples, it will be seen that the genitive after an adjective is sometimes translated by other words besides *of, in,* or *in respect to,* though the relation which it denotes remains the same. Cf. 211, R. 12.

REMARK 1. The following classes of adjectives, which, as denoting a relation to a thing, are called *relative adjectives* (§ 104, 13), are frequently limited by a genitive; viz. (1.) *Verbals* in *ax;* as, *căpax, ĕdax, fĕrax, fŭgax, pervĭcax, tĕnax,* etc.—(2.) *Participials* in *ns,* and a few in *tus,* with their compounds; as, *ămans, appĕtens, cŭpiens, effĭciens, pătiens, impătiens, sitiens;—consultus, doctus, sŏlūtus.*—(3.) Adjectives denoting *desire* or *aversion;* as, *ăvārus, ăvĭdus, cŭpĭdus, stŭdiōsus ; fastĭdiōsus :—participation;* as, *particeps, affinis, consors, exsors, expers, inops :—knowledge, experience, capacity,* and their contraries; as, *callĭdus, compos, conscius, gnārus, ignārus, pĕrītus, impĕrītus, impos, pŏtens, impŏtens, prūdens, imprūdens, expertus, inexpertus, conscius, inscius, nescius, insŏlens, insŏlĭtus, insuētus, rŭdis, sollers :—memory* and *forgetfulness;* as, *mĕmor, immĕmor,* etc.:—*certainty* and *doubt,* as, *certus, incertus, ambĭguus, dŭbius, suspensus :—care* and *negligence;* as, *anxius, sollicĭtus, prōvĭdus, imprōvĭdus, sēcūrus :—fear* and *confidence,* as, *păvĭdus, timĭdus, trĕpĭdus, impăvĭdus, fīdens, interrĭtus :—guilt* and *innocence;* as, *noxius, reus, suspectus, compertus, manĭfestus, innoxius, innŏcens, insons :—plenty* and *want;* as, *ăbundans, plēnus, dives, sătus, largus, inops, ĕgēnus inānis, pauper, parcus, sŏlūtus, văcuus.*

(a.) In the poets and later prose writers, many other adjectives, particularly those which express mental emotions, are in like manner limited by a genitive, especially by *ănĭmi, ingĕnii, mentis, iræ, militiæ, belli, labōris, rērum, ævi, futūri, morum,* and *fidei.*

REM. 2. The limiting genitive, by a Greek construction, sometimes denotes a *cause* or *source,* especially in the poets; as, *Lassus* māris, *et* viūrum, militiæque. Hor. *Fessus* viæ. Stat. *Fessus* māris. Hor. *Attŏnĭtus* serpentis. Sil. *Mens intĕrrĭta* lēti. Ovid.

REM. 3. Participles in *us, when used as such,* take after them the same case as the verbs from which they are derived; as, Se *ămans,* Loving himself. Cic. *Māre* terram *appĕtens.* Id.

§ 213. SYNTAX.—GENITIVE AFTER ADJECTIVES. 215

REM. 4. Instead of the genitive, denoting *of*, *in*, or *in respect to*, a different construction is sometimes used after many of these adjectives; as,

(1.) An infinitive or a subjunctive clause; as, *Certus* Ire, Determined *to go*. Ovid. *Cantāre pĕrīti*. Virg. *Fēlicior* unguēre *tēla*. Id. *Anxius* quid facta ŏpus sit. Sall. *l'īre mĕmor* quam sis ævi brĕvis. Hor.—So *aliĕnus*, *avīdus*, *callīdus*, *cŭpīdus*, *firmus*, *frĕquens*, *gnārus*, *impŏtens*, *inops*, *lætus*, *largus*, *līber*, *pollens*, *mĕmor*, *dŭbius*, etc.

(2.) An accusative with a preposition; as, Ad rem *ăvīdior*. Ter. *Avīdus* in direptiŏnes. Liv. *Anĭmus cāpax* ad præcepta. Ovid. Ad cāsum fortūnamque *fēlix*. Cic. Ad fraudem *callīdus*. Id. *Dīligens* ad custōdiendum. Id. *Neglĭgentior* in patrem. Just. *Vir* ad disciplīnam *pĕrītus*. Cic. Ad bella *rŭdis*. Liv. *Pŏtens* in res bellicas. Id. *Alăcer* ad mălĕficia. Cic. Inter bellum *et* pācem *nihil nĕdium est*. Id.—So with *ad*, *fertīlis*, *firmus*, *infirmus*, *pŏtens*, *stĕrilis*, etc.— with *in*, *cŭpīdus*, *parcus*, *pŏtens*, *prōdĭgus*, etc.

(3.) An accusative without a preposition, chiefly in the poets; as, *Nūdus* membra, Bare as to his limbs. Virg. Os, hŭmĕrosque deo *simīlis* Id. Cētĕra *fulvus*. Hor. Cuncta *pollens*. Sen. Ag. See § 234, II.

(4.) An ablative with a preposition; as, *Avīdus* in pĕcūniis, Eager in regard to money. Cic. *Anxius* de fāmā. Quint. *Rūdis* in jūre cīvīli. Cic. *Pĕrītus* de agricultūrā Varr. *Prūdens* in jūre cīvīli. Cic. *Reus* de vi. Id. *Pūrus* ab cultu *hūmāno*. Liv. *Certior factus* de re. Cic. *Sollicitus* de re. Id. Sŭper scĕlĕre *suspectus*. Sall. *Inops* ab āmīcis. Cic. *Pauper* in ære. Hor. *Mŏdicus* in cultu. Plin. Ab āquis *stĕrilis*. Apul. *Cōpiōsus* a frūmento. Cic. Ab ĕquitātu *firmus*. Id. So with *in*, *immŏdicus*, *parcus*, *ŭber*:—with *ab*, *aliēnus*, *beātus*, *extorris*, *immūnis*, *inops*, *līber*, *nūdus*, *orbus*, *văcuus*.

(5.) An ablative without a preposition; as, Arte *rŭdis*, Rude in art. Ovid. *Regni* crimine *insons*. Liv. *Compos* mente. Virg. *Prūdens* consilio. Just. *Æger* pĕdibus. Sall. *Præstans* ingĕnio. Cic. *Mŏdicus* sĕvērītāte. Tac. *Nĭhil* insĭdiis *văcuum*. Cic. *Amor et* melle *et* felle *est fēcundissĭmus*. Plaut. *Mĕdius* Pollūce *et* Castōre. Ovid. Cf. Rem. 5.

In many instances, the signification of the accusative and ablative after adjectives differs, in a greater or less degree, from that of the genitive.

REM. 5. As many of the adjectives, which are followed by a genitive, admit of other constructions, the most common use of each, with particular nouns, can, in general, be determined only by recourse to the dictionary, or to the classics. Some have,

(1.) The genitive only; as, *bĕnignus*, *căpax*, *exsors*, *impos*, *impŏtens*, *insătiābīlis*, *irrītus*, *lībĕrālis*, *mŏdicus*, *mŭnĭficus*, *prælargus*, and many others.

(2.) The genitive more frequently; as, *compos*, *consors*, *ĕgēnus*, *exhēres*, *expers*, *fertīlis*, *indīgus*, *inops*, *parcus*, *particeps*, *pauper*, *prōdĭgus*, *prosper*, *stĕrilis*.

(3.) The genitive or ablative indifferently; as, *dīves*, *fēcundus*, *fērax*, *immūnis*, *inānis*, *immŏdicus*, *jējūnus*, *largus*, *nimius*, *ŏpŭlentus*, *pĕrītus*, *plēnus*, *pŏtens*, *pūrus*, *refertus*, *sătur*, *ŭber*, *văcuus*.

(4.) The ablative more frequently; as, *ăbundans*, *aliēnus*, *cassus*, *cōpiōsus*, *ĕxtorris*, *firmus*, *fētus*, *frēquens*, *grăvĭdus*, *grăvis*, *infirmus*, *līber*, *lŏcuples*, *lætus*, *mactus*, *nūdus*, *ŏnustus*, *orbus*, *pollens*, *sătiātus*, *truncus*, *vălĭdus*, *viduus*.

(5.) The ablative only; as, *beātus*, *crĕber*, *densus*, *mŭtīlus*, *tŭmĭdus*, *turgĭdus*.

For the ablative after many of the preceding adjectives, see § 250.

REM. 6. Some adjectives usually limited by a dative, sometimes take a genitive instead of the dative; as, *similis*, *dissimilis*, etc. See § 222, R. 2.

REM. 7. Many adjectives in addition to the genitive or ablative denoting *of* or *in respect to*, take also another case to express a different relation; as, *Mens sibi conscia* recti. Cf. § 222, R. 3. *Conscius* has also sometimes the dative instead of the genitive of the *thing*; as, *conscius* huic făcĭnŏri. Cic.

GENITIVE AFTER VERBS

§ 214. *Sum*, and verbs of *valuing*, are followed by a genitive, denoting *degree of estimation*; as,

A me argentum, quanti *est*, *sūmito*, Take of me so much money as (he) is worth. Ter. *Magni æstimābat pēcūniam*, He valued money greatly. Cic. *Ager nunc plūris est*, *quam tunc fuit.* Id. *Tanti est*, It is worth so much; and, absolutely, It is worth while. Cic. *Hūjus non fācio*, I don't care *that* for it.

REMARK 1. (*a.*) Verbs of valuing are joined with the genitive, when the value is expressed in *a general* or *indefinite* manner by :—

(1.) A neuter adjective of quantity; as, *tanti, quanti, plūris, mĭnŏris, magni, permagni, plūrĭmi, maxĭmi, minĭmi, parvi, tantīdem, quantīcumque, quantīvis, quantĭlĭbet*, but only very rarely *multi* and *mājŏris*.

(2.) The nouns *assis, flocci, nauci, nihĭli, pĭli, tēruncii*, and also *pensi* and *hūjus*.

(*b.*) But if the price or value of a thing is a *definite* sum, or is expressed by a *substantive*, other than *assis, flocci*, etc., it is put in the ablative. Cf. § 252.

REM. 2. The verbs of valuing are *æstĭmo, existĭmo, dūco, fācio, fĭo, hăbeo, pendo, pŭto, depŭto, taxo*. Thus, *Ut* quanti *quisque se ipse fāciat*, tanti *fĭat ab amīcis*, That as much as each one values himself, so much he should be valued by his friends. Cic. *Sed quia parvi id dūcĕret.* Id. *Hŏnōres si magni non pŭtēmus.* Id. *Non assis fācis?* Catull. *Nēque quod dixi*, flocci *existĭmat.* Plaut.

NOTE 1. (*a.*) The phrase *æqui bŏni*, or *æqui bŏnīque fācio*, or *consŭlo*, I take a thing in good part, am satisfied with it, may be classed with genitives of value; as, *Nos æqui bŏnīque fācĭmus.* Liv. So, *Bŏni consŭluit* Plin.—(*b.*) A genitive of price is joined also to *cæno, hăbĭto, dŏceo*, etc.; as, *quanti hăbĭtas?* what rent do you pay for your house or lodging? *quanti dŏcet?* what are his terms in teaching?

NOTE 2. After *æstĭmo*, the ablatives *magno, permagno, parvo, nihĭlo*, are sometimes used instead of the genitive; as, *Dāta* magno *æstĭmas, acceptă* parvo. Sen. *Pro* nihilo, also, occurs after *dūco, hăbeo*, and *pŭto*; and *nihil* with *æstĭmo* and *mŏror.* Cf. § 231, R. 5.

NOTE 3. The neuter adjectives above enumerated, and *hūjus*, may be referred to a noun understood, as *prētii, æris, pondĕris, mŏmenti*; and may be considered as limiting a preceding noun, also understood, and denoting some person or thing; as, *Æstĭmo te magni*, i. e. *hŏmĭnem magni prētii. Scio ejus ordinis auctōrĭtātem semper ăpud te magni fuisse*, i. e. *rem magni mŏmenti.* The words *assis*, etc., may also be considered as depending on an omitted noun; as, *prētio, rei*, etc.

REM. 3. Statements of *price*, also, *when general* or *indefinite*, are put in the genitive after verbs of *buying, selling, letting*, and *hiring*, as,

Mercātōres non tantīdem vendunt, quanti *ēmērunt.* Cic. *Nulla pestis hūmāno gĕnĕri* plūris *stĕtit, quam ira.* Sen.

NOTE 1. Verbs of buying, selling, etc., are *ĕmo, vendo*, the neutral passive, *rĕneo, consto, prōsto*, and *lĭceo*, to be exposed for sale.

NOTE 2. With verbs of buying, selling, etc., the ablatives *magno, permagno, plūrĭmo, parvo, minĭmo*, and *nihĭlo* are often used instead of the genitive; as, *Non potest parvo res magna constāre.* Sen. *Quanti ĕmĕre possum* minĭmo? What is the lowest price I can buy at? Plaut. Sometimes also the adverbs *cāre bĕne*, and *mălē* take the place of the genitive or ablative of price.

§ 215, 216. SYNTAX.—GENITIVE AFTER VERBS. 217

§ 215. (1.) *Misĕreor, misĕresco,* and the impersonals *misĕ-ret, pœnĭtet, pŭdet, tædet,* and *pĭget,* are followed by a genitive of the object in respect to which the feeling is exercised; as,

Misĕrēmĭni sŏciōrum, Pity the allies. Cic. *Misĕrescĭte rēgis,* Pity the king. Virg. *Mea māter, tui me misĕret,* mei *pĭget,* I pity you, and am dissatisfied with myself. Acc. *Eos* ineptiārum *pœnĭtet.* Cic. *Frātris me pŭdet pĭgetque.* Ter. *Me cīvĭtātis* mōrum *pĭget tædetque.* Sall. So the compound *distædet; Haud quod* tui *me, nĕque* dōmi *distædeat.* Plaut.; and the passive; *Numquam suscepti* nĕgōtii *eum pertæsum est.* Nep. Lentitūdĭnis *eōrum pertæsa.* Tac. *Misĕrĭtum est me tuārum* fortūnārum. Ter. *Cāve te* frātrum *misĕreātur.* Cic. *Pŭdet (me)* deōrum hŏminumque, I am filled with shame in reference both to gods and men. Liv.

NOTE 1. *Misĕrescĭt* is sometimes used in the same manner as *misĕret; as, Nunc te misĕrescat* mei. Ter. *Misĕreo,* as a personal verb, also, occurs with a genitive; as, *Ipse sui misĕret.* Lucr.

REMARK. The genitive after the above impersonals seems to depend on some general word constituting the grammatical subject of such verbs, and signifying, *matter, business, fact, case, circumstances, conduct, character,* etc., cf § 211, R. 8, (3); and § 209, R. 3, (4.) Instead of the genitive with its omitted noun, an infinitive or clause with *quod* or with an interrogative particle is sometimes used as a subject; as, *Non me hoc jam* dicĕre *pŭdēbit.* Cic. *Non pœnĭtet me* quantum prōfēcĕrim, I am not dissatisfied with my progress. Id. These verbs have also sometimes a nominative; as, *Me quidem hæc* conditio *non pœnĭtet.* Plaut. *Non te* hæc *pŭdent?* Ter.

NOTE 2. *Misĕret* occurs with an accusative of the object, instead of a genitive; as, *Mĕnĕdēmi* vicem *misĕret me.* Ter. So, also, *Pertæsus* ignāviam *suam.* Suet.

NOTE 3. (*a.*) These impersonals, as active verbs, take also an accusative of the person exercising the feeling which they express. See § 229, R. 6.— (*b.*) And sometimes also the accusative of the *neuter pronouns* and of *nihil,* denoting *to what degree* the feelings are exercised; as, *Sēquĭtur ut* nihil (*sāpĭentem,*) *pœnĭteat.* Cic. Cf. § 232, (3.)

(2.) *Sătăgo* is sometimes followed by a genitive denoting *in what respect;* as,

Is sătăgit rērum *suārum,* He is busily occupied with his own affairs. Ter. This compound is often written separately, and in either case the genitive seems to depend upon *sat.* See § 212, R. 4. *Agĭto,* with *sat,* in like manner, is followed by a genitive; as, *Nunc ăgĭtas sat tūte tuārum* rērum. Plaut.

§ 216. *Rĕcordor, mĕmĭni, rĕmĭniscor,* and *oblīviscor,* are followed by a genitive or accusative of the object remembered or forgotten; as,

Flāgitiōrum *suōrum rĕcordābĭtur.* Cic. *Omnes* grădus *ætātis rĕcordor tuæ,* I call to mind all the periods of your life. Id. *Mĕmĭni* vīvōrum, I am mindful of the living. Id. Nŭmĕros *mĕmĭni,* I remember the measure. Virg. *Rĕmĭnĭsci vĕtĕris* fāmæ. Nep. *Dulces mŏriens rĕmĭniscĭtur* Argos. Virg. *Rĕmĭnĭsci* amīcos. Ovid. *Oblītus* sui. Virg. Injūriārum *oblĭviscĭtur.* Nep. *Oblĭviscor* injūrias. Cic. *Oblĭviscĕre* Graios. Virg.

REMARK 1. (*a.*) When the thing remembered or forgotten is expressed by a neuter pronoun or adjective, it is always put in the accusative. An accusative of the *person* with these verbs is unusual, except that *mĕmĭni,* when referring to a contemporary always takes an accusative of the person; as, Cinnam *mĕmĭni.* Cic.

(*b.*) An infinitive or a dependent clause sometimes follows these verbs; as *Memento mihi suppetias ferre.* Plaut. *Esse quoque in fatis reminiscitur,* affore *tempus, quo mare, etc.* Ovid. *Obliti* quid *decea*t Hor. *Memini te scribere* Cic. *Quæ sum passura recordor.* Ovid.

REM. 2. *Recordor* and *memini, to remember,* are sometimes followed by an ablative with *de;* as, *Petimus ut de suis* liberis *recor dentur.* Cic. *De pallâ memento.* Plaut.

REM. 3. *Memini,* signifying *to make mention of,* has a genitive, or an ablative with *de;* as, *Neque hujus rei meminit, poëta.* Quint. *Meministi* de exsul bus. Cic. With *venit mihi in mentem,* the person or thing may be made the subject of *venit;* as, *Miseræ ubi venit in mentem mortis* metus. Plaut. *Venit hoc mihi in mentem;* or an infinitive or subjunctive clause may supply the place of the subject:—for the genitive with this phrase, as in *Solet mihi in mentem venire illius temporis,* see § 211, R. 8, (6.) The genitive with *recordor* is very rare.

§ 217.
Verbs of *accusing, convicting, condemning,* and *acquitting,* with the accusative of the person, are followed by *a* genitive denoting the *crime;* as,

Arguit me furti, He charges me *with theft. Alterum accusat* probri, He accuses another *of villany. Meipsum* inertiæ condemno. Cic.

REMARK 1. (*a.*) To this rule belong the verbs of

Accusing; *accuso, ago, arcesso, arguo, cito, defero, increpo, incuso, insimulo, postulo,* and more rarely *alligo, anquiro, astringo, capto, increpito, urgeo, interrogo, reum ago* or *facio, alicui diem dico, cum aliquo ago.*—Convicting; *convinco, coarguo, prehendo, teneor, obstringo, obligor.*—Condemning; *damno, condemno, infamo,* and more rarely *judico, noto, plector.*—Acquitting; *absolvo, libero, purgo,* and rarely *solvo.* To the verbs of accusing, etc., may be added the adjectives denoting *guilt* and *innocence,* which likewise take a genitive. Cf. § 213, R. 1, (3.)

(*b.*) The genitives which follow these verbs are, *audaciæ, avaritiæ, cædis, falsi, furti, ignaviæ, impietatis, injuriarum, levitatis, majestatis, maleficii, mendacii, parricidii, peccati, peculatus, probri, proditionis, rei capitalis, repetundarum, sceleris, stultitiæ, temeritatis, timoris, vanitatis, veneficii,* etc.

REM. 2. (*a.*) Instead of the genitive, an ablative with *de* is often used after *accuso, defero, anquiro, arguo, postulo, damno, condemno, absolvo,* and *purgo;* as, *Accusare* de negligentiâ. Cic. *De vi condemnati sunt.* Id. *De repetundis est postulatus.* Id. Sometimes with *in,* after *accuso, coarguo, convinco, teneor,* and *deprehendor;* as, *In quo te accuso* (Cic.); and after *libero,* with *a* or *ab;* as, *A scelere liberati sumus.* Cic. *Accuso* and *damno* with *inter* occur in the phrases *inter sicarios accusare,* etc., to charge with assassination.

(*b.*) With some of the above verbs, an ablative without a preposition is often used; as, *Liberare* culpâ. Cic. *Crimen* quo *argui posset.* Nep. *Proconsulem postulaverat repetundis.* Tac. This happens especially with general words denoting crime; as, *scelus, maleficium, peccatum,* etc.; as, *Me* peccâto *solvo.* Liv. The ablatives *crimine* and *nomine,* without a preposition, are often inserted before the genitive; as, *Arcessere aliquem* crimine *ambitus.* Liv. Nomine *sceleris conjurationisque damnati.* Cic.; and when not so inserted they are to be understood.

(*c.*) Sometimes a clause takes the place of the genitive; as, *Eum accusabant* quod societâtem fecisset. Nep. So the infinitive with the accusative. *Quid? quod me—arguit serum accessisse?* Ovid.

REM. 3. (*a.*) The *punishment* is commonly expressed by the genitive; as, *capitis, mortis, multæ, pecuniæ, quadrupli, octupli;* but sometimes by the ablative; as, *capite, morte, multâ, pecuniâ:* and always by this case when a definite sum is mentioned; as, *quinque tim millibus æris:* or the accusative with *ad* or *in,*

as, *ad pœnam, ad bestias, ad metalla,* in *metallum,* in *expensas;*—sometimes though rarely, in the poets, by the dative; as, *Damnātus* morti. Lucr.—
(*b.*) *Vōti* or *votōrum,* and less frequently *rōto* or *votis damnāri,* signifies 'to be condemned to fulfil one's vow,' and is consequently equivalent to 'to obtain what one wishes.' So also in the active voice, *Damnābis tu quōque vōtis.* Virg. *Perdo* is used by Plautus as a verb of accusing, with *cāpitis; Quem ĕgo căpitis perdam,* will charge with a capital offence. So *căpite* or *căpitis* periclĭtări, Plaut., signifies 'to be in peril of one's life.' With *plecto* and *plector, căput* is used in the ablative only.—(*c.*) *Damni infecti* is put in the genitive (depending upon *nōmine* understood) after *sătisdo, prōmitto, stipŭlāri, reprōmitto,* and *căveo;* as, *Si quis in părĭete dēmōliendo* damni infecti *prōmīsĕrit.* Cic.

Rem. 4. *Accūso, incūso,* and *insĭmŭlo,* instead of the genitive, sometimes take the accusative, especially of a neuter pronoun; as, *Si id me non accūsas.* Plaut. *Quæ me incūsāvĕras.* Ter. *Sic me insĭmŭlāre falsum* facinus. Plaut. See § 231, Rem. 5.

Rem. 5. (*a.*) The following verbs of accusing, etc., are not followed by a genitive of the crime, but, as active verbs, by an accusative:—*cālumnior, carpo, corrĭpio, crīmĭnor, culpo, excūso, multo, pūnio, reprehendo, sŭgillo, taxo, trādūco, vĭtŭpĕro;* as, *Culpāre infēcundĭtātem agrōrum.* Colum. *Excūsāre errōrem et ădōlescentiam.* Liv.

(*b.*) This construction also sometimes occurs with *accūso, incūso, arguo,* and *inarguo;* as, *Ejus āvārĭtiam perfĭdiamque accūsārat.* Nep. *Culpam arguo.* Liv. With *multo,* the punishment is put in the ablative only, without a preposition; as, *Exsĭliis, morte multantur.* Cic.

§ 218.
Verbs of admonishing, with the accusative of the person, are followed by a genitive of the person or thing respecting which the admonition is given; as,

Milĭtes tempŏris *mŏnet,* He admonishes the soldiers of the occasion. Tac. *Admŏnēbat ălium* ĕgestātis, *ălium* cŭpĭdĭtātis *suæ.* Sall.

Note. The verbs of admonishing are *moneo, admŏneo, commŏneo,* and *commŏnĕfăcio.*

Remark 1. Instead of the genitive, verbs of admonishing sometimes have an ablative with *de;* as, De æde *Tellūris me admŏnes.* Cic.—sometimes an accusative of a pronoun or adjective in the neuter gender; as, *Eos* hoc *moneo* Cic. *Illud me admŏneo.* Id.; and in the passive, Multa *admŏnēmur.* Id.—rarely also a noun in the accusative; as, *Eam* rem *nos lŏcus admŏnuit.* Sall.

Rem. 2. Instead of the genitive, verbs of admonishing are also often followed by an infinitive or clause; as, *Sŏror alma mŏnet* succēdĕre Lauso Turnum, His sister admonishes Turnus to take the place of Lausus. Virg. *Mŏnet,* ut suspiciōnes vītet. Cæs. *Sed eos hoc mŏneo,* dēsinant fŭrēre. Cic. *Mŏnet* rătiōnem frūmenti esse hăbendam. Hirt. Immortālia ne spēres *mŏnet* annus. Hor. *Discĭpŭlos* id ūnum *mŏneo,* ut, etc. Quint. *Mŏneo* quid facto ŏpus sit. Ter. See § 273, 2.

§ 219.
Rēfert and *intĕrest* are followed by a genitive of the person or thing whose concern or interest they denote; as,

Hūmānĭtātis rēfert, It concerns human nature. Plin. *Rēfert* omnium *ănĭmadverti in mălos.* Tac. *Intĕrest* omnium *recte făcĕre,* It concerns all to do right. Cic.

Remark 1. Instead of the genitive of the substantive pronouns, the adjective pronouns *mea, tua, sua, nostra,* and *vestra,* are used; as,

Men nihil rēfert, It does not concern me. Ter. *Illud* mea *magni intĕrest,* That greatly concerns me. Cic. *Tua et mea maxĭme intĕrest, te vălēre.* Cic *Măgis* reipūblicæ *intĕrest* quam mea. Id. *Magni intĕrest* Cicĕrōnis, *vel* mea *pŏtius, vel mehercŭle* utriusque, *me intervĕnīre dīcenti.* Id.

NOTE. *Rĕfert* rarely occurs with the genitive, but often with the pronouns *mea, tua*, etc., and most frequently without either such pronoun or a genitive as, *quid rĕfert? magni* or *magnŏpĕre rĕfert.*

REM. 2. In regard to the case of these adjective pronouns, grammarians differ. Some suppose that they are in the accusative plural neuter, agreeing with *commŏda* or the like understood; as, *Intĕrest mea*, i. e. *est inter mea*, It is among my concerns. *Rĕfert tua*, i. e. *rĕfert se ad tua*, It refers itself to your concerns. Others think that they are in the ablative singular feminine, agreeing with *re, causā*, etc., understood, or in the dative. The better opinion seems to be, that they are in the accusative feminine for *meam, tuam, suam*, etc., that *rĕfert* was originally *rem fert*, and that hence the *e* of *rĕfert* is long.

REM. 3. Instead of the genitive, an accusative with *ad* is sometimes used; as, *Ad honōrem meum intĕrest quam primum urbem me vĕnire*. Cic. *Quid id ad me aut ad meam rem rĕfert*. Plaut.—sometimes, though rarely, an accusative without a preposition; as, *Quid te igĭtur rĕtŭlit?* Plaut.—or a dative; as, *Dic quid rĕfĕrat intra nātūræ fines vīventi*. Hor.

REM. 4. The subject of these verbs, or the thing which is of interest or importance, is sometimes expressed by a neuter pronoun; as, *Id mea minime rĕfert.* Ter. *Hoc vĕhĕmenter intĕrest reipŭblĭcæ.* Cic.; and sometimes by an infinitive with its accusative, or *ut*, or an interrogative particle with a subjunctive clause; as, *multum mea intĕrest te esse dilĭgentem*, or *ut dilĭgens sis*, or *utrum dilĭgens sis nec ne*. When the infinitive alone is used with *rĕfert* or *intĕrest*, the preceding subject is understood; as, *omnium intĕrest recte fădĕre*, scil. *se*.

REM. 5. The degree of interest or importance is expressed by adverbs or by neuter adjectives, etc., in the accusative or genitive; as, *măgis, magnŏpĕre, vĕhĕmenter, părum, minĭme*, etc.; *multum, plūs, plūrĭmum, nihil, alĭquid*, etc.; *tantĭ, quanti, magni, permagni, plūris*. But *minĭmo discrimĭne rĕfert* is found in Juv. 6, 123.

§ **220**. Many verbs which are usually otherwise construed, are sometimes followed by a genitive. This rule includes

1. Certain verbs denoting an affection of the mind; *ango, discrŭcior, excrŭcio, fallo, pendeo*, which are followed by *ănimi*; *decĭpior, dēsĭpio, fallor, fastĭdĭo, invideo, miror, vĕreor*; as, *Absurde făcis, qui angas te ănimi*. Plaut. *Me ănimi fallit.* Lucr. *Decĭpitur labōrum.* Hor. *Dēsĭpiēbam mentis.* Plaut. *Justitiæne prius mirer belline labōrum.* Virg.

2. The following, in imitation of the Greek idiom; *abstĭneo, desino, pur*, Hor.; *desisto*. Virg.; *laudo, prohĭbeo*. Sil.; *lĕvo, partĭcĭpo*. Plaut.; *libĕro*. Liv.; *dissolvo*. Tibull.: compare *liber labōrum; ŏpĕrum văcuus; pūrus scĕlĕris*. § 213.

3. Some verbs denoting *to fill, to abound, to want or need, to free*, which are commonly followed by an ablative. Such are *abundo, cāreo, compleo, expleo, implĕo, ĕgeo, indĭgeo, sătūro, obsătūro, scăteo*; as, *Adŏlescentem suæ tĕmĕritātis implet*, He fills the youth with his own rashness. Liv. *Anĭmum explesse* flammæ. Virg. *Egeo consilii.* Cic. *Non tam artis indĭgent quam labōris*. Id. See §§ 249 and 250, (2.)

4. *Pŏtior*, which also is usually followed by an ablative; as, *Urbis pŏtiri*, To make oneself master of the city. Sall. *Pŏtiri regni* (Cic.), *hostium* (Sall.), *rerum*, To make oneself master of the world. Cic. *Pŏtio* (active) occurs in Plautus; as, *Eum nunc pŏtivit servitūtis*, He has made him partaker of slavery. In the same writer, *pŏtītus est hostium* signifies, 'he fell into the hands of the enemy.' So, also, *Aliquem compŏtire prædæ or vōti.* App. So, *Rērum ădeptus est.* Tac. *Dŏmĭnātiōnis ăpisci.* Id. *Regnāvit pŏpŭlōrum.* Hor.

GENITIVE OF PLACE.

§ 221. 1. The name of a town *in which* any thing is said *to be*, or *to be done*, if of the first or second declension and singular number, is put in the genitive; as,

Habitat Milēti, He lives at Miletus. Ter. *Quid Rōmæ fáciam?* What can I do at Rome? Juv. *Hercŭles Tȳri maxĭme cŏlĭtur.* Cic.

NOTE. For the construction of nouns of the third declension or plural number, see § 254. The following appears to be the best explanation that has been given of this diversity of construction, depending solely on the number or declension of the noun. The name of the town 'where' or 'in which' is probably neither in the genitive nor the ablative, but always, as in Greek, in the dative. Since the genitive and dative are alike in the singular of the first declension and the dative and ablative plural are the same in all declensions, such examples as *Rōmæ* and *Athēnis* present no difficulty. In the third declension the dative and ablative singular were anciently alike, and in such ablatives as *Anxŭri*, *Carthāgĭni*, *Lăcĕdæmŏni*, the old form remains, see § 82, Exc. 5, (*c*.) In the second declension there was an old dative in *oi*, as in Greek, which was commonly changed to *o*, but sometimes to *i*: and the latter is still found in *nulli*, *uni*, etc., see § 107, and in the adjective pronouns; as, *illi*, etc.

REMARK 1. Names of islands and countries are sometimes put in the genitive, like names of towns; as, *Ithăcæ virēre*, To live in Ithaca. Cic. *Corcȳræ fuĭmus.* Id. *Cōnon plūrĭmum* Cypri *vixit*, *Tĭmŏtheus* Lesbi. Nep. *Quum Miltiădes dŏmum* Chersŏnēsi *habuit*. Id. *Crētæ jussit considēre Apollo*. Virg. *Rōmæ Nămidĭæque fácinōra ĕjus mĕmŏrat.* Sall.

REM. 2. (*a.*) Instead of the genitive, the ablative of names of towns of the first and second declension and singular number, is sometimes, though rarely, used; as, *Rex Tȳro dēcĕdit*, The king dies at Tyre. Just. *Et Cŏrintho et Athēnis et Lăcĕdæmŏne nunciāta est victōria.* Id. *Pons quem ille Abȳdo fĕcĕrat.* Id. *Hujus exemplar Rōmā nullum hăbēmus.* Vitruv. *Non Libyæ*, non *ante Tȳro*. Virg. For the explanation of this apparent anomaly, see the preceding note; in accordance with which it may be remarked, that the adverbs of place, *ŭbi*, *ibi*, *ibidem*, *ălĭbi*, *alĭcŭbi*, *hic*, *illic*, *istic*, etc., appear from their form to be ancient datives.—(*b.*) When the noun is qualified by an adjective, it is put, not in the genitive, but in the ablative with *in*; as, *In ipsā Alexandriā.* Cic. And poetically without *in*, *Gĕnus Longā nostrum dŏmĭnābĭtur* Albā. Virg.—(*c.*) When *urbs*, *oppĭdum*, *lŏcus*, etc., follow the genitive of place as appositions, they are put in the ablative either with, or, more rarely, without, *in*; as, *Archĭas Antĭŏchĭæ nātus est*, cĕlebri *quondam* urbe. Cic. *Cives Rōmānos Neāpŏli*, in cĕleberrimo oppĭdo *sæpe vidĭmus.* Id. But when *in urbe*, etc., precede the name of a town, the latter also is put in the ablative; as, *In oppĭdo* Citio. Nep.; and but very rarely in the genitive; as, Cassius *in oppĭdo* Antĭŏchĭæ *est*,—in the town of Antioch. Cic., where the genitive depends on *oppĭdo*.

REM. 3. The genitives *dŏmi*, *mīlĭtiæ*, *belli*, and *hŭmi*, are construed like names of towns; as,

Tĕnuit se dŏmi, He staid at home. Cic. *Vir* dŏmi *clārus*. Liv. *Spargit* hŭm *jussos dentes*,—on the ground. Ovid. *Militiæ* and *belli* are thus used, especially when opposed to *dŏmi*; as, *Una semper* militiæ *et* dŏmi *fuĭmus*,—both at home and in the camp. Ter. So *Dŏmi militiæque.* Cic. *Et dŏmi et militiæ.* Id. *Militia dŏmique.* Liv. *Militiæ et dŏmi.* Ter. *Belli dŏmique*, in war and in peace. Hor.

(1.) *Dŏmi* is thus used with the possessives *meæ*, *tuæ*, *suæ*, *nostræ*, *vestræ*, and *aliēnæ*; as, Dŏmi nostræ *vixit*, He lived at my house. Cic. *Apud eum sic fui tamquam* meæ dŏmi. Id. *Sacrifĭcium*, *quod* aliēnæ dŏmi *fĭĕret invisĕre.* Id. But with other adjectives, an ablative, generally with a preposition, is used; as, *In viduā dŏmo.* Ovid. *Paternā dŏmo.* Id. Sometimes also with the possessives; as, *Meā in domo.* Hor. *In dōmo suā.* Nep. So, instead of *hŭmi*, 'upon the ground,' *hunc* is sometimes used, with or without a preposition; as, *In hūmo ărĕnōsā* Ovid. *Sēdēre hūmo nūdā.* Id.

(2.) When a genitive denoting the possessor follows, either *dŏmi* or *in dŏmŏ* is used; as, *Dēprĕhensus* dŏmi *Cæsăris.* Cic. *Dŏmi illius fuisti.* Id. *In dŏmo Cæsăris.* Id. *In dŏmo ejus.* Nep.

(3.) The ablative *dŏmo* for *dŏmi* also occurs, but not in Cicero; as, *Ego in nunc expĕrior* dŏmo. Plaut. *Dŏmo se tĕnēre.* Nep. *Dŏmo abdĭtus.* Suet. *Bello* for *belli* is found in Livy—*Dŏmi bellōque.* So, also, *hŭmo* for *hŭmi ; Strātus hŭmo.* Stat. *Figit* hŭmo *plantas.* Virg.: and in hŭmo *lūmen figit.* Ovid.

(4.) *Terræ* is sometimes used like *hŭmi;* as, *Sacra* terræ *cĕlăvĭmus.* Liv. *Prŏjectus* terræ. Virg. *Ignes terræ condit.* Luc. So, also, *ărēnæ ; Truncum rĕliquit* ărēnæ. Virg.: and *vicinĭæ; Proxĭmæ* vicinĭæ hăbĭtat. Plaut.

(5.) The genitive of names of towns, *dŏmi, milĭtĭæ,* etc., is supposed by some to depend on a noun understood; as, *urbe, oppĭdo, ædĭbus, sōlo, lŏco, tempŏre,* etc., but see a different explanation above in Note.

GENITIVE AFTER PARTICLES.

II. Certain adverbs are followed by the genitive. See § 212, R. 4.

III. The genitive plural sometimes depends on the preposition *tĕnus;* as,

Cūmārum tĕnus, As far as Cumæ. Cœl. *Crūrum tĕnus.* Virg. *Lātĕrum tĕnus.* Id. *Urbium Corcỹræ tĕnus.* Liv.—For the ablative after *tĕnus,* and for the place of the preposition, see § 241, and R. 1.

DATIVE.

§ 222. 1. The dative is the case of reference, as it denotes the object with reference to which the subject acts, or in reference to which it possesses any specified quality ; or, in other words, the object *for* which, to the *benefit* or *loss* of which, any thing *is* or *is done.* Hence, in distinction from the dative of the *end* (§ 227) the dative of reference is called *dativus commŏdi et incommŏdi,* the dative of advantage and disadvantage ; as,

Scrībo vōbis *hunc lībrum,* I write this book *for you. Prōsum* tibi, or Tĭbi *ūtĭlis sum,* I am useful *to you.*

2. Hence the dative of advantage and disadvantage may be used (*a*) with adjectives and particles whose meaning is incomplete unless the object is mentioned in reference to which the quality exists. (*b*) With verbs both transitive and intransitive. If transitive they take an accusative of the nearer and a dative of the remoter object, if intransitive they take a dative only. (*c*) With certain verbs compounded with prepositions, after which the dative is used instead of the case which the preposition, if separate, would govern. (*d*) After a few verbal substantives derived from verbs which govern a dative.

DATIVE AFTER ADJECTIVES.

3. A noun limiting the meaning of an adjective, is put in the dative, to denote the *object* to which the quality is directed ; as,

§ 222. SYNTAX.—DATIVE AFTER ADJECTIVES. 223

Utilis ïgris, Useful to the fields. Juv. *Jūcundus amīcis,* Agreeable to his friends. Virt. *Inimīcus quiēti,* Unfriendly to rest. Id. *Charta inūtilis scribendo,* Paper not useful for writing. Plin.

NOTE. The dative is commonly translated by the prepositions *to* or *for*; but sometimes by other prepositions, or without a preposition.

REMARK 1. Adjectives signifying *useful, pleasant, friendly, fit, like, inclined, ready, easy, clear, equal,* and their opposites, also those signifying *near,* many compounded with *con,* and verbals in *bilis,* are followed by the dative; as,

Felix tuis, Propitious to your friends. Virg. *Oratio ingrata Gallis,* A speech displeasing to the Gauls. Nepos. *Amīcus tyrannidi,* Friendly to tyranny. Nep. *Labōri inhābilis,* Unsuited to labor. Colum. *Patri similis,* Like his father. Cic. *Nihil tam est Lysiae diversum, quam Isocrātes. Aptum tempŏri.* Id. *Malo prŏnus.* Sen. *Promptus seditiōni.* Tac. *Cuivis facile est.* Ter. *Mihi certum est* Cic. *Par fratri tuo.* Id. *Falsa veris finitima sunt.* Id. *Oculi concolōres corpŏri.* Colum. *Multis bonis flēbilis.* Hor. *Mors est terribilis iis, quorum,* etc. Cic.

(a.) The following are some of the adjectives included in Rem. 1, viz. *grātus, acceptus, dulcis, jūcundus, laetus, suāvis; ingrātus, insuāris, injūcundus, molestus, gravis, acerbus, odiōsus, tristis;—ūtilis, inutilis, bonus, salūber, salūtāris, fructuosus; calamitōsus, damnōsus, funestus, noxius, pestifer, perniciōsus, exitiōsus:—amīcus, benevŏlus, cārus, familiāris, aequus, fidus, fidēlis, propitius, secundus; inimīcus, adversus, aemulus, aliēnus, contrarius, infestus, infidus, iniquus, irātus;—aptus, accommŏdātus, apposĭtus, habĭlis, idoneus, opportūnus; ineptus, inhabĭlis, importūnus, inconvēniens;—aequālis, par, impar, dispar, similis, dissimilis, abstmilis, discŏlor:—prōnus, proclivis, propensus, promptus, parātus:—facĭlis, difficĭlis:— apertus, conspicuus, manifestus, perspicuus, obscūrus, certus, compertus, nōtus, ambiguus, dubius, ignōtus, incertus, insolĭtus;—vicīnus, finitĭmus, confinis, contermĭnus, propior, proxĭmus, cognātus, concŏlor, concors, congruus, consanguineus, consentāneus, consŏnus, convēniens, contiguus, continuus, continens.*

(b.) Many adjectives of other significations, including some compounds of *ob, sub,* and *super,* as *obnoxius, obvius, subjectus, supplex,* and *superstes,* are also followed by a dative of the object.

(c.) After verbals in *bilis,* the dative is usually rendered by the preposition *by;* as, *Tibi credibilis sermo,* A speech credible to you, i. e. worthy to be believed by you. Ovid.

(d.) The expression *dicto audiens,* signifying obedient, is followed by the dative; as, *Syracūsāni nobis dicto audientes sunt.* Cic. *Audiens dicto fuit jussis magistrātuum.* Nep. In this phrase, *dicto* is a dative limiting *audiens,* and the words *dicto audiens* seem to form a compound equivalent to *obēdiens,* and, like that, followed by a dative; thus, *Nec plebi nōbis dicto audiens atque obēdiens sit.* Liv. So *dicto obēdiens;* as, *Futūra es dicto obēdiens, annon, patri?* Plaut.

REM. 2. (a.) The adjectives *aequālis, affinis, aliēnus, cognōmĭnis, commūnis, contrārius, fīnis, insuētus, par, dispar, peculiāris, proprius, propinquus, sacer, similis, assimilis, consimilis, dissimilis, socius, vicīnus, superstes, supplex,* and some others, instead of a dative of the object, are sometimes followed by a genitive; as, *Par hujus,* Equal to him. Lucan. *Proprium est oratoris ornate dicere.* Cic. But most of these words, when thus used, seem rather to be taken substantively; as, *Aequālis ejus,* His contemporary. Cic.

(b.) *Similis, assimilis, consimilis, dissimilis, par* and *dispar,* take the genitive, when an internal resemblance, or a resemblance in character or disposition, is to be expressed, and hence we always find *mei, tui, sui, nostri, vestri, similis;* as, *Plūres reges Romuli quam Numae similes.* Liv.

(c.) *Amīcus, inimīcus,* and *familiāris,* owing to their character as substantives, take a genitive even in the superlative; as, *Homo amicissimus nostrōrum hŏminum,*—very friendly to our countrymen. Cic. On the other hand, *hostis,* though a substantive, is sometimes used like an adjective, being modified by an adverb, and taking an object in the dative; as, *Exspectantibus omnibus quisnam esset tam impius, tam demens, tam diis hominibusque* hostis, *qui*, etc. Cf. § 277, R. 1.

REM. 3. Some adjectives with the dative are followed by another case denoting a different relation; as, *Mens sibi conscia* recti, A mind conscious to itself of rectitude. Virg. See § 213, R. 7.

REM. 4. Many adjectives, instead of the dative of the object, are often followed by an accusative with a preposition.

(1.) Adjectives signifying useful, fit, and the opposite, take an accusative of the thing with *ad*, but only a dative of the person; as, *Homo* ad *nullam* rem *utilis*. Cic. *Locus aptus* ad insidias. Id.

(2.) Adjectives denoting motion or tendency, take an accusative with *ad* more frequently than a dative; as, *Piger* ad *poenas*, ad *praemia velox*, Ovid; Ad *aliquem* morbum *proclivior*, Cic.; Ad *omne* facinus *paratus*, Id.; *Pronus* ad fidem, Liv.;—sometimes with *in*; as, *Celer* in pugnam. Sil.

(3.) Many adjectives, signifying an affection of the mind, may have an accusative of the object with *in*, *erga*, or *adversus*, instead of the dative; as, *Fidelis* in filios. Just. *Mater acerba* in *suos* partus. Ovid. *Gratus* erga me. Cic. *Gratum* adversus te. Id. So *Dissimilis* in dominum. Tac.

(4.) Adjectives signifying like, equal, common, etc., when plural, are often followed by the accusative with *inter*; as, Inter se *similes*. Cic. Hæc sunt inter eos *communia*. Id. Inter se *diversi*. Id.

REM. 5. *Propior* and *proximus*, instead of the dative, have sometimes, like their primitive *prope*, an accusative; as, *Quod vitium propius* virtutem *erat*. Sall. *P. Crassus proximus* mare Oceanum *hiemarat*. Cæs. *Ager, qui proximus* finem *Megalopolitarum est*. Liv. Cf. § 238, 1.

REM. 6. (*a*.) Some adjectives, instead of the dative, have at times an ablative with a preposition. Thus, *par, communis, consentaneus, discors,* with *cum*; as, *Quem parem* cum liberis *fecisti*. Sall. *Consentaneum* cum iis litteris. Cic. *Civibus* secum *discors*. Liv. So *alienus* and *diversus* with *a* or *ab*; as, *Alienus* a me, Ter.; A *ratione diversus*, Cic.; or without a preposition; as, *Alienum nostra* amicitia. Id.—(*b.*) *Fretus*, which regularly takes the ablative, is in Livy construed with the dative; as, *fortunae fretus*; nulli rei *fretus*, etc. Cf. § 244.—(*c.*) The participial adjectives *junctus* and *conjunctus*, instead of the dative, take sometimes the ablative either with or without *cum*.

REM. 7. *Idem* is sometimes followed by the dative, chiefly in the poets, as *Jupiter* omnibus *idem*. Virg. *Invitum qui servat, idem facit* occidenti. Hor In the first example, *omnibus* is a dative of the object; in the second, the dative follows *idem*, in imitation of the Greek construction with αὐτός and is equivalent to *quod occidens*, or *quod facit is, qui occidit*. *Similis* is construed in the same manner in Hor. Sat. 1, 3, 122. *Idem* is generally followed not by a case, but by *qui, ac, atque, ut, quasi,* or *quam*; sometimes by the preposition *cum*. Cf. § 207, R. 27, (*d.*) *Similis* and *par* are sometimes, like *idem*, followed by *ac* and *atque*.

REM. 8. Some verbal substantives are followed by the dative, when derived from verbs governing the dative; as, *Justitia est obtemperatio* scriptis legibus institutisque *populorum*. Cic. *Traditio alicujus rei* alteri. Id. *Exprobratio* cuiquam *veteris fortunae*. Liv.

NOTE. A dative of the object often follows *esse* and other verbs, in connection with a predicate nominative or accusative, but such dative is dependent, not on the noun, but on the verb Cf. § 227, R. 4

DATIVE AFTER VERBS.

§ 223. A noun limiting the meaning of a verb, is put in the dative, to denote the *object to* or *for* which any thing is, or is done; as,

Mea domus tibi patet, My house is open *to you.* Cic. *Pars optāre locum tecto,* A part choose a site *for a building.* Virg. *Tibi sēris, tibi mētis,* You sow *for yourself,* you reap *for yourself.* Plaut. *Licet nemini contra patriam ducēre exercitum,* It is not lawful *for any one* to lead an army against his country. Cic. *Hoc tibi promitto,* I promise *you* this. Id. *Hæret lateri letalis arundo.* Virg. *Surdo fabulam narras.* Hor. *Mihi responsum dedit.* Virg. *Sic vos non vobis fertis aratra, bōves.* Id. *Omnibus bonis expedit salvam esse rempublicam.* Cic. *Aptat habendo ensem.* Virg.

NOTE. The dative is thus used after all verbs, whether transitive or intransitive, personal or impersonal, and in both voices, provided their signification admits a reference to a remoter object, for whom or to whose benefit or injury any thing is done. In the passive voice, from their nature, neuter verbs can only be so construed impersonally. Cf. § 142, 1, and § 222, 2.

REMARK 1. The dative after many verbs is rendered not by *to* or *for,* but by other prepositions, or without a preposition. Many intransitive Latin verbs are translated into English by verbs transitive, and the dative after them is usually rendered like the object of a transitive verb.—Most verbs after which the signs *to* and *for* are not used with the dative, are enumerated in this and the following sections.

REM. 2. Many verbs signifying to favor, please, trust, assist, and their contraries, also to command, obey, serve, resist, threaten, and be angry, take a dative of the object.

NOTE. The neuter verbs comprehended in this rule generally express in the verbal form the meaning of those adjectives, which are followed by the dative, (cf. § 222, R. 1,) Thus, (a.) *Illa tibi favet,* She favors *you,* or is favorable *to you.* Ovid. *Mihi placēbat Pompeius, minime displicēbat.* Cic. *Qui sibi fidit.* Hor. *Non licet sui commodi causā nocēre altēri.* Cic. *Non invidētur illi ætāti sed etiam favētur.* Id. *Desperat saluti suæ.* Id. *Neque mihi vestra decrēta auxiliantur.* Sall. *Imperat aut servit collecta pecūnia cuique.* Hor. *Obedire et parēre voluntāti.* Cic. *Quoniam factiōni inimicorum resistēre nequivērit.* Sall. *Mihi minabātur.* Cic. *Irasci inimicis.* Cæs.

(b.) So *Adūlor, assentior, blandior, commodo, faveo, gratificor, grator, gratūlor,* and its verbal *gratulabundus, ignosco, indulgeo, lenocinor, palpor, parco, plaudo, respondeo, studeo, supparasitor; æmulor, incommodo, invideo, noceo, obsum, officio;—arrideo, placeo; displiceo;—credo, fido, confido; despero, diffīdo;—administror, auxilior, medeor, medicor, opitūlor, patrocinor, prosum, subvěnio, succurro; desum, insidior;—impero, mando, moderor, præcipio, tempero; ausculto, morigeror, obedio, obsecundo, obsequor, obtempero, pareo, dicto audiens sum;—ancillor, famulor, ministro, servio, inservio, præstolor;—adversor, refrāgor, obsto, obtrecto, reluctor, renitor, repugno, resisto,* and, chiefly in the poets, *bello, certo, luctor, pugno;—minor, comminor, interminor;—irascor, succenseo, stomāchor.*—To these may be added *æquo, adæquo, convicior, degenero, excello, nubo, suppedito, prævaricor, recipio* (to promise), *renuncio, suadeo, persuadeo, dissuadeo, supplico, vaco, video,* and sometimes *misceo* and *lātēo*:—also the impersonals *accidit, convenit, conducit, contingit, decet, dolet, expedit, libet, licet,* or *lubet, liquet, placet,* etc.—(c.) Intransitive verbs governing a dative are often used impersonally in the passive with the same case; as, *mihi invidētur,* I am envied. *Mihi maledicitur,* I am reviled. *Mihi parcitur,* I am spared. Hor. *Hoc persuadētur mihi,* I am persuaded of this.

(1,) (a.) Many of the above verbs, which, as intransitive, take the dative, sometimes become transitive and are followed by an accusative; as, *adulor, ausculto, blandior, degenero, despero, indulgeo, lateo, medeor, medicor, moderor, obtrecto, præstolor, provideo,* etc.; as, *Adulāri aliquem.* Cic. *Hanc cave degeneres.* Ovid. *Indulgeo me.* Ter. *Hujus adventum præstolans.* Cæs. *Providēre rem frumentariam.* Id.—Sometimes also by a preposition and the ablative or accusative; as, A Stoicis *degenerāvit Panætius.* Cic. *De republica despērāre.* Id. *Obtrectārunt inter se.* Nep.—or by a dependent clause; as, *Quæ desperat tractatu n'essēre posse, relinquit.* Hor.

(b.) Others, as transitive verbs, have, with the dative, an accusative, expressed or understood; as, *impĕro, mando, ministro, minor, comminor, interminor, præcipio, rĕcipio, rēnuncio*, etc.; as, Equĭtes *impĕrat civĭtātĭbus*; where *cōgendos* is perhaps to be supplied, He enjoins upon the states the providing of cavalry. Cæs. See § 274, R. 5. *Ministrāre* victum *alĭcui*. Varr. Dēflagrātĭŏnem *urbi et Itălĭæ tōti mĭnābātur*. Cic.

(c.) *Æquo* and *ădæquo* are construed with the accusative and either the dative or *cum* with the ablative.—*Invĭdeo* takes either a single dative of the person or thing, a dative of the person and an accusative of the thing; as, *Honōrem mihi invĭdent*. Hor.; or, when *invĭdĕre* is used in the sense of *privāre*, a dative of the person and an ablative of the thing; as, *Non invīdērunt laude suā muliĕrĭbus*. Liv. In Horace, by a Greek construction, the genitive is once used instead of the accusative or ablative of the thing; as, *Neque ille sēpŏsĭti cicĕri, nec longæ invĭdet ăvēnæ*.

(d.) *Cēdo*, used transitively, takes a dative of the person and an accusative of the thing; but sometimes the thing is expressed by the ablative; as, *cēdĕre alĭcui possessĭōne hortōrum*. So, also, *concēdo tibi lŏcum*, or *concēdo tibi lŏco*.

(2.) Many verbs which, from their significations, might be included in the above classes, are, as transitive verbs, only followed by an accusative; as, *dēlecto, jŭvo, adjŭvo, adjŭto, lædo, offendo*, etc.—*Jŭbeo* is followed by the accusative with an infinitive, and sometimes by the accusative alone, or the dative with the infinitive or subjunctive; as, *Jŭbeo te bĕne spĕrāre*. Cic. *Lex jŭbet ea quæ făcienda sunt*. Id. *Ubi Brĭtannĭco jussit exsurgĕre*. Tac. Quĭbus *jussĕrat, ut instantĭbus rĕsistĕrent*. Id.—*Fido* and *confido* are often followed by the ablative, with or without a preposition; as, *Fidĕre* cursu. Ovid. Cf. § 245.

§ 224.

Many verbs compounded with these eleven prepositions, *ăd, antĕ, cŏn, ĭn, intĕr, ŏb, post, præ, prō, sŭb*, and *sŭpĕr*, are followed by the dative; as,

Annue cœptis, Be favorable to our *undertakings*. Virg. *Rōmānis equĭtĭbus lĭtĕræ affĕruntur*, Letters are brought *to the Roman knights*. Cic. *Antĕcellĕre omnĭbus*, To excel *all*. Id. *Antĕtŭlit* iræ *rĕlĭgĭōnem*. Nep. *Audetque* viris *concurrĕre virgo*. Virg. *Exercĭtum* exercĭtui, *dŭces* dūcĭbus *compărāre*. Liv. *Imminet* his *aĕr*. Ovid. *Pĕcŏri signum impressit*. Virg. *Nox* prælio *intervĕnit*. Liv. *Interdixit* histrĭōnĭbus *scēnam*. Suet. Meis *commŏdis offĭcis et obstas*. Cic. *Cum se hostium* telis *objĕcissent*. Id. *Posthăbui mea sĕria* lūdo. Virg. *Certāmĭni præsēdit*. Suet. Hibernis *Labiēnum præpŏsuit*. Cæs. Genĭbus *prōcumbĕre*. Ovid. Misĕris *succurrĕre disco*. Virg. Iis *subsĭdia submittĭbat*. Cæs. Timĭdis *supervĕnit Ægle*. Virg.

NOTE 1. This rule implies that the compound retains the meaning of the preposition; and the dative following such compound is then used instead of the case governed by the preposition. When such compounds are transitive they have with the dative an accusative also, like other transitive verbs.

1. *Accēdo, accresco, accumbo, acquiesco, ădæquĭto, adhæreo, adjăceo, adno, adnăto, adsto, adstĭpŭlor, adsum, adversor, affulgeo, allăbor, allūdo, annuo, appāreo, applaude, appropinquo, arrēpo, arrīdeo, aspīro, assentior, assĭdeo, assisto, assuesco, assurgo;—addo, adhĭbeo, adjĭcio, adjungo, admŏveo, adverto, advolvo, affero, affĭgo, allĭgo, appōno, applĭco, aspergo*.

2. *Antĕcēdo, antĕcello, antĕeo, antesto, antĕvĕnio, antĕverto;—antĕfĕro, antĕhăbeo, antĕpōno*.

3. *Cŏhæreo, collūdo, concĭno, congruo, consentio, consŏno, consuesco, convīvo, and*, chiefly in the poets, *coëo, concumbo, concurro, contendo;—confĕro, conjungo, compăro, compōno*.

4. *Incīdo, incŭbo, incumbo, indormio, ingĕmisco, inhæreo, inhĭo, innascor, inultor, insĭdeo, insisto, insto, insulto, insulto, invādo, invigĭlo, illacrĭmo, illūdo, immĭneo, immŏrior, immŏror, impendeo, insum;—immisceo, impertio, impōno, imprĭmo, incĭdo, inclūdo, induo, infĕro, ingĕro, injĭcio, insĕro, inspergo, insuesco, intro*.

5. *Intercēdo, interclūdo, interclūdo, interjăceo, intermīco, intersum, intervĕnio;—interjĭcio, interjĭcio, interpōno*

§ 225.   SYNTAX.—DATIVE AFTER VERBS.   227

6. *Obambŭlo, ŏberro, ŏbĕquĭto, obluctor, obmurmŭro, obrēpo, ohsto, obsisto, obstrēpo, obsum, obtrecto, obvĕnio, obversor, occumbo, occurro, occurso, officio;—obĭuco, objĭcio, offĕro, offundo, oppōno.*
7. *Pı̆stfĕro, posthăbeo, postpōno, postpŭto, postscrĭbo.*
8. *Præcēdo, præcurro, præeo, prælūceo, præmineo, prænĭteo, præsĭdeo, præsum, prævăleo, prævertor;—præfĕro, præficio, præpōno.*
9. *Prŏcumbo, prŏficio, prōpugno, prospicio, prōvideo.*
10. *Succēdo, succresco, succumbo, succurro, sufficio, suffrăgor, subŏleo, subjăceo, subrēpo, subsum, subvĕnio;—subdo, subjĭcio, subjŭgo, submitto, suppōno, substerno.*
11. *Supercurro, superstо, supersum, supervĕnio, supervivo.*

Note 2. In some verbs compounded with prepositions the meaning of the preposition is lost. Such compounds are either not followed by a dative, or the case depends, not on the preposition, but on the signification of the verb. according to § 223.

Remark 1. (a.) Some verbs, compounded with *ăb, dē, ex, circum,* and *contrā,* are occasionally followed by the dative; as, *absum, dēsum, dēlabor, despēro, excĭdo, circumdo, circumfundo, circumjăceo, circumjĭcio, contrādĭco, contrauo;* as, *Serta căpiti dīlapsa,* The garlands having fallen from his head. Virg. *Numqui nummi excĭdērunt tibi?* Plaut. *Tigris urbi circumfundĭtur.* Plin. *Sibi despērans.* Cæs.—(b.) *Circumdo* and *circumfundo* take either an accusative of the thing with a dative of the person, or an ablative of the thing with an accusative of the person; as, *circumdo dŭcui custōdias,* or *circumdo ălĭquem custōdiis. Aspergo, inspergo, dōno, impertio, exuo,* and *induo,* are construed in the same manner. Cf. § 251, R. 2.

Rem. 2. Some verbs of repelling and taking away (most of which are compounds of *ăb, dē,* or *ex*), are sometimes followed by the dative, though more commonly by the ablative; as, *abĭgo, abrŏgo, abscindo, aufĕro, adĭmo, arceo, dēfendo, dēmo, dēpello, dērŏgo, dētrăho, erĭpio, ĕruo, excŭtio, exĭmo, extorqueo, extrăho, exuo, prōhĭbeo, surrĭpio.* Thus, *Nec mihi te ĕripient,* Nor shall they take you from me. Ovid. *Solstitium pĕcŏri dēfendĭte.* Virg. *Hunc arcēbis pĕcŏri.* Id. So rarely *abrumpo, aliēno, fŭror,* and *răpio.*

Rem. 3. Some verbs of differing (compounds of *dī* or *dis*) likewise occur with the dative, instead of the ablative with the preposition *ăb,* or poetically with the ablative alone; as, *differo, discrēpo, discordo, dissentio, dissĭdeo, disto;* as, *Quantum simplex hilărisque nepōti discrēpet, et quantum discordet, parcus ăvāro.* Hor. *Distăbit infīdo scurræ amĭcus.* Hor. *Græcis Tusculanæ statuæ differunt.* Quint. *Cōmœdia differt sermōni.* Hor. So likewise *misceo;* as, *Mista mŏdestiæ grăvitas.* Cic.

Rem. 4. Many verbs compounded with prepositions, especially with *ad, con,* and *in,* instead of the dative, either constantly or occasionally take the case of the preposition, which is frequently repeated. Sometimes, also, a preposition of similar signification is used; as, *Ad primām vōcem timĭdas advertĭtis aures.* Ovid. *Nēmo eum antĕcessit.* Nep. *Saxa vides sōla coalescĕre calce.* Lucr. *Infĕrunt omnia* in ignem. Cæs. *Silex incumbēbat* ad amnem. Virg. *Innīxus mŏtĕrāmĭne nāvis.* Ovid. In Pansam *frătrem innīxus.* Plin. *Confertе hanc pācem* cum illo bello. Cic. In this substitution of one preposition for another, *ad* is used for *in,* and *in* for *ad; ăb* for *ex; ăd, antĕ, contrā,* and *in,* for *ŏb; ad* and *antĕ,* for *pro.*

Rem. 5. Neuter verbs of motion or of rest in a place, when compounded with the prepositions, *ăd, antĕ, cŏn, in,* etc., either take the dative, or, acquiring an active signification, are followed by the accusative; as, *Helvētii rělĭquos Gallos virtūte præcēdunt,* The Helvetii surpass the other Gauls in valor. Cæs. *Ŭterque,* Isocrătem *ætāte præcurrit.* Cic. So *præeo, præsto, præverto, præcello.* See § 233. (3.)

§ 225. I. Verbs compounded with *sătis, bĕne,* and *mălĕ,* are followed by the dative; as,

Et natūrae et lēgĭbus sătisfēcit, He satisfied both nature and the laws. Cic. *Tĭbi dii bĕnĕfăciant omnes,* May all the gods bless you. Plaut. But also, *Amīcum ergā bĕne fēci.* Id. *Mălĕdīcit utrīque.* Hor. So *sătisdo, bĕnĕdīco, mălĕfăcio*.

NOTE. These compounds are often written separately; and the dative always depends not on *sătis, bĕne,* and *mălĕ,* but on the simple verb. So, also, *bĕne* and *mălĕ ălĭcui vōlo;* as, Tĭbi bĕne *ex ănĭmo* vōlo. Ter. Illi *ĕgo ex omnĭbus* optĭme vōlo. Plaut. *Non tĭbi male* vult. Petron. In like manner *vălēre dīco,* aud *văle dīco;* as, *Augustus discēdens e cūriā) sĕdentĭbus singŭlis vălēre dīcēbat.* Suet. Tĭbi *valēdīcēre non licet grātis.* Sen.—In late writers *bĕnĕdĭco* and *mălĕdĭco* sometimes take the accusative.

II. Verbs in the passive voice are sometimes followed by a dative of the agent, chiefly in the poets and the later prose writers; as, *Quidquid in hac causā mihi susceptum est.* Cic. *Neque cernĭtur* ulli, Nor is he seen by any one. Virg. *Nulla tuārum audīta* mihi *nĕque visa sŏrōrum.* Id. *Barbărus hic ĕgo sum, quia non intellĭgor* ulli. Ovid. But the agent after passives is usually in the ablative with *a* or *ab.* See § 248, I.

III. The participle in *dus* is followed by a dative of the agent; as,

Unda omnĭbus *ĕnāvīganda,* The wave over which (we) all must pass. Hor. *Nōbis, cum sĕmel occĭdit brĕvis lux, Nox est perpĕtua ūna dormienda.* Catull. *Adhĭbenda est* nōbis *dīlĭgentia,* We must use diligence. Cic. *Vestĭgia summōrum hŏmĭnum* sibi *tuenda esse dīcit.* Id. *Si vis me flēre, dŏlendum est prīmum* ipsi tibi. Hor. *Făciendum* mihi *pŭtāvi, ut respondērem.* Id.

REMARK 1. The dative is sometimes wanting when the agent is indefinite; as, *Ōrandum est, ut sit mens sāna in corpŏre sāno.* Juv. *Hic vincendum aut mŏriendum, mīlĭtes, est.* Liv. In such examples, *tibi, vōbis, nōbis, hŏmĭnibus,* etc., may be supplied. Cf. § 141, R. 2.

REM. 2. The participle in *dus* sometimes, though rarely, has, instead of the dative of the agent, an ablative with *ā* or *ăb;* as, *Non eos in deōrum immortālium numĕro vĕnĕrandos* a vōbis *et cŏlendŏs pŭtātŭs?* Cic. *Hæc a me in dīcendo præ- tĕreunda non sunt.* Id.—The dative after participles in *dus* is by some referred to § 226.

IV. Verbs signifying *motion* or *tendency* are followed by an accusative with *ăd* or *in;* as,

Ad templum *Pallădis ībant.* Virg. Ad prætōrem *hŏmĭnem traxit.* Cic. *Vergit* ad septemtriōnes. Cæs. In conspectum *vĕnīre.* Nep.

So *curro, dūco, fĕro, festīno, fŭgio, inclīno, lĕgo, mitto, pergo, porto, præcĭpĭto, prŏpĕro, tendo, tollo, vădo, verto.*

REMARK 1. So likewise verbs of *calling, exciting,* etc.; as, *Eorum* ad se *vŏcat.* Virg. *Prōvŏcasse* ad pugnam. Cic. So *ănĭmo, hortor, incĭto, invīto, lăcesso, stĭmŭlo, suscĭto;* to which may be added *attĭneo, conformo, pertĭneo,* and *specto.*

REM. 2. But the dative is sometimes used after these verbs; as, *Clāmor it* cœlo. Virg. *Dum* tĭbi *lītĕrœ meæ vĕniant.* Cic. *Grĕgem vĭrĭdi compellĕre* hĭbisco. Virg. *Sēdĭbus hunc rĕfer ante suis.* Id. After *vĕnio* both constructions are used at the same time; as, *Vēnit* mihi in mentem. Cic. *Vēnit* mihi in suspĭciōnem. Nep. *Eum vēnisse* Germānis in ămīcĭtiam *cognōvĕrat.* Cæs. *Prŏ- pinquo* (to approach) takes the dative only.

REM. 3. Sometimes also verbs signifying motion are followed by an accusative of place without a preposition, a supine in *um,* an infinitive, or an adverb of place; as, Rōmam *prŏfectus est. Ite* dōmum. Rus *ībam.* Lāvīnia *vēnit* lītŏra. Virg. *Neque ĕgo te* dērīsum *vĕnio.* Plaut. *Non nos Libўcos* pŏpŭlāre *pĕnātes vĕnīmus.* Virg. Huc *rĕnit.* Plaut. See §§ 237, 276, II. 271, N. 2.

REM. 4. After *do, scrībo,* or *mitto lītĕras,* the person for whom they are written or to whom they are sent, is put either in the dative or in the accusative with *ad;* as, *Ex eo lŏco* tĭbi *lītĕras ante dĕdĕrāmus.* Cic. *Vulturcius lītĕras sibi* ad Catilīnam *dătas esse, dīcēbat*. Id. *Caesar scrībit* Labiēno *cum*, etc. Caes Ad me *Curius de te scripsit*. Cic. But to give one a letter to deliver is also expressed by *dăre lĭtĕras ălĭcui*, and also the delivery of the letter by the bearer.

§ 226. *Est* is followed by a dative denoting a *possessor*;— the thing possessed being the subject of the verb.

Est thus used may generally be translated by the verb *to have* with the dative as its subject; as, *Est mihi dŏmi păter*, I have a father at home. Virg *Sunt* nōbis *mĭtia pōma*, We have mellow apples. Id. *Grātĭa* nōbis *ŏpus est tuā*, We have need of your favor. Cic. *Innŏcentĭae plus pĕrīcŭli quam hŏnōris est*. Sall. *An nescis longas rēgibus esse mănus?* Ovid. So with an infinitive as the subject, *Nec tibi sit dūros ăcuisse in praelia dentes*. Tib. 4, 3, 3. The first and second persons of *sum* are not thus construed.

REMARK 1. Hence *mihi est nōmen* signifies, I have the name, my name is, or I am called. The proper name is put either in the nominative, the dative, or the genitive. See § 204, R. 8. So also *cognōmen, cognōmentum*, and, in Tacitus, *vŏcābŭlum, est mihi*.—Sometimes, also, a possessive adjective agreeing with *nōmen*, etc., supplies the place of the proper name; as, *Est mihi nōmen* Tarquinium. Gell. *Mercŭrĭāle impŏsuĕre mihi cognōmen*. Hor.

REM. 2. The dative is used with a similar signification after *fŏre, suppĕtit, ăbest, deest*, and *dēfit*; as, *Pauper ĕnim non est*, cui *rērum suppĕtit ūsus*. Hor. *Si mihi caula fŏret, cercōpĭthēcus ĕram*. Mart. *Dēfŭit ars vōbis*. Ovid. *Non dēfŏre* Arsăcĭdis *virtūtem*. Tac. *Lac mihi non dēfit*. Virg. *Hoc ūnum illi abfuit*. Cic.

REM. 3. With the dative of the person after *est* Sallust and Tacitus sometimes join, by a Greek idiom, *vŏlens, căpiens*, and *invītus*; as, *Quia nĕque plēbi mīlĭtĭa vŏlentī* (esse) *pŭtābātur*, Because the common people were not thought to like the war. Sall. *Ut quibusque bellum invitis aut căpientĭbus ĕrat*, According as each liked or disliked the war. Tac.

DATIVE OF THE END OR PURPOSE.

§ 227. *Sum*, and several other verbs, are followed by two datives, one of which denotes the *object to which*, the other the *end for which*, any thing is, or is done; as,

Mihi *maxĭmae est cūrae*, It is a very great care to me. Cic. *Spēro* nōbis *hanc conjunctiōnem* vŏluptāti *fŏre*, I hope this union will afford us pleasure. Id. Mātri *puellam* dōno *dĕdit*. Ter. Fābio laudi *dătum est*. Cic. Vĭtio *id* tibi vertunt. Plaut. *Id* tibi hŏnōri *hăbētur*. Cic. *Mātūrāvit* collēgae vĕnīre auxĭlio. Liv Cui bŏno *fuit?* To whom was it an advantage? Cic.

REMARK 1. The verbs after which two datives occur, are *sum, fŏre, flo, do, dōno, dūco, hăbeo, rĕlinquo, trĭbuo, verto*; also *curro, eo, mitto, prŏficiscor, vĕnio, appōno, assigno, cēdo, comparo, pateo, suppĕdĭto, ĕmo*, and some others.

REM. 2. The dative of the *end* or *purpose* is often used after these verbs, without the dative of the object; as,

Exemplo est formīca, The ant is (serves for) an example. Hor. *Absentium bŏna dīvīsui fuĕre*. Liv. *Rĕlĭquit* pignōri *pŭtāmĭna*. Plaut. *Quae ēsui et pōtui sunt*. Gell. *Esse dĕrīsui*, To be a subject of ridicule. Tac. *Receptui cănĕre*, To sound a retreat. Caes. *Alĭquid dōti dĭcāre*, To set out as dowry. Cic.

REM. 3. (a.) The verb *sum*, with a dative of the end, may be variously rendered; as by the words *brings, affords, serves, does*, etc The sign *for* is often omitted with this dative, especially after *sum* instead of it, *as*, or some other particle, may at times be used; as,

Ignāvia ĕrit tibi *magno dēdĕcŏri,* Cowardice will bring great disgrace to you.
Cic. *Hæc res est* argumento, This thing is an argument, or serves as an argument. Id. *Hoc vitio mihi dant,* This they set down as a fault in me. *Universos cūræ hăbuit.* Suet. *Una res ĕrat magno* ūsui. .... was of great use.
Lucil. *Quod* tibi *magnŏpĕre* cordi *est, mihi vĕhĕmenter displicet,* What is a great pleasure, an object of peculiar interest to you, etc. Id.

(*b.*) Sometimes the words *fit, able, ready,* etc., must be supplied, especially before a gerund or a gerundive; as, *Quum* solvendo *civĭtātes non essent, ...* not able to pay. Cic. *Divites, qui ŏnĕri* fĕrendo *essent.* Liv. *Quæ* restinguendo igni *fŏrent.* Liv. *Rădix ejus est* vescendo. Plin.

REM. 4. Instead of the dative of the end, a predicate nominative or accusative is sometimes used; as, *Nātūrā tu illi* pāter *es,* By nature you are his father. *Amor est* exitium *pĕcŏri* : or the purpose is expressed by the accusative with *ad* or *in* ; as, *Alicui cōmes est ad bellum.* Cic. *Se Rēmis* in clientēlam *dicābant.* Cæs.: or by the ablative with *pro* ; as, *Innŏcentia* pro *mālĭvŏlentiā dūci cœpit.* Sall. *Alcĭbus sunt arbŏres* pro cŭbīlĭbus. Cæs.

REM. 5. Instead, also, of the dative of the end or purpose, *quo ?* to what end ? for what purpose ? why ? sometimes occurs, with an accusative, which generally depends on a verb understood, or with an infinitive or a clause ; as, Quo *mihi* fortūnam, *si non concēditur ūti ?* Hor. Quo *tibi, Pasiphaë, prĕtiōsas sūmĕre* vestes ? Ovid.

REM. 6. After *do* and other similar active verbs an accusative of the purpose is found in apposition; as, *Lătini cŏrōnam auream Jŏvi* dōnum in *Căpĭtōlium mittunt.* Liv. *Alicui* cōmĭtem *esse dătum.* Cic. Cf. § 204, R. 1; and § 230, R. 2.

NOTE. The dative, instead of the accusative, is sometimes used after the infinitive, when a dative precedes, and the subject of the infinitive is omitted; as, *Vōbis nĕcesse est fŏrtĭbus esse* viris. Liv. *Maximo tibi et* civi *et* dūci *ēvādĕre contĭgit.* Val. Max. See §§ 205, R. 6, and 239, R. 1.

DATIVE AFTER PARTICLES.

§ 228. Some particles are followed by the dative of the object ; as,

1. Some adverbs derived from adjectives; as,

Prŏpius Tibĕri *quam* Thermŏpȳlis. Nep. *Proxime* castris, Very near to the camp. Cæs. *Prŏpius* stăbŭlis *armenta tĕnērent.* Virg. *Congruenter* nātūræ, *convĕnienterque vivĕre,* Agreeably to nature. Cic. *Epicūrus quam* sibi *constanter convĕnienterque dicat, um lăbōrat.* Id. Nēmĭni *nimium bĕne est.* Afran. *Mihi nunquam in vitā fuit mēlius.* Hor. *Vivĕre* vitæ *hŏmĭnum amice.* Cic. *Bĕne* mihi, *bĕne* vōbis. Plaut. So, Mihi *obviam vĕnisti.* Cic. *In certāmĭna suevo commĭnus ire viro.* Sil. *Quæstōres prŏvinciæ* mihi *præsto fuĕrunt.* Cic. *Samos est* exadversum Milēto. App.

REMARK. *Prŏpius* and *proxime,* like their primitive *prŏpe,* are sometimes construed with *a* and the ablative; as, *Prŏpe* a meis *ædibus.* Cic. *Stellæ errantes* prŏpius a terris. Id. A Surā proxime *est Philiscum, oppidum Parthōrum.* Plin.

2. Certain prepositions, especially in comic writers; as, *Mihi clam est,* It is unknown to me. Plaut. *Contra nōbis.* Id. But in such instances they seem rather to be used like adjectives.

3. Certain interjections; as, *Hei mihi !* Ah me! Virg. *Væ mihi !* Wo is me! Ter. *Væ victis esse !* Liv. *Væ misĕro mihi.* Plaut. *Hem tibi.* Id. *Ecce tibi.* Cic.

NOTE. (*a.*) The dative of the substantive pronouns seems sometimes nearly redundant, but it always conveys the expression of a lively feeling, and is therefore termed *dătivus ĕthĭcus ;* as,

Fur mihi *es* .... in my opinion. Plaut. *An ille* mihi *liber, cui mulier imperat?* Cic. *Tongilium* mihi *eduxit.* Id. *Ubi nunc* nobis *deus ille magister?* Virg. *Ecce* tibi *Sebōsus!* Cic. *Hem* tibi *talentum argenti! Philippium est.* Plaut. *Sibi* is sometimes subjoined quite pleonastically to *suus*; as, *Suo sibi gladio hunc jugulo.* Plaut. *Ignorans* suo sibi *servit patri.* Id. *Sibi suo tempore.*

(b.) The following phrases also occur with *volo* and a reflexive pronoun: *quid tibi vis?* what do you want? *quid sibi iste vult?* what does he want? *quid vult sibi haec ōrātio?* what does this speech mean? *quid haec sibi dōna volunt?* what is the meaning of these presents? or, what is their object?

ACCUSATIVE.

ACCUSATIVE AFTER VERBS.

§ 229. The object of a transitive verb is put in the accusative; as,

Lēgātos *mittunt*, They send ambassadors. Caes. *Animus mŏvet* corpus, The mind moves the body. Cic. *Da* vēniam hanc, Grant this favor. Ter. Eum *imitāti sunt*, They imitated him. Cic. Piscem *Syri vĕnĕrantur.* Id.

REMARK 1. A transitive verb, with the accusative, often takes a genitive, dative, or ablative, to express some additional relation; as,

Te convinco āmentiae, I convict you of madness. Cic. *Da* lŏcum meliōrĭbus, Give place to your betters. Ter. *Solvit se Teucria* luctu, Troy frees herself from grief. Virg. See those cases respectively.

REM. 2. Such is the difference of idiom between the Latin and English languages, that many verbs considered transitive in one, are used as intransitive in the other. Hence, in translating transitive Latin verbs, a preposition must often be supplied in English; as, *Ut me cāvēret,* That he should beware of me. Cic. On the other hand, many verbs, which in Latin are intransitive, and do not take an accusative, are rendered into English by transitive verbs; as, *Ille mihi fāvet,* He favors me: and many verbs originally intransitive acquire a transitive signification.

REM. 3. The verb is sometimes omitted:—

1. To avoid its repetition; as, *Eventum senātus, quem* (scil. *dāre*) *vidēbĭtur, dăbit.* Liv.

2. The interrogative interjection *quid?* what? depends on *ais* or *censes.* So also *quid vēro? quid igitur? quid ergo? quid enim?* which are always followed by another question, and both questions may be united into one proposition, the first serving merely to introduce the interrogation. With *quid postea? quid tum?* supply *sĕquĭtur.* With *quid quod,* occurring in transitions, *dicam de eo* is omitted, but it may be rendered 'nay,' 'nay even,' 'but now,' 'moreover,' etc., without an interrogation.—*Dicam* is also to be supplied with *quid multa? quid plūra? ne multa; ne multis; ne plūra.* The infinitive *dicĕre* is also sometimes omitted; as, *Nimis multa videor de me.* Cic. *Perge rĕliqua.* Id.

REM. 4. The accusative is often omitted:—

1. When it is a reflexive pronoun; as, *Nox praecipĭtat,* scil. *se* Virg. *Tum prōra āvertit.* Id. *Eo lărātum,* scil. *me.* Hor.

The reflexives are usually wanting after *ăbŏleo, abstineo, accingo, ădaquo, aequo, agglŏmĕro, augeo, cĕlĕro, congĕmĭno, continuo, dĕclīno, dĕcŏquo, dēsino, diffĕro, dūro, ĕrumpo, flecto, dēflecto, făcesso, incipio, inclīno, instauo, irrumpo, jungo, lăvo, laxo, lĕnio, mātūro, mollio, mŏveo, mŭto, pōno, praecipĭto, prōrumpo, quătio, rĕmitto, retracto, sēdo, sisto, stăbŭlo, suppĕdĭto, tardo, tĕneo, tendo, trăhĕio, transmitto, turbo, văris, vergo, verto, dēverto, rĕverto, vestio, vibro;* and more rarely after many others.

2. When it is something indefinite, has been previously expressed in any case, or is easily supplied; as, *Ego, ad quos scribam, nescio,* scil. *lĭtĕras* Cic. *De quo et tĕcum ēgi diligenter, et scripsi ad te.* Id. *Bĕne fēcit Sĭlĭus.* Id. *Dūcit in hostem,* scil. *exercĭtum.* Liv.

REM. 5. An infinitive, or one or more substantive clauses, may supply the place of the accusative after an active verb; as,

Da mihi fallĕre. Hor. *Reddes* dulce lŏqui, *reddes* ridēre decōrum. Id. *Cupis* me esse clēmentem.* Cic. *Athēnienses statuĕrunt* ut nāves conscendĕrent. Id. *Vĕreor* ne a doctis reprĕhendar. Id.*Euœ, Bacche, sŏnat.* Ovid. Sometimes both constructions are united; as, *Di* irum *misĕrantur inānem ambōrum, et tantos mortālibus esse labōres.* Virg.—Respecting the infinitive with and without a subject-accusative after an active verb, see § 270-273; and for the subjunctive after such verbs, see § 273.

(*a*.) In such constructions, the *subject* of the dependent clause is sometimes put in the accusative as the *object* of the leading verb; as, *Nosti* Marcellum, *quam tardus sit,* for *Nosti quam tardus sit* Marcellus. Cic. *Illum, ut vivat, optant.* Ter. *At te ego faciam, ut minus valeas.* Plaut.

(*b*.) An ablative with *de* may also supply the place of the accusative, by the ellipsis of some general word denoting *things, facts,* etc., modified by such ablative; as, *De republicā vestrā paucis accipe.* Sall. Compare a similar omission of a *subject* modified by *de* and the ablative, § 209, R. 3, (2.)

REM. 6. The impersonal verbs of feeling, *misĕret, pœnĭtet, pŭdet, tœdet, pĭget, miscrescit, misĕrētur,* and *pertœsum est,* are followed by an accusative of the person exercising the feeling, and a genitive of the object in respect to which it is exercised. Cf. § 215, (1.); as,

Eōrum nos *misĕret,* We pity them. Cic. The impersonal *Vĕritum est* also occurs with such an accusative; *Quos non est vĕritum pōnĕre,* etc. Cic.

REM. 7. *Jŭvat, dēlectat, fallit, fŭgit, prætĕrit,* and *dĕcet,* with their compounds, take an accusative of the person; as,

Te hilāri ănimo esse valde me *jŭvat,* That you are in good spirits greatly delights me. Cic. *Fŭgit* me *ad te scribĕre.* Cic. *Illud altĕrum quam sit difficile,* te *non fŭgit.* Id. *Nec vero* Cæsărem *fĕfellit.* Cæs. *Fācis, ut te dĕcet.* Ter. So also when used personally; as, *Parvum parva dĕcent.* Hor.; but *dĕcet* often takes the accusative of the person with the infinitive; as, *Hunc macŭlam* nos *dĕcet* effūgĕre. Ter.; and in comic writers a dative; as, Vōbis *dĕcet.* Ter.

For *mea, tua, sua, nostra, vestra,* after *rĕfert* and *intĕrest,* see § 219, R. 1: and for the accusative by attraction, instead of the nominative, see § 206, (6,) (*b*.)

§ **230.** Verbs signifying to name or call; to choose, render or constitute; to esteem or reckon, which in the passive voice have two nominatives, are followed in the active voice by two accusatives, one of the *object* and the other of the *predicate.* Cf. § 210, R. 3, (3.); as,

Urbem *ex Antiŏchi patris nōmine* Antiŏchiam *vŏcāvit,* He called the city Antioch, etc. Just. Lūdos *făcis* me, You make game of me. Plaut. Me consŭlem *fĕcisti.* Cic. Iram *bĕne Ennius* initium *dixit insāniæ.* Id. Ancum Marcium rēgem *pŏpŭlus creāvit.* Liv. Sulpicium accusātōrem *suum numĕrābat, non* compĕtitōrem. Cic. *Quum* vos testes *hăbeam.* Nep.

NOTE 1. The following are among the verbs included in this rule, viz. *appello, dico, nōmino, nuncŭpo, perhibeo, salūto, scribo* and *inscribo, voco; capio, constituo, creo, dēclāro, dēlĭgo, dēsigno, dico, ĕligo, făcio, efficio, instituo, lĕgo, prōdo, reddo, rēnuncio, dūco, dignor, existimo, habeo, jūdico, nŭmĕro, pŭto, rĕpĕrio, intellĭgo, invĕnio, se præbēre* or *præstāre,* etc.

NOTE 2. An ablative with *ex* occurs, though rarely, instead of the accusative of the object; as, *Fortūna me, qui liber fuĕram, servum fēcit,* e summa *infĭmum.* Plaut. Cf. *Qui* recta prāva *faciunt.* Ter.

NOTE 3. An infinitive may supply the place of the objective accusative; as, *Si simŭl asse vŏcat crimen.* Ovid.:—and sometimes of the predicate accusative also; as, *Si repĕrīre vŏcas* āmittĕre certius; *aut si* scīre ūbi sit rĕpĕrīre vŏcas. Id. So also an adjective may supply the place of the predicate accusative; as, *Præbuit se dignum suis majōribus.* Cic. *Cæsărem* certiōrem *făciunt.* Cæs.

REMARK 1. After verbs signifying to esteem or reckon, one of the accusatives is often the subject, and the other the predicate, of *esse* expressed or understood; as,

Eum ăvārum *possŭmus existimāre.* Cic. *Tālem* se impĕrātōrem *præbuit.* Nep. *Præsta* te eum, *qui mihi es cognĭtus.* Cic. Mercūrium *omnium* inventōrem *artium fĕrunt;* hunc *viārum atque itinĕrum* dūcem arbitrantur. Cæs.; or an adjective supplies the place of the predicate accusative; as, *Ne me existimāris ad mănĕs tum* esse prōpensiōrem. Cic.

NOTE 4. Instead of the predicate accusative, (1) *pro* with the ablative sometimes follows *pŭto, dūco,* and *hăbeo,* but denotes only an approximation; as, *Aliquid* pro certo *hăbēre* or *pŭtāre. Ea* pre falsis *dūcit.* Sall. *Aliquem* pro hoste *habēre.* Cæs.—So also *in* with the ablative; as, *Nihil præter virtūtem* in bōnis *habēre.* Cic. *Aliquem* in nŭmĕro *hostium dūcĕre.* Cic.—and the ablative without *in;* as, *Uti vos affīnium* lōco *dūcĕrem.* Sall.—So also *e* or *ex* with the ablative; as, *(Ut) fucĕret quod* e rēpūblīcā fīdēque suā *dūcĕret.* Liv.—Sometimes (2. the genitive; as, Officii *duxit exōrāre filiæ patrem.* Suet. (See § 211, R. 8, (3.) So with a genitive or an ablative of price or value; as, *Pŭtāre aliquem* nihilo. Cic. *Non hăbeo* nauci *Marsum augŭrem.* Enn—and sometimes (3) a dative; as, *Quando tu me hăbes* despĭcātui. Plaut.:—or an adverb; as, Ægre *hăbuit, filium id pro părente ausum.* Liv. And (4) *ad* or *in* with the accusative; as, *Lōca* ad hībernācŭla *lĕgĕre.* Liv. Aliquem in Patres *lĕgĕre.* Id.: or (5) the genitive depending on the ablative of cause, manner, etc.; as, *Qui servitūtem* dēdĭtiōnis nōmine *appellant.* Cæs.

REM. 2. Many other verbs, besides their proper accusative, take a second, denoting a purpose, time, character, etc.

Such are *do, trĭbuo, sūmo, pĕto, pōno, adjungo, ascrībo, cognosco, accio, fingo, significo,* etc.; as,

Quāre ejus fūgæ cōmĭtem *me adjungĕrem.* Cic. *Hŏmĭnum ŏpīnio sōcium me ascrībit tuis laudibus.* Id. *Quos ĕgo sim tŏties jam dēdignāta* mārītos. Virg. *Hunc igĭtur* rēgem *agnoscimus, qui Philippum dēdignātur patrem?* Curt. *Filiam tuam mihi* uxōrem *posco.* Plaut. *Pĕtit hanc Sāturnia* mūnus. Ovid. Such constructions may often be referred to apposition, or to an ellipsis of *esse.*

§ **231.** Verbs of asking, demanding, and teaching, and *cēlo* (to conceal), are followed by two accusatives, one of the person, the other of the thing; as,

Hoc te *vĕhĕmenter rŏgo.* Cic. Illud te *ōro, ut,* etc. Id. *Rŏgo* te numnios, I ask you for money. Mart. *Posce* deos vĕniam, Ask favor of the gods. Virg. *Quum lĕgent quis* mūsĭcam *dŏcuĕrit* Epămĭnondam, When they shall read who taught Epaminondas music. Nep. *Antĭgŏnus iter omnes tŏties cēlat,* Antigonus conceals his route from all. Id. *Dēprĕcāri* deos mǎla. Sen. *Quŏtĭdie Cæsar Æduos frūmentum flăgitāre.* Cæs. Multa deos *ōrans.* Virg.

REMARK 1. This rule includes the verbs of asking and demanding, *flāgĭto, ĕflāgĭto, obsecro, ōro, exōro, contendo, percontor, posco, rĕposco, consŭlo, prĕcor, dēprĕcor, rŏgo,* and *interrŏgo,* which, with the accusative of the person, take the accusative of the neuter pronouns *hoc, id, illud, quod, quid,* more frequently than that of a substantive: of teaching, *dŭceo, edŭceo, dēdŭcro,* and *erŭdio,* which last has two accusatives only in the poets. *Admŏneo* and *consŭlo* are rarely found with two accusatives; as, *Consŭlam hanc rem tuam os.* Plaut. *Eam rem nos lŏcus admŏnuit.* Sall.

REM. 2. Instead of the accusative of the person, verbs of asking and demanding often take the ablative with *ab* or *ex;* as, *Non dēbĕbam* abs te *has litĕras poscĕre.* Cic. *Vĕniam ōrēmus* ab ipso. Virg. *Istud vŏlēbam* ex te *percontāri* Plaut.

REM. 3 (*a.*) Instead of the accusative of the thing, the ablative with *de* is sometimes used; as, *Sic ego te eisdem de rebus interrogem.* Cic. *De itinere hostium sēnātum ēdŏcet.* Sall. *Bassus noster me de hoc libro cēlāvit.* Cic. Cf. § 229 R. 5, (*b.*)—(*b.*) Sometimes also instead of the accusative of the thing an infinitive, or an infinitive or subjunctive clause is used; as, *Deus prēcāri dēbētis,* ut urbem defendant. Cic. *Ut dŏceam Rullum posthac tăcēre.* Id. *Dŏcui* id non fĭĕri posse. Id. *Dŏceant eum* qui vir Sex. Roscius fuĕrit. Id.—(*c.*) With verbs of teaching, the instrument by means of which the art is practised is put in the ablative; as, *Aliquem fĭdibus dŏcēre.* Cic. *Dŏcēre aliquem armis.* Liv. *Litĕrae* may be used either in the accusative or in the ablative; as, *Te litĕras dŏceo.* Cic. *Doctus Graecis litĕris.* Id.

REM. 4. Some verbs of asking, demanding, and teaching, are not followed by two accusatives; as, *exīgo, pĕto, postŭlo, quaero, scitor, sciscitor,* which, with the accusative of the thing, take an ablative of the person with the preposition *ab, de,* or *ex; imbuo, instituo, instruo,* etc., which are sometimes used with the ablative of the thing, generally without a preposition, and are sometimes otherwise construed; as, *Instĭtuĕre aliquem ad dicendum.* Cic.

REM. 5. (*a.*) Many active verbs with the accusative of the person, take also an accusative denoting *in what respect* or *to what degree* the action of the verb is exerted.

(*b.*) The accusative of degree, etc., is commonly *nihil*, a neuter pronoun, or a neuter adjective of quantity; as, *Non quo me aliquid jūvāre posses.* Cic. *Pauca pro tempŏre milites hortātus.* Sall. *Id adjūta me.* Ter. *Něque est te fallĕre* quidquam. Virg. Cf. § 232, (8.)

REM. 6. By a similar construction, *gĕnus* and *sĕcus,* 'sex,' are sometimes used in the accusative, instead of the genitive of quality; as, *Nullas hoc gĕnus vigĭlias vigĭlārunt.* Gell. So, *Omnes mŭliebre* sĕcus. Suet. Cf. 211, R. 6, (4.)

§ 232.

(1.) Some *neuter* verbs are followed by an accusative of kindred signification to their own; as,

Vitam jūcundam vivĕre, To live a pleasant *life*. Plaut. *Mirum somniāvi somnium,* I have dreamed a wonderful *dream*. Id. *Fŭrĕre hunc furōrem*. Virg. *Istum* pugnam *pugnābo.* Plaut. *Pugnāre dicenda Mūsis praelia.* Hor. *Lūsum insŏlentem lŭdĕre.* Id. *Si non servitūtem serviat.* Plaut. *Quēror haud facĭles* questus. Stat. *Jūrāvi vērissĭmum* jusjūrandum. Cic. *Ignōtas jūbet ire* vias. Val. Flacc. So, also, *Ire* exsĕquias, To go to a funeral. Ter. *Ire* suppĕtias, To go to one's assistance. *Ire* infitias, To deny. This expression is equivalent to *infitior*, and may like that take an accusative; as, *Si hoc unum adjunxĕro,* quod *nēmo eat infĭtias.* Nep.: or the accusative with the infinitive; as, *Něque infĭtias imus* Sicĭliam nostram provinciam esse. Liv. *Ut suum* gaudium *gaulĕrēmus.* Cœl. ad Cic. *Profĭcisci magnum* iter. Cic. *Pollux itque rēditque* viam. Virg. This accusative is usually qualified by an adjective.

(2.) Verbs commonly neuter are sometimes used transitively, and are then followed by an accusative.

Accusatives are thus used with *ŏleo* and *săpio,* and their compounds, *redŏleo, resĭpio;* as, *Olet* unguenta, He smells of perfumes. Ter. *Olēre pĕregrinum* To have a foreign smell. Cic. *Orationes rĕdŏlentes* antiquĭtātem. Id. *Mella herbam eam săpiunt,* The honey tastes of that herb. Plin. *Ura picem resĭpĭens.* Id. So, *Sĭtio* honōres. Cic. *Carnem pluit.* Liv. *Claudius* aleam *studiŏsissĭme lūsit.* Suet. *Erumpĕre diu coercĭtam* iram *in hostes.* Liv. *Libros ēvigĭlāre.* Ovid. *Praeĭre* verba. Liv. *Nec vox* homĭnem *sŏnat.* Virg. *Sūdāre* mella. Id. *Morientem nōmĭne clāmat.* Id. *Quis post rina grăvem* milĭtiam *aut pauperiem crepat?* Hor. *Omnes ūna mănet nox.* Id. *Ingrāti ănĭmi* crimen *horreo.* Cic. *Ego meas quēror* fortūnas. Plaut. *Vivĕre* Bacchānālia. Juv. *Pastōrem saltāret uti Cyclōpa, rŏgābat.* Hor. So the passive; *Nunc agrestem* Cyclōpa *mēdĭtur.* Id. *Xerxes quum māre ambŭlāvisset,* terram *nāvigasset.* Cic. *Qui stădium currit.* Id. *Commūnia* jūra *migrāre.* Id. *Te* vŏlo *colloqui.* Plaut. *Ea dissĕrĕre mălui.* Cic.

§ 233.   SYNTAX.—ACCUSATIVE AFTER VERBS.   235

Corydon ardēbat Alexin. Virg. *Stȳgias jūrāvimus undas.* Ovid. *Nāvĭgat æquor* Virg. *Currĭmus æquor.* Id. *Pascuntur sylvas.* Id.

NOTE 1. Accusatives are found in like manner after *ambŭlo, calleo, dōleo, ĕquĭto, fleo, gaudeo, gĕmo, glōrior, horreo, lætor, lātro, nāto, palleo, pāveo, pĕreo, dēpĕreo, prōcēdo, quĕror, rĭdeo, sĭleo, sĭbĭlo, tăceo, trĕmo, trĕpĭdo, vādo, vĕnio,* etc.

(3.) Neuter verbs and sometimes adjectives also may be followed by an accusative denoting *in what respect,* or *to what degree,* the feeling, condition, etc., is manifested; as,

Nihil lībōro. Cic. *Num id lacrĭmat virgo?* Does the maid weep on that account? Ter. *Multa ălia peccat.* Cic. *Quicquid dēlīrant rēges, plectuntur Achīvi.* Hor. *Nec tu* id *indignāri posses.* Liv. *Illud mihi lætandum video.* Cic. *Illud valde tibi assentior.* Id. *Idem glōriāri.* Id. *Hæc glōrians.* Liv. *Hoc stŭde' ūnum.* Hor.—So, Id *ŏpĕram do,* I strive for this. Ter. *Consĭlium pĕtis,* quid *tibi sim auctor.* Cic. *Quod quĭdam auctōres sunt,* Which is attested by some authors. Liv. *Nil nostri misĕrēre?* Virg.—*Nihil Rōmānæ plēbis* similis. Liv. *Sēnātus* nihil *sāne* intentus. Sall. These limiting accusatives have commonly the force of adverbs, particularly *nihil,* which is used like an emphatic *very* in the sense of ' in no way,' ' in no respect.' So *non nihil,* ' to some extent,' ' in some measure.'

NOTE 2. In the above and similar examples, the prepositions *ob, propter, per, ad,* etc., may often be supplied. This construction of neuter verbs is most common with the neuter accusatives *id, quid, quidquam, ălĭquid, quicquid, quod, nihil, nonnĭhil, ĭdem, illud, tantum, quantum, ūnum, multa, pauca, ălia, cētĕra, omnia,* etc. Cf. § 256, R. 16, N.

§ 233.   Many verbs are followed by an accusative depending upon a preposition with which they are compounded.

(1.) Active verbs compounded with *trans, ad,* and *circum,* have sometimes two accusatives, one depending upon the verb, the other upon the preposition; as,

Omnem ĕquĭtātum pontem *transdūcit,* He leads all the cavalry over the bridge. Cæs. *Agēsĭlāus* Hellespontum *cōpias trājēcit.* Nep. *Petrēius* jusjūrandum *ad tgit* Afrānium. Cæs. Roscillum *Pompēius omnia sua præsidia circumdŭxit.* Id So, *Pontus* scŏpŭlos *sŭperjăcit undam.* Virg. So, also, *adverto* and *indūco* with *ănĭmum;* as, Id *ănĭmum advertit.* Cæs. *Id quod* ănĭmum *indūxĕrat paulisper non tēnuit.* Cic. So, also, *injĭcio* in Plautus—*Ego te mănum injĭciam.*

(2.) Some other active verbs take an accusative in the passive voice depending upon their prepositions; as,

Măgĭcas accingier artes, To prepare oneself for magic arts. Virg. In prose writers the *ad* is in such cases repeated; as, *accingi ad consŭlātum.* Liv. *Classis circumvĕlĭtur* arcem. Id. *Quod anguis dŏmi* vectem *circumjectus fuisset.* Cic. *Locum prætervectus sum.* Id.

(3.) Many neuter verbs, especially verbs of motion, or of rest in a place, when compounded with prepositions which govern an accusative, become transitive, and accordingly take an accusative; as,

Gentes quæ măre *illud adjăcent,* The nations which border upon that sea. Nep. *Oblĕquĭtāre* agmen. Curt. *Incēdunt mæstos* lŏcos. Tac. *Transĭlui* flammas. Ovid. *Succēdĕre* tecta. Cic. *Lūdōrum dĭbus,* qui cognĭtĭōnem *intervēnĕrant.* Tac. *Adĭre* provinciam. Suet. *Căveat ne* prœlium *ĭneat.* Cic. *Ingrĕdi* iter *pĕdĭbus* Cic. *Epicŭri horti* quos *mŏdo prætĕrĭbāmus.* Id.

NOTE. To this rule belong many of the compounds of *ambŭlo, cēdo, curro, eo, ĕquĭto, fluo, grădĭor, lābor, no* and *nato, rēpo, sălio, scando, vādo, vĕhor, vĕnio, vŏlo ;—rūbo jăo o, sēdĕs, sisto, sto,* etc., with the prepositions included in § 224. and with *ex.*

REMARK 1. Some neuter verbs compounded with prepositions which govern an ablative, in like manner become transitive, and are followed by an accusative; as,

Nēmĭnem convēni, I met with no one. Cic. Qui sŏcĭĕtātem cŏlĕris. Id. Aversāri hŏnōres. Ovid. Ursi arbōrem āversi dērīpunt. Plin. Edormi crāpŭlam. Cic. Egressus exsĭlium. Tac. Ērādĭtque cĕler rīpam. Virg. Excĕdĕre nŭmĕrum. Tac. Exīre līmen. Ter. Tibur āquæ fertĭle præfluunt. Hor.

REM. 2. After verbs both active and neuter, compounded with prepositions which take an accusative, the preposition is often repeated, or one of similar signification is used; as,

Cæsar se ad nēmĭnem adjunxit. Cic. Multĭtūdĭnem trans Rhēnum in Galliam translūcēre. Cæs.—In Galliam invāsit Antōnĭas. Cic. Ad me ădĭre quondam mēmĭni. Id. Orātor pĕragrat per ănĭmos hŏmĭnum. Id. Ne in sēnātum accēdĕrem. Id. Rēgīna ad templum incēssit. Virg. Juxta gĕnĭtōrem adstat Lāvīnĭa. Id. Fines extra quos ēgrĕdi non possim. Cic. A dative instead of the accusative often follows such compounds, according to § 224. Circum is not repeated.

NOTE. Some verbal nouns and verbal adjectives in bundus are followed by an accusative, like the transitive verbs from which they are derived; as,

Quid tibi huc rĕceptĭo ad te est meum vĭrum? Wherefore do you receive my husband hither to you? Plaut. Quid tibi, mălum, me, aut quid ĕgo ăgam, cūrātĭo 'st? Id. Quid tibi hanc ădĭtĭo est? Id. Quid tibi hanc nōtĭo est, inquam, ămīcam meam? Quid tibi hanc dĭgĭto tactĭo 'st? Id. Hanno vĭtābundus castra hostium consŭlesque. Liv. Mithrĭdātes Rōmānum mĕdĭtābundus bellum. Just. Mīrābundi vānam spĕciem. Liv. Pōpŭlābundus agros. Sisenn. Carnĭfĭcem ĭmāgĭnābundus. App.

§ 234.

A verb in the passive voice has the same government as in the active, except that the accusative of the active voice becomes the nominative of the passive.

NOTE 1. The accusative of the person with the infinitive, after verbs of saying and commanding, may become the subject of the passive voice; as, Active, Dico rēgem esse justum;—Passive, Rex dĭcĭtur justus esse. Act. Jŭbeo te rĕdīre;—Pass. Jŭbĕris rĕdīre: the construction in the passive being the same as though rēgem and te had depended immediately upon dico and jŭbeo.—So, also, when the accusative of the person is the object of the verb and the infinitive stands as the accusative of the thing. Cf. § 270, N.

I. When a verb, which in the active voice takes an accusative both of the person and of the thing, is changed to the passive form, the accusative of the person becomes the nominative, and the accusative of the thing is retained; as,

Rŏgātus est sententĭam, He was asked his opinion. Liv. Interrŏgātus causam. Tac. Sĕgĕtes ălĭmentāque dĕbĭta dīres poscēbātur hŭmus. Ovid. Mōtus dŏcēri gaudet Īŏnĭcos mātūra virgo. Hor. Omnes belli artes ēdoctus. Liv. Nosne hos vĕlĭtos tam diu? Ter. Multa in extis mŏnēmur. Cic.

NOTE 2. The accusative of the thing after doctus and ēdoctus is rare; and after cēlāri it is generally a neuter pronoun; as hoc or id cēlābar; of this I was kept in ignorance; but it is found also with the person in the dative; as, Id Alcĭbĭădi dĭūtĭus cēlāri non pŏtuit. Nep. Alcib. 5. Cēlo, and especially its passive, generally takes de with the ablative.

REMARK 1. (a.) Induo and exuo, though they do not take two accusatives in the active voice, are sometimes followed by an accusative of the thing in

§ 235.   SYNTAX.—ACCUSATIVE AFTER PREPOSITIONS.   237

the passive; as, *Induĭtur ātras* vestes, She puts on sable garments. Ovid. Thōrāca *indūtus.* Virg. *Exūta est Rōma* sĕnectam. Mart. So *indūcor* and *cingor;* as, Ferrum *cingĭtur.* Virg. So *rēcingĭtur* anguem. Ovid.

(*b.*) When two accusatives follow an active verb compounded with *trans* the passive retains that which depends upon the preposition; as, *Belgæ* Rhēnum *antiquitus transducti.* Cæs.

REM. 2. The future passive participle in the neuter gender with *est,* is sometimes, though rarely, followed by an accusative; as, Multa *nōvis rēbus quum sit ăgendum.* Lucr. Quam (viam) *nōbis ingrĕdiendum est.* Cic.

II. Adjectives, verbs, and perfect participles, are sometimes followed by an accusative denoting the *part* to which their signification relates; as,

Nūdus membra, Bare as to his limbs. Virg. Os hŭmĕrosque *deo similis.* Id. *Clāri* gĕnus. Tac. *Trĭbūni* suam vicem *anxii.* Liv. *Trĕmit* artus. Virg. Cētĕra *parce puer bello.* Id. *Sĭbĭla* colla *tŭmentem.* Id. *Explĕri* mentem *nĕquit.* Id. *Grȳnœus ĕrultur* ŏcūlos. Ovid. *Picti* scūta *Lăbĭci.* Virg. *Collis* fronteni *lēnlter fastĭgātus.* Cæs. Animum *incensus.* Liv. *Oblitus* făciem *suo cruōre.* Tac.

REMARK 1. In this construction an ablative is often joined with the perfect participle; as, *Miles fractus* membra *lăbōre.* Hor. Dextĕrum gĕnu *lăpĭde ictus.* Suet. Adversum fĕmur *trăgŭlā grăvĭter ictus.* Liv.

REM. 2. This is a Greek construction, and is usually called the *limiting* or *Greek accusative.* It is used instead of an ablative of limitation, (§ 250,) and occurs most frequently in poetry.

REM. 3. A limiting accusative instead of the ablative is found also in a few ordinary expressions, as in *partim* (for *partem*), *vicem, magnam* and *maxĭmam partem,* instead of *magnā* or *maximā ex parte,* or the adverb *fēre;* as, *Maxĭmam partem lacte vivunt.* Cæs. *Magnam partem ex iambis nostra constat ōrātio.* Cic. Livy has *magna pars,* viz. Nŭmĭdæ, *magna pars* agrestes.—So *cētĕra* and *rĕlĭqua* are joined to adjectives in the sense of *cētĕris,* 'for the rest,' 'in other respects'; as, *Proxĭmum regnum,* cētĕra *ēgrĕgium, ab ūnā parte haud sātis prospĕrum fuit.* Liv. So cētĕra *simĭlis,* cētĕra *bŏnus.* *A te bis terrē* summum *litĕras accēpi.* Cic.—So, also, in the expressions *id tempŏris; id, hoc* or *idem ætātis, illud hōræ,* for *eo tempōre, eā ætāte,* etc.; *id gĕnus, omne gĕnus, quod gĕnus.*

III. Some neuter verbs which are followed by an accusative, are used in the passive voice, the accusative becoming the subject, according to the general rule of active verbs; as,

Tertia vivĭtur ætas. Ovid. *Bellum militābĭtur.* Hor. *Dormĭtur hiems.* Mart. *Multa peccantur.* Cic. *Adĭtur Gnossius Mĭnos.* Sen. *Ne ab omnĭbus circumsistĕrētur.* Cæs. *Hostes invādi posse.* Sall. *Campus obĭtur āquā.* Ovid. *Plūres ineuntur grătiæ.* Cic. *Ea res silētur.* Id.

ACCUSATIVE AFTER PREPOSITIONS.

§ 235. (1.) Twenty six prepositions are followed by the accusative.

These are *ad, adversus* or *adversum, antĕ, ăpŭd, circā* or *circum, circĭter, cĭs* or *cĭtrā, contrā, ergā, extrā, infrā, intĕr, intrā, juxtā, ŏb, pĕnĕs, pĕr, post, pōnĕ, prætĕr, prŏpĕ, proptĕr, sĕcundum, suprā, trans, ultrā;* as,

Ad templum non æquæ Pallădis ibant,—to the temple. Virg. *Adversus hostes,* Against the enemy. Liv. *Germāni qui cis Rhēnum incŏlunt,*—this side the Rhine. Cæs. *Quum tantum rĕsĭdeat intra mūros nŏli.* Cic. *Princĭpio rērum impĕrium pĕnes rēges ĕrat.* Just. *Templum pōnam propter ăquam.* Virg. *Inter ăgendum.* Id. *Ante dōnandum.* Id. Respecting the signification of some of the preceding prepositions see § 195, R. 5, etc.

REMARK 1. *Cis* is generally used with names of p aces; *citra* with other words also; as, *Cis Taurum.* Cic. *Cis Pādum.* Liv. *Paucos cis menses.* Plaut. *Citra Veliam.* Cic. *Citra sătiĕtātem,* Not to satiety. Col. *Citra jŭtigătiōnem.* Cels. *Citra Trŏjāna tempŏra.* Ovid.

REM. 2. *Inter,* signifying *between,* applies to two accusatives jointly, and sometimes to a single plural accusative; as, *Inter me et Scĭpiōnem.* Cic. *Inter nātos et pārentes.* Id. *Inter nos,* Among ourselves. Id. *Inter falcārios,* Among the scythe-makers. Cic. When it denotes time it signifies *during,* and more rarely *at;* as, *Inter ipsum pugnæ tempus.* Liv. *Inter cœnam.* Cic.

REM. 3. *Ante* and *post* are commonly joined with concrete official titles, when used to indicate time, rather than with the corresponding abstract nouns; as, *ante* or *post Cĭcĕrōnem* consŭlem, rather than *ante* or *post* consŭlātum *Cĭcĕrōnis.*

(2.) *In* and *sub,* denoting *motion* or *tendency,* are followed by the accusative; denoting *situation,* they are followed by the ablative; as,

Via dūcit in urbem, The way conducts into the city. Virg. *Noster in* te *ămor.* Cic. *Callĭmăchi ĕpĭgramma in* Cleombrŏtum *est*—on or concerning Cleombrotus. Id. *Exercĭtus sub* jŭgum *missus est,* The army was sent under the yoke. Cæs. *Magna mei sub* terras *ibit imāgo.* Virg. *Mĕdĭā in* urbe, In the midst of the city. Ovid. *In* his *fuit Ariovistus.* Cæs. *Bella sub Ilĭăcis* mœnĭbus *gĕrĕre,* To wage war under the Trojan walls. Ovid. *Sub* nocte *silenti.* Virg.

REM. 4. The most common significations of *in,* with the accusative, are, *into, to, towards, until, for, against, about, concerning,*—with the ablative, *in, on, upon, among.* In some instances, *in* and *sub,* denoting tendency, are followed by the ablative, and, denoting situation, by the accusative; as, *In* conspectu meo audet *rĕnīre.* Phæd. *Nātiōnes quæ in* ămicĭtiam *pŏpŭli Rōmāni,* ditiōnemque *essent.* Id. *Sub* jŭgo *dictātor hostes misit.* Liv. *Hostes sub* montem *consēdisse.* Cæs.

REM. 5. *In* and *sub,* in different significations, denoting neither tendency nor situation, are followed sometimes by the accusative, and sometimes by the ablative; as, *Amor crescit in* hŏras. Ovid. *Hostilem in* mŏdum. Cic. *Quod in bŏno* servo *dici posset.* Id. *Sub eā* condĭtiōne. Ter. *Sub* pœnā *mortis.* Suet.

REM. 6. In expressions relating to time, *sub,* denoting *at* or *in,* usually takes the ablative; as, *Sub ădventu Rōmānōrum.* Liv. *Sub lūce.* Ovid. *Sub tempŏre.* Lucan. Denoting *near, about, just before* or *just after,* it takes the accusative; as, *Sub* lūcem. Virg. *Sub* lūmĭna prīma. Hor. *Sub* hoc *hĕrus inquit.* Id.

REM. 7. *In* is used with neuter adjectives in the accusative in forming adverbial phrases; as, *In ūnĭversum,* In general. *In tōtum,* Wholly. So, *in plēnum; in incertum; in tantum; in quantum; in majus; in mĕlius; in omnia,* in all respects, etc.

(3.) *Sŭpĕr,* when denoting place or time, is followed by the accusative, and sometimes poetically by the ablative; but when it signifies *on, about,* or *concerning,* it takes the ablative. With the accusative *sŭper* signifies *over, above, besides* or *in addition to;* with numerals, *more than;* as,

Sŭper lābentem culmĭna *tecti,* Gliding over the top of the house. Virg. *Sŭper tres mŏdios.* Liv. *Sŭper morbum etiam fămes affēcit exercĭtum.* Id. *Sŭper tĕnĕro prosternit* grămĭne *corpus,* He stretches his body on the tender grass. Virg. *Multa sŭper* Priămo *rŏgĭtans sŭper* Hectŏre *multa,* .... concerning Priam, etc. Id.

REM. 8. The compound *dĭsŭper* is found with the accusative, and *insŭper* with the accusative and the ablative.

(4.) *Subter* generally takes the accusative, but sometimes, in poetry, the ablative; as,

Subter terras, Under the earth. Liv. *Subter densā* testūdĭne. Virg.

(5.) *Clam* is followed by either the accusative or the ablative; as,
Clam vos, Without your knowledge. Cic. *Clam* patrem. Ter. *Clam* matrem suam. Plaut. *Clam* vobis. Cæs. *Neque potest clam me esse.* Plaut. *Clam* uxore meā. Id. Its diminutive *clanculum* is once followed by the accusative, *clanculum* patres. Ter.

REM. 9. The adverbs *versus* or *versum* and *usque* are sometimes annexed to an accusative, principally of place, which depends on *ad* or *in*, and sometimes the preposition is omitted; as, Ad Oceănum *versus proficisci*. Cæs. *Fugam ad se versum.* Sall. In Galliam *versus castra movēre*. Id.—*Usque* ad Nŭmantiam. Cic. *Usque* in Pamphӯliam. Id. Ad noctem *usque*. Plaut.—Brundŭsium *versus.* Cic. Terminos *usque* Libyæ. Just. *Usque* Ennam *profecti*. Cic. *Versus* is always placed after the accusative.—*Usque* occurs more rarely with *sub* and *trans* with the accusative; as, Trans Alpes *usque transfertur*. Cic. *Usque* sub extrēmum *brūmæ* imbrem.—*Versus* also rarely follows *ab*, and *usque* either *ab* or *ex* with the ablative; as, Ab septemtriōne *versus*. Varr. A fundāmento *usque movisti mare*. Plaut. *Usque* ex ultimā Sӯriā. Cic. *Usque* a puĕritiā. Ter. *Usque* a Romŭlo. Cic. *Usque* a māne ad vespĕrum. Plaut.

REM. 10. Prepositions are often used without a noun depending upon them; but such noun may usually be supplied by the mind; as, *Multis* post *annis*, i. e. *post id tempus*. Cic. *Circum Concordiæ*, scil. *ædem*. Sall.

REM. 11. The accusative, in many constructions, is supposed to depend on a preposition understood; as, Quid *opus est plurā?* i. e. *propter quid?* why? i. q. *cur?* or *quăre?* Cic. So, Quid me *ostentem?* Id. But it is not easy, in every case, to say what preposition should be supplied. For the accusative without a preposition after neuter verbs, see § 232. For the accusative of limitation, see § 234, II.

ACCUSATIVE OF TIME AND SPACE.

§ **236.** Nouns denoting duration of time, or extent of space, are put, after adjectives and verbs, in the accusative, and sometimes after verbs in the ablative; as,

Acc. *Appius cæcus* multos annos *fuit*, Appius was blind *many years.* Cic. Biduum *Lāodiceæ fui*. Id. Dies totos *de virtute disserunt*. Id. *Te jam* annum *audientem Cratippum*. Id.—*Decrēvērunt intercălārium* quinque et quadrāginta dies *longum*. Id.—Quum *abessem ab Amāno* iter unius diēi. Id. Tres *pateat cæli spatium non amplius* ulnas. Virg. (Cf. § 256, R. 6.) *A portu* stadia centum e. viginti *processimus*. Cic.—*Duas fossas* quindecim pedes *latas perduxit*,—twc ditches fifteen feet broad. Cæs. *Fossæ* quinos pedes *altæ*. Id. *Forāmina longa* pedes tres semis. Cato. *Orbem olearium crassum* digitos sex *facito*. Id.— Abl. *Vixit* annis undetriginta. Suet. Quatuordecim annis *exsilium tolerāvit*. Tac. Triginta annis *vixit Punetius*. Cic.—*Exercitus Romānus tridui* itinere *abfuit ab amne Tānai*. Tac. *Æsculāpii templum* quinque millibus *passuum distans* Liv.

NOTE 1. The ablative denoting extent of time and space is rarely used by Cicero, and less frequently than the accusative by other writers.

NOTE 2. The accusative denoting extent of space sometimes follows the adverbs *longe, alte*, etc.; as, *Campestris lŏcus alte* duos pedes et sēmissem *infŏdiendus est*. Colum. *Vercingetŏrix lŏcum castris diligit ab Ava*. ico *longe* millia *passuum* sedecim. Cæs.

NOTE 3. (*a*.) *Old*, in reference to the time which a person *has lived*, is expressed in Latin by *nātus*, with an accusative of the time; as, *Decessit A'exander mensem unum, annos tres et triginta nātus*. Just. (*b*.) A person's age may also be expressed without *nātus* by a genitive of the time closely connected with his name, according to § 211, R. 6; as, *Alexander annōrum trium et triginta decessit*. (*c*.) *Older* or *younger* than a certain age is expressed by prefixing to the accusative or genitive of the definite age the adverbs *plus* or *minus*, or the adjectives *major* or *minor*, either with or without *quam*. See § 256, R. 6 and 7.—Sometimes, also, the ablative depends on the comparative; as, *Minor viginti quinque annis natus.* Nep. *Minor triginta annis natu.* Cic. Biennio *quam nos major.* Id. Cf. § 256, R. 16. (1.)

REMARK 1. Nouns denoting time or space, used to limit *other nouns*, are put in the genitive or ablative. See § 211, R. 6.

REM 2. A term of time not yet completed may be expressed by an ordinal number; as, *Nos vicēsimum jam diem patimur hebescĕre aciem horum auctōritātis.* Cic. *Punico bello* duodēcimum annum *Italia urēbātur.* Liv. Hence in the passive, *Nunc tertia viritur ætas.* Ovid.

REM. 3. The accusative or ablative of space is sometimes omitted, while a genitive depending on it remains; as, *Castra quæ abĕrant* bidui, scil. *spătium or spătio.* Cic.

REM. 4. To denote a place by its distance from another, the ablative is commonly used; as, *Millibus passuum sex a Cæsăris castris consēdit.* Cæs.; but sometimes the accusative; as, *Tria passuum* millia *ab ipsa urbe castra posuit.* Liv. The only words used for this purpose in the ablative alone are *spătio* and *intervallo*; as, *Quindĕcim ferme millium* spatio *castra ab Tărento posuit.* Id.

NOTE 4. For *abhinc* and a cardinal number, with the accusative or ablative of past time, see § 253, R. 2. For the ablative denoting difference of time or space, see § 256, R. 16.

REM. 5. A preposition is sometimes expressed before an accusative of time or space, but it generally modifies the meaning; as, *Quem per dĕcem annos aluimus,* .... during ten years. Cic.

REM. 6. When the place from which the distance is reckoned is not mentioned, *ab* is sometimes placed before the ablative of distance, as if this depended on the preposition; as, *A millibus passuum duōbus castra posuērunt,* Two miles from the place, or, Two miles off. Cæs.

REM. 7. An *accusative of weight* also occurs when expressed by *libram* or *libras* in connection with *pondo.* Cf. § 211, R. 6. (4.)

ACCUSATIVE OF PLACE.

§ 237. After verbs expressing or implying motion, the name of the town *in which the motion ends* is put in the accusative without a preposition; as,

Rēgŭlus Carthāginem *rēdiit,* Regulus returned *to Carthage.* Cic. *Cāpuam flectit iter,* He turns his course *to Capua.* Liv. *Calpurnius* Rōmam *prōficiscitur.* Sall. Rōmam *erat nunciātum.* Cic.

REMARK 1. The accusative, in like manner, is used after *iter* with *sum, hăbeo,* etc.; as, *Iter est mihi* Lānŭvium. Cic. *Cæsărem iter habēre* Căpuam. Id And even after *sum* alone; as, *Omnia illa mūnicĭpia, quæ* sunt *a Vibōne* Brundisium. Cic. So with a verbal noun; as, *Adventus* Rōmam. Liv. *Redĭtus* Rōmam. Cic.

REM. 2. (*a.*) The preposition to be supplied is *in,* denoting *to* or *into,* which is sometimes expressed; as, In Ephēsum *abii.* Plaut. *Ad,* before the name of a town, denotes direction towards it; as, *Iter dirigĕre ad Mŭtĭnam.* Cic.; and also its vicinity; as, *Adŏlescentŭlus miles prŏfectus sum ad Căpuam;* i. e. in *castra ad Căpuam.* Id. So, *Lælius cum classe ad Brundĭsium vēnit.* Cæs. *Cæsar ad Gĕnēvam pervēnit.* Id. *Quum ego ad Hēraclĕam accēdĕrem.* Cic.

(*b.*) When *urbs, oppĭdum, lŏcus,* etc., follow the names of towns as appositions, they generally take a preposition; as, *Dēmārātus se contŭlit Tarquinios,* in *urbem Etrūriæ flōrentissimam.* Cic. Ad Cirtam oppidum *iter constituunt.* Sall.— So also when the name of the town is qualified by an adjective; as, *Magnum*

§ 238. SYNTAX.—ACCUSATIVE AFTER ADJECTIVES, ETC. 241

iter ad doctas *profīcīsci cōgor* Athēnas. Prop. But the poets and later prose writers sometimes omit the preposition; as, Ovid, Her. 2, 63.

REM. 3. Instead of the accusative, a dative is sometimes, though rarely, used; as, Carthāgĭni *nuncios mittam*. Hor. Cf. § 225, IV. and R. 2.

REM. 4. *Dŏmus* in both numbers, and *rus* in the singular, are put in the accusative, like names of towns; as,

Ite dŏmum, Go *home*. Virg. *Galli* dŏmos *ăbiĕrant*,—had gone home. Liv. *Rus ĭbo*, I will go into the country. Ter.

NOTE. (*a.*) When *dŏmus* is limited by a genitive or a possessive adjective pronoun, it sometimes takes a preposition: with other adjectives, the preposition is generally expressed; as, *Non introĕo* in nostram dŏmum. Plaut. *Vēnisse* in dŏmum Leccæ. Cic. Ad eam dŏmum *prŏfecti sunt*. Id. In dŏmos sŭpĕras *scandĕre cūra fuit*. Ovid. Rarely, also, when not limited; as, *Sōcrătes philŏsŏpnıam* in dŏmos *intrōduxit*. Cic. So, *lărem suum*. App., or *ad lărem suum*. Cic. *Cărĭcas* in Albense rus *infĕrre*. Plin. Quum in sua rūra *vēnērunt*. Cic. With the possessor's name in the genitive, either *dŏmum* or *in dŏmum* is used; as, *Pompōnii dŏmum vēnisse*. Cic. *In dŏmum Mœlii tēla infĕruntur*. Liv.

(*b.*) *Dŏmus* is sometimes used in the accusative after a verbal noun; as, *Dŏmum rĕdĭtiŏnis spe sublātā*. Cæs. So, *Itio dŏmum*. Cic. Concursus *dŏmum*. Cæs. Cf. R. 1.

REM. 5. (*a.*) Before the names of countries and of all other places in which the motion ends, except those of towns, and *dŏmus* and *rus*, the preposition is commonly used; as, *Ex Asĭā transis* in Eurōpam. Curt. *Te* in Epīrum *vĕnisse gaudeo*. Cic. But it is sometimes omitted; as, *Dēvĕniunt* spēluncam. Virg. *Dēvĕnēre* lŏcos. Id. *Tŭmŭlum antĭquæ Cĕrĕris* sēdemque *sacrātam vēnīmus*. Id. *Ibis Cĕcrŏpios* portus. Ovid. So, also, before names of countries, especially those ending in *us*; as, *Ægyptus, Bospŏrus, Chersŏnēsus, Epīrus, Pĕlŏponnēsus,* etc. So, also, Illyricum *prŏfectus*. Cæs. Măcĕdŏniam *pervēnit*. Liv. Africam *transĭtūrus*. Id. So, Tacitus construes even names of nations, when used, as they often are, for those of countries; as, *Ductus inde Cangos exercĭtus*. Ibēros *ad pātrium regnum pervădit*. So, Virgil, *Nos ibĭmus* Afros.—Pliny has, Insŭlas *Rubri Mări navigant*.

(*b.*) Before the names of small islands the preposition is frequently omitted; as, *Pausănĭam cum classe* Cyprum *mīsĕrunt*. Nep.: but rarely before the names of the larger islands; as, *Sardinia, Britannia, Crēta, Eubœa, Sicilia*.

(*c.*) Before accusatives of any words denoting locality after verbs of motion, the poets omit the preposition; as, Itălĭam—*Lăcinĭăque vēnit* litōra. Virg.— The old accusative *fŏras* is used, like names of towns, to denote the place *whither*, while *fŏris* denotes the place *where*; as, *Vāde* fŏras. Mart. *Exi:* fŏras. Plaut.

ACCUSATIVE AFTER ADJECTIVES, ADVERBS, AND INTERJECTIONS.

§ 238. 1. (*a.*) The adjectives *prŏpior* and *proxĭmus*, with their adverbs *prŏpius* and *proxĭme*, like their primitive *prŏpe*, are often joined with the accusative; as,

Ipse prŏpior montem *suos collŏcat*. Sall. *Crassus* proxĭmus măre Oceănum *hiĕmārat*. Cæs.—*Libyes* prŏpius măre Africum *ăgĭtābant*. Sall. Proxĭme Hispāniam *Mauri sunt*. Id.

(*b.*) The adverbs *pridie* and *postridie* are also often followed by the accusative; as, *Pridie eum diem*. Cic. *Pridie idus*. Id. *Postridie lūdos*. Id.—(*c.*) An accusative sometimes follows *intus* and *cŏmĭnus*; as, *Intus dŏmum*. Plaut. *Agrestes cŏmĭnus* e sues, scil. in. Prop.

REMARK 1. The accusative with *pridie* and *postridie* is by some referred to *ante* and *post* understood. For the genitive after these words, see § 212, R. 4, N. 6.—Respecting *versus*, *usque*, *exadversus* (*-um*) and *secus* with the accusative, see § 195, R. 3; and § 235, R. 3.

REM. 2. The adverb *bĕne*, by the elipsis of *vălēre jŭbeo*, is sometimes followed by the accusative in forms of drinking health; as, *Bĕne vos, bĕne nos, bĕne te, bĕne me, bĕne nostram etiam* Stĕphānium! Plaut. *Bĕne* Messālam, a health to Messala. Tibull. It is also construed with the dative. See § 228, 1.

2. In exclamations, the noun or pronoun which marks the *object of the feeling* is put in the accusative either with or without the interjections, *O! ah! heu! eheu! ecce! en! hem! pro!* or *væ!* as,

En quātuor ārās! ecce duas tibi Daphni! Behold four altars! lo, two for thee, Daphnis! Virg. *Eccum! eccos! eccillum!* for *ecce eum! ecce eos! ecce illum!* Plaut. *O præclārum custōdem!* Cic. *Heu me infēlicem!* Ter. *Pro Deûm hŏmĭnumque* fĭdem! Cic. *Ah me, me!* Catull. *Eheu me miserum!* Ter. *Hem astūtias!* Id. *Væ te!* Plaut. *Væ me!* Sen. *Mĭsĕram me!* Ter. *Hŏmĭnem grăvem et cīvem ēgrĕgium!* Cic. Cf. § 228, 3.

NOTE. The accusative after interjections is supposed to depend on some verb of emotion to be supplied.

SUBJECT-ACCUSATIVE.

§ 239. The subject of the infinitive mood is put in the accusative; as,

Mŏleste Pompeium *id ferre constābat*, That Pompey took that ill, was evident. Cic. *Eos hoc nōmĭne appellāri fas est.* Id. *Miror te ad me nĭhil scrĭbĕre*, I wonder that you do not write to me. Cn. Mag. in Cic. *Campos jŭbet esse pătentes.* Virg.

NOTE 1. In historical writing the present infinitive has sometimes its subject in the nominative. Cf. § 209, R. 5.

REMARK 1. The subject of the infinitive is omitted when it precedes in the genitive or dative case; as, *Est ădŏlescentis mājōres nātu vĕrēri*, scil. *eum.* Cic. *Expĕdit bŏnas esse vōbis,* scil. *vos.* Ter.; and rarely when it precedes in the accusative; as, *Ea pŏpŭlus lætāri et mĕrito dĭcĕre fiĕri;* and also when its place is supplied by a possessive pronoun expressed or understood; as, *Non fuit consĭlium* (meum)—*servīlibus offĭciis* intentum *ætātem ăgĕre* (scil. me). Sal.

REM. 2. A substantive pronoun is also sometimes omitted before the infinitive, when it is the subject of the preceding verb; as, *Pollicĭtus sum susceptūrum* (*esse*), scil. *me*, I promised (that I) would undertake. Ter. *Sed reddĕre posse nĕgābat,* scil. *se.* Virg.

REM. 3. The subject of the infinitive is often omitted, when it is a general word for person or thing; as, *Est ăliud īrācundum esse, ăliud īrātum,* scil. *hŏmĭnem.* Cic. See § 269, R. 1.

REM. 4. The subject-accusative, like the nominative, is often *wanting.* See § 209, R. 3. The subject of the infinitive may be an infinitive or a clause. See § 269, R. 3.

NOTE 2. For the verbs after which the subject-accusative with the infinitive is used see § 272. For the accusative in the predicate after infinitives neuter and passive, see § 210.

VOCATIVE.

§ 240. The vocative is used, either with or without an interjection, in addressing a person or thing.

REMARK 1. The interjections *O, heu,* and *pro (proh),* also *ah, au (hau), ĕhem, ĕho, ehodum, eia (heia), hem, heus, hui, io,* and *ohe,* are followed by the vocative; as,

O formōse puer! O beautiful boy! Virg. *Heu virgo!* Id. *Pro sancte Jūpĭter!* Cic. *Ah stulte!* Ter. *Heus Syre!* Id. *Ohe libelle!* Mart. *Ehodum bŏne vir.* Ter.—*Urbem, mi Rūfe, cōle.* Cic. *Quinctīli Vare, lĕgiōnes redde.* Suet. *Quo mŏritūre ruis?* Hor. *Macte virtŭte esto.* Cic.

REM. 2. The vocative is sometimes omitted, while a genitive depending upon it remains; as, *O misĕræ sortis!* scil. *hŏmines.* Lucan.

NOTE. The vocative forms no part of a proposition, but serves to designate the person to whom the proposition is addressed.

ABLATIVE.

The ablative denotes certain relations of nouns and pronouns, all of which are expressed in English by means of prepositions. In Latin this case is sometimes accompanied by a preposition, and sometimes stands alone. Cf. § 37, 6.

ABLATIVE AFTER PREPOSITIONS.

§ 241. Eleven prepositions are followed by the ablative.

These are *ā, (*or *ăb, abs), absquĕ, dē; cōram, pălam, cum, ex, (ē); sĭnĕ, tĕnŭs, prō,* and *præ;* as,

Ab illo tempŏre, From that time. Liv. *A scrībendo,* From writing. Cic. *Cum exercitu,* With the army. Sall. *Certis de causis,* For certain reasons. Cic. *Ex fŭgā,* From flight. Id. *Pălam pōpŭlo.* Liv. *Sĭne lăbōre.* Cic. *Cūpŭlo tĕnus.* Virg. *Cantābit văcuus cōram lătrōne viātor.* Juv. cf. § 195, 5.

NOTE. Of the prepositions followed by the ablative, five signify removal or separation, viz. *ā (ăb* or *abs), dē, ē* (or *ex), absquĕ* and *sĭnĕ.*

REMARK 1. *Tĕnus* is always placed after its case. It sometimes takes the genitive plural. See § 221, III.—*Cum* is always appended to the ablative of the personal pronouns *me, te, se, nōbis,* and *vōbis,* and commonly to the ablatives of the relative pronoun, *quo, quā, quĭbus,* and *qui.* Cf. § 133, 4, and § 136, R. 1.

REM. 2. The adverbs *prŏcul* and *sĭmul* are sometimes used with an ablative, which depends on the prepositions *a* or *ab,* and *cum* understood; as, *Prŏcul mări,* Far from the sea. Liv. *Sĭmul nōbis hăbĭtat.* Ovid. *Prŏcul dūbio.* Suet. The prepositions are frequently expressed; as, *Prŏcul a terrā.* Cic. *Prŏcul a patriā.* Virg. *Tēcum sĭmul.* Plaut. *Vōbiscum sĭmul.* Cic.—So, rarely, *æque. Qui me in terrā æque fortūnātus ĕrit.* Plaut. Cf. *Nōvi æque omnia tēcum.* Id.

REM. 3. Some of the above prepositions, like those followed by the accusative, are occasionally used without a noun expressed; as, *Quum cōram sŭmus.* Cic. *Cum frātre an* sĭne. Id. Cf. § 235, R. 10.

REM. 4. The ablative follows also the prepositions *in* and *sub,* when they answer to the question 'where?' *super,* when it signifies 'on' or 'concerning', and sometimes *clam* and *subter.* Cf. § 235, (2.)—(5.)

REM. 5. *In* is generally joined with the ablative after verbs of *placing,* as, *pōno, lŏco, collŏco, stătuo, constĭtuo,* and *consĭdo;* as, *Et sŭle tăbentes artus* in *lītŏre pōnunt.* Virg.—So, also, after verbs signifying to *have, hold,* or *regard* as, *hăbeo, dūco, nŭmĕro*, etc.—After verbs of *assembling, concealing*, and *including, in* is followed by either the accusative or the ablative.—After *dīfīgo, inscrībo, insculpo, incīdo*, and *insĕro, in* is usually joined with the ablative.

§ 242. Many verbs compounded with *ăb, dē, ex*, and *sŭper* are followed by an ablative depending upon the preposition; as,

Abesse urbe, To be absent from the city. Cic. *Abīre sēdĭbus*, To depart from their habitations. Tac. *Ut se mălĕdictis non abstīneant*. Cic. *Dētrūdunt nāves scŏpŭlo*, They push the ships from the rock. Virg. *Nāvi ēgressus est*. Nep. *Excēdĕre fīnĭbus*. Liv. *Cæsar prœlio sŭpersēdĕre stătuit*. Cæs. *Trĭbūto ac dēlectu sŭpersessum est*. Cic. So the adjective *extorris*; as, *Extorris patriā, dŏmo*. Sall. And so the verbal *ēruptio*, as, *Mūtĭnā ēruptio*. Cic.

REMARK 1. The preposition is often repeated, or one of similar signification is used; as, *Dētrāhĕre de tuā fāmā numquam cōgĭtāvi*. Cic. *Ex ŏcŭlis ăbĭĕrunt*. Liv. *Exīre* a *patriā*. Cic. *Exīre de vītā*. Id. Cf. § 224, R. 4.

REM. 2. These compound verbs are often used without a noun; but, in many cases, it may be supplied by the mind; as, *Equĭtes dēgressi ad pĕdes* scil. *equis*. Liv. *Abīre ad Deos*, scil. *vītā*. Cic.

REM. 3. Some verbs compounded with *ab, de*, and *ex*, instead of the ablative, are sometimes followed by the dative. See § 224, R. 1 and 2. Some compounds, also, of neuter verbs, occur with the accusative. See § 233, R. 1.

ABLATIVE AFTER CERTAIN NOUNS, ADJECTIVES, AND VERBS.

§ 243. *Opus* and *ūsus*, signifying *need*, usually take the ablative of the thing needed; as,

Auctōrĭtāte tuā nōbis ŏpus est, We need your authority. Cic. *Nunc ănĭmis ŏpus, nunc pectōre firmo*. Virg. *Nāves, quĭbus consŭli ūsus non esset*, Ships, for which the consul had no occasion. Liv. *Nunc vīrĭbus ūsus, nunc mănĭbus răpĭdis*. Virg.

REMARK 1. (*a.*) *Opus* and *ūsus* are sometimes followed by the ablative of a perfect participle; as, *Mātūrāto ŏpus est*, There is need of haste. Liv. *Usus facto est mihi*. Ter. *Ubi summus impĕrātor non ădest ad exercĭtum, citius, quod non facto est ūsus, fit, quam quod facto est ŏpus*. Plaut. After *ŏpus*, a noun is sometimes expressed with the participle; as, *Opus fuit* Hirtio convento,—of meeting or, to meet, § 274, R. 5. Cic. *Opus sibi esse dŏmino ējus invento*. Liv.—or a supine is used; as, *Ita dictu ŏpus est*, It is necessary to say, I must say. Ter. Instead of the ablative with *ŏpus est*, an infinitive, either alone or with a subject accusative, or *ut* with a subjunctive clause, sometimes occurs; as, *Opus est te ănĭmo vălēre*. Cic. *Mĭhi ŏpus est, ut lăvem*. Id.

(*b.*) *Opus* and *usus*, though nouns, are seldom limited by the genitive. In a few passages they are construed with the accusative. See § 211, R. 11.

REM. 2. *Opus* is sometimes the subject and sometimes the predicate of *est; usus*, which seldom occurs except in ante-classic poets, is, with only rare exceptions, the subject only. The person to whom the thing is needful is put in the dative; (§ 226.) With *opus* the thing needed may either be the subject of the verb in the nominative or accusative, or follow it in the ablative; as, *Dux nōbis ŏpus est*. Cic. *Verres multa sibi ŏpus esse aiēbat*. Id.; or, *Dūce nōbis ŏpus est*. The former construction is most common with neuter adjectives and pronouns; as, *Quod non ŏpus est, asse cārum est*. Cato apud Sen.—In the predicate *ŏpus* and *ūsus* are commonly translated 'needful' or 'necessary.' Cf. § 210, R. 4.

NOTE. For the ablative of character, quality, etc., limiting a noun, see § 211, R. 6.

§ **244.** *Dignus, indignus, contentus, præditus,* and *fretus,* are followed by the ablative of the object; as,

Dignus laude, Worthy of praise. Hor. *Vox pŏpŭli* mājestāte *indigna,* A speech unbecoming the dignity of the people. Cæs. *Bestiæ* eo *contentæ non quærunt amplius.* Cic. *Hŏmo* scĕlĕre *præditus.* Id. *Plērĭque* ingĕnio *frēti.* Id.—Sq *Æquum est* me *atque* illo. Plaut.

REMARK 1. The adverb *digne,* in one passage, takes the ablative; *Peccat ŭter nostrum* crŭce *dignius.* Hor.—*Dignor,* also, both as the passive of the obsolete *digno,* and as a deponent verb, is followed by an ablative of the thing. As a deponent it takes also an accusative of the person; as, *Haud ĕquidem* tāli me hŏnōre *dignor.* Virg.—Pass. *Qui* tāli hŏnōre *dignāti sunt.* Cic. Conjŭgio, *Anchisa, Vĕnĕris dignāte* sŭperbo. Virg.—Sometimes as a deponent, instead of the ablative of the thing, it is followed by an infinitive clause; as, *Non ĕgo grammătĭcas* ambīre *tribus et pulpĭta dignor.* Hor. And both *dignor* and *dēdignor* are followed by two accusatives, one of the object the other of the predicate. See § 230, R. 2.

REM. 2. (*a.*) *Dignus* and *indignus* are sometimes followed by the genitive; as, *Suscipe cōgĭtātiōnem dignissimam tuæ* virtūtis. Cic. *Indĭgnus* āvōrum. Virg.; and *dignus* sometimes takes a neuter pronoun or adjective in the accusative; as, *Non me censes scīre* qnid *dignus siem?* Plaut. *Frētus* is in Livy construed with the dative. Cf. § 222, R. 6, (*b.*)

(*b.*) Instead of an ablative, *dignus* and *indignus* often take an infinitive, especially in the passive; as, *Erat dignus* āmāri. Virg.; or a subjunctive clause, with *qui* or *ut*; as, *Dignus* qui impĕret. Cic. *Non sum dignus,* ut fīgam pālum in pariĕtem. Plaut.; or the supine in *u*; as, *Digna atque indigna rĕlātu vōcĭfĕrans.* Virg. *Contentus* is likewise joined with the infinitive; as, *Non hæc aries contenta pāternas* ēdĭdĭcisse *fuit.* Ovid.—So, *Nāres pontum* irrumpĕre *frētæ.* Stat.

§ **245.** I. *Utor, fruor, fungor, pŏtior, vescor,* and their compounds, are followed by the ablative; as,

Ad quem tum Jūno supplex his vōcĭbus *ūsa est,*—addressed these words. Virg. *Frui* vŏluptāte, To enjoy pleasure. Cic. *Fungĭtur* offĭcio, He performs his duty. Id. *Oppĭdo pŏtīti sunt.* Liv. *Vescĭtur* aurā. Virg. His rĕbus *perfruor.* Cic. *Lēgĭbus ăbūti.* Id. *Dēfuncti* impĕrio. Liv. Grăvi ŏpĕre *perfungimur.* Cic. *O tandem* magnis *pĕlăgi dēfuncte* pĕrīclis. Virg.

The compounds are *abūtor, deūtor, perfruor, dēfungor,* and *perfungor.*

NOTE. *Utor* may take a second ablative, as an apposition or a predicate, like the predicate accusative, (§ 230, R. 2), and may then be translated by the verb *to have*; as, *Ille făcĭli* me *ūtētur* patre, He shall have in me an indulgent father. Ter.

REMARK. In early writers these verbs sometimes take an accusative; as, *Quam rem mĕdĭci ūtuntur.* Varr. *Ingĕnium frui.* Ter *Datāmes mīlĭtāre* mūnus *fungens.* Nep. *Gentem ălĭquam* urbem *nostram pŏtitūram pŭtem.* Cic. *Sacras lauros vescar.* Tibull. *In prŏlōgis scrĭbendis* ŏpĕram *ăbūtĭtur.* Ter.—*Pŏtior* is, also, found with the genitive. See § 220, 4.

II. 1. *Nitor, innitor, fīdo* and *confīdo,* may be followed by the ablative without a preposition; as, Hastā *innixus.* Liv. *Fīdĕre* cursu. Ovid. Nātūrā *lŏci confīdēbant.* Cæs.

2. *Misceo* with its compounds takes, with the accusative of the object, the ablative of the thing mingled with; as, *Miscēre pābŭla* sāle. Coll. *Aquas* nectāre. Ovid. *Aēr* multo cālōre *admixtus.* Cic.

3. *Assuesco, assuēfăcio, consuesco, insuesco,* and sometimes *acquiesco,* take either the dative or the ablative of the thing; as, *Aves* sanguine *et prædā assuētæ.* Hor. Nullo offĭcio *aut* disciplīnā *assuēfactus.* Cæs. Cf. § 224.

4. *Vivo* and *ĕpŭlor,* 'to live or feast upon,' are followed by the ablative; as. Dăpĭbus *ĕpŭlāmur ŏpĭmis.* Virg. Lacte *atque pĕcŏre vivunt.* Cæs.

5. *Sto* signifying 'to be filled or covered with,' and also when signifying 'to cost,' is followed by the ablative without a preposition; when signifying 'to persevere in, stick to, abide by,' ' to rest or be fixed on,' it is followed by the ablative either with or without *in;* as, *Jam* pulvĕre *cœlum stāre vident.* Virg.— *Multo* sanguine *ac* vulnĕrĭbus *ea Pœnis victōria stĕtit.* Liv. *Stāre* condĭtiōnĭbus. Cic. *Omnis* in Ascānio *stut cūra pārentis.* Virg.—*Consto,* 'to consist of ' or ' to rest upon,' is followed by the ablative either alone or with *ex, de,* or *in;* as *Constat matĕrĭes* sŏlĭdo corpŏre. Lucr. *Hŏmo* ex ănĭmo *constat et* corpŏre. Cic.

REMARK 1. *Fido, confīdo, misceo, admisceo, permisceo,* and *assuesco* often take the dative.

REM. 2. When a preposition is expressed after the above verbs, *sto, fido, confido, nitor, innītor,* and *assuesco* take *in* or *ad; acquiesco, in;* and *misceo* with its compounds, *cum.*

§ 246. Perfect participles denoting *origin* are often followed by the ablative of the, *source,* without a preposition.

Such are *nātus, prōgnātus, sătus, creātus, crētus, ĕdĭtus, gĕnĭtus, gĕnĕrātus, ortus;* to which may be added *ŏriundus,* descended from.

Thus, *Nāte deā!* O son of a goddess! Virg. *Tantălo prōgnātus,* Descended from Tantalus. Cic. *Sătus Nĕrēĭde,* Sprung from a Nereid. Ovid. *Creātus rēge.* Id. *Alcānŏre crēti.* Virg. *Edĭte rēgĭbus.* Hor. *Dīis gĕnĭte.* Virg. *Argŏlĭco gĕnĕrātus Alēmŏne.* Ovid. *Ortus nullis mājōrĭbus.* Hor. *Cœlesti sĕmĭne ŏriundi.* Lucr.

REMARK 1. The preposition is also rarely omitted after the verbs *creo, gĕnĕro,* and *nascor;* as, *Ut* patre *certo nascĕrēre.* Cic. *Fortes creantur* fortĭbus. Hor.

REM. 2. After participles denoting origin, the preposition *ex* or *de* is usually joined to the name of the mother; and in a few passages *ex* or *ab* is joined to the name of the father; as, *Prōgnāti* ab Dīte *patre.* Cæs. In speaking of one's ancestors *ab* is frequently used; as, *Plērosque Belgas esse ortos* a Germānis. Id.

REM. 3. Origin from a place or country is generally expressed by a patrial adjective; as, *Thrăsўbūlus* Athēniensis, Thrasybulus *of Athens.* Livy often uses *ab;* as, *Turnus Herdōnius* ab Aricĭā. Cæsar prefers the ablative alone; as, *Cn. Magius* Crĕmōnā; and in this manner is expressed the tribe to which a person belongs; as, *Q. Verres* Rōmĭlĭā,—*of the Romilian tribe.*

ABLATIVE OF CAUSE, ETC.

§ 247. Nouns denoting the *cause, manner, means,* and *instrument,* after adjectives and verbs, are put in the ablative without a preposition.

NOTE. The English prepositions with the ablative of cause, manner, means and instrument are *by, with, in,* etc.

1. The *cause.* (1.) Adjectives which have a passive signification, as denoting a state or condition produced by some external cause, may take such cause in the ablative; as,

Campāni fuērunt sŭperbi bŏnĭtāte *agrōrum.* Cic. *Animal* pābŭlo *lœtum.* Sen Prælio *fessi lassique,* Weary and faint with the battle. Sall. *Hŏmĭnes ægr* grăvi morbo. Cic.

(2.) Neuter verbs expressing an action, state or feeling of the subject originating in some external cause, may take that cause in the ablative; as,

Intĕriit fāme, He perished with hunger. *Laude ăliēnā dŏlet.* Cic. *Lætos tuā dignitāte.* Id. *Gawle* tuo bŏno. Id. *Suā victōriā glōriāri.* Cæs. *Agrĭlonĭbus lăbōrant quercēta.* Hor.—So with *bĕne est* and the dative; as, *Mihi bĕne ĕrat non* piscĭbus *urbe pĕtītis, sed* pullo *atque* hædo. Hor. *Ubi illi bĕne sit* ligno, *ăquā călĭdā, cibo, vestīmentis,* etc. Plaut.

NOTE 1. After such adjectives and neuter verbs, a preposition with its case often supplies the place of the simple ablative.

NOTE 2. In exclamations of encouragement or approbation, the defective adjective *macte, macti*, either with or without the imperative of *esse (esto, este, estōte,)* is joined with an ablative of cause, especially with *virtūte*.

NOTE 3. After neuter verbs and adjectives denoting emotions, especially those of *care, grief*, and *sorrow*, the accusative *vicem*, with a genitive or a possessive pronoun, is used, instead of the ablative *vice*, to signify 'for' or 'on account of'; as, *Rēmittimus hoc tibi, ne* nostram vĭcem *irascāris*, That you may not be angry on our account. Liv. Tuam vĭcem *sæpe dŏleo, quod,* etc. Cic. Suam vĭcem *măgis anxius, quam* ejus, *cui auxĭlium ab se pĕtĭbātur.* Liv.

REMARK 1. When the *cause* is a voluntary agent, it is put in the accusative with the preposition *ob, propter,* or *per*; as, *Non est æquum me propter vos dēcipi.* Ter. These prepositions, and *a,* or *ab, de, e* or *ex,* and *præ,* are also sometimes used when the cause is not a voluntary agent; as, Ob ădultĕrium cæsi. Virg. *Nec lŏqui præ mærōre pŏtuit.* Cic.

REM. 2. (*a*.) After active verbs, the *cause*, unless expressed by an ablative in *u* from substantives having no other case; as, *Jussu, rŏgātu* and *admŏnĭtu,* is seldom expressed by the simple ablative, but either by a preposition, or by *causā, grătiā, ergo,* etc., with a genitive; as, *Lēgĭbus* propter mĕtum pāret. Cic. *Ne ob eam rem ipsos dēspicĕret.* Id. *Dōnāri* virtūtis ergo. Id. *Si hoc honōris mei causā suscēpĕris.* Id. But with *causā,* etc., the adjective pronoun is commonly used for the corresponding substantive pronoun; as, *Te abesse* meā causā, *mŏleste fĕro.* Cic. Cf. § 211, R. 3, (*b.*)

(*b.*) When the cause is a state of feeling, a circumlocution is often used with a perfect participle of some verb signifying 'to induce'; as, *Cŭpĭdĭtāte ductus, inductus, incītātus, incensus, inflammātus, impulsus, mōtus, captus,* etc. *Mihi bĕne-vŏlentiā* ductus *trĭbuēbat omnia.* Cic. Livy frequently uses *ab* in this sense; as, *Ab īrā, a spe, ab ŏdio,* from anger, hope, hatred.

2. The *manner*. *Cum* is regularly joined with the ablative of manner, when expressed simply by a noun, not modified by any other word; and also when an adjective is joined with the noun, provided *an additional circumstance*, and not merely an essential character of the action, is to be expressed. Thus:

Cum vŏluptāte *ălĭquem audīre. Verres Lampsăcum vĕnit* cum magnā călămĭtāte *cīvĭtātis.* Cic. Hence also when the connection between the subject and the noun denoting the attribute is only external; as, *Prōcēdĕre* cum veste purpūreā: in distinction from Nūdis pĕdĭbus *incēdĕre;* Aperto căpĭte *sĕdĕre,* etc., which express circumstances or attributes essential to the subject.

But *mŏdus, rătio, mos, rītus,* etc., signifying manner, never take *cum,* and it is omitted in some expressions with other substantives; as, Hoc mŏdo *scripsi; Constĭtuērunt* quā rătiōne *ăgĕrētur; Mōre bestiārum văgāri; Latrōnum* rītu *vīvĕre;* Æquo ănimo *fĕro;* Maximā fĭde *ămicĭtias cōluit.* Summā æquĭtāte *res constĭtuit; Viam* incrēdībĭli cĕlĕrĭtāte *confēcit; Librum* magnā cūrā dīligentiāque *scripsit;* the action of the verb being intimately connected with the circumstance expressed by the ablative. So in some expressions with substantives alone; as, Silentio *prætĕrīre* or *făcĕre ălĭquid;* Lege *ăgĕre;* Jūre and injūriā *făcĕre; Magistrātus* vĭtio *creātus; Recte* et ordine *fit.*

REM. 3. The *manner* is also sometimes denoted by *de* or *ex* with the ablative as, *De* or *ex industriā,* On purpose. Liv. *Ex integro,* Anew. Quint.

3. The *means* and *instrument*. An ablative is joined with verbs of every kind, and also with adjectives of a passive signification, to express the means or instrument; as,

Amīcos observantiā, *rem* parsimōniā *rĕtĭnuit*, He retained his friends by attention, his property by frugality. Cic. *Auro ostrōque dĕcōri.* Virg. *Ægrescit mĕdendo.* Id. *Cornibus tauri, apri* dentibus, morsu *leōnes se tŭtantur.* Cic. *Cassis est* virgis. Id. *Trabs saucia* sĕcūri. Ovid. For the ablative of the means after verbs of *filling*, etc., see § 249, I.

REM. 4. When the means is a person, it is seldom expressed by the simple ablative, but either by *per*, or by the ablative *ŏpĕrā* with a genitive or a possessive pronoun; as, *meā, tuā, suā, ŏpĕrā*, which are equivalent to *per me, per te, per se*, and denote both good and bad services. *Bĕnĕfĭcio meo*, etc., is used of good results only; as, *Bĕnĕfĭcio meo patres sunt.* Sall. But persons are sometimes considered as involuntary agents, and as such expressed by the ablative without a preposition; as, Servos, quibus *silvas publicas dēpŏpŭlātus ĕrat.* Cic.— When *per* is used to express the means, it is connected with external concurring circumstances, rather than with the real means or instrument. Hence we always say *vi oppĭdum cēpit*, but *per vim ei bŏna ērĭpuit.*

REM. 5. The material instrument is always expressed by the ablative without a preposition; as, *Confĭcĕre cervum săgittis ; glădio ălĭquem vulnĕrāre ; trā-jĭcĕre pectus ferro.*

§ 248. The ablative is used with passive verbs to denote the *means* or *agent* by which any thing is effected, and which in the active voice is expressed by the nominative. This ablative is used either with *ab* or without it, according as it is a person or a thing.

I. The *voluntary* agent of a verb in the passive voice is put in the ablative with *a* or *ab*; as,

(In the active voice,) *Clōdius me dīlĭgit*, Clodius loves me (Cic.); (in the passive,) A Clōdio *dīlĭgor*, I am loved by Clodius. *Laudātur* ab his, *culpātur* ab illis. Hor.

REMARK 1. (1.) The general word for persons, after verbs in the passive voice, is often understood; as, *Prŏbĭtas laudātur*, scil. *ab hŏmĭnĭbus.* Juv. So after the passive of neuter verbs; as, *Discurrĭtur.* Virg. *Tōto certātum est corpŏre regni.* Id. Cf. § 141, R. 2.

(2.) The agent is likewise often understood, when it is the same as the subject of the verb, and the expression is then equivalent to the active voice with a reflexive pronoun, or to the middle voice in Greek; as, *Quum omnes in omni gĕnĕre scĕlĕrum vŏlūtentur*, scil. *a se.* Cic.

REM. 2. *Neuter* verbs, also, are sometimes followed by an ablative of the voluntary agent with *a* or *ab*; as,

M. Marcellus pĕriit ab Annĭbăle, M. Marcellus was killed by Hannibal. Plin. *Ne vir* ab hoste *cădat.* Ovid.

REM. 3. The preposition is sometimes omitted; as, *Nec* conjŭge *captus* Ovid. *Cŏlĭtur lĭnĭgĕrā* turbā. Id. *Pĕreat meis excisus* Argīvis. Hor.

For the dative of the agent after verbs in the passive voice, and participles in *dus*, see § 225, II. and III.

II. The *involuntary* agent of a verb in the passive voice, or of a neuter verb, is put in the ablative without a preposition, as the cause, means, or instrument; as, *Maxĭmo* dŏlōre *confĭcior.* Cic. *Frangi* cŭpĭdĭtāte. Id. *Æăcĭdæ* tēlo *jăcet Hector.* Virg.

§ 249. SYNTAX.—ABLATIVE OF CAUSE, ETC. 249

NOTE. The involuntary agent is sometimes personified, and takes *a* or *ab*; as, A võluptātĭbus *dĕsĕri*. Cic. A nātūrā *dătum hŏmĭni vivendi currĭcŭlum.* Id. *Vinci* a võluptāte. Id. *Victus* a lăbōre. Id.

§ **249.** I. A noun denoting the means, by which the action of a verb is performed, is put in the ablative after verbs signifying to *affect* in any way, to *fill, furnish, load, array, equip, endow, adorn, reward, enrich*, and many others.

REMARK 1. This rule includes such verbs as *afficio, aspergo, conspergo, inspergo, respergo, compleo, expleo, impleo, oppleo, repleo, suppleo, cumulo, farcio, refercio, satio exsatio, sătŭro, stipo, constipo, obruo, ŏnĕro, augeo, induo, vestio, armo, orno, circumdo, circumfundo, macto, locupleto, instruo, imbuo, dōno, impertio, rĕmūnĕror, honesto, hŏnōro*, etc.; as,

Terrōre *implētur Africa*, Africa is filled with terror. Sil. *Instruxēre* ĕpūlis *mensas*, They furnished the tables with food. Ovid. *Ut ĕjus ănimum his ŏpīnĭōnĭbus imbuas*, That you should imbue his mind with these sentiments. Cic. *Nāves ŏnĕrant auro*, They load the ships with gold. Virg. *Cūmŭlat altāria dōnis* He heaps the altars with gifts. Id. *Terra se grāmĭne vestit*, The earth clothes itself with grass. Id. *Mollibus ornābat cornua sertis*. Id. *Multo cibo et pōtiōne complĕti*. Cic. *Libros pŭĕrīlĭbus* fābŭlis *rĕfercire*. Id. *Sătiāri* dēlectātiōne *non possum*. Id. *Hŏmĭnes sătŭrāti* hŏnōrĭbus. Id. *Senectus stipāta* stŭdiis *jŭventūtis*. Id. *Me tanto* hŏnōre *hŏnestas*. Plaut. Equis *Africam locuplētāvit*. Colum. *Stŭdium tuum nullā me novā* võluptāte *affēcit*. Cic. *Terram nox obruit* umbris. Lucr.

REM. 2. Several verbs denoting to fill, instead of the ablative, sometimes take a genitive. See § 220, 3.

REM. 3. The active verbs *induo, dōno, impertio, aspergo, inspergo, circumdo*, and *circumfundo*, instead of the ablative of the thing with the accusative of the person, sometimes take an accusative of the thing, and a dative of the person; as, *Cui quum Dēiănīra* tūnĭcam *indusset*. Cic. *Dōnāre* mūnĕra civibus. In the earliest writers *dōno*, like *condōno*, has sometimes two accusatives or an accusative of the person with the infinitive.

II. A noun denoting that in *accordance* with which any thing is, or is done, is often put in the ablative without a preposition; as,

Nostro mōre, According to our custom. Cic. *Institūto suo Cæsar cōpias suas ēduxit*, According to his practice. Cæs. *Id factum* consilio meo,—by my advice. Ter. *Pācem fēcit his* conditiōnĭbus,—on these conditions. Nep.

NOTE. The prepositions *de, ex, pro*, and *secundum* are often expressed with such nouns; as, *Neque est factūrus quidquam nisi* de meo consilio. Cic. Ex consuētūdine *aliquid făcĕre*. Plin. Ep. *Decet quidquid ăgas, ăgĕre* pro vir'.us. Cic. Secundum nātŭram *vivĕre*. Id.

III. The ablative denoting *accompaniment*, is usually joined with *cum*; as,

Văgāmur ĕgentes cum conjŭgĭbus *et* lībĕris, Needy, we wander with our wives and children. Cic. *Sæpe admīrāri soleo* cum *hoc* C. Lælio. Id. *Jūlium* cum *his ad te* līterīs *misi*. Id. *Ingressus est* cum glădio. Id. *Rōmam vēni* cum febri. Cum occăsu *sōlis cōpias ēdūcĕre*,—as soon as the sun set.

REMARK. But *cum* is sometimes omitted before words denoting military and naval forces, when limited by an adjective; as, *Ad castra Cæsăris omnibus* cōpiis *contendĕrunt*. Cæs. *Inde tōto* exercĭtu *profectus*. Liv. *Eōdem dĕcem nārĭbus C. Fŭrius vēnit*. Liv. And sometimes in military language *cum* is omitted, when accompanying circumstances are mentioned, and not persons; as *Castra* clāmōre *invādunt*.

§ **250.** 1. A noun, adjective, or verb, may be followed by the ablative, denoting *in what respect* their signification is taken; as,

Piĕtāte filius, consiliis pārens, In affection a son, in counsel a parent. Cic. *Rēges nōmĭne māgis quam impĕrio*, Kings in name rather than in authority. Nep. *Oppĭdum nōmĭne Bibrax*. Cæs.—*Jūre pĕrītus*, Skilled in law. Cic. *Anxĭus ănĭmo*, Anxious in mind. Tac. *Pĕdĭbus æger*, Lame in his feet. Sall. *Crĭne rŭber*, *nĭger ōre*. Mart. *Fronte lætus*. Tac. *Mājor nātu*. Cic. *Prūdentiā non infĕrior*, *ūsu vēro ĕtiam sŭpĕrior*. Id. *Maxĭmus nātu*. Liv.—*Anĭmo angi*, To be troubled in mind. Cic. *Contrĕmisco tōtā mente et omnĭbus artŭbus*, I am agitated in my whole mind and in every limb. Id. *Captus mente*, Affected in mind, *i. e.* deprived of reason. Id. *Altĕro ŏcŭlo căpĭtur*. Liv. *Ingĕnii laude flōruit*. Cic *Pollĕre nōbilĭtāte*. Tac. *Anĭmōque et corpŏre torpet*. Hor.

REMARK. This may be called the *ablative of limitation*, and denotes the relation expressed in English by 'in respect of,' 'in regard to,' 'as to,' or 'in.'— Respecting the genitive of limitation after adjectives, see § 213;—after verbs, § 220, 1: and respecting the accusative of limitation, see § 231, R. 5; § 232, (3.); and § 234, II.

2. (1.) Adjectives of plenty or want are sometimes limited by the ablative; as,

Dŏmus plēna servis, A house full of servants. Juv. *Dives agris*, Rich in lands. Hor. *Fĕrax sæcŭlum bŏnis artĭbus*. Plin.—*Inops verbis*, Deficient in words. Cic. *Orba frātrĭbus*, Destitute of brothers. Ovid. *Vĭduum arbŏrĭbus sōlum*. Colum. *Nūdus agris*. Hor. For the genitive after adjectives of plenty and want, see § 213, R. 3–5.

(2.) Verbs signifying to abound, and to be destitute, are followed by the ablative; as,

Scătentem belluis pontum, The sea abounding in monsters. Hor. *Urbs rēdundat mīlĭtĭbus*, The city is full of soldiers. Auct. ad Her. *Villa ăbundat porco, hædo, agno, gallĭnā, lacte, cāseo, melle*. Cic.—*Vĭrum qui pĕcūniā ĕgeat*, A man who is in want of money. Id. *Cărēre culpā*, To be free from fault. Id. *Mea ădŏlescentia indĭget illōrum bŏrā existĭmātiōne*. Id. *Abundat audāciā, consilio et rătiōne dĕficĭtur*. Id.

REMARK 1. To this rule belong *ăbundo, exŭbĕro, rĕdundo, scăteo, affluo, circumfluo, diffluo, sŭperfluo, suppĕdĭto, văleo, vĭgeo;—căreo, ĕgeo, indĭgĕo, văco, dĕfĭcior, dĕstĭtuor*, etc.

REM. 2. The *genitive*, instead of the ablative, sometimes follows certain verbs signifying to abound or to want. See § 220, 3.

REM. 3. To do any thing with a person or thing, is expressed in Latin by *făcĕre* with *de*; as, *Quid de Tulliŏlā meā fiet?* Cic ; and more frequently by the simple ablative, or the dative; as, *Quid hoc hŏmĭne* or *huic hŏmĭnī făciātis?* What can you do with this man? Cic. *Nescit quid făciat auro*,—what he shall do with the gold. Plaut. *Quid me fiat parvi penŭlis*, You care little what becomes of me. Ter.—*Sum* is occasionally used in the same manner; as, *Mētum rĕpĕrunt quidnam se fŭtūrum esset*,—what would become of them. Liv.

§ **251.** A noun denoting that of which any thing is deprived, or from which it is freed, removed, or separated, is often put in the ablative without a preposition.

This construction occurs after verbs signifying to *deprive, free, debar, drive away, remove, depart*, and others which imply *separation*.

§ 251. SYNTAX.—ABLATIVE OF CAUSE, ETC.

NOTE. The principal verbs of this class are *arceo, pello, děpello, expello, abdico, interdico, děfendo, děturbo, dějicio, ějicio, absterreo, děterreo, mōveo, ămōveo, dēmōveo, rěmōveo, sěcerno, prŏhĭbeo, sěpăro, exclūdo, interclūdo, ăbeo, exeo, cēdo, děcēdo, discēdo, děsisto, ěvādo, abstĭneo, spŏlio, privo, orbo, lĭběro, expědio, laxo, nūdo, solvo, exsolvo, exŏněro, lěvo, purgo*, to which may be added the adjectives *liber, immūnis, pūrus, văcuus*, and *ălĭēnus*; as,

Nūdantur arbŏres fŏliis, The trees are stripped of leaves. Plin. *Hoc me lĭběra mĕtu*, Free me from this fear. Ter. *Tūne eam phĭlŏsŏphiam sěquěre, quæ spŏliat nos jūdĭcio, privat apprŏbātiōne, orbat sensĭbus?* Cic. *Solvit se Teucria luctu.* Virg. *Te illis sēdĭbus arcēbit.* Cic. Q. *Vārium pellěre possessiōnĭbus cōnātus est.* Id. *·Omnes tribu rěmōti.* Liv. *Lěvāre se ære ălĭēno.* Cic. *Me lěves chŏri sěcernunt pŏpŭlo.* Hor. *Ănĭmus omni liber cūrā et angōre.* Cic. *Utrumque hŏmĭne ălĭēnissĭmum.* Id. When *ălĭēnus* signifies 'averse' or 'hostile to,' it takes the ablative with *ab*, or rarely the dative; as, *Id dīcit, quod illi causæ maxime est ălĭēnum.* Id. In the sense of 'unsuited,' it may also be joined with the genitive; as, *Quis ălĭēnum pŭtet ējus esse dignĭtātis?* Id.—*Alius* too, in analogy with adjectives and verbs of separation, sometimes takes an ablative; as, *Nēve pŭtes ălium săpiente bŏnōque beātum.* Hor.; but this may also be referred to the ablative after comparatives. Cf. § 256, R. 14.

REMARK 1. Most verbs of depriving and separating are more or less frequently followed by *ab, de*, or *ex*, with the ablative *of the thing*, and always by *ab* with the ablative *of the person*; as, *Tu Jūpĭter, hunc a tuis āris arcēbis.* Cic. *Præsĭdium ex arce pěpŭlērunt.* Nep. *Aquam* de agro *pellěre.* Plin. *Ex ingrātā civĭtāte cēděre.* Cic. *Arcem* ab incendio *lĭběrāvit.* Id. *Solvěre bellum* ex cătēnis. Auct. ad Her.—*Sēdes rěmōtas* a Germānis. Cæs. *Se* ab Etruscis *sěcernēre.* Liv.

REM. 2. *Arceo*, in the poets, sometimes takes the dative, see § 224, R. 2., and sometimes an infinitive; as, *Plăgamque sēděre cēdendo arcēbat.* Ovid.—*Prŏhĭbeo* and *děfendo* take either the accusative of the person or thing to be defended, with the ablative of the thing to be warded off—or the reverse—*ălĭquem* or *ălĭquid a pěrīcŭlo*, or *pěrīcŭlum ab ălĭquo*. They are also sometimes construed with the dative, see § 224, R. 2, and sometimes with infinitive or subjunctive clauses. *Prŏhĭbeo* has rarely two accusatives; as, Id te *Jūpĭter prŏhĭbessit.* Plaut.; or poetically the accusative and genitive; as, *Captæ prŏhĭběre Pœnos* āquĭlæ. Sil.—*Interdico* takes the person either in the accusative or the dative, and the thing in the ablative, *ălĭquem* or *ălĭcui* ălĭquā re; as, *Quĭbus quum* āquā *et* igni *interdīxissent.* Cæs.—Instead of the ablative, a subjunctive clause with *ne*, and more rarely with *ut*, sometimes follows *interdico*.—*Absum*, in like manner, takes the ablative with *ab*, and sometimes the dative; as, *Curtæ nescio quid semper ăbest* rei. Hor. Cf. § 224, R. 1.—*Abdico* takes sometimes an ablative, and sometimes an accusative of the thing renounced; as, *Abdĭcāre se* măgistrātu. Cic. *Abdĭcāre* măgistrātum. Sall. In Plautus, *circumdŭco*, to cheat, takes the ablative of the thing. *Interclūdo*, instead of an ablative of the thing with an accusative of the person, sometimes takes an accusative of the thing and a dative of the person; as, *Ītĭněrum angustiæ* multĭtūdĭni fŭgam *interclūsěrant.* Cæs.: and, instead of the ablative of the thing, a subjunctive clause with *quŏmĭnus* occurs: *Interclūdor dŏlōre, quŏmĭnus ad te plūra scrībam.* Cic.

REM. 3. Verbs which signify to *distinguish*, to *differ*, and to *disagree*, are generally construed with *ab*, but sometimes, especially in the poets, with the ablative alone.

NOTE. Verbs signifying to distinguish, etc., are *distinguo, discerno, sěcerno, diffěro, discrěpo, dissĭdeo, disto, dissentio, discordo, ăbhorreo, ălĭēno*, and *ăbălĭēno*.—*Dissentĭo, dissĭdeo, discrěpo*, and *discordo* are construed also with *cum*.—The verbs which signify to *differ* are sometimes construed with the dative; as, *Distat* infido scurræ ămīcus. Hor., and in like manner the adjective *diversus*; as, *Nĭhil est tam Lȳsiæ diversum, quam Isocrātes.* Quint.

ABLATIVE OF PRICE.

§ 252. The *price* or *value* of a thing is put in the ablative, when it is a definite sum, or is expressed by a substantive; as,

Quum te trecentis talentis regi Cotto vendidisses, When you had sold yourself to king Cottus for three hundred talents. Cic. *Vendidit hic auro patriam,* This one sold his country for gold. Virg. *Cibus uno asse venalis.* Plin. *Constitit quis- ringentis millibus.* Varr. *Denis in diem assibus animum et corpus (militum) æstimari.* Tac. *Levi momento æstimare.* Cæs. *Istuc verbum vile est viginti minis.* Plaut. *Asse carum est.* Sen. Ep.

REMARK 1. The verbs which take an ablative of price or value are (1) *æstimo, duco, facio, fio, habeo, pendo, puto, deputo, taxo;* (2) *emo, mercor, vendo, do, veneo, sto, consto, prosto, conduco, loco, valeo, luo,* and *liceo.*—To these must be added others, which express some act or enjoyment for which a certain price is paid; as, *Lavor quadrante.* Triginta millibus *Cælius habitat.* Cic. Vix drachmis *est obsonatus* decem. Ter. *Doceo* talento, etc. So *esse* in the sense 'to be worth'; as, Sextante *sal in Italia erat.*

REM. 2. Respecting the genitive of price or value, when expressed in *a general* or *indefinite* manner, see § 214.

REM. 3. The price of a thing, contrary to the general rule, is often expressed indefinitely by a neuter adjective; as, *magno, permagno, parvo, tantulo, plure, minimo, plurimo, vili, viliori, vilissimo, nimio,* etc.; as, Plure vēnit. Cic. *Conduxit non* magno *domum.* Id. These adjectives refer to some noun understood, as *pretio, ære,* and the like, which are sometimes expressed; as, *Parvo pretio ea vendidisse.* Cic.—The adverbs *bene, pulchre, recte, male, care,* etc., sometimes take the place of the genitive or ablative of price; as, *Bene emere; recte vendere; optime vendere,* etc.

REM. 4. Varro has used *valeo* with the accusative; as, *Denarii dicti, quod denos æris valebant.*

REM. 5. *Muto* and its compounds, *commuto* and *permuto,* are commonly construed like verbs of selling, the thing parted with being put in the accusative, and the thing received in exchange for it, in the ablative; as, *Chaoniam glandem pingui mutavit arista.* Virg. But these cases are often reversed, so that the thing received is put in the accusative and the thing given for it in the ablative; as, *Cur valle permutem Sabina divitias operosiores?* Why should I exchange my Sabine valley for more wearisome riches? Hor.—Sometimes in this construction *cum* is joined with the ablative.

ABLATIVE OF TIME.

§ 253. A noun denoting the *time at* or *within* which any thing is said to be, or to be done, is put in the ablative without a preposition; as,

Die quinto decessit, He died on the fifth day. Nep. *Hoc tempore,* At this time. Cic. *Tertia vigilia eruptionem fecerunt,* They made a sally at the third watch. Cæs. *Ut hieme naviges,* That you should sail in the winter. Cic. *Proximo triennio omnes gentes subegit.* Nep. *Agamemnon cum universa Græcia vix decem annis unam cepit urbem.* Nep.

NOTE 1. The English expression 'by day' is rendered in Latin either by *interdiu* or *die;* 'by night,' by *noctu* or *nocte;* and 'in the evening,' by *vespere* or *vesperi;* see § 82, Exc. 5, (a.) *Ludis* is used for *in tempore ludorum;* and *Saturnalibus, Latinis, gladiatoribus,* for *ludis Saturnalibus,* etc. Other nouns not properly expressing time are used in that sense in the ablative either with or without *in,* as *initio, principio, adventu* and *discessu alicujus, comitiis, 'comitiis, tumultu, ello, pace,* etc.; or *in initio,* etc. But *bello* is more common without *in.* If it is

§ 253.   SYNTAX.—ABLATIVE OF TIME.   253

joined with an adjective or a genitive; as, *Bello Pūnĭco sĕcundo, bello Lătĭnōrum;* and so, also, *pugnā Cannensi.* So we say *in puĕrĭtiā*, but omit *in* with an adjective; as, *extrēmā puĕrĭtiā.* *In* is very rarely used with nouns expressing a certain space of time; as, *annus, dies, hōra*, etc., for the purpose of denoting the time of an event. *In tempŏre* signifies either 'in distress,' or 'in time,' i. e. 'at the right time'; but in both cases *tempŏre* alone is used, and *tempŏre* in the sense of 'early' has even become an adverb, an earlier form of which was *tempŏri* or *tempĕri*, whose comparative is *tempĕrius.*

REMARK 1. When a period is marked by its distance before or after another fixed time, it may be expressed by *ante* or *post* with either the accusative or the ablative.—(*a*) The preposition is regularly placed before the accusative, but after the ablative. If an adjective is used, the preposition is often placed between the adjective and the noun. In this connection the ordinal as well as the cardinal numbers may be used. Hence the English phrase 'after three years,' or 'three years after,' may be expressed in these eight ways; *post tres annos, tribus annis post; post tertium annum, tertio anno post; tres post annos, tribus post annis; tertium post annum, tertio post anno.*

(*b.*) When *ante* or *post* stands last, an accusative may be added to denote the time before or after which any thing took place; as, *Multis annis* post dĕcemviros. Cic. So *Consul factus est annis* post Rōmam condĭtam *trĕcentis duŏdēnōnāgintā.*

NOTE 2. *Post* and *ante* sometimes precede the ablatives, as *ante annis octo; post paucis diēbus;* and also before such ablatives as are used adverbially, as *post aliquanto; ante paulo.*

NOTE 3. *Quam* and a verb are sometimes added to *post* and *ante* in all the forms above specified; e. g. *tribus annis postquam vēnĕrat; post tres annos quam vēnĕrat; tertio anno postquam vēnĕrat; post annum tertium quam vēnĕrat,* etc.; all of which expressions signify 'three years after he had come.' Sometimes *post* is omitted; as, *tertio anno quam vēnĕrat.*

NOTE 4. Instead of *postquam,* 'after,' we may use *ex quo, quum,* or a relative agreeing with the preceding ablative; as, *Ipse octo diēbus,* quibus *has litĕras dăbam, cum Lĕpĭdi cōpias me conjungam;* i. e. in eight days *after* the date of this letter. Planc. in Cic. Fam. *Mors Sex. Roscii* quatriduo, quo *is occisus est, Chrȳsŏgŏno nuntiātur,*—four days *after* he had been killed. Cic. *Quem triduo, quum has dăbam litĕras, exspectābam,*—three days *after* the date of this letter. Planc. in Cic. In such cases *in* is sometimes joined with the ablative; as, *In diēbus paucis, quĭbus hæc acta sunt, mŏrĭtur.* Ter.

REM. 2. The length of time before the present moment may be expressed by *ăbhinc* with the accusative, and, less frequently, the ablative; as, *Quæstor fuisti* ăbhinc annos *quătuordĕcim.* Cic. *Cōmitiis jam* ăbhinc *trīginta* diēbus *habĭtis.* Id. The same is also expressed by *ante* with the pronoun *hic;* as, *ante hos sex menses mălēdixisti mihi,*—six months ago. Phæd. *Ante* is sometimes used instead of *ăbhinc:* and the length of time before is sometimes expressed by the ablative joined with *hic* or *ille;* as, *Paucis his diēbus,* or *paucis illis diēbus,*— a few days ago.

REM. 3. The time at which any thing is done, is sometimes expressed by the neuter accusative *id,* with a genitive; as, *Vēnit id tempŏris.* Cic. So with a preposition; *Ad id dĭĕi.* Gell. See § 212, R. 3.

REM. 4. (*a.*) The time *at* or *within* which any thing is done, is sometimes, with personal subjects, expressed by *de,* with the ablative; as, *De tertiā* vigiliā *ad hostes contendit,*—in the third watch. Cæs. *Ut jŭgŭlent homĭnes surgunt de nocte latrōnes.* Hor. So, also, with *sub;* as, *Ne sub ipsā prŏfectiōre milĭtes oppĭdum irrumpĕrent,*—at the very time of his departure. Cæs. *Sub adventu Romanōrum,* While the Romans were arriving. Id.

(*b.*) The time *within* which any thing occurs, is also sometimes expressed by *intra* with the accusative; as, *Dimĭdium partem nātiōnum subĕgit* intra *vigĭnti* dies. Plaut. Intra *decĭmum* diem, *quam Phĕras vēnĕrat* In less than ten days after. Liv

Rem. 5. The time within which a thing happens, is often expressed by the ablative with *in;* especially (*a*) in connection with numerals; as, *Bis* in die *săturum fiĕri; vix ter* in anno *nuntium audīre;* and (*b*), as in the use of *intra*, to denote that the event happened before the time specified had fully expired.

Rem. 6. Instead of *in pueritiā, ădŏlescentiā, jŭventūte, sĕnectūte*, etc., in stating the age at which a person performed any action, the concretes *puer, ădŏlescens, jŭvĕnis, sĕnex*, etc., are commonly joined to the verb; as, *Cn. Pompeius,* ădŏlescens *se et patrem consilio servāvit.—*So, also, adjectives ending in *ēnārius* are sometimes used in stating the number of years a person has lived; as, *Cĭcĕro sexāgēnārius.*

For the ablative denoting duration of time, see § 236.

ABLATIVE OF PLACE.

§ 254. The name of a town *in which* any thing is said *to be,* or *to be done,* if of the third declension or plural number, is put in the ablative without a preposition ; as,

Alexander Băbўlōne *est mortuus,* Alexander died at Babylon. Cic. *Intĕrĕrit multum—*Thēbis *nūtrītus an* Argis,—whether brought up at Thebes or at Argos. Hor. *Nātus* Tībŭre *vel* Gābiis. Id.

Remark 1. ' In the country ' is expressed by *rūre,* or more commonly by *rūri,* without a preposition; as, *Pater fīlium* rūri *hăbĭtāre jussit.* Cic. With an adjective only *rūre* is used; as, *Interdum nūgāris rūre păterno.* Hor. Cf. § 221, N.

Rem. 2. (*a.*) The preposition *in* is sometimes expressed with names of towns; as, In Philippis *quīdam nunciāvit.* Suet.

(*b.*) Names of towns of the first and second declension, and singular number, and also *dŏmus* and *hūmus,* are in like manner sometimes put in the ablative without *in.* See § 221, R. 2 and R. 3.—So, also, *terrā mărīque,* by land and by sea. *In* is also frequently omitted with *lŏco* and *lŏcis,* especially when joined with an adjective and having the meaning of ' occasion '; as, *Hoc lŏco, multis lŏcis,* etc.—*Libro* joined with an adjective, as *hoc, primo,* etc., is used without *in* when the whole book is meant, and with *in* when only a portion is referred to. An ablative of place joined with *tōto, tōtā, tōtis,* is generally used without *in;* as, *Urbe tōtā gĕmĭtus fit.* Cic. *Tōtā Asiā văgātur.* Id. *Tōtō mări.* Id. But in such cases *in* is sometimes used. So *cunctā Asiā.* Liv.

Rem. 3. Before the names of countries, of nations used for those of countries, and of all other places in which any thing is said to be or to be done, except those of towns, and excepting also the phrases specified in the first and second remarks, the preposition *in* is commonly used; as, *Iphicrātes* in Thrāciā *vixit, Chares* in Sigēo. Nep. *Rūre ĕgo vīventem, tu dicis* in urbe *beātum.* Hor. *Aio hoc fĭĕri* in Græciā. Plaut. In Bactriānis Sogdiānis*que urbes condĭdit.* Lūcus in urbe *fuit.* Virg. But it is sometimes omitted by writers of every class and period; as, *Mīlĭtes stătīvis* castris *hăbēbat.* Sall. *Magnis in laudĭbus fuit tōtā* Græciā. Nep. *Pŏpŭli sensus maxĭme* theātro *et* spectācŭlis *perspectus est.* Cic. *Pompeius se* oppido *tĕnet.* Id. In the poets and later prose writers this omission is of very frequent occurrence not only with names of towns but with ablatives of all nouns answering to the question, where? as, *Nāvīta* vixit puppe *sĕdens.* Ovid. *Ibam forte* Viā *Săcrā.* Hor. Silvisque agrisque viis*que corpŏra fœda jăcent.* Ovid. *Mĕdio* alveo *concursum est.* Liv.*—Fŏris,* out at the door, abroad, is properly an ablative of place ; as, Fŏris *cœnat.* Cic. Cf. § 237, R. 5, (*c.*)

§ 255. 1. After verbs expressing or implying motion, the name of a town *whence* the motion proceeds, is put in the ablative, without a preposition ; as,

Brundĭsio *profécti sŭmus*, We departed from Brundisium. Cic. *Diŏnȳsius tȳrannus* Sȳrācūsis *expulsus Cŏrinthi puĕros dŏcēbat*. Id. *Dēmărātus Tarquĭnios* Cŏrintho *fūgit*. Id. *Accēpi tuas litĕras dătas* Plăcentiā. Id. *Intĕrim* Rōmā *per litĕras certior fit;* scil. *dătas* or *missas*. Sall. J. 82. So, also, after a verbal noun; as, Narbōne *rĕdĭtus*. Cic.

REMARK 1. The ablatives *dŏmo, hŭmo,* and *rūre* or *rūri,* are used, like names of towns, to denote the place whence motion proceeds; as,

Dŏmo *profectus*, Having set out from home. Nep. *Surgit* hŭmo *jŭvĕnis,* The youth rises from the ground. Ovid. Rūre *huc advĕnit*. Ter. *Si* rūri *vivĕret*. Id. Virgil uses *domo* with *unde;* as, *Qui gĕnus? unde dŏmo?* and Livy instead of *dŏmo ăbesse,* has *esse ab dŏmo*. With an adjective, *rūre,* and not *rūri,* must be used.

REM. 2. With names of towns and *dŏmus* and *hŭmus,* when answering the question 'whence?' *ab, ex,* or *de,* is sometimes used; as, *Ab Alexandriā profectus*. Cic. *Ex dŏmo*. Id. *De vitĭfĕrā vēnisse Viennā*. Mart. *Ab hŭmo*. Virg.

REM. 3. (*a.*) With other names of places whence motion proceeds, *ab, ex,* or *de,* is commonly expressed; as, *Me a portu præmisit*. Plaut. *Ex* Asiā *transis in Eurōpam*. Curt. *Ex castris profĭciscuntur*. Cæs. *De Pomptīno,* scil. prædio. Cic.—So, also, before names of nations used for those of countries; as, *Ex Mēdis ad adversāriōrum hibernācŭla pervēnit*. Nep.

(*b.*) But the preposition is sometimes omitted; as, *Litĕræ* Măcĕdŏniā *allātæ*. Liv. *Classis* Cypro *advēnit*. Curt. *Cessissent* loco. Liv. *Ni cite* vicis *et* castellis *proxĭmis subventum fŏret*. Id. *Ite* sacris, *propĕrāte* sacris, *laurumque* căpillis *pōnite*. Ovid. Finibus *omnes prōsiluĕre suis*. Virg. *Adrŏlcunt ingentes* montĭbus *ornos*. Id. This omission of the preposition is most common in the poets and later prose writers.

2. The place *by, through,* or *over* which, after verbs of motion, commonly follows *per;* but frequently also it is put in the ablative without a preposition; as,

Per Thēbas *iter fēcit*. Nep. *Exercĭtum* vădo *transdūcit*. Cæs. His pontĭbus *pābŭlātum mittēbat*. Id. *Tribūni militum* portā Collīnā *urbem intrāvēre sub signis,* mediāque urbe *agmine in* Aventīnum *pergunt*. Liv. *Legiōnes* Penninis Cottiānisque Alpĭbus, *pars* monte Graio, *trādūcuntur*. Tac. *Equĭtes* viā brĕviōre præmīsi. Cic.

ABLATIVE AFTER COMPARATIVES.

§ **256.** 1. When two objects are compared by means of the comparative degree, a conjunction, as *quam, atque,* etc., is sometimes expressed, and sometimes omitted.

2. The comparative degree, when *quam* is omitted, is followed by the ablative of that with which the comparison is made; as,

Nihil est virtūte *formōsius,* Nothing is more beautiful than virtue. Cic. *Quis* C. Lælio *cōmior?* Who is more courteous than C. Lælius? Id.

REMARK 1. The person or thing with which the *subject* of a proposition is compared, is usually put in the ablative; as,

Sidĕre *pulchrior ille est, tu lĕvior* cortice. Hor. *Vilius argentum est* auro, virtūtĭbus *aurum*. Id. *Tullus Hostīlius fĕrōcior* Rōmŭlo *fuit*. Liv. Lacrĭmā *nihil citius ărescit*. Cic. *Quid magis est dūrum* saxo, *quid mollius* undā? Ovid. Hoc *nēmo fuit minus ineptus*. Ter. *Albānum, Mæcēnas, sive* Fălernum *te magis* appŏsitis *delectat*. Hor.

Rem. 2. An object with which a person or thing addressed is compared, is also put in the ablative; as, *O fons Bandūsiæ splendidior vitro!* Hor.

Rem. 3. Sometimes the person or thing with which the subject of a proposition is compared, instead of following it in the ablative, is connected with it by *quam*, and it is then put in the same case as the subject, whether in the nominative or the accusative; as, *Orātio quam hăbītus fuit mĭsĕrābĭlior.* Cic. *Affirmo nullam esse laudem ampliōrem* quam eam. Id. So, also, when an ablative in the case absolute takes the place of the subject; as, *Eōdem* (scil. *dŭce*) *plŭra,* quam grĕgārio mīlīte, *tŏlĕrante.* Tac.

Rem. 4. If the person or thing which is compared with any object is neither the subject of the sentence nor the person addressed, *quam* is commonly used, and the object which follows it is then put in the nominative with *sum,* and sometimes in an oblique case to agree with the object with which it is compared; as, *Mĕliōrem,* quam ego sum, *suppōno tibi.* Plaut. *Ego hŏmĭnem callĭdiōrem vīdi nēmĭnem* quam Phormiōnem. Ter. *Adventus hostium fuit* agris, quam urbi *terrĭbilior.* Liv. *Omnes fontes* æstāte, quam hiëme, *sunt gĕlidiōres.* Plin. Thĕmistoclis *nōmen,* quam Sŏlōnis, *est illustrius.* Cic.—The following example illustrates both the preceding constructions:—*Ut tibi multo majōri,* quam Africānus fuit, *me non multo minōrem* quam Lælium *făcile et in rēpūblĭcā et in ămīcĭtĭā adjunctum esse pătiāre.* Cic.

Rem. 5. (*a.*) The person or thing with which the *object* of an active verb is compared, though usually connected with it by *quam,* (R. 4,) is sometimes put in the ablative, especially in the poets, and frequently also even in prose, if the object is a pronoun, particularly a relative pronoun; as, *Attălo,* quo *grăviōrem inimīcum non hăbui, sŏrōrem dĕdit,* He gave his sister to Attalus, *than whom,* etc. Curt. *Hoc nĭhil grātius făcĕre pŏtes.* Cic. *Causam ĕnim suscĕpisti antīquiōrem memŏriā tuā.* Id. *Exēgi monŭmentum ære pĕrennius.* Hor. *Cur ŏlīvum sanguine vīpĕrīno cautius rĭtat?* Id. *Quid prius dīcam sŏlĭtis părentis* laudibus? Id. *Mājōra* viribus *audes.* Virg. *Nullam sacrā* vīte *prius sĕvēris arbŏrem.* Hor. *Nullos* his *mallem lūdos spectasse.* Id. § 178, 3.

(*b.*) The ablative instead of *quam* is never used with any other oblique case except the accusative, but *quam* is sometimes found, even where the ablative might have been used; as, *Mĕlior tūtiorque est certa pax* quam *spērāta victōria.* Liv. After *quam,* if the verb cannot be supplied from the preceding sentence, *est, fuit,* etc., must be added; as, *Hæc verba sunt M. Varrōnis,* quam fuit *Claudius, doctiōris.* Gell. *Drūsum Germānĭcum mĭnōrem nātu,* quam *ipse* erat, *frātrem āmīsit.* Sen.

Rem. 6. (*a.*) *Minus, plus,* and *amplius* with numerals, and with other words denoting a certain measure or a certain portion of a thing, are used either with or without *quam,* generally as indeclinable words, without influence upon the construction, but merely to modify the number; as, *Non plus quam quătuor millia effūgĕrunt,* not *effūgit.* Liv. *Pictōres antīqui non sunt ūsi plus quam quătuor cŏlōrĭbus,* not *plūrĭbus.* Cic.

(*b.*) *Quam* is frequently omitted with all cases; as, *Mīnus duo millia hŏmĭnum ex tanto exercĭtu effūgĕrunt.* Liv. *Mīlĭtes Rōmāni sæpe plus dīmĭdiāti mensis cĭbāria fĕrēbant.* Cic. *Quum plus annum æger fuisset.* Liv. *Sĕdĕcim non amplius eo anno lĕgiōnĭbus dēfensum imperium est.* Id.

(*c.*) These comparatives, as in the preceding example, are sometimes inserted between the numeral and its substantive, and sometimes, when joined with a negative, they follow both, as a sort of apposition; as, *Quinque millia armātōrum, non amplius, rĕlictum ĕrat præsĭdium,*—a garrison of five thousand soldiers, not more. Liv. So, also, *longius; Cæsar certior est factus, magnas Gallōrum cōpias non* longius millia passuum octo *ab hībernis suīs abfuisse.* Cæs. See § 236.

(*d.*) The ablative is sometimes used with these as with other comparatives; as, *Dies trĭgĭnta aut plus* eo *in nāvi fui.* Ter. Triennio *amplius.* Cic. Hōrā *amplius mōliēbantur.* Id. *Ne longius* triduo *ab castris absit.* Cæs. *Apud Suēvos non longius* anno *rĕmănēre ūno in loco incŏlendi causā lĭcet.* Id. *Quum initio non amplius* duobus millibus *hăbuisset.* Sall.

§ 256.   SYNTAX.—ABLATIVE AFTER COMPARATIVES.   257

REM. 7. *Quam* is in like manner sometimes omitted, without a change of case, after *major, minor*, and some other comparatives; as, *Obsides ne minores octonum denum annorum neu majores quinum quadragenum,..... of not less than eighteen, nor more than forty-five years of age.* Liv. *Ex urbano exercitu, qui minores quinque et triginta annis erant, in naves impositi sunt.* The genitive and ablative, in these and similar examples, are to be referred to § 211, R. 6. *Longius ab urbe* mille *passuum.* Liv. *Annos natus magis quadraginta.* Cic.

REM. 8. When the second member of a comparison is an infinitive or a clause, *quam* is always expressed; as, *Nihil est in dicendo majus quam ut faveat Prætori auditor.* Cic.

REM. 9. Certain nouns, participles, and adjectives,—as *opinione, spe, exspectatione, fide,—dicto, solito,—æquo, credibili, necessario, vero,* and *justo,*—are used in a peculiar manner in the ablative after comparatives; as, *Opinione celerius venturus esse dicitur,*—sooner than is expected. Cæs. *Dicto citius tumida æquora placat,* Quicker than the word was spoken. Virg. *Injurias gravius æquo habere.* Sall.

(*a.*) These ablatives supply the place of a clause; thus, *gravius æquo* is equivalent to *gravius quam quod æquum est.* They are often omitted; as, *Themistocles liberius vivebat,* scil. *æquo.* Nep. In such cases, the comparative may be translated by the positive degree, with *too, quite,* or *rather,* as in the above example—'He lived too freely,' or 'rather freely.' *Voluptas quum major est atque longior, omne animi lumen exstinguit,*—when it is too great, and of too long continuance. Cic. So *tristior,* scil. *solito,* rather sad.

(*b.*) The English word 'still,' joined with comparatives, is expressed by *etiam* or *vel,* and only in later prose writers by *adhuc*; as, *Ut in corporibus magnæ dissimilitudines sunt, sic in animis exsistunt majores* etiam *varietates.* Cic.

REM. 10. (*a.*) With *inferior,* the dative is sometimes used, instead of the ablative; as, *Vir nulla arte cuiquam inferior.* Sall. The ablative is also found; as, *Ut humanos casus virtute inferiores putes.* Cic. But usually *inferior* is followed by *quam*; as, *Timotheus belli laude non inferior fuit,* quam pater. Cic. *Gratia non inferior,* quam qui *umquam fuerunt amplissimi.* Id.

(*b.*) *Qualis,* 'such as,' with a comparative, occurs poetically instead of the relative pronoun in the ablative; as, *Nardo perunctum,* quale *non perfectius meæ liborarint manus*; instead of *quo.* Hor. Epod. 5, 59. *Animæ* quales *neque candidiores terra tulit*; for *quibus.* Id. Sat. 1, 5, 41.

REM. 11. *Quam pro* is used after comparatives, to express disproportion; as, *Prælium atrocius* quam pro numero *pugnantium,* The battle was more severe than was proportionate to the number of the combatants. Liv. *Minor,* quam pro tumultu, *cædes.* Tac.

REM. 12. When two adjectives or adverbs are compared with each other, both are put in the comparative; as, *Triumphus* clarior *quam* gratior, A triumph more famous than acceptable. Liv. *Fortius* quam *felicius bellum gesserunt.* So, also, when the comparative is formed by means of *magis*; as, *Magis audacter quam parate ad dicendum veniebat.* Cic.—Tacitus uses the positive in one part of the proposition; as, *Speciem excelsæ gloriæ* vehementius *quam* caute *appetebat*; or even in both; as, *Claris majoribus quam vetustis.*

REM. 13. (*a.*) *Potius* and *magis* are sometimes joined pleonastically with *malle* and *præstare,* and also with comparatives; as, *Ab omnibus se desertos potius quam abs te defensos esse malunt.* Cic. *Qui* magis *vere vincere quam diu imperare* malit. Liv. *Ut emori* potius *quam servire præstaret.* Cic. *Mihi quævis fuga* potius *quam ulla provincia esset* optatior. Id. *Quis* magis *queat esse beatior?* Virg.

(*b.*) So, also, the prepositions *præ, ante, præter,* and *supra,* are sometimes used with a comparative; as, *Unus præ ceteris fortior exsurgit,* Apul. *Scelere ante alios immanior omnes.* Virg. They also occur with a superlative; as, *Ante* alios *carissimus.* Nep. As these prepositions, when joined with the positive, denote comparison, they seem in such examples to be redundant. See § 127

Rem. 14. *Alius* is sometimes in poetry treated as a comparative, and construed with the ablative instead of *atque* with the nominative or accusative; as, *Nēve pŭtes ălium săpiente bŏnōque beātum.* Hor. *Alius Lȳsippo.* Id. But compare § 251, N.

Rem. 15. By the poets *ac* and *atque* are sometimes used instead of *quam* after comparatives; as, *Quanto constantior īdem in vĭtĭis, tanto lĕvius mĭser ac prior ille, qui,* etc. Hor. *Arctius* atque *hĕdĕrā prōcĕra adstringĭtur ilex.* Id.

Rem. 16. The *degree of difference* between objects compared is expressed by the ablative :—

(1.) Of substantives; as, *Mĭnor ūno* mense, Younger by one month. Hor. Sesquipĕde *quam tu longior,* Taller than you by a foot and a half. Plaut. *Hibernia* dimidio *mĭnor quam Britannia.* Caes. *Dimidio mĭnōris constābit,* It will cost less by half. Cic. *Quam mŏlestum est ūno* digito *plus hăbēre!*....to have one finger more, i. e. than we have, to have six fingers. Id.—but the expression is ambiguous, as it might mean ' to have more than one finger.' *Sŭpĕrat* căpite *et cervīcibus altis.* Virg.

(2.) Of neuter adjectives of quantity and neuter pronouns, in the singular number. Such are *tanto, quanto, quo, eo, hoc, multo, parvo, paulo, nimio, ăliquanto, tantŭlo, altĕro tanto* (twice as much); as, *Multo doctior es patre,* Thou art (by) much more learned than thy father. The relative and demonstrative words, *quanto—tanto, quo—eo,* or *quo—hoc,* signifying ' by how much—by so much,' are often to be translated by an emphatic *the;* us, *Quanto sŭmus sŭpĕriōres,* tanto *nos submissius gĕrāmus,* The more eminent we are, the more humbly let us conduct ourselves: lit. by how much—by so much—. Cic. *Eo grāvior est dŏlor,* quo *culpa est mājor.* Id. But the relative word generally precedes the demonstrative; as, *Quo difficilius,* hoc *praeclārius.* Id. Poetically, also, *quam magis—tam magis* are used instead of *quanto magis—tanto magis.* Virg. Æn. 7, 787: and *quam magis—tanto magis.* Lucr. 6, 459.—*Iter* multo *făcilius,*—much easier. Caes. *Parvo brĕvius,* A little shorter. Plin. Eo *magis,* The more. Cic. Eo *minus.* Id. Istoc *magis vŭpŭlabis,* So much the more. Plaut. *Via* altĕro tanto *longior,*—as long again. Nep. Multo *id maxĭmum fuit.* Liv.

(3.) The ablative of degree is joined not only with comparatives but with verbs which contain the idea of comparison; as, *mălo, praesto, sŭpĕro, excello, antĕcello, antĕcēdo,* and others compounded with *ante;* and also with *ante* and *post,* in the sense of ' earlier ' and ' later '; as, *Multo praestat.* Sall. *Post paulo,* A little after. Id. *Multo ante lūcis adventum,* Long before—. Id. *Multis partibus* is equivalent to *multo;* as, *Nŭmĕro multis partibus esset infĕrior.* Caes.

Note. The accusatives *multum, tantum, quantum,* and *ăliquantum,* are sometimes used instead of the corresponding ablatives; as, *Aliquantum est ad rem ăvidior.* Ter. Multum *imprŏbiōres sunt.* Plaut. Quantum *domo infĕrior,* tantum *glōriā sŭpĕrior ēvăsit.* Val. Max. Cf. § 232, (3.)—So *longe,* 'far,' is frequently used for *multo;* as, Longe *mĕlior.* Virg. Longe *et multum antĕcellĕre.* Cic. So, *pars pĕdis* sesqui *mājor,*—longer by one half. Id.

ABLATIVE ABSOLUTE.

§ 257. A noun and a participle are put in the ablative, called *absolute,* to denote the time, cause, means, or concomitant of an action, or the condition on which it depends; as,

Pȳthăgŏras, Tarquinio regnante, *in Ĭtăliam vēnit,* Pythagoras came into Italy, in the reign of Tarquin. Cic. *Lŭpus,* stimŭlante fāme, *captat ŏvīle,* Hunger inciting, the wolf seeks the fold. Ovid. *Milĭtes, pĕcōre e longinquiōribus vīcis ădacto, extrēmam fāmem sustentābant.* Caes. *Hac ōrātiōne hăbĭtā, conciliam dīmīsit.* Id. *Galli,* re cognĭtā, *obsidiōnem rĕlinquunt.* Id. Virtūte exceptā, *nihil mīcitiā praestăbilius pŭtētis.* Cic.

§ 257.   SYNTAX.—ABLATIVE ABSOLUTE.   259

NOTE 1. The Latin ablative absolute may be expressed in English by a similar construction, but it is commonly better to translate it by a clause connected by *when, since, while, although, after, as,* etc., or by a verbal substantive; as, *Te adjŭvante,* With thy assistance. *Non—nisi te adjŭvante,* Only with thy assistance, or not without thy assistance. *Te non adjŭvante,* Without thy assistance. Cf. § 274, R. 5, (c.)

REMARK 1. This construction is an abridged form of expression, equivalent to a dependent clause connected by *quum, si, etsi, quamquam, quamvis,* etc.

Thus, for *Tarquinio regnante,* the expression *dum Tarquinius regnābat* might be used; for *hac ōrātiōne habĭtā;—quum hanc ōrātiōnem habuisset,* or *quum hœc ōrătio habĭta esset,—concilium dimīsit.* The ablative absolute may always be resolved into a proposition, by making the noun or pronoun the subject, and the participle the predicate.

REM. 2. This construction is common only with present and perfect participles. Instances of its use with participles in *rus* and *dus* are comparatively rare; as,

Cæsăre ventūro, *Phosphŏre, redde diem.* Mart. Irruptūris *tam infestis* nātiōnĭbus. Liv. *Quum concio plausum, meo nōmĭne recĭtando, dedisset,*—when my name was pronounced. Cic. *Quum* immōlandā Iphĭgĕnĭā *tristis Calchas esset.* Id. *Quis est ĕnim, qui, nullis officii præceptis trādendis, philŏsŏphum se audeat dicĕre*—without propounding any rules of duty. Cic. Cf. § 274, R. 5, (c.) and R. 9.

REM. 3. (*a.*) A noun is put in the ablative absolute, only when it denotes a different person or thing from any in the leading clause. Cf. § 274, 3, (*a.*)

(*b.*) Yet a few examples occur of a deviation from this principle, especially with a substantive pronoun referring to some word in the leading clause; as, *Se audiente, scribit Thūcydides.* Cic. *Legio ex castris Varrōnis,* adstante *et* inspectante ipso, *signa sustūlit.* Cæs. *Me dūce, ad hunc vōti finem,* me milite, *veni.* Ovid. So *M. Porcius Căto,* vivo *quŏque* Scipiōne, *allātrāre ejus magnitūdinem solĭtus ērat.* Liv.

NOTE 2. Two participles must not be put together in the ablative absolute agreeing with the same noun. Thus, we may say *Porcia sæpe maritum cogitantem invenĕrat,* but not, *Porcia marīto cōgitante invento.*

NOTE 3. Instead of the ablative absolute denoting *a cause,* an accusative with *ob* or *propter* occurs in Livy and in later writers; as, *Cānōpum condidĕre Spartāni,* ob sĕpultum *illic* rectōrem *nāvis* Cănōpum. Tac. *Decemvĭri libros Sibyllinos inspicĕre jussi sunt* propter terrĭtos homĭnes *nŏvis prōdĭgiis.* Liv.

REM. 4. The ablative absolute serves to mark the time of an action, by reference to that of another action. If the present participle is used, the time of the action expressed by the participle, is the same as that of the principal verb. The perfect participle and the future in *rus,* denote respectively an action as prior or subsequent to that expressed by the principal verb.

Thus in the preceding examples—*Pythăgŏras,* Tarquinio regnante, *in Italiam vēnit,* Pythagoras came into Italy *during the reign of Tarquinius. Galli,* re cognĭtā, *obsidiōnem relinquunt,* The Gauls, *having learned the fact,* abandon the siege. So, *Rex ăpum non nisi* migrātūro exāmine *fŏras prōcēdit,* The king-bee does not go abroad, except *when a swarm is about to emigrate.* Plin.

NOTE 4. *Non prius quam, non nisi, ut, velut,* and *tamquam*, are sometimes joined with the participle; as, *Tiberius excessum Augusti* non prius *palam fecit, quam Agrippa juvene interempto,* —not uutil. Suet. *Galli lati,* ut *explorata victoria, ad castra Romanorum pergunt.* Cæs. *Antiochus,* tamquam *non transituris in Asiam Romanis,* etc. Liv.

REM. 5. (*a.*) The construction of the ablative absolute with the perfect passive participle, arises frequently from the want of a participle of that tense in the active voice.

Thus, for 'Cæsar, having sent forward the cavalry, was following with all his forces,' we find, '*Cæsar,* equitatu præmisso, *subsequebatur omnibus copiis.*'

(*b.*) As the perfect participle in Latin may be used for both the perfect active and the perfect passive participles in English, its meaning can, in many instances, be determined only by the connection, since the agent with *a* or *ab* is generally not expressed with this participle in the ablative absolute, as it is with other parts of the passive voice. Thus, *Cæsar,* his dictis, *concilium dimisit,* might be rendered, ' Cæsar, *having said this,* or *this having been said* (by some other person), dismissed the assembly.'

(*c.*) As the perfect participles of deponent verbs correspond to perfect active participles in English, no such necessity exists for the use of the ablative absolute with them; as, *Cæsar,* hæc locutus, *concilium dimisit.* In the following example, both constructions are united: *Itaque....agros Remorum* depopulati, *omnibus vicis, ædificiisque* incensis. Cæs.

REM. 6. The perfect participles of neuter deponent verbs, and some also of active deponents, which admit of both an active and a passive sense, are used in the ablative absolute; as, *Orta luce.* Cæs. *Vel exstincto vel* elapso animo, *nullum residere sensum.* Cic. *Tam* multis *gloriam ejus* adeptis. Plin. *Litteras ad exercitus, tamquam* adepto principatu, *misit.* Tac.

REM. 7. (*a.*) As the verb *sum* has no present participle, two nouns, or a noun and an adjective, which might be the subject and predicate of a dependent clause, are put in the ablative absolute without a participle; as,

Quid, adolescentulo duce, *efficere possent,* What they could do under the guidance of a youth. Cæs. Me suasore *atque* impulsore, *hoc factum,* By my advice and instigation. Plaut. *Hannibale vivo,* While Hannibal was living. Nep. *Invita Minerva,* in opposition to one's genius. Cic. *Cælo sereno,* when the weather is clear. Virg. *Me ignaro,* without my knowledge. Cic. With names of office, the concrete noun is commonly used in the ablative absolute, rather than the corresponding abstract with *in* to denote the time of an event; as, *Romam venit* Mario consule, He came to Rome in the consulship of Marius. Cic.

(*b.*) The nouns so used as predicates are by some grammarians considered as supplying the place of participles by expressing in themselves the action of a verb. Such are *dux, comes, adjutor* aud *adjutrix, auctor, testis, judex, interpres, magister* and *magistra, præceptor* and *præceptrix*; as, duce natura, in the sense of *ducente natura,* under the guidance of nature; *judice Polybio,* according to the judgment of Polybius.

REM. 8. A clause sometimes supplies the place of the noun; as, *Nondum comperto* quam in regionem venisset rex. Liv. *Audito* venisse nuncium. Tac. Vale *dicto.* Ovid. This construction, however, is confined to a few participles; as, *audito, cognito, comperto, explorato, desperato, nunciato, dicto, edicto.* But the place of such participle is sometimes supplied by a neuter adjective in the ablative: as, Incerto *præ tenebris quid peterent.* Liv. Cf. R. 7, (*a.*) *Haud cuiquam dubio* quin hostium essent. Id. *Juxta periculoso* vera an ficta prometret. Tac.

REM. 9. (1.) The noun in the ablative, like the subject nominative, is sometimes wanting; (*a*) when it is contained in a preceding clause; as, *Atticus Serviliam, Bruti matrem, non minus post mortem ejus, quam* florente, coluit, scil. eo,

i. e Brūto. Nep. (*b*) When it is the general word for person or persons followed by a descriptive relative clause; as, *Hannibal Ibērum copias trajēcit, præmissis*, qui *Alpium transitus speculārentur.* Liv. (*c*) When the participle in the neuter singular corresponds to the impersonal construction of neuter verbs in the passive voice; as, *In amnis transgressu, multum certāto, Bardesānes rēcit.* Tac. *Mihi*, errāto, *nulla vēnia, recte facto, extgua laus prōpōnitur.* Cic. *Quum, nondum pālam facto, rivi mortuique prōmiscue complōrārentur.* Liv. *Nam jam ætāte eā sum, ut nom sict,* peccāto, *mi ignosci æquum;* i. e. *si peccātum fuĕrit.* Ter. Cf. § 274, R. 5, (*b*.)

(2.) So in descriptions of the weather; as, *Tranquillo*, scil. *mări*, the sea being tranquil. Liv. *Sĕrēno*, scil. *cælo*, the sky being clear. Id. *Arānei sĕrēno texunt, nūbilo texunt,*—in clear and in cloudy weather. Plin. Substantives when used thus are to be considered as ablatives of time; as, *Cōmītiis, lŭdis, Circensibus.* Suetonius has used *proscriptiōne* in the sense of 'during the proscription.' So *pāce et Principe.* Tac. Impĕrio *pŏpŭli Rōmāni.* Cæs.

REM. 10. This ablative is sometimes connected to the preceding clause by a conjunction; as, *Cæsar,* quamquam obsīdiōne *Massiliæ* rĕtardante, *brĕvi tāmen omnia subĕgit.* Suet. *Dĕcemviri non* ante, quam perlātis lēgĭbus, *dēpŏsītūros impĕrium esse ai*bant. Liv.

REM. 11. A predicate ablative is sometimes added to passive participles of *naming, choosing,* etc. § 210, (3.); as, *Hasdrūbāle* impĕrātōre *suffecto.* Liv.

CONNECTION OF TENSES.

§ 258. Tenses, in regard to their connection, are divided into two classes—*principal* and *historical.*

A. The principal tenses are, the *present*, the *perfect definite*, and the *two futures.*

B. The historical, which are likewise called the *preterite* tenses (§ 145, N. 2.), are the *imperfect*, the *historical perfect*, and the *pluperfect.*

I. In the connection of leading and dependent clauses, only tenses of the same class can, in general, be united with each other. Hence:—

1. A *principal* tense is followed by the *present* and *perfect definite*, and by the periphrastic form with *sim.* And:—

2. A *preterite* tense is followed by the *imperfect* and *pluperfect*, and by the periphrastic form with *essem.*

NOTE. The periphrastic forms in each class supply the want of subjunctive futures in the regular conjugation.

The following examples will illustrate the preceding rules:—

(*a.*) In the first class. *Scio quid ăgas. Scio quid ēgĕris. Scio quid actūrus sis.*—*Audīvi quid ăgas,* I have heard what you are doing. *Audīvi quid ēgĕris Audīvi quid actūrus sis.*—*Audiām quid ăgas,* etc.—*Audīvĕro quid ăgas,* etc.

(*b.*) In the second class. *Sciēbam quid ăgĕres. Sciēbam quid ēgisses. Sciēbam quid actūrus esses.*—*Audīvi quid ăgĕres,* I heard what you were doing. *Audīvi quid ēgisses. Audīvi quid actūrus esses.*—*Audīvĕram quid ăgĕres,* etc.

The following may serve as additional examples in the first class; viz. of *principal tenses* depending on,

(1.) The PRESENT; as, *Non* sum ita *hĕbes, ut istuc* dicam. Cic. *Quantum dŏlōrem* accēpĕrim, *tu existimāre* pōtes. Id. *Nec* dubito *quin rĕdĭtus ējus reipūblicæ salūt iris* fūtūrus sit. Id.

(2.) The PERFECT DEFINITE; as, *Sătis prōvīsum est, ut ne quid ăgĕre possint.* Id. *Quis mūsīcis, quis huic stŭdio lĭtĕrārum se dēdĭdit, quin omnem illārum artium vim* comprĕhendĕrit. Id. *Dēfectiōnes sōlis prædictæ* sunt, *quæ, quantæ, quando* fūtūræ sint. Id.

(3.) The FUTURES; as, *Sic făcillĭme, quanta ōrātōrum sit, semperque* fuĕrit *paucitas,* jūdīcābit. Id. *Ad quos dies* rĕdĭtūrus sim, scrībam *ad te*. Id. *Si* sciĕris *aspĭdem lătĕre uspiam, et velle ălĭquem imprūdentem sŭper eam assĭdĕre, cūjus mors tibi ĕmŏlŭmentum* factūra sit, *imprŏbe* fēcĕris, *nisi* mŏnŭĕris, *ne* assīdeat. Id.

The following, also, are additional examples in the second class, viz. of *preterite tenses* depending on,-

(1.) The IMPERFECT; as, *Unum illud* extĭmescēbam, *ne quid turpĭter* făcĕrem, *vel jam* effēcissem. Cic. *Non ĕnim* dŭbĭtābam, *quin eas libenter* lectūrus eases. Id.

(2.) The HISTORICAL PERFECT; as, *Vēni in ējus villam ut libros inde* prōmĕrem. Id. *Hæc quum* essent nuntiāta, *Vălĕrius classem extemplo ad ostium flūmĭnis* duxit. Liv.

(3.) The PLUPERFECT; as, *Păvor* cēpĕrat *mīlites, ne mortĭfĕrum esset vulnus*. Liv. *Ego ex ipso* audiĕram, *quam a te lĭbĕrālĭter* essĕt tractātus. Cic. *Non sătis mihi* constĭtĕrat, *cum ăliquāne ănimi mei molestiā, an pŏtius libenter te Athēnis* vīsūrus essem. Id.

REMARK 1. (*a*.) When the present is used in narration for the historical perfect, it may, like the latter, be followed by the imperfect; as, *Lēgātos* mittunt, *ut păcem* impetrārent. Cæs.

(*b*.) The present is also sometimes followed by the perfect subjunctive in its historical sense; as, *Paudĭte nunc Hĕlicōna, deæ, cantusque* mŏvēte, *Qui bello* excīti *rēges, quæ quemque sĕcūtæ* Complērint *campos acies*. Virg.

REM. 2. The perfect definite is often followed by the imperfect, even when a present action or state is spoken of, if it is possible to conceive of it in its progress, and not merely in its conclusion or result; and especially when the agent had an intention accompanying him from the beginning to the end of the action; as, *Fēci hoc*, ut intellĭgĕres, I have done this that you might understand; i. e. such was my intention from the beginning. Sunt *philŏsŏphi et* fuērunt, *qui omnīno nullam hăbĕre* censērent *hūmānārum rerum procūrātiōnem deos*. Cic.

REM. 3. (*a*.) The historical perfect is not regularly followed by the perfect subjunctive, as the latter is not, in general, used in reference to past action indefinite.

(*b*.) These tenses are, however, sometimes used in connection, in the narrative of a past event, especially in Livy and Cornelius Nepos; as, Factum est *ut plus quam collēgæ Miltĭădes* văluĕrit. Nep.

(*c*.) The imperfect and perfect are even found together after the historical perfect, when one action is represented as permanent or repeated, and the other simply as a fact; as, *Adeo nihil* mĭsĕrĭti sunt, *ut incursiōnes* făcĕrent *et Vēios in ănimo* hăbuĕrint *oppugnāre*. Liv.

(*d*.) The historical perfect may even be followed by the present, when a general truth is to be expressed, and not merely one which is valid for the time indicated by the leading verb; as, *Antiŏcho păcem pĕtenti ad priōres condĭtiōnes nihil addĭtum, Africāno prædĭcante, nĕque Rōmānis, si* vincantur, *ănimos mĭnui, nĕque, si vincant, sĕcundis rēbus insōlescĕre*. Just.

REM. 4. (*a*.) As present infinitives and present participles depend for their time upon the verbs with which they are connected, they are followed by such tenses as those verbs may require; as, *Apelles pictōres quŏque eos peccāre* dīcēbat, *qui non sentirent, quid esset sătis*. Cic. *Ad te scripsi, te lĕviter accusans in eo, quod de me cito* credĭdisses. Id.

(*b.*) In like manner the tense of the subjunctive following the infinitive future is determined by the verb on which such infinitive depends; as, *Sol Phaëthonti filio factūrum se esse dixit quicquid optasset.* Cic.

REM. 5. (*a.*) The perfect infinitive follows the general rule, and takes after it a principal or a preterite tense, according as it is used in the definite or in the historical sense; as, *Arbitrāmur nos ea praestĭtisse, quae rătio et doctrīna praescripsĕrit.* Cic. *Est quod gaudeas te in istā lŏca vēnisse, ŭbi ălĭquid săpĕre vĭdērēre.* Id.

(*b.*) But it may sometimes take a different tense, according to Rem. 2; as, *Ita mihi vĭdeor et esse Deos, et quāles essent sătis ostendisse.* Cic.

II. Tenses belonging to different classes may be made dependent on each other, when the sense requires it.

(*a.*) Hence a present or perfect definite may follow a preterite, when the result of a past action extends to the present time; as, *Ardēbat autem Hortensius cŭpĭdĭtāte dīcendi sic, ut in nullo umquam flagrantius stŭdium vīdĕrim;* i. e. that up to this time I have never seen. Cic. And, on the other hand, a preterite may follow a present to express a continuing action in the past; as, *Scītōte oppĭdum esse in Sicĭliā nullum, quo in oppĭdo non isti dēlecta mŭlier ad libīdĭnem osset:* (*esset* here alludes to the whole period of Verres' praetorship.) Cic.

(*b.*) But without violating the rule which requires similar tenses to depend upon each other, the *hypothetical* imperfect subjunctive, may be followed by the present or perfect subjunctive, since the imperfect subjunctive refers to the present time; as, *Mĕmŏrāre possem quĭbus in lŏcis maxĭmas hostium cōpĭas pŏpŭlus Rōmānus parvā mănu fūdĕrit.* Sall. *Possem* here differs from *possum* only by the hypothetical form of the expression.

INDICATIVE MOOD.

§ 259. The indicative is used in every proposition in which the thing asserted is represented as a reality.

NOTE. Hence it is used even in the expression of conditions and suppositions with *si, nisi, etsi,* and *ĕtiamsi,* when the writer, without intimating his own opinion, supposes a thing as actual, or, with *nĭsi,* makes an exception, which, only for the sake of the inference, he regards as actual; as, *Mors aut plāne neglĭgenda est, si omnīno exstinguit ănimum, aut ĕtiam optanda, si ălĭquo eum dēdūcit, ŭbi sit fŭtūrus æternus.* Cic. *Adhuc certe, nĭsi ĕgo insānio, stulte omnia et incaute fĭunt.* Id.—It is likewise used in interrogatives.

REMARK 1. The several tenses have already been defined, and their usual significations have been given in the paradigms. They are, however, sometimes otherwise rendered, one tense being apparently used with the meaning of another, either in the same or in a different mood. Thus,

(1.) (*a.*) The present is often used for the historical perfect in narration, see § 145, I. 3.—(*b.*) It is sometimes used also for the future to denote the certainty of an event, or to indicate passionate emotion. So, also, when the leading sentence contains the present imperative, *si* is often joined with the present instead of the future; as, *dēfende si pŏtes.*—(*c.*) The present is also used for the imperfect or perfect, when it is joined with *dum* ' while '; as, *Dum ĕgo in Sicĭliā* sum, *nulla stătua dījecta est.* Cic. It is even so used by Livy in transitions from one event to another; as, *Dum in Asiā bellum gĕrĭtur, ne in Ætōlis quĭdem quiētæ res fuērunt.* But the preterites are sometimes used with *dum* ' while '; and *dum* ' as long as ' is regularly joined with the imperfect.

(2.) (*a.*) The perfect, in its proper signification, i. e. as a perfect *definite,* denotes an act or state terminated at the present time. Thus Horace, at the close of a work, says, *Exēgi mŏnŭmentum ære pĕrennius*; and Ovid, in like circumstances, *Jamque ŏpus exēgi.* So, also, Panthus in Virgil, in order to denote the utter ruin of Troy, exclaims, Fuimus *Trōes*, fuit *Ilium* i. e. we are no longer Trojans, Ilium is no more.—(*b*.) The perfect *indefinite* or *historical* perfect is used in relating past events, when no reference is to be made to the time of other events; as, *Cæsar Rŭbĭcōnem* transiit, Cæsar crossed the Rubicon. (*c.*) As in the epistolary style the imperfect is used instead of the present, when an incomplete action is spoken of (§ 145, II. 3), so the historical perfect is in like circumstances employed instead of the present, when speaking of a completed action. With both the imperfect and perfect, when so used, however, the adverbs *nunc* and *ĕtiamnunc* may be used instead of *tunc* and *ĕtiamtum*.

(*d.*) The historical perfect is sometimes used for the pluperfect in narration; as, *Sed postquam* aspexi, *illico cognōvi*, But after I (had) looked at it, I recognized it immediately. Ter.—This is the usual construction after *postquam* or *posteāquam*, *ŭbi*, *ŭbi prīmum*, *ut*, *ut prīmum*, *quum prīmum*, *sĭmul*, *sĭmul ut*, *simul ac*, or *sĭmul atque*, all of which have the signification of 'as soon as,' and sometimes after *priusquam*. But when several conditions are to be expressed in past time, the pluperfect is retained after these particles; as, *Idem sĭmŭlac se rĕmisĕrat*, *nĕque causa subĕrat*, *quāre animi lăbōrem perferret*, *luxŭriōsus rĕpĕrĭēbātur*. Nep. So, also, *postquam* is joined with the pluperfect, when a definite time intervenes between events, so that there is no connection between them; as, *Hannibal anno tertio*, *postquam dŏmo* profūgĕrat, *cum quinque nāvĭbus Africam accessit*. Id.—In a very few passages the imperfect and pluperfect *subjunctive* are joined with *postquam*.

(3.) The pluperfect sometimes occurs, where in English we use the historical perfect; as, *Dixĕrat*, *et spissis noctis se condĭdit umbris*, She (had) said, and hid herself in the thick shades of night. Virg. Sometimes, also, it is used for the historical perfect to express the rapidity with which events succeed each other; so, also, for the imperfect, to denote what had been and still was.

(4.) The future indicative is sometimes used for the imperative; as, *Valēbis*, Farewell. Cic. And:—

(5.) The future perfect for the future; as, *Alio lŏco de ōrātŏrum ănimo et injūrĭis* vĭdĕro, I shall see (have seen).... Cic. This use seems to result from viewing a future action as if already done, and intimates the rapidity with which it will be completed.

REM. 2. When a future action is spoken of either in the future, or in the imperative, or the subjunctive used imperatively, and another future action is connected with it, the latter is expressed by the *future* tense, if the actions relate to the same time; as, *Nātūram si* sĕquēmur *dūcem*, *numquam* aberrābĭmus. Cic.; but by the future perfect, if the one must be completed before the other is performed; as, *De Carthāgine vērēri non ante* dēsĭnam, *quam illam excĭsam esse* cognōvĕro. Cic. In English the present is often used instead of the future perfect; as, *Făciam si* pŏtĕro, I will do it, if I can. *Ut sēmentem* fēcĕris, *ita mētes*, As you sow, so you will reap. Cic.

REM. 3. In expressions denoting the propriety, practicability or advantage of an action not performed, the indicative of the preterites (§ 145, N. 2.) is used, where the English idiom would have led us to expect the imperfect or pluperfect subjunctive.

(*a.*) This construction occurs with the verbs *ŏportet*, *nĕcesse est*, *dēbeo*, *convēnit*, *possum*, *dĕcet*, *licet*, *reor*, *pŭto*; and with *par*, *fas*, *cōpia*, *æquum*, *justum*, *consentāneum*, *sătis*, *sătius*, *æquius*, *mĕlius*, *ūtĭlius*, *optābĭlius*, and *optimum—est*, *ĕrat*, etc.

(*b.*) In this connection the imperfect indicative expresses things which are not, but the time for which is not yet past; the historical perfect and the pluperfect indicative, things which have not been, but the time for which is past; as, *Ad mortem te dūci jam prīdem* ŏportĕbat, i. e. thy execution was necessary and is still so; hence it ought to take place. Cic.—*Longe* ūtilius fuit *angustias ădĭtūs occŭpāre*, It would have been much better to occupy the pass. Curt. *Cătilīna ĕrūpit e sĕnātu triumphans gaudio*, *quem omnīno vivum illinc exire non* ŏportuĕrat. Cic.

(c.) In both the periphrastic conjugations, also, the preterites of the indicative have frequently the meaning of the subjunctive; as, *Tam bona constanter præda tenenda fuit*,—ought to have been kept. Ovid. This is more common in hypothetical sentences than in such as are independent.

(d.) The indicative in such connections is retained, even when a hypothetical clause with the imperfect or pluperfect subjunctive is added, and it is here in particular that the indicative preterites of the periphrastic conjugations are employed; as, *Quæ si dubia aut procul essent, tamen omnes bonos reipublicæ consulere decebat*. Sall. *Quodsi Cn. Pompeius privātus esset hoc tempōre, tamen erat mittendus*. Cic.—*Deleri totus exercitus potuit, si fugientes persecuti victōres essent*. Liv. *Quas nisi minimisisset, tormentis etiam dedendi fuerunt*. Cic. *Si te non invenissem, periturus per præcipitia fui*. Petr. But the subjunctive also is admissible in such cases in the periphrastic conjugations.

REM. 4. (1.) The preterites of the indicative are often used for the pluperfect subjunctive, in the conclusion of a conditional clause, in order to render a description more animated. They are so used,

(a.) When the inference has already partly come to pass, and would have been completely realized, if something else had or had not occurred, whence the adverb *jam* is frequently added; as, *Jam fames quam pestilentia tristior erat; ni annonæ foret subventum*,—would have been worse. Liv. The same is expressed by the verb *cœpi* instead of *jam*; as, *Britanni circumire terga vincentium cœperant, ni*, etc. Tac. And without *jam*; *Effigies Pisōnis traxerant in Gemoniās ac divellebant* (would have entirely destroyed them) *ni*, etc. Id.

(b.) The perfect and pluperfect indicative used in this sense, and a thing which was never accomplished is thus, in a lively manner, described as completed; as, *Et peractum erat bellum sine sanguine, si Pompeium opprimere Brundisii (Cæsar) potuisset*. Hor.—The imperfect indicative is rarely used, also, for the imperfect subjunctive, when this tense is found in the hypothetical clause; as, *Stultum erat monēre, nisi fieret*. Quint.—Sometimes, also, the preterites of the indicative are thus used in the *condition;* as, *At fuerat melius, si te puer iste tenebat*. Ovid. See § 261, R. 1.

(2.) 'I ought' or 'I should,' is expressed by the indicative of *debeo*, and *possum* is in like manner often used for *possem*; as, *Possum persequi multa oblectamenta rerum rusticarum, sed*, etc., I might speak of the many pleasures of husbandry, but, etc.; and it is usual in like manner to say, *difficile est, longum est, infinitum est*, e. g. *narrāre*, etc., for, 'it would be difficult,' 'it would lead too far,' 'there would be no end,' etc.

(3.) The indicative is used in like manner after many general and relative expressions, especially after the pronouns and relative adverbs which are either doubled or have the suffix *cumque;* as, *quisquis, quotquot, quicumque, utut, utcumque*, etc., see §§ 139, 5, (3.) and 191, I. R. 1, (b.); as, *Quidquid id est, timeo Danaos et dona ferentes*. Virg. *Quem sors cumque dabit, lucro appone*. Hor. *Sed quoquo modo sese illud habet*. But however that may be. Cic.—In like manner sentences connected by *sive—sive* commonly have the verb in the indicative, unless there is a special reason for using the subjunctive; as, *Sive verum est, sive falsum, mihi quidem ita renunciatum est*. Later writers however use the subjunctive both with general relatives, etc., and with *sive—sive*.

SUBJUNCTIVE MOOD.

§ **260.** The subjunctive mood is used to express an action or state simply as conceived by the mind.

NOTE. The subjunctive character of a proposition depends, not upon its substance, but upon its form. 'I believe,' 'I suppose,' are only conceptions, but my believing and supposing are stated as facts, and, of course, are expressed by means of the indicative. When, on the other hand, I say, 'I should believe,' 'I should suppose,' the acts of believing and supposing are represented not as facts, but as mere conceptions. Hence the verb that expresses the purpose or intention for which another act is performed, is put in the subjunctive, since it expresses only a conception; as, *Edo ut vivam*, I eat that I may live. This mood takes its name from its being commonly used in *subjoined* or dependent clauses attached to the main clause of a sentence by a subordinate connective. In some cases, however, it is found in independent clauses, or in such, at least, as have no obvious dependence.

I. The subjunctive, in some of its connections, is to be translated by the indicative, particularly in *indirect questions*, in clauses expressing a *result*, and after *adverbs of time*; as,

Rŏgas me quid tristis sim,—why I am sad. Tac. *Stellārum tanta est multĭtūdo, ut nŭmĕrāri non* possint,—that they cannot be counted. *Quum Cæsar esset in Galliā*, When Cæsar was in Gaul. Cæs.

II. The subjunctive is used to express what is contingent or hypothetical, including *possibility, power, liberty, will, duty*, and *desire*.

REMARK 1. The tenses of the subjunctive, thus used, have the significations which have been given in the paradigms, and are, in general, not limited, in regard to time, like the corresponding tenses of the indicative. Thus,.

(1.) The present may refer either to present or future time; as, *Mēdiŏcrĭbus et quis* ignoscas *vitiis tĕneor*, I am subject to moderate faults, and such as you may excuse. Hor. *Orat a Cæsăre ut det sibi rĕniam*, He begs of Cæsar that he would give him leave. Cæs.

(2.) The imperfect may relate either to past, present, or future time; as, *Si fāta fuissent ut* cădĕrem, If it had been my fate that I should fall. Virg. *Si possem, sānior* essem, I would be wiser, if I could. Ovid. *Cētĕros* rŭpĕrem *et* prosternĕrem, The rest I would seize and prostrate. Ter.

(3.) The perfect subjunctive has always a reference to present time, and is equivalent to the indicative present or perfect definite; as, Errārim *fortasse*, Perhaps I may have erred. Plin.—When it has a future signification it is not to be accounted a perfect, but the subjunctive of the future perfect. See Rem. 4 and 7, (1.) But compare § 258, R. 1, (*b*.) and R. 3, (*b*.)

(4.) The pluperfect subjunctive relates to past time, expressing a contingency, which is usually future with respect to some past time mentioned in connection with it; as, *Id respondērunt se factūros esse, quum ille vento Aquilōne* vēnisset *Lemnum*.... when he should have come.... Nep.

REM. 2. The imperfects *vellem, nollem*, and *mallem*, in the first person, express a wish, the non-reality and impossibility of which are known; as, *vellem, I* should have wished.—In the second person, where it implies an indefinite person, and also in the third when the subject is an indefinite person, the imperfect subjunctive is used in the sense of the pluperfect, and the condition is to be supplied by the mind. This is the case especially with the verbs, *dico, puto, arbitror, credo*; also with *vĭdeo, cerno*, and *discerno*; as, *Mæstīque* (crĕdĕres *victos*) *rĕdeunt in castra*,—one might have thought that they were defeated. Liv. *Pēcūniæ an fāmæ mĭnus parcĕret, haud facĭle* discernĕres. Sall. *Qui* vĭdēret *equum Trŏjānum intrŏductum, urbem captam* dicĕret. Cic. *Quis umquam* crēdĕret? Id. *Quis* pŭtāret? Id.—The imperfect subjunctive is frequently used, also, for the pluperfect in interrogative expressions; as, *Socrātes quum* rŏgārētur *cūjātem se esse dicĕret, Mundānum, inquit.* Id. *Quod si quis deus* dicĕret, *numquam* pŭtārem *me in Acădēmiā tamquam phĭlŏsŏphum dispŭtātūrum*, If any god had said....I never should have supposed. Cic.

REM. 3. The subjunctive in all its tenses may denote a supposition or concession; as, Vendat *ædes vir bŏnus*, Suppose an honest man is selling a house. Cic. Dixĕrit *Epĭcūrus*, Grant that Epicurus could have said. Id. *Ĭerum anceps pugnæ fŭĕrat fortūna*.—Fuisset, Grant that it might have been. Virg. *Malus civis Cn. Carbo fuit*. Fuĕrit *aliis*, He may have been to others Cic.—This concessive subjunctive is equivalent to *esto ut*.

REM. 4. The present and perfect subjunctive are used in independent propositions to soften an assertion. When so used, they do not differ essentially from the present and future indicative; as, *Forsitan quæratis*, You may perhaps ask. *Vĕlim sic existimes*, I would wish you to think so. *Nēmo istud tibi concēdat*, or *concessĕrit*, No one will grant you that. *Hoc sine ulla dŭbĭtatione confirmavĕrim, ēlŏquentiam rem esse omnium difficillimam*, This I will unhesitatingly affirm. Cic. *Nil ĕgo contŭlĕrim jūcundo sānus āmico.* Hor. The form which is called the perfect subjunctive, when thus used for the future, seems to be rather the subjunctive of the future perfect: see Rem. 7, (1.) *Vŏlo* and its compounds are often so used in the present; as, *Vĕlim obvias mihi litĕras crebro mittas*, I wish that you would frequently send, etc. Cic. The perfect subjunctive is also rarely used in the sense of a softened perfect indicative; as, *Forsitan tĕmĕre fēcĕrim*, I may have acted inconsiderately.

REM. 5. The subjunctive is used in all its tenses, in independent sentences, to express a doubtful question implying a negative answer; as, *Quo eam?* Whither shall I go? *Quo irem?* Whither should I go? *Quo ierim?* Whither was I to have gone? *Quo ivissem?* Whither should I have gone? The answer implied in all these cases is, 'nowhere.' So, *Quis dŭbĭtet quin in virtute divitiæ sint?* Who can doubt that riches consist in virtue? Cic. *Quisquam nūmen Junōnis adōret prætĕrea?* Virg. *Quidni, inquit, mĕmĭnĕrim?* Cic. *Quis vellet tanti nuntius esse mali?* Ovid.

REM. 6. The present subjunctive is often used to express a wish, an exhortation, asseveration, request, command, or permission; as,

Mōriar, si, etc. May I die, if, etc. Cic. *Pĕream, si non*, etc. May I perish, if, etc. Ovid. So, *Ne sim salvus.* Cic. *In mĕdia arma ruāmus*, Let us rush... Virg. *Ne me attingas, scĕleste!* Do not touch me, villain! Ter. *Făciat quod lŭbet*, Let him do what he pleases. Id. The perfect is often so used; as, *Ipse vidĕrit*, Let him see to it himself. Cic. *Quam id recte făciam, vidĕrint săpientes.* Id. *Mĕmĭnĕrimus, ĕtiam adversus infimos justitiam esse servandam.* Id. *Nihil incommŏdo vălētūdinis tuæ fĕcĕris.* Id. *Emas, non quod ŏpus est, sed quod nĕcesse est.* Sen. *Dōnis impii ne plăcāre audeant deos; Plătōnem audiant.* Cic. *Nātūram expellas furca, tămen usque rĕcurret.* Hor.

(*a.*) The examples show that the present subjunctive, in the first person singular, is used in asseverations; in the first person plural, in requests and exhortations; in the second and third persons of the present and sometimes of the perfect, in commands and permissions, thus supplying the place of the imperative, especially when the person is indefinite.

(*b.*) With these subjunctives, as with the imperative, the negative is usually not *non* but *ne*; as, *ne dicas; ne dicat; ne dixĕris*. So, also, *ne fuĕrit*, for *licet ne fuĕrit*.

(*c.*) The subjunctive for the imperative occurs most frequently in the third person. In the second person it is used principally with *ne*; as, *ne dicas*. In the latter case the perfect very frequently takes the place of the present; as, *ne dixĕris*. The subjunctive is also used in the second person, instead of the imperative, when the person is indefinite.

(*d.*) In precepts relating to past time, the imperfect and pluperfect, also, are used for the imperative; as, *Forsitan non nēmo vir fortis dixĕrit*, restitisses, *mortem pugnans oppĕtisses*,—you should have resisted. Cic.

REM. 7. In the regular paradigms of the verb, no future subjunctive was exhibited either in the active or passive voice.

(1.) When the expression of futurity is contained in another part of the sentence, the future of the subjunctive is supplied by the other tenses of that mood, viz. the future subjunctive by the present and imperfect, and the future perfect by the perfect and pluperfect. Which of these four tenses is to be used depends on the leading verb and on the completeness or incompleteness of the action to be expressed. The perfect subjunctive appears to be also the subjunctive of the future perfect, and might not improperly be so called; as,

Tantum mŏneo, hoc tempus si āmīsĕris, *te esse nullum umquam măgis* ĭ *dōneum* rĕpertūrum, I only warn you, that, if you should lose this opportunity, you will never find one more convenient. Cic.

(2.) If no other future is contained in the sentence, the place of the future subjunctive active is supplied by the participle in *rus*, with *sim* and *essem*; as, *Non dŭbĭtat quin brĕvi Trōja* sit pĕrĭtūra, He does not doubt that Troy will soon be destroyed. Cic. In hypothetical sentences the form with *fŭĕrim* takes the place of a pluperfect subjunctive; as, *Quis ĕnim dŭbĭtat, quin, si Săguntīnis impĭgre tŭlissĕmus ŏpem, tōtum in Hispāniam* āversūri *bellum* fŭĕrimus. Liv. The form in *fuissem* occurs also, but more rarely; as, *Appāruit, quantum* excĭtātūra *mōlem vēra* fuisset *clādes, quum,* etc. See *Periphrastic Conjugation,* § 162, 14.

(3.) The future subjunctive passive is supplied, not by the participle in *dus*, but by *fŭtūrum sit* or *esset*, with *ut* and the present or imperfect of the subjunctive; as, *Non dŭbĭto quin* fūtūrum sit, *ut laudētur*, I do not doubt that he will be praised.

PROTASIS AND APODOSIS.

§ 261. In a sentence containing a *condition* and a *conclusion*, the former is called the *protăsis*, the latter the *apodŏsis*.

1. In the *protasis* of conditional clauses with *si* and its compounds, the imperfect and pluperfect subjunctive imply the *non-existence* of the action or state supposed, the imperfect, as in English, implying present time. In the *apodosis* the same tenses of the subjunctive denote what the result would be, or would have been, had the supposition in the protasis been a valid one; as,

Nisi te sătis incitātum esse confīdĕrem, scrībĕrem *plūra*, Did I not believe that you have been sufficiently incited, I would write more (Cic.); which implies that he *does believe*, and therefore *will not write*. *Si Neptūnus, quod Thēseo prōmīsĕrat, non* fēcisset, *Thēseus fĭlĭo Hippŏlȳto non* esset orbātus. Id.

2. The present and perfect subjunctive in the *protasis*, imply the *real* or *possible existence* of the action or state supposed; as,

Si vĕlit, if he wishes, or, should wish, implying that he either does wish, or, at least, may wish. In the apodosis the present or perfect either of the subjunctive or of the indicative may be used.

REMARK 1. The tenses of the *indicative* may also be used in the *protasis* of a conditional sentence with *si*, etc.; as, *Si vāles, bĕne est*. Cic. *Si quis antea mīrābātur quid esset, ex hoc tempŏre mirētur pŏtius*.... Id.—The conjunction *si* in the protasis is often omitted; as, *Lĭbet agros ĕmi. Primum quæro quos agros!* If you will buy lands, I will first ask, etc. But the protasis may be rendered without *if*, and either with or without an interrogation, as, You will buy lands, or, Will you buy lands? The future perfect often occurs in the protasis of such sentences; as, *Cāsus mĕdicusve lĕvārit ægrum ex præcipĭti, māter dēlira nĕcābit*, (Hor.) Should chance or the physician have saved him, the silly mother will destroy him. *Si* is in like manner omitted with the imperfect and pluperfect subjunctive, in supposing a case which is known not to be a real one; as, *Absque te esset, hŏdie numquam ad sōlem occāsum vīvĕrem*. Plaut.

REM. 2. The present and perfect subjunctive differ but slightly from the indicative, the latter giving to a sentence the form of reality, while the subjunctive represents it as a conception, which, however, may at the same time be a reality. The second person singular of the present and perfect subjunctive often occurs in addressing an indefinite person, where, if the person were definite, the indicative would be used; as, *Mĕmōrĭa mĭnuĭtur, nisi eam* exerceas. Cic. When the imperfect or pluperfect is required to denote a past action, the indicative must be used, if its existence is uncertain, as these tenses in the subjunctive would imply its non-existence. In the *oratio obliqua*, when the leading verb is a present or a future the same difference is observed between the tenses of the subjunctive as in hypothetical sentences; but when the leading verb is a preterite the difference between possibility and impossibility is not expressed.

REM. 3. The present and perfect subjunctive are sometimes used, both in the *protasis* and *apodosis* of a conditional sentence, in the sense of the imperfect and pluperfect; as, *Tu, si hic sis, aliter sentias*, If you were here, you would think otherwise. Ter. *Quos, ni mea cura resistat, jam flammae tulerint.* Virg.

REM. 4. The *protasis* of a conditional sentence is frequently not expressed, but implied; as, *Magno mercentur Atridae*, i. e. *si possint*. Virg.; or is contained in a participial clause; as, *Agis, etsi a multitudine victus, gloria tamen omnes vicit.* Just. So, also, when the participle is in the ablative absolute; as, *Donarem tripodas*—*divite me scilicet artium, quas aut Parrhasius protulit, aut Scopas.* Hor. *C. Mucius Porsenam interficere, proposita sibi morte, conatus est.* Cic. It is only in later writers that the concessive conjunctions *etsi, quamquam*, and *quamvis* are expressed with the participle, but *tamen* is often found in the *apodosis*, even in the classic period, when a participial clause precedes as a protasis.

REM. 5. In hypothetical sentences relating to past time, the actions seem often to be transferred in a measure to the present by using the imperfect, either in the protasis or the apodosis, instead of the pluperfect; as, *Quod certe non fecisset, si suum numerum (nautarum) naves haberent.* Cic. *Cimbri si statim infesto agmine urbem petissent, grande discrimen esset.* Flor. Sometimes the imperfect, although the actions are completed, appears both in the protasis and the apodosis.

REM. 6. *Nisi, nisi vero*, and *nisi forte* are joined with the indicative, when they introduce a correction. *Nisi* then signifies 'except'; as, *Nescio; nisi hoc video.* Cic. *Nisi vero*, and *nisi forte*, 'unless perhaps,' introduce an exception, and imply its improbability; as, *Nemo fere saltat sobrius*, nisi forte *insanit*. Cic. *Nisi forte* in the sense of 'unless you suppose,' is commonly used ironically to introduce a case which is in reality inadmissible.

SUBJUNCTIVE AFTER PARTICLES.

A. SUBSTANTIVE CLAUSES.

§ 262. A clause denoting the purpose, object, or result of a preceding proposition, takes the subjunctive after *ut, ne, quo, quin*, and *quominus;* as,

Ea non, ut te instituerem, scripsi, I did not write that in order to instruct you. Cic. *Irritant ad pugnandum, quo fiant acriores*, They stimulate them to fight, that they may become fiercer. Varr.

REMARK 1. *Ut* or *uti*, signifying 'that,' 'in order that,' or simply 'to' with the infinitive, relates either to a purpose or to a result. In the latter case it often refers to *sic, ita, adeo, tam, talis, tantus, is, ejusmodi*, etc., in the preceding clause; as,

Id mihi sic erit gratum, ut gratius esse nihil possit, That will be so agreeable to me, that nothing can be more so. Cic. *Non sum ita hebes, ut istuc dicam.* Id. *Neque tam eramus amentes, ut explorata nobis esset victoria.* Id. Tantum indulsi *d lori, ut eum pietas vinceret.* Nep. *Ita* and *tam* are sometimes omitted; as, *Epaminondas fuit etiam disertus, ut nemo Thebanus ei par esset eloquentia*, instead of *tam disertus.* Id. *Esse oportet ut vivas, non vivere ut edas.* Auct. ad Her. *Sol efficit ut omnia floreant.* Cic.

REM 2. *Ut*, signifying 'even if' or 'although,' expresses a supposition merely as a conception, and accordingly takes the subjunctive as,

Ut dēsint vīres, tămen est laudanda vŏluntas, Though strength be wanting, yet the will is to be praised. Ovid. *Ut*, in this sense, takes the negative *non*; as, *Exercĭtus si pācis nōmen audiĕrit, ut non rĕfērat pĕdem* (even if it does not withdraw) *insistet certe*. Cic.

REM. 3. *Ut*, with the subjunctive denoting a result, is used with impersonal verbs signifying *it happens, it remains, it follows*, etc.; as,

Quī fit, ut nēmo contentus vīvat? How does it happen that no one lives contented? Hor. *Huic contĭgit, ut patriam ex servitūte in libertātem vindĭcāret.* Nep. *Sĕquĭtur igĭtur, ut ĕtiam vitia sint parca.* Cic. *Rĕlĭquum est, ut ĕgŏmet mĭhi consŭlam.* Nep. *Restat igĭtur, ut mōtus astrōrum sit vŏluntārius.* Cic. *Extrēmum illud est, ut te ōrem et obsecrem.* Id.

NOTE 1. To this principle may be referred the following verbs and phrases signifying 'it happens,' viz. *fit, fĭĕri non pŏtest, accĭdit, incĭdit, contingit, ēvĕnit, ūsu vĕnit, occurrit* and *est* (it is the case, or it happens, and hence *esto*, be it that):—and the following, signifying 'it remains,' or 'it follows,' viz. *fŭtūrum, extrēmum, prŏpe, proxĭmum*, and *rĕlĭquum—est, rĕlinquĭtur, sĕquĭtur, restat*, and *sŭpĕrest;* and sometimes *accēdit*.

NOTE 2. *Contingit* with the dative of the person is often joined with the infinitive, instead of the subjunctive with *ut;* as, *Non cuivis hŏmini contingit adīre Corinthum*. Hor. And with *esse* also and other verbs of similar meaning, the predicate (as in the case of *licet*) is often found in the dative.—*Sĕquĭtur* and *efficĭtur*, 'it follows,' have sometimes the accusative with the infinitive and sometimes the subjunctive; and *nascĭtur*, in the same sense, the subjunctive only.

NOTE 3. *Mos* or *mōris est, consuētūdo* or *consuētūdĭnis est*, and *nātūra* or *consuētūdo fert*, are often followed by *ut* instead of the infinitive.—*Ut* also occurs occasionally after many such phrases as *nŏvum est, rārum, nātūrāle, nĕcesse, ūsitātum, mīrum, singŭlāre—est*, etc., and after *æquum, rectum, vērum, ūtĭle, vērisĭmĭle*, and *intĕgrum—est*.

For other uses of *ut*, with the subjunctive, see § 273.

REM. 4. *Ut* is often omitted before the subjunctive, after verbs denoting *willingness* and *permission;* also after verbs of *asking, advising, reminding*, etc., and the imperatives *dic* and *fac;* as,

Quid vis făciam? What do you wish (that) I should do? Ter. *Insāni fĕriant sine litōra fluctus.* Virg. *Tentes dissĭmŭlāre rŏgat.* Ovid. *Id sīnas ōro.* Id. *Se suādĕre, dixit, Pharnăbāzo id nĕgōtii dāret.* Nep. *Accēdat ŏportet actio vāria.* Cic. *Fac cōgĭtes.* Sall. So, *Vĭde ex nāvi effĕrantur, quæ*, etc. Plaut.

Verbs of willingness, etc., are *vŏlo, mālo, permitto, concēdo, pătior, sĭno, lĭcet, vĕto*, etc.; those of asking, etc., are *rōgo, ōro, quæso, mŏneo, admŏnĕo, jŭbeo, mando, pĕto, prēcor, censĕo, suādĕo, ŏportet, nĕcesse est, postŭlo, hortor, cūro, dēcerno, opto, impĕro.*

REM. 5. *Nē*, 'that not,' 'in order that not,' or 'lest,' expresses a purpose negatively; as,

Cūra ne quid ei dēsit, Take care that nothing be wanting to him. Cic. *Nēmo prūdens pūnit, ut ait Plăto, quia peccātum est, sed ne peccētur.* Id. *Ut ne* is frequently used for *ne*, especially in solemn discourse, and hence in laws; as, *Opĕra dētur, ut jūdicia ne fiant.* Id. *Quo ne* is used in the same manner in one passage of Horace. *Missus ad hoc—quo ne per vācuum Rōmāno incurrĕret hostis.*—On the other hand *ut non* is used when a simple result or consequence is to be expressed, in which case *ita, sic, tam* are either expressed or understood as, *Tum forte ægrōtābam, ut ad nuptias tuas vĕnire non possem.* In a few cases, however, *ut non* is used for *ne.— Ut non* is further used, when the negation re-

§ 262.   SYNTAX.—SUBJUNCTIVE AFTER PART. CLES.   271

fers to a particular word or to a part only of the sentence, as in similar cases *si non* must be used, and not *nisi*; as, *Confer te ad Manlium, ut a me non ejectus ad alienos, sed invitatus ad tuos isse videaris.* Cic.

REM. 6. *Nē* is often omitted after *căve*; as,
Căve pūtes, Take care not to suppose. Cic. Compare § 267, R. 3.

REM. 7. After *mĕtuo, tĭmeo, vĕreor*, and other expressions denoting fear or caution, *nē* must be rendered by *that* or *lest*, and *ut* by *that not*.

NOTE 3. To the verbs *mĕtuo, tĭmeo*, and *vĕreor* are to be added the substantives expressing fear, apprehension or danger, and the verbs *tĕrreo, conterreo, dēterreo, căveo*, to be on one's guard, *video* and *observo* in requests (as, *vide, vidēte* and *videndum est*), in the sense of 'to consider'; as,
Milo mĕtuēbat, ne a servis indicārētur, Milo feared that he should be betrayed by his servants. Cic. *Vĕreor, ne, dum minuĕre velim labōrem, augeam.* Id. *Păvor ĕrat, ne castra hostis aggrĕdĕrētur.* Liv. *Illa duo vĕreor, ut tibi possim concēdĕre*, I fear that I cannot grant.... Cic. *Căvendum est ne assentatōribus pătĕfăciāmus aures, neu ădūlāri nos sīnāmus.* Cic. *Vide ne hoc tibi obsit.* *Terruit gentes, grăve ne rediret sēcŭlum Pyrrhae. Multitūdĭnem dēterrent, ne frūmentum conferant.* Caes. *Me mīsĕrum! ne prōna cădas.* Ovid.

NOTE 4. *Nēve* or *neu* is used as a continuative after *ut* and *ne*. It is properly equivalent to *aut ne*, but is also used for *et ne* after a preceding *ut*; as, on the other hand, *et ne* is used after a negation instead of *aut ne*; as, *Lēgem tŭlit, ne quis ante actārum rērum accūsārētur, neve multārētur.* Nep. *Caesar milites non longiōre ōrātiōne cōhortātus, quam uti suae pristinae virtūtis memŏriam retinērent, neu perturbārentur ănĭmo—proelii committendi sĭgnum dēdit.* Caes. *Nēque*, also, is sometimes used for *et ne* after *ut* and *ne*; as, *Ut ea praetermittam, nēque eos appellem.* Cic. *Cur non sancĭtis ne vicinus patrĭcio sit plēbeius, nec eōdem ĭtinĕre eat.* Liv.—*Ne non* is sometimes used for *ut* after verbs of fearing; as, *Tĭmeo ne non impĕtrem*, I fear I shall not obtain it.

REM. 8. The proposition on which the subjunctive with *ut* and *nē* depends, is sometimes omitted; as, *Ut ita dicam.* Cic. *Ne singŭlos nomĭnem.* Liv.

NOTE 5. *Nēdum*, like *ne*, takes the subjunctive; as, *Optĭmis tempŏribus clārissimi viri vim tribūnicium sustinēre non potuērunt*: nēdum *his tempŏribus sine judiciōrum remēdiis salvi esse possīmus*,—still less, etc. Cic. *Ne* is sometimes used in the sense of *nēdum*; as, *Novam eam potestātem* (scil. *tribūnōrum plēbis*) *ēripĕre patrĭbus nostris, ne nunc dulcēdine sēmel capti fĕrant desidĕrium.* Liv.— *Nēdum* without a verb has the meaning of an adverb, and commonly follows a negative; as, *Aegre inermis tanta multĭtūdo, nēdum armāta, sustinēri potest.* Liv. *Ne*, also, is used in the same manner in Cic. Fam. 9, 26.

REM. 9. *Quō*, 'that,' 'in order that,' or, 'that by this means,' especially with a comparative; *non quō*, or *non quod*, 'not that,' 'not as if'; *non quin*, 'not as if not'; which are followed in the apodŏsis by *sed quod, sed quia*, or *sed* alone; and *quōmĭnus*, 'that not,' after clauses denoting hinderance, take the subjunctive; as,
Adjūta me, quo *id fiat facĭlius*, Aid me, that that may be done more easily. Ter. *Non quo rēpublĭca sit mihi quicquam cārius, sed desperātis etiam Hippŏcrătis vĕtat ădhibēre medicīnam.* Cic. *Non quod sōla ornent, sed quod excellant.* Id. *Nĕque recūsāvit, quo mĭnus lēgis poenam subīret.* Nep. *Ego me dicam in cīvili bello negāri esse, non quin rectum esset, sed quia*, etc. Cic. And instead of *non quin* we may say *non quo non, non quod non*, or *non quia non*; and for *non quod, non eo quod*, or *non ideo quod*.

REM. 10. *Quin*, after negative propositions and questions with *quis* and *quid* implying a negative, takes the subjunctive. *Quin* is used,

1. For a relative with *non*, after *nēmo, nullus, nĭhil....est, rĕpĕrītur invēnītur* etc., *vix est, ægre rĕpĕrītur*, etc.; as, *Messānam nēmo vēnit*, quin vīdĕrit, i. e *qui non vidĕrit*, No one came to Messana who did not see. Cic. *Nĕgo ullam pictūram fuisse....*quin conquisĭĕrit, i. e. *quam non*, etc. Id. *Nĭhil est*, quin *mălè narrando* possit *dĕprăcări*. Ter. *Quis est*, quin cernat, *quanta vis sit in sensĭbus?* Cic.

NOTE 6. When *quin* is used for the relative it is commonly equivalent to the nominative *qui, qua, quod*, but it is sometimes used in prose instead of the accusative, and sometimes after *dies* for *quo*, as the ablative of time; as, *Dies fĕre nullus est*, quin *hic Satrius dŏmum meam* ventĭtet, i. e. *quo—non ventĭtet*. Cic.—*Qui non* is often used for *quin*; as, *Quis ĕnim ĕrat*, qui non sciret. Id.; and when *quin* stands for *qui non* or *quod non*, *is* and *id* are sometimes added for the sake of emphasis; as, *Cleanthes nĕgat ullum cibum esse tam grăcem*, quin is *die et nocte concŏquătur*. Cic. *Nĭhil est quod sensum hăbeat*, quin id intĕreat. Id.—So, also, the place of *quin* is supplied by *ut non*; as, *Augustus numquam fīlios suos pŏpŭlo commendărit ut non adjĭcĕret* (without adding) *si mĕrēbuntur*. Suet. And if no negation precedes, or if *non* belongs to a particular word, and not to the verb, *qui non* and *ut non* must of course be used and not *quin*.

2. For *ut non*, 'that not,' or 'without' with a participle, especially after *făcĕre non possum, fiĕri non pŏtest, nulla causa est, quid causae est? nĭhil causa est*; as, *Făcĕre non possum* quin *ad te* mittam, i. e. *ut non*, etc. Cic. *Numquam tam mălè est Sicŭlis*, quin *aliquid făcĕte et commŏde* dīcant. Cic. *Numquam accēdo*, quin *abs te* abeam *doctior*,—without going from you wiser. Ter.

NOTE 7. *Quin* takes the subjunctive also after the negative expressions *non dŭbito, non est dŭbium, non ambĭgo,* I doubt not; *non ăbest; nĭhil, paulum, non procul, haud multum ăbest; non, vix, ægre abstinco; tĕnĕre me*, or *tempĕrāre mĭhi non possum; non impĕdio, non recūso, nĭhil prætermitto*, and the like. In these cases, however, the negation in *quin* is superfluous, and it is generally translated into English by 'that,' 'but that,' or 'to' with an infinitive; as, *Non dŭbito* quin *dŏmi sit*, that he is at home. *Non multum ăbest*, quin *miserrimus sim*, Not much is wanting to make me most wretched. Cic. Hence, as *quin* is not in such cases regarded as a negative, *non* is superadded when a negative sense is required; as, *In quibus non dŭbito* quin *offensiōnem negligentiæ vitāre atque effŭgĕre* non possum. Cic. *Dŭbitandum non est* quin numquam possit *ŭtilĭtas cum honestāte contendĕre*. Id.

NOTE 8. In Nepos, *non dŭbito*, in the sense of 'I do not doubt,' is always followed by the infinitive with the accusative, and the same construction often occurs in later writers but not in Cicero: in the sense of to scruple or hesitate, when the verb following has the same subject, *dŭbito* and *non dŭbito* are generally followed by the infinitive; as, *Cĭcĕro* non dŭbitābat *conjūrātos supplicio afficĕre*.—It may be added that 'I doubt whether' is expressed in Latin by *dŭbito sitne, dŭbito utrum—an, dŭbito sitne—an*, or *dŭbito num, numquid*, for *dŭbito an*, and *dŭbium est an* are used, like *nescio an* with an affirmative meaning.

NOTE 9. *Quin* signifies also 'why not?' being compounded of the old ablative *quī* and *nē*, i. e. *um*, and in this sense is joined with the indicative in questions implying an exhortation; as, Quin *conscendĭmus ĕquos?* Why not mount our horses? In this sense it is also joined with the imperative; as, Quin die *stătim*, Well, tell me: or with the first person of the subjunctive. Hence without being joined to any verb it signifies 'even' or 'rather.'

REM. 11. The principal verbs of hinderance, after which *quŏmĭnus* occurs, and after which *ne*, and, if a negative precedes, *quin* also may be used, are *dĕterreo, impĕdio, intercēdo, obsisto, obsto, offĭcio, prŏhĭbeo, recūso*, and *repugno*. It occurs also after *stat* or *fit per me*, I am the cause, *non pugno, nĭhil mŏror, non contĭneo me*, etc.

NOTE. *Impĕdio, dĕterreo*, and *recūso* are sometimes, and *prŏhĭbeo* frequently followed by the infinitive. Instead of *quŏmĭnus, quo sēcius* is sometimes used.

§ 263.   SYNTAX.—SUBJUNCTIVE AFTER PARTICLES.   273

§ 263.   The particles specified in this section always introduce a sentence containing only a conception of the mind, and are hence joined with the subjunctive.

1. The subjunctive is used after particles of wishing, as *ŭtĭnam*, *ŭtĭ*, *O!* and *O! si;* as,

Ŭtinam minus vitæ cŭpĭdi fuissēmus! O that we had been less attached to life: Cic.   *O si sōlĭtæ quicquam virtūtis* ädesset! Virg.

REMARK. The present and perfect tenses, after these particles, are used in reference to those wishes which are conceived as possible; the imperfect and pluperfect are employed in expressing those wishes which are conceived as wanting in reality. Cf. § 261, 1 and 2.—' Would that not ' is expressed in Latin both by *ŭtĭnam ne* and *ŭtĭnam non*.   *Ŭtinam* is sometimes omitted; as, *Tēcum lūdĕre sicut ipsa possem!* Catull.

B. ADVERBIAL CLAUSES.

2. (1.) *Quamvis,* however; *licet,* although; *tamquam, tamquam si, quăsi, ac si, ut si, vĕlut, vĕlut si, vĕlūti, sĭcŭti,* and *ceu,* as if; *mŏdo, dum,* and *dummŏdo,* provided,—take the subjunctive; as,

Quamvis ille fēlix sit, *tămen,* etc. However happy he may be, still, etc. Cic. *Vēritas* licet *nullum dēfensōrem* obtineat, Though truth should obtain no defender. Id.   *Tamquam clausa* sit *Asia, sic nihil perfertur ad nos.* Id.   *Sed quid ego his testĭbus ūtor,* quăsi *res dŭbia aut obscūra* sit? Id. *Me omnibus rēbus, juxta ac si meus frāter* esse, *sustentāvit,* He supported me in every thing, just as though he were my brother. Id.   *Simĭliter făcĕre eos,—*ut si *nautæ* certārent, *ūter,* etc. Id.   *Absentis Ariŏvisti crūdēlĭtātem,* vĕlut si *cōram ădesset,* horrērent. Cæs.   *Inque sĭnus cāros,* vĕlūti cognoscĕret, *ibat.* Ovid.   Sĭcūti *jurgio* lăcessĭtus fōret, *in sĕnātum vēnit.* Sall.   *Hic vĕro ingentem pugnam,* ceu *cētĕra nusquam bella* fŏrent.   Virg.   *Odĕrint* dum mĕtuant. Att. in Cic.   *Mănent ingĕnia sentĭbus,* mŏdo permăneat *stŭdium et industria.* Cic.   *Omnia hŏnesta negligunt* dummŏdo *pŏtentiam* consĕquantur, They disregard every honorable principle, provided they can obtain power. Id.

NOTE. *Mŏdo, dum,* and *dummŏdo,* when joined with a negation, become *mŏdo ne, dum ne,* and *dummŏdo ne.*

(2.) *Quamvis* (although) is in Cicero joined with a principal tense of the subjunctive; as, *Quamvis non* fuĕris *suāsor, apprŏbātor certe fuisti.* Cic. In later writers it is often used with the indicative; as, *Fēlicem Niŏben,* quamvis *tot fŭnĕra* vīdit.   Ovid.   So also once in Cicero, Quamvis *patrem suum nunquam* vīdĕrat. Rab. Post. 2.

(3.) *Quamvis,* as a conjunction, in the sense of 'however much,' is joined with the subjunctive. So also when its component parts are separated; as, *C. Gracchus dixit, sibi in somnis Ti. frātrem vīsum esse dicĕre,* quam vellet cuno tărētur, *tămen,* etc.— *Quamvis* ' however much,' as an adverb, governs no particular mood.

(4.) *Etsi, tămetsi,* even if, although, and *quamquam,* although, commonly introduce an indicative clause:—*ĕtiamsi* is more frequently followed by the subjunctive. In later prose writers, and sometimes in Cicero and Sallust as well as in the poets, *quamquam* is joined with the subjunctive; as, Quamquam *præsente Lūcullo* lŏquar. Cic.   *Vi rĕgĕre patriam quamquam* possis. Sall. Jug. 3. *Filius* quamquam *Thĕtĭdos mărīnæ Dardănas turres* quătĕret. Hor.

REMARK. The imperfect subjunctive with *ac si,* etc., is used after the present, to denote that in reality the thing is not so, but in that case a hypothetical subjunctive must be supplied; as, *Egnātii rem ut tueāre æque a te pĕto,* ac si *mea nĕgōtia* essent, i. e. *ac pĕtĕrem, si mea nĕgōtia essent,* as I would pray it, etc. Cic.

3. After *antĕquam* and *priusquam*, the imperfect and pluperfect tenses are usually in the subjunctive; the present and perfect may be either in the indicative or subjunctive. The present indicative is commonly used when the action is to be represented as certain, near at hand, or already begun; the subjunctive is used when the thing is still doubtful, and also in general propositions; as,

Ea causa ante mortua est, quam *tu* nātus esses, That cause was dead before you were born. Cic. *Avertit ĕquos*, priusquam *pabŭla* gustassent *Trōjæ, Xanthumque* bibissent. Virg. Priusquam incipias, *consulto ŏpus est*, Before you begin there is need of counsel. Sall.

4. (1.) *Dum, dōnec*, and *quoad*, signifying *until*, are followed by the subjunctive, if they refer to the attainment of an object; as,

Dum *hic vĕniret, lŏcum rĕlinquĕre nōluit*, He was unwilling to leave the place until he (Milo) should come. Cic. *Nihil pŭto tibi esse ūtilius quam oppĕriri* quoad *scire possis, quid tibi āgendum sit*. Id. *Cornu tĕtendit, et duxit longe*, dōnec *curvāta* coīrent *inter se cāpĭta*. Virg.—In the sense of 'as long as,' these particles take the indicative, but Tacitus joins *dōnec* with the subjunctive even when a simple fact is to be expressed.

(2.) *Dum*, while, is commonly used with the indicative present, whatever may be the tense of the principal sentence. Cf. § 259, R. 1, (1.), (a.)

5. *Quum (cum)*, when it signifies a *relation of time*, takes the indicative; when it denotes a *connection of thought*, the subjunctive; as,

Qui non dēfendit injūriam, nĕque rĕpulsat a suis, quum *pŏtest, injuste făcit*. Cic. Quum *recte nāvĭgāri pŏtĕrit, tum nāviges*. Id. *Crēdo tum*, quum *Sicilia flōrēbat ŏpĭbus et cōpiis, magna artifĭcia fuisse in ea insŭlā.* Id. Quum *tot sustineas et tanta nĕgōtia, peccem, si mōrer tua tempŏra*, Since you are burdened with so many and so important affairs, I should do wrong, if I should occupy your time. Hor. Quum *vita sine āmicis mĕtus plēna sit, ratio ipsa mŏnet āmicitias compărāre*. Cic.

REMARK 1. (*a.*) The rule for the use of *quum* may be thus expressed: *Quum temporal* takes the indicative, *quum causal* the subjunctive. Hence, when *quum* is *merely* a particle of time, with no reference to cause and effect, and not occurring in a historical narrative (see Rem. 2), it may be joined with any tense of the indicative. But when it is employed to express the relation of cause and effect, or has the meaning of 'though' or 'although,' it is joined with the subjunctive (*b.*) *Quum*, relating to time, is commonly translated *when, while*, or *after*; referring to a train of thought, it signifies *as, since, though* or *although, because*; but may often be translated *when*.

REM. 2. In narration, *quum*, even when it relates to time, is joined with the imperfect and pluperfect subjunctive, when a historical perfect stands in the principal clause; as,

Gracchus, quum *rem illam in rēligiōnem pŏpŭlo vēnisse* sentīret, *ad sĕnātum rĕtŭlit*. Cic. *Alexander*, quum interēmisset *Clitum, vix mĭnus a se abstĭnuit*. Id.

NOTE. *Quum* temporal, when it expresses an action frequently repeated, may be joined with the pluperfect indicative, and the apodosis then contains the imperfect; as, Quum *antem vir esse corpĕrat*, dābat *se lubŏri*. Cic. Quum *rŏsam vidĕrat, tum incĭpĕre ver* arbitrābātur. Id. Cf. § 264, 12.

REM. 3. *Quum* in the sense of 'while' is joined with the perfect and imperfect indicative, often with the addition of *intĕrea* or *intĕrim*, to express simultaneous occurrences; as, *Citulus cēpit magnum suæ virtūtis fructum*, quum *omnes prope ānā vĭce, in eo ipso eos spem hăbitūros esse*, dixistis. Cic. *Cædĕbātur virgis in mĕdio fŏro Messānæ cīvis Rōmānus, jūdĭces,* quum intĕrea *nulla vox ălia istius mĭsĕri* audiēbātur, *nĭsi hæc: civis Rōmānus sum.* Id.

REM. 4. *Quum,* for the most part preceded by an adverb, as, *jam, nondum, vix, ægre,* or joined with *rĕpente* or *sŭbĭto* is followed by the indicative, especially by the present indicative, to express the beginning of an action. In the cases mentioned in this and the preceding remark, the historians also use *quum* with the historical infinitive.

For the subjunctive after *si* and its compounds, see § 261.

C. ADJECTIVE CLAUSES.

SUBJUNCTIVE AFTER *QUI.*

§ 264. Relatives require the subjunctive, when the clauses connected by them express merely a conception; as, for example, a *consequence,* an *innate quality,* a *cause, motive,* or *purpose.*

1 (*a.*) When the relative *qui,* in a clause denoting a *result* of the character or quality of something specified in the antecedent clause, follows a demonstrative, and is equivalent to *ut* with a personal or demonstrative pronoun, it takes the subjunctive.

NOTE. The demonstratives after which *qui* takes the subjunctive, are *tam* with an adjective, *tantus, tālis, ējusmŏdi, hŭjusmŏdi,* and *is, ille, iste,* and *hic* in the sense of *tālis;* as,

Quis est tam Lyncēus, qui *in tantis tĕnebris nĭhil* offendat? i. e. *ut ille in tantis,* etc., Who is so quick-sighted, that he would not stumble, (or, as not to stumble,) in such darkness. Cic. *Tālem te esse ŏportet,* qui *ab impiōrum cīvium sŏciĕtāte* sējungas; i. e. *ut tu,* etc. Id. *At ea fuit lĕgātio Octāvii,* in quā *pērĭcŭli suspiciō non sŭbesset,* i. e. *ut in eā.* Id. *Nec tămen ĕgo sum* ille *ferreus,* qui *frātris cārissimi mœrōre non* mōvear, i. e. *ut ĕgo non mōvear.* Id. *Non sŭmus* ii, quibus *nihil vērum esse* videātur, i. e. *ut nōbis nihil,* etc. Id. *Nulla gens* tam fēra *est,* cūjus *mentem non* imbuērit *deōrum ŏpĭnio,* i. e. *ut ējus mentem,* etc. Id.

(*b.*) Sometimes the demonstrative word is only implied; as,

Res parva dictu, sed quæ stŭdiis in magnum certāmen excesserit, i. e. *tālis* yuæ....of such a kind that it issued in a violent contest. Cic. *Nunc dĭcis ălĭquid,* ĵnod *ad rem* pertĭneat, i. e. *tāle ut id,* etc. Id. So *quis sum,* for *num tālis sum;* as, *Quis sum, cūjus aures lædi nĕfas* sit? Sen.—In like manner, also, a demonstrative denoting a character or quality, is implied in the examples included in the following rule :—

2. When the relative is equivalent to *quamquam is, etsi is,* or *dummŏdo is,* it takes the subjunctive; as,

Laco, consĭlii quamvis ēgrĕgii, quod *non ipse* afferret, *inĭmīcus,* Laco, an opponent of any measure, however excellent, provided he did not himself propose it. Tac. *Tu ăquam a pūmĭce postŭlas,* qui *ipsus sĭtiat.* Plaut. *Nĭhil mŏlestum,* quod *non* dēsīdĕres, i. e. *dummŏdo id.* Cic.

3. *Quod,* in restrictive clauses, takes the subjunctive; as,

Quod sciam, as far as I know; *quod mĕmĭnĕrim,* as far as I recollect; *quod ĕgo intellĭgam; quod intellĭgi possit; quod conjectūrā prōvĭdēri possit; quod salvā fĭde possim; quod commŏdo tuo fīat,* etc.—*Quĭdem* is sometimes added to the relative in such sentences. *Quod sĭne mŏlestiā tuā* fīat, So far as it can be done without troubling you. Cic. In the phrases *quantum possum, quantum ĕgo per-spĭcio,* on the other hand, the indicative is used.

4. A relative clause, after the comparative followed by *quam*, takes the subjunctive; as,

Major sum, quam cui possit fortūna nŏcēre, i. e. *quam ut mihi*, etc., I am too great for fortune to be able to injure me. Ovid. *Audītā vōce præcōnis mājus gaudium fuit, quam quod ūniversum hŏmines cāpĕreut*, Upon the herald's voice being heard, the joy was too great for the people to contain. Liv.

REMARK 1. The clause annexed by *quam qui* implies an inherent quality or a consequence; so that *quam qui* is equivalent to *quam ut*, which also sometimes occurs. Sometimes the subjunctive follows *quam* even without a relative pronoun; as, *In his litĕris longior fui*, quam *aut* vellem, aut quam *me pŭtāvi fŏre:*—and so frequently with the verbs *velle* and *posse*.

5. A relative clause expressing a *purpose*, *aim*, or *motive*, and equivalent to *ut* with a personal or demonstrative pronoun, takes the subjunctive; as,

Lăcĕdæmŏnii lĕgātos Athēnas misērunt, qui *eum absentem* accūsārent: i. e. *ut illi eum accūsārent*, The Lacedæmonians sent ambassadors to Athens to accuse him in his absence. Nep. *Cæsar ĕquĭtātum omnem præmittit*, qui videant, *quas in partes iter făciant*. Cæs. *Sunt autem multi, qui ĕripiunt āliis*, quod *āliis* largiantur. Cic. *Assĭdue rĕpĕtant*, quas perdant, *Bĕlĭdes undas*. Ovid.

REM. 2. So also with relative adverbs; as, *Lampsăcum ei* (*Thĕmistocli*) *rex dōndrat*, unde *vīnum sūmĕret*, i. e. *ex quā* or *ut inde*, etc. Nep. *Sŭper tăbernācŭlum rĕgis*, unde *ab omnībus conspĭci* posset, *imāgo sōlis crystallo inclūsa fulgēbat*. Curt.

6. A relative clause with the subjunctive after certain indefinite general expressions, specifies the circumstances which characterize the individual or class indefinitely referred to in the leading clause; as,

Fuērunt eā tempestāte, qui dīcĕrent, There were at that time some who said. Sall. *Erant, quibus appĕtentior fāmæ*, vidērētur, There were those to whom he appeared too desirous of fame. Tac. *Sunt, qui censeant, ūna ănĭmum et corpus occidĕre*. Cic. *Erunt, qui existĭmāri vĕlint*. Id. *Si quis ĕrit, qui perpĕtuam ōrātiōnem dēsīdĕret, altĕrā actiōne audiet*. Id. *Vēnient lĕgiōnes, quæ nĕque me ĭnultum nĕque te impūnītum* pātiantur. Tac. So after *est* followed by *quod*, in the sense of 'there is reason why'; as, *Est* quod gaudens, You have cause to rejoice. Plaut. *Est* quod visam *dŏmum*. Id. *Si est* quod dēsit, *ne beātus quĭdem est*. Cic.

NOTE 1. The expressions included in the rule are *est, sunt, ădest, præsto sunt, exsistunt, exŏriuntur, invĕniuntur, rĕpĕriuntur,* (scil. *hŏmines*); *si quis est, tempus fuit, tempus vĕniet*, etc.

REM. 3. The same construction occurs with relative particles used indefinitely; as, *Est* unde *hæc* fiant. *Si est culpam ut Antipho in se* admīsĕrit, If it chance that, etc. Ter. *Est* ūbi *id isto mŏdo* vŭleat. Cic. So *est cur* and *est ut* in the sense of *est cur*; as, *Ille ĕrat*, ut ōdisset *dēfensōrem sălūtis meæ*, i. e. he had reason to hate. Cic. *Non est ĭgĭtur* ut mirandum sit, There is no occasion for wondering. Id.

REM. 4. The above and similar expressions are followed by the subjunctive only when they are indefinite. Hence, after *sunt quĭdam, sunt nonnulli, sunt multi*, etc., when referring to definite persons, the relative takes the indicative; as, *Sunt ōrātiōnes quædam, quas Menocrito* dăbo. Cic.

REM. 5. The indicative is sometimes, though rarely, used after *sunt qui* even when taken indefinitely, especially in the poets; as, *Sunt, quos* jŭvat. Hor *Sunt* qui *ĭta* dīcunt. Sall.

7. A relative clause after a general negative, or an interrogative expression implying a negative, takes the subjunctive; as,

Nēmo est, qui haud intelligat, There is no one who does not understand. Cic. *Nulla res est*, quæ *perferre* possit *continuum labōrem*, There is nothing which can endure perpetual labor. Quint. *Nulla pars est corpŏris*, quæ *non* sit *minor*. Id. *Nĭhil est*, quod *tam misĕros* fŭciat, *quam impiĕtas et scĕlus*. Cic. *In fŏre rix dĕcĭmus quisque est*, qui *ipsus sĕse* noscat. Plaut. *Quis est*, qui *ŭtĭlia* fŭgiat? Who is there that shuns what is useful? Cic. *Quæ lătebra est, in* quam *non* intret *mĕtus mortis?* Sen. *Quid dulcius quam hăbēre*, quicum *omnia* audeas *sic lŏqui ut tēcum?* Cic. (See respecting this use of the indefinite *quicum* rather than the definite *quōcum*, § 136, R. 1.) *An est quisquam*, qui *hoc* ignōret? Is there any one who is ignorant of this? Id. *Numquid est māli, quod non dixĕris?* Ter.

NOTE 2. General negatives are *nēmo, nullus, nĭhil, ūnus non, ălius non, non quisquam, vix ullus, nec ullus*, etc., with *est : vix* with an ordinal and *quisque ; nēgo esse quemquam*, etc. Interrogative expressions implying a negative, are *quis, quid ; qui, quæ, quod, quantus, ŭter, ecquis, numquis, an quisquam, an ăliquis, quŏtus quisque, quŏtus*, etc., with *est? quot, quam multi*, etc., with *sunt?*

NOTE 3. The same construction is used after *non est, nĭhil est, quid est, numquid est*, etc., followed by *quod, cur, quāre*, or *quamobrem*, and denoting 'there is no reason why,' 'what cause is there?' 'is there any reason?' as, Quod timeas, *non est*, There is no reason why you should fear. Ovid. *Nĭhil est, quod adventum nostrum pertimescas.* Cic. *Quid est*, quod *de ējus civĭtāte* dŭbĭtes? Id. *Quæris a me, quid ĕgo Cătĭlinam mĕtuam. Nĭhil, et cūrāvi ne quis mĕtuĕret. Quid est*, cur *virtus ipsa per se non* effĭciat *beātos?* Id.—So after *non hăbeo*, or *nĭhil hăbeo*; as, *Non hăbeo*, quod *te* accūsem. Cic. *Nil hăbeo*, quod ăgam, I have nothing to do. Hor. *Nĭhil hăbeo*, quod ad te scribam. Cic. So without a negative, *De quĭbus* hăbeo *ipse*, quid sentiam. Id. *Causa* or, with *quid* and *nĭhil, causæ*, is sometimes added; as, *Non fuit causa, cur postŭlāres.* Id. *Quid ĕrat causæ, cur mĕtuĕret.* Id.

NOTE 4. (*a.*) The relative clause takes the subjunctive after the expressions included in this and the last rule, only when it expresses the character or quality of the subject of the antecedent clause; and the relative, as in the preceding cases of the relative with the subjunctive, is equivalent to a personal or demonstrative pronoun with *ut*; as, *Nēmo est, qui nesciat*, There is no one who is ignorant, *i. e.* no one is ignorant. Cic. So, *Sunt, qui hoc carpant*, There are some who blame this, *i. e.* some blame this. Vell.

(*b.*) If the relative clause is to be construed as a *part of the logical subject* it does not require the subjunctive; as, *Nĭhil stăbile est, quod infĭdum* est Nothing which is faithless is firm. Cic.

8. (1.) A relative clause expressing the *reason* of what goes before, takes the subjunctive; as,

Peccārisse mĭhi videor, qui *a te* discessĕrim, I think I did wrong in leaving you. Cic. *Inertiam accūsas ădŏlescentium*, qui *istam artem non* ēdiscant, You blame the idleness of the young men, because they do not learn that art. Id. *O fortūnāte ădŏlescens*, qui *tuæ virtūtis Hŏmērum præcōnem* invēnĕris!—in having found. Id. *Cănĭnius fuit mĭrĭfĭcā vigilantiā*, qui *suo tōto consŭlātu somnum non* vĭdĕrit,—since, etc. Id.

(2.) Sometimes, instead of *qui* alone, *ut qui, quippe qui*, or *utpŏte qui*, is used, generally with the subjunctive; as,

Convivia cum patre non inībat, quippe qui *ne in oppidum quidem nisi perrārō* vēnisset. Cic. *Nēque Antōnius prŏcul ăbĕrat*, utpŏte qui *magno exercĭtu* sĕquĕrētur. Sall. But sometimes with the indicative in Sallust and Livy; as, Quippe qui *omnia* vīcĕrat. Sall.

9. After *dignus, indignus, aptus,* and *ĭdōneus*, a relative clause takes the subjunctive; as,

Vĭdētur, qui *ălĭquando* impĕret, dignus esse, He seems to be worthy at some time to command. Cic. *Rustĭci nostri quum jĭdem ălĭcūjus bŏnĭtātem fuĕ laudant, dignum esse dĭcunt*, quicum *in tĕnebris* mĭcet. Id. *Nulla vĭdēbātur aptior per-*

278   SYNTAX.—SUBJUNCTIVE IN INDIRECT QUESTIONS.   § 265

tōna, quæ *de ætāte* lŏquĕrētur. Id. *Pompeius* Idōneus *non est*, qui impetret. Id. *Et rem* Idōneam, *de* quā quærātur, *et hŏmĭnes* dignos, quĭbuscum dissĕrātur, *pŭtant*. Id.

NOTE 5. If the relative clause does not express that of which the person or thing denoted by the antecedent is worthy, its construction is not influenced by this rule. Thus, *Quis servus* libertāte dignus *fuit*, cui *nostra sălus cāra non esset?* The subjunctive is here used according to No. 7 of this section.

NOTE 6. The infinitive frequently follows these adjectives in poetry, though rarely in prose; as, *Et puer ipse fuit* cantāri dignus. Virg.;—and sometimes *ut*; as, *Eras* dignus, ut hăbēres *intĕgram mănum*. Quint.

10. A relative clause, after *ūnus, sōlus, prīmus*, etc., restricting the affirmation to a particular subject, takes the subjunctive; as,

Hæc est ūna *contentio*, quæ *ădhuc* permānsĕrit, This is the only dispute which has remained till this time. Cic. *Vŏluptas est* sōla, quæ *nos* vōcet *ad se, et allĭceat suapte natūrā*, Pleasure is the only thing that, by its own nature, invites and allures us to itself. Id.

11. When the relative refers to a *dependent clause*, it often takes the subjunctive. See § 266.

12. The imperfect and pluperfect subjunctive are used in narration after relative pronouns and adverbs, when a repeated action is spoken of; as,

Semper hăbĭti sunt fortissĭmi, qui *summam impĕrii* pōtīrentur, Those were always accounted the bravest, who obtained the supreme dominion. Nep. Quemcumque *lictor jussu consŭlis* prĕhendisset, *tribŭnus mitti jŭbēbat*. Liv. Ut *quisque maxĭme* labōrāret *locus, aut ipse occurrĕbat, aut ălĭquos mittĕbat*. So after *si quis* or *qui*; as, Si qui *rem mălĭtiōsius* gessisset, *dēdĕcus* existĭmābant. Cic. *Quŏtiens sŭper tāli nĕgōtio* consultāret, *ēdĭtā dŏmūs parte ūtĕbātur*. Tac. *Nec quisquam Pyrrhum, quā* tūlisset *impĕtum, sustĭnēre vălŭit*.—It is sometimes found in like manner after *quum, ŭbi, ut*, and *si* when used in the sense of *quum*, when repeated actions are spoken of; as, *Id* ŭbi dixisset, *hastam in fines eōrum ēmittĕbat*. Liv. Sin *Nŭmĭdæ prŏpius* accessissent, *ĭbi vēro virtūtem ostendĕre*. Sall. Sometimes even the present subjunctive is so used when employed to express things which have happened repeatedly, and still happen (see § 145, I. 2.); as, Ubi *de magnā virtūte et glōriā bŏnōrum* mĕmōres, *quæ sĭbi quisque*, etc. Sall.

NOTE 7. This is called the *indefinite subjunctive*, or *subjunctive of generality*, inasmuch as the action is not referred to a distinct, individual case. The indicative, however, is used in such cases more frequently than the subjunctive.

SUBJUNCTIVE IN INDIRECT QUESTIONS.

§ **265.** Dependent clauses, containing an indirect question, take the subjunctive.

NOTE 1. A question is indirect when its substance is stated in a dependent clause without the interrogative form. Indirect questions generally depend upon those verbs and expressions which commonly take after them the accusative with the infinitive. Cf. § 272. Thus:—

Quālis sit *ănĭmus, ipse ănĭmus nescit*, The mind itself knows not what the mind is. Cic. *Crēdĭbile non est*, quantum scrībam, It is incredible how much I write. Id. Quis *ego* sim, *me rŏgĭtas?* Do you ask me who I am? Plaut. *Ad te* quid scrībam *nescio*. Cic. *Nec* quid scrībam *hăbeo*, Nor have I any thing to write. Id. *Dŏce me*, ŭbi sint *dii*, Inform me where the gods are. Id. *Incertum est*, quo *te* lŏco *mors* exspectet. Sen. Ep. Quam prĭdem *sĭbi hērēdĭtas* vēnisset, *dĭc'et*. Id. *Nunc accĭpe*, quāre dēsĭpiunt *omnes*. Hor. *Id* utrum *illi* sentiant, an *vero* sinûlent, *tu intelliges.* Cic. *Quæro,* num *tu sēnātui causam tuam* permittas. Id *Vides,* ut *altō* stet *nive candĭdum Sōracte.* Hor. *Nescit, vitāne* fruātur, an sit *ăpud mānes.* Ovid.

NOTE 2. All interrogatives whether adjectives, pronouns, or particles, may serve as connectives of clauses containing indirect questions; as,

Quantus, quālis, quŏt, quŏtus, quŏtuplex, ŭter; quis, qui, cŭjas; ŭbi, quō, unde, quā quorsum, quamdiu, quamdŭdum, quamprĭdem, quŏties, cur, quāre, quamobrem, quemadmŏdum, quōmŏdo, ut, quam, quantōpĕre, an, ne, num, utrum, anne, annon.

REMARK 1. The indicative is frequently used in dependent questions, especially in Terence and Plautus and occasionally in later poets; as, *Ilde ávāritia* quid făcit. Ter. So Virg. Ecl. 5, 7. In the best prose writers the indicative generally indicates that the question is direct, or that the sentence is not a question; as, *Quærāmus ŭbi mălĕfĭcium* est, Let us seek there, where the crime actually is. Cic. *Nihil est admīrābilius, quam quōmŏdo ille mortem filii* tŭlit.

REM. 2. In double questions, 'whether—or,' the first may be introduced by *utrum,* or the enclitic *ne,* or without an interrogative particle. Hence there are four forms of double questions,—1. *utrum* (or *utrum ne),—an.* 2. *utrum, —an (anne).* 3. *-ne, —— an.* 4. *-ne, —— -ne;* as, *Multum intěrest,* utrum *laus* imminŭātur, an *sălus dēsĕrātur.* Cic. The interrogative particle *utrum* is not used in a single question; and *num—an* is used only in direct questions. The English 'or not' in the second part, which is used without a verb, is expressed in Latin by *annon* or *necne,* either with or without a verb; but *necne* occurs only in indirect questions; as, *Dii utrum sint,* necue *sint, quæritur.* Cic.—*Ne- ne, an—an,* or *num—num* scarcely occur except in poetical or unclassical language.

REM. 3. *Dŭbito, dŭbium est,* or *incertum est an, dēlibĕro* or *hæsito an,* and especially *haud scio an, nescio an,* though implying some doubt, have generally a sense almost affirmative. Compare § 198, 11, R. (e.)

REM. 4. *Nescio quis,* used nearly in the sense of *ălĭquis,* does not influence the mood of the following verb; as, *Sed cāsu* nescio quo *in ea tempŏra ætas nostra* incidit. Cic. *Lūcus,* nescio quo *cāsu, nocturno tempŏre* incensus est. Nep. So, also, *nescio quōmŏdo,* 'somehow' or 'in some way'; as, *Sed* nescio quōmŏdo, *inhæret in mentĭbus quāsi augŭrium.* Cic. In like manner *mirum quam, mirum quantum, nimium quantum,* and the like, when united to express only one dea, do not affect the m d of the verb; as, *Sāles in dicendo nimium quantum vălent,*—very much. Cic

SUBJUNCTIVE IN INSERTED CLAUSES.

§ **266.** 1. When a dependent proposition containing either an accusative with the infinitive, or a verb in the subjunctive, has a clause connected with it, as an *essential part,* either by a relative, a relative adverb, or a conjunction, the verb of the latter clause is put in the subjunctive; as,

Quid enim pŏtest esse tam perspicuum, quam esse ălĭquod nūmen, quo hæc rēgantur? For what can be so clear as, that there is some divinity by whom, these things are governed? Cic. Here the thing which is stated to be clear is, not merely *esse ălĭquod nūmen,* that there is a god, but also that the world is governed by him. Hence the latter clause, *quo hæc rēgantur* is an essential part of the general proposition. *Illud sic fĕre dēfĭnīri sŏlet, děcōrum id esse, quoa consentāneum sit hŏmĭnis excellentiæ.* Id. *Audiam quid sit, quod Epĭcūrum non* probes, I shall hear why it is that you do not approve of Epicurus Id **Jussī** *ut, quæ vēn'ssent nāves Eubæam pĕtĕrent.* Liv.

REMARK 1. Hence the subjunctive is used in general sentences, in which the class of things mentioned exists only as a conception or idea, while the individual thing has a real existence; as, *Est ĕnim ulcīscendi et pūnĭendi mŏdus, atque haud scio an sătis sit cum* qui lăcessĭĕrit *injūriæ suæ pœnĭtēre*, i. e. each individual offender of the class.

REM. 2. When the principal proposition contains a subjunctive denoting a *result*, after *ĭta, tam, tălis*, etc., the inserted clause has the indicative; as, *Asia vēro tam ŏpĭma est et fertĭlis*, ut—*multĭtūdĭne eārum rērum*, quæ exportantur, *făcĭle omnĭbus terris antĕcellat*. Cic. The same is the case in definitions; as, *Vidēre igĭtur ŏportet, quæ sint convĕnĭentia cum ipso nĕgŏtio, hoc est*, quæ *ab re sēpărāre non possunt*. Cic.—So also explanatory clauses, especially circumlocutions introduced by a relative pronoun, are sometimes found with the indicative; as, *Ităque ille Marius ĭtem exĭmie L. Plōtium dīlexit, cūjus ingĕnio pŭtābat ea*, quæ gessērat, *posse cĕlebrāri*. Cic.

NOTE. To this rule belongs the construction of the *ōrātio oblīqua*, 'indirect discourse,' or 'reported speech,' in which the language of another is presented, not as it was conceived or expressed by him, but in the third person. Thus Cæsar said, 'I came, I saw, I conquered,' is direct,—Cæsar said, that 'he came, saw, and conquered,' is indirect discourse.

2. In the *ōrātio oblīqua*, the main proposition is expressed by the accusative with the infinitive; and dependent clauses connected with it by relatives and particles, take the subjunctive.

Thus, Cicero and Quintilian, in quoting the language of Marcus Antonius make use, the former of the *ōrātio dĭrecta*, the latter of the *ōrātio oblīqua*;—*Antōnius inquit*, '*Ars eārum rērum est*, quæ sciuntur', Antonius says, '*Art belongs to those things which are known.' Cic. Antōnius inquit, artem eārum rērum esse*, quæ sciantur, Antonius says, that 'art belongs to those things which are known.' Quint.

So, *Sōcrătes dīcĕre sŏlēbat, omnes, in eo quod scĭrent, sătis esse ēlŏquentes*, Socrates was accustomed to say, that 'all were sufficiently eloquent in that which they understood'? Cic. *Cāto mīrāri se aiēbat, quod non rīdēret hăruspex, hăruspĭcem quum vīdisset*. Id. *Negat jus esse, qui miles non sit, pugnāre cum hoste*. Id. *Indĭgnābantur ibi esse impĕrium, ŭbi non esset lībertas*. Liv. *Ităque Athēnienses quod hŏnestum non esset, id ne ūtĭle quĭdem* (*esse*) *pŭtāvērunt*. Cic.

REMARK 1. (*a.*) When the subjunctive would be necessary in the *ōrātio dĭrecta*, to denote liberty, power, etc., the same remains in the *ōrātio oblīqua*, and is not changed into the infinitive with an accusa‑ e; as, *Ad hæc Ariŏvistus respondit, quum vellet*, congrĕdĕrētur, To this Ariovist replied, that 'he might meet him when he pleased.' Cæs. In the *ōrātio dĭrecta*, this would be *congrĕ dĭāris*.

(*b.*) The imperative in the *ōrātio dĭrecta* is, in the *ōrātio oblīqua*, changed into the subjunctive; as, *hoc mĭhi dīcĭte*, which in the *ōrātio oblīqua* is, *hoc sibi dīcant*, or *hoc sibi dīcĕrent*, according to the tense of the leading verb.

(*c.*) So also direct questions addressed to the second person, when changed from direct to indirect speech, become subjunctives. Liv. 6, 37.—But such questions when not addressed to the second person are expressed in the *ōrātio oblīqua* by the accusative with the infinitive; as when in direct speech we say, *Etiamsi vĕtĕris contŭmēliæ oblīvisci vĕlim, num possum ĕtiam rĕcentium injūriārum mĕmŏriam dĕpōnĕre?* The *ōrātio oblīqua* will be, *Cæsar respondit* (histor. perf.)—*si vĕtĕris contŭmēliæ oblīvisci vellet, num ĕtiam rĕcentium injūriārum—mĕmŏriam dĕpōnĕre posse?* Cæs. Very rarely the accusative with the infinitive is found in a question of the second person, as in Liv. 6, 17: but the subjunctive in questions of the third person is less uncommon in Cæsar; as, *Quis păti posset?* for *quem păti posse? Quis hoc sibi persuādĕret?* for *quem sibi persuāsūrum?* See § 273, 3.

REM. 2. A writer may state his own past words or thoughts in *ōrātio oblīqua* either preserving the first person, or adopting the third.

REM. 3. When the inserted clause contains the words or sentiments of the subject of the leading clause, all references to him are regularly expressed by the reflexives *sui* and *suus*; as, *Hac necessitāte coactus domino naris qui sit aperit, multa pollicens, si se conservasset.* Nep. And this is equally true when the word to which the pronoun refers is not in reality the grammatical subject, provided it may still be conceived as such; as, *Quum ei in suspiciōnem vēnisset, aliquid in epistōlā de se esse scriptum.* Nep.; for the words, *quum ei in suspiciōnem vēnisset*, are equivalent to *quum suspicārētur*. See § 208, (1.)

REM. 4. The tenses to be used in changing the *ōrātio dīrecta* into the *oblīqua*, depend on the tense of the verb which introduces the quotation, according to the rule, § 258. But when the future perfect would be used in the direct, the pluperfect is necessary in the oblique form; but the perfect is used after the present, perfect definite, or future.

REM. 5. When the connected clause contains merely a descriptive circumstance, or expresses what is independent of the sentiment of the preceding clause, it takes the indicative; as, *Imperāvit Alexander Lÿsippo, ut eōrum equitum, qui apud Grānīcum cēcidĕrant, facĕret stătuas*, Alexander ordered Lysippus to make statues of those horsemen who had fallen at the Granicus. Sometimes, in other cases, when it is evident from the sense, that the connected clause is an essential part of the proposition, the indicative is used, to avoid giving the appearance of contingency to the sentence.

3. A clause connected to another by a relative or causal conjunction, takes the subjunctive, (whatever be the mood of the preceding verb,) when it contains not the sentiment or allegation of the writer, but that of some other person alluded to; as,

Sōcrătes accūsātus est, quod corrumpĕret *juventūtem*, Socrates was accused of corrupting the youth, lit., because (as was alleged) he corrupted the youth. *Deum invocābant*, cujus *ad sōlenne* vēnissent, They invoked the god, to whose solemnities they had come. Liv. *Quos vīcĕris amīcos tibi esse cāve crēdas*, Do not believe that those whom you have conquered are your friends. Here, in the first example, the charge of corrupting the youth is not made by the writer, but by the accusers of Socrates. So, in the second example, the worshippers allege that they have come to attend upon the solemnities of the god. In the last, it is implied by the use of the subjunctive mood, that the belief spoken of is that of the person addressed:—*quos vīcisti* would have been merely an addition of the speaker, by means of which he would have designated the persons whose friendship he was speaking of; and, in general, the *indicative*, in such sentences, is employed in those statements which are independent of the sentiments of the person, to whose thoughts or words allusion is made. Cf. supra, 2, R. 5.

REMARK. In the preceding cases, it is not directly said that the sentiments are those of another than the writer. In Cicero, however, the words *dico*, *puto arbitror*, and the like, are often construed in a similar manner, although, properly speaking, not these verbs, but those in the clauses dependent on them should be in the subjunctive; as, *Quum ĕnim*, *Hannibalis permissu*, *exisset de castris*, *rediit paulo post*, *quod se oblitum nescio quod dicĕret*,...because (as) he said, he had forgotten something. Cic. *Ab Athēniensibus*, *locum sepultūrae intra urbem ut dărent*, *impetrāre non pōtui*, *quod rēligiōne se impēdīri dicērent*. Id.

IMPERATIVE MOOD.

§ 267. The imperative mood is used to express a *command wish, advice*, or *exhortation*; as,

Nosce te, Know thyself. Cic. *Æquam mĕmento servīre mentem*, Remember to preserve an unruffled mind. Hor. *Huc ădes*, Come hither. Virg. *Pasce ed pellas, et potum pastas ăge, et inter agendum occursare capro căvēto.* Id.

(1.) The imperative *present* denotes that an action is to be performed directly or at once; as, *lĕge*, read; *mŏrĕre*, die; or that a state or condition is to continue; as, *vīve*, live.

(2.) The imperative *future* denotes that something is to be done, as soon as something else has taken place; as, *Quum rălētūdĭni tuæ consŭluĕris, tum consūlĭto nāvĭgātĭōni.* Cic. *Prius audīte paucis; quæd quum dixĕro, si plăcuĕrit,* făcĭtōte. Ter. The precedent event is often to be supplied by the mind. Sometimes, especially in poetry, the imperative present is used for the imperative future, and, on the other hand, *scīto* and *scītōte*, from *scio*, are used instead of the imperative present, which is wanting.

(3.) Hence the imperative future is properly used in *contracts, laws, and wills*; and also in *precepts* and *rules of conduct*; as, *Rēgio impĕrio duo sunto, iique consŭles appellantor, mīlĭtiæ summum jus hăbento, nēmīni pārento, illis sālus pŏpŭli suprēma lex esto.* Cic. *Non sătis est pulchra esse poēmăta, dulcia sunto.* Hor. *Ignoscĭto sæpe altĕri, nunquam tibi.* Syr.

REMARK 1. With the imperative, *not* is expressed by *nē*, and *nor* by *nēve*; as,

Ne *tanta ănĭmis* assuescite *bella.* Virg. Ne crēde *cŏlōri.* Id. *Hŏmĭnem mortuum in urbe* ne sĕpĕlīto, nēve ūrīto. Cic.

NOTE. *Non* and *nĕque* occur, though rarely, with the imperative; as, *Vos quŏque non cāris aures ŏnĕrāte lăpillis,* nec *prōdĭte grăves insūto vestĭbus auro.* Ovid. But with the subjunctive used for the imperative *non* and especially *nĕque* are found more frequently. Cf. § 260, R. 6, (*b.*)—In Plautus and Terence *ne* is of common occurrence both with the imperative and with the present subjunctive, and with no difference of meaning; but later poets chiefly use *ne* with the present subjunctive, and *ne* with the imperative only when they speak emphatically. In classical prose writers the periphrastic *nōli* with the infinitive is preferred.

REM. 2. The present and perfect subjunctive are often used instead of both tenses of the imperative, to express a command in a milder form, an exhortation, or an entreaty; as, *Qui ădipisci vēram glōriam vŏlet, justĭtiæ* fungātur *officiis.* Cic. *Quod dŭbĭtas,* ne făcĕris. Plin. Ep. See § 260, II., R. 6. An imperative of the perfect passive is very rarely found; as, *At vos admŏnĭti nostris quŏque cāsĭbus* este. Ovid. Jacta *ālea* esto. Cæs. in Suet. But the subjunctive is more common; as, Jacta sit *ālea.* Sometimes also the future indicative; as, *Sed* vălēbis, *meāque nĕgōtia* vidēbis, *mēque diis jūvantĭbus ante brūnnam* exspectābis, instead of *văle, vĭde, exspecta.* Cic. *Ubi sententiam meam vōbis pĕrēgĕro, tum quĭbus eădem plăcēbunt, in dextram partem tăcĭti* transībĭtis, instead of *transĭtōte.* Liv. With the future the negative is *non.* See § 259, R. 1, (4.)

REM. 3. Sometimes, for the simple affirmative imperative, *cūra* or *cūrāto ut, fac ut,* or *fac* alone is used with the subjunctive; as, Cūra ut *quam prīmum* vēnias, *Come* as soon as possible. *Fac ĕrūdias,* Instruct, or Take care to instruct. Cic. For the negative imperative *fac ne, cāve ne* or *cāve* alone, with the present or perfect subjunctive is used; but especially *nōli* with the infinitive; as, *Nōli pūtāre,* Do not suppose. Cic. *Cāve existĭmes,* Do not think. Id. Nōlīte *id* velle *quod non fĭĕri pŏtest, et* căvēte ne *spe præsentis pācis perpĕtuam pācem* ōmittātis. Id.

INFINITIVE MOOD.

OF THE TENSES OF THE INFINITIVE.

§ 268. 1. The infinitive partakes of the properties of the noun and verb, just as the participle combines the properties of the adjective and verb. It expresses simply the action or state implied in the verb in an abstract manner, without specifying either person, number, or time, and thus merely indicates whether an action is in progress or completed.

2. The tenses of the infinitive denote respectively an action as present, past, or future, in reference to the time of the verbs with which they are connected; as,

Hoc făcĕre possum, I am able to do this. Cic. *Vidi nostros inimicos cŭpĕre bellum*, I saw that our enemies were desiring war. Id. *Nec gĕmĕre aëriā cessābit turtur ab ulmo*, Nor shall the turtle dove cease to coo from the lofty elm. Virg.—*Victōrem rictæ succŭbuisse quĕror*, I complain that the victor has yielded to the vanquished. Ovid. *Se a sĕnibus audisse dicēbant*, They said that they had heard (it) from the old men. Cic. *Audiet cives ăcuisse ferrum jŭrentus*, The youth will hear that the citizens have whetted the sword. Hor.—*Negat sĕse verbum esse factūrum*, He declares that he is not about to speak. Cic. *Postquam audiĕrat non dătum iri filio uxōrem suo*, After he had heard that a wife would not be given to his son. Ter. *Semper existimābĭtis nihil hōrum vos visūros fŏre*, You will always suppose that you are to see none of these things. Cic.

REMARK 1. (*a*.) The present and perfect infinitives are sometimes called respectively the infinitives of *incomplete* and of *completed* action. The present infinitive, however, is sometimes used to denote a completed action. This is the usual construction with *mĕmĭni*; but in such case the speaker transfers himself to the past, and the expression denotes rather a recollection of the progress than of the completion of the action; as, *Hoc me mĕmĭni dicĕre*, I remember *my saying* this. Cic. *Teucrum mĕmĭni Sidōna vēnire*, I remember Teucer's coming to Sidon. Virg. So with *mĕmŏriā tĕneo*. Cic. Phil. 8, 10. *Scrībit* also is construed like *mĕmĭnit*; as, Cic. Off. 3, 2: and after the same analogy, and for the sake of vivid expression Cicero says, *M. Maxĭmum accēpimus făcĭle cŏlāre, tăcēre, dissĭmŭlāre*, etc., though speaking of things which he had not witnessed himself. So, also, with *rĕcordor*;—*Rĕcordor longe omnĭbus ūnum antĕferre Dēmosthĕnem*. Cic. When the action is spoken of simply as a fact, the perfect infinitive is used with *mĕmĭni*; as, *Mĕmĭnistis me ita distribuisse causam*. Cic.

(*b*.) The passive voice having no simple form for expressing the completed state of suffering makes use of the combination of the perfect participle with *esse*; as, *ămātus esse*, to have been loved. When thus combined *esse* loses its own signification of a continued state, and when this state is to be expressed, another infinitive must be chosen; as, *Constrictam jam hōrum conscientiā tĕnēri conjūrātiōnem tuam non vides?* Cic. Sometimes, however, when no ambiguity can arise, *esse* in the usual combination retains its original meaning; as, *Apud Plătōnem est, omnem mōrem Lăcĕdæmŏniōrum inflammātum esse cŭpĭdĭtāte rincendi*. Id. Here *inflammātum esse* expresses a continued or habitual state.—*Fuisse* with the perfect participle denotes a state completed previous to a certain past time; as, *Jŭbet bono ănimo esse; sōpītum fuisse rēgem sŭbĭto ictu*. Liv.

REM. 2. To express the result of an action rather than its progress, the perfect infinitive is sometimes used instead of the present, especially after *satis hăbeo, sătis mihi est, pŭdet, contentus sum, mēlius ĕrit, vŏlo* or a verb of equivalent meaning; as, *Bacchātur vātes, magnum si pectŏre possit excussisse deum*. Virg. *Quum illam nēmo vēlit attigisse*. Plin. The poets use the infinitive perfect where we should expect a present; as, *Tendentes Pēlion impōsuisse Olympo*. Hor.

REM. 3. The present infinitive is also sometimes used for the future, especially when the verb has no future; as, *Dĕsine fāta deûm flecti spĕrāre*, Cease to hope that the fates of the gods will be changed. Virg. *Prōgĕniem Trōjāno a sanguĭne dūci audiĕrat*. Id. *Cras mihi argentum dăre dixit*, i. e. *se dătūrum esse*. Ter. *Căto affirmat se vivo illum non triumphāre*. Cic.

REM. 4. (*a*.) The infinitive future active is formed by a combination of the participle future active with *esse*; as, *ămātūrus esse*; the infinitive future passive by a combination of the supine in *um* with *iri*; as, *ămātum iri*. These future infinitives denote an action or state as continuing. The participle in *rus* which properly expresses intention (see § 162, 14), takes also the infinitive *fuisse* to express a past intention; as, *Scio te scriptūrum fuisse*, I know that you have had the intention to write, whence it was an easy transition to the sense, 'you would have written,' in conditional sentences, when the condition is not fulfilled This infinitive is used especially in the apodosis of hypothetical sentences, where in direct speech the pluperfect subjunctive would be used (cf. § 162, 14, R. 3.); as, *Etiamsi obtemperasset auspiciis, idem eventurum fuisse puto.* Cic. In like manner the infinitive future with *esse* is used in the apodosis of hypothetical sentences instead of the imperfect subjunctive; as, *Libertus, nisi jurasset, scelus se facturum* (esse) *arbitrabatur.* Id.

(b.) Instead of the future infinitive, in both voices, *futurum esse* or *fore*, followed by *ut* and the subjunctive, is often used; the present and imperfect subjunctive, in such cases, denoting an unfinished, the perfect and pluperfect a finished, future action; as, *Numquam putavi fore, ut supplex ad te venirem,* I never supposed (that it would happen) that I should come a suppliant to you. Cic. *Suspicor fore, ut infringatur hominum improbitas.* Id. *Credebam fore, ut epistolam scripsisses.*—So, also, in the passive for a continued state of future suffering the present and imperfect are used; as, *Credo fore, ut epistolam scribatur,* and, *Credebam fore, ut epistola scriberetur.* But to express a completed state in future time the perfect participle is employed; as, *Quos spero brevi tempore tecum copulatos fore.* Cic. *Quod rediret nomine pacis bellum involutum fore.* Id. This construction is necessarily used, when the verb has either no future active participle, or no supine; as, in such case, the regular future infinitive cannot be formed; as, *Spero fore ut sapias.*—*Fore* is found in two passages pleonastically joined with the future participle active, viz. *Te ad me fore venturum.* Cic. Att. 5, 21: and *Quum senatus censeret—libenter facturos fore.* Liv. 6, 42.

REM. 5. (a.) The periphrastic infinitive formed by the future active participle with *fuisse*, denotes a future action contingent upon a condition which was not fulfilled; and, in the *apodosis* of a conditional sentence, corresponds to the pluperfect subjunctive; as, *An censes me tantos labores suscepturum fuisse, si iisdem finibus gloriam meam quibus vitam essem terminaturus?* Do you think that I should have undertaken so great labors if, etc. Cic. *Ut perspicuum sit omnibus, nisi tanta acerbitas injuriae fuisset, numquam illos in eum locum progressuros fuisse,*....that they never would have come into that place. Id.

(b.) *Futurum fuisse* with *ut* and the imperfect subjunctive passive, corresponds to the infinitive *fuisse* with the future participle active in a conditional proposition; as, *Nisi nuncii essent allati, existimabant plerique futurum fuisse, ut oppidum amitteretur,*...that the town would have been lost. Cæs.

(c.) The participle future passive cannot be used to form an infinitive future passive, since it always retains the meaning of necessity, and in this sense has three regular infinitives, *amandum esse, amandum fuisse,* and *amandum fore;* as, *Instare hiemem, aut sub pellibus* habendos *milites fore, aut* differendum esse *in æstatem bellum.* Liv.

REM. 6. In the apodosis of a conditional sentence, the perfect infinitive, like the past tenses of the indicative, (see § 259, R. 4.), sometimes corresponds to the pluperfect subjunctive; as, *(Dixit) sibi vitam filiæ suæ cariorem fuisse, si liberæ ac pudicæ vivere licitum fuisset,* (He said) that the life of his daughter had been dearer to him than his own, if it had been permitted.... Liv. This use of the perfect infinitive is necessary, when the verb has no future participle; as, *Equidem Platonem existimo, si genus forense dicendi tractare voluisset, gravissime et copiosissime potuisse dicere,*—would have been able to speak. Cic.

§ 269.

The infinitive may be regarded either as a verb or as an abstract noun. (a.) As a verb it is used either indefinitely (§ 143, 4), or with a subject of its own, which is put in the accusative, (§ 239). But the infinitive *passive* of neuter and sometimes of active verbs, like the third person singular of that voice, may be used impersonally or without a subject; as, *Vides toto properari litore,* You see a stir is made all along the shore. Virg. See §§ 209 R. 3, (2.), and 239, R. 4. The present infinitive has sometimes, in narration, a subject in the nominative See § 209, R. 5.

(*b.*) As a noun, the infinitive, either alone or with a subject-accusative, has two cases, the nominative and the accusative, and is accordingly used either as the subject or the object of a verb.

THE INFINITIVE AS THE *SUBJECT* OF A VERB

The infinitive, either with or without a subject-accusative, may be the *subject* of a verb; as,

Ad rempūblĭcam pertĭnet me conservāri, It concerns the state that I should be preserved. Cic. *Nunquam est ūtile* peccāre, To do wrong is never useful. Id. *Mājus dēdĕcus est parta* āmittĕre *quam omnīno non* parāvisse. Sall. In the first example *conservāri* with its subject accusative *me* is the subject of *pertĭnet*, and is equivalent to 'my preservation': in the second, *peccāre* is the subject of *est ūtile*. See § 202, 2, and III. R. 2.

REMARK 1. A general truth may be expressed by the infinitive without a subject; as, *Facĭnus est* vincīre *cīvem Rōmānum*, To bind a Roman citizen, or, that one should bind a Roman citizen, is a crime. But in such case the verb *esse* and verbs denoting *to appear*, *to be considered* or *called* (§ 210, R. 3.), require the noun or adjective of the predicate to agree with the implied subject in the accusative; as, *Æquum* est *peccātis vēniam* poscentem *reddĕre rursus*. Hor. *Atticus maxĭmum æstĭmāvit quæstum*, memŏrem *grātumque* cognosci. Nep.

NOTE. The indefinite pronoun *ălĭquem* or *ălĭquos* may in such cases be supplied, and the same indefiniteness may be expressed by *te* or *nos*, cf. § 209, R. 7; but it is still more frequently expressed by the infinitive passive. Hence the sentence *Facĭnus est vincīre cīvem Rōmānum*, may also be expressed by *Facĭnus est* vincīri *cīvem Rōmānum*. So, *Quum vidērent de eōrum virtūte non* despērāri. Nep.—The impersonal verbs *licet, decet, oportet, opus est*, and *necesse est*, when there is no definite subject, are joined with the infinitive active alone; but when there is a subject-accusative, they are connected with the passive construction; as, a c t. *licet hoc facĕre; decet specĭmen capĕre ex hac re*; p a s s. *licet hoc fĭĕri; decet specĭmen cāpi*.

REM. 2. The infinitive, with or without a subject accusative, is often the subject of a proposition, when the substantive verb with a noun, a neuter adjective, or an impersonal verb forms the predicate. Of this kind are *justum, æquum, vērisĭmĭle, consentāneum, ŏpertum—est, erat*, etc., *necesse est, ŏpus est;— appāret, constat, convĕnit, decet, licet, oportet; intellĭgĭtur, perspĭcĭtur*, etc.; as, *Cui verba dāre diffĭcĭle est*. Ter. *Mendācem memŏrem esse oportet*. Quint. *Lēgem brĕvem esse oportet*. Sen. *Constat profecto ad salūtem cīvium* inventas esse leges. Cic. *Non ĕnim me* hoc jam dīcĕre *pudēbit*. Id. See § 209, R. 3, (*b*.), (*a.*)

REM. 3. The infinitive may itself be the subject of an infinitive; as, *Audio non licēre cuiquam in nāve cāpillos dēpōnĕre*. Ter.

REM. 4. The infinitive, with or without a subject accusative, may also be the predicate nominative; as, *Impūne quælĭbet facĕre id est regem esse*. Sall. In this sentence *facĕre* is the subject, and *rēgem esse* is the predicate; for *id*, which only represents by a kind of apposition the clause *impūne quælĭbet facĕre*, can be omitted.

REM. 5. When the infinitive *esse*, (or others of similar meaning, as, *fĭĕri, vivĕre, vitam degĕre, cedĕre, abīre*, etc.), with a predicate adjective (or noun), is joined with *licet*, such predicate is put in the accusative, if the subject-accusative of the infinitive is expressed, and sometimes, even when it is omitted, but more frequently, in the latter case, the predicate adjective or noun is attracted to the dative following *licet*; as, *Ut eum licēat ante tempus* consŭlem fi̇̄eri. Auct. ad Her. *Medios esse jam non licēbit*. Cic. *Si civi Rōmāno bert* esse Gaditānum. Id.—*Licuit enim esse ŏtiōso Themistocli*. Id. *Mihi neglĭgenti esse non licet*. Id. *Sibi vĭtam fĭliæ suā cāriōrem fuisse, si libĕræ ac pudīcæ* ei esse *licĭtum fuisset* (scil. ei). Liv. So also *necesse est* with the predicate in the dative. *Vōbis nĕcesse est* fortĭbus vĭris esse. Liv.—But *lĭcet, ŏportet*, an l *nĕcesse est* are also joined with the subjunctive mood, and hence is derived the construction of *lĭcet* as a conjunction. See § 263, 2.

THE INFINITIVE AS THE *OBJECT* OF A VERB.

§ 270. The infinitive, either with or without a subject-accusative, may be the *object* of a verb; as,

Hæc vitāre *cŭpĭmus*, We desire to avoid this. Cic. *Poëtas omnīno non cōnor* attingĕre, I do not at all attempt to read the poets. Id. Sententiam *vălēre cŭpiērunt*, They desired that the opinion should prevail. Id. *Spēro* te vălēre, I hope that you are well. Id.

NOTE. The infinitive as the object of a verb supplies the place of the accusative of the *thing*, and hence many active verbs besides the infinitive take in the active voice an accusative of the *person*, cf. § 231, R. 3, (*b.*), and in the passive retain the infinitive; as, Consŭles jŭbentur scribĕre exercĭtum. Mūros adīre vĕtĭti sunt. Cf. § 234, I.

REMARK 1. The infinitive alone may also depend upon an adjective, and sometimes upon a noun.

(*a.*) It may depend upon *relative adjectives*, (see § 213, R. 1), which, by the poets, are joined with the infinitive instead of their usual construction with the genitive of the gerund, etc.; as, *Cēdĕre* nescius. Hor. Avĭdi *committĕre pugnam*. Ovid. Cŭpĭdus *mŏrīri*. Id. *Cantāre* perīti *Arcădes*. Virg. Callĭdus *condĕre furto*. Hor. *Quidlĭbet* impŏtens *spērāre*. Id. *Sutrīnas făcĕre* inscius. Varr. Insuētus *vēra audīre*. Liv. Certa *mŏri*. Virg. Fēlīcior *unguĕre tēla*. Virg. So, Audax *omnia perpĕti*, Resolute to endure every thing. Hor. Sollers *ornāre Cȳpassis*, Skilful to adorn. Ovid. Segnes *solvĕre nŏdum*. Hor. Indŏcĭlis *pauperiem pāti*. Id. *Non* lēnis *fāta reclūdĕre*. Id. See § 213, R. 4, (1.)

(*b.*) It may also depend upon adjectives signifying *usefulness, fitness*, etc., which are sometimes by the poets construed with the infinitive instead of the dative; as, (*Tibia*) aspirāre *et* ădesse *chōris ĕrat* ūtĭlis. Hor. *Ætas mollis et* apta rēgi. Ovid. *Fons ĕtiam rīvo* dāre *nōmen* idōneus. Hor. *Frūges* consūmĕre nāti. Id. And after *dignus* and *contentus*; as, Dignus *amāri*. Virg. Cf. § 244, R. 2, (*b.*)

(*c.*) Upon a noun; as, Tempus *est hūjus libri* făcĕre *finem*, It is time to finish this book. Nep. *Init* consilia rēges tollĕre, He devised a plan to destroy the kings. Id. *Ea ĕrat* confessio *căput rērum Rōmam* esse. Liv. Cŭpīdo incessĕrat *Æthiŏpiam* invisĕre. Curt. *Quĭbus in ōtio* vivĕre copia *ĕrat*. Sall. So, *Nec mihi sunt* vīres *inimīcos* pellĕre *tectis*, instead of *pellendis inimīcis*, or *ad pellendos inimīcos*. Ovid.

(*d.*) If for the infinitives depending on nouns or adjectives other nouns were substituted, these last would be put in the genitive, dative, or ablative; and hence such infinitives may perhaps be properly regarded as exceptions to the rule, that the infinitive has but two cases, the nominative and the accusative.

REM. 2. (*a.*) The infinitive with the accusative sometimes stands unconnected, especially in exclamations and indignant interrogations, where *credibĭle est?* or *vērumne est?* may be supplied; as, *Mēne incepto* dēsistĕre *victum?* That I, vanquished, should desist from my undertaking? Virg. *Me misĕrum! te in tantas ærumnas propter me* incĭdisse! Cic.—But *ut*, also, with the subjunctive, either with or without an interrogative particle, may be used to express a question with indignation; as, *Eine* (scil. *patri*) *ĕgo* ut adverser? Liv. *Tu ut unquam te* corrigas? Cic. *Jūdicio* ut *ărător decŭmānum* persĕquātur? Id.; where *fĭĕri pŏtest?* may be supplied.

(*b.*) So, in the *ŏrātio oblīqua*, the words signifying *said, saying*, etc., are often omitted, or implied in a preceding verb or phrase; as, *Id făcile effĭci posse*, *ail. dixit*. Nep. *Quem signum* dătūrum *fŭgientĭbus?* Curt.

§ 271. SYNTAX.—INFINITIVE MOOD. 287

REM. 3. The infinitive is sometimes to be supplied; and *esse* and *fuisse* with a predicate adjective, and also in the compound forms of the infinitive, both active and passive, are commonly omitted, especially after verbs of *saying, thinking, knowing,* and *perceiving;* as, *Vos cognōvi fortes.* Sall. *Quem pulsum nēmŏrāci.* Tac.—So, also, with the infinitive perfect passive when depending on *volo, nolo, cupio,* and *oportet;* as, *Adŏlescenti mōrem gestum ŏportuit.* Ter. *Quod jam pridem factum ŏportuit.* Cic.—Sometimes in a relative clause an infinitive is to be supplied from the finite verb of the main proposition; as, *Quos vōluit omnes interfēcit,* scil. *interfīcĕre.* *Ne illam quidem consĕquuntur, quam pŭtant, grātiam;* i. e. *quam se consĕcūtūros pŭtant.* Cic.

THE INFINITIVE WITHOUT A SUBJECT-ACCUSATIVE.

§ **271.** The infinitive, without a subject-accusative, is used after verbs denoting *ability, obligation, intention* or *endeavor;* after verbs signifying *to begin, continue, cease, abstain, dare, fear, hesitate,* or *be wont;* and after the passive of verbs of *saying, believing, reckoning,* etc.

NOTE 1. To these classes belong *possum, queo, nēqueo, vălĕo, dēbeo; cūro, cōgĭto, dēcerno, stătuo, constĭtuo, instĭtuo, păro; cōnor, nītor, tendo, contendo, tento, mātūro, prŏpĕro, aggrĕdior, persĕvĕro;—căpi, incĭpio, pergo, dēsino, dēsisto, intermitto, parco, rĕcūso; sōleo, assuesco, consuesco, insuesco; audeo, vĕreor, mĕtuo, rĕformido, tĭmĕo, horrĕo, dŭbĭto:—audĭor, crēdor, existĭmor, fĕror, nĕgor, nuntior, perhĭbeor, pŭtor, trādor, jŭbeor, vĭdeor,* and *cōgor.*

NOTE 2. When the preceding verbs are joined with *esse, hăbēri, jŭdĭcāri, vĭdēri,* etc., the predicate noun or adjective is put in the nominative; as, *Solet tristis vĭdēri; aude săpiens esse; capit mihi mŏlestus esse; dēbes esse diligens; pŏtest* liber *esse:* and so also *mĕrētur, scit, didĭcit* liber *esse.*

NOTE 3. The poets, in imitation of the Greeks, use the infinitive after *fūge, aufer, cave, parce, memento; păveo, rēfūgio, quaero, urgeo, lăbōro, ămo, gaudeo, fūro, calleo, sūmo, mitto, rēmitto, pătior, jūro, conjūro, pugno, nātus,* and some other verbs, especially to denote a *wish* or *purpose;* as, *Introiit vidēre.* Ter. *Non te frangĕre persĕquor.* Hor. *Non pŏpŭlāre pĕnātes vĕnimus.* Virg. In this construction, the poets are sometimes imitated by the later prose writers.

REMARK 1. Many of the verbs above enumerated, instead of the infinitive, may be followed by the subjunctive with *ut, ne,* etc.; and with some of them this is the regular construction; as, *Sententiam ne dīcĕret, rĕcūsāvit.* Cic.

REM. 2. The passives *dicor, trādor, fĕror, narror, rĕpĕrior, existĭmor, vĭdeor,* etc., may either be used personally, with the infinitive alone, or impersonally, followed by the accusative with the infinitive. Thus we may say, *Māter Pausāniae eo tempŏre vixisse dicitur,* or, *Dicitur eo tempŏre mātrem Pausāniae vixisse,* The mother of Pausanias is said to have been living....or, It is said that the mother of Pausanias was living.... Nep. The former construction is more common especially with *vĭdeor,* see § 272, R. 6; but the latter is frequent with *nuntiātur,* and very common with the compound tenses, *trāditum est, prōdĭtum est,* etc., and with the participle future passive; as, *crēdendum est, intellĭgendum est,* etc.; as, *Quōrum nēmĭnem tălem fuisse* credendum, etc. Cic.

REM. 3. The infinitive without a subject is used after a verb, only when it denotes an action or state of the subject of that verb.

REM. 4. The verbs *to wish* or *desire, vŏlo, nŏlo, mālo; cŭpio, opto, stŭdeo,* have a twofold construction:—the infinitive without a subject-accusative is used after them, when the subject remains the same; and when followed by *esse, hăbēri,* etc., the predicate-noun or adjective is in the nominative;—but the accusative with the infinitive is used when the subject is changed, or when a reflexive pronoun of the same person follows. We say, therefore, *vŏlo ĕrŭditus fĭĕri,* and on the other hand, *vŏlo te ĕrŭdītum fĭĕri,* and *vŏlo me ĕrŭdītum fĭĕri.* So, *V ŭlo is esse, quem tu me esse vŏluisti.* Cic. *Cŭpio me esse clēmentem, cŭgno—*

me *non dissŏlūtum* vidēri. Id.; or, omitting the pronoun, *cŭpĭc esse* clēmens *nec dissŏlūtus vidēri.*—*Omnis hŏmĭnes qui* sese *stŭdent præstāre cētĕris ănĭmālĭbus,* etc. Sall.

NOTE 4. *Vŏlo* is used with the present infinitive passive; as, *Me ămāri vŏlo*, I wish to be beloved; *hoc vĕlim intellĭgi*, I wish this to be understood; and also with the infinitive perfect passive to denote the eager desire that something should be instantly accomplished; as, *Lēgāti quod ērant appellāti sŭperbius, Cŏrinthum patres vestri*—*exstinctum esse vŏluērunt.* Cic.; but it occurs most frequently with the omission of *esse;* as, *hoc factum vŏlo; nunc illos commŏnĭtos vĕlim:* so, *patriam exstinctam cŭpit.*

NOTE 5. The nominative with the infinitive after verbs of saying, perceiving, etc. (§ 272), is rare even in poetry, and is an imitation of the Greek idiom, which requires the nominative with the infinitive when the same subject remains; as, *Phăsēlus ille, quem vĭdētis, hospĭtes, ait* fuisse *nāvium* celerrimus. Catull. *Quin rēttŭlit Ajax* esse *Jŏvis* nĕpos, instead of *se esse Jŏvis* nĕ*pŏtem* Ovid. *Sensit mĕdios* delapsus *in hostes*, instead of *se dēlapsum esse.* Virg.

THE INFINITIVE WITH A SUBJECT-ACCUSATIVE.

§ 272. The infinitive with a subject-accusative follows verbs of *saying, thinking, knowing, perceiving,* and the like; as,

Vĭdēbat, *id non posse fĭēri,* He saw that that could not be done. Nep. Sentit *ănĭmus, se suā vi, non ălĭēnā, mŏvēri.* Cic. Audīvi *te vĕnire. Me in ējus pŏtestāte* dixi *fŏre.* Id. Affirmant *mīlĭtum jăcēre ănĭmos.* Liv. *Sæpe* vēnit ad aures meas, *te istud nĭmis crēbro dīcĕre.* Cic. *Eam pugnam ad Pērūsiam pugnātam* (*esse*), *quidam* auctōres sunt. Liv.

NOTE 1. This rule includes all such verbs and phrases as denote the exercise of the external senses and intellectual faculties, or the communication of thought to others; as, *audio, vĭdeo, sentio, ănĭmadverto, cognosco, intellĭgo, percĭpio, disco, scio, nescio, censeo, spēro, despēro, cōgĭto, jūdĭco, crēdo, arbĭtror, pŭto, ŏpīnor, dūco, stătuo, mĕmĭni, rēcordor, oblīvīscor, ŏpīnio est, spes est,* etc.;—*dīco, trădo, prŏdo, scrībo, rĕfĕro, narro, nuntio, confirmo, nĕgo, ostendo, indĭco, dŏceo, certiōrem făcio, dēmonstro, perhĭbeo, prōmitto, pollĭceor, spondeo,* etc.; but with most of these a different construction often occurs. See § 273

NOTE 2. The propositions, whose subjects are thus put in the accusative and their verbs in the infinitive, are those which are *directly* dependent on the verbs of saying and perceiving. Respecting the clauses inserted in such dependent propositions, see § 266, 1.

NOTE 3. (*a.*) When a relative clause inserted in a proposition containing the accusative with the infinitive, has the same verb as the proposition in which it is inserted, but such verb is not repeated, the noun which is the subject of the relative clause is also put by attraction in the accusative; as, *Te suspĭcor eisdem rēbus, quĭbus* me ipsum, *commŏvēri.* If the verb is expressed we must say, *eisdem rēbus commŏvēri, quibus* (ĕgo) ipse commŏveor. So, also, in inserted relative clauses where the verb, if expressed, would be in the subjunctive, (see § 266, 2.); as, (*Verres*) *aiĕbat se tantidem æstimasse, quanti* Sācerdōtem, *for quanti Sācerdos æstimasset.* Cic. *Confĭdĭtur se in eā parte fuisse quā te, quā* virum *omni laude dignum* patrem tuum. Id.

(*b.*) The same is the case with the particle *quam* after a comparative, see § 256, R. 5, (*a.*). But sometimes when *quam* connects a clause to a preceding proposition containing the accusative with the infinitive, the same construction follows that precedes *quam*, even when the verb of the latter clause is expressed; as, *Nonne tĭbi affirmāvi quidvis me pŏtius perpessūrum,* quam *ex Itălĭā ad bellum civile* me exiturum; instead of *quam exīrem* or *quam ut exīrem.* Cic.

(*c.*) In long speeches in the *ōrātio obliquā*, relative clauses, having a verb of their own which should properly be in the subjunctive, are put in the accusative with the infinitive, if the relative clause is not subordinate to the one with the infinitive, and which is governed by a verb of saying or perceiving,

§ 272. SYNTAX.—INFINITIVE MOOD. 289

out is rather coördinate with it; in which case the relative is equivalent to the demonstrative with *et*; as, *Nam illōrum urbem ut prōpugnācŭlum oppŏsĭtum esse barbăris, ăpud* quam *jam bis classes rēgias fēcisse naufrăgium*; for *et ăpud eam jam bis*, etc.—In Livy and Tacitus the same construction sometimes occurs even after conjunctions; as after *quum* in the sense of 'while,' see § 263, 5, R. 3; after *quamquam* on account of its absolute signification, see § 198, 4, and after *quia*.

NOTE 4. The personal pronouns, which, with the other moods, are expressed only when they are emphatic, must be always expressed in the accusative with the infinitive. The verbs 'to promise' and 'to hope' are in English usually joined with the infinitive present without a pronoun, but in Latin not only is the pronoun expressed, but the infinitive which follows is in the future; as, 'He promised to come,' is in Latin, *Prōmīsit se ventūrum* (scil. *esse*, see § 270, R. 3). But the infinitive present sometimes occurs after these verbs; as, *Pollicentur obsĭdes dăre*, Cæs. B. G. 4, 21; and the pronoun is occasionally omitted, see § 239, R. 2 and 3.

REMARK 1. When ambiguity would arise from the subject and the object of the verb being both in the accusative, the passive infinitive is substituted for the active, by which means the subject is put in the ablative, or in the accusative with *per*; as, *Ne fando quidem audītum est, crŏcŏdīlum violātum esse ab Ægyptio*; instead of *Ægyptium crŏcŏdīlum violasse*. Cic.

REM. 2. After verbs of saying, thinking, etc., the conjunction *that* is omitted in translating from English into Latin, and the subject of the dependent clause is put in the accusative, and its verb in the infinitive.

REM. 3. The accusative with the infinitive is sometimes rendered into English by a similar form; as, *Si vis* me flēre, If you wish *me to weep*. Hor.; but the dependent clause is more frequently connected to the verb of saying, etc., by the conjunction *that*, and the infinitive translated by the indicative or potential mood; as, *Sentĭmus nĭvem esse albam*, We perceive *that snow is white*. Cic. Sometimes the dependent clause is annexed to the other without the conjunction; as, *Crēdunt se neglĭgi*, They think *they are neglected*. Ter.

REM. 4. A present infinitive corresponds to the imperfect indicative, when with an accusative it follows a preterite tense; as, *Dixit Cæsărem vĕnīre*, He said that Cæsar *was coming*. Cæs. In like manner the perfect infinitive with an accusative after a preterite tense corresponds to the pluperfect indicative; as, *Dixit Cæsărem vĕnisse*, He said that Cæsar *had come*. See § 268, 2.

REM. 5. The present infinitive, after verbs of sense, is often equivalent to the present participle; as, *Surgĕre vĭdet lūnam*, He sees the moon (to rise) rising. Virg. *Arma rŭtilāre vident*. Id. *Vĭdēbis collūcēre făces*. Id. *Nec Zĕphyros audis spīrāre*? Do you not hear the zephyrs blowing? Id. *Sæpe hoc majōres nātu dicĕre audīri*. Cic. The two constructions are sometimes united; as, *Mĕdium vĭdeo discēdĕre cœlum, pălantesque pŏlo stellas*. Virg.

REM. 7 The subject-accusative after verbs of *saying, showing,* and *believing*; as, *dico, nĕgo, trādo, fĕro, mĕmŏro, narro, nuntio, perhibeo, prōdo, scribo, dēmonstro, ostendo, arguo, crēdo, pŭto, existĭmo*, and the like, and also after *jŭbeo, rĕto*, and *prŏhĭbeo*, is regarded also as the accusative of the *object* after these verbs; and hence such verbs are used also in the passive, the accusative of the active voice becoming, as usual, the nominative of the passive. This is especially the case when their subject is indefinite; as, *Dīcunt* (they or people say) *me vĭrum prŏbum esse*, or *dicor vir prŏbus esse*. So, *Vĕtāmur hoc făcĕre*, instead of, *Nos hoc făcĕre vĕtant*. Instead also of the impersonal *vĭdētur* (it appears) followed by the infinitive with its subject-accusative, it is common to say personally, *vĭdeor, vĭdēris*, etc., with the infinitive; as, *vĭdeor errasse*, it appears that I have erred.

25

INFINITIVE AND SUBJUNCTIVE CLAUSES.

§ 273. When the particle *that*, in English, introduces a clause denoting a *purpose*, *object*, or *result*, it is a sign of the subjunctive in Latin, and is to be expressed by *ut*, etc.; but otherwise it is usually the sign of the accusative with the infinitive. Cf. §§ 262 and 272.

1. (*a*.) Verbs of *endeavoring* and *resolving* take after them the infinitive and more rarely the subjunctive, when the subject remains the same; but when the subject is changed, they take the subjunctive only.

NOTE 1. Such are *stătuo, constĭtuo, dēcerno, tento, lăbōro, păro, mĕdĭtor, cūro, nītor, contendo, consĭlium căpio, ănĭmum* or *in ănĭmum indūco*. Cf. § 271, N. 1. After *ŏpĕram do*, I exert myself, *id. hoc*, or *illud ăgo*, 1 endeavor, *nĭhil antīquius hăbeo* or *dūco quam*, nothing is of more importance to me, and *video* for *cūro*, the subjunctive is almost exclusively used.

(*b*.) Verbs of *effecting* are construed with *ut* or *ne* and the subjunctive.

NOTE 2. Such are *făcio, efficio, perficio, ēvinco, pervinco, impetro, assĕquor, consĕquor*, etc. But *făcĕre* 'to effect' occurs in Cic. Brut. 38, in connection with the accusative and infinitive passive.

NOTE 3. Făcio with *ut* is also used as a periphrasis for the indicative; as, *Invītus quidem fēci, ut L. Flāmĭnium e sĕnātu ējĭcĕrem*, for *invītus ējēci*. Cic.—*Fac*, 'suppose' or 'granting,' and *efficĕre*, 'to prove,' take the accusative with the infinitive; but the passive *efficĭtur*, 'it follows,' takes also the subjunctive. —*Făcĕre*, 'to introduce' or 'represent,' is joined with a present or perfect participle; as, *Lælium et Scīpiōnem făcĭmus admīrantes.* Cic. In the passive the accusative also with the infinitive is found, there being no present participle; as, *Isocrătem Plăto laudāri fācit a Sōcrăte.* Cic.

2. Verbs signifying *to request, to demand, to admonish, to advise, to encourage, to command*, and the like, both when the subject remains the same and when it is changed, are followed by the subjunctive with *ut* or *ne*, and only rarely by the infinitive.

NOTE 4. (*a*.) Such are *rŏgo, ōro, prĕcor, pĕto; posco, postŭlo, flăgĭto; mŏneo, admŏneo, commŏneo, hortor, cŏhortor, exhortor, suādeo, persuādeo, instĭtuo,* (I instruct) *impello, cōgo, mando, præscrībo, ēdīco, dēcerno, lēgem do, censeo, perpello, excĭto, incĭto, impĕro*, etc.; as, *Te non hortor sōlum, sed ĕtiam ōro, ut tōta mente in rempūblĭcam incumbas.* Cic.

(*b*.) In the poets and later prose writers the infinitive more frequently follows those verbs without any difference of meaning. The poets even use the infinitive to express a purpose; as, *Prōteus pĕcus ēgit altos vīsĕre montes.* Hor.

(*c*.) *Nuntio, scrībo, mitto*, and even *dīco*, are followed by the subjunctive, when they imply an injunction or intention that something should be done; as, *Hæc ut făcias, scrībo.* Cic.

(*d*.) *Jŭbeo* and *vĕto* commonly take the accusative with the infinitive, but sometimes the subjunctive with or rarely without *ut*. Sometimes, with the infinitive, the person to whom the command is given is omitted, especially when it is either obvious from the nature of the command or indefinite; as, *Castra mūnīre jŭbet*, scil. *mīlĭtes.* Cæs. *Lex recte făcĕre jŭbet*, scil. *hŏmĭnes.* Cic. With the subjunctive the dative of the person sometimes follows *jŭbeo*; as, *Britannĭco jussit, exsurgĕret.* Tac.—*Impĕro* is sometimes followed by the accusative with the infinitive passive; and so also is *censeo*, I vote, or, I ordain. The latter is often construed with the participle in *dus* with *esse* expressed or understood; as, *Carthăgĭnem dēlendam censeo.*

(e.) *Moneo* and *admoneo*, 'I remind,' and *persuadeo*, 'I convince take the accusative with the infinitive.

3. (a.) In the *oratio obliqua*, the construction of the accusative with the infinitive, is exchanged for that of the subjunctive, to denote possibility, liberty, duty, etc.; as,

Virginius unum Ap. Claudium legum expertem esse aiebat: respicerent tribunal homines castellum omnium scelerum. Liv.

(b.) On the contrary, when the subjunctive has been used after a verb of requesting, commanding, etc., the construction often passes into that of the accusative with the infinitive; the verb of saying being considered as implied in the verb of requesting, etc.; as, *Orabat ne se ut parricidam liberum aversarentur: sibi vitam filiæ suā cariorem fuisse, si....* Liv. Cf. § 270, R. 2, (b.)

4. (a.) Verbs which denote *willingness, unwillingness, permission,* and *necessity,* commonly take the infinitive, or the accusative with the infinitive, but sometimes the subjunctive.

NOTE 5. Such are *volo, nolo, malo, opto, permitto, patior, sino, concedo, licet, prohibeo, oportet,* and *necesse est.* Cf. § 271, R. 4. *Volo ut* is used to express a strong emphasis. *Nolo* is not construed with the subjunctive.

(b.) An infinitive passive without a subject is sometimes used with *oportet;* as, *Non oportuit relictas,* scil. *esse ancillas.* Ter. *Ut ut erat,* mansum tamen *oportuit,* scil. *esse.* Id. *Non putabant de tali viro suspicionibus oportere judicari.* Nep.

(c.) Some other verbs which regularly take the accusative with the infinitive after them, are occasionally followed by the subjunctive.

5. *Quod,* 'that,' commonly with the indicative, introduces a substantive clause containing the explanation or ground of the predicate or of some other word in the principal clause.

REMARK. The subjunctive follows *quod* in those cases only in which the clause expresses the view or sentiment of some other person than the writer or speaker. Cf. § 266, 3.

Quod is used:—

(1.) After such expressions as *bene, male, prudenter facio; bene, male fit; evenit, accidit,* and the like; *prætereo, mitto;* and generally *adde, accedit,* etc.; as, *Bene facis,* quod *me adjuvas.*

(2.) To introduce the explanation of a noun, pronoun, or pronominal adverb in the principal clause; as, *Magnum beneficium est naturæ,* quod *necesse est mori.*

(3.) After verbs signifying *an affection of the mind,* and the *outward expression of such feeling;* and also after verbs of *praising, censuring, accusing,* and *thanking.*

NOTE 6. Such are *gaudeo, delector, gratum,* or *jucundum est mihi, angor, doleo, ægre, ... ste,* or *graviter fero, succenseo, pænitet, miror, admiror, glorior, gratulor, gratias ago, queror, indignor,* and others of similar meaning; as, *Scipio sæpe* querebatur, quod *omnibus in rebus homines diligentiores essent, ut,* etc. Cic. *Gaudeo* quod *te interpellavi.* Id. *Quod spiratis,* quod *vocem mittitis,* quod *formas hominum habetis,* indignantur. Liv *Cato mirari se aiebat,* quod *non rideret haruspex, haruspicem quum videret.* Cic.

NOTE 7. After those verbs which express the feeling of joy, grief, etc.; as, *gaudeo, doleo, miror,* the accusative with the infinitive is more commonly found, but those which denote the outward expression of such feeling are more commonly construed with *quod;* but sometimes this distinction is reversed *Gratulor* is commonly joined with *quod.*

NOTE 8. A purely objective proposition is expressed by *quod* only when it depends upon *addo*, (generally in the imperative *adde*), or upon *facio* joined with an adverb; as, *Adde quod pubes tibi crescit omnes.* Hor. *Adde huc quod mercem sine fucis gestat.* Id. *Fēcit hūmānĭter Licinius,* quod *ad me vespĕri vĕnit.* Cic. In all other cases the infinitive is employed in purely objective propositions.

6. By the infinitive, with or without a subject-accusative, a proposition is expressed as a *thought*, so that it resembles an abstract noun; by *quod*, with the indicative or the subjunctive, it is represented simply as a *fact*. To the latter is frequently joined *hoc, id, illud, istud,* or *huc,* etc.; as, *Illud quŏque nĭbis accēdĭt incommŏdum,* quod *M. Jūnius ăbest.* Cic. *Huc accēdĭbat,* quod, etc. Sall. *Quod* generally refers to past time, and hence it is preferable to say, *Grātissĭmum mihi est,* quod *ad me tua mănu scripsisti*; but with the infinitive, *Grātissĭmum mihi est te bĕne vălēre.*

(*a.*) *Quod,* with the indicative, in the sense of *as to*, or *with regard to*, is used at the beginning of a sentence, especially in letters, in repeating an expression of a person for the purpose of answering it; as, *Quod autem me Agămemnŏnem æmŭlāri pŭtas, fallĕris.* Nep. *Quod scrībis te velle scīre, qui sit reipūblicæ stătus. summa dissensio est.* Cic. Sentences thus introduced by *quod* are in no grammatical connection with the verb that follows them. See § 206, (14.)

(*b.*) *Quod* is used in explanatory or periphrastic propositions which refer to a preceding demonstrative pronoun, as *hoc, id,* etc., unless such pronoun be added pleonastically, in the nominative or accusative, to verbs governing the accusative with the infinitive; as, *Mihi quidem videntur homines hac re maxime cĕlluis præstāre,* quod *lŏqui possunt.* Cic.

NOTE 9. The construction of the infinitive resembles, in the following particulars, that of a noun in the singular number and neuter gender :—

(*a.*) Like a noun, it may have an adjective or pronoun agreeing with it; as *Tōtum hoc phĭlŏsŏphāri displicet.* Cic. *Quum vīvĕre ipsum turpe sit nōbis.* Id. *Me hoc ipsum nihil ăgĕre dēlectat.* Id. Meum intelligĕre *nullā pecuniā venio.* Petr. See § 205, R. 8.

(*b.*) It may be followed by a limiting genitive; as, *Cūjus non* dīmĭcāre *fuit vincĕre.* Val. Max.

(*c.*) It may be either the subject or object of a verb. See §§ 209, R. 3, (5,) and 229, R. 5. It may also be used after neuter verbs, like an accusative, depending on a preposition understood; as, *Te* accēpisse *meas litĕras gaudeo.* Ter. See §§ 232, (2,) and 273, 5.

(*d.*) It is also used like a predicate-nominative; as, *Vidēre est* perspĭcĕre *aliquid.* Cic. See § 210.

(*e.*) It may, like a genitive, limit the signification of an adjective or noun. See § 270, R. 1.

(*f.*) It may, like an accusative, depend on a preposition; as, *Aristo et Pyrrho* inter *optĭme* vălēre *et* grăvissĭme ægrŏtāre, *nihil prorsus dīcēbant interesse.* Cic. *Quod crimen dicis præter* ămasse *meum?* Ovid. *Invĕniet nil sibi lĕgātum,* præter plorāre. Hor.

(*g.*) It is used also like an ablative; as, *Audīto rēgem in Sicĭliam* tendĕre. Sall.

(*h.*) Sometimes, also, especially in the poets, it denotes a purpose, like a participle in *dus,* (see § 274, R. 7.); as, *Lōrīcam dōnat* hăbēre *viro.* Virg.; or like a dative of the end, (see § 227.)

PARTICIPLES.

§ 274. 1. Participles are followed by the same cases and constructions as their verbs; as,

§ 274. SYNTAX.—PARTICIPLES. 293

Quidam, poēta *nōmĭnātus*, A certain one, called a poet. Cic. Că'ŭlōrn n *oblīta* *lecena*, The lioness forgetful of her whelps. Virg. *Făventes* rēbus *Carthăgĭniensium*, Favoring the interests of the Carthaginians. Liv. *Tendens ad sīdĕra* palmas. Virg. *Accūsātus* rei *căpĭtālis*. Cic. *Prīmā dīcte* mĭhi *summā dĭcende Cămēnā*. Hor. Omĭna *doctus*. Stat. Cāsus *ăbies rīsūra mărīnos*. Id. *Cărĭtūri* arbōre *montes*. Ovid. *Parcendum est* tĕnĕris. Juv. *Utendum est* ætāte. Ovid. L. *Brūtus* arcens rēdĭtu tўrannum, *in prœlio concĭdit*. Cic.

2. The present, perfect, and future active participles, denote respectively an action which is present, past, or future, in reference to the time of the verb with which they are connected; as,

Simul hoc dīcens *attollit se*. Virg. *Tum ad Thraseam in hortis* ăgentem *missus est*. Tac. *Turnum* fŭgientem *hæc terra vĭdēbit?* Virg. *Qui* missus *ab Argis Itālā consēdĕrat urbe*. Id. *Lāmia mŭnĕre ædĭlĭtātis* perfunctus, *pĕtit prætūram*. Cic. Jussus *cum fĭde pœnas luam*. Hor. *Jŭvĕnis mĕdios* mŏrĭtūrus *in hostes irruit*. Virg. Pĕrĭtūrus *injĕcit sēse in agmen*. Id. *Illa tĭbi* ventūra *bella expĕdiet*. Id.

NOTE. The participle expresses the action or state of the verb, and also marks its complete or incomplete state or condition. Cf. § 144, 1–3. Except, however, in deponent verbs, the Latin language has no active participle denoting a completed action, equivalent to the English 'having written,' nor any passive participle denoting a state of suffering still going on, equivalent to the English present participle 'being loved.'

REMARK 1. The present participle, particularly that of the verb *eo*, sometimes denotes that which is about to be done; as, *Interclūsit hiems, et terruit Auster* euntes, ... as they were on the point of going. Virg. *Nec nos via fallit* euntes. Id.

REM. 2. (*a*.) The present participle, also, sometimes denotes a purpose; as, *Ibant*, ōrantes *vĕniam*,....to sue for favor.... Virg. *Eurўpўlum* scĭtantem ōrācŭla *Phœbi mittĭmus*. Id. (*b*.) It is also used to express a state or condition, where, in English, a substantive is employed with a preposition; as, *ignōrans*, from ignorance; *mĕtuens*, from fear; *consŭlātum pĕtens*, in his suit for the consulship; *omne mălum nascens făcĭle opprĭmĭtur*,—in its origin.

REM. 3. (*a*.) The perfect participle passive, especially in the poets, often denotes the result of a past action, and thus supplies the place of a present participle passive; as, *Nōtus trŏlat pĭceā* tectus *cālĭgĭne*....covered with pitchy darkness. Ovid. Cf. Virg. Æn. 1, 480; 2, 277; 4, 72, 589; 5, 113, 708; 6, 335; Georg. 1, 204. It is often to be translated by a present active participle; as, *Mănu pectus percussa dēcōrum, flăventesque* abscissa *cōmas*, i. e. *percŭtiens, abscindens*. Virg. Tunsæ *pectŏra palmis*. Id. So, also, *sōlĭtus, ausus, fīsus*, and the perfect participles of deponent verbs; as, *Longum cantu* sŏlāta *lăbōrem*. Id. *Vox audītur fractos sŏnĭtus* imĭtāta *tŭbārum*. Id. *Divĭtiăcus Cæsărem* complexus, *obsecrāre cœpit*. Cæs. Concrētos *sanguĭne crīnes gĕrens*. Virg. Tonsis *in vallĭbus*, i. e. quæ tondentur. Id.

(*b*.) The perfect participle of a preceding verb is often used in a succeeding clause, to express the completion of an action; as, *Exercĭtum* fundit *fŭgatque*, fūsum *persĕquĭtur*. Liv. This idiom frequently occurs in Ovid.

REM. 4. *Hăbeo*, with perfect participles denoting *knowledge* and *determination*; as, *cognĭtum, perspectum, percēphensum, comprĕhensum, explōrātum, stătūtum, constĭtūtum, dēlĭbĕrātum, persuāsum mĭhi hăbeo*, etc., forms a periphrasis, like the passive verb in English, and equivalent to *cognōvi, perspexi, percēpi*, etc., instead of the verb of the participle; as, *Clōdii ănĭmum* perspectum or cognĭtum *hăbeo*; for *perspexi*, etc., I perceive, know. *Persuāsum mihi hăbeo* and *persuāsissĭmum hăbeo* are used only in the neuter gender and with an accusative with the infinitive in the sense of *mĭhi persuāsi* or *persuāsum mĭhi est*. When *hăbeo* with any other participle than those above indicated is used, it expresses more than the ordinary perfect active; as, *Quod me hortāris ut absolvam*; hăbeo absŏlūtam *suĭve ĕpos ad Cæsărem*; i. e. I have it ready. Cic. *Do, reddo, cūro*,

25*

těneo, possĭdeo, and *missum făcio*, are sometimes so construed with participles as, Missam *iram făciet*, for *mittet*. Ter. *Hostes victos dăre*, for *vincĕre*. Sall.

REM. 5. (*a*.) The passive participles may supply the place of a verbal noun in *io* or *us*, the perfect being employed to represent an action as completed, and the future when it is conceived as still incomplete; as, *Ante Rōmam condĭtam*, Before the building of Rome. Cic. *Consilia urbis dōlendæ*, Plans for the destruction of the city. Id. See § 275, II. With the limitations about to be made in regard to the nominative, this construction is used in all the cases, and even when they are governed by the prepositions, *ad, ante, ob, post, propter; ab* and *ex*; as, *Hæ litĕræ recĭtātæ magnum luctum frĕērunt*, The reading of this letter. Liv. *Tarentum captum*, The taking of Tarentum. *Ob receptu m Hannĭbălem*, On account of the reception of Hannibal. *Sibi quisque cæsi rēgis expĕtēbat děcus*, The glory of killing, or, of having killed the king. *Propter Africam dŏmĭtam*. Eutrop. *Ante Epămĭnondam nātum*. Nep. *Post Christum nātum*. *Ab condĭtā urbe ad lĭbĕrātam*. Liv. The oblique cases only of participles in *dus* are used in this manner as the nominative denotes necessity, (see Rem. 8,) and even the perfect participle is not thus used in the nominative by Cicero.

(*b*.) The neuter of the perfect passive participle without a noun is used by Livy, as the subject of a proposition; as, Tentātum *per dictătōrem, ut ambo patrĭcii consŭles creārentur, rem ad interregnum perduxit*: i. e. the attempt, or the fact of the attempt being made by the dictator. Compare a similar use of this participle in the ablative, § 257, R. 9, (1.) (*c*.)

(*c*.) The English ' without ' with a verbal substantive; as, ' without writing, without having waited,' etc., is expressed in Latin by means of a negative noun, adjective or particle connected with a participle; as, *Cæsar exercitum numquam per insidĭōsa itĭnĕra duxit*, nisi perspĕcŭlātus *lŏcōrum sĭtus*, without having examined the localities. This form occurs often with the ablative absolute; as, *Athēnienses* non exspectāto *auxilio adversus ingentem Persārum exercĭtum in prælium egrĕdiuntur*, without waiting for assistance. So, nullā præstĭtūtā *die*, Without fixing any time. Cic. *Misĕrum est* nihil perfĭcientem *angi*. Id.

REM. 6. (*a*.) The participle in *rus*, especially with verbs of motion, often denotes intention or purpose; as, *Ad Jŏvem Ammŏnem pergit* consultūrus *de ŏrĭgĭne suā*, He goes to Jupiter Ammon, to consult respecting his origin. Just.

(*b*.) It is also used where in English a clause connected by *since, when, although*, etc., is employed; as, *Plūra lŏcūtūros ăbire nos jussit*, When or although we intended to say more. *Hercŭlem Germāni, itūri in prælium cănunt*. Tac. Hence it is sometimes used, though not by Cicero, to express the inference from a hypothetical proposition; as, *Egrĕdĭtur castris Rōmānus, vallum invāsūrus, ni cōpia pugnæ fĭĕret*. And with the repetition of the preceding verb; as, *Dēdit mihi quantum maxĭme pŏtuit*, dătūrus *amplius, si pŏtuisset*, i. e. ac *dēdisset amplius*. Plin. Ep.

REM. 7. (*a*.) The participle in *dus*, also, denotes a purpose passively, when joined with verbs signifying *to give, to deliver, to agree for, to have, to receive, to undertake*, etc. Such are *do, trādo, tribuo, attribuo, mando, mitto, permitto, concēdo, redimo, condūco, lŏco, hăbeo, accĭpio, suscĭpio, rĕlinquo, cūro, dĭpŏsco rŏgo*; as, *Testāmentum tĭbi trādit lĕgendum*, He delivers his will to you to read. Hor *Attrĭbuit nos* trŭcīdandos *Cŭthēgo*. Cic. *Quod* ūtendum *accēpĕris, reddĭto*. Id. *Conon mūros dĭrŭtos a Lȳsandro* rĕfĭciendos *cūrāvit*,—ordered them to be restored. Nep.

(*b*.) But the same meaning may be expressed actively by means of *ad* and the gerund; as, *Cæsar oppidum* ad diripiendum *milĭtibus concessit*.—The poets sometimes use the infinitive active for the same purpose; as, *Tristĭtiam et mĕtus trādam protervis in mare Caspium* portāre *ventis*. Hor. In prose such use of the infinitive is of exceedingly rare occurrence; as, *Bibĕre dăre*. Cic.

REM. 8. (*a.*) The participle in *dus*, when agreeing with the subject of a sentence, has the signification of *necessity* or *propriety*; sometimes, though rarely, except in later writers, that of *possibility*; as,

Is věnĕrandus a nōbis et cŏlendus est, He should be worshipped and honored by us. Cic. *Dēlenda est Carthāgo*, Carthage must be destroyed. Cato. *Hæc spēranda fuērunt.* Virg. So with *est* used impersonally; as, *Utrum pāce nōbis an bello esset* ūtendum. Cic.

(*b.*) Sometimes, also, when not agreeing with the subject of a sentence, it has this signification; as, *Facta narrābas* dissimulanda *tibi*, You were relating facts which you should have concealed. Ovid. *A. L. Brūto principe hūjus maxime* conservandi *gĕnĕris et nōmĭnis.* Cic.

REM. 9. The participle in *dus*, in its oblique cases, supplies the place of a present participle of the passive voice, to denote a continued or incomplete action; as, *Occŭpātus sum in litĕris scribendis*, in writing letters; literally, in letters which are being written. See § 275, II.—So, also, in the poets both in the nominative and oblique cases; as, *Trīginta magnos* volvendis *mensĭbus orbes impĕrio explēbit.* Virg. Volvenda *dies.* Id. Cf. Volventibus *annis.* Id.

REM. 10. After participles in *dus*, the person by whom a thing must be done, is put in the dative, but in a few passages even of Cicero it is found in the ablative with *ab.* See § 225, III.

REM. 11. The neuter of the participle in *dus*, joined with a tense of *esse* in the periphrastic conjugation (see § 184, 3,) retains the signification of necessity; as, *Audendum est*, We must venture. In early writers and sometimes also in the poets, an accusative of the object is joined with this neuter, if the verb is transitive; as, *Nunc pācem ōrandum, nunc—arma rĕpōnendum, et bellum extiāle cavendum.* Sil. But in classical Latin such accusative is generally changed to the nominative, and the participle is made to agree with it in gender and number. Thus, instead of *virtūtem laudandum est*, we usually find *virtus laudanda est.* The accusative in this connection is used by Cicero in only two passages. *Utendum est* with the ablative occurs more than once in Cicero; as, *Quum suo cuique* jūdicio *sit ūtendum.*

REM. 12. In classical prose the participle in *dus* never has the signification of *possibility*, except when joined with *vix*; as, *Vix optandum nōbis vidēbātur.* Cic. *Vix ērat crēdendum*, i. e. *vix crēdi pŏtĕrat.* Later writers use it in this sense with negative particles, and at a later period it was used with still more frequency in the sense of possibility as well as in that of necessity.

3. (*a.*) A participle is often employed, instead of a verb, in a conditional, explanatory, adversative, relative, or other dependent clause; as,

Cŭrio, ad fŏcum sēdenti (as he was sitting) *magnum auri pondus Samnĭtes attŭlērunt.* Cic. *Trĭdui viam prōgressi, rursus rĕvertērunt*; for, *quum progressi essent.* Cæs. *Diŏnȳsius tȳrannus, Sȳrācūsis* expulsus, *Corinthi puĕros dŏcēbat.* Cic. *Diŏnȳsius, cultros* metuens *tonsōrios, candenti carbōne sibi adūrēbat capillum.* [!] *Risus interdum ita repente ērumpit, ut eum* cūpientis *tĕnĕre nĕquĕāmus.* Id. *Ciconiæ* abĭtūræ *congrĕgantur in loco certo.* Plin.

NOTE 1. If the participle refers to a noun not contained in the leading proposition, it is put with that noun in the ablative absolute. See § 257, R. 3.

NOTE 2. (*a.*) The English clauses most frequently expressed in Latin by means of participles are such as are connected by relatives or by *as, when, after, although, since, because*, etc.; as, *Nēmo observat lūnam nisi* lăbōrantem. Sen. *Ut ŏcŭlus, sic ănĭmus, se non* videns, *ălia cernit*,—though not perceiving itself. Cic. *Servīlius Ahā'a Spūrium Mælium, regnum* appĕtentem, *intĕrēmit*,—because he was aspiring to the sovereignty. Cic.—(*b.*) When a participle is connected with a relative or interrogative it can only be translated by a circumlocution; as, *Non sunt ea bōna dīcenda*, quibus abundantem *licet esse miserrimum*,—which one may possess in abundance, and still be very miserable. Cic. *Sĕnātus absurdum esse dīcēbat, ignōrāre regem*, quid spĕrans aut pŏtens vēnĕrit,—with what hope or request he had come. Liv.

(b.) When two verbs are in English connected by *and*, and the act ons denoted by them are regarded as simultaneous, one of them may be expressed in Latin by the present participle; as, He sits and holds his lute, *Ille (Arion) sēdens cithăram tĕnet*. Ovid. *Simul hoc dicens attollit in ægrum se fĕmur*. Virg. i. e. *hoc dicit et attollit*. But if one of the actions precede the other, the perfect participle must be used; as, Cæsar attacked and defeated the enemy, *Cæsar hostes aggressus fūgārit*. Submersas *obrue puppes*, i. e. *Submerge et obrue*. Virg.—When the English clause would be connected by *although*, the participle is often followed by *tamen*. Later writers in such case join the particles *quamquam, quamvis, etiam* and *vel* with the participle itself; as, *Cæsărem milĭtes, quamvis rĕcūsantem ultro in Africam sunt sĕcūti*. Suet.; and these are sometimes retained in the ablative absolute.—It is only in late Latin that participles are sometimes used in describing persons as possessing certain attributes, e. g. *adstantes, audientes*, for *ii qui adstant, audiunt*, i. e. the bystanders, hearers.

(c.) A participle is used with verbs signifying to *represent* and *perceive*, especially to *see* and *hear*, when the object is described or perceived in a particular state; as, *Apelles pinxit Alexandrum Magnum fulmen tĕnentem*. Plin. In English the *infinitive* is often joined with verbs of seeing and hearing; as, *Audīvi te cănentem*, I heard you sing. *Audīvi te cănĕre*, would be, I heard that you sung. *Vidēmus Pŏlўphēmum vastā se mōle mŏventem*. Virg.

NOTE 3. In many cases, for want of a perfect participle active, and a present participle passive, this construction cannot be used. Thus, *quum āmāvisset* cannot be exchanged for a participle corresponding with the English *having loved*. As the perfect participles of deponent verbs, however, have an active signification, they admit of the participial construction. The want of a perfect active participle may also be supplied by the perfect passive participle in the ablative absolute. See § 257, R. 5.

GERUNDS AND GERUNDIVES.

§ 275. I. Gerunds are governed like nouns, and are followed by the same cases as their verbs; as,

Mĕtus părendi sibi, Fear of obeying him. Sall. *Parcendo* victis, By sparing the vanquished. Liv. *Effĕror stŭdio* patres *vestros vĭdendi*, I am transported with a desire of seeing your fathers. Cic. *Pĕtendi* consŭlātum *grātiā*. Sall. *Vēnit ad rĕcĭpiendum* pecūnias. Varr.

REMARK 1. The gerund is the same in form as the oblique cases of the neuter singular of participles in *dus*, but it has the meaning of the active voice. It is sometimes translated by the present participle with a preposition, and sometimes by a present infinitive active; as, *Consilium Lăcĕdæmŏnem occŭpandi*, A design of occupying, or to occupy, Lacedæmon. Liv.

REM. 2. The gerund is sometimes, though rarely, used in a passive sense; as, *Spes restĭtuendi nulla ĕrat*,—of being restored. Nep. *Athēnas ērŭdiendi grātiā* missus,—for the purpose of being instructed. Just. *Ante dŏmandum*. Virg. *Ades ad* imperandum. Cic.

REM 3. The gerund is in its nature a verbal noun, having only the genitive, dative, ablative, and, after a preposition, the accusative. In its signification it corresponds with the English present participle when used as a verbal noun. Hence, in the oblique cases, it supplies the place of a declinable present infinitive active; but in the accusative there is this difference between the infinitive used as an accusative and the gerund, that the infinitive has simply the power of an abstract noun, whereas the gerund expresses a real action; as, *Multum intĕrest inter dăre* et *accipĕre*. Sen. *Non sōlum ad discendum prŏpensi sŭmus, sed ĕtiam ad dŏcendum*. Cic.

II. When the *object* of an active verb is to be expressed, the participle in *dus* is commonly used in preference to the gerund; the object taking the case in which the gerund, if used, would have been put, and the participle agreeing with it.

Thus, to express 'the design of writing a letter,' which, with the aid of the gerund, would be represented in Latin by *Consīlium scribendi ĕpistŏlam*, the participle in *dus* is commonly substituted for the gerund: and since, in this example, the gerund, (*scribendi*) is in the genitive, the rule requires that, in substituting the participle for the gerund, the object of the gerund (*ĕpistŏlam*) should also be put in the genitive, and that the participle (*scribendus*) should agree with it in gender, number, and case. Hence with the participle the expression is, *Consilium scribendæ ĕpistŏlæ*. Between the two forms of construction there is no difference of signification. So, *Consilia urbis dēlendæ* (Cic.), for *urbem dēlendi*, Plans for destroying the city. *Rĕpărandārum classium causā* (Suet.), for *rĕpărandi classes*. Perpĕtiendo lăbōri *ĭdōneus*. Colum. *Ad defendendam Rōmam ab oppugnandā Cāpuā dūces Rōmānos abstrăhĕre.* Liv.

REMARK 1. The same construction is used with the future passive participles of *ūtor, fruor, fungor, pŏtior,* and rarely of *mĕdeor*, as these verbs were originally followed by the accusative; as, *Ætas ad hæc ūtendā idōnea.* Ter. *Justĭtiæ* fruendæ *causā.* Cic. *In munĕre* fungendo. Id. *Hostes in spem* potiundōrum castrōrum *vēnĕraht*. Cæs. *Aquæ sălūbritāte* mĕdendisque corpŏribus *nōbĭles.* Vell.

REM. 2. When a participle is thus used for a gerund, it is called a *gerundive,* and is usually translated like a gerund. The gerundive cannot be substituted for the gerund, where ambiguity would arise from the gender not being distinguishable. It should therefore not be used when the object of the gerund is a neuter pronoun or adjective; as, Aliquid *făciendi rătio* (Cic.), not *ălicūjus.* *Artem et vēra et falsa dijūdĭcandi* (Id.), not *vērōrum dijūdĭcandōrum:* because it would not be known whether *ălicūjus* and *vērōrum* were masculine or neuter. It is to be remarked, also, that the change of the gerund into the gerundive is less frequent in some writers than in others.

III. Examples of the construction of gerunds, in each of their cases, have been already given, among other nouns, under the heads *Genitive, Dative, Accusative,* and *Ablative.* The following remarks specify in what connections they are used: and when it is said that the gerundive is governed in any of the cases like the gerund, it will of course be understood of the noun which is limited by a gerundive.

REMARK 1. The genitive of gerunds and gerundives may follow either nouns or relative adjectives; as,

Amor hăbendi. Cic. *Patriam spes vĭdendi.* Virg. *Nam hăbet nătūra, ut ăliārum omnium rērum, sic vivendi modum.* Cic. *Barbăra consuetŭdo hŏmĭnum immŏlandōrum.* Id. *Postrēmo Cătilina* dissimŭlandi *causā aut* sui expurgandi, *in senatum rĕnit.* Sall. *Inĭta sunt consĭlia urbis dēlendæ, cĭvium trŭcidandōrum, nōmĭnis Rōmāni* exstinguendi. Id. *Vēnandi stŭdiōsi.* Cic. *Certus eundi.* Virg. *Insuĕtus nāvĭgandi.* Cæs. *Pĕrĭtus cīvĭtātis rĕgendæ.* Nep.

(1.) The nouns after which these genitives most frequently occur are *ămor, ars, causa, consilium, consuetūdo, cŏpia, cŭpĭdĭtas, dēsīdĕrium, diffĭcultas, fĭnis, făcultas, forma, grătia, illĕcebra, lĭbido, lŏcus, licentia, mŏdus, mātēria, mos, occāsio, ŏtium, pŏtestas, rătio, spătium, spes, stŭdium, tempus, ūsus, rĕnia, vis, vŏluntas.*

NOTE 1. With these and other substantives the infinitive also may be used, when with a tense of *sum* they form a periphrasis for a verb which is followed by the infinitive, or supply the place of an adjective of which the infinitive is the subject; as, *Quĭbus ōmnia hŏnesta atque inhŏnesta* vendĕre *mos ĕrat,* With whom it was a custom, or, who were accustomed. Sall. *Tempus est* ăbīre, It is time, i. e. *tempestīvum est*, it is proper to go.

(2.) The relative adjectives, which most frequently take after them these genitives, are such as denote *desire, knowledge, remembrance*, and their contraries; as, *ăvĭdus, cŭpĭdus, stŭdĭōsus, pĕrītus, impĕrītus, insuētus, certus, conscĭus, ignārus, rūdis*, etc. See § 213, R. 1, (3.)

NOTE 2. With the relative adjectives the infinitive is also joined poetically.

(3.) Instead of an accusative after the gerund, or a genitive plural with a gerundive, a noun or pronoun in the genitive plural is sometimes joined with the gerund; as, Exemplōrum *ēlĭgendi pŏtestas*, instead of *exempla ēlĭgendi*, or, *exemplōrum ēlĭgendōrum*. Cic. *Eārum rērum infĭtĭandi rătĭo*. Id. *Făcultas agrōrum condōnandi*. Cic. *Nōmĭnandi istōrum ĕrit cōpia*. Plaut.

(4.) The pronoun *tui* and also the plurals *vestri* and *sui*, even when feminine are joined with the masculine or neuter form of the gerundive in *di*; as, *Quōnĭam tui vĭdendi est cōpia*. Plaut. *Non vĕreor, ne quis hoc me vestri ădhortandi causā magnĭfĭce lŏqui exīstĭmet*. Liv. *In castra vēnērunt sui purgandi causā*.— With the demonstrative pronouns, *ējus, hūjus, illius*, the participle usually agrees, but in two passages of Terence *ējus*, though referring to a woman, has the participle in *di*, not in *dæ*; as, *Ego ējus vĭdendi cŭpĭdus rectā consĕquor*. Ter. *Tui* in the first example and *ējus* in the last are feminine.

(5.) By a Greek idiom the gerund and gerundive, after the verb *sum*, are sometimes found in the genitive denoting a *tendency* or *purpose*, with no noun or adjective on which they can depend; as, *Rēgium impĕrium initio conservandæ lībertātis fuĕrat*. Sall. Sometimes *esse* in some form is to be supplied; as, *Quæ postquam glōrĭōsa mŏdo, nĕque belli patrandi cognōvit*, scil. *esse*. Id. *Causā* or *grātiā* may sometimes be supplied. In some other cases, also, the word on which the gerund in *di* depends is not expressed, and the gerund seems to be used instead of the infinitive; as, *Mănĕat prōvincĭālĭbus pŏtentiam suam tāli mŏdo ostentandi*, scil. *făcultas*. Tac. *Quum hăbērem in ănĭmo* nāvĭgandi, scil. *prŏpŏsĭtum*. Cic.

REM. 2. The dative of gerunds and gerundives is used after adjectives which govern a dative (§ 222), especially after those which signify *usefulness* or *fitness*; and also after certain verbs and phrases, to denote a *purpose*; as,

Charta empŏrētĭca est ĭnūtĭlis scrībendo. Plin. *Căpessendæ reīpūblĭcæ hăbĭlis*. Tac. *Ut nec triumvĭri* accĭpiundo, *nec scrībæ rēfĕrundo suffĭcĕrent*. Liv. *Lŏcum oppĭdo condendo căpĕre*. Id. *Non fuit consĭlium agrum cŏlendo aut vēnando intentum ætātem ăgĕre*. Sall. *Tĭbĕrius quăsi firmandæ vălētūdĭni in Campāniam concessit*. Tac. *Quum solvendo ære ălĭēno reīpūblĭca non esset*. Liv. *Quum solvendo cīvĭtātes non essent*,—were insolvent. Cic.

(1.) The verbs and phrases upon which this dative most frequently depends are, *Stŭdēre, intentum esse, tempus impendĕre, tempus consūmĕre* or *insūmĕre, ŏpĕram dāre, suffĭcĕre, sătis esse, deesse, esse*, signifying *to serve for, to be adequate to*, and, in later writers, on verbs of motion.—The dative of the gerund after *sum* is usually supposed to depend on *ĭdōneus* understood; but see § 227, R. 3.

(2.) The dative of the gerundive, denoting a purpose, is also used after names of office; as, *Dĕcemvĭri* lēgĭbus scrībendis, i. e. the ten commissioners for drawing up a code of laws. Liv. So, *Cōmĭtia* creandis dĕcemvĭris. Id. *Triumvĭros* agro dando *creat*. Id.

(3.) A purpose is more commonly expressed by *ad* and the accusative of the gerund, or by a clause with *ut*, than by the dative; as, *Pĕcus* ad vescendum *hŏmĭnĭbus apta*. Cic.

REM. 3. The accusative of gerunds and gerundives follows the prepositions *ad*, to, or *inter*, during or amid, and sometimes *ante, circa,* or *ob*; as,

Ad pœnitendum *properat, qui cito judicat.* Pub. Syr. *Inter bibendum,* Whilt drinking. Just. *Ad tolerandos facilius* labores. Quint. *Ad castra facienda.* Cic. *Ob absolvendum.* Id.

NYTE. The construction of the gerundive instead of the gerund almost invariably occurs here when the object of the gerund is to be expressed.

REM. 4. The ablative of gerunds and gerundives follows the prepositions *a, (ab), de, e, (ex),* or *in ;* or it is used without a preposition, as the ablative of cause, manner, or means; as,

Aristotelem non deterruit a scribendo. Cic. *Ex assentando.* Ter. *Non videor* a *defendendis hominibus discedere.* Cic. *Crescit* eundo. Virg. *Rem quaerunt* mercaturis faciendis. Cic. *Orationem Latinam legendis nostris efficies plenio rem.* Id.

NOTE 1. This ablative also occurs, though rarely, after *pro* and *cum;* as. *Pro vapulando.* Plaut. *Cum loquendo.* Quint.

NOTE 2. Generally with the ablative of the means, and always with the ablative after a preposition, the gerund, when its object is to be expressed, is changed to the gerundive. In a few passages the ablative of the gerundive is differently construed; as, *Nullum officium referenda gratia magis necessarium est,* instead of *relatione gratiae.* § 256. Cic. *Nec jam possidendis publicis agris contentos esse.* § 244. Liv. *Is finis fuit* ulciscenda *Germanici morte,*—in avenging the death of Germanicus. Tac.; where the ablative seems to imply time. § 253.

SUPINES.

§ 276. Supines, like gerunds, are verbal nouns, having no other cases except the accusative and ablative singular. In certain connections they supply the place of the present infinitive; the supine in *um* having an active and the supine in *u* a passive signification. As in the case of gerunds, we are to regard their construction both as verbs and as nouns. As verbs we are to notice their government, as nouns, their dependence.

I. Supines in *um* are followed by the same cases as their verbs; as,

Non Graiis servitum matribus ibo, I shall not go to serve Grecian matrons Virg. *Te id* admonitum *venio.* Plaut.

II. Supines in *um* follow verbs of motion, and serve to denote the *purpose* of the motion; as,

Cubitum discessimus. Cic. *Ire* dejectum *monumenta regis.* Hor. *Legati venerunt* questum *injurias, et res* repetitum. Liv. *Quum* spectatum *ludos iret.* Nep. So after participles; as, *Patriam* defensum *revocatus.* Nep. Spectatum *admissi.* Hor.

NOTE. The construction of the supine in *um,* considered as a noun, is analogous to that of names of places in answer to the question 'whither?' (§ 237), the notion of *purpose* arising from its verbal character.

REMARK 1. Supines in *um* sometimes follow verbs which do not express motion; as, Do *filiam nuptum.* Ter. *Vos ultum injurias* hortor. Sall.

REM. 2. The supine in *um* with *eo* literally signifies 'I go to do a thing,' and hence 'I intend,' or, 'am going to.' Instances of this use are found in Plautus and Terence and in the prose writers later than Cicero; as, *Mea Glycerium, quid agis? cur te* is perditum? Why are you going to destroy yourself? Plaut. *Bonorum praemia* ereptum eunt. Sall. With *eo* the supine in *um* often forms a periphrasis equivalent to the same mood and tense of the verb from which the supine is form ed; as, *Ne bŏnos omnes* perdĭtum eant (Sall.), for *perdant. Ereptum eunt* (Id.), for *ĕripiunt. Ultum iri* (Tac.), for *ultus est.* Ultum ire *injūrias festinat,* i. e. *ulcisci.* Sall.

REM. 3. The supine in *um* most frequently occurs with the infinitive *īri* with which it forms the future infinitive passive; as, *Brūtum* visum īri *a me pūto.* Cic. In this construction the accusative properly depends upon the supine, and *īri* is used impersonally; 'I suppose that I am going to see Brutus.' § 184, 2, (a.) Its notion of futurity is derived from the proper signification of the active voice, as *perdĭtum īri,* to go to destroy, the idea of intending passing easily into that of futurity.

REM. 4. But to express a purpose Latin writers in general prefer using a gerund or gerundive in the accusative with *ad* or in the genitive with *causā* or *grātiā,* a subjunctive clause with *ut* or *qui,* a present or future active participle, and sometimes poetically an infinitive. See § 275, R. 1, 2: §§ 262, 264, 274, and 271.

III. The supine in *u* is used to limit the meaning of adjectives signifying *wonderful, agreeable, easy* or *difficult, worthy* or *unworthy, honorable* or *base,* and a few others; as,

Mirābĭle dictu! Wonderful to tell, *or* to be told! Virg. *Jūcundum cognĭtu atque audītu,* Pleasant to be known and heard. Cic. *Res factu făcĭlis,* A thing easy to be done. Ter. *Făcĭlia inventu.* Gell. *Incrēdĭbile mĕmŏrātu.* Sall. *Turpia dictu.* Cic. *Optĭmum factu.* Id.

NOTE. The principal supines in *u* in common use are *audītu, cognĭtu, dictu, factu, inventu, mĕmŏrātu* and *nātu,* which occurs in the expressions, *grandis, major, minor, maxĭmus,* and *minĭmus nātu.* In *magno nātu,* of an advanced age, and *maxĭmo nātu filius,* the eldest son, *nātu* is the ablative of a verbal substantive, since neither gerunds nor supines are joined with adjectives.

REMARK 1. The principal adjectives, after which the supine in *u* occurs, are *affābĭlis, arduus, asper, bŏnus, deformis, dignus, indignus, dulcis, dūrus, făcĭlis, diffĭcĭlis, fœdus, grăvis, hŏnestus, horrendus, incrēdĭbĭlis, jūcundus, injūcundus, magnus, mĕmŏrābĭlis, mollis, prŏclīvis, pulcher, rārus, turpis,* and *ŭtĭlis.*

REM. 2. The supine in *u* is used also after the nouns *fas, nĕfas,* and *ŏpus;* as, *Hoc fas est dictu.* Cic. *Nĕfas dictu.* Ovid. *Dictu ŏpus est.* Ter.—In the following examples it follows a verb: *Pŭdet dictu.* Tac. Agr. 32. *Dictu fastidienda sunt.* Val. Max. 9, 13, 2.

REM. 3. As the supine in *u* is commonly translated by a passive form, it is placed under the passive voice; but, in many cases, it may with equal or greater propriety be translated actively. As a noun, its construction may be referred to the ablative of limitation. § 250.

REM. 4. (a.) Instead of the supine in *u,* an infinitive, a gerund or gerundive with *ad,* or a verbal noun in the ablative, and sometimes in the dative or accusative, may be used; as, *Ardua imĭtātu, cētĕrum* cognosci *ūtĭlia.* Val. Max. *Illud autem făcĭle* ad credendum *est.* Cic. *Opus* proscriptiōne *dignum.* Plin. *Aqua* pōtui *jūcunda.* Id. *Făcĭlior* ad intellectum *atque* imĭtātiōnem. Quint. With *ŏpus est* the perfect passive participle is often used instead of the supine in *u;* as, *Opus est* mātūrāto, There is need of haste. Cf. § 243, R. 1.

(b.) The construction with *ad* and the gerund; as, *res făcĭlis ad intelligendum;* or with *sum* and the infinitive active; as, *făcĭle est invĕnīre,* is used by the best writers after *făcĭlis, diffĭcĭlis,* and *jūcundus.* The most common construction of *dignus* is with *qui* and the subjunctive, (§ 264, 9), but the poets and later prose writers have joined it with the infinitive passive.

ADVERBS.

§ **277.** I. Adverbs modify or limit the meaning of verbs, adjectives, and sometimes of other adverbs; as,

Bĕne mŏnes, You advise well. Ter. *Fortissĭme urgentes*, Most v goronsly pressing on. Plin. *Măle narrando*. Ter. *Longe dissĭmilis*. Cic. *Valde bĕne*. Id

REMARK 1. Adverbs may also modify nouns, when they are used as adjectives or participles, and accordingly denote a quality, or when a participle is understood. They are also joined to adjective pronouns, when their adjective-haracter predominates; and sometimes limit the meaning of a preposition; as, *Pŏpŭlus lāte rex*, for *late regnans*,—ruling far and wide. Virg. *Nĭhil admŏdum*, Nothing at all. Cic. *Hŏmo plāne noster*,—entirely ours that is, devoted to us. Id. *Homĕrus plāne ōrātor*. Id. *Admŏdum puella*. Liv. *Lāte tyrannus*. Hor. *Grăribus sŭperne ictibus conflictābantur*, i. e. *sŭperne accĭdentibus*. Tac. *Multā-um circa civitātum*, i. e. neighboring cities. Liv.

REM. 2. (*a*.) Most of the modifications made by adverbs may also be made by means of the various cases of nouns and adjectives, and many modifications may be made by these, for expressing which no adverbs are in use. In general those limitations which are most common can be expressed by adverbs; as, *săpienter* for *cum săpientiā*; *hic* for *in hoc lŏco*; *bĕne* for *in bŏno mŏdo*; *nunc* for *hoc tempŏre*.—(*b*.) The following are examples of other parts of speech used adverbially, viz. *Nĭhil*, 'in no way'; *nonnĭhil*, 'in some measure'; *quidquam*, 'at all'; *ălĭquid*, 'somewhat'; *quid?* 'why?'

REM. 3. A negative adverb, modifying another negative word, destroys the negation; as,

Non părēre nōluit, He was not unwilling to obey. Nep. *Haud ignāra măli*, Not ignorant of evil. Virg. *Haud nĭhil est*, It is something. Ter. *Nec hoc ille non vīdit*, And this he clearly perceived. Cic. So, *nonnulli*, some; *nonnumquam*, sometimes. *Non*, before a negative word, commonly heightens the affirmative sense, while it softens the expression; as, *Hŏmo non indoctus*, i. e. *hŏmo sāne doctus*. *Non sĕmel*, i. e. *sœpius*; *non ignōro, non nescio, non sum nescius*, I know very well. *Qui mortem in mălis pōnit, non pŏtest eam non tĭmēre*,—must needs fear it. Cic.

REM. 4. When the subject and predicate of a proposition are both modified by negative words, and also when the predicate contains two negatives, the proposition is affirmative; as,

Nēmo non vĭdet, Every one sees. Cic. *Neque hæc non ēvēnērunt*, And this inde d took place. So, if both the antecedent and the predicate of a relative claus are negative, the proposition is affirmative; as, *Nēmo est, qui nesciat*, Every body knows. Cic.

REM. 5. *a*.) But in the case of *non* followed by *ne—quidem*, the two negatives do no destroy each other; as, *Non fŭgiŏ ne hos quidem mōres*: and when the ra gative leading proposition has subordinate subdivisions with *nĕque —nĭ*que, *neve—nēve*, or *non—non*, these negative particles are equivalent to *aut —avt*; as, Non *me carmĭnĭbus vincet*, nec *Orpheus*, nec *Linus*. Virg. *Nēmĭnem*, non *re*, non *verbo*, non *vultu dēnĭque offendi*. Cic. *Nullius rei nĕque præs*, nĕque *manceps factus est*. Nep.

(*b*.) In a few passages, however, two negatives in Latin, as in Greek, strengthen the negation, and this exception appears to have been derived from the language of common life; as, *Jūra te* non *nocĭtūram hŏmĭni nēmĭni*. Plaut.

(*c*.) *Nēmo, nullus, nĭhil*, and *numquam* have a different sense according as the *non* is place before or after them; as, *Non nēmo*, some one; *nēmo non*, every one; *non nulls*, some; *nullus non*, every; *non nĭhil*, something; *nihil non*, every thing; *non numquam*, sometimes; *numquam non*, at all times. So, *nusquam non*, every where, but instead of *nonnusquam, alĭcŭbi* is used.

REM. 6. (*a*.) *Non* is sometimes omitted after *non mŏdo* or *non sō-lum*, when followed, in a subsequent clause, by *ne quĭdem*, if both clauses have the same verb, and if the verb is contained in the second clause; as,

Mihi non modo irasci, sed ne dolēre quidem impūne licet, which is equivalent to *Mihi non modo non irasci, sed ne dolēre quidem impūne licet,* or *Mihi non modo irasci, sed dolēre quidem impūne non licet,* Not only am I not permitted to be angry, but not even to grieve with impunity. Cic. *Quum senātui non sōlum juvāre rempublicam, sed ne lūgēre quidem licēret.* Id.

(b.) *Non* is also rarely omitted after *non modo* when followed by *sed* or *vērum,* with *ĕtiam,* and also after *viz:* as, *Qui non modo ea futūra timet, vērum ĕtiam fert, sustinetque præsentia,* Who not only does not fear.... Cic. *Hæc gĕnĕra virtūtum non sōlum in morĭbus nostris, sed vix jam in libris rĕpĕriuntur,* These virtues are not only not found in life, but scarcely in books. Id.

Rem. 7. *Facile,* in the sense of *undoubtedly, clearly,* is joined to superlatives, and words of similar import; as, *Vir ūnus tōtius Græciæ facile doctissĭmus.* Cic. *Homo regiōnis illius virtūte* facile princeps. Id.

Rem. 8. Sentences are often united by means of an adverb which is repeated before each of the connected clauses; as, *modo—modo,* and *nunc—nunc,* (sometimes—sometimes); as, *Modo hoc, modo illud dicit; modo huc, modo illuc volat* Instead of the second *modo* other particles of time are sometimes used; as, *aliquando, nonnumquam, interdum, sæpius, tum* or *deinde.—Partim—partim,* 'partly—partly,' is sometimes used with a genitive or the preposition *ex,* in the sense of *ălii—ălii,* as a nominative in all the genders; as, *Quum partim e nōbis ita timidi sunt, ut,* etc., *partim ita rēpublĭcā āversi, ut,* etc.—*Simul—simul,* 'as well—as,' like *nunc—nunc,* is not found in Cicero.—*Quā—quā* is equivalent to *et—et.—Tum—tum* is used sometimes like *modo—modo,* sometimes like *partim—partim;* as *Erumpunt sæpe vitia amicōrum tum in ipsos amīcos, tum in aliĕnos.* Cic. *Hæc (benĕficia) tum in universam rempublĭcam, tum in singŭlos cives conferuntur.* Id.

Rem. 9. *Quum—tum* is equivalent to *et—et,* except in assigning a greater importance to the second part: hence it must be translated by 'both—and especially,' 'not only—but also,' or 'but more particularly.' Sometimes additional weight is given to the second part by means of *vero, certe, ĕtiam, quŏque, præcipue, imprimis* or *maxime.* This use of *quum—tum* seems to have had its origin in the use of *quum* with the subjunctive and often with the indicative in the protasis, followed by *tum* in the apodosis. When *quum* followed by *tum* serves to express the opposition between single words which have the same verb, it is to be regarded as a complete adverb; as, *Fortūna quum in relĭquis rēbus, tum præcipue in bello plurĭmum pŏtest.* Sometimes the verb stands in the first part of the sentence; as, *Quum omnis arrogantia ŏdiōsa est, tum illa ingēnii atque eloquentiæ multo molestissĭma.* *Tum* is sometimes repeated in the second part of the sentence; as, *Quem pater mŏriens quum tūtōrĭbus et propinquis, tum legĭbus, tum æquitāti magistrātuum, tum jūdĭciis vestris commendātum pūtāvit.* Cic. Sometimes the gradation is, *quum—tum—tum vĕro.*

Rem. 10. *Non modo—sed ĕtiam* (or *non sōlum,* or *non tantum—vĕrum ĕtiam*) generally expresses the transition from less important to more important things, like the English 'not only—but (also)'. The transition from greater to smaller things is expressed by *non modo—sed,* without the *ĕtiam,* which we render in English by 'I will not say—but only,' and in Latin, too, we may say *non dicam* or *non dico—sed;* as, *Quid est enim minus non dico ōrātōris, sed homĭnis.*

Rem. 11. *Tam—quam* expresses a comparison in degree; as, *Nēmo tam multa scripsit,* quam *multa sunt nostra.* With superlatives they are rendered into English by 'the—the' and comparatives; as, *Hernōsus* quam *plurĭmum bibit,* tam *maxime sitit,* The more he drinks, the more he thirsts. Cato. Quam *quisque pessĭme fĕcit,* tam *maxime tūtus est.* Sall.—*Tam—quam quod maxĭme* signifies, 'as much as possible.'—*Non tam—quam* signifies, 'not so much—as,' or 'less—than'; as, *Provincia* non tam *gratiōsa et illustris,* quam *negotiōsa ac molesta.* Cic.

Rem. 12. *Non minus—quam* and *non magis—quam* are equivalent to *æque—ac,* 'as much as,' but in *non magis—quam* the greater weight is attached to the affirmative clause beginning with *quam;* as, *Alexander* non *dūcis* magis quam *militis munia exsĭquĕbātur,* Alexander performed as much the service of a soldier as that of a commander. In this connection *plus* frequently supplies the place of *măgis.*

(*a.*) *Sic* and *ita* are demonstrative adverbs corresponding to the relative *ut.* The restrictive meaning of *ita* (see § 191, R. 5.), is sometimes made more emphatic by the addition of *tămen. Tantus* is used in a like restrictive sense; as, *Præsidii tantum est, ut ne mūrus quidem cingi possit,* i. e. 'only so much.' Caes.

(*b.*) *Ut—ita* or *sic* places sentences on an equality. They may sometimes be translated 'although—still,' or 'indeed—but.'—The adverb *ut,* 'as,' sometimes takes the signification of the conjunction *quod,* 'because'; as, *Atque ille ut semper fuit ăpertissĭmus, non se purgārit.* Cic.

REM. 13. In an enumeration, *primum, deinde, tum, dēnique* are commonly preferred to the numerals, *primum, sĕcundo,* (for *sĕcundum* is not often used), *tertium, quartum,* etc., unless the strict succession of the numbers is required. Sometimes *tum* is used once or twice instead of *deinde,* or the series is extended by *accēdit, huc adde,* etc. Sometimes *dēnique* is followed by *postrēmo* to form the conclusion of a series, but often *dēnique* without the other adverbs concludes a series, and is then equivalent to 'in short' or 'in fine.' See Cic. Cat. 1, 5.

REM. 14. *Mĭnus* is often used for *non*; as, *Nonnumquam ea, quæ prædicta sunt,* minus *ĕvĕniunt.* Cic.—So, *si mĭnus—at,* 'if not—yet;' and *sin mĭnus,* 'but if not,' without a verb, after a preceding *si*; but with *si non* the verb is repeated. —The English 'how little' is in Latin *quam non;* and 'so little,' *ita non* or *ădeo non*; as, *ădeo non cūrābat, quid hŏmĭnes de se lŏquĕrentur.*

REM. 15. *Nunc* always expresses the time actually present, or the time to which a narrator transfers himself for the purpose of making his description livelier. Thus in speaking of the present time we may say, *Nunc prīmum somnia me ēlūdunt* or *ēlūsērunt;* but in a narrative we must say, *Somnia* tunc *prīmum se dīcēbat ēlūsisse.* Compare the use of *hic* and *ille.* See § 207, R. 23, (*c.*)

REM. 16. The conjunction *dum,* 'while,' when added to negatives, becomes an adverb, signifying 'yet'; as, *nondum,* 'not yet'; *necdum,* 'and not yet'; *nullusdum,* 'no one yet'; *nĭhildum,* 'nothing yet.' Hence *vixdum* signifies 'scarcely yet'; as, *Vixdum ĕpistŏlam tuam lēgĕram, quum ad me Curtius vēnit.* Cic.— So, also, the conjunction *nĭsi,* by omitting its verb or uniting it with the leading verb, acquires, after negatives and negative questions, the sense of the adverb 'except,' which is generally expressed by *præterquam* or the preposition *præter,* and must be so expressed when no negative precedes. But the expression 'except that' may be rendered either by *nĭsi quod* or *præterquam quod.*—After *nĭhil ăliud* we may use either *nĭsi* or *quam, nĭsi* referring to *nĭhil* and *quam* to *ăliud.* Hence *nĭhil ăliud nĭsi* signifies 'nothing further,' or 'nothing more,' and *nĭhil ăliud quam,* 'nothing else,' or 'no other thing but this.'

REM. 17. *Ut,* 'as,' in interposed clauses, such as *ut ŏpinor, ut pŭto, ut censeo, ut crēdo,* is frequently omitted. *Crēdo,* used in this manner often takes an ironical sense.

PREPOSITIONS.

II. 1. See respecting the construction of prepositions with the accusative, § 235; and with the ablative, § 241. See, also, for the different meanings of prepositions, § 195, and for their arrangement, § 279, 10.

2. Two prepositions must not be joined in Latin, as they sometimes are in English, with the same noun; as, to speak *for* and *against* a law; or, I have learned this *with,* and, to some extent, *from* him. These sentences may be thus expressed in Latin; *pro lēge et contra lēgem dīcĕre; hæc cum eo, partim ĕtiam ab eo dĭdici.* Those dissyllabic prepositions only, which are sometimes used as adverbs, may follow another, without being joined with a case; as, *Quod aut sĕcundum nātūram esset, aut contra.* Cic. *Cis Pădum ultrăque.* Liv *Cæsar* reverses the order, *Intra extrăque mūnitiōnes.* B. Civ. 3, 72

3. When nouns mutually dependent upon a preposition are in apposition, when they constitute an enumeration without a connective, and when connected by copulative, disjunctive, adversative, or comparative conjunctions, the preposition is not repeated, unless such nouns are to be distinguished from each other, or are emphatic; as,

Quid dīcam de thēsauro *omnium rērum*, memōriā? *Hoc appāret* in bestiis, volucribus, nantibus, agrestibus, cicūribus, fĕris, *ut se ipsæ dīlĭgant.* Cic. *Sæpissĭme* inter me *et* Scipiōnem *de amicitiā dissĕrĕbātur.* Id. *Quid făcĕres si* in aliquam dŏmum villamve *vēnisses?* Id. *Nĭhil* per īram *aut* cŭpĭdĭtātem *actum est.* Id. *Thĕmistŏcles non minus* in rēbus gĕrendis *promptus quam* excōgitandis *ĕrat.* Nep.

4. The monosyllabic prepositions *ab, ad, de, ex,* and *in* are often used before each of two nouns connected by *et,* etc., especially if the qualities denoted by such nouns are to be considered separately. If the nouns are separated by *et—et, nec—nec,* etc., the prepositions must be repeated; as, *Ut eōrum* et in *bellīcis* et in *cīvīlĭbus offĭcĭīs vĭgeat industria.* Cic.—*Inter* is frequently repeated by Cicero after *intĕresse,* and other writers repeat it after other verbs also; as, *Quid* intersit inter *pŏpŭlārem—cīvem, et* inter *constantem, sēvērum et grăvem.* Cic. *Certātum* inter *Ap. Claudium maxime fĕrunt et* inter *P. Dĕcium.* Liv.

5. (*a.*) In poetry a preposition is occasionally omitted with the first of two nouns, and put with the second only; as, *Quæ nĕmŏra, aut quos ăgor in spĕcus,* (Hor.) for, *In quæ nĕmŏra aut in quos spĕcus ăgor.* So, Hor. Ep. 2, 1, 25.—
(*b.*) An ellipsis of a preposition with the relative pronoun sometimes occurs, together with that of the verb belonging to the preceding demonstrative; as, *In eādem ŏpīnĭōne fui, quā rēlĭqui omnes,* (Cic.), properly *in quā rēlĭqui omnes fuĕrunt.*

CONJUNCTIONS.

§ 278. Copulative, disjunctive, and other coördinate conjunctions, connect similar constructions.

NOTE 1. Clauses are similarly constructed, which are mutually independent, whose subjects and verbs are in the same case and mood, and which have either no dependence or a similar dependence on another clause.

NOTE 2. (*a.*) Words have a similar construction, when they stand in the same relation to some other word or words in the sentence. Hence,

(*b.*) Conjunctions connect the same cases of nouns and pronouns, dependent, if the cases are oblique, upon the same government; the same number, case, and gender of adjectives, belonging to the same noun; the same mood of verbs, either independent, or alike dependent; adverbs qualifying the same verbs, adjectives, etc.; and prepositions on which depends the same noun or pronoun; as, *Concĭdunt venti, fŭgĭunt*que *nūbes,* The winds subside, and the clouds disperse. Hor. *Lōcum, quem et non cŏquit sol, et tangit ros.* Varr. *Lūdi dĕcem per dies, facti sunt, nēque res ulla prætermissa est.* Cic. *Vĭdes, ut altā stet nĭve candĭdum Sōracte, nec jam sustineant ŏnus silĕæ lăbōrantes, gĕlūque flūmĭna constĭtĕrint acūto.* Hor. *Intellĭgĭtis et ănĭmum ei præsto fuisse, nec consilium dĕfuisse.* Cic. *Gĕnĕri anĭmantium omni est a nātūrā tribūtum, ut se tueātur, dēclinetque ea, quæ nocĭtūra vĭdeantur.* Id. *Aut nēmo, aut Cāto săpiens fuit.* Id. *Pulvis et* umbra *sūmus.* Hor. *Si tu et Tullia vălētis,* ego et *Cicĕro vălēmus.* Cic. *Aggĕre jacto* turrībusque *constĭtūtis.* Cæs. *Clārus et* honōrātus *vir,* An illustrious and honorable man. Id. *Cæsar Rēmos* cōhortātus, *libĕrălĭter*que *ōrātiōne* prōsĕcūtus. Cæs. *Păter tuus, quem* cōlui *et* dĭlexi. Cic. *Belgæ* spectant in septentriōnem *et* ōrientem sōlem. Cæs. *Nāvĭbus* junctis, *rătĭbus*que *complūrĭbus* factis. Id. *Lĕge, rel lăbellos* redde. Plaut. *Allobrŏges trans Rhŏdănum* vicos possessiōnesque *hăbēbant.* Cæs. *Quum triumphum* ēgĕris, censorque fuĕris, *et* **bb'ĕris lǣ**tus. Id. *Quum ad oppĭdum* accessisset, *castrăque îbi* pōnĕret. Cæs

§ 278. SYNTAX.—CONJUNCTIONS. 305

Ades *ănim et ŏmitte tĭmōrem*. Cic. *Ea* vĭdēre *ac* perspĭcēre *pŏtestis*. Id *Grăvĭter et cōpiōse dīxisse dīcĭtur*. Id. *Cum frātre an* sĭne. Id. Cf. § 277, II. 2. *Cŭi carmĭna cordi, nŭmĕrosque* intendĕre *nervis*. Virg. *Nec* census, *nec clārum nōmen ăvōrum, sed prŏbĭtas magnos ingĕniumque făcit*. Ovid. *Phĭlŏsŏphi nĕgant* quemquam vĭrum *bŏnum esse*, nĭsi săpientem. Cic. *Glōria virtūtem tamquam* umbra *sĕquĭtur*. Id.

REMARK 1. Copulative conjunctions may connect either single words and phrases or entire clauses; the other conjunctions, whether coördinate or subordinate, connect clauses only.

REM. 2. Words thus connected are sometimes in different cases, though in the same construction; as, *Meā et* reīpūblĭcæ *intĕrest*. Cic. (See § 219.) *Sīre es Rōmæ, sive in* Epīro. Id. (See §§ 221 and 254. But see also § 221, Note.) *In Mettii descendat jūdĭcis aures, et patris et nostras*. Hor. See § 211, R. 3. In like manner, *Hannĭbal non ălĭter vinci pŏtuit, quam mŏrā*.

REM. 3. As the subjunctive is often used for the imperative, they may be connected by coördinate conjunctions; as, Disce *nec* invĭdeas. Pers.

REM. 4. Where the purpose of the writer requires it, coördinate conjunctions sometimes connect independent propositions, whose verbs are in different moods; as, *Stŭpōrem hŏmĭnis, vel* dicam *pĕcŭdis*, vidēte. Cic. *Nec sătis scio, nec, si sciam, dicĕre* ausim. Liv.

REM. 5. *Et* is used after *multi* followed by another adjective, where in English 'and' is usually omitted; as, *Multæ* et *magnæ arbōres*, Many large trees. In such cases *et* supplies the place of *et is*, introducing a more accurate description. See § 207, R. 26, (c.)

REM. 6. The conjunction is often omitted; as, (*a*.) When two single words, as comprehending the whole idea, are opposed to each other, as, *vĕlim, nōlim*, whether I would or not; *maxima minĭmā*, the greatest as well as the least; *prīma postrēma*, from the first to the last; *dignos indignos ădīre; īre rĕdīre*, to go to and fro. *Ædĭficiis omnĭbus pūblĭcis prīvātis, sacris prŏfānis sic pĕpercit*. Cic. *Nam glōriam, hŏnōrem, impĕrium bŏnus ignāvus æque sibi exoptant*. Sall. C. 11.

(*b*.) *Et* is very frequently omitted between the names of two colleagues; as, *Consŭles dēclārāti sunt Cn. Pompeius M. Crassus. P. Lentŭlo L. Triārio, quæstōrĭbus urbānis*. Cic. Sometimes, also, when the two persons are not colleagues. It is also occasionally omitted between two words in the oratorical style; as, *Aderant amici, propinqui*. Id.; also with verbs; as, *Adsunt, quĕruntur Sicŭli*. Id. In good prose, if three or more substantives are joined, it is usual either wholly to omit the conjunction or to insert it between each. The following may serve as an example of both cases: *Qui non mŏdo Cūriis, Cătōnĭbus, Pompeiis, antiquis illis, sed his rĕcentĭbus, Mariis et Dīdiis et Cæliis commĕmŏrandis jăcēbant*. This is also the common practice with adjectives and verbs, and hence when *et* has not previously occurred in an enumeration of persons or things, we should not conclude the enumeration with *et ălii, et rĕlĭqui, et cĕtĕra*, etc., but should make use of the adjectives alone, *ălii, rĕlĭqui, cĕtĕra*, etc. But though *et, ac* and *atque* are not used alone in the third or fourth place, yet the enclitic *que* frequently occurs in this position; as, *Prĕcor ut ea res vōbis păcem, tranquillĭtātem, ōtium, concordiamque affĕrat*. Cic. *Et* may be supplied also when two protases introduced by *si* are joined together; where we say 'if—and if,' or 'if—and.' See an example in Cic. Off. 3, 9.

(*c*.) An ellipsis of *ut* is supposed when *ne* precedes and *et, atque*, or *que* is used to continue the sentence, those copulative conjunctions in such case obtaining the meaning of the adversative *sed*; as, *Mŏnēre cœpit Pōrum, ne ultĭma expĕrīri persĕvĕrāret, dĕdĕretque se victōri*. Curt.

REM. 7. Copulative conjunctions are often used, before each of two or more connected words or clauses, in order to mark the connection more forcibly; as, *Et pĕcūnia persuādet, et grātia, et auctōrĭtas dīcentis, et dignĭtas, et postrēma aspectus*. Quint. *Hoc et turpe, nec tămen tūtum*. Cic. *Nĕque nāta est, et æternæ est*. Id. *Et tĭbi et mĭhi vŏluptāti fŏre*. Id. Before clauses the disjunctive cor

26*

junctions are used in a similar manner; as, *Res ipsa* aut *invĭtābit* aut *dĕhortābĭtur.* Id. So, also, *nunc...nunc, simul...simul, partim...partim, quā...quā, tum... tum, quum...tum,* are used before successive clauses.

REM. 8. To connect different names of the same person or thing, *sive* or *seu*, rather than *aut* or *vel*, is employed; as, *Mars sive Māvors.* Cf. § 198, 2, (c.)

REM. 9. Instead of *et* and *ut* with the negatives *nēmo, nihil, nullus,* and *numquam, nĕque* (or *nec*), and *ne* are used with the corresponding affirmative words *quisquam, ullus, umquam,* and *usquam.* But 'in order that no one' is rendered in Latin by *ne quis* and not by *ne quisquam,* see § 207, R. 31, (a.); as, *Horæ quĭdem cēdunt, et dies, et menses, et anni:* nec *pretĕritum tempus* umquam *rĕvertĭtur.* Cic. *Sĕnātus dēcrēvit, dārent ŏpĕram consŭles,* ne quid *respublica dĕtrĭmenti cápĕret.* Cæs.

REM. 10. The conjunctions *igĭtur, vērum, vēruntămen, sed,* and *sed tămen,* indicate a return to the construction of the leading clause, when it has been disturbed by the insertion of another clause. These conjunctions, in such connection, are usually rendered by 'I say,' and sometimes in Latin *inquam* is so used. *Nam* also is occasionally employed in this way and very rarely *ităque.*

REM 11. *Vēro* and *autem* are frequently omitted in adversative clauses, especially in short ones; as, *Vincĕre scit Hannĭbal, victōriā ūti nescit.* Liv. This omission often occurs in describing a progress from smaller to greater things, as in Cic. Cat 1, 1. And it is to be remarked that *non* in the second member of such adversative sentences is used without *et* or *vēro;* as, *alĭēna vitia vĭdet, sua non vĭdet.* But in unreal suppositions or ironical sentences, where the second member contains the truth, *et non* or *ac non* must be used, where we may supply 'rather'; see § 198, 1, (c.); as, *Quăsi nunc id ăgātur,—ac non hoc quærātur.* Cic.

INTERJECTIONS.

Respecting the construction of interjections with the nominative, see § 209 R. 13:—with the dative, § 228, 3:—with the accusative, § 238, 2:—and with the vocative, § 240.

ARRANGEMENT.

I. OF THE WORDS OF A PROPOSITION.

§ 279. 1. In arranging the parts of a proposition in English, after *connectives,* are placed, first, the *subject* and the words which modify or limit it; next, the *verb* and its modifiers; then, the *object* of the verb; and finally, *prepositions* and the words depending upon them. This is called the *logical* or *natural* order.

2. (*a.*) In Latin, either of the four principal parts of a sentence may be placed first, and there is great freedom in the arrangement of the rest, but with this general restriction in prose, that *words which are necessary for the complete expression of a thought should not be separated by the intervention of other words.* In ordinary discourse, especially in historical writing, the following general rule for the arrangement of the parts of a sentence is for the most part observed.

(*b.*) In a Latin sentence, after *connectives,* are placed, first, the *subject* and its modifiers; then, the *oblique cases* and other words which depend upon or modify the verb; and last of all, the *verb.*

§ 279. SYNTAX.—ARRANGEMENT OF WORDS. 307

(*c.*) Hence a Latin sentence regularly begins with the subject and ends with the principal verb of its predicate; as, *Dumnŏrix grātiā et largĭtiōne ăpud Sĕquănos plūrimum pŏtĕrat.* Cæs. But the verb is often not placed at the end of a sentence, especially if the sentence is long, or if too many verbs would be thus brought together at the end. In the familiar style, also, the verb is often placed earlier in the sentence, and in explanatory clauses it is sometimes placed at the very beginning of the proposition, in which case a conjunction is generally added.

(*d.*) It is also to be remarked, as a further modification of the general rule of arrangement, that, in sentences containing the expression of emotion, the word whose emphasis characterizes it as especially affecting the feelings, or as forming a contrast, is placed at the beginning; as, *Cĭto ārescĭt lacrĭma, prœ̆sertim in aliĕnis mălis*, Quickly dries the tear, especially when shed for others' woes. Cic. *Sua vĭtia insĭpientes et suam culpam in sĕnectūtem confĕrunt.* Id.

(*e.*) If there be no *emotive* or *pathetic* word requiring prominence, the place at the end of the proposition is reserved for the *significant* word, that is, the word which is to be most strongly impressed upon the understanding or memory; as, *Gallia est omnis divisa in partes tres.* Cæs. *Quod ante id tempŭs accidĕrat* numquam. Id. *Quod ăliud iter hăbĕrent* nullum. Id. *Quæ virtus ex prŏvĭdendo est appellāta* prūdentia. Cic.

3. (*a.*) Connectives generally stand at the beginning of the clause which they introduce, and with the following *this* is their only position; viz. *et, ĕtĕnim, ac, at, atque, atqui, nĕque* or *nec, aut, vel, sīve, sin, sed, nam, vērum,* and the relatives *quāre, quōcirca,* and *quamobrem.*

(*b.*) Most other connectives generally stand in the first place, but when a particular word is peculiarly emphatic, this word with all that belongs to it stands first, and the conjunction follows it. *Ut,* even when there is no particular emphasis, is commonly placed after *vix, pæne,* and *prŏpe,* and also after the negatives *nullus, nēmo, nihil,* and the word *tantum.* In Cicero, *ĭtăque* stands first and *igĭtur* is commonly placed after the first, and sometimes after several words.

(*c.*) *Autem, ĕnim,* and *vēro* (but), are placed after the first word of the clause, or after the second, when the first two belong together, or when one of them is the auxiliary verb *sum;* as, *Ille* ĕnim *rĕvŏcātŭs rĕsistĕre cæpit.* Cæs. *Ego* vēro vellem, affuisse. Cic. Incrēdĭbĭle est ĕnim, quam sit, etc. Id. They rarely occur after several words; as, *Cur non de integro* autem *dătum.* Id. The enclitics *que, ne, ve,* are usually subjoined to the first word in a clause; but when a monosyllabic preposition stands at the beginning, they are often attached to its case; as, *Rōmam Cĭto dēmigrāvit,* in *fŏrōque esse cæpit;* and this is always the case with *a, ad* and *ob.* So, also, for the sake of euphony, *Apud quosque.* Cic.

(*d.*) *Quĭdem* and *quŏque,* when belonging to single words, are always subjoined to the emphatic word in a clause; as, *Verbo ille reus ĕrat, re* quĭdem vēro *Oppiānĭcus.* Cic. *Me scĭlĭcet maxĭme, sed proxĭme illum* quŏque *fĕfellissem.* Id. In negative sentences, *ne* precedes, and *quĭdem* follows, the emphatic word; as, *Ne ad Cătōnem* quĭdem *prŏvŏcābo.* Cic.—*Quĭdem* is sometimes attracted from the word to which it properly belongs to a neighboring pronoun; as, *Tĭbĭque persuāde, esse te* quĭdem *mĭhi cārissĭmum, sed multo fŏre cāriŏrem,* si, etc., instead of, *te cārissĭmum quĭdem mĭhi esse.*—Prepositions and conjunctions belonging to the word on which the emphasis rests are placed with it between *ne* and *quĭdem;* as, *Ne in fānis* quĭdem. Cic. *Ne si dŭbĭtētur* quĭdem. Id. *Ne quum in Sĭcĭliā* quĭdem *fuit.* Id.; and even *Ne cūjus rei arguĕrētur* quĭdem.— So, also, in Cicero, *non nisi,* 'only,' are separated; and the negative may even be contained in a verb.

(*e.*) The preceding rules respecting the position of connectives are often violated by the poets, who place even the prepositive conjunctions after one or more words of a proposition; as, *Et tu, pŏtes* nam, etc.. Hor. *Vivos et rōdĕret ungues.* Id. They even separate *et* from the word belonging to it, as, *Audīre et vidēor piōs errāre per lūcos.* Id. So, *Auctius* atque *dii mēlius fēcēre.* Id And they sometimes append *que* and *ve* neither to the first word, nor to their proper words in other connections; as, *Messallam terrā dum sĕquĭturque mări,* instead of *terrā mărīque.* Tib. In such arbitrary positions, however, these conjunctions are almost invariably joined to verbs only.

4. When a word is repeated in the same clause, so that one is opposed to, or distinguished from, the other, they must stand together; as, *Hŏmĭnes hŏmĭnĭbus maxĭme ūtĭles esse possunt.* Cic. *Equĭtes* ălii ălio *dilapsi sunt.* Liv. *Lĕgĭtĭmē* virum vir. Virg. Mānus mănum lăvat. Petr. So, also, the personal and possessive pronouns; as, *Sĕquĕre quo tua te nătūra dūcit.* Suum sc *nĕgōtium ăgĕre dīcunt.*

5. Words used antithetically are also placed near each other; as, *Dum tăcent, clāmant.* Cic. *Frăgĭle* corpus ănĭmus *sempĭternus mŏvet.* Id.

6. *Inquam* and often *aio,* introducing a quotation, follow one or more of the words quoted; as, '*Non nosti quid păter,*' inquit, '*Chrȳsippus dīcat.*' Hor. '*Quid,*' aio, '*tua crimĭna prŏdis?*' Ovid. When a nominative is added to *inquit,* it usually follows this verb; as, *Mīhi vĕro,* inquit Cotta, *vĭdētur.* Cic.—*Dīcit* and *dixit* are used like *inquit* only by the poets.

7. (*a.*) The adjective may be placed before or after its noun according as one or the other is emphatic, the more emphatic word being placed before the other. When any thing is dependent on the adjective, it usually follows its noun. When a noun is limited by another noun, as well as by an adjective, the adjective usually precedes both; as, *Ulla* officii *præcepta.* Cic. *Tuum* erga dignĭtātem meam *stŭdium.* Id.

(*b.*) Demonstratives, and the adjectives *prīmus, mĕdius,* etc., when signifying the first part, the middle part, etc., (see § 205, R. 17), usually precede their nouns; as, *Ea* res. Cæs *His ipsis verbis.* Cic. *Mĕdia* nox. Cæs. *Rĕliqua Ægyptus.* Cic.

8. Monosyllables are usually prefixed to longer words with which they are connected; as, *Vir clārissĭmus.* Cic. *Di immortāles. Res innŭmĕrābĭles. Vis tempestātis.* Cæs.

9. (*a.*) When nouns are put in apposition, the one which explains or defines the other is generally put last, unless it is to be made emphatic; as, *Opes irrĭtāmenta mălōrum.* Ovid. Hence names of honors or dignities, and every thing of the nature of a title, are commonly placed after the proper name, as explanatory additions. Thus, especially, the names of changeable Roman dignities; as, *Cĭcĕro* consul; *C. Cūriōni* tribūno plēbis; but also permanent appellations; as, *Ennius* poēta; *Plăto* philŏsŏphus; *Diŏnȳsius* tyrannus; and such epithets as *vir hŏnestissĭmus; homo doctissĭmus.* But the hereditary title *rex* is frequently placed before the name; as, rex *Dēiŏtărus;* and so the title *Impĕrātor* after it became permanent.

(*b.*) In the arrangement of the Roman names of persons, the *prænōmen* stands first, next the *nōmen* or name of the *gens,* third the *cognōmen* or name of the *fămīlia,* and last the *agnōmen;* as, *Publius Cornēlius Scĭpio Africānus.* The prænomen is usually denoted by a letter. In the imperial times the *nōmen* is often either omitted or follows as something subordinate.

10. (*a.*) Oblique cases precede the words on which they depend, but they follow prepositions; as,

Pŏpŭli Rōmāni laus est. Cic. *Laudis ăvĭdi, pĕcūniæ lĭbĕrāles.* Sall. *Cunctis esto bĕnignus,* nulli *blandus,* paucis *fămĭliāris,* omnibus *æquus.* Sen. *Mŏnŭmentum ære pĕrennius.* Hor. *Hanc tibi dōno do.* Ter.—*Ad mĕrīdiem spectans* Cic. *Extra pĕrīcŭlum.* Id.

(*b.*) Genitives depending upon neuter adjectives are commonly placed last, as, *Incerta fortūnæ.* Liv. *Nec tibi plus cordis, sed minus oris inest.* Ovid.

§ 279. SYNTAX.—ARRANGEMENT OF WORDS. 309

REMARK. This rule, so far especially as it relates to genitives, is in a great degree arbitrary, as the position of the governed and governing words depends on the idea to be expressed; thus, *mors patris tui*, contrasts the death with the preceding life; but, *fratris tui mors* distinguishes this case of death from others. Hence we say, *ănĭmi mōtus, ănĭmi morbus, corpŏris partes, terræ mōtus.*—An objective genitive usually follows the word on which it depends; as, *ūnā signĭfĭcātiōne litĕrārum,* by means of a single notice by letters.—When several genitives are dependent on one noun, the subjective genitive commonly precedes and the objective genitive may either precede or follow the governing noun.— The genitive dependent on *causā* or *grātiā*, 'on account of,' regularly precedes these ablatives; as, *glōriæ causā mortem ŏbīre; ēmŏlŭmenti suī grātiā.*

(c.) When a noun which is governed by a preposition, is modified by other words which precede it, the preposition usually stands before the words by which the noun is modified; as, *A prīmā lūce ad sextam hōram.* Liv. *Ad ănĭmi mei laetitiam.* Cic. *Ad bĕne beātēque vivendum.* Id.

(d.) Sometimes, however, the preposition comes between its noun and an adjective or a genitive, by which the noun is modified; as, *Nullā in re.* Cic. *Justis dĕ causis.* Id. *Suos inter æquāles.* Id. *Hanc ob causam.* Id. *Magno cum mĕtu.* Id. *Quā in urbe* Id. *Eā in re.* Id. *Ætātis suæ cum prīmis.* Nep.— So, also, a conjunction may follow the preposition; as, *Post vero Sullæ victōriam.*

(e.) *Per*, in adjurations, is often separated from its case by other words; as, *Per ĕgo te deos ōro.* Ter.—In the poets, other prepositions are sometimes separated in the same manner; as, *Vulnĕra, quæ circum plurĭma mūros accĭpit patrios.* Virg.

(f.) *Tĕnus* and *versus*, and sometimes other prepositions, (cf. § 241, R. 1,) follow their cases, especially when joined with *qui* or *hic*. This occurs most frequently with the prepositions *ante, contra, inter,* and *propter;* more rarely with *circa, circum, pĕnes, ultra* and *adversus;* and with still less frequency with *post, per, ad,* and *de;* as, *quam ante, quem contra, quos inter, quem propter, quos ad, quem ultra, hunc adversus, hunc post, quam circa.*—The preceding prepositions, and more rarely others also, sometimes, especially in the poets and later prose writers, follow nouns and personal pronouns. In such case, if the noun be modified by an adjective or a genitive, the preposition sometimes stands between them, and sometimes follows both; as, *Postes sub ipsos.* Virg. *Rīpam apud Euphrātis.* Tac. *Mărīa omnia circum.* Virg. And more rarely other words intervene; as, *His accensa sŭper.* Id. *Vitiis nēmo sĭne nascĭtur* Hor.

11. Infinitives precede the verbs on which they depend; as,

Jugurtha, ŭbi eos Africā dēcessisse rātus est, nĕque propter lŏci nātūram Cirtam armis expugnāre possit, mœnia circumdat. Sall. *Servīre măgis quam impĕrāre părāti estis.* Id.

12. A word which has the same relation to several words, either precedes or follows them all; as, Vir *grăvis et săpiens.* Cic. *Clārus et hŏnōrātus* vir. Id *In* scriptōrĭbus *lĕgendis et ĭmĭtandis,* or *In lĕgendis imĭtandisque* scriptōrĭbus, but not *In lĕgendis* scriptōribus *et ĭmĭtandis. Quum respondēre nĕque vellet nĕque posset. Habentur et dicuntur tỹranni. Amīcitiam nec ūsu nec rătiōne hăbent cognĭtam.*

13. Relatives are commonly placed after their antecedents, and as near to them as possible; as,

Qui sim, ex eo, quem ad te mīsi, cognosces. Sall. *Lĭtĕras ad te mīsi, per quas grātias tibi ēgi.* Cic.

14. *Quisque* is generally placed after *se, suus, qui,* ordinals and superlatives; us, *Suos* quisque *dĕbet tuēri.* Cic. *Sătis sŭperque est sĭbi suārum* cuique *rērum cūra.* Id. *Sĕvĕritas ănĭmadversiōnis infĭmo* cuique *grātissĭma.* Id. *Maxĭme dĕcet, quod est cŭjusque maxĭme suum.* Id. *Quisque* very rarely begins a proposition.

15. (*a.*) An adverb is usually placed immediately before the word which it qualifies; but if the same word is modified by the oblique case of a noun, the latter commonly follows the adverb; as, Malo *partā* male *dīlābuntur.* Cic. *Nĭhil* tam *aspĕrum nĕque* tam *dĭffĭcĭle esse, quod* non cŭpĭdissĭme *factūri essent.* Sall.—*Impĕrium* făcĭle *iis artĭbus* rĕtĭnētur, *quĭbus ĭnĭtio partum est.* Id. *Sed* maxĭme *ădŏlescentium fămĭliărĭtātes* appētēbat. Id. *Non* tam *in bellis et in præliis,* quam *in prŏmissis et fĭde* firmiŏrem. Cic.—(*b.*) When *non* belongs to a single word of the proposition, it always stands immediately before it ; as, non *te rĕprĕhendo, sed fortūnam.* But if it belongs to the proposition generally, it stands before the verb, and particularly before the finite verb, if an infinitive depends on it; as, *Cur tantŏpĕre te angas, intelligĕre sāne* non possum. Instead of *non dico, nĕgo* is generally used; as, *nĕgāvit eum ădesse.*—The negatives *non, nĕque, nēmo, nullus,* when joined to general negative pronouns or adverbs, such as *quisquam, ullus, umquam,* always precede them though not always immediately; as, *nēmĭni quidquam nĕgāvit; non mĕmĭni me umquam te rĭdisse.* § 207, R. 31.

NOTE 1. In some phrases, custom has established a certain order, which must be observed and imitated; as, *Cīvis Rōmānus, pŏpŭlus Rōmānus, jus cīvīle, æs ălĭēnum, terrā mărīque, Pontĭfex maxĭmus, măgister ĕquĭtum, trĭbūnus mĭlĭtum, trĭbūni mĭlĭtum consŭlāri pŏtestāte, Jŭpĭter optĭmus maxĭmus, via Appia; ne quid respūblĭca dĕtrĭmenti căpĭat.* Cic. The ablatives *ŏpīnĭōne, spe, justo, sŏlĭto,* (see § 256, R. 9), generally precede the comparative.

NOTE 2. Exceptions to the foregoing principles are very numerous. These may arise (*a*) from emphasis; (*b*) from poetic license; and (*c*) from regard to the harmony of the sentence. The following general rule sometimes modifies nearly all the preceding.

16. The emphatic word is placed before the word or words connected with it which are not emphatic.

NOTE 3. The last place is often an emphatic one, except for the verb. When the verb is neither first nor last in a proposition the word before it is emphatic. An adjective, when emphatic, commonly precedes its substantive; when not emphatic, it commonly follows it. But with the demonstrative pronouns the rule is reversed.

NOTE 4. The principal poetical variation in the arrangement of words consists in the separation of the adjective from its noun, and in putting together words from different parts of a proposition.

17. A sentence should not close like a hexameter verse, with a dactyl and spondee; as, *Esse vĭdētur;* nor, in general, with a monosyllable.

18. *Hĭātus* should be avoided; that is, a word beginning with a vowel should not follow a word ending with a vowel.

19. A concurrence of long words or long measures,—of short words or short measures,—of words beginning alike or ending alike,—should be avoided.

II. OF THE ARRANGEMENT OF CLAUSES.

§ **280.** A compound sentence, whose clauses are united as protasis and apodosis, or in which the leading clause is divided by the insertion of one or more subordinate clauses, is called a *period.*

1. (*a.*) In the former kind of period the protasis must precede the apodosis; as, *Quum Pausānias sēmiănĭmis de templo ēlātus esset,* confestim ănĭmam efflāvit, When Pausanias had been carried out of the temple but just alive, he immediately expired. In a period of the latter kind the verb of the principal proposition is placed at the end, and the subordinate clauses between the parts of the leading clause; as, Pausānias, *quum sēmiănĭmis de templo ēlātus esset,* confestim ănĭmam efflāvit, Pausanias, when he had been carried out of the temple but just alive, immediately expired. Nep.

(*b.*) A sentence, such as *Scīpio exercĭtum in Africam trājēcit, ut Hannĭbălem ex Ĭtălĭā dēdūcĕret,* is not periodic in its structure, but it becomes so when we say, *Scipio, ut Hannibălem ex Italiā dēdūcĕret, exercĭtum in Africam trājēcit.* Periods in which the subordinate clause precedes with two conjunctions; as, *Quum igitur Rōmam vĕnisset, stătim impĕrātōrem ădiit,* are made still more strictly periodic by placing first the conjunction which belongs to the whole, and then inserting the subordinate proposition; as, Ităque, *quum Rōmam vēnisset,* stătim impĕrātōrem ădiit.

2. (*a.*) If the verbs of the leading and dependent clauses have the same subject, or the same noun depending on them, they are commonly formed into a period; as, Antigŏnus, *quum adversus Sĕleucum Lysimăchumque dīmicāret,* in proelio occīsus est. Nep. Quem, *ut barbări incendium effūgisse ĕmĭnus vidērunt,* telis missis interfēcērunt. Id.

(*b.*) So, also, when the noun which depends on the verb of the leading clause is the subject of the dependent clause; as, L. Manlio, *quum dictātor fuisset,* M. Pompōnius, trĭbūnus plēbis, diem dixit. Cic.

3. When obscurity would arise from separating the leading subject and verb by dependent words or clauses, they are often placed together at the beginning or end of the sentence; as, Lātæ (sunt) deinde lēges, *non sŏlum quæ regni suspiciōne consŭlem absolvĕrent, sed quæ ădeo in contrārium vertĕrent, ut populārem ětiam fācĕrent.* Liv. The position of the leading verb is also often otherwise varied, from regard to emphasis, to avoid monotony, or to prevent its meeting with the verb of the last dependent clause; but clauses, when so arranged, do not constitute a period.

4. When one clause is interrupted by the introduction of another, the latter should be finished before the first is resumed.

5. Clauses expressing a *cause,* a *condition,* a *time,* or a *comparison,* usually precede the clauses to which they relate.

6. A short clause usually stands before, rather than after, a long one.

III. OF THE CONNECTION OF CLAUSES.

(1.) In connecting propositions, relatives, whether pronouns, pronominal adjectives, or adverbs, are often employed in order to avoid the too frequent recurrence of *et, autem,* and certain other conjunctions. Every relative may be used for this purpose instead of its corresponding demonstrative with *et;* as, *qui* for *et is, quālis* for *et tālis, quo* for *et eo,* etc. They are used also before those conjunctions which are joined with *et* or *autem* at the beginning of a proposition; as, *si, nisi, ut, quum,* etc. (see § 206, (14.); as, *quod quum audīvissem, quod si fēcissem, quod quamvis non ignōrassem,* for *et quum hoc, et si hoc, et quamvis hoc;* or *quum autem hoc,* etc.; and, often, also, where in English no conjunction is used, and even before other relatives; as, *quod qui făcit, eum ĕgo impium jūdīco,* i. e. *et qui hoc fācit,* or, *qui autem hoc făcit.* In the ablative with comparatives the relative is often used as a connective; as, *Cato,* quo *nēmo turi ĕrat prūdentior,* i. e. Cato, who was more prudent than all others.

(2.) In propositions consisting of two members, the relative pronoun is joined grammatically either to the apodosis or to the protasis; with the former in, Qui, *quum ex eo quærĕrētur, cur tam diu vellet esse in vītā,* Nihil hăbeo, inquit, quod accūsem sĕnectūtem. Cic. de Sen. 6. But is more frequent with the protasis or secondary clause; as, A quo quum quærĕrētur, quid maxĭme expedīret, *respondit.* Cic. Off. 2, 25. When it is thus joined with the protasis, the nominative of the demonstrative is supplied with the apodosis from another case of the relative in the protasis, as, in the preceding passage, from the ablative. But for the sake of emphasis the demonstrative may be expressed, and frequently, also, for the sake of clearness; as, *Qui mos quum a postĕriōribus non ĕsset rĕtĕntus,* Arcĕsĭlas eum *rĕvŏcāvit.* Cic. de Fin. 2, 1. The accusative is sometimes to be supplied; as, *Qui (Hērăclĭtus) quŏniam intellĭgi nōluit, ōmittāmus.* Cic. N. D. 3, 14. When the demonstrative precedes, and is followed by a proposition consisting of two members, the relative is attached to the protasis, which is placed first, and not to the leading clause or apodosis; as, *Fa suāsi Pompeio*, quibus ille si pāruisset, *Cæsar tantas ōpes, quantas nunc hăbet, non hăbēret.* Cic. Fam. 6, 6. *Nōli adversus eos me velle dūcĕre,* cum quibus ne contra te arma ferrem, *Italiam rēliqui.* Nep. Att. 4.

(3.) Where in English we use 'however' with the relative; as, He promised me many things, which, however, he did not perform, the Latins made use of the demonstrative with *sed* or *vĕrum*, or the relative alone implying the adversative conjunction; as, *multa mihi prōmīsit*, sed ea *non præstĭtit*, or, *quæ non præstĭtit*, but not *quæ autem* or *quæ vēro. Qui autem* and *qui vēro* are used however in protases, where the relative retains its relative meaning, and there is a corresponding demonstrative in the apodosis; as, *Qui autem omnia bŏna a se ipsis pĕtunt, iis nihil mălum vidēri pŏtest, quod nātūræ nĕcessĭtus affĕrat.* Cic. de Sen. 2.

(4.) In double relative clauses, especially where the cases are different, Cicero frequently for the second relative clause substitutes the demonstrative; as, *Sed ipsius in mente insīdēbat spĕcies pulchrĭtūdĭnis eximia quædam, quam in-tuens,* in eāque dēfixus, *ad*, etc. for *et in quā.* Cic. Orat. 2. And sometimes even when the cases are the same; as, *Quem Phliuntem vēnisse fĕrunt, eumque cum Leonte dissĕruisse quædam.* Cic. Tusc. 5, 3; where *et* alone would have been sufficient.

(5.) From this tendency to connect sentences by relatives arose the use of *quod* before certain conjunctions merely as a copulative. See § 206, (14.)

(6.) *Nĕque* or *nec* is much used by Latin writers instead of *et* and a negation, and may be so used in all cases except when the negative belongs to one particular word; see § 278, R. 9. *Nĕque* or *nec* is added to *ĕnim, vēro*, and *tămen*, where we cannot use 'and.' To these negative expressions a second negative is often joined, in which case *nĕque ĕnim non* is equivalent to *nam; non vēro non*, to *atque ĕtiam*, a stronger *et; nec tămen non*, to *attămen*.

ANALYSIS.

§ 281. I. 1. The analysis of a complex or a compound sentence consists in d— ding it into its several component propositions, and pointing out th— r relation to each other.

2. In resolving a s— ence into its component clauses, the participial constructions equivalent to clauses should be mentioned, and ellipses be supplied See § 203, 4; § 274, 3; and § 257.

3. In a continued discourse the connection and relation of the successive sentences also should be specified.

Rules for the Analysis of Complex and Compound Sentences.

(1.) State whether the sentence is complex or compound. § 201, 11, 12.

(2.) If complex, (1) specify the principal and subordinate clauses. (2) Specify the class to which the subordinate proposition belongs, (§ 201, 7), and (3), its connective, and the class to which such connective belongs, (§ 201, 8 and 9.)

(3.) If compound, specify the principal propositions, with their subordinates, if any they have, as in the case of complex sentences.

II. The analysis of a proposition or simple sentence consists in distinguishing the subject from the predicate, and, in case either of them be compound, in pointing out the simple subjects or predicates of which it is composed, and if complex, in specifying the several modifiers, whether of the essential or subordinate parts.

Rules for the Analysis of a Simple Sentence.

1. Divide it into two parts—the subject and the predicate, § 201, 1—3 If these are simple, the analysis is complete, but if either is compound:—
2. Specify the simple subjects or predicates of which the compound consists.—If either is complex:—
3. Point out the grammatical subject, and the words, phrases, etc. *directly* modifying it.
4. Point out the words, phrases, etc., which modify the direct modifiers of the grammatical subject, and those which modify them, and so on successively, until the relation of each of the words composing the logical subject is specified.
5. Point out the grammatical predicate, and the words, phrases, etc., *directly* modifying it.
6. Point out the words, phrases, etc., which modify the direct modifiers of the grammatical predicate, and those which modify them, and so on successively, until the relation of each of the words composing the logical predicate is specified.

PARSING.

III. Parsing consists in resolving a proposition into the parts of speech of which it is composed, tracing the derivation of each word, and giving the rules of formation and construction applicable to it.

Rules for Parsing.

1. Name the part of speech to which each word belongs, including the subdivision in which it is found.
2. If it is an inflected word:—
 (1.) Name its root or crude form, and decline, compare, or conjugate it.
 (2.) If it is a noun or pronoun, tell its gender, number and case:—if in the nominative or in the accusative with the infinitive, tell its verb:—if in an oblique case depending on some other word, tell the word on which its case depends.
 (3.) If it is an adjective, adjective-pronoun, or participle, tell the word which it modifies.
 (4.) If it is a finite verb or an infinitive with the accusative, tell its voice, mood, tense, number, person, and subject.
3. If it is a conjunction, tell its class and what it connects.
4. If it is a preposition, tell the words whose relation is expressed by it.
5. If it is an adverb, tell its class and what it qualifies.
6. Prove the correctness of each step of the process by quoting the definition or rule of formation or construction on which it depends.

NOTE. The words constituting a proposition are most conveniently parsed in that order in which they are arranged in analysis.

Examples of Analysis and Parsing.

1. *Equus currit*, The horse runs.

Analysis. This is a simple sentence: its subject is *equus*, its predicate is *currit*, both of which are simple. See § 201, 1–3; § 202, 2; and § 203, 2.

Parsing. Equus is a common noun, § 26, 1 and 3; of the 2d decl., § 38; masc. gender, § 28, 1; third person, § 35, 2; its root is *equ-*, § 40, 10; decline it, § 46; it is in the nominative case, singular number, § 35, 1, (*b.*); the subject of *currit*, § 209, (*a.*).—*Currit* is a neuter verb, § 141, II.; of the 3d conjugation, § 149, 2, from *curro*; its principal parts are *curro, cucurri, cursum, currĕre*, § 151, 4; it is from the first root *curr-*; give the formations of that root, § 151, 1; it is in the active voice, § 142, 1; indicative mood, § 143, 1; present tense, § 145, I.; third person, § 147; singular number, § 146; agreeing with its subject-nominative *equus*, § 209, (*b.*).

NOTE. The questions to be asked in parsing *equus* are such as these, Why is *equus* a *noun?* Why a *common* noun? Why of the *second* declension? Why *masculine?* etc.—In parsing *currit*, the questions are, Why is *currit* a *verb?* Why a *neuter* verb? Why of the *third* conjugation? Which are the *principal parts* of a verb? Of what does the *first root* of a verb consist? What parts of a verb are derived from the *first root?* etc. The answer in each case may be found by consulting the etymological rules and definitions.

2. *Sævius ventis ăgĭtātur ingens pīnus*, The great pine is more violently shaken by the winds. Hor.

Analysis. This also is a simple sentence:—its subject is *ingens pīnus*, its predicate *sævius ventis ăgĭtātur*; both of which are complex, § 201, 10, § 202, 6, and § 203, 5.

The grammatical subject is *pīnus*, the pine; this is modified by *ingens*, great, § 201, 2, § 202, 2, and § 202, 6, (3.)

The grammatical predicate is *ăgĭtātur*, is shaken; this is modified by two independent modifiers, *sævius*, more violently, and *ventis*, by the winds, § 203 II. 3 Rem., § 203, I. 1, (2), and (3.)

Parsing. Pīnus is a common noun, § 26, 1 and 3; of the 2d and 4th declensions, § 38 and § 99; feminine gender, § 29, 2; 3d person, § 35, 2; from the root *pīn-*, § 40, 10; (decline it both in the 2d and 4th declensions);—it is found in the singular number, § 35, 1, and the nominative case, the subject of *ăgĭtātur*, § 209, (*a.*).

Ingens is a qualifying adjective of quantity, § 104, 4, and § 205, N. 1; of the 3d decl., § 105, 1, and § 38; of one termination, § 108, and § 111; from the root *ingent-*, § 40, 10; (decline it like *præsens*, § 111, but with only *i* in the ablative, § 113, Exc. 3,);—it is found in the singular number, feminine gender, § 26, R. 4; and nominative case, agreeing with its noun *pīnus*, § 205.

Ăgĭtātur is an active frequentative verb, § 141, I., and § 187, II. 1; of the 1st conjugation, § 149, 2; from the first root of its primitive *ăgo*, § 187, II. 1, (*b.*); (name its principal parts in both voices, see § 151, 4; and give the conjugation of the passive voice, indicative mood, present tense, see § 156,);—it is found in the singular number, § 146; third person, § 147; agreeing with its subject-nominative *pīnus*, § 209, (*b.*).

Sævius is a derivative adverb of manner, § 190, 2–4; in the comparative degree, from the positive *sæve* or *sæviter*, which is derived from the adjective *sævus*, § 194, 1 and 2, and § 192, II. 1, and Exc. 1 and 2; modifying the verb *ăgĭtātur*, by expressing its degree, § 277.

Ventis is a common noun, § 26, 1 and 3; of the 2d declension, § 38; masculine gender, § 46; from the root *vent-*, § 40, 10; (decline it);—it is found in the plural number, § 35, 1; ablative case, modifying *ăgĭtātur* by denoting its means or instrument, § 247.

3. *Mĭthrĭdātes, duārum et vīginti gentium rex, tŏtĭdem linguis jūra dixit*, Mithridates, king of twenty-two nations, pronounced judicial decisions in as many languages. Plin.

Analysis. This also is a simple sentence; its subject is *Mĭthrĭdātes, duārum et vīginti gentium rex*, its predicate is *tŏtĭdem linguis jūra dixit*, both of which are complex, § 201, 10, § 202, 6, and § 203, 5.

§ 281.   SYNTAX.—ANALYSIS AND PARSING.   315

The grammatical subject is *Mithridātes;* this is modified directly by *rex* § 202, I. (1.)
Rex is limited by *gentium*, § 202, I. 1, (2.)
Gentium is limited by the compound addition *duārum* and *viginti* connected coördinately by *et*, § 202, III. 3.
The grammatical predicate is *dixit;* this is limited by *jūra* and *linguis*, the former a simple, the latter a complex addition, as it is modified by *tōtidem* § 203, I. 1, (2.) and II. 1.

Parsing. *Mithridātes* is a proper noun, § 26, 2; of the third declension, § 38; masculine gender, § 28, 1; from the root *Mithridāt-*, § 40, 10; genitive *Mithridātis*, § 73, 1; (decline it in the singular number only, § 95, (*a*.);—it is found in the nominative case, the subject of *dixit*, § 209, (*a*.)
Rex is a common noun—third declension, § 38; masculine gender, § 28, 1; from the root *rēg-*, § 40, 10; genitive *rēgis*, § 78, 2; (decline it);—it is found in the singular number—the nominative case, in apposition to *Mithridātes*, § 204.
Gentium is a common noun from *gens*—third declension—feminine gender, § 62; from the root *gent-*, § 56, I, R. 1; genitive *gentis*, § 77, 2 and (2.); (decline it);—it is found in the plural number—genitive case, § 83, II. 3; limiting *rex* subjectively, § 211 and R. 2.
Duārum is a numeral adjective, § 104, 5; of the cardinal kind, § 117; from *duo, duæ, duo;* from the root *du-;* (decline it, § 118, 1,);—it is found in the plural number, § 118, 2; feminine gender, genitive case, § 26, R. 4; agreeing with its noun *gentium*, § 205.
Et is a copulative conjunction, § 198, 1, connecting *duārum* and *viginti*, § 278.
Viginti is a numeral adjective of the cardinal kind, indeclinable, § 118, 1; limiting *gentium*, § 205.
Dixit is an active verb, § 141, I.; of the third conjugation, § 149, 2; from *dico*, (give the principal parts in the active voice, and its first, second, and third roots, § 150, 4, and § 171, 1;) it is formed from the second root *dix-*, (give the formations of the second root);—it is found in the active voice, § 141, 1; indicative mood, § 143, 1; perfect indefinite tense, § 145, IV. and Rem.; singular number, third person, agreeing with *Mithridātes*, § 209, (*b*.)
Jūra is a common noun, of the third declension, from *jus*, root *jūr-*, § 56, I. R. 1. genitive *jūris*, § 76, Exc. 3; neuter gender, § 26; (decline it);—it is found in the plural number, accusative case, § 40, 8; the object of *dixit*, § 229.
Linguis is a common noun, of the first declension, feminine gender, from *lingua*, root *lingu-*, (decline it);—found in the plural number, ablative case, after *dixit*. § 247.
Tōtidem is a demonstrative pronominal adjective, § 139, 5, (2.) and (3.); indeclinable, § 115, 4; it is in the ablative plural, feminine gender, limiting *linguis*, § 205.

4. *Pausānias, quum semianīmis de templo ēlātus esset, confestim anīmam efflāvit.* Nep. Paus. 4.

Analysis. This is a complex sentence, § 201, 11; consisting of two members, which are so arranged as to constitute a period, § 280, 1.
The principal proposition is, *Pausānias confestim anīmam efflāvit*, § 201, 5.
The subordinate proposition is, *quum (is) semianīmis de templo ēlātus esset*, § 201, 6.
The leading proposition has a simple subject, *Pausānias*, § 202, 2, and a complex predicate, *confestim anīmam efflāvit*, § 203, 3; in which *efflāvit* is the grammatical predicate, § 203, 2; which is modified by *confestim* and *animam*, § 203, I. 1, (2.) and (3.), and II. R. 2., and also by the adverbial clause *quum semianīmis*, etc. § 201, 6 and 7, and § 203, I. 3.
The subordinate proposition, which is connected to the leading clause by the subordinate conjunction *quum*, § 201, 9, has a simple subject, viz. *is* understood, and a complex predicate, *semianīmis, de templo ēlātus esset*, § 203, 3.—
The grammatical predicate is *ēlātus esset*, § 203, 2; which is modified by *semianīmis*, § 203, I. 1, (1.), and *de templo*, § 203, I. 2, and II. Rem. 2.

Parsing. *Pausănias*, a Greek proper noun, § 26, 2;—1st decl., §§ 41 and 44; masc. gender, § 28, 1; root *Pausăni-*; found in sing. num., nom. case, the subject of *efflāvit*, § 209, (*a.*)

Confestim, an adv. of time § 190, 3; limiting *efflāvit*, § 277.

Animum is a com. noun of 1st decl., fem. gender, § 41; from *ănima*, root *ănim-*; (decline it);—it is found in the sing. num., acc. case, the object of *efflāvit*, § 229.

Efflāvit, an act. verb, 1st conj., from *efflo*, compounded of *ex* and *flo*, § 196, 6; (give the principal parts in the act. voice and the three roots);—it is formed from the second root; (give the formations of that root); in the active voice ind. mood, perfect indefinite tense, sing. num., 3d pers., agreeing with *Pausănias*, § 209, (*b.*)

Quum is a temporal conjunction, § 198, 10; connecting the dependent to the principal clause, § 278.

Semiănimis is a predicate adj., of the 3d decl., of two terminations, § 109; (decline it);—it is in the sing. num., masc. gend., nom. case, agreeing with *is* understood, § 210, R. 1, (*a.*)

De is a preposition, expressing the relation between *ēlātus esset* and *templo*, § 195.

Templo is a com. noun, 2d decl., neut. gend., from *templum*, root *templ-* ; (decline it);—in the sing. num., abl. case, after *de*, § 241.

Elātus esset is an irregular active verb, of the third conjugation, § 179; from *effero*, compounded of *ex* and *fero*, § 196, 6; (see *fero* and compounds, § 172); (give the principal parts in both voices, and the 1st and 3d roots);—it is formed from the third root, *elāt-*, (give the formations of that root in the passive voice); in the subjunctive mood, pluperfect tense, § 145, V.; sing. num., third person, agreeing with *is* understood referring to *Pausănias*, § 209, (*b.*)

5. Rōmāna pūbes, *sēdāto tandem păvōre, postquam ex tam turbĭdo die sĕrēna et tranquilla lux rĕdiit, ŭbi văcuam sēdem rēgiam vīdit, etsi sătis crēdēbat patrĭbus, qui proxĭmi stĕtĕrant, sublīmem raptum prŏcellā; tămen, vĕlut orbĭtātis mĕtu icta,* mœstum ăliquamdiu silentium obtinuit. Liv. 1, 16.

Analysis. This is a complex sentence, whose clauses constitute a period, § 280. It is composed of the following members or clauses:—

1. Rōmāna pūbes [tămen] mœstum *ăliquamdiu silentium obtĭnuit*. This is the leading clause. The following are dependent clauses.
2. vĕlut *orbĭtātis mĕtu icta,*
3. *sēdāto tandem* păvōre,
4. *postquam ex tam turbĭdo die* sĕrēna *et tranquilla lux* rĕdiit,
5. *ŭbi văcuam sēdem rēgiam vīdit,*
6. etsi *sătis crēdēbat patrĭbus,*
7. qui *proxĭmi stĕtĕrant,*
8. *sublīmem raptum prŏcellā.*

NOTE 1. In the preceding clauses the predicates are printed in Italics.

NOTE 2. The connective of the 1st clause, is the adversative *tămen*, which is inserted on account of *etsi* intervening between the principal subject and predicate. The connective of the 2d clause is *vĕlut*, of the 4th *postquam*, of the 5th *ŭbi*, of the 6th *etsi*, followed by a clause constituting the protasis, and of the 7th *qui*. The 3d and 8th clauses have no connectives.

(1.) The grammatical subject of the leading clause is *pūbes*, which is limited by *Rōmāna*.—The grammatical predicate is *obtĭnuit*, which is limited by *ăliquamdiu* and *silentium*, and also either directly or indirectly by all the dependent clauses. *Silentium* is itself modified by *mœstum*.

The second, third, fourth, fifth, and sixth clauses are used adverbially to denote the time and other circumstances modifying the principal predicate *silentium obtĭnuit*, § 201, 7.

§ 281.   SYNTAX.—ANALYSIS AND PARSING.   317

(2.) The second is a participial clause, equivalent to *vĕlut* (*ea* scil. *pūbes*, *orbitātis mĕtu icta esset*, § 274, 3, (*a*.)
(3.) The third clause is also participial, and is equivalent to *quum tandem pavor sĕdātus esset*, § 257, R. 1; and hence *pavōre* represents the subject, and *sĕdāto tandem* the predicate—the former being simple, the latter complex.
(4.) The grammatical subject of the 4th clause, which is connected to the leading clause by *postquam*, § 201, 9, is *lux*, which is modified by *sĕrēna* and *tranquilla*.—The grammatical predicate is *rĕdiit*, which is modified by *postquam* and *ex tam turbido die*, § 203, I. 1, (3.), and II. 1.
(5.) The grammatical subject of the fifth clause is *ea* understood.—The grammatical predicate is *vidit*, which is modified by *ūbi* and *vācuam sīdem rēgiam*, § 203, I. 1, (3.) and II. 1.
(6.) The grammatical subject of the sixth clause also is *ea*. Its grammatical predicate is *crēdēbat*, which is modified by *sātis* and *patrĭbus*, § 203, I. (2.) and (3.), and by the 8th clause, II. 3.
(7.) The grammatical subject of the seventh clause is *qui*. Its grammatical predicate is *stĕtērant*, which is modified by *proximi*, § 203, I. (1.) It is an adjective clause, modifying *patrĭbus*, § 201, 7 and 9.
(8.) The grammatical subject of the eighth clause, which has no connective, § 204, Rem., is *eum*, i. e. *Rōmŭlum*, understood. Its grammatical predicate is *raptum* (*esse*), which is modified by *sublimem* and *prŏcellā*.

Parsing. *Rōmāna* is a patrial adjective, § 104, 10, derived from *Rōma*, § 128, 6, (*a*.) and (*e*.); of the 1st and 2d declensions, § 105, 2; fem. gender, sing. number, nom. case, agreeing with *pūbes*, § 205.
Pūbes, a collective noun, § 26, 4; 3d decl., fem. gender, § 62; from the root *pūb-*, § 56, I. R. 6; genitive *pūbis*, § 73, 1; (decline it);—found in the nom. sing., the subject of *obtinuit*, § 209, (*a*.)
Tāmen, an adversative conjunction, § 198, 9, relating to *etsi* in the 6th clause.
Mæstum, a qualifying adj., § 205, N. 1; of the 1st and 2d declensions, neut gender, sing. num., acc. case, agreeing with *silentium*.
Aliquamdiu, an adverb of time, § 191, II.; compounded of *aliquis* and *diu* § 193, 6; and limiting *obtinuit*, § 277.
Silentium, a com. noun, 2d decl., neut. gender, § 46; sing. number, acc. case the object of *obtinuit*, § 229.
Obtinuit, an active verb, of the 2d conj., § 149, 2; from *obtineo*, compounded of *ob* and *tĕneo*, see § 168; (give the principal parts in the act. voice, and the formations of the 2d root, § 157 at the end);—found in the active voice, ind. mood, perf. indef. tense, sing. num., 3d person, agreeing with *pūbes*, § 209, (*b*.)
Vĕlut for *vĕlut si*, an adverb, compounded of *vel* and *ut*, §193, 10; modifying *icta*, and *obtinuisset* understood, (as they would have done if, etc.)
Orbitātis, an abstract noun, § 26, 5; from the primitive *orbus*, § 101, 1 and 2; 3d decl., fem. gender, § 62; from the root *orbitat-*, § 56, I., and R. 1; (decline it);—found in the sing. num., subjective gen. case, limiting *mĕtu*, § 211.
Mĕtu, an abstract noun, 4th decl., masc. gen., § 87; sing. num., abl. case, § 247.
Icta, a perf. part. pass., from the active verb *ico*, of the 3d conj. (give the principal parts in both voices, and decline the participle);—found in the fem. gen., sing. num., nom. case, agreeing with *pūbes*, § 205.
Sĕdāto, a perfect pass. part. from the active verb *sēdo*, of the 1st conj., § 149, 2; (give the principal parts in both voices, § 151, 4; and decline it, § 105, R. 2.);—found in the masc. gender, sing. num., abl. case, agreeing with *pavōre*, § 205.
Tandem, an adverb of time, § 191, II.; modifying *sĕdāto*, § 277.
Pavōre, an abstract noun, § 26, 5, and § 102, 1; (from *pāveo*), 3d decl., masc. gen., § 58; root *pavor*, § 56, II., and § 70, (decline it);—found in the sing. number, abl. case, absolute with *sĕdāto*, § 257.
Postquam, an adverb of time, compounded of *post* and *quam*, § 193, 10; modifying *rĕdiit*, and connecting the 1st and 4th clauses, § 201, 9.
Ex, a preposition, § 195, R. 2.
Tum, an adverb of degree, § 191, R. 2; modifying *turbido*, § 277.

27*

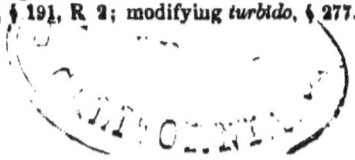

Turbĭdo, an adjective, agreeing with *die*.

Die, a common noun, 5th decl., masc. gender, § 90, Exc. 1.; sing. number abl. case, after the prep. *ex*, § 241.

Sĕrēna, an adj., 1st and 2d decls., fem. gen., sing. num., nom. case, agreeing with *lux*, § 205.

Et, a copulative conjunction, § 198, 1; connecting *sĕrēna* and *tranquilla*, § 278.

Tranquilla, like *sĕrēna*.

Lux, a common noun, 3d decl., fem. gen., § 62; from the root *lūc-*, § 56, I., and R. 2; genitive *lūcis*, § 78, 2.

Rĕdiit, an irregular neuter verb, of the 4th conj., § 176; from *rĕdeo*, compounded of *eo*, § 182, and the inseparable prep. *red*, § 196, (*b*.), 3; (give its principal parts);—found in the ind. mood., perf. indef. tense, sing. num., 3d pers., agreeing with *lux*, § 209, (*b*.)

Ubi, an adverb of time, and like *postquam*, a connective, § 201, 9; and modifying *vidit*, § 277.

Văcuam, an adj., qualifying *sĕdem*.

Sĕdem, a common noun, 3d decl., fem. gen., § 62; from the root *sĕd-*, § 56, I., R. 6; genitive *sēdis*, § 73, 1; (decline it);—found in the sing. num., acc. case, the object of the transitive verb *vidit*, § 229.

Rĕgiam, a denominative adj., § 128, I., 2, (*a.*); from the primitive *rex*, agreeing with *sĕdem*.

Vidit, an active verb, of the 2d conj., (give its principal parts in the active voice, and the formations of the 2d root); found in the active voice, ind. mood, perf. indef. tense, sing. num., 3d pers., agreeing with *ea*, i. e. *pūbes*, understood.

Etsi, a concessive conjunction, § 198, 4; corresponding to the correlative adversative conj. *tămen*, § 198, 4, R. and 9.

Sătis, an adverb of degree, § 191, III., and R. 2; modifying *crēdēbat*, § 27 *t*.

Crēdēbat, an act. verb, § 141, I.; 3d conj., (give the principal parts in the active voice and the formations of the 1st root);—found in the act. voice, ind. mood, imperfect tense, sing. num., 3d person, agreeing with *ea*, scil. *pūbes*, understood.

Patribus, a common noun, § 26, 3; 3d decl., from the root *patr-*, § 56, II., R. 3; gen. *patris*, § 71; masc. gender, § 28, 1; plur. num., dat. case, depending on *crēdēbat*, § 223, R. 2.

Qui, the subject of the 7th clause, is a relative pronoun, § 136; masc. gender, plur. num., agreeing with its antecedent *patribus*, § 206, R. 19, (*a.*); and is nominative to *stĕtĕrant*, § 209, (*a.*).

Proximi, an adj. of the superlative degree, § 126, 1, (compare it); of the 1st and 2d decls., masc. gen., plur. num., nom. case, agreeing with *qui*, § 205, § 210, R. 1, (*a.*) and R. 3, (2.)

Stĕtĕrant, a neuter verb, 1st conj., irregular in its 2d root, § 165; (give its principal parts, and the formations of the 2d root);—found in the act. voice, ind. mood, plup. tense, § 145, V.; 3d person plural, agreeing with its subject *qui*, § 209, (*b.*)

Sublīmem, an adj., of the 3d decl., and two terminations, § 109; masc. gen., sing. num., acc. case, agreeing with *eum*, (i. e. *Rōmŭlum*,) understood and modifying also *raptum esse*, § 205, R. 15.

Raptum (esse), an act. verb, 3d conj.; (give the principal parts in both voices and the formations of the 3d root in the passive voice)—found in the pass. voice, inf. mood, perf. tense; but, following the imperfect, it has the meaning of a pluperfect, § 268, 2, and § 145, V.; depending on *crēdēbat*, § 272.

Prōcellā, a com. noun, 1st decl., fem. gen., sing. num., abl. case, § 247.

PROSODY.

§ 282. Prosody treats of the quantity of syllables, and the laws of versification.

QUANTITY.

1. The quantity of a syllable is the relative time occupied in pronouncing it. Cf. § 13.

2. A syllable is either *short, long,* or *common.*

(*a.*) The time occupied in pronouncing a short syllable is called a *mora* or time.

(*b.*) A long syllable requires two *moræ* or double the time occupied in pronouncing a short one; as, *ămārĕ.*

(*c.*) A common syllable is one which, in poetry, may be made either long or short; as the middle syllable of *tĕnĕbræ.*

3. The quantity of a syllable is either *natural* or *accidental;*—natural, when it depends on the *nature* of its vowel; accidental, when it depends on its *position.*

Thus the *e* in *rĕsisto* is short by nature; while in *rĕstĭti* it is long by its position, since it is followed by two consonants: § 283, IV. On the contrary, the *e* in *dēdūco* is naturally long, but in *dĕerro* it is made short by being placed before a vowel: § 283, I.

4. The quantity of syllables is determined either by certain established *rules,* or by the *authority* of the poets.

Thus it is poetic usage alone that determines the quantity of the first syllables of the following words, viz. *māter, frāter, prāvus, dīco, dūco; păter, ăvus, cădo, măneo, grăvis,* etc.; and hence the quantity of such syllables can be ascertained by practice only or by consulting the gradus or lexicon.

5. The rules of quantity are either *general* or *special.* The former apply alike to all the syllables of a word, the latter to particular syllables.

GENERAL RULES.

§ 283. I. (*a.*) A vowel before another vowel, or a diphthong, is short; as, *e* in *mĕus, i* in *patrĭæ.* Thus,

> Conscĭa mens rectĭ fāmæ mendācĭa rīdet. *Ovid.* F. 4, 311.
> Ipse ĕtĭam exĭmĭæ laudis succensus ămōre. *Virg.* A. 7, 496.

(*b.*) So also when *h* comes between the vowels, since *h* is accounted only a breathing; as, *nĭhil:* (see § 2, 6.) Thus,

> Dē nĭhĭlō nĭhĭl, in nĭhĭlum nil posse rĕvertī. *Pers.* 4, 84.

Exc. 1. (*a.*) *Fīo* has the *i* long, except in *fĭt* and when followed by *er;* as *fīunt, fīēbam.* Thus,

Omnia jam *fīant, fīĕri* quæ posse něgābam. *Ovid.* Tr. 1, 8, 7.

(*b.*) It is sometimes found long even before *er*; as, *fīĕret.* Ter.; *fīĕri.* Plaut and, on the contrary, Prudentius has *fĭŏ* with *i* short.

Exc. 2. (*a.*) *E* is long in the termination of the genitive and dative of the fifth declension, when preceded and followed by *i*; as, *fāciēi.* Thus,

Non rādii sōlis, něque lūcīda tēla *diēi. Lucr.* 1, 148.

(*b.*) In *spĕi, rĕi,* and *fĭdei, e* is short.

NOTE. In Lucretius, the *e* of *rei* is, in a few cases, long, and that of *fīdei* is lengthened once in Lucretius and once in a line of Ennius.

Exc. 3. (*a.*) *A* is long in the penult of old genitives in *aī* of the first declension; as, *aulāī, pictāī.* Cf. § 43, 1.

(*b.*) *A* and *e* are also long in proper names in *aīus, eīus,* or *eīa*; as, *Cāīus Pompēīus, Aquilēīa*; and in the adjectives *Grāīus* and *Vēīus.* Thus,

Æthĕrium sensum, atque *aurāī* simplīcis ignem. *Virg.* A. 6, 747.
Accīpe, *Pompēī,* dēductum carmen ab illo. *Ovid.* Pont. 4, 1, 1.
Necnon cum Věnětis *Aquilēīa* perfūrit armis. *Sil.* 8, 606.

Exc. 4. (*a.*) *I* is common in genitives in *ius;* as, *ūnīus, illīus* Thus,

Illīus et nītīdo stīllent unguenta cāpillo. *Tibull,* 1, 7, 51.
Illīus pūro děstillent tempŏra nardo. *Id.* 2, 2, 7.

(*b.*) But *i* in the genitive of *alter* is commonly short; and in that of *ălīus* it is always long.

Exc. 5. The first vowel of *ēheu* is long; that of *Dīăna, ĭo,* and *ŏhe* is common.

Exc. 6. Greek words retain their original quantities, and hence, in many *Greek* words, a vowel is long, though immediately followed by another vowel; as,

āēr, Achāīa, Achĕlōŭs, dīa, ĕos, Lāertes, and Greek words having in the original a long *e* or *o* (η or ω.) See also § 293, 3.

(1.) Words which, in Greek, are written with *ei* (*ει*) before a vowel, and in Latin with a single *e* or *i*, have the *e* or *i* long; as, *Ænēas, Alexandrīa, Cassiopēa, Clīo, Dārīus, ēlēgīa, Gălătēa, Mēdēa, Mausōlēum, Pēnēlŏpēa, Thālīa, Atrīdes.*

Hence, most adjectives in *eus,* formed from Greek proper names, have the *e* long; as, *Cўthĕrēus, Pēlŏpēus;* and the *e* remains long when *ei* is restored; as, *Pēlŏpēīa.*

Exc. *Acădēmīa, chŏrea, Mălea, plătea,* and some patronymics and patrials in *ēīs;* as, *Nērēīs,* have the penult common.

(2.) Greek genitives in *eos,* and accusatives in *ea,* from nominatives in *eus,* generally shorten the *e*; as, *Orphĕos, Orphĕa;*—but the *e* is sometimes lengthened by the Ionic dialect; as, *Cēphēos, Ilĭŏnēa.*

(3.) Greek words in *ais, ois, aius, eius, oius, aon,* and *ion,* generally lengthen the first vowel; as, *Nāis, Mīnōis, Grāīus, Nērēīus, Mīnōīus, Măchāon, Īxīon.* But *Thĕbāis, Sĭmŏis, Phăon, Deucălīon, Pygmălīon,* and many others, shorten the former vowel.

NOTE 1. Greek words in *aon* and *ion,* with *o* short in the genitive, have the penult long; but with *o* long in the genitive, they have it short; as, *Amўthāon -ăŏnis; Deucălīon, -ōnis.*

§ 283.   PROSODY.—QUANTITY—GENERAL RULES.   321

Note 2. In Greek proper names in *eus* (gen. *eos*), as *Orpheus*, the *eu* in the nominative is always a diphthong in the original, and, with very few exceptions, in the Latin poets.

II. A diphthong is long; as, *aūrum, fœnus, Eubœa, Pompēīus, Orphēū.* Thus,

Infernique lăcus, Æǣaque insŭla Circæ. *Virg.* A. 3, 386.
Thēsaūros ignōtum argenti pondus et aūri. *Id.* A. 1, 359.
Harpyiǣque cōlunt aliǣ, Phineïa postquam. *Id.* A. 3, 212.

Exc. 1. *Præ*, in composition, is short before a vowel; as, *prǣustus, prǣacūtus.* Thus,

Nec tōtā tāmen ille prior prǣeunte cărīnā. *Virg.* A. 5, 186.

In Statius, and Sidonius Apollinaris, it is found long.

Exc. 2. A diphthong at the end of a word, when the next word begins with a vowel, is sometimes made short; as,

Insŭlǣ Ionio in magno, quas dīra Cēlæno. *Virg.* A. 3, 211.

Exc. 3. The diphthongs consisting of *u* followed by a vowel are either long or short; the two vowels thus combined being subject to the same rules of quantity, as their final vowel would be if standing alone; as, *quā, quī, quōrum, quia, quibus, quătio, quēror, æquōr, linguā, sanguis.*

III. A syllable formed by contraction is long; as,

ālius for *alitus; cōgo* for *cŏăgo; nīl* for *nĭhīl; jūnior* for *jŭvēnior.* Thus,

Tītyre cōge pēcus, tu post cārecta lătēbas. *Virg.* E. 3, 20.

IV. A vowel naturally short, before two consonants, a double consonant, or the letter *j*, is long by *position*; as, *ārma, bēllum, āxis, gāza, mājor.* Thus,

Pāscĕre ōpōrtet ōves dēdūctum dīcĕre cărmĕn. *Virg.* E. 6, 5.
Nĕc myrtūs vīncet cŏrȳlos; nĕc laurea Phœbi. *Id.* E. 7, 64.
At nōbis, Pax alma, vĕni, spīcamque tĕnēto. *Tibull.* 1, 10, 67.
Rāra jŭvant: primis sic mājor grătia pōmis. *Mart.* 4, 29, 3.

Note 1. A vowel (other than *i*) before *j* is in reality lengthened by forming a diphthong with it, since *i* and *j* are in fact but one letter. Thus *major* is equivalent to *mai'-or*, which would be pronounced *mi'-yor*. See § 9, 1.

Exc. 1. The compounds of *jŭgum* have *i* short before *j*; as, *bĭjŭgus, quădrījŭgus.* Thus,

Intĕreā bĭjŭgis infert se Lūcăgus albis. *Virg.* A. 10, 575.

Remark. The vowel is long by position, when either one or both of the consonants is in the same word with it; but when both stand at the beginning of the following word, the vowel is either long or short; as,

Tolle mŏras; sempĕr nŏcuit differre părātis. *Lucan.* 1, 281.
Ferte cĭti ferrŭm; dăte tēlă; scandite mūros. *Virg.* A. 9, 37.
Ne tămen ignōrēt, quæ sīt sententiā scripto. *Ovid.*

Note 2. A short vowel at the end of a word, before an initial double consonant or *j* in the following word, is not lengthened.

Note 3. In the comic poets a vowel frequently remains short though followed by two consonants, especially if only one of them is in the same word.

Exc. 2 A vowel *naturally short*, before a mute followed by a liquid, is common; as, ăgris, phărētra, vŏlŭcris, pŏplītes, cŏchlea. Thus,

Et prīmo sĭmĭlis *vŏlŭcri*, mox vēra *vŏlŭcris*. Ovid. M. 13. 607.
Nātum ante ōra *pătris*, *pătrem* qui obtruncat ad āras. Virg. A. 2, 663.
Nox *tĕnĕbras* prŏfert. Phœbus fŭgat inde *tĕnĕbras*. Ovid.

REM. 1. If the vowel before a mute and liquid is *naturally long*, it continues so; as, *sălūbris, ambŭlācrum*.

REM. 2. In *compound* words, of which the former part ends with a mute, and the latter begins with a liquid, a short vowel before the mute is made long by position; as, *ăblŭo, ŏbruo, sŭblĕvo, quamŏbrem*.

REM. 3. A mute and liquid at the beginning of a word seldom lengthen the short vowel of the preceding word, except in the arsis of a foot; as,

Terrasquĕ tractusque mărĭs cœlumque prŏfundum. *Virg*. E. 4, 51.

REM. 4. In Latin words, only the liquids *l* and *r* following a mute render the preceding short vowel common; but, in words of Greek origin, *m* and *n* after a mute have the same effect, as in *Tĕcmessa, Prŏcne, Cўcnus*.

SPECIAL RULES.

FIRST AND MIDDLE SYLLABLES.

I. DERIVATIVE WORDS.

§ **284.** Derivative words retain the quantity of their primitives; as,

by conjugation, ămo, ămat, ămābat, ămāvi, ămātus, etc.; by declension, ămor, ămōris, ămōri, ămōribus, etc.; so, ănĭmal, ănĭmātus, from ănĭma; gĕmĕbundus, from gĕmĕre; fămĭlia, from fămŭlus; māternus, from māter; prŏpinquus, from prŏpe.

NOTE 1. *Lăr, păr, săl*, and *pĕs* in declension shorten the vowel of the nominative; as, *sălis, pĕdis*, etc.

NOTE 2. The vowel of the primitive is sometimes lengthened or shortened in the derivative by the addition or removal of a consonant.

REM. 1. Derivatives from increasing nouns of the second or third declension agree in quantity with the increment of their primitives as,

pŭĕrĭtia, from pŭĕri; virgĭneus, from virgĭnis; sălūber, from sălūtis.

REM. 2. In verbs, the vowels of the derived tenses and of derivative words agree in quantity with the verbal root from which they are formed; as,

mŏvēbam, mŏvēbo, mŏveam, mŏvĕrem, mŏve, mŏvēre, mŏvens, mŏvendus, from *mŏv*, the root of the present, with *ŏ* short;—mōvēram, mōvĕrim, mōvissem, mōvĕro, mōvisse, from *mōv*, the root of the perfect, with *ō* long; mōtūrus and mōtus;—mōto, mōtio, mōtor, and mōtus, -*ūs*, from *mōt*, the root of the supine, with *ō* also long.

REM. 3. (*a*.) *Sŏlūtum* and *vŏlūtum* from *solvo* and *volvo* have the first syllable short, as if from *sŏluo, vŏluo*. So, from *gigno* come *gĕnui, gĕnĭtum*, as if ✢✢ gĕno, and *pŏtui*, from *pŏtis sum (possum)*.

§ 284. PROSODY.—QUANTITY—DERIVATIVE WORDS.   323

(b.) The *a* in *da*, imperative of *do*, is long, though short in other parts of the verb. See § 294, 2.

(c.) The *o* in *pŏsui* and *pŏsitum* is short, though long in *pōno*.

Exc. 1. Perfects and supines of two syllables have the first syllable long, even when that of the present is short; as,

vēni, vīdi, fēci, from vĕnio, vĭdeo, făcio; cāsum, mōtum, vīsum, from cădo, mŏveo, vĭdeo.

Note 3. Such perfects are supposed to have been formed either by the contraction of reduplicated syllables, as *vĕvĕnio*, perf. *vĕvēni*, by syncope *vēēni*, by crasis *vēni*, or by the omission of a consonant, as *vĭdeo*, perf. *vĭdsi*, by sync *pe vīdi*, the vowel retaining the quantity which it had by position.

Note 4. The long vowel of dissyllabic supines probably arose in like manner from syncope and contraction; as, *vĭdeo*, *vĭdsum*, by syncope *vīsum*; *mŏveo*, *mŏvĭtum*, by syncope *mōitum*, by contraction *mōtum*.

(1.) (a.) These seven perfects have the first syllable short :—*bĭbi*, *dĕdi*, *fĭdi*, (from *findo*), *scĭdi*, *stĕti*, *stĭti*, *tŭli*. So also *percŭli*, from *vercello*.

(b.) The first syllable is also short before a vowel (§ 283, l.); as, *rŭi*.

(2.) (a.) These ten supines have the first syllable short:—*cĭtum*, (from *cieo*), *dătum*, *ĭtum*, *lĭtum*, *quĭtum*, *rătum*, *rŭtum*, *sătum*, *sĭtum*, and *stătum*.

(b.) So, also, had the obsolete *fŭtum*, from *fŭŏ*, whence comes *fŭtūrus*.

Exc. 2. (a.) Reduplicated polysyllabic perfects have the first two syllables short; as,

cĕcĭdi, cĕcĭni, tĕtĭgi, dĭdĭci, from cădo, căno, tango, and disco.

(b.) The second syllable of reduplicated perfects is sometimes made long by position; as, *mŏmōrdi*, *tĕtōndi*.—*Cēcĭdi* from *cædo*, and *pĕpēdi* from *pēdo*, retaining the quantity of their first root also have the second syllable long.

Exc. 3. Desiderative verbs in *urio* have the *u* short, though, in the third root of the verbs from which they are formed, it is long; as, *cænătŭrio* from *cænătū*, the third root of *cæno*. So *partŭrio*, *ēsŭrio*, *nuptŭrio*.

Exc. 4. Frequentative verbs, formed from the third root of verbs of the first conjugation, have the *i* short; as, *clāmĭto*, *vŏlĭto*. See § 167, II. 1.

Exc. 5. A few other derivatives deviate from the quantity of their primitives.

1. Some have a long vowel from a short one in the primitive Such are,

Dēni, *from* dĕcem.
Fōmes *and* ⎱ *from*
Fōmentum, ⎰ fŏveo.
Hūmānus, *from* hŏmo.
Lātern.a, *from* lăteo,
Lītera *from* lĭno.
Lex (lēgis), *from* lĕgo.

Mōbĭlis, *from* mŏveo.
Persōna, *from* persŏno.
Rēgŭla *and* ⎱ *from*
Rex (rēgis), ⎰ rĕgo.
Sēcius, *from* sĕcus.
Sēdes, *from* sĕdeo.
Sēmen, *from* sĕro.

Stīpendium, *from* stips (stĭpis).
Suspīcio, ōnis, *from* sus picor.
Tēgŭla, *from* tĕgo.

2. Some have a short vowel from a long one in the primitive Such are,

Dĭcax, *from* dīco.
Dŭx (dŭcis), *from* dūco.
Fĭdes, *from* fīdo.
Lăbo, *from* lābor, *dep. v.*
Lŭcerna, *from* lūceo.

Mŏlestus, *from* mōles.
Năto, *from* nātu. *sup.*
Nŏto, *from* nōtu. *sup.*
ŏdium, *from* ōdi.
Quăsillus, *from* quālus.

Săgax, *from* sāgio.
Sŏpor, *from* sōpio.
Vădum, *from* vādo.
Vĕco, *from* vox (vōcis.)

Note 1. *Dīsertus* comes regularly (by syncope) from *dissertus*, the prefix *dis* being short, § 299, 1. Cf. *dĭrĭmo* and *dĭrĭbeo*, where *s* is changed to *r*. See § 196, (b.) 2.

Note 2. Some other words might, perhaps, with propriety be added to these lists; but, in regard to the derivation of most of them, grammarians are not entirely agreed.

Remark 1. Some of these irregularities seem to have arisen from the influence of syncope and crasis. Thus *mōbĭlis* may have been *mŏvĭbĭlis*; *mōtum*, *mŏvĭtum*, etc.

Rem. 2. Sometimes the vowel in the derived word being naturally short, is restored to its proper quantity by removing one of the consonants which, in the primitive, made it long by position; as, *nŭx*, *nŭcis*. So, when the vowel of the primitive is naturally long, but has been made short before another vowel, it is sometimes restored to its original quantity by the insertion of a consonant: as, *hībernus*, from *hĭems*.

Rem. 3. The first syllable in *lĭquĭdus* is supposed to be common, as coming either from *lĭquor* or *lĭqueo*; as,

Crassāque convēniant *lĭquĭdis*, et *lĭquĭda* crassis. *Lucr.* 4, 1255.

II. COMPOUND WORDS.

§ 285. 1. Compound words retain the quantity of the words which compose them; as,

dēfĕro, of *dē* and *fĕro*; *ădōro*, of *ăd* and *ōro*. So *ăbŏrior*, *ămŏvĕo*, *circŭmĕo*, *cŏmĕdo*, *ēnītor*, *prŏdūco*, *sŭbŏrno*.

2. The change of a vowel or a diphthong in forming the compound does not alter its quantity; as,

concĭdo, from *cădo*; *concīdo*, from *cædo*; *ērĭgo*, from *rĕgo*; *reclūdo*, from *claudo*; *inīquus*, from *æquus*.

Exc. 1. A long syllable in the simple word becomes short in the following compounds:—*agnĭtus* and *cognĭtus*, from *nōtus*; *dĭjĕro* and *pĕjĕro*, from *jūro*; *hŏdie*, from *hōc die*; *nĭhĭlum* and *nĭhĭl*, from *hīlum*; *causĭdĭcus*, and other compounds ending in *dĭcus*, from *dīco*.

Exc. 2. *Imbēcillus*, from *băcillum*, has the second syllable long. The participle *ambītus* has the penult long, from *ītum*, but the nouns *ambĭtus* and *ambĭtio* follow the rule.

Exc. 3. *Innŭba*, *prŏnŭba*, and *subnŭba*, from *nūbo*, have *u* short; but in *connūbium*, it is common.

Exc. 4. *O* final, in the compounds of *do* and *sto*, is common, though long in the simple verbs. § 294, (a.)

Note 1. Prepositions of one syllable, which end in a vowel, are long (§ 294, (a.); those which end in a single consonant are short (§ 299, 1.)—*Trā* from *trans* is long; as, *trādo*, *trādūco*.

Exc. 5. *Pro*, in the following compounds, is short:—*prŏfānus*, *prŏfāri*, *prŏfectŏ*, *prŏfestus*, *prŏfĭciscor*, *prŏfĭteor*, *prŏfŭgio*, *prŏfŭgus*, *prŏcella*, *prŏfundus*, *prŏnĕpos*, *prŏneptis*, and *prŏtervus*. It is common in *procūro*, *profundo*, *propāgo*, *propello*, and *propīno*.—Respecting *præ* in composition before a vowel see § 283, II. Exc. 1.

Rem. 1. The Greek preposition *pro* (before) is short; as, *prŏphēta*. In *proŏgus*, *propōla*, and *propīno*, it is common.

Rem. 2. The inseparable prepositions *di* (for *dis*) and *se* are long; as,

dīdūco, *sēpăro*. Respecting *dīsertus*, see § 284, Exc. 5, 2, N. 1.

REM. 3. (a.) The inseparable preposition *re* or *red* is short; as, *rĕmitto, rĕfĕro, rĕdămo.*

(b.) *Re* is sometimes lengthened in *relīgio, relīquiæ, relīquus, repĕrit, retŭlit, repŭlit, recĭdit, redūcĕre,* where some editors double the consonant following *re*. Cf. § 307, 2. In the impersonal verb *rēfert, re* is long, as coming from *res*.

REM. 4. *A* ending the former part of a compound word, is long the other vowels are short; as,

mālo, quāpropter, trādo, (trans *do*); *nēfas, valēdīco, hujuscēmŏdi; bīceps, trĭdens, omnĭpŏtens, signif̄ico; hŏdie, quandōquidem, philŏsŏphus; dūcenti, lŏcŭples, Trōjŭgēna; Polŭdōrus, Eurŭpŭlus, Thrāsŭbūlus.*

EXC. 1. **A.** *A* is short in *quăsi, eădem,* when not an ablative, and in some Greek compounds; as, *cătăpulta, hexămĕter.*

EXC. 2. **E.** *E* is long in *crēdo, nēmo, nēquam, nēquāquam, nēquidquam, nē quis, nēquitia; mēmet, mēcum, tēcum, sēcum, sēse, vērors, vēsānus, vēnēficus,* and *vīdēlicet;*—also in words compounded with *se* for *sex* or *sēmi;* as, *sēdĕcim, sēmestris, sēnusdius;* but in *selībra* it is found short in Martial.

NOTE 2. (a.) The first *e* in *vīdelicet,* as in *vĭde,* is sometimes made short. See § 295, Exc. 3.

(b.) *E* is common in some verbs compounded with *făcio;* as, *liquefăcio, pătefăcio, rărefăcio, tăbefăcio, tĕpefăcio.*

EXC. 3. **I.** (1.) *I* is long in those compounds in which the first part is declined, (§ 296;) as, *quīdam, quīvis, quīlibet, quantīvis, quantīcumque, tantīdem, unīcuique, eīdem, reīpūblīcæ, utrīque.*

(2.) *I* is also long in those compounds which may be separated without altering the sense, (§ 296;) as, *lūdīmăgister, sīquis, agrīcultūra.*

(3.) *I,* ending the former part of a compound word, is sometimes made long by contraction; as, *tībīcen* for *tībiĭcen,* from *tībia* and *cāno.* See § 283, III.

(4.) *I* is long in *bīgæ, quadrīgæ, īlīcet, scīlīcet.*

(5.) In *īdem,* when masculine, *i* is long; but when neuter, it is short. The *i* of *ŭbīque* and *utrōbīque,* the second in *ĭbīdem,* and the first in *nīmīrum,* are long. In *ŭbicumque,* as in *ŭbi, i* is common.

(6.) Compounds of *dies* have the final *i* of the former part long; as, *bīduum, trīduum, mērīdies, quŏtīdie, quŏtīdiānus, prīdie, postrīdie.*

NOTE 3. In Greek words, *i,* ending the former part of a compound, is short; as, *Callĭmăchus;* unless it comes from the diphthong *ei* (ει), or is made long or common by position.

EXC. 4. **O.** (1.) In compounds, the final *o* of *contro, intro, retro,* and *quando* except *quandŏquidem,*) is long; as, *contrōversia, intrōdūco, retrōcēdo, quandōque.* *O* is long also in *aliōqui* (-*quin*), and *utrōque.*

(2.) *O* is long in the compounds of *quō* and *eo;* as, *quōmŏdo, quōcumque, quōnăm, quōlibet, quōminus, quōcirca, quōvis, quōque* (i. e. *et quo*); *eōdem, eōne;* but in the conjunction *quŏque,* it is short.

(3.) Greek words which are written with an *ōmĕga* (ω) have the *o* long; as, *geōmetra, Mīnōtaurus, lăgōpus.*

EXC. 5. **U.** *U* is long in *Jūpĭter* (*Jŏvis păter*), and *jūdĭco* (*jūs dīco*).

III. INCREMENT OF NOUNS.

§ 286. 1. A noun is said to *increase,* when, in any of its cases, it has more syllables than in the nominative singular; as, *pax, pācis; sermo, sermōnis.* The number of *increments* in any case of a noun is equal to that of its additional syllables.

2. Nouns in general have but one increment in the singular, but *iter*, *sŭpellex*, compounds of *căput* ending in *ps*, and sometimes *jĕcur*, have two increments; as,

ĭter, ĭ-tĭn-ĕ-ris; sŭpellex, sŭ-pel-lec-tĭ-lis; anceps, an-cĭp-ĭ-tis; jĕcur, jĕ-cĭn-ĭ-ris.

REMARK. The double increase of *iter*, etc., in the singular number arises from their coming from obsolete nominatives, containing a syllable more than those now in use; as, *itiner*, etc.

3. The dative and ablative plural of the third declension have one increment more than the genitive singular; as,

rex,	Gen. rē-gis,	D. and Ab. rĕg-ĭ-bus.
sermo,	—— ser-mō-nis,	—— ser-mōn-ĭ-bus.
iter,	—— ĭ-tĭn-ĕ-ris,	—— ĭt-ĭ-nĕr-ĭ-bus.

4. The last syllable of a word is never considered as the increment. If a word has but one increment, it is the penult; if two, the antepenult is called the first, and the penult the second; and if three, the syllable before the antepenult is called the first, the antepenult the second, and the penult the third increment; as,

```
           1        1 2              1 2      1 2 3
        ser-mo, ser-mō-nis, ser-mōn-ĭ-bus; ĭ-ter, ĭ-tĭn-ĕ-ris, ĭt-ĭ-nĕr-ĭ-bus.
```

5. In the third declension, the quantity of the first increment is the same in all the other cases as in the genitive singular; as,

sermōnis, sermōni, sermōnem, sermōne, sermōnes, sermōnum, sermōnĭbus. *Bōbus*, or *būbus*, from *bos, bŏvis*, is lengthened by contraction from *bŏvĭbus*.

NOTE. As adjectives and participles are declined like nouns, the same rules of increment apply to all of them; and so also to pronouns.

INCREMENTS OF THE SINGULAR NUMBER.

OF THE FIRST, FOURTH, AND FIFTH DECLENSIONS.

§ **287.** 1. When nouns of the first, fourth, and fifth declensions increase in the singular number, the increment consists of a vowel before the final vowel, and its quantity is determined by the first general rule with its exceptions, § 283, I.

Thus, *aura*, gen. *aurāi*, § 283, I. Exc. 3, (*a.*): *fructus*, dat. *fructŭi*, § 283, I. (*a.*): *dies*, gen. *diēi*, § 283, I. Exc. 2, (*a.*).

INCREMENTS OF THE SECOND DECLENSION.

2. The increments of the second declension in the singular number are short; as,

gĕner, gĕnĕri; sătur, sătŭri; tĕnĕr, tĕnĕri; vĭr, vĭri. Thus,

Ne, *pŭĕri*, ne tanta ănĭmĭs assuescite bella. *Virg.* A. 6, 833.
Monstra sinunt; *gĕnĕros* externis affōre ab ōris. *Id.* A. 7, 270.

EXC. The increment of *Iber* and *Celtiber* is long. For that of genitives in *ius* see § 283, Exc. 4.

INCREMENTS OF THE THIRD DECLENSION.

3. The increments of the third declension and singular number in *a* and *o* are long; those in *e*, *i*, *u*, and *y*, are short; as,

ănĭmal, ănĭmālis; audax, audācis; sermo, sermōnis; fĕrox, fĕrōcis; ŏpus, ŏpĕris; cĕler, cĕlĕris; mīles, mīlĭtis; supplex, supplĭcis; murmur, murmŭris, dux, dūcis; chlămys, chlămўdis; Styx, Stўgis. Thus,

Prōnăque cum spectent ănĭmālĭa cētĕra terram. *Ovid.* M. 1. 84.
Hæc tum multiplĭci pōpŭlos sermōne replēbat. *Virg.* A. 4, 189.
Incumbent gĕnĕris lapsī sarcīre ruīnas. *Id.* G. 4, 249.
Quālem virgīneo dēmessum pollĭce flōrem. *Id.* A. 11, 68.
Adspĭce, ventōsi cēcĭdērunt murmŭris auræ. *Id.* E. 9, 58.

Exceptions in Increments in A.

1. (*a*.) Masculines in *al* and *ar* (except *Car* and *Nar*) increase short; as, Annĭbal, Annĭbălis; Amilcar, Amilcăris.

(*b*.) *Par* and its compounds, and the following—*ănas, mas, vas* (*vădis*), *baccar, hĕpar, jŭbar, lar, nectar,* and *sal*—also increase short.

2. *A*, in the increment of nouns in *s* with a consonant before it, is short; as, daps, dăpis; Arabs, Arăbis.

3. Greek nouns in *a* and *as* (*ădis, ănis,* or *ătis*) increase short; as, lampas, lampădis; Mĕlas, Mĕlănis; poēma, poēmătis.

4. The following in *ax* increase short:—*ăbax, anthrax, Arctŏphўlax, Atax, Atrax, climax, cōlax, cŏrax,* and *nyctĭcŏrax, drōpax, fax, harpax, pănax, smīlax,* and *stўrax.*—The increment of *Sўphax* is doubtful.

Exceptions in Increments in O.

1. *O*, in the increment of neuter nouns, is short; as,

marmor, marmŏris; corpus, corpŏris; ĕbur, ĕbŏris. But *os* (the mouth), and the neuter of comparatives, like their masculine and feminine, increase long. The increment of *ădor* is common.

2. *O* is short in the increment of Greek nouns in *o* or *on*, which, in the oblique cases, have *omicron*, but long in those which have *omĕga*; as,

Aēdon, Aēdŏnis; Agămemnon, Agămemnŏnis:—Plăto, Plătōnis; Sinon, Sinōnis; Sĭcyon, Sĭcyōnis. Sidon, Orion, and Ægæon, have the increment common.

3. (*a*.) In the increment of gentile nouns in *o* or *on*, whether Greek or barbaric, *o* is generally short; as,

Măcĕdo, Măcedŏnis. So, Amazŏnes, Aŏnes, Myrmidŏnes, Santŏnes, Saxŏnes, Sĕnŏnes, Teutŏnes, etc.

(*b*.) But the following have *o* long:—*Eburōnes, Lacōnes, Iōnes, Nasamōnes, Suessōnes* (or *-iōnes*), *Vettōnes, Burgundiōnes. Britones* has the *o* common.

4. Greek nouns in *or* increase short; as, Hector, Hectŏris; rhētor, rhētŏris; Agēnor, Agēnŏris.

5. Compounds of *pus*, (πούς), as *tripus, pŏlўpus, Œdĭpus,* and also *arbor, mĕmor, bos, compos, impos,* and *lĕpus,* increase short.

6. *O*, in the increment of nouns in *s* with a consonant before it, is short; as,

scrobs, scrŏbis; inops, ĭnŏpis; Dŏlŏpes. But it is long in the increment of *cercops, Cyclops,* and *hydrops*.

7. The increment of *Allobrox, Cappădox,* and *præcox,* is also short.

Exceptions in Increments in E.

1. Nouns in *en, enis* (except *Hymen*), lengthen their increment as, *Sīren, Sīrēnis.* So, *Aniēnis, Nēriēnis,* from *Anio* and *Nerio,* or rather from the obsolete *Anien* and *Nēriēnes*.

2. *Iheres, lŏcŭples, mansues, merces,* and *quies*—also *Iber, ver, lex, rex, ălec* or *ălex* (*hāl-*) *narthex* and *vervex*—*plebs* and *seps*—increase long.

3. Greek nouns in *es* and *er* (except *aër* and *œther*) increase long; as, *magnes, magnētis; crāter, crātēris.*

Exceptions in Increments in I.

1. Nouns and adjectives in *ix,* increase long; as, *victrix, victrīcis fēlix fēlicis.*

EXC. *Cĭlix, Cĭlix, coxendix, fĭlix, fornix, hystrix, lărix, nix, pix, sălix, strix* and rarely *sandix* or *sandyx,* increase short.

2. *Vibex* and the following nouns in *is* increase long:—*dis, glis, lis, vis, Nĕsis, Quĭris,* and *Samnis.* The increment of *Psŏphis* is common.

3. Greek nouns, whose genitive is in *inis* increase long; as, *delphin, delphīnis; Sălămis, Sălămīnis.*

Exceptions in Increments in U.

1. Genitives in *udis, uris,* and *utis,* from nominatives in *us,* have the penult long; as,

pălus, pălūdis; tellus, tellūris; virtus, virtūtis. But *intercus, Ligus* and *pecus pecŭdis,* increase short.

2. *Fur, frux,* (obs.), *lux,* and *Pollux,* increase long.

Exceptions in Increments in Y.

1. Greek nouns whose genitive is in *ynis,* increase long; as, *Trāchyn, Trāchўnis.*

2. The increment of *bombyx, Ceÿx, gryps,* and *mormyr,* is long; that of *Bebrux* and *sandyx* is common.

INCREMENTS OF THE PLURAL NUMBER.

§ 288. 1. A noun in the plural number is said to increase, when, in any case, it has more syllables than in the ablative singular.

REMARK. When the ablative singular is wanting, or its place is supplied by a form derived from a different root, an ablative may, for this purpose, be assumed, by annexing the proper termination to the root of the plural.

2. When a noun increases in the plural number, its penult is called the plural increment; as, *sa* in *mūsārum, no* in *dŏmĭnōrum, pa* in *răpium* and *răpĭbus.*

§ 289, 290. PROSODY.—QUANTITY—INCREMENT OF VERBS. 329

3. In plural increments, *a, e,* and *o,* are long, *i* and *u* are short as,

bŏnārum, ănĭmābus, rērum, rēbus, gĕnĕrōrum, ambōbus; sermōnĭbus, lăcŭbus Thus,

Appia, *longārum,* tĕrĭtur, rēgīna *viārum. Stat.* S. 2, 2, 12.
Sunt lacrўmæ *rērum,* et mentem mortālia tangunt. *Virg.* A. 1, 462.
Atque ălĭi, *quōrum* cōmœdia prisca *virōrum* est. *Hor.* S. 1, 4, 2.
Portŭbus ĕgrĕdior, ventisque *fĕrentĭbus* ūsus. *Ovid.*

IV. INCREMENT OF VERBS.

§ **289.** 1. A verb is said to increase, when, in any of its parts, it has more syllables than in the second person singular of the present indicative active; as, *das, dă-tis; dŏces, dŏ-cē-mus.*

2. The number of increments in any part of a verb is equal to that of its additional syllables. In verbs, as in nouns, the last syllable is never considered the increment. If a verb has but one increment, it is the penult; and this first increment, through all the variations of the verb, except in reduplicated tenses, continues equally distant from the first syllable. The remaining increments are numbered successively from the first; as,

ă-mas,	mŏ-nes,	au-dis,
1	1	1
ă-mā-mus,	mŏ-nē-tur,	au-dī-tis,
1 2	1 2	1 2
ăm-ă-bā-mus,	mŏn-ē-rē-tur,	au-di-ē-bas,
1 2 3	1 2 3	1 2 3 4
ăm-ă-vĕ-rā-mus.	mŏn-ē-bĭm-ĭ-ni.	au-di-ē-băm-ĭ-ni.

3. A verb in the active voice may have three increments; in the passive, it may have four.

4. In determining the increments of deponent verbs, an active voice, formed from the same root, may be supposed.

                     1   1 2
Thus the increments of *læ-tă-tur, læt-ā-bā-tur,* etc., are reckoned from the supposed verb *læto, lætas.*

§ **290.** In the increments of verbs, *a, e,* and *o,* are long; *i* and *u* are short; as,

ămāre, mŏnēre, făcĭtōte, vŏlŭmus, rĕgēbāmĭni. Thus,

Et *cantāre* pāres, et *respondēre* pārāti. *Virg.* E. 7, 5.
Sic ēquīdem *dūcēbam* ănĭmo, rēbarque fŭtūrum. *Id.* A. 6, 690.
Cumque lŏqui pŏtĕrit, mātrem *făcĭtōte* sălūtet. *Ovid,* M. 9, 378.
Scindĭtur incertum stŭdia in contrāria vulgus. *Virg.* A. 2, 39.
Nos nŭmĕrus *sŭmus,* et frŭges consūmĕre nāti. *Hor.* Ep. 1, 2, 27.

(*a.*) *Exceptions in Increments in* A.

The *first* increment of *do* is short; as, *dămus, dăbāmus, dăret, dă-'ūrus, circumdăre, circumdăbāmus.*

(b.) *Exceptions in Increments in* E.

1. *E* before *r* is short in the *first* increment of all the present and imperfect tenses of the third conjugation, and in the *second* increment in *bĕris* and *bĕre*; as,

rĕgĕre (infin. and imperat.), *rĕgĕris* or *rĕgĕre* (pres. ind. pass.), *rĕgĕrem* and *rĕgĕrer* (imp. subj.); *ămābĕris, ămābĕre; mŏnēbĕris, mŏnēbĕre*.

NOTE 1. In *vĕlim, vĕlis*, etc., from *vŏlo*, (second person, regularly *vŏlis*, by syncope and contraction *vīs*), *ĕ* is not an increment, but represents the root vowel *ŏ*, and is therefore short; § 284, and § 178, 1.

2. *E* is short before *ram, rim, ro*, and the persons formed from them; as,

ămāvĕram, ămāvĕrat, ămāvĕrim, mŏnuĕrĭmus, rexĕro, audīvĕritis.

NOTE 2. In verbs which have been shortened by syncope or otherwise, *e* before *r* retains its original quantity; as, *flēram*, for *flēvĕram*.

For the short *e* before *runt*, in the perfect indicative, as, *stĕtĕrunt*, see *Systole*, § 307.

(c.) *Exceptions in Increments in* I.

1. *I* before *v* or *s*, in tenses formed from the second root, is long; as,

pĕtīvi, audīvi, quæsīvit, dīvīsit, audīvĭmus, divīsĭmus, audīvĕram.

2. *I* is long, after the analogy of the fourth conjugation, in the final syllable of the third root of *gaudeo, arcesso, divĭdo, făcesso, lăcesso, pĕto, quæro, rĕcenseo* and *obliviscor;* as,

gāvīsus, arcessītus, divīsus, făcessītus, lăcessītus, pĕtītus, quæsītus, rĕcensītus, oblītus; gāvīsūrus, etc.

3. *I* in the first increment of the fourth conjugation, except in *ĭmus* of the perfect indicative, is long; as,

audīre, audīrem, audītus, audītūrus, pres. *vĕnīmus*, but in the perfect *vēnĭmus*. So in the ancient forms in *ībam, ībo*, of the fourth conjugation; as, *nutrībat, lēnībunt;* and also in *ībam* and *ībo*, from *eo*.

NOTE 3. When a vowel follows, the *i* is short, by § 283; as, *audĭunt, audĭēbam*.

4. *I* is long in the first and second persons plural of subjunctives in *sim, sis, sit*, etc., (§ 162, 1,); as, *sīmus, sītis, vĕlīmus, vĕlītis*, and their compounds; as, *possīmus, adsīmus, mālīmus, nōlīmus*. So also in *nōlīto, nōlīte, nōlītōte*, after the analogy of the fourth conjugation.

5. *I* in *ris, rimus* and *ritis*, in the future perfect and perfect subjunctive, is common; as,

vidĕris, Mart.,*occidĕris*, Hor.; *vidĕrītis* (Ovid), *dēdĕrītis* (Id.); *fēcĕrīmus* (Catull.), *ēgĕrīmus* (Virg.)

(d.) *Exceptions in Increments in* U.

U is long in the increment of supines, and of participles formed from the third root of the verb; as,

sĕcūtus, sŏlūtus, sĕcūtūrus, sŏlūtūrus.

RULES FOR THE QUANTITY OF PENULTIMATE AND ANTEPENULTIMATE SYLLABLES.

I. PENULTS.

§ 291. 1. Words ending in *acus, icus,* and *icum,* shorten the penult; as,

āmārăcus, Ægyptiăcus, rustĭcus, trĭtĭcum, viătĭcum.

Except *Dācus, mērācus, ŏpācus; āmīcus, aprīcus, fīcus, mendīcus, pīcus, postīcus, pūdīcus, spīcus, umbīlīcus, vīcus.*

2. Words ending in *abrum, ubrum, acrum,* and *atrum,* lengthen the penult; as,

candēlābrum, dēlūbrum, lāvācrum, vērātrum.

3. Nouns in *ca* lengthen the penult; as,

ăpŏthēca, cloāca, lactūca, lōrīca, phōca.

Except *ălĭca, brassĭca, dĭca, fŭlĭca, mantĭca, pĕdĭca, pertĭca, scŭtĭca, phălārĭca, tūnĭca, vŏmĭca;* and also some nouns in *ica* derived from adjectives in *icus;* as, *fabrĭca, grammătĭca,* etc. So *mănĭcæ.*

4. Patronymics in *ades* and *ides* shorten the penult; as, *Atlantiădes, Priămĭdes.*

Except those in *ides* which are formed from nouns in *eus* or *ēs* (ης); as, *Atrīdes,* from *Atrēus; Neoclīdes,* from *Neoclēs;* except, also, *Amphiărāĭdes, Bēlĭdes, Amŷclĭdes, Lŷcurgĭdes.*

5. Patronymics and similar words in *ais, eis,* and *ois,* lengthen the penult; as,

Achāis, Chrȳsēis, Mīnōis. Except *Phōcăis* and *Thēbăis.* The penult of *Nĕreis* is common.

6. Words in *do* lengthen the penult; as,

vādo, cēdo, dulcēdo, formīdo, rōdo, testūdo. Except *cădo, dĭvĭdo, ĕdo* (to eat), *comĕdo, Macĕdo, mŏdo, sŏlĭdo, spădo, trĕpĭdo. Rudo* is common.

7. Words in *idus* shorten the penult; those in *udus* lengthen it; as,

callĭdus, herbĭdus, limpĭdus, līvĭdus, perfĭdus; crūdus, lūdus, nūdus, sūdus, ūdus. Except *Idus, fīdus, infīdus, nīdus, sīdus.*

8. Nouns in *ga* and *go* lengthen the penult; as,

sāga, collēga, aurīga, rūga; īmāgo, cālīgo, ærūgo. Except *cālīga, ossīfrăga, tŏga, plăga,* (a region, or a net), *fŭga* and its compounds, *stĕga, eclŏga, ĕgo, harpăgo, lĭgo.*

9. Words in *le, les,* and *lis,* lengthen the penult; as,

crīnāle, mantēle, ancīle; āles, mīles, prōles; annālis, crūdēlis, cīvīlis, cūrūlis.— Except *nūle;*—verbals in *ilis* and *bilis;* as, *ăgĭlis, ămăbĭlis;*—adjectives in *atilis;* as, *umbrātīlis;*—and also, *indŏles, sŏbŏles; pĕriscĕlis, dapsĭlis, grăcĭlis, hŭmĭlis, părĭlis, sĭmĭlis, stĕrĭlis, mūgĭlis, strĭgĭlis.*

10. Words in *elus, ela, elum,* lengthen the penult; as,

phăsēlus, quĕrēla, prēlum. Except *gĕlus, gĕlum, scĕlus.*

11. Diminutives in *olus, ola, olum, ulus, ula, ulum,* also words in

ĭlus, and those in *ulus*, *ula*, and *ulum*, of more than two syllables, shorten the penult; as,

urceŏlus, fīliŏla, lectŭlus, rătiuncŭla, corcŭlum, păbŭlum; rŭtĭlus, garrŭlus, făbŭla. Except *ăsĭlus*.

12. Words in *ma* lengthen the penult; as,

fāma, poēma, rīma, plūma. Except *ănĭma, cŏma, dĕcĭma, lăcrima, victĭma, ădma.*

13. A vowel before final *men* or *mentum* is long; as,

lĕvāmen, grāmen, crīmen, flūmen, jūmentum, ătrāmentum. Except *tămen, cŏlŭmen, Hȳmen, ĕlĕmentum*, and a few verbal nouns derived from verbs of the second and third conjugations; as, *ălĭmentum, dŏcŭmen* or *dŏcŭmentum, ĕmŏlŭmentum, mŏnŭmentum, rĕgĭmen, spĕcĭmen, tĕgĭmen*, etc.

14. Words ending in *imus* shorten the penult; as,

ănĭmus, dĕcĭmus, fĭnĭtĭmus, fortissĭmus, maxĭmus. Except *bīmus, līmus, mīmus, ŏpīmus, quădrīmus, sīmus, trīmus*, and two superlatives, *īmus* and *prīmus*.

NOTE. When an adjective ends in *umus* for *imus*, the quantity remains the same; as, *dĕcŭmus, optŭmus, maxŭmus*, for *dĕcĭmus*, etc.

15. *A, e, o*, and *u*, before final *mus* and *mum*, are long; as,

rāmus, rēmus, extrēmus, prōnus, dūmus, pōmum, vōlēmum. Except *ătŏmus, balsămum, cinnămum, dŏmus, glŏmus, hŭmus, postŭmus, thălămus, tŏmus, călămus, nĕmus.*

16. (*a.*) Words in *na, ne, ni*, and *nis*, lengthen the penult; as,

lāna, ărēna, cărīna, mātrōna, lūna, māne, septēni, octōni, ĭnānis, fīnis, immūnis. Except *advĕna, cottăna, ptĭsăna, mĭna, gĕna, bĕne, sĭne, cănis, cĭnis, jŭvĕnis*; and the following in *ĭna*,—*buccĭna, dŏmĭna, fiscĭna, fēmĭna, fuscĭna, lāmĭna, māchĭna, păgĭna, pătĭna, sarcĭna, tibĭcĭna, trŭtĭna:* and in plur. *ăpĭnæ, nūnæ, nundĭnæ.* So compounds of *gĕno;* us, *indĭgĕna*.

(*b.*) Verbs in *ino* and *inor* shorten the penult; as,

destĭno, fascĭno, inquĭno, sĭno, crimĭnor. Except *festīno, propīno, săgīno, ŏpīnor*, and the compounds of *clino;* as, *inclīno*, etc.

17. (*a.*) Adjectives in *inus*, when they express time, or indicate a material or an inanimate substance, shorten the penult; as,

crastĭnus, diūtĭnus, pristĭnus, pĕrendĭnus: făgĭnus, crŏcĭnus, hyăcinthĭnus, ădămantĭnus, crystallĭnus, ŏlĕăgĭnus, bombȳcĭnus. Except *mātūtīnus, rĕpentīnus, vespertīnus.*

(*b.*) Other adjectives and words in *inus* and in *inum* lengthen the penult; as,

canīnus, bīnus, pĕregrīnus, mărīnus, clandestīnus, sŭpīnus: līnum. Except *ăcĭnus, ăsĭnus, coccĭnus, cŏmĭnus, ĕmĭnus, cŏphĭnus, dŏmĭnus, făcĭnus, fātĭcĭnus, prŏtĭnus, sĭnus, termĭnus, gĕmĭnus, circĭnus, mĭnus, vătĭcĭnus, succĭnum, fascĭnum.*

18. *A, e, o*, and *u*, before final *nus* and *num*, are long; as,

urbānus, sĕrēnus, patrōnus, prōnus, mūnus, trĭbūnus, fānum, vēnēnum, dōnum. Except *ănus*, an old woman, *galbănus, mănus, ŏcĕănus, plătănus, ĕbĕnus, gĕnus, ŭmĭgĕnus, pĕnus, tĕnus, Vĕnus, ŏnus, bŏnus, sŏnus, thrŏnus; lăgănum, peucĕdănum, pŏpănum, tympănum, abrŏtŏnum.*

19. Words ending in *ba, bo, pa*, and *po*, shorten the penult; as,

făba, jŭba, syllăba; bĭbo, cŭbo, prŏbo; ălăpa, lŭpa, scăpha; crĕpo, partĭcĭpo. Except *glēba, scrība, būbo, glūbo, lĭbo, nūbo, scrībo, sīpho, cēpa, cūpa, pāpa, pūpa, rīpa, scōpa, stūpa; cāpo, rēpo, stīpo.*

20. Words in *al*, *ar*, *are*, and *aris*, lengthen the penult; as,

tribūnal, vectīgal: lupānar, pulvīnar; altāre, lāqueāre; nāris. Except *animal, cāpital, cūbital, tōral, jūbar, sălar, măre, bĭmāris, hilāris, canthāris, cappāris, lĕăris.*

21. Before final *ro* or *ror*, *a* and *e* are short; *i*, *o*, and *u*, are long as,

ăro, păro, fĕro, gĕro, sĕro, cĕlĕro, tempĕro, quĕror; mīror, spīro, tīro; auctōro, ignōro, ōro; cūro, dūro, fĭgūro; lūror. Except *dēclāro, pēro, spēro; fōro, mōror, sōror, rōro, fūro, sătūro;* and derivatives from genitives increasing short as, *augŭror, dĕcŏro, mĕmŏro, murmŭro*, etc.; from *augur, augŭris; dĕcus, dĕcŏris*, etc.

22. Before final *rus*, *ra*, *rum*, *e* is short; the other vowels are long; as,

mĕrum, mĕrus, hĕdĕra, sĕrum, cĕtĕrum; cārus, mīrus, mōrus, mūrus, gȳrus; āra, spīra, ōra, nātūra, lōrum.

Except, 1. *austērus, gălērus, plērus, prōcērus, sincērus, sērus, sĕvērus, vērus, crătēra, cēra, pēra, panthēra, stătēra.*

Exc. 2. *barbărus, cinnărus, cămŭrus, canthărus, chŏrus, fŏrus, hellĕbŏrus, nŭrus, ŏpĭpărus, ŏvĭpărus, phosphŏrus, pĭrus, sătȳrus, scărus, spărus, tartărus, tŏrus, zĕphȳrus; amphŏra, ancŏra, cithăra, hăra, lyra, mŏra, purpŭra, philyra, pyra, sătĭra; fŏrum, gărum, părum, suppărum.*

23. Adjectives in *osus* lengthen the penult; as,

fūmōsus, vīnōsus.

24. Nouns in *etas* and *itas* shorten the penult; as,

piĕtas, civĭtas, bonĭtas.

25. Adverbs in *tim* lengthen the penult, those in *iter* and *itus* shorten it; as,

stātim, (constantly), *vīrītim, trĭbūtim; ācrĭter, fundĭtus.* Except *stătim*, (immediately), *affātim.*

26. (*a*.) Words in *ates*, *itis*, *otis*, and in *ata*, *eta*, *ota*, *uta*, lengthen the penult, as,

vātes, pēnātes, vītis, mītis, cāryōtis, Icārĭōtis, pīrāta, mēta, poēta, ălūta, cĭcūta. Except *sĭtis, pŏtis, drăpĕta, nŏta, rŏta.*

(*b*.) Nouns in *ita* shorten the penult; as,

dmĭta, nāvĭta, orbĭta, sēmĭta. Except *pĭtuĭta.*

27. Nouns in *atum*, *itum*, *utum*, lengthen the penult; as,

lupātum, ăcŏnītum, vĕrūtum. Except *dēfrūtum, pulpĭtum, pĕtŏrĭtum, lŭtum* (mud) *compĭtum.*

28. Nouns and adjectives ending in *tus* lengthen the penult; as,

barbātus, grātus, bōlētus, făcētus, crīnītus, pērītus, ægrōtus, tōtus, argūtus, hirsūtus. Except *cătus, lătus,* (-*cris*), *impĕtus, mĕtus, vĕgĕtus, vĕtus; ănhĕlĭtus, dĭgĭtus, grăvĭtus, hālĭtus, hospĭtus, servĭtus, spīrĭtus; antĭdŏtus, nŏtus, quŏtus, tŏtus* (so great); *arbŭtus, pŭtus; inclȳtus;* and derivatives from perfect participles having a short penult; as, *exercĭtus, hăbĭtus.*

29. A penultimate vowel before *v* is long; as,

clāva, ōlīva, dīves, nāvis, cīvis, pāpāver, pāro, privo, ōvum, prāvus, æstīvus fŭgĭtīvus. Except *āvis, brĕvis, grăvis, lĕvis, ŏvis; căvo, grăvo, jŭvo, lăvo, lĕvo, novo; dĭvus, căvus, făvus novus, făvor, păvor, nŏvem.*

30. Words ending in *dex, dix, mex, nix, lex, rex*, lengthen the enult; as,

cŏdex, jūdex; lōdix, rādix; cīmex, pūmex; jūnix; īlex; cārex, mūrex. Except cŭlex, sĭlex, rŭmex.

II. ANTEPENULTS

§ 292. 1. *I* is short in diminutives in *iculus* and *icellus* (a, um) whether nouns or adjectives; as,

vollĭcŭlus, dulcĭcŭlus, crătĭcŭla, pellĭcŭla, mollĭcellus. Except words in which the preceding vowel is short; as, cŭtīcŭla, cănĭcŭla: or in which *i* is long in the primitive; as, cornīcŭla, from cornix, -ĭcis.

2. Numerals in *ginti, ginta, ēni*, and *esĭmus*, lengthen the antepenult; as,

vīginti, quădrāginta, trĭcēni, quinquāgēsĭmus.

3. *O* and *u* before final *lentus* are short; as,

vinŏlentus, fraudŭlentus, pulvĕrŭlentus, trŭcŭlentus.

4. A vowel before final *nea, neo, nia, nio, nius, nium*, is long; as,

ārānea, līnea, cāneo, mānia, pūnio, Fărōnius, patrĭmōnium. Except castănea, tĭnea, mŭneo, mĭneo, mŏnĕo, sĕneo, tĕneo, ignōmĭnia, luscĭnia, vĕnia, lĭnio, rĕnio, ingĕnium, gĕnius, sĕnio, sĕnium; words in *cinium*, as, lēnōcĭnium; and derivatives in *onius*, when *o* in the root of the primitive is short; as, Agāmemnŏnius, from Agămemnon, -ŏnis.

5. Words ending in *areo, arius, arium, erium, orius, orium*, lengthen the antepenult; as,

āreo, cĭbārius, plantārium, dictērium, censōrius, tentŭrium. Except cāreo, vărius, dēsĭdērium, impērium, măgistērium, mĭnistērium.

6. Adjectives in *aticus, atilis*, lengthen the antepenult; as,

ăquātĭcus, plumātĭlis. Except some Greek words in *ăticus*; as, grammătĭcus

7. *I* before final *tudo* is short; as,

altĭtūdo, longĭtūdo.

8. Verbals in *bĭlis* lengthen *a* but shorten *i* in the antepenult; as,

ămābĭlis, mīrābĭlis; crēdĭbĭlis, terrĭbĭlis. In hăbĭlis, *b* belongs to the root.

9. *U* before *v* is short, (except in *Jŭverna*); as,

jŭvĕnis, jŭvĕnālis, jŭvĕnĭlĭtas, flŭvius, dĭlŭvium.

III. PENULT OF PROPER NAMES.

§ 293. 1. Patrials and proper names of more than two syllables, found in the poets with the following terminations, *shorten* the penult:—

ba,	de,	o,[6]	ges,	dus,[13]	ena,[19]	arus,	atus,[22]
ca,	le,[4]	on,[7]	les,	eus,[14]	anes,	erus,[21]	itus,[23]
la,[2]	pe,[5]	os,[8]	lis,[10]	gus,[15]	enes,	yrus,	otus.[24]
be,	re,	er,[9]	bus,	lus,[16]	aris,	asus,	
ce,[3]	al,	mas,	cus,[11]	mus,[17]	yris,	osus,	
che,	il,	ras,	chus,[12]	phus,[18]	asis,[20]	usus,	

§ 293   PROSODY.—QUANTITY—PENULTS.   335

Exceptions.

¹Marīca, Nāsīca.—²Eriphȳla, Messāla, Philōmēla, Suādēla.—³Berenīce.—⁴Eriphȳle, Neōbūle, Perimēle.—⁵Eurōpe, Sīnōpe.—⁶Carthāgo, Cūpāvo, Cūpīdo, Orīgo, Theāno.—⁷Alēmon, Anthēdon, Chalcēdon, Iāson, Philēmon, Polȳpēmon, Sarpēdon, Thermōdon.—⁸Cercȳros, Pēpārēthos, Pharsālos, Scrīphos.—⁹Mēleāger.—¹⁰Bessālis, Eumēlis, Jūvēnālis, Martiālis, Phāsēlis, Stȳmphālis.—¹¹Benācus, Caīcus, Grānīcus, Nūmīcus, Trivīcus.—¹²Ophiūchus.—¹³Abȳdus.—¹⁴Cāphāreus, Enīpeus, Prōmētheus, Phōrōneus, Salmōneus, Oīleus.—¹⁵Cēthōgus.—¹⁶*Names in* -clus, *in* -olus (*except* Æolus, Naubōlus), *in* -bulus, (*except* Bibūlus) Eumēlus, Gætūlus, Iūlus, Massȳlus, Orbēlus, Pharsālus, Sardānāpālus, Stȳmphālus.—¹⁷*Some in* -dēmus *and* -phēmus; *as,* Acādēmus, Polȳphēmus.—¹⁸Scrīphus.—¹⁹Alcmēna, Athēnæ, Cāmēna, Fīdēna, Messēna, Mūrēna, Mycēnæ.—²⁰Amāsis.—²¹Hōmērus, Ibērus.—²²Arātus, Cærātus, Torquātus.—²³Hērāclītus, Hermāphrōdītus.—²⁴Būthrōtus.

2. Proper names of more than two syllables, found in the poets with the following terminations, *lengthen* the penult:—

ana,¹   sa,   num,⁷   tas,   nus,¹²   urus,   etus,¹⁶
ina,²   ta,⁴   tum,   des,⁹   pus,¹³   esus,¹⁵ utus,
ona,³   tæ,⁵   or,⁸   tes,¹⁰   irus,   isus,   ytus,¹⁷
yna,   ene,⁶   nas,   tis,¹¹   orus,¹⁴ ysus,   vus.

Exceptions.

¹Sēquāna.—²Mutīna, Prōserpīna, Ruspīna, Sarsīna.—³Axōna, Matrōna.—⁴Dalmāta, Prochȳta, Sarmāta, Lāpītha.—⁵Galātæ, Jaxāmētæ, Massāgētæ, Macētæ, Saurōmātæ.—⁶Clȳmēne, Hēlēne, Melpōmēne, Nyctīmēne.—⁷Arīmīnum, Drēpānum.—⁸Nūmītor.—⁹Miltīādes, Pȳlādes, Sōtādes, Thūcȳdīdes; *patronymics in* -des, (§ 291, 4,) *and plurals in* -ades.—¹⁰Antīphātes, Chārītes, Eurybātes, Ichnōbātes, Euergētes, Massāgētes, *and all names in* -crates.—¹¹Dercētis.—¹²Apīdānus, Apōnus, Cārānus, Chrȳsōgōnus, Cīmīnus, Clȳmēnus, Concānus, Dardānus, Diādūmēnus, Eārīnus, Erīdānus, Fūcīnus, Hēlēnus, Lībānus, Morīni, Mȳcōnus, Nebrōphōnus, Olēnus, Periclȳmēnus, Rhōdānus, Santōnus, Sēquāni, Stēphānus, Telēgōnus, Termīnus, *and names in* -gonus *and* -xenus.—¹³Œdīpus.—¹⁴Pācōrus, Bospōrus, *and names in* -chorus *and* -phorus; *as,* Stēsīchōrus, Phosphōrus.—¹⁵Ephēsus, Vogēsus, Volēsus.—¹⁶Iāpētus, Tāȳgētus, Vēnētus.—¹⁷Epȳtus, Anȳtus, Eurȳtus, Hippōlȳtus.

3. The penultimate vowel of the following proper names, and adjectives derived from proper names, though followed by a vowel, is long. See § 283, I. Exc. 6.

Æneūs, Æthīon, Achelōus, Achillēus, Alcyōneus, Alexandrīa, Alōeus, Alphēus, Amīnēus, Amphīārāus, Amphīgēnīa, Amphīon, Amȳthāon, Arīon, Anchīseus, Atlantēus, Antīochīa, Biōneus, Cæsārēa, Cālaurēa, Callīōpēa, Cassīōpēa, Cleanthēas, Cȳdōnēus, Cȳmōdōcēa, Cȳthērēa, Dārīus (-ēus), Dēīdamīa, Didȳmāon, Diōmēdēus, Dolīchāon, Echīon, Elēus, Endȳmīōnēus, Enȳo, Eōus, Erēbēus, Erecthēus, Gālātēa, Gigantēus, Hērāclēa (-ēus), Hippōdamīa, Hȳperīon, Ilithȳīa, Imāon, Iōlāus, Iphīgēnīa, Lāōdāmīa, Lātōus, Lesbōus, Lȳcæum, Māchāon, Mausōlēum, Mēdēa, Menēlāus, Methīon, Myrtōus, Ophīon, Orīon, Orīthȳīa, Orphēus, Pallantēum (-us), Pandīon, Paphagēa, Pēnēus, Penthēsīlēa, Phœbēus, Poppēa, Prōtesīlāus, Pȳrēnēus, Sardōus, Thālīa.

NOTE. *Eus* in the termination of Greek proper names, is commonly a diphthong; as, *Alceus, Œneus, Orpheus, Pēleus, Perseus, Prōteus, Thēseus, Tȳdeus,* which are dissyllables; *Brīāreus, Enīpheus, Macāreus, Typhōeus,* which are trisyllables, *Idōmēneus,* etc. Cf. § 283, Exc. 6, Note 2. But in those which in Greek are written υες (*eios*), *eus* forms two syllables; as, *Alphēus.* So also in adjectives in *eus*, whether of Greek or Latin origin; as, *Erēbēus, Erecthēus, Orphēus; aurēus, lignēus.*

QUANTITY OF FINAL SYLLABLES.

I. VOWELS.

MONOSYLLABLES.

§ 294. (a.) All monosyllables, except enclitics, ending in a vowel, are long; as,

ā, āh, dā, stā, ē, dē, mē, tē, sē, nē, rē, ī, fī, hī, quī, nī, sī, O or ōh, dō, prō, prōh, quō, stō, tū.

POLYSYLLABLES.

A *final*.

1. *A* final, in words declined, is short; as, *mŭsă, templă, căpĭtă, Tÿdĕă*. Thus,

Mūsă mihi causas mĕmŏră; quo nūmĭne laeso.... *Virg.* A. 1, 8.

Exc. *A* final is long in the ablative of the first declension, and in the vocative of Greek nouns in *as* and *es*; as,

Mūsā, fundā; O Æneā, O Pallā, O Anchisā.

2. *A* final, in words not declined, is long; as, *ămā, frustrā, anteā, ergā, intrā*. Thus,

Extrā fortūnam est quidquid dōnātur ămīcis. *Mart.* Epig. 5, 42, 7.

Exc. *A* final is short in *eiă, ită, quiă*, and in *pŭtă*, when used adverbially, in the sense of 'for example.' It is sometimes short in the preposition *contră*, and in numerals ending in *ginta*; as, *trīginta*, etc. In *posteă*, it is common.

A final is also short in the names of Greek letters; as, *alphă, bētă*, etc., and in *tărătantără*, the imitated sound of the trumpet.

E *final*.

§ 295. *E* final, in words of two or more syllables, is short; as, *nătĕ, patrĕ, ipsĕ, currĕ, rĕgĕrĕ, nempĕ, antĕ*. Thus,

Incĭpĕ, parvĕ puer, rīsu *cognoscĕrĕ* mātrem. *Virg.* E. 4, 60.

REMARK. The enclitics *-que, -ne, -ve, -ce, -te, -pte*, etc., as they are not used alone, have *e* short, according to the rule; as, *nĕquĕ, hŭjuscĕ, suaptĭ* Cf. § 294, (*a*.)

Exc. 1. *E* final is long in nouns of the first and fifth declensions as,

Calliŏpē, Tÿdīdē, fīdē. So also in the compounds of *rē* and *diē*; as, *quārē, hŏdiē, prĭdiē, postrĭdiē, quŏtĭdiē*, and in the ablative *fāmē*, originally of the fifth declension.

Exc. 2. *E* final is long in Greek vocatives from nouns in *-es*, of the third declension; as, *Achillē, Hippŏmĕnē*; and in Greek neuters plural; as, *cētē, mēlē pĕlăgē, Tempē*.

Exc. 3. In the second conjugation, *e* final is long in the second person singular of the imperative active; as, *dŏcē, mŏnē*;—but it is sometimes short in *căvĕ, vălĕ* and *vĭdĕ*.

§ 296–298. PROSODY.—QUANTITY OF FINAL SYLLABLES. 337

Exc. 4. *E* final is long in adverbs formed from adjectives of the second declension; as,

plăcĭdē, pulchrē, valdē for *vălĭdē, maxĭmē;* but it is short in *bĕnĕ, mălĕ, infernĕ,* and *supernĕ.*

Exc. 5. *Fĕrē, fermē,* and *ŏhē,* have the final *e* long.

I final.

§ 296. *I* final is long; as, *dŏmĭnī, fīlī, classī, dŏcērī, sī.* Thus,

Quid dŏmĭnī făcient, audent cum tălia fūres. *Virg.* E. 3, 16.

Exc. 1. (*a.*) *I* final is common in *mĭhi, tĭbi, sĭbi, ĭbi,* and *ŭbi.*

(*b.*) In *ŭbīque* and commonly in *ĭbīdem* it is long, but in *ŭbĭvis* and *ŭbĭnam* it is short.—(*c.*) In *nĭsi, quăsi,* and *cui,* when a dissyllable, *i* final is common, but usually short. In *ŭtĭnam* and *ŭtĭque,* and rarely, also, in *ŭti,* it is short.

Exc. 2. *I* final is short in the dative singular of Greek nouns of the third declension, which increase in the genitive; as, *Pallădĭ, Minŏĭdĭ, Tēthyĭ.*

Exc. 3. *I* final is short in the vocative of Greek nouns in *-is;* as, *Alexĭ, Daphnĭ, Părĭ.* But it is long in vocatives from Greek nouns in *-is,* (υς) *-entos;* as, *Sĭmoī, Pȳrōī.*

Exc. 4. *I* final is short in Greek datives and ablatives plural in *-si,* or, before a vowel, *-sin:* as, *Dryăsĭ, hērōĭsĭ, Trōăsĭn.*

O final.

§ 297. *O* final, in words of two or more syllables, is common; as, *virgŏ, ămŏ, quandŏ.* Thus,

Ergŏ mĕtu căpĭta Scylla est ĭnĭmīca păterno. *Virg.* Cir. 386.
Ergō sollĭcĭtæ tu causa, pĕcūnia, vītæ es! *Prop.* 3, 5, 1.

Exc. 1. *O* final is long in the dative and ablative singular; as, *dŏmĭnō, regnō, bonō, suō, illō, eō.*

Exc. 2. *O* final is long in ablatives used as adverbs; as, *certō, falsō, mĕrĭtō, vulgō, eō, quō;* and also in *omnīnō,* in *ergō,* 'for the sake of,' and in the interjection *iō.*

REMARK 1. The final *o* of verbs is almost always long in poets of the Augustan age.

REM. 2. In poets subsequent to the Augustan age, final *o* in verbs, in gerunds, and in the adverbs *ădeo, ĭdeo, ergo, sēro, vēro, porro, retro, immo, ĭdcirco, sŭbĭto,* and *postrēmo,* is sometimes short.

Exc. 3. *O* final is short in *cĭto, illĭco, prŏfecto,* and the compounds of *mŏdo;* as, *dummŏdŏ, postmŏdŏ,* etc.; and in *ĕgo* and *hŏmo* it is more frequently short than long.

Exc. 4. *O* final in Greek nouns written with an omega (ω) is long; as, *Clĭō, Dĭdō, Ăthō,* and *Andrŏgeō,* (gen.)

U final.

§ 298. 1. *U* final is long; as, *vultū, cornū. Panthū, dictū, dĭū.* Thus,

Vultū, quo cœlum tempestātesque sĕrēnat. *Virg.* A. 1, 255.

29

Exc. *Indŭ* and *nĕnŭ*, ancient forms of *in* and *non*, have *u* short. *U* is also short in terminations in *ŭs* short, when *s* is removed by elision; as, *cŏntentŭ* for *contentŭs*. See § 305, 2.

Y final.

2. *Y* final is short; as, *Mōlў*, *Tīphў*. Thus,

Mōlў vŏcant sūpĕri: nigrā rādīce tĕnētur. *Ovid.* M. 14, 292.

Exc. *Y* in the dative *Tēthȳ*, being formed by contraction, is long. § 283, III

II. CONSONANTS.

MONOSYLLABLES.

§ **299** 1. Monosyllabic *substantives* ending in a consonant are long; all other monosyllables ending in a consonant are short; as,

sōl, vīr, fūr, jūs, splēn, vēr, fār, lār, Nār, pār, Sēr, fūr, fās, mās, rēs, pēs, Dīs, glīs, līs, vīs, flōs, mōs, rōs, Trōs, ōs, (*ōris*), *dōs, grūs, rūs, lūs ;—nĕc, ĭn, ăn, ăb, ĕd, quĭd, quĭs, quŏt, ĕt;* as,

Ipse dŏcet quĭd ăgam. Făs est ĕt ăb hoste dŏcēri. *Ovid.* M. 4, 428.
Vēr ădeo frondi nĕmōrum, vēr ūtile silvis. *Virg.* G. 2, 323.

NOTE. The rules for the quantity of final syllables ending in a consonant imply that the consonant is single, and that it is preceded by a single vowel. If otherwise the syllable will be long by § 283, IV. and II.

EXC. 1. *Cŏr, fĕl, mĕl, pŏl, vĭr, ŏs* (gen. *ossis*), and probably *vas* (*vădis*), are short.

EXC. 2. *En, nōn, quin, sīn, crās, plūs, cūr,* and *pār*, are long: so also are particles and pronouns ending in *c*, except *nĕc*, which is short, and the pronouns *hic* and *hoc*, in the nominative and accusative, which are common.

EXC. 3. Monosyllabic plural cases of pronouns and forms of verbs in *as, es*, and *is*, are long; as, *hās, quās, hōs, nōs, vōs, quōs, hīs, quīs ;—dās, flēs, stēs, īs, fīs, sīs, vīs;* except *ĕs* from *sum* which is short.

EXC. 4. The abridged imperatives retain the quantity of their root; as, *dīc, dūc*, from *dīco, dūco; făc, fĕr*, from *făcio, fĕro*.

POLYSYLLABLES.

D, L, N, R, T, final.

2. Final syllables ending in *d, l, n, r*, and *t*, are short; as *illŭd, consŭl, carmĕn, pătĕr, căpŭt.* Thus,

Obstŭpuit sĭmŭl ipse, sĭmul perculsus Achātes. *Virg.* A. 1, 513.
Nōmĕn Ariŏnium Sicŭlas implēvĕrăt urbes. *Ovid.* F. 2, 93.
Dum lŏquŏr, horrŏr, hăbet; parsque est mĕmĭnisse dŏlōris. *Id.* M. 9, 291.

EXC. 1. *E* in *liēn* is long.

EXC. 2. In Greek nouns, nominatives in *n* (except those in *on* written with an *omicron*), masculine or feminine accusatives in *an* or *en*, and genitives plural in *on*, lengthen the final syllable; as,

Tītān, Oriōn, Ænēān, Anchīsēn, Calliŏpēn; ĕpĭgrammātōn.

§ 300. PROSODY.—QUANTITY OF FINAL SYLLABLES. 339

Exc. 2. *Aēr*, *æthēr*, and nouns in *ēr* which form their genitive in *ĕris*, lengthen the final syllable; as,

cratēr, *sotēr*. So also *Ibēr*; but the compound *Celtĭber* has sometimes *n* Martial its last syllable short.

REMARK. A final syllable ending in *t*, may be rendered long by a diphthong, by contraction, by syncopation, or by position; as, *aut*, *ăbĭt* for *ăbiit*, *fūmŭĭt*, for *fumāvĭt*, *āmānt*. See § 283, II. III. IV., and § 162, 7, (*d.*)

M *final*.

NOTE Final *m* with the preceding vowel is almost always cut off, when the next word begins with a vowel. See *Ecthlipsis*, § 305, 2.

3. Final syllables ending in *m*, when it is not cut off, are short as,

Quam laudas, plūmā? cocto nūm adest honor idem. *Hor.* S. 2, 2, 28.

REMARK. Hence in composition the final syllables of *cum* and *circum* are short; as, *cŏmĕdo*, *circŭmāgo*.

C *final*.

4. Final syllables ending in *c* are long; as, *ālēc*, *illīc*, *istāc*, *illūc*. Thus,

Illīc indocto primum se exēreuit arcu. *Tib.* 2, 1, 69.

Exc. The final syllable of *dōnĕc* is short; as,

Dōnĕc ĕris fēlix, multos nŭmĕrābis ămīcos. *Ovid.* Trist. 1, 9, 5.

AS, ES, and OS, *final*.

§ 300. Final syllables in *as*, *es*, and *os*, are long; as,

mūsās, piĕtās, āmās, Ænēās, quiēs, sermōnēs, diēs, Pēnĕlŏpēs, dūcentiēs, mŏnēs, hŏnōs, virōs, dŏmĭnōs. Thus,

Hās autem terrās, Itālīque hanc litōris ōram. *Virg.* A. 3, 396.
Si modo dēs illis cultus, simĭlēsque pārātus. *Ovid.* M. 6, 454.

Exc. 1. (*a.*) AS. *As* is short in *ănăs*, in Greek nouns whose genitive ends in *ădis* or *ădos*; as, *Arcăs, Pallăs*; and in Greek accusatives plural of the third declension; as, *hērŏăs, lampădăs*.

(*b.*) *As* is short also in Latin nouns in *as*, *ădos*, formed like Greek patronymics; as, *Appiăs*.

Exc. 2. ES. (*a.*) Final *es* is short in nouns and adjectives of the third declension which increase short in the genitive; as, *hospĕs, limĕs, hĕbĕs*; gen. *hospĭtis*, etc.

(*b.*) But it is long in *ăbiēs, ăriēs, păriēs, Cĕrēs*, and *pēs*, with its compounds *cornipēs, sŏnipēs*, etc.

(*c.*) *Es*, in the present tense of *sum* and its compounds, and in the preposition *pĕnēs*, is short.

(*d.*) *Es* is short in Greek neuters in *es*; as, *căcŏēthĕs*, and in Greek nominatives and vocatives plural from nouns of the third declension, which increase in the genitive; as, *Arcădēs, Trŏēs, Amăzŏnēs*; from *Arcas, Arcădis*, etc.

Exc. 3. OS. (*a.*) *Os* is short in *compŏs, impŏs*, and *ŏs* (*ossis*), with its compound *exŏs* (b.) *Os* is short in Greek nouns and cases written in the original with *omĭcron*; as (1) in all neuters; as, *chaŏs, epŏs, Argŏs*; (2) in all nouns of the second declension; as, *Ilŏs, Tўrŏs, Delŏs*; except those whose genitive is in *ō*, (Greek ω); as, *Athŏs,* gen. *Athō*; (3) in genitives singular of the third declension; as, *Pallădŏs, Těthyŏs,* from *Pallĭs* and *Těthys.*

IS, US, and YS, *final.*

§ **301.** Final syllables in *is, us,* and *ys,* are short; as,

turris, militis, mitis, amatis, amabis, magis; pectŭs, bonŭs, ĕjŭs, ămāmŭs, rursŭs, tĕnĭs; Căpўs, Itўs. Thus,

> Non ăpĭs inde tŭlit collectos sēdŭla flōres. *Ovid.* M. 13, 928.
> Sērĭŭs aut citius sōdem *prŏpĕrāmŭs* ad ūnam. *Id.* M. 10, 33.
> At *Căpўs,* et quōrum mēlior sententia menti. *Virg.* A. 2, 35.

EXC. 1. IS. (*a.*) *Is* is long in plural cases; as,

mūsīs, nōbīs; omnīs, urbīs, (for *omnēs, urbēs*); *quīs,* (for *quēis or quĭbus*). So also in the adverbs *grātīs, ingrātīs,* and *fŏrīs,* which are in reality datives or ablatives plural.

> Et liquidi simul ignis; ut his exordia *primis. Virg.* A. 6, 33.
> Quis ante ōra patrum Trōjæ sub mœnibus altis. *Id.* A. 1, 95.
> Non omnīs arbusta jŭvant, hūmĭlesque myrīcæ. *Id.* E. 4, 2.
> Adde tŏt ēgrĕgias *urbīs,* ŏpĕrumque lăbōrem. *Id.* G. 2, 155.

(*b.*) *Is* is long in the nominative of nouns whose genitive ends in *ītis, īnis,* or *entis;* as, *Samnīs, Salămīs, Simoīs.*

(*c.*) *Is* is long in the second person singular of the present indicative active of the fourth conjugation; as,

audīs, nescīs. So also in the second persons, *fīs, īs, sīs, vīs, vĕlīs,* and their compounds; as, *adsīs, possīs, quamvīs, mālīs, nōlīs,* etc. Cf. § 299, 1, Exc. 3.

(*d.*) *Rīs,* in the future perfect and perfect subjunctive, is common; as, *vidĕrīs.*

EXC. 2. US. (*a.*) *Us* is long in nouns of the third declension which increase long, and in the genitive singular, and the nominative, accusative, and vocative plural of the fourth declension, (§ 89, Rem., and § 283, III.); as,

tellūs, virtūs, incūs;—fructūs. But *pălŭs,* with the *us* short, occurs in Horace, Art. Poet. 65.

(*b.*) *Us* is long in Greek nouns written in the original with the diphthong *ous* (ους) whether in the nominative or genitive; as, nom. *Amāthūs, Opūs, Œdipūs, tripūs, Panthūs;* gen. *Dīdūs, Sapphūs.* But compounds of *pus* (πους), when of the second declension, have *us* short; as, *pŏlўpŭs.*

NOTE. The last syllable of every verse, (except the anapæstic and the Ionic *a minōre*), may be either long or short at the option of the poet.

REMARK. By this is meant, that, although the measure require a long syllable, a short one may be used in its stead; and a long syllable may be used where a short one is required; as in the following verses, where the short syllable *ma* stands instead of a long one, and the long syllable *cu* instead of a short one:—

> Sanguineāque mānu crĕpĭtantia concŭtit armā. *Ovid.* M. 1, 143.
> Nŏn ĕget Mauri jăcŭlīs. nec arcū. *Hor.* Od. 1, 22, 2.

VERSIFICATION.

FEET.

§ 302. A foot is a combination of two or more syllables of a certain quantity.

Feet are either simple or compound. Simple feet consist of two or three syllables; compound feet of four.

I. SIMPLE FEET.

1. *Of two Syllables.*

Spondee,	two long, — —; as,	*fŭndŭnt.*
Pyrrhic,	two short, ⌣ ⌣; as,	*Dĕŭs.*
Trochee, or choree,	a long and a short, — ⌣; as,	*ārmă.*
Iambus,	a short and a long, ⌣ —; as,	*ĕrănt.*

2. *Of three Syllables.*

Dactyl,	a long and two short, — ⌣ ⌣; as,	*cŏrpŏră.*
Anapæst,	two short and a long, ⌣ ⌣ —; as,	*dŏmĭnī.*
Tribrach,	three short, ⌣ ⌣ ⌣; as,	*făcĕrĕ.*
Molossus,	three long, — — —; as,	*cōntēndūnt.*
Amphibrach,	a short, a long, and a short, ⌣ — ⌣; as,	*ămārē.*
Amphimacrus, or Cretic,	a long, a short, and a long, — ⌣ —; as,	*cāstĭtās.*
Bacchius,	a short and two long, ⌣ — —; as,	*Cătōnēs.*
Antibacchius,	two long and a short, — — ⌣; as,	*Rōmānŭs.*

II. COMPOUND FEET.

Dispondee,	a double spondee, — — — —; as,	*cōnflīxērūnt.*
Proceleusmatic,	a double Pyrrhic, ⌣ ⌣ ⌣ ⌣; as,	*hŏmĭnĭbŭs.*
Ditrochee,	a double trochee, — ⌣ — ⌣; as,	*cōmprŏbāvĭt.*
Diiambus,	a double iambus, ⌣ — ⌣ —; as,	*ănăvērănt.*
Greater Ionic,	a spondee and a Pyrrhic, — — ⌣ ⌣; as,	*cōrrēxĭmŭs.*
Smaller Ionic,	a Pyrrhic and a spondee, ⌣ ⌣ — —; as,	*prŏpĕrābănt.*
Choriambus,	a choree and an iambus, — ⌣ ⌣ —; as,	*tērrĭfĭcănt.*
Antispast,	an iambus and a choree, ⌣ — — ⌣; as,	*ădhæsĭssē.*
First epitrit,	an iambus and a spondee, ⌣ — — —; as,	*ămāvērūnt.*
Second epitrit,	a trochee and a spondee, — ⌣ — —; as,	*cōndĭtōrēs.*
Third epitrit,	a spondee and an iambus, — — ⌣ —; as,	*dīscōrdĭās.*
Fourth epitrit,	a spondee and a trochee, — — — ⌣; as,	*āddūxĭstīs.*
First pæon,	a trochee and a Pyrrhic, — ⌣ ⌣ ⌣; as,	*tĕmpŏrĭbŭs.*
Second pæon,	an iambus and a Pyrrhic, ⌣ — ⌣ ⌣; as,	*pŏtēntĭă.*
Third pæon,	a Pyrrhic and a trochee, ⌣ ⌣ — ⌣; as,	*ănĭmātŭs.*
Fourth pæon,	a Pyrrhic and an iambus, ⌣ ⌣ ⌣ —; as,	*cĕlĕrĭtās.*

REMARK. Those feet are called *isochronous*, which consist of equal times as the spondee, the dactyl, the anapæst, and the proceleusmatic, one long time being considered equal to two short.

METRE.

§ 303. 1. *Metre* is an arrangement of syllables and feet according to certain rules.

2. In this general sense, it comprehends either an entire verse, a part of a verse, or any number of verses.

3. Metre is divided into *dactylic, anapæstic, iambic, trochaic, choriambic,* and *Ionic.* These names are derived from the original or fundamental foot employed in each.

4. A *metre* or *measure,* in a specific sense, is either a single foot or a combination of two feet. In the dactylic, choriambic, and Ionic metres, a measure consists of one foot; in the other metres, of two feet. Two feet constituting a measure are sometimes called a *syzygy.*

VERSES.

§ 304. A *verse* is a certain number of feet, arranged in a regular order, and constituting a line of poetry.

1. Two verses are called a *distich;* a half verse, a *hemistich.*

2. Verses are of different kinds, denominated sometimes, like the different species of metre, from the foot which chiefly predominates in them; as, *dactylic, iambic,* etc.;—sometimes from the number of feet or metres which they contain; as, *sēnārius,* consisting of six feet; *octōnārius,* of eight feet; *mŏnŏmĕter,* consisting of one measure; *dĭmĕter,* of two; *trĭmĕter, tetramĕter, pentamĕter, hexamĕter;*—sometimes from a celebrated author who used a particular species; as, *Sapphic, Anacreontic, Alcaic, Asclepiadic, Glyconic, Phalæcian, Sotadic, Archilochian, Alcmanian, Pherecratic, Aristophanic,* etc., from *Sappho, Anacreon, Alcæus, Asclepiādes, Glȳcon, Phalæcus, Sotādes, Archilŏchus, Alcman, Pherecrātes, Aristophānes,* etc.—and sometimes from the particular uses to which they were applied; as, the *prosodiac,* from its use in solemn processions, the *parœmiac,* from its frequent use in proverbs.

3. A verse, with respect to the metres which it contains, may be complete, deficient, or redundant.

(1.) A verse which is complete is called *acatalectic.*

(2.) A verse which is deficient, if it wants one syllable at the end, is called *catalectic;* if it wants a whole foot or half a metre, it is called *brachycatalectic.*

(3.) A verse which wants a syllable at the beginning, is called *acephalous.*

(4.) A verse which has a redundant syllable or foot, is called *hypercatalectic* or *hypermĕter.*

4. Hence, the complete name of every verse consists of three terms—the first referring to the *species,* the second to the *number of metres,* and the third to the *ending;* as, the *dactylic trimĕter catalectic*

§ 305.   PROSODY.—VERSIFICATION—FIGURES.   343

5. A verse or portion of a verse of any kind (measured from the beginning) which contains three half feet, or a foot and a half, is called a *trihēmĭmĕris;* if it contains five half feet, or two feet and a half, it is called a *penthēmĭmĕris;* if seven half feet, or three feet and a half, a *hepthēmĭmĕris;* if nine half feet, or four feet and a half, an *ennehēmĭmĕris.* A portion of a verse consisting of one whole metre and a half, is called a *hēmiŏlius,* as being the half of a *trimeter.*

NOTE. The respective situation of each foot in a verse is called its *place.*

6. SCANNING is the dividing of a verse into the feet of which it is composed.

REMARK. In order to scan correctly, it is necessary to know the quantity of each syllable, and also to understand the following poetic usages, which are sometimes called

FIGURES OF PROSODY.

SYNALŒPHA.

§ 305. 1. *Synalœpha* is the elision of a final vowel or diphthong in scanning, when the following word begins with a vowel.

Thus, *terra antīqua* is read *terr' antīqua; Dardănĭdæ infensi, Dardănĭd' infensi; vento huc, vent' huc.* So,

Quidve mōror? si omnes ūno ordĭne hăbētis Achīvos. *Virg.* A. 2, 102.

Which is scanned thus—

Quidve mōror? s' omnes ūn' ordĭn' hăbētis Achīvos.

(1.) The interjections *O, heu, ah, proh, væ, vah,* are not elided; as,

O et de Lătiă, O et de gente Săbīnā. *Ovid.* M. 14, 832.

REMARK. But *O,* though not elided, is sometimes made short; as,

Te Cōrÿdon O Alexi; trăhit sua quemque vŏluptas. *Virg.* E. 2, 65.

(2.) Other long vowels and diphthongs sometimes remain unelided, in which case, when in the thesis of a foot, they are commonly made short; as,

Victor ăpud răpĭdum Sĭmoënta sŭb *Iliŏ* alto. *Virg.* A. 5, 261.
Anni tempŏre eo *quī* Etēsiæ esse fĕruntur. *Lucr.* 6, 717.
Ter sunt *cōnā'ī* impōnĕre *Pēliŏ* Ossam. *Virg.* G. 1, 281.
Glaucō et *Pănŏpēæ,* et Inŏo Mĕlĭcertæ. *Id.* G. 1, 436.

(3.) Rarely a short vowel, also, remains without elision; as,

Et vēra incessu pătuit deă. Ille ŭbi mātrem.... *Virg.* A. 1, 405.

(4.) Synalœpha in a monosyllable occasionally occurs; as,

Si ad vitŭlam spectas, nihil est, quod pocŭla laudes. *Virg.* E. 3, 48.

For synalœpha at the end of a line, see *Synapheia,* § 307, 3.

ECTHLIPSIS.

2. *Ecthlipsis* is the elision of a final *m* with the preceding vowel, when the following word begins with a vowel. Thus,

O cūras hŏmĭn*um,* O quant*um* est in rēbus Ināne! *Pers.* 1, 1.

Which is thus scanned—

O cūras hŏmin' O quant' est in rēbus Ĭnāne.

Monstr*um* horrend*um*, inforne, ingens, cui lūmen ădemptum. *Virg.* A. 3, 658.

(1.) This elision was sometimes om..tted by the early poets; as,

Corpŏr*um* officium est qu*ĭ*niam prēmēre omnia deorsum. *Lucr.* 1, 363.

See § 299, 2.

(2.) Final *s*, also, with the preceding vowel, is sometimes elided by the early poets before a vowel, and sometimes *s* alone before a consonant; as, *content' atque* (Enn.), for *contentus atque*; *omnibu' rēbus*. (*Lucr.*) So,

Tum *lătĕrāli'* dŏlor, *certissĭmu' nunciu'* mortis. *Lucil.*

REMARK. This elision took place principally in short syllables.

For ecthlipsis at the end of a line, see *Synapheia*, § 307, 3.

SYNÆRESIS.

§ **306.** 1. Synæresis is the contraction into one syllable of two vowels which are usually pronounced separately. Thus,

Aureā percussum virgā, versumque vĕnēnis. *Virg.* A. 7, 190.
Eosdem hăbuit sēcum, quĭbus est ēlāta, căpillos. *Prop.* 4, 7, 7.
Tītyre, pascentes a flūmĭne *reice* căpellas. *Virg.* E. 3, 96.

REMARK 1. So *Phaëthon* is pronounced *Phæthon*; *alveo*, *alvo*; *Orphea*, *Orpha*; *deorsum*, *dorsum*.

(1.) Synæresis is frequent in *ii, iidem, iisdem, dii, diis, dein, deinceps, deinde, deest, deërat, deëro, deërit, deesse*; as,

Præcĭpĭtātur ăquis, et ăquis nox surgit ab *ĭsdem*. *Ovid.* M. 4, 92.
Sint Mæcēnātes; non *deerunt*, Flacce, Mārōnes. *Mart.* 8, 56, 5.

REM. 2. *Cui* and *huic* are usually monosyllables.

(2.) When two vowels in compound words are read as one syllable, the former may rather be considered as elided than as united with the latter; as, e in *anteambŭlo, anteïre, antĕhac, dehinc, mehercŭle*, etc., and *a* in *contraïre*.

(3.) The syllable formed by the union of *i* or *u* followed by another vowel retains the quantity of the latter vowel, whether long or short; as, *ăbĭĕte, ărĭĕte, ăbĭĕgnæ, pārĭĕtĭbus, consĭlĭŭm, fortŭĭtus, Nāsĭdĭēnus, vindēmĭător, omnĭă, gĕnuă, tĕnuĭs, pĭtuĭta, fluvĭōrum*, etc. In such examples, the *i* and *u* are pronounced like initial *y* and *w*; as, *ăbyĕte, păryĕtĭbus, consĭlyum, fortwĭtus, Nāsĭdyēnus, omn-yă, tenwĭs, pĭtwĭta*, etc.; and, like consonants, they have, with another consonant, the power of lengthening a preceding short vowel, as in the above examples.

NOTE. In Statius, the word *tĕnuĭōre* occurs as a trisyllable, in which the three vowels, *uio*, are united in pronunciation; thus, *tĕn-wiŏ-re*.

(4.) Sometimes, after a synalœpha or echthlipsis, two vowels suffer synæresis; as, *stellio et*, pronounced *stell-yet*: consilium *et,—consil-yet*.

(5.) If only one of the vowels is *written*, the contraction is called *crasis*; as, *ĭi, consĭli,* for *dii, consĭlii*.

DIÆRESĬS.

2. *Diærĕsis* is the division of one syllable into two; as,

aulāī, Trŏĭa, sĭlŭa, sŭādent; for aulæ, Troia or Troja, silva, suādent. So, suĕsco for suesco; rĕlĭquŭs for ĕlĭquus; ecquĭs for ecquis; milŭus for milvus, etc., as

§ 307. PROSODY.—VERSIFICATION—FIGURES. 345

Æthēreum sensum, atque aurāï simplicis ignem. Virg. A. 6, 747
Atque ālios ālii irrident, Vĕnĕremque *suādent. Lucr.* 4, 1153.
Grammăticī certant; et ădhuc sub *iūdice* lis est. *Hor.* A. P. 78.
Aurārum et *silŭæ* mētu. *Id.* O. 1, 23, 4.

(1.) So in Greek words originally written with a diphthong (*u* or *ɩ*); as, *ἐλεγεία* for *ĕlĕgīa,* Bacchēīă for *Bacchēa*, Rhœtēlŭs for *Rhœtĕus*, Plēīds for *Pīlās* and also in words of Latin origin; as, *Vēīus* for *Veius, Aquilēīă* for *Aquileiă.*

REMARK. This figure is sometimes called *dialȳsis.*

SYSTOLE.

§ 307. 1. *Systŏle* is the shortening of a syllable which is long by nature or by position; as,

vĭdĕ'n for *vĭdesne,* in which *e* is naturally long; *sătī'n* for *sătisne,* in which *i* is long by position;—*hŏdie* for *hōc die; multĭmŏdis* for *multīs mŏdis.* So,

Dūcĕre *multīmŏdis* vōces, et flectĕre cantus. *Lucr.* 5, 1405.

(1.) By the omission of *j* after *ăb, ăd, ŏb, sŭb,* and *rĕ,* in compound words, those prepositions retain their naturally short quantity, which would otherwise be made long by position; as, *ăbĭci, ădĭcit, ŏbĭcis,* etc. Thus,

Si quid nostra tuis *ădĭcit* vexātio rēbus. *Mart.* 10, 82, 1.

REMARK. In some compounds the short quantity of *ăd* and *ŏb* is preserved before a consonant by the elision of the *d* or *b* of the preposition, as in *ăpĕrio, ŏpĕrio, ŏmitto,* etc.

(2.) The penult of the third person plural of certain perfects is said by some to be shortened by systole; as, *stĕtĕrunt, tŭlĕrunt,* etc.; but others ascribe these irregularities to the errors of transcribers, or the carelessness of writers.

DIASTOLE.

2. *Diastŏle* is the lengthening of a syllable which is naturally short.

(1.) It occurs most frequently in proper names and in compounds of *re;* as, *Prĭāmīdes, rēlĭgio,* etc. Thus,

Hanc tĭbi *Prĭāmīdes* mitto, Lēdæa, sălūtem. *Ovid.* H. 16, 1.
Rēlĭgiōne patrum multos servāta per annos. *Virg.* A. 2, 715.

(2.) Some editors double the consonant after the lengthened *re;* as, *rellĭgio.*
(3.) Diastole is sometimes called *ectăsis.*

SYNAPHEIA.

3. *Synapheia* is such a connection of two consecutive verses, that the first syllable of the latter verse has an influence on the final syllable of that which precedes, either by position, synalœpha, or ecthlipsis. See §§ 283 and 305.

(1.) This figure is most frequent in anapæstic verse, and in the *Ionic a minōre.*

The following lines will illustrate its effect:—

Præceps silvas montesque *fugit*
Citus Actæon. *Sen.*

Here the *i* in the final syllable of *fugit,* which is naturally short, is made long by position before the following consonants, *tc.*

> Omnia Mercŭrio sĭmĭlis, vōcemque cŏlōremque
> Et crīnes flāvos.... *Virg.* A. 4, 558.
> Dissĭdens plēbi nūmĕro beātōrum
> Exĭmit virtus. *Hor.* O. 2, 2, 18.

In the former of these examples, synapheia and synalœpha are combined, *que* being elided before *et* in the following line; in the latter there is a similar combination of synapheia and ecthlipsis.

(2.) By synapheia, the parts of a compound word are sometimes divided between two verses; as,

> .... si non offendĕret ūnum-
> *Quemque* poëtārum līmæ lābor et mŏra... *Hor.* A. P 290.

(3.) In hexameter verse a redundant syllable at the end of a line elided before a vowel at the beginning of the next line, by causing the accent to fall on the second syllable of the concluding spondee, and connecting the two verses by synapheia, excites the expectation of something which is to follow, and often tends to magnify the object; as,

> Quōs sūpĕr- | -ātrā sī- | -lĕx, jăm- | -jăm lāp- | -sūrā că- | -dĕntī- | -*que*
> lūmĭnet assĭmĭlis. *Virg.* A. 6, 602.

REMARK. The poets often make use of other figures, also, which, however, are not peculiar to them. Such are *prosthĕsis, ăphærĕsis, syncŏpe, epenthĕsis, apocŏpe, paragōge, tmēsis, antithĕsis,* and *metathĕsis.* See § 322.

ARSIS AND THESIS.

§ 308. (1.) *Rhythm* is the alternate elevating and depressing of the voice at regular intervals in pronouncing the syllables of verse.

(2.) The elevation of the voice is called *arsis,* its depression *thesis* These terms designate, also, the parts of a foot on which the elevation or depression falls.

1. The natural arsis is on the long syllable of a foot; and hence, in a foot composed wholly of long, or wholly of short syllables, when considered in itself, the place of the arsis is undetermined; but when such foot is substituted for the fundamental foot of a metre, its arsis is determined by that of the latter.

REMARK. Hence, a spondee, in trochaic or dactylic metre, has the arsis on the first syllable; but in iambic or anapæstic metre, it has it on the last.

2. The arsis is either equal in duration to the thesis, or twice as long.

Thus, in the dactyl, — ◡ ◡, and anapæst, ◡ ◡ —, it is equal; in the trochee, — ◡, and iambus, ◡ —, it is twice as long. This difference in the proportionate duration of the arsis and thesis constitutes the difference of rhythm. A foot is said to have the *descending* rhythm, when its arsis is at the beginning, and the *ascending,* when the thesis is at the beginning.

3. The stress of voice which falls upon the arsis of a foot, is called the *ictus.* When a long syllable in the arsis of a foot is resolved into two short ones, the ictus falls upon the former.

NOTE 1. Some suppose that the terms *arsis* and *thesis,* as used by the ancients, denoted respectively the rising and falling of the hand in beating time, and that the place of the thesis was the syllable which received the ictus

NOTE 2. As the ancient pronunciation of Latin is not now understood, writers differ in regard to the mode of reading verse. According to some, the accent of each word should always be preserved; while others direct that the stress of voice should be laid on the arsis of the foot, and that no regard should be paid to the accent.

It is generally supposed that the final letters elided by synalœpha and ecthlipsis, though omitted in scanning, were pronounced in reading verse.

CÆSURA.

§ 309. *Cæsura* is the separation, by the ending of a word, of syllables rhythmically or metrically connected.

Cæsura is of three kinds:—1, of the *foot*; 2, of the *rhythm*; and 3, of the *verse*.

1. Cæsura of the foot occurs when a word ends before a foot is completed; as,

Silves- | -trem tenu- | -i Mu- | -sam medi- | -tāris a- | -vēnā. *Virg.* E. 1, 2.

2. Cæsura of the rhythm is the separation of the arsis from the thesis by the ending of a word, as in the second, third, and fourth feet of the preceding verse.

REM 1. It hence appears that the cæsura of the rhythm is always a cæsura of the foot, as *e. g.* in the 2d, 3d, and 4th feet of the preceding verse; but, on the contrary, that the cæsura of the foot is not always a cæsura of the rhythm, as *e. g.* in the fifth foot of the same verse.

(1.) Cæsura of the rhythm allows a final syllable naturally short, to stand in the arsis of the foot instead of a long one, it being lengthened by the *ictus*; as,

Pectŏrĭ- | -bŭs inhĭ- | -ăns spĭ- | -răntĭă | cōnsŭlĭt | ĕxta. *Virg.* A. 4, 64.

This occurs chiefly in hexameter verse.

REM. 2. Cæsura of the foot and of the verse do not of themselves lengthen a short syllable, but they often coincide with that of the rhythm.

3. Cæsura of the verse is such a division of a line into two parts, as affords to the voice a convenient pause or rest, without injury to the sense or harmony.

REM. 3. The cæsura of the verse is often called the *cæsural pause*. In several kinds of verse, its place is fixed; in others, it may fall in more than one place, and the choice is left to the poet. Of the former kind is the pentameter, of the latter the hexameter.

The proper place of the cæsural pause will be treated of, so far as shall be necessary, under each species of verse.

REM. 4. The effect of the cæsura is to connect the different words harmoniously together, and thus to give smoothness, grace, and sweetness, to the verse.

DIFFERENT KINDS OF METRE.

DACTYLIC METRE.

§ 310. I. A *hexameter* or heroic verse consists of six feet. Of these the fifth is a dactyl, the sixth a spondee, and each of the other four either a dactyl or a spondee; as,

348   PROSODY.—VERSIFICATION—DACTYLIC METRE.   §

Āt tŭbă | tĕrrĭbĭ- | -lĕm sŏnī- | -tūm prŏcŭl | ǣrŏ că- | -nŏrŏ. *Virg.* A. 9, 503.
Intŏn- | -ăt crī- | -nēs lōn- | -gă cēr- | -vīcĕ flū- | ĕbănt. *Tibull.* 3, 4, 27.
Lūdĕrĕ | quǣ vĕl- | -lĕm călă- | -mō pēr- | -mīsĭt ă- | -grēstī. *Virg.* E. 1, 10.

1. The fifth foot is sometimes a spondee, and the verse in such case is called *spondaic*; as,

Cārā dĕ- | -ūm sŭbŏ- | -lēs māg- | -nūm Jŏvīs | Incrē- | -mēntūm. *Virg.* E. 4, 49.

REMARK 1. In such verses, the fourth foot is commonly a dactyl, and the fifth should not close with the end of a word. Spondaic lines are thought to be especially adapted to the expression of grave and solemn subjects.

2. A light and rapid movement is produced by the frequent recurrence of dactyls; a slow and heavy one by that of spondees; as,

Quădrŭpĕ- | -dāntĕ pŭ- | -trēm sŏnī- | -tū quătĭt | ūngŭlă | cāmpum. *Virg.* A. 8, 596.
Illi in- | -tĕr sē- | -sē māg- | -nā vī | brāchĭā tōllunt. *Id.* A. 8, 452.

REM. 2. Variety in the use of dactyls and spondees in successive lines, has an agreeable effect. Hexameter verse commonly ends in a word of two or three syllables, and a monosyllable at the end of a line is generally ungraceful, but sometimes produces a good effect; as,

Stērnĭtūr, | ēxănī- | -mīsquĕ, trĕ- | -mēns prō- | -cūmbĭt hŭ- | -mī bōs. *Virg.* A. 5, 481
Pārtŭrĭ- | -ūnt mōn- | -tēs: nās- | -cētŭr | rīdĭcŭ- | -lūs mūs. *Hor.* A. P. 139.

3. The beauty and harmony of hexameter verse depend much on due attention to the *cæsura*. (See § 309.) A line in which it is neglected is destitute of poetic beauty, and can hardly be distinguished from prose; as,

Rōmǣ | mœnĭā | tūrrŭīt | impĭgĕr | Hānnĭbăl | ārmīs. *Enn.*

4. The cæsural pause most approved in heroic poetry is that which occurs after the *penthemimĕris*, i. e. after the arsis in the third foot. This is particularly distinguished as *the heroic cæsura*. Thus,

Āt dŏmŭs | Intŏrī- | -ōr ‖ rū- | -gălī | splēndĭdă | lūxū. *Virg.* A. 1, 637.

5. Instead of the preceding, a cæsura in the thesis of the third foot, or after the arsis of the fourth, was also approved as heroic; as,

Īnfān- | -dūm rē- | -gīnă ‖ jŭ- | -bēs rĕnŏ- | -vārĕ dŏ- | -lōrem. *Virg.* A. 2, 3.
Indĕ tŏ- | -rō pătĕr | Ænĕ- | -ās ‖ sīc | ōrsŭs ăb | āltŏ. *Id.* A. 2, 2.

REM. 3. When the cæsural pause occurs, as in the latter example, after the *hephthemimĕris*, i. e. after the arsis of the fourth foot, another but slighter one is often found in the second foot; as,

Prīmă tŏ- | -nēt, ‖ plāū- | -sūquĕ vŏ- | -lāt ‖ frĕmĭ- | -tūquĕ sĕ- | -cūndo. *Virg.* A 5, 338.

6. The cæsura after the third foot, dividing the verse into exactly equal parts, was least approved; as,

Cuī nōn | dīctŭs Hȳ- | -lās pŭĕr ‖ ĕt Lā- | -tōnĭă | Dēlos. *Virg.* G. 3, 6.

REM. 4. The cæsural pause between the fourth and fifth feet was considered as peculiarly adapted to pastoral poetry, particularly when the fourth foot was a dactyl, and was hence termed the *bucolic* cæsura; as,

Stānt vītŭ- | -lī ĕt tŭnĕ- | -rīs mū- | -gītĭbŭs ‖ āĕră | cōmplēnt. *Nemes.*

NOTE 1. The cæsura after the arsis is sometimes called the *masculine* or *syllabic* cæsura; that in the thesis, the *feminine* or *trochaic*, as a trochee immediately precedes. When a cæsura occurs in the fifth foot it is usually the trochaic cæsura, unless the foot is a spondee; as,

Frāxĭnŭs | īn sīl- | -vīs pŭl- | -chĕrrĭmă, | pīnŭs īn | hōrtīs. *Virg.* E. 7, 65.

(*a.*) It is to be remarked that two successive trochaic cæsuras in the *second* and *third* feet are, in general, to be avoided, but they are sometimes employed to express irregular or impetuous motion; as,

§ 311.   PROSODY.—VERSIFICATION—DACTYLIC METRE.   349

Ūnă Eu- | -rŭsquĕ Nŏ- | -ăsquĕ rŭ- | -ūnt ĕrĕ- | -bĕrquĕ prŏ-| -cēllīs. *Virg.* A. 1 85.

(*b.*) Successive trochaic cæsuras are, in like manner, to be avoided in the *third* and *fourth* feet, but are approved in the *first* and *second*, in the *fourth* and *fifth*, and in the *first, third* and *fifth*. See Virg. A. 6, 651: 1, 94: and 6, 522.

NOTE 2. In the principal cæsura of the verse poets frequently introduce a pause in the sense, which must be attended to in order to determine the place of the cæsural pause. For in the common place for the cæsura in the third foot there is often a cæsura *of the foot;* while, in the fourth foot, a still more marked division occurs. In this case, the latter is to be considered as the principal cæsura, and distinguished accordingly; as,

Bellī | fĕrrā- | -tōs pŏs- | -tes, ‖ pŏr- | -tāsquĕ rĕ- | -frēgĭt. *Hor.* S. 1, 4, 61.

II. The *Priapēan* is usually accounted a species of hexameter. It is so constructed as to be divisible into two portions of three feet each, having generally a trochee in the first and fourth place, but often a spondee and rarely a dactyl; in the second, usually a dactyl; and an amphimacer and more rarely a dactyl in the third; as,

Ō cŏ- | -lōnĭă | quæ cūpĭs ‖ pōntĕ | lūdĕrĕ | lōngō. *Catull.* 17, 1.

It is, however, more properly considered as choriambic metre, consisting of alternate Glyconics and Pherecratics. See § 316, IV. V. Thus,

Ō cŏ- | -lōnĭă, quæ | cūpĭs
Pōntĕ | lūdĕrĕ lōn- | -go.

NOTE. A regular hexameter verse is termed *Priapēan*, when it is so constructed as to be divisable into two portions of three feet each; as,

Tērtĭă | pārs pā- | -trī dătă ‖ pārs dătă | tērtĭă | mātrī. *Catull.* 62, 64

See above, 6.

§ **311.**   III.   A *pentameter* verse consists of five feet.

REMARK 1. It is generally, however, divided, in scanning, into two hemistichs, the first consisting of two feet, either dactyls or spondees, followed by a long syllable; the last, of two dactyls, also followed by a long syllable; as,

Nātū- | -ræ sĕquī- | -tūr ‖ sēmĭnă | qŭisquĕ sū- | -æ. *Prop.* 3, 7, 20.
Cārmĭnī- | -bŭs vī- | -vĕs ‖ tēmpŭs ĭn | ōmnĕ mĕ- | -īs. *Ovid.*

1. According to the more ancient and correct mode of scanning pentameter verse, it consists of five feet, of which the first and second may each be a dactyl or a spondee; the third is always a spondee; and the fourth and fifth are anapæsts; as,

Nātū- | -ræ sĕquī- | -tūr ‖ sēm- | -ĭnă quĭs- | -quĕ sūæ.
Cārmĭnī- | -bŭs vī- | -vĕs ‖ tēm- | -pŭs ĭn ōm- | -nĕ mĕīs.

2. The cæsura, in pentameter verse, always occurs after the penthemimeris, i. e. at the close of the first hemistich. It very rarely lengthens a short syllable.

3. The pentameter rarely ends with a word of three syllables. In Ovid, it usually ends with a dissyllable.

REM. 2. This species of verse is seldom used, except in connection with hexameter, a line of each recurring alternately. This combination is called *elegiac* verse. Thus,

Flēbĭlĭs ĭndīgnōs, Ēlĕgēiă, sŏlvĕ căpĭllōs.
Ăh nĭmĭs ēx vērō nĕnĕ tĭbī nōmĕn ĕrĭt! *Ovid.* Am. 3, 9, 3.

§ **312.** IV. The *tetrameter a priōre*, or *Alcmanian dactylic tetrameter*, consists of the first four feet of a hexameter, of which the fourth is always a dactyl; as,

Gărrŭlă | pĕr rā- | -mōs, ăvīs | ŏbstrĕpīt. *Sen.* Œd. 454.

V. The *tetrameter a posteriōre*, or *spondaic tetrameter*, consists of the last four feet of a hexameter; as,

Ībĭmŭs, | Ō sŏcĭ- | -ī, cŏmī- | -tēsque. *Hor.* Od. 1, 7, 26.

REMARK. The penultimate foot in this, as in hexameter verse, may be a spondee, but in this case the preceding foot should be a dactyl; as,

Mĕnsō- | -rēm cŏhĭ- | -bēnt Ar- | -chȳtā. *Hor.* Od. 1, 28, 2.

VI. The *dactylic trimeter* consists of the last three feet of a hexameter; as,

Grātō | Pȳrrhă sŭb | āntro. *Hor.* Od. 1, 5, 3.

REMARK. But this kind of verse is more properly included in choriambic metre. See § 316, V.

VII. The *trimeter catalectic Archilochian* consists of the first five half feet of a hexameter, but the first and second feet are commonly dactyls; as,

Pŭlvĭs ĕt | ŭmbră sŭ- | -mus. *Hor.* Od. 4, 7, 16.

VIII. The *dactylic dimeter*, or *Adonic*, consists of two feet, a dactyl and a spondee; as,

Rīsĭt Ā- | -pōllo. *Hor.* Od. 1, 10, 12.

IX. The *Æolic pentameter* consists of four dactyls preceded by a spondee, a trochee, or an iambus. Thus

$$\begin{matrix}-\ -\\-\ \cup\\\cup\ -\end{matrix}\Big| - \cup \cup \Big| - \cup \cup \Big| - \cup \cup \Big| - \cup \cup$$

X. The *Phalæcian pentameter* consists of a dactylic penthimimeris and a dactylic dimeter; as,

Vīsĕ- | -băt gēlĭ- | -dæ ∥ sīdĕră | brūmæ. *Boëthius*.

REMARK. A trochee is sometimes found in the first place and an iambus in the first and second places.

XI. The *Tetrameter Meiurus*, or *Faliscan* consists of the last four feet of a hexameter, except that the last foot is an iambus instead of a spondee; as,

Ŭt nŏvă | frūgĕ grā- | vīs Cĕrēs | ĕat. *Boëthius*.

XII. The *Tetrameter Catalectic* consists of the tetrameter a priore wanting the latter half of the concluding dactyl; as,

Ōmne hŏmĭ- | -nŭm gĕnŭs | īn tĕr- | -rīs. *Boëthius*.

ANAPÆSTIC METRE.

§ **313.** I. The *anapæstic monomēter* consists of two anapæsts; as,

Ŭlŭlās- | -sŏ cănēs. *Sen.*

II. The *anapæstic dimeter* consists of two measures, or four anapæsts; as,

Phărĕtrǣ- | -quē grăvēs | dătĕ sǣ- | -vă fĕrō.... *Sen.*

REMARK 1. The first foot in each measure of anapæstic metre was very often changed to a dactyl or a spondee, and the second foot often to a spondee and, in a few instances, to a dactyl.

REM. 2. Anapæstic verses are generally so constructed that each measure ends with a word, so that they may be written and read in lines of one, two, or more measures.

IAMBIC METRE.

§ **314.** I. 1. The *iambic trimeter*, or *senarius*, consists of three iambic measures, or six iambic feet; as,

Phăsē- | -lūs Il- | -lĕ, | quĕm | vīdē- | -tīs hōs- | -pĭtēs.... *Catull.* 4. 1.

2. The cæsura commonly occurs in the third but sometimes in the fourth foot.

3. The pure iambic measure was seldom used by the Latin poets, but to vary the rhythm spondees were introduced into the first, third, and fifth places. In every foot, also, except the last, which was always an iambus, a long syllable was often changed into two short ones, so that an anapæst or a dactyl was used for a spondee, and a tribrach for an iambus, but the use of the dactyl in the fifth place was very rare; as,

Quō, quō | scĕlĕs- | -tī rŭī- | -tīs? | ŭt | cūr dēx- | -tĕrīs.... *Hor.* Epod. 7, 1.
Ālĭtĭ- | -būs āt- | -quē cănī- | -būs hŏmī- | -cīdam Hēc- | -tŏrĕm.... *Id.* Epod. 17, 12.

4. Sometimes, also, a procelensmatic, or double pyrrhic, was used in the first place for a spondee. The writers of comedy, satire, and fable, admitted the spondee and its equivalents (the dactyl and anapæst) into the second and fourth places, as well as the first, third, and fifth.

5. The following, therefore, is the scale of the Iambic Trimeter:—

1	2	3	4	5	6
ᴗ –	ᴗ –	ᴗ –	ᴗ –	ᴗ –	ᴗ –
ᴗᴗᴗ		ᴗᴗᴗ	ᴗᴗᴗ		
– –		– –			
– ᴗᴗ		– ᴗᴗ		(– ᴗ ᴗ)	
ᴗᴗ –		ᴗᴗ –			

6. In the construction of the Iambic Trimeter an accent should fall on the second syllable of either the third foot or both the second and fourth feet; as,

Ĭbĭs | Lībŭr- | -nĭs ĭn- | tĕr āl- | -tă nā- | -vĭum | .
Ŭtrŭm- | -nĕ jŭs- | -sĭ pĕr- | -sĕquē'- | -mŭr ō- | -tĭum. |

II. The *scazon*, or *choliambus* (lame iambic), is the iambic trimeter, with a spondee in the sixth foot, and generally an iambus in the fifth; as,

Cūr ĭn | thĕā- | -trŭm, Cătō | sĕvē- | -rĕ, vĕ- | -nīstī?
Ăn Ĭdĕ- | ŏ tŭn- | -tŭm vĕn- | -ĕrās, | ŭt ēx- | -īrēs? *Mart.* Ep. 1, 1, 8.

This species of verse is also called *Hipponactic* trimeter, from its inventor Hipponax.

III. The *iambic tetrameter* or *quadrātus*, called also from the number of its feet *octonarius*, a measure used by the comic poets, consists of four iambic measures, subject to the same variations as the iambic trimeter (I.); as,

Nūnc hīc | diēs | ălĭām | vītam āf- | -fērt, ălĭ- | -ōs mŏ- | -rēs pōs- | -tŭlat. *Ter.* A. 1, 2, 18.

REMARK. The cæsura regularly follows the second measure.

IV. The *iambic tetrameter catalectic* or *Hipponactic*, is the iambic tetrameter, wanting the last syllable, and having always an iambus in the seventh place, but admitting in the other places the same variations as the trimeter and tetrameter; as,

Dēprēn- | -să nā- | -vīs īn | mărī, | vēsā- | -nĭēn- | -tĕ vēn- | -to. *Catull.* 25, 13.

V. The *iambic trimeter catalectic* or *Archilochian*, is the iambic trimeter (I.), wanting the final syllable. Like the common iambic trimeter, it admits a spondee into the first and third places, but not into the fifth; as,

Vōcā- | -tūs āt- | -quē nōn | vōcā- | -tūs āu- | -dīt. *Hor.* Od. 2, 18, 40.
Trăhūnt- | -quē sīc- | -căs māch- | -īnæ | cărī- | -nas. *Id.* Od. 1, 4, 2.

VI. The *iambic dimeter* consists of two iambic measures, with the same variations as the iambic trimeter (I.); as,

Fōrtī | sēquē- | -mūr pēc- | -tŏre. *Hor.* Epod. 1, 14.
Cănīdĭ- | -ă trāc- | -tăvīt | dăpēs. *Id.* Epod. 3, 8.
Vīdē- | -rĕ prŏpē- | -răntēs | dŏmum. *Id.* Epod. 3, 62.

REMARK. The iambic dimeter is also called the *Archilochian dimeter*.

The following is its scale:—

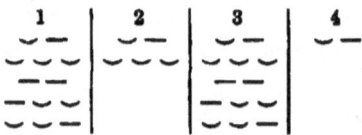

VII. The *iambic dimeter hypermeter*, called also *Archilochian*, is the iambic dimeter, with an additional syllable at the end; as,

Rēdē- | -gĭt īn | vērōs | tĭmŏ- | -rēs. *Hor.* Od. 1, 37, 15.

REMARK. Horace always makes the third foot a spondee.

VIII. The *iambic dimeter acephalous* is the iambic dimeter, wanting the first syllable; as,

Nōn | ĕbūr | nĕque āu- | -rĕum.... *Hor.* Od. 2, 18, 1.

REMARK. This kind of verse is sometimes scanned as a catalectic trochaic meter. See § 315, IV.

IX. The *iambic dimeter catalectic*, or *Anacreontic*, is the iambic dimeter, wanting the final syllable, and having always an iambus in the third foot; as,

Ut tĭ- | grīs ŏr- | -bă gnā- | -tīs. *Sen.* Med. 863.

X. The *Galliambus* consists of two iambic dimeters catalectic, the last of which wants the final syllable.

REMARK 1. It was so denominated from the *Galli* or priests of Cybele, by whom it was used.

REM. 2. In the first foot of each dimeter the anapæst was generally preferred to the spondee. The catalectic syllable at the end of the first dimeter is long, and the second foot of the second dimeter is commonly a tribrach; as,

Sŭpĕr ăl- | -tă vēc- | -tŭs ă- | -tȳs ‖ cĕlĕrī | rătĕ mă- | -rĭa. *Catull*, 63, 1.

REM. 3. The cæsura uniformly occurs at the end of the first dimeter.

TROCHAIC METRE.

§ 315. 1. Trochaic verses bear a near affinity to iambics. The addition or retrenchment of a syllable at the beginning of a pure iambic verse, renders it pure trochaic, and the addition or retrenchment of a syllable at the beginning of a pure trochaic line, renders it pure iambic, with the deficiency or redundancy of a syllable in each case at the end of the verse.

I. The *trochaic tetrameter catalectic* consists of seven feet, followed by a catalectic syllable. In the first five places and very rarely in the sixth, it admits a tribrach, but in the seventh a trochee only. In the *even* places, besides the tribrach, it admits also a spondee, a dactyl, an anapæst, and sometimes a proceleusmatic; as,

Jūssŭs | ēst ĭn | ērmīs | īrĕ : ‖ pūrŭs | īrĕ | jūssŭs | ēst. *Auct. P. Věn.*
Rōmŭ | lĕās | ĭpsī | fēcĭt ‖ cūm Sā- | -bīnĭs | nūptĭ- | -ās. *Id.*
Dănăī | dēs, cō- | -ĭtē; | vēstrās ‖ hĭc dī- | -ēs quæ- | -rĭt mă- | -nŭs. *Sen.*

The following is its scale:—

1	2	3	4	5	6	7	8
— ᴗ	— —	— ᴗ	— —	— ᴗ	— —	— ᴗ	—
ᴗ ᴗ ᴗ	ᴗ ᴗ ᴗ	ᴗ ᴗ ᴗ	ᴗ ᴗ ᴗ	ᴗ ᴗ ᴗ	ᴗ ᴗ ᴗ		
	— ᴗ ᴗ		— ᴗ ᴗ		— ᴗ ᴗ		
	ᴗ ᴗ —		ᴗ ᴗ —		ᴗ ᴗ —		

REMARK 1. The *pure* trochaic verse was rarely used, and the dactyl very rarely occurs in the fourth place. The cæsural pause uniformly occurs after the fourth foot, thus dividing the verse into a complete dimeter and a catalectic dimeter. The comic writers introduced the spondee and its equivalent feet into the odd places.

REM. 2. The complete trochaic tetrameter or *octonarius* properly consists of eight feet, all trochees, subject, however, to the same variations as the catalectic tetrameter; as,

Ĭpsĕ | sūmmīs | sāxīs | fīxŭs | āspĕ- | -rīs, ŏ- | -vīscĕ- | -rātŭs. *Enn.*

II. The *Sapphic* verse, invented by the poetess Sappho, consists of five feet—the first a trochee, the second a spondee, the third a dactyl, and the fourth and fifth trochees; as,

Īntĕ- | -gĕr vī- | -tæ, ‖ scĕlĕ- | -rīsquĕ | pūrŭs. *Hor. Od.* 1, 22, 1.

1. Sappho, and, after her example, Catullus, sometimes made the second foot a trochee.

2. Those Sapphics are most harmonious which have the cæsura after the fifth semi-foot.

NOTE 1. In the composition of the Sapphic stanza, a word is sometimes divided between the end of the third Sapphic, and the beginning of the Adonic which follows; as,

Lābī- | -tŭr rī- | -pā Jŏvĕ | nōn prŏ- | -bāntĕ ux-
ōrĭŭs | āmnĭs. *Hor. Od.* 1, 2, 19.

It has been thought by some that such lines should be considered as one Sapphic verse of seven feet, the fifth foot being either a spondee or a trochee.

NOTE 2. This verse is sometimes scanned as epichoriambic, having an epitrite in the first place, a choriambus in the second, and ending with an iambic sizygy catalectic; thus,

Intĕgĕr vī- | -tæ, scĕlĕrĭs- | -quĕ pūrŭs.

III. The *Phalæcian* verse consists of five feet—a spondee, a dactyl, and three trochees; as,

Nōn ēst | vīvĕrĕ, | sēd vă- | -lērĕ | vītā. *Mart.*

REMARK 1. Instead of a spondee as the first foot, Catullus sometimes uses a trochee or an iambus. This writer also sometimes uses a spondee in the second place.

REM. 2. The *Phalæcian* verse is sometimes called *hendecasyllabic*, as consisting of eleven syllables; but that name does not belong to it exclusively.

IV. The *trochaic dimeter catalectic* consists of three feet, properly all trochees, and a catalectic syllable, but admitting also in the second place a spondee or a dactyl; as,

Nōn ĕ | -būr nĕ- | -que aūrĕ- | -um. *Hor.* Od. 2, 18, 1.
Lēuĭs | ac mŏdī- | -cūm flū- | -ēns
Aūrā, | nēc vēr- | -gēns lā- | -tus. *Sen* (Ed. 887.

NOTE. This measure is the same as the acephalous iambic dimeter (see § 314, VIII.), and it is not important whether it be regarded as iambic or trochaic.

CHORIAMBIC METRE.

§ **316.** (*a.*) In a pure choriambic verse each metre except the last is a choriambus, and the last an Iambic syzygy.

NOTE. A spondee and iambus, i. e. a third epitrite, are sometimes used in place of the Iambic syzygy.

(*b.*) An *epichoriambic* verse is composed of one or more choriambi with some other foot, especially a ditrochee or a second epitrite, joined with it.

I. The *choriambic pentameter* consists of a spondee, three choriambi, and an iambus; as,

Tū nē | quæsĭĕrĭs, | scīrē nĕfās, | quĕm mĭhī, quĕm tĭbī., *Hor.* Od. 1, 11, 1.

II. The *choriambic tetrameter* consists of three choriambi, or feet of equal length, and a Bacchius; as,

Omnĕ nĕmūs | cūm flūvĭīs, | ōmnĕ cănāt | prŏfūudum. *Claud.*

2. In this verse Horace substituted a spondee for the iambus contained in the first choriambus; as,

Tē dēōs ō- | -rō, Sӯbărīn | cūr prŏpĕrēs | āmāndō. *Hor.* Od. 1, 8, 2.

3. Some scan this verse as an epichoriambic tetrameter catalectic, beginning with the second epitrite.

III. 1. The *Asclepiadic tetrameter* (invented by the poet Asclepiădēs) consists of a spondee, two choriambi, and an iambus; as,

Mæcē- | -rās, ătăvĭs ‖ ēdĭtĕ rēg- | -ĭbus. *Hor.* Od. 1, 1, 1.

2. This form is invariably observed by Horace; but other poets sometimes, though rarely, make the first foot a dactyl.

3. The cæsural pause occurs at the end of the first choriambus.

4. This measure is sometimes scanned as a dactylic pentameter catalectic. See § 311, III. Thus,

Mæcē- | -nās, ătă- | vīs ‖ ĕdĭtĕ | rēgĭbūs.

IV. 1. The *choriambic trimeter*, or *Glyconic* (invented by the poet Glyco), consists of a spondee, a choriambus, and an iambus; as,

Sīc tē | dīvă pŏtēns | Cўprī... *Hor.* Od. 1, 3, 1.

2. The first foot is sometimes an iambus or a trochee.

3. When the first foot is a spondee, the verse might be scanned as a dactylic trimeter. Thus,

Sīc tē | dīvă pŏ- | -tēns Cўprī.

V. 1. The *choriambic trimeter catalectic*, or *Pherecratic* (so called from the poet Pherecrātes), is the Glyconic deprived of its final syllable, and consists of a spondee, a choriambus, and a catalectic syllable; as,

Grātō, | Pўrrhă, sŭb ăn- | -trō. *Hor.* Od. 1, 5, 3.

2. The first foot was sometimes a trochee or an anapest, rarely an iambus.

3. When the first foot is a spondee, this measure might be scanned as a dactylic trimeter. See § 312, VI.

4. The Pherecratic subjoined to the Glyconic produces the Priapean verse. See § 310, II.

VI. 1. The *choriambic dimeter* consists of a choriambus and a Bacchīus; as,

Lŷdĭă dīc | pĕr ōmnĕs. *Hor.* Od. 1, 8, 1.

2. This verse is by some called the choriambic dimeter catalectic. Cf. § 316, (a.)

IONIC METRE.

§ 317. I. The *Ionic a majōre*, or *Sotadic*, (from the poet Sotādes), consists of three greater Ionics and a spondee.

1. The Ionic feet, however, are often changed into ditrochees, and either of the two long syllables in those feet into two short ones; as,

Īlās, cūm gĕmĭ- | -nā cōmpĕdĕ, | dēdĭcāt că- | -tēnās,
Sātŭrnē, tī- | -bī Zōīlūs, | ānnŭlōs prī- | -ōrēs. *Mart.*

2. Hence the following is its scale:—

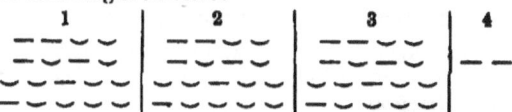

NOTE. The final syllable, by § 301, note, may be short.

II. 1. The *Ionic a minōre* consists generally of verses of three or four feet, which are all smaller Ionics; as,

Pŭĕr ălēs, | tĭbī tĕlās, | ŏpĕrōsæ- | -quĕ Mĭnērvæ... *Hor.* Od. 3, 12, 4.

2. In this verse, as in the anapæstic, no place is assigned to the pause; because, since the metres, if rightly constructed, end with a word, the effect of a pause will be produced at the end of each metre.

COMPOUND METRES.

§ 318. Compound metre is the union of two species of metre in the same verse.

I. The *dactylico-iambic* metre or *Elegiambus* consists of a dactylic penthemimĕris (312, VII.), followed by an iambic dimeter (§ 314, VI.); as,

Scrībĕrĕ | vĕrsīcŭ- | -lōs ‖ ămō- | -rĕ pĕr- | -cŭlsŭm | grăvī. *Hor.* Epod. 11, 2.

II. The *iambico-dactylic* metre or *Iambelegus* consists of the same members as the preceding, but in a reversed order; as,

Nīvĕs- | -quĕ dē- | -dūcŭnt | Jŏvēm: ‖ nūnc mărĕ, | nūnc sīlŭ- | -æ. *Hor.* Epod. 13, 2.

NOTE. The members composing this and the preceding species of verse are often written in separate verses.

III. The *greater Alcaic* consists of an iambic penthemimeris, i. e. of two iambic feet and a long catalectic syllable, followed by a choriambus, and an iambus; as,

Vīdĕs | ūt āl- | -tā ‖ stĕt nīvĕ cān- | -dĭdum. *Hor.* Od. 1, 9, 1.

REMARK 1. The first foot is often a spondee.

REM. 2. The cæsura uniformly occurs after the catalectic syllable.

REM. 3. This verse is sometimes so scanned as to make the last two feet dactyls.

IV. The *dactylico-trochaic* or *Archilochian heptameter*, consists of the dactylic tetrameter *a priōre* (§ 312), followed by three trochees; as,

Sōlvĭtŭr | ācrĭs hī- | -ĕms grā- | -tā vĭcĕ ‖ vĕrĭs | ĕt Fā- | -vōnī. *Hor.* Od. 1, 4, 1.

REMARK. The cæsura occurs between the two members.

V. The *dactylico-trochaic tetrameter* or *lesser Alcaic*, consists of two dactyls, followed by two trochees, i. e. of a dactylic dimeter followed by a trochaic monometer; as,

Lĕvĭā | pĕrsŏnŭ- ‖ -ĕrĕ |.sāxă. *Hor.* Od. 1, 17, 12.

COMBINATION OF VERSES IN POEMS.

§ 319. 1. A poem may consist either of one kind of verse only or of a combination of two or more kinds.

2. A poem in which only one kind of verse is employed, is called *carmen monocōlon;* that which has two kinds, *dicōlon;* that which has three kinds, *tricōlon.*

3. When the poem returns, after the second line, to the same verse with which it began, it is called *distrŏphon;* when after the third line, *tristrŏphon;* and when after the fourth, *tetrastrŏphon.*

4. The several verses which occur before the poem returns to the kind of verse with which it began, constitute a *stanza* or *strophe.*

5. A poem consisting of two kinds of verse, when the stanza contains two verses, is called *dicōlon distrŏphon,* (see § 320, 3); when it contains three, *dicō-*

§ 320. PROSODY.—VERSIFICATION—HORATIAN METRES. 357

Ion tristrŏphon, (Auson. Profess. 21); when four, *dicōlon tetrastrŏphon*, (§ 320, 2); and when five, *dicōlon pentastrŏphon*.

6. A poem consisting of three kinds of verse, when the stanza contains three verses, is called *tricōlon tristrŏphon*, (§ 320, 15); when four, *tricōlon tetrastrŏphon*, (§ 320, 1).

HORATIAN METRES.

§ **320.** The different species of metre used by Horace in his lyric compositions are twenty. The various forms in which he has employed them, either separate or in conjunction, are nineteen, arranged, according to the order of preference given to them by the poet, in the following

SYNOPSIS.

1. Two greater Alcaics (§ 318, III.), one Archilochian iambic dimeter hypermeter (§ 314, VII.), and one lesser Alcaic (§ 318, V.); as,

  Vĭdēs, ŭt āltā stĕt nĭvĕ cāndĭdum
  Sōrāctĕ, nēc jām sŭstĭneānt ŏnŭs
  Sīlvæ lăbōrāntēs, gĕlŭquĕ
   Flūmĭnā cōnstĭtĕrĭnt ăcūto. (*Lib.* 1, 9.)

REMARK. This is called the Horatian stanza, because it seems to have been a favorite with Horace, being used in thirty-seven of his odes.

2. Three Sapphics (§ 315, II.) and one Adonic (§ 312, VIII.); as,

  Jām sătĭs tērrĭs nĭvĭs ātquĕ dīræ
  Grāndĭnĭs mīsĭt pătĕr, ēt, rŭbēntĕ
  Dēxtĕrā sācrās jăcŭlātŭs ārces,
   Tērrŭĭt ūrbem. (*Lib.* 1, 2.)

3. One Glyconic (§ 316, IV.) and one Asclepiadic (§ 316, III.); as,

  Sīc tĕ Dīvă pŏtēns Cўprī,
   Sīc frātrēs Hĕlĕnæ, lūcĭdă sīdĕra... (*Lib.* 1, 3)

4. One iambic trimeter (§ 314, I.) and one iambic dimeter (§ 314, VI.); as,

  Ĭbīs Lĭbūrnīs īntĕr āltă nāvĭum,
   Amīcĕ, prōpŭgnācŭla. (*Epod.* 1.)

5. Three Asclepiadics (§ 316, III.) and one Glyconic (§ 316, IV.); as,

  Scrībĕrĭs Vărĭō fōrtĭs, ēt hōstĭum
  Vīctŏr, Mæŏnĭī cārmĭnĭs ālĭtī,
  Quām rēm cūmquĕ fĕrōx nāvĭbŭs āut ĕquĭs
   Mīlĕs, tĕ dūcĕ, gēssĕrĭt. (*Lib.* 1, 6.)

6. Two Asclepiadics (§ 316, III.), one Pherecratic (§ 316, V.), and one Glyconic (§ 316, IV.); as,

  Dĭānăm, tĕnĕræ, dīcĭtĕ vīrgĭnes:
  Īntōnsŭm, pŭĕrī, dīcĭtĕ Cŷnthĭum,
   Lātōnāmquĕ sŭprēmo
   Dīlēctăm pĕnĭtŭs Jŏvī. (*Lib.* 1, 21)

7. The Asclepiadic (§ 316, III.) alone; as,

  Mæcēnās ătăvīs ēdĭtĕ rēgĭbus. (*Lib.* 1, 1.)

8. One dactylic hexameter (§ 310, I.) and one dactylic tetrameter *a posteriōre* (§ 312, V.); as,

> Laūdābūnt ălĭī clărām Rhŏdŏn, aūt Mĭtўlēnen,
> Aūt Ĕphĕsūm, bĭmărīsvĕ Cŏrīnthĭ... (*Lib.* 1, 7.)

9. The choriambic pentameter (§ 316, I.) alone; as,

> Tū nĕ quæsĭĕrĭs, scīrĕ nĕfās, quĕm mĭhī, quĕm tĭbī... (*Lib.* 1, 11.)

10. One dactylic hexameter (§ 310, I.) and one iambic dimeter (§ 314, VI.); as,

> Nŏx ĕrăt, ĕt cœlō fūlgēbăt lūnă sĕrēno
> Inter mĭnōră sīdĕră. (*Epod.* 15.)

11. The iambic trimeter (§ 314, I.) containing spondees; as,

> Jām, jam ĕffĭcăcī dō mănŭs sciēntĭæ. (*Epod.* 17.)

12. One choriambic dimeter (§ 316, VI.) and one choriambic tetrameter (§ 316, II.) with a variation; as,

> Lȳdĭă, dĭc, pĕr ōmnes
> Tē Dĕŏs ōrō, Sȳbărīn cūr prŏpĕrās āmāndo... (*Lib.* 1, 8.)

13. One dactylic hexameter (§ 310, I.) and one iambic trimeter without spondees (§ 314, I.); as,

> Āltĕră jām tĕrĭtūr bēllīs cīvīlĭbŭs ætas;
> Sŭĭs ĕt īpsă Rōmă vīrĭbŭs rŭit. (*Epŏd.* 16.)

14. One dactylic hexameter (§ 310, I.) and one dactylic penthemimeris (§ 312, VII.); as,

> Dīffŭgĕrĕ nĭvĕs: rĕdĕūnt jăm grămĭnă cāmpīs,
> Ārbŏrĭbūsquĕ cōmæ. (*Lib.* 4, 7.)

15. One iambic trimeter (§ 314, I.), one dactylic trimeter catalectic (§ 312, VII.), and one iambic dimeter (§ 314, VI.); as,

> Pēttī, nĭhĭl mĕ, sĭcŭt āntĕā, jŭvat
> Scrībĕrĕ vērsĭcŭlos,
> Ămōrĕ pērcŭlsūm grăvī. (*Epoa.* 11.)

Note. The second and third lines are often written as one verse. See § 318, 1.

16. One dactylic hexameter (§ 310, I.), one iambic dimeter (§ 314, VI.), and one dactylic penthemimeris (§ 312, VII.); as,

> Hōrrĭdă tēmpēstās cœlūm cōntrāxĭt; ĕt īmbres
> Nĭvēsquĕ dĕdūcŭnt Jŏvem:
> Nūnc mărĕ, nūnc sĭlŭæ... (*Epod.* 13.)

Note. The second and third lines of this stanza, also, are often written as one verse. See § 318, II.

17. One Archilochian heptameter (§ 318, IV.) and one iambic trimeter catalectic (§ 314, V.); as,

> Sōlvĭtūr ācrĭs hĭēms grătā vĭcĕ vērĭs ĕt Făvōnī,
> Trăhūntquĕ sīccās māchĭnæ cărīnas. (*Lib.* 1, 4.)

18. One iambic dimeter acephalous (§ 314, VIII.) and one iambic trimeter catalectic (§ 314, V.); as,

> Nōn ĕbŭr nĕque aūrĕum
> Mĕă rĕnĭdĕt īn dŏmō lăcūnar. (*Lib.* 2, 18.)

19. The Ionic *a minōre* (§ 317, II.) alone; as,

> Mĭsĕrāruṃ ĕst nĕque ămōrī dărĕ lūdŭm, nĕquĕ dūlcī... (*Lib.* 3, 12.)

§ 321. A METRICAL KEY TO THE ODES OF HORACE

Containing, in alphabetic order, the first words of each, with a reference to the numbers in the preceding Synopsis, where the metre is explained.

Æli, vetusto	No. 1	Mollis inertia	No.10
Æquam memento	1	Montium custos	2
Albi, ne doleas	5	Motum ex Metello	1
Altera jam teritur	13	Musis amicus	1
Angustam, amice	1	Natis in usum	1
At, O deorum	4	Ne forte credas	1
Audivere, Lyce	6	Ne sit ancillæ	2
Bacchum in remotis	1	Nolis longa feræ	5
Beatus ille	4	Nondum subacta	1
Cœlo supinas	1	Non ebur neque aureum	18
Cœlo tonantem	1	Non semper imbres	1
Cur me querelis	1	Non usitata	1
Delicta majorum	1	Non vides, quanto	2
Descende cœl.	1	Nox erat	10
Dianam, teneræ	6	Nullam, Vare, sacra	9
Diffugere nives	14	Nullus argento	2
Dive, quem proles	2	Nunc est bibendum	1
Divis orte bonis	5	O crudelis adhuc	2
Donarem pateras	7	O diva, gratum	1
Donec gratus eram tibi	3	O fons Bandusiæ	6
Eheu! fugaces	1	O matre pulchra	1
Est mihi nonum	2	O nata mecum	1
Et ture et fidibus	3	O navis, referent	6
Exegi monumentum	7	O sæpe mecum	1
Extremum Tanaim	5	O Venus, regina	2
Faune, nympharum	2	Odi profanum	1
Festo quid potius die	3	Otium Divos	2
Herculis ritu	2	Parcius junctas	2
Horrida tempestas	16	Parcus Deorum	1
Ibis Liburnis	4	Parentis olim	4
Icci, beatis	1	Pastor quum traheret	5
Ille et nefasto	1	Percicos odi, puer	2
Impios parræ	2	Petti, nihil me	16
Inclusam Danaën	5	Phœbe, silvarumque	2
Intactis opulentior	3	Phœbus volentem	1
Integer vitæ	2	Pindarum quisquis	2
Intermissa, Venus, diu	3	Poscimur: si quid	2
Jam jam efficaci	11	Quæ cura Patrum	1
Jam pauca aratro	1	Qualem ministrum	1
Jam satis terris	2	Quando repostum	4
Jam veris comites	5	Quantum distet ab Inacho	8
Justum et tenacem	1	Quem tu, Melpomene	3
Laudabunt alii	8	Quem virum aut heroa	7
Lupis et agnis	4	Quid bellicosus	1
Lydia, dic, per omnes	12	Quid dedicatum	1
Mæcenas atavis	7	Quid fles, Asterie	6
Mala soluta	4	Quid immerentis	4
Martiis cœlebs	2	Quid obseratis	11
Mater sæva Cupidinum	8	Quid tibi vis	8
Mercuri, facunde	2	Quis desiderio	5
Mercuri, nam te	2	Quis multa gracilis	6
Miserarum est	19	Quo me, Bacche	3

Quo, quo, scelesti ruitis........No. 4	Tu ne quæsiĕris..............No. 9
Quum tu, Lydia................... 3	Tyrrhēna regum.................. 1
Rectius vives.................... 2	Ulla si juris.................... 2
Rogāre longo..................... 4	Uxor paupĕris Ibўci.............. 3
Scribēris Vario.................. 5	Velox amœnum.................... 1
Septimi, Gades................... 2	Vides, ut altā................... 1
Sic te Diva potens............... 3	Vile potābis..................... 2
Solvītur acris hiems.............17	Vitas hinnuleo................... 6
Te maris et terræ................ 8	Vixi puellis..................... 1

The following are the single metres used by Horace in his lyric compositions, viz:—

1. Dactylic Hexameter.
2. Dactylic Tetrameter *a posteriōri*.
3. Dactylic Trimeter Catalectic.
4. Adonic.
5. Trimeter Iambic.
6. Iambic Trimeter Catalectic.
7. Iambic Dimeter.
8. Archilochian Iambic Dimeter Hypermeter.
9. Iambic Dimeter Acephalous.
10. Sapphic.
11. Choriambic Pentameter.
12. Choriambic Tetrameter.
13. Asclepiadic Tetrameter.
14. Glyconic.
15. Pherecratic.
16. Choriambic Dimeter.
17. Ionic *a minōre*.
18. Greater Alcaic.
19. Archilochian Heptameter.
20. Lesser Alcaic.

APPENDIX.

GRAMMATICAL FIGURES.

§ 322. Certain deviations from the regular form and construction of words, are called *grammatical figures*. These may relate either to Orthography and Etymology, or to Syntax.

I. FIGURES OF ORTHOGRAPHY AND ETYMOLOGY.

These are distinguished by the general name of *metaplasm*.

1. *Prosthēsis* is the prefixing of a letter or syllable to a word; as, *gnătus*, for *nătus*; *tĕtŭli*, for *tŭli*. These, however, are rather the ancient customary forms, from which those now in use were formed by aphæresis.

2. *Aphærēsis* is the taking of a letter or syllable from the beginning of a word; as, 'st, for est; *răbōnem*, for *arrăbōnem*.

3. *Epenthēsis* is the insertion of a letter or syllable in the middle of a word; as, *ălĭtŭum*, for *ălĭtum*; *Māvors*, for *Mars*.

4. *Syncŏpe* is the omission of a letter or syllable in the middle of a word; as, *deûm*, for *deōrum*; *meûm factûm*, for *meōrum factōrum*; *sæcla*, for *sæcŭla*; *flesti*, for *flēvisti*; *rēpostus*, for *rēpŏsitus*; *aspris*, for *aspĕris*.

5. *Crasis* is the contraction of two vowels into one; as, *cōgo*, for *oŏăgo*; *nil*, for *nihil*.

6. *Paragōge* is the addition of a letter or syllable to the end of a word; as, *med*, for *me*; *claudier*, for *claudi*.

7. *Apocŏpe* is the omission of the final letter or syllable of a word; as, *mĕn'*, for *mĕne*; *Antŏni*, for *Antōnii*.

8. *Antithĕsis* is the substitution of one letter for another; as, *olli*, for *illi*; *optŭmus*, for *optĭmus*; *afficio*, for *adficio*. *O* is often thus used for *u*, especially after *v*; as, *voltus*, for *vultus*; *servom*, for *servum*. So after *qu*; as, *æquom*, for *æquum*.

9. *Metathĕsis* is the changing of the order of letters in a word; as, *pistris*, for *pristis*.

II. FIGURES OF SYNTAX.

323. The figures of Syntax are *ellipsis, pleonasm, enallăge,* and *hyperbăton*.

1. (*a*.) *Ellipsis* is the omission of some word or words in a sentence; as,

Aiunt, scil. *hŏmines*. *Dārius Hystaspis*, scil. *filius*. *Cŭno*, scil. *ĕgo*. *Quid multa?* scil. *dĭcam*. *Ex quo*, scil. *tempŏre*. *Fĕrina*, scil. *caro*.

(*b*.) Ellipsis includes *asyndĕton, zeugma, syllepsis,* and *prolepsis*.

(1.) *Asyndĕton* is the omission of the copulative conjunction; as, *ăbiit, excessit, ēvāsit, ērūpit* scil. *et*. Cic. This is called in pure Latin *dissŏlūtio*.

(2.) (*a.*) *Zeugma* is the uniting of two nouns or two infinitives to a verb, which, as to its meaning, is applicable to only one of them; as, *Pācem an bellum gĕrens:* (Sall.) where *gĕrens* is applicable to *bellum* only, while *pācem* requires *ăgĕre*. *Semperne in sanguine, ferro, fŭgā versābimur?* (Id.) where the verb does not properly apply to *ferro*.

(*b.*) *Nĕgo* is often thus used with two propositions, one of which is affirmative; as, *Nĕgant Cæsărem mansūrum, postŭlātāque interpŏsita esse,* for *dīcuntque postŭlāta...* Cic. See § 209, Note 4.

(*c.*) When an adjective or verb, referring to two or more nouns, agrees with one, and is understood with the rest, the construction is also sometimes called zeugma, but more commonly syllepsis; as, *Et gĕnus, et virtus, nīsi cum re,* vīlior *algā* est. Hor. *Căper tibi* salvus *et hædi.* Virg. *Quamvis ille niger, quamvis tu candida* esses. Id.

(3.) *Syllepsis* is when an adjective or verb, belonging to two or more nouns of different genders, persons, or numbers, agrees with one rather than another; as, Attŏniti *nŏvĭtāte* pārent Baucis, *timidusque* Philēmon. Ovid. *Prŏcumbit* āterque prōnus *hūmi,* i. e. *Deucălion et Pyrrha.* Id. Sustūllĭmus *mănus et* ĕgo *et* Balbus. Cic. So, Ipse cum frātre *ădĕsse* jussi sŭmus. Id. *Prōjectisque ămĭcŭlo et litĕris.* Curt. See §§ 205, R. 2, and 209, R. 12, (3.) and (7.)

(4. *Prōlepsis* is when the parts, differing in number or person from the w‥ne, are placed after it, the verb or adjective not being repeated; as, *Principes utrinque pugnam cĭebant, ab Sabīnis* Mettius Curtius, *ab Rōmānis* Hostus Hostilius. Liv. *Boni quŏniam convenimus ambo, tu călămos inflāre, ĕgo dicĕre versus.* Virg.

2. (*a.*) *Pleonasm* is using a greater number of words than is necessary to express the meaning; as,

Sic ōre lŏcūta est. Virg. *Qui măgis vĕre vincĕre quam diu impĕrāre* mālit. Liv *Nēmo ūnus.* Cic. *Forte fortūnā.* Id. *Prūdens sciens.* Ter.

(*b.*) Under pleonasm are included *parelcon, polysyndĕton, hendĭădys,* and *periphrăsis.*

(1.) *Părelcon* is the addition of an unnecessary syllable or particle to pronouns, verbs, or adverbs; as, *ĕgŏmet, ăgĕdum, fortassean.* Such additions, however, usually modify the meaning in some degree.

(2.) *Pŏlysyndĕton* is a redundancy of conjunctions; as, *Una Eurusque Nōtusque ruunt crēberque prŏcellis Afrīcus.* Virg.

(3.) *Hendĭădys* is the expression of an idea by two nouns connected by *et* -*que,* or *atque,* instead of a noun and a limiting adjective or genitive; as, *Pătĕris libāmus et* auro, for *aureis pătĕris.* Virg. *Libro et silvestri* sŭbĕre *clausam* for *libro sŭbĕris.* Id. *Cristis et* auro. Ovid. Met. 3, 32.

(4.) *Pĕriphrăsis* or *circumlŏcūtio* is a circuitous mode of expression; as, *Tĕnĕri fœtus ŏvium,* i. e. *agni.* Virg.

3. (*a.*) *Enallăge* is a change of words, or a substitution of one gender, number, case, person, tense, mood, or voice of the same word for another.

(*b.*) Enallăge includes *antimeria, heterōsis, antiptōsis, synĕsis,* and *anacolŭthon.*

(1.) *Antimĕria* is the use of one part of speech for another, or the abstract for the concrete; as, *Nostrum istud* vīvĕre *triste,* for *nostra vīta.* Pers. *Alius* cras. Id. Conjŭgium *vidēbit?* for *conjŭgem.* Virg.

(2.) *Heterōsis* is the use of one form of noun, pronoun, verb, etc., for another. as *Ego quŏque una pereo, quod mihi est cārius,* for *qui mihi sum cārior.* Ter

Rōmānus *prœlio* victor, for *Rōmāni victōres.* Liv. Many words are used by the poets in the plural instead of the singular; as, *colla, corda, ōra,* etc. See § 98. *Me truncus illapsus cĕrĕbro sustŭlĕrat,* for *sustŭlisset.* Hor. See § 259, R. 4.

(3.) *Antiptōsis* is the use of one case for another; as, *Cui nunc cognōmen Iūlo,* for *Iūlus.* Virg. § 204, R. 8. Uxor *invicti Jŏvis esse nescis, for te esse uxŏrem.* Hor. § 210, R. 6.

(4.) *Synēsis*, or *synthĕsis*, is adapting the construction to the *sense* of a word, rather than to its gender or number; as, Sŭbeunt *Tĕgœa* jŭventus *auxilio* tardi. Stat. *Concursus* pōpŭli mīrantium *quid rei est.* Liv. Pars *in crŭcem* acti. Sall. *Uti* illic *est* scĕlus, qui *me perdĭdit?* Ter. *Id* mea *mĭnĭme rĕfert,* qui *sum nătu maxĭmus.* Id. See § 205, R. 3, (1.) and (3.), and § 206, (12.)

(5.) *Anăcŏlūthon* is a disagreement in construction between the latter and former part of a sentence; as, *Nam nos omnes, quibus est ălicunde aliquis objectus labos, omne quod est intĕrea tempus, priusquam id rescitum est,* lucro est. Ter. In this example, the writer began as if he intended to say *lucro hăbĕmus,* and ended as if he had said *nōbis omnibus,* leaving *nos omnes* without its verb.

4. (*a.*) *Hўperbăton* is a transgression of the usual order of words or clauses.

(*b.*) Hўperbăton includes *ănastrŏphe, hystĕron prŏtĕron, hўpallăge, synchŷsis, tmēsis,* and *părenthĕsis.*

(1.) *Anastrŏphe* is an inversion of the order of two words; as, *Transtra per et rēmos,* for *per transtra.* Virg. *Collo dăre brāchia circum,* for *circumdăre.* Id. *Nox ĕrit ūna sŭper,* for *sŭpĕrĕrit.* Ovid. *Et făcit āre,* for *ārĕfăcit.* Lucr.

(2.) *Hystĕron prŏtĕron* is reversing the natural order of the sense; as, *Mŏriāmur, et in mĕdia arma ruāmus.* Virg. *Valet atque vivit.* Ter.

(3.) *Hўpallăge* is an interchange of constructions; as, *In nŏva fert ănimus mūtātas dicĕre formas corpŏra,* for *corpŏra mŭtāta in nŏvas formas.* Ovid. *Dăre classibus Austros,* for *dăre classes Austris.* Virg.

(4.) *Synchŷsis* is a confused position of words; as, *Saxa vŏcant Ităli, mĕdiis quœ in fluctibus, āras,* for *quœ saxa in mĕdiis fluctibus, Ităli vŏcant āras.* Virg.

(5.) *Tmēsis* or *diacŏpe* is the separation of the parts of a compound word; as, *Septem subjecta triōni gens,* for *septentriōni.* Virg. *Quœ me cumque vŏcant terrœ.* Id. *Per mihi, per, inquam, grātum fĕcĕris.* Cic.

(6.) *Părenthĕsis* or *diălŷsis* is the insertion of a word or words in a sentence interrupting the natural connection; as, *Tityre dum rĕdeo,* (brĕvis est via,) *pasce căpellas.* Virg.

REMARK. To the above may be added *archaism* and *Hellenism,* which belong both to the figures of etymology and to those of syntax.

(1.) *Archaism* is the use of ancient forms or constructions; as, *aulāi,* for *aulœ; sĕnāti,* for *sĕnātŭs; fuat,* for *sit; prŏhibesso,* for *prŏhibuĕro; impetrassĕre,* for *impetrātūrum esse; fārier,* for *fāri; nēnu,* for *non; endo,* for *in;—Opĕram ăbūtitur,* for *ŏpĕrā.* Ter. *Quid tibi hanc cūrātio est rem?* Plaut.

(2.) *Hellenism* is the use of Greek forms or constructions; as, *Hĕlĕne,* for *Hĕlĕna; Antiphon,* for *Antipho; aurās* (gen.), for *aurœ; Pallădos, Pallăda,* for *Pallădis, Pallădem; Trŏāsin, Trŏādas,* for *Trŏādibus, Trŏādes;—Abstinĕto irārum.* Hor. *Tempus dĕsistĕre pugnœ.* Virg.

§ **324.** (1.) To the grammatical figures may not improperly be subjoined certain others, which are often referred to in philological works, and which are called

TROPES AND FIGURES OF RHETORIC.

(2.) A rhetorical *figure* is a mode of expression different from the direct and simple way of expressing the same sense. The turning of a *word* from its original and customary meaning, is called a *trope.*

1. (*a.*) A *metaphor* is the transferring of a word from the object to which it properly belongs, and applying it to another, to which that object 1 as some analogy; as, Ridet *ăger*, The field smiles. Virg. *Ætas* aurea, The golden age. Ovid. Naufrăgia *fortūnæ*, The wreck of fortune. Cic. *Mentis* ocŭli, The eyes of the mind. Id. *Virtus ănĭmum glōriæ* stĭmŭlis *concĭtat*. The harshness of a metaphor is often softened by means of *quăsi*, *tanquam*, *quĭdam*, or *ut ita dīcam*; as, *In ūn" vhĭlōsŏphĭā* quăsi tŭbernăcŭlum *vītæ suæ collŏcārunt*. Id. Optĭmum quoddam ... tamquam ădĭpătæ *dictĭōnis gĕnus*. Id.

(*b.*) *Cătachrĕsis* or *ăbūsĭo* is a bold or harsh metaphor; as, Vir *grĕgis ipse căper*. Virg. *Eurus per Sĭcŭlas* ĕquĭtāvit *undas*. Hor.

2. *Metonymy* is substituting the name of an object for that of another to which it has a certain relation; as the cause for the effect, the container for what is contained, the property for the substance, the sign for the thing signified, and their contraries; the parts of the body for certain affections; the possessor for the thing possessed; place and time for the persons or things which they comprise, etc.; as, *Mortāles*, for *hŏmĭnes*. Virg. *Amor dūri* Martis, i. e. *belli*. Id. *Frūges Cĕrĕrem appellāmus, vīnum autem* Libĕrum. Cic. *Cŭpĭo* vĭgĭliam *meam tibi trădĕre*, i. e. *meam cūram*. Id. Pallĭda *mors*. Hor. *Hausĭt* pătĕram, i. e. *vīnum*. Virg. Vīna *cŏrōnant*, i. e. *pătĕram*. Id. *Necte ternos* colōres, i. e. *tria fīla diversi cŏlōris*. Id. *Cēdant* arma *tōgæ*, i. e. *bellum pāci*. Cic. Sæcŭla *mītescent*, i. e. *hŏmĭnes in sæcŭlis*. Virg. *Vīvat Păcūrius vel* Nestŏra tōtum. Juv. *Doctrīnā* Græcia *nos sŭpĕrābat*, for *Græci sŭpĕrābant*. Cic. Păgi centum *Suevōrum ad rīpas Rhēni consēdĕrant*, for *păgōrum incŏlæ*. Cæs. Tempŏra ămīcōrum, for *res advĕrsæ*. Cic. Claudius *lēge prædiātōrĭā vēnālis pĕpendit*, for *Claudii prædium*. Suet. *Vīci ad* Jānum *mĕdium sĕdentes*, for *Jāni vīcum*. Cic.

3. *Synecdŏche* is putting a whole for a part, a genus for a species, a singular for a plural, and their contraries; also the material for the thing made of it, a definite for an indefinite number, etc.; as, Fontem *fĕrēbant*. Id. *Tectum*, for *dŏmus*. Id. *Armāto* mīlĭte *complent*, for *armātis mĭlĭtĭbus*. Id. *Ferrum*, for *glădius*. Id. *Qui Cŏrinthiis* ŏpĕrĭbus *ăbundant*, i. e. *rāsis*. Cic. Urbem, urbem, m *Rūfe*, *cōle*, i. e. *Rōmam*. Cic. Centum *puer artium*, i. e. *multārum*.

4. *Irony* is the intentional use of words which express a sense contrary to that which the writer or speaker means to convey; as, *Salve* bŏne *vir, cūrasti prŏbe*. Ter. Egrĕgiam *vĕro* laudem, *et* spŏlia ampla *rĕfertis, tūque, puerque tuus*. Virg.

5. *Hyperbŏle* is the magnifying or diminishing of a thing beyond the truth; as, *Ipse arduus, altāque pulsat sīdĕra*. Virg. *Ocior Euro*. Id.

6. *Mĕtălepsis* is the including of several tropes in one word; as, *Post ălĭquot ăristas*. Virg. Here *aristas* is put for *messes*, and this for *annos*.

7. (*a.*) *Allegory* is a consistent series of metaphors, designed to illustrate one subject by another; as, *O nāvis, rĕfĕrent in māre te nŏvi fluctus*. Hor.

(*b.*) An obscure allegory or riddle is called an *ænigma*; as, *Dic, quĭbus in terris tres pătĕat cæli spătium non amplius ulnas*. Virg.

8. *Antŏnŏmăsĭa* is using a proper noun for a common one, and the contrary; as, Irus *et est subĭto, qui mŏdo* Crœsus *ĕrat*, for *pauper* and *dīves*. Ovid. So, by periphrasis, *pōtor Rhŏdāni*, for *Gallus*. Hor. *Eversor Carthăgĭnis*, for *Scĭpĭo*. Quint. *Elŏquentiæ princeps*, for *Cĭcero*. Id. Tydīdes, for Diŏmēdes. Virg.

9. *Lĭtŏtes* is a mode of expressing something by denying the contrary; as, *Non laudo*, I blame. Ter. *Non innoxia verba*. Virg.

10. *Antĭphrăsis* is using a word in a sense opposite to its proper meaning, as, *Auri sacra fămes*. Virg.

11. *Euphemism* is the use of softened language to express what is offensive or distressing; as, *Si quid accĭdisset Cæsări*, i. e. *si mortuus esset*. Vell.

12. *Antănaclăsis* or *punning* is the use of the same word in different senses, as, *Quis nĕget* Ænēæ *nātum de stirpe Nĕrōnem? Sustŭlit hic mātrem*, sustŭli *ille patrem*. Epigr. Amāri *jucundum est, si cūrētur ne quid insit* āmāri. Cic.

§ 324. APPENDIX.—TROPES AND FIGURES OF RHETORIC. 365

13. *Anăphŏra* or *ĕpănăphŏra* is the repetition of a word at the beginning of successive clauses; as, Nĭhilne te nocturnum præsĭdĭum pălātĭi, nĭhil urbis vĭgĭlĭæ, nĭhil tĭmor pŏpŭli, etc. Cic. Te, dulcis conjux, te, sōlo in lītŏre sēcum, te, vĕnĭente die, te, dēcēdente, cănēbat. Virg.

14. *Epistrŏphe* is the repetition of a word at the end of successive clauses; as, Pœnos pŏpŭlus Rōmānus justĭtĭā vīcit, armis vīcit, lībĕrālĭtāte vīcit. Cic. In pure Latin this figure is called *conversio*.

15. *Symplŏce* is the repetition of a word at the beginning, and of another at the end, of successive clauses, and hence it includes the anaphŏra and the epistrŏphe; as, Quis lēgem tŭlit? Rullus: Quis mājōrem pŏpŭli partem suffrāgiis prīvāvit? Rullus: Quis cŏmĭtiis præfuit? Idem Rullus. Cic.

16. *Epănălepsis* is a repetition of the same word or sentence after intervening words or clauses. See Virg. Geor. II. 4—7.

17. *Anădĭplōsis* is the use of the same word at the end of one clause, and the beginning of another; as, Sĕquĭtur pulcherrĭmus Astur, Astur ēquo fĭdens. Virg. A. 10, 180. Nunc ētiam audes in hōrum conspectum vĕnīre, vĕnīre audes in hōrum conspectum? Cic. This is sometimes called *ĕpănastrŏphe*.

18. *Epănădĭplōsis* is the use of the same word both at the beginning and end of a sentence; as, Crescit ămor nummi, quantum ipsa pĕcūnia crescit. Juv.

19. *Epănŏdos* or *rēgressio* is the repetition of the same words in an inverted order as, Crūdēlis māter māgis, an puer imprŏbus ille? Imprŏbus ille puer, crūdēlis tu quŏque, māter. Virg.

20. *Epizeuxis* is a repetition of the same word for the sake of emphasis; as, Excĭtāte, excĭtāte eum ab infĕris. Cic. Ah Cōrȳdon, Cōrȳdon, quæ te dēmentia cēpit? Virg. Ibĭmus, ĭbĭmus, utcumque præcēdes. Hor.

21. *Climax* is a gradual amplification by means of a continued anadiplosis, each successive clause beginning with the conclusion of that which precedes it; as, Quæ reliqua spes manet libertātis, si illis et quod libet, licet; et quod licet, possunt; et quod possunt, audent; et quod audent, vobis molestum non est? Cic. This, in pure Latin, is called *grădātio*.

22. *Incrēmentum* is an amplification without a strict climax; as, Făcĭnus est, vincīri cīvem Rōmānum; scĕlus, verbĕrāri; prŏpe parrĭcīdĭum, nĕcāri; quid dīcam in crūcem tolli? Cic.

23. *Pōlyptōton* is the repetition of a word in different cases, genders, numbers, tenses, etc.; as, Jam clĭpeus clĭpeis, umbōne rĕpellĭtur umbo; ense mĭnax ensis, pĕde pes, et cuspĭde cuspis. Stat.

24. *Paregmĕnon* is the use of several words of the same origin, in one sentence; as, Abesse non pŏtest, quin ējusdem hŏmĭnis sit, qui imprŏbos prŏbet, prŏbos imprŏbāre. Cic. Istam pugnam pugnābo. Plaut.

25. *Părŏnŏmăsia* is the use of words which resemble each other in sound as, Amor et melle et felle est fēcundissĭmus. Plaut. Cīvem bŏnārum artium bŏnārum partium. Cic. Amantes sunt āmentes. Ter. This figure is sometimes called *agnŏmĭnātio*.

26. *Hŏmœŏprŏphĕron* or *alliteration* is the use in the same sentence of several words beginning with the same letter; as, O Tīte, tūte Tūti, tĭbi tanta, tȳranne, tŭlisti. Enn. Neu patriæ vălĭdas in viscĕra vertīte vīres. Virg.

27. *Antĭthĕsis* is the placing of different or opposite words or sentiments in contrast; as, Hūjus ōrātiōnis diffĭcillĭma est exĭtum quam princĭpium invĕnīre. Cic. Cæsar bĕnĕfĭciis ac mūnĭfĭcentiā magnus hăbēbātur; integrĭtāte vītæ Cato. Sall.

28. *Oxymōron* unites words of contrary significations, thus producing a seeming contradiction; as, Concordia discors. Hor. Quum tăcent, clāmant. Cic.

29. *Synŏnymia* is the use of different words or expressions having the same import; as, Non fĕram, non pătiar, non sĭnam. Cic. Prōmitto, rĕcĭpio, spondeo. Id.

30. *Părăbŏla* or *Simĭle* is the comparison of one thing with another; as, *Rĕ-pente te, tamquam serpens e lătĭbŭlis, ŏcŭlis ēmĭnentĭbus, inflāto collo, tŭmĭdis cervīcĭbus, intŭlisti.* Cic.

31. *Erōtēsis* is an earnest question, and often implies a strong affirmation of the contrary; as, *Crēdĭtis āvectos hostes?* Virg. *Heu! quæ me æquŏra possunt accĭpĕre?* Id.

32. *Epănorthōsis* or *Correctio* is the recalling of a word, in order to place a stronger or more significant one in its stead; as, *Fīlium ŭnĭcum ădŏlescentŭlum hăbeo: ah! quid dixi? me hăbēre? Imo* hăbui. Ter.

33. *Apŏsiŏpēsis, Rĕtĭcentia,* or *Interruptio,* is leaving a sentence unfinished in consequence of some emotion of the mind; as, *Quos ĕgo—sed mōtos præstat compōnĕre fluctus.* Virg.

34. *Prŏsŏpŏpœia* or *personification* represents inanimate things as acting or speaking, and persons dead or absent as alive and present; as, *Quæ (patria) tēcum, Cătĭlīna, sic ăgit.* Cic. *Virtus sūmit aut pōnit sĕcūres.* Hor.

35. *Apostrŏphe* is a turning off from the regular course of the subject, to address some person or thing; as, *Vi pŏtĭtur; quid non mortālia pectŏra cōgis, auri sacra fāmes!* Virg.

36. *Părăleipsis* is a pretended omission of something, in order to render it more observed. See Cic. Cat. 1, 6, 14.

37. *Epĭphōnēma* or *Acclămātio* is an exclamation or grave reflection on something said before; as, *Tantæ mōlis ĕrat Rōmānam condĕre gentem.* Virg.

38. *Ecphōnēsis* or *Exclămātio* shows some violent emotion of the mind; as, *O tempŏra! O mōres!*

39. *Apŏria, Diăpŏrēsis,* or *Dŭbĭtātio,* expresses a doubt in regard to what is to be said or done; as, *Quos accēdam, aut quos appellem?* Sall.

40. *Prŏlepsis* is the anticipation of an objection before it is made, or of an event before it occurs; as, *Vērum anceps pugnæ fuĕrat fortūna. Fuisset: Quem* mĕtui mōrĭtūra? Virg.

§ 325.

To the figures of rhetoric may be subjoined the following terms, used to designate *defects* or *blemishes* in style:—

1. *Barbarism* is either the use of a foreign word, or a violation of the rules of orthography, etymology, or prosody; as, *rĭgŏrōsus,* for *rĭgĭdus* or *sĕvērus; dommĭnus,* for *dŏmĭnus; davi,* for *dĕdi.*

2. *Solecism* is a violation of the rules of syntax; as, *Vēnus pulcher; vos invĭdēmus.*

3. *Neoterism* is the use of words or phrases introduced by authors living subsequently to the best ages of Latinity; as, *murdrum,* a murder; *constăbŭlārius,* a constable.

4. *Tautology* is a repetition of the same meaning in different words; as, *Jam vos ăciem, et prœlia, et hostem poscĭtis.* Sil.

5. *Amphĭbŏlia* is the use of equivocal words or constructions; as, *Gallus,* Gaul, or a cock. *Aio te, Æăcĭda, Rōmānos vincĕre posse.* Quint.

6. *Idiotism* is a construction peculiar to one or more languages: thus, the ablative after comparatives is a Latinism. When a peculiarity of one language is imitated in another, this is also called *idiotism.* Thus, *Mitte mihi verbum,* instead of *Fac me certiōrem,* is an Anglicism.

ROMAN MODE OF RECKONING.

I. OF TIME.

1. *The Roman Day.*

§ 326. (1.) With the Romans, as with us, the day was either *civil* or *natural*. Their civil day, like ours, extended from midnight to midnight. The natural day continued from sunrise to sunset, as, on the other hand, the night extended from sunset to sunrise. The natural day and night were each divided into twelve equal parts or *hours*, which were consequently of different length, according to the varying length of the days and nights in the successive seasons of the year. It was only at the equinox that the diurnal and nocturnal hours of the Romans were equal to each other, as each was then equal to the twenty-fourth part of the civil day.

(2.) In the Roman camp the night was further divided into four watches (*vĭgĭlĭæ*), consisting each of three Roman hours, the second and fourth watches ending respectively at midnight and at sunrise

2. *The Roman Month and Year.*

(1.) The calendar of the Romans, as rectified by Julius Cæsar, agreed with our own in the number of months, and of the days in each, according to the following table:—

Jānuārius . 31 days.	Maius . . 31 days.	September 30 days.
Februārius 28 or 29.	Jūnius. . 30 "	Octōber . . 31 "
Martius. . . 31 days.	Quintīlis 31 "	Nŏvember 30 "
Aprīlis . . . 30 "	Sextīlis . 31 "	December 31 "

In early times the Roman year began with March, and the names *Quintīlis, Sextīlis, September*, etc., indicated the distance of those months from the commencement of the year. *Quintīlis* and *Sextīlis* were afterwards called *Jūlius* and *Augustus* in honor of the first two emperors. The Romans, instead of reckoning in an uninterrupted series from the first to the last day of a month, had in each month three points or periods from which their days were counted—the *Calends*, the *Nones*, and the *Ides*. The Calends (*Călendæ*), were always the *first* day of the month. The Nones (*Nōnæ*), were the *fifth*, and the Ides (*Idus*), the *thirteenth;* except in March, May, July, and October, when the Nones occurred on the *seventh* day, and the Ides on the *fifteenth*.

(2.) They always counted forward, from the day whose date was to be determined, to the next Calends, Nones, or Ides, and designated the day by its distance before such point. After the first day of the month, therefore, they began to reckon so many days before the Nones; after the Nones, so many days before the Ides; and after the Ides, so many before the Calends, of the next month.

Thus, the second of January was denoted by *quarto Nōnas Jānuārias*, or *Jānuārii*, scil. *die ante:* the third, *tertio Nōnas;* the fourth, *prīdie Nōnas;* and the fifth, *Nōnis*. The sixth was denoted by *octāvo Idus;* the seventh *septimo Idus;* and so on to the thirteenth, on which the Ides fell. The fourteenth was denoted by *undēvigēsimo Călendas Februārias,* or *Februārii;* and so on to the end of the month.

(3.) The day preceding the Calends, Nones, and Ides, was termed *pridie Calendas,* etc., scil. *ante:* in designating the other days, both the day of the Calends, etc., and that whose date was to be determined, were reckoned; hence the second day before the Calends, etc., was called *tertio,* the third *quarto,* etc.

(4.) To reduce the Roman calendar to our own, therefore, when the day is between the Calends and the Nones or between the Nones and the Ides, it is necessary to take one from the number denoting the distance of the given day from the Nones or the Ides, and to subtract the remainder from the number of the day on which the Nones or Ides fell in the given month.

Thus, to determine the day equivalent to *IV. Nonas Jānuārias,* we take 1 from 4, and subtract the remainder, 3, from 5, the day on which the Nones of January fell (i. e. 4—1=3, and 5—3=2): this gives 2, or the second of January, for the day in question. So *VI. Idus Aprilis:* the Ides of April falling upon the 13th, we take (6—1, i. e.) 5 from 13, which leaves 8 (i. e. 6—1=5, and 13—5=8): the expression, therefore, denotes the 8th of April.

(*a.*) In reckoning the days before the Calends, as they are not the last day of the current month, but the first of the following, it is necessary to subtract two from the number denoting the distance of the given day from the Calends of the following month, and to take the remainder from the number of days in the month.

Thus, *XV. Cal. Quintīles* is 15—2=13, and 30—13=17, i. e. the Roman date XV. Cal. Quint. is equivalent to the 17th of June.

(*b.*) To reduce our calendar to the Roman, the preceding method is to be reversed. Thus when the given day is between the Calends and the Nones or between the Nones and the Ides, (unless it be the day before the Nones or the Ides), we are to *add* one to the number denoting the day of the month, according to our reckoning, on which the Nones or Ides fell. But if the day is after the Ides, (unless it be the last day of the month), we must add *two* to the number of days in the month, and then subtract the number denoting the day of the month as expressed in our reckoning. The remainder will be the day before the Nones, Ides or Calends.

Thus to find the Roman date corresponding to the third of April, we have 5+1—3=3; the required date, therefore, is *III. Non. Apr.*—To find the proper Roman expression for our tenth of December we have 13+1—10=4; the date, therefore, is *IV. Id. Dec.*—The Roman expression for the 22d of August, in pursuance of the above rule, is found thus, 31+2—22=11, and the date is *XI Cal. Sept.*

(5.) In leap year, both the 24th and 25th of February were called the sixth before the Calends of March. The 24th was called *dies bisextus,* and the year itself *annus bisextus,* bissextile or leap year.

(*a.*) The day after the Calends, etc., was sometimes called *postridie cālendas,* etc.

(*b.*) The names of the months are properly adjectives, though often used as nouns, *mensis* being understood.

§ 326. APPENDIX.—ROMAN MODE OF RECKONING—TIME.

(6.) The correspondence of our calendar with that of the Romans is exhibited in the following

TABLE.

Days of our months.	MAR. MAI. JUL. OCT.	JAN. AUG. DEC.	APR. JUN. SEPT. NOV.	FEBR.
1	Calendæ.	Calendæ.	Calendæ.	Calendæ.
2	VI. Nonas.	IV. Nonas.	IV. Nonas.	IV. Nonas.
3	V. "	III. "	III. "	III. "
4	IV. "	Pridie "	Pridie "	Pridie "
5	III. "	Nonæ.	Nonæ.	Nonæ.
6	Pridie Non.	VIII. Idus.	VIII. Idus.	VIII. Idus.
7	Nonæ.	VII. "	VII. "	VII. "
8	VIII. Idus.	VI. "	VI. "	VI. "
9	VII. "	V. "	V. "	V. "
10	VI. "	IV. "	IV. "	IV. "
11	V. "	III. "	III. "	III. "
12	IV. "	Pridie "	Pridie "	Pridie "
13	III. "	Idus.	Idus.	Idus.
14	Pridie Id.	XIX. Cal.	XVIII. Cal.	XVI. Cal.
15	Idus.	XVIII. "	XVII. "	XV. "
16	XVII. Cal.	XVII. "	XVI. "	XIV. "
17	XVI. "	XVI. "	XV. "	XIII. "
18	XV. "	XV. "	XIV. "	XII. "
19	XIV. "	XIV. "	XIII. "	XI. "
20	XIII. "	XIII. "	XII. "	X. "
21	XII. "	XII. "	XI. "	IX. "
22	XI. "	XI. "	X. "	VIII. "
23	X. "	X. "	IX. "	VII. "
24	IX. "	IX. "	VIII. "	VI. "
25	VIII. "	VIII. "	VII. "	V. "
26	VII. "	VII. "	VI. "	IV. "
27	VI. "	VI. "	V. "	III. "
28	V. "	V. "	IV. "	Pridie " Mart
29	IV. "	IV. "	III. "	
30	III. "	III. "	Pridie Cal.	
31	Pridie Cal.	Pridie Cal.		

(7.) In leap-year the last seven days of February were reckoned thus:—

23. VII. *Cálendas Martias.*   27. IV. *Cal. Mart.*
24. *bisexto Cal. Mart.*   28. III. "   "
25. VI. *Cal. Mart.*   29. *pridie Cal. Mart.*
26. V.   "   "

(*a.*) Hence in reducing a date of February in leap-year to the Roman date, for the first 23 days we proceed according to the preceding rule in 4, (*b.*), as if the month had only 28 days. The 24th is marked as *bisexto Cal. Mart.*, and to obtain the proper expression for the remaining five days we regard the month as having 29 days. Thus the 27th of February in leap-year is 29+2—27=4, and the proper Roman expression is *IV. Cal. Mart.*

(*b.*) On the other hand, to reduce a Roman date of February in leap-year to our date we reverse the above process, and during the Nones and Ides and until the *VII. Cálendas Martias* we reckon the month to have only 28 days:— *bisexto Cal. Mart.* is set down as the 24th, and for the remaining days designated as *VI. V. IV. III.* and *pridie Cal. Mart.* we reckon the month to have 29 days. Thus *III. Cal. Mart.* is 3—2=1, and 29—1=28, and the given day is equivalent to the 28th of February.

370 APPENDIX.—ROMAN MODE OF RECKONING—MONEY. § 327.

(8.) The Latins not only said *tertio*, *pridie*, etc., *Calendas*, etc., but also *ante diem tertium*, etc., *Calendas*, etc.; and the latter form in Cicero and Livy is far more common than the former, and is usually written thus, *a. d. III. Cal.*, etc.

(9.) The expression *ante diem* was used as an indeclinable noun, and is joined with *in* and *ex*; as, *Consul Latīnas fērias* in ante diem *tertium Idus Sextīlis ēdixit*, The consul appointed the Latin festival for the third day before the Ides of August. Liv. *Supplicātio indicta est* ex ante diem *quintum Idus Octōbres*. Id. So, Ad pridie *Nōnas Maias.* Cic.

(10.) The week of seven days (*hebdŏmas*), was not in use among the Romans under the republic, but was introduced under the emperors. The days of the week were then named from the planets; *dies Sōlis*, Sunday; *dies Lūnæ*, Monday; *dies Martis*, Tuesday; *dies Mercūrii*, Wednesday; *dies Jŏvis*, Thursday; *dies Vĕnĕris*, Friday; *dies Sāturni*, Saturday.

(11.) The term *nundīnæ* (from *nŏvem—dies*) denotes the regular market day at Rome when the country people came into the city; but it is not used for the purpose of denoting the period of eight days intervening between two successive market days.

(12.) The year at Rome was designated by the names of the consuls for that year. Thus Virgil was born, *M. Licinio Crasso et Cn. Pompeio Magno consulibus*, i. e. in the year of the consulship of Crassus and Pompey. But in Roman authors events are often dated from the year in which Rome was founded, which, according to Varro, was in the 753d year before the birth of Christ. This period was designated as *anno urbis condĭtæ*, and by abbreviation, *a. u. c.*, or simply *u. c.*, and sometimes by *a.* alone, before the numerals.

Thus the birth of Virgil was *a. u. c.* 684. To reduce such dates to our reckoning, if the given number is less than 754, we subtract it from the latter number, and the difference is the required year before Christ. The birth of Virgil therefore is 754—684=70 before Christ.—But if the number of the Roman year exceeds 753, we deduct 753 from the given number, and the remainder is the year after Christ. For example, the emperor Augustus died *a. u. c.* 767, and the corresponding year of our era is 767—753=14.

II. TABLES OF MONEY, WEIGHT, AND MEASURE.

Of the As.

§ **327.** The Romans used this word (*As*) to denote, I. The copper coin, whose value (in the time of Cicero) was about one cent and a half of our money. II. The unit of weight (libra), or of measure (jūgĕrum). III. Any unit or integer considered as divisible; as, of inheritances, interest, houses, etc.; whence *ex asse hēres*, one who inherits the whole. The multiples of the *As* are, *Dŭpondius* (*duo pondo*; for the *As* originally weighed a pound), i. e. 2 Asses; *Sestertius* (*sesqui tertius*), i. e. 2½ Asses; *Tressis*, i. e. 3 Asses; *Quatrussis*, i. e. 4 Asses; and so on to *Centussis*, i. e. 100 Asses. The *As*, whatever unit it represented, was divided into twelve parts or *unciæ*, and the different fractions received different names, as follows:

	Uncia.		Uncia.
As	12	Quincunx	5
Deunx	11	Triens	4
Dextans	10	Quādrans, or Tĕruncius	3
Dodrans	9	Sextans	2
Bes	8	Uncia	1
Septunx	7		
Sēmis	6	Sescuncia	1½

§ 327. APPENDIX.—TABLES OF MONEY, WEIGHT, ETC. 371

The *Uncia* was divided in the following manner:—

    1 Uncia contained 2 Sēmunciæ.
        "   "   3 Duellæ.
        "   "   4 Sicīlici.
        "   "   6 Sextŭlæ.
        "   "   8 Drachmæ.
        "   "   24 Scrūpŭla.
        "   "   48 Obŏli.

Roman Coins.

These were the *Tĕruncius*, *Sembella*, and *As* or *Libella*, of copper; the *Sestertius*, *Quinārius* (or *Victōriātus*), and *Dēnārius*, of silver; and the *Aureus* of gold.

				$	Cts.	M.
	The Tĕruncius................			0	0	3.9
2	Tĕruncii make	1	Sembella.........	0	0	7.8
2	Sembellæ "	1	As *or* Libella.....	0	1	5.6
2½	Asses* "	1	Sestertius........	0	3	9
2	Sestertii "	1	Quinārius........	0	7	8
2	Quinārii "	1	Dēnārius.........	0	15	6
25	Dēnārii "	1	Aureus..........	3	90	0

* Sometimes also (in copper) the triens, sextans, uncia, sextŭla, and dŭpondius.

Roman Computation of Money.

Sestertii Nummi.

	$	Cts.	M.
Sestertius (or nummus)	0	3	9
Dĕcem sestertii	0	39	0
Centum sestertii	3	90	0
Mille sestertii (equal to a sestertium)	39	0	0

Sestertia.

Sestertium (equal to mille sestertii).......................	39	0	0
Dĕcem sestertia	390	0	0
Centum, centum sestertia, or centum millia sestertiŭm......	3900	0	0
Dĕcies sestertiŭm, or dĕcies centēna millia nummŭm.......	39000	0	0
Centies, or centies H. S...................................	390000	0	0
Millies H. S..	3900000	0	0
Millies centies H. S.......................................	4290000	0	0

N. B.—The marks denoting a Sestertius nummus are IIS., LLS., IIS., which are properly abbreviations for 2 1-2 *asses*. Observe, also, that when a line is placed over the numbers, *centēna millia* is understood, as in the case of the numeral adverbs; thus, H. S. M̄C. is millies centies IIS.; whereas IIS. MC. is only 1100 Sestertii.

Roman Calculation of Interest.

The Romans received interest on their loans monthly, their highest rate being one per cent. (*centesima*), a month, i. e. 12 per cent a year. As this was the highest rate, it was reckoned as the *as* or unit in reference to the lower rates, which were denominated, according to the usual division of the *as*, *semisses*, *trientes*, *quadrantes*, etc., i. e. the half, third, fourth, etc., of the *as* or of 12 per cent. according to the following table:—

	Per cent. a year.
Asses ūsūræ or centēsimæ	12
Sēmisses ūsūræ	6
Trientes ūsūræ	4
Quadrantes ūsūræ	3
Sextantes ūsūræ	2
Unciæ ūsūræ	1
Quincunces ūsūræ	5
Septunces ūsūræ	7
Besses ūsūræ	8
Dodrantes ūsūræ	9
Dextantes ūsūræ	10
Deunces ūsūræ	11

ROMAN WEIGHTS.

				Oz.	Dwts.	Gr.
	Siliqua			0	0	3.036
3	Siliquæ	make	1 Obŏlus	0	0	9.107
2	Obŏli	"	1 Scrūpŭlum	0	0	18.214
3	Scrūpŭla	"	1 Drachma	0	2	6.643
1½	Drachma	"	1 Sextŭla	0	3	0.857
1½	Sextŭla	"	1 Sicilicus	0	4	13.286
1½	Sicilicus	"	1 Duella	0	6	1.714
3	Duellæ	"	1 Uncia	0	18	5.143
12	Unciæ	"	1 Libra* (As)	10	18	13.714

* The Libra was also divided, according to the fractions of the As, into Deunx, etc.

ROMAN MEASURES FOR THINGS DRY.

				English Corn Measure.			
				Peck.	Gal.	Pint.	Sol. in.
	Ligŭla			0	0	0 1-48	0.01
4	Ligŭlæ	make	1 Cyăthus	0	0	0 1-12	0.04
1½	Cyăthus	"	1 Acētăbŭlum	0	0	0 1-8	0.06
4	Acētăbŭla	"	1 Hēmina	0	0	0 1-2	0.24
2	Hēminæ	"	1 Sextārius	0	0	1	0.48
16	Sextārii	"	1 Modius	1	0	0	7.68

ROMAN MEASURES FOR THINGS LIQUID.

				English Wine Measure.		
				Galls.	Pints.	Sol. in.
	Ligŭla			0	0 1-48	0.117
4	Ligŭlæ	make	1 Cyăthus	0	0 1-12	0.469
1½	Cyăthus	"	1 Acētăbŭlum	0	0 1-8	0.704
2	Acētăbŭla	"	1 Quartārius	0	0 1-4	1.409
2	Quartārii	"	1 Hēmina	0	0 1-2	2.876
2	Hēminæ	"	1 Sextārius*	0	1	5.636
6	Sextārii	"	1 Congius	0	7	4.942
4	Congii	"	1 Urna	3	4 1-2	5.33
2	Urnæ	"	1 Amphŏra (or Quadrantal)	7	1	10.66
20	Amphŏræ	"	1 Cūleus	143	3	11.095

* The *Sextārius* was also divided into twelve equal parts, called *cyăthi*, and therefore the *cālices* were denominated *sextantes, quadrantes, trientes*, according to the number of *cyăthi* which they contained.

N. B.—*Cădus, congiărius,* and *dōlium,* are the names of certain *vessels,* not *measures,* of capacity.

§ 327. APPENDIX.—TABLES OF MONEY, WEIGHT, ETC. 373

ROMAN MEASURES OF LENGTH.

				English paces.	Feet.	Inch. Dec
	Digitus transversus			0	0	0.725 1-4
1 1-5	Digitus	make	1 Uncia	0	0	0.967
3	Unciæ	"	1 Palmus minor	0	0	2.901
4	Palmi minōres	"	1 Pes	0	0	11.604
1 1-4	Pes	"	1 Palmīpes	0	1	2.505
1 1-5	Palmīpes	"	1 Cŭbĭtus	0	1	5.406
1 2-3	Cŭbĭtus	"	1 Grădus	0	2	5.01
2	Grădus	"	1 Passus	0	4	10.02
125	Passus	"	1 Stădium	120	4	4.5
8	Stădia	"	1 Milliārium	967	0	0

ROMAN SQUARE MEASURES.

	Roman sq. feet.	English rods.	Sq. pls.	Sq. feet.
Jūgĕrum (As)	28,800	2	18	250.05
Deunx	26,400	2	10	183.85
Dextans	24,000	2	02	117.64
Dodrans	21,600	1	34	51.42
Bes	19,200	1	25	257.46
Septunx	16,800	1	17	191.25
Sēmis	14,400	1	09	125.03
Quincunx	12,000	1	01	58.82
Triens	9,600	0	32	264.85
Quădrans	7,200	0	24	198.64
Sextans	4,800	0	16	132.43
Uncia	2,400	0	08	66.21

REMARK 1. The Romans reckoned their copper money by *asses*, their silver money by *sestertii*, and their gold money by *aurei* and sometimes by Attic *talents*.

REM. 2. The *as*, as the unit of money, was originally a pound of copper, but its weight was gradually diminished, until, in the later days of the republic, it amounted to only 1-24th of a pound.

REM. 3. (*a.*) The *dēnārius* was a silver coin, originally equal in value to ten *asses*, whence its name; but, after the weight of the *as* was reduced, the *dēnārius* was equal to eighteen *asses*.

(*b.*) The *sestertius*, or sesterce, was one fourth of the *dēnārius*, or two *asses* and a half (*sēmistertius*). The *sestertius* was called emphatically *nummus*, as in it all large sums were reckoned after the coining of silver money.

(*c.*) The *aureus* (a gold coin), in the time of the emperors, was equal to 25 *dēnārii*, or 100 sesterces.

REM. 4. In reckoning money, the Romans called any sum under 2000 sesterces so many *sestertii*; as, *decem sestertii*, ten sesterces; *centum sestertii*, a hundred sesterces.

REM. 5. Sums from 2000 sesterces (inclusive) to 1,000,000, they denoted either by *mille*, *millia*, with *sestertiûm* (gen. plur.), or by the plural of the neuter noun *sestertium*, which itself signified *a thousand* sesterces. Thus they said *quadrāginta millia sestertiûm*, or *quadraginta sestertia*, to denote 40,000 sesterces. With the genitive *sestertiûm*, *millia* was sometimes omitted; as, *sestertiûm centum*, scil. *millia*, 100,000 sesterces.

REM. 6. To denote a million, or more, they used a combination; thus, *dĕcies centēna millia sestertiûm*, 1,000,000 sesterces. The words *centēna millia*, however, were generally omitted; thus, *dĕcies sestertiûm*, and sometimes merely *dĕcies* See § 118, 5. So, *centies*, 10 millions; *millies*, 100 millions.

REX. ¹. Some suppose that *sestertium*, when thus joined with the numeral adverbs, is always the neuter noun in the nominative or accusative singular. The genitive and ablative of that noun are thus used; as, *Decies sestertii dote*, With a dowry of 1,000,000 sesterces. Tac. *Quinquagies sestertio*, 5,000,000 sesterces. Id. But this usage does not occur in Cicero.

ABBREVIATIONS.

§ 328. The following are the most common abbreviations of Latin words:—

A., *Aulus*.	M. T. C., *Marcus Tullius Cicero*.	Q., or Qu., *Quintus*.
C., *Caius*, or *Gaius*.		Ser., *Servius*.
Cn., *Cneïus*.	M., *Manius*.	S., or Sex., *Sextus*.
D., *Decimus*.	Mam., *Mamercus*.	Sp., *Spurius*.
L., *Lucius*.	N., *Numerius*.	T., *Titus*.
M., *Marcus*.	P., *Publius*.	Ti., or Tib., *Tiberius*.

A. d., *ante diem*.	F., *Filius*; as, M. F., *Marci filius*.	Pont. Max., *pontifex maximus*.
A. U. C., *anno urbis conditæ*.	Ictus, *jurisconsultus*.	Pr., *prætor*.
Cal., or Kal., *Calendæ*.	Id., *Idus*.	Proc., *proconsul*.
Cos., *Consul*.	Imp., *imperator*.	Resp., *respublica*.
Coss., *Consules*.	J. O. M., *Jovi, optimo maximo*.	S., *salutem, sacrum*, or *senatus*.
D., *Divus*.	N., *nepos*.	S. D. P., *salutem dicit plurimam*.
D. D., *dono dedit*.	Non., *Nonæ*.	
D. D. D., *dat, dicat, dedicat*, or *dono dicat, dedicat*.	P. C., *patres conscripti*.	S. P. Q. R., *Senatus populusque Romanus*.
	Pl., *plebis*.	
Des., *designatus*.	Pop., *populus*.	S. C., *senatus consultum*.
D. M., *diis manibus*.	P. R., *populus Romanus*.	Tr., *tribunus*.
Eq. Rom., *eques Romanus*.		

To these may be added terms of reference; as, *c., caput*, chapter; *cf., confer*, compare; *l. c., loco citato; l. l., loco laudato*, in the place quoted; *v., versus*, verse.

DIFFERENT AGES OF ROMAN LITERATURE.

§ 329. 1. Of the Roman literature for the first five centuries after the foundation of the city, but few vestiges remain. The writers of the succeeding centuries have been arranged in four ages, in reference to the purity of the language in the period in which they flourished. These are called the *golden, silver, brazen*, and *iron* ages.

2. The golden age is reckoned from the time of Livius Andronicus, about A. U. C. 514, to the death of Augustus, A. U. C. 767, or A. D. 14, a period of a little more than 250 years. The writers of the early part of this age are valued rather on account of their antiquity, and in connection with the history of the language, than as models of style. It was not till the age of Cicero, that Roman literature reached its highest elevation. The era comprehending the generation immediately preceding, and that immediately succeeding, that of Cicero, as well as his own, is the period in which the most distinguished writers of Rome flourished; and their works are the standard of purity in the Latin language.

3. The silver age extended from the death of Augustus to the death of Trajan, A. D. 118, a period of 104 years. The writers of this age were inferior to those who had preceded them; yet several of them are worthy of commendation.

4. The brazen age comprised the interval from the death of Trajan to the time when Rome was taken by the Goths, A. D. 410. From the latter epoch commenced the iron age, during which the Latin language was much adulterated with foreign words, and its style and spirit essentially injured.

5. The body of Latin writings has been otherwise arranged by Dr. Freund, so as to be comprised in three main periods,—the *Ante-classical, Classical,* and *Post-classical.* The ante-classical extends from the oldest fragments of the language to Lucretius and Varro; the classical from Cicero and Cæsar to Tacitus, Suetonius, and the younger Pliny inclusive; the post-classical from that time to the fifth century of our era. The classical Latinity is subdivided into (*a.*) *Ciceronian*, (*b.*) *Augustan*, (*c.*) *post-Augustan*, and to the language of the fourth and fifth centuries he has given the title of *late Latin*.

LATIN WRITERS IN THE DIFFERENT AGES

(From the Lexicon of Facciolatus.)

WRITERS OF THE GOLDEN AGE.

Livius Andronicus.	L. Cornelius Sisenna.	Q. Novius.
Lævius.	P. Nigidius Figūlus.	C. Q. Atta.
C. Nævius.	C. Decius Laberius.	L. Cassius Hemina.
Statius Cæcilius.	M. Verrius Flaccus.	Fenestella.
Q. Ennius.	Varro Atacīnus.	Q. Claud. Quadrigarius.
M. Pacuvius.	Titinius.	Cœlius Antipāter.
L. Accius.	L. Pomponius.	Fabius Pictor.
C. Lucilius.	C. Sempronius Asellio.	Cn. Gellius.
Sex. Turpilius.	Cn. Matius.	L. Piso, and others.
L. Afranius.		

Of the works of the preceding writers, only a few fragments remain.

M. Porcius Cato.	Sex. Aurelius Propertius.	P. Ovidius Naso.
M. Accius Plautus.	C. Sallustius Crispus.	Q. Horatius Flaccus.
M. Terentius Afer.	M. Terentius Varro.	C. Pedo Albinovānus.
T. Lucretius Carus.	Albius Tibullus.	Gratius Faliscus.
C. Valerius Catullus.	P. Virgilius Maro.	Phædrus.
P. Syrus.	T. Livius.	C. Cornificius.
C. Julius Cæsar	M. Manilius.	A. Hurtius, *or* Oppius.
C. Cornelius Nepos.	M. Vitruvius.	P. Cornelius Sevērus.
M. Tullius Cicĕro.		

To these may be added the following names of lawyers, whose opinions are found in the digests:—

Q. Mutius Scævŏla.	M. Antistius Labeo.	Masurius Sabīnus.
Alfenus Varus.		

Of the writers of the golden age, the most distinguished are Terence, Catullus, Cæsar, Nepos, Cicero, Virgil, Horace, Ovid, T. Livy, and Sallust.

WRITERS OF THE SILVER AGE.

A. Cornelius Celsus.
P. Velleius Paterculus.
L. Junius Moderātus Columella.
Pomponius Mela.
A. Persius Flaccus.
Q. Asconius Pediānus.
M. Annæus Senĕca.
L. Annæus Senĕca.
M. Annæus Lucānus.
T. Petronius Arbiter.
C. Plinius Secundus.
C. Silius Italicus.
C. Valerius Flaccus.
C. Julius Solinus.
D. Junius Juvenālis.
P. Papinius Statius.
M. Valerius Martiālis.
M. Fabius Quintiliānus.
Sex. Julius Frontīnus.
C. Cornelius Tacĭtus.
C. Plinius Cœcilius Secundus.
L. Annæus Florus.
C. Suetonius Tranquillus.

The age to which the following writers should be assigned is somewhat uncertain:—

Q. Curtius Rūfus.
Valerius Prŏbus.
Scribonius Largus.
Sulpitia.
L. Fenestella.
Atteius Capīto.

Of the writers of the silver age, the most distinguished are Celsus, Velleius, Columella, the Senecas, the Plinies, Juvenal, Quintilian, Tacitus, Suetonius, and Curtius.

WRITERS OF THE BRAZEN AGE.

A. Gellius.
L. Apuleius.
Q. Septimius Tertulliānus.
Q. Serēnus Sammonĭcus.
Censorīnus.
Thascius Cæcilius Cypriānus.
T. Julius Calpurnius.
M. Aurelius Nemesiānus.
Ælius Spartiānus.
Julius Capitolīnus.
Ælius Lampridius.
Vulcatius Gallicānus.
Trebellius Pollio.
Flavius Vopiscus.
Cœlius Aureliānus.
Flavius Eutropius.
Rhemnius Fannius.
Arnobius Afer.
L. Cœlius Lactantius.
Ælius Donātus.
C. Vettus Juvencus.
Julius Firmĭcus.
Fab. Marius Victorīnus.
Sex. Rūfus, or Rūfus Festus.
Ammiānus Marcellīnus.
Vegetius Renātus.
Aurel. Theodōrus Macrobius.
Q. Aurelius Symmăchus.
D. Magnus Ausonius.
Paulīnus Nolānus.
Sex. Aurelius Victor.
Aurel. Prudentius Clēmens.
Cl Claudiānus.
Marcellus Empirīcus.
Falconia Prŏba.

Of an Age not entirely certain.

Valerius Maximus.
Justīnus.
Terentiānus Maurus.
Minutius Felix.
Sosipăter Charisius.
Flavius Aviānus.

The opinions of the following lawyers are found in the digests:—

Licinius Procŭlus.
Neratius Priscus.
P. Juventius Celsus.
Priscus Jabolēnus.
Domitius Ulpiānus.
Herennius Modestīnus.
Salvius Juliānus.
Caius.
Callistrătus.
Æmilius Papiniānus.
Julius Paulus.
Sex. Pomponius.
Venuleius Saturnīnus.
Ælius Marciānus.
Ælius Gallus, and others

Of the writers of the brazen age, Justin, Terentianus, Victor, Lactantius, and Claudian, are most distinguished.

The age to which the following writers belong is uncertain. The style of some of them would entitle them to be ranked with the writers of the preceding ages, while that of others would place them even below those of the iron age.

§ 329.   APPENDIX.—WRITERS IN DIFFERENT AGES.   377

Palladius Rutilius Taurus Æmiliānus.
Æmilius Mācer.
Messāla Corvīnus.
Vibius Sequester.
Julius Obsèquens.
L. Ampelius.
Apicius Cœlius.
Sex. Pompeius Festus.
Prŏbus (auctor Notārum.)
Fulgentius Planciădes.
Hygīnus.
C. Cæsar Germanĭcus.
P. Victor.
P. Vegetius.

Auctōres Priapeiōrum.
Catalecta Virgilii et Ovidii.
Auctor oratiōnis Sallustii in Cic. et Cicerōnis in Sall.; item illius *Antĕquam iret in exsilium.*
Auctor Epistŏlæ ad Octavium.
Auctor Panegyrĭci ad Pisōnem.
Declamatiōnes quæ tribuuntur Quintiliāno, Porcio Latrōni, Calpurnio Flacco.

Interpres Darētis Phrygii, et Dictyos Cretensis.
Scholiastæ Vetĕres.
Grammatĭci Antīqui.
Rhetŏres Antīqui.
Medĭci Antīqui.
Catalecta Petroniāna.
Pervigilium Venĕris.
Poematia et Epigrammăta vetĕra a Pithæo collecta.
Monumentum Ancyrănum.
Fasti Consulāres.
Inscriptiōnes Vetĕres.

WRITERS OF THE IRON AGE.

Cl. Rutilius Numatiānus.
Servius Honorātus.
D. Hieronўmus.
D. Augustīnus.
Sulpicius Sevērus.
Paulus Orosius.
Cœlius Sedulius.
Codex Theodosiānus.
Martiānus Capella.
Claudiānus Mamertus.
Sidonius Apollināris.

Latīnus Pacātus.
Claudius Mamertīnus, et alii, quorum sunt Panegyrĭci vetĕres.
Alcĭmus Avītus.
Manl. Severīnus Boëthius.
Prisciānus.
Nonius Marcellus.
Justiniāni Institutiōnes et Codex.

Ruf. Festus Aviēnus.
Arātor.
M. Aurelius Cassidōrus.
Fl. Cresconius Corippus.
Venantius Fortunātus.
Isidōrus Hispalensis.
Anonŷmus Ravennas.
Aldhelmus *or* Althelmus.
Paulus Diacŏnus.

32*

INDEX.

The figures in the following Index designate the *Sections* and their divisions: R. stands for *remark*, N for *note*, E. for *exception*, w. for *with*, and pr. for *prosody*.

A, sound of, 7 and 8; nouns in, of 1st decl., 41; gender of, 41; of 3d decl. gender of, 66; genitive of, 68, 2; in acc. sing. of masc. and fem. Greek nouns, 79 and 80; in nom. acc. and voc. plur. of all neuter nouns, adjectives and participles, 40, 8; 83, 1.; 85; 87; 105, 2; verbals in, 102, 6, (c.); change of in compd. verbs, 189; increment in, 3d decl., 287, 3; in plur., 288; of verbs, 290; ending the first part of compds., 285, R. 4; final, quantity of, 294.

A, ab, abs, how used, 195, R. 2, and 10; in composition, 196, I., 1; before the abl. of distance, 236, R. 6; ab, de, or ex, with abl. of depriving, etc., 251, R. 1.

Abbreviations, 328.

Abdico, constr. of, 251, R. 2.

Abest mihi, 226, R. 2; *non multum abest quin*, 262, N. 7.

Abhinc, 253, R. 2.

Ablative, 37; sing. 3d decl., 82; of adjs. of 3d decl., 113; plur. 1st decl., 40, R. 6, and 43; 2d decl., 40, R. 6; 3d decl., 84; 4th decl., 89, 5; used adverbially, 192, I., II.; of character, quality, etc., 211, R. 6; after prepositions, 241; after compd. verbs, 242; after *opus* and *usus*, 243; after *dignus*, etc. 244; after *utor*, etc., 245, I.; after *nitor*, etc., 245, II.; after parts. denoting *origin*, 246; of cause, etc., 247; of means and agent, 248; of means, 249, I.; of accordance, 249, II.; of accompaniment, 249, III.; denoting in what respect, 250; after adjectives of plenty or want, 250, 2, (1.); after verbs of abounding, etc., 250, 2, (2.); after *facio* and *sum*, 250, R. 3; after verbs of depriving, etc., 251; of price, 252; of time when, 253; of place where, 254; of place whence, 255, 1; of place by or through which 255, 2; after comparatives, 256; of degree of difference, 256, R. 16; abl. absolute, 257; how translated, 257, N. 1; equivalent to what, 257, R. 1; only with pres. and perf. parts., 257, R. 2; without a participle, 257, R. 7; with a clause, 257, R. 8; how it marks the time of an action, 256, R. 4; noun wanting, 256, R. 9.

Abounding and wanting, verbs of, with abl. 256 with gen. 220, (3.)

"About to do," how expressed, 162. 14, "about to be done," how expressed, 162. 14, R. 4.

Abstineo, w. abl., 251, N.; *viz or œgre ab stineo, quin*, 262, N. 7.

Abstract nouns, 26; formation from adjs 101; their terminations, 101, 1 and 2, (3.); from verbs. 102.

Abundo, 250, (2.) R. 1.

-abus, dat. and abl. plur. in, 43.

Ac or *atque*, 198, 1, R. (b.) and 2. R.; instead of *quam*, 256, R. 15; *ac si* with subj., 263, 2, and R.

Acatalectic verse, 304, 3. (1.)

Accent in English, 16; place of secondary accent, 16, 1 and 2; in Latin, 14 and 15; of dissyllables, 14. 4; of polysyllables, 14, 4, and 15—written accents, 5, 2, and 14, 2.

Accentuation, 14—16.

Accidents of nouns, 26, 7; of verbs, 141.

Accipio, w. part. in *dus*, 274, R. 7.

Accompaniment, abl. of, 249, III.

Accordance, abl. of, 249, II.

Achivom for *Achivorum*, 53.

-acis, genitives in, 78. 2, (1.)

Accusative, 37; sing., terminal letter of in masculines and feminines, 40, 2; plural, terminal letter of in do., 40, 7; of 3d decl., 79; of Greek nouns, 80; plur. 3d decl., 85; do. of adjs. of 3d decl., 114; neuter in all declensions, sing and plur., 40, 8; in *em* and *im*, 79; of Greek nouns in *im, in, or a*, 79, (b.) and 80; in *idem*, 80, E. 1; in *ym* or *yn*, 80, II.; in *ea*, 80, III.; in *tem, eta, em*, or *en*, 80, IV.; neuter used adverbially, 192. II., 4, and 205, R. 10; acc. after verbs, 229—234; omitted, 229, R. 4; inf. or a clause instead of, 229, R. 5; of a person after *misert* etc., 229, R. 6; after *jurat*, etc., 229, R. 7; after neuter verbs, 232; after compound verbs, 233; after verbal nouns and verbal adjs., 233, N.; of part affected, 234, II.; a limiting acc. instead of the abl in *partim, virem, cetera*, etc., 234, II., R. 3; after prepositions, 235; of time and space, 236; of place, 237; after adverbs and interjections, 238; acc. as subject, 239; acc. of the thing supplied by the inf., 270, N., acc. w. inf., 272; do. exchanged for the subjunctive

INDEX.   379

278, 8.—two accusatives after certain verbs, 230 and 231; acc. of thing retained in passive voice, 234; places supplied by infinitives, 229, N. 2; pred. acc. how supplied, ib. N. 4.

Accusing and acquitting, verbs of, constr., 217, and R. 4.
Accuso, constr., 217, and R. 2—5.
Acephalous verse, 304, 3, (3.)
Acer, declined, 108, I.
Achilles, declined, 86.
Acquiesco, 245, II., 3.
Acute accent, 5, 2, and 14, 2; when used, 14, 3.

Active voice, 141.
Active verb, 141; used impersonally, 184, 2; object of act. verb, 229; two cases after, 229, R. 1; verb omitted, 229, R. 3.
Ad, how used, 195, R. 5; in composition, 196, I. 2; construction of verbs compounded with, 224; *ad* used for *in*, 224, R. 4.
Adde quod, 273, N. 8.
Additions to simple subject, 202, 6, etc.; to simple predicate, 203, 5, etc.
Adeo, adv., 191, R. 5; *adeo non*, 277, R. 14.—verb, constr., 233, 3, and N.
-ades, patronymics in, 100, 1, (a.)
Adest, qui, with subj., 264, 6.
Adhuc locorum, 212, R. 4. N. 4.
Adipiscor, w. gen., 220, 4 *fin.*

Adjectives, 104—131; classes of, 104, 1—15; declension of, 105; of 1st and 2d decls. 105—107; of 3d declension, 108—114; of three terminations, 108; of two terminations, 109, 110; of one termination, 111; their gen. sing., 112; their abl. sing. 113; their nom., acc., and gen. plur., 114; irregular, 115—116; defective, 115; redundant, 116; numeral, 117—121; cardinal, 117, 118; ordinal, 119, 120; multiplicative, 121, 1; proportional, 121, 2; temporal, 121, 3; interrogative, 121, 5; comparison of, 122—127; irregular comparison, 125; defective comparison, 126; derivation of, 128—130; composition of, 131; amplificative, 128, 4; patrial, 128, 6; verbal, 129; participial, 130; composition of 131;—how modified, 202, II., 1, (2.); agreement of, 205; qualifying and limiting, 205, N. 1; modifiers or predicates, 205, N. 2; with two or more nouns, 205, R. 2; with a collective noun, 205, R. 3; sing. with a plur. noun, 205, R. 4; dat. of, for acc. in the predicate of acc. with the inf., 205, R. 6; without a noun, 205, R. 7; with infinitive, a clause, etc., 205, R. 8; in the neuter with gen. of their noun, 205, R. 9, and 212, R. 3; neuter adjs. used adverbially, 205, R. 10; gender of, when used partitively, 205, R. 12; in genitive with possessive adj. or pronoun, 205, R. 13; agreeing with the governing noun instead of the genitive, 205, R. 14; two or more with one noun, 205, R. 16; instead of an adverb, 205. R. 15; first, last, etc. part expressed by the adj. alone, 205, R. 17; agreeing with relative instead of its antecedent, 206, (7.); with gen. 213; w. gen. or abl., 213, R. 5; w. dat., 222; w. gen. or dat., 213, R. 6, and 222, R. 2; of plenty or want with abl., 250; w. inf. 270, R. 1; place of, 279, 7.

Adjective pronouns, 134—139; nature of 132, 5; classes, 134; agreement, 205.
Adjective clauses, 201, 7; how connected, 201, 9.
Adjunctive pronoun, 135, R. 1.
Adjuro and *adjuto*, constr., 223, R. 2, (2.)
Admonishing, verbs of, w. gen. 218; other constructions, 218, R. 1 and 2; 273, N. 4.
Adolescens, its gender, 30; as adj. how compared. 126, 4.
Adorning, verbs of, w. abl., 249.
Adonic verse, 312.
Adulari, constr., 223, R. 2, (b), and (1), (a.)
Adverbial correlatives, 191, F 1;—clauses, 201, 7, 9.
Adverbs, 190, 2—194; primitive, 191; of place and order, 191, I.; correlative, 191, R. 1; of time, 191, II.; of manner, quality, degree, 191, III.; division of, 191, R. 2;—derivation of, 192; numeral, 192, II., 3, and 119; diminutive, 192, IV., R.; composition of, 193; signification of some adverbs of time and manner, 193;—comparison of. 194;—how modified, 277, I.; used as adjectives, 205, R. 11; w. gen. 212, R. 4; w. dat., 228, (1.); w. acc. 238; use of, 277; two negatives, force of, 277, R. 3—5; equivalent to phrases, 277, R. 8; of likeness, as connectives, 278, R. 1; place of 279, 15.
Adversative conjunctions, 198, 9.
Adversus, how used, 195, R. 7.
Æ, how pronounced, 9.
Æqualis, construction of, 222, a. 2.
Æque with abl., 241, R. 2; *æque ac.*, 198, 3, R.
Æqui boni facio or *consulo*, 214, N. 1.
Æquo and *adæquo*, construction of, 214; *æquo*, adj. w. comparatives, 256, R. 9.
Aër, acc. of, 80, R.; pr. 299, R. 3.
Æolic pentameter, 312, IX.
Æs, gender of, 61, 2; gen. of, 73, R. 2.
Æstimo, constr., 214.
Æther, acc., 80, R.; pr. 299, R. 3.
-æus, adjs. in, 128, 6, (A.)
Æquum est, ut, 262. R. 3, N. 2; *æquum erat*, indic. instead of subj., 259, R. 8; *æquum est*, with inf. as subject, 269, R. 2.
Affatim, w. genitive, 212, R. 4.
Affluo, constr., 250, 2, R. 1.
Aficio, constr., 249, R. 1.
Affinis, constr., 222, R. 2, (a.)
Ager, declined, 46.
Agent, verbal nouns denoting, 102, 6; dative of, 225, III., R. 1; 248, R. 1; abl of, 248.
Ages of Roman literature, 329.
Agnitus, pr. 285, 1, E. 1.
Agnominatio, 324, 25.
Ago w. gen. of the crime, 217, R. 1;—*age* w. plur. subject, 183, 10;—*id agere ut*, 273, N. 1.
Agreement defined, 203, III., 6; of adjs., etc., 205; of relatives, 206.
Ai, how pronounced. 9. 1.—*aï*, old gen in, 43; quantity of the *a* in do., 283. E. 3.
Aio, conjugated, 183, 4; *ain'* for *aisne*, *ait*, ellipsis of, 209, R. 4; its place in a sentence, 279, 6.

-al, abl. of nouns in, 82; increment of, 287, E. (A.) 1.
Alcaic verse, 304, 2;—greater, 318, III.; lesser, 318, IV.
Alcmanian verse, 304, 2;—dactylic tetrameter, 312.
Alec, gender of, 66; genitive, 70.
Ales, gender of, 30 and 61, 2; genitive sing., 73, 2; gen. plur., 83, II., R. 2.
Alex, gender of, 65, 2.
Alieno, and *abalieno*, constr., 251, R. 3, and N.
Alienus, constr., 222, R. 1 and 6.
Aliquanto, 127, 2; 256, R. 16, (2.)
Aliquantum, 256, R. 16, N.
Aliquis, declined, 133; how used, 138, 2; 207, R. 30.
Aliquo, w. gen., 212, R. 4, N. 2.
Aliquot, indeclinable, 115, 4; correlative, 121, 5.
Aliquoties, correlative of *quoties*, 121, 5.
-*alis*, adjs. in, 128, 2; how compared, 126, 4; *alis*, old adj., for *alius*, 192, II., 2.
Aliter, from *alis* for *alius*, 192, II., 2.
Alius, how declined, 107; how used, 207, R. 32; *alius—alium*, with plur. verb, 209, R. 11, 4; refers to more than two, 212, R. 2, N. 1, (b.); w. abl., 256, R. 14; pr. 283. 1, R. 4.
Allegory, 324, 7.
Alliteration, 324, 26.
Alphabet, 2, 1.
Alter, how declined, 105, 3; 107, and R. 2; gen. *alterius*, quantity of 283, 1., E. 4, (b.); used for *secundus*, 120, 1; answers to *uter*, 139, 5, (1.), (b.)—*altero tanto*, w. comparatives, 256, R. 16.
Alteruter, 107; 139, 5, (1.), (b.)—*alteruterque*, 107.
Altus and *alto*, w. acc. of space, 236, and N. 2.
Ambi, *amb*, *am*, or *an*, 197, (b.)
Ambio, how conjugated, 182, R. 3.—*ambitus*, pr. 285, 2, E. 2.
Ambo, how declined, 118, R. 1.
Amicus, constr., 222, R. 2. (c.)
Amo, conjugated, 155, 156.
Amphibolia, 325, 5.
Amplificatives, nouns, 100, 4, (a.); adjectives, 104, 12; 128, 4.
Amplius, with or without *quam*, 256, R. 6.
An, 198, 11; use of, 198, 11, R. (d., (e.); 265, R. 2 and 3; *an—an*, 265, R. 2.
Anabasis, 324, 22.
Anacoluthon, 323, 3. (5.)
Anacreontic verse, 304, 2;—iambic dimeter, 314, IX.
Anadiplosis, 324, 17.
Analysis of sentences, 281.
Anapaestic metre, 313; 303;—monometer, 313, I.;—dimeter, 313.
Anaphora, 324, 13.
Anastrophe, 324, 4, (1.)
Anas, gen. of, 72, E. 1; pr. 300, E. 1.
Anceps, gen. of, 112, 2; abl. of, 111 E. 3.
Ancile, 93, 2.
Androgeos, declined, 54, 1.
-*aneus*, adjs. in, 128, 8.
Angor, constr., 273, 5, N. 6.
Animal, declined, 57.

Animans, gender of, 64.
Animo, 250.—*animi* for *animæ*, 220, 1, 213, R. 1, (a.)
Anio, genitive of, 69, E. 2.
Anne, in double questions, 265, R. 2;—*annon*, ib.
Annus, compds. of, 121, 3.
Antanaclasis, 324, 12.
Ante, w. superlatives, 127, 6; in composition, 196, I., 3; construction of verbs compounded with, 224; with titles, 235, R. 2; with comparatives, 256, R. 13, (b.);—*ante* and *post* w. acc. and abl. of time, 253, R. 1; w. *quam* and a verb, 253, N. 3; for *abhinc*, 253, R. 2.
Antecedent, 136; ellipsis of, 206, (3.), (4.), its place supplied by a demonstrative, 206, 3, (a.); in the case of the relative, 206, (6.), (b.); implied in a possessive pronoun, 206, (12); may be a proposition, 206, (13.)
Antecedo and *antecello*, constr., 256, R 16, (3.)
Antepenult, 13; quantity of, 292.
Antequam, constr., 263, 3.
Antimeria, 323, 3, (1.)
Antiphrasis, 324, 10.
Antiptosis, 323, 3, (3.)
Antithesis, 322; 324, 27.
Antonomasia, 324, 8.
-*anus*, adjs. in, 128, 6.
Aorist tense, 145, IV., R.
Apage, 183, 10.
Apertum est, w. inf. as subject, 269, R. 2.
Aphæresis, 322.
Apiscor and *adipiscor*, w. gen., 220.
Aplustre, nom. plur. of, 83 and 94, 4.
Apocope, 322.—Apodosis, 261.
Apollo, gen. of, 69, E. 2.
Aposiopesis, 324, 33.
Apostrophe, 324, 35.
Apparet, w. inf. as subject, 269, R. 2.
Appellative nouns, 26, 3.
Appello, constr., 230, N. 1.
Appetens, w. gen., 213, R. 1, (2.)
Appendix, 322—329.
Apposition, 204; to two or more nouns, 204, R. 5; to nouns connected by *cum*, 204, R. 5, (1.); to proper names of different genders, 204, R. 5, (2.); genitive instead of, 204, R. 6; 211, R. 2, N.; abl. with gen., 204, R. 7; of a proper name with *nomen*, etc., 204, R. 8; of a clause, 204, R. 9; of parts with a whole, 204, R. 10; 212, R. 2, N. 5; place of nouns in apposition, 279, 9.
Apprime, 127, 2; 193.
Aptotes, 94.
Aptus, constr., 222, R. 1 and 4, (1.); *aptus qui*, w. subj., 264, 9; w. gerund, 275, R. 2 and 3.
Apud, 195, R. 6.
-*ar*, nouns in, gender of, 66, 67; genitive of, 70, 71; abl. of, 82; increment of, 287, E. (A.) 1.
Arbitror, in imperf. subj., 260, R. 2.
Arbor (-*os*), gender of, 61.
Arceo, w. abl., 251, R. 2.
Arcesso, constr., 217, R. 1.
Archaism, 323, R., (1.)
Archilochian verse, 304, 2;—penthemimeris, 312;—iambic trimeter, 314, V.; do

INDEX. 381

tiimster, 314, VII.;—heptameter, 318, IV.
Arenœ, as gen. of place, 221, R. 3, (4.)
Argo, genitive of, 69, E. 3.
Argos (-gi), 92, 4.
Arguo, constr., 217, R. 1.
Aristophanic verse, 304, 2.
-arium and *-arius*, nouns and adjs. in, 100, 8; 128, 3; 121, 4.
Arrangement of words, 279; poetical, 279, N 4; of clauses, 280.
Ars, declined, 57.
Arsis and thesis, 308.
Article. wanting in Latin, 41, N.
-as, genitives in, 43; nouns in of 3d decl., gender of, 62; genitive of, 72; gen. plur. of, 83, II., 4; lu acc. plur. of Greek nouns of 3d decl., 85, E. 2.— *-as* and *-anus*, adjs. in, 128, 6; *-as* final, quantity of, 300.
As, value of, 327; how divided, 327;—gender of, 62, E. 1; 72, E. 1; gender of parts ending in *ns*, 64, 2; *assis non habere*, 214, R. 1.
Asclepiadic verse, 304, 2;—tetrameter, 316, III.
Asking, verbs of, with two accs., 231; constr. in the pass., 234, I.
Aspergo, 249. I. and R. 1 and 3.
Aspirate, 3, 1.
Assepuor, ut, 273, N. 2.
-assa for *-avero*, 162, 9.
assuesco and *assuefacio*, w. abl., 245, II.; w. dat., 245, II., R. 1.
Asyndeton, 323, 1, (1.)
-at, roots of nouns in, 56, II., R. 5.
At, conj., 198, 9; *at enim*, *atqui*, 198, 9, (b.)
-atim, adverbs in, 192, I., 1.
Atque, composition and meaning, 198, 1, R. (b.) See *ac*.
Attraction, 206, (6.); 209, N. 6 and R. 8; 210, R. 6; 272, N. 3.
Attribuo. w. participle in *dus*, 274, R. 7.
-atus, adjs. in, 128, 7.
Au, how pronounced, 9, 2 and R. 2.
Auleo, how conjugated, 142, R. 2.
Audio, conjugated, 160; used like *appellor*, 210, N. 2; constr., 272, N. 1; *audes* for *audies*, 183, R. 3;—*audiens*, constr., 222, R. 1.
-aus, nouns in, gender of, 62; genitive of, 76, E. 4.
Ausculto, constr., 222, R. 2, (b.), and (1.), (a.)
Ausim, 183, R. 1.
Aut and *vel*, 198, 2, R. (a.); *aut* and *ve*, 198, 2. R. (d.); *aut—aut*, 198, 2, R. (e.); *au* with the singular, 209, R. 12, (5.)
Autem, 198, 9; its position, 279, 3, c.); ellipsis of. 278, R. 11.
Authority, in prosody, 282, 4.
Auxiliary verb, 153.
-av and *-atu* in the 2d and 3d roots of verbs 164.
Avarus, with gen., 213, R. 1.
Ave, 183, 8.
Avidus. with gen. 213, R. 1; w. gen. of gerund, 275, (2.); w. inf. poetically, 270, R. 1.
-ax, nouns in, gen. of, 78, 2, (1.); adjs. in, 129, 6; verbals in with gen., 213, R. 1.

B.

B, roots of nouns ending in. 56, 1. changed to *p*., 171, 2.
Balneum, plur. *-ea* or *-eœ*, 92, 6.
Barbarism, 325, 1.
Barbiton, declined, 54, 1.
Belle, *bellissime*, 192, IV. R.
Belli, construed like names of towns, 221, R. 3; *bello*, 253.
Bene, derivation, 192, II., 1; constr. of its compounds, 225, I.; *bene est*, w. dat., 228, 1; *bene*, w. acc., 239, R. 2; with verbs of price, 252, R. 3.
-ber, names of months in, how declined, 71 and 108.
Bes, gen. of, 73, E. 2.
Bibi, pr., 284, E., (1.)
Bicorpor, abl. of, 113, E. 2; 115, 1, (a.)
Biduum, *triduum*, etc., *biennium*, etc., 121, 2.
-bilis, adjs. in, 129, 4; how compared, 126, 4; with dative, 222, R. 1.
Bimestris, 113, E. 1.
Bipes, genitive of, 112, 1; abl. of, 113, E. 2; 115, 1, (a.)
Bonus, declined, 105, 2; compared, 125, 5; *boni consulo*, 214, N. 1.
Bos, dat. and abl. plur. of, 84, E. 1; 286, 5; gender of, 30; genitive of, 75, E. 1; gen. plur., 83, II., R. 1.
-br, roots of nouns in, 56, II., R. 3.
Brachycatalectic verse, 304, 3, (2.)
Brazen age of Roman literature, 329, 4.
-brum, verbals in, 102, 5.
Bucolic cæsura, 310, 6, R. 4.
-bulum, verbals in, 102, 5.
-bundus, adjs. in, 129, 1; comparison of, 126, 5; with acc., 233, N.

C.

C, sound of, 10; before *s* in roots of nouns, 56, 1., R. 2; in roots of verbs, 171, 1; gender of nouns in, 66; genitive of, 70; *c* final, quantity of, 299, 4; *C.* for *Caius*, i. q. *Gaius*, 328.
Cœlebs, 112, 2; in abl. sing., 113, E. 2; 115, 1, (a.)
Cæsura, 309; kinds of, 309; in hexameter verse, 310, 3; cæsural pause, 309, 3; in hexameter verse, 4—6; in pentameter verse, 311, 2; in iambic verse, 314, I. and X.; in trochaic verse, 315, 1; in choriambic verse, 316, III.
Calco, change of *a* to *u* in its compds., 189, N. 3.
Calendar, Roman, 326, 6.
Calends, 326.
Callidus, 270, R. 1; 213, R. 1.
Canalis, abl. of, 82, 5, (c.)
Cano receptui, 227, R. 2.
Capax, w. genitive, 213, R. 1. (1.), and R. 5, (1.)
Capio. conjugated, 159; adjs. compound ed of, 112. 2.
Capital letters, how used by the Romans, 2, 2; as numerals, 118, 7.
Caput declined, 57; *capitis* and *capite damnare*, *accusare*, etc., 217, R. 3.

382 INDEX.

Carbasus, plur. *-i* and *-a*, 92, 3.
Cardinal numbers, 117 and 118.
Careo, 250, 2, R. 1.
Carmen, declined, 57.
Caro, gender of, 59, 3; gen. of, 69, ɴ 2; gen. plur., 83, ɪɪ., 5.
Carthagini, in abl. of the place where, 82, ʀ. 5, (c.)
Case-endings, table of, 39.
Cases of nouns, 36 and 37.
Casus recti and *obliqui*, 37, ʀ.
Causā, gratiā, etc. with *meā*, etc., 247, ʀ 2; their place with genitive, 279, ʀ.
Causal conjunctions, 198, 7.
Cause, abl. of, 247; after active verbs, 247, ʀ. 2; acc. of with prepositions, 247, ɴ. 1.
Causo, change of *au* in its compounds, 189, ɴ. 3.
Cave or *cave ne*, w. subj., 267, ʀ. 3; 262, ɴ. 3.
-ce and *-cine*, enclitic, 134, ʀ. 4.
Cedo, constr., 223, ʀ. 2. (1), (d.)
Cedo, imperative, 183, 11.
Celer, how declined, 108; gen. plur., 114, ᴇ. 2.
Celo, with two accs., 231; w. *de*, 231, ʀ. 3.
Censeo, 273, ɴ. 4.
Centena millia, ellipsis of, 118, 5.
-ceps, nouns in, gen. of, 77, ʀ; adjs. in, gender of, 112, 2; abl. of, 113, ᴇ. 2, and ᴇ. 3.
Ceres, genitive, of, 73, ᴇ. 2.
Certe and *certo*, 192. ɴ. 1.
Certus, 213, ʀ. 1; 275, ɪɪɪ., (2.); 270, ʀ. 1.
Cetera and *reliqua* for *ceteris*, 234, ɪɪ., ʀ. 3.
Ceterum, 198, 8, ʀ., (b.)
Ceu, w. subj., 263, 2.
Ch. sound of, 10, 1; when silent, 12, ʀ.; in syllabication, 18, 2.
Character or quality, gen. of, 211, ʀ. 6.
Chaos, 61, ᴇ. 3.
Chelys, declined, 86.
Choliambus, 314, ɪɪ.
Choriambic metre, 316; 303;—pentameter, 316, ɪ.;—tetrameter, 316. ɪɪ.;—trimeter, 316, ɪᴠ.;—trimeter catalectic, 316, ᴠ.;—dimeter, 316, ᴠɪ.
Cicur, gen. plur. of, 114, ᴇ. 2.
Circum, in composition, 196, 4.
Circumdo and *circumfundo*, 249, ʀ 3.
Circumflex accent, 15, 2, and 14; how used, 14, 3.
Cis and *citra*, constr., 235, ʀ. 1.
Citerior, compared, 126. 1.
Citum, pr., 284. ᴇ. 1, (2.)
Clam. constr., 235, (5.)
Clanculum, 192, ɪᴠ., ʀ.; 235, (5.); 126, 1.
Claudo, its compounds, 189, ɴ. 3.
Clause, 201, 13; as the subject of a proposition, 202, ɪɪɪ., ʀ. 2; as an addition to the predicate, 203, ɪɪ., 3; its gender, 34, 4; as the object of a verb, 229, ʀ. 5; in abl. absolute, 256, ʀ. 8; connection of clauses, 198, ɪ. and ɪɪ.; 278, ʀ. 1; 280, ɪɪɪ.; arrangement of. 280; similar clauses, 278, ɴ. 1.
Climax. 324, 21.
Clothing, verbs of, 249, 1.
Cœlestis, abl. of, 113, ᴇ. 1; gen. plur. of, 114, ᴇ. 3.
Cœlum, plur. *cœli*, 92, 4.

Cœno, w. gen. of price, 214, ɴ. 1, (b.)
Cœpi and *cœptus sum*, 183. 2.
Cognate object, 232;—subject, 234, ɪɪɪ.
Cognitus, pr., 285, 2, ᴇ. 1.
Cognomen follows the gentile name, 279, 9, (b.)
Cognominis, abl. of, 113, ᴇ. 1.
Cogo, 273, ɴ. 4.
-cola, compounds in, gen. plur. of, 43, 2
Collective nouns, 26, 4; number of their verbs, 209, ʀ. 11.
Com for *cum* in composition, 196, 5; 197, 5.
Comitiis, as abl. of time, 253, ɴ. 1.
Common, nouns, 26, 3;—gender, 30;—syllables, 282, 2; 283, ɪᴠ., ʀ. 2.
Commoneo and *commonefacio*, constr., 218; 273, ɴ. 4.
Communis, constr., 222, ʀ. 2, (a.) and ʀ 6, (a.)
Commuto, constr., 252, ʀ. 5.
Compar., gen. plur. of, 114, ᴇ. 2.
Comparo, constr., 224, ɴ. 1, 3.
Comparative conjunctions, 198, 3.
Comparative degree, 122, 5; uses of, 122, ʀ. 1, 2, 3; formation of, 124; by *magis*, 127, 1.—comparatives declined, 110; abl. sing. of, 113, 2: w. gen., 212, ʀ. 2,; denotes one of two, 212. ʀ. 2., ɴ. 1; w. abl., 256; used pleonastically, 256, ʀ. 12, 13.
Comparison, 25; of adjs., 122—127; degrees of, 122, 3; terminal, 124;—irregular, 125; defective, 126; by *magis* and *maxime*, 127;—of adverbs, 194.
Complex subject, 202, 1, 3, 6; complex predicate, 203, 1, 3, 5; complex sentence, 201, 11.
Complures, how declined, 110.
Compono. constr., 224, ɴ. 1, 3, and ʀ. 4.
Compos and *impos*, gen. of, 112, 2; abl. of, 113, ᴇ. 2; 115, 1, (a.); pr. 300, ᴇ. 3.
Composition of nouns, 103;—of adjs., 131;—of verbs, 183;—of adverbs, 193.
Compound verbs, how conjugated, 163, 4;—subject, 202, 4;—predicate, 203, 4;—sentence, 201, 12;—metres, 318;—words, in syllabication, 23;—nouns, declension of, 91; how formed, 103; quantity of compd. words, 285.
Con, adjs. compd. with, w. dat., 222, ʀ. 1; verbs compd. with, w. dat., 224; w. *cum*, 224, ʀ. 4.
Concedo, constr., 273, ɴ. 5; 274, ʀ. 7.
Concessive conjunctions, 198, 4.
Concors, and *discors*, gen. of, 112, 2; abl. of, 113, ᴇ. 2.
Concrete, nouns, 26, ʀ. 2.;—adjs., 101, ʀ.; used for abstracts, in expressions of time, 253, ʀ. 6.
Conditio, in abl., 249, ɪɪ.
Conditional conjunctions, 198, 5.
Conduco, with part. in *dus*, 274, ʀ. 7.
Condemning, verbs of, w. gen., 217.
Confero, w. dat, 224, ɴ. 1, 3.
Confido, w. abl., 245, ɪɪ.; w. dat., 245, ʀ. 1
Confit, 183, 12; 180, ɴ.
Confinis, 222, ʀ. 1.
Congruo, 224, ɴ. 1, 3, and ʀ. 4.
Conjugation, 25; 149; first, 155 156 second, 157; third, 158, 159; fourth, 160

of deponent verbs, 161; periphrastic, 162; general rules of, 163; of irregular verbs, 178—182; of defective verbs, 183; of impersonal verbs, 184; regular and irregular verbs in the four conjugations, 164—177.—conjugations, how characterized, 149; remarks on, 162.

Conjunctions, 198; classes of, 198; coördinate, 198, I.; subordinate, 198, II.; enclitics, 198, N. 1; copulative and disjunctive, their use, 278; use of coördinate and subordinate conjs., 193, R. 1; repeated, 278, R. 7; when omitted between adjs., 205, R. 16;—between words opposed, 278, R. 6.

Conjungo, 224, N. 1, 3, and R. 4.
Conjunctus, 222, R. 6.
Conjux, gender of, 30; gen. of, 78, 2, (5.)
Connecting vowel, 150, 5; omitted in 2d root, 163. 2; in verbal nouns, 102, 5, (b.); in verbal adjs., 129, 1 and 4, (b.); in compd. nouns and adjs., 103, R. 1.; 131, N.
Connection of tenses, 258;—of words by conjunctions, 278;—of clauses by do., 278, R. 3.
Connectives, 201. 8, 9; place of, 279, 3.
Conor, 271. N. 1.
Conscius, 213, R. 1; 275, III., (2.)
Consentaneus, w. dat., 222, R. 1, w. abl., 222, R. 6; *consentaneum erat*, the indic. instead of the subj., 259, R. 3, (a.); with inf. as subject, 269, R. 2.
Consentio, w. dat., 224, N. 1, 3.
Consequor, ut, 273, N. 2.
Consido, 241, R. 5.
Consonants, 3, 1; division of, ib.; double, 8, 1, 2; sounds of, 10—12.
Consors, 213, R. 1.
Constat, w. inf. as subject, 269, R. 2.
Constituo, 272. N. 1.
Consto, w. abl., 245, II., 5.
Consuetudo est, constr., 262, R. 3, N. 2.
Consuesco, 245, II., 3.
Contendo, 273, N. 1.
Contentus, w. abl., 244; w. perf. inf., 268, R. 2.
Conterminus, w. dat., 222, R. 1, (a.)
Continens, abl. of, 82, E. 4, (a.)
Continental pronunciation of Latin, 6.
Contingit, conjugation, 184; w. *ut*, 262, R. 3; w. dat. and inf., 262, R. 3, N. 1.
Continuo, 193, II., 1.
Contra, how used, 195, R. 7.
Contracted syllables, quantity of, 283, III.
Contractions in 2d root of verbs, 162, 7.
Convenio, 233, N.
Convenit, the indic. for the subj., 259, R. 3; w. inf. 269, R. 2.
Convinco, 217, R. 1.
Copia est, w. inf., 270, R. 1, (c.)
Copula, 140, 4.
Copulative conjs., 198, 1; repeated, 198, R. (e.)
Cor, gender of, 61; genitive of, 71, R. 2; compds. of, 112, 2.
Correlative adjs., 139, (2.), (3.); 104, 14;—adverbs, 191, R. 1.
Cornu, declined, 87.
Crasis, 306, (5.) and 322.
Crater, genitive of, 71.
Credo, 272, and R. 6;—*crederes*, in the sense of a pluperfect, 260, II., R. 2; —*credendum est*, 271, R. 2.
Creo, nascor, etc., 246, R. 1.
Crime, in genitive after verbs, 217.
Crimine, without a preposition, 217, R. 2, (b.)
Crude form or root, 40, 10.
-*crum*, verbals in, 102, 5.
Cr, initial, 12, 3.
Cui and *huic*, how pronounced, 9, 5; pr. 306, R. 2.
Cujas, how declined, 139, 4, (b.)
Cujus, how declined, 137, 5; *cujusmodi*, etc., 134, R. 5.
-*culum*, verbals in, 102, 5; contracted to -*clum*, 102, 5, (b.)
-*culus*, a, um, diminutives in, 100, 3, and B., 1, 2; 128, 5.
Cum, prep., affixed to abl., 241, R. 1; 133, R. 4; 136, R. 1; how used, 195, R. 11; w. abl. of manner, 247, 2; in composition, 196, 5.
Cum or *quum*, mood of the verb following it, 263, 5.
Cum, 'while,' 263, 5, R. 4.
-*cumque*, used to form general indefinites, 191, R. 1, (b.); 139, 5, R.; composition and meaning, 139, 5, N. 1; sometimes separated from *qui*, etc., 323, 4, (5.)
Cumprimis, its meaning, 193, II., 2.
Cuncti and *omnes*, w. gen. plur. 212, R. 2, N. 6.
-*cundus*, adjs. in, 129, 1.
Cupido, gender of, 59, R. 2.
Cupidus, constr., 213, R. 1; 275, (2.); 270, R. 1.
Cupio, 271, R. 4; *cupiens*, 213, R. 1, (2.)
Curo, 273, N. 1; 274, R. 7; *cura ut*, 267, R. 3.
Curritur, conjugated, 184, 2, (b.)
Custos, gender of, 30; 61, 3; genitive, 75, R. 1.

D.

D final in prosody, 299, 2; before *s* in roots of nouns, 56, R. 1; in roots of verbs, 171, 3, and E. 5.
Da, pr., 284, R. 2, (b.)
Dactylic metre, 310 and 303;—trimeter, 312, VI.;—dimeter, 312, VII.;—hexameter, 310, I. Dactylico-iambic meter, 318, I.; dactylico-trochaic heptameter, 318, IV.;—tetrameter, 318, V.
Dama, gender of, 42, 2.
Damni infecti satisdo, etc., 217, R. 3.
Dative, 37; sing. of 3d decl., 79; plur. always like abl., 40, 6; exceptions in do 1st decl., 43; of 3d decl., 84; of 4th decl., 89, 5; used for predicate nom., 210, N. 3; for gen., 211, R. 5; *commodi et incommodi*, 222, 1 and 2; dative of the end, 227; dat. of the object, after adjs., 222; different constructions instead of, 222, R. 4 and 6; after *idem*, 222, R. 7; after verbs, 223—227; after verbs compounded with *ad, ante*, etc., 224; with *ab, ex, de, circum* and *contra*, 224, R. 1 and 2; with *dis*, 224, R. 3; with *satis, bene* and *male*, 225, I.; dat. of the agent, 225, II.

and III.; of the possessor after *est*, 226; after particles, 228; dat. with the acc., 228, (1.); two datives after *sum*, etc., 227; wanting, 225, III., R.; *dativus ethicus*, 228, N.
Datum, pr., 284, E. 1, (2.)
De, 195, R. 12; with abl. instead of acc., 229, R. 5, (b.); 231, R. 3.
Dea, dat. and abl. plur. of, 43.
Debebat, indic. instead of subj., 259, R. 3.
Decedo, w. abl., 251.
Decerno, 273, N. 1 and 4.
Decet, conjugated, 184; its construction, 229, R. 7; 223, R. 2,(b.); indic. for subj., 259, R. 3.
Declarative sentences, 200, 3.
Declaro, 230, N. 1.
Declension, 38; parts of speech declined, 25, 3; of nouns, 38—40; rules of, 40; first, 41—45; exceptions in do., 43: paradigms of, 41;—second, 46—54; paradigms of, 46; exceptions in do., 52; third, 55—86; paradigms of, 57; exceptions in do., 68—85; fourth, 87—89; paradigms of, 87; exceptions in do., 89; formed by contraction, 89; fifth, 90; paradigms, 90; exceptions in, 90; —of adjs., 1st and 2d, 105—107; third, 108—111;—declensions, how distinguished, 38; tabular view of, 39.
Dedi, pr., 284, 2, E. 1.
Deest mihi, 226, R. 2; pr., 306, 1, R. 1, (1.)
Defective nouns, 94—96;—adjs., 115;— verbs, 183.
Defendo, 251, R. 2.
Defero, w. gen. of the crime, 217, R. 1.
Deficior, w. abl., 250, 2, N. 1.
Defit, 183, 13, and 180, N.; 226, R. 2.
Deflecto, 229, R. 4.
Defungor, 245, 1.
Degree, acc. of, 231, R. 5; 232, (3.)
Degrees of comparison, 122 and 123; inferior degrees, 123, 1; equal degrees, 123, 3; a small degree, 123. 2; superior degrees variously expressed, 127, 2, 3, 4.
Dejero, 189, N. 3; pr., 285, 2, E. 1.
Dein, *deinceps*, *deinde*, pr., 306, 1, R. 1, (1.)
Delectat, conjugated, 184; its construction, 229, R. 7; 223, R. 2.
Delector, w. *quod*, 273, N. 6.
Deligo, w. two accs., 230, N. 1.
-dem, enclitic, 134, R. 6.
Demonstrative adjs., 104, 15; 139, 5, R.; —pronouns, 134; constr. of, 207; in apposition to a clause, R. 22; 206, (3.); used when the reference is not to the subject, 208, (6.); place of, 279, 7; ellipsis of demonstratives before their relatives, 206, (3.), (a.); constr. of dem. adjs., 206, (16.); dem. advs. for dem. pronouns, 206, (20.); dem. pronouns *is*, etc., used for the oblique cases *him*, *her*, etc., 207, R. 20; redundant, 207, R. 21; dem. prons. and advs. announcing a proposition, 207, R. 22.
Demoveo, w. abl., 251, N.
Denarius, value of, 327, R. 3; divisions of, ib.
Denique, its use, 277, I., R. 13.
Denominatives, adjs., 128;—verbs, 187, I.
Deus, gender of, 64, 1; compds. of, 64, 1.
Depello, w. abl., 251, N.

Dependence, defined, 203, III , 3; • tenses, 258.
Dependent or subordinate propositions, 201, 6.
Deponent verbs, 142, R. 4; conjugated, 161; participles of, 162, 17; lists of in 1st conj., 166; 2d conj., 170; 3d conj., 174; 4th conj., 177; increment of, 289, 8.
Deposco, 274, R. 7.
Depriving, verbs of, w. abl., 251.
Derivation of nouns, 100;—of adjs., 128 —of verbs, 187;—of advs., 192.
Derivative words, quantity of, 284.
Deses, gen. of, 112, 1; abl. of, 113, E. 2; defective, 115, 2; compared, 126, 4.
Desiderative verbs, 187, II., 3; 176, N.; quantity of the *u* in, 284, E. 3.
Designo, with two accs., 230, N. 1.
Despero, constr., 224, R. 1.
Desuper and *insuper*, 235, R. 8.
Deterior, compared, 126, 1.
Deterreo, *quin*, *ne*, or *quominus*, 262, R. 11; w. inf. ib. N.
Deturbo, w. abl., 251, N.
Dexter, how declined, 106; how compared, 125, 4.
Deus, declined, 53; *deum* for *deorum*, 53.
Di or *dii*, 53; ellipsis of, 205, R. 7.
-di or *-dis*, see *-dis*.
Diæresis, 306, 2; mark of, 5, 2.
Dialysis, 306, R.
Diana, pr. 282, I., E. 5.
Diastole, 307, 2.
Dico, w. two accs., 230, N. 1; ellipsis of, 229, R. 3, 2; 209, R. 4; 270, R. 2, (b.); w. inf. and acc., 272, N. 1; w. *ut*, 273, 2, (c.); *dicunt*, 'they say,' 209, R. 2, (2.); *dicor*, w. predicate nominative, 210, R. 3, (3.), (a.) and N. 1, cf. 271, R. 2; 272, R. 6; *dic*, imperative, 162, 4.
Dicolon, 819, 2.
Dicto audiens, w. dat., 222, R. 1; *dicto*, w. comparative, 256, R. 9.
-dicus, words ending in, pr., 284, 2, E. 1.
Dido, declined, 86; genitive of, 69, E. 3.
Dies, declined, 90; its gender, 90, R. 1, compds. of with numerals, 121, 3; quantity of, 285, R. 4, E. 3, (6.)
Difference, degree of, how expressed, 25 4, R. 10.
Differo, constr., 251, R. 3, N.; 229, R. 4, 1.
Differing, verbs of, 251, R. 3.
Difficile est, the indic. for the subj., 259, R. 4, (2.); with an inf. as subject, 269, R. 2; with supine in *u*, 276, III., R. 1; w. *ad* and a gerund, 276, III., R. 4.
Digne, w. abl., 244, R. 1.
Dignor, w. abl., 244, R. 1; w. acc. of the person, ib.; w. inf., ib.; w. two accs., ib.
Dignus, w. abl. of the thing, 244; w. gen. 244, R. 2, (a.); w. acc. of neut. pron. or adj., 244, R. 2, (a.); w. inf. or a subj. clause, 244, R. 2, (b.); with relative and subj., 264, 9; w. supine in *u*, 276, III., R. 1.
Dimeter, 304, 2.
Diminutive nouns, 100, 3;—adjs., 104, 11 128, 5;—verbs, 187, II., 4;—adverbs, 192, a
Diphthongs, 4; sounds of, 9; quantity of, 18 4; 283, II.
Diptotes, 94.

Dir for *dis*, 196, (b.), 2.
Dis or *di*, inseparable prep., 196, (b.), 2; construction of some verbs compounded with, 251, R. 3, N.; pr., 285, 2, R. 2.
-dis, genitives in, 77, E. 1; *dis*, adj., gen. plur. of, 114, E. 8.
Discerno, 251, R. 3, N.; in imperf. subj. for pluperf., 260, II., R. 2.
Discolor, abl. of, 113, E. 2.
Discordo and *discrepo*, 251, R. 3, and N.
Disertus, pr., 284, E. 5, 2, N. 1.
Disjunctive conjs., 198, 2.
Dissideo, constr., 251, R. 3, and N.
Dissimilis, 222, R. 1, and R. 2.
Distich, 304.
Distinguo and *disto*, 251, R. 3, and N.
Distributive numbers, 119, 120; gen. plur. of, 105, R. 4; used for cardinal numbers, 120, 4;—for multiplicatives, 120, 4, (b.)
Distrophon, 319, 3.
Diu, compared, 104, 6.
Dives, gen. sing. 112, 1; gen. plur., 114, E. 2; 115, 1, (a.)
Division of words into syllables, 17—23.
Do, 149, E.; w. perf. participles, 274, R. 4; w. participles in *dus*, 274, R. 7; inclement of, 290, E.; 284, E. 4.
-do, nouns in, gender of, 59, 2; genitive of, 69, E. 1.
Doceo, 231, R. 1; w. gen. of price, 214, N. 1.
Doleo, w. *quod*, etc., 273, N. 7.
Dominus, declined, 46.
Domus, declined, 89; different use of *domûs* and *domi*, 89, (a.); constr. of gen., 221, R. 3; of acc., 237, R. 4; of abl., 255, R. 1; 254, R. 2.
Donec, w. subj., 263, 4; pr., 299, 4, E.
Dono, w. abl., 249, I., R. 1; w. two datives, 227, R. 1.
Dos, gen. of, 61, 3; *doti dicare*, 227, R. 2.
Double consonants, 3, 1.
Doubtful gender, 30.
Dubito and *non dubito*, 262, N. 7 and 8; *dubito an*, 198, 11, (e.); *dubito sit ne*, etc., 262, N. 8.
Duco, constr., 214; 227, R. 1; 230, N. 1; *in numero*, or *in loco*, 230, N. 4; *duc*, imperat., 162, 4.
Dudum and *jamdudum*, 191, R. 6.
Duim, *duis*, etc., 162, 1.
Dum, w. subj., 263, 4; *dum ne* and *dummodo ne*, 263, 2, N; *dum*, 'until,' 263, 4, '1.);—'while' 263. 4, (2.)—compounded with a negative, 277, R. 16.
Duntaxat, 193, II., 2.
Duo, declined, 118; *duum* for *duorum*, 118, R. 1.
-dus, participle in, how declined, 103, R. 2; of neuter deponent verbs, 161; with *sum*, 162, 15, neuter in *-dum* with *est*, 274, R. 11; w. dat. of person, 162, 15, R. 5; 225, III.; of dep. verbs, 162, 17, (b.); w. acc., 234, R. 2; its signification. 274, 2, R. 7 and 8; used for a gerund, 275, II.

E.

E, sound of, 7 and 8; *ě* changed to *ŭ* or *i*, 56, R. 4 and 5; nom. in *ě* in 3d decl., 56, I, R. 1, 7; gender of nouns in *e* of 3d decl.,
66; genitive of, 63; abl. of, 82; old lat. in 79; acc. plur. in, 54, 5; nom. plur. in, 83, I., 1; voc. in, 81, R.; in gen. and dat. sing. 5th decl., 90, E. 2; cf 40, 11; advs. in, 192, II.; syncope of in imperf. of 4th conj., 162, 2; increment in *e* of 3d decl., 287, 3; plur., 288; of verbs, 290; *e* ending the first part of a compound word, 285, R. 4; *e* final, quantity of, 295.—*e* or *ex*, prep., see *ex*.
-ea, Greek acc. sing. ending in, 54, 5, and 80, III.
Eapse, etc., 135, R. 3.
Ecce, compounded with demonstrative pronouns, 134, R. 2; w. nom., 209, R. 13; w. acc., 238, 2.
Eccum, *eccillum*, *eccistam*, etc., 134, R. 2; 238, 2.
-ecis, gen. in, 78, (2.)
Ecquis and *ecqui*, how declined, 137, 3, and R. 3; *ecquae* and *ecqua*, 137, 3, R. 4; *ecquis est qui*, 264, 7, N. 2; *ecquid*, interrog. particle, 198, 11, and R. *a* and *b*.
Ecquisnam, 137, 4.
Ectasis, 307, 2, (3.)
Ecthlipsis, 305, 2.
Edepol, 199, R. 3.
Edico, 273, N. 4.
Edim, *edis*, etc., 162, 1.
-edis, gen. in, 73, E. 1 and 112, 1.
Editus, w. abl., 246.
Edo, 'to eat,' conjugated, 181; compds. of, 181, N.
-edo, abstracts in, 101, 1.
Edoceo, w. two accs., 231, R. 1.
Efficio, 273, N. 2;—*efficiens*, w. gen., 213, R. 1, (2.);—*efficitur*, w. *ut*, or the acc. with the inf., 262, R. 3, N. 1.
Effugio, w. acc., 233, R. 1.
Egeo and *indigeo*, 250, 2, R. 1; 220, 3.
-egis, genitives in, 78, 2.
Ego, declined, 133.
Ehru, pr., 283, I., E. 5.
Ei, how pronounced, 9, 1, and R. 1; genitive in, 73, R.; pr., 283, I., E. 6, (1.)
-eia, verbals in, 102, 3.
-eis, fem. patronymics in, 100, 1, (b.)—acc. plur. in, 85, E. 1, and 114, 2.
-eius, pr., 283, I., E. 6, (3.)
Ejus, use of, 208, (6.)
Ejusmodi and *ejusdemmodi*, 139, 5, N. 2
-ela, verbals in, 102, 3.
Elegiac verse, 311, R. 2.
Ellipsis, 323; of pronoun in case of apposition, 204, R. 4; of the noun of an adj., 205, R. 7; 252, R. 3; of the antecedent. 206, (3.) and (4.); of *meus*, etc., 207, R. 38; of nom., 209, R. 2 and 3; of verb, 209, R. 4; 229, R. 3; of a noun limited by a genitive, 211, R. 8; of gen., 211, R. 9; of a partitive, 212. R. 1, N. 3; of subject acc., 229; 269, R. 1; of acc. after transitive verb, 229, R. 4; of prep., 232, (2.); 235, R. 5; 241, R. 4; 248, R. 3; of voc., 240; of *quam*, 256; of participle, in abl. absol., 257, R. 7; of *ut* w. subj., 262, R. 4; of *ne* after *cave*, 262, R. 6; of *non* after *non modo*, etc., 277, R. 6; of conjunctions, 278, R. 6; of *j* in composition, 307; of *centena millia*, 327, R. 6.
-ellus, *a*, *um*, diminutives in, 100, 3, A. 3.

386   INDEX.

-em and *-en*, accs. in, 45, 1; 80, iv.; *-em* in acc. sing. 3d decl., 79, 80.
Em, 252, r. 1.
Emphatic word, its place in a sentence, 279. 2 and 16.
En, interrogative particle, 198, 11, and r. (a.); 137, r. 3; *en*, interjection, 199; w. nom., 209, r. 13; w. acc. 238, 2; *-en*, acc. in, 45, 1; 80, iv.
Enallage, 323, 3.
Enclitics, in accentuation, 15, 3;—conjunctions, 198, n. 1.
Endeavoring, verbs of, 273, 1, (a.)
endus and *-undus*, 163, 20.
English pronunciation of Latin, 6.
Enim and *nam*, 198, 7, and r.; 279, 3, a.) and (c.)
Enimvero, 198, 9, r. (a.)
Ennehemimeris, 304, 5.
Ens, participle, 154, r. 1.
-ensis, adjs. in, 128, 6, (a.)
-entissimus, superlatives in, 126, 8
-enus, adjs. in, 128, 1, (c.)
Eo, conjugated, 182; compds of, 182, r. 3; w. supine in *um*, 276, ii., r. 2; w. two datives, 227, r. 1.
-eo, verbs in of 1st conj., 165. r. 3.
Eo, pron. w. comparatives, 256, r. 10. As adverb of place, w. gen., 212, r. 4. n. 2, (b.)—of degree, w. gen., 212, r. 4. n. 3. As an illative conj., 198, 6.
Eodem, w. gen., 212, r. 4. n. 3.
eos, Greek gen. in, 76, e. 7; 54 5; pr., 353. 1., e. 6, (2.)
Epanadiplosis, 324, 18.
Epanados, 324, 19.
Epanalepsis, 324, 16.
Epanaphora, 324, 15.
Epanastrophe, 324, 17.
Epanorthosis, 324, 32.
Epenthesis, 323, 3.
Epicene nouns, 33.
Epistrophe, 324, 14.
Epizeuxis, 324, 20.
Epulor, with abl., 245, ii., 4.
Epulum, 92, 6.
Equality, how denoted, 123, 3.
Eques, gender of, 31, 2; used collectively, 209, r. 11, (1.), (b.)
Equidem, its composition and use, 191, r. 4.
-er, nouns in, of 2d decl., 46—syncopated, 48, 1; of 3d decl., gender of, 58 and 60; genitive of, 70 and 71; syncopated, 71;— adjectives in, superlative of, 125; annexed to pres. infin. pass., 162, 6.
Erga, how used, 195, r. 7.
-ere, in 3d pers. plur. of perf. indic. active, 162, 8.
-eris, genitives in, 76; 73, e. 2; 74, e. 1; and 112, 1 and 2.
Ergo, w. gen., 147, r. 2, (a.)
Erotesis, 324, 31.
-errimus, superlatives in, 125, 1.
-es, proper names in, 44, 1; *-es* and *-e* in Greek nouns changed to *a*, 45, 3; nouns in of 3d decl. increasing in genitive, gender of, 58; 61; genitive of, 73; genitive of adjs. in, 112; not increasing, gender of, 62; genitive of, 73; in nom., acc., and voc. plur. of

masc. and fem. nouns of 3d decl., 83, 1.; 85; final, sound of, 8, e. 2; quantity of, 300.
Escit, 154, r. 4.
Esse and *fuisse*, ellipsis of, 270, r. 3.
-esso, *-isso* or *-so*, intensives in, 137, ii., b.
Est, w. dat. of a possessor, 226; *est, qui*, with subj., 264, 6; so *est, unde, ubi, cur*, or *ut*, 264, 6, r. 3.
Et and *que*, 198, 1, r. (a.); *et ipse*, 207, r. 27, (b.); ellipsis of *et*, 298, r. 6, (b.); *et is, et id, et is quidem*, 207, r. 26, (c.); *et—et, et—que, et—neque* or *nec*, 198, 1, r. (s.); *et non*, 198, 1, (c.)
Etenim, 198, 7, r. (a.)
Etiam, 198, 1, r. (d.); with comparatives, 256, r. 9, (b.); 127, 3; *etiamnum, etiam tum*, 191, r. 7.
-etis, genitive in, 73; 112, 1.
Etsi and *etiamsi*, constr., 271, r. 2
-etum, derivative nouns in, 100, 7
Etymology, 24—199
Eu, the diphthong, 10, 3; when not a diphthong, 10, 3, r. 3; in voc. sing. of Greek nouns in *eus*, 81.
Euphemism, 324, 11.
Eus, nouns in of 2d decl., 54, 5;—adjs. in, 128, 1 and 2; Greek proper names in, 233, n. 2; gen. of, 76, e. 7; acc. of, 180, iii.
-ev and *-etu*, in 2d and 3d roots of verbs, 167.
Evado, constr., 251, n.
Evenit, conjugated, 184; *evenit ut*, 262, r. 3.
Ex and *e*, prep., how used, 195, r. 2 and 13;—used with partitives instead of the genitive, 212, n. 4; sometimes omitted, 251, and r. 1; *ex quo*, scil. *tempore*, 253, n. 4.
-ex, gender of nouns in, 65, 2.
Exadversus, w. acc., 195, r. 3.
Excedo, w. acc., 233, (3.), n.
Excello, constr., 256, r. 16, (3.)
Excito, w. ut, 273, n. 4.
Excludo, constr., 251, n.
Exeo, constr., 251, n.
Existimo, w. gen., 214; w. two accs., 230, n. 1; *existimor*, constr., 271, r. 2.
Exlex, 112, 2; 196, 1., 6.
Exos, genitive of, 112. 2.
Exosus, 153, 1, n.
Exsistunt qui, w. subj., 264, 6.
Exter, 105, 3, and n.; comparison of, 125, 4.
Expedio, 251, n.; *pedit*, w. dat., 228, r. 2, (b.)
Experior si, 198, 11, (c.)
Expers, w. gen., 213, r. 1, (3.), and r. 5, (2.)
Extemplo, 193, ii., 1.
Extera, how compared, 125, 4; *extremus*, how used, 205, r. 17; *extremum est, ut*, 262, r. 3.
Exuo, constr., 225, r. 2; *exuor*, 234, 1., r. 1.

F.

Fabula, ellipsis of, 29, 2.
Fac, imperative, 152, 4; *fac ut* or *ne*, 267, r. 3; *fac*, 'suppose or granting,' w. acc. and inf., 273, n. 3; pr., 299, e. 4.

Facile, adv., 192, 4, (*b.*); w. superlatives, etc., 277. R. 7.
Facilis, constr., 276, III.. R. 4; 222, R. 1.(*a.*)
Facio and compds., passive of, 180 and N.; changes of *in* the compds., 189, N. 1; w. gen. of value, 214, R. 2; w. two accs., 230, N. 1; w. abl., 250. R. 3; w. *ut* and subj., 273, 1, N. 2 and 3; w. participle, 273, 1; w. *de,* etc., 250, R. 3; *facere non possum quin*, 262, 2; *facere quod,* 273, N. 8; ellipsis of, 209, R. 4; *facere certiorem,* 230, N. 3.
Faliscan verse, 312, XI.
Fallit me, 229, R. 7.
Familia with *pater,* etc., gen. of. 43, 2.
Familiaris, w. dat., 222, R. 1, (*a.*); with gen., 222, R. 1, (*c.*)
Far, its root, 56, II., R. 6; gen. of, 71, E 2; abl., 82, E. 1, (*b.*); 94 and 95.
Fas, gender of, 62, E. 2; 94; *fas erat,* the indic. instead of the subj., 259, R. 3; *fas est,* w. supine in *u,* 276. III., R. 2.
Faxo, faxim and *faxem,* 162, 9, and 183, R. 1.
Faux, genitive of, 78, 2, (5.); but cf. 94, P 50; gen. plur., 83, II., 3.
Faveturn, conjugated, 184. 2. (*b.*) constr. 223.
Fearing, verbs of, w. *ut* and *ne,* 262, R. 7.
Febris, ellipsis of, 205. R. 7, (1.)
Fecundus, w. gen. or abl., 213. R. 5. (3.)
Feet, in poetry, 302; isochronous, 302. R.
Fel, its root, 56. II., R. 6; its genitive, 70, E.; 94.
Felix, declined, 111; 213, R. 4. (1.)
Femina, added to epicene nouns, 133, N.
Feminine nouns, of 1st decl., 41; of 2d decl., 49—51; of 3d decl., 62; exceptions in, 62—65.
Femur, genitive of, 71, 3.
Fer, 162, 4; quantity of, 299, E. 4.
Fero, conjugated, 179; its compds., 172, (p. 134.); *fertur,* constr. of, 271, R. 2.
-ficus, comparison of adjs. in, 125, 3, (*a.*)
Fido; how conjugated, 142. R. 2; w. abl., 245, II.; w. dat., 245, II., R. 1; 223, R. 2.
Fidi, (from *findo*), pr., 284, E. 1, (1.)
Figures of prosody, 305—307; of orthography and etymology, 322; of syntax, 323; of rhetoric. 324.
Filia, dat. and abl. plur., 43.
Filius, voc. sing., 52.
Filling, verbs of, w. abl., 249, I.; w. gen., 250, 3.
Final syllables, quantity of, 294—301;—conjunctions, 198, 8.
Finitimus, w. dat., 222, R. 1, (*a.*)
Fio, conjugated, 180; w. gen. of value, 214, R. 2; w. two datives, 227. R. 1; *fit* and *fieri non potest ut,* 262, R. 3; *fit per me,* 262, R. 11; quantity of *i* in *fio,* 283, E. 1.
Flagito w. two accs., 231. R. 1; w. *ut,* 273, N. 4.
Flecto, used reflexively, 229, R. 4, 1.
Flocci habere, etc., 214, R. 1.
Fluo and *struo,* 2d and 3d roots of, 171, N.
Follow, in what sense used, 263, 9.
Fons, gender of, 64, 1.
Foras and *foris,* 237, R. 5. (*c.*)
Forem, fore, etc., 154. R. 3; 162. 12, (1.); w two datives, 227, R. 1.

Fractional expressions, 121, 6.
Freeing, verbs of, 251.
Frenum, plur. *freni* and *frena,* 92, 5.
Frequens, w. gen. or abl., 213, R. 3. (3.); cf. R. 4, (1.)
Frequentative verbs, 187. II., 1; quantity of *i* in, 284, E. 4.
Fretus, w. abl., 244; w. dat., 222, R. 6; w. inf., 244, R. 2. (*b.*)
Fructus, declined, 87.
Frugi, 115, 4; comparison of, 125 5.
Fruor, w. abl., 245. I.; w. acc., 245, I. R.
Frux, genitive of. 78, 2, (5.): 94.
Fugio, constr., 225, IV.; 210, R. 3, (2); *fuge,* poetically, w. inf., 271, N. 3; *fugit me,* 239, R. 7.
Fui, etc., in compound tenses, 162 12 (1.); *fuisse,* w. perf. pass. participles, 268 R. 1, (*b.*)
Fungor, w. abl., 245, I.; w. acc., 245, R.; 275, II., R. 1.
Fuo, root of *fui,* 154, R. 2 and 3; *futurum,* pr., 284. E. 1, (2.)
Furo, 183, R. 2.
Furor, w. dat. or abl., 224, R. 2.
Future tense, 145, III.; how supplied in the subj., 260, R. 7; future perfect tense, 145, VI.; old form in *so,* 162, 9 and 10; future indic. for imperative, 267, R. 2; 259, R. 1, (4.); fut. imperative, 267, (2.), (3.); future pass. part. w. acc., 234, I., R. 2; fut. perf. for fut., 259, R. 1, (5.)
Futurum esse or *fore, ut,* w. subj., 268 R. 4, (*b.*); *futurum fuisse, ut,* 268, R. 5.

G.

G, sound of, 10; before *s* in roots o nouns, 56, R. 2; in roots of verbs, 171, L and E. 5.
Galliambus, 314, X.
Gaudeo, how conjugated, 142, R. 2; with abl., 247, 1, (2.); w. acc., 232, N. 1; with *quod,* etc., 273, N. 6.
Gemo, w. acc., 232, N. 1.
Gems, gender of names of, 29.
-gena, compounds in, 43, 2.
Gener, declined, 46.
General relatives, 139, 5, R.; how used, 207, R. 29.
General indefinites, 139, 5, R.
Gender, 26, 7 and 27; its divisions, 27; general rules of, 27—34; natural and grammatical, 27; masc. from signification, 28; fem. from do., 29; common and doubtful, 30; epicene, 33; neuter appellatives of persons, 32, 2; of Greek nouns, 34. R. 1: neuter, 34; of 1st decl., 41; exes in 1st decl., 42; of 2d decl., 46; exes. in 2d decl., 49; of 3d decl., 58, 62, and 66; exes. in 3d decl., 59—67; of 4th decl., 87; exes. in 4th decl., 88; of 5th decl., 90; exes. in 5th decl., 90, gender of adjs., 205.
Genero, w. abl., 246, R. 1; *generatus,* w. abl., 246.
Genitive. 37; sing., 1st decl., exes. in, 43; of 3d decl., 68; of adjectives, 3d decl., 112 plur., 1st decl., contracted, 43; 2d decl. do., 53; 3d decl., 83; terminal letters in all the declensions, 40, 5; of adjectives. 3d

decl., 112 and 114; after nouns, 211; its place, 279, R.; what relations it denotes, 211, R 1; subjective and objective, 211, R. 2; of substantive pronouns objective, 211, R. 3; possessive adjective used for, 211, R. 4; dative used for, 211, R. 5; of character or quality, 211, R. 6; of measure, 211, R. 6, and (3.) and (6.): noun limited by, omitted, 211, R. 7; wanting, in the predicate after *sum*, 211, R. 8; in other cases, 211, R. 8, (4.); omitted, 211, R. 9; two genitives, 211, R. 10; gen. after *opus* and *usus*, 211, 11; how translated, 211, R. 12; after partitives, 212; after a neuter adjective or adj. pronoun, 212, R. 3; its place, 279, 10; after adverbs, 212, R. 4; after adjectives, 213; of *cause* or *source*, 213, R. 2; different constructions instead of, 213, R. 4; after *dignus* and *indignus*, 244, R. 2; after verbs, 214—220; after *sum*, and verbs of valuing, 214; of crime, 217; after verbs of admonishing, 218; after verbs denoting an affection of the mind, 220; instead of abl. after verbs of abounding, etc., 220, 3; instead of predicate acc., 230, N. 4; of place, 221; after particles, 221, II., III.; of gerunds, 275, III., R. 1; plur. depending on a gerund, 275, R. 1. (3.); place of, after neuter adjectives, 279, 10.

Genitives, two, limiting the same noun, 211, R. 10.
Genitus, w. abl., 246.
Genius, voc. sing., 52.
Gentium, 212, R. 4, N. 2.
Genus, in acc. instead of the gen. or abl., as, *id genus, omne genus*, etc., 234. 11., n. 2, *fin.*; 209, R. 7, (4.); 231, R. 6; used with the genit. instead of an appositiou, 211, R. 2, N.
Georgicon, 54, 4.
Gero and *fero*, compounds of, in nouns of 2d decl., 47; in adjs. of 1st and 2d decls., 105, 3; not compared, 127, 7.
Gerundives, defined, 275, R. 2; how used, 275, II.
Gerunds, 25, and 148, 2; by what cases followed, 274; and gerundives, genitive of, 275, III., R. 1; nouns which they follow, ib. (1.); adjectives, ib. (2.); after *sum* denoting tendency, 275, (5.); instead of a noun in apposition, 211, R. 2, N.; dat. of, 275, R. 2; acc. of, 275, R. 3; abl. of, 275, R. 4; infin. for, after adj., 270, R. 1, (a.)
Gigno, pr., 284, R. 3.
Gl, *tl*, and *thl*, in syllabication, 18, 3.
Glorior, with abl., 247, 1, (2.); w. acc., 232. N. 1, and (3.)
Glyconic verse, 304, 2; 316, IV.
Gn, initial, 12, R.
Gnarus, w. gen., 213, R. 1; cf. R. 4, (1.)
-go, nouns in, gender of, 59, 2; genitive of, 69. E. 1.
Golden age, of Roman literature, 329, 2.
Government defined, 203. 7.
Grammatical subject, 202, 2; cases of, 202. R. 4; predicate, 203, 2; figures, 322.
Gratia, w. gen., 247, R. 2; its place, 279, R.; *gratias ago*, constr., 273, N 6.
Gratum mihi est, quod, 273, N 6.
Gratuler, constr., 278, N. 7.

Grave accent, 5, 2, and 14, 2; 15, R 8
Gravidus and *gravis*, w. gen. or ab 213, R. 5, (3.)
Greek nouns, gender of, 34, R. 1; terminations of in 1st decl., 44; in 2d decl., 54; terminations of in 3d decl., 55, R.; acc. of in 3d decl., 80; declension of, in do., 86
Greek or limiting acc., 234, R. 2.
Grex, gender of, 65, 2; genitive of, 78, 2, (2.)
Grus, gender of, 30; genitive of, 76, E. 3
Guilt and innocence, adjectives of, with gen., 217, R. 1.

H.

H, its nature, 2. 6; its place in syllabication, 18, 1; before *s* in verbal roots, 171, 1; in prosody, 283, 1., (b.)
Habeo, with two accs., 230, N. 1; *habere in numero* or *in loco*, 230, N. 4; w. gen of value, 214, t. 2; w. abl. of price, 252, R. 1; w. two datives, 227, R. 1; w. participle perf. pass., 274, R. 4; w. participle in *dus*, 274, R. 1, (n.); *habeo, non habeo*, or *nihil habeo, quod*, w. subj., 264, N. 3; *haberi*, w. predicate nom., 210, R. 3, (3.), (c.); 271, N. 2, and R. 4.
Habito, w. gen. of price, 214, N. 1; w abl. of, price, 252, R. 1.
Hac in answer to *qua*? 191, R. 1, (c.)
Hactenus, adv. of place and time, 191, R. 1, (g.)
Hadria, gender of, 42, 2.
Hæc, for *hæ*, 134, R. 1.
Haud, signification and use, 191, R. 3; *haud multum abest quin*, 262, N. 7; *haud scio an*, 198, 11, R. (e.)
Hebes, gen. of, 112, 1; abl. of, 113, E 3; defective, 115, 2.
Hei mihi, 228, 3.
Hellenism, 323. R (2.)
Hem. w. dat., 228, 3; w. acc., 238, 2; w. voc., 240, R. 1.
Hemistich, 304.
Hemiolius, 304, 5.
Hendiadys, 323, 2, (3.)
Ilepar, genit. of, 71; abl. of, 82, E. 1, (b.)
Hephthemimeris, 304, 5.
Heres, gender of, 31, 2; genitive, 78, E. 1.
Heroic cæsura, 310, 4 and 5.
Heros, genitive, 75, 2; acc., 80, R.; dat plur., 84; acc. plur., 85, E. 2; declined, 86
Heteroclite nouns, 93.
Heterogeneous nouns, 34, R. 2; 92.
Heterosis, 323, 3, (2.)
Hexameter verse, 310; Priapean, 310, II.
Hiatus, 279, 18.
Hibernus, pr., 284, E. 5, R. 2.
Hic, prou., declined, 134; distinguished from *ille*, 207, R. 23; *hic—hic*, for *hic—ille*, 207. R. 23, (b.); related in time like *nunc* and *tunc*.
Hic, adv. of place, *hic, hinc, huc*, etc., referring to the place of the speaker, 191, R. 1, (e.); w. gen., 212, R. 4, N. 2, (b.); adv. of time, 191, R. 1, (g.)
Him, her, etc., how expressed in Latin 207, R. 20.

Hipponactic trimeter, 314, II.; tetrameter, 314, IV.
Historical present, 145, I., 3; perfect, 145, IV., R.; for the pluperfect, 259, R. 1, (d.); infinitive, 209, R. 5; tenses. 258.
Hoc, pleonastic, 207, R. 21 and 22; hoc w. partitive gen., 212, R. 3, N. 1; hōc with comparitives, 256, R. 16.
Hodie, pr., 285, 2, E. 1.
Homo, gender of. 31, 2; genitive, 69, E. 2; homo, homines, ellipsis of, 209, R. 2, (2.); 205, R. 7, (1.); 229, R. 4.
Homœopropheron, 324, 26.
Honor, (-os), declined, 57.
Horace, key to the odes of, 321.
Horatian metres, 320.
Horreo, w. inf., 271, N. 1.
Hortor, w. ad, 225, R. 1; w. ut, ne, etc., 273, 2; without ut, 262, R. 4.
Hospes, gender of, 30; formation of nom. sing., 56, I., R. 3; genitive, 73, 2; abl., 113, R. 2; as an adj., 129, 8.
Hostis, w. gen. or dat., 222, R. 2, (c.)
'However' w. a relative, how expressed in Latin, 280, III., (3.)
Huc, w. genitive, 212, R. 4, N. 3, (b.); huccine rerum, 212, R. 4, N. 3.
Humi, constr., 221, R. 3; humo, 254, R. 2; 255, R. 1.
Huic, pronunciation of, 9, 5; pr., 306, R. 2.
Hujus non facio, 214, R. 1.
Hujusmodi, 134, R. 5; w. qui and the subj., 264, 1, N.
Hypallage, 323, 4, (3.)
Hyperbaton, 323, 4.
Hyperbole. 324, 5.
Hypercatalectic or hypermeter verse, 304, 3, (4.)
Hypothetical sentences, 259, R. 3, (c.), (d.), and R. 4; 260, N.; in the inf., 268, R. 4—R. 6.
Hysteron proteron, 323, 4, (2.)

I.

I, its sound, 7 and 8; i and j but one character. 2, 3; i for ii in gen. of 2d decl., 52; i changed to e in forming certain noms., 56, I., R. 3; nouns in i, gender of, 66; genitive of, 68: genitive of Greek nouns in, 73, R.; dat. of 3d decl. in, 79; abl. sing. in, 82; 113; in gen. and dat. sing. of 5th decl., 90, E. 2; i ending the former part of a compound noun or adj. 103, R. 1; 131, N; i in dat. sing. of nine adjs. in us and er, 117; in 1st person sing. of the perf. act., 147, 3; i, the characteristic vowel of the 4th conj., 149, 2; cf. 150, 5; i or e for the Greek u, 283, E. 6, 1.); increment in, 3d decl., 287, 3; plur., 288; of verbs, 290; i final, quantity of, 285, R. 4.; 296.
-ia, abstracts in, 101, 3; in nom., acc. and voc. plur., 83: 85.
-iacus, adjs. in, 128, 1, (d.)
Iambic metre, 314; 303; tetrameter, 314, III; trimeter, 314. I.; catalectic, 314. IV.; dimeter, 314. VI.; hypermeter, 314. VII.; acephalous, 314, VIII.; catalectic, 314, IX.; iambico-dactylic metre, 318, II.

-ianus, adjs. in, 128, 6, (. ⁎.)
-ias, fem. patronymics in 100, 1, (b.)
Ibi, ellipsis of before ubi, 206, (3.), (a.)
-icis, genitives in, 78, 2, (2.) and (3.) 74, E. 2.
-icius, adjs. in, 128, 2; -icius or -itius verbal adjs. in, 129, 5.
Ictus, 308, 3.
-iculus, a, um, diminutives in, 100, 3, R. 1
-icus, adjs. in, 128, 1, (d.), and 2. (a.). and 6, (i.)
Id, before a relative pron., 206, (13.); w. gen., 212. R. 3; id temporis, œtatis, id genus, etc., 234, II., R. 3; 253, R. 3; id ago, constr., 273, N. 1; 207. R. 22; id quod instead of quod. 206. (13.), (b.); as acc. of degree, etc., 232, (3.)
Idem, declined, 134, R. 6; how used, 207, R. 27; w. gen., 212. R. 3; w. dat., 222, R. 7; 207, R. 27, (d.); supplying the place of item, etiam, or tamen, 207, R. 27; idem qui, ac, atque, ut, cum, etc., 207, R. 27, (a.); 222, R. 7; idem—idem, 'at once,' 207, R. 27, (c.); as acc. of degree, 232, (3.)
Ides, 326, 2.
-ides, and -iades, patronymics in, 100, 1, (a.); pr., 291, 4.
Idiotism, 325, 6.
-idis, genitives in, 73, E. 1; 74, E. 2.
Idoneus, qui, 264, 9; 270, R. 1.
-idus, adjs. in, 129, 2.
-iei, in 5th decl., quantity of the e, 288, I., E. 2.
-ies, advs. in, 192, II., 3.
Igitur, 198, 6; its place, 279, 3, (b.) equivalent to 'I say,' 278, R. 10.
Ignarus, w. genitive, 213, R. 1; 275, III. R. 1, (2.)
-ii in genitive contracted, 52; how accented, 14, E.
-ile, derivative nouns in, 100, 9.
-ilis, adjs. in, 129, 4; 128, 4.
Illac, in answer to qua? 191, R. 1, (d.)
Illacrimo, w. dat., 224, N. 1, 4.
Illative conjunctions, 198, 6.
Ille, declined, 134; its uses, 207, R. 20—26; w. quidem, redundant, 207, R. 21; its relation to time, 207, R. 23, (c.); as a pron. of the 3d pers., 207, R. 20; relation of hic and ille, 207, R. 23; ille, qui, w. subj., 264, 1, N.
Illic, pron, how declined, 134, R. 3; illic, illuc, illinc, advs., their reference, 191, R. 1, (e.)
-illimus, superlatives in, 125, 2.
Illiusmodi, 134, 5.
-illo, verbs in, 187, II., 4.
Illud, w. genitive, 212, R. 3, N. 1, (a.); pleonastic, 207, R. 22; as acc. of degree, 232, (3.)
Illudo, w. dat., 224, 4.
-illus, a, um, diminutives in, 100, 3, A. 3.
-im, in acc. sing. 3d decl., 79; 80; im for eum, 134, R. 1; -im, is, etc., in pres. subj. 162, 1; adverbs in, 192, I. and II.
Imbecillus, pr., 284, 2, E. 2.
Imbuo, constr., 231, R. 4.
Imitative verbs, 187, 3.
Immemor, gen. of, 112, 2; abl., 113, E. 3 gen. plur., 114, E. 2.

Immo, 191, R. 3.
Immodicus, w. gen. or abl., 213, R. 5, (3.)
Immunis, w. gen. or abl., 213, R. 5, (3.) cf- 251, N.
-imonium, deriv. nouns in, 100, 6;—and *-imonia*, verbals in, 102, 3.
Impatiens, w. genit., 213, R. 1, (2.)
Impavidus, w. genit., 213, R. 1, (3.)
Impedio, w. *quin*, 262, N. 7; w. *quominus*, 262, R. 11; w. inf., 262, R. 11, N.
Impello, 273. N. 4.
Imperative, 143, 3; its tenses, 145, R. 3; how used, 267, (1.), (2.); irregular, 162, 4 and 5; subj. for imperative 267, R. 2; sing for plur., 209. N 2· used as a noun, 205, R. 8.
Imperfect tense, 145, II.; w. *oportet*, etc., 259, R. 3; the imperf. indic. for plup. subj., 259, R. 4.
Imperitus, w. genit., 213, R. 1, (3.); of gerund, 275, III., R. 1, (2.)
Impero, constr., 273, N. 4; 262, R. 4; w. dat. and acc., 223, R. 2, (1.)
Impersonal verbs, 184; subject of, 184, 2; list of in 2d conj., 169; 184, R. 1; in 1st, 3d, and 4th conj., 184, R. 1; constr. w. gen., 215, 1; 219; w. dat., 223, R. 2, N. (*b.*); w. acc., 229, R. 6 and 7.
Impertio, 249, I., and R. 3; 225, R. 1, (*b.*)
Impetro, *ut*, 273, N. 2.
Impleo, 249, R. 1; 220, 3.
Impono, 241, R. 5.
Impos and *impotens*, w. genit., 213, R. 1, (3.)
Imprimis, 193, II., 2.
Imprudens, *improvidus*, w. genit., 213, R. 1.
Impubes, genitive, 112, 1; abl., 113, E. 2; 115, 1, (*a.*)
Impulsus, w. abl. of cause, 247, R. 2, (*b.*)
-in, roots of nouns in, 56, II., R. 1 and 2; in acc. sing., 79.
In, prep., constr., 235, (2.); signification and use, 195, R. 14; in composition, 196, 7; *in* with abl. instead of predicate acc., 230, N. 4; constr. of verbs compd. with, 224; w. abl. after verbs of placing, holding, regarding, assembling, etc., 241, R. 5; ellipsis of with some ablatives of place, 254 and Rs.; with ablatives of time, 253, N. 1, and R. 5; with names of towns, 254, R. 2 and R. 3.
Inanis, w. genit. or abl., 213, R. 5, (3.)
Incassum. 193, II., 4.
Incedo, 233, (3.), N.; 210, R. 3. (2.)
Inceptive verbs, 187, II., 2; list of, 173.
Incertus, w. genit., 213, R. 1; *incertum est an*, 198, 11, R. (*c.*); 265, R. 3.
Inchoatives, see inceptive verbs.
Incidit ut, 202, R. 3.
Incito, constr., 225, R. 1; *incitatus*, w. abl. of cause, 247, R. 2, (*b.*)
Incipio, w. inf., 271, N. 1.
Inclino, constr., 229, R. 4, 1; 225, IV.
Incommodo, w. dat., 223, R. 2, N. (*b.*)
Increment of nouns, 286; sing. num., 287; plur. num., 288; of verbs, 289.
Incrementum, 324, 22.
Increpo and *increpito*, w. gen., 217, R. 1.
Incumbo, w. dat., 224, 4; w. *ad*, 224, R. 4.
Incuso, w genit., 217, R. 1.

Inde, ellipsis of before *unde*, 206, (3.), (*a*)' *inde loci*, 212, R. 4, N. 4.
Indeclinable nouns, 34; 94;—adjectives. 115. 4.
Indefinite adjectives, 104; 139, 5, R.;— pronouns, 138;—adverbs, 191, R. 4.
Indicative mood. 143, 1; its tenses, 145; how used, 259; tenses used one for another, 259, R. 1–4; indic. of the preterites with *oportet*, etc., 259, R. 3; in inserted clauses, 266, 2, R. 3 and 5; 266. 1, R. 1.
Indico, w. acc. and inf., 272, N. 1.
Indigeo, w. abl., 250, 2, (2.); w. genit 220. 3.
Indignor, constr., 273, 5, N. 6.
Indignus, w. abl. 214; w. genit., 244, R. 2; *indignus qui*, w. subj., 264, 9; w. supine in *u*, 276, III., R. 1.
Indigus, w. genit. or abl., 213, R. 5, (2.)
Indirect questions, subj. in, 265:—indirect reference, 266, 3:—indirect discourse, 268, 1, N. and 2.
Induco, *id animum inducere*, 233, (1.); pass. w. acc., 234, R. 1; *inductus*, w. abl of cause, 247, R. 2, (*b.*)
Indulgeo, constr., 223, (1.), (*a.*)
Induo, w. dat. and acc., 224, 4; w. abl. and acc., 249, I., R. 1; cf. 224, R. 1, (*b.*); *induo* and *exuo*, constr. in pass., 234, R. 1.
-ine or *-ione*, fem. patronymics in, 100, 1,(*b.*)
Ineo, 183, R. 3; *inire consilia*, w. inf., 270, R. 1, (*c.*); 134, III.
Iners, abl. of, 113, E. 3, and R. 1.
Inexpertus, w. genit., 213, R. 1.
Infamo, w. genit. of crime, 217, R. 1.
Infero, 224, 4, and R. 4.
Inferus, comparison of, 125, 4;—*inferior* w. dat., abl., or *quam*, 256, R. 10; *infimus* and *imus*, 205, R. 17.
Infinitive, 143, 4; as a noun, 26, R.; 269; its gender, 34, 4; 205, R. 8; its cases, 269, (*b.*); as an acc., 229, R. 5; 270; as a verb, 269, (*a.*); its tenses, 145, R. 4; old inf. pres. pass. in *-er*, 162, 6;—inf. as logical subj., 202, R. 2; 269; how modified, 203, II., 5; with subject nom., 209, R. 5; for the genitive, 213, R. 4; its subjete, 239; w. dat. instead of acc., 227, N.; construction and meaning of its tenses, 268; inf. as subject of inf., 269. R. 3; as predicate nom., 269, R. 4; *esse*, etc., with *licet* and a predicate noun or adj., case of such predicate, 269, R. 5; poetically after what verbs, 271, A. 3; depending on a verb, 270; 229, R. 5; on an adj. or noun, 270, R. 1; 275, II., R. 1, N. 1; absolute, 270, R. 2; ellipsis of, 270, R. 3; inf. without a subject after what verbs used, 271; with a subject, after what verbs 272; 273; how translated, 272, R. 3; used like a noun, 273, N. 9; its place, 279, 11; inf. pres. for inf. perfect, 268, R. 1; inf. perf. for present, 268, R. 2; pres. for future, 268, R. 3; poet. to denote a purpose, 274, R. 7, (*b.*)
Infinitum est, the indic. for the subj., 259, R. 4, (2)
Infirmus, w. genit. or abl., 213, R. 5, (3.)
Infit, 183, 14, 180, ⋆
Inflection. 25; parts of speech inflected 24. 4.

Ingens, abl. of, 113, R. 3.
Inimicus, w. dat., 222, R. 1; w. genit., 222, R. 2, (c.)
Inis, genitives in, 69, R. 1 and 2.
Initio, "at first," 253, N.
Innitor, 224, R. 4. See also *nitor*.
Innocens and *innoxius*, w. genit. 218, R. 1.
Insatiabilis, w. genit., 213, R. 5, (1.)
Inscius, w. genit., 213, R. 1. (3.)
Inscribo, *insculpo*, and *insero*, constr., 241, R. 5.
Insimulo, w. gen., 217, R. 1.
Insolens and *insolitus*, w. genit., 213, R. 1.
Inops, abl. of, 113, R. 3; 115, 1, (a.); w. genit., 213, R. 1; cf. R. 4, (1.); w. abl., 250, 2, (1.)
Inquam, 183, 5; ellipsis of, 209, R. 4; its position, 279. 6.
Inserted clauses, 266.
Insinuo, constr., 229, R. 4, 1.
Insons, genit. plur. of, 114, R. 3; 115, 1, (a.); w. genit., 213, R. 1.
Inspergo, 249, I., R. 1 and R. 3.
Instar, a diptote, 94.
Instituo, 273, N. 4; 230, N. 1; 231, R. 4; w. inf., 271, N. 1.
Instrument, abl. of, 247, and R. 5; w. verbs of teaching, 231, R. 3, (c.)
Instruo, 231, R. 4.
Insumere tempus, 275, R. 2.
Insuesco, w. dat. or abl. of the thing, 245, II., 3; w. inf., 271, N. 1.
Insuetus, 213, R. 1, (3.); 222, R. 2. (a.); 275. III., (2.); 270, R. 1; 275, III., R. 1, (2.)
Insuper, w. acc. or abl., 235, R. 8.
Integer, w. genit., 213; *integrum est ut*, 262, R. 3, N. 3.
Intelligo, w. two accs., 230, N. 1; w. acc. and inf., 272, N. 1; *intelligitur*, w. inf. as subject, 269, R. 2.
Intention denoted by participle in *rus* with *sum*, 162, 14; 274, R. 6.
Intentus, w. acc. *nihil*, 232, (3.); *intentum esse*, w. dat. of gerund, 275, III., R. 2, (1.)
Inter, use of, 235, 1, R. 2; in composition, 196, I., 8;—w. *se* or *ipse*, 208, (5.); w. gerunds, 275, III., R. 3; instead of partitive gen., 212, R. 3, R. 4; construction of its compds., 224; repeated by Cicero after *interesse*, 277, II., 4.
Intercedo, w. *quin*, *ne*, or *quominus*, 262, R. 11.
Intercludo and *interdico*, 251, N. and R. 2.
Interdico, w. abl., 251. N.
Interdiu or *die*, 253, N. 1.
Interea loci, 212, R. 4, N. 4.
Interest, Roman computation of, 327.
Interest, w. genit., 219; w. *mea*, etc., 219, R. 1; subject cf. 219, R. 4; degree of interest how expressed, 219. R. 5.
Interior, comparison of, 126, 1; *intimus*, 205. R. 17.
Interjections. 199; w. nom., 209, R. 13; w. dat., 222, (3.); w. acc., 238, 2; w. voc., 240; *O*, *heu*, etc., not elided, 305.
Intermitto, w. inf., 271, N. 1.
Interpres, gender of, 30; 61 2; genit. of, 78. 8.
Interritus, w. genit., 213, R. 1 and 2.

Interrogative particles, 198, 11;—adjs. 104, 14; 121, 5; 139, 5, 3;—pronouns, 137. in indirect questions, 137, N.; 265, N. 2;—sentences, 200, 3.
Interrogo, w. two accs., 231, R. 1; constr. in pass., 234, 1.; w. genit. of the crime, 217, R. 1.
Intersum, w. dat., 224, 5.
Intus, w. acc., 338, 1. (b.)
Intra, how used, 195, R. 8; 253. R. 4 (b.)
Intransitive verb, 141. II.; used impersonally in pass. w. dat., 223 N. 1, (c.)
-inus, adjs. in, 128, 1, 2, and 6.
Invado, 233. (3.), N.
Invariable adjs., 122; specified, 127, 7.
Invenio, w. two accs., 230, N. 1; *inveniuntur*, *qui*, w. subj., 264, 6.
Invideo, constr., 223, (1.), (c.); 220, 1 *invidetur mihi*, 223, R. 2, N. (c.)
Invitus, w. dat. of the person, 226, R. 3, *invitâ Minervâ*, 257, R. 7.
Involuntary agent of pass. verb, 248, II., and N.
-io, nouns in, gender of, 59, 1; personal appellatives in, 100, 4, (b.); verbals in, 102, 7; verbs in of 3d conj., 159.
Ionic metre. 317; 303;—*a majore*, 317, I.; —*a minore*, 317, II.
-ior, *-ius*, in terminational comparatives, 124, 1.
Ipse, declined, 135; how used, 135, R. 2; 207, R. 28; used reflexively, 208, (4.); 207, R. 28, (c.); w. *inter*, 208, (5.); *et ipse*, 207, R. 27, (b.); *ipse*, with the inf., 273, N. 9, (a.); *nunc ipsum* and *tum ipsum*, 191, R. 7.
Ipsus and *ipsissimus*, 135, R. 2.
Irascor, w. dat., 223, R. 2, N., (b.)
Iri, w. supine in *um*, 276, II., R. 3.
Iron age of Roman literature, 329, 4.
Irony, 324. 4.
Irregular nouns, 92;—adjs., 115;—verbs, 178—182.
-is, nouns in, gender of, 62; 63; genitive of, 74; *-is* or *-eis* instead of *-es* in acc. plur. of 3d decl., 85, R. 1; abl. of adjs. in *is* used as nouns, 82, R. 4;—used as proper names, 82, R. 4, (b.); *-is* for *-us* in genitive of 4th decl., 89, 2; fem. patronymics in, 100, 1, (b.); ellipsis of in 2d root of verbs, 162, 7, (c.)
Is, pron., declined, 134; how used, 207, R. 26; referring to a clause, 206, (13.); *is* and *ille* with *quidem* used pleonastically, 207, R. 21; *is* for *talis*, 207, R. 26, (b.); 264, 1, N.; *et is*, *atque is*, *isque*, *et is quidem* 207, R. 26, c.); ellipsis of *is*, 207, R. 26, (d.); *is-qui*, 264, 1, N.
Islands, gender of, 29; constr. of names of, 237, R. 5, (b.)
-issimus, *a*, *um*, the terminational superlative, 124, 2.
-isso, verbs in, 187, II., 5.
Iste, how declined, 134; how used, 207 R. 23, 25; *iste qui*, w. subj., 264, 1, N.
Istic, pron., declined, 134, R. 3.
Istic, adv., *istinc*, *istuc*, their reference, 191, R. 1. (c.)
Istiusmodi, 134, R. 5.
-it, roots of nouns in, 56, II., R. 5; in 3d root of 4th conj., 175, of certain verbs of 3d conj., 171, R. 7.

INDEX.

Ita, 191, R 5; 277, R. 12, (a.); *ita non*, 277, R. 14.
Itaque, its meaning, 198, 6, R.; its place, 279, 3, (b.)
Iter, declined, 57; 71, 2; with *sum* and acc. of place, 237, R. 1; increments of, 286, 2.
-iter and *-ter*, advs. in, 192. II. and IV.
-itas, *-ia*, *-itia*, *-ities*, *-itudo*, and *-itus*, abstracts in, 101. 1.
-itis, genitive in, 73; 78, 1; 112, 1.
-ito, frequentatives in, 187, II., 1.
-itius or *-icius*, adjs. in, 129, 5.
Itum, sup., in prosody, 284, E. 1, (2.)
-itus, advs. in, 192, I. and II.; adjs. in, 129, 7.
-ium, verbals in, 102, 2; *-ium* or *-itium*, nouns in, 100, 5.
-ius, genitives in, place of English accent, 15; in what adjs., 107; quantity of the *i*, 283, I., E. 4:—adjs. in, 128, 1, 2, and 5; voc. sing. of patrials and possessives in, 52.
-iv, in 2d roots of verbs, 175; 171, E. 3.
-ivus, adjs. in, 129, 7.

J.

J, vowel before, in prosody, 283, IV., N. 1.
Jaceo, 210, R. 3, (2.); 233, (3.), N.
Jam, with a negative, 191, R. 6; *jamdudum*, ib.
Jecur, genitive of, 71, 3; increments of, 286, 2.
Jejunus, w. gen. or abl., 213, R. 5, (3.)
Jesus, decl. of, 53.
Jocus, plur. *joci* and *joca*, 92, 2.
Jubar, abl. of, 82, E. 1, (b.)
Jubeo, constr., 223, (2.); 273, 2, (d.); 272, R. 6; 262, R. 4; ellipsis of *jubeo valere*, 233, R. 2; *jubeor*, w. inf., 271, N. 1.
Jucundus, constr., 276, III., R. 1 and 4; *jucundum est*, w. *quod*, 273, 5, N. 6.
Judico, w. two accs., 230, N. 1; w. acc. and inf., 272, N. 1; in pass., 210, R. 3, (3.), (c.); *judicari* w. predicate nominative, 271, N. 2.
Jugerum, 93, 1; 94.
Jugum, quantity of its compds., 283, IV., E. 1.
Jungo, constr., 229, R. 4, 1.
Junctus and *conjunctus*, constr., 232, R. 6, (c.)
Jupiter, genitive of, 71; declined, 85.
Jus aliquid facere, without *cum*, 247, 2.
Jus, its compds., 189, N. 3:—*juratus*, with active meaning, 163, 16:—*juro*, poet. w. inf., 71, N. 3.
Jusjurandum, declined, 91.
Justum erat, indic. for subj., 259, R. 3; *justum est* with inf. as subject, 269, R. 2; *justo* after comparatives, 256, R. 9; its place, 279, N. 1.
Jurat, w. acc., 229, R. 7.
Juvenalis, abl. of, 82, E. 4, (b.)
Juvenis, abl. of, 82, R. 4, (b.); 113, E. 2; comparison of, 126, 4; 115, 1, (a.); for *in juventute*, 253, R. 6.
Juxta as an adv., 195, R. 4; *juxta ac* or *atque*, 198, 3, a

K.

K, its use, 2, 4.
Key to the Odes of Horace, 321.
Knowing, verbs of, their construction, 272

L.

L, roots of nouns in, 56, II.; gender of nouns in, 66; genitive of, 70;—final, quantity of, 299, 2.
Laboro, constr., 273, N. 1; poet. w. inf., 271, N. 3.
Labials, 3, 1.
Lac, gender of, 66, E.; genitive of, 70.
Lacesso, constr., 225, R. 1.
Lætor, w. abl., 247, 1, (2.); acc., 232, (5.)
Lætus, w. abl. or gen., 213, R. 5, (4.); cf. R. 4, (1.)
Lampas, declined, 86.
Lapis, declined, 57.
Lar, pr., 234, N. 1.
Largus, w. gen. or abl., 213, R. 5, (3.); cf. R. 4, (1.)
Lars, genitive of, 71.
Lassus, w. genit., 213, R. 2.
Lateo, w. dat. or acc., 223, R. 2, N., (b.), and (1.), (a.)
Latin grammar, its divisions, 1.
Latinis, for *ludis Latinis*, 253, N. 1.
Latus, *altus*, and *longus*, w. acc. of space, 236.
Lavo and *lavo*, scil. *se*, 229, R. 4, 1; *lavo*, w. abl. of price, 252, R. 1.
Laxo, w. abl., 251, N.
Leading clause, subject, and verb, 201. 13.
Lego (*ere*), its form in the compds., 189, N. 2; constr., 230, N. 1.
Lenio, constr., 229, R. 4, 1.
-lentus, adjs. in, 123, 4.
Letters, 2; division of, 3; sounds of, 7 numeral, 118, 7; capital, 2, 2; silent, 12, R. terminal in 3d decl., 55.
Levo, w. abl., 251, N.; w. gen. poet. 220, 2.
Lex, gender, 65, 2; genitive, 78, 2, (2.);—*legem dare*, constr., 273, 2, N. 4;—*lege*, abl. of manner, 247, 2.
Liber, w. abl. or gen., 213, R. 5, (4.); cf. 220, 2; and 251, N.; w. genit., 213, R. 5, (4.); cf. R. 4, (1.)
Libero, w. abl., 251, N.; poetically, w. genit., 220, 2.
Liberalis. w. genit., 213, R. 5, (1.)
Libram and *libras*, 236, R. 7.
Libro, abl. w. adj. without prep., 254, R. 2.
Licentia, w. genit. of gerund, 275, III., R. 1, (1.)
Liceo, w. genit. of price, 214, R. 3: w. abl., 252, R. 1.
Licet, w. dat., 223, R. 2; w. subj. the acc. with the inf., or the inf. alone, 273, 4: 262, R. 4; w. inf. as subject, 269, R. 2; case of the predicate after *licet esse*, etc., 269, R. 5; w. indicative instead of subj., 259, R. 3, (a.) —*licet*, conj. w. subj., 263, 2.
Limiting acc., 234, II.;—abl. 250 and R.
-limus, superlatives in, 125, 2.
Linguals and liquids, 3, 1.

Liquidus, pr., 284, E. 5., R. 8.
-lis, adjs. in, comparison, 125, 2.
Literas dare, scribere or *mittere*, 225, m., R. 4; ellipsis of, 229, R. 4, 2; *literas* or *literis*, after verbs of teaching, 231, R. 3, (c.)
Litotes, 324, 9.
Litum, pr., 284, E. 1, (2.)
Loading, verbs of, w. abl., 249, I.
Locuples, genitive of, 112, 1; abl., 113, E. 2; gen. plur., 114, E. 3; 115, 1, (a.); w. abl. or gen., 213, R. 5, (4.)
Locus, plur. *loci* and *loca*, 92, I., 2; *loco* and *loris*, abl. of place without a preposition, 254, R. 2; *loco*, w. gen. for predicate nom., 210, N. 3; for predicate acc., 230, N. 4; *loci* and *locorum*, 212, R. 4, N. 2 and N. 4; *locus* in apposition to names of towns, 237, R. 2; *loco*, w. gen. of price, 241, R. 5; w. abl. of price, 252, R. 1; w. participles in *dus*, 274, R. 7; w. genitive of gerunds, 275, III. R. 1, (1.)
Logical subject, 202, 3;—predicate, 203, 3.
Long syllable, 282, 2.
Longe, w. comparatives and superlatives, 127, 3; 256, N.; w. acc. of space, 236, N. 1; *longe gentium*, 212, R. 4, N. 2, (b.); *longius* without *quam*, 256, R. 6.
Longitudine, w. genit. of measure, 211, R. 6, (6.)
Longus, w. acc. of space, 236; *longum est*, the indicative instead of the subjunctive, 259, N. 4, (2.)
-ls, genitive of nouns in, 77, 2, (2.)
Ludis, for *in tempore ludorum*, 253, N. 1; 257, R. 9, (2.)
Luo, w. abl., 252, R. 1.

M.

M, roots of nouns ending in, 56, I.; before *d* changed to *n*, 134, N. 1; dropped in the 3d root of certain verbs, 171, R. 6; final, quantity of, 299, 3; elided, 305, 2.
-ma, Greek nouns in, genitive plur. of, 84, E. 2.
Mactus, 115, 5; *macte*, w. abl., 247, 1, N. 2; w. genit., 213, R. 5, (4.)
Magis and *maxime*, use of in forming comparatives and superlatives, 127, 1; pleonastic with *malle*, etc., 256, R. 13.
Magnus, compared, 125, 5; w. supine in *u*, 276, III., R. 1; *magnam partem*, 234, II., R. 3; *magni, parvi*, etc., w. verbs of valuing, 214, R. 1; *magno, parvo*, etc., w. verbs of buying, etc., 252, R. 3.
Male, constr. of its compounds *malefacio, maledico*, etc., 225, I.; *male*, instead of abl. of price, 252, R. 3; *male, bene*, or *prudenter facio; male* or *bene fit*, w. *quod*, 273, 5, (1.)
Malo, conjugated, 178, 3; constr., 273, 4; 262, R. 4; *mallem*, meaning of, 260, II, R. 2; constr. w. abl. like a comparative, 256, R. 16, (3.)
Malus, compared, 125, 5.
Man tu, constr., 223, R. 2. and (1.), (b.); 273, N. 7, (a.); 262, R. 4.
Mane, 94; 192, 3.
Maneo, 210, R. 3, (2.); compds. of, 233, R.), N
Manifestus, w. genit., 213, R. 1.

Manner, advs. of, 191, I.I., abl of 247 with *cum*, 247, 2; w. *de* or *ex*, 247, R. 3.
Manus, gender of, 88; ellipsis of, 205, R 7; *manum injicere*, 233, (1.)
Mare, abl. of, 82, E. 1, (b.); ellipsis of, 205, R. 7.
Mas, gender of, 62, E. 1; genitive, 72, E. 1; genit. plur., 83, II., 3, E.; used to distinguish the sex of epicenes, 33, N.
Masculine nouns of 3d decl., 58; exceptions in, 59—61;—masculine cæsura, 310, N. 1.
Materfamilias, declined, 91.
Materia, w. genit. of gerunds, 275, III., R. 1., (1.)
Material nouns, 26, 6;—adjs., 104, 5
Maturo, scil. *se*, 229, R. 4, 1; w. inf., 271, N. 1.
Me and *mi* for *mihi*, 133, R. 1.
Mea, tua, etc., w. *refert* and *interest*, 219, R. 1 and 2.
Means, abl. of, 247; when a person. 247, R. 4; w. passive verbs, 248.
Measure or metre, 303; Roman measures of length, etc., 327.
Medeor, w. dat., 223, N. (b.); its gerundive, 275, II., R. 1.
Medicor, constr., 223, (1.), (a.)
Meditor, constr., 273, N. 1.
Medius, how translated, 205, R. 17; w. genit., 213; w. inter, 212, R. 4, (2.); w. abl., 213, R. 4, (5.); its place, 279, 7, (b.)
Mel, genitive of, 70, E.; 56, II., R. 6; abl., 82, E. 5, (b.); 94.
Melas, genitive of, 72, E. 2.
Melius fuit and *erat* instead of subj., 259, R. 3; *melius est*, w. dat., 228, 1; *melius erit*, w. perf. inf., 268, R. 2.
Melos, nom. plur. of, 83, 1; 94.
Meme and *mepte*, intensive, 133, R. 2.
Memini, 183, 3; constr., 216; w. present inf., 268, R. 1; w. acc. and inf., 272, N. 1; *memento*, poet. w. inf., 271, N. 3.
Memor, w. genit., 213, R. 1, (3.); w. subj., 213, R. 4.
Memoro, constr., 272, R. 6.
-men, nouns in, gender of, 61, 4, and 66; genitive, 71, 1; *-min* or *-mentum*, verbals in, 102, 4.
Mens; in mentem venit, constr., 216, R. 3.
Mercor, w. abl. of price, 252, R.
-met, enclitic, 133, R. 2; 139, R. 1
Metalepsis, 324, 6.
Metaphor, 324, 1.
Metaplasm, 322, 1.
Metathesis, 322, 9.
Meto, 171, E. 2.
Metonymy, 324, 2.
Metre, 303; how divided, 303, 3; different kinds, 310—317.
Metres, compound, 318; Horatian, 320.
-metros, Greek nouns in, 49, 2.
Metuo, w. *ut* or *ne*, 262, R. 7; w. inf., 271, N. 1.
Meus, voc. sing. masc., 105, R. 3; 139, 1; used reflexively, 139, R. 2; how declined, 139; *meum est*, 211, R. 8, (3.), (a.)
Mi, for *mihi*, 133, R. 1.
Middle voice in Greek, 248, R. 1, (2.)

Mile, Roman, 327.
Miles, declined, 57; gender, 30; 61, 2; genitive, 73, 2; used collectively, 209, R. 11, (1.), (b.); ellipsis of, 205, R. 7.
Military expressions without *cum*, 249, III., R.
Militia, construed like names of towns, 221, R. 3.
Mille, how used, 118, 6; ellipsis of, 327, R 5.
Million, how expressed, 118, 5, (a.); a million sesterces, 327, R. 3.
Min' for *mihine*, 133, R. 1.
-mino, in old imperatives, 162, 5.
Minor and compds, w. acc. and dat., 223, (1) (b.)
Ministro, w. dat., 223, R. 2; and (1.), (b.)
Minus and *minimum*, w. genit., 212, R. 3, N. 1; *minus*, for *non*, 277, I., R. 14; *minus* without *quam*, 250, R. 6.
Miror, conjugated, 161; w. genit. poet., 220. 1; constr., 273, N. 6.
Mirum est ut, 262, R. 3, N. 3; *mirum quam, quantum*, etc., 264, R. 4.
Misceo, how construed, 245, II., 2, and R. 1; 224, R. 3.
Misereor, miseresco, miseret, miseritum est, and *miserescit*, w. gen. of the thing, 215; *miseret*, etc., w. acc. of the person, 215, N. 3; 229, R. 6; and w. acc. of the thing, 215, N. 2; w. acc. of degree, 215, N. 3.
Mitis, declined, 109.
Mitto, w. *ad* or *in*, 225; w. two dats., 227; 273, 2. (c.); w. participle in *dus*, 274, R. 7; w. inf., 271, N. 3; w. *quod*, 273; *missum facio*, 274. R. 4.
Mn. initial, 12, 2, R.
Mobilis, pr., 284, E. 5, R. 1.
Moderor, constr., 223, (1.), (a.).
Modi annexed to pronouns, 134, R. 5; its use, 211, R. 6, (5.)
Modicus, w. genit., 213, R. 5, (1.)
Modified subject, 202, 6; itself modified, 202, III., R. 1;—predicate, 203, 5.
Modify or limit, in what sense used, 202, 4, R.
Modo as abl. of manner, 247, 2.
Modo, conditional conj., 198, 5; w. subj., 263, 2; *modo*, adv., 193, II., 3; *modo ne*, 203, 2. N. 1; *modo—modo*, 277, R. 8.
Modus, w. genit. of gerunds, 275, III., R. 1, (1.)
Mollio, 229, R. 4, 1.
Moleste, ægre or *graviter fero*, w. *quod*, 273, N. 6.
Moneo. conjugated, 157; constr., 218, and R. 1, 2; 273, R. 1; without *ut*, 262, R. 4; w. acc. and inf., 273, N. 4, (e.); in pass., 234, I.
Money, Roman, 327, pp. 370—372.
Monocolon, 319, 2.
Monometer, 304, 2; 313, I.
Monoptotes, 94.
Monosyllables, quantity of, 294, (a.); 299. 1; their place, 279, 8.
Mons, gender of, 64, 1.
Months, Roman, 326, 2; names of, 326; division of, 326, 1; gender of names of, 28; 115, 3; abl. of names in *er* and *is*, 82, E. 2, a)

Moods, 143.
Mora, in prosody, 282, 2.
Mos or *moris est*, constr., 262, N. 2; w genit. of gerunds, 275, III., R. 1, (1.); *more* as abl. of manner without *cum*, 247, 2.
Motion or tendency, verbs of, constr., 225, IV.; 237, R. 3.
Motum, pr., 284, E. 5, R. 1.
Mountains, gender of names of, 28, 3.
Moveo, constr., 229, R. 4. 1; 251, N.; *motus*, w. abl. of cause, 247, R. 2, (b.)
-ms, nouns in, genitive of, 77, 2, (1.)
Multiplicatives, 121, 1.
Multo, (*are*), constr., 217, R. 5.
Multus, compared, 125, 5; *multi et*, how used, 278, R. 5; *multo*, w. comparatives, etc., 127, 3; 256, R. 16; so *multum*, ib., N.; *multum*, w. genitive, 212, R. 3, N. 1; as acc. of degree, 212, (2.); *multus* instead of an adverb, 205, R. 15.
Mus, gender of, 80; 67, 4; genitive, 76, E. 3; genit. plur., 83, II., 3.
Munificus, w. genit., 213, R. 5, (1.)
Mutes, division of, 3, 1; a mute and a liquid in prosody, 283, IV., E. 2.
Mutilus, w. abl., 213, R. 5, (5.)
Muto, constr., 252, R. 5; 229, R. 4, 1.

N.

N, roots of nouns in, 56, n.; nouns in, gender of, 58; 61; genitive of, 70; 71; final, quantity of, 299, E.; dropped in the 3d root of certain verbs, 171, E. 6.
-nactis, genitive of Greek names in, 78, 2, (1.)
Nam and *enim*, 198, 7, R., (a.); place of, 279, 3, (a.) and (c.)
Names of persons, their order, 279, 9, (b.); of nations instead of those of countries 255, R. 3; 237, R. 5.
Narro, w. acc. and inf., 272, N. 1, and R. 6; *narror*, constr., 271, R. 2.
Nascor, w. abl., 246, R. 1; *nascitur*, w. subj., 262, R. 3, N. 2.
Nato, 232, (2.), N. 1; constr. of compds., 233, (3.), N.
Natura fert, constr., 262, R. 3., N. 2.
Naturale est, w. *ut* and the subj., 262, R. 3, N. 3.
Natus, w. abl., 246; *natus*, 'old,' w. acc., 236, N. 3; poet. w. inf., 271, N. 3.
Natu, 94; 250. 1; 126, 4.
Nauci habere, 214, R. 1.
-nĕ, enclitic conjunction, 198, 11; quantity of, 295, R.; as an interrogative particle, 198, 11, R., (c.); its place, 279, 3, (c.)
Nē, adv., the primitive negative particle, 191, III., R. 3, p. 158; w. *quidem*, ib.; 279, 3, (d.); w. subjunctives used as imperatives, ib.; in wishes, asseverations and concessions, ib.; 260, R. 6, (b.) with the imperative, 267, R. 1; *ne multa, ne plura*, etc., 229, R. 3, 2;—in intentional clauses, 262, R. 5; *ne non*, for *ut*, 262, N. 4; ellipsis of, 262, R. 6; *ne*, for *nedum*, 262, N. 5.
Nec or *neque*, 198, 1; *nec non* or *neque non*, ib.; *nec—nec*, with the singular, 209, R. 12, (5.), (a.); *neque*, for *et ne*, after *ut* and *ne*, 262, R. 6, N. 4;—*nec ipse*, 207, R. 27,

INDEX. 395

(b.); nec is, 207, R. 26, (c.); necne or annon, 265, R. 2; necdum, 277, I., R. 16; its place, 279, 3, (a.)
Necesse, defective adj., 115, 5: necesse est ut, etc., 262, R. 3, N. 2; without ut, 262, N. 4; necesse fuit, the indic. for the subj, 259, R. 3; w. inf. as subject, 269, R. 2; w. predicate dat., 269, R. 5; 273, 4.
Necessity, how expressed, 162. 15.
Necessario, after comparatives, 256, R. 9.
Nedum, w. subj., 262, N. 5; without a verb, ib.
Nefas, gender of, 62, E. 2: 94; w. supine in u, 276, III., R. 2.
Negatives, two, their force, 277, R. 3—5; negative joined to the conjunction, as, nec quisquam, nec ullus, etc., instead of et nemo, et nullus, etc., 278, R. 9.
Negligens, constr., 218, R. 4, (2.)
Nego, instead of non dico, 279, 15, (b.); w. acc. and inf., 272, N. 1, and R. 6; negor, w. inf., 271, N. 1.
N gotium, ellipsis of. 211. R. 8, N.
Nemo, 94 and 95: for nullus, 207, R. 31; nemo est qui. 264. 7. N. 2; nemo non, 'every one.' 277, R. 5, (c.)
Nempe, 191. R. 4; 198, 7. R., (a.)
Neoterism, 325, 3.
Nequa and neque, 138, 2.
Nequam, indeclinable, 115, 4; compared, 125, 5.
Neque, see nec; for et non, 198, 1, (c.); neque—neque, or nec—nec, neque—nec, nec —neque, 198. 1. (e.); neque—et, ib.; neque w. general negatives. 279, 15, (b.); neque non, 277, R. 3: neque quisquam, ullus, umquam, etc., 278. R. 9.
Nequeo, how conjugated, 182, N.; w. inf., 271, N. 4.
Ne quis or nequis, how declined, 138, 2; ne quis, instead of ne quisquam, 207, R. 31; 278, R. 9.
Nerio, genitive of, 69, E. 2.
Nescio an, 198, 11, R., (e.); 265, R. 3; nescio quis, 265, R. 4; nescio quomodo, ib.; w. acc. and inf., 272. N. 1.
Nescius, w. genit., 213, R. 1, (3.)
-neus and -nus, adjs. in, 128, 1, (b.)
Neuter, nouns, 34; not found in 1st and 5th decls., 40, 9; of 2d decl., 46; 54; of 3d decl., 65; excs. in, 66; 67; adjs. used adverbially, 205, R. 10, adjs. and adj. prons, w. genit., 212, R. 3; acc. of denoting degree w. another acc. after transitive verbs, 231, R. 5; verbs. 141; form cf, 142, 1: neuter passives, 142. 2; neuter verbs with cognate, etc., subjects, 234, III.; w. cognate acc., 232, (1.); w. acc. of degree, etc., 232, (3.); w. abl. of age it, 248, R. 2; used in personally, 184, 2; in the passive voice, 142. R. 2: participles of, 162, 1: neuters of possessive pronouns and adjs. instead of the genitive of their personal pronouns, or of a corresponding noun, 211, R. 8, (3.), (a.) und (b.)
Neutral passive verbs, 142, 3.
Neve or neu, 198, 8; after ut and ne, 262, N. 4.
Ni or nisi, 198, 5, B., (b.); nisi, 'except,' 201, R. 6; 277, R. 16; nisi quod, ib.; nisi vero, and nisi forte, 'unless perhaps,' ib.

Nihil, nihilum, 94; w. genitive, 212, R. 1; instead of non, 277, R. 2, (b.); 232, (3.) nihil aliud quam or nisi, 277. R. 16: nihil, acc. w. æstimo and moror, 214, N. 2 nihil w. facio, 214; as acc. of degree, 215. N. 3: 232, (3.); nihil est quod, etc., 264. 7. N. 2; nihil abest, quin, 262. N. 7; nihil antiquius habeo or duco quam, w. subj., 273, N. 1; nihildum, 277, I., R. 16.
Nimius, w. genit. or abl., 213, R. 5, (3.)
Nimio, w. comparatives, 256, R. 16; as abl. of price, 252, R. 3.
-nis, nouns in, gender of, 63, 1.
Nitor, w. abl., 245, II.; w. in or ad, 245, II., R. 2; w. inf. or subj., 273, 1, N. 1.
Nix, 56, R. 2; genit. sing., 78, (3.); genit plur., 83, II., 3.
No, constr. of compds. of 233, (3.), N.
Noctu or nocte, 253, N. 1.
Nolo, conjugated, 178. 2; constr., 273, 4; noli w. inf., paraphrasing the imperative, 267, N. and R. 3; nollem, meaning of, 260, II., R. 2.
Nomen est, constr., 226, R. 1; 211, R. 2, N.; nomine, without a prep. before the genitive following verbs of accusing, 217, R. 2, (b.); its place, 279. 9, (b.)
Nominative, 37; construction of. 209; 210; ellipsis of, 209, R. 1 and 2; wanting, 209, R. 3; w. inf., 209, R. 5; after interjections, 209, R. 13; formation in 3d decl. from the root, 56; plural, 3d decl., 83: of adjs. of 3d decl., 114. See Subject-nominative and Predicate-nominative.
Nomino, 230; pass., 210, R. 3, (3.)
Non, 191, R. 3; ellipsis of, after non modo, etc., followed by ne quidem, 277, R. 6; non quo, non quod, non quin, 262, R. 9; non est quod, cur, quare, or quamobrem, w. subj., 264, 7, N. 3; non before a negative word, 277, R. 3;—before ne quidem, 277, R. 6; position of, 279, 15, (b.); non, rare with the imperative, 267, R. 1; difference between non and haud, 191, R. 3: non nemo, non nulli, non nihil, non numquam, different from nemo non, etc., 277, R. 5, (c.); non nihil, to some extent, 232, (3.); nonne, 198, 11, R., (c.); non modo- sed etiam, and non modo—sed, equivalent to non dicam—sed, 277, R. 10; non dubito, non est dubium, non ambigo, non procul, non abest, quin, 262, 2, N. 7; non quo non, non quod non, or non quia non, instead of non quin; non eo quod, non ideo quod, for non quod, 262, R. 9; non priusquam, non nisi, w. abl. absolute, 257, N. 4; nondum, 277, I., R. 16; non in the second member of adversative sentences without et or vero, 278, R. 11; non nisi, separated, 279. 3, (d.)
Nonæ, 'the Nones,' 326, 2.
Nonnullus, pronominal adj., 139, 5, (1.)
Nos, for ego, R. 7.
Nosco, 171, E. 6.
Noster, how declined, 139, 3.
Nostras, how declined, 139, 4, (b.)
Nostrum, how formed, 133, 3; different use of nostrum and nostri, 212, R. 2, N. 2.
'Not' and 'nor,' how expressed with the imperative, 267, R. 1; with subj., 260, R. 6, (b.)

Nouns, 26—103; proper, common, abstract, collective, and material, 26; gender of, 27—34; number of, 35; cases of, 36, 37; declension of, 38—40; nouns of 3d decl., mode of declining, 55; compound, declension of, 91; irregular, 92; variable, 92; defective, in case, 94; in number, 95, 96; sing. and plur. having different meanings, 97; redundant, 99; verbal, 102; derivation of, 100—102; composition of, 103; how modified, 201, III., R. 1; used as adjs., 205, R. 11; extent given to the term noun, 24, R.

Novum est ut, 262, R. 3, N. 2.

Nox, declined, 57; genitive of, 78, 2, (4.); genit. plur., 83, II., 3.

Noxius, w. genit. of the crime. 213. R. 1, (3.); 217, R. 1, (a.); w. dat., 222. R. 1. (a.) *-ns,* participles in, abl. of, 113. 2; when used as nouns, 82. E. 4; nouns in, genit. plur. of, 83, II., 4; genit. sing. of, 77. 2, 2.) and E. 1; participials and participles in, construction of. 213. R. 1 and 3.

Nubilo, scil. *cælo.* 257, 9, (1.)

Nubo, w. dat., 223; quantity of *u* in compds. of, 285, 2, E. 3.

Nudo, w. abl., 251, N.

Nudus, w. abl. or genit., 213. R. 5, (4.); 250. R , (1); w. acc., 213. R. 4, (3.)

Nullus, how declined, 107; a pronominal adj., 139, 5, (1.); for *non,* 205, R. 10; refers to more than two, 212, R. 2, N., (b.) *nullus est, qui,* w. subj., 264, 7. N. 2; *nullus non,* 277, R. 5, (c.); *nullius* and *nullo,* instead of *neminis* and *nemine.* 207, R. 31, (c.); *nullusdum,* 277, I., R. 16.

Num, with its compounds, meaning of, 198, 11, R., (b.); *num—an,* used only in direct questions, 265, R. 2.

Number, 26, 7; of nouns, 35; of verbs, 146; of the verb when belonging to two or more subjects, 209, R. 12; when belonging to a collective noun, 209, R. 11.

Numbers, cardinal, 117, 118; ordinal, 119, 120; distributive, 119, 120; w. genit. plur., 212, R. 2. (4.)

Numerals. adjs., 104, 105; classes of, 117; placed in the relative clause, 206, (7.), (b.); w. genit. plur., 212, R. 2, (4.); letters, 118, 7; adverbs, 119; 192, 3; multiplicative, 121; proportional, temporal, and interrogative, 121.

Nummus, 327, R. 3, (b.)

Numquam non, and *non numquam,* 277, R. 4, (c.)

Numquis, num quis, or *numqui,* etc., how declined, 137, 3; *numquis est qui,* 264, 7, N. 2; *numqua* and *numquæ,* 137, R. 4; *numquid,* as an interrogative particle, 198, 11.

Numquisnam, 137, 4.

Nunc, use of, 277, R. 15; *nunc—nunc,* 277, R. 8; *nunc* and *etiamnunc,* w. imperfect and perfect, 259, R. 1, (b.)

Nuncupo, w. two accs., 230, N. 1; *nuncupor,* 210, R. 3. (3.)

Nundinæ, 326, 2, (11.)

Nuntio, 273, 2, c.); 272, N. 1; pass. w. inf., 271, N. 1; *nuntiatur,* constr., 271, R. 2.

Nuper, mode and *mox,* 191, R. 6.

Nusquam, w. geni.., 212, R. 4, N 2, (b.)

Nux, pr., 284, 8, 5, R. 2.

-nx, nouns in, genitive of, 65, 6, 7.

O.

O, sound of, 7, 8; changed to *u* in forming certain nominatives from the root. 56. I., R. 4, and II., R. 4; nouns in, gender of, 58, 59; genitive of, 69; Greek nouns in, gender of, 59, E. 3; genitive of, 69, E. 3; amplificatives in, 100, 4. (a.); verbals in, 102, 6. (c.); adverbs in, 192; increment in, of 3d decl., 287, 3; of plur., 288; of verbs, 290; final, quantity of. 285, R. 4; 297; sometimes used for *u* after *v,* 322, 8; 53; 178, 1, N.

O, interj. w. nom., 209. R. 15; w. acc., 238. 2; w. voc., 240, R. 1; *O si,* w. subj., 263. 1.

Ob, government of, 195, 4; 275. III.. R. 3; in composition, 196, I., 9; construction of verbs compounded with, 224; of adjs., 222, R. 1, (b.)

Obedio, how formed, 189, N. 3.

Obequito, constr. 233. (3.)

Obro, constr., 233, (3.). N.; pass., 234, III.

Object, of an active verb, 220; the dative of the remote object, 223, N.

Objective genitive, 211, R. 2; after adjs., 213; dat. for objective genitive, 211, R. 5; —prepositions after what, 273, N. 8.

Oblique cases, 37; their place, 279, 10 and 2.

Obliviscor, w. genitive or acc., 216; w. acc. and inf., 272, N. 1.

Obnoxius, w. dat., 222, R. 1, (b.)

Obruo, w. abl., 249, I., R. 1.

Obsecro, w. two accs., 231, R. 1.

Obsequor, obtempero, and *obtrecto,* w. dat, 223, R. 2.

Observo, w. *ut* or *ne,* 262, N. 3.

Obses, gender of, 30; genitive of, 73, E. 1

Obsonor, w. abl. of price, 252, R. 1.

Obsto, and *obsisto, quominus,* etc., 262, R. 11.

Obtemperatio, w. dat., 222, R. 8.

Obtrector, constr., 223, (1.), (a.)

Obvius, w. dat.. 222. R. 1, (b.)

Obviam, w. dat., 228, 1.

Occasio, w. genit. of gerunds, 275, III. R. 1, (1.)

Occumbo, w. dat., 224; w. acc., 224, R. 5.

Occurro, w. dat., 224; w. acc., 233, 8); *occurrit ut,* 262, R. 3, N. 1.

Ocior, comparison of, 126, 1.

-ocis, genitive in, 78, (4.); 112, 2.

Octonarius, 304, 2;—iambic, 314, III.

Odi, 183, 1.

-odis, genitives in, 76, E. 5; 75, E. 1

-odus, Greek nouns in, 49, 2.

Œ, how pronounced, 9; in nom. plur. 2d decl., 54, 2.

Œdipus, genitive of, 76, E. 5.

Œta, gender of, 42.

Officio, w. *quominus,* etc., 262, R. 11.

Ohe, pr., 283, I., E. 5; 295, E. 5.

Oi, how pronounced, 9, 1.

-ois, genitives in, 75, 't. 2; words in, pr 282, I., E. 6, (8.)

Old, how expressed in Latin, 236, N. 3.
Oleo and *redoleo*, w. acc., 232, (2.)
Ollus, for *ille*, whence *olli*, masc. plur. for *illi*, 134, R. 1.
-olus, a. um, diminutives in, 100, 3, A. 2.
-om, for *-um*, 53.
Omission of a letter or syllable, see syncope—of a word, see ellipsis.
Omnes, w. genitive plur., 212, R. 2, N. 6; *omnium*, w. superlatives, 127, 4, N. 2; *omnia*, acc. of degree, 232, (3.)
-on, Greek nouns in, 54, 1; *-ōn* for *-orum*, 54. 4; *-on*, roots in, of 3d decl., 56, II., R. 1; nouns in, of 3d decl., 58 and 61, 5; genit. plur. in, of Greek nouns, 83, II., 6; *-os* and *-on*, nouns in, of 2d decl., changed to *-us* and *-um*, 54, 1.
Onustus, w. abl. or genit., 213, R. 5, (4.)
Operam dare, w. ut, 273, N. 1; w. dat. of gerund, 275, III., R. 2, (1.); w. acc. *id*, 232, (3.);—*operā meā*, equivalent to *per me*, 247, R. 4.
Opinio est, w. acc. and inf., 272, R. 1; *opiniones* after comparatives, 256, R. 9; its place, 279, N. 1.
Opinor, w. acc. and inf., 272, N. 1.
Oportet, w. inf. as its subject, 269, R. 2; w. inf., acc. with the inf., or the subj., 273, N. 5; without *ut*, 262, R. 4.
Oportebat, *oportuit*, the indic. instead of the subj., 259, R. 3, (a.)
Oppido, w. adjs., 127, 2.
Oppidum, in apposition to names of towns, 237, R. 2, (b.)
Oppleo, w. abl., 249, I., R. 1.
Optabilius erat, the indic. instead of the subj.. 259, N. 3.
Optime, instead of abl. of price, 252, R. 3.
Opto, 271, R. 4; 273, 4; *opto*, w. subj., without *ut*, 262, R. 4.
Opulentus w. genit. or abl., 213, R. 5, (3.)
Opus, work, declined, 57; *opus*, need, w. genit. and acc., 211, R. 11; w. abl. of the thing, 243; as subject or predicate of *est*, 243, R. 2; 210, R. 5; w. perfect participle, 243, R. 1; w. supine in *u*, 276, III., R. 2; *opus est*, w. inf. as subject, 269, R. 2.
-or, nouns in, gender of, 58; 61; genit. of, 70; 71; verbals in, 102, 1; 102, 6.
Oratio obliqua, 266, 1, N., and 2; 273, 3; tenses in, 266, R. 4.
Orbo, w. abl., 251, N.
Orbus, w. abl., 250, 2, (1.); or genit., 213. R. 5, (4.)
Order, advs. of, 191, 1.
Ordinal numbers, 119, 120; in expressions of time, 236, R. 2.
Origin, participles denoting, w. abl., 246; from a country expressed by a patrial, 246, R. 3.
-ōris, genitives in, 76; 112, 2; *-ŏris*, genit. in, 75.
-orium, verbals in, 102, 8.
Oriundus, constr., 246.
Oro, w. two accs., 231, R. 1; w. *ut*, *ne*, or inf., 273. 2, N. 4; without *ut*, 262, R. 4.
Orthoepy, 6—23.
Orthography, 2—5; figures of, 322.
Ortus, w. abl., 246.
-os, nouns in, of 2d decl., 54, 1; of 3d decl., gender of, 58 and 61, 3; genit. of, 75; Greek genitives in, 68, 1; final in plural accs., sound of, E. 3; quantity of, 300.
Os, (*oris*), gender of, 61, 3; genit. of, 75; wants genit. plur., 94.
Os, (*ossis*), gender of, 61, 3; genit. of, 75 E. 1.
Ossa, gender of, 42, 1.
Ostendo, w. acc. and inf., 272, N. 1.
-osus, adjs. in, 128, 4.
-otis, genit. in, 75; 112, 2.
'Ought' or 'should,' expressed by indic. of *debeo*, 259, R. 4, (2.)
-ox, nouns in, genit. of, 78, 2, (4.)
Oxymoron, 324, 26.

P.

P, roots of nouns ending in, 56, I.; when inserted after *m* in 2d and 3d roots of verbs, 171, 3.
Pace or in *pace*, 253, N. 1; 257, R. 9, (2.)
Palatals, 3, 1.
Palleo, w. acc., 232, N. 1.
Pan, acc. of, 80, R.
Panthus, voc. of, 54, 5.
Par, abl. of, 82, E. 1, (b.); 113, E. 3; superlative of, 126, 2; w. dat. or genit., 222, R. 2, (a.); w. *cum* and the abl., 222, R. 6; *par erat*, indic. instead of subj., 259, R. 3, (a.); pr., 284, N. 1; *par ac*, 198, 3.
Parabola, 324, 30.
Paradigms, of nouns, 1st decl., 41; 2d decl., 46; 3d decl., 57; 4th decl., 87; 5th decl., 90;—of adjs. of 1st and 2d decl., 105—107; 3d decl., 108—111;—of verbs, *sum*, 153; 1st conj., 155, 156; 2d conj., 157; 3d conj., 158, 159; 4th conj., 160; deponent, 161; periphrastic, conj., 162; defective, 183; impersonal, 184.
Paragoge, 322, 6.
Paratus, constr., 222, R. 4, (2.)
Parco, w. dat., 223, R. 2, N., (a.); *parcitur mihi*, ib., (c.); w. inf., 271, N. 3.
Parcus, w. genit. or abl., 213, R. 5, (2.); w. *in*, 213, R. 4, (2.)
Paregmenon, 324, 24.
Pareleon, 323, 2, (1.)
Parenthesis, 324, 4, (6.)
Pariter ac, 198, 3.
Paro, constr., 273, N. 1; w. inf., 271, N 1.
Paroemiac verse, 304, 2.
Paronomasia, 324, 25.
Pario, compds. of, 163, E. 4.
Parsing, 281, III.
Pars, acc. of, 79, 4; abl. of, 82, E. 6, (a.); ellipsis of, 205, R. 7; its use in fractional expressions, 121, 6; *magnam* and *maximam partem*, 234, II., R. 3; *multis partibus*, 256, R. 16, (3.)
Part, acc. of, 234, II.
Particeps, genit. of, 112, 2; genit. plur of, 114, E. 2; 115, 1, (a.)—w. genit., 213, R. 1, (3.)
Participial adjs., 130;—of perfect tense, meaning of, with tenses of *sum*, 162, 12, (2.); w. genit., 213, R. 1, (2.)
Participles, 25 and 148, 1; in *us*, how declined, 105, R. 2; in *ns*, do., 111; abl. sing of, 113, 2; participles of active verbs, 148

1, (2.); of neuter verbs, 148, 1, (3.); 162, 16; of deponent verbs, 162, 17; of neuter passive verbs, 162, 18; in *-rus*, genit. plur. of, 162, 19; pres. and perf. compounded with *in*, 162, 21; when they become adjs. or nouns, 162, 22; cases of in compd. tenses, 162, 12, 13; sometimes with *esse* indeclinable, 162, 13, (1.); in *-rus* with *sum*, force of, 162, 14; how modified, 202, II., (3.); agreement of. 205; agreement with a predicate nom. instead of the subject, 205, R. 5; gender when used impersonally, 205, R. 18; perfect denoting origin, with abl., 246; in abl. absolute, 256;—passive of naming. etc., with predicate abl., 257, R. 11; their government, 274; their time how determined, 274, 2, and 3; perfect in circumlocution, for abl. of cause, 247, 1, R. 2, (b.); with *habeo*, etc., 274, 2, R. 4; for a verbal noun, 274, 2, R. 5; for clauses, 274, 3.
Participo, poetically, w. genit., 220, 2.
Particles, 190, 1.
Partim, 79, 4: *partim*, w. genit., 212, R. 4; *partim—partim*, w. genit. or *ex*, 277, R. 8.
Partitive nouns, 212, R. 1;—adjs., 104, 9; —partitives with plur. verbs, 209, R. 11; 211, R. 1; w. genit. plur., 212; ellipsis of, 212, R. 2, N. 3; w. acc. or abl., 212, R. 2, N. 4; genit. sing. after neuter adjs. and pronouns, 212, R. 3.
Parts of speech, 24, 2 and 3.
Parum, its meaning, 191, III.; compared, 194, 4; w. genit., 212, R. 4.
Parumper, its meaning, 191, II.
Parvus, compared, 125, 5; *parvi*, w. verbs of valuing, 214, R. 1, (a.), (1.); *parvo*, with comparatives, 256, R. 16; after *æstimo*, 214, R. 2, N. 2; as abl. of price, 252, R. 3.
Pasco, 171, E. 6.
Passive voice, 141, 2; construction of, 234; passive voice with a reflexive pronoun understood as the agent equivalent to the middle voice in Greek, 248, R. 1, (2.); with acc. of the thing 234, 1.
Pateo, w. two dats., 227, R. 1.
Pater, declined, 57.
Pater-familias, etc., how declined, 43, 2.
Pathetic or emotive word, 279, 2, (e.)
Patior, 273, 4; 262, R. 4; *patiens*, w. gen., 213, R. 1, (2.); w. inf., 271, N. 3.
Patrial nouns, 100, 2; in *o*, genitive of, 69, R.;—adjs., 104, 10; 128, 6, (a.); ellipsis of their substantive, 205, R. 7; pronouns, 139, 4.
Patrocinor, w. dat., 223, R. 2.
Patronymics, 100, 1; in *-es*, genit. plur. in *um* instead of *-arum*, 43, 2; in *as* and *is* used as adjs., 205, R. 11; quantity of their penult, 291, 4 and 5.
Pauca, acc. of degree, 232, (3.)
Paulisper, its meaning, 191, II.
Paulo, w. comparatives, 256, R. 16; *paulum abest quin*, 272, N. 7.
Pauper, abl. of, 113, E. 2; defective, 115, 1, (a.); w. genit. or abl., 213, R. 5, (2.)
Pavidus, w. genit., 213, R. 1.
Pavor est ne, etc., 262, N. 3.
Pecus, (-udis), genit. of, 67, E. 3.

Peculiaris, 222, R. 2, (a.)
Pedes, gender of, 31, 2; genit. of, '3, 2, for *pedites*, 209, R. 11, (1.), (b.)
Pejero, pr., 285, 2, E. 1.
Pelagus, gender of, 51; acc. plur of, 54, 5; 94.
Pello, 171, E. 1, (b.); 251, N.
Pendo, w. genit. of value, 214; w. abl. of price, 252, R. 1.
Pensi and *pili habere*, 214, R. 1.
Pentameter verse, 304, 2; 311; 312, IX., X.
Penthemimeris, 304, 5.
Penult, 13; quantity of, 291; of proper names, 293.
Per, its uses, 195, R. 9; 247, 1, R. 1; w. the means when a person, 247, 3, R. 4; in adjurations, 279, 10, (e.); in composition 196, I., 10; *per* compounded with adjectives strengthens their meaning, 127, 2.
Perceiving, verbs of, their construction, 272.
Percipio, w. acc. and inf., 272, N. 1; *perceptum habeo*, instead of *percepi*, 274, R. 4.
Percontor, w. two accs., 231, R. 1.
Perennis, abl. of, 113, E. 1.
Perdo, w. *capitis*, 217, R. 3; *perditum ire*, for *perdere*, 276, II., R. 2.
Perduim, for *perdam*, 162, 1.
Perfect tense, 145, IV.; definite and indefinite, 145, IV. R.; old form in *sim*, 162, 9; quantity of dissyllabic perfects, 284, E. 1.
perfect participles translated actively, 162, 16; both actively and passively, 162, 17, (a.);—of neuter verbs, 162, 18; of impersonal verbs, 184, R. 2; the perf. subj., 260, II., R. 1, (3.); in the connection of tenses, 258; signification of perf. definite, 259, R. 1, (2.), (a.); of perf. indefinite, ib., (b.)—(d.); perf. subj., signification of, 260, II., R. 1, (3.), and R. 4 and 6; in the protasis, 261, 2 and R. 2 and 3; 263, R.; perf. subj. for imperative, 267, R. 2; perf. inf., how used, 268, K. 1, (a.); perf. participle, 274, 2 and N.; supplies the place of a pres. pass. participle, 274, R. 3, (a.); perf. part. of a preceding verb used to express the completion of an action, ib., (b.); w. *habeo*, 274, R. 4; w. *do, reddo, curo*, etc., ib.; supplies the place of a verbal noun, 274, R. 5; used in circumlocution for abl. of cause, 247, R. 2, (b.); neuter perf. pass. participle used as the subject of a verb, 274, R. 5, (b.)
Perficio ut, 273, N. 2.
Pergo, constr., 225, IV.; w. inf., 271, N. 1.
Perhibeo, 230, N. 1; 272, N. 1, and R. 6; *perhibeor*, 210, R. 3, (3.); w. inf., 271, N. 1
Periclitor, capitis or *capite*, 217, R. 3.
Period, 280.
Perinde, 191, III.;—*ac* or *atque*, 198, 3, R
Periphrasis, 323, 2, (4.)
Periphrastic conjugations, 162, 14 and 15
Peritus, 213, R. 1, and R. 4; 275, (2.); 270, R. 1; w. *ad*, 213, R. 4, (2.); 225, III. R. 1, (2.)
Permisceo, 245, II., 2, and R. 1 and 2.
Permitto, 73, 4; w. part. fut. pass., 274, R. 7; w. subj. without *ut*, 262, R. 4.
Permuto, 252, R. 5.
Pernox, genit. of, 112, 2.
Perosus, 188, 1, N.

Porpello, 273, N. 4.
Perpes, in genit. sing., 112, 1; 115, 2.
Persevero, w. inf., 271, N. 1.
Personal pronouns, 132, 4; ellipsis of as subject-nominatives, 209, R. 1; expressed with infinitive, 272, N. 4; —personal terminations of verbs, 147, 3.
Personification, 324, 34
Person of a noun or pronoun, 35, 2; 132, 4, of a verb, 147; used in the imperative, 147, 2; 1st and 2d persons used indefinitely, 209, R. 7; of verbs with nominatives of different persons. 209, R. 12.
Perspectum habeo, instead of *perspexi*, 214, R. 4.
Persuadeo, w. dat., 223, N., (b.); *hoc persuadetur mihi*, 223, N., (c.); —*persuasum mihi habeo*, 274, R. 4.
Pertæsum est, constr., 229, R. 6; 215, (1.) and N. 2.
Pertineo, ellipsis of, 209, R. 4.
Peto, constr., 230, R. 2; 231, R. 4; *peto ut*, 273, N. 4; 262, R. 4
Pes and compds., genit. of, 73, R. 1; 112, 1; abl. of, 113, R. 2; pr., 284, N. 1; 300, E. 2, (b.)
Ph, in syllabication, 18, 2; when silent, 12, R.
Phalecian verse, 304, 2; pentameter, 312, x
Piger, declined, 106; constr., 222, R. 4, (2.)
Piget, w. genit., 215; w. acc., 229, R. 6; participle and gerund of, 184, R. 3.
Pili habere, etc., 214, R. 1.
Place, advs. of, 191, I.; 192, m.; genit. of, 221; acc. of, 237; dat. of, 237, R. 3; place where, abl. of, 254; —whence, abl. of, 255; through which, 255, 2; place of a foot in verse, 309, N.
Plants, gender of their names, 29.
Plaudo, change of *au* in its compds., 189, N. 3.
Plenty or want, adjs. of, w. abl., 250.
Plenus, w. genit. or abl., 213, R. 5, (3.); 250, 2, (1.)
Pleonasm, 323, 2.
-plex, adjs. in, abl. of, 113, E. 3; how declined, 121, 1.
Plerique, w. genit. plur., 212, R. 2, (1.)
Pluperfect tense, 145, v.; old form in *sem*, 162, 9; for the historical perfect, 259, R. 1. (3.)
Plural number, 35, 1; when wanting, 95; nouns only plur., 95; plur. of Greek nouns of 1st decl., 45, 2; do. of 2d decl., 54, 2; —nouns used for singular, 98; *nos* for *ego*, 209, R. 7, (b.); of verbs with collective nouns, 209, R. 11; the plur. of abstract nouns, 95, R.; plur. nouns in apposition to two or more nouns in the singular, 204, R. 5.
Plurimum, w. genit., 212, R. 3; *plurimi* and *plurimo* after verbs of buying, etc., 214, R. 1, (1. and R. 3, N. 2; *plurimo*, abl. of price, 252, R. 3.
Plus, declined, 110; w. genit., 212, R. 3, N. 1, a.; with numerals, etc., with or without *quam*, 256, R. 6; *plus* for *magis*, 277, R. 12; *plure*, abl. of price, 252, R. 3.
Pædena, declined, 57.
Poems, gender of names of, 29.

Pænitet, w. genit., 215; w. subj., 215, R. w. acc. 229, R. 6; participles of, 184, R. 3 w. *quod*, 273, N. 6.
Poësis, declined, 86.
Poetical arrangement of words, 279, 3, (e.); 16, N. 4.
-politanus, adjs. in, 128, 6, (g.)
Pollens, w. genit. or abl., 213, R 5, (4.); cf. R. 4, (1.)
Polliceor, w. acc. and inf., 272, N 1.
Polyptoton, 324, 23.
Polysyndeton, 323, 2, (2.)
Pondo, indeclinable, 94; *pondo libram et libras*, 211, R. 6, (4.); 236, R. 7.
Pono, 171, E. 2; 230, R. 2; 241, R. 5; pr., 284, R. 2, (c.); 229, R. 4, 1.
Posco, w. two accs., 231; 230, R. 2; w. *ut*, etc., 273, N. 4; in pass., 234, I.
Position in prosody, 283, IV.
Positive degree, 122, 4.
Possessive, adjs., 104; pronouns, 139; to what equivalent, 132, 6; how used, 207, R. 36; 211, R. 3; ellipsis of when reflexive, 207, R. 36; used for subjective and possessive genit., 211, R. 3, (b.), and R. 8, (3.), (a.); for objective genit., 211. R. 3, (c.); so possessive adjectives, 211, R. 4, and R. 8, (3.), (b.); *mea*, *tua*, etc., after *refert* and *interest*, 219, R. 1.
Possidro, w. perf. pass. part., 274, R. 4.
Possum, conjugated, 154, R. 7; with superlatives, 127, 4; w. inf., 271, N. 1; *poterat*, the indic. for the subj., 259, R. 3; *possum* for *possem*, 259, R. 4, (2.)
Post, postquam, etc., how pronounced, 8, E. 4; *post*, its case, 195, 4; *post* in composition, 196, 11; 197. 14; constr. of verbs compounded with, 224; with concrete official titles, 233, R. 3; w. acc. and abl of time, 233, R. 1; ellipsis of, 235, N. 3; w. abl like a comparative, 256, R. 16, (3.)
Postea loci, 212, R. 4, N. 4.
Postera, defective, 115, 5; compared, 125, 4; derivation, 130, V.
Posterior and *postremus*, instead of *posterius* and *postremum*, 205, R. 15.
Postquam and *posteaquam*, w. historical perfect instead of pluperfect, 259, R. 1, (2.), (d.)
Postulo, w. two accs., 231, R. 1; w. acc and genit., 217, R. 1; w. *de* or the simple abl., 217, R. 2; w. subj., without *ut*, 262 R. 4.
Potens, w. genit., 213, R. 1, (3.); w. *in* or *ad* and acc., 212, R. 4, (2.)
Potior, w. abl., 245, I.; w. acc., 245, I. R.; w. genit., 220, (4.); *potiundus*, 162, 2 273, II., R. 1.
Potis, defective, 115, 5.
Potius, compared, 194, 4; used pleonastically, 256, R. 13.
Potus, translated actively, 162, 16.
Præ, in composition w. adjs., 127, 2; w verbs, 197; before adjs., 127, 6; constr of verbs compounded with, 224; *præ*, with comparatives, 127, 6; 256, R. 13, (b.)
Præbeo, w. two accs., 230, N. 1.
Præcedo, constr., 233, (3.), and N 224 R. 5.
Præcello, *præeo*, etc., 224, 8, and R. 5.

Præceps, abl. of, 113, R. 2, and E. 1.
Præcipio, constr., 223, (1.), (b.)
Præcipito, 229, R. 4, 1.
Præcipue, præsertim, etc., 193, II. 2.
Præcurro, constr., 224, 8, and R. 5.
Prædium, ellipsis of, 255, R. 3.
Præditus, w. abl., 244.
Præneste, gender of, 66. E., and 29, E.
Prænomen, its place, 279, 9. (b.)
Præpes, genit. sing. of, 112, 1; genit. plur., 114. E. 2.
Præscribo, w. ut, etc., 273, 2, N. 4.
Præsens, declined, 111; abl. of, 113, R. 2.
Præses, gender of, 30; 61, 2; genit. of, 73, E. 1.
Præsto, 233, (3.), and N.; 230, N. 1; 224, 8, and R. 5; 256, R. 16. (3.);—*præsto*, adv., w. dat., 228, 1;—*præsto sunt, qui*, w. subj., 264, 6, N. 1.
Præstolor, w. dat., 223, R. 2. N.; w. acc., 223. (1., (a.)
Præter, w. adjs., 127, 6; w. comparatives, 256, R. 13, (b.); as an adverb, 191, III.
Prætereo, w. quod, 273. 5, (1.)
Præterit, constr. of. 229, R. 7.
Præterquam quod, 277, R. 16.
Præterveho, 233, (2.)
Prævertor, w. dat., 224, 8 and R. 5.
Precor, w. two accs., 231; w. ut, 273, N. 4; *ut* omitted, 262, R. 4.
Predicate, 201; 203;—predicate-nominative, 210; differing in number from the subject-nominative, 210, R. 2; instead of dat. of the end, 227, R. 4; after what verbs, 210, R. 3 and 4; pred. adjs., 210, R. 1; after *esse, haberi, judicari, videri*, etc., 271, N. 2; —predicate-accusative, 210, (b.); dative, 210, (c.); abl., 210, (d.); 257, R. 11.
Prepositions, 195—197; in composition, 196; with nouns, 103; with adjs., 131, 11—13; with verbs, 196; change of in composition, 103, R. 2; 131, R.; 196, (a.); inseparable, 196, (b.); w. accs., 195. 4; 235; w. abl., 195, 5; 241; w. acc. and abl., 195, 6; 235, (2.)—(5.); used as adverbs, 195, R. 4; how modified, 202, II., R. 2; verbs compounded with, w. dat., 224; w. acc., 233; w. abl., 242; compds. of *ad, con*, and *in*, with acc., 224, R. 4; repeated after compds., 224, R. 4; 233, R. 2; how interchanged, ib.; compds. of *ad, ante*, etc., with neuter verbs of motion, 224, R. 5; 233, R. 1; repetition of prepositions, 233, R 2; 277, II., 3 and 4; prepositions of one syllable, pr., 285, 2, N. 1, and E. 5; ellipsis of, 232, (2.); 235, R. 11.; ellipsis of their case, 235, R. 10; their place, 279, 10; quantity of *di, se* and *red*, 285, R. 2 an l 3; put after their case, 279, 10, R., (f.); repeated, 277, II., 4.
Present tense, 145, I.; a principal tense, 259, A.; indicative pres. for historical perf., 259, R. 1, (a.); for the fut., 259, R. 1, (b.); for imperf. or perf. w. *dum*, 259, R. 1, (c.): subj. pres., use of, 260, II., R. 1, (1.); used to soften an assertion, 260, II., R. 4; to express a wish, command, etc., 260, N. 6; 267, R. 2; imperative pres., how used, 145, R. 3; 267, (1.); infinitive pres., how used, 265, R. 1, (a.), and R. 3.; 272, R. 4 and 5; participle pres., how declined, 111, R.; what it

denotes, 274, 2 and N.; denoting something about to be done, 274, R. 1; also a purpose, 274, R. 2, (a.); and a state or condition, 274, R. 2, (b.); present pass. participle, how supplied. 274, R. 9.
Preterites, 145, N. 2; 258, B.; preterites of the indicative used for the pluperfect subjunctive, 259. R. 4. (1.)
Preteritive verbs, 183, I.
Pretii and *pretio*, 214, R. 2, N. 3; ellipsis of, 252, R. 3.
Priapean verse, 310. II.
Price, ablative of, 252; genitive of *tanti*, etc., 214, R. 1.
Pridie, w. genit., 212, R. 4, N. 6;w. acc., 238. 1.
Primus, medius, etc., how translated, 205, R. 17, their place, 279. 7; *prior, primus*, for *prius, primum*, 205. R. 15.
Princeps, genit. of. 112. 2; abl. of, 113, E. 2; 115, 1, (a.); used instead of an adverb of time, 205, R. 15.
Principal parts of a verb, 151, 4;—propositions, 201. 5;—parts of a proposition, 202, 5; tenses, 255. A.
Principio, abl. of time, 253, N.
Priusquam, with what mood, 263, 3.
Privo, w. abl., 251, N.
Pro, constr. of verbs compounded with, 224; w. abl. for predicate nom., 210, N. 3; for predicate acc., 230, N. 4; in composition, quantity of, 285, E. 5, and R. 7; *pro nihilo duco*, etc., 214, R. 2, N. 2; *pro eo* and *proinde ac*, 198, 3, R.
Proclivis, 222, R. 4, (2.); 276, III., R. 1.
Procul, w. abl., 195, R. 3; 241, R. 2
Prodigus, w. genit. or abl., 213, R. 5, (2.) w. *in*, 213, R. 4, (2.)
Prodo, w. acc and inf., 272, N. 1, and R. 6.
Proditur, constr., 271, R. 2.
Proficiscor, w. two datives, 227, R. 1.
Prohibeo, 251, R. 2; w. *quominus*, 262, R. 11; 273, 4; w. genit., 220, 2; w. abl., 251, N.; w. dat. or abl., 224, R. 2; w. acc. and inf., 272, R. 6.
Proinde, adv., 191, III.; *proinde ac*, 198, 3, R.
Prolepsis, 323, 1, (b.) and (4.)
Promitto, constr., 272, N. 4; 217, R. 3, (c.)
Pronouns, 132—139; simple, 132, 2; neuter w. genit., 212, R. 3, N. 1.
Pronominal adjs., 139, 5.
Pronunciation of Latin, 6
Pronus, constr., 222, R. 4. (2.)
Prope est, w. *ut* and the subj., 262, R. 3, N. 1.
Proper nouns, 26, 2; found only in 1st, 2d, and 3d decls., 40, 9.
Propero, w. inf, 271, N. 1.
Propinquo, 225, R. 2.
Propinquus, w. the dat. or genit., 224, R. 2. (a.)
Propior, how compared, 126, 1; *propior* and *proximus*. w. dat., 222, R. 1; w. acc., 222 R. 5; 238. 1; instead of *propius, proxime*, 205, R. 15; *proximum est*, w. *ut* and the subj., 262, R. 3, N. 1
Propius and *proxime*, constr., 238, 1, and R.

Proportional, adj., 121. 2.
Proposition, 201, 1; analysis of, 281.
Proprius, constr., 222, R. 2, (a.)
Prorumpo, constr., 226, R. 4, 1.
Prosodiac verse, 304, 2.
Prosody, 282—321; figures of, 305—307.
Prosopopœia, 324, 34.
Prosper and *prosperus*, 105, N.; w. genit. or abl., 213, R. 5, (2.)
Prosthesis, 322, 1.
Prosto, w. abl. of price, 252, R. 1
Prosum, 154. R. 6.
Provideo, constr., 223, (1.), (a.)
—Protasis and apodosis, 261; import of the different tenses in the protasis and apodosis, 261, 1 and 2.
Providus, w. genit., 213, R. 1, (3.)
Prudens, w. genit., 223, n. 1, (3.)
Ps, initial, 12, R.; —ps, nouns in, genit. of, 77, 2, (1.)
-*pse*, enclitic, 135, R. 3.
Pt, initial, 12, R.
-*pte*, enclitic, 133, R. 2; 139.
Pubes and *impubes*, genit. of, 112, 1; abl. of, 113, R. 2; 115, 1, (a.)
Pudet, w. genit., 215; w. inf., 215; w. acc., 229, R. 6; w. perf. inf., 208, R. 2; w. sup. in u, 276, III., R. 2; participle in *dus*, and gerund of, 184, R. 3.
Puer, instead of *in pueritia*, 253, R. 6.
Pueritia, how used in the abl., 253, N. 1.
Pugnâ, for *in pugnâ*, 253, N. 1; *pugnam pugnare*, 232, (1.)
Pugnatur, conjugated, 184, 2, (b.)
Pulchre, instead of abl. of price, 252, R. 3.
Punctuation, 5.
Punio, constr., 217, R. 5.
Punishment, constr. of words denoting, 217, R. 8.
Purgo, w. genit., 217, R. 1; 220, 2; w. abl., 251, N.
Purpose, denoted by *ut*, etc., with the subj., 262; by participles, 274, 2, R. 2, 6 and 7; by inf., 271; 273, N. 4, (b.); by gerund, 275, III., R. 2, and (1.), (2.); by supine in -*um*, 276, II.
Purus, w. genit. or abl., 213, R. 5, (3.); cf. 251, N.
pus, Greek nouns in, genit. of, 76, R. 5.
Puto, w. genit. of value, 214; w. abl. of price, 252, R. 1; w. two accs., 230, N. 1, and N. 4; w. acc. and inf., 272, N. 1; *putares*, 269, II., R. 2; *putor*, 210, R. 3, (3.), (c.); w. inf., 271, R. 1.

Q.

Qu before *s* in verbal roots, 171, 1
Quâ, adverbial correlative, 191, R. 1.
Quâ—quâ, for *et—et*, 277, R. 8.
Quæro, constr., 231, R. 4; poet. w. inf., 271, N. 3.
Quæso, 183, 7; constr., 262. R. 4.
Qualis, 139, 5, (3.); w. comparatives, 256, R. 10, (b.)
Qualisqualis or *qualiscumque*, 139, 5; 207, R. 29.
Qualis—talis, 206, (16.)
Quam, w. comparatives, 256; w. the superlative, with or without *possum*, 127, 4;
ellipsis of after *plus, minus, amplius*, etc. 256, R. 6 and 7; *quam qui* and superlative after *tam*, 206, (21.); *quam pro*. w. comparatives, 256, R. 11; *quam non*, 277, R. 14; *quam* and a verb after *ante* and *post*, 253, R. 1, N. 3; *quam qui*, w. comparatives and the subjunctive, 264, 4.
Quamquam, peculiar use of, 198, 4. R. constr., 263, 2, (4.); used to connect an abl. absolute, 257, R. 10.
Quamvis, constr., 263, 2, and (2..., (3.)
Quando, quando-quidem, 198, 7, R. (5.)
Quantity, adjs. of, 104, 4; w. genit., 212, R. 3, N. 1; after *sum* and verbs of valuing, 214; adverbs of. w. genit., 212, R. 4.
Quantity, in prosody, 13, 1; marks of, 5, 1; general rules of, 13; 283; special rules of, 284; of penults, 291; of antepenults, 292; of penults of proper names, 293; of final syllables, 294—301; of final vowels, 294—298; of final consonants, 299; of derivative words, 284; of compound words, 285; of increments, 286—290; of Greek words, 283, R. 6.
Quantus, pronom. adj., 139, 5, (3.); *quantus* for *quam*, with *posse* and superlatives, 127, N. 1; constr., 206, (16.); *quanto*, w. comparatives, 256, R. 16; *quantum*, w. genit., 212, R. 3. N. 1; in acc. of degree, 231, R. 5; 232, (3.); 256, R. 16, N.; *quantum possum*, w. indicative, 264, 3 *fin*; *quantus—tantus*. 206, (16.)
Quantuscumque, quantusquantus, quantuluscumque, 139, 5, (3.); w. indicative, 259, R. 4, (3.); *quanticumque*, 207, R. 29.
Quasi, w. subj., 263, 2.
Quatio, constr., 229, R. 4, 1; how changed in its compds., 189, N. 3.
-*que*, its use, 198, 1, R., (a.); *que—et, et—que, que—que*, 198, R., (e.); its place, 279, 3, (c.)
Queis and *quis*, for *quibus*, 136, R. 2.
Queo, how conjugated, 182, N.; w. inf., 271, N. 3.
Queror, w. acc., 232, N. 1; w. *quod*, 273, N. 6.
Qui, declined, 136; *qui* in abl., 136, R. 1; 137, R. 2; interrogative, 137; difference between *qui* and *quis*, 137, 1; person of *qui*, 209, R. 6; w. subj., 264; when translated like a demonstrative, 206, (17.); with *sum* instead of *pro*, 206, (18.); *quicum*, when used, 136, R. 1 *fin*; *qui vero, qui autem*, 280, III., (3.); *ex quo*, for *postquam*, 253, N. 4.
Quia, quod, and *quoniam*, 198, 7, R., (b.)
Quicque and *quicquam*, 138, 3, (a.)
Quicquid, 136, R. 4; acc. of degree, 232, (3.)
Quicumque, how declined, 136, 3, how used, 207, R. 29; w. indic., 259, R. 4, (3.); for *omnis, quivis*, or *quilibet*, 207, R. 29.
Quid, 137; w. genit., 212, R. 3, N. 1, (a.); acc. of degree, 231, R. 5, (a.); 232, (3.); *quid 'why?* 235, R. 11; *quid sibi vult?* 228, N., (b.); *quid est quod?* w. subj., 261, 7, N. 2; *quid est cur?* etc., 264, 7, N. 3; *quid aliud quam?* 209, R. 4; *quid? quid vero? quid igitur? quid ergo? quid enim? quid multa? quid plura?* 229, R. 8, 2.

Quidam, how declined, 138, 5; how used, 207, R. 33.
Quidem, its meaning, 191, R. 4; its place, 279, 3, (d.)
Quilibet, how declined, 138, 5; how used, 207, R. 34.
Quies and compds., gender, 61, 1; genit., 73, 4; 96.
Quin, 198, 8; w. subj., 262, R. 10; for a relative with *non*, ib., 1 and N. 6; for *ut non*, ib., 2; after *non dubito*, etc., *quin*? why not? w. indic., ib., N. 9.
Quippe, 198, 7, R., (b.); *quippe qui*, w. subj. 264, 8, (2.)
Quippiam, 138, 3, (a.)
Quiqui, 136, R. 4.
Quiris, genit. sing., 74, E. 4; genit. plur., 83 11., 5.
Quis, declined, 137; difference of *quis* and *qui*, 137, 1; between *quis* and *uter*, 212, R. 2, N. 1; *quis est qui*? w. subj., 264, 8, (2.); between *quis* and *aliquis*, 207, R. 30, (b.)
Quisnam, *quinam*, how declined. 137, 2.
Quispiam, how declined, 138, 3; how used, 207, R. 30; *quippiam*, w. genit., 212, R. 3, N. 1.
Quisquam, how declined, 138, 3; how used, 207, R. 31; *quicquam* and *quidquam*, w. genit., 212, R. 3; acc. of degree, 231, R. 5, (a.); 232, (3.)
Quisque, how declined, 138, 3; how used, 207, R. 35; with plur. verb, 209, R. 11, (4.); its place, 279, 14; w. a superlative, 207, R. 35, (b.); in apposition, 204, R. 10.
Quisquis, declined, 136, 4; its use, 207, R. 29; difference between *quisquis* and *quicumque*, 207, R. 29; w. indic, 259, R. 4, (3.)
Quivis, how declined, 138, 5; how used, 207, R. 34.
Quo, the correlative adv., 191, R. 1; *quo*, w. a comparative, 256, R. 16, (2.); for *ut eo*, w. subj.. 262, R. 9; as adv. of place, w. genitive, 212, R. 4, N. 2, (b.); *quo mihi hanc rem*, 209, R. 4; 228, R. 5; *quo secius*, 262, R. 11, N.; *quo ne*, 262, R. 5.
Quoad, w. subj., 263, 4; w. *ejus*, 212, R. 4, N. 5.
Quocum, *quacum*, etc., instead of *cum quo*, etc., 241, R. 1.
Quod, causal conj., 198, 7; construction of, 273, 5; refers to past time, 273, (6.); w. subj. of *dico*, *puto*, etc., 266, 3, R.; *quod sciam*, etc., 264, 3; *quod*, referring to a preceding statement, 206, (14); 273, 6, (a.); w. genit., 212, R. 3; before *si*, *nisi*, etc., 206, (14); as acc. of degree, 232, (3.)
Quojus and *quoi*, for *cujus* and *cui*, 136, R. 2.
Quoque and *etiam*, difference between, 198, 1, R., (d.); place of *quoque*, 279, 3, (d.)
Quot, indecl., 115. 4; interrogative, 121, 5; 139, 5, (3.); constr., 206, (16); *quot sunt*, *qui*? 264, 7, N. 2; *quotquot*, w. indic., 259, R. 4, (3.)
Quoteni and *quotus*, interrogative, 121, 5.
Quoties, interrog. adv., 121, 5.
Quotus-quisque, its meaning, 207, R. 35, (a.)
Quum, correlative of *tum*, 191, R. 7; instead of *postquam*, 253, N. 4; — conj., 198, 10: constr., 263, 5, and R. 1—4.

R.

R, before *s* in roots of nouns 16, R. 1; nouns in *r*, genitive of, 70, 71; changed to *s* before *s* and *t*, 171, 3; *r* final, quantity of, 299, 2.
Rapio, w. dat. or abl., 224, R. 2.
Rarum est, *ut*, 262, R. 3, N. 3.
Rastrum, plur. *rastri* or *rastra*, 92, 5.
Ratio, w. genit. of gerunds, 275, III., R. 1, (1.); *ratione*, as abl. of manner, without *cum*, 247, 2.
Ratum est, *ut*, 262, R. 3, N. 2; *ratum pr.*, 284, E. 1, (2.)
-re in 2d person sing. of passive voice, 162, 3.
Re or *red*, inseparable prep., 196, (b.); 197, 18; quantity of, 285, R. 3, (a.)
Reapse, 135, R. 3.
Recens, abl. of, 113, E. 3 and R. 1; also adverb, 192, 4, (b.)
Receptio, constr., 233, R. 2, N.
Recingor, w. acc., 234, R. 1.
Recordor, w. genit. or acc., 216; w. pres. inf., 268, R. 1; w. acc. and inf., 272, N. 1.
Recte, instead of abl. of price, 252, R. 3.
Reckoning, Roman mode of, 326, 327.
Rectum est, *ut*, 262, R. 3, N. 3.
Recuso quin, and *quominus*, 262, N. 7 and R. 11; w. *ne*, 271, R. 1; w. inf., ib., N., and 271, N. 1.
Reddo, w. two accs., 230, N. 1; pass. 210, R. 3, (3), (b.); w. perf. pass. part., 274, R. 4.
Redoleo, w. acc., 232, (2.)
Redundant nouns, 93; adjs., 116; 149, N.; 111, N.; verbs, 185.
Redundo, w. abl., 250, 2, (2.)
Reduplication, 163, R.; of compound verbs, 163, R. 1; of verbs of 1st conj., 165, R. 2; of 2d conj., 168, N. 2; of 3d conj., 171, E. 1, (b.); quantity of, 284, E. 2.
Refero, w. acc. and inf., 272, N. 1.
Refert and *interest*, w. genit., 214; 219; w. the adj. pronouns *mea*, etc., 219, R. 1; w. *ad*, etc., 219, R. 3; *refert*, pr., 285, R. 3.
Refertus, w. genit. or abl., 213, R. 5, (3.)
Reflexive pronouns, 132, 4; 139, R. 2; how used, 208; for demonstratives, 208, (6.); ellipsis of, 229, R. 4; in oratio obliqua, 266, R. 3.
Reformido, w. inf., 271, N. 1.
Regno, w. genit., 220, 4.
Regnum, declined, 46.
Rego, conjugated, 158.
Relative adjs., 104, 13; 139, R.; government of, 213, R. 1; 222, 3; adverbs, w. subj., expressing a purpose, 264, 5, R. 2; used indefinitely, w. subj., 264, R. 3.
Relative pronouns, 136; agreement of, 206, R. 19; ellipsis of, 206, (5.); in the case of the antecedent, 206, (6.), (a.); referring to nouns of different genders, 206, (9.);—to a proposition, 206, (13.); agreeing with a noun implied, 206, (11); number and gender of, when referring to two or more nouns, 206, (15);—relative clauses used as circumlocutions and to express the English 'so called,' 206, (19); relative adverbs for relative pronouns, 206, (20); the relative adjs. *quot*, *quantus*, etc., construction of,

206, (16); *qui* with *sum*, instead of *pro*, 206, 18); person of, 209, R. 6; 206, R. 19;— w. subj., 264; their place, 279, 13; 280, III., (2.); relatives as connectives, 280, III., (1.); 198. II.
Resolving, verbs of, 273, 1, (a.)
Relinquo, w. two datives, 227, R. 1; w. part. in *dus*, 274, R. 7; *relinquitur*, w. *ut* and the subj., 262. R. 3, N. 1.
Reliqua, acc., 234, II., R. 3; *reliquum est ut*, 262, R. 3.
Reminiscor, constr., 216.
Remitto, 229, R. 4, 1.
Removing, verbs of, w. abl., 251.
Remuneror, w. abl., 249, I., R. 1.
Renuncio, w. two accs., 230, N. 1; pass., 210, R. 3, (3.), (b.)
Repeated words, their place, 279, 4.
Repens, abl. of, 113, E. 3.
Reperio, w. two accs., 230, N. 1; —*reperior*, 210, R. 3, (3.), (e.); 271, R. 2; —*reperiuntur, qui*, w. subj., 264, 6.
Repo, constr. of compds. of, 233, (3.), N.
Repono, 241, R. 5.
Reposco, w. two accs., 231, R. 1.
Repugno, with *quominus* or *ne*, 262, R. 11.
Res, declined, 90; use of, 205, R. 7, (2.), N. 1.
Reses, genit. sing. of, 112, 1; defective, 115, 2.
Resipio, w. acc., 232, (2.)
Responsives, case of, 204, R. 11.
Respublica, declined, 91.
Restat, ut, 262, R. 3, N. 1.
Rete, abl. of, 82, E. 1, (b.)
Retracto, constr., 229, R. 4, 1.
Reus, w. genit., 213. R. 1, (3.); *reum agere* or *facere*, w. genit., 217, R. 1.
Rhetoric, figures of, 324.
Rhus, genit. of, 76, E. 3; acc. of, 80, II.
Rhythm, 308, (1.)
Rideo, w. acc., 232, N. 1.
-*rimus*, -*ritis*, quantity of. 290, E., (1.), 4.
-*rimus*, superlatives in, 125, 1.
Ritu, as abl. of manner without *cum*, 247, 2.
Rivers, gender of names of, 28.
-*rix*, verbals in, 102. 6, (a.) See *tor* and *trix*.
Rogo, w. two accs., 231, R. 1; w. *ut*, 273, N. 4; 274, R. 7; without *ut*, 262, R. 4; constr. in pass., 234. 1.
Roman day, 326, 1:—hour, ib.;—month, 326, 2;—names of the months, 326, 2, (1); —calendar table of, 326, 2, (6), p. 369;— week, 326, 2, (10); names of the days of the week, ib.;—year, how designated, 326, 2, 11 ;—money, weights and measures, 327;— tables of weights, etc., 327. pp. 370—373;— coins, 327, p. 371;—interest, how computed, ib.
Root or crude form of words inflected, what and how found, 40, 10; formation of nominative sing. from in 3d decl., 56, 1. and n.
Roots of verbs, 150; general, 150, 1; special, 150, 2; second and third, how formed, 150, 3 and 4; third, how determined when there is no supine, 151, N.; first, its derivatives, 151, 1; irregularities in tenses formed from, 162, 1—6; second, do. 151, 2; irregularities in tenses formed from 162, 7—10; third, do., 151, 3; second and third, formation of, 1st conj., 164—106; 2d conj., 167—170; 3d conj., 171—174; 4th conj., 175—177; second and third irregular, 1st conj., 165; 2d conj., 168; 4th conj, 176.

-*rs*, nouns in, genitive sing. of, 77, 2 (2.); genit. plur. of, 83, II., 4.
Rudis, 213, R. 1, and R. 4. (2.); 275, II., R. 1, (2.)
Rupes, declined, 57.
Rus, construed like names of towns, in acc., 237, R. 4; in abl., 254; 255; cf. 2, E. 5, (b.); *rure*, not *ruri* with an adj., 255, R. 1.
-*rus*, participle in, how declined, 105, R. 2; its signification, 162, 14; 274, 2, R. 6; with *sim* and *essem* serving as future subjunctives, 162, R. 3; with *esse* and *fuisse*, 162, 14, R. 3; 268, R. 4; genitive plur. of, 162, 19; denotes intention, 274, R. 6; used for an English clause connected by 'since, when,' etc., ib.; as an apodosis, ib.
Rutum, pr., 284, E. 1, (2.)

S.

S, sound of, 11; added to some roots of nouns of 3d decl., 56, I.; added to roots of verbs ending in a consonant, 171; used instead of *t* in the 3d root of some verbs, 171, E. 5; inserted in some verbals, 102, 5, (b.); *s* preceded by a consonant, nouns in, gender of, 62; 64; genit. of, 77; final, elided, 305, 2.
Sacer, w. genit. or dat., 222, R. 2, (a.)
Sacerdos, gender of, 30; 61, 3.
Saepe, comparison of, 194, 5.
Sal, 82, E. 1, (b.), and 66, E.; 96, 9; pr., 284, N. 1.
Salio, constr. of compds. of, 233, (3.), N.
Saltem, 198, II., 3.
Saluto, w. two accs., 230, N. 1; *salutor*, w. two nominatives, 210, R. 3, (3.)
Salve, 183, 9.
Samnis, genit. sing., 74, E. 4; genit. plur., 83, II., 5.
Sapio, w. acc., 232, (2.)
Sapphic verse, 304, 2; 315, II.
Sat, indecl., 115, 4; *satis*, w. genit., 212, R. 4; *satis esse*, w. dat. of gerund, 275, III.; R. 2, (1); *satis habeo*, and *satis mihi est*, w. perf. infin., 268, R. 2; *satis erat*, indic. instead of subj., 259, R. 3; degrees of comparison, 126, 4.
Satago, w. genit., 215. 2.)
Satelles, gender of, 30; 61, 2.
Satiatus, w. abl. or genit., 213, R. 5, (3.)
Satisdo, w. *damni infecti*, 217, R. 3, (c.), w. dat., 225, I.
Satisfacio, w. dat., 225, I.
Satum, pr., 284, E. 1, 2.
Saturnalibus, for *ludis Saturnalibus*, 253, N. 1.
Satur, how declined, 105, R. 1; w. genit. or abl., 213, R. 5, (3.)
Saturo, w. abl., 249, I., R. 1; w. genit poet., 220, 3.

Satus, w. abl., 246.
Saying, verbs of, constr., 272; ellipsis of, 270, N. 2. (b.) and 3; implied, 273, 3, (b.); used in the passive, 272, R. 6.
Scando, compds. of, 233, (3.), N.
Scanning, 304, 6.
Scateo, w. abl., 250, 2, (2.), R. 1; with genit. poet., 220, 3.
Scazon, 314, II.
Scidi, pr., 284, E. 1, (1.)
Scilicet, 198, 7, R., (a.)
Scio, w. acc. and inf., 272, N. 1; *scito*, 162, 4.
Scitor and *sciscitor*, constr., 231, R. 4.
-*sco*, verbs in, 187, II.. 2; drop *sc* in 2d and 3d root before *t*, 171. R. 6.
Scribo, 273. 2, (c.); w. two accs., 230, N. 1; w. acc. and inf., 272, N. 1, and R. 6; in pass. w. predicate nominative, 210, N. 3, (3); *scribit*, w. pres. inf. instead of perf., 268. R. 1, (a.)
Se, inseparable prep., 196, (b.)
Se, w. *inter*, 208, 5. See *sui*.
Secerno, 251, N., and R. 2, N.
Secus, for *sexus*, 88, 1; 94; 211, R. 6, (4.); 230, R. 6; adv., 191, III.; w. acc., 195, R. 3.
Sed, 198, 9, R., (a.); its place, 279, 3, (a.); *sed, sed quod, sed quia*, 262, R. 9; *sed, sed tamen*, 278, R. 10; *sed et*, 198, 1, (d.)
Sedeo, 210, R. 3, (2.); compds. of, 233, (3), N.
Sedile, declined, 57.
Sedo, constr., 229, R. 4, 1.
-*sem*, old termination of plup. indic. active, 162, 9.
Semi-deponent verbs, 142, 2.
Senarius, 304, 2; Iambic, 314.
Senex, its degrees of comparison, 126, 4; gender of, 65, 2; genitive of, 78, 2. (2); abl. of, 113, E. 2; 115, 1; for *in senectute*, 253, R. 6.
Sentences, 200; analysis of, 281.
Sentiments of another, in dependent clauses, 266, 3.
Sentio, w. acc. and inf., 272, N. 1.
Separating, verbs of, w. abl., 251.
Separo, w. abl., 251, N.
Sequitur, constr. 262, R. 3, N. 1.
-*sere*, future infin. in, 162. 10.
Sereno, scil. *ca lo*, 257, R. 9, (2.)
Sermo, declined, 57.
Serpens, gender of, 64, 3.
Sese, intensive, 133, R. 2.
Servitutem servire, 232, (1.)
Sestertius, its value, 327, R. 2, (b.); how denoted, ib.; mode of reckoning, ib.; *sestertium*, ib., R. 5—7.
Seu, or *sive*, 198, 2. R., (c.)
Ships, gender of their names, 29.
Short syllable, 282, 2.
Showing, verbs of, constr., 272, R. 6.
Si, how pronounced, 11, E. 1.
-*si* or -*sin*, Greek datives in, 84.
Si, conj., 198, 5; *si* for *num*, 198, 11, R., (s.); *si minus, sin minus* or *sin aliter*, 198, 5, R., (b.); 277, N. 14; ellipsis of in the protasis, 261. R. 1; *si* with the imperfect subj., instead of the pluperfect, 261, R. 5; *si nihil aliud*, 209, R. 4; *si quisquam* and *si ullus*, 207, R. 30, (b.); *si non*, 262, N. 5.

Sibi suo, 228, N., (a.)
Sic, 191, R. 5; 277, R. 12, (a.); pleonastically, 207, R. 22.
Sicuti, w. subj., 263, 2, (1.)
Significant word, in a proposition, 279 2, (e.)
Siem, sies, etc., 154, R. 4.
Silentio præterire or *facere aliquid*, without *cum*, 247, 2.
Sileo, w. acc., 232, N. 1; pres., 234, III.
Silver age of Roman literature, 329. 3.
-*sin*, old termination of perfect indic active, 162, 9.
Similar constructions, 278, N. 1 and 2
Simile, 324, 30.
Similis, w. genit. or dat., 222, R. 2, (a.) w. dat. in imitation of the Greek, 222, R. 7; *similes*, w. inter., 222, R. 4, (4.); w. *ac* and *atque*, 222, R. 7, *fin*.
Simple, subject, 202, 2;—predicate, 203, 2;—sentences, 201, 10.
Simul, w. abl., 195, R. 3; 241, R 2; *simul*—*simul*. 277, R. 8.
Sin, 198, 5; its place, 279, 3, (a.); *sin minus*. 277, R. 14.
Singular number, 35, 1; sing. for plur., 209, R. 11, 1, (b.)
Singulare est ut, 262, R. 3, N. 3.
Singuli, 119.
Sino, 273. 4; 262, R. 4.
Siquidem, 198, 7, R., (b.)
Siquis, how declined, 138, 2; *siquis* and *siquid*, how used, 138, 2, (a.) and (b.); 207, R. 29; *si quis est, qui*, w. subj., 264, 6.
Sis for *si vis*, 183. R. 3.
Sisto, constr., 229, R. 4, 1.
Situm, pr., 284, E. 1, (2.)
Sive or *seu*, 198, 2, R.; 278, R. 8; its place 279, 3, (a.); *sive*—*sive*, w. verb in the indic., 259, R. 4, (3.)
-*so*, -*sim*, -*sem*, old verbal terminations, 162, 9.
Socius, w. genit. or dat., 222, R. 2, (a.)
Sodes, for *si audes*, 183, R. 3.
Solecism, 325, 2.
Soleo, how conjugated, 142, R. 2; w. inf., 271, N. 1.
Solitus, 274, R. 3; *solito*, after comparatives, 256, R. 9; its place, 279, N. 1.
Solum, solummodo, 193, II., 3.
Solus, how declined, 107; w. relative and subj., 264, 10; for *solum*, 205, E. 15.
Solutus, w. genit., 213; w. abl., 251, N ; *solutum*, pr., 284, R. 3.
Solvo, w. abl., 251, N.
Sons, genit. plur. of, 114, E. 3; 115, 1, (a.)
Sospes, genit. of, 112, 1; abl. of, 113, E 2; 115, 1. (a.); 126, 5. (b.)
Sotadic verse, 304. 2; 317, I.
Sounds of the letters, 7—12; of the vowels, 7 and 8; of the diphthongs, 9; of the consonants, 10—12.
Space, acc. and abl. of, 236; ellipsis of, 236, R. 3.
Spatium, w. genit. of gerund, 275, III., R. 1, (1); *spatio* as abl. of space, 236, R. 4.
Specto, constr., 225, R. 1.
Specus, 88, 1.
Spero, w. acc. and inf., 272, N. 1.
Spes est, w. acc. and inf., 272, N. 1

spes, w. genit. of gerunds, 275, II., R. 1, (1.); *spe*, after comparatives, 256, R. 9; its place, 279, N 1.
Spolio, w. abl., 251, N.
Spondaic verse, 310; tetrameter, 312.
Spondeo, 163, R.; w. acc. and inf., 272, N. 1.
Stanza, 319, 4.
Statim, 193, II., 1.
Statuo, 241, R. 5; 278, N. 1; 271, N. 3; 272, N. 1; *statutum habeo*, 274, R. 4.
Statum, pr., 284, E. 1, (2.)
Sterilis, w. genit. or abl., 213, R. 5, (2); w. *ad*, 213, R. 4, (2.)
Steti and *stiti*, pr., 284, E. 1, (1.)
'Still,' w. comparatives, how expressed in Latin, 256, R. 9, (b.)
Stipulor, 217, R. 3, (c.)
Sto, 163, R.; w. genit. of price, 214, R. 3; w. pred. nom., 210, R. 3, (2.); w. abl., 245, II., 5, and R. 2; *stat per me*, construction of, 262, R. 11; compds. of, 233, (3.), N.
Strophe, 319, 4.
Studeo, w. dat., 223. R. 2; with gerund, 275, III., R. 2, (1.); with the inf. with or without an accusative, 271, R. 4; w. *ut*, 273, 4, (a.); w. acc. *id*, 232, (3.)
Studiosus, w. genit., 213, R. 1; 275, III., R. 1, (2.)
Studium, w. genit. of gerunds, 275, II., R. 1, (1.)
Styx, gender of, 28, E.
Suadeo, constr., 273, N. 4; 262, R. 4.
Sub, in composition, force of, 122; government of, 235, (2); constr. of verbs comp. unded with, 224; of adjs., 222, R. 1, (b.)
Subject of a verb, 140; of a proposition, 201; 202; simple, complex, and compound, 202; its place in a sentence, 279, 2; subject of a dependent clause made the object of the leading verb, 229, R. 5, (a.)
Subject-nominative, 209; ellipsis of, 209, R. 1 and 2; when wanting, 209, R. 3; w. inf., 209, R. 5; 239, N. 1; two or more in the singular with a plural verb, 209, R. 12; (2.)
Subject-accusative, 239; ellipsis of, 239, R. 1—3; considered also as the accusative of the object after verbs of saying, showing, and believing, 272, R. 6.
Subjective genitive, 211, R. 2; possessive pronoun used instead of, 211, R. 3.
Subjectus, w. dat., 222, R. 1, (b.)
Subjunctive, 143, 2; its tenses, 145, R. 2; how used, 260—266, and 273; various use of its tenses, 260; how translated, 260, I. and II., R 1; for imperative, 260, R. 6; in impersonal verbs, 184, R. 2; in conditional clauses, 261; after particles, 262 and 263; after *qui*, 264; after relative advs., 264, R. 2; indefinite subj., 264, 12 and N.: in indirect questions, 265; in inserted clauses, 266; in oratio obliqua, 266, 1 and 2; after what verbs used, 273; after adjectives, 213, R. 4; exchanged for acc. w. inf., 273, 3, (b.); subjunctive in doubtful questions, 260, R. 5; in repeated actions after relative pronouns and adverbs, 264, 12

Subito, 193, II., 1.
Subordinate conjunctions, 198, II.; —propositions, 201, 6 and 7.
Substantive, 26—103; substantive pronouns, 132, 138; their gender, 132, 3; declined, 133; as subject nominative, ellipsis of, 209, R. 1; dat. of, redundant, 228, N.; substantive verb, 153; substantive clauses, 201, 7 and 8; 229, R. 5; 231, R. 2, (b.); substantive clause instead of the abl. after *opus est*, 243, R. 1; and after *dignus* and *indignus*, 244, R. 2, (b.)
Subter, constr., 235, (4.)
Subtractive expressions in numerals, 113, 4; 120, 2, 3, and 5.
Succenseo, 223, R. 2; w. *quod*, 273, N. 6.
Sufficio, w. dat. of gerund, 275, III., R. 2, (1.)
Sui, signification of, 132, 4; declined, 133; use of, 208; 266, R. 3; 275, II., R. 1, (4.)
Sultis for *si vultis*, 183. R. 3.
Sum, why called an auxiliary, 153; why substantive, ib.; why the copula, 140, 4; conjugated, 153; compds. of, 154, R. 5—R. 7; w. a genit. of quality, 211, R. 6, (7); in expressions denoting part, property, duty, etc., 211, R. 8, (3); 275, R. 1, (5); denoting degree of estimation, 214; w. dat., 226; with two datives, 227; how translated, 227, R. 3; w. abl. denoting in regard to, 250, R. 3; w. an abl. of place, manner, etc., in the predicate, 210, R. 3, (1); w. dat. of gerund, 275, R. 2, (1); w. abl. of price, 252, R. 1; w. genit. of value, 214; *sunt qui*, w. subj., 264, 6; *sunt quidam*, *nonnulli*, etc., 264, 6, R. 4; ellipsis of as copula, 209, R. 4 *fin.*; of *esse* and *fuisse*, 270, R. 3; *sum* w predicate nom., etc., 210, R. 3, (1); *esse* w predicate nom., 271, N. 2. and R. 4.
Sumo, w. two accs., 230, R. 2; poet. w inf., 271, N. 3.
Supellex, genitive of, 78, 2, (2); abl. of, 82, E. 5, (a.)
Super, constr., 235, (3); of verbs compounded with, 224; of adjs., 222, R. 1, (b.)
Superfluo, w. abl., 250, 2, (2), R. 1.
Superjacio, constr., 233, (1.)
Superlative degree, 122, 6; particular use of, 122 R. 4; formation of, 124; by *maxime*, 127, 1; superlative with *quisque*, 207, R. 35; w. partitive genit., 212, R. 2, and R. 4, N. 7; place of, 296, (7), (b.)
Supero, w. abl., 256, R. 16, (3.)
Supersedeo, w. abl., 242.
Superstes, genit. of, 112, 2; abl. of, 112 E. 2; 115, 1, (a.); 126, 5, (b.); w. genit. or dat., 222, R. 2, (a.)
Supersum, w. dat., 224, 11; *superest ut*, etc., 262, R. 3, N. 1.
Superus, its degrees of comparison, 125, 4; *supremus* or *summus*, 205, R. 17; *summum* used adverbially, 205, R. 10; 234, II., R. 3.
Supines, 25 and 143, 3; few in number, 162, 11; in *um*, by what cases followed, 276, I.; on what verbs dependent, 276, II., w. *eo*, 276, II., R. 2 and 3; supines in *u* after what adjs., 276, III., and R. 1; after *fas*, *nefas*, and *opus*, 276, III., R. 2; of two syllables, quantity of, 284, E. 1.

406   INDEX.

Supra, w. acc., 195; w. adjs., 127, 6; 256, R. 13 (*b*.)
Suppedito, w. two dats., 227, R. 1; 229, R. 4, 1; w. abl., 250, 2, R. 1.
Supplex, genit. plur. of, 114, R. 2; 115, 1, (*a*.); w. dat., 222, R. 1, (*b*.)
Supposition or concession denoted by the tenses of the subj., 260, R. 3.
Surripio, w. dat. or abl., 224, R. 2.
Sus, gender of, 30; 67, E. 4; genit. of, 16, E. 3; dat. and abl. plur., 84. E. 1.
Suscipio, w. participle in *dus*, 274, R. 7.
Suspensus and *suspectus*, w. genit., 213, R. 1.
Suus, use of, 139, R. 2; 208; referring to a word in the predicate, 208, (7); for *hujus* when a noun is omitted, 208, (7.); when two nouns are united by *cum*, 208, (7), (*c*.); denoting fit, etc., 208, (8.)
Syllabic cæsura, 310. N. 1.
Syllabication, 17—23.
Syllables, number of, in Latin words, 17; pure and impure, 80; quantity of first and middle, 284; of penultimate, 291; of antepenultimate, 292; of final, 294.
Syllepsis, 323, 1, (*b*.) and (3.)
Symploce, 324. 15.
Synæresis, 306, 1.
Synalœpha, 305. 1
Synaphela, 307, 3.
Synchysis, 324. 4.
Syncope, 322. 4; in genit. plur. of 1st decl., 43, 2; of 2d decl., 53; in cases of *bos* and *sus*, 83, R. 1 and 84, E. 1; of *e* in oblique cases of nouns in *er* of 2d decl., 48; of 3d decl., 71, E. 1; in perfect, etc., of verbs, 162, 7; see Omission.
Synecdoche, 234, II.; 323, 1, (5.); 324, 3.
Synesis or synthesis, 323, 3, (4.)
Synonymia, 324, 29.
Synopsis of Horatian metres, 320.
Syntax, 1; 200—281.
Systole, 307, 1.
Syzygy, 303, 4.

T.

T, sound of, 12; before *s* in roots of nouns, 56, R. 1; in roots of verbs, 171. 3, and E. 5; nouns in, gender of, 66; genit. of, 78; final, quantity of, 299, 2.
Taceo, w. acc., 232. N. 1.
Tædet, w. genit., 215; w. acc. 229, R. 6.
Tactio w. acc., 233. R. 2, N.
Talma, gender of, 42, 2.
Talis, demonstr. adj., 139, 5, (3.); *talis* followed by *qui* and the subj., 264, 1, N.; ellipsis of, 264, 1, (*b*.); 206, (3), (*a*.); and (16); *talis ac*, 198, 3, R.; *talis—qualis*, 206, (16.)
Tam, 191, R. 5,; *tam—quam*, 277, R. 11; *tam* with an adj. before *qui* and the subj., 264. 1, N.
Tamen, how used. 198, 4. R.
Tametsi, 198, 4. constr., 263, 2, (4.)
Tamquam, w. subj., 263, 2; used like *quidam*, 207, R. 33, (*b*.) *fin*.; w. abl. absolute, 257, N. 4.
Tandem, 191, R. 6.

Tantum, adv., 193, II., 3.
Tantus, demonstrative, 139, 5, (3.); followed by *qui* and the subj., 264, 1, N. ellipsis of. 264, 1, (*b*.); 206, (3.), (*a*.); and 6, *tantus—quantus*, 206, (16); *tanti, quanti,* etc., w. verbs of valuing, 214. R. 1, (1.), *tantum*, w. genit. plur. and plur. verb, 209, R. 11, (3).; *tantum*, w. genit., 212. R. 3, N. 1; *tanti* after *refert* and *interest*, 219, R. 5; *tantum*, acc. of degree, 231, R. 5; 232, '3.); 256, R. 16, N.; *tanto*, w. comparatives, 256. R. 16, (2.)
Tantopere, 191, R. 5.
Tardo, 229, R. 4. 1.
Tautology, 325, 4.
Taxo, constr., 217, R. 5; w. abl. of price, 252, R. 1.
-te, enclitic, 133, R. 2.
Tempe, 83, 1, and 94.
Tempero, 223, R. 2, and (1), (*a*.); *temperare mihi non possum, quin*, 262, N. 7.
Temporal adjs., 104, 6; classes of, 121, 3;—conjunctions, 198, 10.
Tempus, ellipsis of. 205, R. 7; *tempus est,* w. inf., 270, R. 1; *tempus impendere*, 275, III., R. 2; *tempus consumere* Ib.; *tempuris after tum* and *tunc*, 212, R. 2. N. 4; w. *id, hoc,* or *idem*, 234. II., R. 3; *tempore* or *in tempore*, 253. N. 1; w. genit. of gerunds, 275, III., R. 1, (1.)
Tenax, w. genitive, 213, R. 1, (1.)
Tendo, constr., 225, IV.; 229, R. 4, 1; w. inf., 271, R. 1.
Teneo, w. perf. pass. participle, 274, R. 4 *fin*.; *teneri*, perf. pass. part., 268, R. 1, (*b*.)
Tenses, 144; division of, 144, 2 and 3; of the subj., 145, R. 2; of the imperative, 145, R. 3: of the infinitive, 145, R. 4; connection of, 258; principal and historical, 258, A. and B.; of indic. mood, used one for another, 259; future for imperative, 259, R. 1, (4); the preterites of the indic. for the pluperfect subj. In the apodosis of a conditional clause, 259, R. 4; of subj. mood, their use, 260, I., R. 1, and II., R. 1; in protasis and apodosis, 261; of inf. mood, use of, 268; tenses used in epistolary style, 145, II., 3; 259, R. 1, (2.), (*c*.)
Tento, constr., 273, N. 1; w. inf., 271, N. 1.
Tenus, w. genit., 221, III.; w. abl., 241, R. 1; place of, 279, 10; 241, R. 1.
-ter, nouns in, 48, 1; 71.
Teres, in genit. sing., 112, 1; defective. 115, 2; its degrees, 126, 4.
Terminational comparative, and superlative, 124; adjs. without such comparison, 126, 5.
Terminations of inflected words, 40; of nouns, table of. 39; of 1st decl., 41 and 44; of 2d decl., 46; of 3d decl., 55; of 4th decl., 87; of 5th decl., 90; masculine and feminine affixed to the same root. 32, 3; of degrees of comparison in, adjs., 124, 125; in adverbs, 194, 2; personal, of verbs, 147, 3; verbal, 199; table of verbal, 152.
Terræ, as genit. of place, 221, R. 3, (4); *terrā marique*, 254. R. 2; *terrarum*, 212, R. 4, N. 2.
Terreo, w. *ut* or *ne*, 262. N. 8.

Teruncius, 327, p. 371; *eruncii habere*, 214, R. 1.
Tete, intensive, 133, n. 2.
Tetrameter, 304, 2; *a priore*, 312, IV.; *a posteriore*, 312, V.; meiurus, 312, XI.; catalectic, 312, XII.
Tetraptotes, 94.
Tetrastrophon, 319, 3.
Th. in syllabication, 18, 2.
'That,' sign of what moods, 273; instead of a repeated subst., how expressed in Latin, 207, R. 26, (*e*.)
Thesis, in prosody, 308.
Thinking, verbs of, their constr., 272.
Thousands, how expressed in Latin, 118, 5, (*a*.)
Ti, how pronounced, 12.
Tiaras, 45, 3.
Tibi, its pronunciation, 7, R. 1; 19, E.
Tigris, genit. of, 75, 2; acc. of, 80, E. 2; abl. of, 82, E. 2, (*b*.)
Time, advs. of, 191, II.; conjs., 198, 10; acc. of, 236; abl. of, 253; with *de* or *sub*, 253, R. 4; with *intra*, ib.; with *in*, 253, R. 5; expressed by *id* with a genit., 253, R. 3; by the abl. absolute, 257; the concrete noun instead of the abstract title, 257, R. 7; mode of reckoning, 326; table of, 326, 6.
Timeo, 223, R. 2. (1.); w. *ut* or *ne*, 262, R. 7; w. inf., 271, N. 1.
Timidus, w. genit., 213, R. 1.
Tiryns, genit. of, 77, E. 2.
-tis, genit. in, 77, 2; 71, 2.
Titles, place of, 279, 9, (*a*.)
'Too' or 'rather' how expressed in Latin, 122, R. 3; 256, R. 9.
-tor and *-trix*, verbals in, 102, 6; used as adjs., 129, 8.
Tot, indecl., 115, 4; correlative of *quot*, 121, 5; 206, (16); syncope of, before *quot*, 206, 16.)
Totidem, indecl., 115, 4.
Toties, correlative of *quoties*, 121, 5.
Totus, how declined, 107; *toto*, *totā*, abl. without *in*, 254, R. 2; *totus*, instead of an adverb, 205, R. 15.
Towns, gender of names of, 29, 2; constr.; see Place.
-tr, roots of nouns in, 56, II., R. 3.
Traditio, w. dat., 222, R. 8.
Trado, w. acc. and inf., 272, N. 1, and R. 6; w. part. fut. pass., 274, R. 7, (*a*.); *traditur*, constr., 271, R. 2; *trador*, constr., 271, R. 2.
Tranquillo, scil. *mari*, 257, R. 9, (1.)
Trans, constr. of verbs compounded with, 233, 1; in passive, 234, R. 1, (*b*.)
Trajicio, constr., 229, R. 4, 1; 233, (1.)
Transitive verbs, 141; w. acc., 229 · ellipsis of, 229, R. 2.
Trees, gender of names of, 29.
Tres, how declined, 109.
Trepidus, w. genit., 213, R. 1.
Tribuo, w. two datives, 227, R. 1; w. two accs., 230, R. 2; w. part. perf. pass., 274, R. 7, (*a*.)
Tricolon, 319, 2; tricolon tristrophon and tetrastrophon, 319, 6.
Tricorpor, abl. of, 113, E 2; 115, 1.
Tricuspis, abl. of, 113, E. 2.

Trihemimeris, 304, 5.
Trimeter, 304, 2, catalectic, 312 VII.
Tripes, genit. of, 112, 1; abl. of, 113 E. 2.
Triptotes, 94.
Tristrophon, 319, 3.
Trochaic or feminine cæsura, 310, N. 1;— metre, 315 and 303; tetrameter catalectic, 315, I.; dimeter catalectic, 315, IV.; trochaic pentameter or Phalecian, 315, III.
Tropes, 324.
-trum, verbals in, 102, 5.
Truncus, w. abl. or genit., 213, R. 5, (4.)
Tu, declined, 133; in nom. with adj. in voc., 205, R. 15, (*c*.); used indefinitely, 209, R. 7; when expressed, 209, R. 1; *tui*, feminine, with masc. or neuter gerundive, 275, III., R. 1, (4.)
Tum and *quum*, 191, R. 7; *tum—tum*, 277, R. 8; *tum* and *tunc*, difference between, ib.; *tum maxime*, ib.; *tum temporis*, 212, R. 4, N. 4.
Tumultu, as abl. of time, 253, N. 1.
Tunc and *nunc*, 191, R. 7; *tunc temporis*, 212, R. 4, N. 4.
Tumidus and *turgidus*, w. abl., 213, R. 5, (5.)
Turris, declined, 57.
-tus, adjs. in, 126, 7; nouns in, of 3d decl., 76, E. 2; 102, 7.
Tuus, how declined, 139; used reflexively, 139 R. 1; *tua* after *refert* and *interest*, 219, R. 1.

U.

U, sound of, 7 and 8; *u* and *v*, 2, 3; *u* is genit. and voc. of Greek nouns, 54; root of nouns of 3d decl. ending in, 56, I.; dat in, 89; neuters of 4th decl. in, 87; dat. in of 4th decl., 89, 3: in 2d root of verbs, 167 and 171, E. 2; increment in, 3d decl., 287, 3; plur., 288; of verbs, 290; final, quantity of, 298; 285, R. 4; *u* and *itu* in 3d roots of verbs, 167.
Ua, *ue*, etc., pronunciation of, 9, 4 and 5; quantity of, 283, II., E. 3.
Uber, w. genit. or abl., 213, R. 5, (3.)
-ubus, in dat. and abl. plur., 89, 5.
Ubi, genit., 212, R. 4, N. 2; w. indic. perf. instead of pluperf., 259, R. 1, (*d*.); *ubiubi*, 191, R. 1.
-ucis, genitives in, 78, (5); 112, 2.
-udis, genitives in, 76, E. 1.
-uis, genitives in, 76, E. 3.
-uleus, *a*, *um*, diminutives in, 100, 8, c. 1.
Ullus, pronom. adj., 139, 5, (1, (z.); how declined, 107; how used, 207 R. 31.
Ulterior, its degrees, 126, 1; *ultimus* for *ultimum*, 205, R. 15; how translated, 205, R. 17.
Ultrix, gender of, 125, 1, (*b*.)
Ultra, prep., 195, 4; adv., 191, I.
Ultum ire for *ulcisci*, 276, II., R 2.
-ulum, verbals in, 102, 5.
-ulus, *a*, *um*, diminutives in, 100, 8; 128, 5.
-um, genit. plur. in instead of *arum*, 48; instead of *orum*, 53; nouns ending in, 46;

in genit. plur. 3d decl., 83; 114;—advs. in, 192, II., 4, (b.).
Uncia, 327, p. 372.
-undus, participles in, 162, 20.
Unde domo, 255, R. 1.
Umquam, 191, II.; *umquam, usquam, usque, uspiam*, 191, R. 6.
-untis, in genit. of Greek nouns, 76, E. 6.
Unus, declined, 107; when used in plur. 118, R. 2; added to superlatives, 127, N. 2; *unus et alter*, with verbs singular, 209, R. 12; w. relative and subj., 264, 10; for *solum, tantum*, etc., 205, R. 15. (b.); *unum*, as acc. of degree, 232, (3.).
Unusquisque, how declined, 138, 4.
-ur, nouns in, gender of, 66, 67; genit. rf, 70, 71.
-ura, verbals in, 102, 7, R. 2.
Urbs, in apposition to names of towns, 237, R. 2, (b.)
-urio, verbs in, 187, II., b.
-uris, genitives in, 76, E. 3.
-us, nouns in, of 2d decl., 46; exceptions in, 49—51; voc. sing. of, 46, N. and 52; of 3d decl., gender of, 66; 67; genitive of, 76; Greek genit. in, 69, E. 3; nouns in of 4th decl., 87—89; participles in, how declined, 105, R. 2; verbals in, 102, 7; final, quantity of, 301.
Usitatum est, ut, 262, R. 3, N. 3.
Uspiam, usquam, usque, 191, R. 6; *usquam*. w. genit., 212, R. 4, N. 2; *usque*, w. acc., 195, R. 3; 235, R. 9.
Usus, w. abl., 243; *usu venit, ut*, 262, R. 3, N. 1; w. genit. of gerunds, 275, III., R. 1, (1.)
Ut or *uti*, a conj., 198, 8; *ut non* and *ut ne*, ib.; w. subj., 262; its correlatives, 202, R. 1; ellipsis of, 262, R. 4; its meaning after *metuo*, etc., 262, R. 7; *ut non*, 262, R. 5, and R. 6, 2; *ut—ita* or *sic*, 277, R. 12, (b.); *ut*, 'as,' ellipsis of, 277, R. 17; *ut*, 'even if,' and *ut non*, w. subj., 262, R. 2; *ut* with certain impersonal verbs and subj., 262, R. 3; in questions expressing indignation, 270. R. 2, (a.); *ut, ut primum*, etc., with the historical perf., indic., instead of the pluperf., 259, R. 1, (d.); its place, 279, 3, (b.); *ut* after *est* with a predicate adj., 262, R. 3, N. 4; *ut credo, ut puto*, etc., in interposed clauses, 277, I., R. 17; *ut*, 'because,' 277, I., R. 12, (b.); *ut qui*, 264, 8, 2; *ut si*, w. subj., 263, 2; *ut ita dicam*, 207, R. 33, (b.) *fin.*; *ut*, 'as if,' w. abl. absolute, 257, N. 4; *utut*, w. indic., 259, R. 4, (3); ellipsis of *ut* when *ne* precedes and *et*, etc., follow, 278, R. 6, (c.)
Utcumque, w. indic., 259, R. 4, (3.)
Uter, how declined, 107; w. dual genit., 212, R. 2, N. 1.
Utercumque, how declined, 107.
Uterlibet, uterque, and *utervis*, their meaning and declension, 107; 139, 5, (1), (b.); *uterque*, use of, 207, R. 32; *uterque*, w. plur. verb, 209, R. 11, (4.)
Utilis, w. dat., 222, R. 1; 275, III., R. 2; w. ad, 222, R. 4, (1.); *utile est ut*, 262, R. 3, N. 3; *utilis*, w. inf. poetically, 270, R. 1, (b.); 275, R. 2; *utilius fuit*, indic. instead of subj., 259, R. 3; w. supine in *u*, 276, III., R. 1.

Utinam and *uti*, w. subj., 263, 1.
-utis, genitives in, 76, E. 2; 112, 2.
Utor, w. abl., 245; w. acc., 245, I., **I** | w. two ablatives, 245, N.; *utor, fruor*, etc., their gerundives, 275, II., R. 1.
Utpote qui, w. subj., 264, 8, (2.)
Utrique, how used, 107, R. 32, (a.)
Utrum and *utrumne*, 198, 11.
-utus, adjectives in, 128, 7.
-uus, adjectives in, 129, 3.
-ux, nouns in, genit. of, 78, 2, (5.)
Uxor, ellipsis of, 211, R. 7.

V.

V, changed to *u*, 163, 2; sometimes dropped in forming the 2d root of verbs of the 3d conj., 171, E. 4.
Vaco, 250, 2, R. 1.
Vacuus, w. genit. or abl., 213, R. 5, (3.) cf. 251, N.
Vado, constr., 225, IV.; 232, N. 1; 233, (3), N. 1.
Væ, w. dat., 228, 3; w. acc., 238, 2.
Valde, 127, 2.
Valeo, w. abl., 250, 2, R. 1; 252; w. acc., 252, R. 4; *valere* or *vale dico*, w. dat., 225, I., N.; w. inf., 271, N. 1.
Validus, 213, R. 5, (4.)
Valuing, verbs of, 214, R. 2; w. genit., 214; w. abl., 252, R. 1.
Vapulo, 142, R. 3.
Variable nouns, 92; adjs., 122.
Vas, genit. of, 72, E. 1; gender of, 62, E. 1, and E. 2; 93, 2.
-ve, 198, 2, and N. 1, p. 76; place of, 279, 3, (c.)
Vehor, compds of, 233, (3.), N.
Vel, 198, 2; difference between *vel* and *aut*, 198, R.; *vel* w. superlative degree, 127, 4; w. comparatives, 256, R. 9, (b.)
Velim, w. subj. without *ut*, 260, R. 4; 262, R. 4.
Vellem, how used, 260, R. 2.
Velox, constr., 222, R. 4, (2.)
Velut, velut si, veluti, w. subj., 263, 2; *velut*, 'as if,' w. abl. absolute, 257, N. 4.
Venalis, w. abl. of price, 252.
Vendo, w. abl., 252; w. genit., 214, R. 3, N. 1.
Veneo, 142, R. 3; 252; 214, R. 3, N. 1.
Venio, w. two datives, 227, R. 1; w. ad or *in*, 225, IV.; w. dat., 225, R. 2; *venit mihi in mentem*, constr., 211, R. 8, (5): 216, R. 3.
Venitur, conjugated, 184, 2, (b.)
Verbal terminations, 152; nouns, 102; w. acc., 233, R. 2, N.; of place, 237, R. 1; w. dat., 222, R. 8; w. abl. of place, 255; w. genit. of personal pronouns, 211, R. 3, (a.); verbal adjs., 129.
Verbs, 140—189; subject of, 140, 1; active or transitive, 141, I.; neuter or intransitive, 141, II.; neuter passive, 142, 2; neutral passive, 142, 3; deponent, 142, 4; common, 142, 4, (b.); principal parts of, 151, 4; neuter, participles of, 162, 10; inceptive, 173; desiderative, 187, II., 3; 176, N.; irregular, 178—182; defective, 183; re-

INDEX. 409

dundant, 185; verbs spelled alike, or having the same perfect or supine, 186; derivation of, 187; imitative, 187, 3; frequentative, 187, ii.. 1; inceptive, 187, ii., 2; desiderative, 187, ii., 3; diminutive, 187, ii.. 4; intensive, 187, ii., 5; 187, ii., 1, (c.); composition of. 188; changes in composition. 189: compounds from simples not in use. 189, n. 4: agreement of, 209, (b.); ellipsis of, 209, n. 4; person of with qui, 209, n. 6; agreeing with predicate nominative, 209, n. 9; with collective nouns, 209, n. 11; plural with two or more nominatives, 209, n. 12; after uterque, etc., 209, n. 11, 4); after a nominative with cum and the abl., 209, n. 12, (6); after nominatives connected by aut, 209, n. 12, (5); their place in a sentence, 279, 2; in a period, 280.
Vere and vero, 192, 4, n. 1.
Vereor, w. genit. poet., 220, 1; w. ut or ne, 262, n. 7; w. inf., 271, n. 1.
Verisimile est ut, 262, n. 3, n. 3; w. inf. as subject, 269, n. 2.
Veritum est, w. acc., 229, n. 6.
Vero, use of in answers, 192, 4, n. 1; 198, 9, n., (a.); ellipsis of, 278, n. 11; its place, 279. 3, (c.)
Verses, 304; combinations of in poems, 319.
Versification, 302.
Versus, w. acc., 195, n. 3; 235, n. 9; place of, 279, 10, (f.)
Verto, constr., 225, iv.; w. two datives, 227, n. 1; 229, n. 4. 1.
Verum est, ut, 262, n. 3. n. 3; w. inf. as subject, 269, n. 2; verum, conj., 192, 9; its place, 270, 3; verum and verum-tamen, 'I say,' 278, n. 10; verum enimvero, 198, 9, n., (a.); vero after comparatives, 256, n. 9.
Vescor, with abl., 245, i.; with acc., 245, i., n.
Vespere, or -ri, 253, n. 1.
Vester, how declined, 139, 1; vestrūm, 133, 3; used after partitives, 212, n. 2, n. 2.
Vestio, 229, n. 4. 1.
Veto, 273, 2, (d.); 262, n. 4; w. acc. and inf., 272, n. 6.
Vetus, declension of, 112, 2; its superlative, 125, 1; 126, 3.
Via, abl of place without in, 254, n. 3.
Vicem for vice, 247, 1, n. 3.
Vicinia, genit. of place, 221, n. 3, (4.); 212, n. 4, n. 2, (b.)
Vicinus, w. dat. or genit., 222, n. 2, (a.)
Victrix, 115, 1, (b.); how declined as an adj., 129, 8.
Videlicet and scilicet, 198, 7, n., (a.); pr , 285, n. 4, n. 2.
Video, w. acc. and inf., 272, n. 1; w. ut or ne, 262, n. 3; videres, 260, n. 2; video for curo, w. ut, 273, n. 1; videor, constr., 271, n. 2; 272, n. 6.
Viduus, constr., 213, n. 5, (4); 250, 2, (1.)
Vigeo, w. abl., 250, 2, n. 1.
Vigil, abl. of, 113, n. 3; genit. plur of, 114, n. 2; 115, 1, (a.)
Vigiliae, 326, 1, (2.)

Vigilias, vigilare, 232.
Vilis, w. abl. of price, 252.
Vir, how declined, 48, 2.
Virgilius, voc. of, 52; *accent of, 14, n.
Virgo, declined, 57.
Virus, gender of, 51.
Vis, declined, 85; acc. sing. of, 79, 2; abl. sing., 82, n. 2; genit. plur., 83, ii.. 3; 94; vi and per vim, difference between, 247, 3, n. 4; w. genit. of gerunds, 275, iii, n. 1, (1.)
Vitabundus, w. acc., 233, n. 2, n.
Vitam vivere, 232, (1.)
Vitio creati magistratus, 247, 2.
Viro, w. abl., 245, ii., 4; w. pred. nom , 210, n. 3, (2); tertia vivitur aetas, 231, iii.
Vix, with part. fut. pass., 274, n. 12; vixdum, 277, 1., n. 16.
Vocative, 37; sing., its form, 40, 3; plur., 40, 4; ellipsis of, 240, n. 2.
Voco, constr., 225, n. 1; 230, n. 1; pass., 210, n. 3, (3.)
Voices, 141.
Volucer, in genit. plur., 108, n. 2.
Volo, (are), compds. of, 233, (3), n.
Volo, conjugated, 178, 1; w. perf. inf., 268, n. 2; w. perf. part., and ellipsis of esse, 269, n. 3; its construction, 271, n. 4, and n. 4; 273, 4: 262, n. 4; volens, w. dat. of person, 226, n. 3; volo bene and male alicui, 225, i., n.; volo, w. reflexive pron., 228, n., (b.)
Voluntary agent of pass. verbs, 248, i.; ellipsis of, 141, n. 2; 248, i., n. 1; when expressed by per and acc., 247, n. 4; of neuter verbs, 248, n. 2; dative of voluntary agent, 225, ii. and iii.
Volutum, pr., 284, n. 3.
Vos, see tu, 133.
Voti and votorum damnati, 217, n. 3.
Vowels, 3, 1; sounds of, 7 and 8; vowel, before a mute and liquid, its quantity, 13, 6, and 283, iv., n. 2; before another vowel, quantity of, 13, 3, and 283, i.; in Greek words, 283, n. 6; before two consonants, 13, 5, and 283, iv.; ending first part of a compound, quantity of, 285, n. 4.
Vulgus, gender of, 51; 95.
Vultur, gender of, 67.

W.

W, not used in Latin, 2, 4.
Weight, acc. of, 236, n. 7; weights, Roman, 327.
Willingness, verbs of. constr., 273, 4.
Winds, gender of names of, 28.
Wishing, verbs of, constr., 271, n. 4.
Words, division of, 17 -23; arrangement of, 279; gender of as mere words, 34, 3.
Writers in different ages, 329.

X

X, sound of, 12; its equivalents, 3, 2; 56, n. 2; 171, 1; in syllabication, 18, 4; nouns in, gender of, 52 and 65; genitive of, 78, 2.

Y, found only in Greek words, 2, 5; sound of, 7, R. 2; δ, E. 5; nouns in, gender of, 62; genitive of, 69; increment in, 3d decl., 287, 3; final, quautity of, 298; 285, R. 4.
 -*ychis*, in genitive, 78, 2, (6.)
 -*ycis*, genitives in, 78, 2, (6.)
 -*ydis*, genitives in, 77, 1.
Yi, how pronounced, 9, 1; abl. in, 82, N. 6.

-*ygis*, genitives in, 178, 2, (6.)
-*ynos*, Greek genitive in, 71, 2.
-*ys*, nouns in, gender of, 62, 63, E.; genitive of, 77; acc. of, 80, II.; abl. of, 82. E. 6 final, quantity of, 301.
-*yx*, nouns in, gender of, 65, 6.

Z.

Z, found only in words derived from the Greek, 2, 5; its equivalents, 3, 2.
Zeugma 328, 1 (b.) and 2.)

www.ingramcontent.com/pod-product-compliance
Lightning Source LLC
Chambersburg PA
CBHW030553300426
44111CB00009B/966